Communications in Computer and Information Science 1167

Commenced Publication in 2007
Founding and Former Series Editors:
Phoebe Chen, Alfredo Cuzzocrea, Xiaoyong Du, Orhun Kara, Ting Liu, Krishna M. Sivalingam, Dominik Ślęzak, Takashi Washio, Xiaokang Yang, and Junsong Yuan

More information about this series at http://www.springer.com/series/7899

Peggy Cellier · Kurt Driessens (Eds.)

Machine Learning and Knowledge Discovery in Databases

International Workshops of ECML PKDD 2019 Würzburg, Germany, September 16–20, 2019 Proceedings, Part I

Editors
Peggy Cellier
Institut National des Sciences Appliquées
Rennes, France

Kurt Driessens
Maastricht University
Maastricht, The Netherlands

ISSN 1865-0929 ISSN 1865-0937 (electronic)
Communications in Computer and Information Science
ISBN 978-3-030-43822-7 ISBN 978-3-030-43823-4 (eBook)
https://doi.org/10.1007/978-3-030-43823-4

This Springer imprint is published by the registered company Springer Nature Switzerland AG
The registered company address is: Gewerbestrasse 11, 6330 Cham, Switzerland

Preface

The European Conference on Machine Learning and Principles and Practice of Knowledge Discovery in Databases (ECML PKDD) is the premier European machine learning and data mining conference. In 2019, ECML PKDD was held in Würzburg, Germany, during September 16–20.

During the first and last day of the conference, the workshop program allowed a number of specialized and/or new topics to take the fore-front.

A record 46 workshop and tutorial topics were submitted to the 2019 conference. The selection and merging process resulted in 25 workshops taking place over the two days, of which 3 were combined with a tutorial.

The workshop program included the following workshops:

1. The 12th International Workshop on Machine Learning and Music (MML 2019)
2. Workshop on Multiple-aspect analysis of semantic trajectories (MASTER 2019)
3. The 4th Workshop on MIning DAta for financial applicationS (MIDAS 2019)
4. The Second International Workshop on Knowledge Discovery and User Modelling for Smart Cities (UMCit 2019)
5. New Frontiers in Mining Complex Patterns (NFMCP 2019)
6. New Trends in Representation Learning with Knowledge Graphs
7. The Second International Workshop on Energy Efficient Scalable Data Mining and Machine Learning (Green Data Mining)
8. Workshop on Deep Continuous-Discrete Machine Learning (DeCoDeML 2019)
9. Decentralised Machine Learning at the Edge (DMLE 2019)
10. Applications of Topological Data Analysis (ATDA 2019)
11. GEM: Graph Embedding and Mining
12. Interactive Adaptive Learning (AIL 2019)
13. IoT Stream for Data Driven Predictive Maintenance (IoT Steam 2019)
14. Machine Learning for Cybersecurity (MLCS 2019)
15. BioASQ: Large-scale biomedical semantic indexing and question answering
16. The 6th Workshop on Sports Analytics: Machine Learning and Data Mining for Sports Analytics (MLSA 2019)
17. The 4th Workshop on Advanced Analytics and Learning on Temporal Data (AALTD 2019)
18. MACLEAN: MAChine Learning for EArth ObservatioN
19. Automating Data Science
20. The 4th Workshop on Data Science for Social Good (DSSG 2019)
21. The Third Workshop on Advances in managing and mining Large Evolving Graphs (LEG 2019)
22. Data and Machine Learning Advances with Multiple Views (DAMVL 2019)
23. Workshop on Data Integration and Applications (DINA 2019)
24. XKDD Tutorial and XKDD-AIMLAI Workshop
25. The First Workshop SocIaL Media And Harassment (SIMAH 2019)

Of these 25 workshops, 17 workshops decided to select and publish their best papers with Springer. Two workshops were large enough to publish their own proceedings: (i) MIDAS – the 4th Workshop on MIning DAta for financial applicationS and (ii) AALTD – the 4th workshop on Advanced Analytics and Learning on Temporal Data. The 15 other workshops received a total of 200 submitted papers, out of which 70 long and 46 short papers were selected for publication after the conference. These papers are spread over two proceedings volumes.

This two-volume set contains the papers from the following workshops:

1. Automating Data Science
2. XKDD Tutorial and XKDD-AIMLAI Workshop
3. Decentralised Machine Learning at the Edge (DMLE 2019)
4. The Third Workshop on Advances in managing and mining Large Evolving Graphs (LEG 2019)
5. Data and Machine Learning Advances with Multiple Views (DAMVL 2019)
6. New Trends in Representation Learning with Knowledge Graphs
7. The 4th Workshop on Data Science for Social Good (DSSG 2019)
8. The Second International Workshop on Knowledge Discovery and User Modelling for Smart Cities (UMCit 2019)
9. Workshop on Data Integration and Applications (DINA 2019)
10. Machine Learning for Cybersecurity (MLCS 2019)
11. The 6th Workshop on Sports Analytics: Machine Learning and Data Mining for Sports Analytics (MLSA 2019)
12. The First Workshop on SocIaL Media And Harassment (SIMAH 2019)
13. IoT Stream for Data Driven Predictive Maintenance (IoT Stream 2019)
14. The 12th International Workshop on Machine Learning and Music (MML 2019)
15. BioASQ: Large-scale biomedical semantic indexing and question answering

We would like to thank all participants and invited speakers, the workshop organizers and the reviewers, as well as the local organizers for making the workshop program of ECML PKDD 2019 the success that it was. Sincere thanks also goes to Springer for their help in publishing the proceedings.

January 2020

Peggy Cellier
Kurt Driessens

Organization

ECML Workshop Chairs/Editors

Peggy Celier	INSA Rennes, France
Kurt Driessens	Maastricht University, The Netherlands

Individual Workshop Chairs/Editors

Tijl De Bie	UGent, Belgium
Luc De Raedt	KU Leuven, Belgium
Jose Hernandez-Orallo	Universitat Politecnica de Valencia, Spain
Adrien Bibal	University of Namur, Belgium
Tassadit Bouadi	University of Rennes/IRISA, France
Benoît Frénay	University of Namur, Belgium
Luis Galárraga	Inria/IRISA, France
Stefan Kramer	Universität Mainz, Germany
Ruggero G. Pensa	University of Turin, Italy
Michael Kamp	University of Bonn, Germany
Yamuna Krishnamurthy	Rolay Holloway University of London, England
Daniel Paurat	Fraunhofer IAIS, Germany
Sabeur Aridhi	University of Lorraine, France
José Antonio de Macedo	Universidade Federal do Ceará, Brazil
Engelbert Mephu Nguifo	University Clermont Auvergne, France
Karine Zeitouni	Université de Versailles Saint-Quentin, France
Stéphane Ayache	Aix Marseille University, France
Cécile Capponi	Aix-Marseille University, France
Rémi Emonet	Jean-Monnet University, France
Usabelle Guyon	Orsay University, France
Volker Tresp	Ludwig-Maximilians University and Siemens, Germany
Jens Lehmann	Bonn University and Fraunhofer IAIS, Germany
Aditya Mogadala	Saarland University, Germany
Achim Rettinger	Trier University, Germany
Afshin Sadeghi	Fraunhofer IAIS, Germany
Mehdi Ali	Bonn University and Fraunhofer IAIS, Germany
Ricard Gavalda	UPC BarcelonaTech, Spain
Irena Koprinska	University of Sydney, Australia
Joao Gama	University of Porto, Portugal
Rabeah Alzaidy	King Abdullah University of Science and Technology, Saudi Arabia
Marcelo G. Armentano	ISISTAN, CONICET-UNICEN, Argentina
Antonela Tommasel	ISISTAN, CONICET-UNICEN, Argentina

Ludovico Boratto	Eurecat, Barcelona, Spain
Clyde L. Giles	College of Information Sciences and Technology, Pennsylvania State University
Luiza Antonie	University of Guelph, Canada
Peter Christen	The Australian National University, Australia
Erhard Rahm	University of Leipzig, Germany
Osmar Zaïane	University of Alberta, Canada
Annalisa Appice	Università degli Studi di Bari, Italy
Battista Biggio	Università degli Studi di Cagliari, Italy
Donato Malerba	Università degli Studi di Bari, Italy
Fabio Roli	Università degli Studi di Cagliari, Italy
Ibéria Medeiros	Universidade de Lisboa, Portugal
Pedro Ferreira	Universidade de Lisboa, Portugal
Michael Kamp	University of Bonn, Germany
Jesse Davis	KU Leuven, Belgium
Ulf Brefeld	Leuphana University, Germany
Jan Van Haaren	SciSports, The Netherlands
Albrecht Zimmermann	University of Caen, France
Rita Ribeiro	University of Porto, Porto
Albert Bifet	Telecom-ParisTech, France
João Gama	University of Porto, Porto, Portugal
Anders Holst	RISE SICS, Sweden
Sepideh Pashami	Halmstad University, Sweden
Sima Sharifirad	Dalhousie University, Canada
Stan Matwin	Dalhousie University, Canada
Rafael Ramirez	Universitat Pompeu Fabra, Spain
Darrell Conklin	Universidad del País Vasco, Spain
José Manuel Iñesta	Alicante University, Spain
George Paliouras	University of Houston, USA
Anastasia Krithara	NCSR "Demokritos", Greece
Anastasios Nentidis	Aristotle University of Thessaloniki, Greece

Contents – Part I

Decentralized Machine Learning at the Edge

Advances in Managing and Mining Large Evolving Graphs - 3rd Edition (LEG)

Contents – Part II

First Workshop on Categorizing Different Types of Online Harassment Languages in Social Media

IoT Stream for Data Driven Predictive Maintenance

Automating Data Science

The ABC of Data: A Classifying Framework for Data Readiness

Laurens A. Castelijns[1,2,3], Yuri Maas[1,2,3], and Joaquin Vanschoren[1](✉)

[1] Faculty of Mathematics and Computer Science, Eindhoven University of Technology, Eindhoven, The Netherlands
j.vanschoren@tue.nl

[2] School of Law, Tilburg University, Tilburg, The Netherlands

[3] Jheronimus Academy of Data Science, 's-Hertogenbosch, The Netherlands

Abstract. In order to (semi)automate data cleaning and preprocessing, we need a clear and measurable definition of data quality. Data readiness levels have been proposed to fit this need, but they require a more detailed and measurable definition than is given in prior works. We present a practical framework focused on machine learning that encapsulates data cleaning and (pre)processing procedures. In our framework, datasets are classified within bands, and each band introduces more fine-grained terminology and processing steps. Scores are assigned to each step, resulting in a data quality score. This allows teams of people, as well as automated processes, to track and reason about the cleaning process, and communicate the current status and deficiencies in a more structured, well-documented manner.

Keywords: Data quality · Data readiness levels · Data cleaning · Preprocessing · Automated data science

1 Introduction

"Data is the new oil. It is valuable, but if unrefined it cannot really be used. It has to be changed into gas, plastic, chemicals, etc to create a valuable entity that drives profitable activity; so must data be broken down, analyzed for it to have value".

The popular metaphor between data and oil is credited to the British mathematician Clive Humby in 2006. There are many ways in which his analogy might be broken down but Dr. Humby here points out an incontestable truth: Data needs processing.

We pose that data (pre)processing aims to increase *data quality*, and present a practical framework that encapsulates a range of data processing steps to achieve this. Inspired by the concepts introduced by Lawrence in his position paper on *Data Readiness Levels* [13], it examines and structures the technical challenges that, when solved, increase data quality. The resulting framework is used as the theoretical foundation of the software package PyWash [3], a collection of tools used to clean and process datasets to increase their quality.

P. Cellier and K. Driessens (Eds.): ECML PKDD 2019 Workshops, CCIS 1167, pp. 3–16, 2020.
https://doi.org/10.1007/978-3-030-43823-4_1

Raw data usually suffers from a wide range of issues, such as duplicated records, missing values, outliers, typo's, and many other issues that weaken the quality of the data and hinder advanced analysis. This results in machine learning systems learning the wrong things, decreasing their accuracy and making them unreliable at best and plain wrong at worst. Data cleaning is, therefore, an essential task. Data cleaning is often an iterative process that is tailored to the needs and wants of a specific analysis task. Krishnan et al. (2015) conducted a survey that expresses the need for a streamlined data cleaning framework. The question "How do you determine whether the data is sufficiently clean to trust the analysis?" made clear that most of the respondents had no rigorous validation of their data cleaning. In response to this survey the same authors created ActiveClean [12], which describes an iterative cleaning process that selects and cleans some records. After this cleaning, it measures the performance of the dataset on the main analysis to then select and evaluate if more cleaning is necessary. The iterative nature of data cleaning paired with the absence of an evaluation methodology is alarming. Alternating between cleaning data and analyzing data, and using these analysis results to guide the subsequent data cleaning procedures can result in overfitting. Data cleaning procedures are generally under-reported because it is such a 'dirty' process. Often there is no log maintained of data cleaning operations executed whilst these operations can introduce bias into the dataset [11].

Since then, some attempts have been made to set up a data quality framework. "InfoQ" breaks down data analysis into 4 distinct components: analysis goal, available data, utility measure, and data analysis method. The information quality is then assessed using eight dimensions, such as data structure (explained as the type of data and data characteristics) and temporal relevance. The quality of each of these eight dimensions is then assessed separately, often using a rating on a Likert scale. There are multiple approaches to then compute an overall InfoQ score by properly combining this set of eight assessments [7]. For example, Ron Kenett and Marco Reis applied InfoQ to the Chemical Processing Industry and proposed an assessment strategy in which each dimension is weighted to reflect the distinct focal points in different analysis goals [16]. A limitation of InfoQ is that a Likert scale abstracts away from the actual operations that have to be performed to increase data quality. If you were told that a dataset obtained an InfoQ score of 77% it is not clear what kind of deficiencies are present. After sharing the individual Likert scale scores for each dimension it is still unknown what exactly can be done to improve the score (and in what order). Lawrence (2017) recognized the overall lack of terminology in discussions about data quality and proposed an initial set of descriptors for data readiness. The proposal is to split data readiness into three distinct *bands*. The bands are represented by the letters: A, B, and C. Each band contains sub levels: A1 is data of the highest quality and C4 would be data of the worst quality [13]. However, the author refrains from elaborating the bands in greater detail and therefore the bands remain vague. In this paper, we propose one way to further extend, detail and quantify these bands.

2 The Framework

We introduce a framework which streamlines and describes the data cleaning process. The framework splits the cleaning process into multiple distinct categories we likewise call *bands* and it analyzes the dataset to determine in which band it currently is. Datasets that are in a certain band may possess one or more deficiencies which are specified for that band and will negatively influence any analysis, such as machine learning, performed on the dataset. Thus, in order for a dataset to be classified as a higher tier band and be deemed *cleaner*, the issues from the current band have to be resolved.

The bands introduce steps and terminology in the cleaning process that are easy to follow for most practitioners. Teams will be able to communicate, argue and customize the cleaning process to better fit their needs in a structured, potentially well-documented process.

This new way of thinking about data cleaning as a step-by-step process and a standalone part of the whole data process will hopefully save people from rushing through data cleaning, and provide them with useful data quality metrics rather than purely optimizing a final model quality score (e.g. model accuracy). Moreover, it will also help to increasingly automate the process while alleviating overfitting.

2.1 Data Bands

The framework consists of the following bands: C, B, A, AA, and AAA. These represent the different stages of usability that datasets can be in during the process.

Band C (Conceive) refers to the stage that the data is still being ingested. If there is information about the dataset, it comes from the data collection phase and how the data was collected. The data has not yet been introduced to a programming environment or tool in a way that allows operations to be performed on the dataset. The possible analyses to be performed on the dataset in order to gain value from the data possibly haven't been conceived yet, as this can often only be determined after inspecting the data itself.

Band B (Believe) refers to the stage in which the data is loaded into an environment that allows cleaning operations. However, the *correctness* of the data is not fully assessed yet, and there may be errors or deficiencies that would invalidate further analysis. Therefore, analyses performed in this stage are often more cursory and exploratory, such as a exploratory data analysis with visualization methods to ascertain the correctness of the data. Skipping these checks might lead to errors or 'wrong' results and conclusions.

In **band A (Analyze)**, the data is ready for deeper analysis. However, even if there are no more factual errors in the data, the quality of an analysis or machine learning model is greatly influenced by how the data is represented. For instance, operations such as feature selection and normalization can greatly increase the accuracy of machine learning models. Hence, these operations need to be performed before arriving at accurate and adequate machine learning models or analyses. In many cases, these operations can already be automated to a significant degree.

In **band AA (Allow Analysis)**, we consider the context in which the dataset is allowed to be used. Operations in this band detect, quantify, and potentially address any legal, moral or social issues with the dataset, since the consequences of using illegal, immoral or biased datasets can be enormous. Hence, this band is about verifying whether analysis can be applied without (legal) penalties or negative social impact. One may argue that legal and moral implications are not part of data cleaning, but rather distinct parts of the data process. However, we argue that readiness is about learning the ins and outs of your dataset and detecting and solving any potential problems that may occur when analyzing and using a dataset.

Band AAA is the terminus of our framework. Getting into AAA would mean that the dataset is clean. The data is self-contained and no further input is needed from the people that collected or created the data.

2.2 Quality Scores

A dataset has a score between 0 and 1 for each band of our framework, so a dataset can have score 0.9 for band C, 0.8 for band B, 0.10 for A, 0.20 for AA and possibly 0 for band AAA. Datasets start with initial band score values of 0 for every band, as we generally do not know (for certain) which issues the dataset is suffering from that could potentially jeopardize machine learning methods. The dataset is classified in band C at this stage. We then proceed to check and solve all issues from band C. Each band deficiency that is solved or non-existent contributes to the band score of the dataset. Partially checked or solved deficiencies can grant partial weight scores. A dataset will move to the next band only when it has surpassed a certain *threshold* score. This also means that a dataset cannot get a band label of A or above when it has a B.60 score, even if the dataset fulfills all band A requirements.

The threshold scores can be determined by the framework users to determine how thoroughly the dataset has to be cleaned before it is able to proceed to further bands. We have set the default threshold for all bands on 0.85 to allow a dataset to advance while it's not totally perfect, since striving for a perfect dataset may not be achievable or cost-effective in general. The dataset might not be entirely clean when the thresholds are less than 1, as a dataset could advance to the next band (including band AAA) while not every issue has been checked or fixed yet. That said, the thresholds cannot be set too low (e.g., <0.65) as datasets wouldn't be checked properly, which could seriously impact machine learning methods and dataset usability, causing errors and false predictions or estimates.

This terminology makes it easier to track and communicate the cleaning progress to others. This is because others will be able to understand what has to be done when a dataset is currently in band B, but might not know what to do next when only given a list of completed cleaning methods.

3 The Different Levels of Data Readiness

A dataset will be ready for certain operations to be performed on it depending on its band. The bands consist of several weighted dataset deficiencies which reflect what are currently the most important deficiencies that need to be addressed in the current band. An overview of the bands and their deficiencies can be found in Table 1. A description of the bands, the functionality they unlock and their deficiencies are given below. The weights that we have given in Table 1 are advisory weights for a generic dataset without a specific target analysis. In some scenarios, people may decide to use a different weighting. For example, medical applications may prioritize outlier detection, since detecting and investigating anomalies may have greater importance compared to other fields.

Table 1. The framework bands with weights and deficiencies

Band	W	Deficiency
C	40	Parseability
	25	Data storage
	15	Decoding
	10	Data Formats
	10	Disjoint Datasets
B	20	Column Types
	30	Missing Values
	20	Inconsistent Data Entries
	10	Duplicated Records
	20	Meaningful Values
A	20	Interpretable Values
	20	Feature Scaling
	20	Outlier Detection
	30	Feature Selection
	10	Coverage gap detection
AA	40	Legal Violations
	40	Security Risks
	20	Bias Detection
AAA		None

3.1 Band C: Conceive

Band C, and so too the framework, starts with having *access* to files or databases with the actual data. Data access has many problems of its own: datasets may be stored in a remote system with limited access or hidden in a large corporate ecosystem where few know the exact location of the desired dataset, thus human interaction may be required before programmatic access is possible. Having access to the data is a prerequisite to even begin assessing its quality, hence the dataset's score will be 0 until access has been obtained. Such *hearsay data* [13] is therefore outside the scope of our framework.

That said, when we do have access, the data enters band C and tests have to be performed to see if the dataset is compatible with a programming environment or tool. Indeed, data files cannot provide value as is. Some procedures have to be followed before even basic analysis can be done. The aim in band C is to test for, and fix if necessary, the data deficiencies that are described below.

Parseability
There are many different file formats to store a dataset for long-term storage and transport, such as CSV, JSON and plain text. These formats specify how data can be loaded into a programming environment or analysis tool to perform operations. Therefore, making sure that a dataset can be loaded without errors receives a high weight in band C. This also includes the requirement of data access. You may know that a dataset exists, but technical or legal barriers might make it impossible to actually load and use the files.

Data Storage
The dataset needs to be stored in an effective and efficient manner relative to the operations that will have to be performed on the dataset. Getting the data in such a shape is often called *data wrangling*. The storage method does not have to be optimal, so there is no set limit to the runtime of the operations set by this paper. However, all operations of the subsequent bands must be executable. These operations aren't possible when the dataset isn't able to be stored in a way that allows these operations, thus checking how the data is stored is part of band C.

Decoding
The data has to be recognizable as data. This means that the data formatter should be able to use encoding styles that are known and understood by the environment that processes the dataset. The largest problem is that there are many different character encodings, and datasets can use any one of them. Common character encoding formats include ASCII [15], ISO 8859 and UTF-8 [18]. Luckily, automatic encoding detection has long been available [14].

Nevertheless, a system won't be able to use and find meaning in the data if the system is not able to distinguish or relate characters to each other. Thus datasets containing unknown formats cannot reliably be used to perform meaningful operations on. Which is why we classify any such datasets as being in band C.

Data Formats
Datasets are not always stored cleanly in a particular format. Human or technical problems can occur which might result in writing errors during the data collection phase. There are several different ways a data format may break. CSV files could change their separator halfway through the file, a JSON file misplaces a bracket or an ARFF file misses a categorical value. Mistakes happen and when they do, the parsing of data becomes difficult and could lead to unexpected outcomes. Therefore, a system has to check if a dataset has a consistent format and, even though it's not easy, should be able to fix most potential issues. This

is different from being able to load the dataset since an incorrect format may not raise an error, but will change the structure of the dataset.

Disjoint Datasets
Datasets can be divided up into multiple tables over several different files. Since they essentially are just one spread out dataset, any analysis should be performed on the entire dataset, rather than just one subset of it. Performing analysis on partial data can invite bias, and multiple analyses on the different dataset parts may introduce false positive errors and increase result variance.

3.2 Band B: Believe

In band B are datasets that are loaded into memory but still defective in some ways, which means that the data cannot be trusted at this moment. The data must be checked for trustworthiness and correctness of the data itself. After checking for these deficiencies and rectifying them, basic analytics can be used to explore the dataset.

Known and Correct Data Types
Columns should have the correct data type (boolean, integer, float, date, categorical, ordinal, and string). A counterexample would be that a column is labeled as 'integer' while it is effectively a non-ordinal encoding of categorical values (e.g. 1 = blue, 2 = green, 3 = red) [17].

Missing Values Are Identified and Appropriately Dealt with
Missing values are encoded as a variety of characters such as "null", "N/A", "na", "?", and "−1". The data points or features with missing data should be either removed or repaired (e.g. imputed) [1]. However, in some cases it does no harm to keep the missing values as long as they are properly identified.

Redundancy
We need to assess the degree to which there are duplicate records and columns.

Typos and Inconsistent Data Entries
Imagine a column with colors which has 'red' but also 'read'. These values should be fixed or removed if the true value is unclear [9].

Meaningful Values
If possible, variables should be expressed in a unit that is most suitable for machine learning. As a counterexample: a column with the height of people is expressed as a combination of feet and inches and encoded as a string. This can be useless for some machine learning models since no distance metric can be computed. This is also the point where clearly faulty data points -such as a name in a postcode field- should be removed [9].

3.3 Band A: Analyze

In band A are operations that further optimize and clean the data. The data is modified such that it is in a format that is properly suited for machine learning. Data that is not needed is filtered out to reduce overhead and increase accuracy.

Interpretable Values
In is important that we know exactly what each feature (variable) in the data means. Maintaining a codebook [2] with a semantic description as possibly a unit for each feature is a good practice. For instance, if a column is named price but has no currency attached to it, it cannot be clearly interpreted. Knowing the right semantics also enables algorithmic transformation to a more convenient unit if needed [9]. Moreover, this also includes mappings for categorical values when they are encoded numerically, so that it is known what the numeric codes represent.

Feature Scaling
In feature scaling, you transform the data such that it is within a specific range. Some scaling methods such as normalization and standardization also change the distribution of the data. For some machine learning models, it is beneficial to scale the data. Neural networks, for example, are known to converge more quickly on normalized data.

Outlier Detection
As we have cleaned obvious faulty data points in band B, we are now able to search for naturally occurring data points that differ significantly from other observations. Outliers must be dealt with appropriately because not every machine learning model is robust to outliers [10].

Feature Selection
Some features may be redundant, for instance, a column may portray the same information as the column next to it. Removing the column will decrease training time and lower the risk of overfitting [6]. Dimensionality reduction techniques may also be used to represent high-dimensional data in fewer dimensions that facilitate modelling (but decrease interpretability).

Coverage Gap Detection
Data may have gaps such as spatial or temporal coverage gaps, For instance: sensor data was collected for 2 years, but because of a defect in the measurement equipment a part of the data is absent [9].

3.4 Band AA: Allow Analysis

We check the context in which the data is to be used in band AA. Data often originates from real people and is used to make decisions for real people. Thus the information of a dataset has to be placed in context to make sure that any analysis performed on the dataset will be permissible, usable and allowed. This is often not easily measurable, as this requires a lot of metadata from the dataset and from the context of possible analyses and how their results may be used. However, in most cases manual checks should be possible and should be done to ensure a dataset is allowed to be used in the real world.

Legal Violations
Laws and regulations can prevent the allowed usage of a dataset for analysis, even if the dataset was legally collected. This can happen when the data contains

wrong values about the data subjects, or when the dataset is used outside the original scope. Information stored in datasets can also be harmful to the data subjects, even if the contents of the dataset are not leaked or stolen. That's why datasets that violate the GDPR [5] or other privacy regulations can result in large fines being imposed on the company or institution that is creating or using those datasets.

We deem these violations to be very important, both for any data processor and for all subjects within the data. That's why we propose to put a high weight on checking and solving any problems relating to this topic. Note that in many contexts, legal restrictions could inhibit anyone from even loading the data. In that case they would fall in band C (or pre-C).

Security Risks
Data security is a must when performing analyses on sensitive data such as personal data. Datasets containing sensitive information should be secure by design and security systems should already exist at the data collection stage. Consequently, the data should already be secure when entering the data cleaning phase. However, when this is not the case, the data cleaning phase should prioritize the security of the data and transform and/or protect the data in such a way that any insecurities are prevented, either by encrypting the data or by securing the network the data is stored in. This also includes technical security procedures to work with the data [4].

A dataset is often secure because of the security systems around the dataset (e.g. firewalls), not because of the dataset itself. But it is essential that a dataset is protected, that's why we assigned such a high weight for checking the security of a dataset.

Bias Detection
Bias can occur when the data collection samples neglect a portion of the entire population or when it over-samples on a specific portion. Analysis performed on datasets often separates the instances of the dataset into several groups to generalize them and suggest different actions for the different groups. This can become unethical (and illegal) when the groups are created based on discriminatory attributes (either directly or indirectly due to data collection bias). This is especially unethical when the results of the main analysis are used in decision-based applications, since such applications can and will discriminate. Therefore, datasets should be checked before any analysis, and any resulting models should only make predictions on cases that are sufficiently covered by their training data.

Techniques and frameworks exist to detect and eliminate dataset bias during training, and these should be an integral part of the cleaning process [8]. However, it is hard to eliminate *unknown* biases during the cleaning process.

3.5 Band AAA: A Clean Dataset

If a dataset has passed all bands, then it is considered as properly cleaned based on how the thresholds and weights were chosen. As mentioned before, dataset can advance to the next band while not every single issue has been completely solved. Thus a dataset might not be perfectly clean when in band AAA, but it is clean enough such that we can use it in most applications.

Band AAA does not contain any issues and doesn't add any functionality. It is rather an indicator that a dataset has completed the cleaning process and is ready to be effectively used in the determined main analysis.

4 Deployment

As mentioned in the introduction, this framework is used as the theoretical foundation of the practical tool *PyWash* [3]. PyWash is a python package that combines the described framework with a set of (semi)automatic data cleaning and preprocessing methods. The package will analyze datasets, assign band scores, and guide the user to the appropriate tools to import, clean, and export the dataset.

In addition, we built a user interface on top of the python package in the form of a web application to guide the user through the cleaning process. The

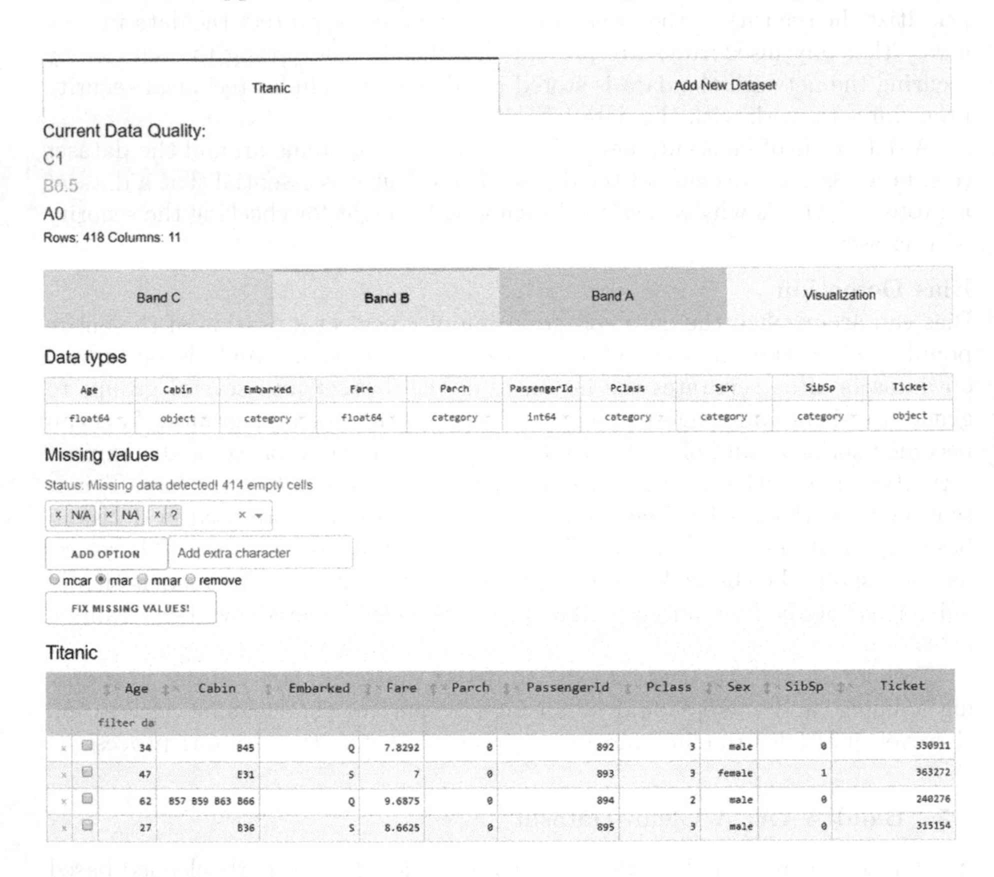

Fig. 1. The PyWash web interface.

interface, shown in Fig. 1, groups the operations for each band into separate color-coded tabs. Loading datasets happens in the tab called 'Band C', which will initially be the only band that is accessible. Band C includes interactions (e.g. forms) to import datasets and merged them together if applicable. Once a dataset is successfully parsed, it will receive a tab at the top of the screen with its name and the other bands will be unlocked. The interface supports multiple datasets being loaded at the same time, with every loaded dataset in a unique tab. When a dataset is selected, a description is shown which includes the data quality score. Below this description, there is a row of buttons which are used to switch between the bands from the framework. Selecting different bands will show the various operations available to fix or investigate the deficiencies that are part of that band. Band B is selected in Fig. 1. Data types are automatically inferred and shown to the user, who can leave them as is, or correct them through a dropdown menu. In the missing value section, an indicator shows whether missing values are detected. Users can also check the data in the shown table add extra characters that indicate a missing value. Missing values can optionally be imputed or removed. At the moment, the user still has to choose between one of four techniques (based on whether the data is missing at random or not), but we hope to automate this further in future work.

Underneath the operations from the selected band, a data table is shown so that the effect of the operations is immediately visible. This table supports

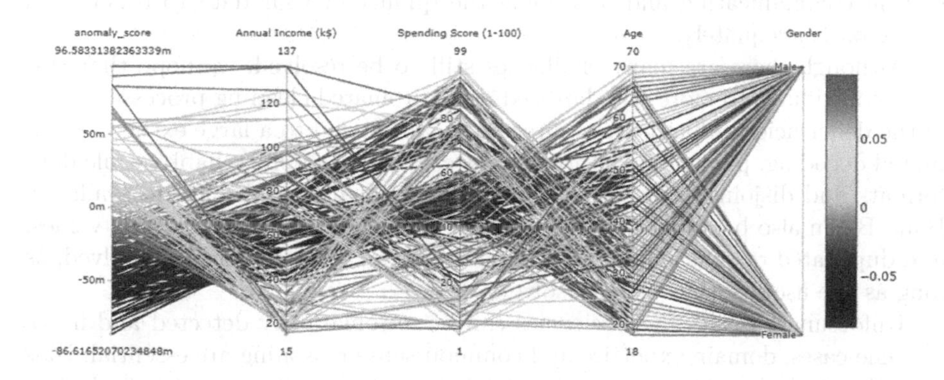

Mall_Customers

		Age	Annual Income (k$)	Gender	Spending Score (1-100)	anomaly_score	prediction
		filter d					
×	☐	32	137	Male	18	0.09658331382363339	1
×	☐	30	137	Male	83	0.08973938934859016	0
×	☐	64	19	Male	3	0.08401876579198053	0
×	☐	45	126	Female	28	0.08274928973733486	0
×	☐	20	16	Female	6	0.06875584617998964	0

Fig. 2. Visualization of outliers in PyWash, color-coded by anomaly score.

row/column deletion, filtering, sorting, and editing. The exporting options will store return the data 'as is', thus including any modifications made in the table (filtering, sorting, etc.). In future work, we also plan to export a log of all cleaning operations with the data export.

The rightmost tab contains a visualization section to help the user with decision making and perform instant exploratory analysis. Figure 2 is an example of a parallel coordinates graph color-coded by an anomaly score computed by an Isolation Forest in band A. The outlier detection adds the columns 'anomaly_score' to the plot and a 'prediction' column to the table indicating which rows are predicted to be outliers. The first row is marked as an outlier and highlighted. Since these columns are added as part of the dataset, we can export them for further analysis with other tools and visualizations.

Our data quality framework, the PyWash package, and the web interface are all open source and we warmly welcome and encourage anyone to help fine-tune the framework and improve the libraries and interfaces.

5 Discussion

The goal of this paper is to streamline the data cleaning process by creating a vocabulary and a framework for automatic data cleaning, such that the data cleaning process becomes an explicit, accountable, reported process. This will help in communicating and describing the quality of your data to others and acting on it adequately.

Although there are many challenges still to be resolved, we hope that this work contributes to more standardized and automated cleaning processes. Most of the deficiencies in band C can already be automated to a large extend. Automated decoding, parsing and storing of datasets can be done reliably, while data formats and disjoint datasets can be detected when enough data is available. Band B can also be automated to some degree since data types, missing values, and duplicated records can be detected and issues can be (partially) resolved, as long as the user specifies how to solve it.

Unfortunately, not all deficiencies can be automatically detected and fixed. In some cases, domain expertise and common sense reasoning are essential. Bias detection tools do exist, but most band AA deficiencies will have to be checked by humans since detecting the context of a dataset is often impossible or unreliable. Therefore, we have taken a human-in-the-loop approach that provides as much guidance and automation as possible, yet leaves many decisions at the discretion of the user.

From a usage perspective, an open challenge is that we have no objective method to determine the weights and thresholds of each band. We have supplied default values, but these will not suffice for everyone since not every dataset and analysis has to meet the same requirements. Also, the framework does not yet encompass every aspect of data preprocessing. For instance, feature construction would be a valuable addition to band A, but much more work is needed to codify it and guide the user in applying it.

However, we do already provide an extensible software framework in which new techniques that automate data cleaning and preprocessing can be implemented and made easily available to anyone. As such, we hope that it will become a test bed for automated data science research in general.

Acknowledgements. The authors would like to thank Neil D. Lawrence for contributing many original ideas and his valuable feedback on the ideas in this paper. We also like to thank Hero de Smeth for contributing to the definition and composition of the bands.

References

1. Allison, P.D.: Missing Data. SAGE, Thousand Oaks (2002)
2. Arslan, R.C.: How to automatically document data with the codebook package to facilitate data reuse. Adv. Methods Pract. Psychol. Sci. **2**, 169–187 (2019). https://doi.org/10.1177/2515245919838783
3. Castelijns, L.A., Maas, Y.: PyWash. (2019). https://github.com/pywash/pywash
4. Dandurand, L., Serrano, O.S.: Towards improved cyber security information sharing. In: 2013 5th International Conference on Cyber Conflict (CYCON 2013), pp. 1–16 (2013)
5. General Data Protection Regulation, European Union, Regulation (EU) 2016/679 (2018). https://gdpr-info.eu/
6. Guyon, I., Elisseeff, A.: An introduction to variable and feature selection. J. Mach. Learn. Res. **3**, 1157–1182 (2003)
7. Kenett, R., Shmueli, G.: Information Quality: The Potential of Data and Analytics to Generate Knowledge. Wiley, Chichester (2017)
8. Khosla, A., Zhou, T., Malisiewicz, T., Efros, A.A., Torralba, A.: Undoing the damage of dataset bias. In: Fitzgibbon, A., Lazebnik, S., Perona, P., Sato, Y., Schmid, C. (eds.) ECCV 2012. LNCS, vol. 7572, pp. 158–171. Springer, Heidelberg (2012). https://doi.org/10.1007/978-3-642-33718-5_12
9. Kim, W., Choi, B.-J., Hong, E.-K., Kim, S.-K., Lee, D.: A taxonomy of dirty data. Data Min. Knowl. Disc. **7**, 81–99 (2003). https://doi.org/10.1023/A:1021564703268
10. Kriegel, H.-P., Kröger, P., Zimek, A.: Outlier detection techniques. In: Tutorial, 16th ACM SIGKDD Conference on Knowledge Discovery and Data Mining, Washington DC (2010)
11. Krishnan, S., Haas, D., Franklin, M.J., Wu, E.: Towards reliable interactive data cleaning: a user survey and recommendations (2016). https://sirrice.github.io/files/papers/cleaning-hilda16.pdf
12. Krishnan, S., Franklin, M.J., Goldberg, K., Wang, J., Wu, E.: ActiveClean: an interactive data cleaning framework for modern machine learning. In: Proceedings of the 2016 International Conference on Management of Data - SIGMOD 2016, pp. 2117–2120. ACM Press, San Francisco (2016). https://doi.org/10.1145/2882903.2899409
13. Lawrence, N.D.: Data Readiness Levels. arXiv:1705.02245 [cs] (2017)
14. Li, S., Momoi, K.: A composite approach to language/encoding detection. In: 19th International Unicode Conference (2001)
15. Patterson, J.B.: Coded Character Sets, History and Development. In: IEE Proceedings E Computers and Digital Techniques, UK, vol. 128, p. 173 (1981). https://doi.org/10.1049/ip-e.1981.0034

16. Reis, M.S., Kenett, R.: Assessing the value of information of data-centric activities in the chemical processing industry 4.0. AIChE J. **64**, 3868–3881 (2018). https://doi.org/10.1002/aic.16203
17. Valera, I., Ghahramani, Z.: Automatic discovery of the statistical types of variables in a dataset. In: Proceedings of the 34th International Conference on Machine Learning, vol. 70, pp. 3521–3529. JMLR.org (2017)
18. Yergeau, F.: UTF-8, a transformation format of ISO 10646 (2003)

Automating Common Data Science Matrix Transformations

Lidia Contreras-Ochando(✉), Cèsar Ferri, and José Hernández-Orallo

Valencian Research Institute for Artificial Intelligence (vrAIn),
Universitat Politècnica de València, Valencia, Spain
{liconoc,jorallo}@upv.es, cferri@dsic.upv.es

Abstract. Programming languages such as R or Python are commonplace in data science projects. However, transforming data is usually tricky and the composition of the right primitives (using the appropriate libraries) to get the most elegant code transformation is not always easy. In this paper, we present the first system that is able to automatically synthesise program snippets in R given an input data matrix and an output matrix, partially filled by the user representing the required transformation. We use the type information given by the dimensions of the matrix primitives (and other constraints) to reduce the combinatorial explosion of primitive compositions. We test the performance of our approach with a set of artificial data and real examples from Stack Overflow questions.

Keywords: Data science automation · Matrix transformation · Inductive programming · R programming language

1 Introduction

Many data scientists use programming languages, such as R or Python, that allow them to manipulate data for analysis. Programming requires multiple skills and the learning process of these languages can be long and frustrating for those people without programming knowledge [8].

Matrices (or data frames) are a very common way of working with data[1]. Matrix algebra can be applied to transform the data or extract a variety of useful information. However, it is quite common that a data scientist knows what kind of transformation she wants to do with a matrix, by just applying it by hand to a few cells of the input and the output matrices, but struggles to find a simple combination (or just a working combination) of operators that produces

[1] https://medium.com/@rathi.ankit/linear-algebra-for-data-science-a9648b9daee0.

This research was supported by the EU (FEDER) and the Spanish MINECO RTI2018-094403-B-C32, and the Generalitat Valenciana PROMETEO/2019/098. L. Contreras-Ochando was also supported by the Spanish MECD (FPU15/03219). J. Hernández-Orallo is also funded by FLI (RFP2-152).

P. Cellier and K. Driessens (Eds.): ECML PKDD 2019 Workshops, CCIS 1167, pp. 17–27, 2020.
https://doi.org/10.1007/978-3-030-43823-4_2

the desired matrix transformation. On other occasions, the data scientist sees an example of the transformation and would like to write a concise piece of code copying that transformation to apply to her own data. Finally, it is also quite common that the data scientist has some code in the same or different language (e.g., using loops) that she wants to transform into a more elegant algebraic matrix transformation.

For instance, consider a data matrix as shown in Fig. 1a and a data scientist who wants to extract the positions of the non-empty values. The data scientist has an idea of what she wants as a result of the transformation (represented in Fig. 1b), but she does not find the right combination or function to do this.

NA	0.30	0.50	NA	NA	NA	NA
NA	NA	NA	0.90	NA	NA	0.40
NA	NA	NA	NA	NA	NA	NA
NA	NA	NA	NA	0.60	NA	NA
NA	NA	NA	NA	NA	NA	NA

(a) Matrix A with empty values.

1	2
1	3
2	4
4	5
2	7

(b) Position (row, column) of non-empty values of A.

Fig. 1. Example of data transformation using matrices. Can you code it?

A data scientist will try with a loop (or a nested loop) or will check Stack Overflow, or will struggle to find a single function that makes the transformation. In the end, she can get the right code for this transformation, but what if the process could be automated with a system that by taking Fig. 1a and b as inputs, could generate an elegant code snippet such as `which(!is.na(A), arr.ind=TRUE)`? Note that in this example there is no similarity whatsoever between input and output. The input is full of real numbers and `NA`s, and the output only has integer numbers, none of them in common with the input. Also, the dimension of the input matrix is 5×7, while the output matrix has dimension 5×2, where the same number of rows is just a coincidence. Is this problem solvable at all? And what if we only give some of the rows (or even a few cells) of the solution?

In this paper, we present a system that is able to induce R programs from: (1) an input data matrix and (2) a partial output matrix filled by the user representing the desired transformation. The system is able to automatically find the operation or set of operations that can be applied to the input to obtain the complete output. Because of the combinatorics of primitives and operations for generating possible transformations, we need to use the characteristics of the input and output matrices, and the primitives themselves, in the form of constraints (dimensions, non-zero values, etc.) in order to reduce the search space. Our system checks that the sequence of compositions is consistent with the dimensions, and completes the output matrix, automatically producing the R code, ready to be inserted in the data science pipeline.

The following section contains an overview of relevant work in programming by example and related areas, and how much this has impacted on languages for data science and the automation of data science in general. Section 3 defines the new problem that we address in this paper, and Sect. 4 presents an enumeration algorithm that is constrained by the matrix dimensions. Section 5 presents some experiments with artificial and real data. Finally, Sect. 6 closes the paper with the applicability of the system and the future work.

2 Related Work

Programming by example (PbE) is a kind of program synthesis or inductive programming [5] in which the system automatically produces programs that match the examples that are provided by a user. Generally, in order to make many PbE applications effective, only a few examples should be sufficient to induce the right solution even when the examples are incomplete. Data transformation using string manipulation domain-specific languages is one of the applications where PbE has been shown very successful (see [1,2,4,7,14,18]): the training data is generated by the user, and we only need a small number of examples. In [6] the authors present a tool for automating the generation of scripts for file manipulation based on string transformations. One of the most recent applications is live programming by example. In this approach and usually via a graphical user interface, programmers receive real-time feedback when writing code. The goal is to use live programming to provide a new way for novice programmers to interact and understand programming, as well as a useful tool for more advanced programmers to develop. In [16] a plug-in for Javascript live coding is presented. The authors use CVC4's Syntax-guided synthesis (SyGuS) algorithm [15].

Most of these systems are focused on string transformations. TaCLe [13] on the other hand, is a system able to reconstruct the formulae used in a data spreadsheet based on a comma-separated file by using the number of cells and constraints to check. However, a tool that is more focused on automatic code generation for data science problems has not been developed yet, covering the different data structures that are common in data science projects and languages, such as matrices, vectors or lists. Two of the most used languages for data science are R[2] and Python[3] [17]. The automation of small but convoluted snippets in these languages could represent an important reduction of the time needed in many data science projects. In this paper we use program synthesis techniques to automatically generate matrix transformation snippets in R, which can be re-used for data preprocessing and postprocessing.

3 Problem Definition

In our approach we assume that there is a set of operations that the user knows and can apply manually to a matrix A in order to obtain a result S. However, the

[2] https://www.r-project.org/.
[3] https://www.python.org/.

operations should be coded in some specific language (in our case, R) and the human needs some assistance to generate the code automatically from a single example. This is the setting that serves as problem formulation:

1. There is an input matrix A, a finite real matrix of size $m \times n$ $(m, n > 0)$.
2. There is also a partially filled matrix B, a finite real matrix of size $m' \times n'$ $(m', n' > 0)$ where only some elements are filled and the rest are empty (represented by '$\cdot$').
3. We look for a function $\hat{f}$ such that $\hat{f}(A) = S$, where S is a finite real matrix of size $m' \times n'$, such that for every non-empty $b_{ij} \in B$ there is $s_{ij} \in S$ such that $b_{ij} = s_{ij}$.
4. The function $\hat{f}$ is expressed as a composition of matrix operations in a given programming language.

As additional criteria we will consider that the representation of $\hat{f}$ in the programming language should be as short as possible, and we will also allow for some precision error ϵ (so that we relax item 3 above with $|b_{ij} - s_{ij}| \leq \epsilon$, instead of $b_{ij} = s_{ij}$). We use the notation $\hat{f}(A) \models_\epsilon B$ to represent this, and say that it *covers* B.

As a basic example, consider the following matrices A and B:

$$A = \begin{bmatrix} 1 & 3 & 5 \\ 4 & 2 & 6 \\ 3 & 8 & 7 \end{bmatrix}$$

$$B = \begin{bmatrix} 8 & 13 & \cdot \end{bmatrix}$$

where A is the input matrix and B the partially-filled output. We try to find $\hat{f}(A) \models_\epsilon B$. In this case the function `colsum` in R, which adds the values columnwise, gives the following matrix S that covers B.

$$S = \begin{bmatrix} 8 & 13 & 18 \end{bmatrix}$$

Note that we look for a system that: (1) works with an input matrix and a partially-filled output matrix, and nothing more, (2) automatically synthesise the composition of primitives in the base programming language that solves the above problem, and (3) export both the complete transformed matrix and the code in R.

As far as we know from the related work seen in the previous section, no other approach is able to solve this problem. This is what we try to do next.

4 Method

The nature of the main criterion used for finding $\hat{f}$, namely the minimisation of the number of primitives involved in the solution, suggests that the problem can be addressed with an enumeration approach. Enumeration is a common approach in other inductive programming scenarios [9–12] but it must always be coupled with some constraints (e.g., types, schemas, etc.) or strong heuristics. In our case, we will use the dimensions of the matrices as the main constraint for reducing the combinatorial explosion.

The number of primitives taken into account for the search is known as the *breadth* (b) of the problem, while the minimum number of such primitives that have to be combined in one solution is known as *depth* (d). Clearly, both depth and breadth highly influence the hardness of the problem, in a way that is usually exponential, $O(b^d)$ [3] affecting the time and resources needed to find the right solution. As said above, for each matrix primitive g we take into account the size of the input and output at any point of the composition, and also some other constraints about minimum size (for instance, calculating correlations requires at least two rows, i.e., $m > 1$).

More formally, for each primitive g we define a tuple $\langle m_{min}, n_{min}, \gamma \rangle$ where m_{min} and n_{min} are the minimum number of rows and columns (respectively) for the input (by default $m_{min} = 1$ and $n_{min} = 1$), and $\gamma : \mathbb{R}^2 \rightarrow \mathbb{R}^2$ is a *type function*, which maps the dimensions of the input matrix to the dimensions of the output matrix. For instance, for $g = \texttt{colSums}$, $\gamma(m,n) = (1,n)$, because g takes a matrix of size $m \times n$ and returns a matrix of size $1 \times n$. Here, $m_{min} = 1$ and $n_{min} = 1$. Similarly, for $g = \texttt{cor}$, $\gamma(m,n) = (n,n)$, because g takes a matrix of size $m \times n$ and returns a matrix of size $n \times n$. Here, $m_{min} = 2$ and $n_{min} = 1$, as we need at least two rows to calculate a correlation.

The whole procedure works as follows (see Algorithm 1):

1. The system can be configured to use a set of primitive functions (G), including for each of them: the minimum values for the size of the input (m_{min}, n_{min}) and the type function γ.
2. For each particular problem to solve, we take the input matrix A and the partially filled matrix B.
3. Being d_{max} the maximum number of operations that can be composed for the transformation, we run the algorithm from $d = 1$ to $d = d_{max}$ building on each iteration all the possible combinations C_d of the form $\{g_1, \ldots, g_d\}$ where each g_i is a function in G.
4. For each combination $\{g_1, \ldots, g_d\}$ in C_d, we take the size of A and we verify if $g_1(A)$ is feasible by its constraints and, in that case, we calculate the output size after g_1 (using its type function γ_1) so producing the input size for the next function g_2 in the combination, and so on for all the primitives. Only if we reach the final g_d and the dimensions of the output matches the dimensions of B, then we really apply the combination $\{g_1, \ldots, g_d\}$ to A and check whether the result covers S, as defined in the previous section. In the positive case, we build $\hat{f}$ as the composition of $\{g_1, \ldots, g_d\}$ and we stop.
5. We repeat this procedure increasing d in each iteration and until $d = d_{max}$ (or the first $\hat{f}$ is found).

As mentioned in the problem formulation we allow for some small precision error ϵ between the cells in S (generated by $\hat{f}$) and the cells that are present in B (and are generated by f).

Algorithm 1
Selecting matrix operations by example

Require: {$A[m \times n]$ *(Input matrix)*}
Require: {$B[m' \times n']$ *(Output matrix partially filled)*}
Require: {BK *(Dataset of matrix functions including in each row the tuple* $\langle g, m_{min}, n_{min}, \gamma \rangle$*)*}
Require: {d_{max} *(Max functions in each solution)*}
Ensure: Find a matrix $S \approx B$

```
d ← 1
found ← False
while !found and d ⩽ d_max do
  C ← permutation(BK, d) {All possible combinations of d functions in BK}
  for all c ∈ C do
    for i ← 1, d do
      valid ← True
      ⟨g, m_min, n_min, γ⟩ ← c[i] {We extract the primitive and its corresponding type function}
      if i = 1 then
        m_input ← m
        n_input ← n
      else
        m_input ← m_output
        n_input ← n_output
      end if
      if m_input < m_min or n_input < n_min then
        valid ← False
        break
      end if
      ⟨m_output, n_output⟩ ← γ(m_input, n_input) {Apply the type function γ to m_input, n_input}
    end for
    if valid and m_output = m' and n_output = n' then
      S ← apply(c, A) {Executes all the functions included in c over the matrix A}
      if S ≈ B then
        found ← True
        break
      end if
    end if
  end for
  d ← d + 1
end while
return c, S
```

---

5 Experiments

We have implemented our system for R, a language and environment for statistical computing and graphics. R operates on named data structures (vectors, matrices, data frames, etc.). In our case, we work with those functions such that input and output are data-related structures (matrices, vectors, etc.). We also take as functions some characteristics that we can extract from the structures (number of rows, number of columns, element on the i position, etc.).

More specifically, we take 45 R functions related to matrices from the *base*[4] and *stats*[5] packages included on R, such as `colMeans(A)`, which computes the

[4] https://stat.ethz.ch/R-manual/R-devel/library/base/html/00Index.html.
[5] https://stat.ethz.ch/R-manual/R-devel/library/stats/html/00Index.html.

Table 1. Example of functions included in the *BK*.

Function	m_{min}	n_{min}	Description
rowSums(A)			Form row sums for numeric values
colSums(A)			Form column sums for numeric values
nrow(A)			Return the number of rows present in A
ncol(A)			Return the number of columns present in A
cor(A)	2		Compute the correlation of A
det(A)			Calculates the determinant of A
is.na(A)			Indicates which elements of Á are missing
!is.na(A)			Indicates which elements of Á are not missing
which(A)			Give the TRUE indices of a logical object
apply(A,1,rev)			Provides a reversed version of A

mean of the columns, or `cor(A)`, which generates the correlation matrix of A. Table 1 shows some of the functions included.

Note that in this preliminary version of the system some functions used (for instance: !, apply...) and some arguments (for instance: 1...) are already added to the functions lists manually for testing. This will be generated dynamically on execution time in future versions.

In order to evaluate the algorithm, we first generate problems and sets of synthetic matrices A for those problems. Next, we test the system with real problems published on Stack Overflow[6].

For replicability and encouraging future research, all the matrices used and the code (also in R) are published on: https://github.com/liconoc/ProgramSynthesis-Matrix.

5.1 Results with Artificial Data

We first have tested the system with synthetic data. For this, we have generated 10 random real matrices of different dimensions $m \times n$ where $m, n \in (2, 10)$. These matrices are filled with numeric values following a uniform distribution between 0 and 100. For each matrix A we have derived 50 random matrices S, generated by combining d random operations to make the true transformation f, where $d = 1..5$ (10 matrices for each d). From every matrix S we generate a matrix B where we replace between 60%..80% of the cells by empty values. In total we have 500 pairs of matrices A, B to test the algorithm with different numbers of operations.

Table 2 shows the accuracy results (percentage of cases where the correct transformation is found). For each value of d (number of operations applied) we can see the correct results, with an overall 95.2% of accuracy.

[6] https://stackoverflow.com/.

5.2 Results with Real Examples

To test our system with real problems, we have used questions and answers from Stack Overflow that are tagged with the r tag and contain matrix transformations. For this, we have used the dataset "R Questions from Stack Overflow" from Kaggle[7], filtering the questions by the title.

Table 2. Number of correct results for matrix transformations using program synthesis with R. d is the number of functions applied to the matrix A.

d	Correct
1	96
2	98
3	94
4	95
5	93
Acc.	95.2%

For instance, one simple question asks to "replace 0's with 1's and vice versa for a diagonal matrix in R". In Fig. 2a and b we can see the original matrix A and the partially filled matrix B used to infer the operation needed to obtain the matrix in Fig. 2c, the expected solution to the problem. The system is able to solve this problem with $d = 1$: $\hat{f} = \texttt{1} - \texttt{A}$.

1.00	0.00	0.00	0.00	0.00
0.00	1.00	0.00	0.00	0.00
0.00	0.00	1.00	0.00	0.00
0.00	0.00	0.00	1.00	0.00
0.00	0.00	0.00	0.00	1.00

(a) Matrix A.

0.00	1.00	1.00	1.00	1.00
.	.	.	.	.
.	.	.	.	.
.	.	.	.	.
.	.	.	.	.

(b) Matrix B.

0.00	1.00	1.00	1.00	1.00
1.00	0.00	1.00	1.00	1.00
1.00	1.00	0.00	1.00	1.00
1.00	1.00	1.00	0.00	1.00
1.00	1.00	1.00	1.00	0.00

(c) Matrix S.

Fig. 2. Matrices A, B and S from the first example of Stack Overflow. In matrix S the 0s have been replaced by 1 and the other way round. For matrix B only the first row is provided.

Our system can also deal with operations related to non-numeric matrices and vectors. For example, another question asks about the "positions of non-NA cells", where one matrix filled with characters can be used as input (see Fig. 3a) and the result is a vector of positions for those values that are not `NA`. With just two filled values, the system is able to solve the problem with $d = 2$: $\hat{f} = \texttt{which(!is.na(A))}$.

[7] https://www.kaggle.com/stackoverflow/rquestions.

a b NA c NA
d e f g h

(a) Matrix A.

1 2 · · · · · ·

(b) Matrix B.

1 2 3 4 6 7 8 10

(c) Matrix S.

Fig. 3. Matrices A,B and S from the example "positions of non-NA cells" from Stack Overflow. Values of matrix A are characters or `NA`. Matrix S is a vector of positions. In matrix B only two values are provided.

A more difficult question asks to "Extract sub-diagonal". Figure 4a shows the A matrix for this example, where S is again a vector of values $S = [2, 6]$, and B only provides a value. In this case, the system produces the function $\hat{f} =$ `diag(A[-1,-ncol(A)])`.

1 4 7
2 5 8
3 6 9

(a) Matrix A.

2 ·

(b) Matrix B.

2 6

(c) Matrix S.

Fig. 4. Matrices A, B and S from the third example "Extract sub-diagonal" from Stack Overflow. Matrix S is a vector with the values of the sub-diagonal of A. In matrix B only one value is provided.

Some examples, however, are not correct. This is because in some cases the cells that are generated are compatible with B but not entirely with S. In these cases more cells filled in B would be needed in order to generate the correct solution.

In total we have tested 15 examples from the dataset and 13 give the correct matrix (see Table 3).

Table 3. Number of correct results for matrix transformations for the examples of Stack Overflow. d is the number of functions applied to the matrix A.

d	Correct
1	6
2	5
3	2
Acc.	86.67%

6 Conclusions and Future Work

The process of generating code automatically can help data scientists when dealing with matrices (or data frames), the most common representation of information in data science projects. When the data scientist is a non-expert in programming (or is obfuscated by some complex transformations), she can now have the resource of producing an example of the input matrix and a few cells of the output matrix, and the system will generate the code for her. This can be used when coding a transformation from scratch, when trying to imitate a transformation seen on a website or a report (or in a different language) or when optimising code (e.g., the data scientist finds a solution using a loop but wonders if there is a more elegant solution in an algebraic form).

In this paper we have presented a new system that is able to generate code in R according to this novel scenario. The system is based on an enumeration approach guided by the number of primitives and pruned by the consistency of the types given by the dimensions of the matrices and the intermediate results.

We have tested our preliminary approach with a synthetic set of 500 matrices and 45 different transformations in R. The results show that the system is able to give the correct result in 95.2% of the cases. We have also tried the system with real examples of problems published on Stack Overflow. In this case, the system achieves 86.7% accuracy. Note that the system could be used interactively, and with some more values, some of these examples could be solved by the system as it is.

As future work we plan to add new characteristics (constraints) over the types (e.g., $m = n$ as input), or over the values (positive values only). We would like to include more primitives from several other packages from R and new data structures apart from matrices. We can also explore more efficient algorithms in such a way we can add constants (arguments for the functions) or multiple pairs of input-output matrices. Of course, the approach can be replicated to synthesise functions from other languages such as Python. Finally, we plan to create a visual interface or an R package to test the system with real users.

References

1. Contreras-Ochando, L., Ferri, C., Hernández-Orallo, J., Martínez-Plumed, F., Ramírez-Quintana, M.J., Katayama, S.: Automated data transformation with inductive programming and dynamic background knowledge. In: Proceedings of the European Conference on Machine Learning and Knowledge Discovery in Databases. ECML PKDD 2019 (2019, to appear)
2. Cropper, A., Tamaddoni-Nezhad, A., Muggleton, S.H.: Meta-interpretive learning of data transformation programs. In: Inoue, K., Ohwada, H., Yamamoto, A. (eds.) ILP 2015. LNCS (LNAI), vol. 9575, pp. 46–59. Springer, Cham (2016). https://doi.org/10.1007/978-3-319-40566-7_4
3. Ferri-Ramírez, C., Hernández-Orallo, J., Ramírez-Quintana, M.J.: Incremental learning of functional logic programs. In: Kuchen, H., Ueda, K. (eds.) FLOPS 2001. LNCS, vol. 2024, pp. 233–247. Springer, Heidelberg (2001). https://doi.org/10.1007/3-540-44716-4_15
4. Gulwani, S.: Automating string processing in spreadsheets using input-output examples. In: Proceedings of 38th Principles of Programming Languages, pp. 317–330 (2011)
5. Gulwani, S., Hernández-Orallo, J., Kitzelmann, E., Muggleton, S.H., Schmid, U., Zorn, B.: Inductive programming meets the real world. Commun. ACM **58**(11), 90–99 (2015)

6. Gulwani, S., Mayer, M., Niksic, F., Piskac, R.: StriSynth: synthesis for live programming. In: 2015 IEEE/ACM 37th IEEE International Conference on Software Engineering, vol. 2, pp. 701–704. IEEE (2015)
7. He, Y., Chu, X., Ganjam, K., Zheng, Y., Narasayya, V., Chaudhuri, S.: Transform-data-by-example (TDE): an extensible search engine for data transformations. Proc. VLDB Endow. **11**(10), 1165–1177 (2018)
8. Jenkins, T.: On the difficulty of learning to program. In: Proceedings of the 3rd Annual Conference of the LTSN Centre for Information and Computer Sciences, vol. 4, pp. 53–58. Citeseer (2002)
9. Katayama, S.: Systematic search for lambda expressions. Trends Funct. Program. **6**, 111–126 (2005)
10. Menon, A., Tamuz, O., Gulwani, S., Lampson, B., Kalai, A.: A machine learning framework for programming by example. In: ICML, pp. 187–195 (2013)
11. Mitchell, T., et al.: Never-ending learning. Commun. ACM **61**(5), 103–115 (2018)
12. Mitchell, T.M., et al.: Theo: A framework for self-improving systems. In: Architectures for Intelligence, pp. 323–355 (1991)
13. Paramonov, S., Kolb, S., Guns, T., De Raedt, L.: TaCLe: learning constraints in tabular data. In: Proceedings of the 2017 ACM on Conference on Information and Knowledge Management. CIKM 2017, pp. 2511–2514. ACM, New York (2017).https://doi.org/10.1145/3132847.3133193
14. Parisotto, E., Mohamed, A.R., Singh, R., Li, L., Zhou, D., Kohli, P.: Neuro-symbolic program synthesis. arXiv preprint arXiv:1611.01855 (2016)
15. Reynolds, A., Tinelli, C.: SyGuS techniques in the core of an SMT solver. arXiv preprint arXiv:1711.10641 (2017)
16. Santolucito, M., Hallahan, W.T., Piskac, R.: Live programming by example. In: Extended Abstracts of the 2019 CHI Conference on Human Factors in Computing Systems, p. INT020. ACM (2019)
17. DataFlair Team: Top 6 Data Science Programming Languages for 2019 (2019). https://data-flair.training/blogs/data-science-programming-languages/
18. Wu, B., Szekely, P., Knoblock, C.A.: Learning data transformation rules through examples: preliminary results. In: Information Integration on the Web, p. 8 (2012)

DeepNotebooks: Deep Probabilistic Models Construct Python Notebooks for Reporting Datasets

Claas Völcker[1(✉)], Alejandro Molina[1], Johannes Neumann[2], Dirk Westermann[2], and Kristian Kersting[1,3]

[1] Machine Learning Group, CS Department, TU Darmstadt, Darmstadt, Germany
c.voelcker@stud.tu-darmstadt.de, {molina,kersting}@cs.tu-darmstadt.de

[2] University Heart and Vascular Center Hamburg, Hamburg, Germany
{jo.neumann,d.westermann}@uke.de

[3] Centre for Cognitive Science, TU Darmstadt, Darmstadt, Germany

Abstract. Machine learning is taking an increasingly relevant role in science, business, entertainment, and other fields. However, the most advanced techniques are still in the hands of well-educated and -funded experts only. To help to democratize machine learning, we propose DeepNotebooks as a novel way to empower a broad spectrum of users, which are not machine learning experts, but might have some basic programming skills and are interested data science. Within the DeepNotebook framework, users feed a cleaned tabular datasets to the system. The system then automatically estimates a deep but tractable probabilistic model and compiles an interactive Python notebook out of it that already contains a preliminary yet comprehensive analysis of the dataset at hand. If the users want to change the parameters of the interactive report or make different queries to the underlying model, they can quickly do that within the DeepNotebook. This flexibility allows the users to interact with the framework in a feedback loop—they can discover patterns and dig deeper into the data using targeted questions, even if they are not experts in machine learning.

1 Introduction

Data science has enjoyed considerable successes in recent years, both in creating more powerful models and broadening the range of potential applications. However, behind all these exceptional success stories, there are troves of human experts, including machine learning and domain experts, statisticians, and computer scientists, among others. These experts focus on different aspects aspect of the data analysis pipeline, from data acquisition and feature engineering to modeling selection, training, and evaluation. As the complexity of each of these tasks increases, even experts can lose track of all the details and nuances of each part of the pipeline. As for non-experts, they might not be aware of best practices nor have a chance to keep track of the rapidly evolving state-of-the-art.

P. Cellier and K. Driessens (Eds.): ECML PKDD 2019 Workshops, CCIS 1167, pp. 28–43, 2020.
https://doi.org/10.1007/978-3-030-43823-4_3

These difficulties have given rise to a new area of research focused on building off-the-shelf machine learning methods that can easily be used by non-experts – automatic machine learning (AutoML).

Indeed, several different approaches to AutoML do already exist, ranging from automatic building blocks for feature engineering [1–3] and model learning [4,5], to automatic reporting as in the Automatic Statistician [6–8] and interactive machine learning notebooks[1]. There is also work on interpreting the computations of modern machine learning models [9–11] as this is of crucial importance to non-experts. However, to the best of our knowledge, there is no framework yet that incorporates modeling, learning, reporting, explainability and interactivity at the same time. The question whether such an exploratory automatic statistician, which is not limited to only investigating a single target variable, is possible, was the seed that grew into the present paper.

Specifically, triggered by the recent successes of deep and tractable probabilistic models, we introduce DeepNotebooks[2]—an interactive system that automatically constructs data reports in the form of Python notebooks using mixed sum-product networks (MSPNs) [12,13]. Similar approaches for modelling heterogeneous data have been explored before [14], leading to the BayesDB system for exploring databases [15]. Instead of exploring a method for approximate inference in databases, DeepNotebooks are built on models for tractable, exact inference for single table data. In addition, they are not only a framework for user interaction with data, but also reporting tool, which performs a preliminary array of common statistical tests. Python notebooks provide an interactive computational environment, in which you can combine code execution, rich text, mathematics, plots, and rich media. A DeepNotebook is therefore not just a data report as it allows non-experts to interactively answer complex queries using tractable inference within the underlying MSPN.

We proceed as follows: We start off by briefly reviewing MSPNs. We then introduce DeepNotebooks. Before concluding, we illustrate them on several datasets, including one on myocardial infarction diagnosis.

2 Automatic Statisticians via Deep Probabilistic Models

The vision of an automatic statistician [6–8] is to build statistical models with minimal input from experts in statistics and machine learning. Probabilistic graphical models (PGMs) [16] are arguably a promising tool for realizing this vision. They can solve many ML tasks by estimating a distribution and then answering probabilistic queries. Consider, e.g. predictive modeling. One may train a PGM and use inference to obtain probabilistic answers to queries; for multi-class classification answering the query $\arg\max_c P(\text{Class} = c|\text{data})$ gives us the most likely class according to our model. Alternatively, we can ask which is

[1] www.h2o.ai/h2o-old/h2o-flow/.

[2] Code available at https://github.com/cvoelcker/DeepNotebooks, an example of a generated DeepNotebooks at https://cvoelcker.github.io/DeepNotebooks/demo/deepnotebook.html.

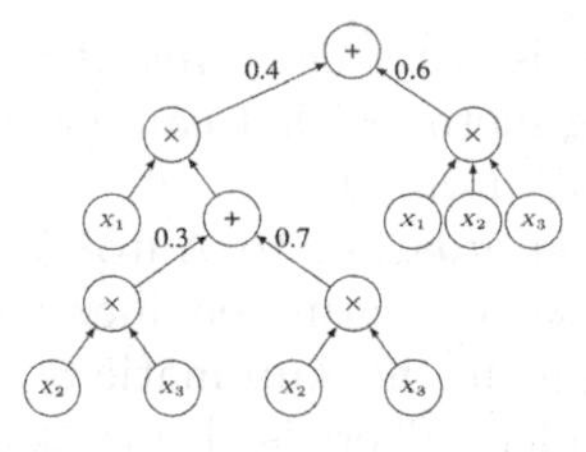

Fig. 1. An example of a valid SPN. Here, x_1, x_2 and x_3 are random variables modelled by histograms. The structure represents the joint distribution $P(x_1, x_2, x_3)$.

the most likely value of any feature: $\arg\max_x P(X = x|\text{evidence})$. Unfortunately, inference in unrestricted PGMs is intractable.

2.1 Deep and Tractable Probabilistic Models

Motivated by the importance of efficient inference for large-scale applications, a substantial amount of work has been devoted to learning probabilistic models for which inference is guaranteed to be tractable. Examples of these model classes include sum-product networks (SPNs) [17] and in particular mixed sum-product networks (MSPNs) [12], hinge-loss Markov random fields [18], and tractable higher-order potentials [19]. In this work, we have focused on SPNs.

Being instances of Arithmetic Circuits (ACs) [20], SPNs are a deep architecture that can represent high-treewidth models [21] and facilitate fast, exact inference for a range of queries in time linear in the network size [17]. They inherit universal approximation properties from mixture models – a mixture model is simply a "shallow" SPN with a single sum node. Consequently, SPNs can represent any prediction function, very much like deep neural networks. However, having exact probabilistic inference at hand offers an advantage not present in other PGMs and deep neural networks. One can compare the probabilities computed by different models and not only solve classification or regression problems, but also do anomaly detection at the same time while taking into account the statistical nature of the data. Also, instead of e.g. classical deep neural networks, SPNs are not only trained to predict the probability of a single target variable. This makes them especially useful in a data exploration context, where the true target of the investigation might not be known prior. Furthermore, any measures based on probabilities such as entropy, mutual information, and information gain can be computed efficiently. In the present paper, we will also show this for Shapley values [10].

2.2 Mixed Sum-Product Networks (MSPNs)

DeepNotebooks resort to MSPNs, as they are currently the only model able to build an SPN structure in a likelihood-agnostic way – using piecewise polynomials to encode the leaf distributions – therefore being suitable for our heterogeneous setting. MSPN learning is also able to deal with missing or unknown values out of the box, by implicit marginalization over the missing features. This makes them applicable in contexts where common imputation methods might not be able to easily fill in a lot of the data.

Representation of MSPNs: Formally, an MSPN is a rooted directed acyclic graph, comprising *sum*, *product*, and *leaf* nodes as seen in Fig. 1. The scope of an MSPN is the set of random variables appearing on the network. More precisely, an MSPN can be defined recursively as follows:

1. a tractable univariate distribution is an MSPN.
2. a product of MSPNs defined over different scopes is an MSPN, and
3. a convex combination of MSPNs over the same scope is an MSPN.

Here, a product node encodes a factorization over independent distributions defined over different random variables, while a sum node stands for a mixture of distributions defined over the same variables. From this definition, it follows that the joint distribution modeled by an MSPN is a valid probability distribution, i.e. each complete and partial evidence inference query produces a consistent probability value [17,22]. This also implies that we can construct multivariate distributions from simpler univariate ones. To build the structure in a likelihood-agnostic way, we make a piecewise approximation to the leaf distributions. In their purest form, piecewise constant functions are often adopted in the form of histograms or staircase functions. More expressive approximations are comprised of mixtures of truncated polynomials and exponentials.

Tractable Inference in MSPNs. To answer probabilistic queries in an MSPN, we evaluate the nodes starting at the leaves. Given some evidence, the probability output of querying leaf distributions is propagated bottom up. For product nodes, the values of the child nodes are multiplied and propagated to their parents. For sum nodes, instead, we sum the weighted values of the child nodes. The value at the root indicates the probability of the asked query.

To compute marginals, i.e., the probability of partial configurations, we set the probability at the leaves for those variables to 1 and then proceed as before. All these operations traverse the tree at most twice and therefore can be achieved in linear time w.r.t. the size of the MSPN.

Learning MSPNs. Existing SPN learning works focus on learning the SPN parameters given a structure [23–25] or jointly learn both the structure and the parameters [26–28]. A particular prominent approach is LearnSPN [29,30], which recursively partitions a data matrix using hierarchical co-clustering. In particular, LearnSPN alternates between partitioning features into independent groups, inducing a product node, and clustering the data instances, inducing a sum node. As the base step, univariate likelihood models for single features are induced. To learn MSPNs, the LearnSPN algorithm is adapted to deal with the lack of parametric forms by performing a partitioning over mixed continuous and discrete data by exploiting a randomized approximation of the Hirschfeld-Gebelein-Rényi Maximum Correlation Coefficient (RDC) [31]. Thus, MSPNs maintain their expressiveness while representing a wide range of statistical data

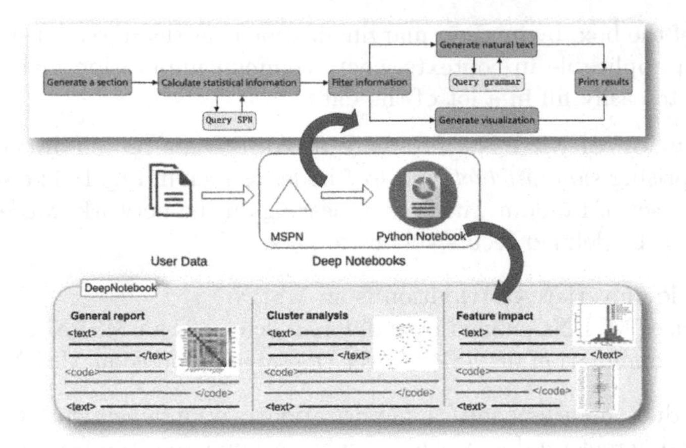

Fig. 2. Illustration of DeepNotebooks. A user feeds data into the system, and an MSPN is trained. The MSPN along with analysis information computed from the MSPN are then embedded into a Jupyter Python notebook, producing an interactive data report that uses the MSPN as "virtual statistical machine".

types, which can even be estimated automatically from data [13], resulting in an automatic exploratory density estimation approach.

3 DeepNotebooks – Constructing Data Reports in the Form of Python Notebooks Based on MSPNs

Generally, the idea behind DeepNotebooks can be defined as follows: *A DeepNoteboook for a dataset D is a Jupyter notebook* [32] *with an embedded (deep) probabilistic model encoding the distribution of D. The model is used used to precompute the cells of the notebook describing the dataset D.*

The workflow of DeepNotebooks is depicted in Fig. 2: A user loads a dataset into the system, which automatically creates a probabilistic model that encodes the distribution of the data, in our case an MSPN. Using the MSPN, the system proceeds without user interaction and performs statistical analysis based on the model. Both the model and the analysis are then stored in a Jupyter notebook, the DeepNotebook. The user then opens the DeepNotebook where they can see the automatically generated report, as well as interact with the model. Changing the parameters of the reports is easy, as well as doing further analysis or even evaluating other datasets with the given model. All those options and more are available to the user from within the DeepNotebook. Each generated DeepNotebook contains three major sections, cf. Fig. 2:

Section 1: a general report on descriptive statistics and feature marginals,
Section 2: an analysis of the clusters encoded by the SPN structure
Section 3: report of the impact of features on conditional probabilities,

Exploring the iris dataset

This report describes the dataset iris and contains general statistical information and an analysis on the influence different features and subgroups of the data have on each other. The first part of the report contains general statistical information about the dataset and an analysis of the variables and probability distributions.
The second part focusses on a subgroup analysis of the data. Different clusters identified by the network are analyzed and compared to give an insight into the structure of the data. Finally the influence different variables have on the predictive capabilities of the model are analyzes.
The whole report is generated by fitting a sum product network to the data and extracting all information from this model.

Report framework created @ TU Darmstadt

Fig. 3. Textual introduction to the DeepNotebook automatically written for Iris.

which are wrapped into natural text produced by templates and by a probabilistic grammar making the report more user-friendly, cf. Fig. 3. Normally, the notebook reports the top 5 results (variables with the highest correlation, variables with the most impact on a prediction), but the user can also provide thresholds for reporting or specify which variables they are specifically interested in. We will now describe each section of a DeepNotebook in more detail.

DeepNotebook Section 1 - General Report. The general report provides a description of the data at hand. It includes descriptive statistics like correlations, dependencies, and mutual information among the random variables. Since the network represents the full joint probability density function of all variables, it allows efficient computation of these common statistical measures. Each calculation only requires one full bottom-up evaluation of the MSPN. The expectations of each variable can be computed by propagating expectations from the leaves to the root and treating each sum node as a weighted sum of expectations. The variable correlations can be computed similarly by recursively evaluating the covariance of the variables at each node. Covariance and correlation are only defined for ordered attributes in the data. Therefore, these measures cannot be computed for all variable combinations when the dataset contains categorical features. For the coupling between a categorical and a continuous variable, the notebook reports the coefficient of variation. For categorical variables without an ordering, normalized mutual information (MI) is reported.

Due to the efficient inference, it is possible to present partial dependency plots [33] for categorical and continuous variables. By default, a DeepNotebook selects all those features, which show a linkage (either due to covariance or MI) above a certain threshold. This can be adapted dynamically by the users according to their specific needs. Similar to the other sections, the notebook also contains a written explanation of the visualization, constructed from the probabilistic grammar shown in Fig. 4.

DeepNotebook Section 2 - Cluster Analysis. The MSPN structure contains an implicit hierarchical clustering due to the sum nodes. A DeepNotebook uses this to explain sub-clusters of the data and to provide descriptions for them. Furthermore, the distribution of variance for each variable between the clusters is calculated and presented. This allows users to understand the different parts of the underlying model better. Intuitively, if a particular cluster explains a large

```
<start>                  ::= <fullClause> | ... omitted for brevity
<fullClause>             ::= <subject_feature> <object_dependency> |
 ↪  <subject_dependency> <object_feature>
<subject_dependency>     ::= There is a {strength} {neg_pos} <dependency> | The model
 ↪  shows a {strength} {direction} <dependency>
<object_feature>         ::= <conjunctionFor> <features?> "{x}" and "{y}"
<subject_feature>        ::= <features?> "{x}" and "{y}" have
<object_dependency>      ::= a {strength} {neg_pos} <dependency>
<conjunctionFor>         ::= between | for
<dependency>             ::= <linear?> dependency | <linear?> relation | <linear?>
 ↪  relationship
<features>               ::= the features
<conjunctionWhile>       ::= , while | , but | . on the other hand
```

Fig. 4. Parts of the grammar used for producing correlation descriptions. Variables with a "?" at the end are randomly included/omitted for variation. Variables in curly brackets are replaced with the computed values from the MSPN.

part of the variance of an interesting feature, this cluster and its constituent nodes are important for a more in-depth analysis.

DeepNotebook Section 3 - Feature Impact. Finally, a DeepNotebook computes different conditional probabilities for important variables and analyzes the influence of the features on predictions. To do this, each categorical variable is treated as a target variable separately, and the SPN is used as a predictive model. These predictions are then analyzed using the methods proposed by Robnik-Šikonja and Kononenko [34], Baehrens et al. [35] and Štrumbelj and Kononenko [36]. These explanation approaches allow the users to understand how different variables change the conditional probability of others and to estimate the importance of a feature for classification. They require only the computation of marginals, or gradients on the network. Due to the graph structure of the MSPN, gradients can be computed by a simple backward pass through the network using automatic differentiation. Marginalization of features is also easy in MSPNs [17]. For more details about the computations, we refer to Sect. 4.

The information is aggregated and normalized to provide an easy overview. Using Baehrens et al. [35]'s approach, the gradients are computed for each point in the original dataset and then normalized. This normalization is important, as the piecewise linear structure of the MSPN can result in very sharp edges with correspondingly large gradients. The normalized gradients represent relative importance for each feature and datapoint. These are then aggregated into one plot per feature and prediction, which describes the relative importance for the prediction. With significant computational resources, users can also use Shapley values [37] to estimate feature importance, which generalize the gradient approach but requires a Monte Carlo sampling step. Overall feature importance for each possible prediction attribute is then summarized using the mean squared distance of each gradient component to zero. This assures that features which never have any local impact on the classification are also assumed to not contribute to the impact globally. Finally, the Shapley values are visualized.

Since DeepNotebooks are Jupyter notebooks, the users can add more cells, access the model and the data, and add arbitrary Python code for further queries and analysis. A DeepNotebook therefore serves as an easy and accessible introduction to a dataset and enables a user to employ the reported results in their own data analytics pipeline later on. The data science loop does not start with an empty but with a pre-filled Python notebook, "programmed" by the machine.

4 Computing Statistical Measures Using MSPNs

Each section of a DeepNotebook provides a different view on the data at hand and is based on statistical measures computed form MSPNs as underlying "virtual statistical machine". Showing how to compute them is one of our main technical contributions.

Computing Covariance Using MSPNs. Calculating the covariance of two variables in a distribution can be decomposed into computing the joint expectation and the marginal expectation of each variable. The graph structure of an SPN allows an algorithm to calculate the moments of a probability function directly from the network, in one bottom-up pass. At a sum node, the moment of the distribution can be calculated as follows: $m_k = \mathbb{E}[x^k] = \sum p_i \mathbb{E}[x^k] = \sum p_i m_i^k$. At a product node, the moments of independent variables are also independent, and therefore the moment of the child nodes can just be combined in a vector. At a leaf node, the moments need to be calculated according to the distributions. In the case of MSPNs, all leaves are piecewise linear density approximations, therefore it is very easy to calculate the required integral for the estimation, since all moments are polynomial functions of the base points. Using the moments as computational blocks, it is possible to compute the correlation matrix in closed form from the covariance matrix of the whole probability density function.

The joint expectation can also be calculated efficiently in a similar manner: First, the means of all leaf nodes are calculated independently. These are then combined at the sum and product nodes in a bottom-up-pass. At a product node, due to the assumption of independence, the joint expectation is equal to the product of the expectation: $\mathbb{E}[xy] = \mathbb{E}[x] \cdot \mathbb{E}[y]$. At a sum node, the expectations are multiplied by the weights and summed together. Finally, the correlation can be obtained by normalizing the covariance matrix by the variances of the features.

Dependencies Among Variables Using the Law of Total Variance. When dealing with general tabular data, it is necessary to deal with categorical variables. In this case, the covariance is not defined, and therefore we use the coefficient of determination as a measure for categorical-continuous variables and the mutual information for categorical-categorical dependence. Both are normalized between 0 and 1 and serve a similar purpose of estimating variable dependency as the correlation. The coefficient of determination between a categorical variable X and a continuous variable Y can be calculated as follows. If the categorical variable is assumed to correspond to clusters in the continuous one, the coefficient shows that the total variance of Y results from adding the intra- and inter-cluster variance:

$$1 = \frac{E[\sigma^2(p(Y|X))]}{\sigma^2(p(Y))} + \frac{\sigma^2(E[p(Y|X)])}{\sigma^2(p(Y))} .$$

The first term approaches zero as the clusters become smaller and more and more separated, while the second term approaches zero if the conditional means of the clusters do not vary significantly. To compute them, we extended the algorithm for computing mean and variance to conditional probabilities in MSPNs.

Compiling Conditional MSPNs from MSPNs. Calculating moments as presented above, marginalizes the MSPNs over and over. We can optimize that by compiling a network that computes the conditional probability function $p(x|y)$. At a product node, the probability of $p(x)$ and $p(y)$ are independent of each other and therefore the conditional probability $p(x|y)$ equals the marginal $p(x)$. The leaf node representing $p_i(y)$ is omitted from the graph. At a sum node, the conditional probability function reads as

$$p(x|y) = p(y)^{-1} \sum_i \alpha_i p_i(x, y) = \sum_i \alpha_i p_i(y) p(y)^{-1} p(x) .$$

The probability $p_i(y)$ for each child serves as an update on the weights of the sum node. This assumes that the probabilities of x and y are independent for each child of the sum node, which is guaranteed if the algorithm is run bottom-up on the network as $p(y)$ has already been removed for all children. After extracting the conditional MSPN, the algorithm detailed above can be run to get the conditional means and variances of the continuous variable. Likewise, one can compute the mutual information:

$$\text{MI}(x, y) = \frac{I(x, y)}{\sqrt{H(x)H(y)}} = \frac{\sum_x \sum_y p(x, y)(\log(p(x, y)) - \log(p(x)p(y)))}{\sqrt{\sum_x p(x)\log(p(x)) \sum_y p(y)\log(p(y))}} .$$

Indeed, mutual information has been used in the context of evaluating (M)SPNs [38], to visualize the connection between two variables. But evaluating the equation above using a numeric method by repeatedly calculating the needed probabilities for continuous features is potentially slow since the probability functions represented by MSPNs can be non-smooth. This is the reason this framework uses correlation for the dependency between continuous variables since approximating the mutual information becomes practically intractable for more complex marginal distributions, which would incur a runtime overhead not feasible in data exploration settings. For categorical variables, where the possible states are finite, and often few, the mutual information can be calculated precisely using the equation above.

Estimating Shapley Explanation Values from MSPNs. SHAP values [10,36] estimate the impact of a feature on a single classification using the game-theoretic concept of Shapley values. These values represent the contribution each feature brings to the outcome of the classification by looking at subsets of features. In general, a complete calculation of these values for a classifier is intractable, because the number of possible subsets of features grows exponentially, but they can be estimated using Monte Carlo sampling [36]. Since MSPNs have a natural way of marginalizing over missing features, this can be done efficiently without using interpolation or summation over missing values.

5 Illustrations of DeepNotebooks

To investigate DeepNotbooks empirically, we implemented the system in Python using the SPFlow library [39] for learning the MSPN. Then we generated DeepNotebooks for four well known UCI datasets [40]. We used the Iris dataset to develop and test all algorithms and descriptions. We then generated DeepNotebooks on the Titanic, Boston Housing and Adult datasets. As a final validation, we generated a DeepNotebook for a real-world medical dataset comprised of information on heart infarct patients, which has not been studied in the context of machine learning or exploratory data analysis before.

Experimental Protocol. The Iris and Boston Housing datasets were used as provided by the sklearn library [41], while the Titanic and Adult datasets were cleaned and preprocessed. Finally, the medical dataset considers diagnosis of myocardial infarction using high-sensitivity troponin I 1-h [42]. The dataset contains a large number of variables and a lot of missing values since not all patients are subject to all test procedures. We filtered this dataset by estimating the 20 most relevant attributes for diagnosis by using gradient tree boosting. We then generated a DeepNotebook to further investigate the relationship of these features to each other and the final diagnosis. For each dataset, we investigated three questions to assess the usability of the report for exploratory data analysis: Does the report reflect patterns in the data as expected from prior knowledge?, are there unexpected results?, and do these reflect genuine information discernible from the data?. Together, these questions aim at deducing whether the generated report provides reasonable insight into the data. Since the datasets are originally intended for classification or regression, we focused on understanding the relationship between the features and the label.

Correlation and Statistical Measures. For all datasets, we found that an overview of the marginal distributions can help the user to assess the general shape of the data quickly. The histograms calculated from the MSPN correspond to empirical histograms of the data, albeit smoothed by the training process.

Figure 5 shows the correlation and determination coefficients for the UCI datasets. For the Boston housing data, the correlation already captures many important relationships within the data. This is to be expected, as the Boston housing data is specifically intended to showcase simple regression models and

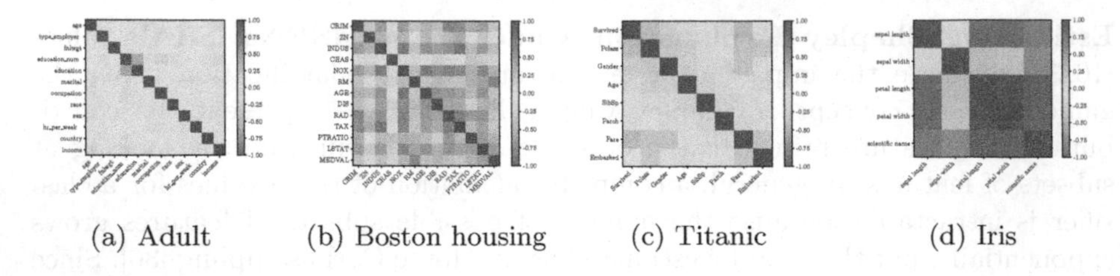

(a) Adult (b) Boston housing (c) Titanic (d) Iris

Fig. 5. MSPN Correlations reported in the DeepNotebooks on four UCI datasets.

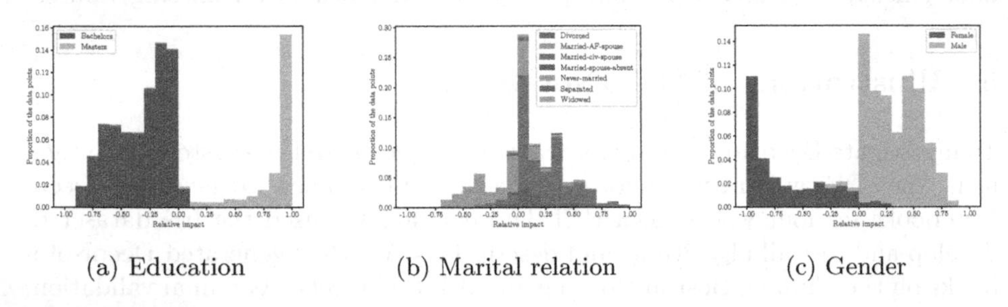

(a) Education (b) Marital relation (c) Gender

Fig. 6. Relative impact of the features with the widest spread on classifying high income in the Adult dataset as reported in the DeepNotebook.

linear correlations. Similarly, the Iris dataset contains a lot of well known dependencies. On the Titanic and Adult dataset, the descriptive statistics are non-informative, since the MSPN finds nearly no correlations within the data. The only significant finding in the Adult data results from two redundant attributes, the "education level" and a numeric representation thereof.

For the medical dataset, the mutual information (not shown here) indicates a clear dependence between the diagnosis and the troponin levels of a patient, which is a well known medical indicator for cardiovascular disease. The troponin levels of a patient at different test times were also clearly correlated with each other and less strongly with most other features, indicating their medical relevance among the tests. Other weaker dependencies do not warrant a closer inspection on the first pass, but might be interesting for a second, more thorough, investigation. Since all features were already selected as being predictive for the diagnosis, this was counter-intuitive, but mutual information and correlation consider only pairwise interactions. This highlights the importance of non traditional statistical tests, like feature importance analysis for prediction.

Explaining Predictions. We found that explaining predictions can highlight variable interactions, which are not directly evident from correlation measures alone. On the Adult dataset, the variable most commonly chosen as the target for classification analysis is the variable "income", which has two possible values, representing a yearly income below or above USD 50,000 respectively. The predictive precision of DeepNotebook for this target was 76.28%. To assess the

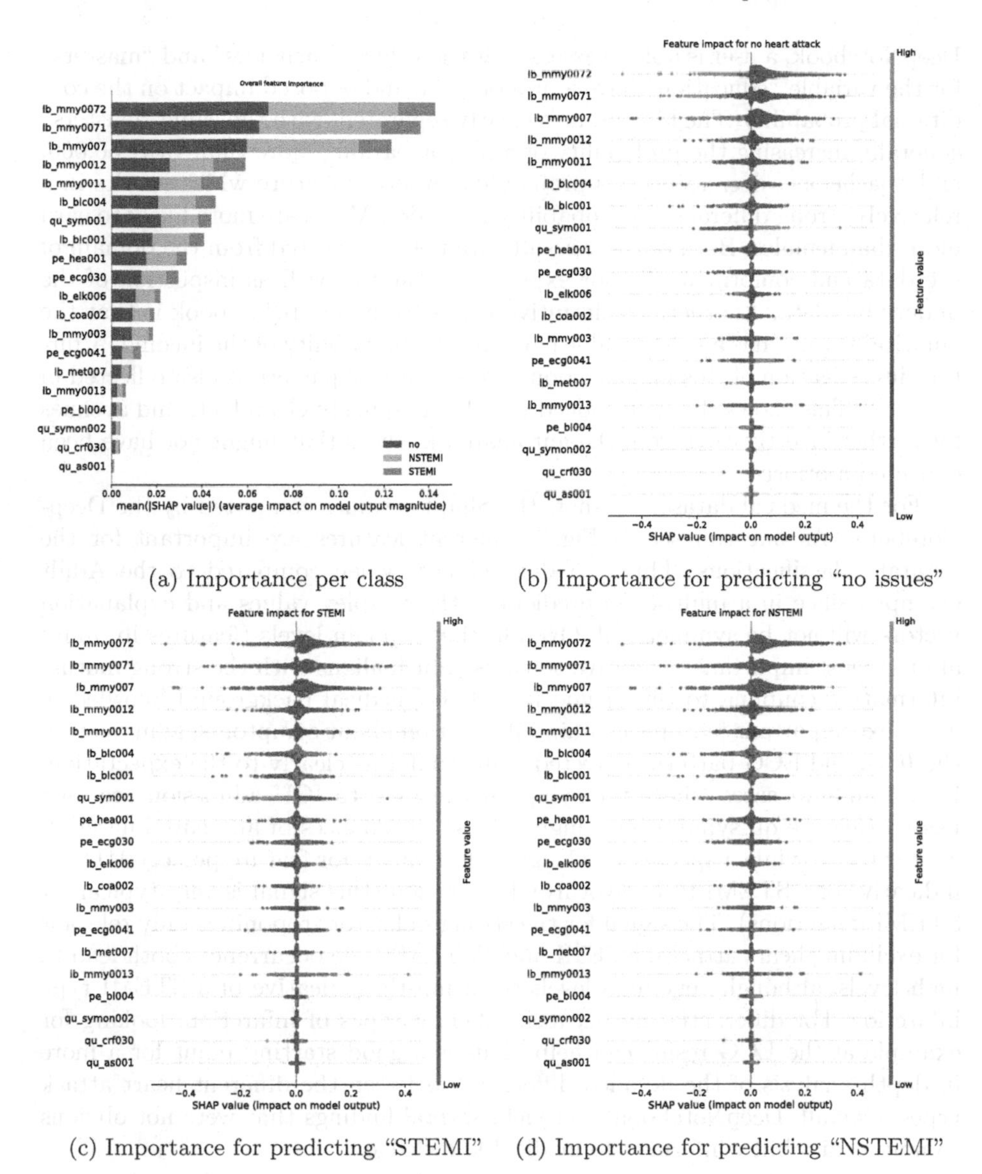

(a) Importance per class (b) Importance for predicting "no issues"

(c) Importance for predicting "STEMI" (d) Importance for predicting "NSTEMI"

Fig. 7. Shapley impact values for the diagnosis prediction on the medical dataset. Grey dots visualize values for other class predictions. (Color figure online)

usefulness of the feature importance and impact measures, this classification was investigated in more detail.

Figure 6 shows that the normalized gradient strengths for these features computed by the DeepNotebook. One can clearly see that "education level", "sex", and "marital status" are informative features for the prediction with a clear impact. Also, by inspecting the visual explanations automatically created in a

DeepNotebook, a user is able to assess that the values "bachelors" and "masters" for the variable "education" have a pronounced, and opposed impact on the conditional probability. The histogram is clearly separated, with the value "masters" generally increasing the probability of a person earning more than USD 50,000, and "bachelors" decreasing this probability. Another feature which results in a relatively strong difference in probability is gender. Males are more likely to earn more than females. Both of these results are not unexpected from the domain of the data and conform with prior expectations and as well as inspection of the underlying data. Another, less intuitive result of the DeepNotebook is that the "marital status" has a recognizable effect on the probability of the income. A further investigation of this phenomenon shows that this pattern is also reflected in the data. This shows that it is indeed possible to quickly glean facts and avenues for further investigation from the automated analysis that might not have been expected a priori.

For the medical dataset we show the Shapley values computed by the DeepNotebook. As one can see in Fig. 7, different features are important for the separate classifications. This is a distinct case when compared to the Adult example, since in a multi-class prediction, the Shapley values and explanation vectors will not be symmetrical. Overall, the troponin levels (features lb_mmy) are the most important predictive features, which aligns with the strong mutual information coupling to the diagnosis and the medical background knowledge. The next important features contain information about symptoms, admission to the ICU, and ECG patterns detected. This conforms clearly to the expectation, for example in cases where the symptoms leading to ICU admission are long passed (feature qu_sym001 with high values) the chances of an acute infarction are far lower, while a specific ECG signal (low values for feature pe_ecg0041) are indicative of a STEMI type myocardial infarction (this signal is very typical for STEMI infarctions). The signal for the strong indicator troponin is only relevant for excluding heart attacks, STEMI and NSTEMI type occurrences both lead to high levels, although very high levels seem mostly indicative of a STEMI type infarction. For differentiating between different types of infarction, looking for example at the ECG result can help. This is a good starting point for a more in depth analysis of the detailed differences between the different heart attack types. Overall, DeepNotebooks can yield several findings that were not obvious to non-medics but conformed to medical knowledge.

6 Conclusions

We have presented DeepNotebooks—a novel way of interacting with data using a deep probabilistic model in the background. The generated reports automatically capture several insights from the data presented in a natural, comprehensible way. The automatic evaluation presented in written and graphical form enables domain experts that are not machine learning experts to get feedback instantly and to explore their data at their own pace. Changing the parameters of the generated report allows a user to choose between an in-depth analysis and a quick overview of the most important patterns. Also, since the data reports are Jupyter notebooks, the results reported are highly interactive and flexible. Overall, the example DeepNotebooks show that they allow one to find patterns in the data, which conform to prior expectation, but also result in novel findings. Given these insights, the user can directly investigate the model and data further using standard Python.

Nevertheless, DeepNotebooks are only a starting point and many things are left to be done. One should extend DeepNotebooks to include other statistical measures. Currently, DeepNotebooks are also specifically focused on analyzing categorical datasets. They should be extended to analyzing regression and time series data. Extending SPNs to provide better or even counterfactual explanations of the underlying model is another interesting avenue. Incorporating other model agnostic or developing similar measures specifically for SPNs could provide additional insight into the predictive capabilities of the network. Likewise, extracting Bayesian and Markov networks from SPNs would also lead to additional insights into the underlying data. Finally, there are many SPN learning algorithms with different properties. A thorough investigation of these, especially concerning how easy they are to use and tune for a non-expert user, would greatly improve the usability of the method for a wide audience.

Acknowledgements. The authors thank the reviewers for their valuable feedback. They also thank Antonio Vergari, Robert Peharz, and Isabel Valera for valuable discussions on DeepNotebooks. They also acknowledge the support of the BMBF project "Artificial intelligence for diagnosis of myocardial infarction" (B19-003 EXT) as well as of the Rhine-Main Universities Network for "Deep Continuous-Discrete Machine Learning" (DeCoDeML). Major parts of the work have been done as part of the B.Sc. thesis of CV [43].

References

1. Lam, H.T., et al.: One button machine for automating feature engineering in relational databases. arXiv preprint arXiv:1706.00327 (2017)
2. Anderson, M.R., et al.: Brainwash: a data system for feature engineering. In: CIDR (2013)
3. Zhou, Y., et al.: Parallel feature selection inspired by group testing. In: Advances in Neural Information Processing Systems, pp. 3554–3562 (2014)
4. Feurer, M., et al.: Efficient and robust automated machine learning. In: Advances in Neural Information Processing Systems, pp. 2962–2970 (2015)
5. Mendoza, H., et al.: Towards automatically-tuned neural networks. In: Workshop on Automatic Machine Learning, pp. 58–65 (2016)
6. Duvenaud, D.K., et al.: Structure discovery in nonparametric regression through compositional kernel search. In: Proceedings of ICML, pp. 1166–1174 (2013)
7. Lloyd, J.R., et al.: Automatic construction and natural-language description of nonparametric regression models. In: Proceedings of AAAI, pp. 1242–1250 (2014)
8. Kim, H., Teh, Y.W.: Scaling up the automatic statistician: scalable structure discovery using gaussian processes. In: AISTATS, pp. 575–584 (2018)

9. Ribeiro, M.T., Singh, S., Guestrin, C.: Why should I trust you? Explaining the predictions of any classifier. In: Proceedings of the 22nd ACM SIGKDD International Conference on Knowledge Discovery and Data Mining, pp. 1135–1144. ACM (2016)
10. Lundberg, S.M., Lee, S.-I.: A unified approach to interpreting model predictions. In: Advances in Neural Information Processing Systems, pp. 4765–4774 (2017)
11. Lapuschkin, S., et al.: Unmasking Clever Hans predictors and assessing what machines really learn. Nat. Commun. **10** (2019). Article no. 1096. https://www.nature.com/articles/s41467-019-08987-4
12. Molina, A., et al.: Mixed sum-product networks: a deep architecture for hybrid domains. In: AAAI (2018)
13. Vergari, A., et al.: Automatic Bayesian density analysis. In: Proceedings of the AAAI Conference on Artificial Intelligence (AAAI) (2019)
14. Mansinghka, V.K., et al.: CrossCat: a fully Bayesian, nonparametric method for analyzing heterogeneous, high-dimensional data. J. Mach. Learn. Res. **17**(138), 1–49 (2016)
15. Mansinghka, V.K., et al.: BayesDB: a probabilistic programming system for querying the probable implications of data. arXiv preprint arXiv:1512.05006 (2015)
16. Koller, D., Friedman, N.: Probabilistic Graphical Models: Principles and Techniques. MIT Press, Cambridge (2009)
17. Poon, H., Domingos, P.: Sum-product networks: a new deep architecture. In: UAI (2011)
18. Bach, S.H., et al.: Hinge-loss Markov random fields and probabilistic soft logic. JMLR **18**, 109:1–109:67 (2017)
19. Tarlow, D., Givoni, I.E., Zemel, R.S.: HOP-MAP: efficient message passing with high order potentials. In: Proceedings of the Thirteenth International Conference on Artificial Intelligence and Statistics. AISTATS 2010, Chia Laguna Resort, Sardinia, Italy, 13–15 May 2010, pp. 812–819 (2010)
20. Choi, A., Darwiche, A.: On relaxing determinism in arithmetic circuits. In: Proceedings of ICML, pp. 825–833 (2017)
21. Zhao, H., Melibari, M., Poupart, P.: On the relationship between sum-product networks and Bayesian networks. In: ICML (2015)
22. Peharz, R., et al.: On theoretical properties of sum-product networks. In: AISTATS (2015)
23. Gens, R., Domingos, P.: Discriminative learning of sum-product networks. In: NIPS (2012)
24. Trapp, M., et al.: Safe semi-supervised learning of sum-product networks. In: UAI (2017)
25. Zhao, H., Poupart, P., Gordon, G.J.: A unified approach for learning the parameters of sum-product networks. In: NIPS, pp. 433–441 (2016)
26. Dennis, A., Ventura, D.: Learning the architecture of sum-product networks using clustering on variables. In: NIPS (2012)
27. Dennis, A., Ventura, D.: Greedy structure search for sum-product networks. In: IJCAI 2015, Buenos Aires, Argentina, pp. 932–938. AAAI Press (2015). ISBN: 978-1-57735-738-4
28. Peharz, R., Geiger, B.C., Pernkopf, F.: Greedy part-wise learning of sum-product networks. In: Blockeel, H., Kersting, K., Nijssen, S., Železný, F. (eds.) ECML PKDD 2013. LNCS (LNAI), vol. 8189, pp. 612–627. Springer, Heidelberg (2013). https://doi.org/10.1007/978-3-642-40991-2_39
29. Gens, R., Domingos, P.: Learning the structure of sum-product networks. In: ICML, pp. 873–880 (2013)

30. Vergari, A., Di Mauro, N., Esposito, F.: Simplifying, regularizing and strengthening sum-product network structure learning. In: Appice, A., Rodrigues, P.P., Santos Costa, V., Gama, J., Jorge, A., Soares, C. (eds.) ECML PKDD 2015. LNCS (LNAI), vol. 9285, pp. 343–358. Springer, Cham (2015). https://doi.org/10.1007/978-3-319-23525-7_21
31. Lopez-Paz, D., Hennig, P., Schölkopf, B.: The randomized dependence coefficient. In: NIPS, pp. 1–9 (2013)
32. Kluyver, T., et al.: Jupyter notebooks - a publishing format for reproducible computational workflows. In: Loizides, F., Schmidt, B. (eds.) Positioning and Power in Academic Publishing: Players, Agents and Agendas, pp. 87–90. IOS Press (2016)
33. Molnar, C.: Interpretable Machine Learning (2018). https://christophm.github.io/interpretable-ml-book/. Accessed 4 June 2019
34. Robnik-Šikonja, M., Kononenko, I.: Explaining classifications for individual instances. IEEE Trans. Knowl. Data Eng. **20**, 589–600 (2008)
35. Baehrens, D., et al.: How to explain individual classification decisions. J. Mach. Learn. Res. **11**, 1803–1831 (2010)
36. Štrumbelj, E., Kononenko, I.: Explaining prediction models and individual predictions with feature contributions. Knowl. Inf. Syst. **41**(3), 647–665 (2013). https://doi.org/10.1007/s10115-013-0679-x
37. Lundberg, S.M., et al.: Explainable machine-learning predictions for the prevention of hypoxaemia during surgery. Nat. Biomed. Eng. **2**(10), 749 (2018)
38. Molina, A., et al.: Mixed sum-product networks: a deep architecture for hybrid domains. In: AAAI (2018)
39. Molina, A., et al.: SPFlow: an easy and extensible library for deep probabilistic learning using sum-product networks (2019). eprint: arXiv:1901.03704
40. Dheeru, D., Taniskidou, E.K.: UCI machine learning repository. Technical report University of California, Irvine, School of Information and Computer Sciences (2017)
41. Pedregosa, F., et al.: Scikit-learn: machine learning in Python. J. Mach. Learn. Res. **12**, 2825–2830 (2011)
42. Neumann, J.T., et al.: Diagnosis of myocardial infarction using a high-sensitivity troponin I 1-hour algorithm. JAMA Cardiol. **1**(4), 397–404 (2016)
43. Völcker, C.: DeepNotebooks - interactive data analysis using sum- product networks. B.Sc. thesis. TU Darmstadt (2018)

HyperUCB: Hyperparameter Optimization Using Contextual Bandits

Maryam Tavakol[1(✉)], Sebastian Mair[2], and Katharina Morik[1]

[1] Technical University of Dortmund, Dortmund, Germany
{maryam.tavakol,katharina.morik}@tu-dortmund.de
[2] Leuphana University of Lüneburg, Lüneburg, Germany
mair@leuphana.de

Abstract. Setting the optimal hyperparameters of a learning algorithm is a crucial task. Common approaches such as a grid search over the hyperparameter space or randomly sampling hyperparameters require many configurations to be evaluated in order to perform well. Hence, they either yield suboptimal hyperparameter configurations or are expensive in terms of computational resources. As a remedy, Hyperband, an exploratory bandit-based algorithm, introduces an early-stopping strategy to quickly provide competitive configurations given a resource budget which often outperforms Bayesian optimization approaches. However, Hyperband keeps sampling iid configurations for assessment without taking previous evaluations into account. We propose HyperUCB, a UCB extension of Hyperband which assesses the sampled configurations and only evaluates promising samples. We compare our approach on MNIST data against Hyperband and show that we perform better in most cases.

Keywords: Hyperparameter optimization · Multi-armed bandits

1 Introduction

The performance of machine learning models highly depends on the choice of the hyperparameters. For many years, grid search was the standard approach for tuning the underlying models. However, with the emergence of more sophisticated models such as in deep learning, grid search is no longer practical due to the large hyperparameter space, and thus simpler approaches such as random search became more desirable and showed to be more effective [2].

Over the last few years, the problem of hyperparameter optimization has been successfully presented as metalearning using Bayesian optimization methods [3,5,10]. Nevertheless, bandit-based approaches exhibit superb performance in many scenarios [8,9]. Li et al. [8] propose a method, called Hyperband (HB), for hyperparameter selection which, in their settings, outperforms Bayesian methods while providing a significant speed-up compared to those competitors. Hyperband is based on the successive halving approach [11] for improving random search by an adaptive allocation of available resources to different configurations.

P. Cellier and K. Driessens (Eds.): ECML PKDD 2019 Workshops, CCIS 1167, pp. 44–50, 2020.
https://doi.org/10.1007/978-3-030-43823-4_4

Algorithm 1. Hyperband

```
   input : R, η
1  initialization: s_max = ⌊log_η R⌋ and B = (s_max + 1)R ;
2  for s ∈ {s_max, s_max − 1, ..., 0} do
3      n = ⌈(B/R) η^s/(s+1)⌉,   r = Rη^(−s);
4      Λ_s = get_hyperparameter_configuration(n);
5      for i ∈ {0, ..., s} do
6          n_i = ⌊nη^(−i)⌋ ,   r_i = rη^i;
7          L(Λ_s) = {run_then_return_val_loss(λ, r_i) | λ ∈ Λ_s};
8          Λ_s = top_k(Λ_s, L(Λ_s), ⌊n_i/η⌋);
9      end
10 end
   output: configuration λ with lowest validation loss seen so far
```

However, Hyperband is an amended version of random search in which there is no learning to guide the search. In addition, despite the fact that Hyperband is highly efficient for finding a good configuration, it does not find an optimum fast enough. Hence, modeling the hyperparameter optimization as a learning problem is more reliable than a search algorithm. Therefore, instead of only sampling iid configurations of hyperparameters as Hyperband does, we propose to leverage the information of previous *batches* in order to pre-evaluate sampled configurations and to discard unpromising ones. This is done by a UCB bandit strategy in a contextual setting.

In this paper, we introduce *HyperUCB*, a model-based bandit framework, to accommodate exploitation into the purely exploratory algorithm of Hyperband. In HyperUCB, the arm selection is carried out by incorporating an Upper Confidence Bound (UCB) strategy [1] to guide the search within the iterations in order to balance exploration vs. exploitation. We further model the arms in a contextual setting which generalizes the model for unseen arms (i.e., configurations). Therefore, we employ a modified version of LinUCB [7] in our approach to achieve a model-based Hyperband for the task of hyperparameter optimization. Empirically, we show that our proposed approach either outperforms Hyperband or performs on par on optimizing the hyperparameters of a deep learning model.

2 Background

2.1 Problem Setting

Let $\mathcal{D} = (\mathcal{X}, \mathcal{Y})$ be a data set and M be a learning algorithm. The data is usually split into a training set for optimizing the parameters of the model, a validation set for optimizing the hyperparameters and a test set for evaluating the overall performance of the model. Assume that $\mathcal{H}$ is the set of all possible hyperparameter configurations, we denote by $\mathcal{L}(\lambda)$ the loss of M using $\lambda \in \mathcal{H}$

on the validation set. The goal is to find the best hyperparameter configuration $\lambda^\star = \arg\min_\lambda \mathcal{L}(\lambda)$, which minimizes the validation loss for a given budget.

2.2 Hyperband

Hyperband (HB) is an anytime search algorithm based on multi-armed bandits to find the best configuration for a machine learning approach given limited resources. The method performs several iterations based on the available resources, and in each iteration repeatedly calls the SuccessiveHalving method [6] for choosing the best ones. Let R be the maximum budget available for training various instances of a model, then Hyperband conducts $s_{max} = \lfloor \log_\eta R \rfloor$ iterations for exploration, where η is the ratio of sampling the best arms.

Hyperband is outlined in Algorithm 1. Note that the evaluation of the hyperparameters $\lambda \in \Lambda_s$ in line 7 can be done in parallel. Within the algorithm, three methods are used. The method `get_hyperparameter_configuration(`n`)` returns a set Λ_s of $n \in \mathbb{N}$ hyperparameter configurations $\{\lambda_1, \ldots, \lambda_n\}$ sampled iid from a given hyperparameter space $\mathcal{H}$ of feasible configurations. Furthermore, by calling `run_then_return_val_loss(`λ, r`)`, we obtain the validation loss $\mathcal{L}(\lambda)$ of configuration λ and resource allocation r. Finally, `top_k(`$\Lambda_s, \mathcal{L}(\Lambda_s), k$`)` returns a subset of Λ_s of size k with the k lowest validation losses given in $\mathcal{L}(\Lambda_s)$.

2.3 Contextual Bandits

The multi-armed bandits in contextual settings benefit from the available information (context) to make a better decision at the time of action (arm) selection. That means, before making a decision, some context is shown to the bandits, and depending on the situation the decision might be different. The context could include the information about the current state, the attributes of the arms, or any other available data. A contextual bandit aims at finding a mapping between the contexts and their corresponding outcomes in order to minimize the total regret. Li et al. [7] propose LinUCB in which the outcome of every arm is modeled as a linear function of the context. In the next section, we present a modified form of LinUCB to design contextual Hyperband.

3 Contextual HyperUCB

In this section, we present our approach to upgrade Hyperband to a contextual bandit method using a UCB strategy. Let $\mathcal{H}$ be the space of all possible hyperparameter configurations for a machine learning approach. We are interested in finding $\lambda^\star \in \mathcal{H}$ that gives the best performance $y^\star$ in terms of the validation loss $\mathcal{L}$ of the model

$$\lambda^\star = \arg\min_\lambda \mathcal{L}(\lambda). \tag{1}$$

We assume that a hyperparameter configuration can be represented by a d-dimensional vector λ and model the contextual bandit as a linear function of

Algorithm 2. HyperUCB

```
   input : R, η, α, γ
 1 initialization (HB): s_max = ⌊log_η R⌋ and B = (s_max + 1)R;
 2 initialization (UCB): θ = 0_{d×1}, X ← ∅_{0×d}, A ← γI_{d×d}, n_0 = η^{s_max};
 3 for s ∈ {s_max, s_max − 1, ..., 0} do
 4     compute n and r as in HB;
 5     Λ_s = top_ucb(get_hyperparameter_configuration(n_0), θ, A, n);
 6     append λ to X  ∀λ ∈ Λ_s and initialize y_λ = 0;
 7     for i ∈ {0, ..., s} do
 8         compute n_i and r_i as in HB;
 9         for λ ∈ Λ_s do
10             A = A + λλ^⊤;
11             y_λ = −run_then_return_val_loss(λ, r_i);
12         end
13         θ = (X^⊤X + γI)^{−1} X^⊤ y ;
14         Λ_s = top_ucb(Λ_s, θ, A, ⌊n_i/η⌋);
15     end
16 end
17 top_ucb (Λ_s, θ, A, n):
18     p_λ = θ^⊤λ + α√(λ^⊤A^{−1}λ)    ∀λ ∈ Λ_s;
19     return top_k(Λ_s, p, n)
```

the configurations. After learning the parameters $\boldsymbol{\theta}$ of the linear model, a new configuration λ can be evaluated as $\hat{y} = \boldsymbol{\theta}^\top \lambda$. The optimization problem in Eq. (1) suggests a lower confidence bound strategy since we aim to minimize $\mathcal{L}$. However, by considering negative loss values $-y$, we can retain the usual upper confidence bound (UCB) strategy since maximizing the negative validation loss $-\mathcal{L}$ is equivalent to minimizing $\mathcal{L}$. The UCB approach trades off exploration and exploitation as it also considers the uncertainty for a specific hyperparameter configuration. The score p_λ is thus obtained from $\boldsymbol{\theta}^\top \lambda + \alpha\sqrt{\lambda^\top A^{-1} \lambda}$, where $A = \boldsymbol{X}^\top \boldsymbol{X} + \gamma \mathbf{I}$ is the regularized design matrix of the configurations with $\gamma \geq 0$ which have been evaluated so far and $\alpha > 0$ is a trade-off parameter.

Algorithm 2 summarizes our approach for HyperUCB. In this algorithm, the bandit model is learned in line 13, and together with the covariance matrix it computes the upper confidence values in two sampling steps. At every iteration, a number of n_0 configurations are randomly sampled as in HB, and from those, the bandit model selects the n most promising ones. The next sampling step is at line 14, where `top_ucb` is performed on the values of p_λ rather than y_λ. Note that the matrix A is updated every time a configuration is chosen, even within an iteration, which leads to a tighter confidence interval for those configurations.

Table 1. Hyperparameters of the multi-layer perceptron.

Hyperparameter	Range	Type
Learning rate	$[0.0001, 1]$	Float
# hidden layers	$\{1, 2, 3, 4, 5\}$	Integer
# neurons	$\{16, 32, \ldots, 512\}$	Integer
Activation	$\{\text{relu}, \text{tanh}, \text{sigmoid}\}$	Categorical

4 Empirical Study

In this section, we evaluate the performance of the HyperUCB strategy compared to Hyperband [8]. The experiments are conducted on the MNIST data which consists of 60,000 training and 10,000 test instances. As a model, we use a simple multi-layer perceptron (MLP) which learns to classify images of handwritten digits. We use the categorical cross entropy as a loss function and the RMSprop optimizer. The validation loss is computed on the hold-out data. Within the MLP we use four hyperparameters which are outlined in Table 1. We determine a minimum budget of one unit of resource which corresponds to 100 mini-batches of size 100. The maximum budget consists of R units of resources, hence $100R$ mini-batches. We use the default value of $\eta = 3$ as specified in Hyperband. Our approach contains two additional parameters: the exploration-exploitation trade-off α and a regularization-weight γ in ridge regression. We select the values of $\alpha = 0.4$ as it gives best performance in [7] and the regularization is set to $\gamma = 0.1$.

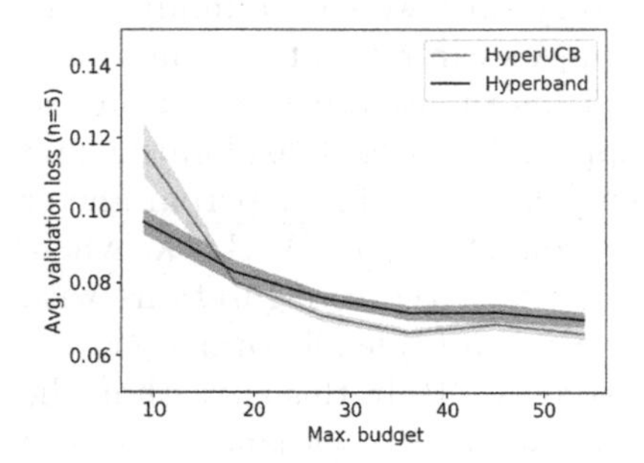

Fig. 1. Performance w.r.t. the budget.

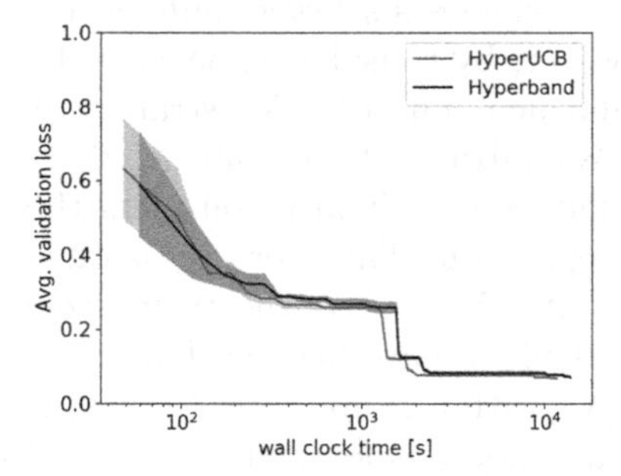

Fig. 2. Performance w.r.t. the time.

Figure 1 shows the validation loss averaged over five independent runs for various maximum budgets including standard errors. With a max. budget higher than 19, HyperUCB outperforms Hyperband as it consistently yields lower validation errors. We credit this finding to the fact that using a higher budget, more rounds are conducted on which the bandit model can learn to discriminate promising from unpromising hyperparameter configurations. This can be hardly done with lower max. budgets due to the lack of training data.

Figure 2 depicts the average validation loss in dependence of computational time, measured in seconds, for a budget of 45. It can be seen that HyperUCB performs on par with Hyperband, meaning it is as fast or faster than Hyperband.

5 Conclusion and Future Work

In this paper, we presented HyperUCB, a contextual extension using a UCB strategy for Hyperband, which is a bandit-based method for hyperparameter optimization. The idea was as follows: Instead of sampling n iid hyperparameter configurations in each round for evaluation, we sampled more configurations, assessed them using a multi-armed bandit with a UCB strategy and only evaluated the n best configurations. This way, we guided the sampling procedure towards more promising configurations and avoided evaluating hyperparameters which are already assumed to yield a high validation error. An experiment on the MNIST data showed that it outperforms the Hyperband baseline for moderate budgets at optimizing several hyperparameters of a multi-layer perceptron.

Further work will utilize the ideas from Tavakol and Brefeld [12], in which the parameters of the bandit model can be learned using kernel methods in the dual space to capture non-linearity. We also plan on extending the experimental setup by adding more baselines, e.g., BO-HB [4] as well as considering multiple hyperparameter optimization scenarios on various data sets and models.

References

1. Auer, P., Cesa-Bianchi, N., Fischer, P.: Finite-time analysis of the multiarmed bandit problem. Mach. Learn. **47**(2–3), 235–256 (2002). https://doi.org/10.1023/A:1013689704352
2. Bergstra, J., Bengio, Y.: Random search for hyper-parameter optimization. J. Mach. Learn. Res. **13**(Feb), 281–305 (2012)
3. Bergstra, J.S., Bardenet, R., Bengio, Y., Kégl, B.: Algorithms for hyper-parameter optimization. In: Advances in Neural Information Processing Systems (2011)
4. Falkner, S., Klein, A., Hutter, F.: BOHB: robust and efficient hyperparameter optimization at scale. In: International Conference on Machine Learning (2018)
5. Hutter, F., Hoos, H.H., Leyton-Brown, K.: Sequential model-based optimization for general algorithm configuration. In: Coello, C.A.C. (ed.) LION 2011. LNCS, vol. 6683, pp. 507–523. Springer, Heidelberg (2011). https://doi.org/10.1007/978-3-642-25566-3_40
6. Jamieson, K., Talwalkar, A.: Non-stochastic best arm identification and hyperparameter optimization. In: Artificial Intelligence and Statistics (2016)
7. Li, L., Chu, W., Langford, J., Schapire, R.E.: A contextual-bandit approach to personalized news article recommendation. In: Proceedings of the 19th International Conference on World Wide Web (2010)
8. Li, L., Jamieson, K., DeSalvo, G., Rostamizadeh, A., Talwalkar, A.: Hyperband: a novel bandit-based approach to hyperparameter optimization. J. Mach. Learn. Res. **18**, 6765–6816 (2018)

9. Shang, X., Kaufmann, E., Valko, M.: A simple dynamic bandit algorithm for hyper-parameter tuning. In: Workshop on Automated Machine Learning at International Conference on Machine Learning (2019)
10. Snoek, J., Larochelle, H., Adams, R.P.: Practical Bayesian optimization of machine learning algorithms. In: Advances in Neural Information Processing Systems (2012)
11. Sparks, E.R., Talwalkar, A., Haas, D., Franklin, M.J., Jordan, M.I., Kraska, T.: Automating model search for large scale machine learning. In: Proceedings of the Sixth ACM Symposium on Cloud Computing (2015)
12. Tavakol, M., Brefeld, U.: A unified contextual bandit framework for long- and short-term recommendations. In: Ceci, M., Hollmén, J., Todorovski, L., Vens, C., Džeroski, S. (eds.) ECML PKDD 2017. LNCS (LNAI), vol. 10535, pp. 269–284. Springer, Cham (2017). https://doi.org/10.1007/978-3-319-71246-8_17

Learning Parsers for Technical Drawings

Dries Van Daele[1(✉)], Nicholas Decleyre[2], Herman Dubois[2], and Wannes Meert[1]

[1] Department of CS, KU Leuven, Leuven, Belgium
dries.vandaele@cs.kuleuven.be
[2] Saint-Gobain Mobility | Engineered Components (Seals), Kontich, Belgium

Abstract. From a set of technical drawings, we learn a parser program to interpret the tabular data contained in such a drawing. This enables automatic reasoning and learning on top of a database of technical drawings. For example to help designers find or complete designs more easily.

Keywords: Inductive Logic Programming · Technical drawings

1 Introduction

Technical drawings are the main method in engineering to (visually) communicate how a new machine or component functions or is constructed. They are the result of a design process starting from a set of specifications that the final product needs to comply with. This design process follows a number of strict and soft rules (e.g., material choice as a function of temperature). Figure 1 shows a typical example containing both a 2D and 3D visualisation of the object, and a material list in tabular form specifying its parts and properties. They are carefully crafted documents that act as key deliverables at the end of a design process. As such, they contain a wealth of information. Furthermore, information is laid out according to generally applied conventions.

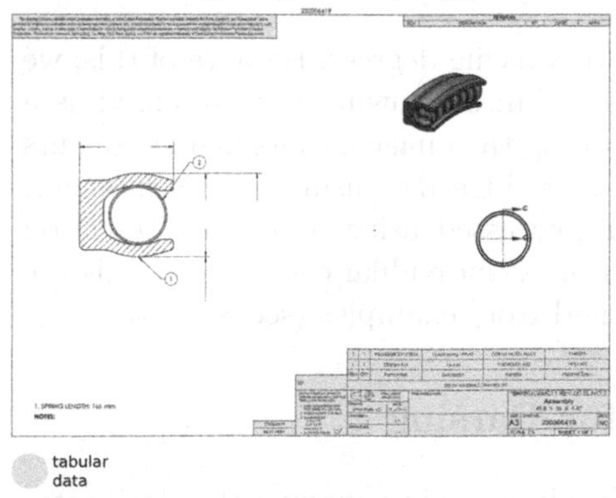

Fig. 1. A technical drawing with highlighted tabular data

Engineering companies have a large database of previous designs, potentially going back decades. They are often underutilized because previous designs can only be search for by title or by a limited set of textual annotations. Ideally, however, this database can also be used to: (1) given a technical drawing, finding other relevant drawings in a large database of previous designs; (2) given a partial description, finding designs that would complete the partial design. In this work we present an approach that can extract the knowledge in a technical

P. Cellier and K. Driessens (Eds.): ECML PKDD 2019 Workshops, CCIS 1167, pp. 51–56, 2020.
https://doi.org/10.1007/978-3-030-43823-4_5

drawing and thus improve the search capabilities significantly to achieve the aforementioned tasks.

To be able to use the data encapsulated in technical drawings, we need to parse the information contained in them, and translate this to a representation that can be handled by automated systems. Furthermore, such a system should be able to deal with both recent digital drawings and historical analog drawings. The latter is important because a great amount of information is captured in legacy drawings. Ideally, extracting the information can be done using a parser, thus a small computer program. The main challenge is that writing and maintaining such a parser is a time-consuming and expensive task. Furthermore, it is error prone since this requires an expert to explain subtle rules to an analyst or a programmer. The approach we present here will learn such parsers directly from expert feedback on the original drawing and allow its output to be used in automated tasks such as searching relevant designs.

We apply Inductive Logic Programming (ILP) to extract structured information from technical drawings, and propose a bootstrapping approach that boosts performance during multitask learning. The feedback used for learning takes the form of annotated technical drawings. Providing such annotations is a trivial task for domain experts. The required number of drawings that need to be annotated is mainly dependent on the number of variations or templates that need to be recognized. Fortunately, since all technical drawings within an organisation are expected to be (loosely) based on a limited set of templates, the number of drawings that need to be annotated is also limited.

In this work we introduce two contributions. First, we introduce the use of ILP to learn parsers from data and expert knowledge to interpret a technical drawing and produce a formal representation. Second, we introduce a novel bootstrapping learning strategy for ILP. The efficacy of this method is demonstrated in experiments on a real-world data set.

2 Identifying Technical Drawing Elements

Archived technical drawings are digitized to varying degrees. Because of this, we consider as a baseline the case where the technical drawing is represented as a bitmap image. A first step involves partitioning the image into its main segments using DBSCAN [2]. The resulting segments are identified using a CNN classifier. Segments identified as tables are further processed using a contour detection algorithm [4]. This enables the extraction of all individual cells. These cells are further processed by a *parser* that is learned from examples (see Sect. 3).

3 Inductive Logic Programs for Parsing

The data contained in a technical drawing is laid out in a manner that facilitates human interpretation. Tabular data in particular tends to have its data organised both spatially and through explicit annotation. Common examples of spatial structuring involve assigning related cells to common rows or columns, while assigning unrelated cells to different subtables or distant cells. Particularly useful are cells that contain unambiguous keywords such as attribute names. These are helpful to gain insight in the structure of a table. They serve as anchors to cells that are less distinctive on their own but can be described relatively to anchored cells.

The application at hand does not only require us to parse a table, but also demands that we learn how to interpret its spatial organisation. A small computer program is required to parse these custom drawings. Programming a parser for each type of drawing is not only an expensive and time consuming task to build and maintain, but also prone to errors. Various errors are potentially introduced while programming a parser. First, the structure of such technical drawings needs to be explained to a non-expert, i.e. a programmer, who interprets the instructions. Second, the tables are typically not simple rectangular tables. They thus require a non-trivial parser that is difficult to understand. Third, a design can change over time requiring periodic maintenance and lead to software erosion. Ideally, these parsers would thus be programmed automatically based on the expert's knowledge. This is possible by means of machine learning techniques that learn programs from examples. The examples in this setting are obtained by annotating technical drawings, a task that is trivial for a domain expert.

The highly relational nature of tabular data and the ease with which tables can sensibly be navigated by visiting adjacent cells suggests the use of Inductive Logic Programming. ILP systems are particularly suitable for learning small programs from complex input data. Two advantages of learning programs using ILP we benefit from in this work are the ability to learn recursive definitions (e.g., row n is defined by row $n+1$) and to reuse learned target labels (e.g., first learning what a header row is helps to define what a content row is).

3.1 Standard ILP

An inductive logic programming system learns from relational data a set of definite clauses. Given background knowledge B, positive examples E^+ and negative examples E^-, it attempts to construct a program H consisting of definite clauses such that $B \wedge H$ entail all, or as many as possible, examples in E^+, and none, or as few as possible, of those in E^-.

We thus need to supply three types of inputs. First, a set of training data, examples E, that contains the properties to describe a cell in a technical drawing. An example can be:

- *Cell text:* The textual contents of each cell. Tesseract 4.0 is used to recognize cell contents [3].
- *Cell location:* The cell's bounding box information (i.e. (x, y) coordinates and cell width and height).

Second, a label for each cell (e.g., author, bill of materials, quantity). A cell can be annotated with multiple labels (e.g., a cell can be a quantity in the bill of materials). Depending on which target label we want to learn, we split the set of examples E in a tuple (E^+, E^-) where E^+ contains the examples associated with a cell that has the target label and E^- those examples that do not. For standard ILP, the learning task is defined for one target label, so we repeat the standard ILP task for each label in the set of labels.

Third, we can provide background knowledge B that contains generally applicable knowledge for the problem at hand and remains unchanged across examples. In this case we provide:

- *Relative cell positions.* Relations capturing which cells are adjacent to each other, and in which direction (horizontally or vertically) based on their bounding boxes.
- *Numerical order.* The successor relationship. Although not essential, it is useful for learning concise, recursive rules.

The output of ILP, the program H, is a set of definite clauses of the form '`author(A) :- cell_contains(A, drawn)`' which can be read as the rule 'Cell A contains the author if it contains the word 'drawn''.

3.2 ILP with Bootstrapping

It is expected that learning programs to properly parse the target labels in P will prove simple for some targets and more challenging for others. We propose a bootstrapping extension that supports the construction of sophisticated programs by allowing them to employ the simpler ones in their definition. This is loosely inspired by the ideas raised in [1], but applied to the ILP setting.

This corresponds to a variation of the previously discussed ILP set-up where a dependency graph G is used. The nodes in this directed acyclic graph each represent a possible target label and the edges represent dependencies between those labels. A dependency indicates that one target label might have a natural description in function of another. Although we allow for this dependency graph to be specified manually, our method defaults to a fully automated approach where standard ILP is first applied to learn programs for each target. Then targets are ranked according to the ascending F_1 score of their programs on the training data. Each target in the list then has all subsequent targets as its dependencies. Finally, ILP with bootstrapping learns targets in the order specified by a correct evaluation order of G, and extends the background knowledge B for each target with the programs constructed to parse its dependent target labels. When learning program H using bootstrapping to capture a particular target label l, we define its extended background knowledge $B' = B \wedge (\bigwedge_{i \in descendants(G,l)} H_i)$, where H_i is the program trained for target label i.

4 Experiments

4.1 Learning Set-Up

The ILP system Aleph is used to learn possibly recursive programs that parse the chosen targets from the tabular data, ranging from the document's author

	ITEM	QTY	Partnumber	Description	Material	Material Spec.
1:	2	1	V5DM0008C0114*0254	Coiled spring with HT	COBALT NICKEL ALLOY	FSS0010
0:	1	1	230306419JA	Jacket	FLUOROLOY A02	HP5A102

EP

LIST OF MATERIALS OR PARTS LIST

UNLESS OTHERWISE SPECIFIED DIMENSIONS ARE IN MILLIMETERS AND [ ] ARE IN INCHES
1. DWG INTERPRETATION PER ASME Y14.5M-1994
2. BREAK EDGES 0.25 MAX.
3. TOLERANCES X.X ± 0.76 X.XX ± 0.25 ANGLES ± 2°
4. SURFACE FINISH 1.6

FIRST ANGLE PROJECTION

PREPARED FOR

DRAWN DriveWorks V01 DATE 19 Jul 2016

CHECKED --- -/-/-

APPROVED --- -/-/-

TBAFB0106M011 REV.00 SL.NO.2

Assembly

49.8 X 56 X 4.87

SIZE A3 DWG NO. 230306419 REV. NC

SCALE: 2:3 SHEET 1 OF 1

230306419

NEXT ASSY.

(a) A table excerpt from a technical drawing. Its header and materials are highlighted.

```
% Materials hypothesis
materials(A,B) :-
    zero(A),
    above_below(B,C),
    header(C).

materials(A,B) :-
    succ(C,A),
    above_below(B,D),
    materials(C,D).

% Header hypothesis
header(A) :-
    above_below(A,B),
    cell_contains(B, 'LIST').
```

(b) header/1 covers any cell located directly above a cell containing the word 'LIST'. materials/2 parses the indexed parts of the materials table. Its first argument is the index and its second argument represents the cell. materials/2 consists of two clauses. The first clause anchors the table by considering row 0 to consist of the cells above the header. It employs header/1 in its definition. The second, recursive clause indicates that the index is incremented for each row located above another.

Fig. 2. Figure a provides an illustration of the materials table and its header. Listing b shows the associated program learned using bootstrapping.

and its approval date to the attributes covered in the materials table and its indexed components.

Training data consists of a set of fully labeled technical drawings. A custom data labeling tool with a web-based graphical interface was constructed to support domain experts in labeling drawings.

Using this tool, 30 technical drawings with on average 50 cells were labeled with 14 different labels. For each target label, examples that contain that label form its positive example set, while negative examples are automatically derived by taking the complement of all possible examples for that target with its positive example set.

The labeled data is split in a training set consisting of 10 drawings, and a test set containing the remaining 20. Since the choice of training data can heavily affect the capability for finding rules that properly generalize, experiments are repeated 5 times on random samples of the training data. Because the order in which training examples are presented can also affect the rules identified by the coverage-based algorithm employed by Aleph, repeat experiments are performed even when all training data is available for learning, as a sample then corresponds to a different order in which the examples are presented to the learner.

4.2 Results

Figure 3 visualizes the performance with which cell labels and their appropriate index are correctly identified. This shows that only a few annotated designs are required for the bootstrapping method to learn perfect parsers for all labels whereas standard ILP fails to learn a perfect parser. Furthermore, it highlights how ILP with bootstrapping compared to Standard ILP is less sensitive to overfitting when presented with additional training data. This robustness of ILP with bootstrapping lends itself well to incremental learning. Both subtle and drastic variations in template design can be handled by providing the learner with a representative sample as training data. Learning perfect parsers for simple labels such as author or approval date can be achieved by both standard ILP and the bootstrap method with only a few training examples. More interesting is to look at the most complicated label, the indexed components (*materials* in Fig. 2a). The best performing program constructed using standard ILP consists of 14 clauses and yields 17 false negatives. Bootstrap learning, however, succeeds at learning a completely accurate, concise program (see Fig. 2b) whenever more than three technical drawings are provided in the training set. The poor performance when using only a few drawings is due to poor generalization. More specific, in these drawings the materials tables provided for training each consisted only of a single component and there was no pressure on the inductive learner to learn the recursive rule necessary to capture the rows of larger tables.

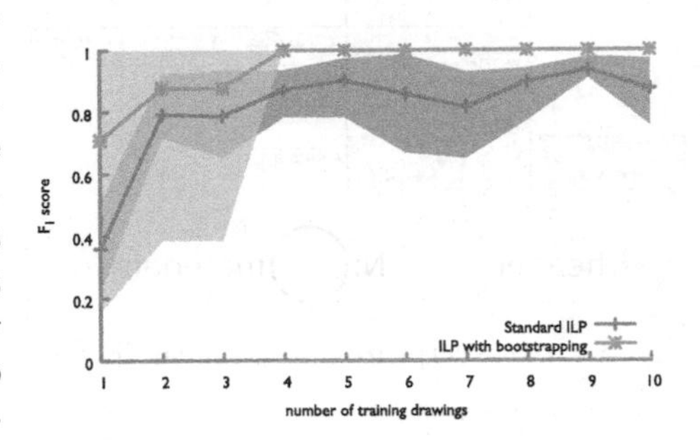

Fig. 3. The performance measured using the F_1 score of programs learning materials/2. Min/max shading is included to indicate the range of performance between the best and worst-performing program over 5 repetitions.

References

1. Dechter, E., Malmaud, J., Adams, R.P., Tenenbaum, J.B.: Bootstrap learning via modular concept discovery. In: Proceedings of the Twenty-Third International Joint Conference on Artificial Intelligence, IJCAI 2013, pp. 1302–1309. AAAI Press (2013)
2. Ester, M., Kriegel, H.P., Sander, J., Xu, X.: A density-based algorithm for discovering clusters a density-based algorithm for discovering clusters in large spatial databases with noise. In: Proceedings of the Second International Conference on Knowledge Discovery and Data Mining, KDD 1996, pp. 226–231. AAAI Press (1996)
3. Smith, R.: An overview of the tesseract OCR engine. In: Proceedings of the Ninth International Conference on Document Analysis and Recognition, ICDAR 2007, vol. 2, pp. 629–633. IEEE Computer Society, Washington (2007)
4. Suzuki, S., Abe, K.: Topological structural analysis of digitized binary images by border following. Comput. Vis. Graph. Image Process. **30**(1), 32–46 (1985)

Meta-learning of Textual Representations

Jorge G. Madrid[1], Hugo Jair Escalante[1,2(✉)], and Eduardo Morales[1]

[1] Computer Science Department, INAOE, Puebla, Mexico
{jgmadrid,hugojair,emorales}@inaoep.mx

[2] Computer Science Department, CINVESTAV, Zacatenco, Mexico City, Mexico

Abstract. Recent progress in AutoML has lead to state-of-the-art methods (e.g., AutoSKLearn) that can be readily used by non-experts to approach *any* supervised learning problem. Whereas these methods are quite effective, they are still limited in the sense that they work for tabular (matrix formatted) data only. This paper describes one step forward in trying to automate the design of supervised learning methods in the context of text mining. We introduce a meta learning methodology for automatically obtaining a representation for text mining tasks starting from raw text. We report experiments considering 60 different textual representations and more than 80 text mining datasets associated to a wide variety of tasks. Experimental results show the proposed methodology is a promising solution to obtain highly effective off the shell text classification pipelines.

Keywords: Text mining · Meta-features · Text classification

1 Introduction

Nowadays, the success of machine learning systems relies on the knowledge of human-experts that according to their experience design and test multiple models extensively to select the best modeling option. Although effective, this strategy is not only time consuming but also impractical since an expert is not always available. This has motivated the increasing demand for easy-to-use automated machine learning solutions. In this context, AutoML is the field of research aiming to generate machine learning models without any human supervision. Recent progress in AutoML has lead to quite effective and competitive solutions when dealing with tabular (matrix formatted) data, see e.g., [5,7,16]. However, these techniques are still limited in the sense that they require the user to transform raw data into a tabular representation. This step relies heavily on the expertise of users.

Text classification is one of the most studied tasks in Natural Language Processing (NLP), this is because of the number of applications that can be

This work was partially supported by CONACyT under grant *Aprender Objetos de Internet para Buscarlos con un Robot*, ID: CB-250938.

P. Cellier and K. Driessens (Eds.): ECML PKDD 2019 Workshops, CCIS 1167, pp. 57–67, 2020.
https://doi.org/10.1007/978-3-030-43823-4_6

approached as text classification problems (e.g. sentiment analysis, topic labeling, spam detection, and author profiling among others). Many techniques for pre-processing, feature extraction, feature selection and document representation have been developed over the last decades. Despite all this progress by the NLP community, it is still an expert who designs the pipeline for text classification systems that includes one or many of such techniques, each of which usually requiring the fine-tuning of hyperparameters.

In this work we take a step towards the automated generation of the classification pipelines for text classification by focusing on the representation. Thus, our goal is to automate the process of determining the best representation to approach a text classification task starting from raw text. Unlike other data types, language/text provides an unstructured and rich source of information, hence selecting the adequate representation for text will have a direct impact on the performance of text mining solutions. In fact, representing texts has been one of the most studied venues in NLP. We propose a meta-learning solution to automatically determine the best representation given a dataset of raw text. This is a first step towards the full automation of the generation of text classification pipelines. We propose a number of meta features some of which are extracted directly from raw text, and most of them not used before for meta-learning. We report experimental results considering 60 textual representations and more than 80 text mining tasks. Our results show that the proposed meta features successfully characterize text mining tasks and that an AutoML solution for text mining (AutoText) is feasible. Our work is among the first to approach text classification via meta-learning from raw data and it is by far the largest study on meta learning in the context of text mining.

2 Related Work

In the context of text mining, few works have explored the automated selection of different parts of classification pipelines. With experiments in the Reuters-21578 corpus, Lam and Lai [11] proposed to characterize documents with 9 (meta) features and to predict the classification error of different models using data from a previous phase, thus recommending a classification model. More recently, [19] searched for text representations with Bayesian Representation [15]. Their search space was limited to only word n-grams and experiments were performed in 8 datasets: 4 sentiment analysis tasks and 4 topic classification tasks. Nevertheless, they outperformed every linear classifier reported until their publication date. Despite their limited scope, given the lack of data and computational resources of the time, this work represents one of the first meta-learning approaches for text classification.

Other works have explored different meta-learning approaches for text classification in small-scale, for example, Gomez et al. [9] addressed the problem with evolutionary computation methods and using 11 meta-features. In a broader approach Ferreira and Brazdil [6] recommend *pipelines* with Active Testing Method, in their work they also present statistical analysis of 48 preprocessing methods and 8 classifiers.

Another related work is that by [14] where a set of features derived from the text was proposed for characterizing short-text corpora in the context of clustering. Although the goal of such reference was to characterize the harness of text corpora and not AutoML, such work is relevant because their features inspired some of the meta-features considered in this paper. In Sect. 3 we describe how we combined this set of features with other proposed ones for characterizing text collections in the context of automatic text mining.

Meta-learning has been studied for a while in the broad machine learning context [1–3,17,18]. However, it is only recently that it has become a mainstream topic, this mainly because of its successes in several tasks. For instance, Feurer et al. [8] successfully used a set of meta-features to warm-start a hyperparameter optimization technique in the popular state-of-the-art AutoML solution *Autosklearn*. Likewise, the success of deep learning together with the difficulty in defining appropriate architectures and hyperparameters for users, has motivated a boom on neural architecture search, where meta-learning is becoming common [4].

In this paper we propose a novel approach to meta-learning of text representations. We propose a novel set of meta-features, comprising standard meta-features from the machine learning literature, features that have been used for other problems than meta-learning and novel meta-features that have not been used previously. Some of which are derived directly from raw text and aim at capturing complex language patterns. We approach the problem of recommending textual representations. Whereas this problem has been addressed in previous work, such references have considered only a few representations and a very limited number of meta-features (up to 11).

To the best of our knowledge this is the largest scale study on meta-learning in the context of text mining. Whereas results are promising, please note that this is only a first step towards the ultimate goal of automating the text mining process.

3 Recommending Textual Representations

We introduce a meta-learning method that takes as input the labeled raw text from a corpus associated to a text classification task and automatically selects a representation. The method recommends vector representations for text classification tasks based on which one worked best for *similar* tasks. In order to do so we define a set of meta-features and perform extensive experiments on 81 different text classification tasks. Although this approach is common within meta-learning [17], it has not been widely explored for text classification. In fact, previous work (see Sect. 2) has considered small subsets of generic meta-features.

Table 1 sums up the feature extraction methods that with some preprocessing processes or hyper-parameters gives a total of 60 representations, while not exhaustive, our work is the first to consider representations not only based on simple features, but also those based on topic modeling, embeddings, and semantic analysis, we also included a representation based on the word percentage of categories from LIWC2007 dictionary. Furthermore, the output of our method can be useful for both human experts designing text classification pipelines and for complementing other optimization methods for AutoML (e.g. it can be used for warm-starting Bayesian Optimization [8] for a wider search space of text representations or easily combined with existing AutoML solutions).

Table 1. Representations considered

Features	Hyper-parameters
N-grams	[words, char], stop_words[None, 'English'], range[1, 3], weight[bi, tf, tfidf]
LDA	stop_words[None, 'English']
LSA	stop_words[None, 'English'], weight[tf, tfidf]
LIWC [13]	categories[64]
W2V [12]	pre_trained[True, False], vector[mean, sum], dimension[300]

The proposed method comprises 2 stages, an offline phase where it *learns how to learn* and a predicting phase where it uses the data collected in phase 1 to recommend a text representation for classifying.

A human-expert uses knowledge acquired in the past when a new task is presented, equivalently, *meta-learning* imitates this reasoning. Our method applies meta-learning to learn from the performance of different representations on a number of corpora. Namely, we defined 72 meta-features to characterize 81 text corpora and performed an exhaustive search for the performance of 60 representations. A *knowledge base* is built associating the performance of each representation with a task, described by the vector of meta-features. Traditionally, meta-features extract meta-data from a dataset such as statistics of its distribution or simple characteristics like the number of classes and attributes, in our proposed set we contemplate this type of features as well as other attributes extracted directly from the raw text. The proposed meta-features are described below. For clarity we have divided them in groups.

- **General meta-features.** The *number of documents* and the *number of categories.*
- **Corpus hardness.** Most of these originally used in [14] to determine the hardness of short text-corpora.
  Domain broadness. Measures related to the thematic broadness/narrowness of words in documents. We included measures based on the vocabulary length and overlap: *Supervised Vocabulary Based (SVB)*, *Unsupervised Vocabulary Based (UVD)* and *Macro-averaged Relative Hardness (MRH).*
  Class imbalance. Class Imbalance (CI) ratio.
  Stylometry. Stylometric Evaluation Measure (SEM)
  Shortness. Vocabulary Length (VL), Vocabulary Document Ratio (VDR) and average *word length.*
- **Statistical and information theoretic.** We derive meta-features from a document-term matrix representation of the corpus.

min, max, average, standard deviation, skewness, kurtosis, ratio average-standard deviation, and entropy of: vocabulary distribution, documents-per-category and words-per-document:
Landmarking. 70% of the documents are used to train 4 simple classifiers and their performance on the remaining 30% was used based on the intuition that some aspects of the dataset can be inferred: *data sparsity - 1NN, data separability - Decision Tree, linear separability - Linear Discriminant Analysis, feature independence Naïve Bayes.* The *percentage of zeros* in the matrix was also added as a measure for sparsity.
Principal Components (PC) statistics. Statistics derived from a PC analysis: *pcac* from [9]; for the first 100 components, the same statistics from documents per category and their *singular values sum, explained ratio and explained variance*, and for the first component its *explained variance.*

- **Lexical features.** We incorporated the distribution of parts of speech tags. We intuitively believe that the frequency of some lexical items will be higher depending on the task associated to a corpus, for instance a corpus for sentiment analysis may have more adjectives while a news corpus may have less. We tagged the words in the document and computed the average number of *adjectives, adpositions, adverbs, conjunctions, articles, nouns, numerals, particles, pronouns, verbs, punctuation marks* and *untagged words* in the corpus.
- **Corpus readability.** Statistics from text that determine readability, complexity and grade from textstat library[1]: *Flesch Reading Ease, SMOG grade, Flesch-Kincaid grade level, Coleman-Liau index, automated readability index, Dale-Chall readability score, the number of difficult words, Linsear Write formula, Fog scale,* and *estimated school level to understand the text.*

Apart from general, statistical and PC based, the rest of the listed features have not been used in a meta-learning context. After the offline phase takes place, for a new task the same meta-features are extracted and compared with the prior knowledge, to recommend a representation. We considered 4 strategies that leverage learned experiences and make predictions for a new task, these are described below

(1) Using directly the representation with best performance of the *nearest* corpus. This strategy directly follows the idea of finding the most similar task in order to know what model will work best. The euclidean distance is used to determine the *similarity* between the new task and those in the knowledge base. This approach can also be seen as classifying unseen tasks with a Nearest Neighbors algorithms using only 1 neighbor, in which case each of the 60 representations constitutes a class.
(2) Predicting the representation as a classification problem, where each representation is a class and every prior task is a sample represented by its 72 meta-features. In this case every sample was labeled with the representation with best performance as its class, thus, the problem is to select the *correct* class finding patterns among the tasks and using 81 samples for training.

[1] https://github.com/shivam5992/textstat.

Since the dimensionality of this problem is big given the number of samples available this isn't an easy task, so we tested different classification models. In the end, a Random Forest was selected as the classifier for this strategy. Hyper-parameters of this RF model are listed in Table 2.

(3) Predicting the performance for every representation and selecting the one with the smallest error. In this strategy 60 different regression models are needed, one for each representation, they are trained using the performance of each representation for the different tasks, the objective is to correctly predict the performance for each representation given a new task (described by the same 72 meta-features). As for (2) several models were trained and compared, finally, a Random Forest Regressor was found to work best.

(4) Predicting the rank of each representation and selecting the one with best predicted rank. 60 regression models are trained with performances in 81 different tasks. Given a new task the 60 trained models predict the expected rank for each representation, the results are ordered and the representation with lowest rank is recommended. Like before we compared various regression models and again regression with Random Forest was selected (see Table 3).

Table 2. Hyper-parameter for the Random Forest Classifier used in strategy (2).

Hyper-parameter	Value
Estimators	200
Quality criteria	Gini
Max depth	Unlimited
Min features	2
Max features	$\sqrt{\lvert features \rvert}$

Table 3. Hyper-parameter for the Random Forest Regressor used in strategies (3) and (4).

Hyper-parameter	Value
Estimators	200
Quality criteria	Mean absolute error
Max depth	Unlimited
Min features	2
Max features	$\lvert features \rvert$

For strategies 2–4 different classification and regression models were tested, a Random Forest classifier was selected for strategy 2 and Random Forest regressor for both strategies 3 and 4. Once the representation is chosen, an SVM classifier with linear kernel is used in every case to train and make predictions with the new corpus.

4 Experiments and Results

For the experimental evaluation we collected 81 publicly available text corpora, each associated with a different classification task, most of which can be categorized as one of 6 common NLP tasks: authorship attribution, author profiling, topic/thematic classification, irony and deception detection. Some of these datasets are commonly used for benchmarks in text classification (e.g. Amazon, Dbpedia, 20NGs) while others have been used in competitions. After processing each corpus to share the same format and codification we extracted the 72 meta-features for each of the 81 collections. To accelerate the meta-feature extraction process we limited the number of documents to 90,000 per category. The resultant matrix of size 81×72 comprises our *knowledge base* characterizing multiple corpora.

In an offline phase, for each classification task every representation was used for training and testing a classification model, the *performance* of each representation was calculated with 3-fold Cross validation, they were also ranked from best (1) to worst (60).

We evaluated the 4 meta-learning strategies with unseen tasks following a leave-one-out setting, using the results from 60 representations in the rest of the tasks as knowledge to decide which representation to recommend. The objective for the strategies, then, is to select what in exhaustive search was found to be the *best* representation. We compared the average performance achieved by our strategies in 5 runs against the best solution found and the average performance of all of the considered representations. Table 4 shows the average performance for each strategy after 5 runs in terms of the average accuracy and average rank. Figure 1 depicts the performance of our method and the baselines in 9 corpora (we selected these representative corpora to cover a wide variety of tasks and because they are well known benchmarks).

Table 4. Average accuracy [0, 1] and average rank [60, 1] of different strategies in 81 corpus, the last row indicates the number of times the best representation was predicted. (1) Nearest corpus, (2) classification, (3) performance regression, (4) rank prediction.

Method	Best	(1)	(2)	(3)	(4)	Random
Avg accu	77.06 ± 0	73.75 ± 0	$\mathbf{75.25 \pm 0.12}$	73.34 ± 0.34	$\mathbf{75.20 \pm 0.07}$	68.45 ± 0
Avg rank	1.00 ± 0	14.20 ± 0	$\mathbf{8.71 \pm 0.46}$	14.30 ± 1.31	$\mathbf{8.51 \pm 0.34}$	30.30 ± 0
# of 1s	81.00 ± 0	17.00 ± 0	$\mathbf{25.80 \pm 0.45}$	4.20 ± 0.84	14.80 ± 0.84	0.00 ± 0

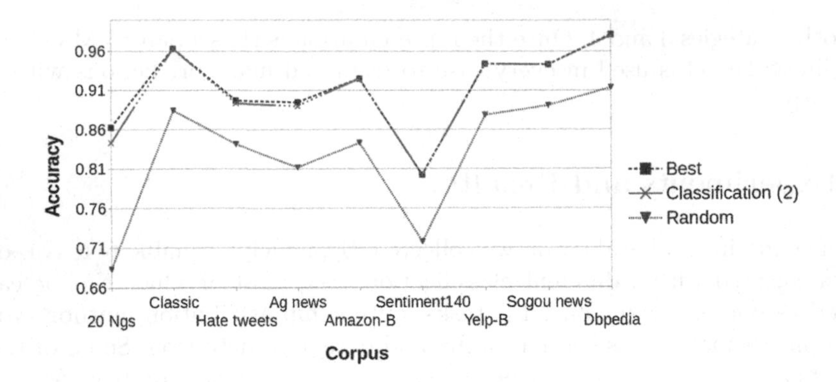

Fig. 1. Accuracy of (2) in 9 selected corpora.

The 4 strategies clearly outperform selecting a *random* representation (we illustrate this by averaging the results of all the representations). While in terms of average ranking they could be closer to the optimal, the average accuracy of (2) and (4) strategies was only 2% behind the best. (2) also found the best representation 35% of the time. Results show strong evidence that our meta-learning approach finds relations between corpora and pipeline performances that exploits prior knowledge for the autonomous classification of texts (Table 5).

From the 72 proposed meta-features we tested different subsets according to their Gini importance from the Random Forest used in strategy (2). A subset of 38 meta-features improved our results relatively by 8% with (2) and 38% with (1) in terms of average ranking. We also compared this subset against a subset comprised of 19 *traditional* meta-features used in related work. Using strategy (2) our subset outperformed the *traditional* one by almost 0.8% in average accuracy and 3 places in average rank. The results also showed a significant difference between both subsets ($p < .001$ Student's t-test). The subset of 38 meta-features is detailed in Table 6.

Table 5. Results after meta-feature selection

Method	(1)	(2)	(3)	(4)
Avg accu	75.16 ± 0	$\mathbf{75.39 \pm 0.13}$	73.57 ± 0.14	75.16 ± 0.05
Avg rank	8.68 ± 0	$\mathbf{8.00 \pm 0.47}$	14.42 ± 0.53	9.05 ± 0.25
# of 1s	$\mathbf{27.00 \pm 0}$	$\mathbf{26.44 \pm 0.56}$	6.40 ± 1.34	16.00 ± 0.87

In addition, we compared our strategies with commonly used representations such as pre-trained Word2Vec and Bag-of-Words outperforming them in average by 9% and 3% respectively, Fig. 2 depicts this comparison (between strategy (4) and W2V) in the 9 corpora we selected. Despite the robustness of such common representations their performance can usually be improved by fine tuning some

Table 6. 38 Meta-features selected by Gini importance

Meta-feature selection
average word length
document per category:
min
max
average
standard deviation
average/stdev
entropy
word per document:
average
skewness
entropy
Imalance Degree
SEM
UVB
SVB
MRH_J
VDR
max vocabulary
average vocabulary
sd vocabulary
skweness vocabulary
avg/stdev vocabulary
pca:
singular values sum
explained ratio
explained variance
explained variance (1)
pca max
pca skewness
pca kurtosis
data sparsity
data separability
linear separability
% of zeros
% of adpositions
% of adverbs
% of conjunctions
% of nouns
% of numbers
% of untagged words
difficult words

of their hyper-parameters or they are largely outperformed by another, as shown in the results the strategies are able to find these improvements.

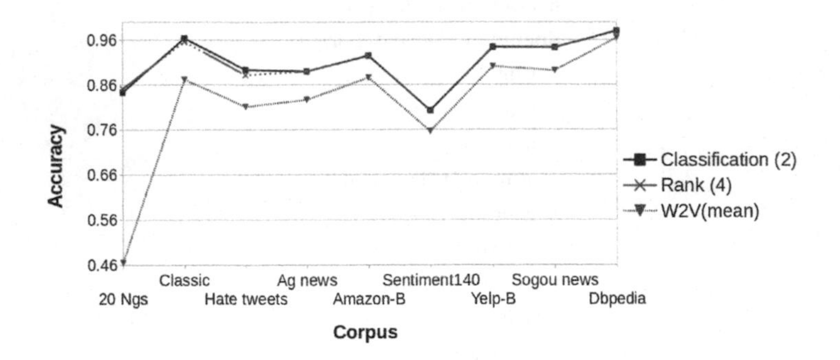

Fig. 2. Accuracy comparison between (2), (4) and Word2Vec in 9 corpora.

5 Conclusion and Future Work

We introduced a meta-learning method that takes as input a corpus and without human intervention builds a model to solve a text classification task focusing on the selection of a vector-based representation. The results show empirically that this approach is able to characterize tasks and approximate an optimal representation. Our work can not only recommend a single representation but also the best n representations using one of the strategies proposed to rank them, these can later be used to *warm-start* an optimization technique allowing us to expand the search space and, like in similar works on different fields [10], ideally finding pipelines that perform better than those designed by humans. Our also work comprises a first step towards the automated recommendation of full text classification pipelines. The source code of our method is available under an open source license at: https://github.com/jorgegus/autotext.

References

1. Bengio, Y.: Gradient-based optimization of hyperparameters. Neural Comput. **12**(8), 1889–1900 (2000)
2. Bergstra, J.S., Bardenet, R., Bengio, Y., Kégl, B.: Algorithms for hyper-parameter optimization. In: Advances in Neural Information Processing Systems, pp. 2546–2554 (2011)
3. Bozdogan, H.: Model selection and Akaike's information criterion (AIC): the general theory and its analytical extensions. Psychometrika **52**(3), 345–370 (1987)
4. Elsken, T., Metzen, J.H., Hutter, F.: Neural architecture search: a survey. J. Mach. Learn. Res. **20**(55), 1–21 (2019)
5. Escalante, H.J., Montes, M., Sucar, L.E.: Particle swarm model selection. J. Mach. Learn. Res. **10**, 405–440 (2009). http://dl.acm.org/citation.cfm?id=1577069.1577084

6. Ferreira, M.J., Brazdil, P.: Workflow recommendation for text classification with active testing method. In: Workshop AutoML 2018@ ICML/IJCAI-ECAI (2018)
7. Feurer, M., Klein, A., Eggensperger, K., Springenberg, J., Blum, M., Hutter, F.: Efficient and robust automated machine learning. In: Advances in Neural Information Processing Systems, pp. 2962–2970 (2015)
8. Feurer, M., Springenberg, J.T., Hutter, F.: Initializing Bayesian hyperparameter optimization via meta-learning. In: Twenty-Ninth AAAI Conference on Artificial Intelligence (2015)
9. Gomez, J.C., Hoskens, S., Moens, M.F.: Evolutionary learning of meta-rules for text classification. In: Proceedings of the Genetic and Evolutionary Computation Conference Companion, pp. 131–132. ACM (2017)
10. Guyon, I., et al.: Analysis of the AutoML challenge series 2015–2018. In: Hutter, F., Kotthoff, L., Vanschoren, J. (eds.) Automated Machine Learning. TSSCML, pp. 177–219. Springer, Cham (2019). https://doi.org/10.1007/978-3-030-05318-5_10
11. Lam, W., Lai, K.Y.: A meta-learning approach for text categorization. In: Proceedings of the 24th Annual International ACM SIGIR Conference on Research and Development in Information Retrieval, pp. 303–309. ACM (2001)
12. Mikolov, T., Chen, K., Corrado, G., Dean, J.: Efficient estimation of word representations in vector space. arXiv preprint arXiv:1301.3781 (2013)
13. Pennebaker, J.W., Boyd, R.L., Jordan, K., Blackburn, K.: The development and psychometric properties of LIWC2015. Technical report (2015)
14. Pinto, D.: On clustering and evaluation of narrow domain short-text corpora. Ph.D., UPV (2008)
15. Snoek, J., Larochelle, H., Adams, R.P.: Practical Bayesian optimization of machine learning algorithms. In: Advances in Neural Information Processing Systems, pp. 2951–2959 (2012)
16. Thornton, C., Hutter, F., Hoos, H.H., Leyton-Brown, K.: Auto-WEKA: combined selection and hyperparameter optimization of classification algorithms. In: Proceedings of the 19th ACM SIGKDD International Conference on Knowledge Discovery and Data Mining, KDD 2013, pp. 847–855. ACM, New York (2013). https://doi.org/10.1145/2487575.2487629. http://doi.acm.org/10.1145/2487575.2487629
17. Vanschoren, J.: Meta-learning. In: Hutter, F., Kotthoff, L., Vanschoren, J. (eds.) Automated Machine Learning. TSSCML, pp. 35–61. Springer, Cham (2019). https://doi.org/10.1007/978-3-030-05318-5_2. http://automl.org/book
18. Vilalta, R., Drissi, Y.: A perspective view and survey of meta-learning. Artif. Intell. Rev. **18**(2), 77–95 (2002)
19. Yogatama, D., Kong, L., Smith, N.A.: Bayesian optimization of text representations. In: Proceedings of the 2015 Conference on Empirical Methods in Natural Language Processing, pp. 2100–2105 (2015)

ReinBo: Machine Learning Pipeline Conditional Hierarchy Search and Configuration with Bayesian Optimization Embedded Reinforcement Learning

Xudong Sun(✉), Jiali Lin(✉), and Bernd Bischl(✉)

Department of Statistics, Ludwig Maximillian University of Munich, Munich, Germany
Xudong.Sun@stat.uni-muenchen.de, linjialideu@gmail.com, bernd_bischl@gmx.net

Abstract. Machine learning pipeline potentially consists of several stages of operations like data preprocessing, feature engineering and machine learning model training. Each operation has a set of hyper-parameters, which can become irrelevant for the pipeline when the operation is not selected. This gives rise to a hierarchical conditional hyper-parameter space. To optimize this mixed continuous and discrete conditional hierarchical hyper-parameter space, we propose an efficient pipeline search and configuration algorithm which combines the power of Reinforcement Learning and Bayesian Optimization. Empirical results show that our method performs favorably compared to state of the art methods like Auto-sklearn, TPOT, Tree Parzen Window, and Random Search.

Keywords: Bayesian Optimization · Reinforcement Learning · Conditional hierarchy search · AutoML

1 Introduction

Over the past years, Machine Learning (ML) has achieved remarkable success in a wide range of application areas, which has greatly increased the demand for machine learning systems. However, an efficient machine learning algorithm crucially depends on a human expert, who has to carefully design the pipeline of the machine learning system, potentially consisting of data preprocessing, feature filtering, machine learning algorithm selection, as well as identifying a good set of hyper-parameters. As there are a large number of possible alternatives of models as well as hyper-parameters, the need for automated machine learning (AutoML) has been growing, which is supposed to automatically generate a data analysis pipeline with machine learning methods and parameter settings that

X. Sun and J. Lin—Equal contribution.

P. Cellier and K. Driessens (Eds.): ECML PKDD 2019 Workshops, CCIS 1167, pp. 68–84, 2020.
https://doi.org/10.1007/978-3-030-43823-4_7

are optimized for a given data set, in order to make machine learning methods available for non-expert users.

Since hyper-parameters of a machine learning model have a large influence on the performance of the model, hyper-parameter optimization becomes a critical part of an AutoML system. Popular hyper-parameter optimization methods include Sequential Bayesian Optimization, which iterates between fitting surrogate models that predict model performance, and using them to make choices about which configurations to investigate.

However, the composition of the machine learning pipelines also plays a vital role in the performance of AutoML systems. Choosing different data preprocessing or feature engineering techniques as well as choosing different machine learning models for a specific dataset could potentially result in considerable performance differences. The joint optimization of the pipeline search and its associated hyper-parameters configuration could essentially reside under the umbrella of Combined Algorithm Selection and Hyperparameter optimization (CASH) problem [31], where Algorithm corresponds to the pipeline and Configuration corresponds to the hyper-parameters associated with the pipeline. The pipelines and hyper-parameters reside in a conditional hierarchical space, where some hyper-parameters only become valid when the corresponding pipeline is present. For example, Fig. 1 illustrates such a situation when the data preprocessing and feature engineering operations are selected, which correspond to an incomplete pipeline, one out of three machine learning algorithms need to be chosen (indicated by dashed edges) to complete the pipeline, the corresponding hyper-parameters (indicated by solid edges) of an algorithm only become valid when the algorithm is selected.

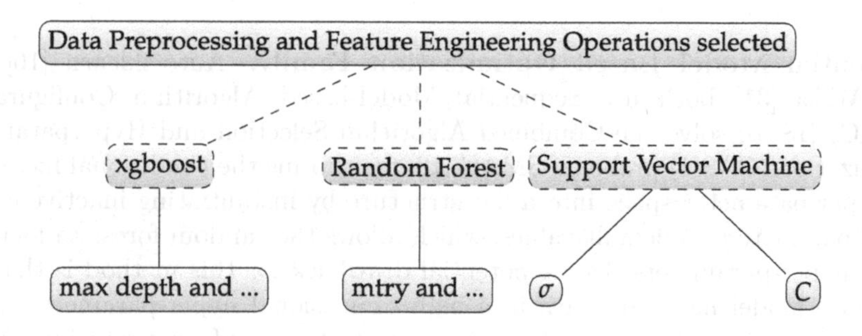

Fig. 1. Example of conditional hierarchical space

To optimize the conditional hyper-parameters space jointly with the pipeline it is attached to, we embed Bayesian Optimization in the Reinforcement Learning process, and dub the method ReinBo, which means Machine Learning Pipeline search and configuration with Reinforcement Learning and Bayesian Optimization. Note that ReinBo can solve not only CASH problems, but also any mixed discrete and continuous conditional hierarchical space optimization, which is left for future work.

Our major contributions are:

- Inspired by Hierarchical Reinforcement Learning [14], we transform the conditional hierarchical hyper-parameter optimization problem into subtasks of pipeline selection and hyper-parameter optimization, which circumvents the conditional constraint and reduces the search dimension.
- To our best knowledge, we are the first to embed Bayesian Optimization (BO) into Reinforcement learning, specifically Q Learning [32] for collaborative joint search of pipelines and hyper-parameters, which is different from using BO for policy optimization [12], and also different from using BO for hyper-parameter fine tuning after an optimal pipeline is selected by a reinforcement learning based AutoML framework [33].
- We provide an open source light weight R language implementation with benchmark codes[1] for the R Machine Learning community which could run efficiently on a personal computer, and takes much less resources (IO, disk space for example) compared to other AutoML softwares.

In the following section, we review related works and discuss the differences to our method. In Sect. 3, we explain our method in detail and also shed light to connections with Hyperband [22]. In Sect. 4, we benchmark our method by comparing it with several state of the art methods.

2 Related Work

In this section, we try to classify the current popular AutoML solutions into a taxonomy and discuss the differences of each individual work with ours.

Sequential Model Based Optimization Family. Auto-sklearn [16] and Auto-Weka [31] both use Sequential Model-based Algorithm Configuration (SMAC) [18] to solve the Combined Algorithm Selection and Hyperparameter optimization (CASH) problem. SMAC [18] transforms the conditional hierarchical hyper-parameter space into a flat structure by instantiating inactive conditional parameters to default values, which allows the random forest to focus on active hyper-parameters [18]. A potential drawback for this method is that the surrogate model needs to learn in a high dimensional hyper-parameter space, which might need a large sample of observations to be sufficiently trained, while in practice, running machine learning algorithm is usually very expensive. Tree Parzen Window (TPE) [7], however, tackles the conditional hierarchical hyper-parameter space using a tree like Parzen Window to construct two density estimators on top of a tree like hyper-parameter set. Expected improvement induced from lower and upper quantile density estimators is used to select new candidate proposals from points generated by Ancestral Sampling.

[1] https://github.com/compstat-lmu/paper_2019_ReinBo.

Tree-Based Genetic Programming. TPOT [25] automatically designs and optimizes machine learning pipelines with a genetic programming [3] algorithm. The machine learning operators are used as genetic programming primitives, which will be combined by tree-based pipelines and the Genetic Programming algorithm is used to evolve tree-based pipelines until the best pipeline is found. Similar methods also include Recipe [27]. However, this family of methods does not scale well [24]. In this paper, we aim for an AutoML system that could give a valuable configured pipeline within limited time.

Monte Carlo Tree Search Alike. ML-Plan [24] is an AutoML system, built upon a Hierarchical Task Network, which uses a Monte Carlo Tree Search like algorithm to search for pipelines and also configure the pipeline with hyper-parameters. Task is expanded based on best-first search, where the score is estimated by a randomized depth first search by randomly trying different subtree possibilities on a Hierarchical Task Network. To ensure exploration, ML-Plan gives equal possibility to the starting node in a Hierarchical Task Network and then uses a best-first strategy for searching at the lower part of the network. Potential drawback for this method is that the hyper-parameter space is discretized, which might essentially lose good candidates in continuous spaces since large continuous hyper-parameter spaces would be essentially hard to discretize.

Reinforcement Learning Based Neural Network Architecture Search. This family of methods are usually not termed as AutoML systems but rather Neural Architecture Search. For instance, MetaQNN [2] uses Q-learning to search convolutional neural network architectures. The learning agent is trained to sequentially choose CNN layers using Q-learning with an ϵ-greedy exploration strategy and the goal is to maximize the cross-validation accuracy. In [35], instead of using Q-learning, the authors use Recurrent Neural Networks as the reinforcement learning policy approximator to generate variable strings to represent various neural architecture forms. The reward-function is designed to be the validation performance of the constructed network. The reinforcement learning policy is trained with gradient descent algorithm, specifically REINFORCE. The architecture elements being searched are very similar to MetaQNN. Inspired from [35], we also assume the machine learning pipeline to be optimized could be represented by a variable length string, but our work is different from [35] in that we use both Deep Q-learning and Tabular Q-learning. More importantly, compared with both [2] and [35], which optimize the neural architecture, the elements of the architecture are mostly factor variables like layer type or discretized elements like filter size, while in this paper, we deal heavily with continuous hyper-parameters (The C and σ for a rbf kernel Support Vector Machine). To jointly optimize the discrete pipeline choice and associated continuous hyper-parameters, we embed Bayesian Optimization inside our reinforcement learning agent.

Other Reinforcement Learning Based Methods. In [33], the authors also combine pipeline search and hyper-parameter optimization in a reinforcement learning process based on the PEORL [34] framework, however, the hyper-parameter is randomly sampled during the reinforcement learning process, an extra stage is needed to sweep the hyper-parameters using hyper-parameter optimization techniques, while in our work, hyper-parameter optimization is embedded in the reinforcement learning process. Alpha3M [15] combined MCTS and recurrent neural network in a self play [28] fashion, however, it seems that Alpha3M does not perform better than the state of the art AutoML systems. For example, out of all the 6 OpenML datasets they have used to compare with state of the art AutoML systems, Alpha3M only shows a clear improvement on 1 dataset (spectf) against Auto-sklearn [16] and TPOT [25], according to Fig. 4 in [15]. Furthermore, it is not clear to us how the hyper-parameters are set and if Bayesian Optimization is used. The implementation of Alpha3M takes advantage of the GPUs [15] for the fast performance while our method has a light weight implementation which efficiently runs with CPU and does not necessarily need Neural Networks.

3 Method

3.1 Towards ReinBo

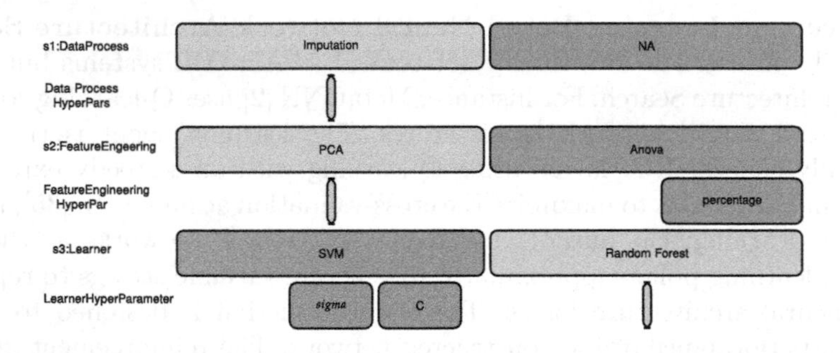

Fig. 2. Illustrative example of selected pipeline and associated hyper-parameters (Color figure online)

As shown in Fig. 2, we assume that a machine learning pipeline potentially consists of 3 stages (s1 through s3 in the figure), which include data preprocessing (imputations, NA and more), feature engineering (Principal Component Analysis for feature transform, Anova for feature filtering and more), and machine learning model selection (learner like SVM, Random Forest). Specifically, we use operation "NA" to indicate that no operation would be done in the stage in question. Figure 2 just serves as a toy but working example for ReinBo, in practice, there are a lot more operations available. A particular operation has associated hyper-parameters (for instance the percentage of selected features in Anova feature filtering). In Fig. 2, dark color filled cells (NA, Anova, SVM) represent selected operations and their associated active hyper-parameters (percentage, sigma, C), while hyper-parameters for inactive operations are not drawn in the figure.

Observing from Fig. 2, along with Fig. 1, we could think of the pipeline selection and configuration problem as a two-phase process. During the first phase, a planning algorithm guides the agent to choose a path which corresponds to an unconfigured pipeline. This is similar to a multi-armed bandit problem, where each path corresponds to one arm, while difference lies in that the agent can not directly pull a discrete arm but have to pull across several consecutive discrete arm groups (each arm group corresponds to a stage in Fig. 2) and the agent only gets reward after choosing one of arms from the last group. The second phase is similar to contextual bandit with continuous action space (corresponding to hyper-parameters), where the context is which path from the first phase has been selected.

We model the first phase as a reinforcement learning episode, where a particular operation in stage i is treated as action a_i, taken upon corresponding state s_i. State s_i could be represented by actions taken up to the current stage for example. The pipeline search problem is then to find an optimal policy π to decide which operation (action) to take at a particular state. The action value function $Q(s, a)$ at each state tells us how favorable a particular operation is. We use $\mathcal{A}_{s_i}$ to denote the space of legal actions at state s_i. Suppose a roll-out of states trajectory for one composition (episode) is $s_1, \ldots, s_K$, the corresponding space of pipeline could be denoted by $\prod_{i=1}^{K} \mathcal{A}_{s_i}$, where K is the total number of stages and we use $\prod$ to denote the Cartesian Product. For a more general notation, we use $\mathcal{A}(S_i, \Phi_{a_i})$ to denote the space of actions, together with configurable hyper-parameters when the state is S_i at stage i.

We search for potentially better hyper-parameters in the second phase with Bayesian Optimization. Aside from the pipeline itself, each concrete operation (action a_i) at stage i is configurable by a set of hyper-parameters Φ_{a_i}. Φ_{a_i} can be hyper-parameters set for a preprocessor like the ratio of variance to keep in PCA or hyper-parameters set for a machine learning model like the C and σ hyper-parameter for SVM. Thus a configured pipeline search space would be $\prod_{i=1}^{K} \mathcal{A}(S_i; \Phi_{a_i})$ where we use Φ_{a_i} to denote the conditional hyper-parameter space at stage i.

The connection point between reinforcement learning and Bayesian Optimization lies in the reward function design in the reinforcement learning part. During the composition process, there is no signal available to judge how good a current uncompleted pipeline is until the final learner (classifier) is configured with hyper-parameters and trained on the data. At the starting point, different pipelines are tried out randomly, which corresponds to an untrained exploration policy π. A completed pipeline with a joint non-conditional hyper-parameter search space is optimized with Bayesian Optimization for a few steps. The best negative loss is then used as a reward at the end of an episode to guide the reinforcement learning agent towards a better policy. The environment uncertainty only comes with the stochastic reward, while the transition from current state to next state through action is deterministic. We choose to use Q-learning [32] to optimize the policy where we have tried the Tabular Q-learning and Deep Q-learning [23]. We find out that the Tabular Q-learning works better than Deep Q-learning. For space constraint, the latter is not discussed in detail in this work.

We need Bayesian Optimization to optimize the hyper-parameters in a fine grained level with limited budget, but also want to give budget preference to those promising pipelines. To circumvent the complexity of conditional and hierarchical relationship between hyper-parameters and pipeline, we use reinforcement learning to choose a pipeline and let Bayesian Optimization tune the hyper-parameters. We model the variation of the same pipeline with different hyper-parameters as the environment uncertainty. By using separate surrogate model for each pipeline, we circumvent the risk of mistakenly modeling improper dependent structure between different hyper-parameters, at a minor cost of maintaining those searched pipelines surrogate model as dictionary in memory.

3.2 Connections to Hyperband

The idea of only using a few steps of Bayesian Optimization is inspired by Hyperband [22], where the trade-off between aggressively exploring more configurations and giving each configuration more resources to be validated is solved by grid searching. Instead, in this paper, we do not need the grid search, promising pipelines will get a higher probability to be selected by our reinforcement learning agent which means these pipelines get more chances to be evaluated by the Bayesian Optimization process. The trade-off between exploitation and exploration is naturally resolved by an ϵ-greedy policy, and by annealing ϵ from a large value to a small value, we encourage more exploration at the beginning. Compared to Hyperband, our method selects the budgets allocated for a particular pipeline automatically, the effectiveness of our strategy could then rely on the recent success of reinforcement learning in different areas.

3.3 Connection and Extension to Hierarchical Reinforcement Learning

Hierarchical Reinforcement Learning (hrl) [4] is proposed to tackle the curse of dimensionality in Reinforcement Learning [20]. Although the Option approach [4] is more popular, our method has a close connection to the MAXQ subtask approach [14], which divides a task recursively into subtasks and decompose the value function accordingly. The current version of ReinBo can be treated as a special case of the MAXQ task decomposition, where we have two tasks of pipeline selection and hyper-parameter configuration. However, in the current version, most states are not shared between these two tasks, so there is no need to use MAXQ hrl algorithm to solve the problem. But our method can be naturally extended to a hrl version when our design space of pipeline allow shared state between the two subtasks. We leave it as future work to optimize such complicated pipelines using Hierarchical Reinforcement Learning.

3.4 Procedures of ReinBo

As shown in Algorithm 1, we first initialize a policy π for the agent which can be represented by neural network or a Q-table initialized with certain strategy, coupled with an exploration mechanism like the ϵ-greedy strategy. During the roll-out, initial populations of pipelines get sampled, with the corresponding hyper-parameter space $\Lambda(\prod a_i) = \prod_i \Phi_{a_i}$ to be optimized by Bayesian Optimization for several steps, where Λ means extracting the hyper-parameter set from a pipeline. The corresponding surrogate model is stored in the dictionary $\mathcal{R}$ for future episode if the same pipeline gets rolled out again. The performance of the pipeline on validation data will be used to serve as feedback signal or reward to the reinforcement learning agent to conduct policy iteration.

Algorithm 1. ML ReinBo

Require: dataset $\mathcal{D}$, pipeline operators and hyper-parameters candidates
  Initialize Policy π
  Initialize Surrogate Dictionary $\mathcal{R} \leftarrow \emptyset$ with pipeline as key
  while Budget not reached **do**
    Roll-out an **unconfigured** pipeline $\prod a_i$ according to policy π
    Extract hyper-parameters set for the ground pipeline $\Lambda(\prod a_i) = \prod_i \Phi_{a_i}$
    Reward $R \leftarrow$ BO_PROBE($\prod a_i, \Lambda, \mathcal{R}$)
    Update Policy π with reinforcement learning algorithm with reward R
  end while

Once an unconfigured pipeline is constructed at the end of the episode, running Bayesian Optimization could be beneficial in searching for a more favorable hyper-parameter setting. However, Bayesian Hyperparameter Optimization with large budgets could be rather expensive. Instead, we optimize hyper-parameters for an unconfigured pipeline only for several iterations. For example, we take the number of iterations to be 2 or 3 times the dimension of hyper-parameter space, which means that hyper-parameter spaces with higher dimension will get more sampling budgets. After each episode, the current best configuration's performance for this pipeline in question is used as reward. The next time the same pipeline is sampled, the surrogate model could be retrieved from the dictionary $\mathcal{R}$ to facilitate further search using Bayesian Optimization. We dub the hyper-parameter search process as BO_PROBE, with details shown in Algorithm 2.[2] If an unconfigured pipeline is not sampled yet, an initial design is generated to facilitate an initial surrogate model.

[2] To save budgets, when an unconfigured pipeline does not improve after a number of trials of BO_PROBE, it can also be suspended for future evaluation.

Algorithm 2. BO_PROBE($\prod a_i, \Lambda, \mathcal{R}$)

Require: Surrogate Dictionary $\mathcal{R}$ with pipeline as key
  if $\mathcal{R}\{\prod_i a_i\} = \emptyset$ **then**
    generate initial design of size n^{init} hyper-parameter configurations $\{\phi_j\}_{1:n^{init}}$ for surrogate model with corresponding hyper-parameters set $\Lambda(\prod a_i)$.
    for j in $1 : n^{init}$ **do**
      evaluate the pipeline with ϕ_j to get predicative accuracy y_j
    end for
    initialize surrogate model $\mathcal{R}\{\prod_i a_i\}$ by fitting $\{(\phi_j, 1 - y_j)\}_{1:n^{init}}$
  end if
  for k in $1 : n^{probe}$ **do**
    propose new configuration ϕ_k according to surrogate model $\mathcal{R}\{\prod a_i\}$
    evaluate new configuration to get accuracy y_k to update model $\mathcal{R}\{\prod a_i\}$
  end for
  return $y^* \leftarrow$ best accuracy until now

4 Experiments

4.1 Implementation, Comparison Methods and Setups

Our initial implementation for ReinBo is based on R machine learning packages *mlr* [10], *mlrCPO* [8] for pipeline construction and *mlrMBO* [11] for Bayesian Optimization. The R package *parabox*[3] is implemented for this project to specify conditional hierarchical hyper-parameter space and provides the conditional ancestral sampling (random search in conditional hyper-parameter space). The R package *rlR*[4] is implemented for reinforcement learning where the user could implement a custom environment as input. All python packages are invoked with the R-Python interface *reticulate* [1].

To evaluate the performance of our proposed method, we compare the performance of ReinBo with several state of the art AutoML systems, as well as several conditional hyper-parameter space tuning methods running on top of our R implementation, in order to reduce implementation and search space confounding factors. We compare against Auto-sklearn [16] and TPOT [25] (TPOT with two search spaces to reduce confounding[5]), both based on *scikit-learn* [26]. ML-Plan [24] is not included due to lack of detailed documentation and examples online when experiment is conducted. Additionally, we compare against hyper-parameter optimization techniques which preserve the hierarchical conditional structure, including Tree-structured Parzen Estimator (TPE) [7] used in *Hyperopt* [6], and Random Search with conditional Ancestral Sampling (self implemented in R package *parabox*). Random Search remains a very strong baseline in a lot of machine learning hyper-parameter optimization scenarios [5].

[3] https://github.com/smilesun/parabox.
[4] https://github.com/smilesun/rlR.
[5] We also selected a matching search space of Autosklearn according to Table 1 but still get worse results than Reinbo.

Evaluation Criteria. As warned in [24], many state of the art AutoML systems seem to have missed to deal with the risk of overfitting. Therefore, in the experiment part, we focus on evaluating the generalization capability of the selected pipeline empirically. To avoid any potential confusion from synonyms, we use D^{opt} to represent the part of a dataset fed into a given AutoML system and use D^{test} to represent the locked out part [29] of the same dataset used to test the generalization capacity. The split of D^{opt} and D^{test} is done by Cross Validation, which means for a dataset D, $D = D^{opt} \bigcup D^{test}$ and $D^{opt} \bigcap D^{test} = \emptyset$. To create the D^{opt} and D^{test} split, we use 5-fold cross-validation (*CV5*), which corresponds to the outer loop of Nested Cross Validation (*NCV*) [13]. We take the aggregated mmce (mean miss-classification error) across the 5-fold iterations over each D^{test} as ultimate performance measure.

As of optimization on D^{opt}, instead of using running time as budget, we use the number of configuration evaluations as the unit of budget, to circumvent effects of hardware and network load variations, etc. For each D^{opt}, we assign a budget of 1000 times of *CV5* equivalents (5000 times model training) to each AutoML algorithm, which corresponds to the inner loop of *NCV* [13].

Other Setups. To account for different AutoML systems data input format incompatibility problem, we conduct dummy encoding to categorical features beforehand. Aiming for a light weight implementation, in the experiment, we limit our choice of pipeline components for ReinBo. We compose a pipeline in 3 stages, with potential operations/actions at each stage listed in Table 1. Associated hyper-parameters with an unconfigured pipeline are listed in Table 2. We call the components and associated hyper-parameters the pipeline pool. The same pipeline pool is used for ReinBo, TPE and Random Search.

For Auto-sklearn, Meta-learning and ensemble are disabled, the resampling strategy is set to be *CV5*, stop criteria is changed to budget instead of time and all other configurations are kept default. We have contacted the author of Autosklearn through Github for the right use of the API to ensure the above configuration is satisfied. For TPOT (version 0.9), the default configuration space contains a lot of operators while the light version provides only fast models and pre-processors. The light TPOT is therefore less time-consuming but it could probably lead to lower accuracy in consequence. For this reason, we compare ReinBo with both TPOT with the default configuration and TPOT with light configuration, and we call them TPOT and TPOT-light respectively. TPOT is configured to allow equal amount of budgets with all methods being compared and other configurations are left to be default.

Datasets. We experimented on a set of standard benchmarking datasets of high quality collected from OpenML-CC18[6] [9] and Auto-Weka [30], which are rather well-curated from many thousands and have diverse numbers of classes, features, observations, as well as various ratios of the minority and majority class size. Summary of these datasets is listed in Table 3.

[6] https://www.openml.org/s/99.

Table 1. List of pipeline operations. An operation of "NA" here is used to indicate that no operation would be taken in the corresponding stage. Please refer to *mlrCPO* documentation for the detailed meaning of these operators.

	Stage	Operation/action				
1	DataPreprocess	Scale(default)	Scale(center=FALSE)	Scale(scale=FALSE)	SpatialSign	NA
2	Feature engineering	Pca	FilterKruskal	FilterAnova	FilterUnivariate	NA
3	Classifier	kknn	ksvm	ranger	xgboost	naiveBayes

Table 2. List of hyper-parameters to the operations in Table 1. "p" in the column "Range" indicates the number of features of the original dataset. We invite the user to refer to the R packages *mlrCPO* and *mlr* documentations for the exact meaning of operation, hyper-parameters, etc.

Operation	Parameter	Type	Range
Anonva, Kruskal, Univariate	perc	numeric	(0.1, 1)
Pca	rank	integer	(p/10, p)
kknn	k	integer	(1, 20)
ksvm	C	numeric	$(2^{-15}, 2^{15})$
ksvm	sigma	numeric	$(2^{-15}, 2^{15})$
ranger	mtry	integer	(p/10, p/1.5)
ranger	sample.fraction	numeric	(0.1, 1)
xgboost	eta	numeric	(0.001, 0.3)
xgboost	max_depth	integer	(1, 15)
xgboost	subsample	numeric	(0.5, 1)
xgboost	colsample_bytree	numeric	(0.5, 1)
xgboost	min_child_weight	numeric	(0, 50)
naiveBayes	laplace	numeric	(0.01, 100)

4.2 Experiment Results

In Fig. 3, we compare the mmce (1-Accuracy) of each method with boxplot over the datasets listed in Table 3 across 10 statistical replications. Additionally, we list numerical results in Table 4 with statistical test, where each numerical value represents the aggregated mean mmce over the statistical replications. Underline in each row indicates the smallest mean value over the corresponding dataset. The bold-faced values indicate that the corresponding algorithm does not perform significantly worse than the underlined algorithm on the corresponding dataset based on Mann-Whitney U test. As shown in Table 4, ML-ReinBo has boldfaces for 8 of 10 datasets followed by much less boldfaces from other methods.

In Table 5, we compare win (significantly better), lose and tie (neither significantly better nor worse) relationships according to the test. As shown in Table 5,

Table 3. List of OpenML datasets for experiment. Columns are the OpenML task_id and name, the number of classes (nClass), features (nFeat) and observations (nObs), as well as the ratio of the minority and majority class sizes (rMinMaj).

task_id	Name	nClass	nFeat	nObs	rMinMaj
14	mfeat-fourier	10	77	2000	1.00
23	cmc	3	10	1473	0.53
37	diabetes	2	9	768	0.54
53	vehicle	4	19	846	0.91
3917	kc1	2	22	2109	0.18
9946	wdbc	2	31	569	0.59
9952	phoneme	2	6	5404	0.42
9978	ozone-level-8hr	2	73	2534	0.07
146817	steel-plates-fault	7	28	1941	0.08
146820	wilt	2	6	4839	0.06

ReinBo has won TPOT on 5 datasets and performed worse than TPOT for only one dataset. And not surprisingly, TPOT has performed considerably better than TPOT-light in the empirical experiments since TPOT-light has smaller search space with only fast models and preprocessors. ReinBo also performs much better than Random Search and TPE, where ReinBo has significantly won them on 5 and 6 tasks respectively and lost only on 1 task. Compared to ReinBo, Auto-sklearn has won only once and behaved worse than ReinBo on 3 of 10 datasets.

Table 4. Average performance (mmce) of algorithms across 10 statistical replications with different seeds. In each run the aggregated mmce based over the outer loop of *NCV* is taken as performance measure for each algorithm. Each value in this table is the mean value of the aggregated mmce values across 10 replications and the best mean value for each dataset is underlined. The bold-faced values indicate that the algorithm does not perform significantly worse than the underlined algorithm on the corresponding dataset based on Mann-Whitney U test.

Dataset	Auto-sklearn	TPE	TPOT	TPOT-light	Random	ReinBo	Underlined algorithm
mfeat-fourier	0.1412	0.1542	0.1451	0.1489	0.1580	**0.1278**	ReinBo
cmc	**0.4470**	**0.4485**	**0.4457**	**0.4506**	**0.4500**	**0.4485**	TPOT
diabetes	0.2483	**0.2436**	0.2452	**0.2413**	**0.2455**	**0.2395**	ReinBo
vehicle	**0.1679**	0.2117	0.1784	0.2057	0.2020	**0.1621**	ReinBo
kc1	0.1421	**0.1351**	**0.1380**	0.1438	**0.1353**	0.1387	TPE
wdbc	**0.0299**	0.0348	0.0353	**0.0264**	0.0341	**0.0271**	TPOT-light
phoneme	**0.0902**	**0.0920**	**0.0893**	0.1016	**0.0912**	**0.0905**	TPOT
ozone-level-8hr	**0.0588**	0.0601	**0.0577**	0.0603	0.0598	**0.0578**	TPOT
steel-plates-fault	0.2041	0.2330	**0.1985**	0.2601	0.2146	0.2141	TPOT
wilt	0.0132	0.0159	0.0141	0.0164	0.0161	**0.0123**	ReinBo

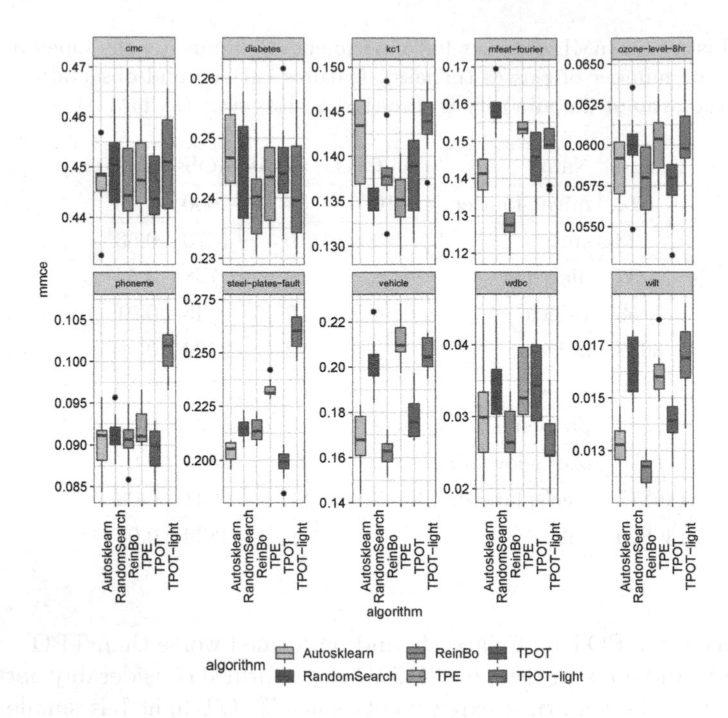

Fig. 3. Boxplots showing the distribution of aggregated mmce achieved by each algorithm within 10 statistical replications.

Meanwhile, ReinBo has comparatively short box ranges in most cases as shown in Fig. 3. Hence, we would conclude that ReinBo performed better and more stably than other algorithms in our empirical experiments. Besides comparing the final performance, it is also interesting to look into the machine learning pipelines suggested by an AutoML system. The frequencies of the operators in the pipelines suggested by ReinBo are listed in Table 6.

Running Time. Figure 4 shows the average running time each algorithm takes to complete one experiment, which corresponds to a Nested Cross Validation (*NCV*) process. It can be seen that Auto-sklearn is the most time-consuming

Table 5. Win-Lose-Tie comparison between ReinBo and other algorithms on benchmarking datasets based on Mann-Whitney U test (significance level $\alpha = 0.05$).

		Random_search	TPE	Auto-sklearn	TPOT-light	TPOT
ReinBo	Win	5	6	3	7	5
	Tie	4	3	6	3	4
	Lose	1	1	1	0	1

Table 6. Frequency of operators suggested by ReinBo. During empirical experiments there are 500 pipelines in total suggested by ReinBo at the end of optimization process. The frequency (Freq.) and relative frequency (Relative freq.) of each operator selected in best pipelines are shown here.

Preprocess	Freq.	Relative freq.	Feature engineering	Freq.	Relative freq.	Classifier	Freq.	Relative freq.
Scale(default)	259	51.8%	FilterAnova	210	42.0%	ksvm	276	55.2%
Scale(scale=FALSE)	106	21.2%	FilterKruskal	139	27.8%	ranger	201	40.2%
Scale(center=FALSE)	67	13.4%	PCA	63	12.6%	kknn	12	2.4%
NA	36	7.2%	Univariate	46	9.2%	xgboost	10	2.0%
SpatialSign	32	6.4%	NA	42	8.4%	naiveBayes	1	0.2%

algorithm in our empirical experiments. Although TPOT-light is the fastest algorithm, it resulted in worse performance because it contains only fast operators. Our proposed ReinBo algorithm spent less time than Random Search and state of the art AutoML systems TPOT and Auto-sklearn in average.

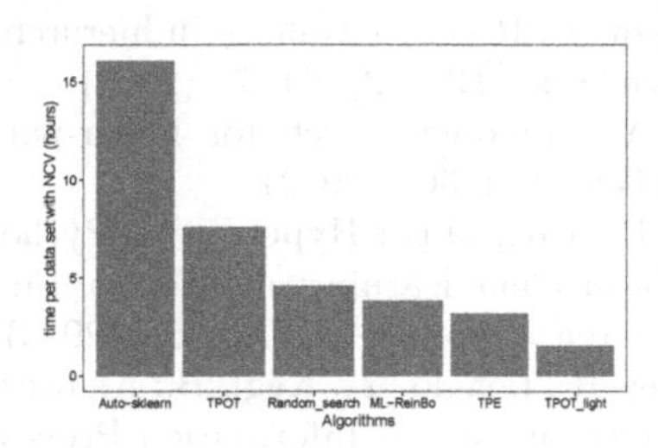

Fig. 4. Comparison of average running time of each algorithm per data set with *NCV*

5 Summary and Future Work

We present a new AutoML algorithm ReinBo by embedding Bayesian Optimization into Reinforcement Learning. The Reinforcement Learning takes care of pipeline composition, and Bayesian Optimization takes care of configuring the hyper-parameters associated with the composed pipeline. ReinBo is inspired by Hyperband and previous efforts in AutoML by considering the trade-off of assigning resources to a particular configuration and exploring more configurations as a reinforcement learning problem, where the learned policy solves the trade-off automatically. Experiments show our method has a considerable improvement compared to other state of the art systems and methods. For future work, it would be interesting to include meta learning into our system, which does not only learn how to construct a pipeline and configure it for a dataset in question, but also how to generalize the learned policy to a wide range of datasets by learning jointly on the meta features. Additionally, it would be nice to see how ReinBo performs on jointly optimizing neural architecture and continuous hyper-parameters like learning rate and momentum, as well as applications like Computer Vision [19] and semantic web based Recommendation Systems [21] where pipeline might play a role. Multi-Objective Bayesian Optimization [17] for hyper-parameter tuning would also be future direction.

Acknowledgement. Janek Thomas gave us many helpful suggestions, Martin Binder and Florian Pfisterer helped us with mlrCPO and auto-sklearn setup.

References

1. Allaire, J., Ushey, K., Tang, Y.: Reticulate: interface to 'Python' (2019). https://CRAN.R-project.org/package=reticulate. R package version 1.11.1
2. Baker, B., Gupta, O., Naik, N., Raskar, R.: Designing neural network architectures using reinforcement learning. In: International Conference on Learning Representations (2017)
3. Banzhaf, W., Nordin, P., Keller, R.E., Francone, F.D.: Genetic Programming: An Introduction, vol. 1. Morgan Kaufmann, San Francisco (1998)
4. Barto, A.G., Mahadevan, S.: Recent advances in hierarchical reinforcement learning. Discrete Event Dyn. Syst. **13**(1–2), 41–77 (2003)
5. Bergstra, J., Bengio, Y.: Random search for hyper-parameter optimization. J. Mach. Learn. Res. **13**(Feb), 281–305 (2012)
6. Bergstra, J., Yamins, D., Cox, D.D.: Hyperopt: a Python library for optimizing the hyperparameters of machine learning algorithms. In: Proceedings of the 12th Python in Science Conference, pp. 13–20. Citeseer (2013)
7. Bergstra, J.S., Bardenet, R., Bengio, Y., Kégl, B.: Algorithms for hyper-parameter optimization. In: Advances in Neural Information Processing Systems, pp. 2546–2554 (2011)
8. Binder, M.: mlrCPO: composable preprocessing operators and pipelines for machine learning (2019). https://CRAN.R-project.org/package=mlrCPO. R package version 0.3.4-2
9. Bischl, B., et al.: OpenML benchmarking suites and the openml100. arXiv preprint arXiv:1708.03731 (2017)
10. Bischl, B., et al.: mlr: machine learning in R. J. Mach. Learn. Res. **17**(170), 1–5 (2016). http://jmlr.org/papers/v17/15-066.html
11. Bischl, B., Richter, J., Bossek, J., Horn, D., Thomas, J., Lang, M.: mlrMBO: a modular framework for model-based optimization of expensive black-box functions. arXiv preprint arXiv:1703.03373 (2017)
12. Brochu, E., Cora, V.M., De Freitas, N.: A tutorial on Bayesian optimization of expensive cost functions, with application to active user modeling and hierarchical reinforcement learning. arXiv preprint arXiv:1012.2599 (2010)
13. Cawley, G.C., Talbot, N.L.: On over-fitting in model selection and subsequent selection bias in performance evaluation. J. Mach. Learn. Res. **11**(Jul), 2079–2107 (2010)
14. Dietterich, T.G.: Hierarchical reinforcement learning with the MAXQ value function decomposition. J. Artif. Intell. Res. **13**, 227–303 (2000)
15. Drori, I., et al.: AlphaD3M: machine learning pipeline synthesis. In: AutoML Workshop at ICML (2018)

16. Feurer, M., Klein, A., Eggensperger, K., Springenberg, J., Blum, M., Hutter, F.: Efficient and robust automated machine learning. In: Advances in Neural Information Processing Systems, pp. 2962–2970 (2015)
17. Horn, D., Dagge, M., Sun, X., Bischl, B.: First investigations on noisy model-based multi-objective optimization. In: Trautmann, H., et al. (eds.) EMO 2017. LNCS, vol. 10173, pp. 298–313. Springer, Cham (2017). https://doi.org/10.1007/978-3-319-54157-0_21
18. Hutter, F., Hoos, H.H., Leyton-Brown, K.: Sequential model-based optimization for general algorithm configuration. In: Coello, C.A.C. (ed.) LION 2011. LNCS, vol. 6683, pp. 507–523. Springer, Heidelberg (2011). https://doi.org/10.1007/978-3-642-25566-3_40
19. Zhang, J., Guo, L., Yang, S., Sun, X., Li, X.: Detecting Chinese calligraphy style consistency by deep learning and one-class SVM. In: 2017 2nd International Conference on Image, Vision and Computing (ICIVC), pp. 83–86. IEEE (2017)
20. Kulkarni, T.D., Narasimhan, K., Saeedi, A., Tenenbaum, J.: Hierarchical deep reinforcement learning: integrating temporal abstraction and intrinsic motivation. In: Advances in Neural Information Processing Systems, pp. 3675–3683 (2016)
21. Kushwaha, N., Sun, X., Singh, B., Vyas, O.: A lesson learned from PMF based approach for semantic recommender system. J. Intell. Inf. Syst. **50**(3), 441–453 (2018)
22. Li, L., Jamieson, K., DeSalvo, G., Rostamizadeh, A., Talwalkar, A.: Hyperband: a novel bandit-based approach to hyperparameter optimization. J. Mach. Learn. Res. **18**(1), 6765–6816 (2017)
23. Mnih, V., et al.: Human-level control through deep reinforcement learning. Nature **518**(7540), 529 (2015)
24. Mohr, F., Wever, M., Hüllermeier, E.: ML-plan: automated machine learning via hierarchical planning. Mach. Learn. **107**(8–10), 1495–1515 (2018)
25. Olson, R.S., Moore, J.H.: TPOT: a tree-based pipeline optimization tool for automating machine learning. In: Workshop on Automatic Machine Learning, pp. 66–74 (2016)
26. Pedregosa, F., et al.: Scikit-learn: machine learning in Python. J. Mach. Learn. Res. **12**, 2825–2830 (2011)
27. de Sá, A.G.C., Pinto, W.J.G.S., Oliveira, L.O.V.B., Pappa, G.L.: RECIPE: a grammar-based framework for automatically evolving classification pipelines. In: McDermott, J., Castelli, M., Sekanina, L., Haasdijk, E., García-Sánchez, P. (eds.) EuroGP 2017. LNCS, vol. 10196, pp. 246–261. Springer, Cham (2017). https://doi.org/10.1007/978-3-319-55696-3_16
28. Silver, D., et al.: Mastering the game of go without human knowledge. Nature **550**(7676), 354 (2017)
29. Sun, X., Bommert, A., Pfisterer, F., Rähenfürher, J., Lang, M., Bischl, B.: High dimensional restrictive federated model selection with multi-objective Bayesian optimization over shifted distributions. In: Bi, Y., Bhatia, R., Kapoor, S. (eds.) IntelliSys 2019. AISC, vol. 1037, pp. 629–647. Springer, Cham (2020). https://doi.org/10.1007/978-3-030-29516-5_48
30. Thornton, C., Hutter, F., Hoos, H.H., Leyton-Brown, K.: Auto-WEKA: automated selection and hyper-parameter optimization of classification algorithms. CoRR abs/1208.3719 (2012). http://arxiv.org/abs/1208.3719
31. Thornton, C., Leyton-Brown, K.: Auto-WEKA: automated selection and hyper-parameter optimization of classification algorithms (2012)
32. Watkins, C.J., Dayan, P.: Q-learning. Mach. Learn. **8**(3–4), 279–292 (1992)

33. Yang, F., Gustafson, S., Elkholy, A., Lyu, D., Liu, B.: Program search for machine learning pipelines leveraging symbolic planning and reinforcement learning. In: Banzhaf, W., Spector, L., Sheneman, L. (eds.) Genetic Programming Theory and Practice XVI. GEC, pp. 209–231. Springer, Cham (2019). https://doi.org/10.1007/978-3-030-04735-1_11
34. Yang, F., Lyu, D., Liu, B., Gustafson, S.: PEORL: integrating symbolic planning and hierarchical reinforcement learning for robust decision-making. arXiv preprint arXiv:1804.07779 (2018)
35. Zoph, B., Le, Q.V.: Neural architecture search with reinforcement learning. arXiv preprint arXiv:1611.01578 (2016)

Supervised Human-Guided Data Exploration

Emilia Oikarinen[1(✉)], Kai Puolamäki[1], Samaneh Khoshrou[2], and Mykola Pechenizkiy[2]

[1] Department of Computer Science, University of Helsinki, Helsinki, Finland
{emilia.oikarinen,kai.puolamaki}@helsinki.fi

[2] Department of Computer Science, Eindhoven University of Technology, Eindhoven, The Netherlands
{s.khoshrou,m.pechenizkiy}@tue.nl

Abstract. An exploratory data analysis system should be aware of what a user already knows and what the user wants to know of the data. Otherwise it is impossible to provide the user with truly informative and useful views of the data. In our recently introduced framework for human-guided data exploration (Puolamäki et al. [20]), both the user's knowledge and objectives are modelled as distributions over data, parametrised by tile constraints. This makes it possible to show the users the most informative views given their current knowledge and objectives. Often the data, however, comes with a class label and the user is interested only of the features informative related to the class. In non-interactive settings there exist dimensionality reduction methods, such as supervised PCA (Barshan et al. [1]), to make such visualisations, but no such method takes the user's knowledge or objectives into account. Here, we formulate an information criterion for *supervised human-guided data exploration* to find the most informative views about the class structure of the data by taking both the user's current knowledge and objectives into account. We study experimentally the scalability of our method for interactive use, and stability with respect to the size of the class of interest. We show that our method gives understandable and useful results when analysing real-world datasets, and a comparison to SPCA demonstrates the effect of the user's background knowledge. The implementation will be released as an open source software library.

1 Introduction and Related Work

Exploratory data analysis (EDA) is a long studied topic [24]. More often than not, the data is so high-dimensional that it is not possible for a user to view it at once. This problem can be solved, e.g., by various *dimensionality reduction* (DR) methods that attempt to embed the data in a lower-dimensional manifold so that a chosen metrics is preserved as accurately as possible [15]. The main drawback in almost all DR methods is that the criteria by which dimensionality is reduced are often fixed, or at least it is not clear *how to take into account what the*

P. Cellier and K. Driessens (Eds.): ECML PKDD 2019 Workshops, CCIS 1167, pp. 85–101, 2020.
https://doi.org/10.1007/978-3-030-43823-4_8

user already knows and what are the objectives of the user when computing the embedding; see [23] for a survey of recent work on interactive DR. EDA systems also incorporate *visual* and *interactive* components, and visual interactive EDA has applications in different contexts, e.g., in item-set mining and subgroup discovery [3,8,16], information retrieval [22], and network analysis [4].

One approach to incorporate the user's knowledge to EDA is to model this as a distribution over datasets—*background distribution*—and then show the user an embedding that gives the user as much information as possible that the user did not already know. One of the original works in modelling the background distribution using randomisation was [11], and in [6] maximum entropy distributions were used. In both of these works the users can encode their knowledge as constraints. Later, these ideas have been realised as parts of working EDA systems with DR methods able to show the user what the user does not already know and able to absorb the relations the user has learned from the data, see, e.g., [5,12,13,18,19,21,25]. The drawback in all of these works is, however, that the *EDA process is unguided*: the user is shown something she or he does not know and what is therefore by definition always a surprise. Recently, we solved this problem in [20] by allowing the user to formulate also her or his *objectives* in terms of the relations of attributes the user is interested in. This allows the user to *guide the exploration to patterns of interest.*

Often, however, the user is not interested in all possible features of the data, but only in features that are informative, e.g., of a given class label. *Supervised DR* methods try to find an embedding that shows only the features of the data that are informative in such cases. Typical examples of supervised DR, such as Fisher's discriminant analysis [9], metric learning [26], sufficient dimensionality reduction [10], and supervised PCA [1] are however all based on a fixed embedding criteria. User interaction in guiding data exploration has been considered in the context of database management systems, e.g., in [7], where the user tells the system which samples are relevant and which are not, allowing the system to incrementally lead the user to explore towards interesting data areas. However, to the best of our knowledge there are no earlier approaches that take into account *both the human's subjective background knowledge and allow for supervised dimensionality reduction.*

Contributions. The objective of this work is to propose a method of supervised DR for interactive EDA systems that take both the user's background knowledge and the user's objectives into account. Our contributions are as follows: (i) An information criterion for *supervised human-guided data exploration*, where we can find the most informative views about the class structure of the data. (ii) An experimental study of scalability for interactive use, and stability with respect to the size of the class of interest. (iii) A demonstration showing that our method gives understandable and useful results when analysing real-world datasets.

Organisation. We provide a recap of the necessary concepts of the human-guided data exploration framework proposed in [20] in Sect. 2. In Sect. 3 we extend and modify the framework from [20] into a supervised setting. In Sect. 4 we evaluate

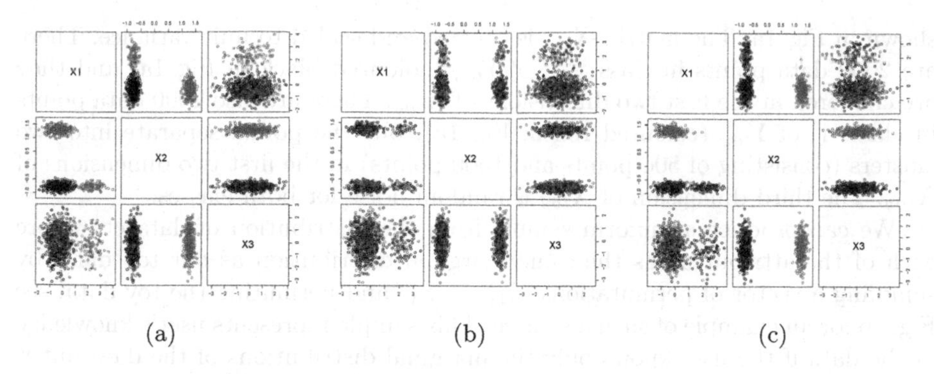

(a) (b) (c)

Fig. 1. Samples drawn from the distribution of datasets where each attribute has the same marginal distribution as the toy data Z_{toy}, see Examples 1 and 2 for details. Class attribute Y_{toy} shown with colour: class '1' in red and class '−1' in black. A sample of 1000 data points plotted for illustration. Here Z_{toy} is permuted using (a) a vector of identity permutations (i.e., the plot shows Z_{toy}) (b) a vector of random permutations (i.e., the plot shows an unconstrained permutation of Z_{toy}) (c) a vector of permutations allowed by tile t from Example 2. (Color figure online)

the scalability of our method for interactive use using crafted datasets. We also provide real-life data use cases demonstrating the utility of our method. We present our conclusions and directions for further work in Sect. 5.

2 Background

We start by introducing our notation and providing a brief recap to *human-guided data exploration* (HGDE) framework proposed in [20]. For now, we assume that X is a real-valued $n \times m$ data matrix (dataset) and $Y \in L^n$ a vector of class labels in L. Here $X(i,j)$ (resp. $Y(i)$) denotes the ith element (in column j). Each column $X(\cdot, j)$, $j \in [m]$, is an *attribute* in the dataset, where we used the shorthand $[m] = \{1, \ldots, m\}$. Let $Z = (X|Y)$ denote the $n \times m'$ where $m' = m+1$ data matrix obtained by augmenting X with Y.

A *permutation* of matrix Z is defined as follows.

Definition 1 (Permutation). *Let $\mathcal{P}$ denote the set of permutation functions of length n such that $\pi : [n] \mapsto [n]$ is a bijection for all $\pi \in \mathcal{P}$, and denote by $(\pi_1, \ldots, \pi_{m'}) \in \mathcal{P}^{m'}$ the vector of column-specific permutations. A permutation $\widehat{Z}$ of the data matrix Z is then given as $\widehat{Z}(i,j) = Z(\pi_j(i), j)$.*

When permutation functions are sampled uniformly at random, we obtain a uniform sample from the distribution of datasets where each of the attributes has the same marginal distribution as the original data.

Example 1. We will use a running example throughout the paper to illustrate the main concepts. Our artificial toy data Z_{toy} consists of a three dimensional matrix $X_{toy} \in \mathbb{R}^{n \times 3}$ and a binary class attribute $Y_{toy} \in \{-1, 1\}^n$, where $n = 4000$, shown in Fig. 1a. The matrix X_{toy} is centred and scaled to unit variance. There are 2000 data points in class '−1' of Y_{toy} (coloured black in Fig. 1a) and they are clustered in the first two dimensions of X_{toy}. There are also 2000 data points in class '1' of Y_{toy} (coloured red in Fig. 1a), but the points separate into two clusters (consisting of 500 points and 1500 points) in the first two dimensions of X_{toy}. The third dimension of X_{toy} is random noise for both classes.

We can produce a uniform sample from the distribution of datasets where each of the attributes has the same marginal distribution as our toy data, by sampling a vector of permutations $(\pi_1, \ldots, \pi_4)$ and permuting the toy data, see Fig. 1b for an example of such a sample. This sample represents user's knowledge of the data if the user knows only the marginal distributions of the data but is unaware of any relations between the class and the attributes.

We will next parametrise this distribution with *tiles* preserving the relations[1] in the data matrix Z for a subset of rows and columns: a tile is a tuple $t = (R, C)$, where $R \subseteq [n]$ and $C \subseteq [m']$. In an unconstrained case, there are $(n!)^{m'}$ allowed vectors of permutations. The tiles constrain the allowed permutations as follows.

Definition 2 (Tile constraint). *Given a tile $t = (R, C)$, the vector of permutations $(\pi_1, \ldots, \pi_{m'}) \in \mathcal{P}^{m'}$ is allowed by t iff the following condition is true for all $i \in [n]$, $j \in [m']$, and $j' \in [m']$:*

$$i \in R \wedge \{j, j'\} \subseteq C \implies \pi_j(i) \in R \wedge \pi_j(i) = \pi_{j'}(i).$$

Given a set of tiles T, $(\pi_1, \ldots, \pi_{m'})$ is allowed iff it is allowed by all $t \in T$.

A tile defines a subset of rows and columns, and the rows in this subset are permuted by the same permutation function in each column in the tile. In other words, the *relations between the attributes inside the tile are preserved* (such as correlations etc.). Notice that the identity permutation is always an allowed permutation. Now, the sampling problem can be formulated as follows.

Problem 1 (Sampling problem). Given a set of tiles T, draw samples uniformly at random from vectors of permutations in $\mathcal{P}^{m'}$ allowed by T.

The sampling problem is trivial when the tiles are non-overlapping. In the case of overlapping tiles, one can always merge tiles to obtain an equivalent set of non-overlapping tiles (i.e., a *tiling*) as shown in [20].

Example 2. Let us consider again the toy data Z_{toy} and define a tile constraint $t = (R, C)$ as follows. Let R be the set of points from class '1' that are separated from the points in class '−1' along the second attribute in X_{toy}, i.e., the larger of the two red clusters, and let $C = \{1, 2, 4\}$, i.e., the first two attributes of X_{toy} and the class attribute Y_{toy}. Now, if we permute Z_{toy} using a vector of permutations allowed by t, we obtain a sample data in which the relations inside the tile are preserved. An example of such a data sample is shown in Fig. 1c. This distributions models the case where the user is aware that the points in the tile are in class '1' and that they form a cluster in attributes $X1$ vs. $X2$.

[1] We use the general term *relation* for any structure in data that can be controlled using the constrained permutation scheme, e.g., correlation or cluster structure.

Focusing Exploration Using Hypotheses. The tile constraints can also be used to specify the relations in which the user is interested [20]. The so-called *hypothesis tilings* define the items R and attributes C of interest, and the relations between the attributes that the user is interested in through a partition of C. To simplify the presentation here, we will make the assumption that the user is interested in *all* relations between all the attributes. This restricted setting reduces to *unguided data exploration*, where the user is interested in all unknown inter-attribute relations in the data. Notice that the HGDE framework allows the user to define more general hypotheses in a flexible way (see [20] for details) and our current approach is compatible with the more general hypothesis as well.

The intuition is that we model two distributions over data sets: (i) the one which models what the user can learn of the interesting relations in the data (formalised by HYPOTHESIS 1), and (ii) the other which models what the user already knows of the interesting relations in the data (formalised by HYPOTHESIS 2). The dimensionality reduction problem is then to find a direction $v \in \mathbb{R}^m$ in which the two distributions differ the most, using a suitable objective function. In [20], e.g., the objective in DR was essentially to find the direction maximising variance, which will by definition give a user a view (projection) that is the most informative. More formally, let us thus consider the following hypotheses:

- HYPOTHESIS 1: there are relations in data between all the attributes, and
- HYPOTHESIS 2: there are no relations in data between any of the attributes.

Now, a distribution p_1 conforming to HYPOTHESIS 1 can be characterised using the tile $t_1 = ([n], [m'])$, which restricts the set of allowed vectors of permutations so that every column (attribute) has to be permuted using the same permutation. On the other hand, a distribution p_2 conforming to HYPOTHESIS 2 can be characterised using the set of tiles $\{([n], \{j\}) \mid j \in [m']\}$, which places no restrictions on the set of allowed vectors of permutations, i.e., every column (attribute) is permuted independently.

The knowledge of the user concerning relations in the data is described by tiles defined by the user during exploration process (user tiles), which are merged into the both of the hypothesis tilings. The process is iterative in the sense that after the user adds more constraints, a new direction v is sought. While the permutation-based randomisation scheme is general to all data types, the projection pursuit in [20] is restricted to real-valued data, and reduces to *principal component analysis* (PCA) when the user has initially no background knowledge and the hypotheses cover all the data.

Example 3. In Fig. 2a the projection of the real-valued part X_{toy} to the first two principal components is shown, which corresponds to the most informative projection in the HGDE framework when the user has no background knowledge and the hypotheses cover all the data. While this projection provides the view to data maximising variance, it is not very useful in case if the user was interested in, e.g., the class '1'.

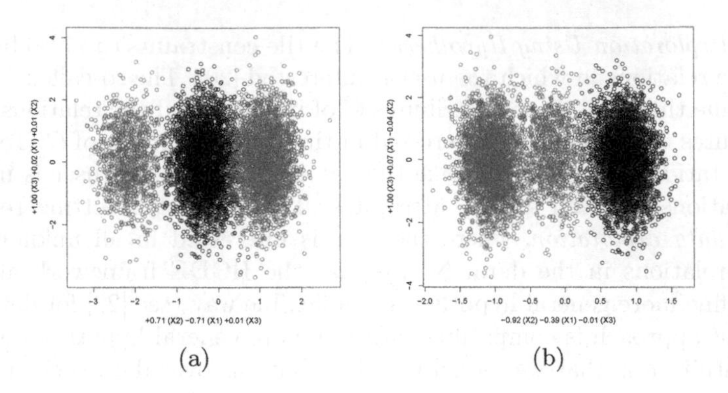

Fig. 2. Toy data Z_{toy} projected into first two principal components using PCA (a) and SPCA (b). Colors as in Fig. 1. (Color figure online)

3 Supervised Exploration

Example 3 shows that the most informative projection in the HGDE framework does not take into account the class information, which is by no means surprising, since only the real-valued part of the data was used. We now extend the HGDE framework to a supervised setting, i.e., instead of looking for directions in which the distributions corresponding to hypotheses differ the most in general, we are interested in finding directions which give most information about a class.

Example 4. Let us assume that a user is interested in class '1' in our toy data Z_{toy}. One alternative could be to use supervised PCA (SPCA) [1]. In Fig. 2b we provide a projection obtained performing SPCA on X_{toy} with delta-kernel for Y_{toy}. Clearly, the x-axis separates the data with respect to Y_{toy}. However, if we assume that the user already has some background knowledge about the data, e.g., the user knows the relations formulated in terms of tile t from Example 2, this projection becomes less informative and there is no direct way to incorporate the user's knowledge into SPCA.

As a further observation, we note that when there is only a single target attribute (as it is the case with our present work), the resulting optimisation problem in SPCA involves a rank-1 matrix, and thus only the first component contains meaningful information.

We formulate now our *main problem*, i.e., how to find the direction $v \in \mathbb{R}^m$ that is the most informative with respect to a particular class $c \in L$. We will use two hypotheses, HYPOTHESIS 1 and HYPOTHESIS 2, formulated as described in Sect. 2. Furthermore, we assume that the tile constraints used to represent the background knowledge of a user are merged into both hypotheses, and when we refer to HYPOTHESIS 1 and HYPOTHESIS 2, we always assume that the current user tiles are merged into both.

Problem 2 (Main problem). Given distribution p_1 conforming to HYPOTHESIS 1 and p_2 conforming to HYPOTHESIS 2 together with a class $c \in L$, find the direction $v \in \mathbb{R}^m$ providing the most information about the class c, i.e., the direction v in which p_1 and p_2 differ the most in terms of c.

Let $X_{Y=c}$ denote the restriction of the real-valued part X of $Z = (X|Y)$ to those rows i for which $Y(i) = c$. Our problem can then be formalised as finding a direction v in which $X_{Y=c}$ and $X'_{Y'=c}$ differ most by some suitable measure, where $Z = (X|Y)$ and $Z' = (X'|Y')$ have been sampled from p_1 and p_2, respectively. Thus, to solve Problem 2, we need a function that measures how well the class c is separated in p_1 and p_2 in a direction v.

We want to choose a measure that will separate the distributions as much as possible *visually*. To illustrate what we mean by this, consider, e.g., a case where distributions p_i^v, $i \in \{1, 2\}$, are defined by a uniform distribution plus a narrow peak[2] at $x_i(v) \in [-1, 1]$ to direction v. We would want to find a measure that is largest when the distance between the peaks $|x_1(v) - x_2(v)|$ is maximised. From information-theoretic view an obvious alternative would be Kullback-Leibler divergence between distributions p_i^v, but, in fact, it is insensitive to the distance between peaks. Thus, we choose to use the numerically more stable *L1-norm between cumulative distributions.* For example, in the case of p_1^v and p_2^v this measure is maximised for v for which the distance between the peaks is the largest.

Definition 3. *Given distributions p_1 and p_2 and a class of interest $c \in L$, the difference between p_1 and p_2 with respect to c in direction $v \in \mathbb{R}^m$ is computed using the L1-distance between the empirical cumulative distribution functions for the real-valued parts of samples $Z = (X|Y)$ and $Z' = (X'|Y')$ from p_1 and p_2, respectively, restricted to c and projected to v:*

$$f(Z, Z', c, v) = ||F(X_{Y=c}v) - F(X'_{Y'=c}v)||_1, \quad (1)$$

where $F(x) : \mathbb{R}^n \mapsto [0, 1]$ is the empirical cumulative distribution function for the set of values in vector x.

Now, given a sample Z from the distribution p_1 conforming to HYPOTHESIS 1 and a sample Z' from the distribution p_2 conforming to HYPOTHESIS 2, we obtain the solution to Problem 2 by finding the direction v maximising $f(Z, Z', c, v)$:

$$v^* = \arg\max_{v \in \mathbb{R}^m} f(Z, Z', c, v). \quad (2)$$

In visualisations where we use two-dimensional scatterplots, we find the second dimension of the scatterplot by optimising the same objective while requiring the direction to be orthogonal to the first dimension. We will solve the optimisation problem above in practice using the standard quasi-Newton solver in R with random initialisation and default settings (i.e., the general-purpose `optim`

[2] More formally defined by $p_i^v(t) = U_{1+\sigma}(t)/2 + U_\sigma(t - x_i(v))/2$, where $U_a(t) = 1/(2a)$ if $-a \le t \le a$ and $U_a(t) = 0$ otherwise, at the limit of small σ or $\sigma \to 0^+$.

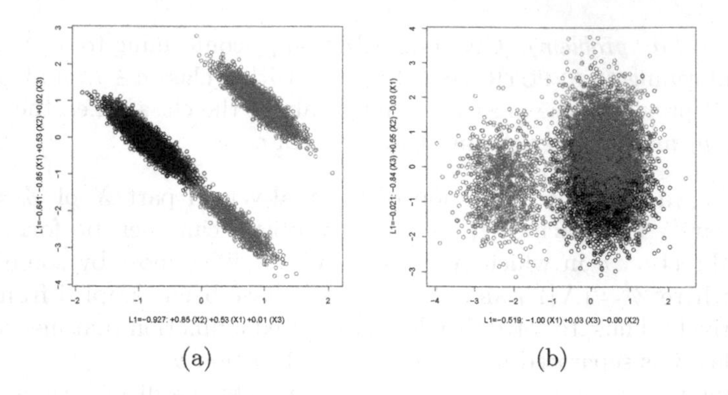

(a) (b)

Fig. 3. The most informative projection about class ‘1’ for the toy data Z_{toy} without background knowledge (a) and using the tile t constraint from Example 2 as background knowledge (b). Colors as in Fig. 1. (Color figure online)

function in `R` with `method="BFGS"`). This approach proved to be sufficiently efficient for the data sizes typical for visual exploratory data analysis (in the order of thousands data points), as demonstrated in the experimental evaluation.

Example 5. We now apply Definition 3 to find the most informative view to the user with respect to class ‘1’. Assuming no initial background knowledge, the datasets shown in Fig. 1a, b are examples of data samples from the distributions p_1 and p_2, respectively. By solving Eq. (2) we obtain the projection in Fig. 3a. The difference between the distributions is maximised along the x-axis, and we observe that the class ‘1’ consists of two group of points. We can now add this observation to the background knowledge[3], e.g., by using the tile t from Example 2. Because the tile is added to *both* HYPOTHESIS 1 and HYPOTHESIS 2, the information we have learned is reflected in both distributions, and any samples conforming to the updated hypotheses will not differ in terms of the relations constrained by t. The most informative projection for Z_{toy} with the background knowledge (tile t) is shown in Fig. 3b. This projection is different to Fig. 3a, and we see that the most informative direction (x-axis) separates the data items in class ‘1’ for which we did not yet add background knowledge from the rest of the data.

4 Experimental Evaluation

In this section we first consider the scalability (in terms of the dimensions of the data) and stability (in case the class contains only a few samples) of the method presented in this paper. After this, we present use cases of exploration of relations in data relevant for a class. The experiments were performed with a

[3] In an interactive setting, the selection of data items would be easy from the scatterplot. For the selection of attributes, one can use, e.g., the method from [20, Sec. 2.4].

single-threaded R 3.5.0 implementation on a MacBook Pro laptop with a 3.1 GHz Intel Core i5 processor.[4]

Datasets. In the experiments, we utilise the following datasets. We scale the real-valued variables to zero mean and unit variance.

The GERMAN socio-economic dataset [3, 12] contains records from 412 administrative districts in Germany. Each district is represented by 46 attributes describing socio-economic and political aspects in addition to the *type* of the district (rural/urban), area name/code, state, *region* (East, West, North, South) and the geographic coordinates of each district centre. The socio-ecologic attributes include, e.g., population density, age and education structure, economic indicators, and the proportion of the workforce in different sectors. The political attributes include election results of the five major political parties (CDU/CSU, SPD, FDP, Green, and Left) in the German federal elections in 2005 and 2009, as well as the voter turnout. We exclude the election results from 2005, the area code and coordinates of the districts, and all non-numeric variables except those for *region* and *type*. This results in 32 real-valued attributes and two class variables (*region* and *type*) used in our experiments.

The British National Corpus (BNC) [2] is one of the largest annotated text corpora freely available in full-text format. The texts are annotated with information such as author gender, age, and target audience, and all texts have been classified into *genres* [14]. We use a preprocessed data from [21] in which the vector-space model (word counts) is computed using the first 2000 words from each text belonging to one the four main *genres* in the corpus ('prose fiction', 'transcribed conversations', 'broadsheet newspaper', 'academic prose') as done in [17]. The BNC dataset has word counts for 1335 texts and the attributes are

Table 1. Median wall clock running time for the synthetic data with varying number of rows (n) and columns (m). We give the time to generate the hypothesis tilings, add three random tiles, and generate the data samples conforming to the hypotheses (t_{model}) and the time to find the most informative view (t_{view}), i.e., to solve Eq. (2).

n	m	t_{model} (s)	t_{view} (s)
500	16	0.01	0.97
	32	0.01	2.26
	64	0.02	8.15
	128	0.03	66.15
1000	16	0.02	1.23
	32	0.02	3.97
	64	0.04	18.91
	128	0.06	92.83

n	m	t_{model} (s)	t_{view} (s)
2000	16	0.03	2.03
	32	0.05	7.57
	64	0.07	32.38
	128	0.12	114.76
4000	16	0.09	4.54
	32	0.11	12.78
	64	0.16	45.05
	128	0.26	140.35

[4] Code and data available at https://github.com/edahelsinki/shgde.

the 100 words with highest counts. The class attribute contains classification of each text into one of the 4 main *genres*.

The Kaggle Telco customer CHURN dataset[5] contains information of 7043 customers with 21 attributes (18 categorial and 3 real-valued) including information about services of the customer, customer account, and demographic information. The task is to predict the value of binary class attribute 'churn' (whether the customer has left within the last month). We transform all the categorical attributes (except 'churn') using one-hot encoding, which creates a column for every label of every attribute and the presence (or absence) of a label is indicated by 1 (or 0). Note that variables with many labels are implicitly given more weight in the one-hot encoding. To overcome this effect, we scale the binary data in groups, that is, all columns that originate from the same attribute are scaled to have a total variance of 1. Finally, we drop 11 rows containing 'NA' for attribute 'total charges', and end up with 7032 rows and 46 columns.

4.1 Scalability

We started by evaluating the scalability of our method on synthetic data with $m \in \{16, 32, 64, 128\}$ dimensions and $n \in \{500, 1000, 2000, 5000\}$ data points. We generated the datasets similarly to [18]. The data points are scattered around 10 randomly drawn cluster centroids. We used the clusters to form a binary class attribute (by assigning the cluster centres closest to each other into same class). We added $k = 3$ random tiles as background knowledge: for each tile the rows were selected by taking the data points from one of the 10 clusters, and for the columns we randomly selected $[2..m]$ columns.

We report in Table 1 the median wall clock running times. We can observe that the time t_{model} to generate the hypothesis tilings, add three random tiles, and generate the data samples conforming to the hypotheses is negligible, i.e., we can update our hypotheses and obtain new samples very fast. The time t_{view} to find the most informative direction, i.e., to solve Eq. (2) scales roughly as $O(nm^{2..3})$. Even with our unoptimised R implementation the running times

Table 2. Stability experiment. In columns avg(f), sd(f), and sd(f)/avg(f) we report the average of each of these over the six different classes used.

c_{min}	k	avg(f)	sd(f)	sd(f)/avg(f)
100	0	2.03	0.070	0.042
	3	1.79	0.068	0.045
500	0	2.01	0.036	0.028
	3	1.80	0.034	0.028
1000	0	2.00	0.023	0.022
	3	1.78	0.026	0.023

[5] Available at https://www.kaggle.com/blastchar/telco-customer-churn.

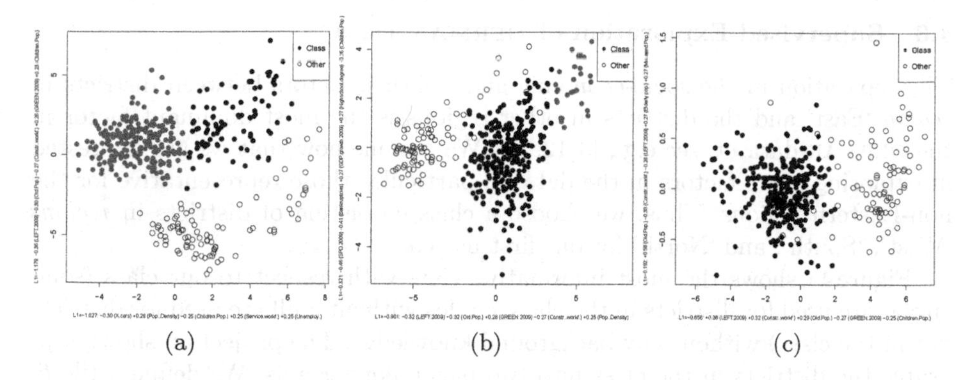

Fig. 4. Supervised exploration of the GERMAN data w.r.t. a class consisting of the districts in regions 'West', 'South', and 'North'. (a) The most informative projection with no background knowledge. (b) The most informative projection with tile t_1^g as background knowledge. (c) The most informative projection with tiles t_1^g and t_2^g as background knowledge. See Sect. 4.3 for details of selections shown in red. (Color figure online)

are at the order of 10 s for reasonably sized datasets. We note that for visual exploration the size of the data n should be reasonable and, it should be down-sampled as needed. Hence, the time complexity will be asymptotically constant with respect to n. The time complexity with respect the dimensionality m could be controlled by first reducing the dimensionality of the data, e.g., by PCA or by random projections, or by relaxing the convergence criteria of the numerical optimisation.

4.2 Stability

When the class of interest has only a few items, the effect of a particular sample from the distribution conforming to HYPOTHESIS 2 to the direction that is optimal for Eq. (2) is potentially large. This potential instability caused by the sampling can be controlled by taking several samples from the distributions and concatenating them, thus making the sample used to solve Eq. (2) large enough. To study this effect, we used the GERMAN dataset, taking the districts from each *region* and of each *type* as classes (6 cases in total, the class sizes varying between 64 and 290) and added $k \in \{0, 3\}$ random clusters as the background knowledge. Then, we computed mean value and the standard deviation of Eq. (1) in the optimal direction for 10 samples for each $c_{\min} \in \{100, 500, 1000\}$. Here, the number of samples needed s was computed as $s = \lceil c_{\min}/|\{i \mid Y(i) = c\}|\rceil$. Looking at the ration of standard deviation and the mean in Table 2, we observe that setting $c_{\min} \geq 500$ suffices for practical purposes. For the remaining experiments we use this value.

4.3 Supervised Exploration of GERMAN Data

The separation in the socio-economic and political factors between districts in *region* 'East' and the districts in other regions is the most dominant factor in the GERMAN dataset, see e.g., [3,12,20]. We assume now that we are interested in exploring other factors in the data, in particular those representative for the non-Eastern regions. Thus, we choose a class consisting of districts in *regions* 'West', 'South', and 'North' for our first use case.

Figure 4a shows the most informative view with respect to our class (solid circles are used for districts in the class, circles without a fill are used for districts not in the class) without any background knowledge. The projection shown separates the districts in the class into two parts along x-axis. We define a tile t_1^g to add this observation into the background knowledge. We select the districts coloured red in Fig. 4a for the rows, and all attributes for the columns.[6] Looking at the distribution of *region* (North = 46, South = 108, West = 78) and *type* (Urban = 7, Rural = 225) attributes for this selection we observe that we have defined a tile constraint for a set of mainly rural districts.

Figure 4b shows the most informative view the class given t_1^g as background knowledge. We obtain a different projection and observe the districts coloured red in Fig. 4b have higher values along x-axis than the rest of the districts. From the distribution of *region* (North = 4, South = 15, West = 11) and *type* (Urban = 25, Rural = 5) attributes for this selection we observe that these are mainly urban districts from the class. We add this observation into the background knowledge by defining a tile t_2^g. The rows in t_2^g are those coloured red in Fig. 4b, and for columns we include all attributes. Figure 4c then shows the most informative view with respect to the class given both t_1^g and t_2^g as background knowledge, demonstrating the division between the Eastern districts and the rest.

To understand the utility of the views shown, we compute values of the measure f in Eq. (1) using samples from the distributions conforming

Table 3. The GERMAN data use case. The value of f from Eq. (1) for different projection vectors v and cases of background knowledge.

GERMAN	No background	Tile t_1^g	Tiles t_1^g, t_2^g
v_0	**1.627**	0.148	0.073
v_1	1.079	**0.901**	0.641
v_2	1.115	0.880	**0.656**
v_{spca}	1.306	0.739	0.555
v_{pca}	1.336	0.417	0.322

[6] For simplicity, we use the set of all attributes as the columns in the tiles in explorations of the GERMAN and BNC datasets. In [20, Sec. 2.4] we provide a principled way for selecting a subset of columns most relevant for a selection of rows, which could be used in a more subtle exploration.

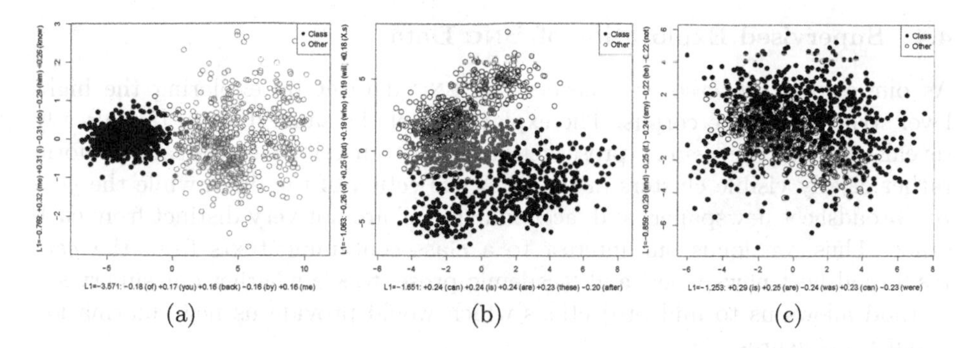

Fig. 5. Supervised exploration of the BNC data w.r.t. a class consisting of the texts from the *genres* 'broadsheet newspaper' and 'academic prose'. (a) The most informative projection with no background knowledge. (b) The most informative projection when tile t_1^{bnc} is added to the background knowledge. (c) The most informative projection when tiles t_1^{bnc} and t_2^{bnc} are added to the background knowledge. See Sect. 4.4 for details of selections coloured red. (Color figure online)

to HYPOTHESIS 1 and HYPOTHESIS 2 given the background knowledge. We have three cases: no background knowledge (0 tiles), background knowledge represented using tile t_1^g (1 tile), and background knowledge represented using tiles t_1^g and t_2^g (2 tiles). For each case we compute the direction in optimising the measure f, i.e., a solution to Eq. (2), denoting these by v_i where i corresponds to the number of tiles in the background knowledge. For comparison, we also compute the first PCA and SPCA projection vectors, denoted by v_{pca} and v_{spca}, respectively. Then, we calculate the value for f in different cases. The results are presented in Table 3. We notice that the value of the measure f indeed is always the highest, when the projection vector matches the background knowledge (highlighted in the table), as expected. This shows that the views presented are indeed the most informative ones given the current background knowledge. We also notice that PCA and SPCA projection vectors are less informative in terms of the measure f.

Table 4. The BNC data use case. The value of f from Eq. (1) for different projection vectors v and cases of background knowledge.

BNC	No background	tile t_1^{bnc}	tiles t_1^{bnc}, t_2^{bnc}
v_0	**3.571**	0.589	0.247
v_1	1.708	**1.651**	1.103
v_2	1.513	1.480	**1.253**
v_{spca}	3.561	0.572	0.241
v_{pca}	3.488	0.520	0.206

4.4 Supervised Exploration of BNC Data

As our second use case we consider the BNC dataset by exploring the high-level structure of the corpus. The exploration of the same data in [21] already reveals us that the *genres* 'prose fiction' and 'transcribed conversations' form rather clearly visible clusters in the PCA projection of the data, while the *genres* 'broadsheet newspaper' and 'academic prose' are not very distinct from each other. Thus, we focus our interest to a class containing texts from the *genres* 'broadsheet newspaper' and 'academic prose' to see whether our supervised method allows us to find projections which would provide us new information about these genres.

Figure 5a shows the most informative view with respect to the class (solid circles are used for texts belonging to the class, circles without a fill are used for the texts not in the class). The projection shown clearly separates the texts with respect to our class. We define a tile constraint t_1^{bnc}, by selecting the points with x-axis value greater than zero (coloured red in Fig. 5a) for the rows, and all attributes for the columns. The selection contains 144 texts from *genre* 'transcribed conversations', 413 from 'prose fiction', and 12 texts from *genre* 'broadsheet newspaper'. Thus, we add a tile constraint covering mostly texts outside the class, making this way explicit to the system that we already know the main features of the texts not in our class. Figure 5b shows the most informative view after t_1^{bnc} has been added to the background knowledge. We observe that the texts in the class seem to separate in the direction along y-axis. By selecting the points with higher values in y-axis (coloured red in Fig. 5b) in our class, we observe that these are mainly texts from *genre* 'broadsheet newspaper' (211 texts), the remaining 10 texts are from *genre* 'academic prose'. Thus, this view shows us how the two genres in our class are separated. If we now add a tile constraint t_2^{bnc} for this selection (taking again all attributes as the columns), we obtain the view shown in Fig. 5c, in which some outliers could be potentially studied further.

Similarly to the GERMAN data use case, we provide the value of the measure f for each projection vector in Table 4, and compare these to the first PCA and SPCA projection vectors. Here we observe, that both PCA and SPCA provide a direction with a very similar interestingness value to our method when there is no background knowledge. However, with background knowledge, the situation changes and our approach provides clearly more interesting views given the class.

4.5 Identification of Churners

Finally, we explore the CHURN data. The problem of identifying possible *churners*, i.e., customers likely to cancel a subscription to a service, has become a popular use case in business domain, because retaining one customer costs much less than gaining a new one. Churn prediction problem is typically addressed with off-the-shelf machine learning and statistical approaches which usually do not use any domain expert knowledge. In this example, our goal is to demonstrate how our method can help to put the domain-specific knowledge into better use.

We can use our framework to find the most informative direction with respect to the class containing customers who churn.

Now, let us assume that the domain experts have already identified from their previous experiences that 'monthly charge' and 'total charges' are the most salient features that cause customer to churn. We will use this background knowledge in the exploration, i.e., we add a tile t_{chu} covering attributes 'monthly charge', 'total charges', and 'churn' and all the rows in the data to the background distribution. The most informative direction in this case has the highest (absolute) weights for the attributes 'tech support = no', 'online security = no', and 'internet service = fiber optic'.

We can compare this set of five features (i.e., 'total charges', 'monthly charges', 'tech support', and 'online security' and 'internet service') identified by the user to the whole set of features in the data, when classifying churners using the *non-preprocessed dataset*. Here we use fitted binary classification decision tree with 10-fold cross validation for the classification, and measure the performance with misclassification error (ME) and false positives (FP) rate. We observe, that using the user identified 5-feature set (ME = 0.263, FP = 0.127) the performance that is at least as good as using the full 20-feature set (ME = 0.264, 0.133), and even marginally better in terms of false positives rate. This demonstrates the potential human-guided exploration approach for a real-world dataset, in particular in a scenario in which a high false positive rate is a major concern.

5 Conclusions

In this paper we proposed a method for *supervised dimensionality reduction* for interactive EDA systems that take the user's background knowledge and objectives into account. We defined an information criterion, which allows us to find the most informative views about the class structure of data by taking the user's current knowledge and objectives into account. In the experimental evaluation we demonstrated that our method gives understandable and useful results when analysing real-world datasets. Taking the user's background knowledge into account matters, as the use of the updating background knowledge allows an EDA system to show the user currently unknown and relevant projection to the data.

For potential future directions we note that our method could potentially be used for *human-guided classification* by using an updating class of interest, instead a fixed one. Initially, all items would belong to the class of interest, and the user is shown the most informative projection. The user could then identify set(s) of data items and classify them, and a new projection could be shown for an updated class of interest containing the data items unclassified so far. Moreover, the knowledge of the user of the found sets of data items could be added into the background knowledge. We also plan to implement our method in an interactive data analysis tool, and study how the optimisation problem in Eq. (2) can be solved more efficiently in practice. For a better interpretability of the views, we could consider, e.g., sparse projection vectors.

Acknowledgements. We thank Buse Gül Atli for discussions and help. Supported by the Academy of Finland (decisions 326280 and 326339). This work is part of the research programme Commit2Data, specifically the RATE-Analytics project NWO628 003 001 (partly) financed by the Dutch Research Council.

References

1. Barshan, E., Ghodsi, A., Azimifar, Z., Jahromi, M.Z.: Supervised principal component analysis: visualization, classification and regression on subspaces and submanifolds. Pattern Recogn. **44**(7), 1357–1371 (2011)
2. The British National Corpus, v. 3 (BNC XML Edition). Distributed by Oxford University Computing Services on Behalf of the BNC Consortium (2007). http://www.natcorp.ox.ac.uk/
3. Boley, M., Mampaey, M., Kang, B., Tokmakov, P., Wrobel, S.: One click mining: interactive local pattern discovery through implicit preference and performance learning. In: KDD-IDEA, pp. 27–35 (2013)
4. Chau, D., Kittur, A., Hong, J., Faloutsos, C.: Apolo: making sense of large network data by combining rich user interaction and machine learning. In: CHI, pp. 167–176 (2011)
5. De Bie, T., Lijffijt, J., Santos-Rodriguez, R., Kang, B.: Informative data projections: a framework and two examples. In: ESANN, pp. 635–640 (2016)
6. De Bie, T.: Maximum entropy models and subjective interestingness: an application to tiles in binary databases. Data Min. Knowl. Discov. **23**(3), 407–446 (2011)
7. Dimitriadou, K., Papaemmanouil, O., Diao, Y.: AIDE: an active learning-based approach for interactive data exploration. IEEE Trans. Knowl. Data Eng. **28**(11), 2842–2856 (2016)
8. Dzyuba, V., van Leeuwen, M.: Interactive discovery of interesting subgroup sets. In: Tucker, A., Höppner, F., Siebes, A., Swift, S. (eds.) IDA 2013. LNCS, vol. 8207, pp. 150–161. Springer, Heidelberg (2013). https://doi.org/10.1007/978-3-642-41398-8_14
9. Fisher, R.A.: The use of multiple measurements in taxonomic problems. Ann. Eugen. **7**, 179–188 (1936)
10. Globerson, A., Tishby, N.: Sufficient dimensionality reduction. J. Mach. Learn. Res. **3**, 1307–1331 (2003)
11. Hanhijärvi, S., Ojala, M., Vuokko, N., Puolamäki, K., Tatti, N., Mannila, H.: Tell me something I don't know: randomization strategies for iterative data mining. In: KDD, pp. 379–388 (2009)
12. Kang, B., Lijffijt, J., Santos-Rodríguez, R., De Bie, T.: Subjectively interesting component analysis: data projections that contrast with prior expectations. In: KDD, pp. 1615–1624 (2016)
13. Kang, B., Lijffijt, J., Santos-Rodríguez, R., De Bie, T.: SICA: subjectively interesting component analysis. Data Min. Knowl. Disc. **32**(4), 949–987 (2018). https://doi.org/10.1007/s10618-018-0558-x
14. Lee, D.W.: Genres, registers, text types, domain, and styles: clarifying the concepts and navigating a path through the BNC jungle. Lang. Learn. Technol. **5**(3), 37–72 (2001)
15. Lee, J.A., Verleysen, M.: Nonlinear Dimensionality Reduction. Springer, New York (2007). https://doi.org/10.1007/978-0-387-39351-3

16. van Leeuwen, M., Cardinaels, L.: VIPER – visual pattern explorer. In: Bifet, A., et al. (eds.) ECML PKDD 2015. LNCS (LNAI), vol. 9286, pp. 333–336. Springer, Cham (2015). https://doi.org/10.1007/978-3-319-23461-8_42
17. Lijffijt, J., Nevalainen, T.: A simple model for recognizing core genres in the BNC. In: Studies in Variation, Contacts and Change in English, vol. 19 (2017)
18. Puolamäki, K., Kang, B., Lijffijt, J., De Bie, T.: Interactive visual data exploration with subjective feedback. In: Frasconi, P., Landwehr, N., Manco, G., Vreeken, J. (eds.) ECML PKDD 2016. LNCS (LNAI), vol. 9852, pp. 214–229. Springer, Cham (2016). https://doi.org/10.1007/978-3-319-46227-1_14
19. Puolamäki, K., Papapetrou, P., Lijffijt, J.: Visually controllable data mining methods. In: ICDMW, pp. 409–417 (2010)
20. Puolamäki, K., Oikarinen, E., Henelius, A.: Guided visual exploration of relations in data sets. arXiv preprint arXiv:1905.02515 (2019)
21. Puolamäki, K., Oikarinen, E., Kang, B., Lijffijt, J., Bie, T.D.: Interactive visual data exploration with subjective feedback: an information-theoretic approach. In: ICDE, pp. 1208–1211 (2018)
22. Ruotsalo, T., Jacucci, G., Myllymäki, P., Kaski, S.: Interactive intent modeling: information discovery beyond search. CACM **58**(1), 86–92 (2015)
23. Sacha, D., et al.: Visual interaction with dimensionality reduction: a structured literature analysis. IEEE Trans. Visual Comput. Graphics **23**(1), 241–250 (2017)
24. Tukey, J.W.: Exploratory Data Analysis. Addison-Wesley, Reading (1977)
25. Vartak, M., Rahman, S., Madden, S., Parameswaran, A., Polyzotis, N.: SeeDB: efficient data-driven visualization recommendations to support visual analytics. PVLDB **8**(3), 2182–2193 (2015)
26. Xing, E.P., Jordan, M.I., Russell, S.J., Ng, A.Y.: Distance metric learning with application to clustering with side-information. In: NIPS, pp. 521–528 (2003)

SynthLog: A Language for Synthesising Inductive Data Models (Extended Abstract)

Yann Dauxais, Clément Gautrais(✉), Anton Dries, Arcchit Jain, Samuel Kolb, Mohit Kumar, Stefano Teso, Elia Van Wolputte, Gust Verbruggen, and Luc De Raedt

Department of Computer Science, KU Leuven, Celestijnenlaan 200A, Leuven, Belgium
{Yann.Dauxais,Clement.Gautrais,Anton.Dries,Arcchit.Jain,Samuel.Kolb, Mohit.Kumar,Stefano.Teso,Elia.Vanwolputte,Gust.Verbruggen, Luc.Deraedt}@cs.kuleuven.be

Abstract. We introduce SynthLog, an extension of the probabilistic logic programming language ProbLog, for synthesising inductive data models. Inductive data models integrate data with predictive and descriptive models, in a way that is reminiscent of inductive databases. SynthLog provides primitives for learning and manipulating inductive data models, it supports data wrangling, learning predictive models and constraints, and probabilistic and constraint reasoning. It is used as the back-end of the automated data scientist approach that is being developed in the SYNTH project. An overview of the SynthLog philosophy and language as well as a non trivial example of its use, is given in this paper.

Keywords: Automated data science · Inductive databases · Probabilistic programming

1 Introduction

Automated data science has received a lot of attention in the last decade [2], and has been recognized as an important challenge and solutions promise to democratize data science and make it available to non-expert end-users. Most current approaches tackle the problem of automatically constructing the best prediction pipeline [6,7]. These approaches typically target expert end-users, that can understand most of the steps in the pipeline. In contrast, the SYNTH framework wants to democratize data science and make it available to the naive end-user. The central setting in SYNTH is that of autocompletion in spreadsheets [4]. Spreadsheets are used ubiquitously and the autocompletion task consists of predicting the next cell and value that the user wants to fill out, of course, under the

Y. Dauxais, C. Gautrais and A. Dries—Have contributed equally.

P. Cellier and K. Driessens (Eds.): ECML PKDD 2019 Workshops, CCIS 1167, pp. 102–110, 2020.
https://doi.org/10.1007/978-3-030-43823-4_9

assumption that there are sufficient regularities in the data to enable meaningful predictions.

The autocompletion task constitutes the front-end of the SYNTH framework, and it is easy to see how this can be included in spreadsheet software such as Excel. The back-end, however, consists of the SynthLog language that should support the underlying data science processes and components. This includes tools to automate various steps in data science, from data wrangling to predictive modeling and constraint learning. But rather than viewing this as a data science workflow or pipeline, SYNTH has the SynthLog language that allows the knowledgeable user to define and steer the data science process in a declarative manner. It is this language that we briefly introduce and illustrate in the present note. SynthLog builds on the inductive database idea [8] in that we are looking for a small and non-trivial set of primitives that supports data science processes. Rather than building on top of databases [9], however, SynthLog extends the probabilistic programming language ProbLog that already supports deductive and probabilistic inference, learning and (a limited form of) constraint processing, which are all important for data science.

The idea that SynthLog borrows from inductive databases is that it should treat models (such as predictors or constraints) as first class citizens, that is, SynthLog should support manipulating, constructing, using, and learning such models. Indeed, SynthLog should not only allow to handle the inputs and outputs of the data science components, but also to reason about which models should be learned, used or combined for a particular dataset or task. The models will be represented as SynthLog theories, which are essentially ProbLog programs, consisting of a set of probabilistic facts and clauses. Combining data science components then corresponds to performing operations on theories: adding/deleting facts, adding/deleting clauses, and combining theories.

In Sect. 2, we introduce the main contribution of this paper: the SynthLog language. Then, in Sect. 3, we present a case-study illustrating how SynthLog can be used to bridge many components of data science: from data wrangling to constraints.

2 Introduction to SynthLog

SynthLog is a language for supporting automated data science processes. It allows to construct and manipulate inductive data models. An *Inductive Data Model (IDM)* consists of (1) a set of data models (DM) that specifies an adequate data structure for the dataset (like a database), and (2) a set of inductive models (IMs), that is, a set of patterns and machine learning models (like classifiers) that have been discovered in the data. While the DM can be used to retrieve information about the dataset and to answer questions about specific data points, the IMs can be used to make predictions, find inconsistencies and redundancies, etc. IDMs integrate data and inductive models in a SynthLog *theory*.

SynthLog is built on top of the ProbLog probabilistic programming language. It essentially assumes that both the data models and the inductive models are

ProbLog programs, and allows to refer to and manipulate such models by means of a new ProbLog operator. As SynthLog manipulates both data and inductive models, it borrows ideas from inductive databases that also consider both data and inductive models as first class citizens. For example, SynthLog follows the mantra of inductive databases that requires the closure property to be satisfied [3,8]. In the SynthLog context this means that the result of any operation must be a theory, and thus must be a ProbLog program. At the same time, as each theory is a ProbLog program, SynthLog supports deductive and probabilistic reasoning, a form of answer set programming (through DTProbLog [1]) and machine learning. We first introduce ProbLog on a simple example, and then introduce the notion of a theory.

2.1 ProbLog by Example

ProbLog [5] is a probabilistic logic programming language, that extends Prolog by adding probabilistic primitives and inference. Let us take the example (from [5]) of a small social network, where smoking behavior depends on friendship among people.

```
1 0.4::asthma(X) :- smokes(X).
2 0.3::smokes(X).
3 0.2::smokes(X) :- friend(X,Y), smokes(Y).
4 friend(1,2). friend(2,1). friend(2,4). friend(3,2). friend(4,2).
5 query(asthma(2)).
```

For example, the first rule states that somebody that smokes has a probability of 40% to have asthma. Likewise, the second rule states that any person has a 30% chance of smoking. The query corresponds to the answer we want to get: we want to know the probability that person 2 has asthma. In this case, the result is 0.15.

As SynthLog extends ProbLog, which extends Prolog, a basic knowledge of Prolog and ProbLog is assumed in the remainder of this paper. For the interested reader, a more detailed presentation of ProbLog is available[1].

2.2 SynthLog Theories

We now extend ProbLog with the notion of a theory. Each theory will consist of a ProbLog program and it will be possible to define theories through the scope operator `':'/2`. For example, the fact `theory(a):knowledge(1)` states that the theory or ProbLog program identified by `theory(a)` contains the fact `knowledge(1)`.

The following SynthLog listing defines various theories:

```
1     constraints:(a:-b).
2     data:b.
3     global:X :- constraints:X; data:X.
4     query(global:_).
```

[1] https://dtai.cs.kuleuven.be/problog/index.html.

In this case, the clause `a:-b` is defined in the theory `constraints` and is interpreted as `constraints:a :- constraints:b`. Beyond the syntactic sugar allowing to factorize the theory name in each terms in a clause, such representation allows to share constraints between theories and automatically interpret them. In this example, the `global` theory is the union of the `constraints` and `data` theories. `global` contains the fact `b` and the clause `a:-b`. Thus, `global:a` can be inferred. To support the inductive database aspect of SynthLog, and to allow for further manipulating inductive models, theories can be loaded from or stored in a database or file.

2.3 A Language for Data Science

To facilitate the use of SynthLog as a language dedicated to data science, several predicates are introduced to infer properties of relational datasets, build classifiers and learn or apply constraints on theories. SynthLog supports the definition of custom predicates, that take a theory (i.e. an inductive data model) as input and returns a theory as output. Many tasks fit within that framework: learners typically take data as input to output a model, data wrangling takes data as input and outputs data, applying a predictor requires data and model as input and outputs data. Some of these custom predicates are detailed in the next section.

3 Case Study: Auto-Completion

Table 1. Data representing the historical sales of an ice-cream factory.

Type	Country	June	July	August	Total	Profit
Vanilla	BE	610	190	670	1470	1
Banana	BE	170	690	520	1380	1
Chocolate	BE	560	320	140	1020	1
Banana	DE	610	640	320	1570	0
Speculaas	BE	300	270	290	860	0
Chocolate	FR	430	350	300	1080	1

Table 2. Data representing the sales of an ice-cream factory, with missing profit.

Type	Country	June	July	August	Total	Profit
Banana	DE	250	650	630	1530	
Chocolate	NL	210	280	270	760	

In this Section, we show how SynthLog can tackle a classic challenge in data science: automatically filling missing values in a spreadsheet. More precisely, these missing values are predicted with inductive models. The auto-completion task has been identified as a simple, yet challenging task, that illustrates the core of the SYNTH framework [4].

This case study shows that SynthLog successfully use both predictors, such as logistic regression; and probabilistic rules to infer the most likely missing values. We can therefore build on the large literature of the automation of predictor learning [7], while also providing an easy way to add user knowledge in the inference process. We also illustrate how inductive database ideas are used to store and query models depending on the task at hand. We use a toy dataset emulating sales of an ice-cream factory. The data is shown in Tables 1 and 2, with missing profit for the two rows in Table 2. It will be inferred using logistic regression combined with user defined constraints. The code performing the auto-completion is presented below:

```
1  magic_cells:X :- load_csv('magic_ice_cream.csv', X).
2  missing_data_cells:X :- load_csv('magic_test1.csv', X).
3
4  magic_tables:X :- detect_tables(magic_cells, X).
5  missing_data:X :- detect_tables(missing_data_cells, X).
6
7  magic_models:X :-sklearn_predictor(magic_tables,
8      'linear_model.LogisticRegression',
9      [column('T1',3), column('T1',4)], [column('T1',6)], X).
10
11 magic_predict:X :- magic_models:predictor(Y),
12     magic_models:source(Y, column('T1', 3)),
13     magic_models:source(Y, column('T1', 4)),
14     predict(missing_data,Y,[column('T1',3),column('T1',4)],X).
15
16 final_pred:table_cell('T1', X, 7, V) :-
17     magic_predict:cell_pred(X, Y, V, _).
18
19 magic_constraints:
20     (0.7::table_cell(T,X,7,0):- table_cell(T,X,5,V), V<300).
21 magic_constraints:table_cell('T1', X, Y, V) :-
22     missing_data:table_cell('T1', X, Y, V).
23
24 combined_pred:table_cell(T,X,Y,V) :-
25     magic_constraints:table_cell(T,X,Y,V);
26     final_pred:table_cell(T,X,Y,V).
27
28 query(combined_pred:_).
```

In **Line 1**, we create the theory *magic_cells* from a csv file containing the data in Table 1, by using the custom predicate `load_csv/2`. Details about the custom predicates and their exact behavior are presented in Appendix A. Likewise, **Line 2** creates the theory *missing_data_cells* by loading the data represented in Table 2.

The rest of the program manipulates these 2 theories using SynthLog primitives and custom predicates to perform wrangling, prediction and inference. For example, **Lines 4 and 5** perform wrangling, by using the custom predicate `detect_tables/2`. More precisely, in **Line 4**, `detect_tables/2` transforms the theory *magic_cells* to output the theory *magic_tables*. The new theory *magic_tables* contains the same data as the theory *magic_cells* (i.e. the data from Table 1), but uses a different data model. Indeed, `detect_tables/2` takes a cell based data model and transforms it into a table based data model. Details of this transformation are given in Appendix A. In this simple example, wrangling is straightforward, as the data is already nicely formatted. However, `detect_tables/2` still provides information about cell types and detects headers.

From the theory *magic_tables*, the custom predicate `sklearn_predictor/5` learns an inductive model (**Lines 7 to 9**). More precisely, it learns a logistic regression model[2] that predicts column 6 of Table T1 (the Table depicted in Table 1) from columns 3 and 4 of Table T1. The theory *magic_predict* contains this newly learned inductive model. The theory *magic_predict* also contains additional information about the learned inductive model: on which theory was it learned, using which columns and what type of inductive model it is. Keeping track of all these information allows us to easily query any model, hence treating them as first class citizens.

Lines 11 to 13 query an inductive model by manipulating the theory *magic_predict*. To retrieve an inductive model, we simply specify its properties: it is a predictor and was trained on columns 3 and 4 from Table T1. If several inductive models in *magic_predict* satisfy these requirements, they are all used. SynthLog therefore handles models following the inductive database idea of treating them as first class citizens. Then, **Line 14** applies the queried inductive model on the theory *missing_data* to create the new theory *magic_predict*, using the custom predicate `predict/4`. The theory *magic_predict* contains probabilistic facts representing the predictions of the logistic regression.

Lines 16 and 17 create the theory *final_pred* by selecting a sub-part of the theory *magic_predict*, using a simple ProbLog rule. **Lines 19 and 20** create a new inductive model, by storing a user-defined rule in the theory *magic_constraints*. This rule states that if column 5 of Table T in row X has a value below 300, then column 7 (profit) of Table T in row X has a value of 0 with probability 0.7. In this simple case, this rule could be specified by a user. However, SynthLog supports learning such rules through the use of custom predicates. **Lines 21 and 22** add a sub-part of theory *missing_data* to the theory *magic_constraints*. Since the theory *magic_constraints* now contains `table_cell` predicates, the rule defined in Line 20 will automatically trigger, hence creating the probabilistic fact `0.7::table_cell(T,X,7,0)` when applicable.

Finally, **Lines 24 to 26** create the theory *combined_pred* by performing the union of sub-parts from the theories *magic_constraints* and *final_pred* through the `';'/2` operator of ProbLog. As SynthLog combines probabilistic facts from *final_pred* with the probabilistic rule from *magic_constraints* to create *final_pred*,

[2] We use the scikit-learn library: https://scikit-learn.org/stable/index.html.

probabilistic inference has to be performed. Because SynthLog extends ProbLog, it relies on its probabilistic inference mechanism to soundly combine both theories. As in ProbLog, the query of **Line 28** determines what probabilistic facts the program should infer. In this case, we query for the theory *final_pred* to infer the cell values of Table 2, by combining the logistic regression predictions with the user defined rule. The result is shown in Table 3.

Overall we have seen that SynthLog manipulates theories by using either custom predicates or native ProbLog operators. This simple way of manipulating theories is nonetheless powerful, as the resulting program is performing complex inference, taking into account predictive models and rules, while remaining simple to read.

Table 3. Data (from Table 2) with filled profit values and probability on predictions

Type	Country	June	July	August	Total	Profit	Probability
Banana	DE	250	650	630	1530	0	0.04
Banana	DE	250	650	630	1530	1	0.96
Chocolate	NL	210	280	270	760	0	0.46
Chocolate	NL	210	280	270	760	1	0.54

4 Conclusion

We have introduced SynthLog, a declarative language for synthesising Inductive Data Models (IDM). IDMs integrate data and inductive models in a SynthLog theory. Theories can also be seen as ProbLog programs, consisting of probabilistic facts and clauses. Assembling data science components corresponds to manipulating theories, hence making SynthLog a language suitable for automating data science. As SynthLog is an extension of ProbLog, it natively supports probabilistic reasoning and we have illustrated through a use case how SynthLog can use probabilistic inference to effortlessly combine results from different type of models (predictors and constraints).

Having a language to assemble data science components, based on probabilistic logic, opens new possibilities. First, the inherent uncertainty of data and inductive models can be leveraged to perform probabilistic inference and provide predictions that reflect our confidence in our data and inductive models. Second, SynthLog handles different types of inductive models. More specifically, it handles rules or constraints along with other machine learning models. Hence, SynthLog provides a great opportunity to bridge user interaction and model learning through a unique language.

In the SYNTH framework, SynthLog is also first step towards the automation of data science. Indeed, with a single language combining all data science components, we can tackle the more challenging task of learning to learn, that is learning which SynthLog programs are suitable to automatically solve the data science task at hand.

Finally, the further development of SynthLog will likely require the development of new implementation techniques to support fast inference and learning. This will allow smoother user interaction and the analysis of larger datasets.

Acknowledgements. This work has received funding from the European Research Council (ERC) under the European Union's Horizon 2020 research and innovation programme (grant agreement No. [694980] SYNTH: Synthesising Inductive Data Models).

Appendix A: SynthLog Custom Predicates Documentation

- `load_csv/2`: loads the content of a csv file in a theory
  - Input
    - csv file
  - Output: Theory with predicates:
    - `cell/3`: row id, column id and value of each cell
- `detect_tables/2`: calls a data wrangler [10] to detect tables in the spreadsheet
  - Input
    - Theory with `cell/3` predicates
  - Output: Theory with predicates:
    - `table/5`: table id, top left row, top left column, height, width
    - `table_cell/4`: table id, row id, column id and value of each cell
    - `table_cell_type/4`: table id, row id, column id and type of each cell
    - `table_header/5`: table id, column id, name, type, list of unique values
- `sklearn_predictor/5` learns a scikit-learn predictor
  - Input
    - Theory with `table_cell/4` predicates
    - Inductive model type (from scikit-learn models)
    - List of columns to use as features
    - List of columns to predict
  - Output: Theory with predicates:
    - `sklearn_predictor/1`: inductive model
    - `target/2`: inductive model, predicted column
    - `source/2`: inductive model, feature column
- `predict/5` makes prediction using a previously trained model
  - Input
    - Theory with `table_cell/4` predicates
    - Inductive model
    - List of columns to use as features
    - List of columns to predict
  - Output: Theory with predicates:
    - `cell_pred/4`: table id, row id, column id and value of each cell
    - `predictor/1`: inductive model
    - `source/2`: inductive model, feature column
    - `confidence/2`: inductive model, confidence score

References

1. Van den Broeck, G., Thon, I., Van Otterlo, M., De Raedt, L.: DTProbLog: a decision-theoretic probabilistic Prolog. In: Twenty-Fourth AAAI Conference on Artificial Intelligence (2010)
2. De Bie, T., De Raedt, L., Hoos, H.H., Smyth, P.: Automating data science (dagstuhl seminar 18401). Schloss Dagstuhl-Leibniz-Zentrum fuer Informatik (2019)
3. De Raedt, L.: A perspective on inductive databases. ACM SIGKDD Explor. Newslett. **4**(2), 69–77 (2002)
4. De Raedt, L., Blockeel, H., Kolb, S., Teso, S., Verbruggen, G.: Elements of an automatic data scientist. In: Duivesteijn, W., Siebes, A., Ukkonen, A. (eds.) IDA 2018. LNCS, vol. 11191, pp. 3–14. Springer, Cham (2018). https://doi.org/10.1007/978-3-030-01768-2_1
5. Dries, A., et al.: ProbLog2: probabilistic logic programming. In: Bifet, A., et al. (eds.) ECML PKDD 2015. LNCS (LNAI), vol. 9286, pp. 312–315. Springer, Cham (2015). https://doi.org/10.1007/978-3-319-23461-8_37
6. Feurer, M., Klein, A., Eggensperger, K., Springenberg, J., Blum, M., Hutter, F.: Efficient and robust automated machine learning. In: Advances in Neural Information Processing Systems, pp. 2962–2970 (2015)
7. Hutter, F., Kotthoff, L., Vanschoren, J. (eds.): Automated Machine Learning: Methods, Systems, Challenges. Springer, Cham (2018). https://doi.org/10.1007/978-3-030-05318-5. http://automl.org/book
8. Imielinski, T., Mannila, H.: A database perspective on knowledge discovery. Commun. ACM **39**(11), 58–64 (1996)
9. Malec, M., Khot, T., Nagy, J., Blasch, E., Natarajan, S.: Inductive logic programming meets relational databases: an application to statistical relational learning. In: Inductive Logic Programming (ILP) (2016)
10. Verbruggen, G., De Raedt, L.: Automatically wrangling spreadsheets into machine learning data formats. In: Duivesteijn, W., Siebes, A., Ukkonen, A. (eds.) IDA 2018. LNCS, vol. 11191, pp. 367–379. Springer, Cham (2018). https://doi.org/10.1007/978-3-030-01768-2_30

The autofeat Python Library for Automated Feature Engineering and Selection

Franziska Horn[1(✉)], Robert Pack[2], and Michael Rieger[2]

[1] Machine Learning Group, Technische Universität Berlin, Marchstr. 23, 10587 Berlin, Germany
cod3licious@gmail.com
[2] BASF SE, Carl-Bosch-Str. 38, 67056 Ludwigshafen, Germany
{robert.pack,michael.rieger}@basf.com

Abstract. This paper describes the autofeat Python library, which provides a scikit-learn style linear regression model with automated feature engineering and selection capabilities. Complex non-linear machine learning models such as neural networks are in practice often difficult to train and even harder to explain to non-statisticians, who require transparent analysis results as a basis for important business decisions. While linear models are efficient and intuitive, they generally provide lower prediction accuracies. Our library provides a multi-step feature engineering and selection process, where first a large pool of non-linear features is generated, from which then a small and robust set of meaningful features is selected, which improve the prediction accuracy of a linear model while retaining its interpretability.

Keywords: AutoML · Feature engineering · Feature selection · Explainable ML

1 Introduction

More and more companies aim to improve production processes with data science and machine learning (ML) methods, for example, by using a ML model to better understand which factors contribute to higher quality products or greater production yield. While advanced ML models such as neural networks (NN) might, theoretically, in many cases provide the most accurate predictions, they have several drawbacks in practice. First of all, with many hyperparameters to set, these model can be difficult and time consuming to fit, which is only aggravated by the current shortage of ML specialists in industry. Second, in many cases there is not enough data available in the first place to train a low bias/high variance model like a NN, for example, because comprehensive data collection pipelines are not yet fully implemented or because obtaining individual data points is expensive, e.g., when it takes several days to produce a single product. Last but not least, the insights generated by a ML analysis need to

P. Cellier and K. Driessens (Eds.): ECML PKDD 2019 Workshops, CCIS 1167, pp. 111–120, 2020.
https://doi.org/10.1007/978-3-030-43823-4_10

be communicated to others in the company, who want to use these results as a basis for important business decisions [30]. While great progress has been made to improve the interpretability of NNs, e.g., by using layer-wise relevance propagation (LRP) to reveal which of the input features contributed most to a neural net's prediction [1,2,25], this is in practice still not sufficient to convince those with only a limited understanding of statistics. Especially when dealing with data collected from physical systems, using a plausible model might even be more important than getting small prediction errors [22].

To avoid these shortcomings of NNs and other non-linear ML models, in practice we find it necessary to rely mostly on linear prediction models, which are intuitive to understand and can be trained easily and efficiently even on very small datasets. Of course, employing linear models generally comes at the cost of a lower prediction accuracy. Therefore, inspired by the SISSO algorithm [28], we propose a framework to automatically generate several tens of thousands of non-linear features from the original inputs and then carefully select the most informative of them as additional input features for a linear model. We have found that this approach leads to sufficiently accurate predictions on real world data while providing a transparent model that has a high acceptance rate amongst non-statisticians in the company and therefore provides the possibility to positively contribute to important business decisions.

To make this framework more accessible to other data scientists, our implementation is publicly available on GitHub.[1] The rest of the paper is structured as follows: After introducing some related work in the area of automated feature engineering and selection, we describe our approach and the `autofeat` Python library in detail (Sect. 2). We then report experimental results on several datasets (Sect. 3) before concluding the paper with a brief discussion (Sect. 4).

1.1 Related Work

Feature construction frameworks generally include both a feature engineering, as well as a feature selection component [21]. One of the main differences between feature construction approaches is whether they first generate an exhaustive feature pool and then perform feature selection on the whole feature set (which is also the strategy `autofeat` follows), or if the set of features is expanded iteratively, by evaluating at each step whether the inclusion of the new features would improve the prediction accuracy. Both approaches have their drawbacks: The first approach is very memory intensive, especially when starting off with a large initial feature set from which the additional features are constructed via various transformations. With the second approach, important features might be missed if some variables are eliminated too early in the feature engineering process and can therefore not serve to construct more complex, possibly helpful features. Furthermore, depending on the strategy for including additional features, the whole process might either be very time intensive, if at each step a model is trained and evaluated on the feature subset, or can fail to include (only)

[1] https://github.com/cod3licious/autofeat.

the relevant features, if a simple heuristic is used for the feature evaluation and selection.

Most existing feature construction frameworks follow the second, iterative feature engineering approach: The FICUS algorithm [21] uses a beam search to expand the feature space based on a simple heuristic, while the FEADIS algorithm [9] and Cognito [18] use more complex selection strategies. A more recent trend is to use meta-learning, i.e., algorithms trained on other datasets, to decide whether to apply specific transformation to the features or not [16,17,26]. While theoretically promising, we could not find an easy to use open source library for any of these approaches, which makes them essentially irrelevant for practical data science use cases.

The well-known `scikit-learn` Python library [29] provides a function to generate polynomial features (e.g. x^2), including feature interactions (e.g. $x_1 \cdot x_2, x_1^2 \cdot x_2^3$). Polynomial features are a subset of the features generated by `autofeat`, yet, while they might be helpful for many datasets, in our experience with `autofeat`, a lot of times the ratios of two features or feature combinations turn out to be informative additional features, which can not be generated with the `scikit-learn` method. The `scikit-learn` library also contains several options for feature selection, such as univariate feature scoring, recursive feature elimination, and other model-based feature selection approaches [13,19]. Univariate feature selection methods consider each feature individually, which can lead to the inclusion of many correlated features, like those contained in the feature pool generated by `autofeat`. The more sophisticated feature selection techniques rely on the use of an external prediction model that provides coefficients indicating the importance of each feature. However, algorithms such as linear regression get numerically unstable if the number of features is larger than the number of samples, which makes these approaches impractical for feature pools as large as those generated by `autofeat`.

One popular Python library for automated feature engineering is `featuretools`, which generates a large feature set using "deep feature synthesis" [15]. This library is targeted towards relational data, where features can be created through aggregations (e.g. given some customers (data table 1) and their associated loans (in table 2), a new feature could be the sum of each customer's loans), or transformations (e.g. time since the last loan payment). A similar approach is also implemented by the "one button machine" [20]. The strategy followed by `autofeat` is somewhat orthogonal to that of `featuretools`: It is not meant for relational data, found in many business application areas, but was rather built with scientific use cases in mind, where e.g. experimental measurements would instead be stored in a single table. For this reason, `autofeat` also makes it possible to specify the units of the input variables to prevent the creation of physically nonsensical features.

Another Python library worth mentioning is `tsfresh` [6,7], which provides feature engineering methods for time series, together with a univariate feature selection strategy. However, while `autofeat` can be applied to a variety of datasets, the features generated by `tsfresh` only make sense for time series data, as they are constructed, e.g., using rolling windows.

To the best of our knowledge, there does not exist a general purpose open source library for automated feature engineering and selection, which is why we felt compelled to share our work.

2 Automated Feature Engineering and Selection with `autofeat`

The `autofeat` library provides the `AutoFeatRegression` model, which automatically generates and selects additional non-linear input features given the original data and then trains a linear regression model with these features. The model provides a familiar `scikit-learn` [29] style interface, as demonstrated by a simple usage example, where `X` corresponds to a $n \times d$ feature matrix and `y` to an n-dimensional target vector (both NumPy arrays [27] and Pandas DataFrames [23] are supported as inputs):

```
# instantiate the model
model = AutoFeatRegression()
# fit the model and get a pandas DataFrame with the original,
# as well as the additional non-linear features
df = model.fit_transform(X, y)
# predict the target for new test data points
y_pred = model.predict(X_test)
# compute the additional features for new test data points
# (e.g. as input for a different model)
df_test = model.transform(X_test)
```

In the following, we describe the feature engineering and selection steps happening during a call to `AutoFeatRegression.fit()` or `AutoFeatRegression.fit_transform()` in more detail. The `autofeat` library requires Python 3 and is pip-installable.

2.1 Construction of Non-linear Features

Additional non-linear features are generated in an alternating multi-step process by applying user selectable non-linear transformations to the features (e.g. $\log(x)$, $\sqrt{x}$, $1/x$, x^2, x^3, $|x|$, $\exp(x)$, 2^x, $\sin(x)$, $\cos(x)$) and combining pairs of features with different operators $(+, -, \cdot)$. This results in an exponentially growing feature space, e.g., with only three original features, the first feature engineering step (applying non-linear transformation) results in about 20 new features, the second step (combining features), results in about 350 new features, and after a third step (again applying transformations), the feature space has grown to include over 7000 features. As this may require a fair amount of RAM depending on the number of original input features, the data points can be subsampled before computing the new features. In practice, performing only two or three feature engineering steps is usually sufficient.

The new features are computed using the SymPy Python library [24], which automatically simplifies the generated mathematical expressions and thereby makes it possible to exclude redundant features. If the original features are provided with physical units, only 'legal' new features are retained, e.g., a feature representing a temperature would not be subtracted from a feature representing a volume of something. This is implemented using the Pint Python library,[2] which is additionally used to compute several dimensionless quantities from the original features using the Buckingham π-theorem [5]. If categorical features are included in the original features, these are transformed into one-hot encoded vectors using the corresponding `scikit-learn` model and not considered for the main feature engineering procedure.

2.2 Feature Selection

After having generated several thousands of features (often more than data points in the original dataset), it is now indispensable to carefully select only those features that contribute meaningful information when used as input to a linear model. To this end, we employ a multi-step feature selection approach (Fig. 1). In addition to the `AutoFeatRegression` model, the library also provides only this feature selection part alone in the `FeatureSelector` class, which again provides a `scikit-learn` style interface.

Individual features can provide redundant information or they might seem uninformative by themselves yet proof useful in combination with others. Therefore, instead of ranking the features independently by some criterion, it is advantageous to use a wrapper method that considers multiple features at once to select a promising subset [13]. For this we use the Lasso LARS regression model [3,10,12] provided in the `scikit-learn` library, which yields sparse weights based on which the features can be filtered. However, with more features than data points, a linear regression model is numerically unstable. Therefore, the features are first ranked based on their absolute correlation with the target residual [11] and the model is only trained on the highest ranked features. Then, to include further features capturing the not yet explained parts of the target variable, these steps are repeated multiple times, where in each iteration the regression model is used to compute a new target residual.

To identify a more robust set of features, this feature selection process can be repeated multiple times using subsamples of the data. The resulting set of features is then filtered by imposing a significance threshold: For this, a Lasso LARS regression model is trained on the selected features, as well as a random permutation of all features. The final set of features is then determined by choosing only those of the real features with a regression coefficient larger than the largest coefficient of the random noise features. After this multi-step selection process, typically only a few dozen of the several thousand engineered features are retained and used to train the final model. For new test data points, the `AutoFeatRegression` model can then either generate predictions directly, or a

[2] https://pint.readthedocs.io/en/latest/.

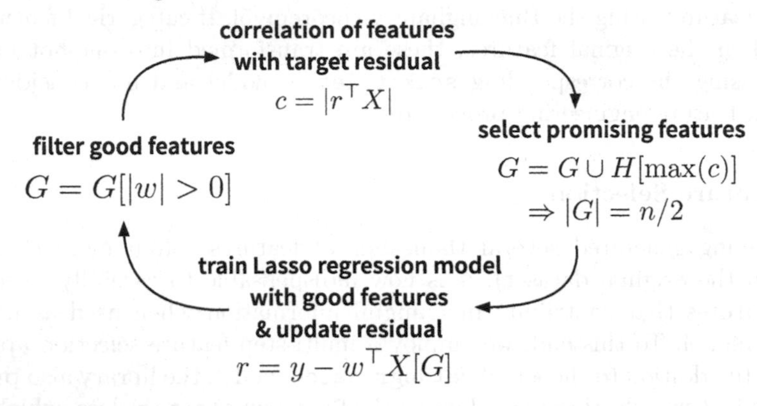
Input:
feature matrix (mean=0, std=1): $X \in \mathbb{R}^{n \times d}$
residual to be explained: $r = y \in \mathbb{R}^{n \times 1}$
candidate features: $H = \{x_1, ..., \log(x_2 + x_3)\}$
good features: $G = \{\}$
Do until convergence of G:
correlation of features with target residual
$c = |r^\top X|$
select promising features
$G = G \cup H[\max(c)]$
$\Rightarrow |G| = n/2$
train Lasso regression model with good features & update residual
$r = y - w^\top X[G]$
filter good features
$G = G[|w| > 0]$

Fig. 1. The heart of our feature selection algorithm. Given the feature matrix X with all candidate features H, the aim is to select a few informative features (G) that explain the target variable y. The set of good features G is adapted until a stable set of features is reached. First, promising features are identified by computing the correlation between the features and the target residual, and G is extended by those features with the largest absolute correlation until G contains up to $n/2$ features (to guarantee numerical stability in the following regression step). Next, the currently selected good features are used to train a Lasso LARS regression model, based on which the target residual is updated and the good features are filtered by retaining only those with a non-zero regression weight.

DataFrame with the new features can be computed for all data points and used to train other models.

By examining the coefficients of the regression model (possibly normalized by the standard deviation of the corresponding features, in case these are not of comparable magnitudes), the most prominent influencing factors related to higher or lower values of the target variable can be identified.

3 Experimental Results

To give an indication of the performance of the `AutoFeatRegression` model in practice, compared to other non-linear ML algorithms, we test our approach on five regression datasets (Table 1), provided in the `scikit-learn` package (*diabetes* and *boston*) or obtainable from the UCI Machine Learning Repository.[3] For further details on the experiments, including the hyperparameter selection of the other models, please refer to the corresponding Jupyter notebook in the GitHub repository.

Table 1. Overview of datasets, including the number of samples n and number of original input features d.

Dataset	n	d	Prediction task
diabetes [10]	442	10	Disease progression one year after baseline
boston [14]	506	13	Median housing values in suburbs of Boston
concrete [31]	1030	8	Compressive strengths of concrete mixtures
airfoil [4]	1503	5	Sound pressure levels of airfoils in a wind tunnel
wine quality [8]	6497	12	Red & white wine quality from physiochemical tests

While on most datasets, the `AutoFeatRegression` model does not quite reach the state-of-the-art performance of a random forest regression model (Table 2), it clearly outperforms standard linear ridge regression, while retaining its interpretability. Across all datasets, with one feature engineering step, `autofeat` generated between 0 and 4 additional features, while with two and three steps, it produced on average 22 additional features (Table 3). Most of the selected features are ratios or products of (transformed) features (Table 4).

Table 2. R^2 scores on the training and test folds of different datasets for ridge regression (RR), support vector regression (SVR), random forests (RF), and the `autofeat` regression model with one, two, or three feature engineering steps (AFR1-3). Best results per column are in boldface.

	Diabetes		Boston		Concrete		Airfoil		Wine quality	
	Train	Test	Train	Test	Train	Test	Train	Test	Train	Test
RR	0.541	0.383	0.736	0.748	0.625	0.564	0.517	0.508	0.293	0.310
SVR	0.580	0.320	0.959	**0.882**	0.933	0.881	0.884	0.851	0.572	0.411
RF	**0.598**	0.354	**0.983**	0.870	**0.985**	**0.892**	**0.991**	**0.934**	**0.931**	**0.558**
AFR1	0.556	0.396	0.829	0.802	0.800	0.732	0.544	0.532	0.296	0.310
AFR2	0.539	**0.402**	0.886	0.818	0.903	0.859	0.879	0.866	0.348	0.365
AFR3	0.597	0.395	0.929	0.035	0.898	0.858	0.876	0.855	0.346	0.348

With only a single feature engineering step, the `AutoFeatRegression` model often only performs slightly better than ridge regression on the original features.

[3] http://archive.ics.uci.edu/ml/index.php.

Table 3. Number of engineered (eng) and selected (sel) additional features for each dataset from an `autofeat` regression model with one, two, or three feature engineering steps (AFR1-3).

	Diabetes		Boston		Concrete		Airfoil		Wine quality	
	eng	sel	eng	sel	eng	sel	eng	sel	eng	sel
AFR1	50	3	64	4	34	2	22	3	63	0
AFR2	1781	6	2945	13	873	30	333	39	2797	19
AFR3	33661	7	52513	23	12360	25	2239	35	53684	20

Table 4. Most frequently selected features across all datasets for one, two, or three feature engineering steps (AFR1-3). Only the non-linear transformations $\log(x)$, $\sqrt{x}$, $1/x$, x^2, x^3, $|x|$, and $\exp(x)$ were applied during the feature engineering steps.

AFR1	$1/x$, x^3, x^2, $\exp(x)$
AFR2	$\sqrt{x_1}/x_2$, $1/(x_1 x_2)$, x_1/x_2, x_1^3/x_2, x_1^2/x_2, $\exp(x_1)\exp(x_2)$, $\exp(x_1)/x_2$, $\sqrt{x_1}\sqrt{x_2}$, $\sqrt{x_1}x_2^3$, $x_1\log(x_2)$, $\log(x_1)/x_2$, $x_1^3 x_2^3$, $x_1^3 x_2$, $x_1^3\log(x_2)$, ...
AFR3	x_1^3/x_2^3, $\exp(\sqrt{x_1}-\sqrt{x_2})$, $1/(x_1^3 x_2^3)$, $\sqrt{x_1 x_2}$, $1/(x_1+x_2)$, x_1/x_2^2, $1/(\sqrt{x_1}-\log(x_2))$, $\lvert\sqrt{x_1}-\log(x_2)\rvert$, $\exp(\log(x_1)/x_2)$, $\log(x_1)^2/x_2^2$, $\lvert\log(x_1)+\log(x_2)\rvert$, ...

With three feature engineering steps, on the other hand, the model can overfit on the training data (as indicated by the discrepancy between the training and test R^2 scores), because the complex features do not only explain the signal, but also the noise contained in the data. However, the only dataset where this is a serious problem here is the *boston* dataset, where over 50k features were generated in the feature engineering process, while less than 500 data points were available for feature selection and model fitting, which means overfitting is somewhat to be expected.

4 Conclusion

In this paper, we have introduced the `autofeat` Python library, which includes an automated feature engineering and selection procedure to improve the prediction accuracy of a linear regression model by using additional non-linear features. The regression model itself is based on the Lasso LARS regression from `scikit-learn` and provides a familiar interface. During the model fit, a vast number of non-linear features is generated from the original features and a few of these are selected in an elaborate iterative process to optimally explain the target variable. By combining a linear model with complex non-linear features, a high prediction accuracy can be achieved, while retaining a transparent model that yields traceable results as a basis for business decisions made by non-statisticians.

The `autofeat` library was developed with scientific use cases in mind and is especially useful for heterogeneous datasets, e.g., containing sensor measurements with different physical units. It should not be seen as a competitor for the existing feature engineering libraries `featuretools` or `tsfresh`, which would be the first choice when dealing with relational business data or time series respectively.

We have demonstrated on several datasets that the `AutoFeatRegression` model significantly improves upon the performance of a linear regression model and sometimes even outperforms other non-linear ML models. While the model can be used for predictions directly, it might also be beneficial to use the generated features as input to train other ML models. By adapting the kinds of transformations applied in the feature engineering process, as well as the number of feature engineering steps, further insights can be gained with respect to how which of the input features influences the target variable, as well as the complexity of the system as a whole.

References

1. Arras, L., Horn, F., Montavon, G., Müller, K.R., Samek, W.: "What is relevant in a text document?": an interpretable machine learning approach. PLOS ONE **12**(8), e0181142 (2017)
2. Bach, S., Binder, A., Montavon, G., Klauschen, F., Müller, K.R., Samek, W.: On pixel-wise explanations for non-linear classifier decisions by layer-wise relevance propagation. PLOS ONE **10**(7), e0130140 (2015)
3. Baraniuk, R.G.: Compressive sensing [lecture notes]. IEEE Signal Process. Mag. **24**(4), 118–121 (2007)
4. Brooks, T.F., Pope, D.S., Marcolini, M.A.: Airfoil self-noise and prediction. Technical report, NASA RP-1218 (1989)
5. Buckingham, E.: On physically similar systems; illustrations of the use of dimensional equations. Phys. Rev. **4**(4), 345 (1914)
6. Christ, M., Braun, N., Neuffer, J., Kempa-Liehr, A.W.: Time series feature extraction on basis of scalable hypothesis tests (tsfresh-a python package). Neurocomputing **307**, 72–77 (2018)
7. Christ, M., Kempa-Liehr, A.W., Feindt, M.: Distributed and parallel time series feature extraction for industrial big data applications. arXiv preprint arXiv:1610.07717 (2016)
8. Cortez, P., Cerdeira, A., Almeida, F., Matos, T., Reis, J.: Modeling wine preferences by data mining from physicochemical properties. Decis. Support Syst. **47**(4), 547–553 (2009)
9. Dor, O., Reich, Y.: Strengthening learning algorithms by feature discovery. Inf. Sci. **189**, 176–190 (2012)
10. Efron, B., Hastie, T., Johnstone, I., Tibshirani, R., et al.: Least angle regression. Ann. Stat. **32**(2), 407–499 (2004)
11. Fan, J., Lv, J.: Sure independence screening for ultrahigh dimensional feature space. J. Roy. Stat. Soc. B (Stat. Methodol.) **70**(5), 849–911 (2008)
12. Friedman, J., Hastie, T., Tibshirani, R.: Regularization paths for generalized linear models via coordinate descent. J. Stat. Softw. **33**(1), 1 (2010)

13. Guyon, I., Elisseeff, A.: An introduction to variable and feature selection. J. Mach. Learn. Res. **3**, 1157–1182 (2003)
14. Harrison Jr., D., Rubinfeld, D.L.: Hedonic housing prices and the demand for clean air. J. Environ. Econ. Manag. **5**(1), 81–102 (1978)
15. Kanter, J.M., Veeramachaneni, K.: Deep feature synthesis: towards automating data science endeavors. In: 2015 IEEE International Conference on Data Science and Advanced Analytics, DSAA 2015, Paris, France, 19–21 October 2015, pp. 1–10. IEEE (2015)
16. Katz, G., Shin, E.C.R., Song, D.: ExploreKit: automatic feature generation and selection. In: 2016 IEEE 16th International Conference on Data Mining (ICDM), pp. 979–984. IEEE (2016)
17. Khurana, U., Samulowitz, H., Turaga, D.: Feature engineering for predictive modeling using reinforcement learning. In: Thirty-Second AAAI Conference on Artificial Intelligence (2018)
18. Khurana, U., Turaga, D., Samulowitz, H., Parthasrathy, S.: Cognito: automated feature engineering for supervised learning. In: 2016 IEEE 16th International Conference on Data Mining Workshops (ICDMW), pp. 1304–1307. IEEE (2016)
19. Kursa, M.B., Rudnicki, W.R., et al.: Feature selection with the boruta package. J. Stat. Softw. **36**(11), 1–13 (2010)
20. Lam, H.T., Thiebaut, J.M., Sinn, M., Chen, B., Mai, T., Alkan, O.: One button machine for automating feature engineering in relational databases. arXiv preprint arXiv:1706.00327 (2017)
21. Markovitch, S., Rosenstein, D.: Feature generation using general constructor functions. Mach. Learn. **49**(1), 59–98 (2002). https://doi.org/10.1023/A:1014046307775
22. Martius, G., Lampert, C.H.: Extrapolation and learning equations. arXiv preprint arXiv:1610.02995 (2016)
23. McKinney, W., et al.: Data structures for statistical computing in Python. In: Proceedings of the 9th Python in Science Conference, Austin, TX, vol. 445, pp. 51–56 (2010)
24. Meurer, A., et al.: SymPy: symbolic computing in Python. PeerJ Comput. Sci. **3**, e103 (2017)
25. Montavon, G., Samek, W., Müller, K.R.: Methods for interpreting and understanding deep neural networks. Digital Signal Processing **73**, 1–15 (2018)
26. Nargesian, F., Samulowitz, H., Khurana, U., Khalil, E.B., Turaga, D.S.: Learning feature engineering for classification. In: IJCAI, pp. 2529–2535 (2017)
27. Oliphant, T.E.: A Guide to NumPy, vol. 1. Trelgol Publishing, Spanish Fork (2006)
28. Ouyang, R., Curtarolo, S., Ahmetcik, E., Scheffler, M., Ghiringhelli, L.M.: SISSO: a compressed-sensing method for identifying the best low-dimensional descriptor in an immensity of offered candidates. Phys. Rev. Mater. **2**(8), 083802 (2018)
29. Pedregosa, F., et al.: Scikit-learn: machine learning in Python. J. Mach. Learn. Res. **12**(Oct), 2825–2830 (2011)
30. Ribeiro, M.T., Singh, S., Guestrin, C.: "Why should I trust you?": explaining the predictions of any classifier. In: Proceedings of the 22nd ACM SIGKDD International Conference on Knowledge Discovery and Data Mining, San Francisco, CA, USA, 13–17 August 2016, pp. 1135–1144 (2016)
31. Yeh, I.C.: Modeling of strength of high-performance concrete using artificial neural networks. Cem. Concr. Res. **28**(12), 1797–1808 (1998)

The Extended Dawid-Skene Model
Fusing Information from Multiple Data Schemas

Michael P. J. Camilleri[1(✉)] and Christopher K. I. Williams[1,2]

[1] School of Informatics, University of Edinburgh, Edinburgh, UK
michael.p.camilleri@ed.ac.uk
[2] Alan Turing Institute, London, UK

Abstract. While label fusion from multiple noisy annotations is a well understood concept in data wrangling (tackled for example by the Dawid-Skene (DS) model), we consider the extended problem of carrying out learning when the labels themselves are not consistently annotated with the same schema. We show that even if annotators use disparate, albeit related, label-sets, we can still draw inferences for the underlying full label-set. We propose the Inter-Schema AdapteR (ISAR) to translate the fully-specified label-set to the one used by each annotator, enabling learning under such heterogeneous schemas, without the need to re-annotate the data. We apply our method to a mouse behavioural dataset, achieving significant gains (compared with DS) in out-of-sample log-likelihood (-3.40 to -2.39) and F1-score (0.785 to 0.864).

Keywords: Multi-schema learning · Crowdsourcing · Annotations · Behavioural characterisation · Probabilistic modelling · Data wrangling

1 Introduction

Machine learning is based on learning from examples [2]. This often requires human annotations, e.g. class labels for image classes in ImageNet [12]. However, human labelling is error prone and consequently, methods such as the Dawid-Skene (DS) model [5] have been developed to estimate individual error rates and draw inferences on the true label from multiple annotators, see e.g. [11,20].

In this paper, we are interested in the extended problem of carrying out such learning when the annotations have been carried out under different schemas, and in so doing, help to automate the data wrangling and cleaning portion of data science. Given a 'complete' set of possible labels, we consider the scenario where the annotations for different samples are performed using different subsets (schemas) of this 'complete' label-set. A schema can be obtained, for example, by aggregating labels together to produce fewer, coarser labels, or by singling out one label to annotate and lumping all the others together (i.e. 'One-vs-Rest'). This is a common data wrangling problem in scientific analysis where the actual nature of the research question is being formulated: for example, in labelling animal behaviour, scientists may realise half-way through data collection that

P. Cellier and K. Driessens (Eds.): ECML PKDD 2019 Workshops, CCIS 1167, pp. 121–136, 2020.
https://doi.org/10.1007/978-3-030-43823-4_11

a certain activity is rich enough that it warrants splitting into multiple labels. Alternatively, due to the expertise of certain annotators, they may be directed to focus on specific subsets of activity, and clumping all others.

The challenge we address here is how to draw inferences about the underlying complete label-set, despite being provided with annotations which make use of different labelling schemas. Normally, this would not be possible without re-annotating the entire data-set (which is often expensive) or simply discarding older data (which is wasteful in limited data scenarios). Our contribution is to show that with the appropriate formulation, learning from all the data can indeed be achieved by adding an Inter-Schema AdapteR (ISAR) which allows us to translate the full label-set to the one used by a given annotator. Furthermore, we demonstrate the applicability and effectiveness of our method for behavioural annotation, using both simulated and actual data.

The rest of our paper is structured as follows. In Sect. 2 we define the data wrangling problem we tackle and propose our solution, and then compare our approach to related work (Sect. 3). Subsequently we describe a concrete problem which motivated our model in Sect. 4, and in Sect. 5 report experimental results under various scenarios. We conclude with a discussion of the merits of the model and proposed future extensions.

2 Problem and Model Definition

We start by defining a 'complete' set of labels $L = \{1, ..., |L|\}$ encompassing all possible classes/feature values, which we will refer to as the 'full label-set'. However, we consider the case where the observations are drawn from a reduced sub-set of L. That is, given $|S|$ different label-sets/schemas, denoted L_s for $s \in \{1, ..., |S|\}$, different samples are labelled according to different schemas. Each L_s may contain labels from L and/or groupings thereof, as illustrated in Fig. 1.

To motivate our problem consider the task of documenting the behaviour of an individual according to a discrete set of labels. A number of annotators are

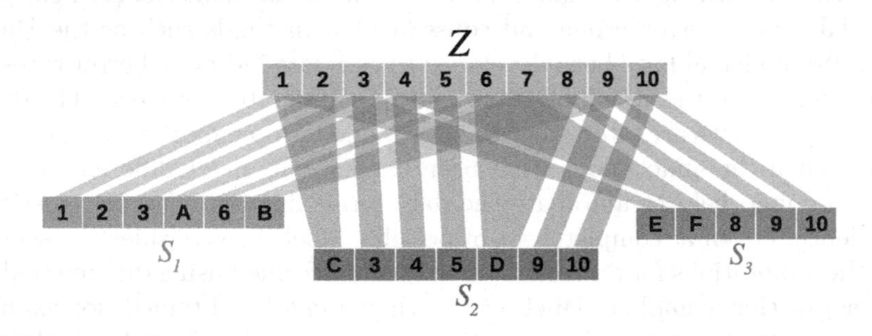

Fig. 1. An example scenario with ten labels, and three schemas (colour-coded), showing how super-labels (enumerated **A** through **F**) are constructed from the full label-set. Note that while the above super-labels encompass contiguous labels, this is only for clarity and need not be the case.

tasked to do this, but their annotations are not restricted to a single schema (for the reasons enumerated above). Our aim is to collate their labels so that we get a posterior belief over the true behavioural state, and to do so while constructing a global rather than a single model per-schema, thus sharing statistical strength across the entire data-set. This helps to automate the data wrangling process, as opposed to re-annotating the data using a consistent schema. In what follows, we first describe the DS model, which can be used to solve the problem under the constraint of a single schema, and then show how using ISAR we can achieve an Extended DS model for dealing with multiple schemas.

2.1 Model Definition

The standard DS model appears in Fig. 2a. The categorical variable Z represents the true behaviour of the individual, and is parametrised by the prior π over the full label-set (indexed by z). U_k is the *observed* annotation provided by each annotator k, and models the observer error-rate through a Conditional Probability Table (CPT) ($|U| = |Z| = |L|$):

$$\psi_{k,u,z} \equiv P\left(U_k = u|Z = z\right), \tag{1}$$

where the subscripts indicate indexing in the respective dimension.

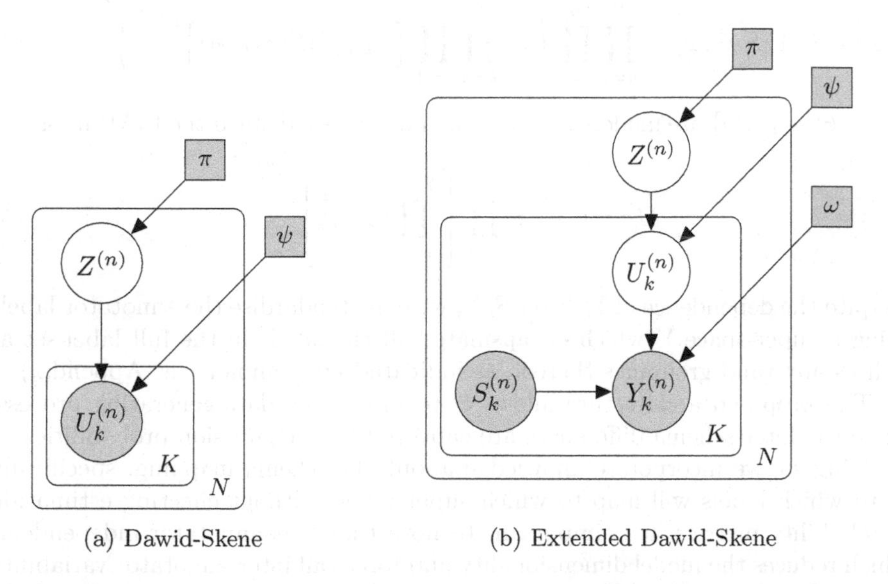

Fig. 2. Multi-annotator label fusion with the (a) DS and (b) Extended DS (using ISAR adapter) models.

In our setup (Fig. 2b), however, U_k is 'corrupted' by the schema: i.e. we only observe Y_k whose domain is conditioned by the schema S_k. Y_k is another discrete variable representing the annotator's assigned label contingent on which schema $S_k^{(n)}$ is currently active: i.e. $|Y_k^{(n)}| = |L_{S_k^{(n)}}|$. Consider for example that each annotator is an expert in only a handful of behaviours: thus we opt to ask the annotator to only label observations of the activity that they know about. For each annotator k, Y_k spans only those behaviours plus a special Not In Schema (NIS) label, which groups together the remaining behaviours. We assume knowledge of $S_k^{(n)}$ (i.e. which schema is used), a valid assumption in our application domain. The mapping from U to Y (conditioned on S) is modelled by the Inter-Schema AdapteR (ISAR) CPT ω:

$$\omega_{y,u,s} = P\left(Y = y | U = u, S = s\right). \tag{2}$$

For our purposes, ω is *fixed* and *deterministic*: i.e. all entries are either 1 or 0, and encode expert knowledge about which labels in L map to the same L_s. This gives a very intuitive way to construct the mapping, as governed by:

$$\omega_{y,u,s} = \begin{cases} 1 & \text{if } u \text{ is one of the states captured by } y \text{ under } s, \\ 0 & \text{otherwise.} \end{cases} \tag{3}$$

If we assume a one-hot-encoding of the variables (such that a particular manifestation is indicated by indexing the respective variable dimension), we can represent our model by the following joint distribution:

$$P(Z, U, Y | S; \Theta, \omega) = \prod_{n=1}^{N} \prod_{z=1}^{|L|} \left(\pi_z \prod_{k=1}^{K} \prod_{u=1}^{|L|} \left\{ \psi_{k,u,z} M_\omega^{(n)}\left(k, u\right) \right\}^{U_{k,u}^{(n)}} \right)^{Z_z^{(n)}}, \tag{4}$$

where $\Theta = \{\pi, \psi\}$ are model-parameters, and we have defined the ISAR message:

$$M_\omega^{(n)}\left(k, u\right) \equiv \prod_{s=1}^{|S|} \left[\prod_{y=1}^{|Y^{(n)}|} \omega_{y,u,s}^{Y_{k,y}^{(n)}} \right]^{S_{k,s}^{(n)}}. \tag{5}$$

Despite the dependence of $Y_k^{(n)}$ on $S_k^{(n)}$, we can standardise the annotator labels using a super-space Y which encapsulates all the labels in the full label-set as well as any valid groupings thereof, as indicated by Lemma 1 (see Appendix).

The proposed architecture allows Θ to model the data-generating process, while the inter-schema differences are captured by the emission probabilities ω. In doing so, we incorporate knowledge about the schema mapping, specifically as to which labels will map to which super-labels without effecting estimation of reliability metrics. It is important to note that ω is annotator-independent, which reduces the model dimensionality and forces all inter-annotator variability to be incorporated in ψ. Due to the ISAR adapter, the Extended DS model is able to infer more accurate statistics about the distribution of the full label-set, even in cases where the signal is very sparse (such as one vs rest schemas, see 5.4 below). Despite being deterministic, ω does not preclude multiple latent states mapping to any super-label, and hence, the model is rich enough to capture the inherent uncertainty over the latent state.

2.2 Training the Model

Training the model involves learning the parameters π and ψ (ω is fixed). We add a *Log Prior* to the log of the joint likelihood (Eq. 4), and compute Maximum-A-Posteriori (MAP) rather than Maximum-Likelihood (MLE) estimates for π and ψ, thus reducing the risk of overfitting. We use conjugate Dirichlet priors:

$$Dir(\pi|\alpha^{\pi}) \equiv \frac{1}{\beta(\alpha^{\pi})} \prod_{z=1}^{|Z|} \pi_z^{\alpha_z^{\pi}-1}, \qquad Dir(\psi_{k,z}|\alpha_{k,z}^{\psi}) \equiv \frac{1}{\beta(\alpha_{k,z}^{\psi})} \prod_{u=1}^{|U|} \psi_{k,u,z}^{\alpha_{k,u,z}^{\psi}-1}.$$

We derive an Expectation Maximisation (EM) algorithm [8] to infer the parameters. During the E-step, we need to compute two expectations:

$$\gamma_z^{(n)} \equiv \left\langle Z_z^{(n)} \right\rangle = \frac{\pi_z M_{\psi}^{(n)}(z)}{\sum_{z'=1}^{|Z|} \pi_{z'} M_{\psi}^{(n)}(z')}, \tag{6}$$

and

$$\rho_{k,u,z}^{(n)} \equiv \left\langle Z_z^{(n)} U_{k,u}^{(n)} \right\rangle = \frac{\pi_z M_{\omega}^{*(n)}(k,u,z) M_{\psi}^{*(n)}(k,z)}{\sum_{z'=1}^{|Z|} \left(\pi_{z'} M_{\psi}^{(n)}(z')\right)}, \tag{7}$$

where $M_{\omega}^{(n)}$ is as defined before (Eq. 5), with messages:

$$M_{\omega}^{*(n)}(k,u,z) \equiv \ \psi_{k,u,z} M_{\omega}^{(n)}(k,u), \tag{8}$$

$$M_{\psi}^{(n)}(z) \ \equiv \ \prod_{k'=1}^{K} \sum_{u'=1}^{|U|} M_{\omega}^{*(n)}(k',u',z), \tag{9}$$

$$M_{\psi}^{*(n)}(k,z) \equiv \frac{M_{\psi}^{(n)}(z)}{\sum_{u=1}^{|U|} M_{\omega}^{*(n)}(k,u,z)}. \tag{10}$$

The M-Step involves maximising the expected complete data log-likelihood with respect to each of the unknown parameters π and ψ:

$$\hat{\pi}_z = \frac{\sum_{n=1}^{N} \gamma_z^{(n)} + \alpha_z^{\pi} - 1}{N + \sum_{z'=1}^{|Z|} \alpha_{z'}^{\pi} - |Z|}, \tag{11}$$

and

$$\hat{\psi}_{k,u,z} = \frac{\sum_{n=1}^{N} \rho_{k,u,z}^{(n)} + \alpha_{k,u,z}^{\psi} - 1}{\sum_{n=1}^{N} \sum_{u'=1}^{|U|} \rho_{k,u',z}^{(n)} + \sum_{u'=1}^{|U|} \alpha_{k,u',z}^{\psi} - |U|}. \tag{12}$$

The full derivations are available in [3].

As regards computational complexity, we note that the ISAR adapter acts as a message function in graphical modelling terms, and given that ω is fixed and both Y and S are observed, M_{ω} can be computed once and used throughout the optimisation: moreover, being a merely indexing operation, it is linear in the number of samples. As regards estimation of the other parameters, each EM step scales linearly in the number of samples and annotators, and quadratically in the size of the super-schema.

3 Related Work

Our approach towards automating information fusion and thus streamlining the data-wrangling process is concerned with probabilistic inference from incompletely specified data. In this respect, ISAR is related to the general Transfer Learning (TL) field, specifically in learning across feature-spaces. Our solution is novel in that it is applied to an 'unsupervised' learning scenario, and rather than focusing on learning the mapping between feature spaces – refer to [10] for a review – we take the problem one step further through our interpretation of the different schemas (using domain knowledge about the specific problem), which allows us to collate information across label-spaces in an efficient manner.

Another perspective comes from Multi-Task Learning (MTL) [19]. To relate to this literature we can view each label schema as a "task", but the analogy is not perfect. In multi-task learning one aims to improve the learning of a model for each task by using knowledge contained in all or some of the tasks, while in our case, we typically consider a single task but the feature-space is only partially observed (by way of the schema). We do share a similar goal of sharing statistical strength across schemas (rather than across tasks): by using ISAR we seek to *fuse* the information from all annotators (who may be using different schemas) in order to draw inferences for the 'complete' label-set (rather than one 'task' at a time), and hence is a step beyond the standard MTL setting.

Our schema mapping can be viewed as "data coarsening" as discussed in [6]: however, our problem setup is different and applied to categorical rather than continuous data. Cour *et al.* [4] have addressed a similar problem, using a discriminative rather than generative method, but only applied for supervised learning.

One may be inclined to cast our problem into the hierarchical classification framework [13], particularly Hierarchical Multi-label Classification (HMlC) [17] due to the apparent 'multi-label' aspect of the mapping together with the two-level nature. While hierarchical classification seeks to structure the space of labels hierarchically according to a fixed taxonomy, we stress that contrary to multi-label classification, in our setting, there is a single valid label, but there is uncertainty on which one it is (due to the coarse labelling imposed by the schema). Moreover, while we seek mandatory leaf-node predictions [13], we do not require specification of the full label hierarchy for each sample which to our knowledge has not been tackled before. Finally, our model focuses on handling multiple annotators and their uncertainty.

4 Description of the Data

We tested our Extended DS on a social behaviour-phenotyping data-set for caged mice, obtained from the Medical Research Council, Harwell Institute, Oxfordshire (MRC Harwell) as documented in [1]. This consists of 27.5 h of annotated behaviour of various mice kept in cages of three. Each 30-min segment was individually labelled by two or three annotators from a pool of eleven individuals, with responsibility for annotating changing between segments.

Labelling involves specifying the start/end-times of exhibited behaviours, which periods are then aligned to 1-s boundaries. The data contains periods for which no label is given ('unlabelled samples'): this is because the annotators were explicitly instructed not to annotate observations if they cannot be coerced to any of the available behaviours or if they were unsure about it. The annotations follow one of four schemas (denoted **I**, **II**, **III** and **IV**), containing the labels shown in Fig. 3. The schemas are consistent within a segment (i.e. all annotators use the same schema) but change between segments. The goal of the study is to infer the 'true' latent behaviour of the mice given the observations, which can then be used for example in the analyse of phenotype differences between strains (although in this paper, all wild-type strains were used). In this scenario, the need for a holistic model is even more significant since some labels are missing entirely from some schemas, and hence a model trained solely on data from a particular schema would miss potentially significant behaviour.

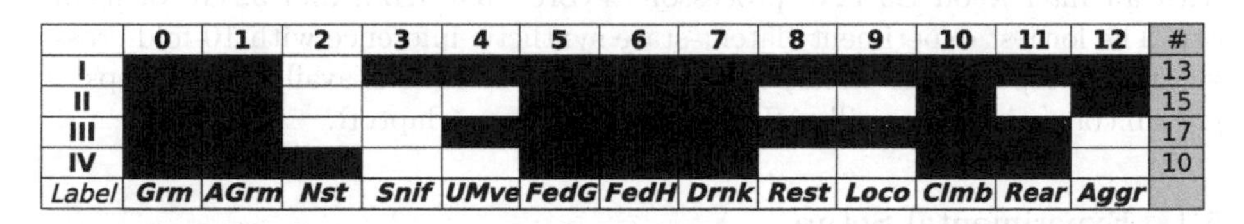

Fig. 3. The behavioural annotation schemas used in this project, with *black* cells indicating which labels (numerical representation, top row) are present in which schema (first column). The last row, marked *(Label)* is our short-hand notation for referring to the labels while the last column indicates the number of segments in our data-set corresponding to each schema.

Since the schemas used did not have an explicit label to indicate a behaviour not in the label-set (NIS), we had to infer this from the unlabelled data. We distinguish between two cases of such samples:

1. Informative Unlabelling, which arises from the observed behaviour not being in the schema (translating to NIS), *and*
2. Missing Data, i.e. where the annotator was unsure about how to label a behaviour.

We assign NIS only to those time-points where all responsible annotators do not give a label, treating all other unlabelled samples as Missing at Random

(MAR) [7]. This is based on the assumption that in our laboratory setting, the annotators are adequately trained, and hence, the probability of all responsible annotators not providing a label is close to insignificant. This was indeed verified by recording the fraction of time-points with no labelling by schemas, and saw that this is correlated with the schema (dropping to ≈ 0 for Schemas I and III).

5 Experimental Analysis

We now document the empirical results which serve to illustrate the validity of the ISAR method. Specifically we seek to answer two questions: (a) can such a model be learnt under the condition of disparate schemas, *and, if so,* (b) is there merit to using ISAR over just discarding incompatibly annotated data? To this end, we report two main experiments. Lacking any ground truth in the real data, we first evaluate the observed-data log-likelihood under both our Extended DS and individual DS models trained on each schema in Sect. 5.2. Next we analyse the ability of our model to learn the true data-generating process by evaluating the predictive performance on synthetic data for which ground-truth is available (Sect. 5.3). We also provide results on parameter recovery (Sect. 5.4) as well as an information-theoretic analysis of the schema adapter (Sect. 5.5). In all our tests (except for the parameter recover), we train on a portion of the data and report measures on 'unseen' data using cross-validation.

All experiments were carried out on a desktop running Ubuntu Linux (18.04), with an Intel Xeon E3-1245 processor (4-cores, 3.5 GHz), and 32 Gb of memory. The longest experiment (latent-state synthetic inference with 10-fold cross-validation, repeated 20 times) took about 6 h. The code is available at: https://github.com/michael-camilleri/ISAR-Inter_Schema_AdapteR.

5.1 Experimental Setup

We explored training the models from multiple random restarts. However, extensive testing indicated that starting from a diagonally-biased emission matrix (ψ) provided consistently better validation-set likelihoods: paired t-test with 164 DoF yielded a t-statistic of 2.90 ($p = 0.004$) when compared to the best of 30-random restarts. We hence initialised ψ as a strongly diagonal matrix by adding a uniform matrix of 0.01 entries to the Identity matrix, and then normalising across u to produce valid probabilities. This encodes our belief that most annotators are consistent in their labelling (i.e. most of the probability mass is on the diagonal). It also provides the added benefit that the latent-states are 'naturally' identifiable, avoiding the 'label-switching' issue [14] in the latent space since it biases the search in the vicinity of the identity permutation. The prior π was initialised to the uniform distribution (i.e. all states equally likely). In all cases, we used symmetric Dirichlet priors ($\alpha = 2$) on the parameters π and ψ.

5.2 Likelihood-Based Evaluation on Real Data

We evaluate our architecture on the task of inferring latent mouse-behaviour from noisy annotations, and compare it to the DS baseline trained independently per schema. Lacking ground-truths, we score the models using the log-likelihood on out-of-sample data, with 11-fold cross-validation[1] (training on ten and evaluating metrics on the remaining one). When training the DS model, the individual schemas were augmented with the NIS label, to provide an equivalent observed sample-space, and allow for a like-with-like likelihood comparison between the two models. The folds were engineered to be as uniform in size as possible while separating different mice in different folds to achieve more generalisable performance measures. We: (a) use fixed-folds, to provide a fair comparison between models, *and* (b) report/compare measures on a per-segment basis, since the DS architecture can only be trained on a single schema at a time.

Table 1 reports schema-averages (across segments) for the per-sample log-likelihood (where the log-likelihood is divided by the number of samples), and the global average (computed across all segments). All likelihoods are higher (better) in the ISAR case, indicating the ability of the model to share statistical strength across the schemas, including learning about annotators which would otherwise not be observed in some schemas. Specifically, a paired t-test with 54 DoF (55 segments) indicated a significant increase in validation-set log-likelihood for the ISAR model as compared to the DS model: the result yielded a t-statistic of 5.78 ($p = 3.89 \times 10^{-7}$).

Table 1. Validation average log-likelihoods (higher is better)

	Schema				Mean	Std
	I	II	III	IV		
DS	−3.27	−3.23	−2.65	−5.07	−3.40	1.20
ISAR	**−2.68**	**−2.29**	**−2.48**	**−2.01**	**−2.39**	**0.82**

5.3 Latent State Inference in Synthetic Data

While the real data lacks ground-truth of the latent mouse behaviour, we can simulate data using the parameters learnt above (to be as realistic as possible) and evaluate the MAP ‘predictive’ performance on it. Note that in this scenario, we cannot compare ISAR to the DS model trained individually per-schema, since in every schema, DS does not have knowledge of the entire label-set. In effect, the DS model cannot be used in such a scenario to give true predictions. A naive alternative is to clump together all the samples as if they come from the same schema, and treat NIS as missing data. This is based on the clearly incorrect assumption that the missing data is MAR and can thus be ignored, which will in general lead to inferior results. It does however provide a baseline comparison.

[1] The 11 is due to the natural groupings of segments in the available data.

In order to test the merits of ISAR under a number of statistical conditions, we performed a study in which we simulated different data generation conditions. The full details of the experimental procedure as well as the results are given in Appendix B: below we report the case on the statistics which most closely match our dataset. We ran the experiment 20 times, with 10-fold cross-validation in each run and report the macro-averaged F1-score (computing F1-score for each class independently and then averaging [9, p. 185]) and predictive log-likelihood (log-likelihood assigned to the true label) in Table 2. We prefer the macro-averaged F1 score over accuracy, as we have high class imbalance, but care about each label equally. Note how in both metrics ISAR shows consistently and (statistically) significantly better performance.

Table 2. Macro F1 and predictive log-likelihood for the ISAR and DS models applied to synthetic data.

	Log-likelihood			Macro F1		
	Mean	Std	p-value	Mean	Std	p-value
DS	−0.61	0.09	6.1×10^{-16}	0.785	0.02	3.2×10^{-26}
ISAR	**−0.35**	**0.04**		**0.864**	0.02	

5.4 Parameter Recovery from Synthetic Data

Another indicator of performance is the ability of our architecture to learn the 'true' parameters which generate the data. We again generated synthetic data from known fixed values for $\Theta = \{\pi, \psi\}$ (obtained from the parameters trained on the real-data), and trained our model on it. While space precludes us from a full treatment of these results here, we observed convergence towards the same π identified by using the full schema (up to 2.3% error) even in extreme one-vs-rest schemas where the annotator only provides the presence/absence of a single label: ψ was estimated to within 11.3% of the true values under the MRC Harwell schemas. More details are provided in Appendix C.

5.5 Analysis of Mutual Information

We sought to explain the relative performance of the ISAR architecture in terms of the Mutual Information (MI) $\mathbf{I}(Z;Y)$ between the latent state Z and sets of observations Y from different schemas on the model fitted from the real data. When using more than one schema we can also compute the Redundancy $R(Z;Y)$ [15] between Z and Y, where:

$$R(Z;Y) \equiv \sum_{s=1}^{|S|} \mathbf{I}(Z;Y_s) - \mathbf{I}\left(Z;Y_1,...,Y_{|S|}\right) \tag{13}$$

Table 3. Mutual Information **I** and Redundancy R between the observations and the latent behaviour, under the effect of the different schemas. The statistics are reported across annotators.

	$\mathbf{I}(Z;\boldsymbol{Y})$			$R(Z;\boldsymbol{Y})$		
	Mean	Min	Max	Mean	Min	Max
$Y = U$	1.48	1.39	1.56			
I	1.48	1.39	1.56			
II	0.87	0.73	0.93			
III	1.47	1.38	1.56			
IV	0.95	0.90	0.99			
I+III	1.73	1.67	1.78	1.22	1.09	1.34
II+IV	1.10	1.06	1.15	0.72	0.60	0.80
I+III+IV	1.78	1.71	1.82	2.12	1.93	2.29
All	1.79	1.72	1.82	2.98	2.73	3.21

The resulting measures are shown in Table 3. We consider first the MI for individual schemas in Table 3 (top). Note how schema **I** yields the same MI as if we had access to the full label-set: this is because in **I** there is only one missing label, and hence the model correctly identifies NIS with that label. Looking at the individual schemas, we see that those with a smaller number of labels coded as NIS have a higher mutual information.

We next consider combinations of the schemas, a subset of which appear in Table 3. That is we potentially have observations from up to four schemas for the same underlying latent state. The table shows that (as expected) increasing the number of schemas yields higher mutual information, up to the maximum from using all four schemas. We can also measure the redundancy of the different schemas. This shows that the schemas are redundant (rather than synergistic), which makes sense given the way the model is constructed.

6 Conclusions

In this paper we have presented a novel and effective solution to inferring latent variables from observations across different but related label-spaces (schemas). We developed an inter-schema adapter (ISAR), that allows us to build a holistic model and share statistical strength across disparately-labelled portions of the data-set. We validated our model under both simulated and real-world conditions, for a behaviour annotation task. The ISAR model improved on the baseline DS in terms of log-likelihood with an increase from -3.40 to -2.39. In simulated data, ISAR achieved a 10% increase in macro F1-score.

While above we assume that the samples are independent and identically distributed (IID), we can easily extend the unsupervised model to the temporal modelling domain: indeed, we investigated such an extension in [3]. We have constructed the schema adapter from knowledge of the schemas and how labels are mapped; however, it could be interesting to consider *learning* the adapter if this information were not known.

Our model focused on the problem of inter-annotator variability under inconsistent schemas. However, due to the 'plugin' nature of our adapter, the model is amenable to extensions which take into account for example task difficulty [18] or shared latent-structure across the annotators [16].

Acknowledgements. We thank our collaborators at the Medical Research Council, Harwell Institute, Oxfordshire, especially Dr Sara Wells, Dr Pat Nolan, Dr Rasneer Sonia Bains and Dr Henrik Westerberg for providing and explaining the data set. MC's work was supported in part by the EPSRC Centre for Doctoral Training in Data Science, funded by the UK Engineering and Physical Sciences Research Council (grant EP/L016427/1) and the University of Edinburgh. The work of CW was supported in part by The Alan Turing Institute under the EPSRC grant EP/N510129/1.

Ethical Approval. While none of the authors were involved in the data collection, all procedures and animal studies in the behavioural-characterisation data-set used were carried out in accordance with the Animals (Scientific Procedures) Act 1986, UK, Amendment Regulations 2012 (SI 4 2012/3039) as indicated in [1].

A Extended Proofs

Lemma 1. *Let* $Y_k^{'(n)}$ *be a 1-Hot encoded variable, where the sample-space is denoted* $L_{S^{(n)}}$*: i.e. this may vary between samples/annotators. This is equivalent to representing* $Y_k^{(n)}$ *by a fixed sample-space, where the probability of emitting* $Y_y^{(n)}$ *for some* $y \notin L_{S^{(n)}} = 0$.

Proof.

$$M_\omega^{(n)}(k,u) = \prod_{s=1}^{|S|}\left[\prod_{y=1}^{|Y|} \omega_{y,u,s}^{Y_{k,y}^{(n)}}\right]^{S_{k,s}^{(n)}} = \prod_{s=1}^{|S|}\left[\prod_{y \in Y^{(n)}} \omega_{y,u,s}^{Y_{k,y}^{(n)}} \prod_{y \notin Y^{(n)}} \omega_{y,u,s}^{Y_{k,y}^{(n)}}\right]^{S_s^{(n)}}. \quad (14)$$

However, for the second set of products, $Y_{k,y}^{(n)} = 0$ by definition, since it is never observed. Hence,

$$M_\omega^{(n)}(k,u) = \prod_{s=1}^{|S|}\left[\prod_{y \in Y^{(n)}} \omega_{y,u,s}^{Y_{k,y}^{(n)}} \times 1\right]^{S_{k,s}^{(n)}} = \prod_{s=1}^{|S|}\left[\prod_{y \in Y^{(n)}} \omega_{y,u,s}^{Y_{k,y}^{(n)}}\right]^{S_{k,s}^{(n)}}. \quad (15)$$

Note that while we do not require that $\omega_{y,u,s} = 0 \; \forall y \notin L_{S^{(n)}}$, this is enforced to avoid the model expending probability mass on impossible combinations.

B Additional Comparisons between ISAR and DS

We evaluated the Extended and baseline DS models through the macro F1-score, raw accuracy and predictive log-likelihood in synthetic experiments. While the F1 and likelihood scores provide the best comparison, the accuracy is also reported as a more challenging baseline to beat (since it is generally easy to achieve high accuracy using poor models on very unbalanced datasets such as ours). In each experiment, we simulated 20 independent runs, and evaluated the metrics on a hold-out set using 10-fold cross validation. For most of the experiments, we used a *reduced* data-set size of 60 segments of 100 samples each, allowing us to test various conditions quickly (we show that this alone does not significantly impact our results, see first and second rows of Table 4). We tested the effect of a *uniform* distribution over latent-states, Π sampled (once) from a *Dirichlet* prior with $\alpha = 10$ as well as schema distributions *Biased* towards the less informative ones (in the ratio 1:10:1:10). Note that in this latter case, the number of segments was increased to 80 (since otherwise certain schemas do not appear in some folds). p-Values corresponding to paired t-tests with 19-Degrees of Freedom (DoF) (20 independent runs) are reported in all cases.

Table 4. Predictive log-likelihood, F1 and accuracy for the ISAR and DS models under different conditions. In the interest of avoiding clutter, we omit p-Values for the accuracy, but in all cases, it was less than 1×10^{-16}.

		Log-likelihood			Macro F1			Accuracy (%)	
		Mean	Std	p-value	Mean	Std	p-value	Mean	Std
Realistic	DS	-0.61	0.09	6.1×10^{-16}	0.785	0.02	3.2×10^{-26}	82.5	2.13
	ISAR	**-0.35**	**0.04**		**0.864**	0.02		**84.5**	**1.95**
Reduced	DS	-0.60	0.09	1.0×10^{-14}	0.757	0.02	2.5×10^{-14}	82.6	2.05
	ISAR	**-0.37**	**0.04**		**0.803**	0.02		**84.3**	**1.84**
Uniform	DS	-0.92	0.08	8.0×10^{-24}	0.726	0.02	1.9×10^{-21}	73.8	1.99
	ISAR	**-0.38**	**0.04**		**0.840**	0.02		**83.4**	**1.89**
Dirichlet	DS	-0.94	0.07	1.6×10^{-24}	0.727	0.02	2.2×10^{-23}	73.8	1.83
	ISAR	**-0.36**	**0.04**		**0.835**	0.02		**84.8**	**1.75**
Biased	DS	-1.83	0.21	3.6×10^{-19}	0.533	0.02	1.6×10^{-24}	35.7	2.32
	ISAR	**-0.82**	**0.15**		**0.667**	**0.01**		**69.3**	**1.21**
Biased & Uniform	DS	-1.60	**0.11**	9.1×10^{-10}	0.585	0.02	5.5×10^{-19}	62.5	**1.05**
	ISAR	**-0.82**	0.37		**0.709**	0.02		**71.9**	1.34

C Parameter Recovery Curves

We carried out simulation experiments of the ability of the model to recover the 'true' parameters, under a number of scenarios. In each case, datasets were generated according to the parameters as learnt from the MRC Harwell data, and subsequently we retrained the model from scratch, using successively larger portions of the dataset. Each experiment was repeated 20 times, with noisy perturbation

($\sim$Unif[0, 0.05]) in the underlying prior/emission probabilities. We evaluated the quality of the estimate with the Relative Absolute Deviation (RAD) between the true Θ and learnt $\hat{\Theta}$ parameters, using the mean magnitude of individual probabilities as the normaliser:

$$RAD = \frac{|\hat{\Theta} - \Theta| \times 100\%}{mean(\Theta)}.$$

We prefer this over the KL-Divergence as it is more readily interpretable.

In the first case (Fig. 4) we experimented with an extreme scenario where each schema indicates only the presence/absence of a single label (i.e. a One-vs-Rest schema). To reduce the complexity of the problem, we generated data using the first six of the original 11 annotators, seven of the original 13 labels, and with maximum sample sizes of 500 segments of 100 time-points each. Annotators and schemas were drawn from uniform distributions. We investigated scenarios where (a) all responsible annotators use the same schema within a sample, and (b) annotators may use different schemas even within the same sample.

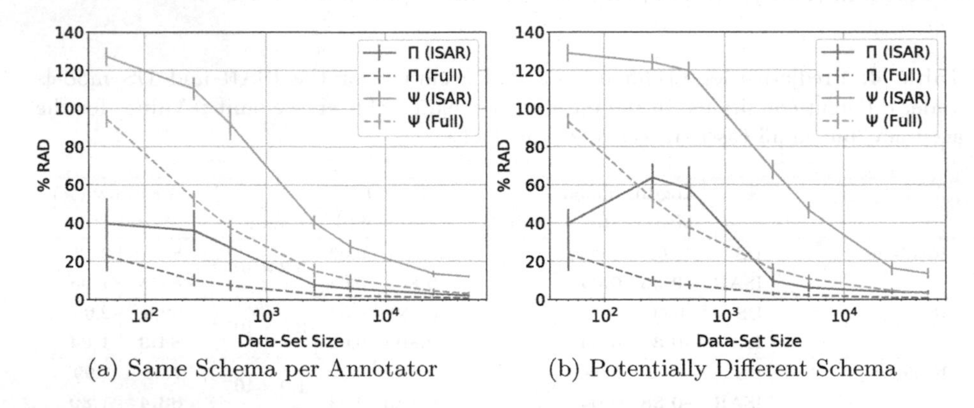

(a) Same Schema per Annotator (b) Potentially Different Schema

Fig. 4. RAD as a function of data-set size for the One-vs-Rest schemas. The error-bars indicate one standard deviation across runs. The initial increase in error in (b) is due to the interplay between the 'prior' counts becoming insignificant, but there not being enough data to get a true estimate of the probabilities (due to label imbalance).

In the second case we used the same setup as in the real data, i.e. the four schemas in the MRC Harwell dataset, the full annotator/label-set and the full data-set size. This is shown in Fig. 5.

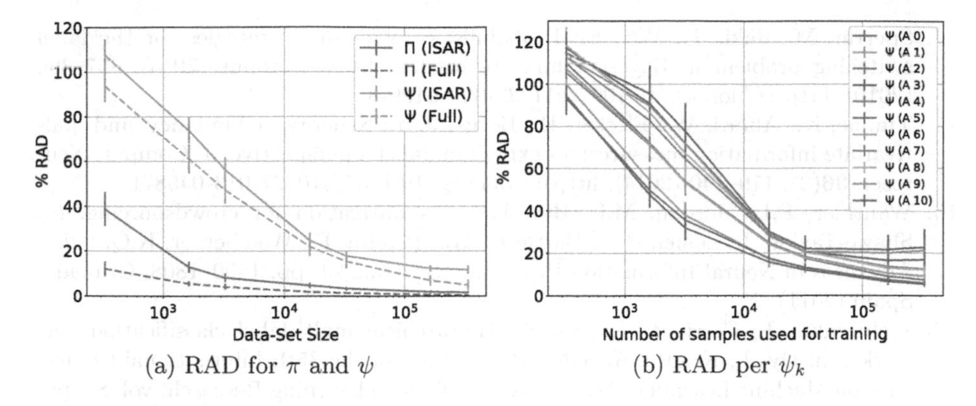

(a) RAD for π and ψ (b) RAD per ψ_k

Fig. 5. RAD for simulation runs based on actual data parameters.

References

1. Bains, R.S., et al.: Analysis of individual mouse activity in group housed animals of different inbred strains using a novel automated home cage analysis system. Front. Behav. Neurosci. **10**, 106 (2016). https://doi.org/10.3389/fnbeh.2016.00106
2. Bishop, C.M.: Pattern Recognition and Machine Learning. Springer, New York (2006)
3. Camilleri, M.P.J.: Modelling annotator variability across feature spaces in the temporal analysis of behaviour. M.Sc. dissertation, University of Edinburgh (2018)
4. Cour, T., Sapp, B., Taskar, B.: Learning from partial labels. J. Mach. Learn. Res. **12**, 1501–1536 (2011)
5. Dawid, A.P., Skene, A.M.: Maximum likelihood estimation of observer error-rates using the EM algorithm. Appl. Stat. **28**(1), 20–28 (1979). https://doi.org/10.2307/2346806
6. Heitjan, D.F., Rubin, D.B.: Ignorability and coarse data. Ann. Stat. **19**(4), 2244–2253 (1991). https://doi.org/10.1214/aos/1176348396
7. Little, R.J.A., Rubin, D.B.: Statistical Analysis with Missing Data, 2nd edn. Wiley, Hoboken (2002). https://doi.org/10.1214/aos/1176348396
8. McLachlan, G.J., Krishnan, T.: The EM Algorithm and Extensions, 2E, Wiley Series in Probability and Statistics, vol. 54, 2 edn. Wiley, Hoboken (2008). https://doi.org/10.1002/9780470191613
9. Murphy, K.P.: Machine Learning: A Probabilistic Perspective. MIT Press, Cambridge (2012)
10. Pan, S.J., Yang, Q.: A survey on transfer learning. IEEE Trans. Knowl. Data Eng. **22**(10), 1345–1359 (2010). https://doi.org/10.1109/TKDE.2009.191
11. Raykar, V.C., et al.: Learning from crowds. J. Mach. Learn. Res. **11**(Apr), 1297–1322 (2010)
12. Russakovsky, O., et al.: ImageNet large scale visual recognition challenge. Int. J. Comput. Vis. **115**(3), 211–252 (2015). https://doi.org/10.1007/s11263-015-0816-y
13. Silla Jr., C.N., Freitas, A.A.: A survey of hierarchical classification across different application domains. Data Min. Knowl. Discov. **22**(1–2), 31–72 (2011). https://doi.org/10.1007/s10618-010-0175-9

14. Sperrin, M., Jaki, T., Wit, E.: Probabilistic relabelling strategies for the label switching problem in Bayesian mixture models. Stat. Comput. **20**(3), 357–366 (2010). https://doi.org/10.1007/s11222-009-9129-8
15. Timme, N., Alford, W., Flecker, B., Beggs, J.M.: Synergy, redundancy, and multivariate information measures: an experimentalist's perspective. J. Comput. Neurosci. **36**(2), 119–140 (2014). https://doi.org/10.1007/s10827-013-0458-4
16. Wauthier, F.L., Jordan, M.I.: Bayesian bias mitigation for crowdsourcing. In: Shawe-Taylor, J., Zemel, R.S., Bartlett, P.L., Pereira, F., Weinberger, K.Q. (eds.) Advances in Neural Information Processing Systems 24, pp. 1800–1808, Granada, Spain (2011)
17. Wehrmann, J., Cerri, R., Barros, R.: Hierarchical multi-label classification networks. In: Dy, J., Krause, A. (eds.) Proceedings of the 35th International Conference on Machine Learning. Proceedings of Machine Learning Research, vol. 80, pp. 5075–5084. PMLR (2018)
18. Whitehill, J., Ruvolo, P., Wu, T., Bergsma, J., Movellan, J.: Whose vote should count more: optimal integration of labels from labelers of unknown expertise. In: Bengio, Y., Schurrmans, D., Lafferty, J.D., Williams, C.K.I., Culotta, A. (eds.) Advances in Neural Information Processing Systems 22, vol. 22, pp. 2035–2043. Curran Associates, Inc. (2009)
19. Zhang, Y., Yang, Q.: A survey on multi-task learning. arXiv, pp. 1–20, July 2017
20. Zhou, D., Bian, J., Zheng, S., Zha, H., Giles, C.L.: Exploring social annotations for information retrieval. In: Proceeding of the 17th International Conference on World Wide Web, WWW 2008, pp. 715–724. ACM Press, New York (2008). https://doi.org/10.1145/1367497.1367594

Towards Automated Configuration of Stream Clustering Algorithms

Matthias Carnein[1(✉)], Heike Trautmann[1], Albert Bifet[2], and Bernhard Pfahringer[2]

[1] University of Münster, Münster, Germany
{carnein,trautmann}@wi.uni-muenster.de
[2] University of Waikato, Hamilton, New Zealand
{abifet,bernhard}@waikato.ac.nz

Abstract. Clustering is an important technique in data analysis which can reveal hidden patterns and unknown relationships in the data. A common problem in clustering is the proper choice of parameter settings. To tackle this, automated algorithm configuration is available which can automatically find the best parameter settings. In practice, however, many of our today's data sources are data streams due to the widespread deployment of sensors, the internet-of-things or (social) media. Stream clustering aims to tackle this challenge by identifying, tracking and updating clusters over time. Unfortunately, none of the existing approaches for automated algorithm configuration are directly applicable to the streaming scenario. In this paper, we explore the possibility of automated algorithm configuration for stream clustering algorithms using an ensemble of different configurations. In first experiments, we demonstrate that our approach is able to automatically find superior configurations and refine them over time.

Keywords: Stream clustering · Automated algorithm configuration · Algorithm selection · Ensemble techniques

1 Introduction

One of the hardest challenges for data scientists is to find a suitable algorithm as well as appropriate parameter settings to solve a given problem. This is even more challenging when working with data streams which do not allow re-evaluations and a posteriori optimisation. In addition, data streams can change over time and parameters need to be adapted accordingly. These problems considerably prevent the widespread adoption of stream mining algorithms in the real-world. A popular tool in stream mining are stream clustering algorithms which aim to identify and track clusters, i.e. groups of similar objects in a stream [5]. In this paper we propose an innovative, ensemble-based approach that allows to automatically find and adapt optimal parameters for data stream clustering algorithms. In each iteration, promising configurations are used to sample new

P. Cellier and K. Driessens (Eds.): ECML PKDD 2019 Workshops, CCIS 1167, pp. 137–143, 2020.
https://doi.org/10.1007/978-3-030-43823-4_12

ones that can replace inferior configurations. In first experiments, we demonstrate that our approach can considerably improve clustering results. To the best of our knowledge, this is the first attempt to apply automated algorithm configuration to data streams as well as stream clustering.

2 Automated Algorithm Configuration

Automated algorithm configuration aims at automatically determining the best parameter settings for a given scenario [8,9]. Popular approaches for this are `SMAC` [7] or `irace` [10]. Unfortunately, none of these approaches is directly applicable to the streaming scenario. These algorithms are mostly set-based and do not focus on single instances. In addition, they require multiple evaluations of the data and usually require static and stationary data without concept drift. This would require to apply the parameter configuration a posteriori [4] or on an initial sample of the stream which is both undesirable.

In this paper, we transfer the idea of automated algorithm configuration to stream clustering. Similar challenges and prior work can be found in the algorithm *selection* and stream *classification* literature. In [12], for example, the authors create an ensemble of different stream classification algorithms. All algorithms are trained simultaneously on the same data stream. The stream is divided into windows of specified size and for every window, meta-features such as standard deviation or entropy are computed. Based on these features and the performance of the classifiers, a meta-classifier is trained to predict which classifier is most suited to classify the next window. In [11,13], the `BLAST` algorithm is introduced which uses the same ensemble strategy and inspired this work conceptually. However, instead of using a meta-classifier it always selects the classifier which performed best on the last window to predict the next window.

3 Automated Configuration of Stream Clustering Algorithms

In this section we propose `confStream`, an ensemble-based approach for automated algorithm configuration in stream clustering, focusing on the online phase of the algorithm, i.e. optimising the micro-cluster representation. In particular, our aim is to maintain, adapt and improve an ensemble of different configurations over time. For this, our algorithm requires a given starting configuration as well as predefined parameter ranges. The main idea of `confStream` is summarised in Fig. 1. In order to apply the ensemble strategy, we process the stream in windows of fixed size h. Observations within a window are processed one by one and used to train all algorithms in the ensemble simultaneously. At the end of the window, the clustering performance of every configuration is evaluated (Step 1). For example, the Silhouette Width measures for an observation i, the average similarity to observations in its own cluster $a(i)$ and compares it to the average similarity to its closest clusters $b(i)$. It is defined as: $s(i) = (b(i) - a(i))/(\max\{a(i), b(i)\})$. While the Silhouette Width is state-of-the-art, there are also other evaluation measures which are equally applicable here. In order to evaluate our ensemble, we compute the average Silhouette Width for all observations of the last window for the different configurations. The clustering algorithm that performed best becomes the active clusterer or *incumbent* for the next iteration. The incumbent represents the current clustering result of the ensemble and will be used throughout the next window.

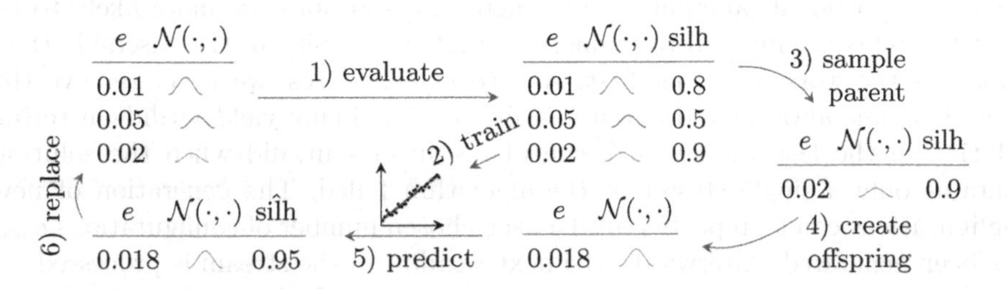

Fig. 1. The performance of algorithms in the ensemble is evaluated and used to train a regression model. Afterwards, one algorithm is sampled to create an offspring. If its predicted performance is high enough, it replaces one of the algorithms in the ensemble.

In a next step, the configurations of the algorithms and their performances are used to train a regression model (Step 2). The regression model is supposed to learn how well certain configurations perform. This is later used in order to determine whether a new configuration is promising and should be incorporated into the ensemble. In our case, we use an Adaptive Random Forest (ARF) regression as proposed in [6]. The ARF is a natural choice, since it is a streaming algorithm which can be trained over time. In order to generate new configurations, one configuration is sampled from the ensemble as a parent (Step 3). The sampling is performed proportionally to the performance of the algorithms such that better performing configurations are more likely to be selected.

The selected configuration is then used as a parent in order to derive a new configuration from it (Step 4). For this, we use a similar strategy as `irace` [10]. In particular, every parameter i of every configuration has an associated truncated normal distribution $\mathcal{N}(\mu_i, \sigma_i)$ with expectation μ_i and standard deviation σ_i. In order to sample a new parameter value, we place the expectation of the distribution at the position of the parent. The distribution has an upper bound U and a lower bound L which are set to the boundaries of the parameter range. The standard deviation σ_i is initialised with $(U - L)/2$ for every parameter and slowly reduced over time. For this, we use a fading strategy which exponentially decreases the standard deviation over time: $\sigma_{t+1} = \sigma_t \cdot 2^{-\lambda}$. The underlying idea is that the configuration will converge to the optimum over time and the smaller standard deviation allows to explore this area better. To account for concept drift, we occasionally explore the full parameter range by resetting the standard deviation to its initial value with a probability p. While we only consider continuous parameters here, the approach could be extended to categorical parameters, e.g. by drawing a new value from a list of probabilities where the probability of the winning category is increased [10].

Next, the performance of the new configuration is predicted based on the regression model (Step 5). If the size of the ensemble is smaller than e_{size} the new configuration is added directly to the ensemble. If the ensemble is full but the predicted performance is better than a performance in the ensemble, the new configuration can be incorporated into the ensemble (Step 6). For this, we use proportional sampling again, where bad solutions are more likely to be replaced. This is supposed to maintain a higher diversity in the ensemble than removing the worst solutions first. As two special cases, we never remove the incumbent and always remove solutions first which did not yield a valid clustering solution in the last window. We consider solutions invalid when the solution contains only a single cluster or the algorithm failed. The generation of new configurations can be repeated until a user-chosen number of configurations e_{new} has been generated. Afterwards, the next window of the stream is processed. In summary, our approach has 5 main parameters itself: the window size h, the fading parameter λ, the ensemble size e_{size}, the number of new configurations e_{new} and the exploration probability p. We note that our ensemble approach is slower than running individual algorithms. Nevertheless, in our experiments the algorithm was fast enough to work in real-time since the algorithms can be trained in parallel.

4 Evaluation

In order to evaluate our approach we implemented a proof-of-concept in Java[1] as a clustering algorithm for the MOA framework [2]. For our analysis, we consider a simple configuration scenario for the `DenStream` [3] algorithm, one of the most popular stream clustering algorithms [5]. First, we evaluate the performance of `DenStream`'s default configuration $\epsilon = 0.02$, $\beta = 0.2$, $\mu = 1$. We then compare this with our ensemble approach, where we start with the same configuration but optimise the distance threshold ϵ in its full value range $[0, 1]$. We set the ensemble size $e_{\text{max}} = 25$, fading $\lambda = 0.05$, reset probability $p = 0.001$ and evaluate the solutions every $h = 1000$ data points. After each window, we create $e_{\text{new}} = 10$ new configurations. In order to evaluate the quality of the clustering algorithms, we use the Silhouette Width. Since we want to evaluate cluster quality over time, we evaluate the quality for windows of 1000 observations in our experiments. We evaluate both algorithms, i.e. the default parametrisation of `DenStream` vs. the configured version `confStream`, using a Random Radial Basis Function (RBF) stream [1], `sensor` stream[2], and `covertype` data set[3]. All data sets are popular choices in the (stream) clustering literature.

[1] Implementation available at: https://www.matthias-carnein.de/confStream.
[2] Dataset available at: http://db.csail.mit.edu/labdata/labdata.html.
[3] Dataset available at: http://archive.ics.uci.edu/ml/datasets/Covertype.

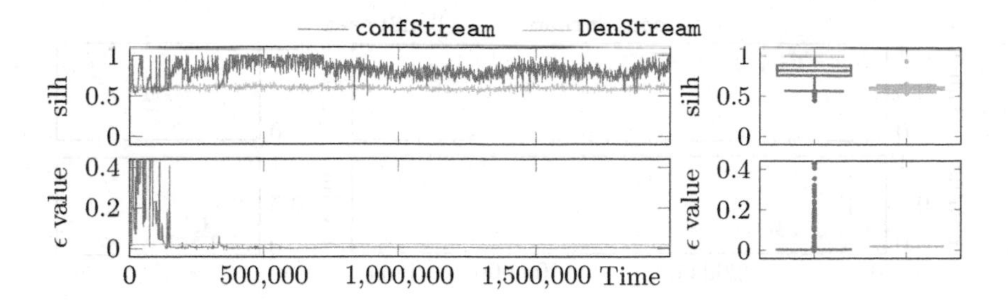

Fig. 2. Development of Silhouette Width and ϵ parameter for the `Random RBF` stream

Figure 2 shows the Silhouette Width for every window of the `Random RBF` stream. The boxplot on the right summarises the range of values. It is obvious, that our ensemble approach quickly improves the default configuration and remains superior for the vast majority of the stream. When observing the development of the ϵ parameter in our ensemble, it becomes obvious how `confStream` first explores a large range of values. Over time, the algorithm reduces the standard deviation of the distributions in order to explore promising regions further before settling on roughly $\epsilon = 0.005$. Note that this is similar to the initial configuration of $\epsilon = 0.02$. Nevertheless, the performance is vastly improved which also highlights how sensitive stream clustering algorithms are to different configurations.

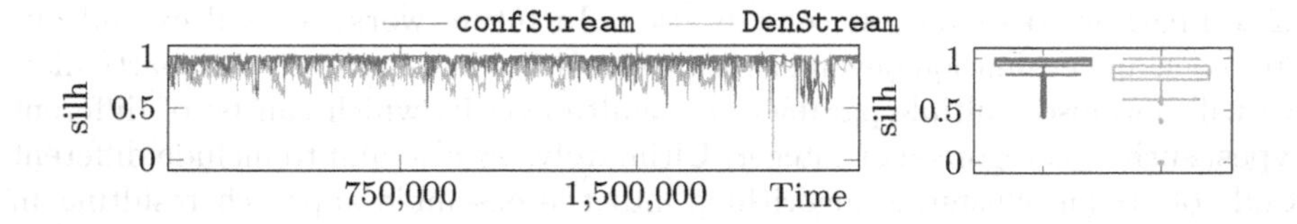

Fig. 3. Silhouette Width for the `sensor` stream

For the other data sets, we observe similar trends. Figure 3 shows the results for the `sensor` data stream. Again, `confStream` quickly improves upon the initial configuration and yields better results with a near-perfect median silhouette width of 0.98. While the default configuration also yields a good results, it is stronger affected by concept drift in the data stream. In particular, the `sensor` data set exhibits a periodic pattern of day and night. `confStream` is less affected by this since it adapts to the changing scenarios. For the `covertype` data set the difference is most obvious. Using the default configuration, `DenStream` is not able to produce a single valid solution with at least two clusters throughout the entire stream. While `confStream` starts with the same initial configuration, it quickly adapts and is able to produce very high quality (Fig. 4). This also shows in the development of the parameter value which quickly changes from the initial value $\epsilon = 0.02$ and explores more suitable values between $\epsilon = 0.1$ and $\epsilon = 0.2$.

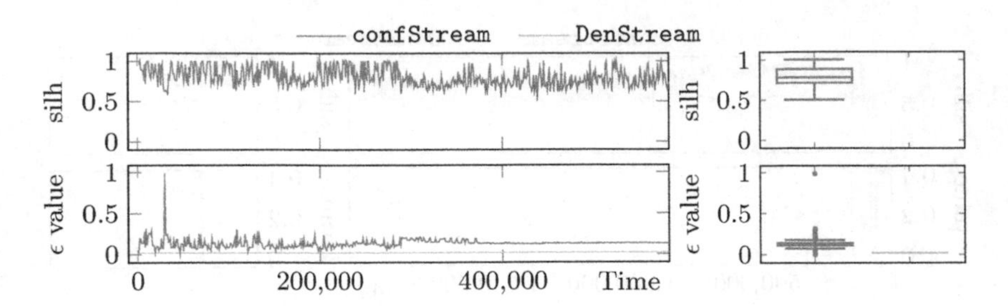

Fig. 4. Development of Silhouette Width and ϵ parameter for the `covertype` data set

Overall, these initial results show that our ensemble strategy produces vastly better clustering solutions than the default configuration. In particular, changes and improvements are made over time which allow for adapting to stream characteristics and/or unsuitable starting configurations.

5 Outlook and Conclusion

In this paper we explored the possibility of automated algorithm configuration for stream clustering. By training an ensemble of algorithms in parallel and deriving new configurations from promising solutions, we are able to efficiently adapt the configuration over time. Results for a configuration problem with one parameter have shown to improve the overall clustering result considerably in comparison to its default configuration. In future work, we will extend our approach and evaluation beyond a single algorithm and parameter. In particular, we will optimise multiple parameters simultaneously, which can be of different types, such as categorical or integer. Ultimately, we also aim to include different kinds of stream clustering algorithms into the ensemble approach resulting in per-instance algorithm selection and configuration on streaming data.

References

1. Bifet, A., Gavalda, R., Holmes, G., Pfahringer, B.: Machine Learning for Data Streams with Practical Examples in MOA. MIT Press, Cambridge (2018)
2. Bifet, A., Holmes, G., Kirkby, R., Pfahringer, B.: MOA: massive online analysis. J. Mach. Learn. Res. **11**, 1601–1604 (2010)
3. Cao, F., Ester, M., Qian, W., Zhou, A.: Density-based clustering over an evolving data stream with noise. In: Proceedings of the Conference on Data Mining (SIAM 2006), pp. 328–339 (2006)
4. Carnein, M., Assenmacher, D., Trautmann, H.: An empirical comparison of stream clustering algorithms. In: Proceedings of the ACM International Conference on Computing Frontiers (CF 2017), pp. 361–365. ACM (2017)
5. Carnein, M., Trautmann, H.: Optimizing data stream representation: an extensive survey on stream clustering algorithms. Bus. Inf. Syst. Eng. **61**(3), 277–297 (2019). https://doi.org/10.1007/s12599-019-00576-5

6. Gomes, H.M., Barddal, J.P., Ferreira, L.E.B., Bifet, A.: Adaptive random forests for data stream regression. In: Proceedings of the 26th European Symposium on Artificial Neural Networks (ESANN 2018) (2018)
7. Hutter, F., Hoos, H.H., Leyton-Brown, K.: Sequential model-based optimization for general algorithm configuration. In: Coello, C.A.C. (ed.) LION 2011. LNCS, vol. 6683, pp. 507–523. Springer, Heidelberg (2011). https://doi.org/10.1007/978-3-642-25566-3_40
8. Hutter, F., Kotthoff, L., Vanschoren, J. (eds.): Automated Machine Learning. TSSCML. Springer, Cham (2019). https://doi.org/10.1007/978-3-030-05318-5
9. Kerschke, P., Hoos, H.H., Neumann, F., Trautmann, H.: Automated algorithm selection: survey and perspectives. Evol. Comput. (ECJ) **27**(1), 3–45 (2019)
10. López-Ibáñez, M., Dubois-Lacoste, J., Pérez Cáceres, L., Stützle, T., Birattari, M.: The irace package: iterated racing for automatic algorithm configuration. Oper. Res. Perspect. **3**, 43–58 (2016)
11. van Rijn, J.N., Holmes, G., Pfahringer, B., Vanschoren, J.: Having a blast: meta-learning and heterogeneous ensembles for data streams. In: Proceedings of the 2015 IEEE International Conference on Data Mining (ICDM 2015), pp. 1003–1008 (2015)
12. van Rijn, J.N., Holmes, G., Pfahringer, B., Vanschoren, J.: Algorithm selection on data streams. In: Džeroski, S., Panov, P., Kocev, D., Todorovski, L. (eds.) DS 2014. LNCS (LNAI), vol. 8777, pp. 325–336. Springer, Cham (2014). https://doi.org/10.1007/978-3-319-11812-3_28
13. van Rijn, J.N., Holmes, G., Pfahringer, B., Vanschoren, J.: The online performance estimation framework: heterogeneous ensemble learning for data streams. Mach. Learn. **107**(1), 149–176 (2017). https://doi.org/10.1007/s10994-017-5686-9

Advances in Interpretable Machine Learning and Artificial Intelligence & eXplainable Knowledge Discovery in Data Mining (AIMLAI-XKDD)

Effect of Superpixel Aggregation on Explanations in LIME – A Case Study with Biological Data

Ludwig Schallner[1], Johannes Rabold[2(✉)], Oliver Scholz[1], and Ute Schmid[2]

[1] Fraunhofer IIS/EZRT, Fürth, Germany
[2] Cognitive Systems, University of Bamberg, Bamberg, Germany
johannes.rabold@uni-bamberg.de

Abstract. End-to-end learning with deep neural networks, such as convolutional neural networks (CNNs), has been demonstrated to be very successful for different tasks of image classification. To make decisions of black-box approaches transparent, different solutions have been proposed. LIME is an approach to explainable AI relying on segmenting images into superpixels based on the Quick-Shift algorithm. In this paper, we present an explorative study of how different superpixel methods, namely Felzenszwalb, SLIC and Compact-Watershed, impact the generated visual explanations. We compare the resulting relevance areas with the image parts marked by a human reference. Results show that image parts selected as relevant strongly vary depending on the applied method. Quick-Shift resulted in the least and Compact-Watershed in the highest correspondence with the reference relevance areas.

Keywords: Explainable AI · Superpixel · LIME

1 Introduction

Especially in visual domains, deep Convolutional Neural Networks (CNNs) have shown their superior capabilities for object classification tasks such as semantic segmentation [7]. For CNNs, as well as for other deep learning architectures, crucial requirements for real-world applications are that the learned classifiers (a) make accurate predictions and (b) that the systems' decision making is transparent and comprehensible to humans [10,15]. Explanations of a system's decision making process can help machine learning experts to uncover unwanted biases. Additionally, for domain experts without a background in machine learning, explanations are crucial for being able to understand and trust the propositions of a classifier [10]. Applications in the medical or pharmaceutical fields particularly require the trust of the end user, since a physician will not trust the decision of a black-box unless this decision is comprehensible.

In the context of image classifications, many approaches for visual explanations have been proposed [22], such as LRP (Layer-wise Relevance Propagation, [2]) or LIME (Local Interpretable Model-Agnostic Explanations, [15]). For

P. Cellier and K. Driessens (Eds.): ECML PKDD 2019 Workshops, CCIS 1167, pp. 147–158, 2020.
https://doi.org/10.1007/978-3-030-43823-4_13

explaining image classifications, LIME relies on segmentation of the image into superpixels, that is on similarity based grouping of pixels into larger structures based on local features [4]. LIME by default applies the specific superpixel algorithm Quick-Shift. The segmentation of an image into superpixels is crucial for the generation of the explanation in LIME since perturbation of superpixels is used to identify which of the image areas has been relevant for a specific class decision. Therefore, we were interested in exploring whether different superpixel approaches have a significant impact on the kind of visual explanations generated by LIME. Furthermore – in the case of differences between the superpixel approaches – it is also of interest how similar these results are to reference assessments generated by a humans based on relevance.

As an application domain we focus on biological data which come in a huge variety of image types – from fine grained microscopic images to holistic images of plants and animals. Our two case studies focused on applications from the medical and biological field, namely the detection of malaria parasites in thin blood smear images [13] and the detection of stress in tobacco plants used for pharmaceutical purposes [17].

In the following, we will first recapitulate the basic concepts of LIME. Afterwards, we will introduce a variety of superpixel approaches which are well known in computer vision. Furthermore, we present the malaria domain and evaluation results – showing differences of LIME's relevance explanation for the considered superpixel approaches and similarity to the relevance selection. Additionally, we shortly present and discuss the tobacco domain. We conclude with a short discussion and further work to be done.

2 Visual Explainability with LIME

LIME [15] is an explanation framework for the decision of any machine learning classifier. In the original implementation it is capable of processing classifiers that either have text, images or tabular data as input. In this work we focus on the explanation of decisions for classifiers that process image data. The output of LIME therefore is a set of connected pixel patches along with a weighting for each patch. These weights indicate how strong a patch is correlated with the classifier decision.

Given a classifier f and an image instance x, LIME outputs the weights w for all pixel patches x' of the image x. w can be seen as coefficients for a linear model that acts as a surrogate for the possibly complex decision boundary of f. This linear model g should approximate the decision boundary in the locality of x. To achieve this, first a pool $\mathcal{Z}$ with size N (user defined constant) of perturbed versions (in the following named z') of x' is generated. For images, this is achieved by randomly removing patches from the image and replacing them with the mean color of the patch or with some chosen color (default is grey). Every instance of $\mathcal{Z}$ consists of the triples $\langle z_i', f(z_i), \pi_x(z_i)\rangle$ with $f(z_i)$ being the classification result of f for the perturbed version z_i' in the image space and $\pi_x(z_i)$ being a proximity measure that indicates how different the perturbed version is from the original instance. This measure is used to enforce locality for the linear model g. The weights w are ultimately found through K-Lasso, a procedure that is based on the regression method Lasso [18]. The input is the pool $\mathcal{Z}$ and a user defined feature limit K which is the number of patches the user wants in its explanation.

3 Superpixel Methods

Pixels, which are used to represent images in grid form, do not represent a natural representation of the depicted scene. If a single image pixel is viewed, neither its origin in the original image nor its semantic meaning can be determined. This results from the process of creating digital images. Pixels are artefacts that are created by the process of taking and creating the digital image [14].

In comparison, the origin and semantic meaning of a superpixel can be determined. A superpixel is a local grouping or combination of pixels based on common properties, such as the color value (See Fig. 1). The advantages of superpixels can be summarized as follows [14]:

- Lower complexity: Although the superpixel algorithm must be applied first to enable the name-giving groupings of pixels, this process reduces the complexity of the image due to the small number of entities. In addition, subsequent steps based on these superpixels require significantly less processing power.
- Significant entities: Individual pixels are not very meaningful. However, pixels in a superpixel group share properties such as texture or color distribution. Through this embedding, superpixels gain an expressiveness.
- Marginal information loss: superpixel approaches tend to oversegmentation. Thus, important areas are differentiated, but also insignificant ones. However, this apparent disadvantage basically has the positive aspect of only a minor loss of information.

3.1 Felzenszwalb

The algorithm of Felzenszwalb and Huttenloch (FSZ) [3] is to be categorized as a graph-based approach and can be described as an edge-oriented method. The approach has a complexity of $\mathcal{O}(M\ log\ M)$.

First, the algorithm calculates a gradient between two adjacent pixels. This is weighted according to the characteristic properties of the pixels, for example based on the color and brightness of the individual pixels. Subsequently, individual segments - the seed for future superpixels - are formed per pixel. The aim of this process is to make the differences between the gradients within the segment as small as possible but make the differences as large as possible for adjacent segments. The resulting superpixels should neither be too small or too large. However, this algorithm lacks a direct influence on the size and number of superpixels. This usually results in a very irregular size and shape distribution [3].

(a) Felzenszwalb (b) Quickshift (c) SLIC (d) Compact-Watershed

Fig. 1. Superpixel approaches in comparison. Source: original photo by Baptist Standaert on Unsplash

3.2 Quick-Shift

Quick-Shift (QS) is an algorithm LIME uses by default, it is described in detail in [20]. Its uses a so-called *mode-seeking* segmentation scheme to generate superpixels. This approach moves each point x_i to the next point which are higher density (P), which causes an increase in the density. QS does not have the possibility of controlling neither the number nor the size of the superpixels.

3.3 SLIC

As the name Simple Linear Iterative Clustering (SLIC) [1] suggests, this superpixel algorithm belongs to the group of cluster-based algorithms. SLIC uses the well-known K-Means algorithm [8] as a basis, but there are essential differences:

- The search space ($2S \times 2S$) is limited proportional to the size of the superpixel ($S \times S$). This significantly reduces the number of distance calculations.

- In addition, the complexity is independent of the number of superpixels k, whereby SLIC has a complexity of $\mathcal{O}(N)$.
- Furthermore, a weighted distance measure (see Eq. 1) combines the spatial (d_s) and color (d_c) proximity.
- In addition, the control of compactness and size of the superpixels is ensured by a parameter (m).

$$D = \sqrt{d_c^2 + (\frac{d_s}{S})^2 m^2} \tag{1}$$

With the parameters k the desired number of superpixels is defined. The cluster process starts with the initialization of k cluster centers (mathematically: $C_k = [l_k, a_k, b_k, x_k, y_k]^T$), which are scanned by a regular grid with a distance of S pixels. By $S = \sqrt{N/k}$ approximately even superpixels are guaranteed. Next, the centers are shifted in the direction of the position of the smallest gradient within a 3×3 range. This is done, among other things, to avoid placing a superpixel at an edge.

Then each pixel i is assigned to the nearest cluster center whose search area ($2S \times 2S$) overlaps with the position of the superpixel ($S \times S$). The nearest cluster center is determined by the distance measure D (see Eq. 1).

Then the average $[l\ a\ b\ x\ y]^T$ vector of the pixels belonging to each cluster center is calculated by an update step for each cluster center and adopted as the new cluster center. Finally, a residual error E between the new and the old cluster center is determined. The assignment and calculation step can be repeated until the residual error reaches a threshold value ($E \leq Threshold$). Finally, all unconnected pixels are added to a nearby superpixel.

3.4 Compact-Watershed

The Compact-Watershed (CW) [11] algorithm is an optimized – respectively a more compact – version of the superpixel algorithm Watershed [9]. As input a gradient image is used. Because the grey-tone of each pixel is considered as an altitude, the input can be seen as a topographical surface. Then this surface gets continuously flooded, resulting in watershed with catchment basins. During this process over-segmentation may occur. For prevention, so called markers are used [9]:

1. The set of markers (for each one a different label) where the flooding should begin has to be chosen.
2. A priority queue will be created and collects the neighboring pixels of each marked area. Each pixel is graded a priority level which corresponds with the gradient magnitude of the pixel.
3. The pixel with the highest level of priority, gets pulled out of the priority queue. This pixel gets labeled with the same label as its neighbors if all of its neighbors are already labeled. The neighbor pixels who are not yet marked and are not contained in the priority queue are pushed into this queue.

4. Repeat the previous step (3) until the priority queue is empty.

Those pixel who are still not labeled after the priority queue is empty are the watershed lines.

Compact-Watershed is derived from the original Watershed algorithm resulting in more compact superpixels in terms of size and extension. This is achieved by using a weighted distance measure between Euclidean distance of a pixel from the superpixel's seed point and the difference of the pixel's grey value compared to the seed pixel's grey value.

4 Case Studies

4.1 Malaria

Malaria is a parasitic infectious disease. It is predominantly transmitted by anopheles mosquitoes, but can also be transmitted from person to person. This happens for example by blood transfusion, organ transplantation or by sharing injection needles [12,21]. Malaria killed 435,000 people in 2017. Of these 266,000 were children under 5 years of age [21].

A network trained for the detection of malaria in cells and whose results are comprehensible by LIME thus has a great benefit in the application in the field of diagnosis of malaria. For this purpose a ResNet50 [6] was trained (see Table 4 for the hyperparameters), the results are shown in Table 1.

The malaria data set [13] consists of blood smear images of the most used diagnostic tool Rapid Diagnostic Tests (RDT) [21]. The data are divided into two classes: positive and negative malaria labeled cells. In particular, the relatively large number and equally distributed (50%–50%) of training examples (26,758 total) promise a good basis for a meaningful network to assess whether a cell is infected with malaria or not (Fig. 2).

Table 1. Model results for the malaria model

Metric	Value
Training accuracy	97.8182%
Training loss (cross entropy)	0.0573
Validation accuracy	96.5167%
Validation loss (cross entropy)	0.0970
Test accuracy	96.3715%
Test loss (cross entropy)	0.1069

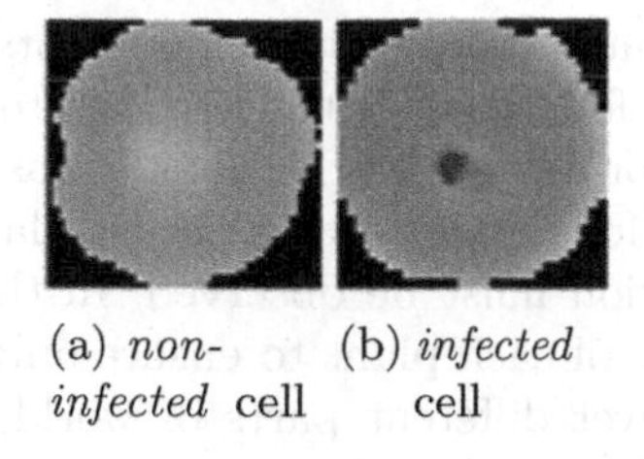

(a) *non-infected* cell (b) *infected* cell

Fig. 2. Examples of the malaria dataset

Experiments. To enable an objective comparison of the superpixel approaches, the Jaccard-Coefficient [5] was calculated, which indicates the similarity of two sets. The similarity measure is determined between the results of the different superpixel approaches and the respective average relevant area of the decision. The relevant area per image is selected manually selects the indicator, which is most relevant to the decision making process (Fig. 3).

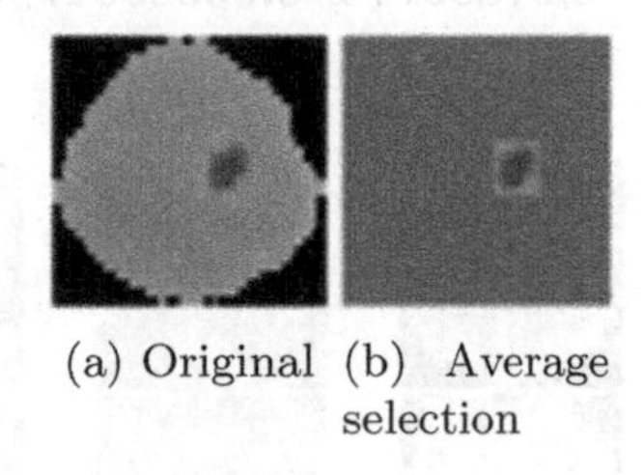

(a) Original (b) Average selection

Fig. 3. Original blood smear image from the malaria data set, as well as the corresponding average selection

For the comparability of the results, 100 images of infected cells were selected from the test data set of the malaria blood smear images. To make it easier to select, only images with a single malaria indicator were selected. Of these 100 images, 85 were classified by the network as *infected* (*true positive*). The remaining 15 were classified as *not-infected* (false negative). Table 2 shows the result of the Jaccard-Coefficient for the respective superpixel approach with the *true positive* classified explanations, where only the most important feature for the network's decision (see Fig. 4) is displayed. All of the superpixel methods were optimized to the given case to maximize the average Jaccard-Coefficient, hence the optimized Quick-Shift version. This was done so that all of the superpixel approaches would be compared on a fair level.

4.2 Tobacco Plants

Tobacco is a significant plant used in biopharmaceutical production using genetically modified (GM) plants. Two important reasons are its ability to produce biomass quickly and minimum risk of food chain contamination because of the fact that tobacco is not a food crop [19]. It is able to produce proteins which can be used for treatment or diagnosis of various diseases. However, if plants are used to produce medicine for human use, strict regulations present in the field of pharmaceutical production must be observed. In this context it is desirable to monitor the health state of each plant to ensure only healthy plants are used for drug production, however different parts of world regulate pharmaceutical production of GM plants differently [16].

Table 2. Jaccard coefficient of the different superpixel methods

Superpixel method	Mean value	Variance	Standard deviation
Felzenszwalb	0.85603243	0.03330687	0.18250170
Quick-Shift	0.52272303	0.04613085	0.21478094
Quick-Shift optimized	0.88820585	0.00307818	0.05548137
SLIC	0.96437629	0.00014387	0.01199452
Compact-Watershed	**0.97850773**	**0.00003847**	**0.00620228**

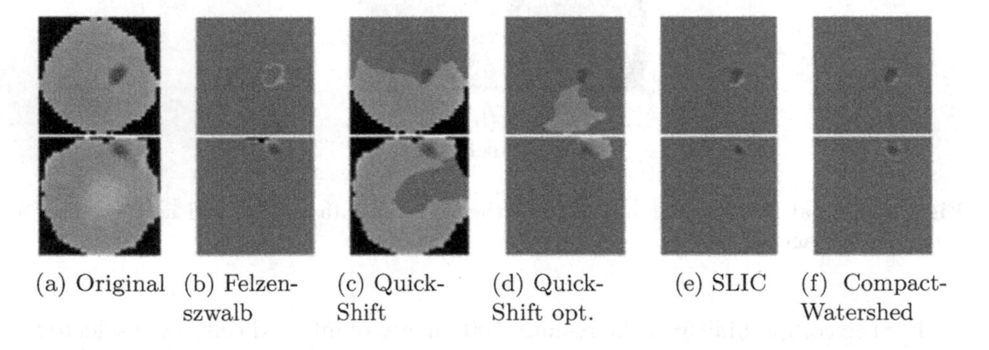

(a) Original (b) Felzenszwalb (c) Quick-Shift (d) Quick-Shift opt. (e) SLIC (f) Compact-Watershed

Fig. 4. LIME results for true positive predicted malaria infected cells

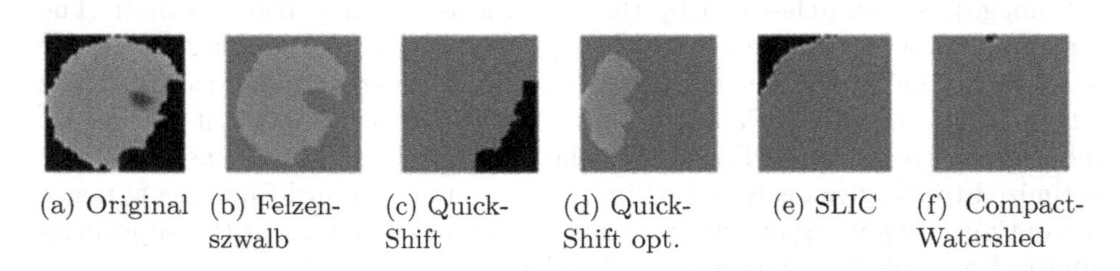

(a) Original (b) Felzenszwalb (c) Quick-Shift (d) Quick-Shift opt. (e) SLIC (f) Compact-Watershed

Fig. 5. LIME results for false positive predicted malaria infected cells

Stocker et al. have investigated various methods to classify stress in tobacco plants using non neuronal AI approaches [17]. Figure 6 shows sample images of healthy and stressed tobacco plants. We use the same tobacco data set as a

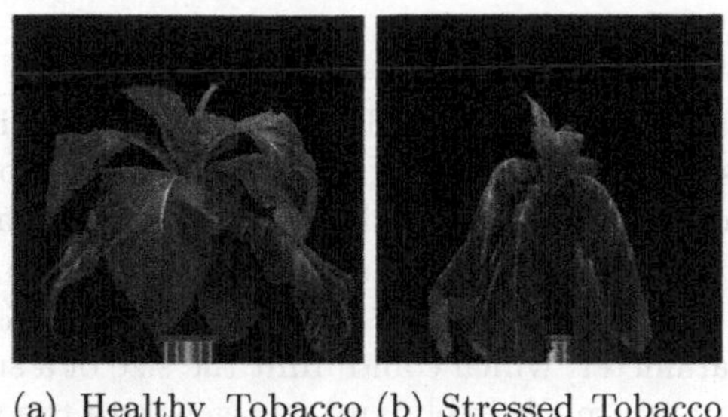

(a) Healthy Tobacco plant (b) Stressed Tobacco plant

Fig. 6. Examples of the tobacco plant dataset

case study to assess the suitability of CNNs for stress classification again using LIME to provide insights into the classification process. For the training the same ResNet50 as for the malaria dataset was used. The only difference was that, to prevent overfitting, the last layers were unfrozen during the training of the tobacco trainingsset. The tobacco data set consists of 700 images total divided into two classes, healthy and stressed. Only 81 images of stressed plants are contained in the data set, so expectations of a good classification result were limited.

Table 3 shows the trained model results on the tobacco plant data set. These clearly already show that the results should not be trusted to begin with, so we decided to discontinue work on this case study for the time being.

Table 3. Model results for tobacco plants

Metric	Value
Training accuracy	91.2577%
Training loss	0.4459
Test accuracy	50%
Test loss	0.7524

Table 4. Hyperparameter for the training of both models

Hyperparameter	Value
Epochs	50
Batch size	32
SGD learning rate	0,0001
SGD momentum	0,90
SGD nesterov	Ja
Dropout	0,50
L2-regulation	0,0001

5 Discussion

In the following, the experiments with LIME from the previous chapter, their results and the possible improvement of the visual explainability are discussed (see Table 2). Although FSZ is an older algorithm compared to the other approaches considered, still good results were achieved. Surprisingly, *QS*, the standard algorithm of LIME, is surpassed by about 33.33%. Since FSZ itself does not have any parameter, which could limit the size of a superpixel, it seems that LIME can act pretty much freely and can generate the superpixels purely based on relevance regarding explainability. A good example for such a case is the explanation from LIME for the false positive classification shown in Fig. 5. In contrast to the other superpixel methods explored though FSZ's decision for *not infected* is more comprehensible. However the variance and standard deviation for the true positive examples, indicates the similarity vary significantly and with FSZ the results are not stable and may sometimes show regions as relevant for the decision which are actually not important. This for example is the case for the first result from LIME while using FSZ (see Fig. 4).

The optimized version of QS, remarkably achieved an improvement of 36.55% compared to the standard version of LIME. Additionally it performs slightly better than FSZ - with an improvement of 3.22% - and the variance and standard deviation are also lower, which indicates the results are more stable than with FSZ and the unoptimized QS version.

SLIC makes it possible to influence the actual size of the superpixels through a parameter. Consequently, the higher similarity measure with over 44.17% compared to QS and over 7.62% compared to the optimized version of QS, is not surprising. Additionally, a lower variance and standard deviation was achieved. These results show that SLIC has advantages over QS due to showing a better correspondence between superpixels and relevant areas.

The last superpixel approach compared with QS was CW. Like SLIC it supports influencing the compactness of the resulting superpixels. In comparison to all other superpixel approaches CW yielded the best results. This approach achieved an improvement of 45.58% over the standard QS and an improvement of 9.03% over the optimized QS version. It also significantly reduces the variance and standard deviation. This indicates there is a very correspondence over all the 85 images.

6 Conclusion

Our results suggest that tailoring of the superpixel approach - whether by an optimized version of QS or by FSZ, SLIC or CW - to the task will improve the visual explainability of LIME. Therefore a selecting a suitable algorithm for LIME can be beneficial and should be considered. With the exception of QS the remaining approaches segment fewer irrelevant areas of an image (see Fig. 4). It was also observed that CW achieved the best results.

In applications where large area and uneven features are to be emphasized, an approach like CW would possibly do worse because it divides the input into very small, evenly sized superpixels. FSZ, which generates superpixels in significantly different sizes, may even achieve the best results in such application areas. Consequently, the finding that CW does give the best results in malaria is not universally valid and the superpixel approaches should be evaluated by experts in different application areas. Another conclusion is that superpixel methods other than QS are more suitable for LIME.

Since the area of pharmaceutical and agricultural applications is an emerging research area for applying machine learning to digital plant phenotyping tasks, we plan to continue pursuing the ideas begun in the tobacco case study. We suspect that an objective assessment of plant health will yield better results if based on 3D data, because the habitus of a plant should then be represented more realistically than in a purely texture based 2D analysis as in the tobacco case study. Furthermore, the number of training images in said case study was insufficient, so the goal will be to generate a greater data set containing 3D scans of plants to continue research on this subject.

References

1. Achanta, R., Shaji, A., Smith, K., Lucchi, A., Fua, P., Süsstrunk, S.: SLIC superpixels compared to state-of-the-art superpixel methods. IEEE Trans. Pattern Anal. Mach. Intell. **34**(11), 2274–2282 (2012)
2. Bach, S., Binder, A., Montavon, G., Klauschen, F., Müller, K.R., Samek, W.: On pixel-wise explanations for non-linear classifier decisions by layer-wise relevance propagation. PLoS ONE **10**(7), e0130140 (2015)
3. Felzenszwalb, P.F., Huttenlocher, D.P.: Efficient graph-based image segmentation. Int. J. Comput. Vision **59**(2), 167–181 (2004). https://doi.org/10.1023/B:VISI.0000022288.19776.77
4. Fulkerson, B., Vedaldi, A., Soatto, S.: Class segmentation and object localization with superpixel neighborhoods. In: 2009 IEEE 12th International Conference on Computer Vision, pp. 670–677. IEEE (2009)
5. Jaccard, P.: Lois de distribution florale dans la zone alpine. Bull. Soc. Vaudoise Sci. Nat. **38**, 69–130 (1902)
6. He, K., Zhang, X., Ren, S., Sun, J.: Deep residual learning for image recognition. CoRR abs/1512.03385 (2015)
7. Krizhevsky, A., Sutskever, I., Hinton, G.E.: ImageNet classification with deep convolutional neural networks. In: Advances in Neural Information Processing Systems, pp. 1097–1105 (2012)
8. Lloyd, S.: Least squares quantization in PCM. IEEE Trans. Inf. Theory **28**(2), 129–137 (1982)
9. Meyer, F.: Color image segmentation. In: 1992 International Conference on Image Processing and Its Applications, pp. 303–306 (1992)
10. Muggleton, S.H., Schmid, U., Zeller, C., Tamaddoni-Nezhad, A., Besold, T.: Ultra-strong machine learning: comprehensibility of programs learned with ILP. Mach. Learn. **107**(7), 1119–1140 (2018). https://doi.org/10.1007/s10994-018-5707-3
11. Neubert, P., Protzel, P.: Compact watershed and preemptive SLIC: on improving trade-offs of superpixel segmentation algorithms. In: 2014 22nd International Conference on Pattern Recognition (ICPR), pp. 996–1001 (2014)

12. Nocht, B., Mayer, M.: Die Malaria: Eine Einführung in Ihre Klinik, Parasitologie und Bekämpfung. Springer, Heidelberg (1936). https://doi.org/10.1007/978-3-642-91256-6. s.l., zweite erweiterte auflage edn
13. Rajaraman, S., et al.: Pre-trained convolutional neural networks as feature extractors toward improved malaria parasite detection in thin blood smear images. PeerJ **6**, e4568 (2018)
14. Ren, X., Malik, J.: Learning a classification model for segmentation (2003)
15. Ribeiro, M.T., Singh, S., Guestrin, C.: Why should i trust you? Explaining the predictions of any classifier. In: Proceedings of the 22nd ACM SIGKDD International Conference on Knowledge Discovery and Data Mining, pp. 1135–1144. ACM (2016)
16. Spök, A., Twyman, R.M., Fischer, R., Ma, J.K., Sparrow, P.A.: Evolution of a regulatory framework for pharmaceuticals derived from genetically modified plants. Trends Biotechnol. **26**(9), 506–517 (2008)
17. Stocker, C., Uhrmann, F., Scholz, O., Siebers, M., Schmid, U.: A machine learning approach to drought stress level classification of tobacco plants. In: LWA, pp. 163–167 (2013)
18. Tibshirani, R.: Regression shrinkage and selection via the lasso. J. Roy. Stat. Soc.: Ser. B (Methodol.) **58**(1), 267–288 (1996)
19. Tremblay, R., Wang, D., Jevnikar, A.M., Ma, S.: Tobacco, a highly efficient green bioreactor for production of therapeutic proteins. Biotechnol. Adv. **28**(2), 214–221 (2010)
20. Vedaldi, A., Soatto, S.: Quick shift and kernel methods for mode seeking. In: Forsyth, D., Torr, P., Zisserman, A. (eds.) ECCV 2008. LNCS, vol. 5305, pp. 705–718. Springer, Heidelberg (2008). https://doi.org/10.1007/978-3-540-88693-8_52
21. World Health Organization, et al.: World malaria report 2018 (2018)
22. Zhang, Q.S., Zhu, S.C.: Visual interpretability for deep learning: a survey. Front. Inf. Technol. Electron. Eng. **19**(1), 27–39 (2018). https://doi.org/10.1631/FITEE.1700808

Global Explanations with Local Scoring

Mattia Setzu[1(✉)], Riccardo Guidotti[2], Anna Monreale[1], and Franco Turini[1]

[1] University of Pisa, Pisa, Italy
mattia.setzu@phd.unipi.it, {anna.monreale,franco.turini}@unipi.it
[2] ISTI-CNR, Pisa, Italy
riccardo.guidotti@isti.cnr.it

Abstract. Artificial Intelligence systems often adopt machine learning models encoding complex algorithms with potentially unknown behavior. As the application of these "black box" models grows, it is our responsibility to understand their inner working and formulate them in human-understandable explanations. To this end, we propose a rule-based model-agnostic explanation method that follows a local-to-global schema: it generalizes a global explanation summarizing the decision logic of a black box starting from the local explanations of single predicted instances. We define a scoring system based on a rule relevance score to extract global explanations from a set of local explanations in the form of decision rules. Experiments on several datasets and black boxes show the stability, and low complexity of the global explanations provided by the proposed solution in comparison with baselines and state-of-the-art global explainers.

Keywords: Explainable AI · Rule-based explainer · Decision system

1 Introduction

The adoption of machine learning models in Artificial Intelligence (AI) has found application in increasingly sensitive and diverse areas such as speech recognition, image classification, biology, and medicine. When approaching a machine learning classifier, one has to take into consideration several potential issues such as overfitting, fragility to adversarial attacks, and over-parameterization. These well-known weaknesses highlight the underlying complexity of the generalization problem and have been addressed by several scholars in the field which leverage other learning tools, such as distillation and dataset enriching [7,11].

A recent prominent research area is that of Explainable AI, which instead of addressing the model complexity in a *ante-hoc* fashion, subsumes it in human-understandable *explanations*. In this setting the objective is to *explain* the decisions of "black box" machine learning classifiers [6]. Explanations are a powerful tool which enables model inspection [22], validation [5], and human-in-the-loop systems [14]. Explainability also gained attention from institutional bodies which recently put into law the *General Data Protection Regulation* (GDPR). Besides

P. Cellier and K. Driessens (Eds.): ECML PKDD 2019 Workshops, CCIS 1167, pp. 159–171, 2020.
https://doi.org/10.1007/978-3-030-43823-4_14

giving people control over their personal data, the GDPR provides restrictions for automated decision-making processes. It introduces a right to meaningful' explanation: an individual has the right to obtain "meaningful information about the logic involved" when automated decision making takes place [17,19,24].

In spite of the common interest and effort in the explainability field, the formal definition of what an explanation is remains an open question [18]. However, the research community is converging towards a small set of families of explanations (Sect. 2). With respect to tabular data, that is the focus of our work, explanations can take the form of: prototypes [3,13], that is samples representative of some cluster of interest; sets of relevant features [1,12]; or decision rules [23,27]. In our work, we focus on rule-based explanations. Single-instance explanations, also known as *local* explanations, have shown promising results in approximating the behavior and motivating the decisions of black box models, and seldom they are able to outperform *global* interpretable-by-design models.

In light of these results we introduce the *local-to-global* problem (Sect. 3), a generalization problem which aims to relax the locality constraints of single-instance explanations [19]. It is based on the idea of deriving a global explanation by subsuming local logical rules. We propose to address this problem with a *scoring system* which subsumes a given set of local interpretable decision rules into a smaller set, then it is used to perform predictions and to describe the overall logic of the black box model (Sect. 4). In particular, we aim to derive explanations with a good trade-off among the following properties. *Conciseness*, which describes the succinctness of an explainable model: a concise model is composed of a small number of rules. *Completeness* which identifies the validity boundaries of explanations: complete models provide the user with explanations for a large number of instances. Finally, *complexity* which measures the inherent complexity of an explanation. We attempt to take into account these properties in the scoring system by defining a local *Rule Relevance Score* (RRS). We empirically show the effectiveness of the proposed explanation method explaining the decisions of two different black box models on four datasets in which each entry represents a human (Sect. 5). The local-to-global scoring system using the RRS, thanks to the aforementioned properties, is able to compete with and outperforms a set of baselines and explainable-by-design models.

2 Related Work

We report in this section some of the most relevant explainability techniques with a focus on our area of application, tabular dataset. Our scope is rule-based classifiers and rule generation/selection algorithms.

There are two main actors in an explainability problem: an opaque classifier, also called *black box* whose behavior must be explained, and a dataset to train the explainable model [6]. Explanation algorithms and models can be split into two branches of *local* and *global* explanation method [10]. The former provides explanations on the model behavior on a single prediction while the latter provides explanations on the whole model behavior. In this setting, local explainability problems operate on an available dataset comprised of a single instance. Local explanation algorithms tend to focus either on a neighborhood or on a candidate approach. Given a black box, a distance measure, and a record x, neighborhood approaches generate a synthetic neighborhood of x, then exploits an interpretable algorithm (such as a decision tree or a rule-based classifier) to extract a local explanation from it. LIME [22] and LORE [9] tackle the neighborhood generation through input perturbation and genetic algorithms, respectively. Candidate approaches instead focus on greedily exploring the problem space. ANCHORS [23] generates a starting one-premise rule, then iteratively adds relevant premises by leveraging multi-bandit algorithms. Global explanation algorithms instead leverage the whole dataset and try to explain the overall logic of the black box classifier with explainable-by-design models. TREPAN [4] for instance, is a revised decision tree, and tries to jointly optimize gain ratio and fidelity to the given black box. This feature allows to reduce erroneous splits and dampen overfitting in the deeper levels of the tree.

While the methods previously discussed try to approximate either the local or global behavior of a black box, interpretable classifiers are explainable by design [8,10] and are meant to substitute it in the classification task. However, at the cost of their interpretability comes a generally lower performance than those of black boxes. Decision trees like C4.5 [20] are probably the most notorious family of interpretable models. Another large family is the one of rule-based classifiers like FOIL [21] and CPAR [27] that operate by iteratively generating detailed rulesets. Restricting ourselves to rule-based algorithms, there are several recent proposals in the literature. Decision sets [15] and MUSE [16] optimize an objective function balancing accuracy and complexity of the output ruleset, thus yielding a set of sorted and mutually exclusive rules. In [26] the authors introduce the Scalable Bayesian Rule Lists (SBRL), i.e., a Bayesian model to filter a given ruleset. The authors set up a prior distribution over the output ruleset bounded in number of premises per rule and size of the ruleset. The posterior is then addressed with a probabilistic scheme. A Bayesian formulation is also applied by the Falling Rule Lists [25], where the ruleset is updated with random operations such as premise swapping, replacement, addition and removal. Finally, CORELS [2] introduces an algorithmically bounded ruleset construction procedure with a strong emphasis on optimality.

The explanation methods reviewed above operate by either generating local (LORE, ANCHORS) or global rules (CPAR, FOIL, CORELS, SBRL, etc.). The problem we address is instead that of subsuming a set of local rules to a set of global ones guaranteeing high affordability with the black box and a low complexity in the explanation for a better understanding. Note that the problem we deal with extracts explanations from other explanation, rather than directly from the data, as it is the case for the above global models. As a consequence, to the best of the our knowledge, our proposal is conceptually different from all those existing in the literature. However, in the experiment section we try to exploit existing methods as a replacement of the proposed one.

3 Problem Formulation

We first recall basic notations on classification and explanation. Afterwards, we define the *local-to-global explanation problem* for which we propose a solution.

We name *black box* b a not interpretable classification model, such as a neural network or a random forest. It is defined as a function $b : \mathcal{X}^{(m)} \rightarrow \mathcal{Y}$ which maps records x from a feature space $\mathcal{X}^{(m)}$ with m input features to a decision y in a target space[1] $\mathcal{Y}$. We write $b(x) = y$ to denote the decision y predicted by b, and $b(X) = Y$ as a shorthand for $\{b(x) \mid x \in X\} = Y$. An instance x consists of a set of m attribute-value pairs (a_i, v_i), where a_i is a feature (or attribute) and v_i is a value from the domain of a_i. We assume that b can be queried at will. Given b and an instance x for which the outcome $b(x) = y$ has to be explained, we model a *local* explanation e of such decision as a decision rule $r = p \rightarrow y$, where each premise $p_i \in p$ is associated to a feature a_i and a range $[v_i^{(l)}, v_i^{(u)}]$. We can now formalize the *local-to-global* explanation problem as follows:

Definition 1 (Local-to-Global Explanation). *Let b be a black box classifier, $X = \{x_1, \dots, x_n\}$ a set of instances and $R = \{r_1, \dots, r_n\}$ a set of the rule-based local explanations of b for all the instances in X. The* local-to-global explanation problem *consists in deriving from R an interpretable rule-based classifier approximating the* global *behavior of b.*

Therefore, starting from a set of *local* explanations, our objective is to find a *global* interpretable classifier from which is possible to understand the overall logic followed by the black box for taking its decision.

4 Scoring Methods and Rule Relevance Score

In this section, we describe a *scoring system* for solving the local-to-global explanation problem. The proposed approach can be summarized as follows. Given a set of rules R as local explanation of a black box classifier b, the *scoring system* calculates a *score* for each rule $r_i \in R$. Then, it *prunes out* the rules with a score lower than a given threshold. The resulting set of rules $R^* \subseteq R$ is the global explanation approximating the behavior of the black box b.

In particular, our target is to select a small set of rules sufficiently large and precise to approximate the black box b, i.e., to extract from R a subset R^* rewarding the following properties. Firstly, generality: we wish for rules to be general, and hence applicable to large subsets of the dataset. The more general a rule set is, the larger the probability that a record in the dataset can be explained by it. Secondly, high accuracy: naturally, we wish for the predictions of the rule set to be accurate. Lastly, "outliers accuracy". The results in [27] suggest that, in the solution space, accuracy and coverage are involved in a trade-off relationship. We wish to reward rules which capture rule-outliers, i.e., rules able to explain

[1] Without loss of generality, in our study we restrict to binary decisions, but the problem can also be faced for multi-class decisions.

records matched by few other rules, as they are outliers in the solution space of explanations. Moreover, rewarding such rules allows us to reduce the overlap between rules and to discard a large chunk of the most "obvious" rules. Measures embedding these properties can act as a proxy for model completeness, as highly general rule sets lower the probability of occurring in non-explainable records. As a side-effect, fixed the rule set, general models tend to be simpler, since the more complex and detailed an explanation is, the lower its generality. Therefore, the effectiveness of the scoring system lies in the definition of a scoring function implementing the above properties.

In this proposal, we define the *Rule Relevance* Score (RRS). The proposed scoring formulation accounts for the required generality and accuracy constraints by weighting them in a tunable linear sum:

$$\text{RRS}_{R,X} = \alpha_1 \cdot c + \alpha_2 \cdot s + \alpha_3 \cdot a + \alpha_4 \cdot \widetilde{c} + \alpha_5 \cdot \widetilde{a} \quad (1)$$

where c is a *coverage score*, s is a *sparsity* score, a is an association score, $\widetilde{c}$ is a *prediction coverage* score, $\widetilde{a}$ is a *prediction association* score, and $\alpha_1, \ldots, \alpha_5$ are tunable weights[2]. Coverage and sparsity act as a proxy for model complexity: the longer a rule is, the lower its coverage. It also follows that high-coverage rulesets yield highly complete models: the larger the ruleset coverage, the more records can be explained. Score vectors are computed on a given ruleset R and validation set X. Next, we detail each component of RRS defined in Eq. 1.

4.1 Coverage

Given a rule $r = p \rightarrow y$ and a dataset X, we define the *coverage* of the rule r on X as the set of records $x \in X$ that satisfy the premise of the rule, i.e.,

$$\Gamma(r, X) = \{x \in X \mid \forall a_i \in p,\ (a_i, v_i) \in x.\ v_i^{(l)} \leq v_i < v_i^{(u)}\}. \quad (2)$$

In addition, we call the inverse of the coverage function of a record the *associated ruleset* of a record, that is the set of rules satisfied by the record. Moreover, we extend the notion of coverage to that of *perfect coverage* of a rule r with target y, that is the subset of records covered and correctly predicted by r:

$$\widetilde{\Gamma}(r, X) = \{x \in X \mid x \in \Gamma(r, X) \wedge b(x) = y\}. \quad (3)$$

The definition of *perfect associated ruleset* of a record is analogous to the non-perfect version and replaces the coverage function with its perfect extension.

We turn the above sets into the scores of the RRS formula as follows. Given a ruleset R, the *coverage matrix* $C_{R,X}$ of R over X is a binary matrix such that $C_{R,X}[i,j] = 1$ if and only if the i-th rule in R covers the record j, i.e., if $x_j \in \Gamma(R, \{x_j\})$.

[2] We adopt default unitary weights of $\alpha_i = 0.2$ to balance the score vectors in a linear non-weighted sum.

It is then straightforward to define both the *coverage score* vector $c_{R,X}$ and *association score* vector $c^{-1}_{R,X}$ as the ratio of covered records and the ratio of the covering ruleset, respectively:

$$c_{R,X} = 1/|X| \cdot C_{R,X} \cdot \mathbb{1}, \quad c^{-1}_{R,X} = 1/|R| \cdot \mathbb{1}^T \cdot C_{R,X} \tag{4}$$

where $\mathbb{1}$ is a column vector of appropriate size and 1 entries. The coverage score vector accounts for the normalized coverage of the records, while the association score vector accounts for the coverage of the rules.

4.2 Associated Rule Coverage

In order to accommodate also "outlier coverage", i.e., the coverage of rare records, we apply product between the $c_{R,X}$ and $c^{-1}_{R,X}$, resulting in the *associated rule-coverage score* vector $a_{R,X}$:

$$a_{R,X} = C_{R,X}(c^{-1}_{R,X})^{-1}. \tag{5}$$

This score captures, for each rule, the average associated rule set cardinality of its covered records. Hence, rules covering less-covered records will tend to have a large associated rule-coverage.

We define the perfect coverage matrix $\widetilde{C}_{R,X}$ using the $\widetilde{\Gamma}$ operator, and in line with Eqs. 4 and 5 we name $\widetilde{c}_{R,X}$ and $\widetilde{a}_{R,X}$ the *perfect coverage score* and *perfect associated rule-coverage* of the RRS formula.

4.3 Sparsity

Coverage is not necessarily the unique measure to account for the coverage of a ruleset. We also account for the distance among the records covered by a rule with an average pairwise distance of the covered records. Let D_X be the pairwise symmetric distance matrix in which element (i, j) holds the distance between record i and record j, we define *sparsity* as:

$$s_{R,X} = 1/D_X \cdot C_{R,X} \cdot D_X. \tag{6}$$

4.4 Model Explanation and Prediction

The model explanation is comprised of two phases: a *pruning* phase, which extracts a global set of rules from a set of local ones, and a *prediction* phase, which employs the global set of rules to classify a given instance.

Pruning. Given a set R of local rules, and a validation set X, we calculate the RRS vector. Then, we extract a subset of rules R^* from R by pruning out the rules having a RRS lower than a threshold. As a threshold, we adopt a percentile of the values in the RRS vector. Formally, given β we prune R to R^* by removing all $r \in R$ with score lower than the βth percentile. The ruleset R^* represents the global interpretation of the black box b explained by the scoring system RRS.

Prediction. Given a set of relevant rules R^* and a record x, we adopt the Laplacian schema introduced in [27]. Given a record x, the set of relevant rules R^* and a validation set X, the prediction of R^* on x is the prediction of the rule with the highest Laplacian accuracy in the associated ruleset of x.

5 Experiments

In this section we present an array of experiments showing the validity of the proposed solution[3]. In particular, we show the effectiveness of the scoring system using RRS in subsuming an optimal set of rules with respect to baseline scores and to state-of-the-art rule-based explainable by design methods.

Table 1. Dataset cardinality and encoded dimensionality.

Dataset	Training	#Local explanations	Dimensionality
adult	39,072	9,768	109
churn	3,332	2,333	79
compas	7,213	1,544	19
german	999	299	60

5.1 Experimental Setting

We selected a set of standard binary classification tasks with datasets preprocessed in a one-hot format[4]: `adult` is a dataset on future income prediction[5]; `churn` is a Kaggle dataset on telephone plan subscription prediction[6]; `compas` is a dataset on recidivism prediction[7]; `german` is a dataset on creditor prediction[8]. We split each dataset in a stratified fashion: 80% is used for training the black box classifiers, and we explain the remaining 20%, namely X. Table 1 reports basic information about the datasets[9]. As black box classifiers, we report experiments[10] explaining a Neural Network (NN) and a Random Forest (RF). As initial set of local rules R we adopt the explanation rules extracted using the local-explanation method LORE [9] on the dataset X. As validation set, we adopt the test set X from which we extract the local explanations.

In order to evaluate the requirements reported in the previous section, we validate the explanation methods using the following measures.

[3] Code available at github.com/msetzu/rule-relevance-score.
[4] Missing values were replaced by mean and mode according to the feature type.
[5] https://archive.ics.uci.edu/ml/datasets/adult.
[6] https://www.kaggle.com/becksddf/churn-in-telecoms-dataset.
[7] https://github.com/propublica/compas-analysis.
[8] https://archive.ics.uci.edu/ml/datasets/statlog+(german+credit+data).
[9] The reported dimensionality refers to the one-hot encoding applied.
[10] RF trained with scikit-learn, three-layer NN trained with keras.io.

- *fidelity*$(X, R, b) \in [0, 1]$, the fidelity of the interpretable model with respect to a given black box b on a dataset X. It indicates how well the interpretable model mimics the black box.
- *coverage*$(X, R) \in [0, 1]$ the normalized coverage of the interpretable model R on the given dataset X, i.e., $c_{R,X}$. It indicates how many records the interpretable model is able to deal with.
- *hmean*$(X, R, b) \in [0, 1]$ the *harmonic score*, that is the harmonic mean of fidelity and coverage, striking a balance between the two.
- *size*$(R) \in [0, +\infty)$, the conciseness of the interpretable model in terms of cardinality of the ruleset R, i.e., $|R|$.
- *len*$(R) \in [0, +\infty)$, the complexity of the interpretable model in terms of average number of conditions in the premises of the rules in R.

As *baselines*, we compare the proposed RRS, with a trivial fidelity-based scoring schema FS, and with a coverage-based scoring schema CS. In practice, we replace the RRS adopted in the pruning phase of the proposed scoring system with FS or CS. Moreover, we compare the RRS scoring schema against global rule-based state-of-the-art[11] explainable-by-design classifiers: CPAR [27], CORELS [2] and SBRL [26]. In addition, we prove that the global rules, extracted by these classifiers and provided as input to the RRS scoring system, do not guarantee the same performance of the local rules.

5.2 Rule Relevance Score vs. Fidelity and Coverage Scores

In this section, we show the importance of using a compound score like RRS in the pruning phase of the scoring system instead of trivial scores like FS or CS.

Figure 1 shows how *fidelity*, *coverage* and *harmonic score* varies when varying the pruning percentile threshold β for the various datasets using the NN black box classifier. Results using the RF as black box are close to those obtained using the NN and are not reported due to lack of space.

Regardless of the score RRS, FS or CS, most datasets show increasingly higher *fidelity* on higher pruning factors. We attribute this behavior to a large number of poorly performing rules which sway the ensemble towards the wrong prediction. FS shows the highest and the most stable *fidelity* across pruning factors. This pattern is probably due to the low usage of each rule. RRS and CS show almost no difference in terms of *fidelity* with a slight increase, indicating that (i) the fidelity score does not play a crucial role in the pruning, (ii) the coverage may hinder the prediction performance on lower pruning factors.

The differences between FS, RRS and CS grow significantly when *coverage*, and hence *harmonic score*, is measured. While both RRS and CS display a stable trend, FS dips in coverage between the 50th and 80th percentile, regardless of the dataset. As suggested in the *fidelity* analysis, *coverage* does not seem to correlate with *fidelity*. We notice that the decrease in *coverage* in FS does not correlate with a decrease in *fidelity*. This suggests that most of the rules in R and therefore

[11] For CPAR, CORELS and SBRL we adopt the default hyperparameter setting.

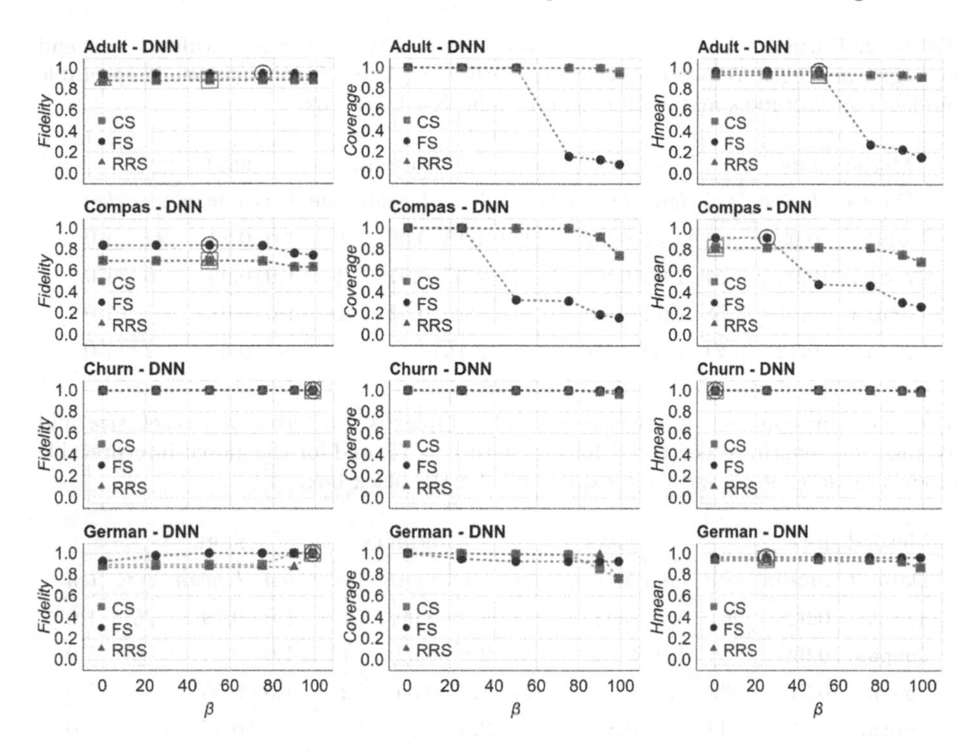

Fig. 1. Fidelity, coverage and harmonic score for RRS, FS and CS on local explanations extracted from a NN, for the different datasets varying the pruning percentile threshold β. The highest score is highlighted by a double marker.

in R^* are not useful in prediction, and thus, that the fidelity measure strongly relies on the default rule with majority target label.

5.3 Local vs Global Rules

In this section we compare the RRS scoring schema against the global rule-based classifiers: CPAR, CORELS and SBRL. Tables 2 and 3 report the *harmonic score*, and ruleset *size* as a proxy of *conciseness* (the lower the better) and average rule length as a proxy for *complexity* (the lower the better) of the interpretable models for the NN and RF explanations, respectively. On the one hand, we have the scoring system with RRS subsuming the best local rules; on the other hand, we have the global rules from the explainable by design algorithms. RRS shows the highest *harmonic score* at the cost of a not very low complexity and conciseness. On the NN rules, CPAR has an overall lower harmonic score, and higher complexity and conciseness than RRS. On the RF rules, instead, there is not a clear winner. Viceversa, CORELS, and SBRL provide a low-complexity highly concise model at the cost of the harmonic score. Finally, it is worth to underline that RRS displays consistent and stable performance across all the metrics independently from the dataset or the black box.

Table 2. Harmonic score, conciseness and complexity (in terms of ruleset *size* and average rule length, respectively) for RRS with $\beta = 75$, and for the global interpretable models CPAR, CORELS and SBRL explaining the NN black box.

Method	RRS			CPAR			CORELS			SBRL		
Dataset	*hmean*	*size*	*len*	*hmean*	*size*	*len*	*hmean*	*size*	*len*	*hmean*	*size*	*len*
adult	0.93	331	2.74	0.90	299	4.15	0.00	1	1.0	0.84	24	1.0
compas	0.99	51	1.90	0.83	94	2.37	0.91	3	1.0	0.99	6	1.0
churn	0.81	58	2.62	0.77	2247	3.08	0.53	1	1.0	0.08	7	1.0
german	0.92	21	1.80	0.75	26	2.19	–	–	–	0.00	2	1.0

Table 3. Harmonic score, conciseness and complexity (in terms of ruleset *size* and average rule length, respectively) for RRS with $\beta = 75$, and for the global interpretable models CPAR, CORELS and SBRL explaining the RF black box.

Method	RRS			CPAR			CORELS			SBRL		
Dataset	*hmean*	*size*	*len*	*hmean*	*size*	*len*	*hmean*	*size*	*len*	*hmean*	*size*	*len*
adult	0.92	361	5.2	0.92	85	2.3	0.00	1	1.0	0.29	26	1.0
compas	0.92	56	1.9	0.84	130	2.8	0.92	1	1.0	0.24	6	1.0
churn	0.91	82	2.8	0.83	44	2.7	0.36	2	1.0	0.55	5	1.0
german	0.82	30	2.0	0.83	18	2.3	–	–	–	0.47	6	1.0

In Fig. 2 we show that if we replace the local rules in the RRS scoring system with the global rules extracted by CPAR, CORELS and SBRL there is a clear drop in the performance with respect to RRS. Analyzing the fidelity and coverage we observe that several methods show sub-par fidelity regardless of the rule filtering, and in some cases, they fail in generating output rules (CORELS on `german`), with CPAR being the best method after the scoring system with RRS. We attribute the poor performance of CORELS and SBRL to the low number of rules generated (see Tables 2 and 3 for $\beta = 0$).

5.4 Qualitative Evaluation

In this section, we explore the rules employed by the RRS scoring system, CPAR, CORELS and SBRL to explain the decision of a sample of instances. In particular, we consider two instances x_1 adn x_2 from the `compas` dataset for which using the RF as black box we have $b(x_1) = High$ and $b(x_2) = Low$.

x_1 = {age = 25, priors count = 0, days before arrest = 1, is recidive, is violent recidive, not 2-years recidive, length of stay = 1, age ∈ [25, 45], sex = Male, race = african, charge = grave}

x_2 = {age = 47, priors count = 23, days before arrest = 1, is recidive, is not violent recidive, not 2-years recidive, length of stay = 403, age ∈ [25, 45], sex = Male, race = african, charge = not grave}

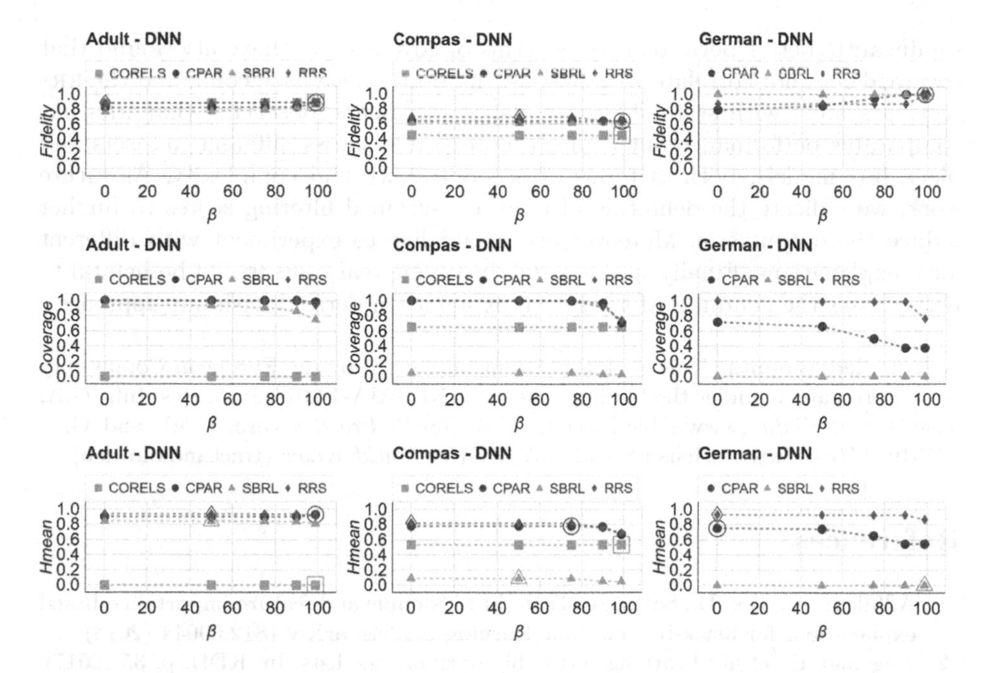

Fig. 2. Fidelity, coverage and harmonic score for RRS on local explanations and global methods for NN, for the different datasets varying the pruning percentile threshold β. The highest score is highlighted by a double marker.

We report in the following the rules selected to explain the black box decision.

x_1
- RRS `{priors count` $\in$ `[0, 4], is recidive, age` $<$ `25}` $\rightarrow$ `High`
- CPAR `{priors count` $\in$ `[0, 4], is recidive}` $\rightarrow$ `High`
- CORELS `{age` $<$ `45, priors count` $\notin$ `[18, 34]}*` $\rightarrow$ `High`
- SBRL `{is violent recid}` $\rightarrow$ `High`

x_2
- RRS `{age` $>$ `45}` $\rightarrow$ `Low`
- CPAR `{priors count` $>$ `15}` $\rightarrow$ `Low`
- CORELS `{age` $>$ `45}` $\rightarrow$ `Low`
- SBRL `{is recid}` $\rightarrow$ `Low`

We notice that while all methods are able to capture significant features (age, priors count, past recidivism), RRS leverages longer and more detailed rules than CPAR. This behavior is also empirically supported by the data shown in Tables 2 and 3 and is due to the local input rules, which are longer than the global ones. We leave the study of the effect of input length on RRS and human-subject experiments for future study.

6 Conclusion

In this paper, we have proposed a scoring system for explaining the global behavior of a black box classifier starting from a set of local explanations in the form of rules. To guarantee high performance and to account for important properties when selecting the most relevant rules, we have defined the rule relevance score (RRS). We have compared RRS to baseline scores finding comparable fidelity and significantly better performances in terms of coverage. We have also found that coverage does not correlate with fidelity. In addition, we have compared the RRS scoring system with state-of-the-art global explainers, observing that RRS has comparable performance but is much more stable across different datasets and black box models, both in terms of accountability and complexity. As future work, we indicate the definition of more fine-grained filtering scores to further reduce the output size. Moreover, we would like to experiment with different local explanations. Finally, a case study involving real users would be helpful to better asses the goodness of the global explanation derived with our approach.

Acknowledgements. This work is partially supported by the European Community H2020 programme under the funding schemes: INFRAIA-1-2014-2015: Res. Infr. G.A. 654024 *SoBigData* (www.sobigdata.eu), G.A. 78835 *Pro-Res* (prores.eu), and G.A. 825619 *AI4EU* (www.ai4eu.eu), and G.A. 780754 *Track&Know* (trackandknow.eu).

References

1. Adhikari, A., Tax, D., Satta, R., Fath, M.: Example and feature importance-based explanations for black-box machine learning models. arXiv:1812.09044 (2018)
2. Angelino, E., et al.: Learning certifiably optimal rule lists. In: KDD, p. 35 (2017)
3. Bien, J., et al.: Prototype selection for interpretable classification. AAS **5**(4), 2403–2424 (2011)
4. Craven, M., Shavlik, J.W.: Extracting tree-structured representations of trained networks. In: NIPS 1995, pp. 24–30 (1995)
5. Dodge, J., et al.: Explaining models: an empirical study of how explanations impact fairness judgment. In: IUI, pp. 275–285 (2019)
6. Freitas, A.: Comprehensible classification models: a position paper. SIGKDD **15**(1), 1–10 (2014)
7. Frosst, N., et al.: Distilling a neural network into a decision tree. arXiv:1711 (2017)
8. Guidotti, R., Soldani, J., Neri, D., Brogi, A., Pedreschi, D.: Helping your docker images to spread based on explainable models. In: Brefeld, U., et al. (eds.) ECML PKDD 2018. LNCS (LNAI), vol. 11053, pp. 205–221. Springer, Cham (2019). https://doi.org/10.1007/978-3-030-10997-4_13
9. Guidotti, R., et al.: Local rule-based explanations of black box decision systems. CoRR, abs/1805.10820 (2018)
10. Guidotti, R., Monreale, A., Ruggieri, S., Turini, F., Giannotti, F., Pedreschi, D.: A survey of methods for explaining black box models. CSUR **51**(5) (2018). Article no. 93
11. Hinton, G., et al.: Distilling the knowledge in a neural network. arXiv:1503.02531 (2015)
12. Ish-Horowicz, J., Udwin, D., Flaxman, S., Filippi, S., Crawford, L.: Interpreting deep neural networks through variable importance. arXiv:1901.09839 (2019)
13. Krishnan, R., Sivakumar, G., Bhattacharya, P.: Extracting decision trees from trained neural networks. Pattern Recogn. **32**(12), 1999–2009 (1999)
14. Lage, I., Ross, A.S., Gershman, S.J., Kim, B., Doshi-Velez, F.: Human-in-the-loop interpretability prior. In: NIPS 2018, pp. 10180–10189 (2018)
15. Lakkaraju, H., Bach, S.H., Leskovec, J.: Interpretable decision sets: a joint framework for description and prediction. In: SIGKDD, pp. 1675–1684 (2016)

16. Lakkaraju, H., Kamar, E., Caruana, R., Leskovec, J.: Faithful and customizable explanations of black box models. In: AIES (2019)
17. Malgieri, G., Comandé, G.: Why a right to legibility of automated decision-making exists in the GDPR. Int. Data Priv. Law **7**(4), 243–265 (2017)
18. Mittelstadt, B., et al.: Explaining explanations in AI. arXiv:1811.01439 (2018)
19. Pedreschi, D., Giannotti, F., Guidotti, R., Monreale, A., Ruggieri, S., Turini, F.: Meaningful explanations of Black Box AI decision systems. In: AAAI (2019)
20. Quinlan, J.R.: C4.5: Programs for Machine Learning. Elsevier, Amsterdam (2014)
21. Quinlan, J.R., Cameron-Jones, R.M.: FOIL: a midterm report. In: Brazdil, P.B. (ed.) ECML 1993. LNCS, vol. 667, pp. 1–20. Springer, Heidelberg (1993). https://doi.org/10.1007/3-540-56602-3_124
22. Ribeiro, M.T., Singh, S., Guestrin C.: "Why should i trust you?" Explaining the predictions of any classifier. In: KDD, pp. 1135–1144 (2016)
23. Ribeiro, M.T., Singh, S., Guestrin, C.: Anchors: high-precision model-agnostic explanations. In: AAAI 2018, pp. 1527–1535 (2018)
24. Wachter, S., et al.: Why a right to explanation of automated decision-making does not exist in the GDPR. IDPL **7**(2), 76–99 (2017)
25. Wang, F., Rudin, C.: Falling rule lists. In: AISTATS (2015)
26. Yang, H., et al.: Scalable Bayesian rule lists. In: ICML, pp. 3921–3930 (2017)
27. Yin, X., Han, J.: CPAR: classification based on predictive association rules. In: SIAM, pp. 331–335 (2003)

Adversarial Robustness Curves

Christina Göpfert, Jan Philip Göpfert(✉), and Barbara Hammer

Bielefeld University, Bielefeld, Germany
jgoepfert@techfak.uni-bielefeld.de

Abstract. The existence of adversarial examples has led to considerable uncertainty regarding the trust one can justifiably put in predictions produced by automated systems. This uncertainty has, in turn, lead to considerable research effort in understanding adversarial robustness. In this work, we take first steps towards separating robustness analysis from the choice of robustness threshold and norm. We propose robustness curves as a more general view of the robustness behavior of a model and investigate under which circumstances they can qualitatively depend on the chosen norm.

1 Introduction

Robustness of machine learning models has recently attracted massive research interest. This interest is particularly pronounced in the context of deep learning. On the one hand, this is due to the massive success and widespread deployment of deep learning. On the other hand, it is due to the intriguing properties that can be demonstrated for deep learning (although these are not unique to this setting): the circumstance that deep learning can produce models that achieve or surpass human-level performance in a wide variety of tasks, but completely disagree with human judgment after application of imperceptible perturbations [13]. The ability of a classifier to maintain its performance under such changes to the input data is commonly referred to as *robustness to adversarial perturbations.*

In order to better understand adversarial robustness, recent years have seen the development of a host of methods that produce adversarial examples, in the white box and black box settings, with specific or arbitrary target labels, and varying additional constraints [3,7,8,11,12]. There has also been a push towards training regimes that produce adversarially robust networks, such as data augmentation with adversarial examples or distillation [1,4,6,10]. The difficulty faced by such approaches is that robustness is difficult to measure and quantify: even if a model is shown to be robust against current state of the art attacks, this does not exclude the possibility that newly devised attacks may be successful [2]. The complexity of deep learning models and counter-intuitive nature of some phenomena surrounding adversarial examples further make it challenging to understand the impact of robust training or the properties that determine whether a model is robust or non-robust. Recent work has highlighted

C. Göpfert and J. P. Göpfert—Equal contribution.

P. Cellier and K. Driessens (Eds.): ECML PKDD 2019 Workshops, CCIS 1167, pp. 172–179, 2020.
https://doi.org/10.1007/978-3-030-43823-4_15

settings where no model can be simultaneously accurate and robust [14], or where finding a model that is simultaneously robust and accurate requires optimizing over a different hypothesis class than finding one that is simply accurate [9]. These examples rely on linear models, as they are easy for humans to understand. They analyze robustness properties for a fixed choice of norm and, typically, a fixed disadvantageous perturbation size (dependent on the model). This raises the question: "How do the presented results depend on the choice of norm, choice of perturbation size, and choice of linear classifier as a hypothesis class?"

In this contribution, we:

- propose *robustness curves* as a way of better representing adversarial robustness in place of "point-wise" measures,
- show that linear classifiers are not sufficient to illustrate all interesting robustness phenomena, and
- investigate how robustness curves may depend on the choice of norm.

2 Definitions

In the following, we assume data $(x, y) \in X \times Y$, $X \subseteq \mathbb{R}^d$, are generated i.i.d. according to distribution P with marginal P_X. Let $f : X \to Y$ denote some classifier and let $x \in X$. The *standard loss* of f on P is

$$L(f) := P(\{(x, y) : f(x) \neq y\}). \tag{1}$$

Let $n : X \to \mathbb{R}^+$ be some norm, let $\varepsilon \geq 0$ and let

$$B_n(x, \varepsilon) := \{x' : n(x - x') \leq \varepsilon\}. \tag{2}$$

Following [14], we define the ε-*adversarial loss* of f regarding P and n as

$$L_{n,\varepsilon}(f) := P(\underbrace{\{(x, y) : \exists x' \in B_n(x, \varepsilon) : f(x') \neq y\}}_{=:A_\varepsilon^n}). \tag{3}$$

We have $L_{n,0}(f) = L(f)$. Alternatively, we can exclude from this definition any points that are initially misclassified by the model, and instead consider as adversarial examples all points where the model changes its behavior under small perturbations. Then the ε-*margin loss* is defined as

$$L'_{n,\varepsilon}(f) := P_X(\{x : \exists x' \in B_n(x, \varepsilon) : f(x') \neq f(x)\}). \tag{4}$$

$L'_{n,\varepsilon}$ is the weight of all points within an ε-margin of a decision boundary. We have $L'_{n,0}(f) = 0$.

There are two somewhat arbitrary choices in the definition in Eqs. (3) and (4): the choice of ε and the choice of the norm n. The aim of this contribution is to investigate how ε and n impact the adversarial robustness.

3 Robustness Curves

As a first step towards understanding robustness globally, instead of for an isolated perturbation size ε, we propose to view robustness as a function of ε. This yields an easy-to-understand visual representation of adversarial robustness in the form of a *robustness curve.*

Definition 1. *The* robustness curve *of a classifier f, given a norm n and underlying distribution P, is the curve defined by*

$$r_{f,n,P} : [0, \infty) \to [0, 1] \tag{5}$$

$$\varepsilon \mapsto L_{n,\varepsilon}(f). \tag{6}$$

The margin curve *of f given n and P is the curve defined by*

$$r'_{f,n,P} : [0, \infty) \to [0, 1] \tag{7}$$

$$\varepsilon \mapsto L'_{n,\varepsilon}(f). \tag{8}$$

Commonly chosen norms for the investigation of adversarial robustness are the ℓ_1 norm (denoted by $\|\cdot\|_1$), the ℓ_2 norm (denoted by $\|\cdot\|_2$), and the ℓ_∞ norm (denoted by $\|\cdot\|_\infty$). In the following, we will investigate robustness curves for these three choices of n.

[14] propose a distribution P_1 where $y \overset{\text{u. a. r.}}{\sim} \{-1, +1\}$ and

$$x_1 = \begin{cases} 1 & \text{w. p. } p \\ -1 & \text{w. p. } (1-p) \end{cases} \qquad x_2, \ldots, x_{d+1} \overset{\text{i. i. d.}}{\sim} \mathcal{N}(\eta y, 1). \tag{9}$$

For this distribution, they show that the linear classifier $f_{\text{avg}}(x) = \text{sign}(w^T x)$ with $w = (0, 1/d, \ldots, 1/d)$ has high accuracy, but low ε-robustness in ℓ_∞ norm for $\varepsilon \geq 2\eta$, while the classifier $f_{\text{rob}}(x) = \text{sign}(w^T x)$ with $w = (1, 0, \ldots, 0)$ has high ε-robustness for $\varepsilon < 1$, but low accuracy. [9] proposes a distribution P_2 where $y \overset{\text{u. a. r.}}{\sim} \{-1, +1\}$ and

$$x_i = \begin{cases} y & \text{w. p. } 0.51 \\ -y & \text{w. p. } 0.49 \end{cases} \tag{10}$$

where the linear classifier $f_s(x) = \text{sign}(w^T x)$ with $w = \mathbf{1}_d$ has high accuracy, but low ε-robustness in ℓ_∞ norm for $\varepsilon \geq \frac{1}{2}$. Figure 1 shows margin curves and robustness curves for P_1 and f_{avg}, P_1 and f_{rob} and P_2 and f_s.

4 The Impact of n

The curves shown in Fig. 1 seem to behave similarly for each norm. Is this always the case? Indeed, if f is a linear classifier parameterized by normal vector w and offset b, denote by

$$d_n((w, b), x) = \min\{n(v) : \exists p : x = p + v, \langle w, p \rangle + b = 0\} \tag{11}$$

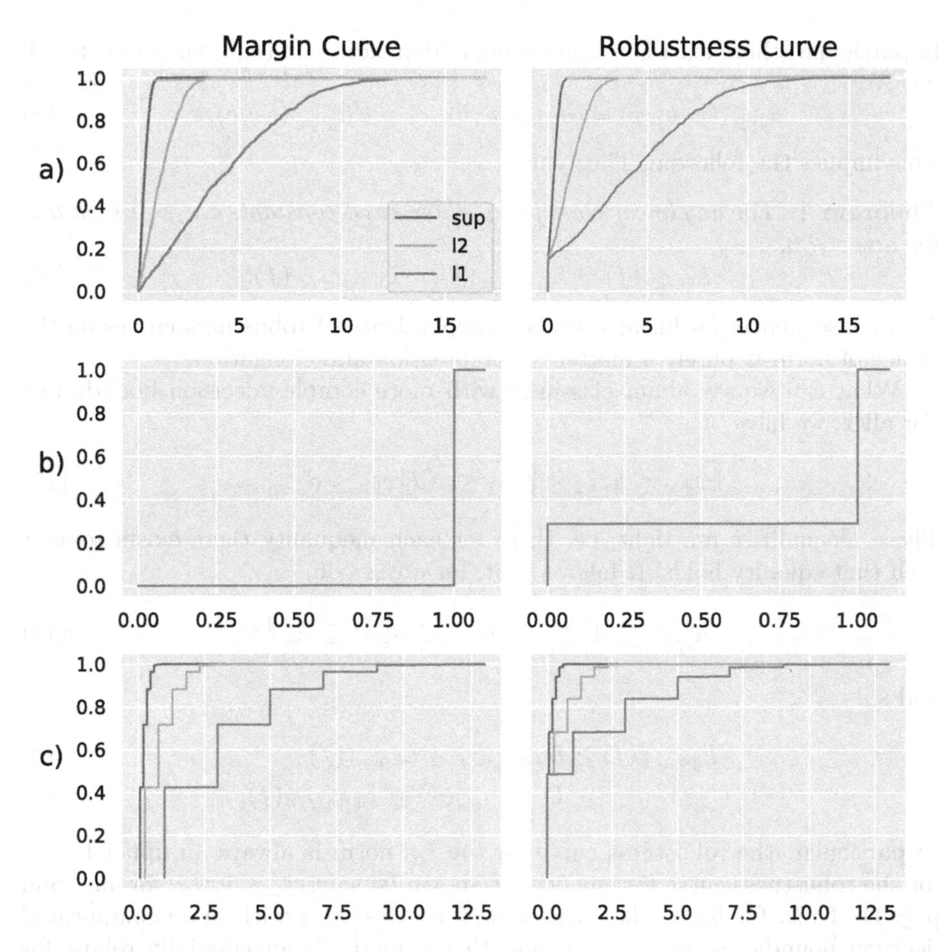

Fig. 1. Margin curves and robustness curves for several examples of distributions and linear models from the literature. Row (a) shows curves for classifier f_{avg} and distribution P_1. Row (b) shows curves for classifier f_{rob} and distribution P_1. In this case, all three curves are identical and thus appear as one. Row (c) shows curves for classifier f_s and distribution P_2.

the shortest distance between (w, b) and x in norm n. Then a series of algebraic manipulations yield

$$d_{\|\cdot\|_1}((w,b),x) = \frac{|b + \langle w, x\rangle|}{\|w\|_\infty}, \tag{12}$$

$$d_{\|\cdot\|_2}((w,b),x) = \frac{|b + \langle w, x\rangle|}{\|w\|_2}, \tag{13}$$

$$d_{\|\cdot\|_\infty}((w,b),x) = \frac{|b + \langle w, x\rangle|}{\|w\|_1}. \tag{14}$$

In particular, there exist constants c and c' depending on (w, b) such that for all $x \in X$,

$$d_{\|\cdot\|_1}((w,b),x) = c d_{\|\cdot\|_2}((w,b),x) = c' d_{\|\cdot\|_\infty}((w,b),x) \tag{15}$$

This implies the following Theorem:

Theorem 1. *For any linear classifier f, there exist constants $c, c' > 0$ such that for any $\varepsilon \geq 0$,*

$$L_{\|\cdot\|_1,\varepsilon}(f) = L_{\|\cdot\|_2,\varepsilon/c}(f) = L_{\|\cdot\|_\infty,\varepsilon/c'}(f). \tag{16}$$

As a consequence, for linear classifiers, dependence of robustness curves on the choice of norm is purely a matter of compression and elongation.

What can we say about classifiers with more complex decision boundaries? For all x, we have

$$\|x\|_\infty \leq \|x\|_2 \leq \|x\|_1 \leq \sqrt{d}\|x\|_2 \leq d\|x\|_\infty. \tag{17}$$

These inequalities are tight, i.e. there for each inequality there exists some x such that equality holds. It follows that, for any $\varepsilon > 0$,

$$A_{\varepsilon/d}^{\|\cdot\|_\infty} \subseteq A_{\varepsilon/\sqrt{d}}^{\|\cdot\|_2} \subseteq A_\varepsilon^{\|\cdot\|_1} \subseteq A_\varepsilon^{\|\cdot\|_2} \subseteq A_\varepsilon^{\|\cdot\|_\infty} \tag{18}$$

and so

$$L_{\|\cdot\|_\infty,\varepsilon}(f) \geq L_{\|\cdot\|_2,\varepsilon}(f) \geq L_{\|\cdot\|_1,\varepsilon}(f) \tag{19}$$

$$\geq L_{\|\cdot\|_2,\varepsilon/\sqrt{d}}(f) \geq L_{\|\cdot\|_1,\varepsilon/d}(f). \tag{20}$$

In particular, the robustness curve for the ℓ_∞-norm is always an upper bound for the robustness curve for any other ℓ_p-norm (since $\|x\|_p \leq \|x\|_\infty$ for all x and $p \geq 1$). Thus, for linear classifiers as well as classifiers with more complicated decision boundaries, in order to show that a model is adversarially robust for any fixed norm, it is sufficient to show that it exhibits the desired robustness behavior for the ℓ_∞-norm. On the other hand, in order to show that a model is *not* adversarially robust, showing this for the ℓ_∞ norm does not necessarily imply the same qualities in another norm, as the robustness curves may be strongly separated in high-dimensional spaces, both for linear and non-linear models.

Contrary to linear models, for more complicated decision boundaries, robustness curves may also exhibit *qualitatively* different behavior. This is illustrated in Fig. 2. The decision boundary in each case is given by a quadratic model in 2-dimensional space: $f(\boldsymbol{x}) = \text{sign}(x_1^2 - x_2)$. In the first example, we construct a finite set of points, all at ℓ_2-distance 1 from the decision boundary, but at various ℓ_1 and ℓ_∞ distances. For any distribution concentrated on a set of such points, the ℓ_2-robustness curve jumps from zero to one at a single threshold value, while the ℓ_1- and ℓ_∞-robustness curves are step functions with the height of the steps determined by the distribution across the points and the width determined by the variation in ℓ_1 or ℓ_∞ distances from the decision boundary. The robustness curves in this example also exhibit, at some points, the maximal possible separation by a factor of $\sqrt{d}$ (note that $d = 2$) while touching in other points.

In the second example, we show a continuous version of the same phenomenon, with points inside and outside the parabola distributed at constant ℓ_2-distance from the decision boundary, but with varying ℓ_1 and ℓ_∞ distances. As a result, the robustness curves for different norms are qualitatively different. The third example, on the other hand, shows a setting where the robustness curves for the three norms are both quantitatively and qualitatively similar.

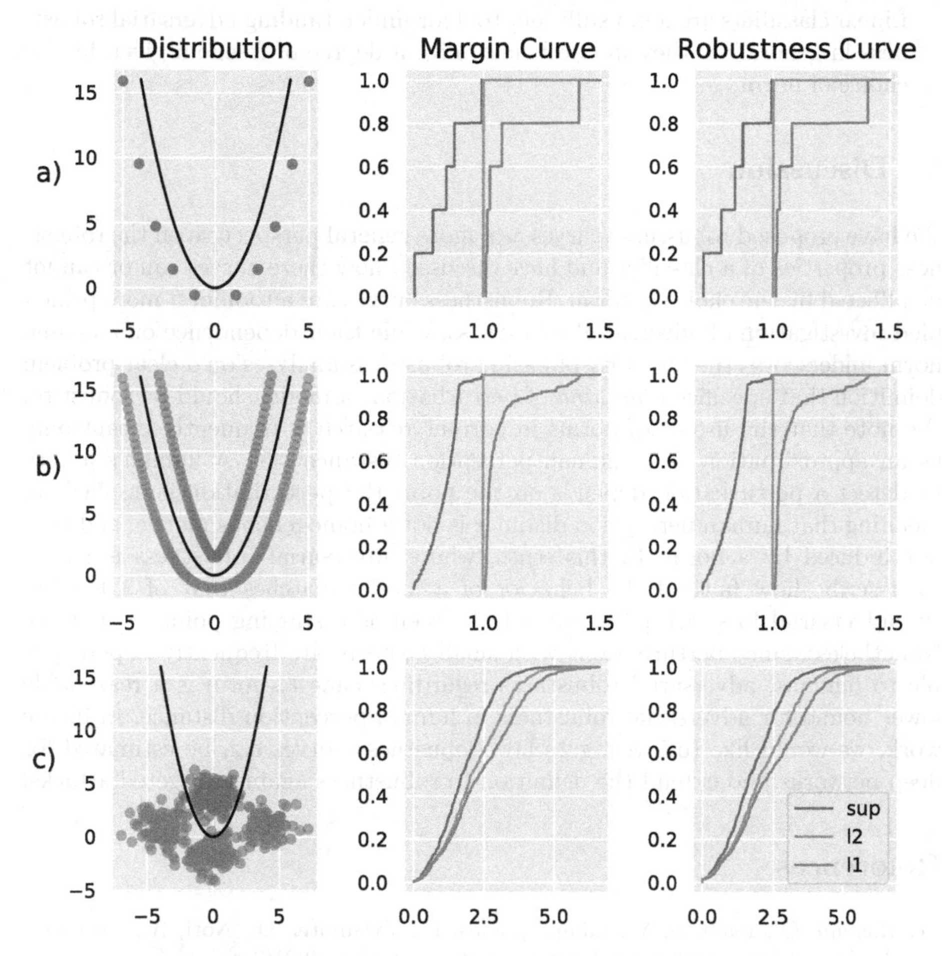

Fig. 2. Margin curves and robustness curves for $f(\boldsymbol{x}) = \mathrm{sign}(x_1^2 - x_2)$ and three different underlying distributions, illustrating varying behavior of the robustness curves for different norms. In rows (a) and (b), the robustness curves are qualitatively different, while they are almost identical in row (c). Note that in these examples, robustness curves and margin curves are nearly identical, as the standard loss of f is zero or close to zero in all cases.

These examples drive home two points:

- The robustness properties of a classifier may depend both quantitatively and qualitatively on the norm chosen to measure said robustness. When investigating robustness, it is therefore imperative to consider which norm, or, more broadly, which concept of closeness best represents the type of perturbation to guard against.
- Linear classifiers are not a sufficient tool for understanding adversarial robustness in general, as they in effect neutralize a degree of freedom given by the choice of norm.

5 Discussion

We have proposed robustness curves as a more general perspective on the robustness properties of a classifier and have discussed how these curves can or cannot be affected by the choice of norm. Robustness curves are a tool for a more principled investigation of adversarial robustness, while their dependence on a chosen norm underscores the necessity of basing robustness analyses on a clear problem definition that specifies *what kind* of perturbations a model should be robust to. We note that the use of ℓ_p norms in current research is frequently meant only as an approximation of a "human perception distance" [5]. A human's ability to detect a perturbation depends on the point the perturbation is applied to, meaning that human perception distance is not a homogeneous metric, and thus not induced by a norm. In this sense, where adversarial robustness is meant to describe how faithful the behavior of a model matches that of a human, the adversarial loss in Eq. (3) can only be seen as a starting point of analysis. Nonetheless, since perturbations with small ℓ_p-norm are frequently imperceptible to humans, adversarial robustness regarding some ℓ_p-norm is a reasonable lower bound for adversarial robustness in human perception distance. In future work, we would like to investigate how robustness curves can be estimated for deep networks and extend the definition to robustness against targeted attacks.

References

1. Bastani, O., Ioannou, Y., Lampropoulos, L., Vytiniotis, D., Nori, A., Criminisi, A.: Measuring neural net robustness with constraints (2016)
2. Carlini, N., Wagner, D.A.: Towards evaluating the robustness of neural networks. In: 2017 IEEE Symposium on Security and Privacy (SP), pp. 39–57 (2017). https://doi.org/10.1109/sp.2017.49
3. Goodfellow, I.J., Shlens, J., Szegedy, C.: Explaining and harnessing adversarial examples (2014)
4. Gu, S., Rigazio, L.: Towards deep neural network architectures robust to adversarial examples (2014)
5. Göpfert, J.P., Wersing, H., Hammer, B.: Adversarial attacks hidden in plain sight (2019)

6. Huang, R., Xu, B., Schuurmans, D., Szepesvari, C.: Learning with a strong adversary (2015)
7. Kurakin, A., Goodfellow, I.J., Bengio, S.: Adversarial examples in the physical world (2016)
8. Kurakin, A., Goodfellow, I.J., Bengio, S.: Adversarial machine learning at scale (2016)
9. Nakkiran, P.: Adversarial robustness may be at odds with simplicity (2019)
10. Papernot, N., McDaniel, P., Wu, X., Jha, S., Swami, A.: Distillation as a defense to adversarial perturbations against deep neural networks. In: 2016 IEEE Symposium on Security and Privacy (SP), May 2016. https://doi.org/10.1109/sp.2016.41
11. Papernot, N., McDaniel, P.D., Goodfellow, I.J., Jha, S., Celik, Z.B., Swami, A.: Practical black-box attacks against deep learning systems using adversarial examples (2016)
12. Su, J., Vargas, D.V., Sakurai, K.: One pixel attack for fooling deep neural networks (2017). https://doi.org/10.1109/tevc.2019.2890858
13. Szegedy, C., et al.: Intriguing properties of neural networks (2014)
14. Tsipras, D., Santurkar, S., Engstrom, L., Turner, A., Madry, A.: Robustness may be at odds with accuracy. In: International Conference on Learning Representations (2019). https://openreview.net/forum?id=SyxAb30cY7

Enriching Visual with Verbal Explanations for Relational Concepts – Combining LIME with Aleph

Johannes Rabold(✉), Hannah Deininger, Michael Siebers, and Ute Schmid

Cognitive Systems, University of Bamberg, Bamberg, Germany
johannes.rabold@uni-bamberg.de

Abstract. With the increasing number of deep learning applications, there is a growing demand for explanations. Visual explanations provide information about which parts of an image are relevant for a classifier's decision. However, highlighting of image parts (e.g., an eye) cannot capture the relevance of a specific feature value for a class (e.g., that the eye is wide open). Furthermore, highlighting cannot convey whether the classification depends on the mere presence of parts or on a specific spatial relation between them. Consequently, we present an approach that is capable of explaining a classifier's decision in terms of logic rules obtained by the Inductive Logic Programming system Aleph. The examples and the background knowledge needed for Aleph are based on the explanation generation method LIME. We demonstrate our approach with images of a blocksworld domain. First, we show that our approach is capable of identifying a single relation as important explanatory construct. Afterwards, we present the more complex relational concept of towers. Finally, we show how the generated relational rules can be explicitly related with the input image, resulting in richer explanations.

Keywords: XAI · Deep learning · Inductive Logic Programming

1 Introduction

Explainable Artificial Intelligence (XAI) mostly refers to visual highlighting of information which is relevant for the classification decision of a given instance [9,19]. In general, the mode of an explanation can be visual, but also verbal or example-based [13]. Visual explanations have been introduced to make black-box classifiers such as (deep) neural networks more transparent [9,18,19]. In the context of white-box machine learning approaches, such as decision trees or Inductive Logic Programming (ILP) [16], it is argued that these models are already transparent and interpretable by humans [16]. In the context of ILP it has been shown that a local verbal explanation can easily be generated from symbolic rules with a template-based approach [20].

For image classification tasks, it is rather obvious that visual explanations are helpful for technical as well as for domain experts: Information about what

P. Cellier and K. Driessens (Eds.): ECML PKDD 2019 Workshops, CCIS 1167, pp. 180–192, 2020.
https://doi.org/10.1007/978-3-030-43823-4_16

pixels or patches of pixels most strongly contribute to a class decision can help to detect model errors which might have been caused by non-representative sampling. Highlighting can also support domain experts to assess the validity of a learned model [18]. In general, an explanation can be characterized as useful, if it meets the principles of cooperative conversations [13]. These pragmatic aspects of communication are described in the Gricean maximes [8] which encompass the following four categories: (1) quality – explanations should be based on truth or empirical evidence; (2) quantity – be as informative as required; (3) relation – explanations should communicate only relevant information; (4) manner – avoidance of obscurity and ambiguity. We argue that visual explanations can in general not avoid obscurity and ambiguity since they cannot or only partially capture the following kinds of information:

- **Feature values:** Visual highlighting can explain that a specific aspect of an entity is informative for a specific class – e.g., that an emotion is expressed near the eye. However, the relevant information is whether the eye is wide open or the lid is tightened [21].
- **Negation:** While approaches like LRP [19] allow to visualize which pixels have a negative contribution to the classification, it is not generally possible to inform that the absence of a feature or object is relevant. E.g., it might be relevant to explain that a person is not classified as a terrorist because he or she does not hold a weapon (but a flower).
- **Relations:** If two parts of an image are highlighted, it is not possible to discriminate whether the conjunction (e.g., there is a green block and a blue block) or a more specific relation (e.g., the green block is on the blue block) is relevant.

ILP approaches [14] can capture all three kinds of information because the models are expressed as first-order Horn clauses. Relational concepts such as *grandparent(X, Y)* [15] or mutagenicity of chemical structures [23] can be induced. Furthermore, classes involving relations, such as the Michalski Train Domain [15], can be learned. Here, the decision whether a train is east- or west-bound depends on relational information of arbitrary complexity, e.g., that a waggon with six wheels needs to be followed by a waggon with an open top.

Recently, there have been proposed several deep learning approaches to tackle relational concepts, such as the differentiable neural computer [7], RelNNs [10], or RelNet [2]. In contrast to ILP, these approaches depend on very large sets of training examples and the resulting models are black-box. A helpful explanation interface should be able to take into account visual/image-based domains as well as abstract/graph-based domains. The model agnostic approach of LIME [18] provides linear explanations based on sets of super-pixels or words. This is not sufficient when more expressive relational explanations are necessary. Current focus of our work is to provide relational explanations for black-box, end-to-end classifiers for image-based domains. We believe that for image-based domains, a combination of visual and verbal explanations is most informative with respect to the Gricean maximes. Psychological experiments also give evidence that humans strongly profit from a combination of visual and verbal explanations [12].

In a previous study [17], we could show that relational symbolic explanations (Prolog rules) can be generated by combining the ILP approach Aleph [22] with LIME [18]. However, simple visual concepts have been pre-defined and

(a) A house, because three windows left of each other.

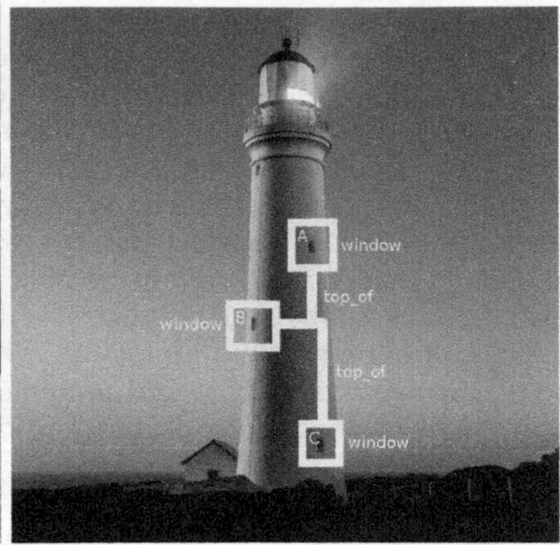

(b) A tower, because three windows on top of each other.

Fig. 1. Combining visual and symbolic explanations for house in contrast to tower. Photo of house by Pixasquare, photo of lighthouse by Joshua Hibbert, both on Unsplash

used as input to Aleph and not extracted automatically. In the following, we present an extension of [17] covering end-to-end image classification with a convolutional neural network (CNN) [11], partitioning images into sub-structures, as well as automatic extraction of visual attributes and spatial relations. Local symbolic explanations are learned with Aleph, providing logical descriptions of original and perturbed images. Finally, local symbolic explanations are related to visual highlighting of informative parts of the image to provide a combined visual-symbolic explanation. The symbolic explanation can be transformed in a verbal one with a template-based approach as demonstrated in [20]. An illustrative example is given in Fig. 1. Here the concept of house is explained by the fact that three windows are next to each other. This information is given by identifying three relevant parts of the image, naming them (A, B, C), labeling them as windows (which might be done by another automatic image classification or by the user) and stating the spatial relation between the objects using the `left_of` relation. This example also demonstrates an important aspect of symbolic explanations: Which attributes and relations are useful to explain why some object belongs to some class depends on the contrasting class [5].

In the next section, we introduce the core concepts for our approach. Then we present a significantly extended version of the LIME-Aleph algorithm [17]. We demonstrate the approach on images of a blocksworld domain. In a first experiment we show that LIME-Aleph is capable of identifying a single relation (`left_of(block1, block2)`) as relevant for the learned concept. In a second experiment, we demonstrate that more complex relational concepts such as `tower` can be explained. Finally we show how the fusion of visual and symbolic explanations might be realized.

2 Explaining Relational Concepts with LIME-Aleph

2.1 Core Concepts

The ILP System Aleph. To find symbolic explanations for relational concepts we use Aleph [22]. Aleph infers a logic theory T given a set of positive (E^+) and negative (E^-) examples. An example is represented by the target predicate (e.g. `stack(e1).` or `not stack(e2).`) together with additional predicates (e.g. `contains(b1, e1).`) as background knowledge (BK). Predicates in BK are used to build the preconditions for the target rules. Aleph is based on specific-to-general refinement search. It finds rules covering as many positive examples as possible, avoiding covering negative ones. Search is guided by modes which impose a language bias. The general algorithm is [22]:

1. As long as positive exist, select one. Otherwise halt.
2. Construct the most-specific clause that entails the selected example and is within the language constraints
3. Find a more-general clause which is a subset of the current literals in the clause.
4. Remove covered by the current clause.
5. Repeat from step 1.

An example of a rule from T in Prolog is `stack(Stack) :- contains(Block1, Stack), contains(Block2, Stack), on(Block2, Block1).`
Denoting that a `stack` is defined by one block on top of another.

LIME's Identification of Informative Super-Pixels. LIME (**L**ocal **I**nterpretable **M**odel-Agnostic **E**xplanations) is an approach to explain the decision result of any learned model [18]. Explanations state the parts of an instance that are positively or negatively correlated to the class. It works by creating a simpler, local surrogate model around the instance to be explained. In case of an image, the explanation is a set of connected pixel patches called *super-pixels*.

Let x be an image and x' be the binary vector that states whether super-pixels $x'_i \in x'$ are switched on or off (see below). LIME finds a sparse linear model $g(x')$ that locally approximates the unknown decision function $f(x)$ represented by a black-box classifier. It effectively finds the coefficients $\boldsymbol{w}$ for the super-pixel representations being variables in a simplified linear model. This is done by generating a pool of perturbed examples z' by taking the original super-pixel representation x' and randomly selecting elements in a uniformly distributed fashion. That way, images z are obtained with some super-pixels still original and some altered according to a transform function h effectively removing the information they contained (Switching them off). Each sample z' (The binary vector indicating if super-pixels are switched off in this sample) is stored in a sample pool $\mathcal{Z}$ along with the classifier result $f(z)$ and a distance measure $\pi_x(z)$ that expresses the distance of the perturbed example z to the original image x. For images this can be the Mean Squared Error. The distance is needed for the linear model to be locally faithful to the original function $f(x)$ and thus has to be minimized. The "un-faithfulness" of the model g to the black-box model

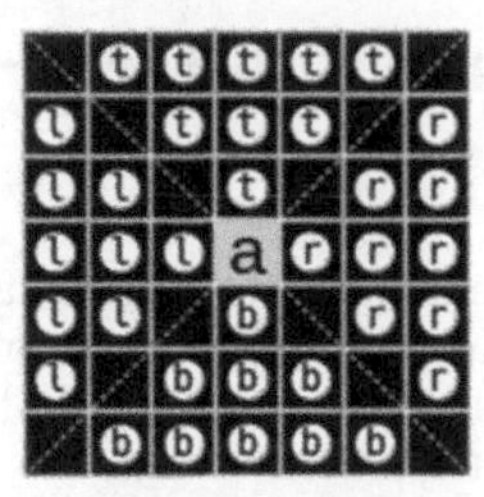

(a) All positions in the image, where a block has to be located in order to be left, right, top, or bottom of block a.

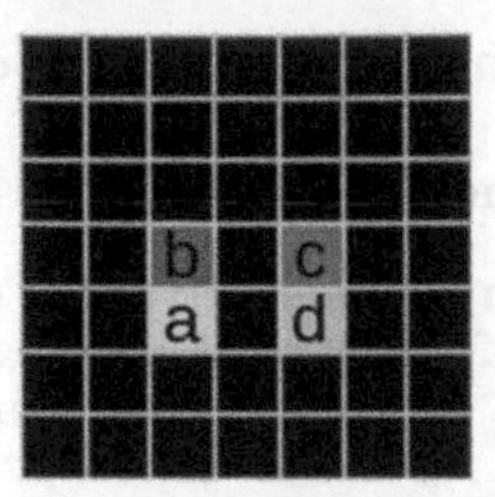

(b) for the relations **on** and **under**, illustrated with **on(b,a)**, **on(c,d)**, resp. **under(a,b)** and **under(d,c)**.

Fig. 2. Diagrams to show the different concepts of the relations used. (Color figure online)

f with respect to the distance measure $\pi_x(z)$ is expressed with the following formula [18]:

$$\mathcal{L}(f, g, \pi_x) = \sum_{z,z' \in \mathcal{Z}} \pi_x(z)(f(z) - g(z'))^2.$$

The goal is to find the coefficients $\boldsymbol{w}$ for g that minimize this un-faithfulness $\mathcal{L}$. The coefficients ultimately translate back to weights for the super-pixels. LIME uses K-Lasso to find the weights [3].

The original LIME uses the algorithm Quick Shift [25] to find super-pixel. It imposes an irregular pixel mask over the input image that segments it in terms of pixel similarity. The segmentation is performed in a 5D space consisting of the image space and the color space. Quick Shift is only one of several segmentation algorithms that are available for LIME. They all share the attribute of imposing an irregular mask over an image. In many domains, this irregularity is not wanted. For the domain used in this paper it is preferable to use a segmentation algorithm that divides an image into a regular grid with square cells.

2.2 Extraction of Image Parts and Their Relations

Based on image segmentation into a grid of super-pixels i with domain-specific cell size, a set of attributes A_i for cells and spatial relations between cells can be automatically extracted. Attributes A_i are taken from a pool of attributes $\mathcal{A}$. An example for an attribute in $\mathcal{A}$ is the mean color of i in the RGB color space. To find a human-comprehensible name, the nearest color according to the Euclidean distance in a pool of commonly known color names is assigned. Other extractable attributes are the size or the general location in the image. The coordinates of the center point of i are stored for spatial reasoning. Extracted attributes are converted into predicates for BK. The attribute that a given super-pixel `SP` is blue is represented as `has_color(SP, blue)`.

Spatial relations can be defined between pairs of super-pixels. To restrict the number of pairs, we need a pre-selection S of super-pixels that might be relevant for the concept. LIME's $\boldsymbol{w}$ describe the magnitude of relevance for either the true classification (positive weight) or the counter-class (negative weight). By introducing a user-defined constant k, we restrict how many super-pixels the selection S should contain, taking the k super-pixels with the highest values in $\boldsymbol{w}$. Spatial relations $r : S \times S$ are drawn from a pre-defined pool $\mathcal{R}$. For this work, we use the relations `left_of`, `right_of`, `top_of`, `bottom_of` as well as relations that represent an immediate adjacency in the regular grid mentioned earlier, namely `on` and `under`. Relations are defined with respect to the center coordinates of the super-pixels in S. Figure 2 sketches the underlying semantics of these relations. It is possible to include additional relations as long as they are automatically extractable and their inverses are defined in the image space. In domains with super-pixels that differ in size, a `larger` relation between super-pixels could be defined. Also, a `not_equal` relation can be considered.

2.3 Learning Rules for Relational Concepts via Aleph

To generate symbolic relational explanations for visual domains, we combine LIME's super-pixel weighting with Aleph's theory generation. The input into LIME-Aleph is an image x and a model f returning class probability estimations for x. Currently our approach is only applicable for explaining one class in contrast to all other classes, effectively re-framing the original classification as a concept learning problem. The output of LIME-Aleph is a theory T of logic rules describing the relations between the super-pixels that lead to the class decision.

LIME's explanation relies on that linear surrogate model which contains the set of super-pixels with the highest positive weights for the true class. When dealing with the question which relations contribute most to the classification, identifying the most informative super-pixels has to be replaced by identifying the most informative *pairs* of super-pixels. Instead of turning super-pixels on and off, LIME-Aleph inverts extracted relations between super-pixels and observes the effects on the classification. Algorithm 1 shows our approach. Given the selection S of super-pixels together with the extracted attributes, our approach first finds all relations $R \subseteq \mathcal{R}$ that hold between them. For every relation $r(i, j) \in R$, a new perturbed example z from the image space is created by flipping the super-pixels i and j in the image space. To generate a new example for Aleph, the resulting perturbed image is first put through the classifier f. If the estimator $f(z)$ exceeds a threshold θ for the class we want to explain, a new positive example is declared. Otherwise, the example is declared negative. All relations holding for the perturbed image are written in the BK characterizing this example. The initial positive example for Aleph is always generated for the unaltered constellation.

Algorithm 1. Explanation Generation with LIME-Aleph.

1: **Require:** Instance $x \in X$
2: **Require:** Classifier f, Selection size k, Threshold θ
3: **Require:** Attribute pool $\mathcal{A}$, Relation pool $\mathcal{R}$
4: $S \leftarrow LIME(f, x, k)$ ▷ Selection of k most important super-pixels.
5: $A \leftarrow$ extract_attribute_values$(S, \mathcal{A})$ ▷ Find all attribute values A_i for all $i \in S$.
6: $R \leftarrow$ extract_relations$(S, \mathcal{R})$ ▷ Find all relations $r : S \times S$ between all $i \in S$.
7: $E^+ \leftarrow \{\langle A, R \rangle\}$
8: $E^- \leftarrow \{\}$
9: **for each** $r(i, j) \in R$ **do**
10: $z \leftarrow$ flip_in_image(x, i, j) ▷ Flip the super-pixels in the image space.
11: $r' \leftarrow r(j, i)$ ▷ Obtain new predicate for the BK by flipping parameters.
12: $R' \leftarrow R \setminus \{r\} \cup \{r'\}$ ▷ All relations in the BK; also the altered one.
13: $R' \leftarrow calculate\_side\_effects(R', r')$ ▷ Re-calculate relations that are affected by the flipped relation.
14: $c' \leftarrow f(z)$ ▷ Obtain new estimator for the perturbed image.
15: **if** $c' \geq \theta$ **do** ▷ If estimator reaches threshold, add new positive example.
16: $E^+ \leftarrow E^+ \cup \{\langle A, R' \rangle\}$
17: **else** ▷ Else, add negative example.
18: $E^- \leftarrow E^- \cup \{\langle A, R' \rangle\}$
19: **end for**
20: $T \leftarrow$ Aleph(E^+, E^-) ▷ Obtain theory T with Aleph.
21: **return** T

3 Experiments and Results

We investigate the applicability of LIME-Aleph in a blocksworld domain consisting of differently colored squares that can be placed in a regular-grid world. For a first investigation, we decided to focus on artificially generated images rather that real world domains.

3.1 An Artificial Dataset for Relational Concepts

We implemented a generator to create a huge variety of positive and negative example images for different blocksworld concepts. All generated images are of size 32×32 pixels consisting of a single-colored red background, containing constellations of colored squares of dimension 4×4 pixels. The squares are single-colored (excluding red) with color-channel values either being set to 0.0 or 0.8. The squares are placed into the image according to an 8×8 uniform grid. Positive examples are generated by first randomly placing a reference square. Then, the other squares are placed randomly following the relation conventions shown in Fig. 2. For the experiments we restricted $\mathcal{A} = \{$`color`$\}$ with attribute values in $\{$`cyan, green, blue`$\}$ and $\mathcal{R} = \{$`left_of, right_of, top_of, bottom_of, on, under`$\}$.

3.2 Training a Black-Box Model

To obtain a black-box model for image classification, we used a small convolutional neural network [11] which we trained from scratch with commonly known best-practice hyper-parameters. The network consists of two convolution layers with kernel size 2×2 and ReLU activations. Each layer learns 16 filters to be able to robustly recognize the colored squares. After flattening the output, the convolution layers are followed by 2 fully connected layers each with a ReLU activation. The first layer consists of 256 neurons, the second one of 128 neurons. A small amount of dropout is applied past each layer to cope with potential overfitting [24]. The network does not contain a pooling layer. That way, fewer location information is lost in aggregation during the learning process which we believe is crucial for preserving spatial relationships (see [6] p. 331). For the experiments, we generated perfectly balanced datasets with 7.000 training-, 2000 validation- and 1000 test-images for both the concept and the counter-examples. We trained the networks for a maximum of 10 epochs with early stopping if the validation loss did not decrease after 5 epochs.

3.3 Experiment 1: Single Relation Concept

The concept for the first experiment can be described by the single relation that a green square is left of a blue square in an image x. Figure 3 shows two positive examples (a, b) and one negative example (c). After the full 10 epochs, the accuracy on the validation set reached `93.47%`. For Fig. 3a the classifier gave the estimator for the concept to be `89.83%`. For Fig. 3b the estimator was `94.18%`. The estimator output for belonging to the concept for Fig. 3c was `0.28%` showing that the network is able to discriminate the positive and negative examples. To generate explanations for these three images, each image is separately fed into LIME. The number of kept super-pixels k is set to 3. We choose this value for k because we were aware that there are 2 squares in the image that are distinguishable from the background. One additional super-pixel was taken to generate a richer pool for selection S containing also some background. In general, for many domains it is not that easy to estimate good values for k. So in most of the cases it is preferable to over-estimate the value to not lose information for the explanation.

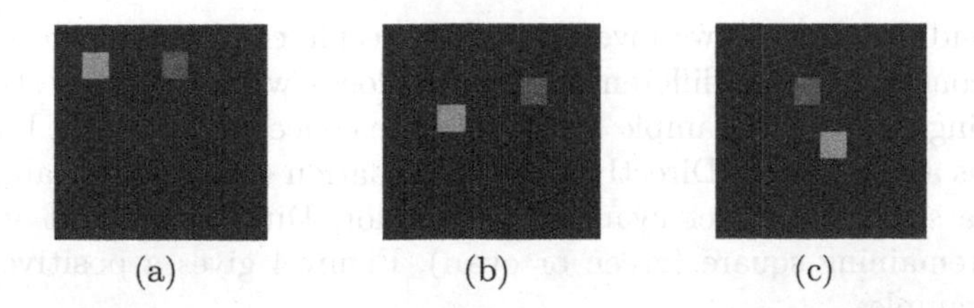

Fig. 3. Positive (a, b) and negative (c) for the first experiment. (Color figure online)

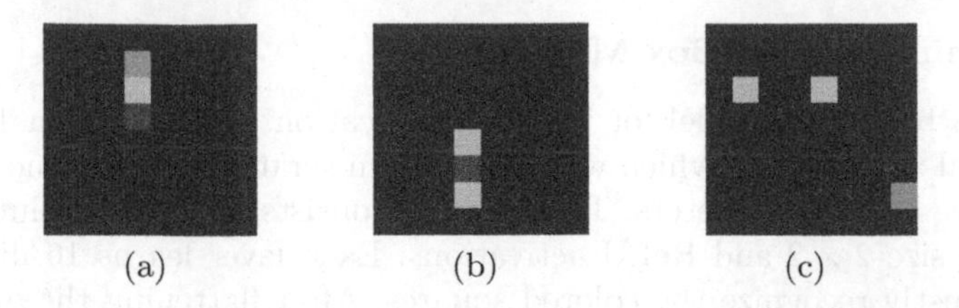

Fig. 4. Positive (*a*) and negative (*b*, *c*) for the tower experiment. (Color figure online)

Finally, a symbolic explanation is generated with LIME-Aleph. We describe the procedure for the positive example Fig. 3a. First, Algorithm 1 extracts the colors of the selected super-pixels and the relations between them. Then, all the relations get flipped one after the other to produce the example set and BK for Aleph. The original example Fig. 3a is used as the seed for a set of perturbed versions of the image. Threshold θ indicates whether the perturbed example is classified positive or negative. Based on the final validation accuracy of the trained f and from the estimator for the original Fig. 3a, it was set to $\theta = 0.8$. For example Fig. 3a 3 positive and 4 negative examples were created. From these 7 examples, Aleph induced a theory T consisting of a single rule with accuracy of 100%:

```
concept(A) :- contains(B,A), has_color(B,green), contains(C,A),
                 has_color(C,blue), left_of(B,C).
```

The learned rule accurately resembles the construction regulation of the wanted concept; a green square has to be left of a blue square in an example A. Also, this explanation matches the input image.

For Fig. 3b we used the same hyper-parameters ($k = 3, \theta = 0.8$). Again, Aleph came up with an accuracy of 100% and a rule structurally different, but conveying the same concept as the first rule:

```
concept(A) :- contains(B,A), has_color(B, blue), contains(C,A),
                has_color(C, green), left_of(C,B).
```

3.4 Experiment 2: Tower Concept

In the second experiment, we investigated a specific concept of towers. Positive examples consist of three differently colored blocks with a given restriction on their stacking order. An example belongs to the concept `tower`, if a blue square is present as a foundation. Directly on the foundation (one grid cell above) there has to be a square of either cyan or green color. Directly on that square has to be the remaining square (green or cyan). Figure 4 gives a positive and two negative examples.

We again trained the CNN for 10 epochs. The final validation accuracy was 98.70%. The original estimator for example Fig. 4a gave $f(a) = 94.88\%$. We first set $k = 3$ being the smallest selection of which we know can contain a tower.

Again setting $\theta = 0.8$, LIME-Aleph came up with 5 positive and 6 negative examples (accuracy 81.82%) and the following rule:

```
concept(A) :- contains(B,A), has_color(B,cyan), contains(C,A),
                          on(B,C).
```

This rule expresses the fact, that the cyan square can not be the foundation. When setting the selection size $k = 4$, we let an additional background super-pixel be part of S. The resulting rule is:

```
concept(A) :- contains(B,A), has_color(B,cyan), contains(C,A),
              has_color(C,blue), top_of(B,C).
```

This rule captures the fact, that a cyan block has to be above a blue one. The generated explanations are only partial representations of the intended concept. The symbolic explanations capture relevant aspects, but are too general.

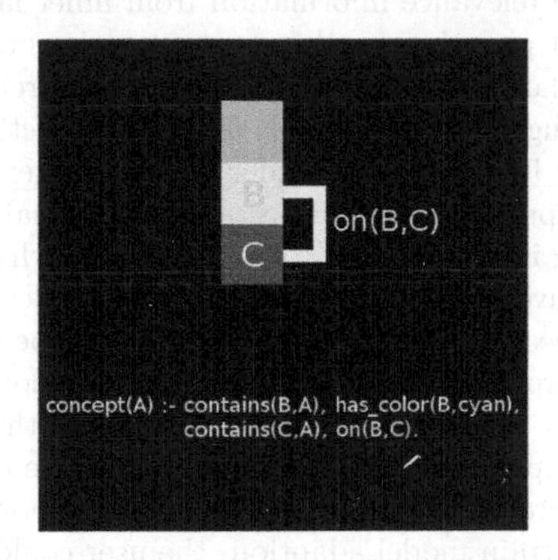

Fig. 5. An example for the combination of visual and verbal explanations. Here it is explained, why and where this particular image shows evidence for belonging to the concept tower.

4 Bringing Together Visual and Symbolic Explanations

The generated rules give explanations in symbolic form which can be re-written into verbal statements. We postulate that helpful explanations for images should relate highlighting of relevant parts of the image with explicit symbolic information of attributes and relations. In this section we give an example on how this fusion might look like. Let us take the tower example from Sect. 3.4. In Fig. 5, the output of standard LIME is given with the 3 most important super-pixels matching the expected region in the image. Additionally, the relation from the instantiated rule from the experiment for $k = 3$ is given. Since cyan is the only square that is mentioned in the rule, we take it as a reference. The relation on links the cyan square to another unknown square below. This relation is shown explicitly in the image by connecting the two squares and writing the instantiated relation.

5 Conclusion and Further Work

We proposed an approach to extract symbolic rules from images which can be used to explain classifier decisions in a more expressive way than visual highlighting alone. For a simple artificial domain we gave a proof of concept for our approach LIME-Aleph. The work presented here significantly extends [17] by providing a method of automated extraction of visual attributes and spatial relations from images. As a next step we want to also let the explanative power be evaluated by humans. Also we plan to cover real world image datasets like explaining differences between towers and houses as shown in Fig. 1. The challenge here is to come up with arbitrarily placeable segmentations that are easily interchangeable. While our algorithm relies on a regular grid, in an image "in the wild", the semantic borders of sub-objects can be irregular in shape and not easily be flipped in order to test for different relations. One idea to cope with this problems is to use relevance information from inner layers in a CNN (e.g., with LRP, [19]) to first pinpoint small important regions and sub-objects, then super-imposing a standardized selection shape (square, circle, etc.) over the pixel values to find interchangeable super-pixels for filling selection S.

In general, it might be useful to consider a variety of explanation formats to accommodate specific personal preferences and situational contexts. For example, visual highlighting is a quick way to communicate what is important while verbal explanations convey more details. Likewise, examples which prototypically represent a class and near-miss counter-examples could be used to make system decisions more transparent [1]. Explanations might also not be a one-way street. In many domains, it is an illusion that the labeling of the training is really a ground truth. For example, in medical diagnosis, there are many cases where not even experts agree. Therefore, for many practical applications, learning should be interactive [4]. To constrain model adaption, the user could mark-up that parts of an explanation which are irrelevant or wrong. Such a cooperative approach might improve the joint performance of the human-machine-partnership.

References

1. Adadi, A., Berrada, M.: Peeking inside the black-box: a survey on explainable artificial intelligence (XAI). IEEE Access **6**, 52138–52160 (2018)
2. Bansal, T., Neelakantan, A., McCallum, A.: RelNet: end-to-end modeling of entities & relations. In: NIPS Workshop on Automated Knowledge Base Construction (AKBC) (2017)
3. Efron, B., Hastie, T., Johnstone, I., Tibshirani, R.: Least angle regression. Ann. Stat. **32**(2), 407–499 (2004)
4. Fails, J.A., Olsen Jr, D.R.: Interactive machine learning. In: Proceedings of the 8th International Conference on Intelligent User Interfaces, pp. 39–45. ACM (2003)
5. Gentner, D., Markman, A.B.: Structural alignment in comparison: no difference without similarity. Psychol. Sci. **5**(3), 152–158 (1994)
6. Goodfellow, I., Bengio, Y., Courville, A.: Deep Learning. MIT Press, Cambridge (2016)

7. Graves, A., et al.: Hybrid computing using a neural network with dynamic external memory. Nature **538**, 471–476 (2016)
8. Grice, H.P.: Logic and conversation. In: Cole, P., Morgan, J. (eds.) Syntax & Semantics, vol. 3, pp. 41–58. Academic Press (1975)
9. Gunning, D.: Explainable artificial intelligence (XAI) (2017). https://www.darpa.mil/attachments/XAIProgramUpdate.pdf
10. Kazemi, S.M., Poole, D.: RelNN: a deep neural model for relational learning. In: McIlraith, S.A., Weinberger, K.Q. (eds.) Proceedings of the Thirty-Second AAAI Conference on Artificial Intelligence, AAAI 2018, New Orleans, Louisiana, USA, 2–7 February 2018, pp. 6367–6375. AAAI Press (2018)
11. Krizhevsky, A., Sutskever, I., Hinton, G.E.: ImageNet classification with deep convolutional neural networks. In: 26th Annual Conference on Neural Information Processing Systems, NIPS, Lake Tahoe, NV, 3–6 December 2012, pp. 1106–1114 (2012)
12. Mayer, R.E., Sims, V.K.: For whom is a picture worth a thousand words? Extensions of a dual-coding theory of multimedia learning. J. Educ. Psychol. **86**(3), 389–401 (1994)
13. Miller, T.: Explanation in artificial intelligence: insights from the social sciences. Artif. Intell. **267**, 1–38 (2019)
14. Muggleton, S., De Raedt, L.: Inductive logic programming: theory and methods. J. Log. Program. **19–20**, 629–679 (1994). Special Issue on 10 Years of Logic Programming
15. Muggleton, S.H., Lin, D., Tamaddoni-Nezhad, A.: Meta-interpretive learning of higher-order dyadic datalog: predicate invention revisited. Mach. Learn. **100**(1), 49–73 (2015). https://doi.org/10.1007/s10994-014-5471-y
16. Muggleton, S.H., Schmid, U., Zeller, C., Tamaddoni-Nezhad, A., Besold, T.: Ultra-strong machine learning: comprehensibility of programs learned with ILP. Mach. Learn. **107**(7), 1119–1140 (2018). https://doi.org/10.1007/s10994-018-5707-3
17. Rabold, J., Siebers, M., Schmid, U.: Explaining black-box classifiers with ILP – empowering LIME with aleph to approximate non-linear decisions with relational rules. In: Riguzzi, F., Bellodi, E., Zese, R. (eds.) ILP 2018. LNCS (LNAI), vol. 11105, pp. 105–117. Springer, Cham (2018). https://doi.org/10.1007/978-3-319-99960-9_7
18. Ribeiro, M.T., Singh, S., Guestrin, C.: Why should i trust you? Explaining the predictions of any classifier. In: Proceedings of the 22nd ACM SIGKDD International Conference on Knowledge Discovery and Data Mining, pp. 1135–1144. ACM (2016)
19. Samek, W., Wiegand, T., Müller, K.R.: Explainable artificial intelligence: Understanding, visualizing and interpreting deep learning models. ITU J. ICT Discov. **1**(1), 39–48 (2018). Special Issue 1 - The Impact of Artificial Intelligence (AI) on Communication Networks and Services
20. Siebers, M., Schmid, U.: Please delete that! Why should i? Explaining learned irrelevance classifications of digital objects. KI **33**(1), 35–44 (2019). https://doi.org/10.1007/s13218-018-0565-5
21. Siebers, M., Schmid, U., Seuß, D., Kunz, M., Lautenbacher, S.: Characterizing facial expressions by grammars of action unit sequences-a first investigation using ABL. Inf. Sci. **329**, 866–875 (2016)
22. Srinivasan, A.: The Aleph Manual (2004). http://www.cs.ox.ac.uk/activities/machinelearning/Aleph/

23. Srinivasan, A., Muggleton, S.H., Sternberg, M.J., King, R.D.: Theories for mutagenicity: a study in first-order and feature-based induction. Artif. Intell. **85**(1–2), 277–299 (1996)
24. Srivastava, N., Hinton, G., Krizhevsky, A., Sutskever, I., Salakhutdinov, R.: Dropout: a simple way to prevent neural networks from overfitting. J. Mach. Learn. Res. **15**(1), 1929–1958 (2014)
25. Vedaldi, A., Soatto, S.: Quick shift and kernel methods for mode seeking. In: Forsyth, D., Torr, P., Zisserman, A. (eds.) ECCV 2008. LNCS, vol. 5305, pp. 705–718. Springer, Heidelberg (2008). https://doi.org/10.1007/978-3-540-88693-8_52

Quantifying Model Complexity via Functional Decomposition for Better Post-hoc Interpretability

Christoph Molnar(✉), Giuseppe Casalicchio, and Bernd Bischl

Department of Statistics, LMU Munich, Ludwigstr. 33, 80539 Munich, Germany
christoph.molnar@stat.uni-muenchen.de

Abstract. Post-hoc model-agnostic interpretation methods such as partial dependence plots can be employed to interpret complex machine learning models. While these interpretation methods can be applied regardless of model complexity, they can produce misleading and verbose results if the model is too complex, especially w.r.t. feature interactions. To quantify the complexity of arbitrary machine learning models, we propose model-agnostic complexity measures based on functional decomposition: number of features used, interaction strength and main effect complexity. We show that post-hoc interpretation of models that minimize the three measures is more reliable and compact. Furthermore, we demonstrate the application of these measures in a multi-objective optimization approach which simultaneously minimizes loss and complexity.

Keywords: Model complexity · Interpretable machine learning · Explainable AI · Accumulated Local Effects · Multi-objective optimization

1 Introduction

Machine learning models are optimized for predictive performance, but it is often required to understand models, e.g., to debug them, gain trust in the predictions, or satisfy regulatory requirements. Many post-hoc interpretation methods either quantify effects of features on predictions, compute feature importances, or explain individual predictions, see [17,24] for more comprehensive overviews. While model-agnostic post-hoc interpretation methods can be applied regardless of model complexity [30], their reliability and compactness deteriorates when models use a high number of features, have strong feature interactions and complex feature main effects. Therefore, model complexity and interpretability are deeply intertwined and reducing complexity can help to make model interpretation more reliable and compact. Model-agnostic complexity measures are needed to strike a balance between interpretability and predictive performance [4,31].

Contributions. We propose and implement three model-agnostic measures of machine learning model complexity which are related to post-hoc interpretability. To our best knowledge, these are the first model-agnostic measures that

P. Cellier and K. Driessens (Eds.): ECML PKDD 2019 Workshops, CCIS 1167, pp. 193–204, 2020.
https://doi.org/10.1007/978-3-030-43823-4_17

describe the global interaction strength, complexity of main effects and number of features. We apply the measures to different datasets and machine learning models. We argue that minimizing these three measures improves the reliability and compactness of post-hoc interpretation methods. Finally, we illustrate the use of our proposed measures in multi-objective optimization.

2 Related Work and Background

In this section, we introduce the notation, review related work, and describe the functional decomposition on which we base the proposed complexity measures.

Notation: We consider machine learning prediction functions $f : \mathbb{R}^p \mapsto \mathbb{R}$, where $f(x)$ is a prediction (e.g., regression output or a classification score). For the decomposition of f, we write $f_S : \mathbb{R}^{|S|} \mapsto \mathbb{R}$, $S \subseteq \{1, \ldots, p\}$, to denote a function that maps a vector $x_S \in \mathbb{R}^{|S|}$ with a subset of features to a marginal prediction. If subset S contains a single feature j, we write f_j. We refer to the training data of the machine learning model with the tuples $\mathcal{D} = \{(x^{(i)}, y^{(i)})\}_{i=1}^n$ and refer to the value of the j-th feature from the i-th instance as $x_j^{(i)}$. We write X_j to refer to the j-th feature as a random variable.

Complexity and Interpretability Measures: In the literature, model complexity and (lack of) model interpretability are often equated. Many complexity measures are model-specific, i.e., only models of the same class can be compared (e.g., decision trees). Model size is often used as a measure for interpretability (e.g., number of decision rules, tree depth, number of non-zero coefficients) [3,16,20,22,31–34]. Akaikes Information Criterion (AIC) and the Bayesian Information Criterion (BIC) are more widely applicable measures for the trade-off between goodness of fit and degrees of freedom. In [26], the authors propose model-agnostic measures of model stability. In [27], the authors propose explanation fidelity and stability of local explanation models. Further approaches measure interpretability based on experimental studies with humans, e.g., whether humans can predict the outcome of the model [8,13,20,28,35].

Functional Decomposition: Any high-dimensional prediction function can be decomposed into a sum of components with increasing dimensionality:

$$f(x) = \overbrace{f_0}^{\text{Intercept}} + \overbrace{\sum_{j=1}^{p} f_j(x_j)}^{\text{1st order effects}} + \overbrace{\sum_{j<k}^{p} f_{jk}(x_j, x_k)}^{\text{2nd order effects}} + \ldots + \overbrace{f_{1,\ldots,p}(x_1, \ldots, x_p)}^{\text{p-th order effect}} \quad (1)$$

This decomposition is only unique with additional constraints regarding the components. Accumulated Local Effects (ALE) were proposed in [1] as a tool for visualizing feature effects (e.g., Fig. 1) and as unique decomposition of the prediction function with components $f_S = f_{S,ALE}$. The ALE decomposition is unique under an orthogonality-like property described in [1].

The ALE main effect $f_{j,ALE}$ of a feature $x_j, j \in \{1, \dots, p\}$ for a prediction function f is defined as

$$f_{j,ALE}(x_j) = \int_{z_{0,j}}^{x_j} \mathbb{E}\left[\frac{\partial f(X_1, \dots, X_p)}{\partial X_j}\middle| X_j = z_j\right] dz_j - c_j \tag{2}$$

Here, $z_{0,j}$ is a lower bound of X_j (usually the minimum of x_j) and the expectation $\mathbb{E}$ is computed conditional on the value for x_j and over the marginal distribution of all other features. The constant c_j is chosen so that the mean of $f_{j,ALE}(x_j)$ with respect to the marginal distribution of X_j is zero, so that the ALE components sum to the full prediction function. By integrating the expected derivative of f with respect to X_j the effect of x_j on the prediction function f is isolated from the effects of all other features. ALE main effects are estimated with finite differences, i.e., access to the gradient of a prediction function is not required (see [1]). We base our proposed measures on the ALE decomposition, because ALE are computationally cheap (worst case $O(n)$ per main effect), they can be computed sequentially instead of simultaneously, they do not require knowledge of the joint distribution, and several software implementations exist [2,25].

3 Functional Complexity

In this section, we motivate complexity measures based on functional decomposition. Based on Eq. 1, we decompose the prediction function into a constant (estimated as $f_0 = \frac{1}{n}\sum_{i=1}^{n} f(x^{(i)})$), main effects (estimated by ALE), and a remainder term containing interactions (i.e., the difference between the full model and constant + main effects).

$$\underbrace{f(x) = f_0 + \sum_{j=1}^{p} \overbrace{f_{j,ALE}(x_j)}^{\text{MEC: How complex?}} + \overbrace{IA(x)}^{\text{IAS: Interaction strength?}}}_{\text{NF: How many features were used?}} \tag{3}$$

This arrangement of components emphasizes a decomposition of the prediction function into a main effect model and an interaction remainder. We can analyze how well the main effect model itself approximates f by looking at the magnitude of the interaction measure IAS. The average main effect complexity (MEC) captures how many parameters are needed to describe the one-dimensional main effects on average. The number of features used (NF) describes how many features were used in the full prediction function.

3.1 Number of Features (NF)

We propose an approach based on feature permutation to determine how many features are used by a model. We regard features as "used" when changing a feature changes the prediction. If available, the model-specific number of features is preferable. The model-agnostic version is useful when the prediction function is only accessible via API or when the machine learning pipeline is complex.

The proposed procedure is formally described in Algorithm 1. To estimate whether the j-th feature was used, we sample instances from data $\mathcal{D}$, replace their j-th feature values with random values from the distribution of X_j (e.g., by sampling x_j from other instances from $\mathcal{D}$), and observe whether the predictions change. If the prediction of any sample changes, the feature was used.

Algorithm 1. Number of Features Used (NF)

Input: Number of samples M, data $\mathcal{D}$
1 NF = 0
2 **for** $j \in 1, \ldots, p$ **do**
3 Draw M instances $\{x^{(m)}\}_{m=1}^M$ from dataset $\mathcal{D}$
4 Create $\{x^{(m)*}\}_{m=1}^M$ as a copy of $\{x^{(m)}\}_{m=1}^M$
5 **for** $m \in 1, \ldots, M$ **do**
6 Sample $x_j^{(new)}$ from $\{x_j^{(i)}\}_{i=1}^n$ with the constraint that $x_j^{(new)} \neq x_j^{(m)}$
7 Set $x_j^{(m)*} = x_j^{(new)}$
8 **if** $f(x^{(m)*}) \neq f(x^{(m)})$ *for any* $m \in \{1, \ldots, M\}$ **then** $NF = NF + 1$.
9 **return** NF

We tested the NF heuristic with the Boston Housing data. We trained decision trees (CART) with maximum depths $\in \{1, 2, 10\}$ leading to 1, 2 and 4 features used and an L1-regularized linear model with penalty $\lambda \in \{10, 5, 2, 1, 0.1, 0.001\}$ leading to 0, 2, 3, 4, 11 and 13 features used. For each model, we estimated NF with sample sizes $M \in \{10, 50, 500\}$ and repeated each estimation 100 times. For the elastic net models, NF was always equal to the number of non-zero weights. For CART, the mean absolute differences between NF and number of features used in the trees were 0.300 ($M = 10$), 0.020 ($M = 50$) and 0.000 ($M = 500$).

3.2 Interaction Strength (IAS)

Interactions between features mean that the prediction cannot be expressed as a sum of independent feature effects, but the effect of a feature depends on values of other features [24]. We propose to measure interaction strength as the scaled approximation error between the ALE main effect model and the prediction function f. Based on the ALE decomposition, the ALE main effect model is defined as the sum of first order ALE effects:

$$f_{ALE1st}(x) = f_0 + f_{1,ALE}(x_1) + \ldots + f_{p,ALE}(x_p)$$

We define interaction strength as the approximation error measured with loss L:

$$IAS = \frac{\mathbb{E}(L(f, f_{ALE1st}))}{\mathbb{E}(L(f, f_0))} \geq 0 \tag{4}$$

Here, f_0 is the mean of the predictions and can be interpreted as the functional decomposition where all feature effects are set to zero. IAS with the $L2$ loss equals 1 minus the R-squared measure, where the true targets y_i are replaced with $f(x^{(i)})$.

$$IAS = \frac{\sum_{i=1}^{n}(f(x^{(i)}) - f_{ALE1st}(x^{(i)}))^2}{\sum_{i=1}^{n}(f(x^{(i)}) - f_0)^2} = 1 - R^2$$

If $IAS = 0$, then $L(f, f_{ALE1st}) = 0$, which means that the first order ALE model perfectly approximates f and the model has no interactions.

3.3 Main Effect Complexity (MEC)

To determine the average shape complexity of ALE main effects $f_{j,ALE}$, we propose the main effect complexity (MEC) measure. For a single ALE main effect, we define MEC_j as the number of parameters needed to approximate the curve with piece-wise linear models. For the entire model, MEC is the average MEC_j over all main effects, weighted with their variance. Figure 1 shows an ALE plot (= main effect) and its approximation with two linear segments.

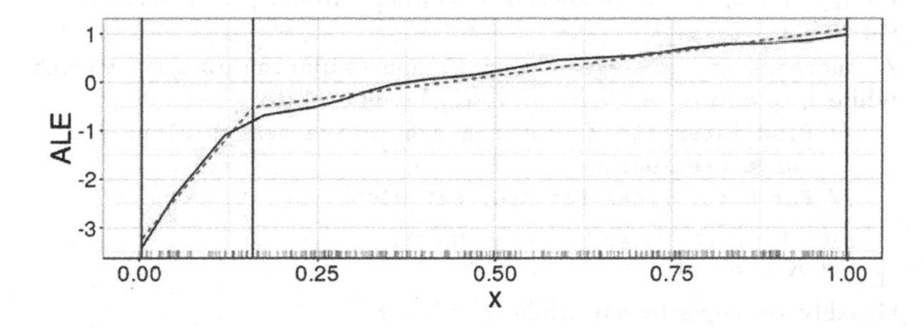

Fig. 1. ALE curve (solid line) approximated by two linear segments (dotted line).

We use piece-wise linear regression to approximate the ALE curve. Within the segments, linear models are estimated with ordinary least squares. The breakpoints that define the segments are found by greedy and exhaustive search along the interval boundaries of the ALE curve. Greedy here means that we first optimize the first breakpoint, then the second breakpoint with the first breakpoint fixed and so on. We measure the degrees of freedom as the number of non-zero coefficients for intercepts and slopes of the linear models. The approximation allows some error, e.g., an almost linear main effect may have $\text{MEC}_j = 1$, even if dozens of parameters would be needed to describe it perfectly. The approximation quality is measured with R-squared (R^2), i.e., the proportion of variance of $f_{j,ALE}$ that is explained by the approximation with linear segments. An approximation has to reach an $R^2 \geq 1 - \epsilon$, where ϵ is the user defined maximum approximation error. We also introduced parameter max_{seg}, the maximum number of segments. In the case that an approximation cannot reach an $R^2 \geq 1 - \epsilon$

with a given max_{seg}, MEC$_j$ is computed with the maximum number of segments. The selected maximum approximation error ϵ should be small, but not too small. We found ϵ between 0.01 and 0.1 visually meaningful (i.e. a subjectively good approximation) and used $\epsilon = 0.05$ throughout the paper. We apply a post-processing step that greedily sets slopes of the linear segments to zero, as long as $R^2 \in \{1 - \epsilon, 1\}$. The post-processing potentially decreases the MEC$_j$, especially for models with constant segments like decision trees. MEC$_j$ is averaged over all features to obtain the global main effect complexity. Each MEC$_j$ is weighted with the variance of the corresponding ALE main effect to give more weight to features that contribute more to the prediction. Algorithm 2 describes the MEC computation in detail.

Algorithm 2. Main Effect Complexity (MEC).

Input: Model f, approximation error ϵ, max. segments max_{seg}, data $\mathcal{D}$
1 Define $R^2(g_j, f_{j,ALE}) := \sum_{i=1}^n (g_j(x_j^{(i)}) - f_{j,ALE}(x_j^{(i)}))^2 / \sum_{i=1}^n (f_{j,ALE}(x_j^{(i)}))^2$
2 **for** $j \in \{1, \ldots, p\}$ **do**
3 Estimate $f_{j,ALE}$
`// Approximate ALE with linear model`
4 Fit $g_j(x_j) = \beta_0 + \beta_1 x_j$ predicting $f_{j,ALE}(x_j^{(i)})$ from $x_j^{(i)}$, $i \in 1, \ldots, n$
5 Set $K = 1$
`// Increase nr. of segments until approximation is good enough`
6 **while** $K < max_{seg}$ *AND* $R^2(g_j, f_{j,ALE}) < (1 - \epsilon)$ **do**
`// Find intervals` Z_k `through exhaustive search along ALE curve breakpoints`
`// For categorical feature, set slopes` $\beta_{1,k}$ `to zero`
7 $g_j(x_j) = \sum_{k=1}^{K+1} \mathbb{I}_{x_j \in Z_k} \cdot (\beta_{0,k} + \beta_{1,k} x_j)$
8 Set $K = K + 1$
9 Greedily set slopes to zero while $R^2 > 1 - \epsilon$
`// Sum of non-zero coefficients minus first intercept`
10 $MEC_j = K + \sum_{k=1}^{K} \mathbb{I}_{\beta_{1,k} > 0} - 1$
11 $V_j = \frac{1}{n} \sum_{i=1}^n (f_{j,ALE}(x^{(i)}))^2$
12 **return** $MEC = \frac{1}{\sum_{j=1}^p V_j} \sum_{j=1}^p V_j \cdot MEC_j$

4 Application of Complexity Measures

In the following experiment, we train various machine learning models on different prediction tasks and compute the model complexities. The goal is to analyze how the complexity measures behave across different datasets and models. The dataset are: Bike Rentals [10] (n = 731; 3 numerical, 6 categorical features), Boston Housing (n = 506; 12 numerical, 1 categorical features), (down-sampled) Superconductivity [18] (n = 2000; 81 numerical, 0 categorical features) and Abalone [9] (n = 4177; 7 numerical, 1 categorical features).

Table 1. Model performance and complexity on 4 regression tasks for various learners: linear models (lm), cross-validated regularized linear models (cvglmnet), kernel support vector machine (ksvm), random forest (rf), gradient boosted generalized additive model (gamboost), decision tree (cart) and decision tree with depth 2 (cart2).

Learner	Bike				Boston housing				Superconductivity				Abalone			
	MSE	MEC	IAS	NF	MSE	MEC	IAS	NF	MSE	MEC	IAS	NF	MSE	MEC	IAS	NF
cart	905974	1.2	0.07	6	26.6	1.9	0.12	4	329.0	1.0	0.27	8	5.9	2.8	0.09	3
cart2	1307619	1.0	0.01	2	34.6	1.7	0.02	2	431.4	1.0	0.27	3	6.6	3.0	0.02	1
cvglmnet	686320	1.2	0.00	9	27.7	1.0	0.00	9	349.3	1.0	0.00	45	5.2	1.0	0.00	7
gamboost	531245	1.6	0.00	8	16.5	2.5	0.00	10	362.1	2.1	0.00	17	5.3	1.1	0.00	4
ksvm	403762	1.6	0.04	8	16.4	1.7	0.09	13	268.5	2.2	0.22	81	4.6	1.0	0.11	8
lm	636956	1.5	0.00	9	23.0	1.0	0.00	13	330.2	1.0	0.00	81	4.9	1.0	0.00	8
rf	460362	1.8	0.06	9	12.0	2.4	0.11	13	180.8	2.9	0.21	81	4.6	1.7	0.29	8

Table 1 shows performance and complexity of the models. As desired, the main effect complexity for linear models is 1 (except when categorical features with 2+ categories are present as in the bike data), and higher for more flexible methods like random forests. The interaction strength (IAS) is zero for additive models (boosted GAM, (regularized) linear models). Across datasets we observe that the underlying complexity measured as the range of MEC and IAS across the models varies. The bike dataset seems to be adequately described by only additive effects, since even random forests, which often model strong interactions show low interaction strength here. In contrast, the superconductivity dataset is better explained by models with more interactions. For the abalone dataset there are two models with low MSE: the support vector machine and the random forest. We might prefer the SVM, since main effects can be described with single numbers ($MEC = 1$) and interaction strength is low.

5 Improving Post-hoc Interpretation

Minimizing the number of features (NF), the interaction strength (IAS), and the main effect complexity (MEC) improves reliability and compactness of post-hoc interpretation methods such as partial dependence plots, ALE plots, feature importance, interaction effects and local surrogate models.

Fewer Features, More Compact Interpretations. Minimizing the number of features improves the readability of post-hoc analysis results. The computational complexity and output size of most interpretation methods scales with $O(\text{NF})$, like feature effect plots [1,14] or feature importance [6,11]. As demonstrated in Table 2, a model with fewer features has a more compact representation. If additionally $IAS = 0$, the ALE main effects fully characterize the prediction function. Interpretation methods that analyze 2-way feature interactions scale with $O(\text{NF}^2)$. A complete functional decomposition requires to estimate $\sum_{k=1}^{NF} \binom{NF}{k}$ components which has a computational complexity of $O(2^{NF})$.

Less Interaction, More Reliable Feature Effects. Feature effect plots such as partial dependence plots and ALE plots visualize the marginal relationship between a feature and the prediction. The estimated effects are averages across instances. The effects can vary greatly for individual instances and even have opposite directions when the model includes feature interactions.

In the following simulation, we trained three models with different capabilities of modeling interactions between features: a linear regression model, a support vector machine (radial basis kernel, C = 0.05), and gradient boosted trees. We simulated 500 data points with 4 features and a continuous target based on [15]. Figure 2 shows an increasing interaction strength depending on the model used. More interaction means that the feature effect curves become a less reliable summary of the model behavior.

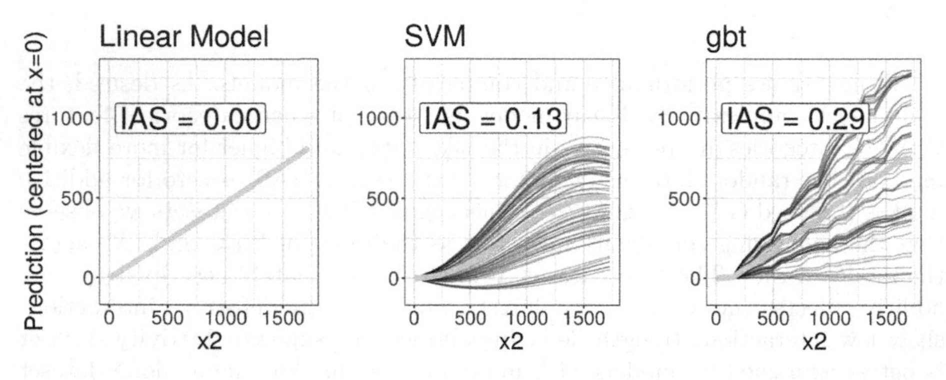

Fig. 2. The higher the interaction strength in a model (IAS increases from left to right), the less representative the partial dependence plot (light thick line) becomes for individual instances represented by their individual conditional expectation curves (dark thin lines).

The Less Complex the Main Effects, the Better Summarizable. In linear models, a feature effect can be expressed by a single number, the regression coefficient. If effects are non-linear the method of choice is visualization [1,14]. Summarizing the effects with a single number (e.g., using average marginal effects [23]) can be misleading, e.g., the average effect might be zero for U-shaped feature effects. As a by-product of MEC, there is a third option: Instead of reporting a single number, the coefficients of the segmented linear model can be reported. Minimizing MEC means preferring models with main effects that can be described with fewer coefficients, offering a more compact model description.

6 Application: Multi-objective Optimization

We demonstrate model selection for performance and complexity in a multi-objective optimization approach. For this example, we predict wine quality (scale from 0 to 10) [7] from the wines physical-chemical properties such as alcohol and residual sugar of 4870 white wines. It is difficult to know the desired compromise between model complexity and performance before modeling the data. A solution is multi-objective optimization [12]. We suggest searching over a wide spectrum of model classes and hyperparameter settings, which allows to select a suitable compromise between model complexity and performance.

We used the mlrMBO model-based optimization framework [19] with ParEGO [21] (500 iterations) to find the best models based on four objectives: number of features used (NF), main effect complexity (MEC), interaction strength (IAS) and cross-validated mean absolute error (MAE) (5-fold cross-validated). We optimized over the space of following model classes (and hyperparameters): **CART** (maximum tree-depth and complexity parameter cp), **support vector machine** (cost C and inverse kernel width sigma), **elastic net** regression (regularization alpha and penalization lambda), **gradient boosted trees** (maximum depth, number of iterations), **gradient boosted generalized additive model** (number of iterations nrounds) and **random forest** (number of split features mtry).

Results. The multi-objective optimization resulted in 27 models. The measures had the following ranges: MAE 0.41–0.63, number of features 1–11, mean effect complexity 1–9 and interaction strength 0–0.71. For a more informative visualization, we propose to visualize the main effects together with the measures in Table 2. The selected models show different trade-offs between the measures.

Table 2. A selection of four models from the Pareto optimal set, along with their ALE main effect curves. From left to right, the columns show models with (1) lowest MAE, (2) lowest MAE when $MEC = 1$, (3) lowest MAE when $IAS = \leq 0.2$, and (4) lowest MAE with $NF \leq 7$.

	gbt (maxdepth:8, nrounds:269)	svm (C:23.6979, sigma:0.0003)	gbt (maxdepth:3, nrounds:98)	CART (maxdepth:14, cp:0.0074)
MAE	0.41	0.58	0.52	0.59
MEC	4.2	1	4.5	2
IAS	0.64	0	0.2	0.2
NF	11	11	11	4
fixed.acidity				
volatile.acidity				
citric.acid				
residual.sugar				
chlorides				
free.sulfur.dioxide				
total.sulfur.dioxide				
density				
pH				
sulphates				
alcohol				

7 Discussion

We proposed three measures for machine learning model complexity based on functional decomposition: number of features used, interaction strength and main effect complexity. Due to their model-agnostic nature, the measures allow model selection and comparison across different types of models and they can be used as objectives in automated machine learning frameworks. This also includes "white-box" models: For example, the interaction strength of interaction terms in a linear model or the complexity of smooth effects in generalized additive models can be quantified and compared across models. We argued that minimizing these measures for a machine learning model improves its post-hoc interpretation. We demonstrated that the measures can be optimized directly with multi-objective optimization to make the trade-off between performance and post-hoc interpretability explicit.

Limitations. The proposed decomposition of the prediction function and definition of the complexity measures will not be appropriate in every situation. For example, all higher order effects are combined into a single interaction strength measure that does not distinguish between two-way interactions and higher order interactions. However, the framework of accumulated local effect decomposition allows to estimate higher order effects and to construct different interaction measures. The main effect complexity measure only considers linear segments but not, e.g., seasonal components or other structures. Furthermore, the complexity measures quantify machine learning models from a functional point of view and ignore the structure of the model (e.g., whether it can be represented by a tree). For example, main effect complexity and interaction strength measures can be large for short decision trees (e.g. in Table 1).

Implementation. The code for this paper is available at https://github.com/compstat-lmu/paper_2019_iml_measures. For the examples and experiments we relied on the mlr package [5] in R [29].

Acknowledgements. This work is funded by the Bavarian State Ministry of Science and the Arts in the framework of the Centre Digitisation.Bavaria (ZD.B) and supported by the German Federal Ministry of Education and Research (BMBF) under Grant No. 01IS18036A. The authors of this work take full responsibilities for its content.

References

1. Apley, D.: Visualizing the effects of predictor variables in black box supervised learning models. arXiv preprint arXiv:1612.08468 (2016)
2. Apley, D.: ALEPlot: accumulated local effects (ALE) plots and partial dependence (PD) plots. CRAN (2017)
3. Askira-Gelman, I.: Knowledge discovery: comprehensibility of the results. In: Proceedings of the Thirty-First Hawaii International Conference on System Sciences, vol. 5, pp. 247–255. IEEE (1998)
4. Bibal, A., Frénay, B.: Interpretability of machine learning models and representations: an introduction. In: Proceedings on ESANN, pp. 77–82 (2016)

5. Bischl, B., et al.: mlr: Machine learning in R. J. Mach. Learn. Res. **17**(170), 1–5 (2016)
6. Casalicchio, G., Molnar, C., Bischl, B.: Visualizing the feature importance for black box models. In: Berlingerio, M., Bonchi, F., Gärtner, T., Hurley, N., Ifrim, G. (eds.) ECML PKDD 2018. LNCS (LNAI), vol. 11051, pp. 655–670. Springer, Cham (2019). https://doi.org/10.1007/978-3-030-10925-7_40
7. Cortez, P., Cerdeira, A., Almeida, F., Matos, T., Reis, J.: Modeling wine preferences by data mining from physicochemical properties. Decis. Support Syst. **47**(4), 547–553 (2009)
8. Dhurandhar, A., Iyengar, V., Luss, R., Shanmugam, K.: TIP: typifying the interpretability of procedures. arXiv preprint arXiv:1706.02952 (2017)
9. Dua, D., Graff, C.: UCI machine learning repository (2017). http://archive.ics.uci.edu/ml
10. Fanaee-T, H., Gama, J.: Event labeling combining ensemble detectors and background knowledge. Prog. Artif. Intell. **2**, 113–127 (2014). https://doi.org/10.1007/s13748-013-0040-3
11. Fisher, A., Rudin, C., Dominici, F.: All models are wrong but many are useful: variable importance for black-box, proprietary, or misspecified prediction models, using model class reliance. arXiv preprint arXiv:1801.01489 (2018)
12. Freitas, A.A.: Comprehensible classification models: a position paper. ACM SIGKDD Explor. Newsl. **15**(1), 1–10 (2014)
13. Friedler, S.A., Roy, C.D., Scheidegger, C., Slack, D.: Assessing the local interpretability of machine learning models. arXiv preprint arXiv:1902.03501 (2019)
14. Friedman, J.H.: Greedy function approximation: a gradient boosting machine. Ann. Stat. **29**(5), 1189–1232 (2001)
15. Friedman, J.H., et al.: Multivariate adaptive regression splines. Ann. Stat. **19**(1), 1–67 (1991)
16. Fürnkranz, J., Gamberger, D., Lavrač, N.: Foundations of Rule Learning. Springer, Heidelberg (2012). https://doi.org/10.1007/978-3-540-75197-7
17. Guidotti, R., Monreale, A., Ruggieri, S., Turini, F., Giannotti, F., Pedreschi, D.: A survey of methods for explaining black box models. ACM Comput. Surv. (CSUR) **51**(5), 93 (2018)
18. Hamidieh, K.: A data-driven statistical model for predicting the critical temperature of a superconductor. Comput. Mater. Sci. **154**, 346–354 (2018)
19. Horn, D., Bischl, B.: Multi-objective parameter configuration of machine learning algorithms using model-based optimization. In: 2016 IEEE Symposium Series on Computational Intelligence (SSCI), pp. 1–8. IEEE (2016)
20. Huysmans, J., Dejaeger, K., Mues, C., Vanthienen, J., Baesens, B.: An empirical evaluation of the comprehensibility of decision table, tree and rule based predictive models. Decis. Support Syst. **51**(1), 141–154 (2011)
21. Knowles, J.: ParEGO: a hybrid algorithm with on-line landscape approximation for expensive multiobjective optimization problems. IEEE Trans. Evol. Comput. **10**(1), 50–66 (2006)
22. Lakkaraju, H., Kamar, E., Caruana, R., Leskovec, J.: Interpretable & explorable approximations of black box models. arXiv preprint arXiv:1707.01154 (2017)
23. Leeper, T.J.: Interpreting regression results using average marginal effects with R's margins. CRAN (2017)
24. Molnar, C.: Interpretable Machine Learning (2019). https://christophm.github.io/interpretable-ml-book/
25. Molnar, C., Bischl, B., Casalicchio, G.: iml: An R package for interpretable machine learning. JOSS **3**(26), 786 (2018)

26. Philipp, M., Rusch, T., Hornik, K., Strobl, C.: Measuring the stability of results from supervised statistical learning. J. Comput. Graph. Stat. **27**(4), 685–700 (2018)
27. Plumb, G., Al-Shedivat, M., Xing, E., Talwalkar, A.: Regularizing black-box models for improved interpretability. arXiv preprint arXiv:1902.06787 (2019)
28. Poursabzi-Sangdeh, F., Goldstein, D.G., Hofman, J.M., Vaughan, J.W., Wallach, H.: Manipulating and measuring model interpretability. arXiv preprint arXiv:1802.07810 (2018)
29. R Core Team: R: A Language and Environment for Statistical Computing. R Foundation for Statistical Computing, Vienna, Austria (2018)
30. Ribeiro, M.T., Singh, S., Guestrin, C.: Model-agnostic interpretability of machine learning. arXiv preprint arXiv:1606.05386 (2016)
31. Rüping, S., et al.: Learning interpretable models. University in Dortmund (2006). http://d-nb.info/997491736
32. Schielzeth, H.: Simple means to improve the interpretability of regression coefficients. Methods Ecol. Evol. **1**(2), 103–113 (2010)
33. Ustun, B., Rudin, C.: Supersparse linear integer models for optimized medical scoring systems. Mach. Learn. **102**(3), 349–391 (2015). https://doi.org/10.1007/s10994-015-5528-6
34. Yang, H., Rudin, C., Seltzer, M.: Scalable Bayesian rule lists. In: Proceedings of the 34th International Conference on Machine Learning, vol. 70, pp. 3921–3930. JMLR.org (2017)
35. Zhou, Q., Liao, F., Mou, C., Wang, P.: Measuring interpretability for different types of machine learning models. In: Ganji, M., Rashidi, L., Fung, B.C.M., Wang, C. (eds.) PAKDD 2018. LNCS (LNAI), vol. 11154, pp. 295–308. Springer, Cham (2018). https://doi.org/10.1007/978-3-030-04503-6_29

Sampling, Intervention, Prediction, Aggregation: A Generalized Framework for Model-Agnostic Interpretations

Christian A. Scholbeck(✉), Christoph Molnar, Christian Heumann, Bernd Bischl, and Giuseppe Casalicchio

Department of Statistics, Ludwig-Maximilians-University Munich, Ludwigstr. 33, 80539 Munich, Germany
christian.scholbeck@stat.uni-muenchen.de

Abstract. Model-agnostic interpretation techniques allow us to explain the behavior of any predictive model. Due to different notations and terminology, it is difficult to see how they are related. A unified view on these methods has been missing. We present the generalized SIPA (sampling, intervention, prediction, aggregation) framework of work stages for model-agnostic interpretations and demonstrate how several prominent methods for feature effects can be embedded into the proposed framework. Furthermore, we extend the framework to feature importance computations by pointing out how variance-based and performance-based importance measures are based on the same work stages. The SIPA framework reduces the diverse set of model-agnostic techniques to a single methodology and establishes a common terminology to discuss them in future work.

Keywords: Interpretable Machine Learning · Explainable AI · Feature Effect · Feature Importance · Model-Agnostic · Partial Dependence

1 Introduction and Related Work

There has been an ongoing debate about the lacking interpretability of machine learning (ML) models. As a result, researchers have put in great efforts developing techniques to create insights into the workings of predictive black box models. Interpretable machine learning [15] serves as an umbrella term for all interpretation methods in ML. We make the following distinctions:

(i) *Feature effects or feature importance:* Feature effects indicate the direction and magnitude of change in predicted outcome due to changes in feature values. Prominent methods include the individual conditional expectation (ICE) [9] and partial dependence (PD) [8], accumulated local effects (ALE) [1], Shapley values [19] and local interpretable model-agnostic explanations (LIME) [17]. The feature importance measures the importance of a feature

P. Cellier and K. Driessens (Eds.): ECML PKDD 2019 Workshops, CCIS 1167, pp. 205–216, 2020.
https://doi.org/10.1007/978-3-030-43823-4_18

to the model behavior. This includes variance-based measures like the feature importance ranking measure (FIRM) [10,20] and performance-based measures like the permutation feature importance (PFI) [7], individual conditional importance (ICI) and partial importance (PI) curves [4], as well as the Shapley feature importance (SFIMP) [4]. Input gradients were proposed by [11] as a model-agnostic tool for both effects and importance that essentially equals marginal effects (ME) [12], which have a long tradition in statistics. They also define an average input gradient which corresponds to the average marginal effect (AME).

(ii) *Intrinsic or post-hoc interpretability:* Linear models (LM), generalized linear models (GLM), classification and regression trees (CART) or rule lists [18] are examples for intrinsically interpretable models, while random forests (RF), support vector machines (SVM), neural networks (NN) or gradient boosting (GB) models can only be interpreted post-hoc. Here, the interpretation process is detached from and takes place after the model fitting process, e.g., with the ICE, PD or ALEs.

(iii) *Model-specific or model-agnostic interpretations:* Interpreting model coefficients of GLMs or deriving a decision rule from a classification tree is a model-specific interpretation. Model-agnostic methods such as the ICE, PD or ALEs can be applied to any model.

(iv) *Local or global explanations:* Local explanations like the ICE evaluate the model behavior when predicting for one specific observation. Global explanations like the PD interpret the model for the entire input space. Furthermore, it is possible to explain model predictions for a group of observations, e.g., on intervals. In a lot of cases, local and global explanations can be transformed into one another via (dis-)aggregation, e.g., the ICE and PD.

Motivation: Research in model-agnostic interpretation methods is complicated by the variety of different notations and terminology. It turns out that deconstructing model-agnostic techniques into sequential work stages reveals striking similarities. In [14] the authors propose a unified framework for model-agnostic interpretations called SHapley Additive exPlanations (SHAP). However, the SHAP framework only considers Shapley values or variations thereof (KernelSHAP and TreeSHAP). The motivation for this research paper is to provide a more extensive survey on model-agnostic interpretation methods, to reveal similarities in their computation and to establish a framework with common terminology that is applicable to all model-agnostic techniques.

Contributions: In Sect. 4 we present the generalized SIPA (sampling, intervention, prediction, aggregation) framework of work stages for model-agnostic techniques. We proceed to demonstrate how several methods to estimate feature effects (MEs, ICE and PD, ALEs, Shapley values and LIME) can be embedded into the proposed framework. Furthermore, in Sects. 5 and 6 we extend the framework to feature importance computations by pointing out how variance-based (FIRM) and performance-based (ICI and PI, PFI and SFIMP) importance measures are based on the same work stages. By using a unified notation, we also reveal how the methods are related.

2 Notation and Preliminaries

Consider a p-dimensional feature space $\mathcal{X}_P = \mathcal{X}_1 \times \cdots \times \mathcal{X}_p$ with the feature index set $P = \{1, \ldots, p\}$ and a target space $\mathcal{Y}$. We assume an unknown functional relationship f between $\mathcal{X}_P$ and $\mathcal{Y}$. A supervised learning model $\hat{f}$ attempts to learn this relationship from an i.i.d. training sample that was drawn from the unknown probability distribution $\mathcal{F}$ with the sample space $\mathcal{X}_P \times \mathcal{Y}$. The random variables generated from the feature space are denoted by $X = (X_1, \ldots, X_p)$. The random variable generated from the target space is denoted by Y. We draw an i.i.d. sample of test data $\mathcal{D}$ with n observations from $\mathcal{F}$. The vector $x^{(i)} = (x_1^{(i)}, \ldots, x_p^{(i)}) \in \mathcal{X}_P$ corresponds to the feature values of the i-th observation that are associated with the observed target value $y^{(i)} \in \mathcal{Y}$. The vector $x_j = (x_j^{(1)}, \ldots, x_j^{(n)})^\top$ represents the realizations of X_j. The generalization error $GE(\hat{f}, \mathcal{F})$ corresponds to the expectation of the loss function $\mathcal{L}$ on unseen test data from $\mathcal{F}$ and is estimated by the average loss on $\mathcal{D}$.

$$GE(\hat{f}, \mathcal{F}) = \mathbb{E}\left[\mathcal{L}(\hat{f}(X_1, \ldots, X_p), Y)\right]$$

$$\widehat{GE}(\hat{f}, \mathcal{D}) = \frac{1}{n} \sum_{i=1}^{n} \mathcal{L}(\hat{f}(x_1^{(i)}, \ldots, x_p^{(i)}), y^{(i)})$$

A variety of model-agnostic techniques is used to interpret the prediction function $\hat{f}(x_1, \ldots, x_p)$ with the sample of test data $\mathcal{D}$. We estimate the effects and importance of a subset of features with index set S ($S \subseteq P$). A vector of feature values $x \in \mathcal{X}_P$ can be partitioned into two vectors x_S and $x_{\setminus S}$ so that $x = (x_S, x_{\setminus S})$. The corresponding random variables are denoted by X_S and $X_{\setminus S}$. Given a model-agnostic technique where S only contains a single element, the corresponding notations are $X_j, X_{\setminus j}$ and $x_j, x_{\setminus j}$.

The partial derivative of the trained model $\hat{f}(x_j, x_{\setminus j})$ with respect to x_j is numerically approximated with a symmetric difference quotient [12].

$$\lim_{h \to 0} \frac{\hat{f}(x_j + h, x_{\setminus j}) - \hat{f}(x_j, x_{\setminus j})}{h} \approx \frac{\hat{f}(x_j + h, x_{\setminus j}) - \hat{f}(x_j - h, x_{\setminus j})}{2h}, \quad h > 0$$

A term of the form $\hat{f}(x_j + h, x_{\setminus j}) - \hat{f}(x_j - h, x_{\setminus j})$ is called a finite difference (FD) of predictions with respect to x_j.

$$FD_{\hat{f},j}(x_j, x_{\setminus j}) = \hat{f}(x_j + h, x_{\setminus j}) - \hat{f}(x_j - h, x_{\setminus j})$$

3 Feature Effects

Partial Dependence (PD) and Individual Conditional Expectation (ICE): First suggested by [8], the PD is defined as the dependence of the prediction function on x_S after all remaining features $X_{\setminus S}$ have been marginalized out [9]. The PD is estimated via Monte Carlo integration.

$$PD_{\hat{f},S}(x_S) = \mathbb{E}_{X_{\setminus S}}\left[\hat{f}(x_S, X_{\setminus S})\right] = \int \hat{f}(x_S, X_{\setminus S})\, d\mathcal{P}(X_{\setminus S}) \tag{1}$$

$$\widehat{PD}_{\hat{f},S}(x_S) = \frac{1}{n}\sum_{i=1}^{n} \hat{f}(x_S, x_{\setminus S}^{(i)})$$

The PD is a useful feature effect measure when features are not interacting [8]. Otherwise it can obfuscate the relationships in the data [4]. In that case, the individual conditional expectation (ICE) can be used instead [9]. The i-th ICE corresponds to the expected value of the target for the i-th observation as a function of x_S, conditional on $x_{\setminus S}^{(i)}$.

$$\widehat{ICE}_{\hat{f},S}^{(i)}(x_S) = \hat{f}(x_S, x_{\setminus S}^{(i)})$$

The ICE disaggregates the global effect estimates of the PD to local effect estimates for single observations. Given $|S| = 1$, the ICE and PD are also referred to as ICE and PD curves. The ICE and PD suffer from extrapolation when features are correlated, because the permutations used to predict are located in regions without any training data [1].

Accumulated Local Effects (ALE): In [1] ALEs are presented as a feature effect measure for correlated features that does not extrapolate. The idea of ALEs is to take the integral with respect to X_j of the first derivative of the prediction function with respect to X_j. This creates an accumulated partial effect of X_j on the target variable while simultaneously removing additively linked effects of other features. The main advantage of not extrapolating stems from integrating with respect to the conditional distribution of $X_{\setminus j}$ on X_j instead of the marginal distribution of $X_{\setminus j}$ [1]. Let $z_{0,j}$ denote the minimum value of x_j. The first order ALE of the j-th feature at point x is defined as:

$$\begin{aligned} ALE_{\hat{f},j}(x) &= \int_{z_{0,j}}^{x} \mathbb{E}_{X_{\setminus j}|X_j}\left[\frac{\partial \hat{f}(X_j, X_{\setminus j})}{\partial X_j}\middle| X_j = z_j\right] dz_j - constant \\ &= \int_{z_{0,j}}^{x} \left[\int \frac{\partial \hat{f}(z_j, X_{\setminus j})}{\partial z_j}\, d\mathcal{P}(X_{\setminus j}|z_j)\right] dz_j - constant \end{aligned} \tag{2}$$

A constant is subtracted in order to center the plot. We estimate the first order ALE in three steps. First, we divide the value range of x_j into a set of intervals and compute a finite difference (FD) for each observation. For each i-th observation, $x_j^{(i)}$ is substituted by the corresponding right and left interval boundaries. Then the predictions with both substituted values are subtracted in order to receive an observation-wise FD. Second, we estimate local effects by averaging the FDs inside each interval. This replaces the inner integral in Eq. (2). Third, the accumulation of all local effects up to the point of interest replaces the outer integral in Eq. (2), i.e., the interval-wise average FDs are summed up.

The second order ALE is the bivariate extension of the first order ALE. It is important to note that first order effect estimates are subtracted from the second order estimates. In [1] the authors further lay out the computations necessary for higher order ALEs.

Marginal Effects (ME): MEs are an established technique in statistics and often used to interpret non-linear functions of coefficients in GLMs like logistic regression. The ME corresponds to the first derivative of the prediction function with respect to a feature at specified values of the input space. It is estimated by computing an observation-wise FD. The average marginal effect (AME) is the average of all MEs that were estimated with observed feature values [2]. Although there is extensive literature on MEs, this concept was suggested by [11] as a novel method for ML and referred to as the input gradient. Derivatives are also often utilized as a feature importance metric.

Shapley Value: Originating in coalitional game theory [19], the Shapley value is a local feature effect measure that is based on a set of desirable axioms. In coalitional games, a set of p players, denoted by P, play games and join coalitions. They are rewarded with a payout. The characteristic function $v : 2^p \rightarrow \mathbb{R}$ maps all player coalitions to their respective payouts [4]. The Shapley value is a player's average contribution to the payout, i.e., the marginal increase in payout for the coalition of players, averaged over all possible coalitions. For Shapley values as feature effects, predicting the target for a single observation corresponds to the game and a coalition of features represents the players. Shapley regression values were first developed for linear models with multicollinear features [13]. A model-agnostic Shapley value was first introduced in [19].

Consider the expected prediction for a single vector of feature values x, conditional on only knowing the values of features with indices in K ($K \subseteq P$), i.e., the features $X_{\setminus K}$ are marginalized out. This essentially equals a point (or a line, surface etc. depending on the power of K) on the PD from Eq. (1).

$$\mathbb{E}_{X_{\setminus K}}\left[\hat{f}(x_K, X_{\setminus K})\right] = \int \hat{f}(x_K, X_{\setminus K})\, d\mathbb{P}(X_{\setminus K}) = \widehat{PD}_{\hat{f},K}(x_K) \tag{3}$$

Equation (3) is shifted by the mean prediction and used as a payout function $v_{PD}(x_K)$, so that an empty set of features ($K = \varnothing$) results in a payout of zero [4].

$$\begin{aligned} v_{PD}(x_K) &= \mathbb{E}_{X_{\setminus K}}\left[\hat{f}(x_K, X_{\setminus K})\right] - \mathbb{E}_{X_{K \cup (P \setminus K)}}\left[\hat{f}(X_K, X_{\setminus K})\right] \\ &= \widehat{PD}_{\hat{f},K}(x_K) - \widehat{PD}_{\hat{f},\varnothing}(x_\varnothing) \\ &= \widehat{PD}_{\hat{f},K}(x_K) - \frac{1}{n}\sum_{i=1}^{n} \hat{f}(x_K^{(i)}, x_{\setminus K}^{(i)}) \end{aligned}$$

The marginal contribution $\Delta_j(x_K)$ of a feature value x_j joining the coalition of feature values x_K is:

$$\Delta_j(x_K) = v_{PD}(x_{K \cup \{j\}}) - v_{PD}(x_K) = \widehat{PD}_{\hat{f},K \cup \{j\}}(x_{K \cup \{j\}}) - \widehat{PD}_{\hat{f},K}(x_K)$$

The exact Shapley value of the j-th feature for a single vector of feature values x corresponds to:

$$\begin{aligned}\widehat{Shapley}_{\hat{f},j} &= \sum_{K \subseteq P \setminus \{j\}} \frac{|K|!(|P|-|K|-1)!}{|P|!} \Delta_j(x_K) \\ &= \sum_{K \subseteq P \setminus \{j\}} \frac{|K|!(|P|-|K|-1)!}{|P|!} \left[\widehat{PD}_{\hat{f},K\cup\{j\}}(x_{K\cup\{j\}}) - \widehat{PD}_{\hat{f},K}(x_K)\right]\end{aligned}$$

Shapley values are computationally expensive because the PD function has a complexity of $\mathcal{O}(N^2)$. Computations can be sped up by Monte Carlo sampling [19]. Furthermore, in [14] the authors propose a distinct variant to compute Shapley values called SHapley Additive exPlanations (SHAP).

Local Interpretable Model-Agnostic Explanations (LIME): In contrast to all previous techniques which are based on interpreting a single model, LIME [17] locally approximates the black box model with an intrinsically interpretable surrogate model. Given a single vector of feature values x, we first perturb x_j around a sufficiently close neighborhood while $x_{\setminus j}$ is kept constant. Then we predict with the perturbed feature values. The predictions are weighted by the proximity of the corresponding perturbed values to the original feature value. Finally, an intrinsically interpretable model is trained on the weighted predictions and interpreted instead.

4 Generalized Framework

Although the techniques presented in Sect. 3 are seemingly unrelated, they all work according to the exact same principle. Instead of trying to inspect the inner workings of a non-linear black box model, we evaluate its predictions when changing inputs. We can deconstruct model-agnostic techniques into a framework of four work stages: sampling, intervention, prediction, aggregation (SIPA). The software package `iml` [16] was inspired by the SIPA framework.

We first sample a subset (**sampling stage**) to reduce computational costs, e.g., we select a random set of available observations to evaluate as ICEs. In order to change the predictions made by the black box model, the data has to be manipulated. Feature values can be set to values from the observed marginal distributions (ICEs and PD or Shapley values), or to unobserved values (FD based methods such as MEs and ALEs). This crucial step is called the **intervention stage**. During the **prediction stage**, we predict on previously intervened data. This requires an already trained model, which is why model-agnostic techniques are always post-hoc. The predictions are further aggregated during the **aggregation stage**. Often, the predictions resulting from the prediction stage are local effect estimates, and the ones resulting from the aggregation stage are global effect estimates.

In Fig. 1, we demonstrate how all presented techniques for feature effects are based on the SIPA framework. Although LIME is a special case as it is based

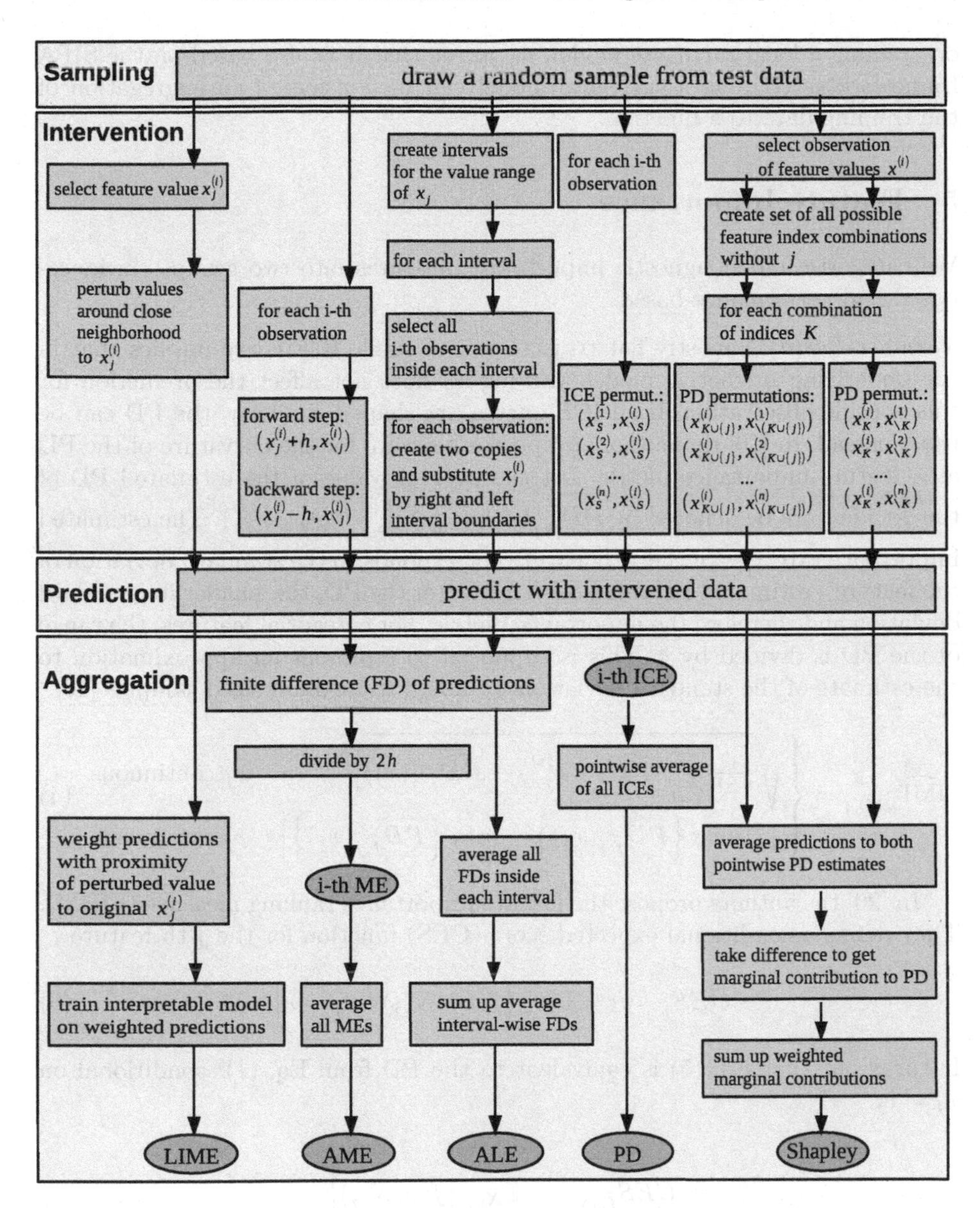

Fig. 1. We demonstrate how all presented model-agnostic methods for feature effects are based on the SIPA framework. For every method, we assign each computational step to the corresponding generalized SIPA work stage. Contrary to all other methods, LIME is based on training an intrinsically interpretable model during the aggregation stage. We consider training a model to be an aggregation, because it corresponds to an optimization problem where the training data is aggregated to a function. For reasons of simplicity, we do not differentiate between the actual functions or values and their estimates.

on training a local surrogate model, we argue that it is also based on the SIPA framework as training a surrogate model can be considered an aggregation of the training data to a function.

5 Feature Importance

We categorize model-agnostic importance measures into two groups: variance-based and performance-based.

Variance-Based: A mostly flat trajectory of a single ICE curve implies that in the underlying predictive model, varying x_j does not affect the prediction for this specific observation. If all ICE curves are shaped similarly, the PD can be used instead. In [10] the authors propose a measure for the curvature of the PD as a feature importance metric. Let the average value of the estimated PD of the j-th feature be denoted by $\overline{\widehat{PD}}_{\hat{f},j}(x_j) = \frac{1}{n}\sum_{i=1}^{n} \widehat{PD}_{\hat{f},j}(x_j^{(i)})$. The estimated importance $\widehat{\text{IMP}}_{\widehat{PD},j}$ of the j-th feature corresponds to the standard deviation of the feature's estimated PD function. The flatter the PD, the smaller its standard deviation and therefore the importance metric. For categorial features, the range of the PD is divided by 4. This is supposed to represent an approximation to the estimate of the standard deviation for small to medium sized samples [10].

$$\widehat{\text{IMP}}_{\widehat{PD},j} = \begin{cases} \sqrt{\frac{1}{n-1}\sum_{i=1}^{n}\left[\widehat{PD}_{\hat{f},j}(x_j^{(i)}) - \overline{\widehat{PD}}_{\hat{f},j}(x_j)\right]^2} & x_j \text{ continuous} \\ \frac{1}{4}\left[max\left\{\widehat{PD}_{\hat{f},j}(x_j)\right\} - min\left\{\widehat{PD}_{\hat{f},j}(x_j)\right\}\right] & x_j \text{ categorial} \end{cases} \tag{4}$$

In [20] the authors propose the feature importance ranking measure (FIRM). They define a conditional expected score (CES) function for the j-th feature.

$$CES_{\hat{f},j}(v) = \mathbb{E}_{X_{\setminus j}}\left[\hat{f}(x_j, X_{\setminus j}) \mid x_j = v\right] \tag{5}$$

It turns out that Eq. (5) is equivalent to the PD from Eq. (1), conditional on $x_j = v$.

$$\begin{aligned} CES_{\hat{f},j}(v) &= \mathbb{E}_{X_{\setminus j}}\left[\hat{f}(v, X_{\setminus j})\right] \\ &= PD_{\hat{f},j}(v) \end{aligned}$$

The FIRM corresponds to the standard deviation of the CES function with all values of x_j used as conditional values. This in turn is equivalent to the standard deviation of the PD. The FIRM is therefore equivalent to the feature importance metric in Eq. (4).

$$\widehat{FIRM}_{\hat{f},j} = \sqrt{Var(\widehat{CES}_{\hat{f},j}(x_j))} = \sqrt{Var(\widehat{PD}_{\hat{f},j}(x_j))} = \widehat{\text{IMP}}_{\widehat{PD},j}$$

Performance-Based: The permutation feature importance (PFI), originally developed by [3] as a model-specific tool for random forests, was described as a model-agnostic one by [6]. If feature values are shuffled in isolation, the relationship between the feature and the target is broken up. If the feature is important for the predictive performance, the shuffling should result in an increased loss [4]. Permuting x_j corresponds to drawing from a new random variable $\tilde{X}_j$ that is distributed like X_j but independent of $X_{\setminus j}$ [4]. The model-agnostic PFI measures the difference between the generalization error (GE) on data with permuted and non-permuted values.

$$PFI_{\hat{f},j} = \mathbb{E}\left[\mathcal{L}(\hat{f}(\tilde{X}_j, X_{\setminus j}), Y)\right] - \mathbb{E}\left[\mathcal{L}(\hat{f}(X_j, X_{\setminus j}), Y)\right]$$

Let the permutation of x_j be denoted by $\tilde{x}_j$. Consider the sample of test data $\mathcal{D}_j$ where x_j has been permuted, and the non-permuted sample $\mathcal{D}$. The PFI estimate is given by the difference between GE estimates with permuted and non-permuted values.

$$\begin{aligned} \widehat{PFI}_{\hat{f},j} &= \widehat{GE}(\hat{f}, \mathcal{D}_j) - \widehat{GE}(\hat{f}, \mathcal{D}) \\ &= \frac{1}{n}\sum_{i=1}^{n} \mathcal{L}(\hat{f}(\tilde{x}_j^{(i)}, x_{\setminus j}^{(i)}), y^{(i)}) - \frac{1}{n}\sum_{i=1}^{n} \mathcal{L}(\hat{f}(x_j^{(i)}, x_{\setminus j}^{(i)}), y^{(i)}) \end{aligned} \quad (6)$$

In [4] the authors propose individual conditional importance (ICI) and partial importance (PI) curves as visualization techniques that disaggregate the global PFI estimate. They are based on the same principle as the ICE and PD. The ICI visualizes the influence of a feature on the predictive performance for a single observation, while the PI visualizes the average influence of a feature for all observations. Consider the prediction for the i-th observation with observed values $\hat{f}(x_j^{(i)}, x_{\setminus j}^{(i)})$ and the prediction $\hat{f}(x_j^{(l)}, x_{\setminus j}^{(i)})$ where $x_j^{(i)}$ was replaced by a value $x_j^{(l)}$ from the marginal distribution of observed values x_j. The change in loss is given by:

$$\Delta\mathcal{L}^{(i)}(x_j^{(l)}) = \mathcal{L}(\hat{f}(x_j^{(l)}, x_{\setminus j}^{(i)})) - \mathcal{L}(\hat{f}(x_j^{(i)}, x_{\setminus j}^{(i)}))$$

The ICI curve of the i-th observation plots the value pairs $(x_j^{(l)}, \Delta\mathcal{L}^{(i)}(x_j^{(l)}))$ for all l values of x_j. The PI curve is the pointwise average of all ICI curves at all l values of x_j. It plots the value pairs $(x_j^{(l)}, \frac{1}{n}\sum_{i=1}^{n} \Delta\mathcal{L}^{(i)}(x_j^{(l)}))$ for all l values of x_j. Substituting values of x_j essentially resembles shuffling them. The authors demonstrate how averaging the values of the PI curve results in an estimation of the global PFI.

$$\widehat{PFI}_{\hat{f},j} = \frac{1}{n}\sum_{l=1}^{n}\frac{1}{n}\sum_{i=1}^{n} \Delta\mathcal{L}^{(i)}(x_j^{(l)})$$

Furthermore, a feature importance measure called Shapley feature importance (SFIMP) was proposed in [4]. Shapley importance values based on model

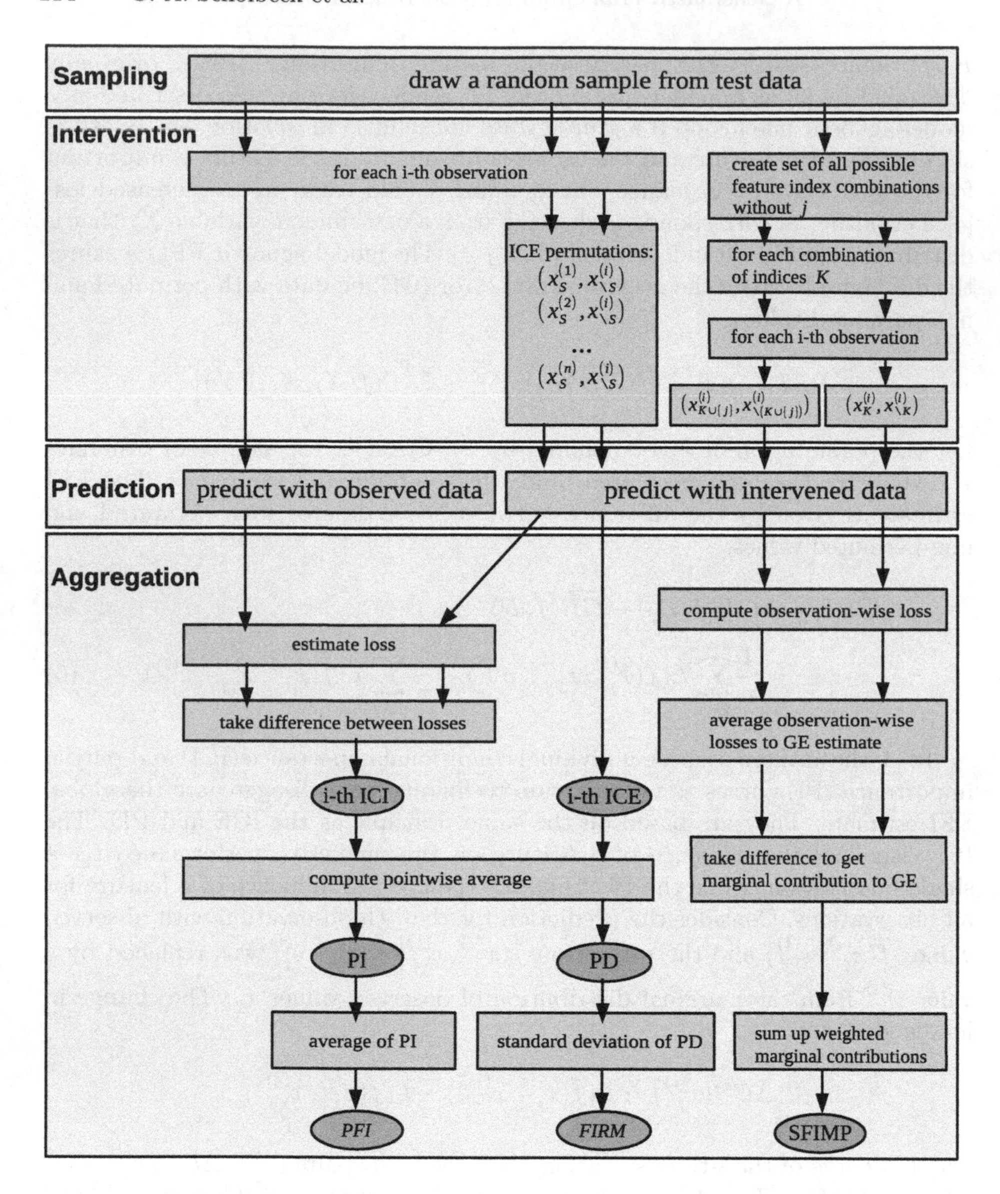

Fig. 2. We demonstrate how importance computations are based on the same work stages as effect computations. In the same way as in Fig. 1, we assign the computational steps of all techniques to the corresponding generalized SIPA work stages. Variance-based importance measures such as FIRM measure the variance of a feature effect, i.e., we add a variance computation during the aggregation stage. Performance-based importance measures such as ICI, PI, PFI and SFIMP are based on computing changes in loss after the intervention stage. For reasons of simplicity, we do not differentiate between the actual functions or values and their estimates.

refits with distinct sets of features were first introduced by [5] for feature selection. This changes the behavior of the learning algorithm and is not helpful to evaluate a single model, as noted by [4]. The SFIMP is based on the same computations as the Shapley value but replaces the payout function with one that is sensitive to the model performance. The authors define a new payout $v_{GE}(x_j)$ that substitutes the estimated PD with the estimated GE. This is equivalent to the estimated PFI from Eq. (6).

$$v_{GE}(x_j) = \widehat{GE}(\hat{f}, \mathcal{D}_j) - \widehat{GE}(\hat{f}, \mathcal{D}) = \widehat{PFI}_{\hat{f},j} = v_{PFI}(x_j)$$

We can therefore refer to $v_{GE}(x_j)$ as $v_{PFI}(x_j)$ and regard the SFIMP as an extension to the PFI [4].

6 Extending the Framework to Importance Computations

Variance-based importance methods measure the variance of feature effect estimates, which we already demonstrated to be based on the SIPA framework. Therefore, we simply add a variance computation during the aggregation stage. Performance-based techniques measure changes in loss, i.e., there are two possible modifications. First, we predict on non-intervened or intervened data (prediction stage). Second, we aggregate predictions to the loss (aggregation stage). In Fig. 2, we demonstrate how feature importance computations are based on the same work stages as feature effect computations.

7 Conclusion

In recent years, various model-agnostic interpretation methods have been developed. Due to different notations and terminology it is difficult to see how they are related. By deconstructing them into sequential work stages, one discovers striking similarities in their methodologies. We first provided a survey on model-agnostic interpretation methods and then presented the generalized SIPA framework of sequential work stages. First, there is a sampling stage to reduce computational costs. Second, we intervene in the data in order to change the predictions made by the black box model. Third, we predict on intervened or non-intervened data. Fourth, we aggregate the predictions. We embedded multiple methods to estimate the effect (ICE and PD, ALEs, MEs, Shapley values and LIME) and importance (FIRM, PFI, ICI and PI and the SFIMP) of features into the framework. By pointing out how all demonstrated techniques are based on a single methodology, we hope to work towards a more unified view on model-agnostic interpretations and to establish a common ground to discuss them in future work.

Acknowledgments. This work is supported by the Bavarian State Ministry of Science and the Arts as part of the Centre Digitisation.Bavaria (ZD.B) and by the German Federal Ministry of Education and Research (BMBF) under Grant No. 01IS18036A. The authors of this work take full responsibilities for its content.

References

1. Apley, D.W.: Visualizing the effects of predictor variables in black box supervised learning models. arXiv e-prints arXiv:1612.08468, December 2016
2. Bartus, T.: Estimation of marginal effects using margeff. Stata J. **5**(3), 309–329 (2005)
3. Breiman, L.: Random forests. Mach. Learn. **45**(1), 5–32 (2001)
4. Casalicchio, G., Molnar, C., Bischl, B.: Visualizing the feature importance for black box models. In: Berlingerio, M., Bonchi, F., Gärtner, T., Hurley, N., Ifrim, G. (eds.) ECML PKDD 2018. LNCS (LNAI), vol. 11051, pp. 655–670. Springer, Cham (2019). https://doi.org/10.1007/978-3-030-10925-7_40
5. Cohen, S., Dror, G., Ruppin, E.: Feature selection via coalitional game theory. Neural Comput. **19**(7), 1939–1961 (2007)
6. Fisher, A., Rudin, C., Dominici, F.: Model class reliance: variable importance measures for any machine learning model class, from the "Rashomon" perspective. arXiv e-prints arXiv:1801.01489, January 2018
7. Fisher, A., Rudin, C., Dominici, F.: All models are wrong but many are useful: variable importance for black-box, proprietary, or misspecified prediction models, using model class reliance. arXiv e-prints arXiv:1801.01489, January 2018
8. Friedman, J.H.: Greedy function approximation: a gradient boosting machine. Ann. Stat. **29**(5), 1189–1232 (2001)
9. Goldstein, A., Kapelner, A., Bleich, J., Pitkin, E.: Peeking inside the black box: visualizing statistical learning with plots of individual conditional expectation. J. Comput. Graph. Stat. **24**, 44–65 (2013)
10. Greenwell, B.M., Boehmke, B.C., McCarthy, A.J.: A simple and effective model-based variable importance measure. arXiv e-prints arXiv:1805.04755, May 2018
11. Hechtlinger, Y.: Interpretation of prediction models using the input gradient. arXiv e-prints arXiv:1611.07634, November 2016
12. Leeper, T.J.: Margins: marginal effects for model objects (2018)
13. Lipovetsky, S., Conklin, M.: Analysis of regression in game theory approach. Appl. Stoch. Models Bus. Ind. **17**(4), 319–330 (2001)
14. Lundberg, S.M., Lee, S.I.: A unified approach to interpreting model predictions. In: Guyon, I., et al. (eds.) Advances in Neural Information Processing Systems, vol. 30, pp. 4765–4774. Curran Associates, Inc., New York (2017)
15. Molnar, C.: Interpretable Machine Learning (2019). https://christophm.github.io/interpretable-ml-book/
16. Molnar, C., Bischl, B., Casalicchio, G.: iml: an R package for interpretable machine learning. JOSS **3**(26), 786 (2018)
17. Ribeiro, M.T., Singh, S., Guestrin, C.: Why should I trust you?: explaining the predictions of any classifier. In: Knowledge Discovery and Data Mining (KDD) (2016)
18. Rudin, C., Ertekin, Ş.: Learning customized and optimized lists of rules with mathematical programming. Math. Program. Comput. **10**(4), 659–702 (2018). https://doi.org/10.1007/s12532-018-0143-8
19. Štrumbelj, E., Kononenko, I.: Explaining prediction models and individual predictions with feature contributions. Knowl. Inf. Syst. **41**(3), 647–665 (2013). https://doi.org/10.1007/s10115-013-0679-x
20. Zien, A., Krämer, N., Sonnenburg, S., Rätsch, G.: The feature importance ranking measure. In: Buntine, W., Grobelnik, M., Mladenić, D., Shawe-Taylor, J. (eds.) ECML PKDD 2009. LNCS (LNAI), vol. 5782, pp. 694–709. Springer, Heidelberg (2009). https://doi.org/10.1007/978-3-642-04174-7_45

Learning and Interpreting Potentials for Classical Hamiltonian Systems

Harish S. Bhat(✉)

Applied Mathematics Unit, University of California, Merced, USA
hbhat@ucmerced.edu

Abstract. We consider the problem of learning an interpretable potential energy function from a Hamiltonian system's trajectories. We address this problem for classical, separable Hamiltonian systems. Our approach first constructs a neural network model of the potential and then applies an equation discovery technique to extract from the neural potential a closed-form algebraic expression. We demonstrate this approach for several systems, including oscillators, a central force problem, and a problem of two charged particles in a classical Coulomb potential. Through these test problems, we show close agreement between learned neural potentials, the interpreted potentials we obtain after training, and the ground truth. In particular, for the central force problem, we show that our approach learns the correct effective potential, a reduced-order model of the system.

Keywords: Neural networks · Equation discovery · Hamiltonian systems

1 Introduction

As a cornerstone of classical physics, Hamiltonian systems arise in numerous settings in engineering and the physical sciences. Common examples include coupled oscillators, systems of particles/masses subject to classical electrostatic or gravitational forces, and rigid bodies. For integer $d \geq 1$, let $\mathbf{q}(t) \in \mathbb{R}^d$ and $\mathbf{p}(t) \in \mathbb{R}^d$ denote, respectively, the position and momentum of the system at time t. Let T and V denote kinetic and potential energy, respectively. Our focus here is on classical, separable systems that arise from the Hamiltonian

$$H(\mathbf{p}, \mathbf{q}) = T(\mathbf{p}) + V(\mathbf{q}). \tag{1}$$

In this paper, we consider the problem of learning or identifying the potential energy V from data $(\mathbf{q}(t), \mathbf{p}(t))$ measured at a discrete set of times. We assume

This work was performed under the auspices of the U.S. Department of Energy by Lawrence Livermore National Laboratory under Contract DE-AC52-07NA27344 and was supported by the LLNL-LDRD Program under Project No. 19-ERD-009. LLNL-PROC-779792.

P. Cellier and K. Driessens (Eds.): ECML PKDD 2019 Workshops, CCIS 1167, pp. 217–228, 2020.
https://doi.org/10.1007/978-3-030-43823-4_19

T is known. To motivate this problem, consider the setting of m interacting particles in three-dimensional space; here $d = 3m$. Suppose that we are truly interested in a reduced set of variables, e.g., the position and momentum of one of the m particles. Let us denote the reduced-order quantities of interest by $(\widetilde{\mathbf{q}}(t), \widetilde{\mathbf{p}}(t)) \in \mathbb{R}^{2\widetilde{d}}$. The direct approach is to integrate numerically the $6m$-dimensional system of differential equations for the full Hamiltonian (1) and then use the full solution $(\mathbf{q}(t), \mathbf{p}(t))$ to compute $(\widetilde{\mathbf{q}}(t), \widetilde{\mathbf{p}}(t))$. While such an approach yields numerical answers, typically, *it does not explain* how the reduced-order system evolves dynamically in time. If we suspect that $(\widetilde{\mathbf{q}}(t), \widetilde{\mathbf{p}}(t))$ itself satisfies a Hamiltonian system, we can search for a potential $\widetilde{V}(\widetilde{\mathbf{q}})$ that yields an accurate, reduced-order model for $(\widetilde{\mathbf{q}}(t), \widetilde{\mathbf{p}}(t))$. If $\widetilde{V}$ is interpretable, we can use it to explain the reduced system's dynamics—*here we mean interpretability in the sense of traditional models in the physical sciences, which are written as algebraic expressions*, not as numerical algorithms. We can also use the reduced-order model to simulate $(\widetilde{\mathbf{q}}(t), \widetilde{\mathbf{p}}(t))$ directly, with computational savings that depend on $d/\widetilde{d}$.

There is a rapidly growing literature on machine learning of potential energies in computational/physical chemistry, e.g., [1–3,9,10]. As in these studies, the present work uses neural networks to parameterize the unknown potential. A key difference is that, in the present work, we apply additional methods to interpret the learned neural potential. There exists a burgeoning, recent literature on learning interpretable dynamical systems from time series, e.g., [4–6,8,12], to cite but a few. We repurpose one such method—SINDy (sparse identification of nonlinear dynamics)—to convert the learned neural potential into a closed-form algebraic expression that is as interpretable as classical models. We apply only one such method for accomplishing this conversion into an algebraic expression; we hope that the results described here lead to further investigation in this area.

2 Approach

Assume $T(\mathbf{p}) = \sum_{i=1}^{d} M_{ii}^{-1} p_i^2$ where M is a diagonal mass matrix. Then, from (1), we can write Hamilton's equations:

$$\dot{\mathbf{q}} = M^{-1}\mathbf{p} \tag{2a}$$

$$\dot{\mathbf{p}} = -\nabla V(\mathbf{q}). \tag{2b}$$

Let the training data consist of a set of R trajectories; the j-th such trajectory is $\{\mathbf{q}_i^j, \mathbf{p}_i^j\}_{i=0}^{N}$. Here $(\mathbf{q}_i^j, \mathbf{p}_i^j)$ denotes a measurement of $(\mathbf{q}(t), \mathbf{p}(t))$ at time $t = ih$ for fixed $h > 0$. We choose this equispaced temporal grid for simplicity; this choice is not essential. Because we treat the kinetic energy T as known, we assume that the training data consists of (possibly noisy) measurements of a system that satisfies (2a). We now posit a model for V that depends on a set of parameters $\boldsymbol{\theta}$. For instance, if we model V using a neural network, $\boldsymbol{\theta}$ stands for the collection of all network weights and biases. Then we use (2b) to form an empirical risk loss

$$L(\boldsymbol{\theta}) = \frac{1}{RN} \sum_{j=1}^{R} \sum_{i=0}^{N-1} \left\| \frac{\mathbf{p}_{i+1}^j - \mathbf{p}_i^j}{h} + \nabla_{\mathbf{q}} V(\mathbf{q}_i^j; \boldsymbol{\theta}) \right\|^2. \tag{3}$$

Let $\tau = Nh$ denote the final time in our grid. Note that (3) approximates $E\left[(1/\tau)\int_{t=0}^{t=\tau} \|\dot{\mathbf{P}}(t) + \nabla_{\mathbf{Q}} V(\mathbf{Q}(t); \boldsymbol{\theta})\|^2 \mathrm{dt}\right]$, the expected mean-squared error of a random trajectory $(\mathbf{Q}(t), \mathbf{P}(t))$ assumed to satisfy (2a).

We model V using a dense, feedforward neural network with $L \geq 2$ layers. Because we train with multiple trajectories, the input layer takes data in the form of two tensors—one for $\mathbf{q}$ and one for $\mathbf{p}$—with dimensions $N \times R \times d$. The network then transposes and flattens the data to be of dimension $NR \times d$. Thus begins the potential energy function part of the network (referred to in what follows as the *neural potential*), which takes a d-dimensional vector as input and produces a scalar as output. Between the neural potential's d-unit input layer and 1-unit output layer, we have a number of hidden layers. In this model, we typically choose hidden layers to all have ν units where $1 \leq \nu \leq d$. As these architectural details differ by example, we give them below.

Note that the loss (3) involves the gradient of V with respect to the input $\mathbf{q}$. We use automatic differentiation to compute this gradient. More specifically, in our IPython/Jupyter notebooks (linked below), we use the `batch_jacobian` method in TensorFlow. This is easy to implement, fast, and accurate up to machine precision.

The trained network gives us a neural potential $\widehat{V} : \mathbb{R}^d \to \mathbb{R}$. To interpret $\widehat{V}$, we apply the SINDy method [5]. We now offer a capsule summary of this technique. Suppose we have a grid $\{\mathbf{x}^k\}_{k=1}^K$ of points in $\mathbb{R}^d$. We use the notation $\mathbf{x}^k = (x_1^k, \ldots, x_d^k)$. We evaluate $\widehat{V}$ on the grid, resulting in a vector of values that we denote by $\mathbf{V}$. We also evaluate on the grid a library of J candidate functions $\xi^j : \mathbb{R}^d \to \mathbb{R}$ for $1 \leq j \leq J$; each such evaluation results in a vector Ξ^j that we take to be the j th column of a matrix Ξ. In $d = 1$, examples of candidate functions are $\{1, x, x^2, \ldots\}$ or $\{1, x^{-1}, x^{-2}, \ldots\}$. In $d = 2$, an example is $\{1, x_1, x_2, x_1^2, x_1 x_2, x_2^2, \ldots\}$. Each candidate function is simply a scalar-valued function on $\mathbb{R}^d$.

Equipped with the $K \times 1$ vector $\mathbf{V}$ and the $K \times J$ matrix Ξ, we solve the regression problem

$$\mathbf{V} = \Xi \boldsymbol{\beta} + \epsilon \tag{4}$$

for the $J \times 1$ vector $\boldsymbol{\beta}$ using an iteratively thresholded least-squares algorithm. The algorithm has one constant hyperparameter, $\lambda > 0$. The algorithm is then succinctly described as follows: (i) estimate $\boldsymbol{\beta}$ using ordinary least squares, and then (ii) reset to zero all components of $\boldsymbol{\beta}$ that are less than the threshold λ. Once components of $\boldsymbol{\beta}$ are reset to zero, they stay frozen at zero. We then repeat steps (i) and (ii) until $\boldsymbol{\beta}$ stabilizes to its converged value.

As shown recently [13], this algorithm converges in a finite number of steps to an approximate minimizer of $\|\mathbf{V} - \Xi\boldsymbol{\beta}\|^2 + \lambda^2 \|\boldsymbol{\beta}\|_0$. Here $\|\boldsymbol{\beta}\|_0$ denotes the number of nonzero entries of $\boldsymbol{\beta}$. Hence, increasing the parameter λ leads to a more sparse set of coefficients $\boldsymbol{\beta}$. Once we have fit the regression model in this way, we obtain an interpretable model of $\widehat{V}$, specifically:

$$\widehat{V}(\mathbf{x}) = \sum_{j=1}^{J} \beta_j \xi^j(\mathbf{x}) + \epsilon. \tag{5}$$

If $\boldsymbol{\beta}$ is highly sparse, most of the coefficients β_j will be zero. Suppose that the candidate functions ξ^j are well-known functions such as positive or negative powers of the coordinates x_i of the input $\mathbf{x}$. In this case, the right-hand side will be a relatively short algebraic expression that is as interpretable as most potential energy functions routinely encountered in classical physics. The norm of ϵ here captures the error in this sparse approximation of $\widehat{V}$. In general, one chooses λ to balance the sparsity of $\boldsymbol{\beta}$ with the quality of the approximation $\|\epsilon\|$.

3 Tests

We now describe a series of increasingly complex tests that demonstrate the proposed method. For each such model, we use either exact solutions or fine-scale numerical integration to create a corpus of time series measurements. Using the time series, we train a neural potential energy model, which we then interpret using SINDy. We use NumPy/SciPy or Mathematica for all data generation, TensorFlow for all neural network model development/training, and the `sindyr` package [7] in R to interpret the neural potential. In what follows, the mass matrix M in (2) is the identity unless specified otherwise. In all cases, we train the neural network using gradient descent. We are committed to releasing all code/data at https://github.com/hbhat4000/learningpotentials.

3.1 Simple Harmonic Oscillator

The first model we consider is the simple harmonic oscillator ($d = 1$) with Hamiltonian

$$H(q, p) = \frac{p^2}{2} + \frac{q^2}{2}. \tag{6}$$

Exact trajectories consists of circles centered at the origin in (q, p) space. For training data, we use $R = 10$ such circles; for $1 \leq i \leq 10$, the i-th circle passes through an initial condition $(q(0), p(0)) = (0, i)$. We include $N = 1000$ steps of each trajectory, recorded with a time step of 0.01, in the training set. Here our goal is to check how closely the neural potential $\widehat{V}(q)$ can track the true potential $V(q) = q^2/2$. We take the neural potential model to have two hidden layers, each with 16 units and tanh activations. We train for 50000 steps at a learning rate of 0.01.

In Fig. 1, we plot both the trained neural potential $\widehat{V}$ (in red) and the true potential $V(q) = q^2/2$ (in black). When plotting $\widehat{V}$, we have subtracted a constant bias (the minimum obtained value of $\widehat{V}$) so that the curve reaches a minimum value of zero. Note that this constant bias is completely unimportant for

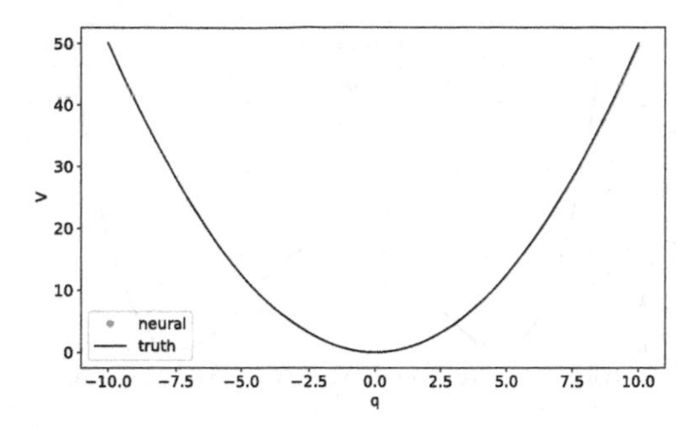

Fig. 1. For the simple harmonic oscillator (6), after adjusting a constant bias, the neural potential $\widehat{V}(q)$ closely matches the true potential $V(q) = q^2/2$. (Color figure online)

physics, as only ∇V appears in Hamilton's equations (2) and the loss (3). However, the constant bias does lead us to include an intercept in the regression model (4), i.e., to include 1 in the set of candidate functions for SINDy. We follow this practice in all uses of SINDy below.

We apply SINDy to the learned potential $\widehat{V}(q)$ with candidate functions $\{1, q, q^2, q^3\}$. In the following test, and in fact throughout this paper, we start with $\lambda = 1$ and tune λ downward until the error $\|\epsilon\|$—between the neural network potential $\widehat{V}(q)$ and the SINDy-computed approximation—drops below 10^{-10}. We find that with $\lambda = 0.04$, the estimated system is

$$\widehat{V}(q) \approx \beta_0 + \beta_2 q^2 \tag{7}$$

with $\beta_0 \approx -49.18$ and $\beta_2 \approx 0.4978$. We see that $\widehat{V}$ closely tracks the true potential $V(q) = q^2/2$ up to the constant bias term, which can be ignored.

3.2 Double Well

Let us consider a particle in a double well potential ($d = 1$)

$$V(q) = x^2(x-2)^2 - (x-1)^2. \tag{8}$$

We take the kinetic energy to be $T(p) = p^2/2$. We now use explicit Runge-Kutta integration in Mathematica to form three training sets:

- Training set $\mathcal{T}_1$ includes $R = 10$ trajectories with random initial conditions $(q(0), p(0))$ chosen uniformly on $[-1, 1]^2$, one of which has sufficiently high energy to visit both wells.
- Training set $\mathcal{T}_2$ consists of $R = 2$ trajectories, each of which starts and stays in an opposing well. The first trajectory has initial condition $(q(0), p(0)) = (3, 0)$ while the second has initial condition $(q(0), p(0)) = (-1, 0)$. These $q(0)$ values are symmetric across $q = 1$, the symmetry axis of $V(q)$.
- Training set $\mathcal{T}_3$ has only $R = 2$ trajectories that stay in the left well only.

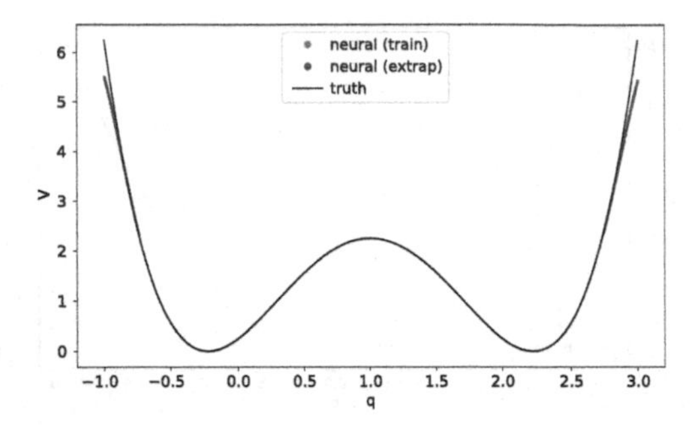

Fig. 2. For the double well potential (8), the neural potential $\widehat{V}(q)$ trained on $\mathcal{T}_1$ closely matches the true potential $V(q)$. This training set includes one high-energy trajectory that visits both wells. In red, we plot $V(q)$ for $q \in \mathcal{T}_1$; in green, we plot $V(q)$ for $q \in [-1,3] \setminus \mathcal{T}_1$. Potentials were adjusted by a constant bias so that they both have minimum values equal to zero. (Color figure online)

For each trajectory, we record 5001 points at a time step of 0.001. We take the neural potential model to have two hidden layers, each with 16 units and tanh activations. For each training set $\mathcal{T}_m$, we train for 50000 steps at a learning rate of 0.01.

We seek to understand how the choice of training set $\mathcal{T}_m$ affects the ability of the neural potential $\widehat{V}$ to track the true potential (8). We plot and discuss the results in Figs. 2 and 3. Overall, the neural potentials trained using $\mathcal{T}_1$ and $\mathcal{T}_2$ match $V(q)$ closely—both on the training set and extrapolated to the rest of the interval $-1 \leq q \leq 3$. Clearly, the neural potential trained using $\mathcal{T}_3$ only captures one well and does not extrapolate correctly to the rest of the domain.

Let $\widehat{V}^m(q)$ denote the neural potential trained on $\mathcal{T}_m$. We now apply SINDy to the output of each $\widehat{V}^m$ only on its respective training set $\mathcal{T}_m$, with candidate functions $\{1, q, q^2, q^3, q^4, q^5, q^6\}$. For reference, the ground truth $V(q)$ can be written as $V(q) = -1 + 2q + 3q^2 - 4q^3 + q^4$. Adjusting λ downward as described above, we find with $\lambda = 0.5$ the following algebraic expressions:

$$\widehat{V}^1(q) \approx -8.138 + 2.0008q + 3.0009q^2 - 4.0009q^3 + 1.0001q^4$$
$$\widehat{V}^2(q) \approx -6.061 + 2.0032q + 3.0054q^2 - 4.0148q^3 + 0.9748q^4$$
$$\widehat{V}^3(q) \approx -6.165 + 1.9909q + 2.9991q^2 - 3.9886q^3 + 0.9955q^4$$

Noting that the constant terms are irrelevant, we note here that *all three models agree closely with the ground truth.* The agreement between V and the algebraic forms of $\widehat{V}^1$ and $\widehat{V}^2$ was expected. We find it somewhat surprising that SINDy, when applied to the output of $\widehat{V}^3$ on its training set $\mathcal{T}^3$, yields a quartic polynomial with two wells.

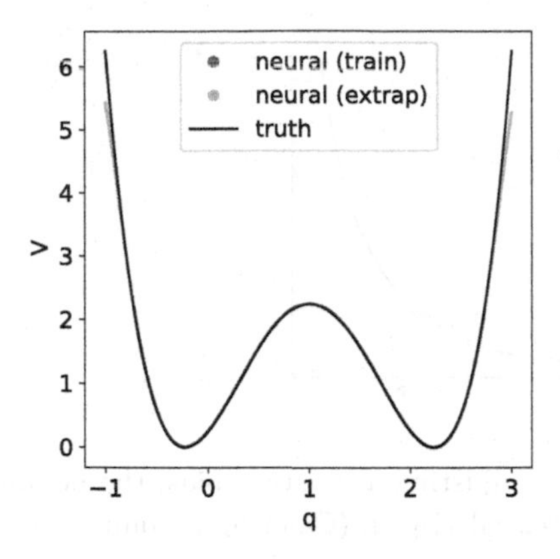

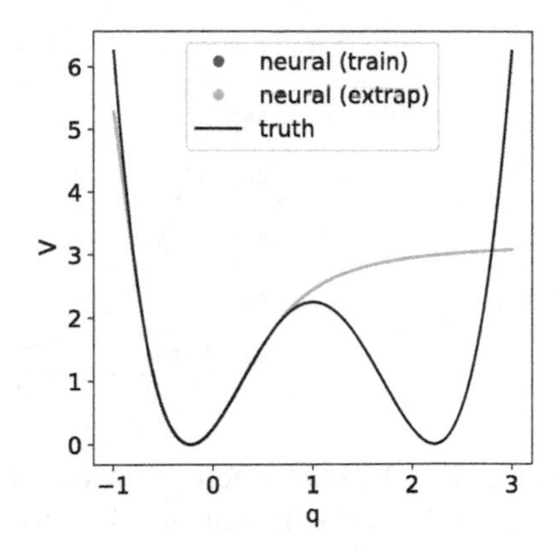

Fig. 3. For the double well potential (8), we train neural potentials $\widehat{V}(q)$ using, in turn, the training sets $\mathcal{T}_2$ (left) and $\mathcal{T}_3$ (right). We plot in red $\widehat{V}(q)$ only for the values of q covered by the respective training sets; in green, we extrapolate $\widehat{V}(q)$ to values of q that are not in the respective training sets. Since $\mathcal{T}_2$ includes two trajectories, one from each well, the neural potential captures and extrapolates well to both wells. Conversely, because $\mathcal{T}_3$ only includes trajectories that stay in one well, the neural potential completely misses one well. Potentials were adjusted by a constant bias so that they all have minimum values equal to zero. (Color figure online)

3.3 Central Force Problem

We consider a central force problem for one particle ($d = 3$) with Hamiltonian

$$H(\mathbf{q}, \mathbf{p}) = \frac{\|\mathbf{p}\|^2}{2} + \|\mathbf{q}\|^{-1} + (10 - \|\mathbf{q}\|)^{-1}. \tag{9}$$

The norm here is the standard Euclidean norm. Using explicit Runge-Kutta integration in Mathematica, we generate $R = 1$ trajectory with random initial condition $(\mathbf{q}(0), \mathbf{p}(0))$ chosen uniformly on $[-1, 1]^6$. Using this trajectory, we compute $r(t) = \|\mathbf{q}(t)\|$ as well as $\dot{r}(t) = dr/dt$. We save the $(r(t), \dot{r}(t))$ trajectories at $N = 20001$ points with a time step of 0.001. We then search for a reduced-order ($d = 1$) model with Hamiltonian

$$H(r, \dot{r}) = \frac{\dot{r}^2}{2} + \widetilde{V}(r), \tag{10}$$

where $\widetilde{V}(r)$ is a neural potential. We take the neural potential model to have two hidden layers, each with 16 units. We train for 500000 steps at a learning rate of 10^{-3}, first using exponential linear unit activations $\psi(x) = \begin{cases} x & x \geq 0 \\ \exp(x) - 1 & x < 0. \end{cases}$ We then initialize the neural network using the learned weights/biases and retrain using softplus activations $\phi(x) = \log(1 + \exp(x))$—this activation was chosen to enable series expansions of $\widehat{V}(r)$, as described in greater detail below. Prior to retraining, we also change the network by adding

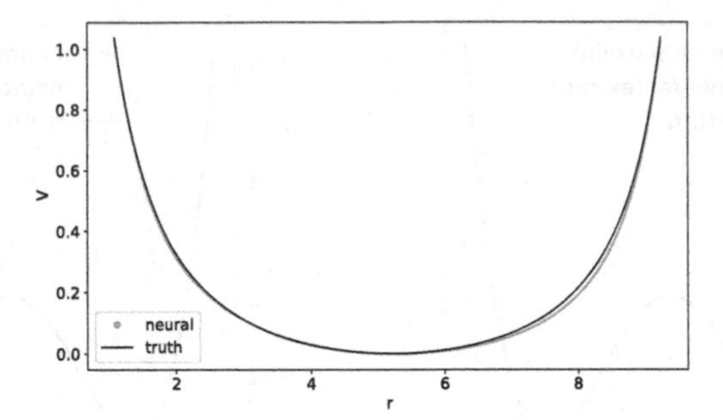

Fig. 4. For the central force problem (10), after adjusting a constant bias, the neural potential $\widehat{V}(r)$ closely matches the effective potential $V_{\text{eff}}(r)$. (Color figure online)

an exponential function to the output layer—we incorporate this function to better model the steep gradients in the potential near $r = 0$ and $r = 10$. When we retrain, we take 500000 steps at a learning rate of 10^{-3}. We carry out the training in two stages because training directly with softplus activations and exponential output failed.

For this problem, classical physics gives us an *effective potential*

$$V_{\text{eff}}(r) = r^{-1} + (10 - r)^{-1} + \ell^2/(2r^2). \tag{11}$$

where ℓ is a conserved quantity determined from the initial condition. In Fig. 4, we plot both the trained neural potential $\widehat{V}$ (in red) and the effective potential $V_{\text{eff}}(r)$ (in black). After adjusting for the constant bias term, we find close agreement.

We then exported the weight and bias matrices to Mathematica, forming the neural potential model

$$\widehat{V}(r) = W_3\phi(W_2\phi(W_1 r + b_1) + b_2) + b_3. \tag{12}$$

Unlike ψ, the softplus activation ϕ is amenable to series expansion via symbolic computation. In particular, since we can see that the effective potential $V_{\text{eff}}(r)$ is a rational function, we explored Padé expansions of $\widehat{V}(r)$. These attempts were unsuccessful in the sense that we did not obtain models of $\widehat{V}(r)$ that are any more interpretable than the compositional form of (12).

Turning to SINDy, we formed a library of candidate functions

$$\{1, r^{-1}, r^{-2}, r^{-3}, (10 - r)^{-1}, (10 - r)^{-2}, (10 - r)^{-3}\}.$$

Adjusting λ in the same manner described above, we find that with $\lambda = 0.15$, the estimated model is

$$\widehat{V}(r) \approx \beta_0 + \beta_1 r^{-1} + \beta_2 r^{-2} + \beta_4 (10 - r)^{-1} \tag{13}$$

Here $\beta_0 \approx -0.2384$, $\beta_1 \approx 1.005$, $\beta_2 \approx 0.4461$, and $\beta_4 \approx 0.9723$. We see from the form of $V_{\text{eff}}(r)$ given above that β_1 and β_4 are both close to the ground truth values of 1. Note that for the trajectory on which the system was trained, we have $\ell^2/2 \approx 0.4655$. Hence β_2 has an error of less than 4.2%. This demonstrates a successful application of SINDy to interpret the neural potential as a rational function; this interpretation of $\widehat{V}$ is itself close to V_{eff}.

3.4 Charged Particles in Coulomb Potential

We now consider two oppositely charged particles ($d = 6$) subject to the classical Coulomb electrostatic potential. We take the mass matrix to be $M = \text{diag}(1, 1/2)$. The kinetic energy is $T(\mathbf{p}) = \mathbf{p}^T M^{-1} \mathbf{p}/2$. If we partition $\mathbf{q} = (\mathbf{q}_1, \mathbf{q}_2)$ where $\mathbf{q}_i$ is the position of the i-th particle, then the potential is

$$V(\mathbf{q}) = -\frac{1}{4\pi} \frac{1}{\|\mathbf{q}_1 - \mathbf{q}_2\|}. \tag{14}$$

Here we apply the Störmer-Verlet algorithm, a symplectic method, to generate $R = 1000$ trajectories, each with $N = 10001$ points recorded at a time step of 0.001. Each trajectory starts with random initial conditions $(\mathbf{q}(0), \mathbf{p}(0))$ chosen from a standard normal. For this problem, our goal is to use the data to recover V. We train two different neural potential models with increasing levels of prior domain knowledge:

1. We first set up the neural network's input layer to compute from $\mathbf{q}$ the difference $\mathbf{q}_1 - \mathbf{q}_2 \in \mathbb{R}^3$; the neural potential then transforms this three-dimensional input into a scalar output. The neural network here has 8 hidden layers, each with 16 units and tanh activations. Using only 800 of the $R = 1000$ trajectories, we first train using the first 100 points from each of the 800 trajectories, taking 500000 steps at a learning rate of 0.01. Again restricting ourselves to the 800 training trajectories, we then use the next 100 points, followed by the next 100 points, etc., each time taking 500000 steps at a learning rate of 0.01. As the training loss was observed to be sufficiently small (≈ 0.006021), we halted training.
   In Fig. 5, we plot both training (left) and test (right) results. The training results are plotted with the first 1000 points of the 800 trajectories used for training, while the test results are plotted with the first 1000 points of the 200 held out trajectories. For both plots, we subtracted the maximum computed value of $\widehat{V}$ (on each respective data set). In each plot, we plot $\widehat{V}$ (on all points $\mathbf{q}$ in the training and test sets) versus $r = \|\mathbf{q}_1 - \mathbf{q}_2\|$.
   Overall, we see reasonable agreement between the neural potential and the ground truth. Note that the neural network is essentially tasked with discovering that it should compute the inverse of the norm of $\mathbf{q}_1 - \mathbf{q}_2$. We suspect that this function of $\mathbf{q}_1 - \mathbf{q}_2$ may be somewhat difficult to represent using a composition of activation functions and linear transformations as in (12). Despite training for a large number of steps, there is noticeable variation in neural potential values for large r.

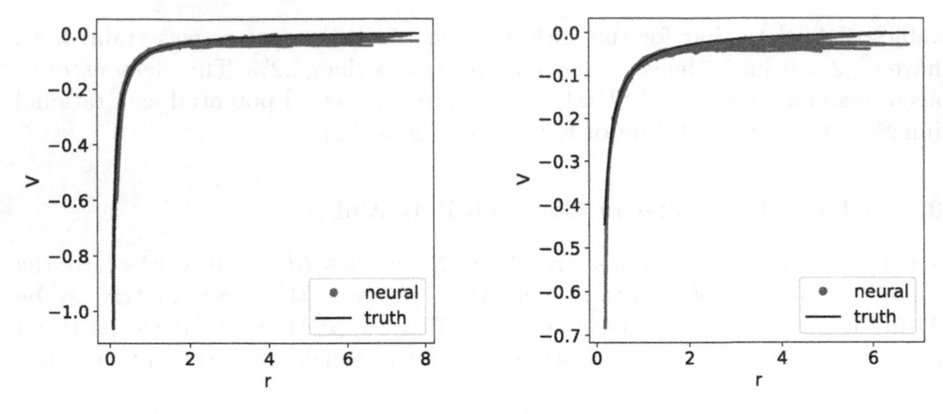

Fig. 5. Here we plot both training (left) and test (right) results for the Coulomb problem (14). For both plots, we have subtracted a constant bias, the maximum value of the neural potential on the data set in question. These results are for a neural potential $\widehat{V}$ that is a function of the difference $\mathbf{q}_1 - \mathbf{q}_2$ between the two charged particles' positions; for each $\mathbf{q}$ in the training and test sets, we plot $\widehat{V}(\mathbf{q}_1 - \mathbf{q}_2)$ versus $r = \|\mathbf{q}_1 - \mathbf{q}_2\|$. We also plot the true potential (14) versus r. Both training and test plots show reasonable agreement between the neural potential and the ground truth.

We now apply SINDy to $\widehat{V}$ (on the training set) using candidate functions $\{1, r^{-1}, r^{-2}, r^{-3}\}$. Adjusting λ as described above, we find with $\lambda = 0.04$, the approximation

$$\widehat{V}(r) \approx \beta_0 + \beta_1 r^{-1} \tag{15}$$

with $\beta_0 \approx 0.7602$ and $\beta_1 \approx -0.06911$. For comparison, the ground truth coefficient of r^{-1} is $-(4\pi)^{-1} \approx -0.07958$.

2. We then rearchitect the network to include a layer that takes the input $\mathbf{q}$ and computes the norm of the difference $\|\mathbf{q}_1 - \mathbf{q}_2\|$; the rest of the neural potential is then a scalar function of this scalar input. Here the neural network has 8 hidden layers, each with 8 units and tanh activations. We train for 50000 steps with learning rate of 0.05. Note that here, for training, we use $N = 5001$ time steps of only 100 trajectories.

   In Fig. 6, we plot both training (left) and test (right) results. The training results are plotted with the first 5001 points of the 100 trajectories used for training, while the test results are plotted with a completely different set of 100 trajectories, each of length 5001 For both plots, we subtracted the minimum computed value of $\widehat{V}$ (on each respective data set). In each plot, we compute $\widehat{V}$ on all points $\mathbf{q}$ in the training and test sets, and then plot these $\widehat{V}$ values versus $r = \|\mathbf{q}_1 - \mathbf{q}_2\|$.

   To generate an interpretable version of $\widehat{V}$ (on the training set), we apply SINDy with candidate functions $\{1, r^{-1}, r^{-2}, r^{-3}\}$. Adjusting λ as described above, we find with $\lambda = 0.05$, the approximation

$$\widehat{V}(r) \approx \beta_0 + \beta_1 r^{-1} \tag{16}$$

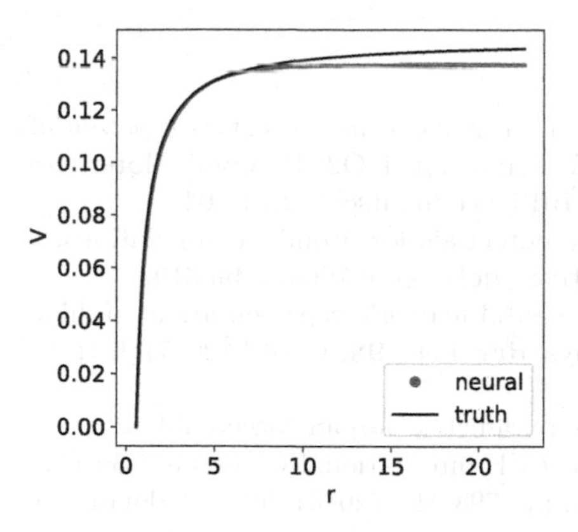

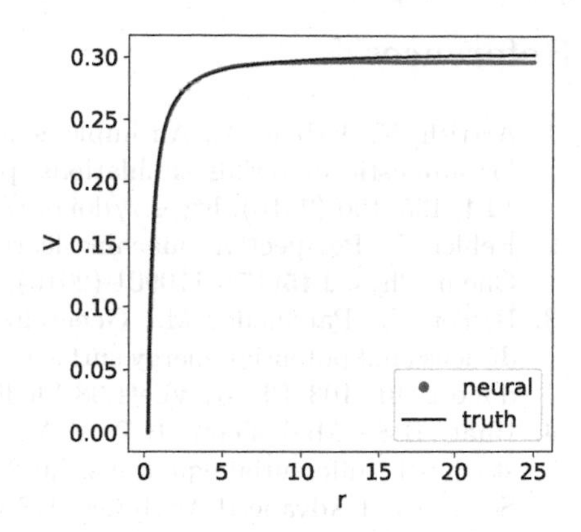

Fig. 6. Here we plot both training (left) and test (right) results for the Coulomb problem (14). For both plots, we have subtracted a constant bias, the maximum value of the neural potential on the data set in question. These results are for a neural potential $\widehat{V}$ that is a function of the distance $r = \|\mathbf{q}_1 - \mathbf{q}_2\|$ between the two charged particles; for each $\mathbf{q}$ in the training and test sets, we plot $\widehat{V}(r)$ versus $r = \|\mathbf{q}_1 - \mathbf{q}_2\|$. We also plot the true potential (14) versus r. Both training and test plots show excellent agreement between the neural potential and the ground truth.

with $\beta_0 \approx 2.267$ and $\beta_1 \approx -0.07792$. This computed value of β_1 is less than 2.1% away from the ground truth value of $-(4\pi)^{-1}$; the error for the earlier approximation (15) was just over 13.1%.

Incorporating prior knowledge that the potential should depend only on r dramatically improves the quality of the learned potential. Essentially, we have eliminated the need for the neural network to learn the norm function. We outperform the results from Fig. 5 using a less complex network, trained for fewer steps and a larger learning rate. Comparing with Fig. 5, we see that Fig. 6 features reduced variation in $\widehat{V}(r)$ for large r, and improved test set results as well.

4 Conclusion

We conclude that, for the examples we have explored, our approach does lead to accurate potentials that can themselves be approximated closely by interpretable, closed-form algebraic expressions. In ongoing/future work, we plan to apply the techniques described here to high-dimensional systems for which reduced-order (i.e., effective) potentials are unknown. We also seek to extend our method to quantum Hamiltonian systems. While we have focused here on clean data from known models, we are also interested in learning potentials from noisy time series. We expect that by adapting the method of [11], we will be able to simultaneously filter the data and estimate an interpretable neural potential.

References

1. Artrith, N., Urban, A.: An implementation of artificial neural-network potentials for atomistic materials simulations: performance for TiO2. Comput. Mater. Sci. **114**, 135–150 (2016). https://doi.org/10.1016/j.commatsci.2015.11.047
2. Behler, J.: Perspective: machine learning potentials for atomistic simulations. J. Chem. Phys. **145**(17), 170901 (2016). https://doi.org/10.1063/1.4966192
3. Behler, J., Parrinello, M.: Generalized neural-network representation of high-dimensional potential-energy surfaces. Phys. Rev. Lett. **98**, 146401 (2007). https://doi.org/10.1103/PhysRevLett.98.146401
4. Bhat, H.S., Madushani, R.W.M.A.: Nonparametric adjoint-based inference for stochastic differential equations. In: 2016 IEEE International Conference on Data Science and Advanced Analytics (DSAA), pp. 798–807 (2016). https://doi.org/10.1109/DSAA.2016.69
5. Brunton, S.L., Proctor, J.L., Kutz, J.N.: Discovering governing equations from data by sparse identification of nonlinear dynamical systems. Proc. Natl. Acad. Sci. **113**(15), 3932–3937 (2016)
6. Dale, R., Bhat, H.S.: Equations of mind: data science for inferring nonlinear dynamics of socio-cognitive systems. Cogn. Syst. Res. **52**, 275–290 (2018)
7. Dale, R., Bhat, H.S.: sindyr: Sparse Identification of Nonlinear Dynamics (2018). https://CRAN.R-project.org/package=sindyr. r package version 0.2.1
8. Duncker, L., Bohner, G., Boussard, J., Sahani, M.: Learning interpretable continuous-time models of latent stochastic dynamical systems. In: Chaudhuri, K., Salakhutdinov, R. (eds.) Proceedings of the 36th International Conference on Machine Learning, Proceedings of Machine Learning Research, PMLR, Long Beach, California, USA, 09–15 June 2019, vol. 97, pp. 1726–1734 (2019). http://proceedings.mlr.press/v97/duncker19a.html
9. Hansen, K., et al.: Machine learning predictions of molecular properties: accurate many-body potentials and nonlocality in chemical space. J. Phys. Chem. Lett. **6**(12), 2326–2331 (2015). https://doi.org/10.1021/acs.jpclett.5b00831
10. Ramakrishnan, R., Hartmann, M., Tapavicza, E., von Lilienfeld, O.A.: Electronic spectra from TDDFT and machine learning in chemical space. J. Chem. Phys. **143**(8), 084111 (2015). https://doi.org/10.1063/1.4928757
11. Raziperchikolaei, R., Bhat, H.S.: A block coordinate descent proximal method for simultaneous filtering and parameter estimation. In: Chaudhuri, K., Salakhutdinov, R. (eds.) Proceedings of the 36th International Conference on Machine Learning, Proceedings of Machine Learning Research, PMLR, Long Beach, California, USA, 09–15 June 2019, vol. 97, pp. 5380–5388 (2019). http://proceedings.mlr.press/v97/raziperchikolaei19a.html
12. Sahoo, S., Lampert, C., Martius, G.: Learning equations for extrapolation and control. In: Dy, J., Krause, A. (eds.) Proceedings of the 35th International Conference on Machine Learning, Proceedings of Machine Learning Research, PMLR, Stockholmsmässan, Stockholm Sweden, 10–15 July 2018, vol. 80, pp. 4442–4450 (2018). http://proceedings.mlr.press/v80/sahoo18a.html
13. Zhang, L., Schaeffer, H.: On the convergence of the SINDy algorithm. arXiv e-prints arXiv:1805.06445, May 2018

Finding Interpretable Concept Spaces in Node Embeddings Using Knowledge Bases

Maximilian Idahl(✉), Megha Khosla, and Avishek Anand

L3S Research Center, Hannover, Germany
{idahl,khosla,anand}@l3s.de

Abstract. In this paper we propose and study the novel problem of explaining node embeddings by finding embedded human interpretable subspaces in already trained unsupervised node representation embeddings. We use an external knowledge base that is organized as a taxonomy of human-understandable concepts over entities as a guide to identify subspaces in node embeddings learned from an entity graph derived from Wikipedia. We propose a method that given a concept finds a linear transformation to a subspace where the structure of the concept is retained. Our initial experiments show that we obtain low error in finding fine-grained concepts.

Keywords: Interpretability · Node embeddings · Conceptual spaces

1 Introduction

Representations of nodes in a graph or node embeddings have proven useful in many applications such as question answering [1], dialog systems [14], recommender [21] systems and knowledge-base completion [15]. The core idea behind *node representation learning* (NRL) [4,10,22] approaches is to distill the high-dimensional discrete representation of nodes into a dense vector embedding using dimensionality reduction methods, which optionally not only incorporate the graph structure, but also features attached to nodes. These representations can be seen as features extracted from only the topology or from both the topology and the available node attributes. The dense representations thereby learnt form a latent feature space where the basis or dimensions are non-interpretable.

Consequently, in spite of their success, there is a lack of an understanding of what the latent dimensions encode in terms of existing human knowledge. This is problematic for downstream tasks requiring interpretability, since using such embeddings results in the input already being non-interpretable. For aiding interpretability and utility of these embeddings in downstream application scenarios we initiate an inquiry into presence of *interpretable* or human understandable subspaces in the learnt feature representation space of these graph embeddings. We ask the fundamental question: *What do node embeddings encode in terms of*

P. Cellier and K. Driessens (Eds.): ECML PKDD 2019 Workshops, CCIS 1167, pp. 229–240, 2020.
https://doi.org/10.1007/978-3-030-43823-4_20

human world knowledge? Recent works in interpretability for learning on structured data either focus on generating interpretable embeddings or explaining the predictions made by a classifier to which embeddings form the input [26]. But none of these methods provide insights into the embedding itself, a problem which we propose and study in this work.

We take an alternate view on interpretability of node embeddings in that we want to find sub-spaces in the embedding space corresponding to human-understandable concepts. Our main contribution is in finding interpretable sub-spaces in the latent feature representation space and thus characterizing the behavior of node representations when projected into these interpretable spaces. This has two distinct advantages – first we do not compromise on the effectiveness of these embeddings as we post-hoc analyze the presence of interpretable spaces in the already learned representation space. Secondly, we ground the interpretable space to existing world knowledge in the form of knowledge bases.

To this extent, in this work, we use external knowledge bases (KB) to learn conceptual spaces for corresponding characteristics that can be attributed to a given node. In particular, we assume that we have an input graph of labelled or named nodes. As a use case we focus on a hyperlink graph of named entities. We observe that KBs like YAGO [7] encode human understandable concepts organized in a taxonomy which can be used as the source of world knowledge assuming that the nodes/entities in the input graph are also present in the taxonomy. In principle one can use any input graph and KB as long as the input graph node names are grounded in the KB. Having extracted the possible concepts from the taxonomy, we then propose methods to explain a node embedding in terms of the applicability of various concepts. For example, a node named *Albert Einstein* could be explained by concepts like *Theoretical physicists*, *Scientists* etc.

We propose two simple algorithms, SAS and CSD, to explain node embeddings in terms of concepts and provide promising first results for pre-trained embeddings corresponding to two unsupervised random walk based node embedding methods, namely, DeepWalk [22] and LINE [24]. We show that our second approach CSD that projects a node embedding to a common learnt concept space distinguishes the applicable and non applicable concepts better than our first approach which operates in the original embedding space.

2 Related Work

Supervised learning approaches are either *interpretable by design* [3,13,25] or explanations can be generated in a post-hoc manner after the model is trained [12,19,23]. Post-hoc methods for interpretability either operate introspectively (full access to the model parameters) [12,19] or are model agnostic [23]. We operate in the model introspective interpretable regime where we assume full access to the model parameters. For other notions of interpretability and a more comprehensive description of the approaches we point the readers to [5].

Methods focussing on building interpretable representations include MEmbER [8] which learns entity embeddings using max-margin constraints to encode the desideratum that (salient) properties of entities should have a simple geometric representation in the entity embedding. Jameel and Schockaert [9] propose a method which learns a vector-space embedding of entities from Wikipedia and constrains this embedding such that entities of the same semantic type are located in some lower-dimensional subspace. Minervini et al. [18] leverage equivalence and inversion axioms during the learning of knowledge graph embeddings, by imposing a set of model dependent soft constraints on the predicate embeddings. Post-hoc methods include GNN-Explainer [26] which provides interpretations for GNN predictions on link prediction, node classification and graph classification tasks. The interpretations are tied to specific tasks. We, on the other hand, propose to understand the node representations directly in terms of user provided conceptual categories.

Unlike the above works we focus on explaining the node vector representation itself which might have been obtained using an arbitrary embedding method.

3 Preliminaries

In this section we give a brief overview of YAGO and node embedding methods used in this work.

3.1 Knowledge Graphs

As a source of *concepts* or human understandable world knowledge we use the YAGO [7] knowledge base (KB), which was automatically constructed from Wikipedia. Typically, each article in Wikipedia becomes an entity in the knowledge base (e.g., since Albert Einstein has an article in Wikipedia, Albert Einstein is an entity in YAGO). Each entity is organized into a taxonomy of classes. In addition, every entity is an instance of one or multiple classes and every class (except the root class) is a subclass of one or multiple classes. therefore yielding a hierarchy of classes – the *YAGO taxonomy.*

Each class name is of the form `<wordnet_XXX_YYY>` or `<wikicat_XXX_YYY>`, where XXX is the name of the concept (e.g., singer), and YYY is the WordNet 3.0 synset id of the concept (e.g., 110599806). For example, the class of singers is `<wordnet_singer_110599806>`. Additionally, each class is connected to its more general class by the `rdfs:subclassOf` relationship.

Not all Wikipedia categories correspond to classes in YAGO. The lowest layer of the taxonomy is the layer of instances. Instances comprise individual entities such as rivers, people, or movies. For example, the lowest layer contains `<Elvis_Presley>`. Each instance is connected to one or multiple classes of the higher layers by the relationship rdf:type. For example, for entity Albert_Einstein we have:

`<Albert_Einstein> rdf:type <wikicat_Nuclear_physicist>`.

One can therefore walk from the instance up to its class by `rdf:type`, and then further up by `rdfs:subclassOf`. In Sect. 4 we will provide details about how the concepts derived from the taxonomy are used as explanations for node embeddings.

3.2 Node Embeddings

Node representations or node embeddings can be understood as the set of features extracted from the graph topology and (if given) node attributes. The present set of techniques for node representation learning generally fall into one of these categories: (1) random walk based [4,10,22,24], (2) matrix factorization based [2,20] or (3) deep learning or Graph Neural Network (GNN) based [6,11]. In this section we describe briefly the two random walk based approaches which we employ in this work. In future we will investigate our methods using a general set of unsupervised and semi-supervised embedding approaches.

The basic idea behind random walk based embedding techniques is to transform the graph into a collection of node sequences, in which, the occurrence frequency of a node-context pair measures the structural distance between them. *DeepWalk* [22] was the first method to exploit random walk techniques to build sentence like structures from graphs to train a *SkipGram* model [17]. It employs truncated random walks to create vertex sequences, which are later used in a word2vec fashion to learn vertex embeddings given its context. For a graph G, it samples uniformly a random vertex v as the root of the random walk W_v. A walk samples uniformly from the neighbors of the last vertex visited until the maximum length t is reached. For each $v_i \in W_v$ and for each $u_k \in W[j-c : j+c]$ (c is the window size), (v_j, u_k) forms a vertex-context training pair (similar to word -context pair in word embeddings). The objective is then to maximize the probability of observing u_k given the representation of v_j. LINE [24] optimizes first order proximity (i.e. embeds nodes sharing a link closer) and second order proximities (embeds nodes closer if they have similar neighborhoods) using an SGNS (Skip-gram with negative sampling) objective function [16]. Similar to DeepWalk, it can be understood as sampling random walks of length 1 and uses vertices sharing an edge as training pairs.

4 Research Questions and Our Approach

We propose a general approach for post-hoc interpretability of node representation learned by an unsupervised or semi-supervised method. We bring in a completely new perspective of interpretability of extracted features of nodes by using external knowledge to determine the concepts that a given representation encodes. More precisely, we use Wikipedia entity graph, $G = (V, E)$, as the input graph, where the nodes are Wikipedia pages and the edges correspond to the hyperlinks between them. We employ DeepWalk and LINE to generate embeddings for all $v \in V$. We ignore the edge direction to learn the embeddings. We also recall that the present topic of this work is to define and validate interpretability on node embeddings and the choice of embeddings methods is therefore arbitrary. Let Φ_v represent the embedding vector corresponding to v. We ponder over the following question:

RQ 1 *What concepts do these embeddings encode?*

As the embeddings are usually generated only considering the structure of the graph or/and node attributes, an embedding vector Φ_v encodes the concepts which it shares with its neighborhood (neighborhood here depends on the employed embedding method). Consider, for example, an entity *Barack Obama*, which could be understood as sharing characteristics with other *Presidents* and *Nobel Prize winners. Presidents* and *Nobel Prize winners* here are the human understandable world knowledge or concepts. Rather than characterizing nodes in terms of their neighbors, we in this work use these implicit human understandable concepts to characterize an embedding vector. In particular, for a given embedding vector Φ_v and a concept c, we assign a score $\mathcal{S}(\Phi_v, c) \in \mathcal{R}$ which quantifies the characteristic c of the embedding Φ_v. Roughly speaking, the score measures the amount of the characteristic that an embedding vector possesses.

The challenge here is that often only the graph structure or sometimes the node attributes are also available but there are no explicit concepts provided. We therefore ask the following question:

RQ 2 *How can explicit concepts be constructed given an input graph with named vertices?*

In order to generate possible concepts related to an entity, we propose the use of external knowledge base like YAGO (see also Sect. 3.1), which provides a hierarchy of concepts related to any given node, say v in the graph. These concepts form the characteristics of v. The user can then query the encoding of possible concepts in the trained node embedding. For example, a user may ask how much the embedding vector corresponding to *Barack Obama* encodes *American Presidents* and *Scientists.* One might assume that the Obama's embedding vector should not have anything to do with the concept *Scientists,* which might not be true as the underlying graph might put Obama in close proximity with other Nobel Prize winners who are also Scientists. Having defined or collected concepts from external knowledge bases, the next natural question is:

RQ 3 *For a given embedding vector, Φ_v and a concept c, how can we score the applicability of c to Φ_v ?*

To quantify the applicability of concept corresponding to an embedding or to explain an embedding in terms of the applicable and not applicable concepts, we propose two algorithms: Simple Aggregation Strategy (SAS) and Concept Space Discovery (CSD).

4.1 Simple Aggregation Strategy

The first approach uses a simple aggregation strategy to build concept representations from the representations of the nodes (from the training set) to which the concept is applicable (test nodes are held out). In particular, we first compute a vector representing the given concept by taking the element-wise mean of all the embedding vectors corresponding to nodes to which the concept applies, excluding the query nodes. This vector defines the *concept center*. To score a query node, we compute the L2 distance between its embedding vector and the concept center.

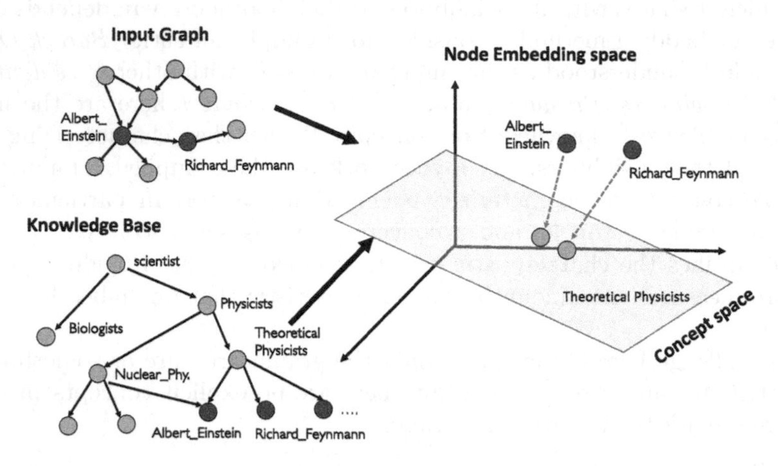

Fig. 1. Extracting concept spaces

4.2 Concept Space Discovery (CSD)

The second algorithm is more involved and explicit, in the sense that for each concept c it learns a linear transformation, which is used to project the node vectors into a more restricted space for c, that we call *concept space*. The original embedding vectors are projected into this new space to extract their effective representations which best encode the given concept (refer Fig. 1). We learn the parameters for this transformation on triplets of entities, using triplet loss. Let a be the entity node (also called anchor node) which is a direct descendant of concept c, p be some sibling of a in the taxonomy and n be the negative example, i.e., an entity which is not a sibling of a in the taxonomy. For any node v, let Φ_v represent the corresponding embedding vector. The triplet loss $\mathcal{L}(a, p, n)$ is then defined as follows.

$$\mathcal{L}(a, p, n) = max\{d(\Phi_a, \Phi_p) - d(\Phi_a, \Phi_n) + m, 0\} \tag{1}$$

where $d(\Phi_x, \Phi_y) = ||x - y||_2$ and m is a margin specific to the negative entity in a triplet. We set this margin to be the distance from the target concept to the lowest common ancestor concept shared by the positive and the negative entity, i.e. negative entities that are conceptually close to the positive entity have lower margins and ones that are conceptually far away have higher margins. We refer to negative entities with low margins as soft negatives and to negative entities with high margins as hard negatives. An illustrative example for computing margin is provided in Fig. 2.

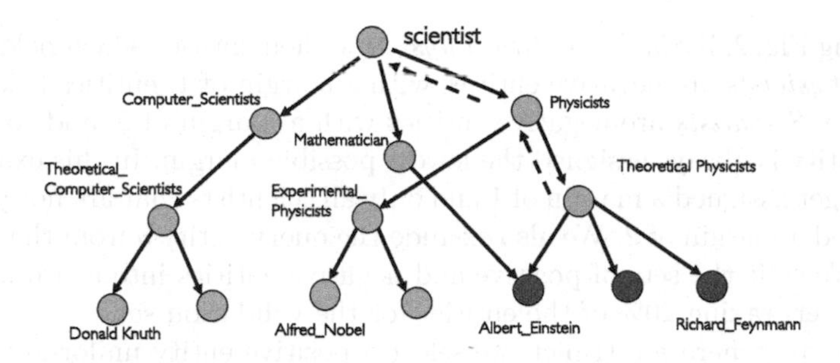

Fig. 2. Margin for triplet loss is determined by the similarity in the taxonomy graph. The margin between Albert Einstein and Donald Knuth is 2, where as the margin between Albert Einstein and Alfred Nobel is 1.

Score Computation. The scoring of how much a concept applies to a query entity is analogous to the first approach, but of course operates in the *concept space*. That is, for a given concept c and the positive entities (the training set) corresponding to the concept, we first compute their projections into common concept space and then compute the mean of the resulting projected vectors to represent the concept. Again for a given query node, we first compute its projection into the concept space and the final score is then given by the L2 distance between the concept vector and the query projection. Lower the score, better is the concept encoded by the query node. Note that both loss function and scoring make use of the same distance metric, the L2 distance.

5 Experiments

5.1 Data Acquisition

We conduct our experiments on the Wikipedia entity graph, where the nodes are Wikipedia pages and the edges correspond to the hyperlinks between them. In addition, we use the type hierarchy of YAGO as the KB and consider all leaves under a concept node as belonging to the concept, as described in Sect. 3.1.

5.2 Methodology

Given a query entity q and a start concept c_{start} we learn concept spaces for c_{start} and its sibling concepts in the taxonomy. Note that we limit the number of concepts due to computation (Some concepts have a large number of siblings). For each selected concept, we a learn a concept representation as described in Sect. 4. Below we give more details about the training employed in our second approach CSD.

For CSD where we use triplet loss function to learn the concept space we choose positive and negative examples as follows. For each concept c, the set of positive entities (examples) consists of all entities contained in c. Next, we rank all ancestor concepts of c by the margin, which is the distance of the concept to *c*. Following Fig. 2, if *c* is *Theoretical Physicists*, then entities which belong to the concept *Physicists* are negative entities with a margin of 1, entities belonging to the concept *Scientists* are negative entities with a margin of 2, and so on. Note that an entity is always assigned the lowest possible margin. In this example, all physicists get assigned a margin of 1 and only all scientists that are not physicists get assigned a margin of 2. We also exclude the query entity q from the sampling process. We split the sets of positive and negative entities into a training and a validation set, taking 20% of the entities for the validation set.

In order to generate a triplet, we select a positive entity uniformly from the set of positive samples. An anchor entity is selected in the same way, with respect to the anchor not being the same entity as the chosen positive one. Next, we select a margin m uniformly from the available margins in the set of negative entities. Then, we select a negative entity uniformly from the negative samples corresponding to margin m. To train one concept space, we sample a total of ten thousand triplets. We then train the linear transformation using Stochastic Gradient Descent with Momentum for 100 epochs, with a mini batch size of 16 and a leaning rate of 0.001. We stop the training early if the validation loss does not improve over 5 epochs. After training, we score the query entity as described in Sect. 4 corresponding to our two approaches.

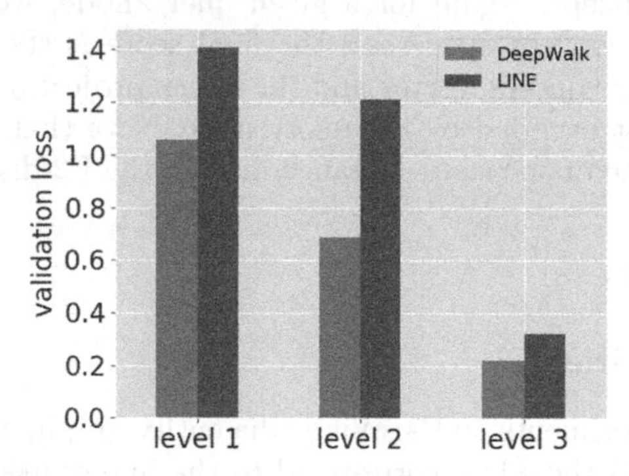

Fig. 3. Mean validation losses for training concept space projections for concepts of different hierarchy levels. Level 1 includes concepts high up in the hierarchy, namely *person*, *organization* and *country*. The second level includes *scientist*, *educational institution* and *countries in Europe*. Level 3 then covers the more fine-grained concepts *theoretical physicist*, *university or college in Germany* and *states of Germany*.

6 Results

In Fig. 3 we show the errors corresponding to each concept level for different node embedding approaches (DeepWalk and LINE). Concepts at a higher level, as expected, exhibit higher error but the error reduces to a small value for more specific concepts. It is interesting to observe that it is easier to find interpretable concept spaces in DeepWalk as opposed to LINE. In this regard DeepWalk can be in some sense regarded as more interpretable than LINE.

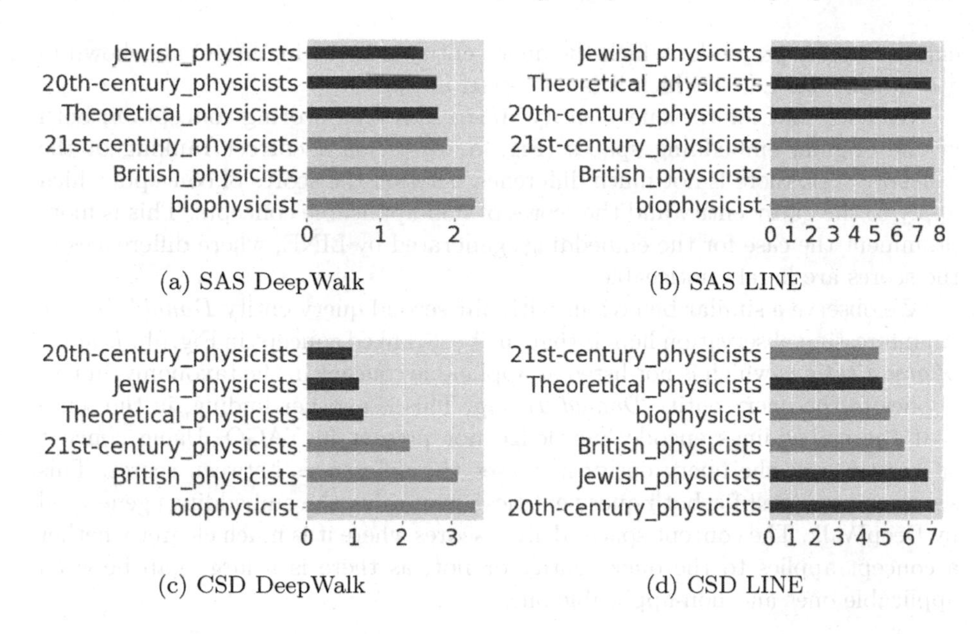

Fig. 4. Concept ranking for Albert Einstein (Color figure online)

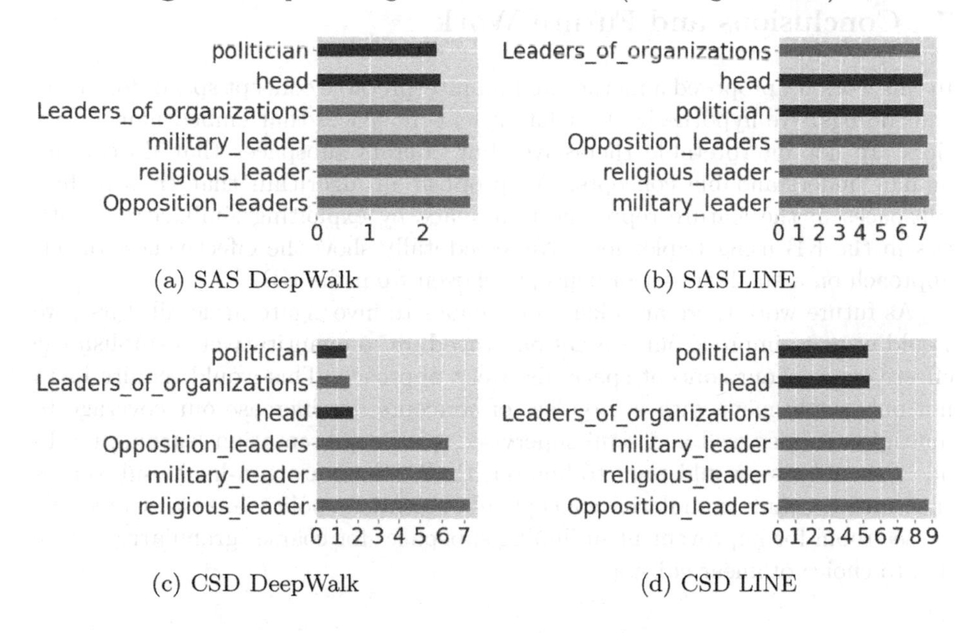

Fig. 5. Concept ranking for Donald Trump (Color figure online)

Figures 4 and 5 show the scores of different concepts for the query entities *Albert Einstein* and *Donald Trump*, respectively. We recall that lower the score $\mathcal{S}(\Phi_v, c)$, more is the applicability of c towards the embedding vector Φ_v or the entity v. Concepts under which the query entity is listed in YAGO are shown in green, concepts under which it is not listed in red.

We note that for the query entity *Albert Einstein*, scoring concepts in both of the original embedding spaces (Fig. 4a, b) yields a correct ranking of the concepts. Yet, there is not much difference between the scores of concepts which apply to the query entity and the scores of non-applicable concepts. This is more prominent the case for the embeddings generated by LINE, where differences in the scores are barely noticeable.

We observe a similar behaviour with our second query entity *Donald Trump*. An interesting observation here is that the best ranked concept in Fig. 5b, *Leaders of organizations* which is not listed as applicable concept in the taxonomy, in fact applies to the query entity *Donald Trump*. This is another finding, in the sense that the embeddings encode knowledge not present in YAGO. Using concept spaces to score the query entity increases the differences between scores. This seems to work well for both query entities when using the embeddings generated by DeepWalk. The concept spaces deliver scores where it is much clearer whether a concept applies to the query entity or not, as there is a large gap between applicable ones and non-applicable ones.

7 Conclusions and Future Work

In this work we proposed a method to find interpretable concept spaces for graph embeddings. We hypothesize that latent feature spaces that embed named vertices are not interpretable themselves but contain subspaces that do contain human understandable concepts. We propose an algorithm that tries to find subspaces in the feature representation space by exploiting similarity of entities in the KB using triplet loss. We anecdotally show the effectiveness of our approach on a small subset of concepts chosen from the KB.

As future work there are plenty of avenues to investigate in detail. First, we would want to improve our evaluation procedure to quantitatively establish the effectiveness of our concept space discovery approach. This would require us to not only experiment with a large set of concepts but increase our coverage to multiple unsupervised and semi-supervised node representation learning methods. Secondly, we would want to find out that if there are non-linear sub spaces that encode coarse-granularity concepts like scientists, politicians etc. Currently, we see room for improvement in finding subspaces for coarser granularity topics due to choice of linear subspaces.

References

1. Bordes, A., Chopra, S., Weston, J.: Question answering with subgraph embeddings. arXiv preprint arXiv:1406.3676 (2014)
2. Cao, S., Lu, W., Xu, Q.: GraRep: learning graph representations with global structural information. In: CIKM, pp. 891–900. ACM (2015)

3. Caruana, R., Lou, Y., Gehrke, J., Koch, P., Sturm, M., Elhadad, N.: Intelligible models for healthcare: predicting pneumonia risk and hospital 30-day readmission. In: Proceedings of the 21th ACM SIGKDD International Conference on Knowledge Discovery and Data Mining, pp. 1721–1730. ACM (2015)
4. Grover, A., Leskovec, J.: node2vec: scalable feature learning for networks. In: SIGKDD, pp. 855–864. ACM (2016)
5. Guidotti, R., Monreale, A., Ruggieri, S., Turini, F., Giannotti, F., Pedreschi, D.: A survey of methods for explaining black box models. ACM Comput. Surv. (CSUR) **51**(5), 93 (2018)
6. Hamilton, W., Ying, Z., Leskovec, J.: Inductive representation learning on large graphs. In: NIPS, pp. 1024–1034 (2017)
7. Hoffart, J., Suchanek, F.M., Berberich, K., Lewis-Kelham, E., De Melo, G., Weikum, G.: Yago2: exploring and querying world knowledge in time, space, context, and many languages. In: Proceedings of the 20th International Conference Companion on World Wide Web, pp. 229–232. ACM (2011)
8. Jameel, S., Bouraoui, Z., Schockaert, S.: Member: max-margin based embeddings for entity retrieval. In: Proceedings of the 40th International ACM SIGIR Conference on Research and Development in Information Retrieval, pp. 783–792. ACM (2017)
9. Jameel, S., Schockaert, S.: Entity embeddings with conceptual subspaces as a basis for plausible reasoning. In: Proceedings of the Twenty-Second European Conference on Artificial Intelligence, pp. 1353–1361. IOS Press (2016)
10. Khosla, M., Leonhardt, J., Nejdl, W., Anand, A.: Node representation learning for directed graphs. In: ECML-PKDD (2019)
11. Kipf, T.N., Welling, M.: Semi-supervised classification with graph convolutional networks. arXiv preprint arXiv:1609.02907 (2016)
12. Koh, P.W., Liang, P.: Understanding black-box predictions via influence functions. arXiv preprint arXiv:1703.04730 (2017)
13. Letham, B., Rudin, C., McCormick, T.H., Madigan, D., et al.: Interpretable classifiers using rules and Bayesian analysis: building a better stroke prediction model. Ann. Appl. Stat. **9**(3), 1350–1371 (2015)
14. Ma, Y., Crook, P.A., Sarikaya, R., Fosler-Lussier, E.: Knowledge graph inference for spoken dialog systems. In: 2015 IEEE International Conference on Acoustics, Speech and Signal Processing (ICASSP), pp. 5346–5350. IEEE (2015)
15. Meilicke, C., Fink, M., Wang, Y., Ruffinelli, D., Gemulla, R., Stuckenschmidt, H.: Fine-grained evaluation of rule- and embedding-based systems for knowledge graph completion. In: Vrandečić, D., et al. (eds.) ISWC 2018. LNCS, vol. 11136, pp. 3–20. Springer, Cham (2018). https://doi.org/10.1007/978-3-030-00671-6_1
16. Mikolov, T., Chen, K., Corrado, G., Dean, J.: Efficient estimation of word representations in vector space. CoRR abs/1301.3781 (2013). http://arxiv.org/abs/1301.3781
17. Mikolov, T., Sutskever, I., Chen, K., Corrado, G.S., Dean, J.: Distributed representations of words and phrases and their compositionality. In: NIPS, pp. 3111–3119 (2013)
18. Minervini, P., Costabello, L., Muñoz, E., Nováček, V., Vandenbussche, P.-Y.: Regularizing knowledge graph embeddings via equivalence and inversion axioms. In: Ceci, M., Hollmén, J., Todorovski, L., Vens, C., Džeroski, S. (eds.) ECML PKDD 2017. LNCS (LNAI), vol. 10534, pp. 668–683. Springer, Cham (2017). https://doi.org/10.1007/978-3-319-71249-9_40

19. Montavon, G., Lapuschkin, S., Binder, A., Samek, W., Müller, K.R.: Explaining nonlinear classification decisions with deep taylor decomposition. Pattern Recogn. **65**, 211–222 (2017)
20. Ou, M., Cui, P., Pei, J., Zhang, Z., Zhu, W.: Asymmetric transitivity preserving graph embedding. In: SIGKDD, pp. 1105–1114. ACM (2016)
21. Palumbo, E., Rizzo, G., Troncy, R., Baralis, E., Osella, M., Ferro, E.: An empirical comparison of knowledge graph embeddings for item recommendation. In: DL4KGS@ ESWC, pp. 14–20 (2018)
22. Perozzi, B., Al-Rfou, R., Skiena, S.: Deepwalk: online learning of social representations. In: SIGKDD, pp. 701–710. ACM (2014)
23. Ribeiro, M.T., Singh, S., Guestrin, C.: Why should I trust you?: explaining the predictions of any classifier. In: Proceedings of the 22nd ACM SIGKDD International Conference on Knowledge Discovery and Data Mining, pp. 1135–1144. ACM (2016)
24. Tang, J., Qu, M., Wang, M., Zhang, M., Yan, J., Mei, Q.: Line: large-scale information network embedding. In: WWW, pp. 1067–1077 (2015)
25. Xu, K., et al.: Show, attend and tell: neural image caption generation with visual attention. In: International Conference on Machine Learning, pp. 2048–2057 (2015)
26. Ying, R., Bourgeois, D., You, J., Zitnik, M., Leskovec, J.: GNN explainer: a tool for post-hoc explanation of graph neural networks. arXiv preprint arXiv:1903.03894 (2019)

Local Interpretation Methods to Machine Learning Using the Domain of the Feature Space

Tiago Botari[1(✉)], Rafael Izbicki[2], and Andre C. P. L. F. de Carvalho[1]

[1] Institute of Mathematics and Computer Sciences, University of São Paulo, São Carlos, SP, Brazil
tiagobotari@gmail.com,
andre@icmc.usp.br

[2] Department of Statistics, Federal University of São Carlos, São Carlos, SP, Brazil
rafaelizbicki@gmail.com

Abstract. As machine learning becomes an important part of many real world applications affecting human lives, new requirements, besides high predictive accuracy, become important. One important requirement is transparency, which has been associated with model interpretability. Many machine learning algorithms induce models difficult to interpret, named black box. Black box models are difficult to validate. Moreover, people have difficulty to trust models that cannot be explained. Explainable artificial intelligence is an active research area. In particular for machine learning, many groups are investigating new methods able to explain black box models. These methods usually look inside the black models to explain their inner work. By doing so, they allow the interpretation of the decision making process used by black box models. Among the recently proposed model interpretation methods, there is a group, named local estimators, which are designed to explain how the label of particular instance is predicted. For such, they induce interpretable models on the neighborhood of the instance to be explained. Local estimators have been successfully used to explain specific predictions. Although they provide some degree of model interpretability, it is still not clear what is the best way to implement and apply them. Open questions include: how to best define the neighborhood of an instance? How to control the trade-off between the accuracy of the interpretation method and its interpretability? How to make the obtained solution robust to small variations on the instance to be explained? To answer these questions, we propose and investigate two strategies: (i) using data instance properties to provide improved explanations, and (ii) making sure that the neighborhood of an instance is properly defined by taking the geometry of the domain of the feature space into account. We evaluate these strategies in a regression task and present experimental results that show that they can improve local explanations.

Keywords: Interpretability · Local estimation · Machine learning

P. Cellier and K. Driessens (Eds.): ECML PKDD 2019 Workshops, CCIS 1167, pp. 241–252, 2020.
https://doi.org/10.1007/978-3-030-43823-4_21

1 Introduction

Machine learning (ML) algorithms have shown high predictive capacity for model inference in several application domains. This is mainly due to recent technological advances, increasing number and size of public dataset repositories, and development of powerful frameworks for ML experiments [1–6]. Application domains where ML algorithms have been successfully used include image recognition [7], natural language processing [8] and speech recognition [9]. In many of these applications, the safe use of machine learning models and the users' right to know how decisions affect their life [10] make the interpretability of the models a very important issue. Many currently used machine learning algorithms induce models difficult to interpret and understand how they make decisions, named black boxes. This occurs because several algorithms produce highly complex models in order to better describe the patterns in a dataset.

Most ML algorithms with high predictive performance induce black box models, leading to inexplicable decision making processes. Black box models reduce the confidence of practitioners in the model predictions, which can be a obstacle in many real world applications, such as medical diagnostics [11], science, autonomous driving [12], and others sensitive domains. In these applications, it is therefore important that predictive models are easy to interpret.

To overcome these problems, many methods that are able to improve model interpretation have been recently proposed; see e.g. [13,14] for details. These methods aim at providing further information regarding the predictions obtained from predictive models. In these methods, interpretability can occur at different levels: (i) on the dataset; (ii) after the model is induced; and (iii) before the model is induced [15]. We will focus our discussion on methods for model interpretability that can be applied after the induction of a predictive model by a ML algorithm; these are known as *agnostic methods*.

Model-agnostic interpretation methods are a very promising approach to solve the problem of trust and to uncover the full potential of ML algorithms. These methods can be applied to explain predictions made by models induced by *any* ML algorithm. Some well known model-agnostic interpretation methods are described in [16–20]. Perhaps the most well known interpretation method is LIME [18], which allows local explanations for classification and regression models. LIME has been shown to present a very good capability to create local explanations. As a result, LIME has been used to interpret models induced by ML algorithms in different application domains. However, it it still not clear how to make some decisions when implementing and applying LIME and related methods. Some questions that arise are:

(i) How to best define the neighborhood of an instance?
(ii) How to control the trade-off between the accuracy of the interpretation model and its interpretability?
(iii) How to make the obtained solution robust to small variations on the instance to be explained?

A good local explanation for a given instance $\mathbf{x}^*$ needs to have high fidelity to the model induced by a ML algorithm in the neighborhood of $\mathbf{x}^*$. Although this neighborhood is typically defined in terms of Euclidean distances, ideally it should be supported by the dataset. Thus, the sub-domain used to fit the local explanation model (*i.e.*, a model used to explain the black box model) should reflect the domain where the black model model was induced from. For instance, high-dimensional datasets often lie on a submanifold of $\mathbb{R}^d$, in which case defining neighborhoods in terms of the Euclidean distance is not appropriate [21–24]. To deal with this deficiency, we address issue (i) by creating a technique that samples training points for the explanation model along the submanifold where the dataset lies (as opposed to Euclidean neighborhoods). We experimentally show that this technique provides a solution to (iii).

In order to address (ii), we observe that a good local explanation is not necessarily a direct map of the feature space. For some cases, the appropriate local description of the explanation lies on specific properties of the instance. These instance properties can be obtained through a transformation of the feature space. Thus, we address issue (ii) by creating local explanations on a transformed space of the feature space. This spectrum of questions should be elaborated by the specialists of the specific application domain.

In this work, we focus on performing these modifications for regression tasks. However, these modifications can be easily adapted for classification tasks. In Sect. 2.1, we discuss the use of instance properties, how to deal with the trade-off between explanation complexity and the importance of employing a robust method as an explanatory model. In Sect. 2.2, we describe how to improve the local explanation method using the estimation of the domain of feature space. In Sect. 3, we apply our methodology to a toy example. Finally, Sect. 4 presents the main conclusions from our work and describes possible future directions.

2 Model Interpretation Methods

2.1 Local Explanation Through Instance Properties

A crucial aspect for providing explanations to predictive models induced by ML algorithms is the relevant information to the specific knowledge domain. In some cases, a direct representation of the original set of features of an instance does not reflect the best local behavior of a prediction process. Hence, other instance properties can be used to create clear decision explanations. These properties can be generated through a map of the original features space, *i.e.*, a function of the input $\mathbf{x}$. Moreover, these instance properties can increase the local fidelity of the explanation with the predictive model. This can be easily verified when the original feature space is highly limited and providing poor information on the neighborhood of a specific point. This case is illustrated by Fig. 1(a).

In order to provide a richer environment to obtain a good explanation, the interpretable model should be flexible to possible questions that an user want to instigate the ML model. Given that the possible explanations are mapped using

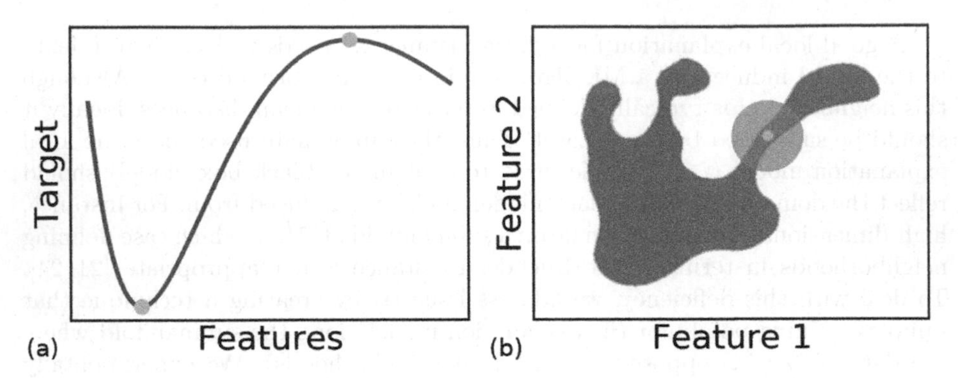

Fig. 1. (a) An example where a linear regression of the original features would provide little information regarding the model prediction. The blue continuous line represents the predictive model output as a function of the input, and the red circles represent two critical points of the curve. A local linear regression of the original feature space will produce a limited explanation in the neighborhood of the two critical points. (b) Representation of a domain of a two-dimensional feature problem where the plane defined by the two features is not fully covered. A local sampling can be used to create explanations on the neighborhood of the instance (red circle) that belongs to the correct task domain (blue region) (i.e., the intersection of the orange circle with the blue region) rather than on the orange circle (Color figure online).

specific functions of the feature space, we can create an interpretable model using

$$g(\mathbf{x}) = \alpha_0 + \sum_{i=1}^{N} \alpha_i f_i(\mathbf{x}) \tag{1}$$

where $\mathbf{x}$ represents the original vector of features, α_i are the coefficients of the linear regression that will be used as an explanation, and $f_i(.)$ are known functions that map $\mathbf{x}$ to the properties (that is, questions) that have a meaningful value for explaining a prediction, or that are necessary to obtain an accurate explanation.

Once f_i's are created, the explainable method should choose which of these functions better represent the predictions made by the original model locally. This can be achieved by introducing an $L1$ regularization in the square error loss function. More precisely, let h be a black-box model induced by a ML algorithm and consider the task of explaining the prediction made by h at a new instance $\mathbf{x}$. Let $\mathbf{x}'_1, \ldots, \mathbf{x}'_M$ be a sample generated on a neighborhood of $\mathbf{x}$. The local explanation can be found by minimizing (in α)

$$\mathbf{L} = \sum_{k=1}^{M} (h(\mathbf{x}'_k) - g(\mathbf{x}'_k))^2 + \sum_{i=1}^{N} \lambda_i |\alpha_i| \;, \tag{2}$$

where the first term is the standard square error between the induced model and the explanatory model and the second term is the penalization over the explanatory terms. The value of λ_i can be set to control the trade-off among the explanatory terms. For instance, if some explanatory terms (f_i) are more difficult to interpret, then a larger value can be assigned to λ_i.

In order to set the objective function (Eq. 2), one must be able to sample in a neighborhood of $\mathbf{x}$. To keep consistency over random sampling variations on the neighborhood of $\mathbf{x}$, we decided to use a linear robust method that implements the L_1 regularization (see [25]). This robust linear regression solves some of the problems of instability of local explanations [26].

Additionally, a relevant question is how to define a meaningful neighborhood around $\mathbf{x}$. In the next section we discuss how this question can be answered in an effective way.

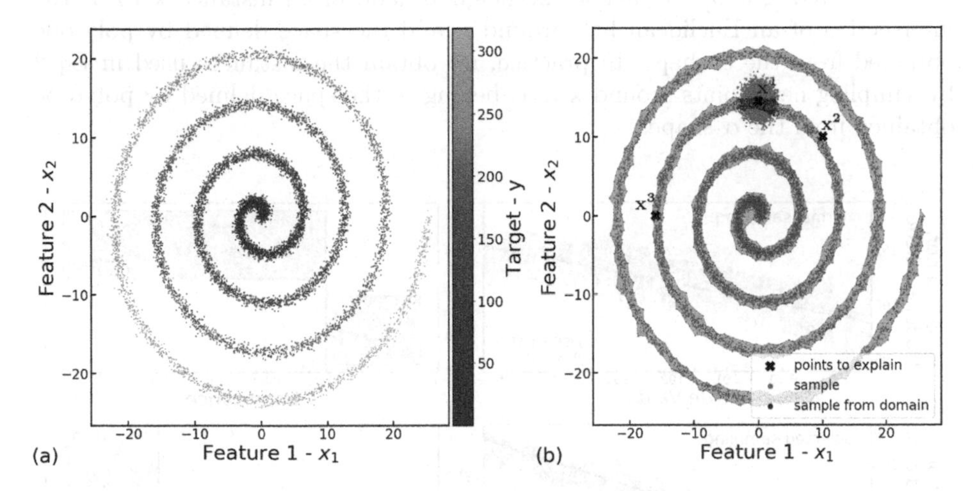

Fig. 2. A graphical bi-dimensional representation of the spiral toy model described by Eq. 3. (a) Original data where the colors represent the target value (y). (b) The domain of feature space (manifold), the blue points represent the original data, the pink polygon is the estimate of the manifold using α-shape ($\alpha = 1.0$), the black crosses represent the instances to be explained ($\mathbf{x}_{exp}$) (details in Sect. 3.1 - $\mathbf{x}^1 = (0.0, 14.5)$, $\mathbf{x}^2 = (10.0, 10.0)$ and $\mathbf{x}^3 = (-16.0, 0.0)$), gray points represent a sample from a normal distribution around the $\mathbf{x}_{exp}$, and the red points correspond to the sample that belong to the estimated domain (Color figure online).

2.2 Defining Meaningful Neighborhoods

Feature Space. The training data used by a ML algorithm defines the domain of the feature space. In order to obtain a more reliable explanation model, we can use the estimated domain of the feature space for sampling the data needed to obtain this model via Eq. 2, $\mathbf{x}'_1, \ldots, \mathbf{x}'_M$. This approach improves the fidelity and accuracy of the model when compared to standard Euclidean neighborhoods used by other methods [18]. The estimation of the feature domain is closely related to the manifold estimation problem [27]. Here, we show how this strategy works by using the α-shape technique [28,29] to estimate the domain of the feature space.

α-shape. The α-shape is a formal mathematical definition of the polytope concept of a set of points on the Euclidean space. Given a set of points $S \subset \mathbb{R}^d$ and a real value $\alpha \in [0, \infty)$, it is possible to uniquely define this polytope that enclose S. The α value defines an open hypersphere H of radius α. For $\alpha \to 0$, H is a point, while for $\alpha \to \infty$, H is an open half-space. Thus, an α-shape is defined by all k-simplex, $\{k \in \mathbb{Z} | 0 \leq k \leq d\}$, defined by a set of points $s \in S$ where there exist an open hypersphere H that is empty, $H \cap S = \emptyset$, and $\partial H \cap s = s$. In this way, the α value controls the polytope details. For $\alpha \to 0$, the α-shape recovered is the set of points S itself, and for $\alpha \to \infty$, the convex hull of the set S is recovered [28,29]. We define the neighborhood of an instance $\mathbf{x}$ to be the intersection of an Euclidean ball around $\mathbf{x}$ and the space defined by polytope obtained from the α-shape. In practice, we obtain the instances used in Eq. 2 by sampling new points around $\mathbf{x}$ that belong to the space defined by polytope obtained from the α-shape.

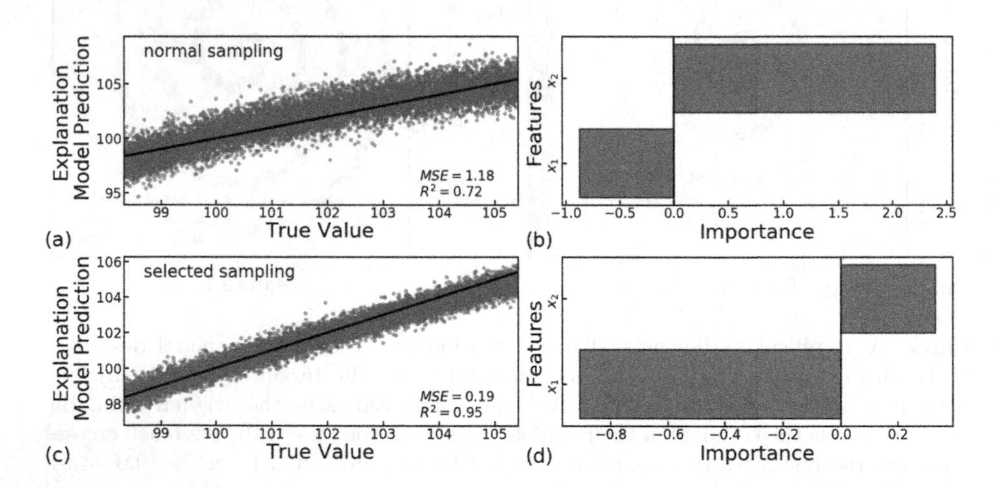

Fig. 3. Comparison of prediction performed by the explanation model and the true value of the spiral length using a data set not used during the induction of the model by a ML algorithm. The explanation model was generated for point $\mathbf{x}^1 = (0.0, 14.5)$. Figures (a) and (c) show the true label y *versus* the explanation model prediction. The black line represents the perfect matching between the two values. Figures (b) and (d) show the importance of the features obtained by the explanation model. Normal sampling strategy ((a) and (b)): MSE = 1.18; R^2 = 0.72. Selected sampling ((c) and (d)): MSE = 0.19; R^2 = 0.95.

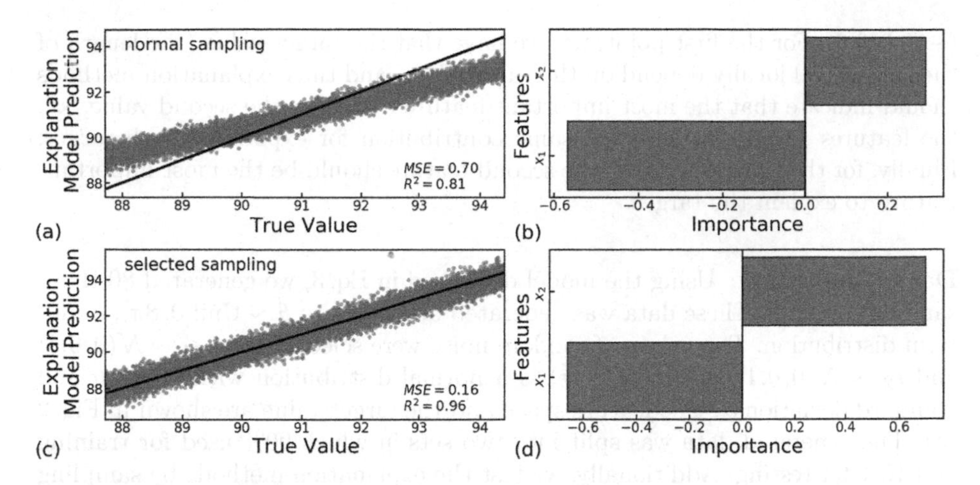

Fig. 4. Comparison of prediction performed by the explanation model and the true value of the spiral length using a data set not used during training of the ML model. The explanation model was generated for point $\mathbf{x^2} = (10.0, 10.0)$. Figures (a) and (c) show the true label y *versus* the explanation model prediction. The black line represents the perfect matching between the two values. Figures (b) and (d) show the importance of the features obtained by the explanation model. Normal sampling strategy ((a) and (b)): MSE $= 0.70$; $R^2 = 0.81$. Selected sampling ((c) and (d)): MSE $= 0.16$; $R^2 = 0.96$.

3 Results for a Toy Model: Length of a Spiral

In this section, we present an application of our proposed methodology for a toy model in which the data is generated along a spiral. For such, we use the Cartesian coordinates of the spiral on the plane as features.

3.1 Definition

We explore the toy model described by

$$x_1 = \theta\cos(\theta) + \epsilon_1 \qquad x_2 = \theta\sin(\theta) + \epsilon_2 \tag{3}$$
$$y = \frac{1}{2}\left[\theta\sqrt{1+\theta^2} + \sinh^{-1}\theta\right]$$

where x_1 and x_2 are the values that form the feature vector $\mathbf{x} = (x_1, x_2)$, θ is a independent variable, ϵ_i, $i \in \{1, 2\}$, is a random noise, and the target value is given by y, the length of the spiral. This toy model presents some interesting features for our analysis, such as the feature domain over the spiral and the substantial variance of the target value when varying one of the features coordinate while keeping the other one fixed.

Instances for Investigation. We investigate the explanation for 3 specific instances of our toy model: $\mathbf{x^1} = (0.0, 14.5)$, $\mathbf{x^2} = (10.0, 10.0)$ and $\mathbf{x^3} =$

(−16.0, 0.0). For the first point, $\mathbf{x^1}$, we have that the target value (the length of the spiral) will locally depend on the value of x_1 , and thus explanation methods should indicate that the most important feature is x_1. For the second value, $\mathbf{x^2}$, the features x_1 and x_2 have the same contribution for explaining such target. Finally, for the third point, $\mathbf{x^3}$, the second feature should be the most important feature to explain the target.

Data Generation: Using the model described in Eq. 3, we generated 80 thousand data points. These data was generated according to $\theta \sim$ Unif$[0, 8\pi]$, a uniform distribution. The values of random noise were selected from $\epsilon_1 \sim \mathcal{N}(0, 0.4)$ and $\epsilon_2 \sim \mathcal{N}(0, 0.4)$, where $\mathcal{N}(\mu, \sigma)$ is a normal distribution with mean μ and standard deviation σ. The feature space and the target value are shown in Fig. 2 (a). The generated data was split into two sets in which 90% used for training and 10% for testing. Additionally, we test the explanation methods by sampling three sets of data in the neighborhoods of $\mathbf{x^1}$, $\mathbf{x^2}$, and $\mathbf{x^3}$.

Model Induction Using a ML Algorithm: We used a decision tree induction algorithm (DT) in the experiments. We used the Classification and Regression Trees (CART) algorithm implementation provided by the scikit-learn [5] library. The model induced by this algorithm using the previously described dataset had as predictive performance $MSE = 24.00$ and $R^2 = 0.997$.

Determining the α-shape of the Data: For this example, we applied the α-shape technique using $\alpha = 1.0$. The value of α can be optimized for the specific dataset at hand; see [29] for details. The estimation of the domain using the α-shape is illustrated by Fig. 2(b).

3.2 Local Explanation

The local explanation was generated though a linear regression fitted to a data generated over the neighborhood of the point for which the explanation was requested ($\mathbf{x_{exp}}$). We use the linear robust method available on the scikit-learn package [5].

Explanation for Instance $\mathbf{x^1} = (0.0, 14.5)$: The obtained explanation using the standard sampling approach (hereafter *normal sampling*) presents low agreement with true value of the spiral length (Fig. 3(a)). We also noticed that this explanation is unstable with respect to sampling variations (even though we use a robust method to create the interpretation), and indicates that the best feature to explain the ML algorithm locally is x_2 (Fig. 3(b)). This description is inaccurate (see discussion in Section **Instances for Investigation**). On the other hand, when the sampling strategy is performed over the correct domain of the feature space (hereafter *selected sampling*), we obtain an explanation method with high predictive accuracy (i.e., that accurately reproduces the true target value - Fig. 3(c)). Moreover, the feature that best explains such prediction is x_1 (Fig. 3(d)), which is in agreement with our expectation.

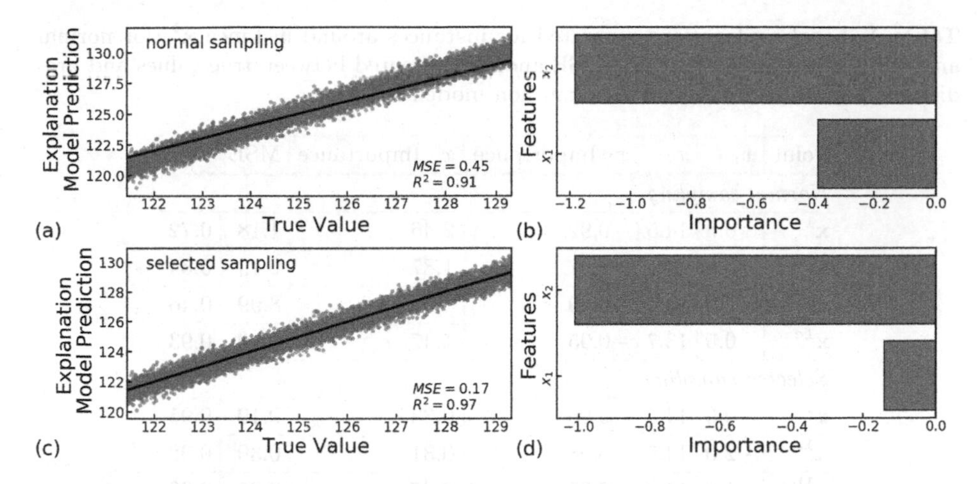

Fig. 5. Comparison of prediction obtained by the explanation model and the true value of the spiral length using a data set not used during training of the ML model. The explanation model was generated for point $\mathbf{x^3} = (-16.0, 0.0)$. Figures (a) and (c) show the true label y *versus* the explanation model prediction. The black line represents the perfect matching between the two values. Figures (b) and (d) show the importance of the features obtained by the explanation model. Normal sampling strategy ((a) and (b)): MSE = 0.45; $R^2 = 0.91$. Selected sampling ((c) and (d)): MSE = 0.17; $R^2 = 0.97$.

Explanation for Instances $\mathbf{x^2} = (\mathbf{10.0}, \mathbf{10.0})$ and $\mathbf{x^3} = (-\mathbf{16.0}, \mathbf{0.0})$: We also analyzed the other two points to demonstrate the capability of the selected sampling to capture the correct feature importance. For the instance $\mathbf{x^2}$, the features importance is almost equally divided between the two features (Fig. 4). For the instance $\mathbf{x^3}$, the most important feature is x_2, with importance of -1.0 (Fig. 5). In the case of $\mathbf{x^3}$, the normal sampling strategy produced a good explanation (Fig. 5(b)). However, we noticed that this result is unstable due to random variation in the sampling. All results presented here are in agreement with our discussion in Section **Instances for Investigation**.

3.3 Robustness of Explanations

Good explanation models for $\mathbf{x}*$ should be stable to small perturbations around $\mathbf{x}*$. To illustrate the stability of our method, we generated explanations for instances in the neighborhood of $\mathbf{x^1}$: $\mathbf{x^{1a}} = (-2.0, 14.5)$, $\mathbf{x^{1b}} = (1.0, 14.0)$ and $\mathbf{x^{1c}} = (0.5, 13.7)$. Table 1 shows that the explanations created for these points using selected sampling are compatible with those for $\mathbf{x^1}$. On the other hand, the normal sampling strategy is unstable. These results demonstrate that using the domain defined by the feature space can improve the robustness of a local explanation of an instance.

Table 1. Local explanations generated for instances around instance $\mathbf{x^1}$: for normal and selected sampling strategies. MSE and R^2 measured between true values and predictions performed by the local explanation model.

Point	x_1	x_2	x_1 Importance	x_2 Importance	MSE	R^2
Normal sampling						
$\mathbf{x^1}$	0.0	14.5	−0.92	2.46	1.18	0.72
$\mathbf{x^{1a}}$	−2.0	14.5	−1.07	1.87	6.19	0.64
$\mathbf{x^{1b}}$	1.0	14.0	−0.89	3.91	8.99	0.46
$\mathbf{x^{1c}}$	0.5	13.7	−0.95	1.47	1.09	0.93
Selected sampling						
$\mathbf{x^1}$	0.0	14.5	−0.96	0.33	0.19	0.95
$\mathbf{x^{1a}}$	−2.0	14.5	−0.98	0.31	0.30	0.98
$\mathbf{x^{1b}}$	1.0	14.0	−0.97	0.07	0.21	0.99
$\mathbf{x^{1c}}$	0.5	13.7	−0.96	0.39	0.39	0.99

4 Conclusion

In order to increase trust and confidence on black box models induced by ML algorithms, explanation methods must be reliable, reproducible and flexible with respect to the nature of the questions asked. Local agnostic-model explanations methods have many advantages that are aligned with these points. Besides, they can be applied to any ML algorithm. However, the standard of the existing agnostic methods present problems in producing reproducible explanation, while maintaining accuracy to the original model. To overcome these limitations, we developed new strategies to overcome them. For such, the proposed strategies address the following issues: (i) estimation of the domain of the feature space in order to provide meaningful neighborhoods; (ii) use of different penalization level on explanatory terms; and (iii) employment of robust techniques for fitting the explanatory method.

The estimation of the domain of the features space should be performed and used during the sampling step of local interpretation methods. This strategy increases the accuracy of the local explanation. Additionally, using robust regression methods to create the explainable models is beneficial to obtain stable solutions. However, our experiments show that robust methods are not enough; the data must be sampled taking the domain of the feature space into account, otherwise the generated explanations can be meaningless.

Future work includes testing other methods for estimating manifolds such as diffusion maps [30] and isomaps [31], extending these ideas to classification problems, and investigating the performance of our approach on real datasets.

Acknowledgments. The authors would like to thank CAPES and CNPq (Brazilian Agencies) for their financial support. T.B. acknowledges support by Grant 2017/06161-7, São Paulo Research Foundation (FAPESP). R. I. acknowledges support by Grant

2017/03363 (FAPESP), 2019/11321-9 (FAPESP), and Grant 306943/2017-4 (CNPq). The authors acknowledge Grant 2013/07375-0 - CeMEAI - Center for Mathematical Sciences Applied to Industry from São Paulo Research Foundation (FAPESP). T.B. thanks Rafael Amatte Bizao and Frederik Hvilshøj for review and comments.

References

1. Dua, D., Graff, C.: UCI machine learning repository (2017)
2. Deng, J., Dong, W., Socher, R., Li, L.-J., Li, K., Fei-Fei, L.: ImageNet: a large-scale hierarchical image database. In: CVPR 2009 (2009)
3. Vanschoren, J., van Rijn, J.N., Bischl, B., Torgo, L.: OpenML: networked science in machine learning. SIGKDD Explor. **15**(2), 49–60 (2013)
4. Abadi, M., et al.: TensorFlow: large-scale machine learning on heterogeneous systems (2015). Software available from tensorflow.org
5. Pedregosa, F., et al.: Scikit-learn: machine learning in Python. J. Mach. Learn. Res. **12**, 2825–2830 (2011)
6. Paszke, A., et al.: Automatic differentiation in pytorch. In: NIPS-W (2017)
7. Szegedy, C., et al.: Going deeper with convolutions. In: Proceedings of the IEEE Conference on Computer Vision and Pattern Recognition, pp. 1–9 (2015)
8. Xu, K., et al.: Show, attend and tell: neural image caption generation with visual attention. In: International Conference on Machine Learning, pp. 2048–2057 (2015)
9. LeCun, Y., Bengio, Y., Hinton, G.: Deep learning. Nature **521**(7553), 436 (2015)
10. 2018 reform of eu data protection rules
11. Caruana, R., Lou, Y., Gehrke, J., Koch, P., Sturm, M., Elhadad, N.: Intelligible models for healthcare: predicting pneumonia risk and hospital 30-day readmission. In: Proceedings of the 21th ACM SIGKDD International Conference on Knowledge Discovery and Data Mining, pp. 1721–1730. ACM (2015)
12. Bojarski, M., et al.: End to end learning for self-driving cars. arXiv preprint arXiv:1604.07316 (2016)
13. Gilpin, L.H., Bau, D., Yuan, B.Z., Bajwa, A., Specter, M., Kagal, L.: Explaining explanations: an overview of interpretability of machine learning. In: 2018 IEEE 5th International Conference on Data Science and Advanced Analytics (DSAA), pp. 80–89. IEEE (2018)
14. Molnar, C.: Interpretable Machine Learning (2019). https://christophm.github.io/interpretable-ml-book/
15. Lipton, Z.C.: The mythos of model interpretability. arXiv preprint arXiv:1606.03490 (2016)
16. Friedman, J.H.: Greedy function approximation: a gradient boosting machine. Ann. Stat. **29**, 1189–1232 (2001)
17. Fisher, A., Rudin, C., Dominici, F.: All models are wrong but many are useful: variable importance for black-box, proprietary, or misspecified prediction models, using model class reliance. arXiv preprint arXiv:1801.01489 (2018)
18. Ribeiro, M.T., Singh, S., Guestrin, C.: "Why should I trust you?": explaining the predictions of any classifier. In: Proceedings of the 22nd ACM SIGKDD International Conference on Knowledge Discovery and Data Mining, San Francisco, CA, USA, 13–17 August 2016, pp. 1135–1144 (2016)
19. Lundberg, S., Lee, S.-I.: An unexpected unity among methods for interpreting model predictions. arXiv preprint arXiv:1611.07478 (2016)

20. Štrumbelj, E., Kononenko, I.: Explaining prediction models and individual predictions with feature contributions. Knowl. Inf. Syst. **41**(3), 647–665 (2013). https://doi.org/10.1007/s10115-013-0679-x
21. Aswani, A., Bickel, P., Tomlin, C., et al.: Regression on manifolds: estimation of the exterior derivative. Ann. Stat. **39**(1), 48–81 (2011)
22. Lee, A.B., Izbicki, R.: A spectral series approach to high-dimensional nonparametric regression. Electron. J. Stat. **10**(1), 423–463 (2016)
23. Izbicki, R., Lee, A.B.: Nonparametric conditional density estimation in a high-dimensional regression setting. J. Comput. Graph. Stat. **25**(4), 1297–1316 (2016)
24. Izbicki, R., Lee, A.B.: Converting high-dimensional regression to high-dimensional conditional density estimation. Electron. J. Stat. **11**(2), 2800–2831 (2017)
25. Owen, A.B.: A robust hybrid of lasso and ridge regression. Contemp. Math. **443**(7), 59–72 (2007)
26. Alvarez-Melis, D., Jaakkola, T.S.: On the robustness of interpretability methods. arXiv preprint arXiv:1806.08049 (2018)
27. Wasserman, L.: Topological data analysis. Annu. Rev. Stat. Appl. **5**, 501–532 (2018)
28. Edelsbrunner, H., Kirkpatrick, D., Seidel, R.: On the shape of a set of points in the plane. IEEE Trans. Inf. Theory **29**(4), 551–559 (1983)
29. Edelsbrunner, H.: Alpha shapes-a survey. Tessellations Sci. **27**, 1–25 (2010)
30. Coifman, R.R., Lafon, S.: Diffusion maps. Appl. Comput. Harmonic Anal. **21**(1), 5–30 (2006)
31. Tenenbaum, J.B., De Silva, V., Langford, J.C.: A global geometric framework for nonlinear dimensionality reduction. Science **290**(5500), 2319–2323 (2000)

Measuring Unfairness Through Game-Theoretic Interpretability

Juliana Cesaro(✉) and Fabio Gagliardi Cozman(✉)

Escola Politécnica da Universidade de São Paulo, USP, São Paulo, Brazil
{juliana.cesaro,fgcozman}@usp.br

Abstract. One often finds in the literature connections between measures of fairness and measures of feature importance employed to interpret trained classifiers. However, there seems to be no study that compares fairness measures and feature importance measures. In this paper we propose ways to evaluate and compare such measures. We focus in particular on SHAP, a game-theoretic measure of feature importance; we present results for a number of unfairness-prone datasets.

Keywords: Group and individual fairness · Interpretability · Feature importance · Shapley value

1 Introduction

Machine learning algorithms have been used in a range of applications, from decisions about bank loans to criminal sentencing. Due to concerns about algorithmic fairness [4,12], several metrics have been created to detect bias injustice across groups [8,10] or individuals [7,9] or both [25]. It has been suggested that measures of feature importance can identify failure of fairness [1,26,27] as feature importance can indicate that a feature has a larger effect that it should have [19,21,24,30].

There seems to be no study that verifies whether feature importance measures are indeed useful in assessing fairness. Moreover, no study about the (supposed) connection between the two kinds of measures seems to be available. This paper proposes a simple scheme to evaluate the relationship between feature importance and fairness measures, by comparing measures on a dataset with and without bias removal technique.

The contributions of this paper are: (i) a framework to evaluate the merits of feature importance in assessing fairness, based on comparing the variation of results with and without application of reweighing; and (ii) a study across four standard datasets, where the results obtained through feature importance are compared with fairness measures. We focused on reweighing techniques to remove bias [14] and SHAP to measure feature importance [20].

The first author has been supported by Magazine Luiza. The second author has been partially supported by CNPq grant 312180/2018-7.

P. Cellier and K. Driessens (Eds.): ECML PKDD 2019 Workshops, CCIS 1167, pp. 253–264, 2020.
https://doi.org/10.1007/978-3-030-43823-4_22

In the next section we review various metrics concerning fairness and interpretability; we introduce a few twists to emphasize their connection. Later we describe our proposals and experiments.

2 Background

In this section we summarize definitions of fairness, techniques for bias removal, and tools to measure feature importance that are related to interpretability.

2.1 Defining Fairness

Definitions of fairness can be divided into two major categories: group fairness and individual fairness. These definitions quantify the relationship between an "unprivileged" and a "privileged" group.

In this paper we assume that there is a unique *sensitive* feature A that differentiates the privileged group from the unprivileged one. And we assume that that value zero for this feature signals the unprivileged group, while value one indicates the privileged group. The target output has values $\{0, 1\}$, where 1 is the desirable class, such as good credit score, and 0 is the undesirable class.

Group fairness is obtained when the privileged and the unprivileged groups are treated the same. One possible way to quantify group fairness is to use *disparate impact* [8]:

$$disp\_impact = P(\hat{Y} = 1|A = 0)/P(\hat{Y} = 1|A = 1), \tag{1}$$

where $\hat{Y}$ is the predicted outcome and A is the sensitive feature. Equation (1) must be close to one to indicate fairness; other values indicate unequal treatment through feature A.

Another measure of group fairness is based on predicted and actual outcomes as captured by *equality of opportunity* [10]:

$$equal\_opport = P(\hat{Y} = 1|A = 0, Y = 1) - P(\hat{Y} = 1|A = 1, Y = 1), \tag{2}$$

where Y is the actual outcome. Expression (2) should be close to zero; other values indicate unequal treatment.

Approaches that aim at equalizing relationships between groups may increase unfairness amongst individuals. Consider for instance a job application setting: to equalize relationship between groups one may select less qualified candidates from the unprivileged group. Individual-level fairness then makes sense.

Individual fairness requires similar individuals to receive similar classification outcomes. For instance, *consistency* compares a model prediction of an instance x to its k-nearest neighbors, $kNN(x)$ [29]:

$$consistency = 1 - \frac{1}{N}\sum_{n=1}^{N}\left|\hat{y}_n - \frac{1}{k}\sum_{j \epsilon kNN(x'_n)} \hat{y}_j\right|. \tag{3}$$

Note that we here introduced a small change to the original formulation of consistency: instead of calculating kNN for the input x, we use x', where the latter refers to the input x with the removal of the sensitive feature. Expression (3) must be close to one to indicate fairness.

In this paper we employ the three definitions presented above in our experiments: disparate impact (1), equality of opportunity (2) and consistency (3).

2.2 Removing Bias

Techniques that attempt to remove bias from a model can be divided into three categories: ones that preprocess data before a classifier is trained [8,13,29]; ones that operate inprocessing, where the model is optimized at training time [15]; and ones that explores postprocessing of the model prediction [10]. In this paper we adopt a preprocessing methodology called **reweighing** [14] that aims at improving group fairness, as it is a well-known technique that requires no hyper-parameters (thus allowing us to avoid lengthy digressions into parameter tuning). In addition, reweighting does not change the features as other methods do [8,29].

Reweighing assigns weights to the points in the training dataset to reduce bias. Every random unlabeled data object X is assigned a weight:

$$W(X) = \frac{P_{exp}(A = X(A) \wedge Y = X(Y))}{P_{obs}(A = X(A) \wedge Y = X(Y))}, \tag{4}$$

where P_{obs} is the observed probability, P_{exp} is the expected probability and A is the sensitive feature. Lower weights are assigned to instances that the privileged class favors. This approach is restricted to a single binary sensitive attribute and a binary classification problem.

2.3 Feature Importance

We can divide techniques that explain the behavior of machine learning algorithms in two main groups: global approaches that aim at understanding the behavior of the model as a whole [18] and local approaches that interpret individual predictions [19–21]. In this paper we choose a local approach called SHAP, which has the advantage of ensuring three important properties: local accuracy, missingness and consistency. We use a local approach because if the methodology were used in practice, it is important that it be able to provide justification for a certain generated result, which would allow to assess whether the prediction was fair.

SHAP (SHapley Additive exPlanations) [20] produces a local explanation for each prediction of a given classifier. Using insights from game theory, SHAP can explain prediction of any machine learning model and unifies concepts of several previous methods [2,5,17,21–23,30].

SHAP approximates locally the function to be explained, which we call f, by a linear function g such that

$$f(x) = g(x') = \phi_0 + \sum_{i=0}^{M} \phi_i x'_i,$$

where x' is again the modified input and each weight ϕ_i is called a SHAP value, given by

$$\phi_i = \sum_{S \subseteq N \setminus \{i\}} \frac{|S|!(M - |S| - 1)!}{M!} [f_x(S \cup \{i\}) - f_x(S)], \tag{5}$$

where S is the set of non-zero entries in x' and N is the set of all input features.

SHAP values satisfy a few properties. *Local accuracy* requires the result of the explanation model g for an input x to be equal to the prediction of the model desired to explain f. *Missingness* requires features missing in the input to be given no importance. Finally, recall that *consistency* states that if a change in the model occurs so that a feature has larger impact on the result, the importance of that feature should not decrease.

In this paper we mostly focus on a unique sensitive feature A in the model, but with the graphical results provided by the SHAP framework one can understand influences that go far beyond that. For instance, one can investigate how the input of each feature impacts the output, analyze relations between variables, and verify which variables exert a greater influence on the model result.

We selected two types of graphs that influences detected by SHAP: dependence plots and summary plots [19].

Dependence plots represent the effect of a single feature in the model output. To represent this relation the plot shows in the x-axis the value of the feature and the y-axis shows the SHAP value of the same feature. SHAP dependence plots also let one visualize the effect of the feature with the strongest interaction (calculated by SHAP interaction values). These effects are shown by coloring from low (blue) to high (red) each dot in the graph with the value of an interacting feature. Examples of these graphs are shown later in Fig. 4.

Summary plot sorts features by global impact on the model, calculated as

$$G_j = \frac{1}{N} \sum_{i=1}^{N} \mid \phi_j^i \mid . \tag{6}$$

Each dot in the graph represents the SHAP value of that feature. Examples are shown later in Fig. 5.

3 Proposal

In this section we propose techniques that will allow us to compare fairness measures and results obtained through SHAP. It should be noted that simply computing SHAP values will not help us doing it: SHAP values are computed by datapoint, whereas fairness measures capture the whole behavior of a classifier. Hence the need for novel ideas as proposed here.

To evaluate fairness we resort, first, to global impact of each feature (Expression (6)) as we focus on the ranking of the feature in a list of features ordered by descending global values. Besides looking at global impact, we also employ the following measure:

$$D_j = \frac{1}{N_k}\sum_{k=1}^{N_k}\phi_j^k - \frac{1}{N_l}\sum_{l=1}^{N_l}\phi_j^l, \tag{7}$$

where k represents unprivileged group and l privileged group, and each ϕ is a SHAP value. A value of D_j close to one indicates fairness, while a negative value favors the privileged group and a positive value favors the unprivileged one.

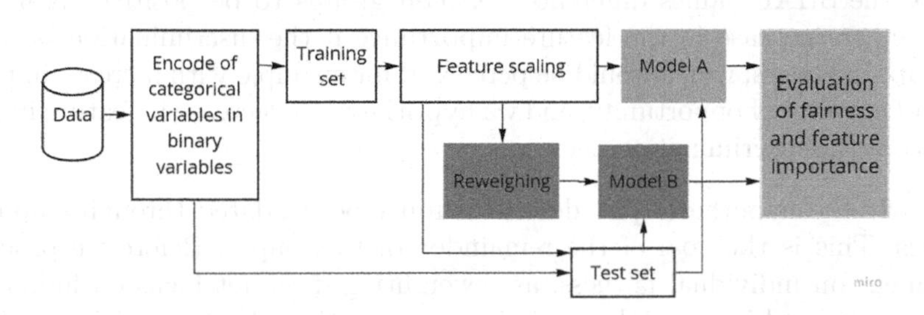

Fig. 1. Fairness through feature importance: the model in red was trained with a fairness-sensitive dataset; the model in blue had bias removed. (Color figure online)

Figure 1 summarizes the steps in assessing fairness through feature importance. An initial step in the workflow is the encoding of categorical variables in the dataset, followed by data split into 80% – 20% train-test sets and a standardization of features.

Then there are two possible paths: the red box indicates training directly with the model, and the blue box indicates an additional step of de-biasing before model training (through reweighting). Finally, results obtained from feature importance and fairness measures are compared.

More precisely, we compare the results by evaluating how fairness and feature importance measures vary as bias varies. When bias is present, we expect discrimination to appear in fairness measures (disparate impact and consistency smaller than one, and equality of opportunity smaller than zero), while we expect feature importance measures to display a negative SHAP value difference between privileged and unprivileged groups.

Note that reweighting focuses on group fairness; consequently, we can expect three scenarios concerning group fairness, as we now analyze:

- **Equality between groups**: This scenario is characterized by disparate impact close to one and equality of opportunity to zero. We hypothesize that privileged and unprivileged groups get similar importance, which should be reflected in their mean SHAP values getting closer and in some reduction in feature importance with a global SHAP value close to zero.
- **Favoring the privileged group**: This scenario is characterized by increase of disparate impact and equality of opportunity. However, disparate impact

would remain smaller than one and equality of opportunity negative. We hypothesize a decrease in SHAP value difference, but the value would remain negative. We also hypothesize a decrease in importance of the sensitive feature.

- **Favoring the unprivileged group**: This scenario is characterized by inversion of importance between groups, which would be perceived with disparate impact result greater than one or equality of opportunity positive. We hypothesize the SHAP values difference between groups to be positive. While we expect an increase in the feature importance if the discrimination between groups increases, which would be perceived for example with increase in module of equality of opportunity, and we hypothesize a decrease in feature importance if the discrimination decreases.

Clearly the hypotheses just described must be validated through empirical analyses. This is the goal of the remainder of this paper. Before we proceed, a comment on individual fairness: as reweighting does not focus on individual fairness, it is hard in principle to say how reweighting affects consistency (later we show that the relationship between these techniques is significant and actually somewhat surprising).

4 Experiments

To test our proposed scheme and the hypotheses outlined at the end of the previous section, we applied Logistic Regression, Random Forests and Gradient Boosting to four unfairness-prone datasets (using the scikit-learn library[1]). The study was limited to one binary sensitive attribute and a binary classification problem, due to limitations in reweighing and in some fairness measures. However, the methodology used to obtain feature importance could be applied to any classifier, and the sensitive variable could be of any type.

All tests were done using the same hyperparameters. The AIF-360[2] library was used to apply reweighing and to calculate disparate impact and equality of opportunity metrics. We use the kNN implementation of sckit-learn to compute the consistency metric.

All datasets and techniques are available in a github repository[3].

4.1 Datasets

Four datasets often analyzed with respect to fairness were used: Adult, German, Default and COMPAS datasets. Adult, German and Default datasets were obtained from the UCI repository [6] and the COMPAS dataset from ProPublica [12]. The Adult dataset [16] contains information from the 1994 census database. The objective is to predict whether income is larger 50K dollars per

[1] http://scikit-learn.org.
[2] https://aif360.mybluemix.net.
[3] https://github.com/cesarojuliana/feature_importance_fairness.

year. We consider gender as the sensitive attribute, following Ref. [15]. The German dataset contains information about bank account holders, and the goal is to classify each holder as good or bad credit risk. We use age as the sensitive attribute as in Ref. [13]. The Default dataset [28] contains information from credit card clients in Taiwan from April 2005 to September 2005. The objective is to predict default of their customers. We use the gender as the sensitive attribute as in [3]. The COMPAS dataset [12] contains data from criminal defendants in Broward County, Florida, which objective is to predict recidivism over a two-year period. We use the same filter as in Ref. [11]. The sensitive attribute is race, being selected Caucasian as the privileged group.

We remove the variable *fnlwgt* from Adult dataset, because this variable does not aggregate information to the problem goal. In the Default dataset we excluded *id* variable for the same reason. For the COMPAS dataset we use only the following variables: *race*, *age*, *c_charge_degree*, *v_score_text*, *sex*, *priors_count*, *days_b_screening_arrest*, *v_decile_score*, *two_year_recid*, *is_recid*.

4.2 Results and Discussion

In Fig. 2, in the x-axis *lr* means Logistic Regression, *rf* means Random Forest and *gbm* means Gradient Boosting. The y-axis carries the names of fairness and feature importance measures. The red line shows results without reweighing and the blue line shows results with reweighing. The results were separated in four columns according to the used dataset. In Fig. 3 we can see the relation between variation in fairness measures with feature importance measures in the y-axis and the x-axis respectively. The unfilled markers represents results without reweighing, and the filled markers results with reweighing. The markers in red show results for Adult dataset, in green for COMPAS dataset, in blue for German dataset, and in black for Default dataset. Legends indicate both the dataset and abbreviation of the used model.

In this section we will classify the results according to the three scenarios described previously: *equality between groups*, *favoring the privileged group* and *favoring the unprivileged group*. This classification is made based on the fairness results, and we hypothesized about what would be the feature importance result. We will compare whether the assumptions made actually occurred.

From the results we see that when reweighing is applied, disparate impact, equality of opportunity and difference in SHAP value between groups had a variation greater than or equal to zero. Furthermore, in several cases equality of opportunity and difference in SHAP value changed from negative to positive value; there was no case where disparate impact changes to a value greater than one with reweighing. With exception of the COMPAS results, in all other cases there was an decrease in feature importance with reweighing.

In the COMPAS results we perceived the following peculiarity with reweighing: increased in consistency and in feature importance. In COMPAS we also note the scenario of favoring the privileged group with Random Forest and with Gradient Boosting. However, this case had the unexpected result of increasing in feature importance probably due to variation in consistency.

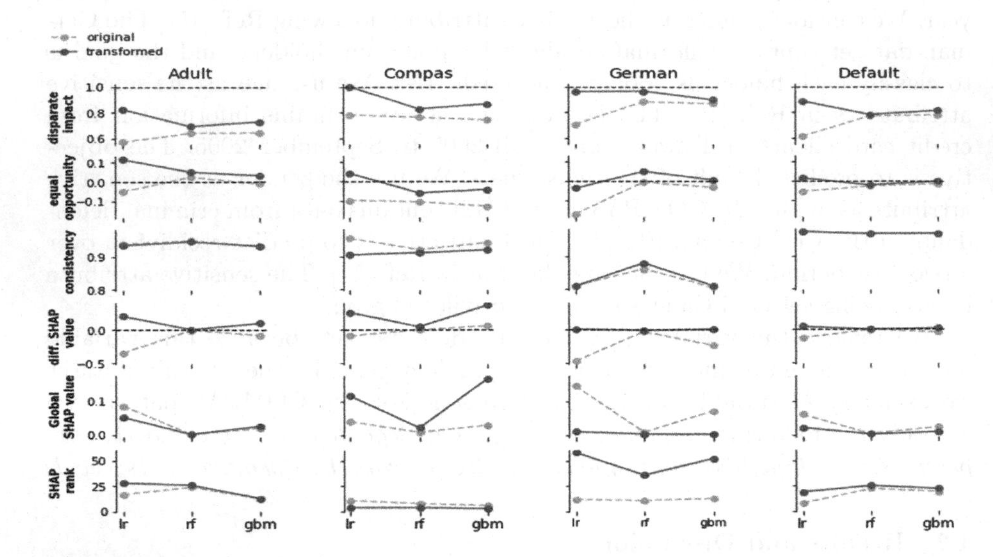

Fig. 2. Evaluation of fairness on test set for four datasets: Adult, COMPAS, German and Default, for three types of models: Logistic Regression, Random Forest and Gradient Boosting. Fairness is evaluated according to several definitions so as to capture both group and individual fairness.

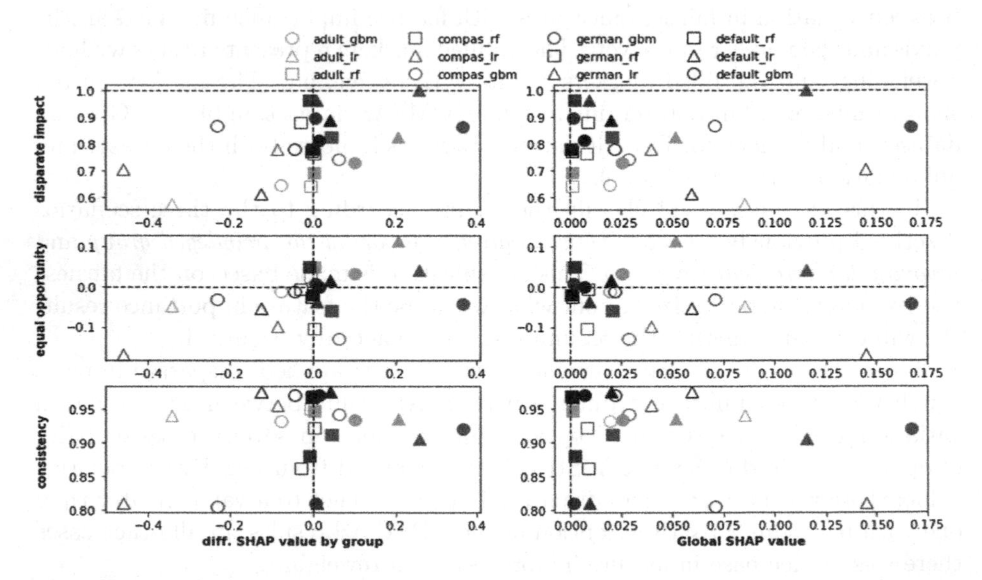

Fig. 3. Comparison between fairness and feature importance measures, performed with four datasets (Adult, COMPAS, German and Default) and with three types of models (Logistic Regression, Random Forest and Gradient Boosting). The unfilled markers represents results without reweighing, and the filled markers results with reweighing.

The scenario of equality between groups can be seen in the Default datatset and German dataset with Gradient Boosting. In all cases we see that equality of opportunity was very close to zero, but disparate impact was not close to one. In this situation, feature importance measures behaved as expected, SHAP values difference and feature importance approached zero.

We find the scenario of favoring the privileged group in Adult dataset with Logistic Regression and Random Forest, COMPAS with Logistic Regression and German with Random Forest. Only with Adult dataset there is no variation in consistency, and in this situation we see the expected scenario where equality of opportunity ranged from a negative to a positive value.

Results demonstrate two important facts. First, there is a direct relation between SHAP value difference and equality of opportunity, which is much more significant than the relationship with disparate impact. This is most evident from Fig. 3. Second, the relation of feature importance is inverse with consistency. In the results where there was a decrease in consistency, we note that the impact of consistency dominates feature importance (rather than the effect of increase in equality of opportunity).

Thus we reach our main conclusion in this empirical study: feature importance measures are connected *both* with consistency and equality of opportunity. Consequently we see that feature importance measures do quantify *both* group and individual fairness.

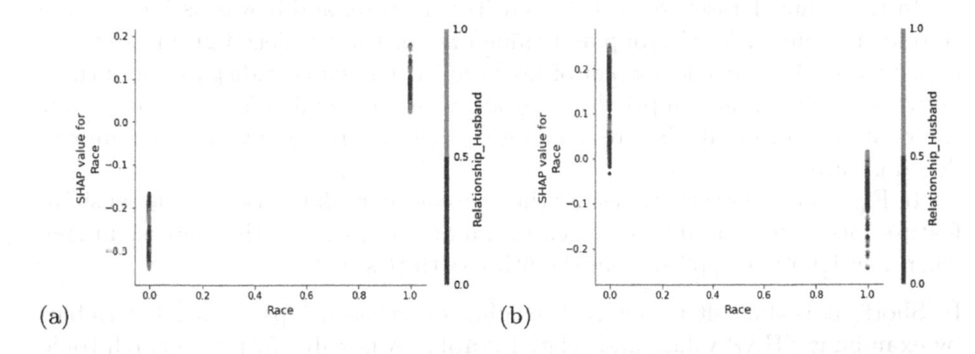

Fig. 4. SHAP dependence plot of a Logistic Regression trained with Adult dataset. The sensitive feature is race, where value one refers to white and value zero to non white. In y-axis is the SHAP value attributed to race. In (a) the model was trained with the original data, and we can see that it associated higher SHAP values with the white group, indicating discrimination in the dataset. In (b) reweighing was applied to reduce unfairness caused by race; we note that the relationship was reversed and non white became the group favored by the model according to SHAP values.

In the remainder of this section we present some additional remarks on the graphs that are provided by graphs build with SHAP values and on the insights that one may get from them. Basically, these graphs allow us to note implicit relationships between variables. Furthermore, they display the overall effect of *any* variable in the model by varying its input.

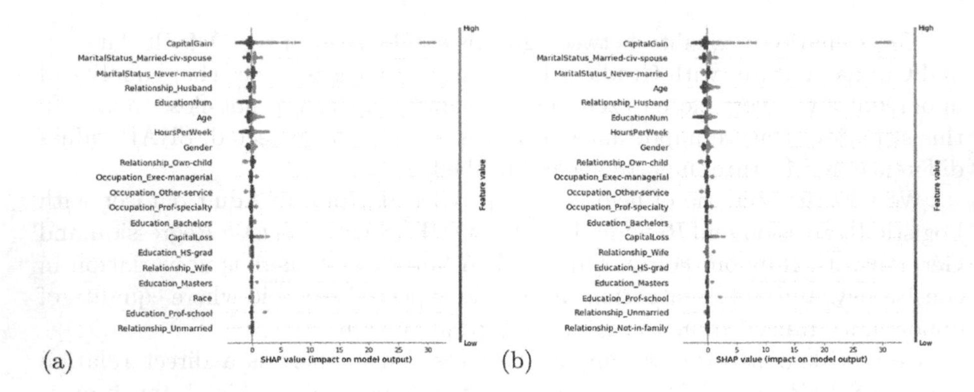

Fig. 5. SHAP summary plots of Logistic Regression trained with Adult dataset not applying (a) and applying (b) reweighing so as to reduce unfairness caused by race. We can see that without reweighing the rank position of race was 17th. When reweighing is applied the position decreases, and race is no longer among the twenty most important features.

For example, Figs. 4 and 5 show results obtained with Logistic Regression in the Adult dataset, with and without reweighing. Figure 4 shows dependence plots, and Fig. 5 shows summary plots.

In the Adult dataset, race is the sensitive feature, and it was assigned value zero for the unprivileged group and value one for the privileged group. Figure 4 depicts a partial dependency plot of Logistic Regression that displays unfairness between privileged and unprivileged group when reweighing is not applied, but the relation is inverted when reweighing is applied (greatly favoring the unprivileged group).

In Fig. 5 we can see that, besides the decrease in rank position of the sensitive feature race, other variables changed in importance, such as the increase in *Age* when reweighing is applied from the 6th to 4th position.

In Short: It is difficult to get real insights on relationships amongst variables by examining SHAP values and related graphs. A possible future research topic would be to extract such insights automatically.

5 Conclusion

We presented a framework that compares fairness definitions (group or individual) with results based on feature importance as quantified by SHAP. The basic idea is to examine how fairness definitions vary by changing the effect of the sensitive feature on the model (this was done here with reweighing). Experiments show that feature importance measures can identify group and individual fairness in the model. Certainly this is a preliminary effort that must be refined and extended in a variety of ways, but we feel that it is a valuable contribution due to the absence of similar analyses in the literature.

In particular, further work is needed to remove some important restrictions. We have focused on binary sensitive features and two-class classification problems. Such restrictions must be lifted. In future work we intend to study other interpretability techniques that are based on feature importance. This would allow us to determine whether some methodologies work better for some definitions of fairness than others. Furthermore, we want to extend the tests to other techniques that remove bias besides reweighting. Another promising extension of this work would be to evaluate the visualization techniques that must be used to present results. SHAP graphs speed up the perception of relationships between variables, but additional insights would be welcome.

References

1. Adebayo, J., Kagal, L.: Iterative orthogonal feature projection for diagnosing bias in black-box models (2016)
2. Bach, S., et al.: On pixel-wise explanations for non-linear classifier decisions by layer-wise relevance propagation. PloS one **10**(7) (2015)
3. Berk, R., et al.: A convex framework for fair regression (2017)
4. Dastin, J.: Amazon scraps secret AI recruiting tool that showed bias against women (2018). https://reut.rs/2Od9fPr
5. Datta, A., Sen, S., Zick, Y.: Algorithmic transparency via quantitative input influence: theory and experiments with learning systems (2016)
6. Dua, D., Taniskidou, E.K.: UCI machine learning repository (2018). https://archive.ics.uci.edu/ml
7. Dwork, C., Hardt, M., Pitassi, T., Reingold, O., Zemel, R.S.: Fairness through awareness (2011)
8. Feldman, M., Friedler, S.A., Moeller, J., Scheidegger, C., Venkatasubramanian, S.: Certifying and removing disparate impact. In: ACM SIGKDD International Conference on Knowledge Discovery and Data Mining, pp. 259–268. ACM, New York (2015)
9. Gupta, S., Kamble, V.: Temporal aspects of individual fairness (2018)
10. Hardt, M., Price, E., Srebro, N.: Equality of opportunity in supervised learning. In: International Conference on Neural Information Processing Systems, pp. 3323–3331 (2016)
11. Angwin, J., Larson, J., Mattu, S., Kirchner, L.: How we analyzed the compas recidivism algorithm (2016). https://www.propublica.org/article/how-we-analyzed-the-compas-recidivism-algorithm
12. Angwin, J., Larson, J., Mattu, S., Kirchner, L.: Machine bias (2016). https://www.propublica.org/article/machine-bias-risk-assessments-in-criminal-sentencing
13. Kamiran, F., Calders, T.: Classifying without discriminating (2009)
14. Kamiran, F., Calders, T.: Data preprocessing techniques for classification without discrimination. Knowl. Inf. Syst. **33**, 1–33 (2012). https://doi.org/10.1007/s10115-011-0463-8
15. Kamishima, T., Akaho, S., Asoh, H., Sakuma, J.: Fairness-aware classifier with prejudice remover regularizer. In: Learning and Knowledge Discovery in Databases, pp. 35–50 (2012)
16. Kohavi, R.: Scaling up the accuracy of Naive Bayes classifiers: a decision-tree hybrid. In: International Conference on Knowledge Discovery and Data Mining, pp. 202–207 (1996)

17. Lipovetsky, S., Conklin, M.: Analysis of regression in game theory approach. Appl. Stochast. Mod. Bus. Ind. **17**(4), 319–330 (2001)
18. Louppe, G., Wehenkel, L., Sutera, A., Geurts, P.: Understanding variable importances in forests of randomized trees. In: Advances in Neural Information Processing Systems, vol. 26, pp. 431–439 (2013)
19. Lundberg, S.M., Erion, G.G., Lee, S.I.: Consistent individualized feature attribution for tree ensembles (2018)
20. Lundberg, S.M., Lee, S.I.: A unified approach to interpreting model predictions. In: Advances in Neural Information Processing Systems, vol. 30, pp. 4765–4774 (2017)
21. Ribeiro, M.T., Singh, S., Guestrin, C.: "Why should i trust you?": explaining the predictions of any classifier (2016)
22. Saabas, A.: Interpreting random forests (2014). http://blog.datadive.net/interpreting-random-forests
23. Shrikumar, A., Greenside, P., Kundaje, A.: Learning important features through propagating activation differences (2017)
24. Sliwinski, J., Strobel, M., Zick, Y.: A characterization of monotone influence measures for data classification (2017)
25. Speicher, T., et al.: A unified approach to quantifying algorithmic unfairness: measuring individual & group unfairness via inequality indices (2018)
26. Tan, S., Caruana, R., Hooker, G., Lou, Y.: Distill-and-compare: auditing black-box models using transparent model distillation, pp. 303–310 (2018)
27. Wadsworth, C., Vera, F., Piech, C.: Achieving fairness through adversarial learning: an application to recidivism prediction (2018)
28. Yeh, I., Lien, C.H.: The comparisons of data mining techniques for the predictive accuracy of probability of default of credit card clients (2009)
29. Zemel, R., Wu, Y., Swersky, K., Pitassi, T., Dwork, C.: Learning fair representations. In: International Conference on Machine Learning, pp. 325–333 (2013)
30. Štrumbelj, E., Kononenko, I.: Explaining prediction models and individual predictions with feature contributions (2013)

LioNets: Local Interpretation of Neural Networks Through Penultimate Layer Decoding

Ioannis Mollas(✉), Nikolaos Bassiliades, and Grigorios Tsoumakas

Aristotle University of Thessaloniki, 54124 Thessaloniki, Greece
{iamollas,nbassili,greg}@csd.auth.gr

Abstract. Technological breakthroughs on smart homes, self-driving cars, health care and robotic assistants, in addition to reinforced law regulations, have critically influenced academic research on explainable machine learning. A sufficient number of researchers have implemented ways to explain indifferently any black box model for classification tasks. A drawback of building agnostic explanators is that the neighbourhood generation process is universal and consequently does not guarantee true adjacency between the generated neighbours and the instance. This paper explores a methodology on providing explanations for a neural network's decisions, in a local scope, through a process that actively takes into consideration the neural network's architecture on creating an instance's neighbourhood, that assures the adjacency among the generated neighbours and the instance. The outcome of performing experiments using this methodology reveals that there is a significant ability in capturing delicate feature importance changes.

Keywords: Explainable · Interpretable · Machine learning · Neural networks · Autoencoders

1 Introduction

Explainable artificial intelligence is a fast-rising area of computer science. Most of the research in this area is currently focused on developing methodologies and libraries for interpreting machine learning models for two main reasons: (a) increased use of black box machine learning models, such as deep neural networks, in safety-critical applications, such as self-driving cars, health care and robotic assistants, and (b) radical law changes empowering ethics and human rights, which introduced the right of users to an explanation of machine learning models' decisions that concern them.

Local Explanators are methods aiming to explain individual predictions of a particular model. LIME [18] is a state-of-the-art methodology that first constructs a local neighbourhood around a given new unlabeled instance, by perturbing the instance's features, and then trains a simpler transparent decision model to extract the features' importance. Subsequent model agnostic methods like Anchors [19], X-SPELLS [12] and LORE [8] focused on generating better neighbourhoods.

P. Cellier and K. Driessens (Eds.): ECML PKDD 2019 Workshops, CCIS 1167, pp. 265–276, 2020.
https://doi.org/10.1007/978-3-030-43823-4_23

This paper is concerned with generating better neighbourhoods too. However, it focuses on neural network models in particular, in contrast to the *model agnostic* local explanators mentioned in the previous paragraph that can work with any type of machine learning model. Our approach is inspired by the following observation: small changes at the input layer might lead to large changes at the penultimate layer of a (deep) neural network, based on which the final decision of the network is taken. We hypothesize that creating neighbourhoods at the penultimate layer of the neural network instead, could lead to better explanations.

To investigate this intuitive research hypothesis, we introduce our approach, dubbed LioNets (Local Interpretation Of Neural nETworkS through penultimate layer decoding). LioNets constructs a local neighbourhood at the penultimate layer of the neural network and records the network's decisions for this neighbourhood. However, in order to build a transparent local explanator, we need to have input representations at the original input space. To achieve this, LioNets trains a decoder that learns to reconstruct the input examples from their representations at the penultimate layer of the neural network. Taking together, the neural network model and the decoder resemble an autoencoder.

For the evaluation of LioNets, a set of experiments have been conducted, whose code is available at GitHub repository "LioNets"[1]. The results show that LioNets can lead to more precise explanations than LIME.

2 Background and Related Work

In order to be able to present LioNets architecture, this section will provide a sequence of definitions concerning the matter of explainable machine learning, autoencoders and knowledge distillation.

2.1 Explainable Machine Learning

Explainable artificial intelligence is a broad and fast-rising field in computer science. Recent works focus on ways to interpret machine learning models. Thus, this paper will focus on explainable machine learning. An accurate definition is the following:

> "An interpretable system is a system where a user cannot only see but also study and understand how inputs are mathematically mapped to outputs. This term is favoured over "explainable" in the ML context where it refers to the capability of understanding the work logic in ML algorithms" [1].

There are several dimensions that can define an interpretable system according to [9]. One interesting dimension is the *scope* of interpretability. There are two different scopes. An interpretable system can provide global or/and local

[1] https://github.com/iamollas/LioNets.

explanations for its predictions. Global explanations can present the structure of the whole system, while local explanations are focused on particular instances.

In the same paper, they are also presenting the desired features of any interpretable system. Those are:

- **Interpretability**: Interpretability measures how much comprehensible is an explanation. In fact, there is not a formal metric because for every problem we measure different attributes.
- **Accuracy**: The accuracy, and probably other metrics, of the original model and the accuracy of the explanator.
- **Fidelity**: Fidelity describes the mimic ability of the explanator, namely the ability of the explanator on providing the same results as the model it explains for specific instances.

2.2 Autoencoders

Autoencoders is a growing area within deep learning [13]. An autoencoder is an unsupervised learning architecture and can be expressed as a function

$$f : X \rightarrow X. \tag{1}$$

Autoencoder networks are widely used for reducing the dimensionality of the input data. They initially encode the original data into some latent representation and subsequently reconstruct the original data by decoding this representation to the original dimensions. The most common varieties of autoencoders are the three following:

- **Vanilla**: A three-layered neural network with one hidden layer.
- **Multilayer**: A deeper neural network with more than one hidden or recurrent layers. For example Variational Autoencoders [11,17].
- **Convolutional**: Used for image or textual data. In practice, the hidden layers are not fully connected, but convolutional layers.

2.3 Related Work

As already mentioned, LIME [18] is a state-of-the-art method for explaining predictions. It follows a simple pipeline. It generates a neighbourhood of a specific size for an instance by choosing randomly to put a zero value in one or more features of every neighbour. Then the cosine similarity of each neighbour with the original instance is measured and multiplied by one hundred. This constitutes the weight on which the simple linear model will depend on for its training. Thus, the most similar neighbours will have more impact on the training process of the linear model. A disadvantage of LIME is in sparse data. Due to the perturbation method that takes place on the original space, LIME can only generate 2^n different neighbours, where n the number of non-zero values. For example, in textual data, in a sentence of six words represented as a vector of four thousand features, where each feature corresponds to a word from the vocabulary, the non-zero features are only six. Hence, only $2^6 = 64$ different neighbours can be generated. However, LIME will create a neighbourhood of five thousand instances by randomly sampling through the 64 unique neighbours.

X-SPELLS [12] is a forthcoming solution providing model agnostic local explanations to black boxes dealing with sentiment analysis problems. The core idea of this work is to generate neighbourhoods for instances, which they will contain semantically correct synthetic neighbours, using techniques similar to paraphrasing. By creating such neighbourhoods, using variational autoencoders [11,17] to create new examples in the latent space, the goal is to present some of these neighbours to the user as the explanation. To accomplish this, they train a decision tree on the neighbourhood with labels assigned from the black box and subsequently they are extracting the exemplars.

Another set of methodologies in explaining decision systems, and specifically neural networks, are using Knowledge Distillation [7,10]. Those methods are trying to explain globally the whole structure and the predictions of a deep neural network, by distilling its knowledge to a transparent system. This idea originates by the Dark Knowledge Distillation [20], which is trying to enhance the performance of a shallow network (the student) through the knowledge of a deeper and more complex network (the teacher).

3 LioNets

This section presents the full methodology and architecture of LioNets. LioNets consist of four fundamental sub-architectures, which are visible in Fig. 1 at points 1, 2, 6 and 11. The main part of such system is the neural network, which will work as the predictor. A decoder based on the predictor is the second part. Finally, a neighbourhood generation process and a transparent predictor are the last two mechanisms. Hence, the following process should be executed.

3.1 Neural Network Predictor

For a given dataset, a neural network with a suitable fine-tuned architecture is being trained on this dataset. The output layer is by design in the same length as the number of classes of the classification problem. This process is similar to other supervised methodologies of building and training a neural network for classification tasks, which defines a function $f : X \rightarrow Y$.

3.2 Encoder and Decoder

When the training process of the neural network is over, a duplicate it is created. Then removing the last layer of this copy model and labelling every other layer as untrainable, the foundations for the autoencoder have been defined. Actually, these foundations would be the encoder, the first half of the autoencoder, thus only the decoder part is missing. By building successfully the decoder part and training it, the first two stages for Lionets' completion are achieved. Although, this is the most

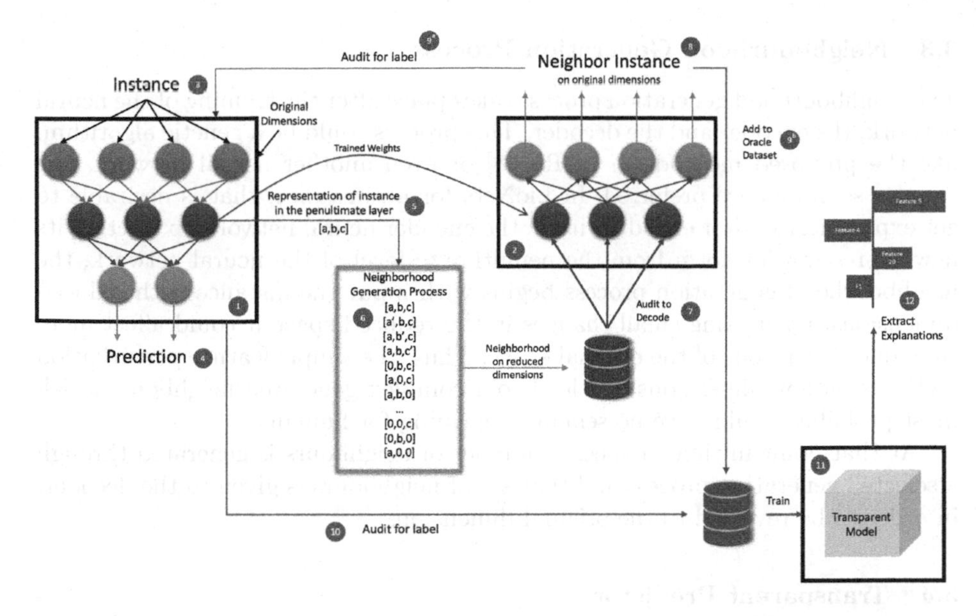

Fig. 1. LioNets' architecture. In this flow chart, the four fundamental mechanisms of LioNets are visible. In point 1 there is the predictor, while in point 2 the decoder. In point 3 there is the neighbourhood generation process and in point 4 the transparent model.

difficult stage to complete since it is not easy to successfully train autoencoders, especially when the first half of the autoencoder is untrainable. Another approach is to build the autoencoder firstly and afterwards to extract the layers in order to create the encoder, decoder and predictor networks.

Mathematically those neural networks can be expressed via these functions:

$$Encoder\colon X \rightarrow Z, \tag{2}$$

$$Decoder\colon Z \rightarrow X, \tag{3}$$

$$Autoencoder\colon X \rightarrow X, \tag{4}$$

$$Predictor\colon X \rightarrow Y. \tag{5}$$

By keeping the encoder part untrainable with stable weights, it guarantees that the generated neighbourhood is transforming from the reduced dimensions to the original dimensions with a decoder, which was trained with the original architecture of the neural network. That process will produce a more representative neighbourhood for the instance, without any semantic meaning to humans.

The academic community has extensively explored ways to create better neighbourhoods for an instance, but every methodology was focused on generating new instances in the level of the input. In this work, the generation processes take place to the latent representation of the encoded input.

3.3 Neighbourhood Generation Process

The neighbourhood generation process takes place after the training of the neural network, the encoder and the decoder. This process could be a genetic algorithm, like the proposed methods in LORE [8] or even another neural network, but simpler solutions are preferred. In LioNets for an instance, that is desirable to get explanations, after encoding it via the encoder neural network, extracting its new representation form from the penultimate level of the neural network, the neighbourhood generation process begins with input the instance with reduced dimensions. By making small changes in the reduced space it could affect more than one dimensions of the original space. Thus, the simple feature perturbation methods on low dimensions will lead to a complex generated neighbour, which most probably would have no semantic meaning for humans.

At that point in time, a specific number of neighbours is generated through a selected generation process and that set of neighbours is given to the decoder, in order to be reversed to the original dimensions.

3.4 Transparent Predictor

By the end of the neighbourhood generation stage, the neighbourhood dataset is almost complete. The only missing part is the neighbours' labels. Thus, the neural network is predicting each instance of the neighbourhood dataset assigning labels to every neighbour, in the form of probabilities. Afterwards, the final dataset with the neighbours and their labels are given as training data to any transparent regression model. The ultimate goal is to overfit that model to the training data.

4 Evaluation

The following section is presenting the setup for the experiments. The data preprocessing methods for two different datasets are described, alongside with the neural network models preparation and the neighbourhood generation process. Finally, there is a discussion about the results of the experiments.

4.1 Setup

Our experiments involve two textual binary classification datasets. The first one concerns the detection of hateful YouTube comments[2] [3] and contains 120 hate and 334 non-hate comments. The second dataset deals with the detection of spam SMS messages [2] and contains 747 spam and 4.827 ham (non-spam) messages. The pre-processing of these datasets consists of the following steps for each document:

- Lowercasing,
- Stemming and Lemmatisation through WordNet lemmatizer [14] and Snowball stemmer [15],

[2] https://intelligence.csd.auth.gr/research/hate-speech-detection.

- Phrases transformations (Table 1),
- Removal of punctuation marks,
- Once again, Stemming and Lemmatisation.

Table 1. Phrases and words transformations.

"what's"	to	"what is"
"don't"	to	"do not"
"doesn't"	to	"does not"
"that's"	to	"that is"
"aren't"	to	"are not"
"'s"	to	"is"
"isn't"	to	"is not"
"%"	to	"percent"
"e-mail"	to	"email"
"i'm"	to	"i am"
"he's"	to	"he is"
"she's"	to	"she is"
"it's"	to	"it is"
"'ve"	to	"have"
"'re"	to	"are"
"'d"	to	"would"
"'ll"	to	"will"

Then, for transforming the textual data to vectors a simple term frequency-inverse document frequency [21] (TF-IDF) vectorization technique is taking place.

Afterwards, the neural network predictor for these experiments consists of six layers (Fig. 2a) and it has 'binary_crossentropy' as loss function. The encoder has five layers, which we extract from the predictor and the decoder has four layers as well (Fig. 2b), which we train using 'categorical_crossentropy' loss function. The autoencoder is the combination of the encoder and the decoder.

In this set of experiments, a simple generation process via features perturbation methods is applied. Specifically, the creation of neighbours for an instance emerges by multiplying one feature value at a time with 0 and 2^z, $z \in \{-2, -1, 1, 2\}$. Concisely, the above process generates instances which are different in only one dimension in their latent representation.

As soon as the neighbourhood is acquired, every neighbour is transformed via the decoder to the original dimensions. Then, the transformed neighbourhood is given as input to the predictor to predict the class probabilities. Finally, combining the output of the predictor with the transformed neighbourhood a new oracle dataset has been created.

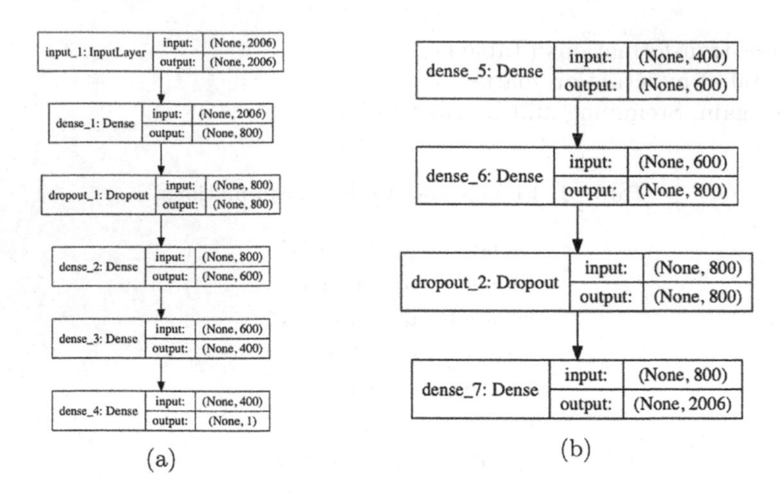

Fig. 2. The predictor's architecture (a) and the decoder's architecture (b).

```
input: neighbourhood
output: X, y
transformed_neighbourhood = decoder.predict(neighbourhood)
class_probabilities = predictor.predict(transformed_neighbourhood)
X = transformed_neighbourhood, y = class_probabilities
```

Algorithm 1.1. Oracle dataset synthesis

The last step is to train a transparent model with this oracle dataset. It might be useful to check the distribution of probabilities of this dataset and if needed to transform it to have a normal distribution. In these experiments, the transparent model chosen is a Ridge Regression model. By training this model, the coefficients of the features are extracted and transformed into explanations, presented as features' weights in the x-axis of the following figures.

```
input: X, y, instance, feature_names
transparent_model = Ridge().fit(X,y)
coef = transparent_model.coef_
plot_explanation(coef*instance, feature_names)
```

Algorithm 1.2. Explaining an instance

4.2 Results on the Hate Speech Dataset

We take the following YouTube comment from the hate speech dataset as an example: "aliens really, Mexicans are people too". The true class of this comment is *no hate*. According to the neural network, the probability of the *hate* class is approximately 0.00208.

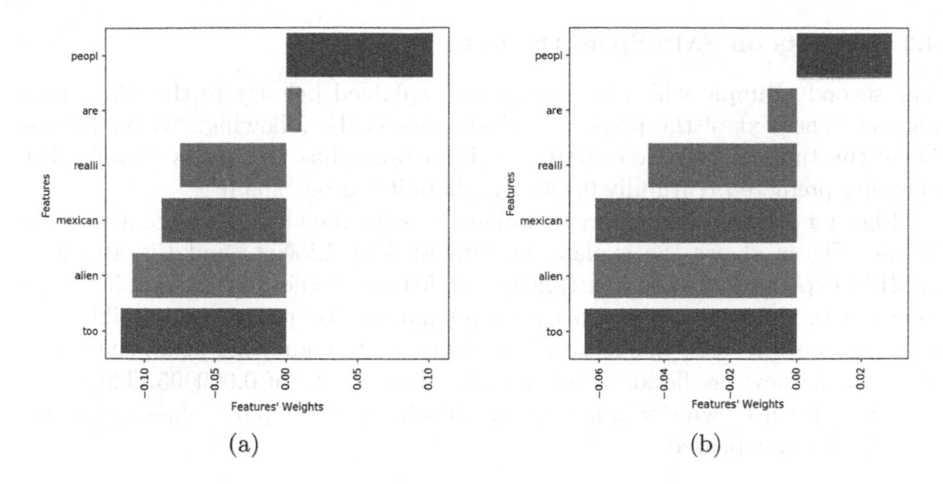

Fig. 3. Explanation plots of a hate speech instance via (a) LioNets and (b) LIME.

Figure 3 visualizes the explanation of the neural network's decision via LioNets (Fig. 3a) and LIME (Fig. 3b). At first sight, they appear similar. Their main difference is that they assign the feature's "are" contribution to different classes. By removing this word from the instance the neural network predicts 0.00197, which is a lower probability. Thus, it is clear that the feature "are" it was indeed contributing to the "Hate Speech" class for this specific instance as LioNets explained.

Although to support LioNets explanations, the generated neighbourhoods' distances from the original instance computed and presented in Table 2. As it seems the neighbours generated by LIME on original space, in this example, when are encoded to the reduced space are further to the neighbours generated by LioNets in the encoded space. However, when the LioNets' generated neighbours are transformed back to the original space, are more distant to the original instance in comparison to LIME's neighbours, but that is the assumption that has been made through the beginning of these experiments. It is critical to mention at this point, that these distances measured with neighbours generated by changing only one feature at a time.

Table 2. Neighbourhood distances for instance of hate speech dataset.

	Euclidean distance
LIME: generated on original space	0.3961
LIME: encoded	0.9444
LioNets: generated on encoded space	0.2163
LioNets: decoded to original space	0.7635

4.3 Results on SMS Spam Dataset

The second example which is going to be explained belongs to the SMS spam dataset. The text of the preprocessed instance is the following: "Wife.how she knew the time of murder exactly". This instance has true class "ham". The classifier predicted truthfully 0.00014 probability to be "spam".

Figure 4 presents two different explanations for the classifier's prediction. As before, Fig. 4a shows the explanation provided by LioNets and Fig. 4b shows LIME's explanation. The contribution of feature "wife" to the prediction is assigned to different classes in each explanation. To prove the stability and robustness of LioNets, this feature is removed and by auditing again the neural network the new prediction is lower with a probability of 0.000095. Thus, it is clear that feature "wife" was indeed contributing to the "spam" class as LioNets explained and captured.

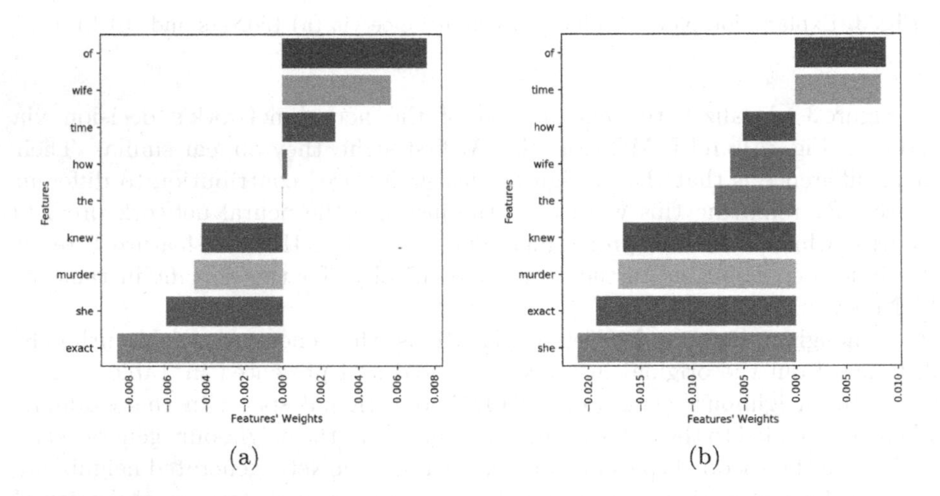

Fig. 4. Explanation plots of SMS spam instance using LioNets (a) and LIME (b).

Like before, the neighbourhoods' distances from the original instance are computed and presented in Table 3. As it seems the neighbours generated by LIME on original space, by projecting them into the encoded space, are more distant to the encoded instance, compared to the neighbours generated by LioNets directly in the encoded space.

Table 3. Neighbourhood distances for instance of SMS spam collection.

	Euclidean distance
LIME: generated on original space	0.3184
LIME: encoded	0.8068
LioNets: generated on encoded space	0.3459
LioNets: decoded to original space	0.7875

5 Conclusion

In summary, the LioNets architecture provides valid explanations for the decisions of a neural network that are comparable to other state-of-the-art techniques, while at the same time it guarantees better adjacency between the generated neighbours of an instance because the generation of the neighbours is performed on the penultimate layer of the network. In addition, LioNets can create better, larger and more representative neighbourhoods, because the generation process takes place at the encoded space, where the instance has a dense representation. These are the main points of creating and using LioNets on decision systems like neural networks.

One main disadvantage of LioNets is that it is focused only on explaining neural networks, thus it is not a model agnostic method. Moreover, the overall process of building LioNets is harder than training neural network predictors, because they demand the training of a decoder, which is a difficult task.

Future work plans include testing the LioNets methodology on different variations of encoders and decoders and implementing more complex neighbourhood generation and neighbours selection processes. In addition, we would like to explore different transparent models for explaining the instances, such as rule-based models [5], decision tree models [4,16] and models based on abstract argumentation [6]. Lastly, we plan to evaluate LioNets based on human subject experiments.

Acknowledgment. This paper is supported by the European Union's Horizon 2020 research and innovation programme under grant agreement No 825619. AI4EU Project (https://www.ai4eu.eu).

References

1. Adadi, A., Berrada, M.: Peeking inside the black-box: a survey on explainable artificial intelligence (XAI). IEEE Access **6**, 52138–52160 (2018). https://doi.org/10.1109/ACCESS.2018.2870052. https://ieeexplore.ieee.org/document/8466590/
2. Almeida, T.A., Hidalgo, J.M.G., Yamakami, A.: Contributions to the study of SMS spam filtering: new collection and results. In: Proceedings of the 11th ACM Symposium on Document Engineering, pp. 259–262. ACM (2011)
3. Anagnostou, A., Mollas, I., Tsoumakas, G.: Hatebusters: a web application for actively reporting YouTube hate speech. In: IJCAI (2017). http://www.inach.net/index.php
4. Breiman, L., Friedman, J.H., Olshen, R., Stone, C.: Classification and regression trees. Biometrics **40**(3), 17–23 (1984)
5. Clark, P., Niblett, T.: The CN2 induction algorithm. Mach. Learn. **3**(4), 261–283 (1989). https://doi.org/10.1007/BF00116835
6. Dung, P.M.: On the acceptability of arguments and its fundamental role in nonmonotonic reasoning, logic programming and n-person games. Artif. Intell. **77**(2), 321–357 (1995). https://doi.org/10.1016/0004-3702(94)00041-X. http://www.sciencedirect.com/science/article/pii/000437029400041X

7. Frosst, N., Hinton, G.: Distilling a neural network into a soft decision tree. arXiv preprint arXiv:1711.09784, November 2017
8. Guidotti, R., Monreale, A., Ruggieri, S., Pedreschi, D., Turini, F., Giannotti, F.: Local rule-based explanations of black box decision systems. arXiv preprint arXiv:1805.10820, May 2018
9. Guidotti, R., Monreale, A., Ruggieri, S., Turini, F., Giannotti, F., Pedreschi, D.: A survey of methods for explaining black box models. ACM Comput. Surv. **51**(5), 1–42 (2018). https://doi.org/10.1145/3236009. http://dl.acm.org/citation.cfm?doid=3271482.3236009
10. Hinton, G., Vinyals, O., Dean, J.: Distilling the knowledge in a neural network. arXiv preprint arXiv:1503.02531, March 2015
11. Kingma, D.P., Welling, M.: Auto-encoding variational Bayes. arXiv preprint arXiv:1312.6114 (2013)
12. Lampridis, O.P.: Explaining sentiment prediction by generating exemplars in the latent space. Undergraduate thesis, Aristotle University of Thessaloniki, School of Informatics (2019)
13. Liu, W., Wang, Z., Liu, X., Zeng, N., Liu, Y., Alsaadi, F.E.: A survey of deep neural network architectures and their applications. Neurocomputing **234**, 11–26 (2017). https://doi.org/10.1016/j.neucom.2016.12.038. https://linkinghub.elsevier.com/retrieve/pii/S0925231216315533
14. Miller, G.A.: WordNet: a lexical database for english. Commun. ACM **38**(11), 39–41 (1995)
15. Porter, M.F.: Snowball: a language for stemming algorithms, October 2001. http://snowball.tartarus.org/texts/introduction.html. Accessed 11 March 2008
16. Quinlan, J.R.: C4.5: Programs for Machine Learning. Elsevier, Amsterdam (2014)
17. Rezende, D.J., Mohamed, S., Wierstra, D.: Stochastic backpropagation and approximate inference in deep generative models. arXiv preprint arXiv:1401.4082 (2014)
18. Ribeiro, M.T., Singh, S., Guestrin, C.: "Why should I trust you?": explaining the predictions of any classifier. In: Proceedings of the 22nd ACM SIGKDD International Conference on Knowledge Discovery and Data Mining - KDD 2016, February 2016. https://arxiv.org/abs/1602.04938
19. Ribeiro, M.T., Singh, S., Guestrin, C.: Anchors: high-precision model-agnostic explanations. In: Thirty-Second AAAI Conference on Artificial Intelligence (2018). www.aaai.org
20. Sadowski, P., Collado, J., Whiteson, D., Baldi, P.: Deep learning, dark knowledge, and dark matter, August 2015. http://proceedings.mlr.press/v42/sado14.html
21. Sparck Jones, K.: A statistical interpretation of term specificity and its application in retrieval. J. Doc. **28**(1), 11–21 (1972)

Decentralized Machine Learning at the Edge

Decentralized Machine Learning at the Edge

Many of today's parallel machine learning algorithms were developed for tightly coupled systems like computing clusters or clouds. However, the volumes of data generated from machine-to-machine interaction, by mobile phones or autonomous vehicles, surpass the amount of data that can be realistically centralized. Thus, traditional cloud computing approaches are rendered infeasible. To scale parallel machine learning to such volumes of data, computation needs to be pushed towards the edge, that is, towards the data generating devices. By learning models directly on the data sources—which often have computational power of their own, for example, mobile phones, smart sensors, and vehicles-network communication can be reduced by orders of magnitude. Moreover, it enables raining a central model without centralizing privacy-sensitive data. This workshop aims to foster discussion, discovery, and dissemination of novel ideas and approaches for decentralized machine learning.

The second international workshop on Decentralized Machine Learning at the Edge (DMLE'19) was held in Würzburg, Germany in conjunction with ECML PKDD. The workshop included a keynote by Dr. Ingo Thon (Siemens AG) followed by technical presentations, a hardware demo, and a poster session. The workshop was attended by around 40 people.

The accepted papers presented interesting novel aspects of decentralized machine learning, especially in the context of edge computing, including hardware aspects of physically decentralized systems. We want to thank the authors for their valuable contributions, great presentations, and lively and fruitful discussions. We would also like to thank the DMLE'19 program committee, whose members made the workshop possible with their rigorous and timely review process. Finally, we would like to thank ECML PKDD for hosting the workshop and the workshop chairs, Peggy Cellier and Kurt Driessens for their valuable support.

Organization

DMLE'19 Chairs

Michael Kamp	Monash University
Yamuna Krishnamurthy	Royal Holloway University of London
Daniel Paurat	Fraunhofer IAIS

Program Committee

Stefan Wrobel	Fraunhofer IAIS
Jochen Garke	Fraunhofer SCAI
Mario Boley	Monash University
Christian Bauckhage	Fraunhofer IAIS
Janis Keuper	Fraunhofer ITWM
Sandy Moens	University of Antwerp
Dino Oglic	King's College, London
Michael Mock	Fraunhofer IAIS
Sven Giesselbach	Fraunhofer IAIS
Tim Wirtz	Fraunhofer IAIS
Pascal Welke	University of Bonn
Rafet Sifa	Fraunhofer IAIS
Linara Adilova	Fraunhofer IAIS
Dorina Weichert	Fraunhofer IAIS

Distributed Generative Modelling with Sub-linear Communication Overhead

Nico Piatkowski(✉)

Fraunhofer IAIS, ME Group, Sankt Augustin, Germany
nico.piatkowski@iais.fraunhofer.de

Abstract. Pushing machine learning towards the edge, often implies the restriction to ultra-low-power (ULP) devices with rather limited compute capabilities. Generative models estimate the data generating probability mass $\mathbb{P}^*$ which can in turn be used for various tasks, including simulation, prediction/forecasting, and novelty detection. Whenever the actual learning task is unknown at learning time or the task is allowed to change over time, learning a generative model is the only viable option. However, learning such models on resource constrained systems raises several challenges. Recent advances in exponential family learning allow us to estimate sophisticated models on highly resource-constrained systems. Nevertheless, the setting in which the training data is distributed among several devices in a network with presumably high communication costs has not yet been investigated. We close this gap by deriving and exploiting a new property of integer models. More precisely, we present a model averaging scheme whose communication complexity is sub-linear w.r.t. the parameter dimension d, and provide an upper bound on the global loss. Experimental results on benchmark data show, that the aggregated model is often on par with the non-distributed global model.

Keywords: Distributed learning · Undirected models · Integer models · Model averaging

1 Introduction

When data is collected at various physical locations, we are faced with several opportunities regarding the subsequent data processing. Data might be partitioned in several different ways. Two prototypical scenarios are depicted in Fig. 1. In the horizontal scenario, the full data is distributed instance-wise over multiple devices. This happens due to storage or privacy restrictions. For vertically distributed data, different devices measure different features of the same instance. This does not imply that those features are independent. An example are large industrial processes, where measurement hardware itself is distributed. Here, we consider case (a), i.e., the same data generating process can be observed at multiple locations. Approaches for case (b) can be found in [14].

P. Cellier and K. Driessens (Eds.): ECML PKDD 2019 Workshops, CCIS 1167, pp. 281–292, 2020.
https://doi.org/10.1007/978-3-030-43823-4_24

The most obvious option to address horizontal data distribution is to send the data to a central server. This comes of course with a huge communication overhead and a loss of privacy. To address these issues, we may aggregate the collected data to reduce the communication. Moreover, data points can be perturbed [4] to increase the privacy of the data source. However, we still have to send a significant amount of data over the network. Instead of sending the raw, aggregated, or perturbed data, an alternative is to learn the model directly at the edge, i.e., where the data is actually generated. In this scenario, models are updated whenever new data arrives at the device. If a convergence criterion is met, e.g., based on distributed convex thresholding [16], the models of all devices are collected and aggregated, to arrive at a global solution that can benefit from the complete data. Such an aggregation can be carried out by Radon machines [8]. However, we will resort to a simple averaging operation that is reminiscent of Bayesian model averaging [5].

A huge set of machine learning techniques can potentially be applied in this setting. Here, we restrict ourselves to generative probabilistic models for discrete data, which can used for various tasks, including simulation, prediction/forecasting, and novelty detection. Moreover, these models are statistically sound, in the sense that they allow for consistent estimation of the data generating probability mass. This is especially interesting when the actual learning task is unknown at learning time or the task is allowed to change over time.

Learning a model close to where the data is actually generated, often implies the restriction to ultra-low-power (ULP) devices with rather limited compute capabilities. Especially in the distributed or federated learning settings, edge devices are subject to strong resource constraints. Communication efficiency [9] and computational burden [2,13] must be reduced, in order to get along with the available hardware. Here, we will resort to integer undirected models [11,13] which provide a complete framework for learning and inference under heavy resource constraints. Nevertheless, the setting in which the training data is distributed among several devices in a network with presumably high communication costs has not yet been investigated in the context of integer undirected models. We close this gap by deriving and exploiting a new property of integer models. More precisely, we show that integer models have a high intrinsic sparsity. Based on this observation, we present a model averaging scheme whose communication complexity is sub-linear w.r.t. the parameter dimension d.

2 Notation and Background

Let us summarize the notation and background necessary for the subsequent development. The Kullback-Leibler divergence between two probability mass functions $\mathbb{P}$ and $\mathbb{Q}$ is defined by $\mathrm{KL}[\mathbb{Q}||\mathbb{P}] = \sum_{\boldsymbol{x}\in\mathcal{X}} \mathbb{Q}(\boldsymbol{x})(\log \mathbb{Q}(\boldsymbol{x}) - \log \mathbb{P}(\boldsymbol{x}))$, which is never negative and zero if and only if $\mathbb{P} = \mathbb{Q}$. The set $\mathbb{N}$ contains all non-negative integers.

a)

	id	$\boldsymbol{X}_1$	$\boldsymbol{X}_2$	$\boldsymbol{X}_3$	$\boldsymbol{X}_4$
I	1	$\boldsymbol{x}_1^1$	$\boldsymbol{x}_2^1$	$\boldsymbol{x}_3^1$	$\boldsymbol{x}_4^1$
	2	$\boldsymbol{x}_1^2$	$\boldsymbol{x}_2^2$	$\boldsymbol{x}_3^2$	$\boldsymbol{x}_4^2$
II	3	$\boldsymbol{x}_1^3$	$\boldsymbol{x}_2^3$	$\boldsymbol{x}_3^3$	$\boldsymbol{x}_4^3$
	4	$\boldsymbol{x}_1^4$	$\boldsymbol{x}_2^4$	$\boldsymbol{x}_3^4$	$\boldsymbol{x}_4^4$

b)

	III		IV	
id	$\boldsymbol{X}_1$	$\boldsymbol{X}_2$	$\boldsymbol{X}_3$	$\boldsymbol{X}_4$
1	$\boldsymbol{x}_1^1$	$\boldsymbol{x}_2^1$	$\boldsymbol{x}_3^1$	$\boldsymbol{x}_4^1$
2	$\boldsymbol{x}_1^2$	$\boldsymbol{x}_2^2$	$\boldsymbol{x}_3^2$	$\boldsymbol{x}_4^2$
3	$\boldsymbol{x}_1^3$	$\boldsymbol{x}_2^3$	$\boldsymbol{x}_3^3$	$\boldsymbol{x}_4^3$
4	$\boldsymbol{x}_1^4$	$\boldsymbol{x}_2^4$	$\boldsymbol{x}_3^4$	$\boldsymbol{x}_4^4$

Fig. 1. Two prototypical scenarios for data distribution of an exemplary data set with $n = 4$ features (columns) and $N = 4$ data points (rows). Left: Horizontal distribution. The data points are distributed among devices I and II. Right: Vertical distribution. The features are distributed among devices III and IV.

2.1 Undirected Models

An undirected graph $G = (V, E)$ consists of $n = |V|$ vertices, connected via edges $(v, w) \in E$. A clique C is a fully-connected subset of vertices, i.e., $\forall v, w \in C : (v, w) \in E$. The set of all maximal cliques of G is denoted by $\mathcal{C}$. Here, any undirected graph represents the conditional independence structure of some n-dimensional random variable $\boldsymbol{X}$ [15]. To this end, we identify each vertex $v \in V$ with a random variable $\boldsymbol{X}_v$ taking values in the state space $\mathcal{X}_v$. The random vector $\boldsymbol{X} = (\boldsymbol{X}_v : v \in V)$, with probability mass function (pmf) $\mathbb{P}$, represents the random joint state of all vertices in some arbitrary but fixed order, taking values $\boldsymbol{x}$ in the Cartesian product space $\mathcal{X} = \bigotimes_{v \in V} \boldsymbol{X}_v$. If not stated otherwise, $\mathcal{X}$ is a discrete set. Moreover, we allow to access these quantities for any proper subset of variables $S \subset V$, i.e., $\boldsymbol{X}_S = (\boldsymbol{X}_v : v \in S)$, $\boldsymbol{x}_S$, and $\mathcal{X}_S$, respectively. According to the Hammersley-Clifford theorem [6], the probability mass of $\mathcal{X}$ factorizes over positive functions $\psi_C : \mathcal{X} \to \mathbb{R}_+$, one for each maximal clique of the underlying graph,

$$\mathbb{P}(\boldsymbol{X} = \boldsymbol{x}) = \frac{1}{Z} \prod_{C \in \mathcal{C}} \psi_C(\boldsymbol{x}_C) , \tag{1}$$

normalized via $Z = \sum_{\boldsymbol{x} \in \mathcal{X}} \prod_{C \in \mathcal{C}} \psi_C(\boldsymbol{x}_C)$. Due to positivity of ψ_C, it can be written as an exponential, i.e., $\psi_C(\boldsymbol{x}_C) = \exp(\langle \boldsymbol{\theta}_C, \phi_C(\boldsymbol{x}_C) \rangle)$ with sufficient statistic $\phi_C : \mathcal{X}_C \to \mathbb{R}^{|\mathcal{X}_C|}$. Here, we assume the use of overcomplete sufficient statistic, i.e., for discrete data, $\phi_C(\boldsymbol{x}_C)$ is a $|\mathcal{X}_C|$-dimensional "one-hot" vector, where the single 1 entry indicates the specific state $\boldsymbol{x}_C$ of the clique C. Thus, $\psi_C(\boldsymbol{x}_C) = \exp(\langle \boldsymbol{\theta}_C, \phi_C(\boldsymbol{x}_C) \rangle) = \exp(\boldsymbol{\theta}_{C=\boldsymbol{x}_C})$. The full joint pmf can then be written in the famous exponential family form $\mathbb{P}(\boldsymbol{X} = \boldsymbol{x}) = \exp(\langle \boldsymbol{\theta}, \phi(\boldsymbol{x}) \rangle - A)$ with $\boldsymbol{\theta} = (\boldsymbol{\theta}_C : C \in \mathcal{C})$, $\phi(\boldsymbol{x}) = (\phi_C(\boldsymbol{x}_C) : C \in \mathcal{C})$, and log-partition function $A = \log Z = \log \sum_{\boldsymbol{x}} \exp(\langle \boldsymbol{\theta}, \phi(\boldsymbol{x}) \rangle)$.

The parameters of exponential family members are estimated by minimizing the negative average log-likelihood $\ell(\boldsymbol{\theta}; \mathcal{D}) = -(1/|\mathcal{D}|) \sum_{\boldsymbol{x} \in \mathcal{D}} \log \mathbb{P}_{\boldsymbol{\theta}}(\boldsymbol{x})$ for some data set $\mathcal{D}$ via first-order numeric optimization methods. $\mathcal{D}$ contains samples from $\boldsymbol{X}$, and it can be shown that the estimated probability mass converges to the data generating distribution $\mathbb{P}^*$ as the size of $\mathcal{D}$ increases.

In the context of horizontally distributed data (Fig. 1a), we assume the existence of k data sets $\mathcal{D}_1, \mathcal{D}_2, \ldots, \mathcal{D}_k$, each generated by $\mathbb{P}^*$, and collected by one of k distributed devices.

2.2 Integer Undirected Models

Pushing machine learning towards the edge, i.e., towards the data generating devices, often translates to pushing machine learning to devices with heavily restricted resources. To facilitate the application of undirected models on such devices, we consider an integer version of $\psi_C(\boldsymbol{x}_C)$ [13]:

$$\bar{\psi}_C(\boldsymbol{x}_C) = 2^{\langle \bar{\boldsymbol{\theta}}_C, \phi_C(\boldsymbol{x}_C) \rangle} \tag{2}$$

with $\bar{\boldsymbol{\theta}} \in \mathbb{N}^d$. Let us shortly recap the different layers of approximation that are involved in integer undirected model: (1) The mere base change from exp to 2 is not an approximation at all—the exponential family of densities can be formulated equivalently with any arbitrary base. (2) The restriction to parameter vectors in $\mathbb{N}^d$ is indeed an approximation. However, it can be shown that the error w.r.t. the model likelihood is bounded—the best integer model is not arbitrarily far away from the best real-valued solution. (3) Probabilistic inference is per se possible in the integer domain, e.g., via belief propagation [10] or Gibbs sampling. To circumvent issues with numerical stability, we use an approximate message passing scheme, called bit-length propagation [11]. In general, we assume that the underlying conditional independence structure G is a tree. If not, we employ the junction tree algorithm [15].

Using integer models has several convenient implications for ultra-low-power systems. First of all, it can be shown that approximate maximum likelihood estimation can be carried out without the need for floating point co-processing units [11]. This reduces both, the required chip-size as well as the power consumption of the underlying hardware: Evaluating (2) reduces to a mere bit-shift instead of a rather costly (in terms of clock-cycles) evaluation of the transcendental function exp. Indeed, having $\langle \bar{\boldsymbol{\theta}}_C, \phi_C(\boldsymbol{x}_C) \rangle > \omega$ results in an overflow during bit-shifting on systems with word-size ω. However, it was shown in [11] that overflows can be prevented by using specialized inference algorithms and data structures. The actual parameter learning is carried out by an integer gradient descent technique that is guaranteed to output a (locally) optimal integer solution.

Second, empirical results show [11,13], that only a few (≈ 3) bits for each model parameter suffice to achieve practical results in terms of prediction accuracy and approximate marginals probabilities. Technically, learning is carried out over $\{0, 1, \ldots, 2^b - 1\}^d$ instead of the full $\mathbb{N}$—a fact that is always true on practical hardware—where b is a hyper-parameter. Hence, storing and communicating the learned model $\bar{\boldsymbol{\theta}}$ requires less than 10% of bits compared to an ordinary model with 64 bit encoding.

Third, it can be shown that the parameter vector of exponential family models with overcomplete sufficient statistic is *never* dense, i.e., at least $|\mathcal{C}|$ model parameters are guaranteed to be zero. We exploit and improve this fact in the sequel and use it to devise a distributed learning scheme with sub-linear communication overhead.

3 Distributed Integer Undirected Models

We will now go through a series of theoretical insights which will eventually lead to a new distributed learning scheme for integer undirected models. But before we start, let us stress the meaning of "sub-linear" in the context of exponential family models. As said in the introduction, the easiest solution is to send the raw data to a central server and perform learning there. Having observed N_i n-dimensional data points at device i, this amounts to $nN_i\omega$ transmitted bits, assuming word-size ω. In this extreme case, no computational resources are required at the data source but at the cost of maximum communication complexity. One could tend to say that communicating less than $\mathcal{O}(nN_i\omega)$ is "sub-linear". However, in case of exponential family models, neither sending nor storing the full amount of data is required at all—the model parameters can be learned from an aggregated version of the data set. To see this, consider the objective function of the integer model:

$$\begin{aligned}\ell(\boldsymbol{\theta};\mathcal{D}) &= -\frac{1}{|\mathcal{D}|}\sum_{\boldsymbol{x}\in\mathcal{D}}\log_2\mathbb{P}_{\boldsymbol{\theta}}(\boldsymbol{x}) = -\frac{1}{|\mathcal{D}|}\sum_{\boldsymbol{x}\in\mathcal{D}}\log_2 2^{\langle\boldsymbol{\theta},\phi(\boldsymbol{x})\rangle - A_2(\boldsymbol{\theta})}\\ &= -\frac{1}{|\mathcal{D}|}\sum_{\boldsymbol{x}\in\mathcal{D}}\langle\boldsymbol{\theta},\phi(\boldsymbol{x})\rangle - A_2(\boldsymbol{\theta}) = A_2(\boldsymbol{\theta}) - \langle\boldsymbol{\theta},\frac{1}{|\mathcal{D}|}\sum_{\boldsymbol{x}\in\mathcal{D}}\phi(\boldsymbol{x})\rangle \end{aligned} \tag{3}$$

Setting $\boldsymbol{\mu} = {}^1\!/_{|\mathcal{D}|}\sum_{\boldsymbol{x}\in\mathcal{D}}\phi(\boldsymbol{x})$, we see that $\ell(\boldsymbol{\theta};\mathcal{D}) = A_2(\boldsymbol{\theta}) - \langle\boldsymbol{\theta},\boldsymbol{\mu}\rangle = \ell(\boldsymbol{\theta};\boldsymbol{\mu})$, i.e., $\boldsymbol{\theta}$ can be learned from the average sufficient statistic $\boldsymbol{\mu}$—access to the raw data set $\mathcal{D}$ is not required. Assuming a process that generates new data points in some fixed time intervals, it is straightforward to update $\boldsymbol{\mu}$ as a running average. Thus, in case of exponential family models, transmitting $\boldsymbol{\mu}$ and $|\mathcal{D}|$ to some central server is equivalent to transmitting the full data set. This implies that sub-linearity requires a communication complexity that is strictly less than d—the dimension of $\phi(\boldsymbol{x})$ and $\boldsymbol{\theta}$. To achieve this, we first exploit a property of the one-hot encoding that underlies $\phi(\boldsymbol{x})$.

Theorem 1 (Overcomplete models are always sparse). *Denote the number of non-zeros by* $\|\boldsymbol{\theta}\|_0 = \sum_{i=1}^{d}|\boldsymbol{\theta}_i|^0$ *with* $0^0 = 0$, *and let* $\boldsymbol{\theta}\in\mathbb{R}^d$ *with* $\|\boldsymbol{\theta}\|_0 = d$ *be the dense parameter vector of some exponential family member with overcomplete sufficient statistic* ϕ. *Then, there is* $\boldsymbol{\theta}'\in\mathbb{R}^d$ *such that* $\mathbb{P}_{\boldsymbol{\theta}} = \mathbb{P}_{\boldsymbol{\theta}'}$ *and*

$$\|\boldsymbol{\theta}'\|_0 \leq \|\boldsymbol{\theta}\|_0 - |\mathcal{C}| < \|\boldsymbol{\theta}\|_0 = d$$

Proof. Exponential family models with overcomplete sufficient statistics are shift-invariant w.r.t. each clique parameter vector [11]. Recall that $\boldsymbol{\theta}$ is defined as the concatenation of the parameter vectors of all cliques. Consider the d-dimensional vector $S_C(\alpha)$ which is zero everywhere, except for the positions of the parameters that belong to the clique C—at these positions, we put the value α. For the proof, explicit knowledge about these positions it not required. The only important fact is that some arbitrary subset of the d dimensions contains the parameters for clique C. Now, consider the vector $\boldsymbol{\theta}' = \boldsymbol{\theta} + S_C(\alpha)$. We have

$$\mathbb{P}_{\boldsymbol{\theta}'}(\boldsymbol{x}) = \frac{\exp(\langle \boldsymbol{\theta}', \phi(\boldsymbol{x})\rangle)}{\sum_{\boldsymbol{x}'} \exp(\langle \boldsymbol{\theta}', \phi(\boldsymbol{x}')\rangle)} = \frac{\exp(\langle \boldsymbol{\theta}, \phi(\boldsymbol{x})\rangle + \alpha)}{\sum_{\boldsymbol{x}'} \exp(\langle \boldsymbol{\theta}, \phi(\boldsymbol{x}')\rangle + \alpha)} = \mathbb{P}_{\boldsymbol{\theta}}(\boldsymbol{x})$$

The equality in the middle holds because $\langle S_C(\alpha), \phi(\boldsymbol{x})\rangle = \alpha$ for all $\boldsymbol{x} \in \mathcal{X}$. This is, in fact, a direct implication of ϕ's overcompleteness. The above result is called *shift-invariance.*

Let $\boldsymbol{\theta}_{C,1}$ be the first parameter of each clique's parameter vector. We construct the vector $\boldsymbol{\theta}' = \boldsymbol{\theta} + \sum_{C \in \mathcal{C}} S_C(-\boldsymbol{\theta}_{C,1})$. Shift-invariance holds for each C, and thus $\mathbb{P}_{\boldsymbol{\theta}'}(\boldsymbol{x}) = \mathbb{P}_{\boldsymbol{\theta}'}(\boldsymbol{x})$. By assumption, $\boldsymbol{\theta}$ is dense, i.e., $\|\boldsymbol{\theta}\|_0 = d$. By construction, $\boldsymbol{\theta}'$ must have at least $|\mathcal{C}|$ zero-values. $\|\boldsymbol{\theta}'\|_0 \leq \|\boldsymbol{\theta}\|_0 - |\mathcal{C}|$ holds with equality if all d dimensions of $\boldsymbol{\theta}$ have a different value. □

The above theorem guarantees that any exponential family member with overcomplete sufficient statistic has an optimal parameter with at least $|\mathcal{C}|$ zero-entries. This result arises from overcompleteness and has not yet any specific connection to our integer models. Based on this result, we provide the following genuine new insight:

Theorem 2 (Integer models are sparser). *Let $\boldsymbol{\theta} \in \{1, \ldots, 2^b - 1\}^d$ be the dense parameter vector of some integer exponential family member with overcomplete sufficient statistic ϕ. Let further $|\mathcal{X}_{C_{\min}}|$ be the smallest clique state space. Then, if b is chosen such that $2^b - 1 < |\mathcal{X}_{C_{\min}}|$, there exists $\boldsymbol{\theta}'$ such that $\mathbb{P}_{\boldsymbol{\theta}} = \mathbb{P}_{\boldsymbol{\theta}'}$ and*

$$\|\boldsymbol{\theta}'\|_0 \leq \|\boldsymbol{\theta}\|_0 - 2|\mathcal{C}| < \|\boldsymbol{\theta}\|_0 = d$$

Proof. By assumption, there are less parameter values than clique states. Thus, each clique parameter vector $\boldsymbol{\theta}_C$ must contain one parameter value z at least twice. Again, we exploit shift-invariance to subtract z from each parameter in $\boldsymbol{\theta}_C$ which generates at least 2 zero values. This procedure is applied to all cliques $C \in \mathcal{C}$ to end up with a parameter vector $\boldsymbol{\theta}'$ that contains at least $2|\mathcal{C}|$ zeros. □

Thus the number of zero-parameters is increased by at least a factor of 2. The same idea cannot be applied to ordinary (non-integer) exponential families—there, all real-valued parameters will be different with probability 1.

Our new result tells us that integer models have not only computational benefits but also non-trivial implications when the learned integer model has to be transmitted. The final step is the aggregation of independent local models. For simplicity, we restrict ourselves to plain model averaging. Assuming that the underlying network allows for broadcasts, this operation can be carried out locally in each device. If no broadcast is available, we can send each model to a designated central node that carries out the aggregation. Clearly, model averaging involves some error, due to the non-linearity of the exponential family. However, the following corollary raises some hope that the averaged model is not too bad.

Lemma 1 (Upper bound on the loss). *Let $\boldsymbol{\theta}^i \in \mathbb{R}^d$ for $i = 1, 2, \ldots, k$ be the parameter vector of the model learned on the i-th device. Let further $\hat{\boldsymbol{\theta}} = \sum_{i=1}^{k} \alpha^i \boldsymbol{\theta}^i$ with $\alpha_i > 0$ and $\sum_{i=1}^{k} \alpha^i = 1$ be the corresponding model average. Then, for any arbitrary data set $\mathcal{D}$, we have*

$$\ell(\hat{\boldsymbol{\theta}}; \mathcal{D}) \leq \sum_{i=1}^{k} \alpha_i \ell(\boldsymbol{\theta}^i; \mathcal{D})$$

Proof. The negative log-likelihood is convex. The result is thus a direct corollary of Jensen's inequality. □

At a first glace, this result seems odd, since it suggests that the global model average is *better* than the local models. It is important to understand that the negative log-likelihoods on the right-hand-side are computed w.r.t. the (global) data set $\mathcal{D}$, and not w.r.t. the local sets $\mathcal{D}_i$. The local model's loss can be arbitrarily large on $\mathcal{D}$ which explains why this inequality holds. However, in the joint limit of $|\mathcal{D}_i| \to \infty$ for $i = 1, \ldots, k$, all local data sets are equivalent and the inequality will turn into an equality. In practice, we want to explore the space "in between", where a finite amount of data has been observed at each device, but the individual local models are still similar to each other. The pairwise distances between local average sufficient statistics can be bounded by a function of the available data.

Lemma 2 (Distance between expected statistics). *Let $\boldsymbol{X}$ be a random variable with state space $\mathcal{X}$, $\mathcal{D}_i$ and $\mathcal{D}_j$ two pairwise independent data sets with samples from $\boldsymbol{X}$, and $\phi : \mathcal{X} \to \mathbb{R}^d$ some function. Denote the estimated expectation of $\phi(\boldsymbol{X})$ w.r.t. $\mathcal{D}_i$ by $\boldsymbol{\mu}^i = \frac{1}{|\mathcal{D}_i|} \sum_{\boldsymbol{x} \in \mathcal{D}_i} \phi(\boldsymbol{x})$ and likewise for $\boldsymbol{\mu}^j$. Then,*

$$\|\boldsymbol{\mu}^i - \boldsymbol{\mu}^j\|_\infty \leq 2\sqrt{\frac{(c+1)\log d}{2|\mathcal{D}'|}} = \epsilon$$

with probability of at least $\delta = (1 - 2\exp(-c \log d))^2$ for any $c > 0$. D' is the smaller of the two data sets $\mathcal{D}_i$ and $\mathcal{D}_j$.

Proof. $\boldsymbol{\mu}^i$ is unbiased due to $\mathbb{E}[\boldsymbol{\mu}^i] = \frac{1}{|\mathcal{D}_i|} \sum_{\boldsymbol{x} \in \mathcal{D}_i} \mathbb{E}[\phi(\boldsymbol{X})] = \boldsymbol{\mu}^*$. According to Hoeffding's inequality [7],

$$\mathbb{P}(|\boldsymbol{\mu}^i{}_l - \mathbb{E}[\boldsymbol{\mu}^i]_l| > t) \leq 2\exp(-2|\mathcal{D}|t^2)$$

Algorithm 1: Distributed ULP-Learning of Generative Models

input k local data sets, one per device; desired (ϵ, δ)-pair; parameter width b
output Global model $\hat{\boldsymbol{\theta}} = (1/k)\sum_{i=1}^{k} \boldsymbol{\theta}^i$ (Lemma 1)
1: **for** all devices $i = 1, 2, \ldots, k$ in parallel **do**
2: **if** New data arrives **then**
3: Update($\boldsymbol{\mu}^i$) (Eq. 3)
4: $\boldsymbol{\theta}^i \leftarrow \arg\min_{\boldsymbol{\theta} \in \{0,1,\ldots,2^b-1\}^d} \ell(\boldsymbol{\theta}; \boldsymbol{\mu}^i)$
5: **end if**
6: **if** $|\mathcal{D}_i|$ is large enough to satisfy (ϵ, δ) (Lemma 2) **then**
7: Sparsify($\boldsymbol{\theta}^i$) (Theorem 2)
8: Broadcast($\boldsymbol{\theta}^i$)
9: **return**
10: **end if**
11: **end for**

for all $t > 0$. Since this holds for any dimension l, we can apply the union bound to get

$$\mathbb{P}(\exists l \in [d] : |\boldsymbol{\mu}^i{}_l - \boldsymbol{\mu}^*_l| > t) \leq 2\exp(-2|\mathcal{D}|t^2 + \log d) .$$

We set $t = \sqrt{(c+1)\log d/(2|\mathcal{D}|)}$. Thus $\|\boldsymbol{\mu}^i - \boldsymbol{\mu}^*\|_\infty \leq \sqrt{\frac{(c+1)\log d}{2|\mathcal{D}_i|}}$ with probability at least $1 - 2\exp(-c\log d)$. Indeed, the same holds for $\boldsymbol{\mu}^j$. Finally, we apply the triangle inequality to derive $\|\boldsymbol{\mu}^i - \boldsymbol{\mu}^j\|_\infty \leq \|\boldsymbol{\mu}^i - \boldsymbol{\mu}^*\|_\infty + \|\boldsymbol{\mu}^j - \boldsymbol{\mu}^*\|_\infty$. Since both events are independent, the final inequality has probability of at least $\delta = (1 - 2\exp(-c\log d))^2$. □

Increasing c makes the probability δ larger, at the cost of an increased distance ϵ. The lemma can help us to decide when local models are "good enough": Informally, $\boldsymbol{\theta}^i$ and $\boldsymbol{\theta}^j$ will approach each other when $\boldsymbol{\mu}^i$ and $\boldsymbol{\mu}^j$ are approaching each other. We will make use of this intuition without providing a proof. However, the relation between $\boldsymbol{\theta}$ and $\boldsymbol{\mu}$ can be made explicitly by proof techniques provided in [1]. Here, we choose ϵ and δ to determine the number of samples that is required at each device for all local models being similar with high probability.

The final distributed learning procedure is provided in Algorithm 1. There, evaluating the stopping criterion requires knowledge about the amount of data that has been collected by each device—this number could be transmitted in a recurring manner. Here, for simplicity, we assume that data arrives synchronously at the devices and that all devices are started at the same point in time. Hence, all models will collect the same number of data points.

Note that the global model $\hat{\boldsymbol{\theta}}$ is likely to be non-integer. The resulting model average can be rounded to recover an integer solution. This, however, involves an additional approximation error [11]. Instead, we scale local models by $\log 2$, which results in a base-change back to exp. The scaled output $(\log 2)\hat{\boldsymbol{\theta}}$ is thus the parameter of an ordinary (non-integer) exponential family member. Algorithm 1 can hence be re-interpreted as a method that recovers an ordinary exponential family from a set of integer models.

4 Experimental Demonstration

We perform numerical experiments to assess the proposed method. More precisely, we to answer the following questions:

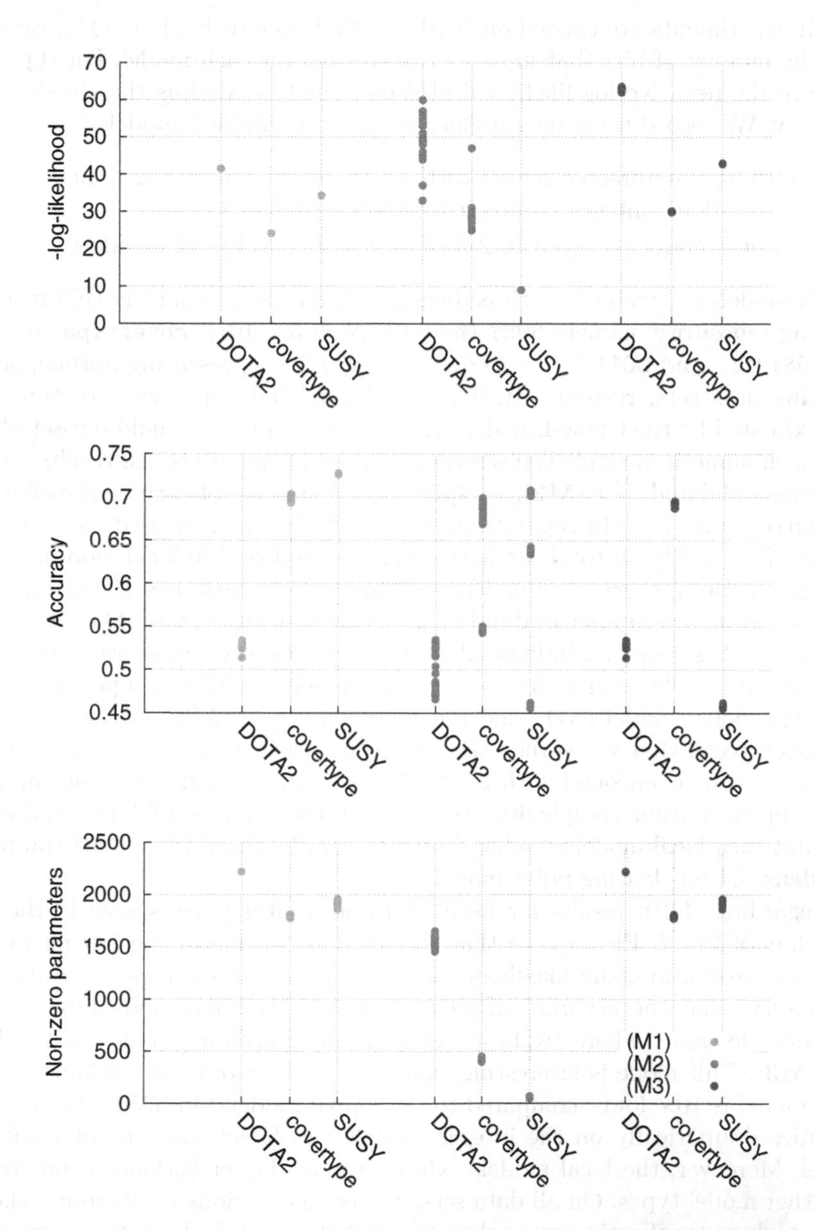

Fig. 2. Experimental results on three benchmark data sets. Each point represents the outcome of a single cross-validation fold. Top: Negative average log-likelihood $\ell(\boldsymbol{\theta}; \mathcal{D})$. Mid: Classification accuracy. Bottom: Number of non-zero values for each learned parameter vector $\boldsymbol{\theta}$, i.e., $\|\boldsymbol{\theta}\|_0$. All three plots share the same key. Best viewed in color.

(**Q1**) What is the improvement w.r.t. communication complexity on real data sets?
(**Q2**) How does the averaged model perform, compared to the global model and the individual local models?

All experiments are carried out with the PX framework[1]. For (**Q1**), we measure the number of bits that must be transmitted for each model. For (**Q2**), we measure the negative log-likelihood of each model, as well as the classification accuracy. We record these measurements for three different models:

(**M1**) Ordinary undirected model with access to the full training data.
(**M2**) $k = 10$ local integer undirected models with $b = 3$.
(**M3**) Scaled model average $(\log 2)\hat{\boldsymbol{\theta}}$ of all $k = 10$ local (**M2**) models.

All models are trained on three benchmark data sets from the UCI machine learning repository, namely SUSY ($n = 19$, $N = 5 \times 10^6$), covertype ($n = 55$, $N = 581012$), and DOTA2 ($n = 117$, $N = 102944$)—representing normal, small, and tiny data sets, respectively. The conditional independence structure G is approximated by the Chow-Liu algorithm [3], computed on a hold-out set of size 10^4. Each numeric variable is discretized into its 10-quantiles. All results are 10-fold cross-validated. For (**M2**), we split the training set of each cross-validation fold further into $k = 10$ separate data sets which are then used as local data sets $\mathcal{D}_1, \mathcal{D}_2, \ldots, \mathcal{D}_k$. In total, we have 10 global models, 100 local modes, and 10 averaged models, where each model averaging is performed over 10 local models.

The results are summarized in Fig. 2. Let us first investigate (**Q1**). The third plot in Fig. 2 shows the individual model sizes for each cross-validation run. As asserted by Theorem 2, the local integer models exhibit a superior sparsity while the global model (**M1**) and the averaged model (**M3**) are mostly dense. Moreover, recall that we learned the integer models with $b = 3$, i.e., each model parameter can be encoded with 3 bits. Combining the higher sparsity and the lower representation complexity, we see that the number of bits required to transmit each local model is reduced by a factor of almost 40 on SUSY compared to a dense 64 bit floating point model.

Regarding (**Q2**), results for likelihood and accuracy are shown in the first two plots of Fig. 2. Please note that the likelihood-value of the integer models is an approximation, the likelihood-values of the other model types are exact. We observe that the accuracy of all models on DOTA2 and covertype is qualitatively the same, where (**M1**) achieves the best accuracy, followed by (**M2**) and (**M3**). This alone is interesting, since the amount of data available to each local model is 10× lower compared to the global model. On SUSY, the accuracy degrades dramatically on the integer models and hence also on the combined model. Moreover, the local models exhibit a much larger variance compared to the other model types. On all data sets, we see that various local models show a much higher classification error than the global model. Indeed, the accuracy of

[1] http://randomfields.org/px.

the aggregated model depends strongly on the local model's quality. The classification results for the (**M3**) model on DOTA2 and covertype are almost indistinguishable from the global (**M1**) model, while the accuracy on SUSY breaks down. The results for the likelihood show similar effects. However, we see that accuracy and likelihood are not strongly coupled. The likelihood of (**M2**) and (**M3**) is much worse than those of (**M1**) models, the corresponding classification results are yet similar.

5 Conclusion

Based on new theoretical findings about the sparsity of integer undirected models, we proposed a new scheme for the distributed learning of generative exponential family models. Theoretical and experimental results certify that our method has a sub-linear communication complexity—a fraction of bits which are required to transmit the dense models is sufficient to reconstruct a full-fledged exponential family model. In many cases, the reconstructed models exhibit a similar classification performance as non-distributed (global) models. Our scheme can thus serve as the basis for many practical distributed solutions.

Moreover, our results provide several new research opportunities: First, our scheme can be easily combined with recent latent variable models [12] and hence, opens the path for distributed probabilistic deep learning. Second, the stopping criterion and the averaging scheme suggest some room for improvement. Our Hoeffding-bound-based stopping criterion is very pessimistic and requires a very large number of samples to guarantee that all local models are similar with high probability. It shall be investigated if convex thresholding [16] delivers any benefit over the stopping criterion that was derived from Lemma 2. Finally, the results presented in [8] suggest, that the model aggregation based on Radon points delivers a higher quality compared to plain model averaging. We should hence employ radon machines instead of plain model averaging to aggregate the local models.

Acknowledgments. This research has been funded by the Federal Ministry of Education and Research of Germany as part of the competence center for machine learning ML2R (01S18038A).

References

1. Bradley, J.K., Guestrin, C.: Sample complexity of composite likelihood. In: International Conference on Artificial Intelligence and Statistics (AISTATS), pp. 136–160 (2012). http://proceedings.mlr.press/v22/bradley12.html
2. Caldas, S., Konecný, J., McMahan, H.B., Talwalkar, A.: Expanding the reach of federated learning by reducing client resource requirements. CoRR abs/1812.07210 (2018). http://arxiv.org/abs/1812.07210
3. Chow, C., Liu, C.: Approximating discrete probability distributions with dependence trees. IEEE Trans. Inf. Theory **14**(3), 462–467 (1968). https://doi.org/10.1109/TIT.1968.1054142

4. Duchi, J.C., Jordan, M.I., Wainwright, M.J.: Privacy aware learning. J. ACM **61**(6), 38:1–38:57 (2014). https://doi.org/10.1145/2666468
5. Fragoso, T.M., Bertoli, W., Louzada, F.: Bayesian model averaging: a systematic review and conceptual classification. Int. Stat. Rev. **86**(1), 1–28 (2018). https://doi.org/10.1111/insr.12243
6. Hammersley, J.M., Clifford, P.: Markov fields on finite graphs and lattices. Unpublished manuscript (1971)
7. Hoeffding, W.: Probability inequalities for sums of bounded random variables. J. Am. Stat. Assoc. **58**(301), 13–30 (1963)
8. Kamp, M., Boley, M., Missura, O., Gärtner, T.: Effective parallelisation for machine learning. In: Advances in Neural Information Processing Systems (NIPS), pp. 6480–6491 (2017). http://papers.nips.cc/paper/7226-effective-parallelisation-for-machine-learning
9. Konecný, J., McMahan, H.B., Yu, F.X., Richtárik, P., Suresh, A.T., Bacon, D.: Federated learning: strategies for improving communication efficiency. CoRR abs/1610.05492 (2016). http://arxiv.org/abs/1610.05492
10. Pearl, J.: Probabilistic Reasoning in Intelligent Systems: Networks of Plausible Inference. Morgan Kaufmann Publishers, Burlington (1988)
11. Piatkowski, N.: Exponential families on resource-constrained systems. Ph.D. thesis, TU Dortmund, Germany (2018). http://hdl.handle.net/2003/36877
12. Piatkowski, N.: Hyper-parameter-free generative modelling with deep Boltzmann trees. In: European Conference on Machine Learning and Principles and Practice of Knowledge Discovery in Databases (ECMLPKDD) (2019)
13. Piatkowski, N., Lee, S., Morik, K.: Integer undirected graphical models for resource-constrained systems. Neurocomputing **173**, 9–23 (2016). https://doi.org/10.1016/j.neucom.2015.01.091
14. Stolpe, M.: Distributed analysis of vertically partitioned sensor measurements under communication constraints. Ph.D. thesis, TU Dortmund, Germany (2017). http://hdl.handle.net/2003/35815
15. Wainwright, M.J., Jordan, M.I.: Graphical models, exponential families, and variational inference. Found. Trends Mach. Learn. **1**(1–2), 1–305 (2008). https://doi.org/10.1561/2200000001
16. Wolff, R.: Distributed convex thresholding. In: Symposium on Principles of Distributed Computing (PODC), pp. 325–334 (2015). https://doi.org/10.1145/2767386.2767387

Distributed Learning of Neural Networks with One Round of Communication

Mike Izbicki[1(✉)] and Christian R. Shelton[2]

[1] Claremont McKenna College, Claremont, CA, USA
mike@izbicki.me
[2] UC Riverside, Riverside, CA, USA
cshelton@cs.ucr.edu

Abstract. The *optimal weighted average* (OWA) is an algorithm for distributed learning of linear models. It achieves statistically optimal theoretical guarantees with only a single round of communication [3]. This paper introduces the *non-linear OWA* (NOWA) algorithm, which extends the linear OWA into the non-linear setting of neural networks. Due to the difficulty of proving theoretical results in this more complex setting, NOWA loses the theoretical guarantees of the OWA algorithm. Nevertheless, we show that NOWA works well empirically. We follow an evaluation procedure introduced by McMahan et. al. [16] for federated learning and show significantly improved results on a simple MNIST baseline task.

1 Introduction

Existing distributed learning algorithms fall into one of two categories:

Interactive algorithms require many rounds of communication between machines. Representative examples include [4,7,11,13,18,22]. The appeal of interactive algorithms is that they enjoy the same statistical performance as standard sequential algorithms. But, interactive algorithms have three main disadvantages. First, these algorithms are slow when communication latency is the bottleneck. An extreme example occurs in the *federated learning* environment proposed by [16], which uses cell phones as the computational nodes. Recent work in this setting has studied how to only communicate between nodes when doing so would proveably decrease loss [7]. Second, these algorithms require special implementations. They are not easy for non-experts to implement or use, and in particular they do not work with off-the-shelf statistics libraries provided by (for example) Python, R, and Matlab. Third, because of the many rounds of communication, any sensitive information in the data is likely to leak between machines.

Non-interactive algorithms require only a single round of communication. Each machine independently solves the learning problem on a small subset of data, then a master machine merges the solutions together. These algorithms solve all the problems of interactive ones: they are fast when communication

P. Cellier and K. Driessens (Eds.): ECML PKDD 2019 Workshops, CCIS 1167, pp. 293–300, 2020.
https://doi.org/10.1007/978-3-030-43823-4_25

is the main bottleneck; they are easy to implement with off-the-shelf statistics packages; and they are robust to privacy considerations. The downside is worse statistical performance. A growing body of work analyzes the popular naive averaging merging procedure under special conditions [14,17,19–21], and develops more robust merging procedures [1,5,6,10,12,23]. All of these estimators are either statistically sub-optimal or have computationally intractable merge procedures.

The *optimal weighted average* (OWA) [2,3] is a recently proposed non-interactive estimator with statistically optimal guarantees. OWA's merge procedure uses a second round of optimization over a tiny fraction of the data. Because the fraction of data is small, it presents negligible computational burden, but OWA is still able to achieve the optimal sequential statistical error rates in the non-interactive setting. The downside of OWA is that it only works for linear models. In this paper, we develop an algorithm called NOWA that extends OWA into the nonlinear setting. The next section introduces OWA in the original linear setting, and then Sect. 3 describes the NOWA extension. Section 4 shows preliminary experiments with NOWA on the MNIST dataset. We see that the standard naive averaging algorithm commonly used in federated learning performs significantly worse in this simple task than NOWA.

2 Warmup: The Linear OWA

2.1 Problem Statement

Let $\mathcal{Y} \subseteq \mathbb{R}$ be the space of response variables, $\mathcal{X} \subseteq \mathbb{R}^d$ be the space of covariates, and $\mathcal{W} \subseteq \mathbb{R}^d$ be the parameter space. We assume a linear model where the loss of data point $(\mathbf{x}, y) \in \mathcal{X} \times \mathcal{Y}$ given the parameter $W \in \mathcal{W}$ is denoted by $\ell(y, \mathbf{x}^\top W)$. We define the true loss of parameter vector W to be $\mathcal{L}^*(W) = \mathbb{E}\ell(y; \mathbf{x}^\top W)$, and the optimal parameter vector $W^* = \arg\min_{W \in \mathcal{W}} \mathcal{L}^*(W)$. We do not require that the model be correctly specified, nor do we require that ℓ be convex with respect to W. Let $Z \subset \mathcal{X} \times \mathcal{Y}$ be a dataset of mn i.i.d. observations. Finally, let $r : \mathcal{W} \to \mathbb{R}$ be a regularization function (typically the L1 or L2 norm) and $\lambda \in \mathbb{R}$ be the regularization strength. Then the regularized empirical risk minimizer (ERM) is

$$\hat{W}^{erm} = \arg\min_{W \in \mathcal{W}} \sum_{(\mathbf{x},y) \in Z} \ell(y, \mathbf{x}^\top W) + \lambda r(W). \tag{1}$$

Assume that the dataset Z has been partitioned onto m machines so that each machine i has dataset Z_i of size n, and all the Z_i are disjoint. Then each machine calculates the local ERM

$$\hat{W}_i^{erm} = \arg\min_{W \in \mathcal{W}} \sum_{(\mathbf{x},y) \in Z_i} \ell(y, \mathbf{x}^\top W) + \lambda r(W). \tag{2}$$

Notice that computing $\hat{W}_i^{erm}$ requires no communication with other machines. Our goal is to merge the $\hat{W}_i^{erm}$s into a single improved estimate.

To motivate our OWA merge procedure, we briefly describe a baseline procedure called *naive averaging*:

$$W^{ave} = \frac{1}{m}\sum_{i=1}^{m} \hat{W}_i^{erm}. \tag{3}$$

Naive averaging is simple to compute but has only limited theoretical guarantees. Recall that the quality of an estimator $\hat{W}$ can be measured by the estimation error $\|\hat{W} - W^*\|_2$, and we can use the triangle inequality to decompose this error as

$$\|\hat{W} - W^*\|_2 \le \|\hat{W} - \mathbb{E}\hat{W}\|_2 + \|\mathbb{E}\hat{W} - W^*\|_2. \tag{4}$$

We refer to $\|\hat{W} - \mathbb{E}\hat{W}\|_2$ as the variance of the estimator and $\|\mathbb{E}\hat{W} - W^*\|_2$ as the bias. McDonald et al. [14] show that the W^{ave} estimator has lower variance than the estimator $\hat{W}_i^{erm}$ trained on a single machine, but the same bias. Zhang et al. [20] extend this analysis to show that if $\hat{W}_i^{erm}$ is a "nearly unbiased estimator," then naive averaging is optimal. But Rosenblatt and Nadler [17] show that in high dimensional regimes, all models are heavily biased, and so naive averaging is suboptimal. All three results require ℓ to be convex in addition to other technical assumptions. The OWA estimator relaxes these assumptions and achieves better error bounds.

2.2 The Full OWA

To motivate the OWA estimator, we first present a less efficient estimator that uses the full dataset for the second round of optimization. Define the matrix $\hat{W} : \mathbb{R}^{d\times m}$ to have its ith column equal to $\hat{W}_i^{erm}$. Now consider the estimator

$$\hat{W}^{owa,full} = \hat{W}\hat{V}^{owa,full}, \tag{5}$$

where

$$\hat{V}^{owa,full} = \operatorname*{arg\,min}_{V\in\mathbb{R}^m} \sum_{(\mathbf{x},y)\in Z} \ell\left(y, \mathbf{x}^\top \hat{W}V\right) + \lambda r(\hat{W}V). \tag{6}$$

Notice that $\hat{W}^{owa,full}$ is just the empirical risk minimizer when the parameter space $\mathcal{W}$ is restricted to the subspace $\hat{\mathcal{W}}^{owa} = \text{span}\{\hat{W}_i^{erm}\}_{i=1}^m$. In other words, the $\hat{V}^{owa,full}$ vector contains the optimal weights to apply to each $\hat{W}_i^{erm}$ when averaging. Figure 1 shows graphically that no other estimator in $\hat{\mathcal{W}}^{owa}$ can have lower regularized empirical loss than $\hat{W}^{owa,full}$.

2.3 The OWA Estimator

The OWA estimator uses fewer data points in the second round of optimization. Recall that in a linear model, the amount of data needed is proportional to the problem's dimension. Since the dimension of the second round is a fraction m/d smaller than the first round, only an m/d fraction of data is needed for the same accuracy.

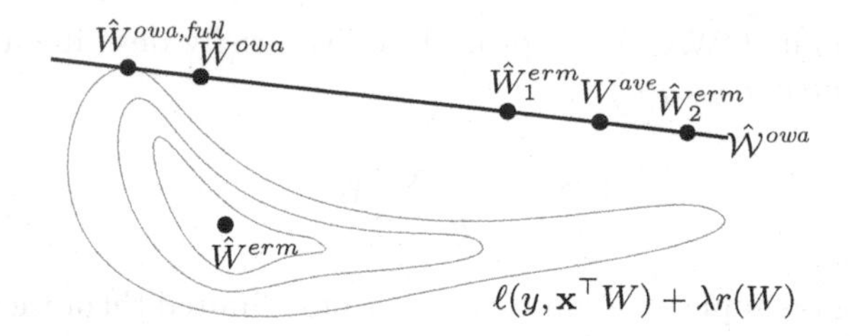

Fig. 1. $\hat{W}^{owa,full}$ is the estimator with best loss in $\hat{\mathcal{W}}^{owa}$, and $\hat{W}^{owa}$ is close with high probability.

Formally, let Z^{owa} be a set of m^2n/d additional data points sampled i.i.d. from the original data distribution. Thus the total amount of data the OWA estimator requires is $mn + m^2n/d$. Whenever $m/d \leq 1$, this expression simplifies to $O(mn)$, which is the same order of magnitude of data in the original problem. The OWA estimator is then defined as

$$\hat{W}^{owa} = \hat{W}\hat{V}^{owa}, \tag{7}$$

where

$$\hat{V}^{owa} = \underset{V \in \mathbb{R}^m}{\arg\min} \sum_{(\mathbf{x},y) \in Z^{owa}} \ell\left(y, \mathbf{x}^\top \hat{W} V\right) + \lambda r(\hat{W} V). \tag{8}$$

OWA's merge procedure is more complicated than the naive averaging merge procedure, but still very fast. Notice that the projected data points $\mathbf{x}^\top \hat{W}$ have dimensionality $m \ll d$, and there are only m^2n/d of them. Because the optimization uses a smaller dimension and fewer data points, it takes a negligible amount of time. Izbicki and Shelton [3] show an experiment where the first round of optimizations takes about a day, and the second optimization takes about a minute.

3 The Non-linear OWA (NOWA)

The intuition of the NOWA algorithm is that we apply the OWA algorithm to each layer of a neural network independently. Unfortunately, the notation is much messier in this scenario due to the need to keep track of many indices.

3.1 Problem Setting

We now extend our notation to include neural networks with multiple hidden layers. In particular, we continue to use subscripts to denote different machines (and let i range over the machines), but we also introduce superscripts to denote different network layers (and let j range over the layers).

Formally, assume our network architecture has p layers. For each layer $j \in \{1, ..., p\}$, there is an associated dimension $d^{(j)} \in \mathbb{N}$, activation function $\sigma^{(j)}$:

$\mathbb{R}^{d^{(j)}} \to \mathbb{R}^{d^{(j)}}$, and weight matrix $W^{(j)} : \mathbb{R}^{d^{(j)} \times d^{(j-1)}}$. The input to the network is a vector $\mathbf{x} \in \mathbb{R}^{d^{(0)}}$. The output of layer j is then recursively given by

$$f^{(j)}(\mathbf{x}) : \mathbb{R}^{d^{(j)}} = \begin{cases} \mathbf{x} & j = 0 \\ \sigma^{(j)}(W^{(j)} f^{(j-1)}(\mathbf{x})) & j > 0 \end{cases} \tag{9}$$

and $f^{(p)}(\mathbf{x})$ is the final output of the network. In supervised learning problems, we are given a dataset $Z \subset \mathbb{R}^{d^{(0)}} \times \mathbb{R}^{d^{(p)}}$ with mn data points, and our goal is to solve

$$\hat{W}^{erm} = \arg\min_{W} \sum_{(\mathbf{x},y) \in Z} \ell(y, f^{(p)}(\mathbf{x})) + \lambda r(W), \tag{10}$$

where ℓ is the loss function and r is the regularization function. We divide Z into m disjoint smaller datasets $\{Z_1, ..., Z_m\}$ each with n points. Each dataset Z_i is transfered to processor i, which solves the local learning problem

$$\hat{W}_i^{erm} = \arg\min_{W} \sum_{(\mathbf{x},y) \in Z_i} \ell(y, f^{(p)}(\mathbf{x})) + \lambda r(W). \tag{11}$$

Each machine solves (11) without communicating with other machines using any optimizer appropriate for the network architecture and data. Our goal is to develop a merge procedure that combines the W_a local parameter estimates into a single global parameter estimate with small loss.

3.2 The Merge Procedures

In this non-linear setting, the naive averaging merge procedure for the jth layer is given by

$$W^{ave,(j)} = \frac{1}{m} \sum_{i=1}^{m} \hat{W}^{erm,(j)}{}_i. \tag{12}$$

Google's recent federated learning architecture uses naive averaging to merge models together that have been independently trained on users' cellphones [16].

We will define an improved merge procedure based on a weighted average of the local parameter estimates. This requires some tensor notation for each layer j in the network, we define the 3rd-order tensor $W^{stacked^{(j)}} : \mathbb{R}^m \times \mathbb{R}^{d^{(j)}} \times \mathbb{R}^{d^{(j-1)}}$, where the (a, b, c)th component of $W^{stacked^{(j)}}$ is defined to be the (b, c)th component of $\hat{W}^{erm,(j)}{}_i$. In words, $W^{stacked^{(j)}}$ is the 3rd-order tensor constructed by stacking the local parameter estimates $\hat{W}^{erm,(j)}{}_a$ along a new axis. We also define the function $\texttt{contract} : (\mathbb{R}^m, \mathbb{R}^m \times \mathbb{R}^{d^{(j)}} \times \mathbb{R}^{d^{(j-1)}}) \to \mathbb{R}^{d^{(i)}} \times \mathbb{R}^{d^{(j-1)}}$ to be the tensor contraction along the first dimension. That is, if $V : \mathbb{R}^m$, then the (b, c)th component of $\texttt{contract}(V, W^{stacked^{(j)}})$ is equal to $\sum_{a=1}^{m} V(a) \hat{W}^{erm,(j)}{}_a(b, c)$. In particular, if each component of V equals $1/m$, then $\texttt{contract}(V, W^{stacked^{(j)}}) = \frac{1}{m} \sum_{a=1}^{m} \hat{W}^{erm,(j)}{}_a = W^{ave,(j)}$.

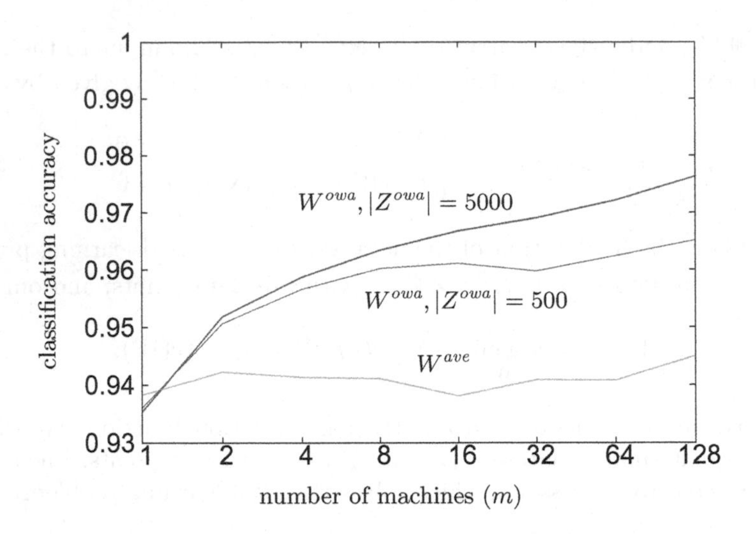

Fig. 2. The performance of the naive averaging estimator used in McMahan et al. [16] is constant as we add more machines, but the performance of the NOWA estimator increases.

In our *non-linear optimal weighted average* (NOWA) merge procedure, we first construct the modified neural network

$$f^{mod,(j)}(\mathbf{x}) : \mathbb{R}^{d^{(j)}} = \begin{cases} \mathbf{x} & j = 0 \\ \sigma^{(j)}(W^{mod,(j)} f^{mod,(j-1)}(\mathbf{x})) & j > 0 \end{cases} \tag{13}$$

where

$$W^{mod,(j)} = \texttt{contract}(V^{(j)}, W^{stacked^{(j)}}). \tag{14}$$

We then select a small subset of the data Z^{owa} (i.e. $|Z^{owa}| \ll |Z|$) and train the network f^{mod} over only the parameters $V^{(j)}$. That is, we solve the optimization problem

$$V^{owa} = \arg\min_{V} \sum_{(\mathbf{x},y)\in Z^{owa}} \ell(y, f^{mod,(p)}(\mathbf{x})) + \lambda r(V). \tag{15}$$

The parameter matrices $W_i^{owa} = \texttt{contract}(V^{owa,(j)}, W^{stacked^{(j)}})$ can then be used in the original neural network. Intuitively, we need only a small number of data points in the optimization of (15) because the number of parameters is significantly smaller than in the original optimization (10). That is, the dimension of V^{owa} is much less than the dimension of $\hat{W}^{erm}$. When the network contains no hidden layers, then the NOWA procedure reduces to the OWA procedure described above.

4 Experiments

McMahan et al. [16] evaluated the naive averaging merge procedure on the MNIST dataset, and we perform a similar experiment here. We train the LeNet neural network [9] provided by TensorFlow's standard tutorial using the Adam optimizer and dropout. We performed no hyperparameter tuning and simply used the default hyperparameters provided by TensorFlow.

We perform our experiment using a cluster of 128 machines. MNIST contains a training set 55,000 data points, and each machine receives a subset of the data containing either 429 or 430 data points. The 10 class labels are evenly distributed throughout the original training set, but we made no effort to ensure they were evenly distributed throughout the subsets. That means on average, each machine has access to only 43 examples from each class, but most machines will have significantly fewer examples for some classes. Under such an extreme paucity of data, it is unlikely for a single machine to be achieve high classification accuracy.

Figure 2 shows the classification accuracy as the number of machines used varies from 2 to 128. (Each experiment is repeated 5 times, and the average is shown.) Since the number of data points per machine is fixed, adding more machines adds more data, so we should expect the classification accuracy to increase for a good merge procedure. We see that the NOWA algorithm significantly outperforms naive averaging. The NOWA algorithm does not perform as well as the oracle network trained on all the data (which has > 0.99 accuracy). This is because of the difficulty of the local learning problems, which average only 42 instances of each class.

5 Discussion

The original papers on federated learning [8,15,16] perform several rounds of naive averaging to improve performance. In each round, the average from the previous round is used to initialize the optimization of each worker node. This procedure can easily be extended to use the NOWA merge procedure instead of naive averaging. Since NOWA's weighted averaging procedure performs better than naive averaging in a single round, a multi-round version of NOWA will likely perform better than a multi-round version of naive averaging. The second round of optimization used in NOWA is particularly negligible in the federated setting because this optimization can be performed in the data center on dedicated machines. Therefore, using NOWA in a federated setup would provide no additional burden to the node machines, which are typically severely computationally limited devices like cell phones.

References

1. Han, J., Liu, Q.: Bootstrap model aggregation for distributed statistical learning. In: NeurIPS (2016)
2. Izbicki, M.: Divide and conquer algorithms for faster machine learning. PhD thesis, UC Riverside (2017)
3. Izbicki, M., Shelton, C.R.: Distributed learning of non-convex linear models with one round of communication. In: ECML-PKDD (2019)

4. Jaggi, M., et al.: Communication-efficient distributed dual coordinate ascent. In: NeurIPS (2014)
5. Jordan, M.I., Lee, J.D., Yang, Y.: Communication-efficient distributed statistical inference. arXiv preprint arXiv:1605.07689 (2016)
6. Kamp, M., Boley, M., Missura, O., Gärtner, T.: Effective parallelisation for machine learning. In: NeurIPS (2017)
7. Kamp, M., et al.: Efficient decentralized deep learning by dynamic model averaging. In: Berlingerio, M., Bonchi, F., Gärtner, T., Hurley, N., Ifrim, G. (eds.) ECML PKDD 2018. LNCS (LNAI), vol. 11051, pp. 393–409. Springer, Cham (2019). https://doi.org/10.1007/978-3-030-10925-7_24
8. Konečný, J., McMahan, H.B., Yu, F.X., Richtárik, P., Suresh, A.T., Bacon, D.: Federated learning: strategies for improving communication efficiency. arXiv preprint arXiv:1610.05492 (2016)
9. LeCun, Y., et al.: Lenet-5, convolutional neural networks
10. Lee, J.D., Liu, Q., Sun, Y., Taylor, J.E.: Communication-efficient sparse regression. JMLR **18**(5), 115–144 (2017)
11. Li, M., Andersen, D.G., Park, J.W.: Scaling distributed machine learning with the parameter server. In: OSDI (2014)
12. Liu, Q., Ihler, A.T.: Distributed estimation, information loss and exponential families. In: NeurIPS (2014)
13. Ma, C., Smith, V., Jaggi, M., Jordan, M.I., Richtárik, P., Takáč, M.: Adding vs. averaging in distributed primal-dual optimization. In: ICML (2015)
14. McDonald, R., Mohri, M., Silberman, N., Walker, D., Mann, G.S.: Efficient large-scale distributed training of conditional maximum entropy models. In: NeurIPS (2009)
15. McMahan, H.B., Moore, E., Ramage, D., Arcas, B.A.y.: Federated learning of deep networks using model averaging. CoRR (2016)
16. McMahan, H.B., Moore, E., Ramage, D., Samson, S., Arcas, B.A.y.: Communication-efficient learning of deep networks from decentralized data (2017)
17. Rosenblatt, J.D., Nadler, B.: On the optimality of averaging in distributed statistical learning. Inf. Infer. **5**(4), 379–404 (2016)
18. Smith, V., Forte, S., Ma, C., Takáč, M., Jordan, M.I., Jaggi, M.: Cocoa: a general framework for communication-efficient distributed optimization. JMLR **18**(1), 8590–8638 (2018)
19. Wang, S.: A sharper generalization bound for divide-and-conquer ridge regression. In: AAAI (2019)
20. Zhang, Y., Wainwright, M.J., Duchi, J.C.: Communication-efficient algorithms for statistical optimization. In: NeurIPS (2012)
21. Zhang, Y., Duchi, J.C., Wainwright,. M.J.: Divide and conquer kernel ridge regression. In: COLT (2013)
22. Zhao, S.-Y., Xiang, R., Shi, Y.-H., Gao, P., Li, W.-J.: Scalable composite optimization for learning on spark. In: AAAI, Scope (2017)
23. Zinkevich, M., Weimer, M., Li, L., Smola, A.J.: Parallelized stochastic gradient descent. In: NeurIPS (2010)

Decentralized Learning with Budgeted Network Load Using Gaussian Copulas and Classifier Ensembles

John Klein[1(✉)], Mahmoud Albardan[1], Benjamin Guedj[2,3], and Olivier Colot[1]

[1] Univ. Lille, CNRS, Centrale Lille, UMR 9189 - CRIStAL - Centre de Recherche en Informatique Signal et Automatique de Lille, 59000 Lille, France
{john.klein,mahmoud.albardan,olivier.colot}@univ-lille.fr
[2] Inria Lille - Nord Europe, Lille, France
benjamin.guedj@inria.fr
[3] University College London, London, UK

Abstract. We examine a network of learners which address the same classification task but must learn from different data sets. The learners cannot share data but instead share their models. Models are shared only one time so as to preserve the network load. We introduce DELCO (standing for Decentralized Ensemble Learning with COpulas), a new approach allowing to aggregate the predictions of the classifiers trained by each learner. The proposed method aggregates the base classifiers using a probabilistic model relying on Gaussian copulas. Experiments on logistic regressor ensembles demonstrate competing accuracy and increased robustness in case of dependent classifiers. A companion python implementation can be downloaded at https://github.com/john-klein/DELCO.

Keywords: Decentralized learning · Classifier ensemble · Copulas

1 Introduction

Big data is both a challenge and an opportunity for supervised learning. It is an opportunity in the sense that we can train much more sophisticated models and automatize much more complex tasks. It is a challenge in the sense that conventional learning algorithms do not scale well when either the number of examples, the number of features or the number of class labels is large. On more practical grounds, it becomes also infeasible to train a model using a single machine for both memory and CPU issues.

Decentralized learning is a setting in which a network of interconnected machines are meant to collaborate in order to learn a prediction function. Each node in the network has access to a limited number of training examples. Local training sets may or may not be disjoint and the cost of transferring all data to

P. Cellier and K. Driessens (Eds.): ECML PKDD 2019 Workshops, CCIS 1167, pp. 301–316, 2020.
https://doi.org/10.1007/978-3-030-43823-4_26

a single computation node is prohibitive. The cost of transfer should be understood in a general sense. It can encompass the network traffic load or the risk to violate data privacy terms. Decentralized learning is a framework which is well suited for companies or public institutions that wish to collaborate but do not want to share their data sets (partially of entirely).

There are several subfields in the decentralized learning paradigm that depend on the network topology and the granted data transfer budget. When any pairwise connection is allowed and when the budget is high, some well established algorithms can be adapted with limited effort to the decentralized setting. For instance, in deep neural networks [4], neural units can exchange gradient values to update their parameters as part of the backpropagation algorithm. This implies that some nodes are used just for training some given neural units or layers and do not have local training sets. The nodes that have training data must train the first layer and share their parameters. In the end, the amount of transferred data may in this case be greater than the entire training data transfer to a single node. When each node is meant to train a model from its private data set but nodes can only exchange symmetrically information with their one-hop neighbors in the network, Giannakis et al. [10] explain that the global optimization of the sum of losses over training data can be broken into several local optimization problems on each node. Since many training algorithms rely essentially on such an optimization problem, the method is rather generic. It also has the advantage that no training data has to be shared and that the distributed optimization can converge to the same parameter estimates as the global one. On the downside, the algorithm is iterative and the amount of transferred data cannot be anticipated. A similar decentralized learning problem is addressed in [9] where an approximate Bayesian statistical solution is proposed.

In this article, we place ourselves in a context where the amount of transferred data must be anticipated and no training examples can be shared. We assume a fully connected topology allowing each node to share its trained base classifier with every other node as well as with a central node which will aggregate models. Local training phases do not have to be synchronized. Ensemble methods or multiple classifier systems are good candidates to operate in such a form of decentralized learning. Indeed, many such methods do not require that the base learners, *i.e.* those trained on each local node, have to collaborate at training time.

In the central node, we train a probabilistic model to aggregate the base classifiers. We investigate a model relying on conditional probabilities of classifier outputs given the true class of an input (whose estimation can be decentralized without difficulty). These distributions are used as building blocks to classify unseen examples as those maximizing class probabilities given all classifiers outputs [3,13]. The originality of our approach consists in resorting to copula functions to obtain a relatively simple model of joint conditional distributions of the local base classifier outputs given the true class.

The next section presents the classifier aggregation problem and existing approaches addressing this issue. Section 2 gives an outline of our new ensemble method. We first present this method in a centralized setting for simplicity. Its deployment in a decentralized setting is explained in the final subsection of this very section. Section 3 assesses the performances of this new ensemble method on both synthetic and real challenging data sets as compared to prior arts.

1.1 Combining Classifiers

Let Ω denote a set of ℓ class labels $\Omega = \{c_1, \ldots, c_\ell\}$, where each element c_i represents one label (or class). Let $\mathbf{x}$ denote an input (or example) with d entries. Most of the time, $\mathbf{x}$ is a vector and lives in $\mathbb{R}^d$ but sometimes some of its entries are categorical data and $\mathbf{x}$ lives in an abstract space $\mathbb{X}$ which does not necessarily have a vector space structure. For the sake of simplicity, we suppose in the following of this article that $\mathbf{x}$ is a vector.

A classification task consists in determining a prediction function $\hat{c}$ that maps any input $\mathbf{x}$ with its actual class $y \in \Omega$. This function is obtained from a training set $\mathcal{D}_{\text{train}}$ which contains pairs $\left(\mathbf{x}^{(i)}, y^{(i)}\right)$ where $y^{(i)}$ is the class label of example $\mathbf{x}^{(i)}$. The cardinality of the training set is denoted by n_{train}. We usually also have a test set $\mathcal{D}_{\text{test}}$ which is disjoint from $\mathcal{D}_{\text{train}}$ to compute unbiased estimates of the prediction performance of function $\hat{c}$. The size of $\mathcal{D}_{\text{train}} \cup \mathcal{D}_{\text{test}}$ is denoted by n.

Given m classifiers, the label y assigned by the kth classifier to the input $\mathbf{x}$ is denoted by $\hat{c}_k(\mathbf{x})$. In the usual supervised learning paradigm, each $\hat{c}_k$ is typically obtained by minimizing a weighted sum of losses incurred by deciding $\hat{c}_k\left(\mathbf{x}^{(i)}\right)$ as compared to $y^{(i)}$ for each data point in the training set or by building a function that predicts $y^{(i)}$ in the vicinity of $\mathbf{x}^{(i)}$ up to some regularity conditions. Once we have trained multiple classifiers, a second algorithmic stage is necessary to derive an ensemble prediction function $\hat{c}_{\text{ens}}$ from the set of classifiers $\{\hat{c}_1, \ldots, \hat{c}_m\}$.

Early attempts to combine classifiers focused on deterministic methods relying on voting systems [27] and Borda counts [12]. In later approaches [14, 15], some authors started to formalize the classifier aggregation problem in probabilistic terms when base classifier outputs are estimates of probabilities $p(y|\mathbf{x})$. It is also possible to probabilistically combine classifiers without assuming that base classifiers rely themselves on probabilistic models. Indeed, we can picture the set of classifier predictions as entries of some vector $\mathbf{z}(\mathbf{x}) = \left[\hat{c}_1(\mathbf{x}), \ldots, \hat{c}_m(\mathbf{x})\right]^T$. Regarding these vectors as new inputs, we resort to a decision-theoretic framework. Under 0–1 loss, the optimal decision rule (in terms of expected loss) is

$$\hat{c}_{\text{ens}}(\mathbf{x}) = \underset{y \in \Omega}{\arg\max}\, p(y|\mathbf{z}(\mathbf{x})). \tag{1}$$

Suppose we select n_{val} training examples from $\mathcal{D}_{\text{train}}$ to build a validation set $\mathcal{D}_{\text{val}}$ and let $\mathcal{D}'_{\text{train}} = \mathcal{D}_{\text{train}} \setminus \mathcal{D}_{\text{val}}$. We can train functions $\hat{c}_1$ to $\hat{c}_m$ using $\mathcal{D}'_{\text{train}}$ and compute predictions for each member of the validation set. So we can build n_{val} vectors $\mathbf{z}^{(i)}$ and use their labels $y^{(i)}$ to infer the parameters of the conditional distributions $p(y|\mathbf{z})$. In the next subsection, we detail such inference methods.

Let alone probabilistic approaches, another possibility is to use the set of pairs $\left(\mathbf{z}^{(i)}, y^{(i)}\right)$ to train a second stage classifier. This approach is known as stacking [25] and has gained in popularity in the past decade as several machine learning competitions were won by stacked classifiers [16]. There are many other multiple classifier systems or ensemble methods in the literature but few of them are applicable in a decentralized setting. In particular, boosting [7] requires each ensemble component to see all data and bagging [2] consists in drawing bootstrap samples of training data so they would both require greater amounts of data transfer than simply sending all data to a single machine. To get a broader picture of the landscape of classifier combination and ensemble methods, we refer the reader to [26].

Stacking is also used in [20] along with correlation analysis in order to account for correlation in classifier predictions. Taking into account these correlations is the most important added value of the copula based probabilistic model that we introduce in Sect. 2. The approach in [20] corresponds to a discriminative model while ours is a generative model of aggregation. It is not adapted to the decentralized setting as it involves a singular value decomposition of a matrix with $n \times m \times \ell$ entries which is prohibitive and propagates big data bottlenecks on the aggregation side.

1.2 A Probabilistic Model of Aggregation

In this subsection, we present several approaches for inferring the parameters of the multinomial conditional distributions $p\left(y|\hat{c}_1\left(\mathbf{x}\right)\right), \ldots, \hat{c}_m\left(\mathbf{x}\right))$. These approaches are essentially due to Dawid and Skene [3] and were promoted and further developed by Kim and Ghahramani [13] in the context of classifier combination; see also [24] for a Bayesian committee algorithm tailored for Gaussian processes. Inferring parameters of multinomial distributions may not seem challenging at first sight. The problem is that, we need to solve ℓ^m such inference problems so the complexity of the problem does not scale well w.r.t. both ℓ and m. Applying Bayes formula, we have

$$p\left(y|\hat{c}_1(\mathbf{x}), \ldots, \hat{c}_m(\mathbf{x})\right) \propto p\left(\hat{c}_1(\mathbf{x}), \ldots, \hat{c}_m(\mathbf{x})|y\right) \times p\left(y\right). \tag{2}$$

The estimation of class probabilities is easy but again, the estimation of conditional joint distributions $p\left(\hat{c}_1(\mathbf{x}), \ldots, \hat{c}_m(\mathbf{x})|y\right)$ has the same complexity as the estimation of the posterior.

Linear complexity can be achieved by making conditional independence assumptions that allow each conditional joint distribution to factorize as the product of its marginals, that is

$$p\left(y|\hat{c}_1(\mathbf{x}), \ldots, \hat{c}_m(\mathbf{x})\right) \propto p\left(y\right) \times \prod_{i=1}^{m} p\left(\hat{c}_i(\mathbf{x})|y\right). \tag{3}$$

In this approach, the parameters of $m+1$ multinomial distributions need to be estimated which does not raise any particular difficulty. Unfortunately, the independence assumption is obviously unrealistic: the classifier outputs are likely to be highly correlated. Indeed, examples that are difficult to classify correctly for classifier $\hat{c}_i$ are usually also difficult to classify correctly for any other classifier $\hat{c}_j$, $j \neq i$. The dependence between classifiers has its roots in several causes, such as learning on shared examples, use of classifiers of the same type, correlation between training examples. This accounts for the fact that misclassifications for each $\hat{c}_k$ occur most of the time with the same inputs. In spite of this, we will see that this approach achieves nice classification accuracy on several occasions. We believe this is explained by the same reason as the one behind naive Bayes classifier[1] efficiency. This model is an efficient technique although it also relies on unrealistic independence assumptions. Indeed, the inadequacy of these assumptions is compensated by a dramatic reduction of the number of parameters to learn making the technique less prone to overfitting.

Let us formalize the inference problem in a more statistical language to present further developments allowing to infer parameters in (3). The classification output $\hat{c}_k$ of the kth classifier is a random variable and the conditional distribution of $\hat{c}_k$ given $Y = y$ is multinomial: $\hat{c}_k|y \sim \text{Mult}\left(\boldsymbol{\theta}_y^{(k)}\right)$ with $\boldsymbol{\theta}_y^{(k)}$ a parameter vector of size ℓ: $\boldsymbol{\theta}_y^{(k)} = \left[\theta_{y,1}^{(k)} \dots \theta_{y,\ell}^{(k)}\right]^T$. In other words, the success/failure probabilities of the kth classifier are the parameters $\theta_{y,i}^{(k)} = p\left(\hat{c}_k = i|y\right)$. The random variable Y representing class labels has a multinomial distribution as well: $Y \sim \text{Mult}\left(\boldsymbol{\gamma}\right)$ and $\boldsymbol{\gamma}$ is another vector of parameters of size ℓ. Let $\mathcal{D}_{\text{agg}}$ denote the data set whose elements are tuples $\left(\hat{c}_1\left(\mathbf{x}^{(i)}\right), \dots, \hat{c}_m\left(\mathbf{x}^{(i)}\right), y^{(i)}\right)$ for $\left(\mathbf{x}^{(i)}, y^{(i)}\right) \in \mathcal{D}_{\text{val}}$. Under classifier independence assumptions, the likelihood writes

$$p\left(\mathcal{D}_{\text{agg}}|\boldsymbol{\theta}_1^{(1)}, \dots, \boldsymbol{\theta}_\ell^{(m)}, \boldsymbol{\pi}\right) = \prod_{i=1}^{n_{\text{val}}} \gamma_{y^{(i)}} \prod_{k=1}^{m} \theta_{y^{(i)}, i_k}^{(k)}, \tag{4}$$

where $i_k = \hat{c}_k\left(\mathbf{x}^{(i)}\right)$. Maximum likelihood estimates of $\boldsymbol{\gamma}$ and each $\boldsymbol{\theta}_y^{(k)}$ are known in closed form and can be easily computed. Kim and Ghahramani [13] propose a Bayesian treatment consisting of using hierarchical conjugate priors on the parameters of all conditional distributions $p\left(c_k|y\right)$ as well as on the class distribution $p\left(y\right)$. The conjugate priors for $\boldsymbol{\theta}_y^{(k)}$ and $\boldsymbol{\gamma}$ are Dirichlet: $\boldsymbol{\theta}_y^{(k)} \sim \text{Dir}\left(\boldsymbol{\alpha}_y^{(k)}\right)$ and $\boldsymbol{\gamma} \sim \text{Dir}\left(\boldsymbol{\beta}\right)$. A second level of priors is proposed for the parameters $\boldsymbol{\alpha}_y^{(k)}$. The conjugate prior distribution of each $\boldsymbol{\alpha}_y^{(k)}$ is exponential. Gibbs and rejection sampling are then used to infer these parameters.

Finally, Kim and Ghahramani [13] also extend this model in order to take into account dependencies between classifiers. They propose to use a Markov random field as a model of classifier output interactions. The main limitation of this method is the high computational cost induced by MCMC and rejection sampling. In the next section, we introduce a copula-based model that allows to grasp classifier dependency without resorting to an MCMC step.

[1] This probabilistic approach can actually be regarded as a form of stacking in which the second stage classifier is a naive Bayes classifier.

2 Method Outline

In this section, we present a new ensemble method allowing to build the decision function $\hat{c}_{\text{ens}}$ from (2) without resorting to some conditional independence assumption. We propose a Gaussian copula model for the conditional joint distributions $p(\hat{c}_1(\mathbf{x}), \ldots, \hat{c}_m(\mathbf{x})|y)$. We start by giving elementary background on copulas and later explain how they can be efficiently implemented in a decentralized learning setting.

2.1 Copulas

An m-dimensional copula function Cop : $[0;1]^m \to [0;1]$ is a cumulative distribution with uniform marginals. The growing popularity of these functions stems from Sklar's theorem which asserts that, for every random vector $\mathbf{L} \sim f$, there exist a copula Cop such that $F = \text{Cop} \circ \mathbf{G}$ where F is the cumulative version of distribution f and $\mathbf{G}$ is a vector whose entries are the cumulative marginals $G_k(a) = F(\infty, \ldots, \infty, a, \infty, \ldots, \infty)$ for any a in the k-dimensional domain of f.

When F is continuous, the copula is unique. When we deal with discrete random variables as in our classification problem, the non-uniqueness of the copula raises some identifiability issues [6,8]. Without denying the importance of these issues, we argue that, from a pattern recognition standpoint, what essentially matters is to learn a model that generalizes well. For instance, there are also identifiability issues for neural networks [23] which do not prevent deep nets to achieve state-of-the-art performance in many applications.

In this article, we investigate parametric copula families to derive a model for the conditional joint distributions $p(\hat{c}_1(\mathbf{X}), \ldots, \hat{c}_m(\mathbf{X})|y)$ where $\mathbf{X}$ is the random vector capturing input uncertainty. Parametric copulas with parameters vector λ are denoted by Cop_λ. A difficulty in the quest for an efficient ensemble method is that we must avoid working with cumulative distributions because the computational cost to navigate from cumulative to non-cumulative distributions is prohibitive. We can compute Radon-Nikodym derivatives of $\text{Cop}_\lambda \circ \mathbf{G}$ w.r.t. a reference measure but again since we work in a discrete setting we will not retrieve closed form expression for f for an arbitrary large number of classifiers. As a workaround, we propose to embed each discrete variable $\hat{c}_k(\mathbf{X})|y$ in the real interval $[0;\ell[$. Let $f_y : \mathbb{R}^m \to \mathbb{R}^+$ be a probability density (w.r.t. Lebesgue) whose support is $[0;\ell[^m$ and such that for any $\mathbf{z} \in \Omega^m$, we have $f_y(\mathbf{a}) = p(\hat{c}_1(\mathbf{X}) = z_1, \ldots, \hat{c}_m(\mathbf{X}) = z_m|y)$ for any vector $\mathbf{a}$ in the unit volume $\mathcal{V}_\mathbf{z} = [z_1 - 1; z_1[\times \ldots \times [z_m - 1; z_m[$. This means that f_y is piecewise constant and it can be understood as the density of some continuous random vector whose quantized version is equal in distribution to the tuple $(\hat{c}_1(\mathbf{X})|y, \ldots, \hat{c}_m(\mathbf{X})|y)$. Moreover, if $f_y^{(i)}$ is the ith marginal density of f_y, we also have $f_y^{(i)}(a) = p(\hat{c}_1(\mathbf{X}) = z|y)$ for any $a \in [z-1; z[$ and any $z \in \{1; \ldots; \ell\}$.

For any $\mathbf{z} \in \Omega^m$, according to this continuous random vector vision of the problem, we can now thus write

$$p\left(\hat{c}_1 = z_1, \ldots, \hat{c}_m = z_m | y\right) = \mathrm{cop}_\lambda\left(\mathbf{u}\right) \times \prod_{i=1}^{m} p\left(\hat{c}_i = z_i | y\right), \tag{5}$$

$$\mathbf{u} = \left[F_{1,y}\left(z_1\right), \ldots, F_{m,y}\left(z_m\right)\right] \tag{6}$$

where cop_λ is the density of Cop_λ and $F_{i,y}$ is the cumulative distribution of variable $\hat{c}_i\left(\mathbf{X}\right)|y$. This construction is not dependent in the (arbitrary) way in which the elements of Ω are indexed.

Among parametric copula families, the only one with a closed form density for arbitrary large m is the Gaussian copula. The density of a Gaussian copula [28] is given by

$$\mathrm{cop}_\lambda\left(\mathbf{u}\right) = \frac{1}{|\mathbf{R}|^{1/2}} \exp\left(-\frac{1}{2}\mathbf{v}^T \cdot \left(\mathbf{R}^{-1} - \mathbf{I}\right) \cdot \mathbf{v}\right), \tag{7}$$

where $\mathbf{R}$ is a correlation matrix, $\mathbf{I}$ is the identity matrix and $\mathbf{v}$ is a vector with m entries such that $v_k = Q\left(u_k\right)$ where Q is the quantile function of a standard normal distribution. The copula parameter in this case is the correlation matrix. Estimating the entries of this matrix is not trivial. We will therefore choose a simplified model and take $\mathbf{R} = \lambda\mathbf{1} + (1-\lambda)\mathbf{I}$ where $\mathbf{1}$ is the all-one matrix. In this model, each diagonal entry of $\mathbf{R}$ is 1 and each non-diagonal entry is λ. The dependency between classifier outputs is regulated by λ which is a scalar living in $\left(\frac{-1}{m-1}; 1\right)$. We also make the assumption that correlation matrices are tied across conditionings on $Y = y$. The $m \times \ell$ cumulative distributions $F_{i,y}$ are evaluated using estimates of the vectors $\boldsymbol{\theta}_y^{(i)} = \left[p\left(\hat{c}_i = c_1|y\right) \ldots p\left(\hat{c}_i = c_\ell|y\right)\right]^T$.

Observe that when $\lambda = 0$, the copula density is constant one and the proposed model boils down to the independent case (3). Since our model is a generalization of (3), this latter is referred to as the independent copula-based ensemble in the remainder of this article but it should be kept in mind that it is a prior art.

2.2 New Ensemble Method

Now that we have introduced all the ingredients to build our new ensemble method, let us explain how it can be implemented efficiently in practice. The only crucial remaining problem is to tune the parameter λ of the parametric copula. This parameter summarizes the dependency information between each pair of random variables $\left(\hat{c}_k\left(\mathbf{X}\right)|y\,;\,\hat{c}_{k'}\left(\mathbf{X}\right)|y\right)$.

Since we have only one parameter to set, we can use a grid search on the interval $\left(\frac{-1}{m-1}; 1\right)$ using the validation set and select $\hat{\lambda}$ as the value achieving maximal accuracy on this validation set. In the experiments, we use an evenly spaced grid (denoted grid_λ) containing 101 values. In the sequel, our approach will be referred to as Decentralized Ensemble Learning with COpula (DELCO). The pseudo-code for DELCO is given in Algorithm 1.

Algorithm 1. DELCO (training)

Data: $\mathcal{D}_{\text{train}}$, n_{val}, grid$_\lambda$ and $\{\text{train-alg}_k\}_{k=1}^m$
Select n_{val} data points from $\mathcal{D}_{\text{train}}$ to build $\mathcal{D}_{\text{val}}$
$\mathcal{D}'_{\text{train}} \leftarrow \mathcal{D}_{\text{train}} \setminus \mathcal{D}_{\text{val}}$
for $k \in \{1, \dots, m\}$ **do**
  Run train-alg$_k$ on $\mathcal{D}'_{\text{train}}$ to learn $\hat{c}_k$
for $y \in \{1, \dots, \ell\}$ **do**
  $\gamma_y \leftarrow \frac{1+\sum_{i=1}^{n_{\text{val}}} \mathbb{I}_y(y^{(i)})}{\ell + n_{\text{val}}}$
  for $k \in \{1, \dots, m\}$ **do**
    for $j \in \{1, \dots, \ell\}$ **do**
      $\theta_{y,j}^{(k)} \leftarrow \frac{1+\sum_{i=1}^{n_{\text{val}}} \mathbb{I}_y(y^{(i)}) \mathbb{I}_j(\hat{c}_k(\mathbf{x}^{(i)}))}{\ell + \sum_{i=1}^{n_{\text{val}}} \mathbb{I}_y(y^{(i)})}$
      $F_{k,y}(j) \leftarrow [1 - \mathbb{I}_0(j)] \times F_{k,y}(j-1) + \theta_{y,j}^{(k)}$
for $\lambda \in grid_\lambda$ **do**
  Obtain $\hat{c}_{\text{ens}}$ by substituting (5) in (2) and then (2) in (1), and using $\hat{c}_1, \dots, \hat{c}_m, \boldsymbol{\gamma}, \boldsymbol{\theta}_1^{(1)}, \dots, \boldsymbol{\theta}_\ell^{(m)}$ and λ
  $\text{Acc}(\lambda) \leftarrow \frac{\sum_{i=1}^{n_{\text{val}}} \mathbb{I}_{y^{(i)}}(\hat{c}_{\text{ens}}(\mathbf{x}^{(i)}))}{n_{\text{val}}}$
$\hat{\lambda} \leftarrow \arg\max_{\lambda \in \text{grid}_\lambda} \text{Acc}(\lambda)$
Obtain $\hat{c}_{\text{ens}}$ by substituting (5) in (2) and then (2) in (1), and using $\hat{c}_1, \dots, \hat{c}_m, \boldsymbol{\gamma}, \boldsymbol{\theta}_1^{(1)}, \dots, \boldsymbol{\theta}_\ell^{(m)}$ and $\hat{\lambda}$
return $\hat{c}_{ens}$

In Algorithm 1, $\mathbb{I}_x$ denotes the indicator function of the singleton $\{x\}$. The vectors of parameters $\boldsymbol{\gamma}$ and $\left\{\boldsymbol{\theta}_1^{(1)}, \dots, \boldsymbol{\theta}_\ell^{(m)}\right\}$ are estimated using the Laplace add-one smoothing which is the conditional expectation of the parameters given the data in a Dirichlet-multinomial model. As opposed to maximum likelihood estimates, it avoids zero counts which are numerically speaking problematic. It is also recommended to maximize the log-version of (1) which is numerically more stable.

Finally, one can optionally retrain the classifiers on $\mathcal{D}_{\text{train}}$ after $\hat{\lambda}$ is estimated. Since $\mathcal{D}_{\text{train}}$ is larger then $\mathcal{D}'_{\text{train}}$, it allows training algorithms to converge to possibly slightly better decision functions. Training them initially on $\mathcal{D}_{\text{train}}$ is however ill-advised as the parameter estimates would be biased. In the next section, where we present numerical results, we use this optional step.

2.3 Dencentralized DELCO

In the previous paragraphs, we presented our new ensemble method in the centralized setting first for simplicity. It can be adapted to the decentralized setting described in the introduction with little efforts. To achieve decentralized learning with DELCO, each local private data set needs to be separated in a local training set and a local validation set. After all locally trained models are exchanged between all nodes, each node computes the confusion matrix of each base classifier using its local validation set. These matrices are sent to the central node which just needs to average and normalize them to obtain the estimates of vectors $\boldsymbol{\theta}_y^{(i)}$. Similarly, vector $\boldsymbol{\gamma}$ can be estimated by sending to the central node the number of examples belonging to each class. Finally, grid search can also be implemented in the same fashion. The central node can send the global estimates of $\boldsymbol{\theta}_y^{(i)}$ and $\boldsymbol{\gamma}$ to each node. Each node can then perform grid search using its local validation set, compute accuracies and send them back to the central node which will average them. Note that the number and the cost of transfers through the network are known before starting to train.

3 Numerical Experiments

In this section, the performance of DELCO is assessed in terms of classification accuracy and robustness. Situations in which aggregation performance discrepancies are most visible usually occur when there is diversity [11,17] in the trained base prediction functions $\hat{c}_i$. Among other possibilities [1,18,19,21], one way to induce diversity consists in distributing data points across the network of base classifiers in a non-iid way, that is, each base classifiers only sees inputs that belong to a given region of the feature space. This is a realistic situation as the data stored in a network node might be dependent on the geographic location of this node for instance.

Furthermore, we chose to combine base classifiers with limited capacity, *i.e.* *weak* classifiers as in boosting [7], so that the aggregated model has a significantly larger capacity allowing to discover better decision frontiers. We decided to use logistic regression on each local data set as this algorithm yields a linear decision frontier. Also, logistic regression has the advantage to have no hyperparameter to tune making the conclusions from the experiments immune to this issue. This is also the reason why we do not use a regularized version of this algorithm.

In each experiment, 10% of the data are used for validation, i.e. $n_{\text{val}} = \frac{n_{\text{train}}}{10}$. We compare DELCO to the following state-of-the-art or reference methods:

- classifier selection based on accuracies,
- best base classifier,
- weighted vote combination based on accuracies,
- stacking,
- centralized classifier trained on all data,
- the independent copula ensemble (equivalent to (3)).

Each method relying on base classifier accuracies uses estimates obtained from the validation set. The validation set is also used as part of stacking to generate inputs for the second stage training. We also use a logistic regression for this second stage and input entries are predicted classes from each

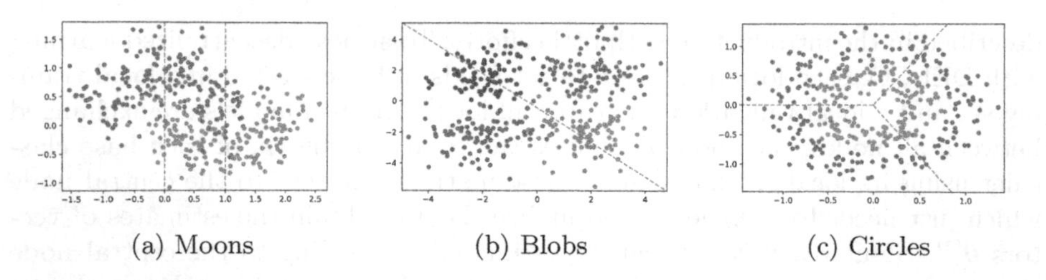

(a) Moons (b) Blobs (c) Circles

Fig. 1. Synthetic data sets and their partitions into feature space regions ($n = 400$).

base classifier. Stacking is applicable if the validation set is shared across learners. The best base classifier and the centralized classifier are relevant references to assess the quality of the aggregation. Concerning DELCO, we examine the simplified Gaussian copula where the copula hyperparameter is estimated by grid search from the validation set. In a reproducible research spirit, we provide a python implementation of DELCO and other benchmarked methods (https://github.com/john-klein/DELCO).

3.1 Synthetic Data

Using synthetic data sets is advantageous in the sense that, in the test phase, we can generate as many data as we want to obtain very reliable estimates of classification accuracies. We examine three different data generation processes from the sklearn library [22]: Moons, Blobs and Circles. Each of these processes yields non-linearly separable data sets as illustrated in Fig. 1.

The Moons and Circles data sets are binary classification problems while Blobs involves three classes. For each problem, the data set is partitioned into disjoint regions of the input space as specified in Fig. 1 and consequently we combine two base classifiers for the Blobs data set and three base classifiers for the others. Also, in each case, input vectors live in $\mathbb{R}^2$.

The Moons data set consists in two half-circles to which a Gaussian noise is added. For each half-circle, one of its extremal point is the center of the other half-circle. The covariance matrix of the noise in our experiment is $0.3\times\mathbf{I}$ where $\mathbf{I}$ is the identity matrix. Before adding this noise, we also randomized the position of sample points on the half circle using a uniform distribution while the baseline sklearn function samples such points with fixed angle step. The Blobs data set is also obtained using a slightly different function than its sklearn version. It generates a data set from four 2D Gaussian distributions centered on each corner of a centered square whose edge length is 4. Each distribution covariance matrix is $\mathbf{I}$. The examples generated by the distributions whose expectations are $(-2;-2)$ and $(2;2)$ are assigned to class c_0. Each remaining Gaussian distribution yields examples for either class c_1 or c_2. Finally, the Circles data set consists in sampling with fixed angle step two series of points from centered circles with radius 0.5 and 1. A Gaussian noise with covariance matrix $0.15 \times \mathbf{I}$ is added to these points. The python code for the synthetic data set generation is also online.

Table 1. Classification accuracies for several synthetic data sets. ($n_{\text{train}} = 200$ in the left table, $n_{\text{train}} = 400$ in the right table)

Method	Moons	Blobs	Circles
Clf. selection	79.25% std. 3.51%	72.34% std. 0.37%	62.38% std. 0.32%
Best clf.	79.25% std. 1.67%	72.34% std. 0.36%	62.38% std. 0.32%
Weighted vote	84.60% std. 2.20%	82.43% std. 11.02%	50.50% std. 0.05%
Stacking	81.07% std. 3.89%	69.87% std. 5.37%	70.20% std. 8.08%
Indep. copula	83.46% std. 2.91%	91.14% std. 7.27%	79.32% std. 6.70%
DELCO Gauss. copula	80.57% std. 4.68%	93.15% std. 4.83%	84.49% std. 4.51%
Centralized clf.	84.99% std. 0.55%	88.49% std. 0.42%	50.02% std. 0.49%
Optimal	91.50% std. 0%	95.50% std. 0%	94.50% std. 0%

Method	Moons	Blobs	Circles
Clf. selection	79.67% std. 2.14%	72.43% std. 0.27%	62.50% std. 0.05%
Best clf.	80.66% std. 1.08%	72.45% std. 0.22%	62.50% std. 0.06%
Weighted vote	87.83% std. 1.19%	78.72% std. 9.96%	50.50% std. 0%
Stacking	85.32% std. 4.08%	71.70% std. 2.61%	78.19% std. 6.95%
Indep. copula	86.43% std. 3.28%	93.78% std. 2.48%	84.54% std. 4.45%
DELCO Gauss. copula	86.75% std. 3.07%	94.39% std. 0.96%	86.39% std. 1.11%
Centralized clf.	85.22% std. 0.45%	88.72% std. 0.42%	50.01% std. 0.50%
Optimal	91.50% std. 0%	95.50% std. 0%	94.50% std. 0%

To evaluate the accuracy of a classifier or classifier ensemble trained on a data set drawn from any of the above mentioned generating processes, we drew test points from the same process until the Clopper-Pearson confidence interval of the accuracy has length below 0.2% with confidence probability 0.95. For each generating process, we repeated this procedure 3000 times to estimate the expected accuracy across data set draws.

The estimated expected accuracies and the estimated accuracy standard deviations are given for each classification method of the benchmark in Table 1 for $n_{\text{train}} = 200$ and $n_{\text{train}} = 400$. In these experiments, one of the copula-based methods is the top 2 method for the Moons data set and is the top 1 for the Blobs and Circles data sets. Most importantly, both copulas based method are obviously more robust since they never perform poorly on any data set. While the weighted vote method is the top 1 for Moons data set, it completely crashed on the Circles data set and converges to a random classifier.

Another result which is surprising at first sight, is that the centralized classifier is sometimes outperformed by some decentralized ensembles. This is actually well explained by the deterministic way in which input spaces are partitioned. Indeed, the partitions are cleverly chosen so that a combination of linear decision frontiers fits intuitively a lot better the data than a single linear separation does. In other words, ensembles have a larger VC dimension and visit a larger hypotheses set. One may wonder to which extent it would be possible to purposely partition data sets in such a relevant way to reproduce such conditions in more general situations. This is however beyond the scope of this article in which we address decentralized learning, a setting where we take distributed data as is and we cannot reorganize them.

There are three situations in which significant performance discrepancies are observed between DELCO and the independent copula. The first one is the

Table 2. Real data set specifications

Name	Size n	Dim. d	Nbr. of classes ℓ	Data type	Source
20newsgroup	18846	100 (after red.)	20	Text	Sklearn
MNIST	70000	784	10	Image	Sklearn
Satellite	6435	36	6	Image features	UCI repo. (Statlog)
Wine	6497	11	2 (binarized)	Chemical features	UCI repo. (Wine Quality)
Spam	4601	57	2	Text	UCI repo. (Spam)
Avila	10430	10	2 (binarized)	Layout features	UCI repo. (Avila)
Drive	58509	48	11	Current statistics	UCI repo. (Sensorless Drive Diagnosis)
Particle	130064	50	2	Signal	UCI repo. (MiniBooNE particle identification)

Moons data set when $n_{\text{train}} = 200$. We argue that DELCO fails to correctly estimate the parameter λ as performance levels are reversed when $n_{\text{train}} = 400$ and the validation set has now 40 elements instead of 20.

The other situations are the Circles data set when either $n_{\text{train}} = 200$ or $n_{\text{train}} = 400$. In this case, we see that the independent copula-based ensemble fails to keep up with DELCO regardless of how many points the validation set contains. In conclusion, DELCO does offer increased robustness as compared to the independent copula model provided that the validation set size allows to tune correctly λ. Remember that when $\lambda = 0$, both models coincide, so if we have enough data and if being independent is really what works best, then there is no reason why we should not obtain $\hat{\lambda} = 0$.

3.2 Real Data

To upraise the ability of the benchmarked methods to be deployed in a decentralized learning setting, we also need to test them on sets of real data. Since decentralized learning is essentially useful in a big data context, we chose eight from moderate to large public data sets. The specifications of these data sets are reported in Table 2.

Example entries from the 20newsgroup data set are word counts obtained using the term frequency - inverse document frequency statistics. We reduced the dimensionality of inputs using a latent semantic analysis [5] which is a standard practice for text data. We kept 100 dimensions. Also, as recommended, we stripped out each text from headers, footers and quotes which lead to overfitting. Besides, for the Wine and Avila datasets, the number of class labels is originally 10 and 12 respectively. We binarized these classification tasks because some classes have very small cardinalities making it impossible for each node to have access to at least one example of this class. Aggregating base classifiers trained w.r.t different subsets of class labels goes behind the scope of this paper and will be touched in future works. In the Wine data set, class labels are wine

Table 3. Classification accuracies (with standard deviations) for several real data sets. ($m = 10$ nodes)

Method	20newsgroup	MNIST	Satellite	Wine	Spam	Avila	Drive	Particle
Clf. selection	37.35%	66.26%	77.83%	63.23%	85.26%	60.76%	58.58%	81.28%
	std. 1.38%	std. 1.57%	std. 2.04%	std. 5.51%	std. 1.31%	std. 3.80%	std. 2.77%	std. 1.07%
Best clf.	38.25%	67.24%	79.10%	64.83%	86.60%	62.79%	58.77%	81.81%
	std. 0.68%	std. 0.76%	std. 1.16%	std. 4.75%	std. 1.32%	std. 2.24%	std. 2.60%	std. 0.32%
Weighted vote	50.17%	82.46%	81.99%	62.89%	89.61%	63.50%	70.42%	81.10%
	std. 0.65%	std. 1.54%	std. 0.80%	std. 4.35%	std. 0.83%	std. 2.51%	std. 2.75%	std. 0.72%
Stacking	14.47%	41.47%	70.16%	66.44%	89.42%	65.06%	46.27%	81.95%
	std. 1.13%	std. 2.90%	std. 3.35%	std. 3.20%	std. 1.16%	std. 4.97%	std. 3.30%	std. 0.52%
Indep. copula	49.19%	85.77%	83.21%	61.38%	89.70%	63.89%	85.45%	81.56%
	std. 0.64%	std. 1.30%	std. 0.68%	std. 5.82%	std. 1.07%	std. 4.83%	std. 1.31%	std. 2.88%
DELCO	49.06%	85.86%	82.99%	65.06%	89.35%	64.26%	85.45%	83.04%
Gauss. copula	std. 0.64%	std. 1.17%	std. 0.83%	std. 3.01%	std. 1.18%	4.25%	std. 1.31%	std. 1.68%
Centralized clf.	58.19%	90.65%	83.16%	73.83%	92.26%	68.23%	74.95%	81.95%
	std. 0.36%	std. 0.33%	std. 0.40%	std. 0.57%	std. 0.52%	std. 0.44%	std. 0.59%	std. 0.52%

quality scores. Two classes are obtained by comparing scores to a threshold of 5. In the avila dataset, class labels are middle age bible copyist identities. The five first copyists are grouped in one class and the remaining ones in the other class.

Unlike synthetic data sets, we need to separate the original data set into a train set and a test set. To avoid a dependency of the reported performances w.r.t train/test splits, we perform 2-fold cross validation (CV). Also, we shuffled at random examples and repeated the training and test phases 100 times.

To comply with the diversity condition, we distributed the training data over network nodes using the following procedure: for each data set, for each class,

1. apply principal component analysis to the corresponding data,
2. project this data on the dimension with highest eigenvalue,
3. sort the projected values and split them into m subsets of cardinality n_i/m where n_i is the proportion of examples belonging to class c_i.

Each such subset is sent to only one node (the node being chosen arbitrarily). We argue that this way of splitting data is somehow adversarial because some nodes may see data that are a lot easier to separate than it should and will consequently not generalize very well. Average accuracies over random shuffles and CV-folds are given in Table 3 for $m = 10$ nodes.

In most experiments, decentralized ensemble methods have difficulties to compete with a centralized classifier. This is presumably because PCA-based data splits do not allow to discover better decision frontiers. However, for the Drive and Particle datasets, it is remarkable that the copula-based approaches achieve higher accuracies than the centralized classifier.

Most importantly, we see that one of the copula-based method is always either the top 1 decentralized method or the top 2 which is in line with the robustness observed in the synthetic data set experiments. When the Gaussian copula is

Table 4. Classification accuracies (with standard deviations) for several real data sets. ($m = 10$ base classifiers. 6 of them are identical ones.)

Method	20newsgroup	MNIST	Satellite	Wine	Spam	Avila	Drive	Particle
Clf. selection	45.90%	73.20%	79.60%	62.37%	86.91%	58.83%	64.18%	81.40%
	std. 0.70%	std. 0.54%	std. 1.03%	std. 4.95%	std. 2.20%	std. 4.88%	std. 2.84%	std. 0.86%
Best clf.	46.11%	73.26%	80.23%	63.30%	87.42%	61.24%	64.31%	81.68%
	std. 0.69%	std. 0.55%	std. 0.75%	std. 4.32%	std. 1.89%	std. 2.98%	std. 2.83%	std. 0.33%
Weighted vote	47.07%	75.14%	79.79%	61.87%	86.94%	58.27%	65.80%	79.87%
	std. 0.66%	std. 0.64%	std. 0.69%	std. 4.62%	std. 2.48%	std. 4.49%	std. 2.63%	std. 1.74%
Stacking	14.25%	36.69%	70.61%	64.91%	89.35%	61.29%	40.17%	80.43%
	std. 1.08%	std. 2.13%	std. 3.05%	std. 2.79%	std. 1.47%	std. 4.89%	std. 4.60%	std. 1.43%
Indep. copula	47.49%	76.37%	81.50%	62.13%	87.20%	58.28%	71.28%	81.56%
	std. 0.67%	std. 0.64%	std. 0.87%	std. 4.90%	std. 2.41%	std. 4.50%	std. 2.52%	std. 0.74%
DELCO	47.04%	77.97%	82.00%	64.65%	89.43%	60.93%	72.10%	83.15%
Gauss. copula	std. 0.89%	std. 0.62%	std. 0.84%	std. 2.70%	std. 1.56%	std. 3.48%	std. 2.26%	std. 1.70%
Centralized clf.	59.41%	90.77%	83.15%	73.83%	92.26%	61.29%	74.94%	88.49%
	std. 0.39%	std. 0.14%	std. 3.05%	std. 0.57%	std. 0.52%	std. 4.88%	std. 0.59%	std. 2.60%

outperformed by the independent copula, the maximal absolute accuracy discrepancy is 0.37%. However, when the independent copula is outperformed by the Gaussian one, the maximal absolute accuracy discrepancy is 3.68%.

To better upraise the added value brought by DELCO, we performed another experiment in which six out of the ten base classifiers are replaced by six copies of a majority vote ensemble relying on those six base classifiers. In this situation, there is clearly a strong dependency among base classifiers. Since copulas are meant to capture dependency information, a better fit should be achieved by the Gaussian copula. This is indeed confirmed by the corresponding average accuracies which are reported in Table 4.

In this second series of results, we see that performance discrepancies between DELCO and the independent copula are much larger. Except for the 20newsgroup data set, the Gaussian copula always achieves higher accuracies than the independent copula. DELCO is the top one decentralized method for 5 datasets and the top 2 for the remaining ones[2]. Classifier selection methods are immune to the artificially added dependency because, by construction, they are idempotent methods. They are nevertheless still outperformed by ensemble methods.

4 Conclusion

In this paper, we introduce a new ensemble method that relies on a probabilistic model. Given a set of trained classifiers, we evaluate the probabilities of each classifier output given the true class on a validation set. We use a Gaussian copula to retrieve the joint conditional distributions of these latter which allow to build an ensemble decision function that consists in maximizing the probability of the true class given all classifier outputs.

[2] We consider that DELCO and weighted vote have equal level of performances for the 20newsgroup data set.

We motivate this new approach by showing that it fits a decentralized learning setting which is a modern concern in a big data context. The approach is validated through numerical experiments on both synthetic and real data sets. We show that a Gaussian copula based ensemble achieves higher robustness than other ensemble techniques and can compete or outperform a centralized learning in some situations.

In future works, we plan to investigate other estimation techniques for the copula parameter than grid search which is suboptimal. In particular, we would like to set up a Bayesian approach to that end. This would also allow us to observe if tying the correlation matrices is too restrictive or not. More complex correlation matrix patterns will also be examined. Also, other copula models will tested and the sensitivity of the method w.r.t the chosen copula family will be studied.

References

1. Ali, K.M., Pazzani, M.J.: On the link between error correlation and error reduction in decision tree ensembles. Citeseer (1995)
2. Breiman, L.: Bagging predictors. Mach. Learn. **24**(2), 123–140 (1996). https://doi.org/10.1007/BF00058655
3. Dawid, A.P., Skene, A.M.: Maximum likelihood estimation of observer error-rates using the EM algorithm. Appl. Stat. **28**, 20–28 (1979)
4. Dean, J., et al.: Large scale distributed deep networks. In: Advances in Neural Information Processing Systems, pp. 1223–1231 (2012)
5. Deerwester, S., Dumais, S.T., Furnas, G.W., Landauer, T.K., Harshman, R.: Indexing by latent semantic analysis. J. Am. Soc. Inf. Sci. **41**(6), 391 (1990)
6. Faugeras, O.P.: Inference for copula modeling of discrete data: a cautionary tale and some facts. Depend. Model. **5**(1), 121–132 (2017)
7. Freund, Y., Schapire, R.E.: A decision-theoretic generalization of on-line learning and an application to boosting. J. Comput. Syst. Sci. **55**(1), 119–139 (1997)
8. Genest, C., Nešlehová, J.: A primer on copulas for count data. ASTIN Bull.: J. Int. Actuar. Assoc. **37**(2), 475–515 (2007)
9. Gholami, B., Yoon, S., Pavlovic, V.: Decentralized approximate Bayesian inference for distributed sensor network. In: Proceedings of the Thirtieth AAAI Conference on Artificial Intelligence, pp. 1582–1588. AAAI Press (2016)
10. Giannakis, G.B., Ling, Q., Mateos, G., Schizas, I.D., Zhu, H.: Decentralized learning for wireless communications and networking. In: Glowinski, R., Osher, S.J., Yin, W. (eds.) Splitting Methods in Communication, Imaging, Science, and Engineering. SC, pp. 461–497. Springer, Cham (2016). https://doi.org/10.1007/978-3-319-41589-5_14
11. Hansen, L.K., Salamon, P.: Neural network ensembles. IEEE Trans. Pattern Anal. Mach. Intell. **10**, 993–1001 (1990)
12. Ho, T.K., Hull, J.J., Srihari, S.N.: Decision combination in multiple classifier systems. IEEE Trans. Pattern Anal. Mach. Intell. **16**(1), 66–75 (1994)
13. Kim, H.C., Ghahramani, Z.: Bayesian classifier combination. In: Artificial Intelligence and Statistics, pp. 619–627 (2012)
14. Kittler, J., Hatef, M., Duin, R., Matas, J.: On combining classifiers. IEEE Trans. Pattern Anal. Mach. Intell. **20**(3), 226–238 (1998)

15. Kittler, J., Alkoot, F.M.: Sum versus vote fusion in multiple classifier systems. IEEE Trans. Pattern Anal. Mach. Intell. **25**(1), 110–115 (2003)
16. Koren, Y.: The bellkor solution to the netflix grand prize. Netflix Prize Doc. **81**, 1–10 (2009)
17. Krogh, A., Vedelsby, J.: Neural network ensembles, cross validation, and active learning. In: Advances in Neural Information Processing Systems, pp. 231–238 (1995)
18. Maclin, R., Shavlik, J.W., et al.: Combining the predictions of multiple classifiers: using competitive learning to initialize neural networks. In: IJCAI, pp. 524–531. Citeseer (1995)
19. Merz, C.J.: Dynamic learning bias selection. In: Proceedings of the Fifth International Workshop on Artificial Intelligence and Statistics, Ft. Lauderdale, FL, pp. 386–395 (1995, Unpublished)
20. Merz, C.J.: Combining classifiers using correspondence analysis. In: Advances in Neural Information Processing Systems, pp. 591–597 (1998)
21. Opitz, D.W., Shavlik, J.W.: Generating accurate and diverse members of a neural-network ensemble. In: Advances in Neural Information Processing Systems, pp. 535–541 (1996)
22. Pedregosa, F., et al.: Scikit-learn: machine learning in Python. J. Mach. Learn. Res. **12**, 2825–2830 (2011)
23. Sontag, E.D.: A learning result for continuous-time recurrent neural networks. Syst. Control Lett. **34**(3), 151–158 (1998)
24. Tresp, V.: A Bayesian committee machine. Neural Comput. **12**(11), 2719–2741 (2000)
25. Wolpert, D.H.: Stacked generalization. Neural Netw. **5**(2), 241–259 (1992)
26. Wozniak, M., Grana, M., Corchado, E.: A survey of multiple classifier systems as hybrid systems. Inf. Fusion **16**, 3–17 (2014). Special Issue on Information Fusion in Hybrid Intelligent Fusion Systems
27. Xu, L., Krzyzak, A., Suen, C.Y.: Methods of combining multiple classifiers and their applications to handwriting recognition. IEEE Trans. Syst. Man Cybern. **22**, 418–435 (1992)
28. Zezula, I.: On multivariate gaussian copulas. J. Stat. Plan. Inference **139**(11), 3942–3946 (2009). Special Issue: The 8th Tartu Conference on Multivariate Statistics & The 6th Conference on Multivariate Distributions with Fixed Marginals

Decentralized Recommendation Based on Matrix Factorization: A Comparison of Gossip and Federated Learning

István Hegedűs[1(✉)], Gábor Danner[1], and Márk Jelasity[1,2]

[1] University of Szeged, Szeged, Hungary
ihegedus@inf.u-szeged.hu
[2] MTA SZTE Research Group on Artificial Intelligence, Szeged, Hungary

Abstract. Federated learning is a well-known machine learning approach over edge devices with relatively limited resources, such as mobile phones. A key feature of the approach is that no data is collected centrally; instead, data remains private and only models are communicated between a server and the devices. Gossip learning has a similar application domain; it also assumes that all the data remains private, but it requires no aggregation server or any central component. However—one would assume—gossip learning must pay a price for the extra robustness and lower maintenance cost it provides due to its fully decentralized design. Here, we examine this natural assumption empirically. The application we focus on is making recommendations based on private logs of user activity, such as viewing or browsing history. We apply low rank matrix decomposition to implement a common collaborative filtering method. First, we present similar algorithms for both frameworks to efficiently solve this problem without revealing any raw data or any user-specific parts of the model. We then examine the aggregated cost in both cases for several algorithm-variants in various simulation scenarios. These scenarios include a real churn trace collected over mobile phones. Perhaps surprisingly, gossip learning is comparable to federated learning in all the scenarios and, especially in large networks, it can even outperform federated learning when the same subsampling-based compression technique is applied in both frameworks.

1 Introduction

Mobile phones represent a key source of data and a very important platform not only for running pre-trained models but also for learning [17]. This is because collecting data centrally has become more and more problematic over the past few years due to novel data protection rules [7] as well as the increasing public

This study was supported by the Hungarian Government and the European Regional Development Fund under the grant number GINOP-2.3.2-15-2016-00037 ("Internet of Living Things") and by the Hungarian Ministry of Human Capacities (grant 20391-3/2018/FEKUSTRAT).

P. Cellier and K. Driessens (Eds.): ECML PKDD 2019 Workshops, CCIS 1167, pp. 317–332, 2020.
https://doi.org/10.1007/978-3-030-43823-4_27

awareness to privacy issues. For this reason, there is an increasing interest in methods that keep the raw data on the device and process it using distributed algorithms.

Google introduced *federated learning* to answer this challenge [10,12]. Not unlike the well-known parameter server architecture [6], a server maintains the current model and regularly distributes it to the workers who in turn calculate a gradient update and send it back to the server, where the updates are aggregated. In federated learning, this framework is optimized so as to minimize communication between the server and the workers. For this reason, the local update calculation is more thorough, and compression techniques can be applied when uploading the updates to the server. *Gossip learning* has also been proposed to address the same challenge [9,14]. This approach is fully decentralized, no parameter server is necessary. Nodes exchange and aggregate models directly. Since no infrastructure is required, and there is no single point of failure, gossip learning enjoys a significantly *cheaper scalability and better robustness* than centralized approaches.

However, it is not clear whether gossip learning is competitive in terms of convergence time and communication cost. To shed light on this question, we carry out an empirical comparison of the two approaches. To do this, we implement a recommender system in both paradigms, based on low-rank matrix decomposition. The gossip learning implementation is based on our previous work [9]. We propose a federated learning implementation as well, following the same design, but adapted to the centralized communication pattern. Also, inspired by [10], we apply subsampling to reduce communication in both approaches.

The result of our comparison is that gossip learning is in general comparable to the centrally coordinated federated learning approach, and in some scenarios it actually outperforms federated learning. One should obviously not jump to conclusions based on one empirical study, but our results suggest that fully decentralized algorithms perhaps deserve more attention in the future.

To sum up our key original contributions in the present study: (1) we propose an efficient collaborative filtering method for federated learning; (2) we improve several details of our previous solution [9] as well including the introduction of coordinate-based age parameters to manage aggregation and the application of an optimized version of subsampling to gossip learning; and (3) we compare the two methods empirically based on a realistic churn trace collected by the application Stunner [2].

We are aware of only two (at the time of writing, unpublished) studies that address the specific problem of recommender systems in federated learning. The first is based on the idea of meta-learning [4]. Here, it is assumed that the devices have enough data to learn a model based only on local data. Then, federated learning is used to find the optimal hyperparameters for the algorithm, using the devices to calculate gradients for the hyperparameters. We are interested in scenarios where there is not much local data, so meta-learning is not an option. The second study is closer to our approach [1] in spirit. However the authors assume a different setup with only implicit binary feedback as data (e.g., a movie was watched or not). Due to this, their input data is a dense matrix (there are no ratings labeled as "unknown") so compressed communication is more problematic. We focus on modeling only the known ratings (a small minority of all ratings) and make predictions based on these. Also, the optimization algorithm they approximate is alternating least squares with a federated gradient optimization step in the inner loop, while we use simple SGD which is more robust to failure and asynchrony.

We note that both approaches offer mechanisms for explicit privacy protection, apart from the basic feature of not collecting data. In federated learning, Bonawitz et al. [3] describe a secure aggregation protocol, whereas for gossip learning one can apply the methods described in [5]. Here, we are concerned only with the efficiency of the different communication patterns and do not compare security mechanisms.

The outline of the paper is as follows. In Sect. 2, we describe the low rank matrix decomposition problem, formulated as a machine learning problem. Here, we also present the key ideas to solve this problem in a decentralized setting. In Sect. 3, we describe the basics of solving the problem with federated learning while in Sect. 4 we present the gossip learning algorithm for the same problem. In Sect. 5 we present the key details of the learning algorithm that are common to both approaches. These include the details of the update rule, the subsampling technique, and the initialization. Finally, in Sect. 6, we present our empirical results.

2 Rank-k Matrix Approximation

Here, we present the problem definition in the form of a model and a corresponding loss function. We also describe our approach and main assumptions—common to both federated learning and gossip learning—regarding the optimization of the model.

2.1 Problem Definition

The problem of rank-k matrix approximation [11] is defined in the following way. Let $A \in \mathbb{R}^{m\times n}$ be a matrix that contains our data (for example, user ratings of items such as movies, songs, or locations). The goal is to find two matrices $X \in \mathbb{R}^{m\times k}$ and $Y \in \mathbb{R}^{n\times k}$ that minimize the error function

$$J(X,Y) = \frac{1}{2}\left\|A - XY^T\right\|_F^2 = \frac{1}{2}\sum_{i=1}^{m}\sum_{j=1}^{n}(a_{ij} - \sum_{l=1}^{k} x_{il}y_{jl})^2. \quad (1)$$

We consider the matrix XY^T an optimal rank-k approximation of A. Note that the rank of X and Y^T (and therefore XY^T) is at most k. Usually a k much smaller than m and n is chosen to significantly compress the data. X and Y^T can be interpreted as high level features (e.g. genres of movies and tastes of users) that compactly represent the original data.

Often in practice we have only partial information regarding A; that is, some values in A might be unknown. As an important generalization of the problem above, here we are looking for a rank-k decomposition that approximates only the known values. A common approach is to minimize the error function

$$J(X,Y) = \frac{1}{2} \sum_{(i,j)\in I} (a_{ij} - \sum_{l=1}^{k} x_{il}y_{jl})^2 + \frac{\lambda}{2} \|X\|_F^2 + \frac{\lambda}{2} \|Y\|_F^2, \tag{2}$$

where I contains the indices of the known values of A. We can then use the decomposition XY^T to approximate the unknown values in A, since XY^T is fully defined. Note the here we also included additional regularization terms and the regularization parameter λ. This helps stabilize the optimization process in a machine learning context.

Another practical technique used is to add bias terms to the model. The bias terms $b \in \mathbb{R}^{m\times 1}$ and $c \in \mathbb{R}^{1\times n}$ are incorporated into the model via the loss function

$$J(X,Y,b,c) = \frac{1}{2} \sum_{(i,j)\in I} (a_{ij} - b_i - c_j - \sum_{l=1}^{k} x_{il}y_{jl})^2 + \frac{\lambda}{2} \|X\|_F^2 + \frac{\lambda}{2} \|Y\|_F^2. \tag{3}$$

For example, in a recommender system, the bias can represent the fact that some users tend to give higher or lower scores than others, and some movies tend to get higher or lower scores. Intuitively, the bias represents average scores, and X and Y represent relative differences. This often enhances the prediction performance. With bias, the approximation of A (both known and unknown values) is given by $XY^T + b\mathbf{1}_n + c^T\mathbf{1}_m$ where $\mathbf{1}_k$ is a row vector of k ones.

2.2 Optimization Approach

Our targeted application environment consists of a potentially large set of personal devices holding private data. We follow the approach in our previous paper [9] and we will adapt the same approach to federated learning. We shall assume that each row in matrix A is stored on exactly one device. We shall also assume that each device will host exactly one row. This setup covers applications where one row of the matrix belongs to one user and the devices belong to exactly one user, as in the case of mobile phones. One matrix row can naturally represent any kind of private user activity, such as watching movies. We should add though that if more than one row is stored on a device, the algorithms are still applicable.

The main idea is that matrix X will also be stored in a similar manner; that is, every device will store the row of X that belongs to the row of A stored on the device. This way, the matrix X that contains information about the users is completely private, every device knows only its own row. However, the entire matrix Y will be shared among all the devices. This is safe, because matrix Y contains only user-independent information about all the items the users might consume.

Algorithm 1. Federated Learning Master

```
1: (t, Y, c) ← initY()
2: loop
3:     (t̃, Ỹ, c̃) ← (0_n, 0_{n,k}, 0_n)
4:     for every node i in parallel do        ▷ non-blocking (in separate thread(s))
5:         send (t, Y, c) to i
6:         receive (t', Y', c') from i        ▷ model gradient
7:         (t̃, Ỹ, c̃) ← (t̃ + t', Ỹ + Y', c̃ + c')
8:     end for
9:     wait(Δ_f)                              ▷ the round length
10:    for j ← 1...n do
11:        if t̃_j ≠ 0 then
12:            Y_j ← Y_j + Ỹ_j/t̃_j
13:            c_j ← c_j + c̃_j/t̃_j
14:            t_j ← t_j + 1
15:        end if
16:    end for
17: end loop
```

The gradient of Y computed by a single user may leak private data. In federated learning, Bonawitz et al. [3] describe a secure aggregation protocol with additional measures to prevent this kind of information leakage. In gossip learning, one can apply the secure distributed mini-batch methods described in [5]. We do not include such additional techniques in our present study.

Using the loss function defined in Eq. (3), and assuming that every device has a copy of Y, the gradient of both its own row of X and the global matrix Y can be computed by each device locally, w.r.t. the local row of A. Devices can use these gradients to update their own row of X locally. Therefore, all we need to take care of is to somehow aggregate the gradients of Y over the devices and then redistribute new versions of Y. Federated learning and gossip learning offer two, rather different alternative solutions to this problem. (Note that the bias vectors b and c are handled similarly to X and Y, respectively.)

3 Federated Learning

Here, we present the well-known federated learning algorithm [10,12], adapted to the problem of rank-k matrix decomposition.

In this framework, there is a master node that runs Algorithm 1, and several worker nodes that execute Algorithm 2. The master first initializes the global model (t, Y, c) that contains matrix Y, the bias vector c and an *age vector* t. For each row j, t_j counts how many times Y_j and c_j have been updated. Having a separate counter for each row is necessary because there can be a very different number of examples for each item, and thus there can be a different number of updates applied to each row (see below).

Similarly, each worker node initializes its private model (x_i, b_i) that contains its own row of X, x_i, and the corresponding bias b_i. After initialization, in every

Algorithm 2. Federated Learning Worker

1: $(x_i, b_i) \leftarrow$ initX()
2:
3: **procedure** ONRECEIVEMODEL($\widetilde{t}, \widetilde{Y}, \widetilde{c}$)
4: $((t, Y, c), (x_i, b_i)) \leftarrow$update$((\widetilde{t}, \widetilde{Y}, \widetilde{c}), (x_i, b_i), a_i)$ ▷ a_i: the local ratings
5: $(t', Y', c') \leftarrow (t - \widetilde{t}, Y - \widetilde{Y}, c - \widetilde{c})$
6: send (compress(t', Y', c')) to master
7: **end procedure**

round, the master sends the global model to all the workers. The workers then update the received global model and their own local user model using the local ratings, and they then send the (potentially compressed) model gradient to the master. In this message to the master, the vector t' can contain only ones and zeros, indicating which rows of Y (and elements of c) were updated. At the end of each round, the server updates the global model with the average of the received gradients.

Each row Y_j (and value c_j) will typically have different associated $\widetilde{t}_j$ values depending on how many valid (non-missing) values are there in the matrix column A_j, and also on which clients manage to send a message to the master in the given round. We can think of $\widetilde{t}_j$ as the effective mini-batch size corresponding to updating Y_j and c_j. Thus, by normalizing with $\widetilde{t}_j$, we effectively perform parallel mini-batch updates on Y_j and c_j.

Note that in the federated learning framework it is typically assumed that the workers are synchronized; that is, the master has to wait until all (or most of) the nodes send a gradient in the given round and, most importantly, the workers have to wait as well for the next globally aggregated model from the master to process. Although asynchronous distributed learning is common, federated learning also seeks to handle the non-uniform sampling of training data, which is expected to make asynchronous implementations less stable.

The methods UPDATE, COMPRESS, INITX and INITY shall be explained in detail in Sect. 5. Note that the same methods are used in gossip learning as well.

4 Gossip Learning

In gossip learning, there is no master node. All the participants are equivalent, and form a P2P network [14]. All the nodes run Algorithm 3. The nodes first initialize their own copy of the global model (t, Y, c) as well as the private model (x_i, b_i). Then, in each cycle, they send their (potentially compressed) copy of the global model to a random online neighbor in the P2P network. Upon receiving a model, the node merges it into its own, then updates both the resulting merged new global model and the local model, using the local ratings.

As mentioned above, methods UPDATE, COMPRESS, INITX and INITY shall be explained in detail in Sect. 5. Note that the same methods are used by federated learning as well.

Algorithm 3. Gossip Learning

```
1: (t, Y, c) ← initY()
2: (x_i, b_i) ← initX()
3: loop
4:     wait(Δ_g)
5:     p ← selectPeer()
6:     send (compress(t, Y, c)) to p
7: end loop
8:
9: procedure onReceiveModel(t̃, Ỹ, c̃)
10:     (t, Y, c) ←merge((t, Y, c), (t̃, Ỹ, c̃))
11:     ((t, Y, c), (x_i, b_i)) ←update((t, Y, c), (x_i, b_i), a_i)
12: end procedure
```

Algorithm 4. Various versions of the merge function

```
1: procedure mergeNone((t, Y, c), (t̃, Ỹ, c̃))
2:     return (t̃, Ỹ, c̃)
3: end procedure
4:
5: procedure mergeAverage((t, Y, c), (t̃, Ỹ, c̃))
6:     for j ← 1 . . . n do
7:         if t̃_j ≠ 0 then
8:             w ← t̃_j / (t_j + t̃_j)
9:             t_j ← max(t_j, t̃_j)
10:            Y_j ← (1 − w)Y_j + wỸ_j
11:            c_j ← (1 − w)c_j + wc̃_j
12:        end if
13:    end for
14:    return (t, Y, c)
15: end procedure
```

Method MERGE, however, is specific to gossip learning, and it is responsible for aggregating the updates computed at the devices. Possible implementations of this method are listed in Algorithm 4. The first option is not to perform any aggregation, in which case different versions of the global model perform random walks in the network independently. The other option is to take the average of the two models row by row, weighted by the corresponding elements of the age vectors so that the more converged copy has a larger effect.

An important effect of this weighted merging technique is that the freshly initialized rows of the model of any newly joined node are ignored. This is because if a row has never been updated, then the age is zero for the given row. The new model will be assigned the maximum of the two merged ages. This is a conservative heuristic that performed better in our preliminary experiments than possible alternatives such as the sum of the two ages. Note that the age of the

Algorithm 5. Model initialization

```
 1: procedure INITX()
 2:     for d ← 1...k do
 3:         x_d ← rand() · √((R_max − R_min)/k)          ▷ rand() ~ U(0,1)
 4:     end for
 5:     b ← R_min/2
 6:     return (x, b)
 7: end procedure
 8:
 9: procedure INITY()
10:     for j ← 1...n do
11:         t_j ← 0
12:         (Y_j, c_j) ←initX()
13:     end for
14:     return (t, Y, c)
15: end procedure
```

different rows can differ significantly because the number of known ratings for different items typically has a large variance.

Since gossip learning uses a P2P network, we have to make our assumptions about this network explicit. We assume that there is a membership service in our system. This service provides unique identities to the participants that might include public and private keys for public key cryptography that are tied to the network address of the node. The membership service also offers peer sampling, accessed through method SELECTPEER. That is, all the nodes are assumed to have access to addresses of live nodes from the network. In practice, peer sampling can have a decentralized implementation that can be dynamic [16] or it can be based on a static network with random neighbors [15] that is able to handle NAT devices as well. It can also be implemented as a centralized service. Ideally, the neighbors returned by the peer sampling service should be uniform random samples of the live nodes, but in practice it suffices if the network has good mixing when, for example, the neighbors are sampled from a fixed overlay network graph.

5 Shared Methods

Here, we present those methods that are used by both federated learning and gossip learning. Let us begin with the initialization methods in Algorithm 5. Both X and Y are initialized with uniform random numbers from the range $[0, \sqrt{(R_{\max} - R_{\min})/k}]$, and the initial bias is set to $R_{\min}/2$, where $R_{\max}$ and $R_{\min}$ are the largest and the smallest possible ratings, respectively. This ensures that when a prediction $x_i Y_j^T + b_i + c_j$ is made using initial values, the result falls in the range $[R_{\min}, R_{\max}]$.

As for learning, both models use a stochastic gradient descent (SGD) update rule with the fixed learning rate η (see Algorithm 6). The age vector t is incremented in positions corresponding to updated rows of Y (that is, for those items

Algorithm 6. Model update rule

```
1: procedure UPDATE((t, Y, c), (x_i, b_i), a_i)
2:     for all j where a_ij is defined do
3:         t_j ← t_j + 1
4:         err ← a_ij − x_i Y_j^T − b_i − c_j
5:         (Y_j, x_i) ← ((1 − ηλ)Y_j + η · err · x_i, (1 − ηλ)x_i + η · err · Y_j)
6:         c_j ← c_j + η · err
7:         b_i ← b_i + η · err
8:     end for
9:     return ((t, Y, c), (x_i, b_i))
10: end procedure
```

Algorithm 7. Various versions of the compress function

```
1: procedure COMPRESSNONE(t, Y, c)
2:     return (t, Y, c)
3: end procedure
4:
5: procedure COMPRESSSUBSAMPLING(t, Y, c)
6:     U ← {1, ..., n}
7:     D ← {j ∈ U | a_ij is defined}
8:     J_d ← random subset of D of size min(s, |D|)
9:     J_u ← random subset of (U \ D) of size (s − |J_d|)
10:    for all j ∈ J_d ∪ J_u do
11:        t'_j ← t_j
12:        Y'_j ← Y_j
13:        c'_j ← c_j
14:    end for
15:    return (t', Y', c')          ▷ we assume a sparse vector representation
16: end procedure
```

that the user rated). The update rule simply follows from the partial derivatives of (3). Note that this version of the update rule uses a constant learning rate, but other implementations might also use the age vector passed to the update method.

Let us now turn to the compression methods. In this study, we focus on subsampling as a simple compression technique. That is, only s rows of Y are sent along with the corresponding elements of t and c, where s is the compression parameter (see Algorithm 7). Subsampling is performed randomly without replacement from the updated rows (that is, those rows where the corresponding rating is known) and, if there is still room left, from the remaining, non-updated rows. Note that sending non-updated rows in fact makes sense because in such cases the given node might act as a forwarding agent. In other words, such rows might be useful for the recipient nodes.

6 Experiments

Here, we present our simulation experiments with gossip learning and federated learning over the MovieLens database in several scenarios.

Table 1. The main properties of the MovieLens data sets and algorithm parameters

	100K	1M	10M
# users (m)	943	6,040	69,878
# movies (n)	1,682	3,952	10,677
# ratings	100,000	1,000,209	10,000,054
Density	6.3%	4.2%	1.3%
Training/Test	90.57%/9.43%	93.96%/6.04%	93.01%/6.99%
Time period	20.09.97–22.04.98	25.04.00–28.02.03	09.01.95–05.01.09
$\eta/\lambda/k$	$10^{-2}/10^{-1}/5$	$10^{-2}/10^{-1}/5$	$10^{-2}/10^{-1}/5$
Message size	0.6 Mbit	1.5 Mbit	4.1 Mbit

6.1 Datasets

The MovieLens data sets [8] were collected by the GroupLens Research Project at the University of Minnesota. The data was collected through the MovieLens website (movielens.org) over various periods of time, depending on the size of the set. The main properties of the MovieLens data sets are shown in Table 1 and Fig. 1. Each data set is split into a training matrix and a test matrix in such a way that for each user, there are either 0 or 10 defined values in the test matrix. Each row of the training matrix (representing the ratings of a given user) was assigned to a unique node in the simulation experiments.

6.2 System Model

In our simulations, fixed random 20-out graphs were used as the overlay network. The number of nodes was equal to the number of users in the given data set. In the churn-free scenario, every node stayed online for the whole experiment. A real availability trace, gathered from smartphones, was used in the churn scenario. A message was considered successfully delivered if and only if both the sender and the receiver remained online during the transfer. Peer selection (method SELECTPEER) returned online nodes only.

The nodes had the same upload and download bandwidths. The motivation for this was that it is likely that in a real application there will be a low, uniform, configured bandwidth cap. The server had infinite bandwidth (which favors federated learning, as gossip learning does not use a server). The transfer time of a

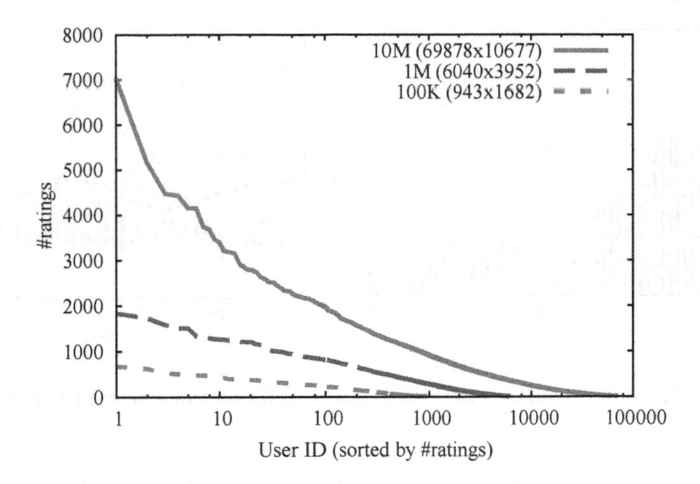

Fig. 1. Visualization of the distribution of the number of rated items per user. Users are sorted according to the number of their rated items for all three databases.

full model was assumed to be 1728 s (irrespective of the data set used) in the low bandwidth scenario, and 172.8 s in the high bandwidth scenario. This allowed for around 100 and 1000 iterations over the course of 48 h, respectively.

The cycle length parameters Δ_g and Δ_f were set so that the two approaches fully utilized the available bandwidth. In our case this also means that the two algorithms transfer the same amount of data overall in the network in the same amount of time, making comparisons of convergence dynamics fair. The gossip cycle length Δ_g is exactly the transfer time of a model, which is proportionally smaller when compression is used. The cycle length Δ_f of federated learning is the round-trip time, that is, the sum of the upload and download times. In this case, only the upstream transfer is compressed.

Note that we use rather low bandwidth settings because in the churn scenario if the transfer is very fast, the network hardly changes during the learning process, the models are learned over an effectively static subset of the nodes. Slower transfer is more challenging, because more transfers fail, just like in the case of very large machine learning models such as deep neural networks. (This issue is completely irrelevant in the churn-free scenario, since the dynamics are identical apart from the scale of time.)

6.3 Smartphone Traces

We used a trace collected by STUNner, a locally developed, openly available smartphone application [2]. In short, the app monitors and collects information about the battery level, charging status, bandwidth, and NAT type.

The trace contains time series spanning varying lengths of time, originating from 1191 different users. Based on the UTC hour of day, we split the data into 2-day segments (with a one-day overlap), resulting in 40,658 segments altogether.

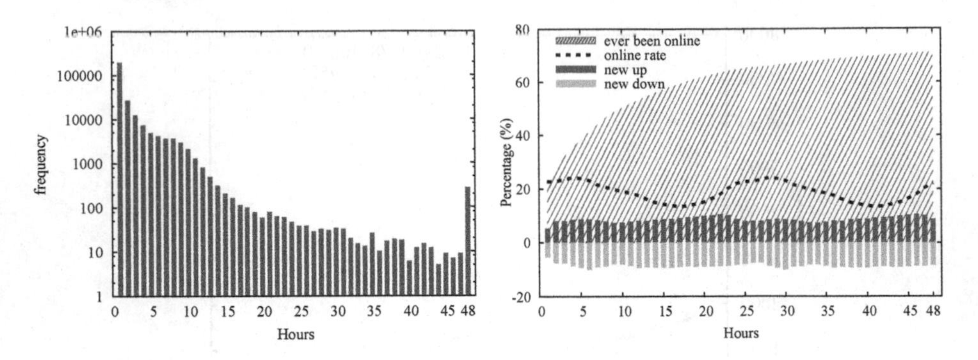

Fig. 2. Online session length histogram (left) and device churn (right).

Using this, we can simulate a virtual 48-hour period by assigning a segment to each simulated node.

To make our algorithm phone and user friendly, we consider a device to be online (available) when it has been on a charger and connected to the Internet (with a bandwidth of at least 1 Mbit/s) for at least a minute, therefore we do not use battery power at all.

The main properties of the trace are shown in Fig. 2. The plot on the right illustrates churn by showing what percentage of the nodes left, or joined the network (at least once) in any given hour. Notice that at any given moment about 20% of the nodes are online. The mean online session length is 81.368 min.

6.4 Hyperparameters

The learning rate η and regularization parameter λ were optimized in the churn-free, low-bandwidth, uncompressed scenario. The resulting values are $\eta = 10^{-2}$ and $\lambda = 10^{-1}$, as shown in Table 1. We used rank-5 factorization.

6.5 Results

We used PeerSim [13] for the simulations. We measured performance with the help of the root-mean-square deviation

$$\mathrm{RMSE} = \sqrt{\frac{1}{|T|} \sum_{i,j \in T} (r_{i,j} - x_i y_j^T)^2},$$

where $R \in \mathbb{R}^{m \times n}$ is the test matrix, and T is the set of indices defined in R. In the case of gossip learning, the error is calculated using the models stored in the currently online nodes and the corresponding rows of R. In the case of federated learning, the aggregated global model is used instead of the local ones. Figure 3 contains our results without churn, and Fig. 4 shows the same experiments over the smartphone trace. The evaluated algorithms are

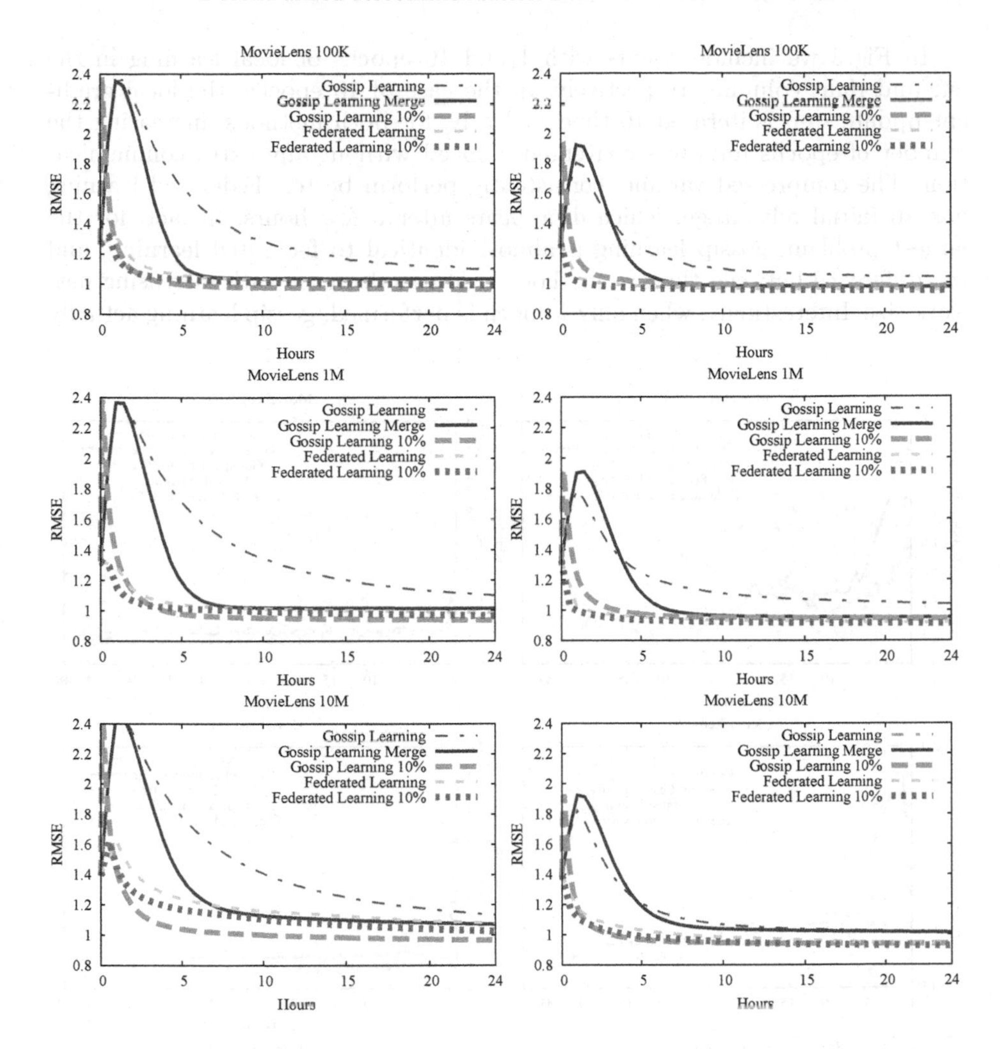

Fig. 3. Churn-free scenario with 1 epoch (left) and 10 epochs (right).

Gossip Learning: no merging and no subsampling. Here, the cycle length equals the time needed for one full model transmission.

Gossip Learning Merge: with merging but no subsampling, so the cycle length is still one full transmission.

Gossip Learning 10%: with merging and subsampling with $s = n/10$. Here, the cycle length corresponds to 0.1 full transmissions.

Federated Learning: no subsampling, so the cycle length corresponds to two full transmissions: upload and download.

Federated Learning 10%: the uploaded model is subsampled with $s = n/10$, so the cycle length corresponds to 1.1 full transmissions.

In Fig. 3 we include results with 1 and 10 epochs of local learning in the left and right columns, respectively. In the case of 10 epochs, the local gradient update step is iterated 10 times. Clearly, for both methods, increasing the number of epochs improves convergence speed without any extra communication. The compressed variants consistently perform better. Federated learning has an initial advantage, which disappears after a few hours. In fact, for the largest problem, gossip learning is almost identical to federated learning, and the difference between the two methods seems to decrease with increasing network size. Interestingly, when only 1 epoch is performed, gossip learning actually

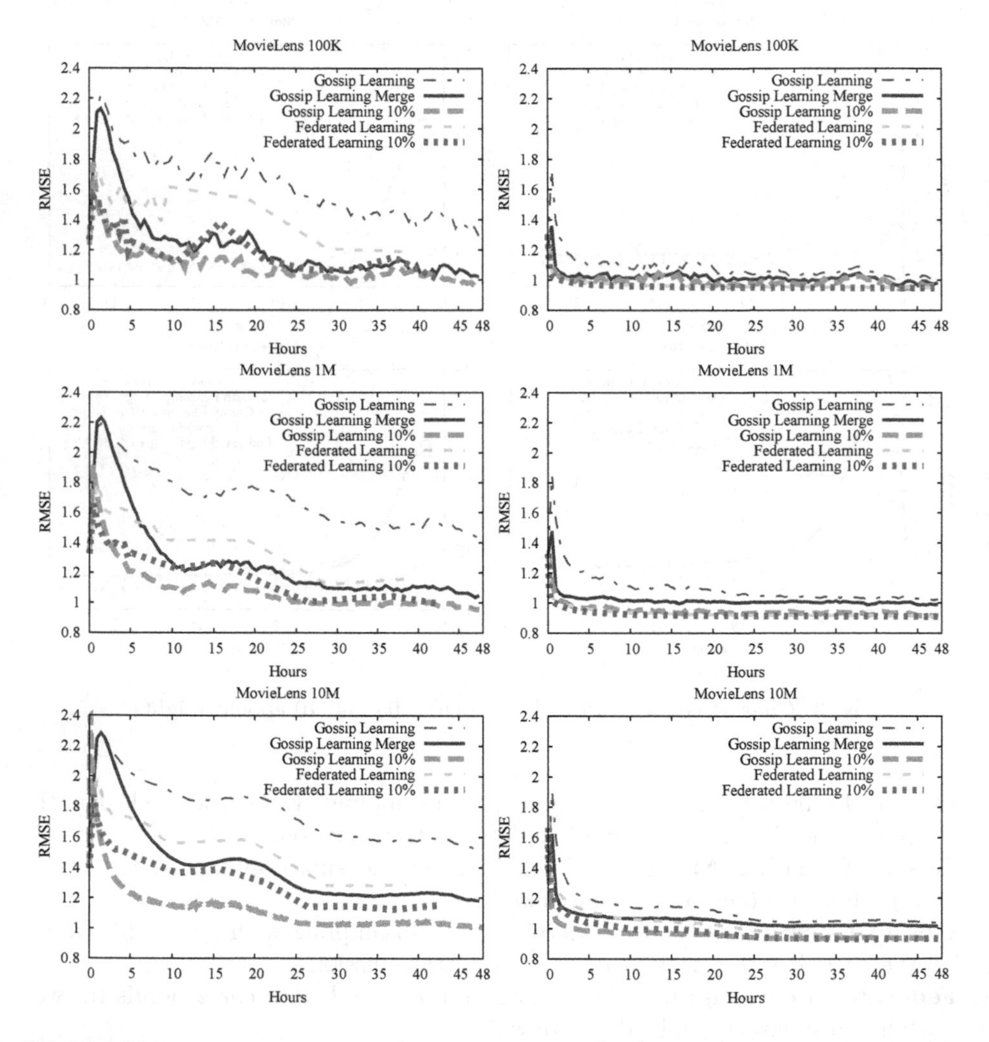

Fig. 4. Churn trace scenario with low bandwidth (left) and $10\times$ higher bandwidth (right).

outperforms federated learning by a significant margin especially on the largest network.

In Fig. 4 we ran one local epoch in each experiment, but the plots on the right show the effect of speeding up communication. Faster communication results in a dramatically better performance, simply because the convergence speed is able to "beat" the speed of churn. Apart from this observation, the other conclusions are similar, namely compression helps both methods and gossip learning performs relatively better in larger networks. Overall, federated learning and gossip learning have a very similar performance, despite the disadvantage of gossip learning of not relying on a central server for aggregation and broadcast.

7 Conclusions

In this study, our main goal was to explore the differences between federated learning and gossip learning over a collaborative filtering task. Since gossip learning does not rely on central servers, one might expect it to pay a performance penalty in terms of convergence speed, when given the same communication budget.

Our main conclusion based on our empirical study is that federated learning does not seem to have a clear performance advantage. In fact, in certain scenarios gossip learning proved to be preferable. Obviously, the design space for both protocols is very large, and there are many possibilities for improving the communication efficiency in both paradigms. It is also a non-trivial question of how one should model communication constraints and costs, since this depends on many factors. However, it is interesting, and perhaps non-trivial, that gossip learning is clearly comparable in performance. This might motivate further research into fully decentralized methods that otherwise have clear benefits such as a very low cost of entry that is not dependent of the network size, or the robustness due to the lack of any critical components.

References

1. Ammad-ud-din, M., et al.: Federated collaborative filtering for privacy-preserving personalized recommendation system. CoRR abs/1901.09888 (2019). http://arxiv.org/abs/1901.09888
2. Berta, Á., Bilicki, V., Jelasity, M.: Defining and understanding smartphone churn over the internet: a measurement study. In: Proceedings of the 14th IEEE International Conference on Peer-to-Peer Computing (P2P 2014). IEEE (2014). https://doi.org/10.1109/P2P.2014.6934317
3. Bonawitz, K., et al.: Practical secure aggregation for federated learning on user-held data. In: NIPS Workshop on Private Multi-Party Machine Learning (2016)
4. Chen, F., Dong, Z., Li, Z., He, X.: Federated meta-learning for recommendation. CoRR abs/1802.07876 (2018). http://arxiv.org/abs/1802.07876
5. Danner, G., Berta, Á., Hegedűs, I., Jelasity, M.: Robust fully distributed minibatch gradient descent with privacy preservation. Secur. Commun. Netw. **2018**, 6728020 (2018). https://doi.org/10.1155/2018/6728020

6. Dean, J., et al.: Large scale distributed deep networks. In: Proceedings of the 25th International Conference on Neural Information Processing Systems, NIPS 2012, vol. 1, pp. 1223–1231. Curran Associates Inc., USA (2012). http://dl.acm.org/citation.cfm?id=2999134.2999271
7. European Commission: General data protection regulation (GDPR) (2018). https://ec.europa.eu/commission/priorities/justice-and-fundamental-rights/data-protection/2018-reform-eu-data-protection-rules
8. Harper, F.M., Konstan, J.A.: The movielens datasets: history and context. ACM Trans. Interact. Intell. Syst. **5**(4), 19:1–19:19 (2015). https://doi.org/10.1145/2827872
9. Hegedűs, I., Berta, Á., Kocsis, L., Benczúr, A.A., Jelasity, M.: Robust decentralized low-rank matrix decomposition. ACM Trans. Intell. Syst. Technol. **7**(4), 62:1–62:24 (2016). https://doi.org/10.1145/2854157
10. Konecný, J., McMahan, H.B., Yu, F.X., Richtárik, P., Suresh, A.T., Bacon, D.: Federated learning: Strategies for improving communication efficiency. In: Private Multi-Party Machine Learning (NIPS 2016 Workshop) (2016)
11. Koren, Y., Bell, R., Volinsky, C.: Matrix factorization techniques for recommender systems. Computer **42**(8), 30–37 (2009). https://doi.org/10.1109/MC.2009.263
12. McMahan, B., Moore, E., Ramage, D., Hampson, S., y Arcas, B.A.: Communication-efficient learning of deep networks from decentralized data. In: Singh, A., Zhu, J. (eds.) Proceedings of the 20th International Conference on Artificial Intelligence and Statistics. Proceedings of Machine Learning Research, vol. 54, pp. 1273–1282. PMLR, Fort Lauderdale, 20–22 April 2017
13. Montresor, A., Jelasity, M.: Peersim: A scalable P2P simulator. In: Proceedings of the 9th IEEE International Conference on Peer-to-Peer Computing (P2P 2009), pp. 99–100. IEEE, Seattle, September 2009. https://doi.org/10.1109/P2P.2009.5284506. http://www.inf.u-szeged.hu/~jelasity/cikkek/p2p09.pdf, extended abstract
14. Ormándi, R., Hegedűs, I., Jelasity, M.: Gossip learning with linear models on fully distributed data. Concurr. Comput.: Pract. Exp. **25**(4), 556–571 (2013). https://doi.org/10.1002/cpe.2858
15. Roverso, R., Dowling, J., Jelasity, M.: Through the wormhole: low cost, fresh peer sampling for the internet. In: Proceedings of the 13th IEEE International Conference on Peer-to-Peer Computing (P2P 2013). IEEE (2013). https://doi.org/10.1109/P2P.2013.6688707
16. Tölgyesi, N., Jelasity, M.: Adaptive peer sampling with newscast. In: Sips, H., Epema, D., Lin, H.-X. (eds.) Euro-Par 2009. LNCS, vol. 5704, pp. 523–534. Springer, Heidelberg (2009). https://doi.org/10.1007/978-3-642-03869-3_50
17. Wang, J., Cao, B., Yu, P.S., Sun, L., Bao, W., Zhu, X.: Deep learning towards mobile applications. In: IEEE 38th International Conference on Distributed Computing Systems (ICDCS), pp. 1385–1393, July 2018. https://doi.org/10.1109/ICDCS.2018.00139. https://arxiv.org/pdf/1809.03559.pdf

Ring-Star: A Sparse Topology for Faster Model Averaging in Decentralized Parallel SGD

Mohsan Jameel(✉), Josif Grabocka, Mofassir ul Islam Arif, and Lars Schmidt-Thieme

Information Systems and Machine Learning Lab, University of Hildesheim, Universitätsplatz 1, 31141 Hildesheim, Germany
{mohsan.jameel,josif,mofassir,schmidt-thieme}@ismll.uni-hildesheim.de

Abstract. In decentralized distributed systems the data resides on the compute devices, which are connected through a high latency network that can adversely impact the communication cost. In such systems, it is desirable to employ a training regime that is inherently decentralized, where learning algorithms operate on local hosts using only the local data partitions. To ensure their convergence to a joint model, the parameters of the local models have to be regularly averaged. As each averaging operation incurs network communication costs, the right balance has to be found between either communication intensive dense averaging operations or sparse averaging operations which slows down the convergence. We propose a hierarchical two-layer sparse communication topology, a ring of fully-connected meshes of workers that communicate with each other (*Ring-Star*). *Ring-Star* allows a principled trade-off between the convergence speed and communication overhead and is well suited to loosely coupled distributed systems. We demonstrate on an image classification task and a batch stochastic gradient descent learning (SGD) algorithm that our proposed method shows similar convergence behavior as *Allreduce* while having lower communication cost of *Ring*.

Keywords: Decentralize sparse topology · Model averaging · Distributed stochastic gradient descent · Deep learning

1 Introduction

Mini-batch Stochastic Gradient Descent is often employed for training deep learning models in distributed settings, as each instance of data can be processed in parallel, which is useful in speeding up the learning process. The most widely used distributed learning approaches focus mainly on using centralized training procedures [4,7], which are based on a parameter server (PS) framework. However, the centralized approaches are not suited for the computing environment, where data cannot be centralized and the central server can become a bottleneck due to the underlying network characteristics [8]. Decentralized training procedures [8,9] are proposed to scale on loosely connected, high latency computing

P. Cellier and K. Driessens (Eds.): ECML PKDD 2019 Workshops, CCIS 1167, pp. 333–341, 2020.
https://doi.org/10.1007/978-3-030-43823-4_28

systems. In these procedures, workers are sparsely connected to each other forming a *Ring* topology. For synchronization, each worker averages its model with two neighboring workers. Decentralized approaches are motivated by control systems and wireless sensor network research, which solve a global consensus problem. These procedures show a significant reduction in the communication overhead. However, sparse averaging increases the parameter variance between workers, which is termed as "network error" in the literature [1,13]. The "network error" or variance is large in the early stages of optimizing a non-convex objective and frequent averaging helps to reduce the variance. Despite being communication efficient, decentralized training procedures suffer from high network error, which increases with an increasing number of workers. On the other hand, a grand averaging step, like *Allreduce* [2], incurs zero network error but is a communication inefficient operation, especially in a high latency network.

The competing objectives of reducing communication overhead, while keeping the network error as small as possible is a challenging task, which requires designing a topology that benefits from both worlds. In this paper we analyze different characteristics of decentralized topologies and design a sparse topology that balances trade-off between communication cost and network error. The main contributions of this paper are (1) a new *Ring-Star* topology for a decentralized parallel SGD that balances network error and communication overhead, and (2) detailed analysis of different design choices for designing a sparse topology. The empirical evaluations on an image classification task show, superior convergence behavior of *Ring-Star* as compared to communication efficient *Ring* based topologies. As a result *Ring-Star* achieves better final test accuracy than *Ring* and *RingRandom* in same wall clock time.

2 Decentralized Model Averaging

2.1 Problem Formulation

Decentralized distributed settings consist of a set of distributed workers $\mathcal{V} = \{1, \cdots, V\}$, where each worker $v \in \mathcal{V}$ holds a local model $\hat{y}(\mathbf{x}; \theta_v)$, with model parameters $\theta_v \in \mathbb{R}^K$ and runs a mini-batch SGD to update its model parameters by sampling a mini-batch $\mathcal{B}_v \subset \mathcal{D}_v$ from the local shard of data $\mathcal{D}_v$.

$$\theta_v^{t+1} = \theta_v^t - \eta \frac{1}{|\mathcal{B}_v|} \sum_{(\mathbf{x},y)\in\mathcal{B}_v} \nabla\mathcal{L}(y, \hat{y}(\mathbf{x}; \theta_v^t)) \tag{1}$$

where $\mathcal{L}(\cdot,\cdot)$ is a loss function. Typical loss functions include the cross entropy loss, square loss, hinge loss etc. These workers periodically synchronize their models by averaging over the models learned by other workers. Given a weight matrix $\mathbf{W} \in \mathbb{R}^{V\times V}$, the averaging step at worker v can be defined as:

$$\bar{\theta}_v^t = \sum_{v'\in\mathcal{V}} \mathbf{W}_{v,v'} \theta_{v'}^t \tag{2}$$

The weight matrix (or mixing matrix) $\mathbf{W}$ is symmetric and $\mathbf{W1} = \mathbf{1}$, where $\mathbf{1}$ denotes a vector of all ones. The weight matrix $\mathbf{W}$ defines the influence of the averaging step in Eq.(2) at each worker. In a dense averaging scheme, such as *Allreduce* [2], each worker gets the model average of all other workers at each averaging step, whereas in a sparse scheme, such as *Ring* [8], each worker averages over two neighboring workers. The weight matrices for *Allreduce* and *Ring* schemes are given as:

$$\mathbf{W}_{Allreduce} = \begin{pmatrix} \frac{1}{V} & \cdots & \frac{1}{V} \\ \vdots & \ddots & \vdots \\ \frac{1}{V} & \cdots & \frac{1}{V} \end{pmatrix}, \mathbf{W}_{Ring} = \begin{pmatrix} \frac{1}{3} & \frac{1}{3} & 0 & \cdots & 0 & \frac{1}{3} \\ \frac{1}{3} & \frac{1}{3} & \frac{1}{3} & 0 & \cdots & \\ 0 & \frac{1}{3} & \frac{1}{3} & \frac{1}{3} & 0 & \cdots \\ & \ddots & \ddots & \ddots & & \\ & \cdots & 0 & \frac{1}{3} & \frac{1}{3} & \frac{1}{3} \\ \frac{1}{3} & 0 & \cdots & 0 & \frac{1}{3} & \frac{1}{3} \end{pmatrix}$$

2.2 Designing a Sparse Topology

To design a sparse topology that incurs a lower communication cost and at the same time has lower network error, we define the average-age matrix and the communication overhead as design characteristics of the topology. The average-age matrix $\mathbf{H}$ holds the information about how old the contribution of a worker u is to a worker v. Given the weight matrix $\mathbf{W}$, the average-age matrix $\mathbf{H}$ can be defined as the shortest path between the workers, which measures the number of averaging steps required to average over the model from any other worker. The second important characteristic of topology is the communication cost, which can be defined, following [11], as $\Upsilon\alpha + \Pi\beta$, where Υ is the number of handshakes, α is the latency, Π is the size of data transferred, and β is the bandwidth. The importance of latency in high latency networks cannot be understated as it can cause a performance bottleneck.

Table 1. Comparison of characteristics of different topologies.

Topology	Averaging step	Communication cost	Average age
Allreduce [2]	Dense	$2(V-1)\alpha + 2K\beta$	$O(1)$
Ring [8]	Sparse	$2\alpha + 2K\beta$	$O(V)$
RingRandom [9]	Sparse	$2\alpha + 2K\beta$	$O(log(V))$
Ring-Star (proposed)	Sparse	$(2(L-1)+2)\alpha + 2K\beta$	$O(G)$ or $O(log(G))$

2.3 Existing Topologies

The *Allreduce* (AR) topology [2] is a dense averaging scheme used for training deep learning models. In this scheme, every worker requires a single averaging step to get the contributions of all other workers, therefore the age matrix $\mathbf{H}$ has one. A disadvantage, however, inherent to this topology is the high communication cost, which for the most optimized implementation still requires $O(V)$ handshakes. The total communication cost incurred by *Allreduce* is $(V-1)\alpha + 2K\beta$, which becomes more pronounced in high latency network as latency grows in V, where V is the number of workers.

The *Ring* (R) topology proposed in [8] has a sparse averaging scheme, where at an averaging step each worker only averages with its two adjacent neighboring workers. This sparse connectivity incurs a very low communication cost of $2\alpha + 2K\beta$ per communication round. However, due to a sparse averaging, a worker on average has to take $O(V)$ averaging steps before it gets the contribution from its furthest neighbor, which causes high network error, requiring more iterations for a model to converge.

The *RingRandom* (RR) topology proposed in [9], improves the averaging steps by averaging randomly with a neighbor that is $2^i + 1$ hops away, where i is an integer between 0 and $log(V) - 1$. They also introduce a bipartite partitioning of the workers, where workers in an *active* group initiate the communication, whereas a *passive* group worker only responds to the request. These random re-links connect any pair of workers in $O(log(V))$ steps. The communication overhead is the same as the *Ring* topology, i.e. $2\alpha + 2K\beta$ per communication round.

2.4 *Ring-Star*: A Sparse Topology

The existing topologies discussed above either incur a high communication overhead or suffer from a low averaging operation which results in a high network error. Keeping in view these characteristics, we propose the *Ring-Star* topology that aims to reduce their disadvantages. In our proposed *Ring-Star* (RS) topology, distributed workers are divided into local groups and a worker from each group is selected as a *Delegate*. The *Delegate* is responsible for averaging models from the local group as well as exchange the group average with two neighboring *Delegates* (similar to a *Ring* topology). After the averaging step, each worker in the connected group gets the average of the two neighboring groups. Let the size of the local group be L then the size of the *Delegates Ring* becomes $G = V/L$. This significantly reduces the average age in $\mathbf{H}$, as each worker requires $O(G)$[1] averaging steps to get contribution from the furtherest worker, and speeds-up the information propagation among workers. *Ring-Star* incurs $((2(L-1)+2)\alpha+2K\beta$ communication cost, where $O(L)$ handshakes are required for local group averaging and two more handshakes are required for averaging between two *Delegates*. *Ring-Star* is a sparse topology, in which, after the averaging step each worker gets the contribution of a subset of workers, and it has a significantly different communication pattern from dense *Allreduce* [2,6], where after the averaging step each worker gets the contribution from all other workers. The characteristics of *Ring-Star* and other topologies are summarized in Table 1.

[1] replacing *Ring* for *Delegates* with *RingRandom* will give $O(log(G))$.

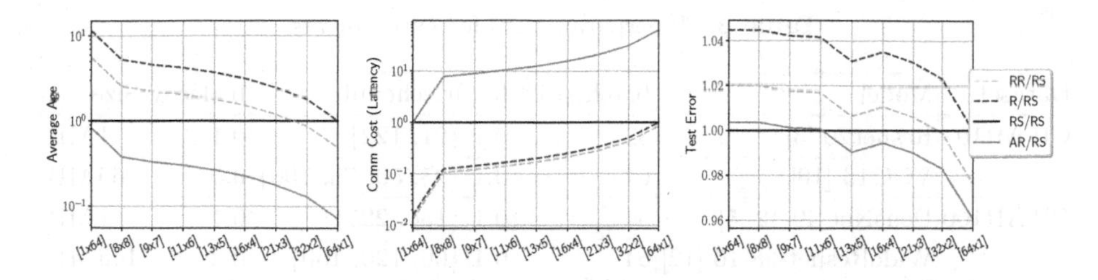

Fig. 1. Analysis of different group configurations for *Ring-Star*.

The group configuration of *Ring-Star*, i.e. $[G \times L]$, controls the sparsity in $\mathbf{W}$ and is a tunable parameter. We designed an experiment by training Resnet20 on the CIFAR10 dataset using 64 workers to analyze the effect of choosing the $[G \times L]$ on average age, communication cost and final test accuracy, and we have used the "Relative Gain"[2] $\in \mathbb{R}^+$ to compare *Ring-Star* and other topologies. Figure 1 shows that *Ring-Star* has better "Relative Gain" in average age over *Ring* and *RingRandom*, whereas it has a lower communication cost as compared to *Allreduce*. The test error of *Ring-Star* is also lower than *Ring* and *RingRandom* across different group configurations. It is also shown that choosing $L = 1$ retrieves the *Ring* topology and $L = V$ retrieves the *Allreduce* topology.

3 Experiments

In this section, we empirically investigate the effect of sparse topologies on the decentralized training of deep convolution neural networks for an image classification task. We selected well-known CIFAR10 and CIFAR100 as evaluation datasets for our experiments, which consists of 32×32 color images with 10 and 100 classes respectively and split into 50K train-set and 10K test-set. The deep learning models and hyperparameters for our experiments are summarized in Table 2. The models are implemented in PyTorch and the distributed framework is implemented using mpi4py. The experimental setup consists of nodes on the Google Cloud Platform (GCP), where each node is a "n1-standard-64" instance with Intel Xeon E5 v3 (Haswell) 64 vCPUs, 240 GB of memory, 1000GB SSD storage, and 4 Nvidia P100 GPUs. The nodes are connected through a 10Gbit/s Ethernet interconnect.

3.1 Convergence Behavior of Difference Topologies with Respect to Epochs

Experiments on CIFAR10: We looked at the convergence behaviors of different topologies on the CIFAR10 dataset by varying the number of workers. Figures 2(a) and (b) summarize the results on the CIFAR10 datasets for

[2] "Relative Gain" is a ratio between *Ring-Star* and other topologies, i.e. $\frac{AR}{RS} > 1$ indicates *Ring-Star* is better than *Allreduce* and $\frac{AR}{RS} < 1$ indicates otherwise.

Table 2. Hyperparameters for experiments

Dataset	Model	batch_size[a]	lr	lr_schedule	lr_decay	Size
CIFAR10	Resnet20 [3]	32	0.1	{81, 122}	0.1	1 MB
	VGG16 [10]	64	0.1	{25, 50, 75, 100}	0.5	60 MB
CIFAR100	DensNet-40-12 [5]	64	0.1	{150, 225}	0.1	1 MB
	WideResnet-28-10 [12]	64	0.1	{60, 120, 160}	0.2	146 MB

[a]The warmup learning rate scaling technique as described in [2] is employed for stabilizing the learning process for large batch sizes i.e $B_{\text{global}} = V \times B$.

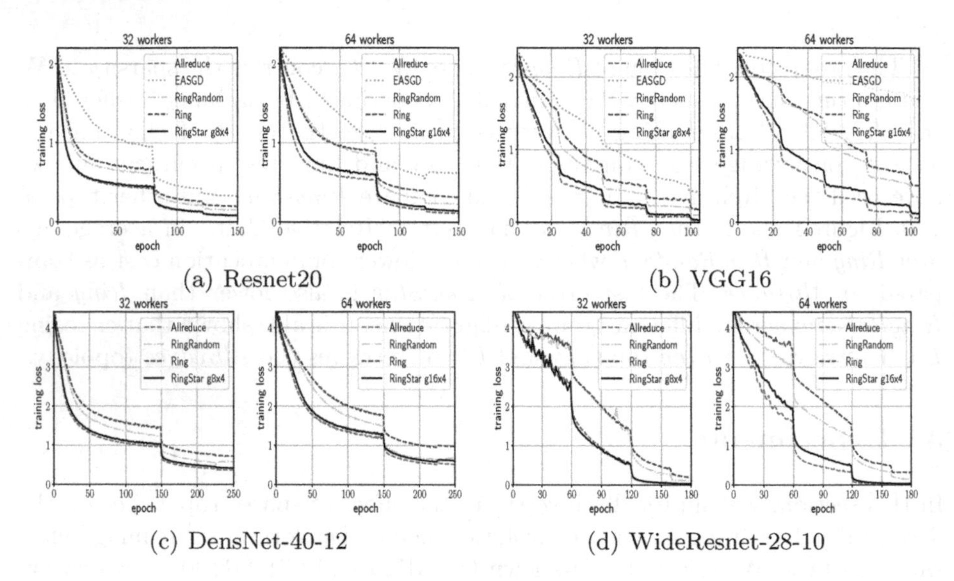

(a) Resnet20 (b) VGG16

(c) DensNet-40-12 (d) WideResnet-28-10

Fig. 2. Epoch-wise convergence behavior of different topologies on the CIFAR10 (a–b) and CIFAR100 (c–d) training using 32 and 64 workers.

Resnet20 and VGG16 respectively. The *Allreduce* and *Ring-Star* consistently show better performance across both the models. It can be seen that *Ring-Star* learning curves follow closely the *Allreduce* learning curves. The impact of fast averaging over all the workers becomes more pronounced as the number of workers is increased. The more sparsely connected workers in *Ring* and *RingRandom* have more divergence among the local models, and they tend to converge to the worst local optima. To overcome this issue, Lian et al. [9] decreased the learning rate for *Ring* and *RingRandom* earlier than *Allreduce* in their experiments for the number of workers ≥32 to stabilize the optimization. The final test accuracies in Table 3 also show a similar trend, where *Allreduce* and *Ring-Star* achieved the best test accuracy with minimum effect of increasing the number of workers. *EASGD* [14] performs the worst among all methods.

Experiments on CIFAR100: In this section, we present results on the CIFAR100 dataset. In these experiments, we choose complex workloads i.e.

Table 3. Comparison of test accuracy for the CIFAR10 experiments.

Model	Workers	*Allreduce*	*Ring-Star*	*RingRandom*	*Ring*	*EASGD* [14]
Resnet20	16 [4 × 4]	91.98%	91.93%	91.68%	91.59%	90.76%
	32 [8 × 4]	91.58%	91.42%	90.82%	90.70%	86.68%
	64 [16 × 4]	90.90%	90.50%	89.44%	87.32%	81.32%
VGG16	16 [4 × 4]	91.89%	91.57%	91.61%	91.43%	89.323%
	32 [8 × 4]	91.77%	91.44%	90.19%	89.71%	83.726%
	64 [16 × 4]	91.47%	91.25%	88.74%	86.04%	–

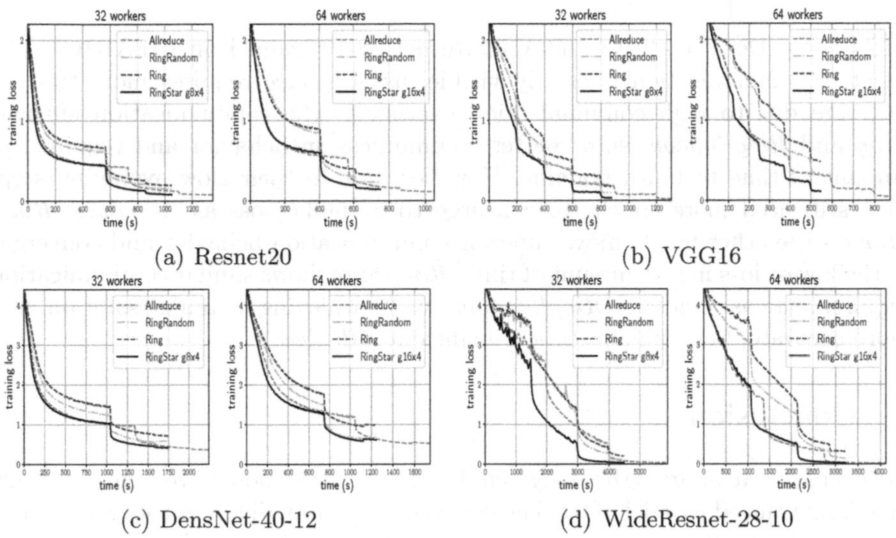

(a) Resnet20 (b) VGG16

(c) DensNet-40-12 (d) WideResnet-28-10

Fig. 3. Time-wise convergence behavior of different topologies on the CIFAR10 (a–b), and CIFAR100 (c–d) training using 32 and 64 workers.

DensNet-40-12 and WideResnet-28-10. Figures 2(c) and (d) summarize the results on the CIFAR100 datasets for DensNet-40-12 and WideResnet-28-10 respectively. The results show similar trends in the learning curves as for the CIFAR10 dataset. The hybrid *Ring-Star* is shown to perform at par with *Allreduce* in terms of final test accuracy (Table 4) as well as speed of convergence, whereas *Ring* and *RingRandom* suffers from a slow averaging step, which leads to slower learning.

3.2 Convergence Behavior of Difference Topologies with Respect to Time

In the second set of experiments, we analyze the convergence speed with respect to time. The comparisons of convergence with respect to time is presented in Figs. 3(a) and (b) for Resnet20 and VGG16 trained on CIFAR10, and Figs. 3(c)

Table 4. Comparison of test accuracy for the CIFAR100 experiments.

Model	Workers	*Allreduce*	*Ring-Star*	*RingRandom*	*Ring*
DensNet-40-12	16 [4×4]	71.59%	71.61%	71.11%	71.09%
	32 [8×4]	71.31%	71.24%	69.37%	67.91%
	64 [16×4]	71.25%	71.19%	68.70%	66.01%
WideResnet-28-10	16 [4×4]	78.86%	78.73%	78.49%	78.10%
	32 [8×4]	78.26%	78.31%	77.18%	76.37%
	64 [16×4]	78.15%	78.20%	76.23%	74.77%

and (d) for DensNet-40-12 and WideResnet-28-10 trained on CIFAR100. The effect of communication is clearly visible, as *Allreduce* requires more time to converge due to high communication overhead. The communication efficient *Ring* and *RingRandom* show better communication behavior and require less amount of time to finish training. However, due to their slow averaging step, they still need more epochs to converge to a similar loss as *Allreduce*. *Ring-Star* on the other hand enjoys superior communication behavior and converges to the lowest loss in less amount of time. *Ring-Star* shows similar communication requirements as *Ring* and *RingRandom*, while achieving a similar solution as a more accurate, but communication inefficient *Allreduce*.

4 Conclusion

In this paper we address the design choices for a sparse model averaging strategy in a decentralized parallel SGD. The detailed analysis of different topologies show the importance of averaging age, communication overhead and variance among workers, and how it could effect the overall learning behavior of the deep learning model. We propose a hierarchical two-layer sparse communication topology, a ring of fully-connected meshes of workers that communicate with each other (*Ring-Star*). *Ring-Star* allows a principled trade-off between convergence speed and communication overhead and is well suited to loosely coupled distributed systems. We demonstrate on an image classification task and a batch stochastic gradient descent learning (SGD) algorithm that our proposed method shows similar convergence behavior as *Allreduce* while having lower communication cost of *Ring*.

References

1. Bijral, A.S., Sarwate, A.D., Srebro, N.: Data-dependent convergence for consensus stochastic optimization. IEEE Trans. Autom. Control **62**(9), 4483–4498 (2017)
2. Goyal, P., et al.: Accurate, large minibatch SGD: training imagenet in 1 hour. CoRR abs/1706.02677 (2017)
3. He, K., Zhang, X., Ren, S., Sun, J.: Deep residual learning for image recognition. In: CVPR 2016, pp. 770–778 (2016)

4. Ho, Q., et al.: More effective distributed ml via a stale synchronous parallel parameter server. In: NIPS 2013, pp. 1223–1231 (2013)
5. Huang, G., Liu, Z., van der Maaten, L., Weinberger, K.Q.: Densely connected convolutional networks. In: CVPR 2017, pp. 2261–2269 (2017)
6. Jia, X., et al.: Highly scalable deep learning training system with mixed-precision: training imagenet in four minutes. CoRR abs/1807.11205 (2018)
7. Li, M., Andersen, D.G., Smola, A.J., Yu, K.: Communication efficient distributed machine learning with the parameter server. In: NIPS 2014, pp. 19–27 (2014)
8. Lian, X., Zhang, C., Zhang, H., Hsieh, C.J., Zhang, W., Liu, J.: Can decentralized algorithms outperform centralized algorithms? A case study for decentralized parallel stochastic gradient descent. In: NIPS 2017, pp. 5330–5340 (2017)
9. Lian, X., Zhang, W., Zhang, C., Liu, J.: Asynchronous decentralized parallel stochastic gradient descent. In: ICML 2018, pp. 3049–3058 (2018)
10. Simonyan, K., Zisserman, A.: Very deep convolutional networks for large-scale image recognition. CoRR abs/1409.1556 (2014)
11. Thakur, R., Rabenseifner, R., Gropp, W.: Optimization of collective communication operations in MPICH. Int. J. High Perform. Comput. Appl. **19**(1), 49–66 (2005)
12. Zagoruyko, S., Komodakis, N.: Wide residual networks. In: Proceedings of the British Machine Vision Conference (BMVC), pp. 87.1–87.12 (2016)
13. Zhang, J., Sa, C.D., Mitliagkas, I., Ré, C.: Parallel SGD: when does averaging help. In: Optimization in Machine Learning Workshop ICML (2016)
14. Zhang, S., Choromanska, A.E., LeCun, Y.: Deep learning with elastic averaging SGD. In: NIPS 2015, pp. 685–693 (2015)

Hardware Acceleration of Machine Learning Beyond Linear Algebra

Sascha Mücke(✉), Nico Piatkowski, and Katharina Morik

AI Group, TU Dortmund, Dortmund, Germany
sascha.muecke@tu-dortmund.de
http://www-ai.cs.tu-dortmund.de

Abstract. Specialized hardware for machine learning allows us to train highly accurate models in hours which would otherwise take days or months of computation time. The advent of recent deep learning techniques can largely be explained by the fact that their training and inference rely heavily on fast matrix algebra that can be accelerated easily via programmable graphics processing units (GPU). Thus, vendors praise the GPU as *the* hardware for machine learning. However, those accelerators have an energy consumption of several hundred Watts. In distributed learning, each node has to meet resource constraints that exceed those of an ordinary workstation—especially when learning is performed at the edge, i.e., close to the data source. The energy consumption is typically highly restricted, and relying on high-end CPUs and GPUs is thus not a viable option. In this work, we present our new quantum-inspired machine learning hardware accelerator. More precisely, we explain how our hardware approximates the solution to several NP-hard data mining and machine learning problems, including k-means clustering, maximum-a-posterior prediction, and binary support vector machine learning. Our device has a worst-case energy consumption of about 1.5 W and is thus especially well suited for distributed learning at the edge.

Keywords: Hardware acceleration · Machine learning · FPGA

1 Introduction

Hardware acceleration for machine learning usually refers to GPU implementations that can do fast linear algebra to enhance the speed of numerical computations. This, however, includes the implicit assumptions that (1) the learning problem can actually benefit from fast linear algebra, i.e., the most complex parts of learning and inference can be phrased in the language of matrix-vector calculus. And (2), learning is carried out in an environment where energy supply, size, and weight of the system are mostly unrestricted. The latter assumption is indeed violated when learning has to be carried out at the edge, that is, on the device that actually measures the data.

P. Cellier and K. Driessens (Eds.): ECML PKDD 2019 Workshops, CCIS 1167, pp. 342–347, 2020.
https://doi.org/10.1007/978-3-030-43823-4_29

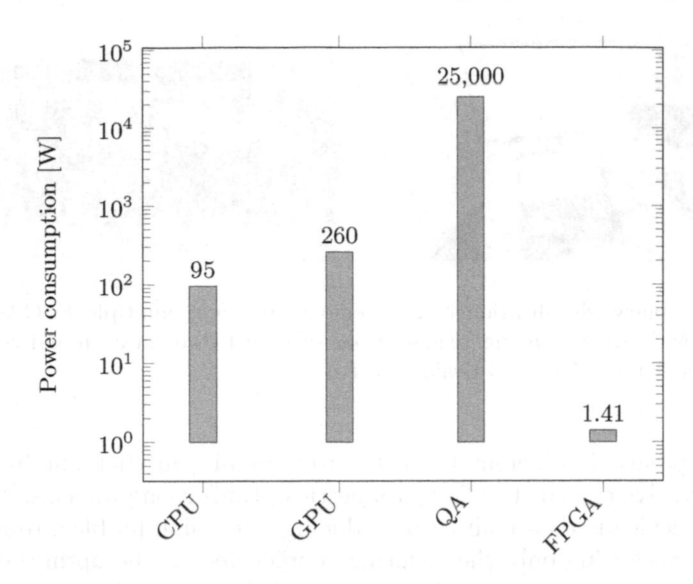

Fig. 1. Power consumption of different hardware solutions for machine learning; CPU: Intel Core i7-9700K, GPU: Nvidia GEFORCE RTX 2080 Ti, QA (Quantum Annealer): D-Wave 2000Q, FPGA: Kintex-7 KC705

Especially in the distributed or federated learning settings, edge devices are subject to strong resource constraints. Communication efficiency [6] and computational burden [3,7] must be reduced, in order to get along with the available hardware. One way to address these issues are efficient decentralized learning schemes [5]. However, the resource consumption of state-of-the-art hardware accelerators are often out of reach for edge devices.

We thus present a novel hardware architecture that can be used as a solver at the core of various data mining and machine learning techniques, some of which we will explain in the following sections. Our work is inspired by the so-called *quantum annealer*, a hardware architecture for solving discrete optimization problems by exploiting quantum mechanical effects. In contrast to GPUs and quantum annealers, our device has a highly reduced resource consumption. The power consumption of four machine learning accelerators is shown in Fig. 1. For the CPU and GPU, we provide the thermal design power (TDP), whereas the FPGA's value is the total on-chip power, calculated using the Vivado Design Suite[1]. We see that the actual peak consumption of CPUs and GPUs exceeds the energy consumption of our device by several orders of magnitude. Moreover, we provide the estimated energy consumption of the D-Wave 2000Q quantum annealer. The annealer optimizes the exact same objective function as our device, but the cooling and magnetic shielding required for its operation leads to an enormous energy consumption, which is very impractical for real applications at its current stage. Hence, its low resource requirements and versatility makes our device the ideal hardware accelerator for distributed learning at the edge.

[1] https://www.xilinx.com/products/design-tools/vivado.html.

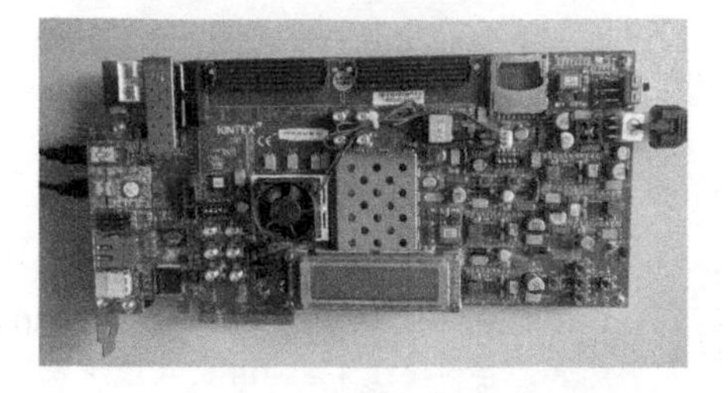

Fig. 2. Exemplary visualization of the demo setup; *left:* multiple FPGAs (Kintex-7, Artix-7) with accompanying visualizations of board configuration and convergence results; *right:* Kintex-7 KC705 Evaluation Kit

Our approach is different to GPU programming in that our hardware is designed to solve a fixed class $\mathcal{C}$ of parametric optimization problems. "Programming" our device is then realized by reducing a learning problem to a member of $\mathcal{C}$ and transferring only the resulting coefficients β. The optimization step, e.g. model training, is performed entirely on the board, without any additional communication cost.

In our demo setup (shown in Fig. 2) we will showcase several machine learning tasks in a live setting on multiple devices, accompanied by live visualizations of the learning progress and the results.

The underlying idea of using a non-universal compute-architecture for machine learning is indeed not new: State-of-the-art quantum annealers rely on the very same problem formulation. There, optimization problem are encoded as potential energy between *qubits* – the global minimum of a loss function can be interpreted as the quantum state of lowest energy [4]. The fundamentally non-deterministic nature of quantum methods makes the daunting task of traversing an exponentially large solution space feasible. However, their practical implementation is a persisting challenge, and the development of actual quantum hardware is still in its infancy. The latest flagship, the *D-Wave 2000Q*, can handle problems with 64 fully connected bits[2], which is by far not sufficient for realistic problem sizes.

Nevertheless, the particular class of optimization problems that quantum annealers can solve is well understood which motivates its use for hardware accelerators outside of the quantum world.

2 Boolean Optimization

A *pseudo-Boolean function* (PBF) is any function $f : \mathbb{B}^n \mapsto \mathbb{R}$ that assigns a real value to a fixed-length binary vector. Every PBF on n binary variables can be uniquely expressed as a polynomial of some degree $d \leq n$ with real-valued coefficients [2]. *Quadratic Unconstrained Binary Optimization* (QUBO) is the

[2] https://www.dwavesys.com/sites/default/files/mwj_dwave_qubits2018.pdf.

problem of finding an assignment $\boldsymbol{x}^*$ of n binary variables that is minimal with respect to a second degree Boolean polynomial:

$$\boldsymbol{x}^* = \arg\min_{\boldsymbol{x}\in\mathbb{B}^n} \sum_{i=1}^{n}\sum_{j=1}^{i} \beta_{ij}\boldsymbol{x}_i\boldsymbol{x}_j$$

It has been shown that all higher-degree pseudo-Boolean optimization problems can be reduced to quadratic problems [2]. For this reason a variety of well-known optimization problems like (Max-)3SAT and prime factorization, but also ML-related problems like clustering, maximum-a-posterior (MAP) estimation in Markov Random Fields and binary constrained SVM learning can be reduced to QUBO or its *Ising*-variant (where $\boldsymbol{x} \in \{-1, +1\}^n$). In our demo, we will explain the impact of different reductions in terms of runtime and quality of different learning tasks.

3 Evolutionary QUBO Solver

If no specialized algorithm is known for a particular hard combinatorial optimization problem, randomized search heuristics, like simulated annealing or *evolutionary algorithms* (EA), provide a generic way to generate good solutions.

Inspired by biological evolution, EAs employ recombination and mutation on a set of "parent" solutions to produce a set of "offspring" solutions. A loss function, also called *fitness function* in the EA-context, is used to select those solutions which will constitute the next parent generation. This process is repeated until convergence or a pre-specified time-budget is exhausted [8].

Motivated by the inherently parallel nature of digital circuits, we developed a highly customizable $(\mu + \lambda)$-EA architecture on FPGA hardware implemented using the VHDL language[3]. Here, "customizable" implies that different types of FPGA hardware, from small to large, can be used. This is done by allowing the end-user to customize the maximal problem dimension n, the number of parent solutions μ, the number of offspring solutions λ and the number of bits per coefficient β_{ij}. In case of low-budget FPGA, this allows us to either allocate more FPGA resources for parallel computation (μ and λ) or for the problem size (n and β). We will show how to generate and run chip designs for low-budget as well as high-end devices in our demo.

4 Exemplary Learning Tasks

"Programming" our devices reduces to determining the corresponding coefficients β and uploading them to the FPGA via our Python interface. We will explain how this is done for various machine learning tasks, two of which we will explain below:

A prototypical data mining problem is k-means clustering which is already NP-hard for $k = 2$. To derive β for a 2-means clustering problem, we use the

[3] https://www.ics.uci.edu/~jmoorkan/vhdlref/Synario%20VHDL%20Manual.pdf.

method devised in [1], where each bit indicates whether the corresponding data point belongs to cluster 1 or cluster 2—the problem dimension is thus $n = |\mathcal{D}|$. The coefficients are then derived from the centered Gramian $\boldsymbol{G}$ over the mean adjusted data. To keep as much precision as possible, we stretch the parameters to use the full range of b bits before rounding, so the final formula is $\beta_{ij} = \lfloor \alpha \boldsymbol{G}_{ij} + 0.5 \rfloor$ with $\alpha = (2^{b-1} - 1)/\max_{i,j} |\boldsymbol{G}_{ij}|$. Exemplary results on the UCI data sets *Iris* and *Sonar* are shown in Fig. 3 (top).

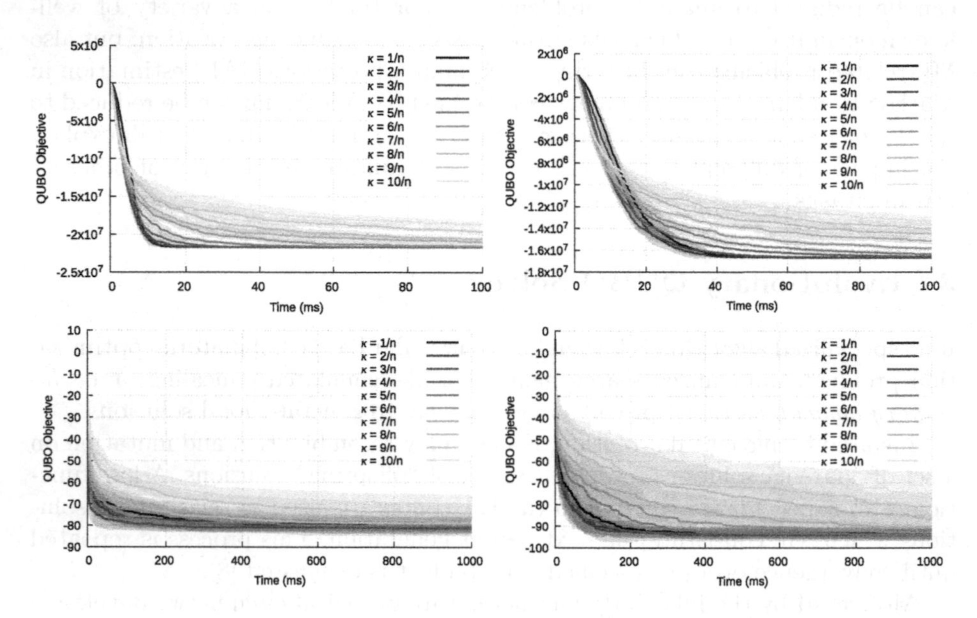

Fig. 3. QUBO loss value over time with different mutation rates, each averaged over 10 runs. Uncertainty indicated by transparent areas. Top-left: 2-means on *Iris* ($n = 150$, $d = 4$). Top-right: 2-means on *Sonar* ($n = 208$, $d = 61$). Bottom-left: MRF-MAP with edge encoding. Bottom-right: MRF-MAP with vertex encoding.

Another typical NP-hard ML problem is to determine the most likely configuration of variables in a Markov Random Field, known as the MAP prediction problem [9]. Similar to efficiency differences between programs for classical universal computers, providing a different QUBO problem encoding has implications for the efficiency of our device. To demonstrate this effect, we will perform a live comparison of different encodings in terms of convergence behavior.

One possible solution for the MRF-MAP problem is to encode the assignments of all X_v as a concatenation of one-hot encodings

$$(X_1 = x_1^{i_1}, \ldots, X_m = x_m^{i_m}) \mapsto \underbrace{0\ldots010\ldots0}_{|\mathcal{X}_1|}\ldots\underbrace{0\ldots010\ldots0}_{|\mathcal{X}_m|},$$

where $m = |V|$ and x_k^i is the i-th value in $\mathcal{X}_k$. The weights $-\theta_{uv=xy}$ are encoded into the quadratic coefficients; if two different bits belong to the same variable encoding, a penalty weight is added between them to maintain a valid one-hot. The negative sign is added to turn MAP into a minimization problem.

For a different possible solution, we may assign bits $b_{uv=xy}$ to all non-zero weights $\theta_{uv=xy}$ between specific values x, y of two variables X_u, X_v, indicating that $X_u = x$ and $X_v = y$. Again, to avoid multiple assignments of the same variable we introduce penalty weights between pairs of edges. We can see in Fig. 3 (bottom) that both approaches lead to a different convergence behavior.

In addition to k-means and MRF-MAP, the demo will include binary SVM learning, binary MRF parameter learning, and others.

A video demonstrating how to use our system by solving a clustering problem can be found here: https://youtu.be/Xj5xx-eO1Mk.

References

1. Bauckhage, C., Ojeda, C., Sifa, R., Wrobel, S.: Adiabatic quantum computing for kernel k=2 means clustering. In: Proceedings of the LWDA 2018, pp. 21–32 (2018)
2. Boros, E., Hammer, P.L.: Pseudo-Boolean optimization. Discret. Appl. Math. **123**(1–3), 155–225 (2002)
3. Caldas, S., Konecný, J., McMahan, H.B., Talwalkar, A.: Expanding the reach of federated learning by reducing client resource requirements. CoRR abs/1812.07210 (2018). http://arxiv.org/abs/1812.07210
4. Kadowaki, T., Nishimori, H.: Quantum annealing in the transverse Ising model. Phys. Rev. E **58**(5), 5355 (1998)
5. Kamp, M., et al.: Efficient decentralized deep learning by dynamic model averaging. In: Berlingerio, M., Bonchi, F., Gärtner, T., Hurley, N., Ifrim, G. (eds.) ECML PKDD 2018. LNCS (LNAI), vol. 11051, pp. 393–409. Springer, Cham (2019). https://doi.org/10.1007/978-3-030-10925-7_24
6. Konecný, J., McMahan, H.B., Yu, F.X., Richtárik, P., Suresh, A.T., Bacon, D.: Federated learning: strategies for improving communication efficiency. CoRR abs/1610.05492 (2016). http://arxiv.org/abs/1610.05492
7. Piatkowski, N., Lee, S., Morik, K.: Integer undirected graphical models for resource-constrained systems. Neurocomputing **173**, 9–23 (2016)
8. Schwefel, H.-P., Rudolph, G.: Contemporary evolution strategies. In: Morán, F., Moreno, A., Merelo, J.J., Chacón, P. (eds.) ECAL 1995. LNCS, vol. 929, pp. 891–907. Springer, Heidelberg (1995). https://doi.org/10.1007/3-540-59496-5_351
9. Wainwright, M.J., Jordan, M.I., et al.: Graphical models, exponential families, and variational inference. F+ Trends Mach. Learn. **1**(1–2), 1–305 (2008)

Advances in Managing and Mining Large Evolving Graphs - 3rd Edition (LEG)

LEG - Advances in Managing and Mining Large Evolving Graphs (3rd Edition)

Workshop Description

The aim of the workshop "Managing and mining Large Evolving Graphs" (LEG) is to bring together active scholars and practitioners of dynamic graphs. Graph models and algorithms are ubiquitous of a large number of application domains, ranging from transportation to social networks, semantic web, or data mining. However, many applications require graph models that are time dependent. For example, applications related to urban mobility analysis employ a graph structure of the underlying road network where the traffic density and speed continuously change over time. Therefore, the time a moving object takes to cross a path segment typically depends on the starting instant of time. This dynamicity makes it more challenging to mine temporal and graph patterns, yet this task is essential to study such structures. The same holds in other contexts, such as social networks.

In this workshop, we aim to discuss the problem of mining large evolving graphs, since many real world applications deal with large volumes of data. Managing and analysing large evolving graphs is very challenging and requires sophisticated methods and techniques for creating, storing, accessing, processing, and mining such large evolving graphs. These techniques typically require a distributed environment, because centralized approaches do not scale in a Big Data scenario. Contributions will clearly point out answers to one of these challenges focusing on large-scale graphs.

Description of the Workshop's Topic and its Goals

The workshop seeks papers with important new insights and experiences on knowledge discovery aspects with dynamic and large-scale time-dependent graphs. The goal is to shed light on the questions mentioned above, related to the knowledge discovery process. Topics of interest include, but are not limited to, the following linked topics, with regards to mining process:

- Large scale graph analysis
- Theoretical foundation of time-dependent and large scale graphs (LEG)
- Construction and maintenance of LEG
- Data quality in LEG
- Data integration in LEG
- Indexing techniques for LEG
- Distributed algorithms & navigational query processing
- LEG data mining: frequent pattern, similarity, cluster analysis, predictive learning
- Trajectory mining in LEG

- Probabilistic LEG
- Applications related to LEG
- Algorithms on LEG

We have received eleven submissions and we have accepted six as full papers and 1 as short paper. Each paper received three reviews. Five full papers are published in this proceedings. The workshop also included the invited talk "*Efficient Structural Embeddings in Large Time-varying Networks*" from Danai Koutra, Computer Science and Engineering University of Michigan.

Organization

Program Chairs

Sabeur Aridhi	LORIA/Inria NGE, University of Lorraine, France https://members.loria.fr/SAridhi/
José Antonio de Macedo	Universidade Federal do Ceará, Fortaleza, Brazil https://josemacedo.github.io/
Engelbert Mephu Nguifo	LIMOS, Université Clermont Auvergne, France http://www.isima.fr/mephu
Karine Zeitouni	DAVID, Université de Versailles Saint-Quentin, France http://www.david.uvsq.fr/zeitouni

Program Committee

Radu Ciucanu	LIFO, Université d'Orléans, France
Wajdi Dhifli	Institute of Systems & Synthetic Biology, Université de Lille, France
Chiara Renso	ISTI-CNR, Italy
Remy Cazabet	LIRIS, Université de Lyon, France
José Antonio de Macedo	Universidade Federal do Ceará, Fortaleza, Brazil
Zoubida Kedad	DAVID, Université de Versailles Saint-Quentin, France
Ticiana L. Linhares	Universidade Federal do Ceará, Fortaleza, Brazil
Malika Smail-Tabbone	LORIA, University of Lorraine, France
Sabeur Aridhi	LORIA, University of Lorraine, France
Engelbert Mephu Nguifo	LIMOS, Université Clermont Auvergne, France
Karine Zeitouni	DAVID, Université de Versailles Saint-Quentin, France
Ana-Paula Appel	IBM Research, Brazil
Raja Chiky	ISEP Paris, France
Renato Cunha	IBM, Brazil
Issam Falih	LIMOS, Université Clermont Auvergne, France
Alberto Montresor	University of Trento, Italy
Vincent Oria	New Jersey Institute of Technology, USA
Fabio Porto	National Laboratory of Scientific Computation, Brazil
Jan Ramon	Katholieke Universiteit Leuven, Belgium
Yannis Velegrakis	University of Trento, Italy

Detecting Stable Communities in Link Streams at Multiple Temporal Scales

Souâad Boudebza[1(✉)], Rémy Cazabet[2], Omar Nouali[3], and Faiçal Azouaou[1]

[1] Ecole nationale Supérieure d'Informatique, BP 68M, 16309 Oued-Smar, Alger, Algeria
s_boudebza@esi.dz

[2] Univ Lyon, Universite Lyon 1, CNRS, LIRIS UMR5205, 69622 Lyon, France

[3] Division de Recherche en Théorie et Ingénierie des Systèmes Informatiques, CERIST, Rue des Frères Aissiou, Ben Aknoun, Alger, Algeria

Abstract. Link streams model interactions over time in a wide range of fields. Under this model, the challenge is to mine efficiently both temporal and topological structures. Community detection and change point detection are one of the most powerful tools to analyze such evolving interactions. In this paper, we build on both to detect stable community structures by identifying change points within meaningful communities. Unlike existing dynamic community detection algorithms, the proposed method is able to discover stable communities efficiently at multiple temporal scales. We test the effectiveness of our method on synthetic networks, and on high-resolution time-varying networks of contacts drawn from real social networks.

1 Introduction

In recent years, studying interactions over time has witnessed a growing interest in a wide range of fields, such as sociology, biology, physics, etc. Such dynamic interactions are often represented using the snapshot model: the network is divided into a sequence of static networks, i.e., snapshots, aggregating all contacts occurring in a given time window. The main drawback of this model is that it often requires to choose arbitrarily a temporal scale of analysis. The link stream model [9] is a more effective way for representing interactions over time, that can fully capture the underling temporal information.

Real world networks evolve frequently at many different time scales. Fluctuations in such networks can be observed at yearly, monthly, daily, hourly, or even smaller scales. For instance, if one were to look at interactions among workers in a company or laboratory, one could expect to discover clusters of people corresponding to *meetings* and/or *coffee breaks*, interacting at **high frequency** (e.g., every few seconds) for **short periods** (e.g., few minutes), *project members*

This work was supported by the ACADEMICS grant of the IDEXLYON, project of the Universite de Lyon, PIA operated by **ANR-16-IDEX-0005**, and of the project **ANR-18-CE23-0004** of the French National Research Agency (ANR).

P. Cellier and K. Driessens (Eds.): ECML PKDD 2019 Workshops, CCIS 1167, pp. 353–367, 2020.
https://doi.org/10.1007/978-3-030-43823-4_30

interacting at medium frequency (e.g., once a day) for medium periods (e.g., a few months), *coordination groups* interacting at low frequency (e.g., once a month) for longer periods (e.g., a few years), etc.

An analysis of communities found at an arbitrary chosen scale would necessarily miss some of these communities: low latency ones are invisible using short aggregation windows, while high frequency ones are lost in the noise for long aggregation windows. A multiple temporal scale analysis of communities seems therefore the right solution to study networks of interactions represented as link streams.

To the best of our knowledge, no such method exists in the literature. In this article, we propose a method having roots both in the literature on change point detection and in dynamic community detection. It detects what we call **stable communities**, i.e., *groups of nodes* forming a *coherent community* throughout a *period of time*, at a given *temporal scale.*

The remainder of this paper is organized as follows. In Sect. 2, we present a brief review of related works. Then, we describe the proposed framework in detail in Sect. 3. We experimentally evaluate the proposed method on both synthetic and real-world networks in Sect. 4.

2 Related Work

Our contribution relates to two active body of research: (i) dynamic community detection and (ii) change point detection. The aim of the former is to discover groups of nodes that persist over time, while the objective of the latter is to detect changes in the overall structure of a dynamic network. In this section, we present existing work in both categories, and how our proposed method relates to them.

2.1 Dynamic Community Detection

The problem of detecting communities in dynamic networks has attracted a lot of attention in recent years, with various approaches tackling different aspects of the problem, see [16] for a recent survey. Most of these methods consider that the studied dynamic networks are represented as sequences of snapshots, with each snapshot being a well formed graph with meaningful community structure, see for instance [5,12]. Some other methods work with interval graphs, and update the community structure at each network change, e.g., [3,17]. However, all those methods are not adapted to deal with link streams, for which the network is usually not well formed at any given time. Using them on such a network would require to first aggregate the links of the stream by choosing an arbitrarily temporal scale (aggregation window).

2.2 Change Point Detection

Our work is also related to research conducted on change point detection considering community structures. In these approaches, given a sequence of snapshots, one wants to detect the periods during which the network organization and/or the community structure remains stable. In [15], the authors proposed the first change-point detection method for evolving networks that uses generative network models and statistical hypothesis testing. Wang et al. [19] proposed a hierarchical change point detection method to detect both inter-community (local change) and intra-community (global change) evolution. A recent work by Masuda et al. [11] used graph distance measures and hierarchical clustering to identify sequences of system state dynamics.

From those methods, our proposal keeps the principle of stable periods delimited by change points, and the idea of detecting changes at local and global scales. But our method differs in two directions: (*i*) we are searching for stable individual communities instead of stable graph periods, and (*ii*) we search for stable structures at multiple levels of temporal granularity.

3 Method

The goal of our proposed method is (*i*) to detect stable communities (*ii*) at multiple scales without redundancy and (*iii*) to do so efficiently. We adopt an iterative approach, searching communities from the coarser to the more detailed temporal scales. At each temporal scale, we use a three step process:

1. **Seed Discovery**, to find relevant community seeds at this temporal scale.
2. **Seed Pruning**, to remove seeds which are redundant with communities found at higher scales.
3. **Seed Expansion**, expanding seeds in time to discover stable communities.

We start by presenting each of these three steps, and then we describe the method used to iterate through the different scales in Sect. 3.4.

Our work aims to provide a general framework that could serve as baseline for further work in this field. We define three generic functions that can be set according to the user needs:

- **CD**(g), a static community detection algorithm on a graph g.
- **QC**(N, g), a function to assess the quality of a community defined by the set of nodes N on a graph g.
- **CSS**(N_1,N_2), a function to assess the similarity of two sets of nodes N_1 and N_2.

See Sect. 3.5 on how to choose proper functions for those tasks.

We define a stable dynamic community c as a triplet $c = (N, p, \gamma)$, with $c.N$ the list of nodes in the community, $c.p$ its period of existence defined as an interval, e.g., $c.p = [t_1, t_2]$[1] means that the community c exists from t_1 to t_2, and $c.\gamma$ the temporal granularity at which c has been discovered.

We denote the set of all stable dynamic communities $\mathcal{D}$.

[1] We use right open intervals such as a community starting at t_x and another one ending at the same t_x have an empty intersection, which is necessary to have coherent results when handling discrete time steps.

3.1 Seed Discovery

For each temporal scale, we first search for interesting seeds. A temporal scale is defined by a granularity γ, expressed as a period of time (e.g.; 20 min, 1 h, 2 weeks, etc.). We use this granularity as a window size, and, starting from a time t_0 – by default, the date of the first observed interaction – we create a cumulative graph (snapshot) for every period $[t_0, t_0+\gamma[$, $[t_0+\gamma, t_0+2\gamma[$, $[t_0+2\gamma, t_0+3\gamma[$, *etc.*, until all interactions belong to a cumulative graph. This process yields a sequence of static graphs, such as $G_{t_0,\gamma}$ is a cumulated snapshot of link stream G for the period starting at t_0 and of duration γ. G_γ is the list of all such graphs.

Given a static community detection algorithm CD yielding a set of communities, and a function to assess the quality of communities QC, we apply CD on each snapshot and filter promising seeds, i.e., high quality communities, using QC. The set of valid seeds $\mathcal{S}$ is therefore defined as:

$$\mathcal{S} = \{\forall g \in G_\gamma, \forall s \in CD(g), QC(s,g) > \theta_q\} \quad (1)$$

With θ_q a threshold of community quality.

Since community detection at each step is independent, we can run it in parallel on all steps, this is an important aspect for scalability.

3.2 Seed Pruning

The seed pruning step has a twofold objective: (*i*) reducing redundancy and (*ii*) speed up the multi-scale community detection process. Given a measure of structural similarity CSS, we prune the less interesting seeds, such as the set of filtered seeds $\mathcal{FS}$ is defined as:

$$\mathcal{FS} = \{\forall s \in \mathcal{S}, \forall c \in \mathcal{D}, (CSS(s.N, c.N) > \theta_s) \vee (s.p \cap c.p = \{\emptyset\}) \quad (2)$$

Where $\mathcal{D}$ is the set of stable communities discovered at coarser (or similar, see next section) scales, $s.p$ is the interval corresponding to the snapshot at which this seed has been discovered, and θ_s is a threshold of similarity.

Said otherwise, we keep as interesting seeds those that are not redundant topologically (in term of nodes/edges), OR not redundant temporally. A seed is kept if it corresponds to a situation never seen before.

3.3 Seed Expansion

The aim of this step is to assess whether a seed corresponds to a *stable* dynamic community. The *instability* problem has been identified since the early stages of the dynamic community detection field [1]. It means that the same algorithm ran twice on the same network after introducing minor random modifications might yield very different results. As a consequence, one cannot know if the differences observed between the community structure found at t and at $t+1$ are due to structural changes or to the instability of the algorithm. This problem is usually solved by introducing smoothing techniques [16]. Our method use a similar approach, but instead of comparing communities found at step t and $t-1$, we check whether a community found at t is still relevant in previous and following steps, recursively.

More formally, for each seed $s \in FS$ found on the graph $G_{t,\gamma}$, we iteratively expand the duration of the seed $s.d = [t, t+\gamma[$ (where t is the time start of this duration) at each step t_i in both temporal directions ($t_i \in (...[t-2\gamma, t-\gamma[, [t-\gamma, t]; [t+\gamma, t+2\gamma[, [t+2\gamma, t+3\gamma]...)$) as long as the quality $QC(s.N, G_{t_i,\gamma})$ of the community defined by the nodes $s.N$ on the graph at $G_{t_i,\gamma}$ is good enough. Here, we use the same similarity threshold θ_s as in the seed pruning step. If the final duration period $|s.p|$ of the expanded seed is higher than a duration $\theta_p\gamma$, with θ_p a threshold of stability, the expanded seed is added to the list of stable communities, otherwise, it is discarded. This step is formalized in Algorithm 1.

Algorithm 1: Forward seed expansion. Forward temporal expansion of a seed s found at time t of granularity γ. The reciprocal algorithm is used for *backward* expansion: $t+1$ becomes $t-1$.

Input: $s, \gamma, \theta_p, \theta_s$
1 $t \leftarrow t^{start} | s.p = [t^{start}, t^{end}[$;
2 $g \leftarrow G_{t,\gamma}$;
3 $p \leftarrow [t, t+\gamma[$;
4 **while** $QC(s.N, g) > \theta_s$ **do**
5 $\quad s.p \leftarrow s.p \cup p$;
6 $\quad t \leftarrow t+\gamma$;
7 $\quad p \leftarrow [t, t+\gamma[$;
8 $\quad g \leftarrow G_{t,\gamma}$;
9 **end**
10 **if** $|s.p| \geq \theta_p\gamma$ **then**
11 $\quad \mathcal{D} \leftarrow \mathcal{D} \cup \{s\}$;
12 **end**

In order to select the most relevant stable communities, we consider seeds in descending order of their QC score, i.e., the seeds of higher quality scores are considered first. Due to the pruning strategy, a community of lowest quality might be pruned by a community of highest quality at the same granularity γ.

3.4 Multi-scale Iterative Process

Until then, we have seen how communities are found for a particular time scale. In order to detect communities at multiple scales, we first define the ordered list of studied scales Γ. The largest scale is defined as $\gamma^{max} = |G.d|/\theta_p$, with $|G.d|$ the total duration of the dynamic graph. Since we need to observe at least θ_p successive steps to consider the community stable, γ^{max} is the largest scale at which communities can be found.

We then define Γ as the ordered list:

$$\Gamma = [\gamma^{max}, \gamma^{max}/2^1, \gamma^{max}/2^2, \gamma^{max}/2^3, ..., \gamma^{max}/2^k] \tag{3}$$

With k such as $\gamma^{max}/2^k > \theta_\gamma >= \gamma^{max}/2^{k+1}$, θ_γ being a parameter corresponding to the finest temporal granularity to evaluate, which is necessarily data-dependant (if time is represented as a continuous property, this value can be fixed at least at the sampling rate of data collection).

This exponential reduction in the studied scale guarantees a limited number of scales to study.

The process to find seeds and extend them into communities is then summarized in Algorithm 2.

Algorithm 2: Multi-temporal-scale stable communities finding. Summary of the proposed method. See corresponding sections for the details of each step. G is the link streams to analyze, $\theta_q, \theta_s, \theta_p, \theta_\gamma$ are threshold parameters.

```
   Input: G, θq, θs, θp, θγ
1  D ← {∅};
2  Γ ←studied_scales(G, θγ) ;
3  for γ ∈ Γ do
4      S ← Seed_Discovery(γ, CD, QC, θq);
5      FS ←Seed_Pruning(S, CSS, θs);
6      for s ∈ FS do
7          Seed_Expansion(s, γ, θp, θs);
8      end
9  end
```

3.5 Choosing Functions and Parameters

The proposed method is a general framework that can be implemented using different functions for CD, QC and CSS. This section provides explicit guidance for selecting each function, and introduces the choices we make for the experimental section.

Community Detection - CD. Any algorithm for community detection could be used, including overlapping methods, since each community is considered as an independant seed. Following literature consensus, we use the Louvain method [2], which yields non-overlapping communities using a greedy modularity-maximization method. The louvain method performs well on static networks, it is in particular among the fastest and most efficient methods. Note that it would be meaningful to adopt an algorithm yielding communities of good quality according to the chosen QC, which is not the case in our experiments, as we wanted to use the most standard algorithms and quality functions in order to show the genericity of our approach.

Quality of Communities - QC. The QC quality function must express the quality of a set of nodes w.r.t a given network, unlike functions such as the modularity, which express the quality of a whole partition w.r.t a given network.

Many such functions exist, like *Link Density* or *Scaled Density* [7], but the most studied one is probably the *Conductance* [10]. Conductance is defined as the ratio of (i) the number of edges between nodes inside the community and nodes outside the community, and (ii) the sum of degrees of nodes inside the community (or outside, if this value is larger). More formally, the conductance ϕ of a community C is:

$$\phi(C) = \frac{\sum_{i \in C, j \notin C} A_{i,j}}{Min(A(C), A(\bar{C}))}$$

Where A is the adjacency matrix of the network, $A(C) = \sum_{i \in C} \sum_{j \in V} A_{i,j}$ and $\bar{C}$ is the complement of C. Its value ranges from 0 (Best, all edges starting from nodes of the community are internal) to 1 (Worst, no edges between this community and the rest of the network). Since our generic framework expects good communities to have QC scores higher than the threshold θ_q, we adopt the definition $QC = $1-conductance.

Community Seed Similarity - CSS. This function takes as input two sets of nodes, and returns their similarity. Such a function is often used in dynamic community detection to assess the similarity between communities found in different time steps. Following [5], we choose as a reference function the Jaccard Index. Given two sets A and B, it is defined as: $J(A, B) = \frac{|A \cap B|}{|A \cup B|}$

3.6 Parameters

The algorithm has four parameters, $\theta_\gamma, \theta_q, \theta_s, \theta_p$, defining different thresholds. We explicit them and provide the values used in the experiments.

1. θ_γ is data-dependant. It corresponds to the smallest temporal scale that will be studied, and should be set at least at the collection rate. For synthetic networks, it is set at 1 (the smallest temporal unit needed to generate a new stream), while, for SocioPatterns dataset, it is set to 20 s (the minimum length of time required to capture a contact).
2. θ_q determines the minimal quality a seed must have to be preserved and expanded. The higher this value, the more strict we are on the quality of communities. We set $\theta_q = 0.7$ in all experiments. It is dependent on the choice of the QC function.
3. θ_s determines the threshold above which two communities are considered redundant. The higher this value, the more communities will be obtained. We set $\theta_s = 0.3$ in all experiments. It is dependent on the choice of the CSS function.
4. θ_p is the minimum number of consecutive periods a seed must be expanded in order to be considered as stable community. We set $\theta_s = 3$ in all experiments. The value should not be lower in order to avoid spurious detections due to pure chance. Higher values could be used to limit the number of results.

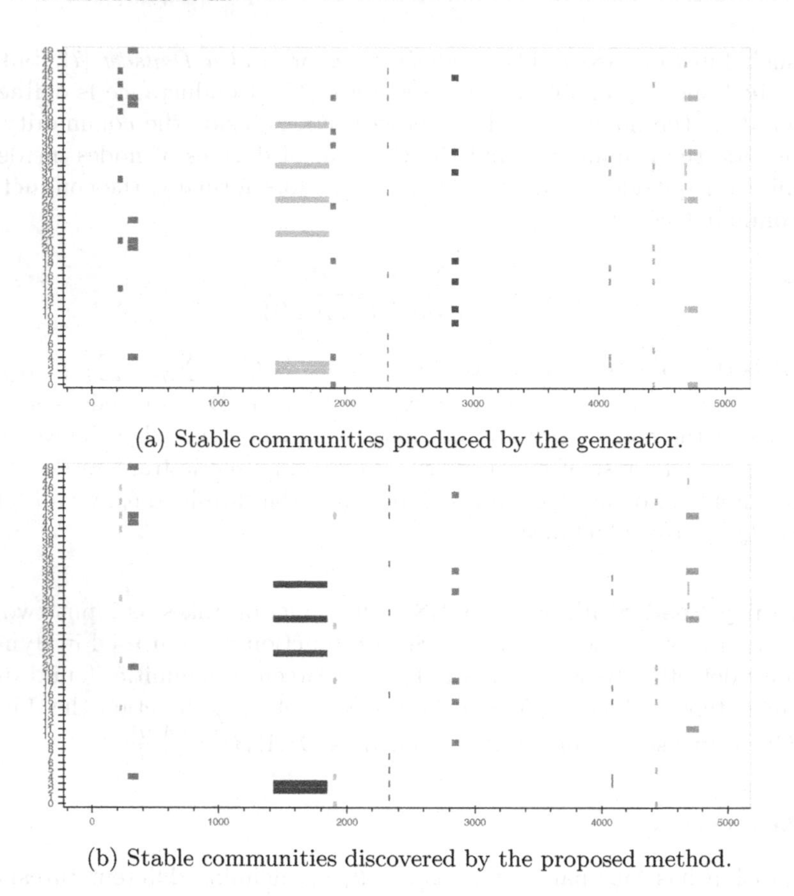

(a) Stable communities produced by the generator.

(b) Stable communities discovered by the proposed method.

Fig. 1. Visual comparison between planted and discovered communities. Time steps on the horizontal axis, nodes on the vertical axis. Colors correspond to communities and are randomly assigned. We can observe that most communities are correctly discovered, both in terms of nodes and of duration. (Color figure online)

4 Experiments and Results

The validation of our method encompasses three main aspects: (*i*) the validity of communities found, and (*ii*) the multi-scale aspect of our method, (*iii*) its scalability. We conduct two kinds of experiments: on synthetic data, on which we use planted *ground-truth* to quantitatively compare our results, and on real networks, on which we use both qualitative and quantitative evaluation to validate our method.

4.1 Validation on Synthetic Data

To the best of our knowledge, no existing network generator allows to generate dynamic communities at multiple temporal scale. We therefore introduce a simple solution to do so. Let us consider a dynamic network composed of T steps and N different nodes. We start by adding some random noise: at each step, an Erdos-Renyi random graph [4] is generated, with a probability of edge presence equal to p. We then add a number SC of random stable communities. For each community, we attribute randomly a set of $n \in [4, N/4]$ nodes, a duration $d \in [10, T/4]$ and a starting date $s \in [0, T-d]$. n and d are chosen using a logarithmic probability, in order to increase variability. The temporal scale of the community is determined by the probability of observing an edge between any two of its nodes during the period of its existence, set as $10/d$. As a consequence, a community of duration 10 will have edges between all of its nodes at every step of its existence, while a community of length 100 will have an edge between any two of its nodes only every 10 steps in average.

Since no algorithm exists to detect communities at multiple temporal scales, we compare our solution to a baseline: communities found by a static algorithm on each window, for different window sizes. It corresponds to *detect & match* methods for dynamic community detection such as [5]. We then compare the results by computing the overlapping NMI as defined in [8], at each step. For those experiments, we set $T = 5000, N = 100, p = 10/N$. We vary the number of communities SC.

Table 1. Comparison of the average NMI scores (over 10 runs) obtained for the proposed method (*Proposed*) and for each of the temporal scales ($\gamma \in \Gamma$) used by the proposed method, taken independently.

t_scale (γ)	5	10	20	30	40	50
Proposed	**0.91**	**0.78**	**0.69**	**0.69**	**0.62**	**0.54**
1666	0.41	0.32	0.24	0.23	0.15	0.19
833	0.36	0.30	0.29	0.27	0.23	0.25
416	0.39	0.40	0.36	0.34	0.32	0.33
208	0.46	0.45	0.40	0.42	0.41	0.37
104	0.47	0.48	0.44	0.46	0.45	0.42
52	0.45	0.47	0.45	0.47	0.47	0.45
26	0.35	0.35	0.38	0.42	0.42	0.41
13	0.28	0.26	0.30	0.31	0.32	0.31
6	0.17	0.16	0.19	0.19	0.20	0.19
3	0.12	0.09	0.11	0.10	0.12	0.11
1	0.05	0.03	0.04	0.03	0.05	0.04

Figure 1 represents the synthetic communities to find for $SC = 10$, and the communities discovered by the proposed method. We can observe a good match, with communities discovered throughout multiple scales (short-lasting and long-lasting ones). We report the results of the comparison with baselines in Table 1. We can observe that the proposed method outperforms the baseline at every scale in all cases in term of average NMI.

The important implication is that the problem of dynamic community detection is not only a question of choosing the right scale through a window size, but that if the network contains communities at multiple temporal scale, one needs to use an adapted method to discover them.

4.2 Validation on Real Datasets

We validate our approach by applying it to two real datasets. Because no ground truth data exists to compare our results with, we validate our method by using both quantitative and qualitative evaluation. We use the quantitative approach to analyze the scalability of the method and the characteristics of communities discovered compared with other existing algorithms. We use the qualitative approach to show that the communities found are meaningful and could allow an analyst to uncover interesting patterns in a dynamic datasets.

The datasets used are the following:

- **SocioPatterns** primary school data [18], face-to-face interactions between children in a school (323 nodes, 125 773 interaction).
- **Math overflow** stack exchange interaction dataset [14], a larger network to evaluate scalability (24 818 nodes, 506 550 interactions).

Qualitative Evaluation. For the qualitative evaluation, we used the primary school data [18] collected by the SocioPatterns collaboration[2] using RFID devices. They capture face-to-face proximity of individuals wearing them, at a rate of one capture every 20 s. The dataset contains face-to-face interactions between 323 children and 10 teachers collected over two consecutive days in October 2009. This school has 5 levels, each level is divided into 2 classes (A and B), for a total of 10 classes.

No community ground truth data exists to validate quantitatively our findings. We therefore focus on the descriptive information highlighted on the SocioPatterns study [18], and we show how the results yielded by our method match the course of the day as recorded by the authors in this study.

In order to make an accurate analysis of our results, the visualization have been reduced to one day (the second day), and we limited ourselves to 4 classes (1B, 2B, 3B, 5B)[3]. 120 communities are discovered in total on this dataset. We created three different figures, corresponding to communities of length respectively (i) less than half an hour, (ii) between half an hour and 2 h, (iii) more than 2 h. Figure 2 depicts the results. Nodes affiliations are ordered by class, as marked on the right side of the figure. The following observations can be made:

- Communities having the longest period of existence clearly correspond to the class structure. Similar communities had been found by the authors of the original study using aggregated networks per day.

[2] www.sociopatterns.org.

[3] Note that full results can be explored online using the provided notebook (see conclusion section).

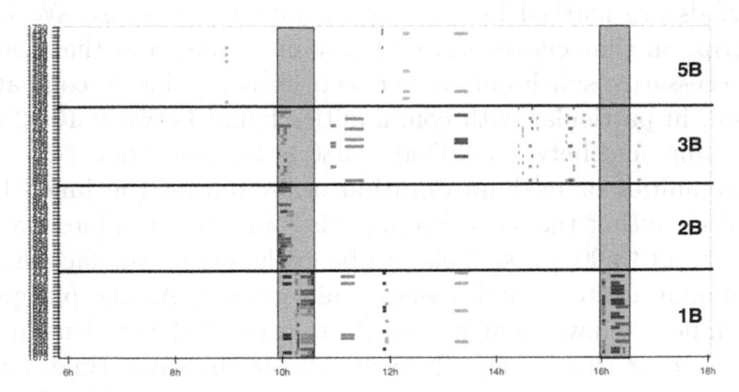

(a) Second day, length<30min. Grey vertical areas correspond to most likely break periods.

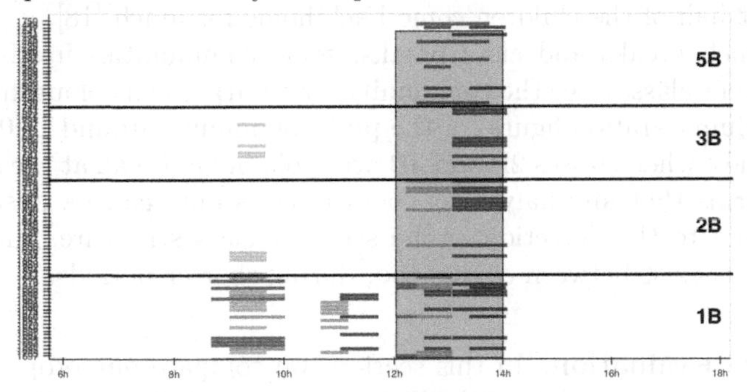

(b) Second day, 30min<length<2hours. Grey vertical area corresponds to the lunch break

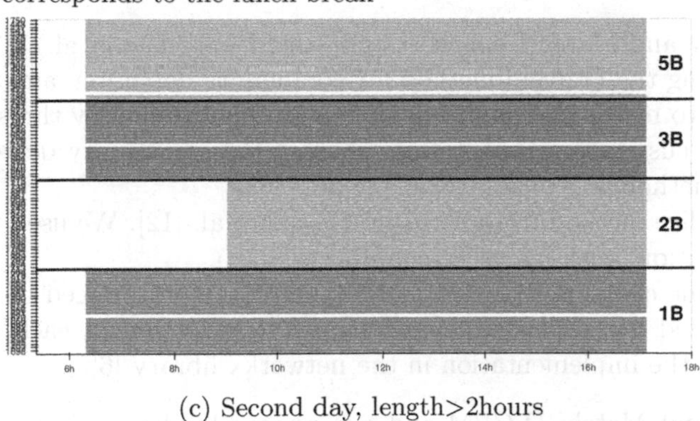

(c) Second day, length>2hours

Fig. 2. Stable communities of different lengths on the SocioPatterns Primary School Dataset. Time on the horizontal axis, children on the vertical axis. Colors are attributed randomly. (Color figure online)

- Most communities of the shorter duration are detected during what are probably breaks between classes. In the original study, it had been noted that break periods are marked by the highest interaction rates. We know from data description that classes have 20/30 min breaks, and that those breaks are not necessarily synchronized between classes. This is compatible with observation, in particular with communities found between 10:00 and 10:30 in the morning, and between 4:00 and 4:30 in the afternoon.
- Most communities of medium duration occur during the lunch break. We can also observe that the most communities are separated into two intervals, 12:00–13:00 and 13:00–14:00. This can be explained by the fact that children have a common canteen, and a shared playground. As the playground and the canteen do not have enough capacity to host all the students at the same time, only two or three classes have breaks at the same time, and lunches are taken in two consecutive turns of one hour. Some children do not belong to any communities during the lunch period, which matches the information that about half of the children come back home for lunch [18].
- During lunch breaks and class breaks, some communities involve children from different classes, see the community with dark-green colour during lunch time (medium duration figure) or the pink community around 10:00 for short communities, when classes 2B and 3B are probably in break at the same time. This confirms that an analysis at coarser scales only can be misleading, as it leads only to the detection of the stronger class structure, ignoring that communities exist between classes too, during shorter periods.

Quantitative Evaluation. In this section, we compare our proposition with other methods on two aspects: scalability, and aggregated properties of communities found. The methods we compare ourselves to are:

- An Identify and Match framework proposed by Greene et al. [5]. We implement it using the Louvain method for community detection, and the *Jaccard coefficient* to match communities, with a minimal similarity threshold of 0.7. We used a custom implementation, sharing the community detection phase with our method.
- The multislice method introduced by Mucha et al. [12]. We used the authors implementation, with interslice coupling $\omega = 0.5$.
- The dynamic clique percolation method (D-CPM) introduced by Palla et al. [13]. We used a custom implementation, the detection in each snapshot is done using the implementation in the networkx library [6].

For Identify and Match, D-CPM and our approach, the community detection phase is performed in parallel for all snapshots. This is not possible for Mucha et al., since the method is performed on all snapshots simultaneously. On the other hand, D-CPM and Indentify and Match are methods with no dynamic smoothing.

Figure 3 presents the time taken by those methods and our proposition, for each temporal granularity, on the Math Overflow network. The task

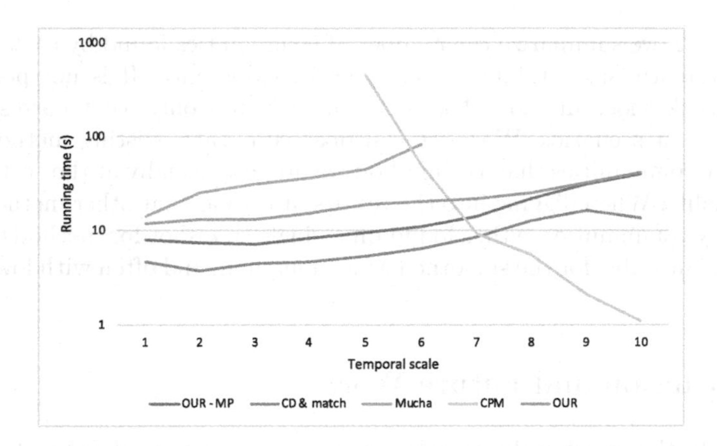

Fig. 3. Speed of several dynamic community detection methods for several temporal granularities, on the Math Overflow dataset. Missing points correspond to computation time above 1000 s. Temporal scales correspond to window sizes and are divided by 2 at every level, from 1 = 67 681 200 s (about 2 years) to 10 = 132 189 s (about 36 h). OUR and OUR-MP corresponds to our method using or not multiprocessing (4 cores)

accomplished by our method is, of course, not comparable, since it must not only discover communities, but also avoid redundancy between communities in different temporal scales, while other methods yield redundant communities in different levels. Nevertheless, we can observe that the method is scalable to networks with tens of thousands of nodes and hundreds of thousands of interactions. It is slower than the Identify and Match (CD&Match) approach, but does not suffer from the scalability problem as for the two other ones (D-CPM and Mucha et al.). In particular, the clique percolation method is not scalable to large and dense networks, a known problem due to the exponential growth in the number of cliques to find. For the method by Mucha et al., the scalability issue is due to the memory representation of a single modularity matrix for all snapshots.

Table 2. Average properties of communities found by each method (independently of their temporal granularity). #Communities: number of communities found. Persistence: number of consecutive snapshots. Size: number of nodes. Stability: average Jaccard coefficient between nodes of the same community in successive snapshots. Density: average degree/size-1. Q: 1-Conductance (higher is better)

Method	#Communities	Persistance	Size	Stability	Density	Q
OUR	179	3.44	10.89	1.00	0.50	0.91
CD& MATCH	29846	1.21	5.50	0.97	0.42	0.96
CPM	3259	1.87	5.37	0.51	0.01	0.53
MUCHA	1097	15.48	9.72	0.62	0.38	0.85

In Table 2, we summarize the number of communities found by each method, their persistence, size, stability, density and conductance. It is not possible to formally rank those methods based on these values only, that correspond to vastly different scenarios. What we can observe is that existing methods yield much more communities than the method we propose, usually at the cost of lower overall quality. When digging into the results, it is clear that other methods yield many noisy communities, either found on a single snapshot for methods without smoothing, unstable for the smoothed Mucha method, and often with low density or Q.

5 Conclusion and Future Work

To conclude, this article only scratches the surface of the possibilities of multiple-temporal-scale community detection. We have proposed a first method for the detection of such structures, that we validated on both synthetic and real-world networks, highlighting the interest of such an approach. The method is proposed as a general, extensible framework, and its code is available[4,5] as an easy to use library, for replications, applications and extensions.

As an exploratory work, further investigations and improvements are needed. Heuristics or statistical selection procedures could be implemented to reduce the computational complexity. Hierarchical organization of relations – both temporal and structural–between communities could greatly simplify the interpretation of results.

References

1. Aynaud, T., Guillaume, J.L.: Static community detection algorithms for evolving networks. In: 8th International Symposium on Modeling and Optimization in Mobile, Ad Hoc, and Wireless Networks, pp. 513–519. IEEE (2010)
2. Blondel, V.D., Guillaume, J.L., Lambiotte, R., Lefebvre, E.: Fast unfolding of communities in large networks. J. Stat. Mech: Theory Exp. **2008**(10), P10008 (2008)
3. Boudebza, S., Cazabet, R., Azouaou, F., Nouali, O.: OLCPM: an online framework for detecting overlapping communities in dynamic social networks. Comput. Commun. **123**, 36–51 (2018)
4. Erdös, P., Rényi, A.: On random graphs i. Publ. Math. Debr. **6**, 290–297 (1959)
5. Greene, D., Doyle, D., Cunningham, P.: Tracking the evolution of communities in dynamic social networks. In: 2010 International Conference on Advances in Social Networks Analysis and Mining, pp. 176–183. IEEE (2010)
6. Hagberg, A., Swart, P., Chult, D.S.: Exploring network structure, dynamics, and function using networkX. Technical report, Los Alamos National Lab. (LANL), Los Alamos, NM, USA (2008)

[4] The full code is available at https://github.com/Yquetzal/ECML_PKDD_2019.

[5] An online notebook to test the method is available at https://colab.research.google.com/github/Yquetzal/ECML_PKDD_2019/blob/master/simple_demo.ipynb.

7. Labatut, V., Orman, G.K.: Community structure characterization. In: Alhajj, R., Rokne, J. (eds.) Encyclopedia of Social Network Analysis and Mining, pp. 1–13. Springer, New York (2017). https://doi.org/10.1007/978-1-4614-7163-9
8. Lancichinetti, A., Fortunato, S., Kertész, J.: Detecting the overlapping and hierarchical community structure in complex networks. New J. Phys. **11**(3), 033015 (2009)
9. Latapy, M., Viard, T., Magnien, C.: Stream graphs and link streams for the modeling of interactions over time. CoRR abs/1710.04073 (2017)
10. Leskovec, J., Lang, K.J., Dasgupta, A., Mahoney, M.W.: Community structure in large networks: natural cluster sizes and the absence of large well-defined clusters. Internet Math. **6**(1), 29–123 (2009)
11. Masuda, N., Holme, P.: Detecting sequences of system states in temporal networks. Sci. Rep. **9**(1) (2019). https://doi.org/10.1038/s41598-018-37534-2
12. Mucha, P.J., Richardson, T., Macon, K., Porter, M.A., Onnela, J.P.: Community structure in time-dependent, multiscale, and multiplex networks. Science **328**(5980), 876–878 (2010)
13. Palla, G., Barabási, A.L., Vicsek, T.: Quantifying social group evolution. Nature **446**(7136), 664 (2007)
14. Paranjape, A., Benson, A.R., Leskovec, J.: Motifs in temporal networks. In: Proceedings of the Tenth ACM International Conference on Web Search and Data Mining, pp. 601–610. ACM (2017)
15. Peel, L., Clauset, A.: Detecting change points in the large-scale structure of evolving networks. CoRR abs/1403.0989 (2014)
16. Rossetti, G., Cazabet, R.: Community discovery in dynamic networks: a survey. ACM Comput. Surv. (CSUR) **51**(2), 35 (2018)
17. Rossetti, G., Pappalardo, L., Pedreschi, D., Giannotti, F.: Tiles: an online algorithm for community discovery in dynamic social networks. Mach. Learn. **106**(8), 1213–1241 (2017)
18. Stehlé, J., et al.: High-resolution measurements of face-to-face contact patterns in a primary school. PLOS ONE **6**(8) (2011). https://doi.org/10.1371/journal.pone.0023176
19. Wang, Y., Chakrabarti, A., Sivakoff, D., Parthasarathy, S.: Fast change point detection on dynamic social networks. In: Proceedings of the 26th International Joint Conference on Artificial Intelligence, IJCAI 2017, pp. 2992–2998. AAAI Press (2017)

A Comparative Study of Community Detection Techniques for Large Evolving Graphs

Lauranne Coppens, Jonathan De Venter, Sandra Mitrović[(✉)], and Jochen De Weerdt

Research Center for Information Systems Engineering (LIRIS), KU Leuven, Leuven, Belgium
sandra.mitrovic@kuleuven.be

Abstract. Community detection has recently received increased attention due to its wide range of applications in many fields. While at first most techniques were focused on discovering communities in static networks, lately the focus has shifted toward evolving networks because of their high relevance in real-life problems. Given the increasing number of the methods being proposed, this paper explores the current availability of empirical comparative studies of dynamic methods and also provides its own qualitative and quantitative comparison with the aim of gaining more insight in the performance of available methods. The results show that no single best performing community detection technique exists, but rather, the choice of the method depends on the objective and dataset characteristics.

Keywords: Dynamic community detection · Large evolving graphs · RDyn

1 Introduction

Community detection techniques in complex networks are a well-covered topic in academic literature nowadays as identifying meaningful substructures in complex networks has numerous applications in a vast variety of fields ranging from biology, mathematics, and computer science to finance, economics and sociology. A majority of the literature covers static community detection algorithms, i.e. algorithms used to uncover communities in static networks. However, real-world networks often possess temporal properties as nodes and edges can appear and disappear, potentially resulting in a changed community structure. Consequently, researchers have recently taken a keen interest in community detection algorithms that can tackle dynamic networks. Given the increasing number of the methods being proposed, a systematic comparison of both their algorithmic and performance differences is required so as to be able to select a suitable method for a particular community discovery problem. Nonetheless, newly proposed community detection methods for dynamic graphs are typically compared with only

P. Cellier and K. Driessens (Eds.): ECML PKDD 2019 Workshops, CCIS 1167, pp. 368–384, 2020.
https://doi.org/10.1007/978-3-030-43823-4_31

very few methods in settings aiming to demonstrate superiority of the proposed method. Consequently, the setup and results of these comparisons might contain an unconscious bias towards one's own algorithm. As such, a well-founded and extensive comparative analysis of dynamic community detection (DCD) techniques is missing in the current literature. This is not surprising given the many different aspects which come into play when comparing DCD methods: different underlying network models, different community definitions, different temporal segments used for detecting communities, different community evolution events tracked etc.

To bridge this literature gap, we perform a qualitative and quantitative comparison of DCD techniques. To this end, we adopt the classification system of Cazabet and Rossetti [1] to provide a concise framework within which the comparison is framed. For our qualitative comparison, we focus on relevant community detection characteristics like community definition used, ability to detect different type of communities and community evolution events as well as computational complexity. For quantitative analysis we report computational time and partition quality in terms of NF1 statistics, on 900 synthetic RDyn [7] and one real-world DBLP dataset [25]. Results showcase that no single best performing community technique exists. Instead, the choice of the method should adapt to the dataset and the final objective.

2 Methodology for Unbiased Comparison of Dynamic Community Detection Methods

In this section we provide details of our comparative study which basically consists of three parts: first, shortlisting candidate algorithms to be compared, second, analyzing their algorithmic characteristics and, third, performing the empirical analysis.

2.1 Algorithm Selection

Given the soundness and completeness of Cazabet and Rossetti's classification framework [1], we opt for using this framework as a steering wheel in the process of method selection. Within this framework, three large types of dynamic algorithms for searching communities are distinguished: (1) those that only consider the current state of the network (instant-optimal); (2) those that only consider past and present clustering and past instances of the network topology (temporal trade-off); (3) those that consider the entire network evolution available in the data, both past and future clustering (cross-time).

In an applied setting, neglecting previous states of the network oftentimes leads to sub-optimal solutions. Additionally, it is realistic to assume that communities will be updated using data that become available periodically. Consequently, no future information will be available at time t. With this in mind, we opt for focusing on temporal trade-off algorithms. Within Cazabet and Rossetti's framework, these are further subdivided into four categories: Global Optimization (denoted originally as 2.1), Rule-Based Updates (2.2), Multi-Objective

Optimization (2.3) and Network Smoothing (2.4). For each subcategory, at least one representative is chosen. Additionally, the list of compared algorithms is complemented by more recently published techniques, which, in turn, are also classified in the four previously mentioned categories.

Moreover, three characteristics are instrumental in the selection. Firstly, the algorithm has to be able to detect communities in evolving graphs. Secondly, the algorithm would preferably be able to detect overlapping communities to ensure a realistic partitioning in social network problems. Thirdly, the capability of extracting community evolution events is a desired trait with the goal of having realistic partitions that incorporate as much available information as possible in the partitioning process. Finally, some algorithms will be included as benchmark algorithms in order to compare results with previously performed comparative analyses.

2.2 Qualitative Analysis

The qualitative analysis is based on the comparison of algorithmic characteristics. In particular, comparison is performed with respect to the following six questions:

1. How does the method search for communities? In other words, which of the categories within the framework of Cazabet and Rossetti does it fit in (if any)?
2. What community definition is adopted (modularity, density, conductance...)?
3. How efficient the method is? That is, what is its computational complexity?
4. Which community evolution events can the method track (birth, death, merge, split, growth, contraction, continuation, resurgence)?
5. Can the method find overlapping communities?
6. Can the method find hierarchical communities?

2.3 Empirical Analysis Setup

Given their different characteristics, to provide a fair comparison, selected DCD methods are benchmarked based on both synthetic and real-life datasets. As synthetic datasets, 9 different RDyn graphs [7] were created by varying the number of nodes to 1000, 2000 and 4000 and the communities size distribution parameter α to be 2.5, 3 and 3.5. Larger α makes the sizes of communities relatively larger, more dispersed, while smaller makes the differences between community sizes smaller, more uniform. The rate of node appearance and vanishing is fixed to 0.05 and 0.02 respectively. The appearance rate is slightly larger than the vanishing rate in an attempt to mimic a slowly growing graph which could resemble, for instance, a customer base where customers enter, remain for a (long) while, and churn. For each of the 9 different RDyn graphs, 100 RDyn instances are created, yielding 900 graphs in total. The specific number 100 was arbitrarily chosen but is used to account for variations in the results.

As for the real-life dataset, the co-authorship graph from [25] was used. This dataset was originally extracted from DBLP database and for purposes of this analysis, was further limited to data from 1971 to 2002. Resulting dataset has 850 875 nodes, which represent 303 628 unique authors, and 1 656 873 edges.

To measure the relative performance of the different algorithms, two metrics were chosen. On the one side, the quality of the partition is measured by Normalized F1-statistics (NF1) and on the other side, the efficiency of the algorithm is reported in terms of the computation time.

3 Results

In this section we provide results of each of the three phases of our comparative analysis: algorithm selection, qualitative and quantitative analysis.

3.1 Algorithm Selection

For the broad selection, the initial list of 51 papers on DCD methods was used [6,13–18,20–23,27–65]. It was obtained by supplementing 32 temporal trade-off algorithms [6,13–15,17,21,22,24,27–50] from [1] with 19 algorithms not included in the aforementioned survey [16,18,20,23,51–65] that nonetheless possess interesting characteristics with regards to community and evolution extraction. Figure 1 illustrates the relevance of adding those 19 papers as it ensures the inclusion of more recent methods.

After this list of algorithms was compiled, the three algorithm-specific characteristics mentioned before were compared in order to select the approximately ten most promising algorithms that will be compared qualitatively and empirically. Following the analysis mentioned above, 13 algorithms were selected to be compared, as follows.

Partition Update by Global Optimization (2.1). This category contains algorithms that incrementally update and find communities by globally optimizing a metric such as modularity, density or other utility functions. Two methods represent this category in the analysis. Firstly, D-GT is a game-theory based algorithm proposed in [13] for dynamic social networks. The technique considers nodes as rational agents, maximizes a utility function and finds the optimal structure when a Nash equilibrium is reached. Secondly, Updated BGL is a modularity based incremental algorithm designed by [14]. It is more time-efficient than its modularity-based peers that do not rely on community updating. Both D-GT and Updated BGL are capable of tracking community evolution events.

Partition Update by Set of Rules (2.2). This category seems to be the most promising in terms of efficiency and accuracy for algorithms that take into account past information. The algorithms belonging to this category all consider a list of historic network changes in order to update the network's partitioning. AFOCS is an algorithm designed for performing well in mobile networks, such as online social networks, wireless sensor networks and Mobile Ad Hoc Networks [15]. The technique is able to uncover overlapping communities in an efficient way by incrementally updating the communities based on past information. It avoids the recalculation of communities at each time step, by identifying community evolution events based on four network changes, namely the appearance of a new node or edge and the removal of an edge or node. The algorithm applies different rules on how to update communities depending on which events occur. HOC-Tracker is a technique designed to detect hierarchical and overlapping communities in online social networks [16]. The approach detects community evolution by comparing significant evolutionary changes between consecutive time steps, reducing the number of operations to be performed by the algorithm. The algorithm identifies active nodes, which are nodes that (dis)appear or are linked to an edge that (dis)appears, and compares those nodes' neighborhoods with their previous time step to reassign nodes to new communities if necessary. TILES, is an online algorithm that identifies overlapping communities by iteratively recomputing a node's community membership in case of a new interaction [17]. The approach is capable of singling out community evolution events such as birth, death, merge, split, growth and contraction. OLCPM is an online, deterministic and DCD method based on clique percolation and label propagation [18]. OLCPM, unlike CPM (Clique Percolation Method) [19], works by updating communities by looking at some predefined events resulting in improved computation times. OLCPM is able to detect overlapping communities in temporal networks. Finally, DOCET [20] incrementally updates overlapping dynamic communities after it finds an initial community structure. It can track community evolution events.

Informed CD by Multi-objective Optimization (2.3). The two previous categories updated partitions by looking at past communities. Informed community detection algorithms, on the other hand, calculate the communities from scratch in each time step. The algorithm tries to balance partition quality and temporal partition coherence or in other words, the current network structure and past partitions. A disadvantage of these kinds of approaches is the computational power necessary to execute the algorithm. An advantage is its temporal independence, potentially resulting in more stable outcomes. In informed community detection by multi-objective optimization, the partition at time t is detected by optimizing a certain metric, e.g. modularity, density. Two algorithms will represent this category in the evaluation. FacetNet was a pioneer in detecting communities in an unified process, in contrast with a two-step approach, where evolution events can be uncovered together with the partitioning [6]. Consequently, FacetNet is used as a benchmark approach in many papers introducing algorithms with similar capabilities. The approach finds communities based on non-negative matrix factorization and iteratively updates the network structure to balance the current partitioning fit and historical cost function. A disadvantage of the technique is that the number of communities is fixed and should be determined by the user. DYNMOGA [21], unlike FacetNet, balances the current partitioning fit and cost function simultaneously and, therefore, does not need a preference parameter with regard to maximizing partition quality and minimizing the historical cost or clustering drift. It optimizes a multi-objective problem and automatically determines the optimal trade-off between cluster accuracy and clustering drift. Neither FacetNet or DYNMOGA are capable of detecting overlapping communities.

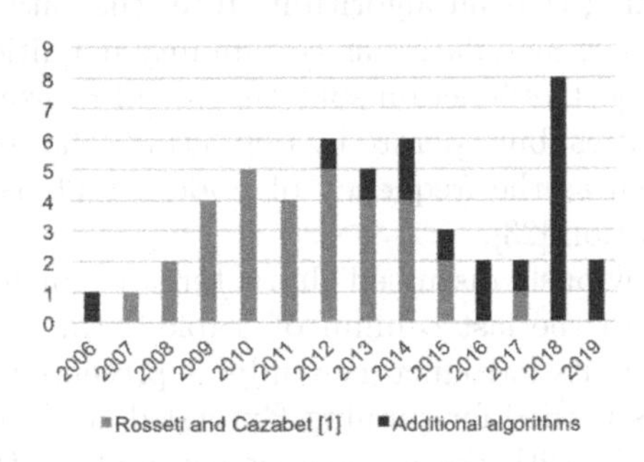

Fig. 1. Analyzed papers by year.

Informed CD by Network Smoothing (2.4). ECSD proposed by [22] is a particle-and-density based evolutionary clustering method that is capable of determining the number of communities itself. The method detects the network's structure and evolutionary events by trading off historic quality and snapshot quality, similar to the previous subcategory. The difference, however, is that ECSD finds its clusters by temporally smoothing data instead of results.

Other Benchmarks. Within this final category of methods introduced for comparison purposes we consider two algorithms: DEMON and iLCD. DEMON introduced in [23] (and extended in [26]) is a technique that is able to hierarchically detect overlapping communities but cannot, unlike all previous methods, identify community evolution events. iLCD [24], in previous empirical comparisons, is repeatedly shown to perform worse in terms of partition quality and computation speed with regards to other tested algorithms (e.g. FacetNet). It will be interesting to evaluate or verify the relative performance of these methods.

3.2 Qualitative Results

The first aspect that stands out is the larger presence of algorithms that update communities by a set of rules (2.2) not only in our final selection, but, likewise, among the more recently proposed methods, such as AFOCS, HOCTracker, OLCPM and DOCET which are also more focused on performing in dynamic social environments.

The second aspect that attracted our attention was the fact that nearly none of the analyzed algorithms focused in particular on the detection of hierarchical communities. Moreover, even though it was expected that hierarchy would be a relevant factor, it was generally not even mentioned whether an algorithm was capable of detecting hierarchical communities. On the other hand, detecting overlapping communities in social networks was oftentimes considered as necessity in current literature.

Thirdly, it is striking that all algorithms from the categories that optimize an objective function use modularity as community definition. Algorithms that do not optimize an objective function sometimes still utilize a metric as a guide to search for communities, but operate by exploiting other characteristics of the network topology, such as the frequency of node neighbors by labeling nodes, done by label propagation [23].

An overview of previously discussed characteristics for selected methods can be found in Table 1. In the last column of Table 1, time complexity per each method, as provided by its introductory study, is presented. It can be seen that the required resources needed for running Extended BGL, LabelRankT, ECSD and iLCD grow linearly with the number edges, making these algorithms the most efficient ones. Next, FacetNet's computation time grows proportional with its number of edges and communities, DYNMOGA scales log-linearly with the number of nodes and DEMON is dependent on the number of nodes and the maximum degree. Finally, TILES, AFOCS, HOCTracker and DOCET appear to be the most complex algorithms as their computation time is expected to grow quadratically with the number of nodes, which is particularly problematic for large graphs. It cannot be derived whether the complexity is closely related to the category the algorithm belongs to Category 2.2., however, seems to be most complex.

In the context of social networks (and not only these), the knowledge of what types of community evolution events occur at which moments in time can be valuable information in order to understand what is happening with the network structure over time. Currently, the literature recognizes eight community evolution events, namely birth, death, merge, split, growth, contraction, continue and resurgence of a community, although, obviously, not every method is able to detect all of them. Therefore, for each of the methods which do support community evolution tracking (see column "Evolution" in Table 1), it is worth investigating further which in particular event(s) the tracking refers to. As can be seen from Table 2, several remarks can be made along these lines.

Table 1. Comparison of **dynamic** methods based on observed characteristics and their time complexity (last column). "CS Type" stands for category in Cazabet and Rossetti's framework. A "-" denotes that methods do not search communities by optimizing a metric, but operate by exploiting characteristics of network topology. Notation used for time complexity: n, m, c, g - number of nodes, edges, communities and generations respectively, K - maximum degree, α - degree distribution parameter, RQ_{ttl} - expected average size of interactions processed during interaction removal phase, $|U|$ - number of nodes to be updated.

CS Type	Method	Definition	Overlap	Evolution	Hierarchy	Time complexity
2.1	D-GT	Modularity	?	✓	?	-
	Extended BGL	Modularity	?	✓	?	O(m)
2.2	TILES	-	✓	✓	?	$O(\|n(c_u + c_v)\| + RQ_{ttl}\|U\|^2)$
	AFOCS	Density	✓	✓	?	$O(n^2)$
	HOCTracker	Density	✓	✓	✓	$O(n^2)$
	OLCPM	Modularity	✓	✓	?	-
	DOCET	-	✓	✓	?	$O(n^2)$
	LabelRankT	-	✗	✓	?	$O(m)$
2.3	FacetNet	Modularity	✗	✓	?	$O(m \cdot c)$
	DYNMOGA	Modularity	✗	✓	?	$O(gn \cdot log(n))$
2.4	ECSD	Modularity	✗	✓	?	$O(m)$
Other	Demon	-	✓	✗	✓	$O(nK^{3-\alpha})$
	iLCD	-	✓	✓	?	$O(m)$

Firstly, it is remarkable that the event resurgence cannot be detected by any of the selected algorithms, nor by any of the other algorithms that were analyzed, even though the event has been included in the literature, among others by [1]. Similarly, the event continue is rarely mentioned explicitly. It might be the case that continue is implied/detected when no event occurs and is therefore not mentioned by the authors.

Secondly, the algorithms, such as OLCPM, HOCTracker and DOCET, that were included in addition to the survey by [1] because they were more recent and possessed good features for social network community detection, can detect most of the events community evolution events. Only resurgence cannot be detected by any of the methods which we assume is due to the fact that detecting resurgence requires more than two timestamps which is not the case with methods from category 2.2, in general.

Thirdly, some algorithms, such as Extended BGL, ECSD and iLCD, only track events that are linked with the emergence of nodes and not their disappearance.

3.3 Quantitative Results

In this section we present the empirical results on synthetic dataset, RDyn, and real-world dataset, DBLP, in terms of partition quality (NF1) and computation times (secs).

Synthetic Graph (RDyn)

Table 2. Tracking of community evolution events by selected algorithms. "CS Type" stands for category in Cazabet and Rossetti framework. Question marks denote that the algorithm is able to detect community evolution events, but the original papers do not specify which ones explicitly.

CS Type	Method	Birth	Death	Merge	Split	Growth	Contraction	Continue	Resurgence
2.1	D-GT	✓	✓	✗	✗	✓	✓	✓	✗
	Extended BGL	✓	✗	✓	✗	✓	✗	✓	✗
2.2	TILES	✓	✓	✓	✓	✓	✓	✗	✗
	AFOCS	?	?	?	?	?	?	?	?
	HOCTracker	✓	✓	✓	✓	✓	✓	✗	✗
	OLCPM	✓	✓	✓	✓	✓	✓	✓	✗
	DOCET	✓	✓	✓	✓	✓	✓	✗	✗
	LabelRankT	✗	✓	✓	✓	✗	✗	✗	✗
2.3	FacetNet	?	?	?	?	?	?	?	?
	DYNMOGA	✓	✓	✓	✓	✓	✓	✗	✗
2.4	ECSD	✓	✗	✓	✗	✓	✗	✗	✗
Other	Demon	✗	✗	✗	✗	✗	✗	✗	✗
	iLCD	✓	✗	✓	✗	✓	✗	✗	✗

Partition Quality. The results of partition quality in terms of NF1 measure are provided in Table 3. The best performing algorithm is HOCTracker followed by iLCD and DEMON which only slightly differ from each other. Next, OLCPM is the second worst performer followed by Tiles who ended up having very poor results in terms of NF1. In general, the community size distribution parameter and the number of nodes do not have a trend that influences the partition quality. The impact of these variables differs algorithm to algorithm.

HOCTracker returns the highest NF1 values for $\alpha = 3$ and the lowest for $\alpha = 2.5$. However, it also exhibits much higher standard deviations associated with each group of RDyn instances, especially in comparison with iLCD and OLCPM. Note that standard deviation in Table 3 is not the standard deviation of the mean NF1 across every RDyn instance of one of the nine RDyn categories, but represents the average standard deviation of all NF1 measures within one RDyn instance. Even though the small standard deviation values in iLCD could be interpreted as method consistency (thus in its advantage), closer investigation revealed that oftentimes a lot of nodes where not assigned to a community for a specific graph resulting in NF1 scores of 0 for those communities and consequently for their graphs. If NF1 mean is 0 than the standard deviation is either close to 0 or 0. This can be seen in Fig. 2. OLCPM and iLCD appear to classify algorithms quite well once the algorithm succeeds at assigning the majority of the nodes.

Scalability. As can be seen from Table 4, the best performing algorithm on synthetic dataset in terms of execution times is iLCD, followed by TILES, DEMON,

OLCPM and lastly HOCTracker. Remarkably, the group with $\alpha = 3$ takes the longest to execute across all sizes with the exception of OLCPM on the (1000, 3) graph where (1000, 2.5) requires the longest time. Although this observation is very notable, there is no reasonable explanation why this occurs. It can be concluded that specific characteristics can have a significant impact on the time required to analyze a graph but we refrain from specifying a specific relation between community size distribution and execution times.

Another interesting observation is that within each size group, the graphs with relatively large differences in community sizes ($\alpha = 3.5$) often require the least time to analyze. If they are not the fastest their performance is rather similar to the fastest.

According to literature, iLCD scales with the number of edges in a graph. However, this is not reflected in the execution times. For OLCPM, it was observed that the execution time is very variable. For the $\alpha = 2.5$, the execution times for 1000 and 4000 are almost equal. For 2000 nodes it only takes 75% of the time used for the former. An anomaly can clearly be observed for OLCPM, the average execution time for the (2000, 2.5) and (2000, 3.5)-instances group takes less time than their (1000, 2.5) and (1000, 3.5) despite having double the number of nodes and approximately edges. This observation cannot be attributed to a specific aspect of the algorithm. As expected, DEMON was found to scale with the number of nodes and the average degree distribution parameter (kept constant on all instances of RDyn). At last, HOCTracker performed the worst which was not unsurprising as it scales in a quadratic way.

Real-World Graph (DBLP). Three algorithms were run on the DBLP dataset: DEMON, iLCD and TILES. HOCTracker returns an OutOfMemoryException when trying to run it on the DBLP dataset, which demonstrates the unsuitability of the algorithm for large graphs. OLCPM runs itself into a loop on the DBLP dataset. We also suspect the method unsuitability for large datasets as this phenomenon did not occur on the RDyn dataset and the test in its introductory paper encompassed only small datasets (<10 000 nodes).

To analyze the performance of DEMON, iLCD and TILES each partitioning is benchmarked with the resulting partitioning of each of the other algorithms as ground truth. From the results, in Table 5, it can be observed that, on average, TILES is the worst and DEMON the best performing algorithm. Even though DEMON is the best performing algorithm, it needs significantly more computation time 3099.48 s on DBLP dataset as compared to TILES requiring 1436.71 s and iLCD which is the fastest with only 55.73 s. Figure 3 shows the evolution of mean NF1 scores of the three different methods for each year from 1971 to 2002. A general trend can be observed: as time progresses and more nodes and edges are introduced, the NF1 values drop significantly, however, not at the same pace for every algorithm. While TILES starts as the worst-performing algorithm in the earlier timestamps and thus smaller graphs, it ends up being the most performing one once the graph size exceeds 35 000 nodes (1991).

4 Related Work

A plethora of studies focusing purely on comparing algorithms for static community detection methods can be found in the literature [3,8–12]. In contrast, to the best of our knowledge, there are no studies that focus purely on the empirical comparison of DCD algorithms. Instead, in the studies which introduce new DCD algorithms or new dynamic benchmark graphs, authors typically benchmark their own method with few others with the aim to showcase that their technique performs better with regard to peers.

Table 3. Mean NF1 results and the associated standard deviations of benchmarked algorithms on RDyn dataset. The highest scores per different number of nodes and alpha are underlined while the best averages are boldfaced. "CS Type" stands for category in Cazabet and Rossetti framework.

CS Type	Method	Alpha	Nodes							
			1000		2000		4000		Avg.	
			Mean	Std.	Mean	Std.	Mean	Std.	Mean	Std.
2.2	TILES	Avg.	0.2002	0.2035	0.1961	0.1967	0.2087	0.1954	0.2017	0.1985
		2.5	0.1951	0.2068	0.1969	0.1994	0.2188	0.2017	0.2036	0.2026
		3	0.2033	0.2026	0.1882	0.1971	0.1953	0.1960	0.1954	0.1985
		3.5	0.2022	0.2010	0.2043	0.1934	0.2131	0.1882	0.2066	0.1941
	HOCTracker	Avg.	**0.4600**	0.2596	**0.4236**	0.2397	0.3852	0.2355	0.4236	0.2402
		2.5	0.3839	0.2570	0.4095	0.2443	0.3605	0.2474	**0.4070**	0.2447
		3	0.5346	0.2536	0.4493	0.2442	0.4352	0.2272	**0.4515**	0.2440
		3.5	0.4469	0.2675	0.4096	0.2298	0.3714	0.2229	**0.4101**	0.2309
	OLCPM	Avg.	0.3132	0.0243	0.3118	0.0206	0.3257	0.0192	0.3169	0.0213
		2.5	0.3006	0.0262	0.3173	0.0201	0.3274	0.0202	0.3151	0.0222
		3	0.3222	0.0253	0.3043	0.0225	0.3227	0.0190	0.3163	0.0223
		3.5	0.3171	0.0212	0.3143	0.0189	0.3270	0.0182	0.3196	0.0194
Other	DEMON	Avg.	0.4022	0.3059	0.3664	0.2962	0.3687	0.2970	0.3788	0.2996
		2.5	0.3987	0.3135	0.3615	0.2974	0.3846	0.2956	0.3814	0.3021
		3	0.3952	0.3001	0.3543	0.2898	0.3396	0.2996	0.3624	0.2964
		3.5	0.4136	0.3041	0.3857	0.3021	0.3845	0.2957	0.3944	0.3006
	iLCD	Avg.	0.3961	0.0170	0.3797	0.0125	**0.3968**	0.0097	0.3908	0.0130
		2.5	0.3838	0.0205	0.3826	0.0133	0.4018	0.0106	0.3894	0.0147
		3	0.3999	0.0159	0.3677	0.0131	0.3826	0.0090	0.3829	0.0126
		3.5	0.4054	0.0145	0.3908	0.0109	0.4071	0.0094	0.4012	0.0115

The situation is slightly better with respect to benchmark graphs, where a vast body of literature is available. Although the most prominently used benchmark graphs Girvan-Newman (GN) [4] and Lancichinetti-Fortunato-Radicchi (LFR) [2] are not suited for temporal community discovery, to this end, their extensions in [6] and [5] respectively, were proposed. Next, RDyn, a framework for generating dynamic networks along with time-dependent ground-truth partitions with tunable qualities, was introduced in [1].

To gain better insight in how the mentioned sporadic comparisons of DCD algorithms and/or dynamic benchmark graphs have been performed, in the context of this literature review, we considered a selection of 51 papers on

Table 4. Average computation time (in sec) over 100 RDyn instances per each benchmarked algorithm (the shortest boldfaced). "CS Type" stands for category in Cazabet and Rossetti framework.

CS Type	Method	Computation time (sec)			
		Alpha	Nodes		
			1000	2000	4000
2.2	TILES	2.5	3.43	5.45	7.47
		3	3.53	6.05	8.42
		3.5	3.45	5.48	7.73
	HOCTracker	2.5	46.12	77.77	152.00
		3	49.61	94.22	214.44
		3.5	43.96	78.62	166.25
	OLCPM	2.5	39.92	30.69	41.74
		3	37.48	69.27	56.40
		3.5	32.79	29.37	45.55
Other	DEMON	2.5	11.34	18.68	30.42
		3	11.77	20.8	35.02
		3.5	10.38	16.81	28.98
	iLCD	2.5	**1.94**	**2.35**	**2.74**
		3	**2**	**2.53**	**3.08**
		3.5	**1.98**	**2.37**	**2.81**

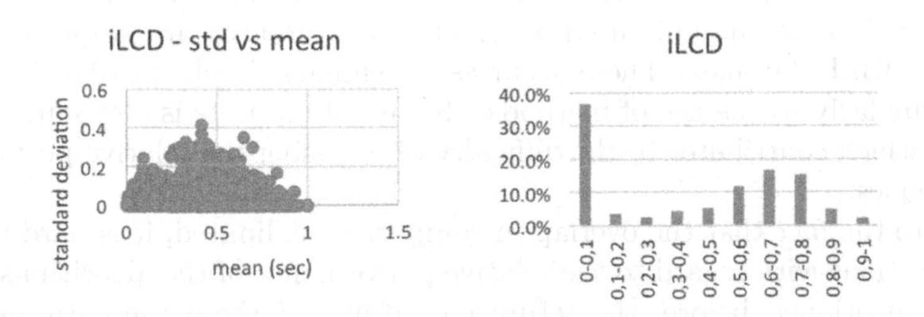

Fig. 2. NF1 mean vs. standard deviation for iCLD on synthetic data.

DCD methods. The first remarkable finding is that 12 out of 51 papers did not include a single comparison with peer algorithms [28,33,35,40,41,44,45,48–50,52,56], while 39 did. A closer investigation of these 39 papers revealed 57 algorithms out of 82 were only benchmarked once. On the other hand, the most frequently referenced algorithm is FacetNet [6]. The second interesting finding is that authors seem to use various datasets for comparison, as they often include synthetic graphs and/or real-world graphs. In the assessed papers, 1 made use of only synthetic graphs [32], 32 used only real graphs [13,14,16,22,27,28,30,31,33,34,36–41,44,45,48–52,54–57,59–63] and 17 used

Table 5. The mean NF1 results and the associated standard deviations when running DEMON, iLCD and TILES (rows) and using them as ground truth (columns) on DBLP dataset.

Method	Ground truth						
	TILES		DEMON		iLCD		Avg
	Mean	Std.	Mean	Std.	Mean	Std.	
TILES	1.0000	0.0000	0.5840	0.3211	0.5941	0.3182	0.5891
DEMON	0.5369	0.2612	1.0000	0.0000	0.7612	0.2817	**0.6490**
iLCD	0.5117	0.2685	0.6619	0.3116	1.0000	0.0000	0.5868

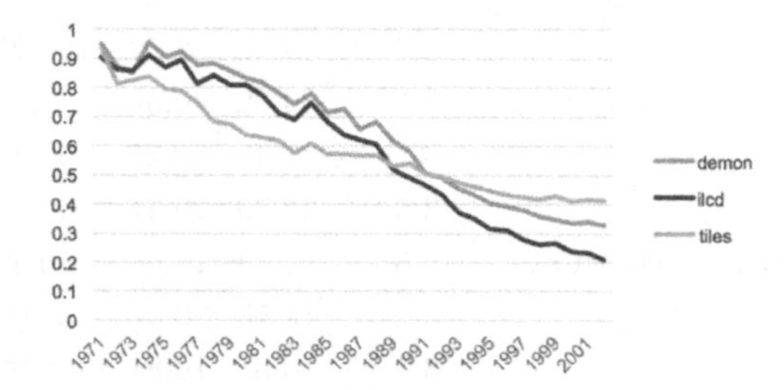

Fig. 3. Mean NF1 results for 1971–2002.

both [6,15,17,18,20,21,23,24,29,42,43,46,47,53,58,64,65]. In the 49 papers that used real graphs 47 different real graphs were introduced. A little over half of the datasets are only used once. The most popular are graphs extracted from the DBLP database. These occur as benchmark graphs in 19 of 51 papers. Hence, similarly to the use of methods, the use of datasets is also fairly heterogeneous which contributes to the difficulty of assessing the relative performance of techniques.

Due to the fact that the overlap in comparison is limited, it is hard to make any deductions with regard to the relative performance of the algorithms. Moreover, as mentioned before, the setup and results of these comparisons might contain an unconscious bias towards the proposed algorithm. This shows the relevance of this study.

5 Conclusion

Dynamic community detection has numerous applications in different fields and as such is extensively studied in the current literature. Nevertheless, a systematic and unbiased comparison of these methods is still missing. Therefore, in this paper we made steps towards scrutinizing algorithms and performing fairly both qualitative and quantitative comparisons on synthetic as well as real-life evolving graphs. The qualitative analysis included an overall set of characteristics relevant for (social) community detection such as community definition used, the ability to track community life-cycle events, overlapping and hierarchical communities, and the time complexity. For the empirical analysis, several limiting factors such as unavailable/poorly documented source code and inability to run methods on large graphs led to a narrower set of compared methods. Nevertheless, 900 synthetic, evolving graphs of various sizes and community size distributions and the most frequently used real-world DBLP dataset were used for a thorough analysis.

Undoubtedly, the field of community detection techniques that act on evolving graphs is characterized by its inherent heterogeneity in all its aspects. As such, there is no single best performing community technique, but rather, the choice and the performance depends on the objective and dataset characteristics. For future work, we envision an even more extensive empirical evaluation.

References

1. Rossetti, G., Cazabet, R.: Community discovery in dynamic networks: a survey. ACM Comput. Surv. **51**, 1–37 (2018)
2. Lancichinetti, A., Fortunato, S., Radicchi, F.: Benchmark graphs for testing community detection algorithms. Phys. Rev. E - Stat. Nonlinear Soft Matter Phys. **78**, 046110 (2008)
3. Lancichinetti, A., Fortunato, S.: Community detection algorithms: a comparative analysis. Phys. Rev. E - Stat. Nonlinear Soft Matter Phys. **80**, 056117 (2009)
4. Newman, M.E.J., Girvan, M.: Finding and evaluating community structure in networks. Phys. Rev. E - Stat. Nonlinear Soft Matter Phys. **69**, 026113 (2004)
5. Greene, D., Doyle, D., Cunninngham, P.: Tracking the evolution of communities in dynamic social networks. In: Proceedings of the International Conference on Advances in Social Networks, pp. 1–18 (2011)
6. Lin, Y.-R., Chi, Y., Zhu, S., Sundaram, H., Tseng, B.L.: Analyzing communities and their evolutions in dynamic social networks. ACM Trans. Knowl. Discov. Data **3**(2), 1–31 (2009)
7. Rossetti, G.: RDyn: graph benchmark handling community dynamics. J. Complex Netw. **4**, 893–912 (2017)
8. Danon, L., Dìaz-Guilera, A., Duch, J., Arenas, A.: Comparing community structure identification. J. Stat. Mech: Theory Exp. **9**, 219–228 (2005)
9. Harenberg, S., et al.: Community detection in large-scale networks: a survey and empirical evaluation. Wiley Interdiscip. Rev. Comput. Stat. **6**(6), 426–439 (2014)
10. Yang, Z., Algesheimer, R., Tessone, C.J.: A comparative analysis of community detection algorithms on artificial networks. Sci. Rep. **6**(1), 30750 (2016)
11. Wagenseller, P., Wang, F., Wu, W.: Size matters: a comparative analysis of community detection algorithms. IEEE Trans. Comput. Soc. Syst. **5**, 951–960 (2018)
12. Zhao, Z., Zheng, S., Li, C., Sun, J., Chang, L., Chiclana, F.: A comparative study on community detection methods in complex networks. J. Intell. Fuzzy Syst. **35**, 1077–1086 (2018)
13. Alvari, H., Hajibagheri, A., Sukthankar, G.: Community detection in dynamic social networks: a game-theoretic approach. In: Proceedings of the 2014 IEEE/ACM International Conference on Advances in Social Networks Analysis and Mining, ASONAM 2014, pp. 101–107 (2014)

14. Shang, J., et al.: A real-time detecting algorithm for tracking community structure of dynamic networks, vol. 12 (2014)
15. Nguyen, N.P., Dinh, T.N., Tokala, S., Thai, M.T.: Overlapping communities in dynamic networks: their detection and mobile applications. In: Mobicom, pp. 85–96 (2011)
16. Bhat, S.Y., Abulaish, M.: HOCTracker: tracking the evolution of hierarchical and overlapping communities in dynamic social networks. IEEE Trans. Knowl. Data Eng. **27**(4), 1013–1019 (2015)
17. Rossetti, G., Pappalardo, L., Pedreschi, D., Giannotti, F.: Tiles: an online algorithm for community discovery in dynamic social networks. Mach. Learn. **106**(8), 1213–1241 (2017)
18. Boudebza, S., Cazabet, R., Azouaou, F., Nouali, O.: OLCPM: an online framework for detecting overlapping communities in dynamic social networks. Comput. Commun. **123**, 36–51 (2018)
19. Gergely, P., Imre, D., Illés, F., Tamás, V.: Uncovering the overlapping community structure of complex networks in nature and society. Nature **435**(m), 814–818 (2005)
20. Wang, Z., Li, Z., Yuan, G., Sun, Y., Rui, X., Xiang, X.: Tracking the evolution of overlapping communities in dynamic social networks. Knowl.-Based Syst. **157**, 81–97 (2018)
21. Folino, F., Pizzuti, C.: Multiobjective evolutionary community detection for dynamic networks. In: Proceedings of the 12th Annual Conference on Genetic and Evolutionary Computation, pp. 535–536 (2010)
22. Kim, M.-S., Han, J.: A particle-and-density based evolutionary clustering method for dynamic networks. Proc. VLDB Endow. **2**(1), 622–633 (2009)
23. Coscia, M., Rossetti, G., Giannotti, F., Pedreschi, D.: DEMON: a local-first discovery method for overlapping communities, pp. 615–623 (2012)
24. Cazabet, R., Amblard, F., Hanachi, C.: Detection of overlapping communities in dynamical social networks. In: Proceedings of the 2010 2nd IEEE International Conference on Socical Computing PASSAT 2010 2nd IEEE International Conference on Privacy, Security and Risk Trust, no. August, pp. 309–314 (2010)
25. Demaine, E., Hajiaghayi, M.: DBLP graphs (BigDND: dynamic network data) (2019). http://projects.csail.mit.edu/dnd/DBLP/
26. Coscia, M., Rossetti, G., Giannotti, F., Pedreschi, D.: Uncovering hierarchical and overlapping communities with a local-first approach. ACM Trans. Knowl. Discov. Data **9**(1), 1–27 (2014)
27. Aynaud, T., Guillaume, J.-L.: Static community detection algorithms for evolving networks. In: Ad Hoc Wireless Networks, pp. 513–519 (2010)
28. Bansal, S., Bhowmick, S., Paymal, P.: Fast community detection for dynamic complex networks. Commun. Comput. Inf. Sci. **116**, 196–207 (2011). https://doi.org/10.1007/978-3-642-25501-4_20
29. Görke, R., Maillard, P., Staudt, C., Wagner, D.: Modularity-driven clustering of dynamic graphs. In: Festa, P. (ed.) SEA 2010. LNCS, vol. 6049, pp. 436–448. Springer, Heidelberg (2010). https://doi.org/10.1007/978-3-642-13193-6_37
30. Miller, K., Eliassi-Rad, T.: Continuous time group discovery in dynamic graphs. In: Networks Learning with Graphs, pp. 1–7 (2009)
31. Agarwal, M.K., Ramamritham, K., Bhide, M.: Real time discovery of dense clusters in highly dynamic graphs: identifying real world events in highly dynamic environments, vol. 5, no. 10, pp. 980–991 (2012)

32. Cazabet, R., Amblard, F.: Simulate to detect: a multi-agent system for community detection. In: Proceedings of the 2011 IEEE/WIC/ACM International Conference on Web Intelligence and Intelligent Agent Technology, IAT 2011, vol. 2, September, pp. 402–408 (2011)
33. Duan, D., Li, Y., Li, R., Lu, Z.: Incremental K-clique clustering in dynamic social networks. Artif. Intell. Rev. **38**(2), 129–147 (2012)
34. Falkowski, T., Barth, A., Spiliopoulou, M.: DENGRAPH: a density-based community detection algorithm. In: WI 2007 Proceedings of the IEEE/WIC/ACM International Conference on Web Intelligence, pp. 112–115 (2007)
35. Görke, R., Hartmann, T., Wagner, D.: Dynamic graph clustering using minimum-cut trees. In: Dehne, F., Gavrilova, M., Sack, J.-R., Tóth, C.D. (eds.) WADS 2009. LNCS, vol. 5664, pp. 339–350. Springer, Heidelberg (2009). https://doi.org/10.1007/978-3-642-03367-4_30
36. Lee, P., Lakshmanan, L.V.S., Milios, E.E.: Event evolution tracking from streaming social posts (2013)
37. Ma, H.S., Huang, J.W.: Cut: community update and tracking in dynamic social networks. In: Proceedings of the 7th Workshop on Social Network Mining and Analysis, pp. 1–8 (2013)
38. Nguyen, N.P., Dinh, T.N., Xuan, Y., Thai, M.T.: Adaptive algorithms for detecting community structure in dynamic social networks. In: Proceedings of the IEEE INFOCOM, pp. 2282–2290 (2011)
39. Xie, J., Chen, M., Szymanski, B.K.: LabelRankT: incremental community detection in dynamic networks via label propagation (2013)
40. Zakrzewska, A., Bader, D.A.: A dynamic algorithm for local community detection in graphs. In: Proceedings of the 2015 IEEE/ACM International Conference on Advances in Social Networks Analysis and Mining, ASONAM 2015, no. 5, pp. 559–564 (2015)
41. Crane, H., Dempsey, W.: Community detection for interaction networks, pp. 1–29 (2015)
42. Gong, M.G., Zhang, L.J., Ma, J.J., Jiao, L.C.: Community detection in dynamic social networks based on multiobjective immune algorithm. J. Comput. Sci. Technol. **27**(3), 455–467 (2012)
43. Görke, R., Maillard, P., Schumm, A., Staudt, C., Wagner, D.: Dynamic graph clustering combining modularity and smoothness. J. Exp. Algorithmics **18**(April), 1.1–1.29 (2013)
44. Kawadia, V., Sreenivasan, S.: Sequential detection of temporal communities by estrangement confinement. Sci. Rep. **2**, 794 (2012)
45. Sun, Y., Tang, J., Han, J., Gupta, M., Zhao, B.: Community evolution detection in dynamic heterogeneous information networks. In: Proceedings of the Eighth Workshop on Mining and Learning with Graphs, MLG 2010, pp. 137–146 (2010)
46. Tang, L., Liu, H., Zhang, J., Nazeri, Z.: Community evolution in dynamic multi-mode networks. Tetrahedron Lett. **45**(9), 1903–1906 (2004)
47. Yang, T., Chi, Y., Zhu, S., Gong, Y., Jin, R.: Detecting communities and their evolutions in dynamic social networks— a Bayesian approach. Mach. Learn. **82**(2), 157–189 (2011). https://doi.org/10.1007/s10994-010-5214-7
48. Zhou, D., Councill, I., Zha, H., Giles, C.L.: Discovering temporal communities from social network documents. In: Proceedings of the IEEE International Conference on Data Mining, ICDM, pp. 745–750 (2007)
49. Guo, C., Wang, J., Zhang, Z.: Evolutionary community structure discovery in dynamic weighted networks. Phys. A Stat. Mech. Appl. **413**, 565–576 (2014)

50. Xu, K.S., Hero, A.O.: Dynamic stochastic blockmodels: statistical models for time-evolving networks. In: Greenberg, A.M., Kennedy, W.G., Bos, N.D. (eds.) SBP 2013. LNCS, vol. 7812, pp. 201–210. Springer, Heidelberg (2013). https://doi.org/10.1007/978-3-642-37210-0_22
51. Li, J., Huang, L., Bai, T., Wang, Z., Chen, H.: CDBIA: a dynamic community detection method based on incremental analysis. In: 2012 International Conference on Systems and Informatics (ICSAI2012), pp. 2224–2228 (2012)
52. Chakrabarti, D., Kumar, R., Tomkins, A.: Evolutionary clustering. In: Proceedings of the 12th ACM SIGKDD International Conference on Knowledge Discovery and Data Mining, KDD 2006, p. 554 (2006)
53. Hu, Y., Yang, B., Lv, C.: A local dynamic method for tracking communities and their evolution in dynamic networks. Knowl.-Based Syst. **110**, 176–190 (2016)
54. Ilhan, N., Oguducu, I.G.: Community event prediction in dynamic social networks. In: 2013 12th International Conference on Machine Learning and Applications, pp. 191–196 (2013)
55. Appel, A.P., Cunha, R.L.F., Aggarwal, C.C., Terakado, M.M.: Temporally evolving community detection and prediction in content-centric networks. In: Berlingerio, M., Bonchi, F., Gärtner, T., Hurley, N., Ifrim, G. (eds.) ECML PKDD 2018. LNCS (LNAI), vol. 11052, pp. 3–18. Springer, Cham (2019). https://doi.org/10.1007/978-3-030-10928-8_1
56. Tajeuna, E.G., Bouguessa, M., Wang, S.: Modeling and predicting community structure changes in time evolving social networks. IEEE Trans. Knowl. Data Eng. **31**, 1166–1180 (2018)
57. Zhao, Z., Li, C., Zhang, X., Chiclana, F., Viedma, E.H.: An incremental method to detect communities in dynamic evolving social networks. Knowl.-Based Syst. **163**, 404–415 (2019)
58. Jiao, P., Wang, W., Jin, D.: Constrained common cluster based model for community detection in temporal and multiplex networks. Neurocomputing **275**, 768–780 (2018)
59. Cheraghchi, H.S., Zakerolhosseini, A.: Toward a novel art inspired incremental community mining algorithm in dynamic social network. Appl. Intell. **46**(2), 409–426 (2017). https://doi.org/10.1007/s10489-016-0838-3
60. Sun, H., et al.: IncOrder: incremental density-based community detection in dynamic networks. Knowl.-Based Syst. **72**, 1–12 (2014)
61. Said, A., Abbasi, R.A., Maqbool, O., Daud, A., Aljohani, N.R.: CC-GA: a clustering coefficient based genetic algorithm for detecting communities in social networks. Appl. Soft Comput. J. **63**, 59–70 (2018)
62. Li, Z., Liu, J., Wu, K.: A multiobjective evolutionary algorithm based on structural and attribute similarities for community detection in attributed networks. IEEE Trans. Cybern. **48**(7), 1963–1976 (2018)
63. Asadi, M., Ghaderi, F.: Incremental community detection in social networks using label propagation method. In: Conference of Open Innovations Association (FRUCT), pp. 13–16, November 2018
64. Li, Y., He, K., Kloster, K., Bindel, D., Hopcroft, J.: Local spectral clustering for overlapping community detection. ACM Trans. Knowl. Discov. Data **12**(2), 1–27 (2018)
65. Zhang, C., Zhang, Y., Wu, B.: A parallel community detection algorithm based on incremental clustering in dynamic network. In: Procedings of the 2018 IEEE/ACM International Conference on Advances in Social Networks Analaysis and Mining, ASONAM 2018, pp. 946–953 (2018)

Dynamic Joint Variational Graph Autoencoders

Sedigheh Mahdavi(✉), Shima Khoshraftar(✉), and Aijun An(✉)

Department of Electrical Engineering and Computer Science,
York University, Toronto, Canada
{smahdavi,khoshraf,aan}@eecs.yorku.ca

Abstract. Learning network representations is a fundamental task for many graph applications such as link prediction, node classification, graph clustering, and graph visualization. Many real-world networks are interpreted as dynamic networks and evolve over time. Most existing graph embedding algorithms were developed for static graphs mainly and cannot capture the evolution of a large dynamic network. In this paper, we propose Dynamic joint Variational Graph Autoencoders (Dyn-VGAE) that can learn both local structures and temporal evolutionary patterns in a dynamic network. Dyn-VGAE provides a joint learning framework for computing temporal representations of all graph snapshots simultaneously. Each auto-encoder embeds a graph snapshot based on its local structure and can also learn temporal dependencies by collaborating with other autoencoders. We conduct experimental studies on dynamic real-world graph datasets and the results demonstrate the effectiveness of the proposed method.

Keywords: Graph representation · Network embedding · Generative model · Dynamic networks · Variational autoencoder

1 Introduction

Many real world data can be formulated as graphs to represent complex relationships among the objects in the data. Dealing with high dimensional graph structures is a highly challenging task for many machine learning algorithms. Graph embedding methods are helpful to reduce the high dimensionality of graph data by learning low-dimensional features as latent representations. Many embedding algorithms [1–4,8,12,13,18,24,25,27,31,35,37] have been proposed to capture different characteristics of a network and they provide effective ways to extract low-dimensional latent representations of graphs.

Most of the embedding approaches are designed as static methods, assuming that the nodes and edges in the graph are fixed. However, real networks are often dynamic, consisting of vertices and edges that may occur and disappear at different time points. In modeling a dynamic network, it is essential to take temporal dependencies and changes into account for characterizing evolving nodes and edges. Capturing these temporal factors requires a dynamic model

P. Cellier and K. Driessens (Eds.): ECML PKDD 2019 Workshops, CCIS 1167, pp. 385–401, 2020.
https://doi.org/10.1007/978-3-030-43823-4_32

that can learn the evolution track of a dynamic network over time. A dynamic network is often represented as a sequence of static graph snapshots over time. Some attempts have been made to develop a dynamic model for leaning temporal low-dimensional latent representations of graph snapshots [9,10,22,23,34,39–41]. A simple traditional method for obtaining the embedding vectors of a graph snapshot is computing embedding vectors in each timestamp separately. Then, the graph embedding vectors across all timestamps are aligned and placed in a same vector space.

Alignment methods raise two main issues. First, some learned embedding vectors are invariant to transformations and it is not possible to place embedding vectors of all graph snapshots in the same latent space. Second, such methods need to solve a separate optimization problem for finding transformation functions. In [41], the authors proposed a joint matrix factorization-based optimization function which can jointly find embedding vectors across time without the alignment step. The problem of this joint optimization function is a non-convex and non-linear optimization problem with a large number of variables. Recently, different types of deep autoencoders have been proposed to solve complex nonlinear functions [13,25,36]. Among the autoencoders, variational graph auto-encoder (VGAE) [18] is an effective static embedding method which is a deep generative model by variational inference. Similar to other static graph embedding methods, it is not designed for the dynamic setting. Joint deep learning models have recently achieved great success in many learning tasks such as multi-task learning and domain adaptation [6], multimodal network embedding [38], video description generation [26], image-text representation [15], and clustering [7]. These joint deep leaning models aim to learn dependencies and similarities among some target tasks by joining their goals together. As a dynamic network includes temporal dependencies among all graph snapshots, the intuition of join deep learning motivates us to develop a joint autoencoder based on VGAE.

In this paper, we propose a joint dynamic Variational autoencoder (DynVGAE) which simultaneously learns latent representations of the graphs at all timestamps. To the best of our knowledge, this is the first study on developing a deep joint learning for dynamic network representations. We first assign a specific variational autoencoder with a modified learning function for each graph snapshot. This learning framework jointly learns latent variables of each graph and captures evolving patterns among graphs by sharing learned latent variables during the training iterations. The main contributions of this work are:

- We introduce a joint learning approach, which is the first study to extract the dynamic network representation with collaboration among graph autoencoders. During the training steps, each autoencoder can collaborate with other autoencoders of previous graph snapshots.
- We define a novel probabilistic smoothness term in the loss function to align latent spaces across time, which provides a transfer learning strategy to adjust learned latent spaces.

- We conducted experiments on dynamic real-world datasets, which show that the proposed joint method can significantly improve the state of the art.

The rest of the paper is organized as follows. The related works are discussed in Sect. 2. In Sect. 3, we describe our proposed architecture. The experiments are detailed in Sect. 4. Conclusions and future work are presented in Sect. 5.

2 Related Work

In this section, we describe related work on static, dynamic, and joint deep learning methods.

2.1 Static Graph Embeddings

Network embedding for static graphs has been well studied in recent years [1,2, 8,12–14,18,25,27,31]. Conventional static network embedding methods include DeepWalk [27], Node2vec [12], LINE [31] and SDNE [36]. [12,27,31] are based on random walks and utilize random walks for capturing the neighborhood of the nodes in a graph inspired by advances in natural language processing. The main difference among these methods is related to the special kind of random walk they exploit. In [27] and [12], uniform random walks and BFS/DFS-like random walks are used, respectively. Another type of graph embedding methods [13,18,25,36] is based on adjacency matrices of graphs. In [36], the first-order and second-order proximity is used to represent the network structure. In [25] a jointly optimized adversarial framework is proposed for network embeddings. In this framework, the method first learns the topology of the graph and then forces the latent codes to be similar to a prior distribution.

2.2 Dynamic Graph Embeddings

Temporal network representation is a challenging problem as it needs to consider the evolutionary structure of graphs over time. There have been some recent efforts to tackle the problems in dynamic network embedding [9–11,19,22,23,34,40,41]. [40] uses the triadic closure process to learns changes in the structure of graphs. This method is specifically designed for undirected graphs. [10] is a deep learning model that initialized a graph model with weights from models of previous graphs to create the desired alignment among temporal embeddings. In [41] a joint matrix factorization method was proposed that learns a temporal latent space model for dynamic networks by developing local and incremental block-coordinate gradient descent algorithms. In [9], the authors proposed a deep learning method that captures the transition model of dynamic networks using dense and recurrent layers. dyngraph2vecAE, dyngraph2vecRNN and dyngraph2vecAERNN are three variations in [9]. dyngraph2vecAE models the changes in graphs using multiple fully connected layers. Then, dyngraph2vecRNN is presented as it has less parameters and takes into consideration the long term dependencies in graphs using an LSTM structure. In dyngraph2vecAERNN, the dimension of input vectors to LSTM is reduced by inputting node representation vectors into LSTM rather than sparsed vectors.

2.3 Joint Deep Learning Methods

Recently, many algorithms have been proposed to jointly learn embeddings for different applications. In [6], a joint learning framework was developed for multiple tasks. The authors designed a neural network model with shared branches for extracting information of common features and local branches for learning features of each task. For visual semantic embeddings, Pan et al. [26] introduced a long short-term memory with a visual-semantic embedding architecture which simultaneously learns the semantic sentence and video content. A joint convolutional autoencoder was proposed in [7] for the clustering task by jointing clustering and embedding tasks. Ren et al. [28] introduced a joint representation for image-text embedding task using the visual information in the text model. A joint embedding was introduced in [38] for coupled networks. Each network transfers some relevant information to other networks for learning intra-network edges in these networks. Huang et al. [15] proposed a deep joint embedding which incorporates the link information and multimodal contents together to obtain embedding for social media.

3 Method

A dynamic network is represented as a time-ordered sequence of static graphs, $G_1, G_2, \ldots, G_T$, where T is the number of time steps. The graph at time t is denoted by $G_t = (V_t, E_t)$ with a set V_t of $|V|$ vertices and an edge set E_t that may change in the time interval $[0, T]$. The dynamic graph embedding can be formulated as a temporal mapping function $f_t : A_t \rightarrow Z_t$ which finds a low-dimensional latent representation Z_t for graph G_t with an adjacency matrix A_t. In this section, we first review the static variational graph autoencoder briefly and then propose a novel dynamic graph embedding method, which we call Dynamic joint Variational Graph Autoencoders (Dyn-VGAE).

3.1 Static Variational Graph Autoencoder (SVGAE)

The overall architecture of SVGAE consists of two components: a variational graph convolutional network encoder and a probabilistic decoder [40]. The variational graph encoder is defined by an inference model, which encodes the observed graph data into stochastic low-dimensional latent variables (Z). The variational graph decoder is designed by a generative model, which decodes latent variables into the distribution of the observed graph data. Let $G = (V, E)$ denote a graph with an adjacency matrix A and the content features X, where V and

E are nodes and edges of the graph. Variational graph convolutional encoder is constructed as follows:

$$GCN(X, A) = (D^{-1/2}AD^{-1/2})f_R((D^{-1/2}AD^{-1/2})XW_0)W_1$$
$$f_R(t) = Relu(t) = max(0, t)$$

where D is a degree matrix. Weight matrices are W_i and first-layer parameters W_0 are shared between $GCN_\mu(X, A)$ and $GCN_\sigma(X, A)$. The generative process is characterized by an inner product between latent variables:

$$p(A|Z) = \prod_{i=1}^{N}\prod_{j=1}^{N} p(A_{i,j}|z_i, z_j),$$
$$with\, p(A_{i,j} = 1|z_i, z_j) = sigmoid(z_i^T, z_j)$$

The inference process is modeled by a two-layer graph convolutional network (GCN) [17] (Variational Graph Encoder):

$$q(Z|X, A) = \prod_{i}^{N} q(z_i|X, A), with\, q(z_i|X, A) = \mathcal{N}(z_i|\mu_i, diag(\sigma_i^2))$$

where $N = |V|$, μ and σ are parameters of the Gaussian distribution $q(.)$, $\mu = GCN_\mu(X, A)$ is the matrix of mean vectors, and $log\sigma = GCN_\sigma(X, A)$. The variational autoencoder is trained by maximizing the variational lower bound $L_{VLBO} = E_{q(Z|X,A)}[logp(A|Z)] - KL[q(Z|X, A)||p(Z)]$, where $KL[p(.)||q(.)]$ is the Kullback-Leibler (KL) divergence between $p(.)$ and $q(.)$. The L_{VLBO} is usually optimized via stochastic gradient descent, using the reparameterization trick to estimate the gradient.

3.2 Dynamic Joint Variational Graph Autoencoders (Dyn-VGAE)

Let $G_1, G_2, \ldots, G_T$ denote a dynamic network with a series of adjacency matrices $A_1, A_2, \ldots, A_T$. Dyn-VGAE aims to obtain a low dimensional latent representation of each graph G_t. This representation preserves both the local topology and the structure of a static graph snapshot G_t and also captures its evolutionary pattern from the previous time steps. In the proposed joint framework, each graph G_t has its own model (the variational autoencoder $VGAE_t$) which is similar to SVGAE except that it has a different learning loss function. The joint learning function encourages all autoencoders to collaborate together for obtaining similar parameters (latent representations). We describe the algorithm in detail below.

Autoencoder Model for Graph G_t. The encoder of a graph snapshot G_t with an adjacency matrix A_t and the content features X_t is modeled by a two-layer GCN:

$$q_t(Z_t|X_t, A_t) = \prod_{i}^{N_t} q_t(z_i^t|X_t, A_t),$$
$$with\; q_t(z_i^t|X_t, A_t) = \mathcal{N}(z_i^t|\mu_{t,i}, diag(\sigma_{t,i}^2))$$

The probabilistic decoder of $VGAE_t$ is:

$$p_t(A_t|Z_t) = \prod_{i=1}^{N_t}\prod_{j=1}^{N_t} p_t(A_{i,j}^t|z_i^t, z_j^t),$$

$$with\ p_t(A_{i,j}^t = 1|z_i^t, z_j^t) = sigmoid((z_i^t)^T, z_j^t).$$

Similar to the static variational autoencoder, $VGAE_t$ optimizes the variational lower bound for learning the current latent representation by minimizing the loss function as follows:

$$\begin{aligned} min\ L_{V_t} = & E_{q_t(Z_t|X_t,A_t)}[logp_t(A_t|Z_t)] \\ & -\mathcal{KL}[q_t(Z_t|X_t,A_t)||p_t(Z_t)] \end{aligned}$$

A general assumption of a dynamic network is [10,22,29,40] that changes are smooth and continuous in a short duration (length l) [40]. Thus, the key question here is how an associated encoder for graph G_t can learn aligned embedding vectors with embedding vectors of other graphs in a dynamic network. We change the learning process in which the autoencoder $VGAE_t$ can be joint with other autoencoders of previous graphs during the training process.

By collaborating with other prior autoencoders, each autoencoder is able to transfer temporal dependencies from previous latent spaces to the current latent space. The parameters of $VGAE_t$ are obtained by a modified loss function which has a temporal smoothness dependency term for aligning the latent space of graph G_t with l prior snapshots. By assuming change smoothness, we force the current latent representations to be similar to the previous latent vectors by minimizing the difference between two distributions of the current latent space and a temporal Gaussian random walk [29]. The temporal Gaussian random walk is defined based on latent representations of the previous graphs in l prior times. For simplicity, first we explain our method by assuming the length l is equal to two. This means the current latent space (Z_t) of the graph G_t should be similar to only the previous latent space (Z_{t-1}); then we will extend l to a general length. This temporal Gaussian random walk (q_W^t) can be defined as a Gaussian distribution with the mean Z_{t-1}:

$$q_W^t = \mathcal{N}(Z_{t-1}, \sigma^2)$$

where σ^2 is considered as Gaussian noise with a fixed standard deviation [29]. Temporal smoothness dependency term $\mathcal{L}_s^t$ is defined as the Kullback-Leibler ($\mathcal{KL}$) divergence among q_W^t and $q(Z_t|X_t, A_t)$:

$$\mathcal{L}_s^t = \mathcal{KL}[q_t(Z_t|X_t, A_t)||q_W^t]$$

$\mathcal{L}_s^t$ prevents the current latent vectors from being placed very far from latent vectors in the previous timestamps. Then, the final learning loss function can be formulated by combining the variational learning function $\mathcal{L}_v^t$ and temporal smoothness dependency term $\mathcal{L}_s^t$:

$$min\ \mathcal{L}_C^t = \mathcal{L}_v^t + \gamma\mathcal{L}_s^t$$

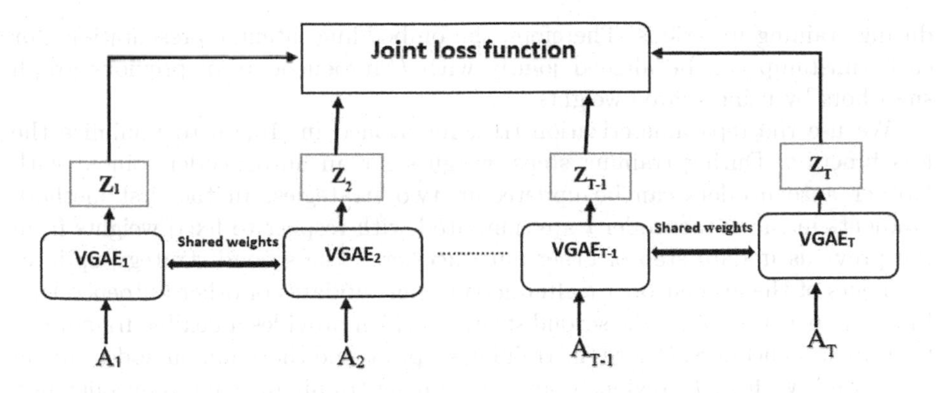

Fig. 1. Joint framework for graphs $G_1, G_2, \ldots, G_T$ with a series of adjacency matrices $A_1, A_2, \ldots, A_T$

where the hyperparameter γ controls the importance of the two losses. The term $\mathcal{L}_v^t$ learns latent representations of the graph G_t by minimizing the distance between the model prediction $p(.)$ and the target variable $q(.)$. The additional smoothness term $\mathcal{L}_s^t$ forces latent representations to be aligned with prior latent representations of the graph G_t. For $l > 2$, $\mathcal{L}_v^t$ can be formulated as follows:

$$\mathcal{L}_s^t = \sum_{i=t}^{t-l} \mathcal{KL}[q_t(Z_t|X_t, A_t)||q_W^i]$$

Joint Dynamic Graph Autoencoders Framework. The joint learning framework is shown in Fig. 1. Consider $G_1, G_2, \ldots, G_T$ as a dynamic network, we assign T autoencoders $VGAE_1, VGAE_2, \ldots, VGAE_T$ for all graphs. All loss learning functions of these autoencodres can be jointly collaborated while each autoencoder can focus on its own task to learn its own graph latent representations. The joint loss learning function can be formulated as the summation of the loss function of all autoencoders:

$$\begin{aligned} min \sum_{i=1}^{T} \mathcal{L}_C^i &= \sum_{i=1}^{T} \mathcal{L}_v^i + \gamma \mathcal{L}_s^i \\ &= \sum_{i=1}^{T} [\prod_{j=1}^{N_i} \prod_{k=1}^{N_i} p_i(A_{j,k}^i | z_j^i, z_k^i) + \\ &\sum_{j=i}^{i-l} \mathcal{KL}[q_i(Z_i|X_i, A_i)||q_W^j]] \end{aligned}$$

Each autoencoder is trained to learn latent variables specific to a graph and extract temporal dependencies among graphs by sharing learned latent variables during training iterations. Therefore, the embedding latent representations for each timstamp can be aligned jointly with l autoencoders of previous graph snapshots by using shared weights.

We use the reparameterization trick mentioned in [16,18] to minimize the loss function. During training steps, weights for an autoencoder jointed with l other autoencoders can be updated in two strategies. In the first method, gradients in the autoencoder t are computed with respect to fixed weights from the previous update step of other autoencoders. The second strategy updates gradients of the autoencoder t after getting new updates of other autoencoders. In this paper, we choose the second strategy which provides a flexible framework to train autoencoders. Before the training step, we find the common nodes among each graph with its l previous graphs, so during training each autoencoder just needs to share learned weights for common nodes. The proposed joint framework is very practical because the gradient of the additional smoothing term can be easily computed similar to the KL term in the variational autoencoder. Also, the framework is trivially parallelizable and each autoencoder just needs to cooperate with only l autoencoders where l is considered as a short period of time.

4 Experiments

We performed the evaluation of our method on multiple real-world datasets from various domains on node classification, link prediction and receommendation tasks. The findings of our experiments are reported as follows.

4.1 Baselines

The models for comparison are listed below:

- **DeepWalk** [27]**:** DeepWalk is a static network embedding method based on uniform random walks.
- **Node2vec** [12]**:** This method is a static network representation algorithm utilizing breadth-first-search (BFS) or depth-first-search (DFS) based random walks and skipgram.
- **SVGAE** [18]**:** This is a variational graph autoencoder model that works for static graphs. SVGAE is an inference-based graph embedding model that encodes the observed graphs into their respective distribution.
- **dynAE** [10]**:** dynAE stands for dyngraph2vecAE, a dynamic network embedding method based on dyngraph2vec. It utilizes deep learning models with multiple fully-connected layers to model interconnections of nodes.
- **dynAERNN** [10]**:** dynAERNN is the short form we used for dyngraph2vecAERNN. This is another variant of the dyngraph2vec method, which is a dynamic representation learning method. It feeds previously learned representations to LSTMs to generate embedding vectors.

For each static baseline method, we apply the static baseline method independently to each graph snapshot G_t in a dynamic network.

4.2 Experiment Settings

We run our experiments on DeepWalk and Node2vec with $(p, q) = (1, 1)$ and $(p, q) = (0.5, 1)$, respectively. The number of random walks per node is set to 10. For dynAE and dynAERNN, we used the default parameters in the publicly available source code [10,11]. The parameters of SVGAE and Dyn-VGAE are similar to [18]. Their autoencoder model structure consists of 32 dimensional hidden layers and 16 dimensional latent variables. For training, we used the Adam optimizer, the learning rate is 0.01, and number of epochs are 200. Dyn-VGAE1 is Dyn-VGAE with $l = 1$ and in Dyn-VGAE2, $l = 2$.

Table 1. Macro-F1 and Micro-F1 scores for node classification

Method	Acm		Dblp	
	mac-f1	mic-f1	mac-f1	mic-f1
node2vec	0.3775	0.5221	0.3768	0.5185
DeepWalk	0.3532	0.502	0.3815	0.5245
SVGAE	0.3896	0.5664	0.4224	0.5227
dynAE	0.3699	0.5237	0.3675	0.479
dynAERNN	0.402	0.5581	0.3876	0.4959
Dyn-VGAE1	0.4048	0.575	0.439	0.5283
Dyn-VGAE2	**0.4402**	**0.5896**	**0.4716**	**0.5356**

Table 2. AUC scores for link prediction

Method	Hep-th	AS	St-Ov
node2vec	0.973137	0.91305	0.59249
DeepWalk	0.97238	0.91219	0.58776
SVGAE	0.97499	0.91974	0.65437
dynAE	0.87834	0.7969	0.52017
dynAERNN	0.93851	0.83913	0.56149
Dyn-VGAE1	**0.98236**	0.92981	**0.74065**
Dyn-VGAE2	0.97754	**0.93187**	0.69466

4.3 Node Classification

In node classification tasks, each node in a graph has a class label. We predict the class label for the nodes in graph G_t using previous graphs in the stream from 0 to $t - 1$ based on the approach mentioned in [10]. Our classification method is logistic regression. We used two measures, Micro-f1 and Macro-f1, for evaluating our method. The results are presented in Table 1. The datasets are as follows:

- **Dblp** [32,33]: Dblp is the main coauthorship network of researches in various fields with 90k nodes and 749k edges over 18 years (2000–2017). There are two class labels for nodes: (1) database and data mining (VLDB, SIGMOD, PODS, ICDE, EDBT, SIGKDD, ICDM, DASFAA, SSDBM, CIKM, PAKDD, PKDD, SDM and DEXA) (2) computer vision and pattern recognition (CVPR, ICCV, ICIP, ICPR, ECCV, ICME and ACM-MM).
- **Acm** [32,33]: The Acm dataset has the same characteristics as the Dblp dataset. The timespan of Acm is considered as 16 years (2000–2015).

Based on the results, it is evident that our approach outperforms the baselines in both Acm and Dblp datasets. Specially, Macro-F1 scores are significantly better than the closest benchmarks and our performance gain is above other methods in terms of Micro-F1 scores. From the results, it can been seen that on both Acm and Dblp datasets, increasing the effect of previous graphs by extending l in Dyn-VGAE2 improves the overall results. The reason is that in coauthorship datasets the changes between consecutive snapshots are smooth and the research area of authors is fixed in a short period of time.

4.4 Link Prediction

One of the main graph mining tasks is link prediction as it shows the effectiveness of the edge embeddings in predicting unseen edges. We predict edges in graph G_t using previous learned embeddings of graph G_{t-1} mentioned in [10]. For this task, the reconstruction scores are computed similar to [18] and we report the average AUC (area under ROC curve) scores over time from 1 to T for all datasets in Table 2. The evaluation was performed on the following three datasets.

- **Hep-th** [20]: This is the coauthorship network of researchers in high energy physics theory conference with 34k nodes, 421k edges, 60 time points.
- **AS** [20]: Autonomous Systems are the communication network between users in BGP. It contains 6k nodes, 13k edges and 100 time steps.
- **St-Ov** [20]: This dataset shows the user interactions in the Math Overflow website. This dataset consists of 14k nodes and 195k edges over 58 time points.

The results show that Dyn-VGAE achieves the highest AUC in all the three datasets. In AS and St-Ov, our approach outperforms the benchmark methods by a significant margin. This highlights that our method effectively learns the dynamic representations in these datasets. Similarly, the results of our method on the Hep-th dataset are better than those of other methods. The effects of increasing l for AS and Hep-th are not that significant while this is not the case in St-Ov. In the St-Ov dataset, graph snopshots have less common edges. Therefore, its results with smaller l's are better.

Table 3. Analysis of parameter γ for node classification

Dataset	γ	mac-f1	mic-f1
Dblp	0.5	0.4386	0.5288
	1.5	0.4377	0.5299
	2	0.4362	0.529
Acm	0.2	0.3992	0.5714
	1.2	0.4028	0.5754
	1.5	0.4004	0.5776

4.5 Recommendation Task

Recommendation is a challenging task, especially in dynamic graphs. A recommendation task aims to suggest potential relations to users in many networks such as coauthorship, communication, and interaction networks. For example, in the coauthorship network **Hep-th**, we recommend co-authors to researchers by learning their embeddings over time. In [42], temporal recommendation is defined as recommending new connections for a node at time t by using obtained embeddings from previous time points. Here, we use the learned embedding at time $t-1$ to rank nodes for recommending top-k possible relations for the graph G_t. Our ranking score is based on the cosine similarity of embedding vectors of nodes. We use Precision@k and Recall@k as evaluation measures where the value k varies from 2 to 10. The number of nodes is different for each k because we select common nodes of consecutive times with more than k neighbors. Tables 5, 6 and 7 show the average Precision@k and Recall@k over time from 1 to T for three datasets: the coauthorship network **Hep-th**, communication network **AS**, and interaction user network **St-ov**. From the results, it can be seen that Dyn-VGAE performs better than other compared methods on **Hep-th** and **St-ov**; it obtains higher Precision@k and Recall@k for all different k values. However, the performance of Dyn-VGAE decreases on **AS** and dynAERNN performs the

Table 4. Analysis of parameter γ for link prediction

Dataset	γ	AUC
Hep-th	0.7	0.98186
	1	0.98031
	1.2	0.97773
AS	0.2	0.92283
	0.5	0.92858
	1.2	0.92766
St-Ov	0.5	0.75342
	0.7	0.72256
	1	0.72064

Table 5. Precision and Recall for recommendation on AS dataset

Method		k=2	k=3	k=4	k=5	k=6	k=7	k=8	k=9	k=10
node2vec	Recall	0.214669	0.334204	0.367184	0.394506	0.407605	0.416419	0.425321	**0.429238**	**0.4371**
	Precision	0.388217	0.543356	0.640374	0.696155	0.739523	0.759523	0.769879	**0.781488**	**0.785693**
DeepWalk	Recall	0.220448	0.338428	0.368539	0.394732	0.407542	0.415795	0.423611	0.42708	0.434744
	Precision	0.395229	0.547698	0.64106	0.695375	0.737814	0.756948	0.76571	0.776629	0.780256
SVGAE	Recall	0.273485	0.263785	0.273485	0.294505	0.306035	0.315532	0.321633	0.32235	0.318589
	Precision	0.494758	0.432536	0.494758	0.540298	0.576909	0.596037	0.603462	0.610673	0.604129
dynAE	Recall	0.243241	0.260874	0.249538	0.340724	0.363635	0.430242	0.027614	0.425404	0.424393
	Precision	0.484355	0.519891	0.58471	0.675628	0.669945	0.667173	0.064773	0.764048	0.763721
dynAERNN	Recall	**0.294509**	**0.358547**	**0.375264**	**0.409208**	**0.445241**	**0.481598**	**0.436302**	0.432607	0.43122
	Precision	**0.501646**	**0.555114**	**0.670827**	**0.712004**	**0.786749**	**0.794443**	**0.776476**	0.773307	0.771579
Dyn-VGAE1	Recall	0.165353	0.253836	0.26011	0.280628	0.291986	0.301531	0.307532	0.31024	0.315377
	Precision	0.30464	0.416175	0.47301	0.516912	0.551996	0.570365	0.57744	0.586087	0.588087
Dyn-VGAE2	Recall	0.16685	0.260054	0.269341	0.290558	0.302173	0.312019	0.317569	0.319883	0.325352
	Precision	0.308355	0.426376	0.487754	0.53296	0.56928	0.588481	0.595397	0.604296	0.606698

Table 6. Precision and Recall for recommendation on Hep-th dataset

Method		k=2	k=3	k=4	k=5	k=6	k=7	k=8	k=9	k=10
node2vec	Recall	0.32482	0.465231	0.55624	0.585563	0.609622	0.646217	0.569039	0.598079	0.547933
	Precision	0.44415	0.585353	0.67445	0.726131	0.739472	0.766933	0.68246	0.687628	0.630987
DeepWalk	Recall	0.315802	0.468277	0.550393	0.572584	0.607141	0.627954	0.568508	0.594742	0.545312
	Precision	0.433653	0.586132	0.668169	0.709337	0.736379	0.745321	0.681347	0.683836	0.628118
SVGAE	Recall	0.378678	0.511046	0.580978	0.600192	0.614316	0.643828	0.567718	0.551842	0.549033
	Precision	0.510663	0.643486	0.703221	0.720982	0.751181	0.763746	0.682238	0.685163	0.632336
dynAE	Recall	0.337487	0.059347	0.530609	0.57412	0.575352	0.558555	0.5437	0.537371	0.528373
	Precision	0.452566	0.073831	0.644052	0.688662	0.685259	0.666084	0.649728	0.640798	0.601132
dynAERNN	Recall	0.373237	0.508547	0.562752	0.599208	0.605728	0.581598	0.565275	0.557373	0.544694
	Precision	0.501881	0.635114	0.665775	0.722004	0.722058	0.694443	0.675759	0.664076	0.620038
Dyn-VGAE1	Recall	0.389606	0.522072	0.591764	0.602518	0.627004	0.645771	0.581532	0.608694	0.55852
	Precision	0.521951	0.646657	0.714264	0.743664	0.76054	0.766375	0.697046	0.699577	0.642631
Dyn-VGAE2	Recall	**0.39046**	**0.522811**	**0.59121**	**0.602739**	**0.626602**	**0.64676**	**0.581511**	**0.610082**	**0.560516**
	Precision	**0.522826**	**0.647528**	**0.713929**	**0.743913**	**0.760167**	**0.767543**	**0.697636**	**0.701501**	**0.645338**

Table 7. Precision and Recall for recommendation on St-Ov dataset

Method		k=2	k=3	k=4	k=5	k=6	k=7	k=8	k=9	k=10
node2vec	Recall	0.199371	0.170521	0.151717	0.142989	0.128116	0.125163	0.120154	0.116243	0.113564
	Precision	0.343357	0.271554	0.229346	0.207767	0.185266	0.17563	0.163032	0.154961	0.148131
DeepWalk	Recall	0.199072	0.170562	0.151378	0.142644	0.126195	0.122637	0.118336	0.119307	0.115129
	Precision	0.342977	0.271374	0.228719	0.207191	0.182268	0.172017	0.161157	0.158638	0.150188
SVGAE	Recall	0.200822	0.170041	0.155608	0.144517	0.131738	0.128646	0.125685	0.122943	0.121674
	Precision	0.34631	0.274437	0.236112	0.212186	0.191121	0.181621	0.171127	0.164683	0.15869
dynAE	Recall	0.088628	0.077637	0.067938	0.062643	0.05903	0.054914	0.054631	0.053159	0.049165
	Precision	0.158084	0.125986	0.104936	0.093048	0.085407	0.077678	0.074203	0.071328	0.064948
dynAERNN	Recall	0.108056	0.094056	0.082202	0.077242	0.071827	0.067795	0.066443	0.065219	0.064853
	Precision	0.191947	0.152271	0.127425	0.114656	0.104315	0.095892	0.09075	0.087338	0.084257
Dyn-VGAE1	Recall	**0.204545**	**0.177749**	**0.160533**	**0.151073**	**0.13851**	**0.136031**	**0.134245**	**0.133499**	**0.135583**
	Precision	**0.352988**	**0.284164**	**0.244354**	**0.222065**	**0.202489**	**0.193704**	**0.185364**	**0.181157**	**0.179375**
Dyn-VGAE2	Recall	0.20165	0.173873	0.157185	0.147463	0.134296	0.128952	0.128332	0.126622	0.127372
	Precision	0.347869	0.277905	0.238164	0.21595	0.194931	0.182753	0.174999	0.170079	0.166873

Table 8. Analysis of parameter γ for recommendation

Dataset	a		k=2	k=3	k=4	k=5	k=6	k=7	k=8	k=9	k=10
Hep-th	0.6	Recall	0.389327	0.523287	0.594644	0.604486	0.628978	0.647625	0.582096	0.609569	0.561969
		Precision	0.521504	0.648319	0.717725	0.746177	0.762935	0.768519	0.698145	0.701224	0.64713
	1	Recall	0.388978	0.522966	0.592967	0.603635	0.629609	0.649588	0.58224	0.609715	0.558395
		Precision	0.52145	0.648012	0.715753	0.745351	0.763854	0.770862	0.698341	0.701171	0.643245
	1.2	Recall	0.389843	0.522133	0.592613	0.603883	0.628463	0.64613	0.581418	0.606744	0.559629
		Precision	0.522121	0.647054	0.715439	0.745214	0.761996	0.766968	0.697532	0.698231	0.644725
AS	0.2	Recall	0.17086	0.266335	0.276734	0.297303	0.309268	0.317995	0.323751	0.325599	0.332499
		Precision	0.314745	0.436361	0.499391	0.544163	0.581436	0.599712	0.607367	0.616013	0.620238
	0.5	Recall	0.170643	0.264457	0.273346	0.293521	0.305441	0.314985	0.320376	0.322351	0.32855
		Precision	0.313586	0.432619	0.493706	0.53772	0.574147	0.593054	0.59961	0.607748	0.611074
	1.2	Recall	0.160112	0.247704	0.251588	0.270774	0.281948	0.290562	0.29635	0.298402	0.3036
		Precision	0.296535	0.405931	0.458814	0.500643	0.53471	0.551478	0.558458	0.565753	0.56792
St-Ov	0.5	Recall	0.20672	0.18231	0.167141	0.162219	0.14719	0.144816	0.142089	0.140077	0.14082
		Precision	0.35675	0.291245	0.253335	0.236867	0.213672	0.20471	0.194035	0.188426	0.185214
	0.7	Recall	0.203847	0.175776	0.158857	0.149699	0.135384	0.130333	0.129943	0.129038	0.129972
		Precision	0.351087	0.281454	0.241279	0.219523	0.197625	0.186804	0.17955	0.174856	0.171854
	1	Recall	0.204545	0.177749	0.160533	0.151073	0.13851	0.136031	0.134245	0.133499	0.135583
		Precision	0.352988	0.284164	0.244354	0.222065	0.202489	0.193704	0.185364	0.181157	0.179375

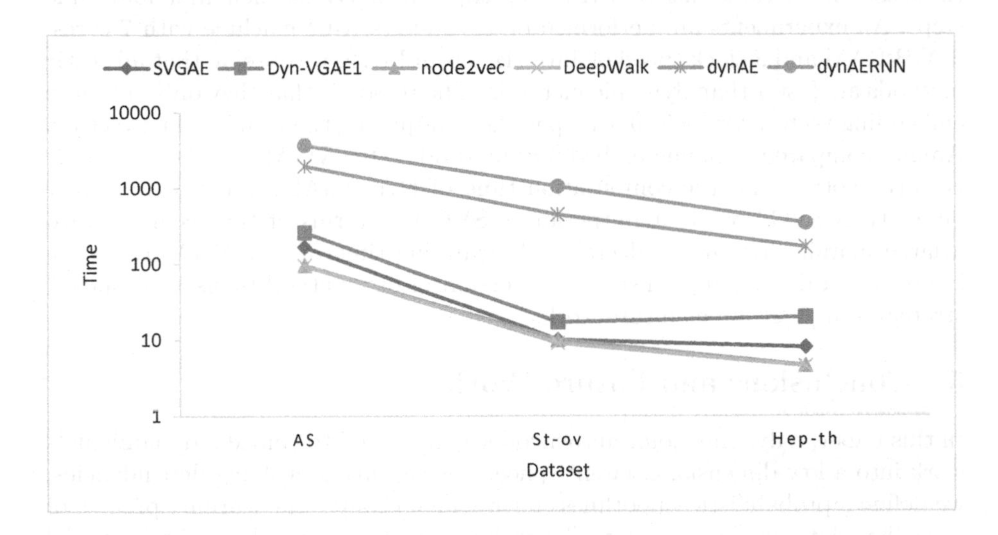

Fig. 2. Computation time of embedding methods for the four timestamps on each dataset.

best. Also, we can see that Dyn-VGA1 performs better than Dyn-VGA2 on the dataset **St-ov** due to characteristics of this dataset. As mentioned previously, the reason is that on this dataset considering smaller length l is more suitable as we observed the same behaviour for the link predication task. It is worth mentioning that as the numbers of nodes for different k's are different, we cannot see a decreasing trend by increasing k for either Precision@k or Recall@k.

4.6 The Effect of Temporal Smoothness γ

We study the effect of γ on the performance of Dyn-VGAE. The parameter γ can be fine-tuned to balance the weights of the local structure of the graph and the effect of previous graphs based on the data and the requirement of the task. We examine how the changes in γ can affect the results. We vary α from 0 to 3. If $\gamma = 0$, the dynamic representations are only learning the local structure of the graph. By increasing the value of γ, we force the learned latent space of the graph to be aligned with the space of previous graphs. Our experiments show that Dyn-VGAE has the best performance when $\gamma \in [0.1, 2.5]$ and it starts decreasing for $\gamma > 2.5$. We report the results of our analysis for three values of γ for each dataset in Tables 3, 4 and 8 for Dyn-VGAE with $l = 1$. We observe the same behavior for Dyn-VGAE with $l = 2$.

4.7 Time Complexity Analysis

We compare our method with all baseline models in terms of running time (in seconds) on three datasets AS, Hep-th, and St-Ov at their first four time steps. All experiments are performed on a windows X-64 machine with 7 cores, 64 GB RAM and a clock speed of 3.6 GHz. From Fig. 2, we observe that all static methods are faster than dynamic methods. The reason is that they only compute embedding vectors for each time step without adjusting these embedding vectors. Among compared dynamic embedding methods, Dyn-VGAE1 is the fastest. It is worth noting that the computation time of Dyn-VGAE1 is not significantly larger than SVGA while it outperforms SVGA in terms of the accuracy with a large margin. To further decrease the running time of Dyn-VGAE1, we are interested in developing a distributed version of our method by using proposed strategies in [5,21,30] as future work.

5 Conclusions and Future Work

In this paper, a dynamic joint autoencoder is proposed to embed a dynamic network into a low-dimensional latent space. For capturing evolving dependencies, we define a probabilistic smoothness term which changes the learning process of a graph variational autoencoder. The proposed joint framework provides a model where autoencoders can share their learned latent vectors across time stamps. The basic idea of the approach is the sharing of learned information of the current graph snapshot with previous graph snapshots for common nodes while each autoencoder works on its own specific graph. Dyn-VGAE simultaneously learns the latent representations of a dynamic network and aligns them across time. The experimental results show that Dyn-VGAE can significantly outperform the state-of-the-art methods on the node classification, link predication, and recommendation tasks. In the future, we are interested in applying different variants of joint deep learning architectures to extract the dynamic latent space of a dynamic network and developing a distributed model to increase the speed of training. Also, we will investigate a joint approach for other deep graph embedding methods.

References

1. Cai, H., Zheng, V.W., Chang, K.C.C.: A comprehensive survey of graph embedding: problems, techniques, and applications. IEEE Trans. Knowl. Data Eng. **30**(9), 1616–1637 (2018)
2. Cao, S., Lu, W., Xu, Q.: GraRep: learning graph representations with global structural information. In: Proceedings of the 24th ACM International on Conference on Information and Knowledge Management, pp. 891–900. ACM (2015)
3. Cao, S., Lu, W., Xu, Q.: Deep neural networks for learning graph representations. In: Thirtieth AAAI Conference on Artificial Intelligence (2016)
4. Cui, P., Wang, X., Pei, J., Zhu, W.: A survey on network embedding. IEEE Trans. Knowl. Data Eng. **31**, 833–852 (2018)
5. Dean, J., et al.: Large scale distributed deep networks. In: Advances in Neural Information Processing Systems, pp. 1223–1231 (2012)
6. Epstein, B., Meir, R., Michaeli, T.: Joint autoencoders: a flexible meta-learning framework. In: Berlingerio, M., Bonchi, F., Gärtner, T., Hurley, N., Ifrim, G. (eds.) ECML PKDD 2018. LNCS (LNAI), vol. 11051, pp. 494–509. Springer, Cham (2019). https://doi.org/10.1007/978-3-030-10925-7_30
7. Ghasedi Dizaji, K., Herandi, A., Deng, C., Cai, W., Huang, H.: Deep clustering via joint convolutional autoencoder embedding and relative entropy minimization. In: Proceedings of the ICCV, pp. 5736–5745 (2017)
8. Goyal, P., Ferrara, E.: Graph embedding techniques, applications, and performance: a survey. Knowl.-Based Syst. **151**, 78–94 (2018)
9. Goyal, P., Hosseinmardi, H., Ferrara, E., Galstyan, A.: Capturing edge attributes via network embedding. IEEE Trans. Comput. Soc. Syst. **5**(4), 907–917 (2018)
10. Goyal, P., Kamra, N., He, X., Liu, Y.: DynGem: deep embedding method for dynamic graphs. In: IJCAI International Workshop on Representation Learning for Graphs (2017)
11. Goyal, P., Rokka Chhetri, S., Mehrabi, N., Ferrara, E., Canedo, A.: DynamicGEM: a library for dynamic graph embedding methods. arXiv preprint arXiv:1811.10734 (2018)
12. Grover, A., Leskovec, J.: node2vec: scalable feature learning for networks. In: Proceedings of the 22nd ACM SIGKDD, pp. 855–864. ACM (2016)
13. Hamilton, W., Ying, Z., Leskovec, J.: Inductive representation learning on large graphs. In: Advances in Neural Information Processing Systems, pp. 1024–1034 (2017)
14. Hamilton, W.L., Ying, R., Leskovec, J.: Representation learning on graphs: methods and applications. arXiv preprint arXiv:1709.05584 (2017)
15. Huang, F., Zhang, X., Li, C., Li, Z., He, Y., Zhao, Z.: Multimodal network embedding via attention based multi-view variational autoencoder. In: Proceedings of the 2018 ACM on International Conference on Multimedia Retrieval, pp. 108–116. ACM (2018)
16. Kingma, D.P., Welling, M.: Auto-encoding variational bayes. arXiv preprint arXiv:1312.6114 (2013)
17. Kipf, T.N., Welling, M.: Semi-supervised classification with graph convolutional networks. arXiv preprint arXiv:1609.02907 (2016)
18. Kipf, T.N., Welling, M.: Variational graph auto-encoders. Stat **1050**, 21 (2016)
19. Kumar, S., Zhang, X., Leskovec, J.: Learning dynamic embeddings from temporal interactions. arXiv preprint arXiv:1812.02289 (2018)

20. Leskovec, J., Krevl, A.: {SNAP Datasets}:{Stanford} large network dataset collection (2015)
21. Liu, J., Dutta, J., Li, N., Kurup, U., Shah, M.: Usability study of distributed deep learning frameworks for convolutional neural networks (2018)
22. Mahdavi, S., Khoshraftar, S., An, A.: dynnode2vec: scalable dynamic network embedding. In: 2018 IEEE Big Data, pp. 3762–3765. IEEE (2018)
23. Nguyen, G.H., Lee, J.B., Rossi, R.A., Ahmed, N.K., Koh, E., Kim, S.: Continuous-time dynamic network embeddings. In: Companion of the The Web Conference 2018 on The Web Conference 2018, pp. 969–976. International World Wide Web Conferences Steering Committee (2018)
24. Ou, M., Cui, P., Pei, J., Zhang, Z., Zhu, W.: Asymmetric transitivity preserving graph embedding. In: Proceedings of the 22nd ACM SIGKDD International Conference on Knowledge Discovery and Data Mining, pp. 1105–1114. ACM (2016)
25. Pan, S., Hu, R., Long, G., Jiang, J., Yao, L., Zhang, C.: Adversarially regularized graph autoencoder for graph embedding. In: Proceedings of the 27th IJCAI, pp. 2609–2615. AAAI Press (2018)
26. Pan, Y., Mei, T., Yao, T., Li, H., Rui, Y.: Jointly modeling embedding and translation to bridge video and language. In: Proceedings of the IEEE Conference on Computer Vision and Pattern Recognition, pp. 4594–4602 (2016)
27. Perozzi, B., Al-Rfou, R., Skiena, S.: Deepwalk: online learning of social representations. In: Proceedings of the 20th ACM SIGKDD, pp. 701–710. ACM (2014)
28. Ren, Z., Jin, H., Lin, Z., Fang, C., Yuille, A.: Joint image-text representation by gaussian visual-semantic embedding. In: Proceedings of the 24th ACM International Conference on Multimedia, pp. 207–211. ACM (2016)
29. Sarkar, P., Moore, A.W.: Dynamic social network analysis using latent space models. In: Advances in Neural Information Processing Systems, pp. 1145–1152 (2006)
30. Simonyan, K., Zisserman, A.: Very deep convolutional networks for large-scale image recognition. arXiv preprint arXiv:1409.1556 (2014)
31. Tang, J., Qu, M., Wang, M., Zhang, M., Yan, J., Mei, Q.: Line: large-scale information network embedding. In: Proceedings of the 24th WWW, pp. 1067–1077. International World Wide Web Conferences Steering Committee (2015)
32. Tang, J., Zhang, J., Yao, L., Li, J.: Extraction and mining of an academic social network. In: Proceedings of the 17th WWW, pp. 1193–1194. ACM (2008)
33. Tang, J., Zhang, J., Yao, L., Li, J., Zhang, L., Su, Z.: ArnetMiner: extraction and mining of academic social networks. In: Proceedings of the 14th ACM SIGKDD, pp. 990–998. ACM (2008)
34. Trivedi, R., Farajtbar, M., Biswal, P., Zha, H.: Representation learning over dynamic graphs. arXiv preprint arXiv:1803.04051 (2018)
35. Tu, C., Zhang, W., Liu, Z., Sun, M., et al.: Max-margin deepwalk: discriminative learning of network representation. In: IJCAI, pp. 3889–3895 (2016)
36. Wang, D., Cui, P., Zhu, W.: Structural deep network embedding. In: Proceedings of the 22nd ACM SIGKDD, pp. 1225–1234. ACM (2016)
37. Wang, X., Cui, P., Wang, J., Pei, J., Zhu, W., Yang, S.: Community preserving network embedding. In: Thirty-First AAAI Conference on Artificial Intelligence (2017)
38. Xu, L., Wei, X., Cao, J., Yu, P.S.: Embedding of Embedding (EOE): joint embedding for coupled heterogeneous networks. In: Proceedings of the Tenth ACM International Conference on Web Search and Data Mining, pp. 741–749. ACM (2017)
39. Yu, W., Cheng, W., Aggarwal, C.C., Zhang, K., Chen, H., Wang, W.: NetWalk: a flexible deep embedding approach for anomaly detection in dynamic networks. In: Proceedings of the 24th ACM SIGKDD, pp. 2672–2681. ACM (2018)

40. Zhou, L., Yang, Y., Ren, X., Wu, F., Zhuang, Y.: Dynamic network embedding by modeling triadic closure process. In: Thirty-Second AAAI (2018)
41. Zhu, L., Ver Steeg, G., Galstyan, A.: Scalable link prediction in dynamic networks via non-negative matrix factorization (2018)
42. Zuo, Y., Liu, G., Lin, H., Guo, J., Hu, X., Wu, J.: Embedding temporal network via neighborhood formation. In: Proceedings of the 24th ACM SIGKDD, pp. 2857–2866. ACM (2018)

Evolution Analysis of Large Graphs with Gradoop

Christopher Rost[1(✉)], Andreas Thor[2(✉)], Philip Fritzsche[1(✉)], Kevin Gomez[1(✉)], and Erhard Rahm[1(✉)]

[1] University of Leipzig, Leipzig, Germany
{rost,fritzsche,gomez,rahm}@informatik.uni-leipzig.de
[2] Leipzig University of Applied Sciences, Leipzig, Germany
andreas.thor@htwk-leipzig.de

Abstract. The temporal analysis of evolving graphs is an important requirement in many domains. We are therefore extending the distributed graph analysis framework Gradoop and its graph data model to support temporal graph analysis. This paper contains an overview of our work in progress and an example use case from the financial domain demonstrating the flexibility of the temporal graph model and its operators.

Keywords: Temporal graph analysis · Distributed analytical workflow · Temporal Property Graph Model

1 Introduction

Temporal graphs represent the evolution of entities and relationships among them throughout time. Many real-world scenarios dynamically change over time, e.g., friendships and likes in social networks, citations and authorship affiliations in literature or transactions between accounts in the financial domain [8]. Instead of neglecting this prevailing time dimension by using a static graph model, it is better to represent the continuously changing network in a temporal graph data model to enable studying the effect of time on the graph [18]. Since many existing graph database systems [3,9,13], graph processing frameworks [4,6,7,10] and graph query languages [2,5,14] concentrate on managing and querying static graphs, there is a lack of native support of the additional time-domain, e.g., to study how communities or paths change over time or to retrieve a snapshot from a past state of the graph.

Sahu et al. show in [17] that graphs maintained and analyzed by companies of all scales have common characteristics. Besides the presence of a wide variety of entities, graphs in practice are very large (containing often over billions of edges) and therefore the need for scalable systems to handle these large graphs is existent. Besides, the biggest part of the graphs used by the companies contain frequent changes (i.e., vertices and edges are added, deleted or updated over time), and all changes are stored permanently in the dataset.

P. Cellier and K. Driessens (Eds.): ECML PKDD 2019 Workshops, CCIS 1167, pp. 402–408, 2020.
https://doi.org/10.1007/978-3-030-43823-4_33

To deal with these characteristics, we developed a temporal property graph model that enables modeling a graph with bitemporal time semantics as well as a set of operators to build distributed analysis workflows considering the additional time dimensions in the graph. The model and its operators are implemented in Gradoop [10,11], an open-source framework[1] for distributed graph analysis based on Apache Flink [4]. After giving an overview of Gradoop's temporal extension we show its expressiveness by composing new and existing operators to answer an analytical question from a use-case of the financial domain.

2 A Brief Overview of Gradoop's Temporal Extension

Gradoop is an implementation of the Extended Property Graph Model (EPGM) and supports many generic operators on graphs (for pattern matching, grouping, etc.) that can be used within workflows for graph analysis. Workflows representing graph analytical programs can be expressed in a declarative domain-specific language called *GrALa* for distributed execution. Since the EPGM is built on top of Apache Flink's Dataset-API, each Gradoop operator is based on a subset of Flink's transformations (map, flatmap, join, etc.) to achieve a parallel execution and scalability to large graphs. It combines and extends features of graph analytical systems with the benefits of distributed graph processing.

Extension of Data Model: Many applications require time-dependent graph models. We therefore developed the Temporal Property Graph Model (TPGM) [15,16] that extends Gradoop's EPGM by adding additional time attributes *from* and *to*, each for valid and transaction time semantics, to the schema of vertices, edges and logical graphs. This approach offers a flexible representation of temporal graphs with bitemporal time semantics where the time can be empty, a timestamp or a time interval. A graph of this model contains all historical and rollback information and therefore allows retrieving valid snapshots from the past, present or future for the application time dimension or past and present states from the transaction time domain. An important advantage of our extension is its backward compatibility to the original EPGM since every existing Gradoop operator (that builds upon the EPGM) can be applied to one or more temporal graphs by disregarding the temporal information of the graph elements. A more detailed description of the TPGM and its operators is given in [15].

Extension of Existing Gradoop Operators: Operators such as *transformation*, *aggregate*, *subgraph*, *grouping* and *pattern matching* may benefit from the temporal extension of EPGM. For example, the *subgraph* operator can identify all vertices and edges where the validity range exceeds a limit. Similarly, the *pattern matching* operator can extract all subgraphs where the query pattern is valid at a given point in time.

Introduction of New Temporal Operators: We introduce *snapshot* and *difference* as specific temporal operators of the TPGM. The *snapshot* operator

[1] https://github.com/dbs-leipzig/gradoop.

allows retrieving a valid state of the entire temporal graph either at a specific point in time or a subgraph that is valid during a given time range by providing a temporal predicate function. Such predicate functions are adopted from the SQL standard for temporal databases [12]. The *difference* operator computes the changes between two snapshots X and Y by determining the union of X and Y and annotating each vertex and edge if it appears in Y only (i.e., if it has been added), in X only (deleted) or in both X and Y (persistent). Following the philosophy of GRADOOP, both operators were implemented on top of Apache Flink: *snapshot* employs Flink's *filter* transformation while *difference* is based on the *flatMap* transformation. Implementation details of these operators and benchmark results exposing a good scalability can be found in [15].

Support of Time-Specific Grouping and Aggregation: The temporal extension of GRADOOP's *grouping* operator offers a flexible mechanism to group (summarize) vertices and edges, which belong to a given time instance. Users can either define their own or use predefined functions to extract keys from a vertex or edge on which to group. Any information of a graph element can be used including all temporal information, such as the day of the week on which the validity of an edge begins or the rounded duration of a vertex validity. Additionally, multiple aggregate functions can be specified to compute aggregates within a vertex or edge group and store them as a new property on the super-vertex (the vertex representing the group) or super-edge respectively. Not only properties can be aggregated, but also information from the additional time dimensions of the graph. For example, the earliest or latest beginning of an edges validity or the average, minimum or maximum vertex duration can be calculated. The resulting grouped graph is again temporal, i.e., the valid times of the super-vertices and -edges are defined by the earliest beginning and latest ending of the elements that are responsible to the group.

Since timestamp values can be analyzed and grouped at different granularities (e.g. year, month, day, hour, minute etc.), time properties inherently lead to hierarchically organized dimensions. Graph summaries determined by the *grouping* operator can thus be additionally "rolled-up" on the time hierarchy to have aggregations on multiple levels of time-granularity. A detailed description of graph grouping with GRADOOP including the roll-up feature and predefined aggregate functions can be found in our GitHub wiki[2].

3 Temporal Graph Analysis Using Gradoop: A Use Case

Supporting graph analysis at large scale is necessary in various domains like Internet-of-Things (IoT), finance, and web to perform risk analysis, customer profiling, etc. In addition, time plays an important role in such analysis since analysts want to know, e.g., how a specific result of their query looks in the past or changes over time. As a result, a graph processing system has to offer a flexible and rich library of functionalities and algorithms to support a wide range of analysis respecting the additional time dimension.

[2] https://github.com/dbs-leipzig/gradoop/wiki.

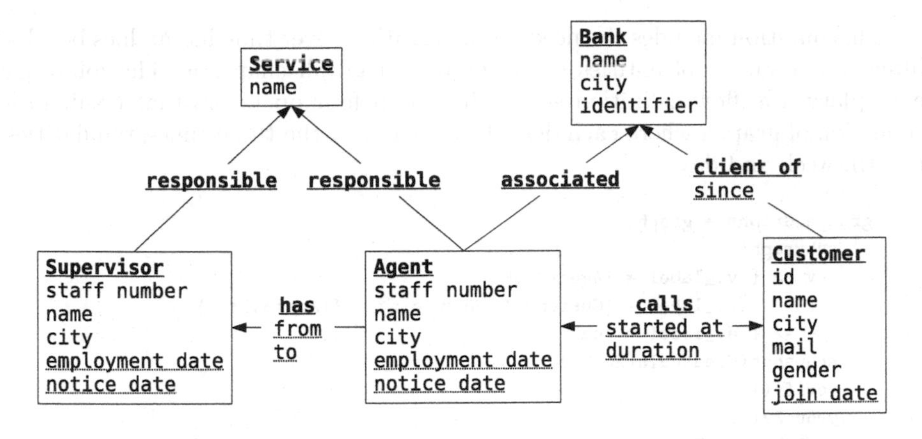

Fig. 1. Simplified example of a call center network from the financial domain. Underlined properties contain temporal information that can be used to define the temporal attributes of our model.

To show the expressiveness and flexibility of Gradoop and its temporal model among its declarative operator principle, we choose a business case from the customer relationship management domain. Specifically, the scenario deals with interactions in a call center for 25 banks of the banks association of Turkey [1]. More than 7,500 agents are employed in about 16 service types (e.g., card, stock, ATM, online banking, etc.). Per month, about 46 million incoming calls are answered by agents, 24 million calls are outgoing calls to customers. These entities and their relations form a huge heterogeneous network that continuously evolves. Figure 1 shows a simplified example of the resulting graph schema. It includes different types of vertices (entities), like *Bank* and *Customer*, as well as edges (relations), like a *call* representing the telephone call between customers and call center agents. Each element includes a variety of properties describing it with additional information, e.g., an *Agent* vertex has a defined *staff number*, a *name* and *city*. We can put all the collected data in our temporal property graph model. Properties containing temporal information (e.g., the *started at* and *duration* properties of the *calls* edge) can be directly mapped to the valid-time attributes of the model, to enable various time-related analysis.

In the following, we study how an analytical question of this use case can be processed. We will utilize the modularity of our temporal graph operators as well as operators from the reference EPGM implementation and compose them within a simple but powerful workflow to show a way to answer them.

What is the average duration of calls per month, week and day between agents of different cities and customers of Istanbul, where both agents and customers joined the bank in 2018?

This question includes the need for aggregations over time hierarchies besides filters for a subset of entities on an extracted graph snapshot. The following exemplary workflow definition shows the use of four operators that result in a collection of graphs where each describes one out of the three time-granularities month, week and day.

```
1  groupedGraphs = graph
2    .subgraph(
3       v -> { v._label = 'Agent' OR
4             (v._label = 'Customer' AND v.city = 'Istanbul' )},
5       e -> { e._label = 'calls'})
6    .snapshot(CreatedIn(2018))
7    .verify()
8    .groupBy(
9       [Label(), Property('city')],                          // V group keys
10      [Count()],                                            // V aggregates
11      [Month(from), Week(from), Day(from)] BY ROLLUP,      // E group keys
12      [AvgDuration(), Count()]);                            // E aggregates
```

The initial *subgraph* operator (line 2–5) applies a filtering using the given vertex and edge predicates to get a subgraph that contains only *Agent* vertices and *Customer* vertices with a property *city* that is equal to the string *Istanbul.* This operator is part of the EPGM. To receive customers that joined a bank in 2018, we apply the newly developed TPGM *snapshot* operator (line 6) with a predefined predicate. Since the result of the *snapshot* operator can contain dangling edges (i.e., their source or target vertices are not contained in the result set), we apply the *verify* operator (line 7) to remove these from the graph. The final *grouping* operator (line 8–12) summarizes the graph. The vertices will be grouped by their label and the property *city* (line 9). A property with the count is added to each grouped vertex as a result of the given *Count()* vertex aggregate function. The edges representing the calls are grouped by month, week and day of the calls beginning timestamp (from) through the usage of time-specific value transformation functions of the same name (line 11). Since we want to know the average call duration, the predefined aggregate function *AvgDuration()* is specified in addition to the *Count()* aggregate function (line 12). Equivalent to the vertices, new properties storing the aggregates are added to each super-edge.

The additional *BY ROLLUP* (line 11) leads to three different aggregations comparable to SQL. First, the graph will be grouped by day, then by week and besides, by the month of the call's beginning. This leads to deeper insights into the evolution of the number and average duration of calls between agents of different cities and customers from the city Istanbul. The resulting three graphs are contained in a graph collection, which is the result of our workflow and exemplified in Fig. 2. The collection can be stored or visualized by one of GRADOOP's data sinks. Further, an analyst may use the *subgraph* operator again to filter this result for periods with a very low or high average call duration.

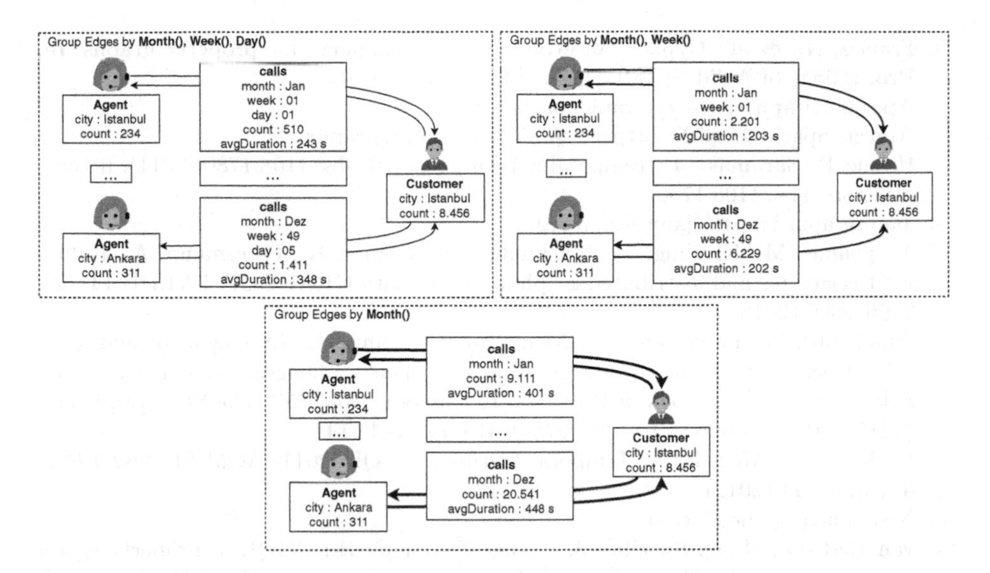

Fig. 2. The resulting temporal graph collection from the given example workflow. Each multi-edge graph represents one temporal granularity. For example, the edges of the lower graph are grouped by the month of their beginning timestamp. For simplicity, each grouped graph contains only a tiny subset of agents and call edges without temporal data. Practically, 24 edges (twelve for each direction) exist between the grouped customer vertex and agents of a certain city within the lower graph.

4 Conclusions

We reported work in progress on temporal graph analysis with the distributed graph analytics framework GRADOOP. We introduced the Temporal Property Graph Model (TPGM) that extends GRADOOP's graph data model. The new temporal operators and further extensions enable a flexible answering of time-oriented analytical questions on evolving graphs, e.g., by chaining several operators. We demonstrated the use of declarative workflows for a time-related use case scenario of the financial domain. The described extensions are already implemented and available in GRADOOP. In future work, we plan further temporal operators and algorithms to increase the functionality for temporal graph analytics.

References

1. The banks association of turkey: statistical report. http://www.tbb.org.tr/en/banks-and-banking-sector-information/statistical-reports/20
2. Angles, R., et al.: G-CORE: a core for future graph query languages. In: Proceedings of ACM SIGMOD, pp. 1421–1432 (2018)
3. Arangodb. https://www.arangodb.com/
4. Apache Flink. https://flink.apache.org/

5. Francis, N., et al.: Cypher: an evolving query language for property graphs. In: Proceedings of ACM SIGMOD, pp. 1433–1445 (2018)
6. Apache Giraph. https://giraph.apache.org/
7. Apache Spark GraphX. https://spark.apache.org/graphx
8. Holme, P., Saramäki, J.: Temporal networks. CoRR abs/1108.1780 (2011). http://arxiv.org/abs/1108.1780
9. Janusgraph. https://janusgraph.org/
10. Junghanns, M., Kießling, M., Teichmann, N., Gómez, K., Petermann, A., Rahm, E.: Declarative and distributed graph analytics with GRADOOP. PVLDB **11**(12), 2006–2009 (2018)
11. Junghanns, M., Petermann, A., Neumann, M., Rahm, E.: Management and analysis of big graph data: current systems and open challenges. In: Zomaya, A.Y., Sakr, S. (eds.) Handbook of Big Data Technologies, pp. 457–505. Springer, Cham (2017). https://doi.org/10.1007/978-3-319-49340-4_14
12. Kulkarni, K., Michels, J.: Temporal features in SQL: 2011. ACM SIGMOD Rec. **41**(3), 34–43 (2012)
13. Neo4j. https://neo4j.com/
14. van Rest, O., Hong, S., Kim, J., Meng, X., Chafi, H.: PGQL: a property graph query language. In: Proceedings of the Fourth International Workshop on Graph Data Management Experiences and Systems, p. 7. ACM (2016)
15. Rost, C., Thor, A., Rahm, E.: Analyzing temporal graphs with GRADOOP. Datenbank-Spektrum **19**(3), 199–208 (2019). https://doi.org/10.1007/s13222-019-00325-8
16. Rost, C., Thor, A., Rahm, E.: Temporal graph analysis using GRADOOP. In: Meyer, H., Ritter, N., Thor, A., Nicklas, D., Heuer, A., Klettke, M. (eds.) Proceedings of BTW Workshops, pp. 109–118 (2019). https://doi.org/10.18420/btw2019-ws-11
17. Sahu, S., Mhedhbi, A., Salihoglu, S., Lin, J., Özsu, M.T.: The ubiquity of large graphs and surprising challenges of graph processing: extended survey. VLDB J. (2019). https://doi.org/10.1007/s00778-019-00548-x
18. Wang, Y., Yuan, Y., Ma, Y., Wang, G.: Time-dependent graphs: definitions, applications, and algorithms. Data Sci. Eng. **4**(4), 352–366 (2019). https://doi.org/10.1007/s41019-019-00105-0

MHDNE: Network Embedding Based on Multivariate Hawkes Process

Ying Yin[1(✉)], Jianpeng Zhang[1], Yulong Pei[2], Xiaotao Cheng[1], and Lixin Ji[1]

[1] Information Engineering University, Zhengzhou, China
15883880517@163.com

[2] Eindhoven University of Technology, Eindhoven, The Netherlands

Abstract. With the evolution of the network, the interactions among nodes in networks make networks exhibit dynamic properties. Mining the rich information behind dynamic networks is of great importance for network analysis. However, most of the existing network embedding methods focus on static networks which ignore the dynamic properties of networks. In this paper, we propose a novel approach MHDNE (Multivariate hawkes process network embedding) to learn the representations of nodes in dynamic networks. The key idea of our approach is to integrate the historical edge information as well as network evolution properties into the formation process of edges based on Hawkes process. By integrating the multivariate Hawkes process into network embedding, MHDNE resolves the issue that the existing methods cannot effectively capture both of the historical information and evolution process of dynamic networks. Extensive experiments demonstrate that the embeddings learned from the proposed MHDNE model can achieve better performance than the state-of-the-art methods in downstream tasks, such as node classification and network visualization.

Keywords: Network embedding · Dynamic network · Hawkes process · Ternary closure theory

1 Introduction

In the era of big data, how to analyze contemporary networks is an urgent problem to be solved. The research on complex networks can help us deal with applications such as node classification, link prediction, community discovery and so on. With the development of machine learning, network embedding, also named network representation learning, serves as a bridge connecting networked data analysis and traditional machine learning. It maps nodes in a network to low-dimensional spaces in order to form low-dimensional dense vectors that can be used as the input of traditional machine learning models to conduct the downstream tasks.

The existing network embedding methods mostly model static networks without dynamic attributes, that is, they assume that nodes and their edges in the

P. Cellier and K. Driessens (Eds.): ECML PKDD 2019 Workshops, CCIS 1167, pp. 409–421, 2020.
https://doi.org/10.1007/978-3-030-43823-4_34

networks don't change with time. The early static network embedding methods were mainly based on the matrix decomposition [2,18], which have high computational complexity and cannot adapt to the growing large-scale networks. With the development of artificial intelligence, Perozzi et al. proposed the classic Deepwalk algorithm [16] to apply neural networks to network embedding which is based on the Word2vec [12] model in natural language processing. Grover et al. proposed the Node2vec algorithm [8] to modify the random walk process of Deepwalk, which preserves both of the homogeneity and isomorphism of the networks by combining breadth-first search and depth-first search. Deepwalk and Node2vec algorithm are based on the Word2vec framework, which has a three-layer shallow neural network at its core. With the development of deep learning, Wang et al. proposed the SDNE algorithm [21] to apply the deep neural network to network embedding. The semi-supervised deep learning model preserves the local information as well as the global information in the networks through the first-order similarity module and the second-order similarity module. The GraphGAN model [22] proposed by Wang et al. and the ANE model [4] proposed by Dai et al. adopt the generative adversarial nets [6] to network embedding, which greatly improved the robustness of static network embeddings.

In recent years, the representation learning for static networks has gradually matured. However, as the network evolves over time, new edges may appear and expired edges may disappear. The evolving interactions among the nodes in networks make networks exhibit dynamic properties. The addition of time information makes the networks more complex, and dynamic networks often have large scales. The research on dynamic network is of great significance to solve practical application problems, such as community detection [1,17] and link prediction [11]. Traditional dynamic network representation methods take snapshots of dynamic networks at specific times to process which is equivalent to split the dynamic network into multiple static network sequences. Thus, the static network embedding models can be extended to handle dynamic networks. Most of the existing dynamic network embedding methods are derived from the static network embedding models: Inspired by the static network embedding method based on matrix eigenvalue decomposition, Li et al. proposed DANE algorithm [10] to capture the evolving patterns of network structures and attribute information. DANE updates the current node embeddings based on the node embeddings obtained from the previous time. DHPE algorithm [24] preserved the high-order proximity based on generalized singular value decomposition and updated the node embeddings dynamically based on matrix perturbation theory. In addition to dynamic network embedding methods based on matrix decomposition, there are some dynamic network embedding methods extended from classic static network embedding methods, for instance, DNE algorithm [5] which extends the LINE model [19] to dynamic network embedding and DynGEM algorithm [7] which is based on the SDNE model. These snapshot-based embedding methods often ignore the network evolution patterns. Besides, the embedding methods which only process dynamic information on the snapshots are relatively coarse-grained. The HTNE algorithm [25] proposed by Zuo et al.

leverages the Hawkes process to model the formation process of neighbor nodes, which provides a novel idea of dynamic network embedding. However, IITNE only takes the influence of historical neighbor nodes on current node embeddings into account, while ignoring the impact of network evolution properties.

Therefore, to overcome the drawbacks of the existing methods, this paper proposes MHDNE (Multivariate hawkes process dynamic network embedding) model to learn the dynamic network embedding. MHDNE integrates the historical edge information as well as network evolution properties to model the formation process of edges based on Hawkes process. The main contributions of this paper are summarized as follows:

(1) We propose a novel approach for dynamic network embedding which preserves the impacts of historical information on the current network based on the Hawkes process.
(2) The MHDNE model proposed in this paper considers the historical edge information as well as the network evolution properties, which captures the influence of historical information on the formation of current edges comprehensively.
(3) Experimental results on real-world networks demonstrate that the embedding vectors learned from the proposed MHDNE model can achieve better performances than the state-of-the-art methods in node classification and network visualization.

2 Problem Definition

In this section, we formulate the problem of dynamic network embedding and give necessary definitions used throughout this paper as follows:

Definition 1 (Dynamic network). A dynamic network within time T can be defined as a collection $G = \{G^1, G^2, ..., G^T\}$ containing a series of network snapshots. The snapshot at time $t (0 < t < T)$ can be denoted as $G^t = (V_t, E_t)$, where V_t and E_t denote the set of nodes and edges at time t respectively.

Definition 2 (Dynamic network embedding). Given a dynamic network $G = \{G^1, G^2, ..., G^T\}$, we map nodes in the snapshots to the low-dimensional space so that nodes can be represented as vectors. And the temporal and structural information can be preserved in the low-dimensional vector space.

Definition 3 (Ternary closure). The ternary closure generally refers to: two people who have common friends in a social circle are more likely to become good friends in the future. That is, if nodes a and b connect to the same node c in a network, edge between a and b is likely to form. The ternary closure theory affects the formation of networks which is an important characteristic reflecting the network evolution mechanism.

Definition 4 (Hawkes process). The Hawkes process, as a special linear self-excited point process, is widely used in economic analysis, social analysis, and geographic prediction. In the Hawkes process, the occurrence of new events is not only affected by the internal properties of the events, but also the historical events occurring at the previous moments. The generation intensity function of a new event can be defined as follows:

$$\lambda(t) = \gamma_t + \sum_{t_s<t} \varphi(t - t_s) \tag{1}$$

Where γ_t indicates the base intensity of a new event, showing the spontaneous event occurring intensity at time t. $\varphi(t - t_s)$ indicates the influence of historical events on the occurrence of new event which continuously decays with time. $\varphi(t-t_s)$ can be expressed as $\varphi(t-t_s) = \alpha\delta(t, t_s)$, where α denotes the excitation intensity of the historical events to the current event, $\delta(t, t_s)$ denotes the time decay coefficient of the historical event.

3 The Proposed Framework: MHDNE

In this section, first we generalize the MHDNE framework, and then we describe the core components of MHDNE in details. Finally, we introduce the model optimization.

3.1 MHDNE Framework

The framework of the MHDNE model proposed in this paper is shown in Fig. 1. First, we model the edge formation process in the dynamic network as two temporal sequences L_1 and L_2 which contain historical edge information and network evolution information, respectively. Then, based on the temporal sequences, we apply the Hawkes process to model the new edge formation process to integrate the historical information of the dynamic network as well as the evolution properties into the node embeddings.

3.2 Component Description

The formation of a dynamic network is a process with continuous emergence and disappearance of edges, so the formation of edges can be regarded as temporal point process. We can define the generation of edges as events in this process. And they form in two ways: one is that the edge exists in the historical moment and is preserved at the current moment. The other is that the edge never appears in the historical moment but forms at the current moment in the evolution process. These two kinds of edge generating ways are respectively related to the following two edge formation sequences.

- **Historical edge sequence:** in a dynamic network, if there is an edge between nodes m and n at time t_i. the edge can be denoted as a time-stamped tuple (e_m^n, t_i). Then, the edges between nodes m and n within time T can be modeled as a temporal sequence $L_1 = (e_m^n, t_1) \longrightarrow (e_m^n, t_2) \longrightarrow ... \longrightarrow (e_m^n, t_T)$.

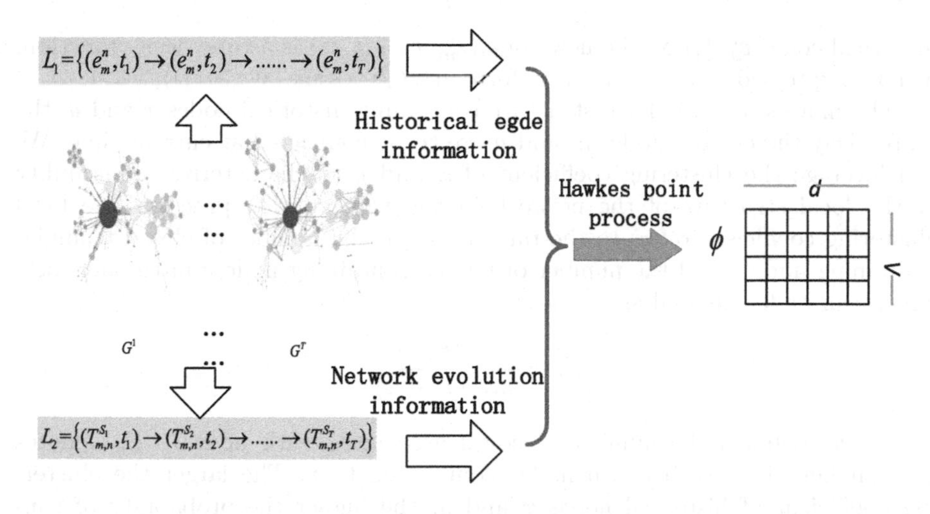

Fig. 1. The framework of MHDNE.

Intuitively, nodes that have more interactions in the history tend to form edge at the current moment. Therefore, the generation intensity of the edge containing nodes m and n at the current time is affected by the historical edge (e_m^n, t_i).

- **Open triangle sequence:** if there is a common neighbor k between nodes m and n at time t, the formed open triangle can be denoted as a triple (e_m^k, e_k^n, t). All of the open triangles composed of nodes m, n, and all of their common neighbors S at time t can be represented as a set $(T_{m,n}^S, t)$. Then, an open triangle sequence within time T can be modeled as a temporal sequence $L_2 = (T_{m,n}^{S_1}, t_1) \longrightarrow (T_{m,n}^{S_2}, t_2) \longrightarrow ... \longrightarrow (T_{m,n}^{S_T}, t_T)$. It can be known from the ternary closure theory that even if there is no edge between nodes m and n in history, if the two nodes have common neighbors, they tend to connect in the process of network evolution.

Since Hawkes process [9] well captures the exciting effects of historical information on the current events, we adapt it to model the edge formation process of nodes m and n based on the historical edge sequence L_1. The generation intensity function for the arrival event (e_m^n, t) can be formulated as:

$$\lambda_{e_m^n}^1(t) = \gamma_{m,n} + \sum_{t_s<t} \alpha_{e_x^y} \delta(t, t_s) \tag{2}$$

where $\lambda_{e_m^n}^1(t)$ indicates the probability of forming edge between node m and n at time t, $\gamma_{m,n}$ indicates the base intensity of forming edge between nodes m and n at time t.The base intensity $\gamma_{m,n}$ reflects the essential relationship between node m and n, Which can be denoted as the negative Euclidean distance between the embeddings of node m and n. i.e., $\gamma_{m,n} = -\|v_m - v_n\|$, v_m and v_n are the embeddings of node m and n respectively. x and y indicates the corresponding historical nodes of node m and n respectively. $\alpha_{e_x^y}$ denotes the influence of the historical edge (e_x^y, t_s) on the new edge (e_m^n, t). $\delta(t, t_s)$ is a time decay function, usually expressed as an exponential form $\delta(t, t_s) = exp(-\theta(t - t_s))$.

The more stable the local structure containing historical nodes x and y, the more likely the current nodes m and n are to be connected at current time. We can leverage the clustering coefficient of x and y to characterize the stability of the local structure of the network in the time-varying process. The local clustering coefficient refers to the ratio between the number of closed triangles containing node r and the number of triples containing node r in the network, which can be formulated as:

$$C_r = \frac{2E_r}{m_r(m_r - 1)} \tag{3}$$

where m_r denotes the number of edges associated with node r, E_r denotes the number of edges between nodes connecting to r. The larger the clustering coefficient of historical nodes x and y, the higher the probability of connecting edges between current nodes m and n. Thus, we can denote $\alpha_{e_y^x}$ as $\alpha_{e_y^x} = C_x C_y g(v_x, v_y)$, the Eq. 2 can be updated as follows.

$$\lambda_{e_m^n}^1(t) = g(v_m, v_n) + \sum_{t_s < t} C_x C_y g(v_x, v_y) \delta(t, t_s) \tag{4}$$

In addition to the fact that the connected edges appeared in history will appear at the current time with a certain probability, in the process of network evolution, it can be known from the ternary closure theory [23] that nodes with common neighbors in history tend to be connected at the current time. That is, when there is historical event (e_m^k, e_k^n, t_s), the probability of occurring new event (e_m^n, t) will increase. Similarly, we can use the local clustering coefficients of nodes to measure the intensity of this influence: the greater the clustering coefficients of nodes, the stronger the ternary closure process nearby, and the greater the probability of generating new event (e_m^n, t). Meanwhile, the more common neighbors two nodes have, the more likely they are to connect. And the closer the historical event (e_m^k, e_k^n, t_s) is to the current time, the greater the probability of generating edge (e_m^n, t). Therefore, Eq. 4 can be updated to:

$$\lambda_{e_m^n}(t) = g(v_m, v_n) + \sum_{t_s < t} (C_x C_y g(v_x, v_y) \delta(t, t_s) + \sum_{(e_m^k, e_k^n, t_s) \in L_2} C_k g(v_k', v_k) \delta(t, t_s)) \tag{5}$$

where $g(v_k', v_k)$ is the negative Euclidean distance between the current common neighbor k' and the historical common neighbor k in the mapping space. It can be seen from Eq. 5, $\lambda_{e_m^n}(t)$ may be a negative value, and the probability of generating new edges should be a positive value. Therefore, we take the index value of $\lambda_{e_m^n}(t)$ as the final probability, namely $\hat{\lambda}_{e_m^n}(t) = exp(\lambda_{e_m^n}(t))$.

Based on the Hawkes process, given the relevant historical edge sequence L_1 and the open triangle sequence L_2, we can obtain the probability of generating edge (e_m^n, t) between node m and n at time t as follows.

$$P(n|m, H(L_1, L_2)) = \frac{\hat{\lambda_{e_m^n}}(t)}{\sum_{n^* \in V, e_m^{n^*} \in E} \hat{\lambda_{e_m^n}}(t)} \tag{6}$$

3.3 Model Optimization

For all nodes in the network, the likelihood function of the model can be denoted as follows.

$$logl = \sum_{m \in V} \sum_{n \in V, e_m^n \in E} logP(n|m, H(L_1, L_2)) \tag{7}$$

In order to reduce the computational complexity of the algorithm, we use the negative sampling method [13] to optimize the algorithm. The probability that a node is selected as a negative sample is related to the frequency at which it appears in the sequence, so we get samples according to the degree distribution of nodes. According to [13], the sampling probability of node v_i can be denoted as follows.

$$P(v_i) = \frac{f(v_i)^{\frac{3}{4}}}{\sum_{j=1}^{K} f(v_i)^{\frac{3}{4}}} \tag{8}$$

Based on the historical edge information and the ternary closure property, the objective function of generating new edge (e_m^n, t) can be denoted as follows.

$$O(X) = log\sigma(\hat{\lambda_{e_m^n}}(t)) + \sum_{i=1}^{K} E_{v_i \sim P(v)}[-log\sigma(\hat{\lambda_{e_m^{v_i}}}(t))] \tag{9}$$

where K is the number of negative samples. $\sigma(x)$ is the sigmoid function.

Commonly, we adopt Stochastic Gradient Descent method [3] to optimize the objective function in Eq. 9. Algorithm 1 shows the core of our method.

Algorithm 1. MHDNE

Input: The dynamic information network $G = \{G^1, G^2, ..., G^T\}$, embedding dimension d, parameter θ, time step h.
Output: The latent node embeddings $X \in R^{V \times d}$.
1: Initialize X
2: **for** epoch in len(epochs) **do**
3: **for** batch(L_1, L_2) **do**
4: Calculate the influence of historical information and network evolution information on the current edge according to equation 5.
5: Select negative samples Neg_{EK} according to equation 8.
6: compute the objective function $O(X)$ according to equation 9.
7: update gradients $X = X - \eta \frac{\partial O(X)}{O(X)}$
8: **end for**
9: **end for**

4 Experiments

In this section, we validate the effectiveness of our model on two real-world datasets as shown in Table 1. First, we introduce the datasets and baseline methods we used in our experiments in details, and then we conduct downstream tasks: node classification and visualization. Finally, we analyze the parameter sensitivity of θ.

4.1 Datasets

- **DBLP** [14]: the DBLP dataset contains a large amount of information about computer science publications. We built the dynamic network in our experiment through the co-author relationships of 28,085 authors in ten research fields over ten years. The categories of authors are the research field in which they published the most papers.
- **Epinions** [20]: the Epinions dataset consists of comment information, user ID, product ID, and timestamp information. In our experiment, 21575 users belonging to five categories in ten years were extracted from the subset of Epinions dataset, and we build edges between users who comment on the same product. The categories of users are determined by the categories of the products they comment the most.

The detailed information of the two datasets is shown in Table 1.

Table 1. Datasets in experiments.

Datasets	Nodes	Edges	Class	Type	Average clustering coefficient
DBLP	28085	236894	10	Undirected	0.715648
Epinions	21575	2590798	5	Undirected	0.153612

4.2 Baseline Methods

In this paper, MHDNE algorithm is compared with the following three baseline algorithms:

- **Avg Deepwalk algorithm**: we conduct Deepwalk algorithm on different snapshots to get node embeddings in different time.
- **STWalk algorithm** [15]: STWalk performs space-walk and time-walk on the constructed graphs which can capture the spatio-temporal behavior of nodes.
- **HTNE algorithm** [25]: HTNE performs the dynamic network embedding based on the Hawkes process which can capture both the historical and current information from the perspective of neighbor nodes sequences.

4.3 Downstream Tasks

In this section, we carry out downstream tasks such as node classification and visualization to verify the feasibility and effectiveness of the proposed dynamic network representation method MHDNE. The experimental default parameters are set as follows: the vector dimension is 128, the negative sample number is 5, and the gradient drop learning rate is 0.01. In the algorithm using random walk and skip-gram model, the random walk length is 50, the number of walks is 100, and the window size is 10.

A. Classification

We conduct node classification task on the DBLP and Epinions datasets, the embeddings learned from different methods were classified by a linear SVM classifier. We repeat classification experiment ten times and take the average of Micro-F1 and Macro-F1 scores as the final classification results. The experimental results are shown in Tables 2 and 3.

We set the training set size varying from 15% to 90%. We can see from the Tables 2 and 3, the MHDNE algorithm proposed in this paper performs better than the baseline methods in node classification on the DBLP and Epinions datasets. On the DBLP dataset, when the training set is 75%, the MHDNE

Table 2. Multi-class node classification results in DBLP dataset.

Metric	Method	15%	30%	45%	60%	75%	90%
Micro-F1	Avg Deepwalk	0.6180	0.6253	0.6285	0.6310	0.6334	0.6371
	STWalk	0.6270	0.6336	0.6413	0.6540	0.6594	0.6586
	HTNE	0.6402	0.6521	0.6559	0.6594	0.6603	0.6559
	MHDNE	**0.6685**	**0.6724**	**0.6792**	**0.6890**	**0.6975**	**0.6856**
Macro-F1	Avg Deepwalk	0.6193	0.6297	0.6302	0.6390	0.6389	0.6323
	STWalk	0.6302	0.63820.6	476	0.6550	0.6598	0.6612
	HTNE	0.6427	0.6584	0.6627	0.6583	0.6613	0.6594
	MHDNE	**0.6711**	**0.6793**	**0.6801**	**0.6850**	**0.6983**	**0.6926**

Table 3. Multi-class node classification results in Epinions dataset.

Metric	Method	15%	30%	45%	60%	75%	90%
Micro-F1	Avg Deepwalk	0.5279	0.5302	0.5386	0.5321	0.5391	0.5302
	STWalk	0.5271	0.5327	0.5367	0.5409	0.5465	0.5497
	HTNE	0.5689	0.5786	0.5796	0.5803	0.5851	0.5867
	MHDNE	**0.5964**	**0.5970**	**0.6054**	**0.6127**	**0.6089**	**0.6103**
Macro-F1	Avg Deepwalk	0.5321	0.5343	0.5392	0.5441	0.5486	0.5467
	STWalk	0.5386	0.5401	0.5427	0.5489	0.5504	0.5526
	HTNE	0.5703	0.5794	0.5828	0.5864	0.5893	0.5907
	MHDNE	**0.5989**	**0.6054**	**0.6086**	**0.6154**	**0.6121**	**0.6128**

algorithm has the highest scores of Macro-F1 and Micro-F1, which are 3.72%–6.41%, 3.70%–5.94% higher than the comparison algorithms respectively. On the Epinions dataset, when the training set is 60%, the MHDNE algorithm has the highest scores of Macro-F1 and Micro-F1, which are 3.24%–8.06% and 2.90%–7.13% higher than the comparison algorithms. It can be seen from the experimental results that the integration of network historical information into current node embeddings is beneficial to improve the quality of embeddings. Especially when we integrate the historical edge information and the network evolution properties into network embedding, the obtained node embeddings perform better in classification.

B. Network visualization

We leverage the t-SNE algorithm to visualize the representation vectors of 2500 authors from four fields (Data Mining, Artificial Intelligence, Information Retrieval and Computer Vision.) in the DBLP dataset into the 2-dimensional space. We use different colors to indicate different research area. Specifically, we use purple dot to represent "Data Mining", blue dot to represent "Artificial Intelligence", orange dot to represent "Information Retrieval", green dot to represent "Computer Vision". Figure 2 demonstrates the visualization results of node embeddings obtained by different algorithms.

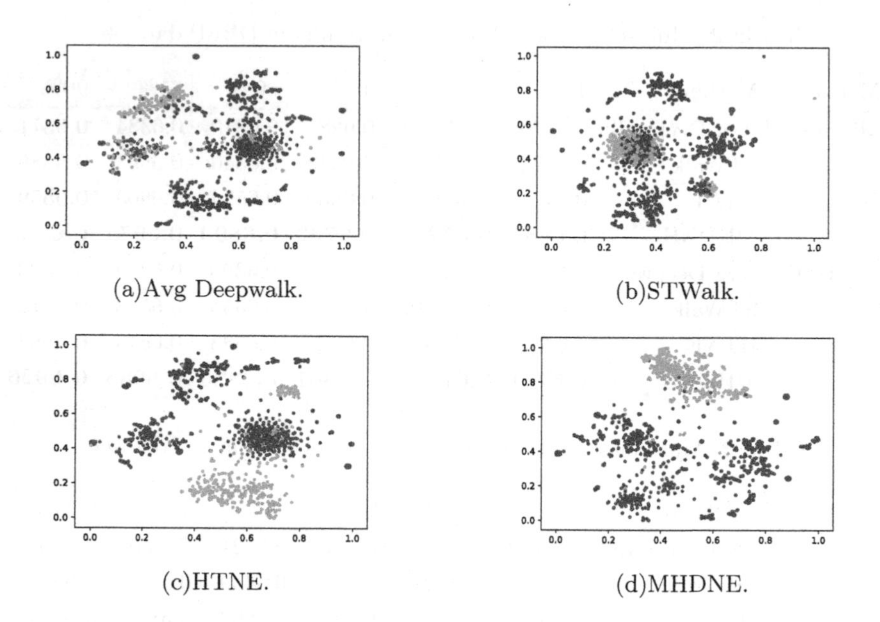

Fig. 2. Visualization of authors from four research areas.

As can be seen from the Fig. 2: the Avg Deepwalk algorithm can only map the authors in the "Artificial Intelligenc" field to an independent community, and the authors in the other three domains are confused; the STWalk algorithm maps authors in the "Data Mining" and "Computer Vision" domain to relatively scattered locations, failing to preserve the properties of such kind of nodes; the HTNE algorithm can Map part of authors in the fields of "Artificial Intelligence", "Information retrieval" and "Computer Vision" to different communities, but map some authors in these three fields to the "Data Mining" field; compared with other algorithms, the proposed MHDNE algorithm can map authors into different communities and there are clear margins among different areas.

The visualization results indicate that the historical information combined with network evolution information in our method can help us do community detection. This is because the formation of a community is often related to historical information, which can assist us in discovering communities. The embeddings generated by our method MHDNE integrate historical information and network evolution information, which can preserve the community information better. Therefore, the embeddings learned by our method MHDNE perform better than other baseline methods in visualization.

5 Parameter Sensitivity

The time decay function can be expressed in exponential form $\delta(t, t_s) = exp(-\theta(t - t_s))$, where θ is the time decay coefficient excited by historical events. We observe the changes of classification accuracy with θ varying from 0.01 to 1 to analyze the parameter sensitivity. We conduct the node classification on DBLP and Epinions, and set the training set to 75%. From Eq. 2, it can be known that: the larger the value of θ is, the smaller the influence of historical events on current events. The experimental results are shown in Fig. 3, from which it can be seen that the optimal value of parameter θ is different from each other in two datasets. On the DBLP dataset, when setting θ to 0.2, the classification accuracy obtained is the highest; when $0.2 < \theta < 0.4$, the classification accuracy remains basically unchanged; when $\theta > 0.4$, the classification accuracy decreases slightly with the increase of θ; On the Epinions dataset, when setting θ to 0.3, the node classification accuracy is the highest; when $\theta > 0.4$, the classification accuracy greatly decreases with the increase of θ.

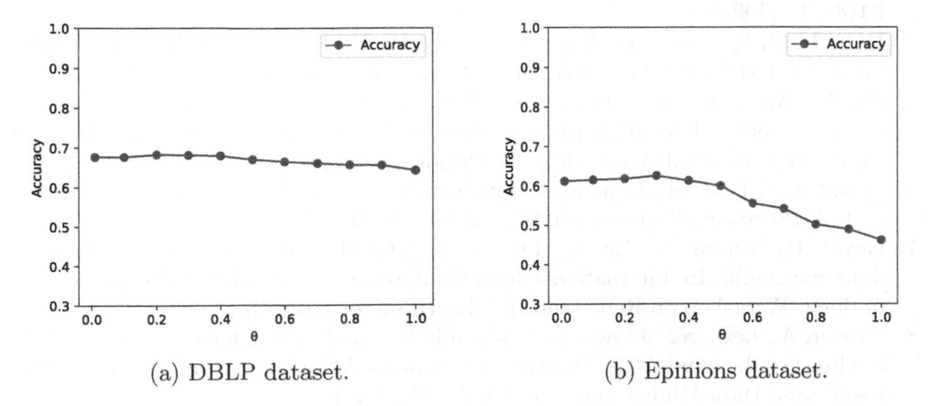

(a) DBLP dataset. (b) Epinions dataset.

Fig. 3. Sensitivity of θ on DBLP and Epinions dataset.

The main reason for the different experimental results on the two datasets is that the DBLP dataset is composed of authors and their co-author relationship, and the co-author relationships between authors will not change much in a short time. Therefore, the historical information of DBLP dataset has a small degree of time decay, and the value of θ should be small. However, Epinions dataset constitutes social network through users and their comment behaviors, and its historical information has a large time decay degree, so θ should be large.

6 Conclusion

To combine the dynamic properties of contemporary networks into network embedding, we proposed a dynamic network embedding method based on Hawkes process (MHDNE). Since the node embedding vectors learned by our model capture both the historical structure information and evolution mechanism, they perform well in the downstream tasks such as node classification and network visualization. At present, the research on network dynamic properties is still in its infancy, our method only takes the dynamic properties of homogeneous networks into account. However, networks in our real life may have both dynamic and heterogeneous features. How to take the rich heterogeneous information into the dynamic network embedding is the next research focus.

References

1. Appel, A.P., Cunha, R.L.F., Aggarwal, C.C., Terakado, M.M.: Temporally evolving community detection and prediction in content-centric networks. In: Berlingerio, M., Bonchi, F., Gärtner, T., Hurley, N., Ifrim, G. (eds.) ECML PKDD 2018. LNCS (LNAI), vol. 11052, pp. 3–18. Springer, Cham (2019). https://doi.org/10.1007/978-3-030-10928-8_1
2. Belkin, M., Niyogi, P.: Laplacian eigenmaps and spectral techniques for embedding and clustering. In: Advances in Neural Information Processing Systems, pp. 585–591 (2002)
3. Bottou, L.: Stochastic gradient learning in neural networks. Proc. Neuro-Nımes **91**(8), 12 (1991)
4. Dai, Q., Li, Q., Tang, J., Wang, D.: Adversarial network embedding. In: Thirty-Second AAAI Conference on Artificial Intelligence, pp. 2167–2174 (2018)
5. Du, L., Wang, Y., Song, G., Lu, Z., Wang, J.: Dynamic network embedding: an extended approach for skip-gram based network embedding. In: International Joint Conferences on Artificial Intelligence Organization, pp. 2086–2092 (2018)
6. Goodfellow, I., et al.: Generative adversarial nets. In: Advances in Neural Information Processing Systems, pp. 2672–2680 (2014)
7. Goyal, P., Kamra, N., He, X., Liu, Y.: DynGEM: deep embedding method for dynamic graphs. In: International Joint Conference on Artificial Intelligence (International Workshop on Representation Learning for Graphs) (2018)
8. Grover, A., Leskovec, J.: node2vec: scalable feature learning for networks. In: Proceedings of the 22nd ACM SIGKDD International Conference on Knowledge Discovery and Data Mining, pp. 855–864. ACM (2016)

9. Hawkes, A.G.: Spectra of some self-exciting and mutually exciting point processes. Biometrika **58**(1), 83–90 (1971)
10. Li, J., Dani, H., Hu, X., Tang, J., Chang, Y., Liu, H.: Attributed network embedding for learning in a dynamic environment. In: Proceedings of the 2017 ACM on Conference on Information and Knowledge Management, pp. 387–396. ACM (2017)
11. Li, T., Jiawei, Z., Philip, S.Y., Yan, Z., Yonghong, Y.: Deep dynamic network embedding for link prediction. IEEE Access **6**(99), 29219–29230 (2018)
12. Mikolov, T., Chen, K., Corrado, G., Dean, J.: Efficient estimation of word representations in vector space. In: International Conference on Learning Representations (Workshop) (2013)
13. Mikolov, T., Sutskever, I., Chen, K., Corrado, G.S., Dean, J.: Distributed representations of words and phrases and their compositionality. In: Advances in Neural Information Processing Systems, pp. 3111–3119. ACM (2013)
14. Moreira, C., Calado, P., Martins, B.: Learning to rank academic experts in the DBLP dataset. Expert Syst. **32**(4), 477–493 (2015)
15. Pandhre, S., Mittal, H., Gupta, M., Balasubramanian, V.N.: STWalk: learning trajectory representations in temporal graphs. In: Proceedings of the ACM India Joint International Conference on Data Science and Management of Data, pp. 210–219. ACM (2018)
16. Perozzi, B., Al-Rfou, R., Skiena, S.: DeepWalk: online learning of social representations. In: Proceedings of the 20th ACM SIGKDD International Conference on Knowledge Discovery and Data Mining, pp. 701–710. ACM (2014)
17. Rossetti, G., Cazabet, R.: Community discovery in dynamic networks: a survey. ACM Comput. Surv. **51**(2), 1–35 (2018)
18. Roweis, S.T., Saul, L.K.: Nonlinear dimensionality reduction by locally linear embedding. Science **290**(5500), 2323–2326 (2000)
19. Tang, J., Qu, M., Wang, M., Zhang, M., Yan, J., Mei, Q.: Line: large-scale information network embedding. In: Proceedings of the 24th International Conference on World Wide Web, pp. 1067–1077. International World Wide Web Conferences Steering Committee (2015)
20. Tang, J., Gao, H., Liu, H.: mTrust: discerning multi-faceted trust in a connected world. In: Proceedings of the Fifth ACM International Conference on Web Search and Data Mining, pp. 93–102. ACM (2012)
21. Wang, D., Cui, P., Zhu, W.: Structural deep network embedding. In: Proceedings of the 22nd ACM SIGKDD International Conference on Knowledge Discovery and Data Mining, pp. 1225–1234. ACM (2016)
22. Wang, H., et al.: GraphGAN: graph representation learning with generative adversarial nets. In: Thirty-Second AAAI Conference on Artificial Intelligence, AAAI-2018 Conference Committee, pp. 2508–2515 (2018)
23. Zhou, L., Yang, Y., Ren, X., Wu, F., Zhuang, Y.: Dynamic network embedding by modeling triadic closure process. In: Thirty-Second AAAI Conference on Artificial Intelligence (2018)
24. Zhu, D., Cui, P., Zhang, Z., Pei, J., Zhu, W.: High-order proximity preserved embedding for dynamic networks. IEEE Trans. Knowl. Data Eng. **30**(11), 2134–2144 (2018)
25. Zuo, Y., Liu, G., Lin, H., Guo, J., Hu, X., Wu, J.: Embedding temporal network via neighborhood formation. In: Proceedings of the 24th ACM SIGKDD International Conference on Knowledge Discovery & Data Mining, pp. 2857–2866. ACM (2018)

Data and Machine Learning Advances with Multiple Views

Workshop on Data and Machine Learning Advances with Multiple Views

Workshop Description

Recent years have witnessed new frameworks and algorithms able to deal with multiple views, such as Multiple Kernel Learning, Boosting, Co-regularized, Deep approaches. Such algorithms come from the Machine Learning community and find applications in many different areas, such as Multimedia Indexing, Computer Vision, Bio-informatics and Neuro-imaging. Multiview learning, naturally enough, emphasises the potential benefits of learning through collaboration with multiple sources of data (e.g. video document can be described through images, sound, motion, text).

The workshop on Data and Machine Learning Advances with Multiple Views built upon successful previous machine learning workshops on multiview learning or connections between ML and applications, such as Machine Learning techniques for processing multimedia content (ICML 2005), Learning with multiples views (ICML 2005), Learning from multiples sources (NIPS 2008), Learning from multiples sources with applications to robotics (NIPS 2009), Multiview learning and multimedia (ECML'2014), Multimodal Learning (NIPS 2015), Multi-View Representation Learning (ICML'2016), Multimodal Learning and Applications (CVPR'2018 and 2019).

The goal of the workshop was to bring together theoretical and applicative communities around multiview learning, which could lead to significant contributions and exchanges between Machine Learning and natural fields of applications such as biology, computer vision, marketing, ecology and health. This workshop dedicated the morning session to invited and contributed presentations on multi-view theory, algorithms and real-world multi-view datasets and tasks. In the afternoon, a hackathon on a multi-view dataset was organized where attendants tackled a multi-view learning problem on a real-world dataset.

These proceedings contain four contributed papers from the workshop. Audebert et al. present a neural network system for multimodal document classification, capable of learning both from image and word embeddings. Karami presents a novel nonlinear multi-view model where the deep neural network is leveraged to model complex latent representation underlying the multi-view data. Pereira et al. put forward a manifold mixing method for learning from multiple sources in a stacked regularization framework, demonstrating robust performance on experimental data. Finally, the paper by Pölsterl et al. introduces wide an deep neural network for multi-view learning with applications in survival analysis in Alzheimer's disease.

The programme chairs would like to thank all the to contributors to the oral presentation programme and the hackathon, as well as all members of the scientific programme committee and the organization committee.

Organization

Program Chairs

Cécile Capponi	Aix-Marseille University, France
Juho Rousu	Aalto University, Finland

Program Committee

Stéphane Ayache	Aix-Marseille University, France
Sahely Bhadra	Indian Institute of Technology, Palakkad, Kerala, India
Cécile Capponi	Aix-Marseille University, France
Ludovic Denoyer	Facebook FAIR, Paris, France
Isabelle Guyon	Orsay University, Saclay, France
Amaury Habrard	Jean-Monnet University, Saint-Etienne, France
Riikka Huusari	Aix-Marseille University, France
Hachem Kadri	Aix-Marseille University, France
Stéphane Marchand-Maillet	University of Geneva, Switzerland
Juho Rousu	Aalto University, Finland
Shiliang Sun	East China Normal University, Shangai, China
Sylvain Takerkart	Aix-Marseille University, France
Paul Villoutreix	Turing Center (Centuri), Marseille, France

Organizing Committee

Stéphane Ayache	Aix-Marseille University, France
Cécile Capponi	Aix-Marseille University, France
Rémi Emonet	Jean-Monnet University, Saint-Etienne, France
Isabelle Guyon	Orsay University, Saclay, France

Multimodal Deep Networks for Text and Image-Based Document Classification

Nicolas Audebert, Catherine Herold(✉), Kuider Slimani, and Cédric Vidal

Quicksign, 38 rue du Sentier, 75002 Paris, France
{nicolas.audebert,catherine.herold,kuider.slimani,
cedric.vidal}@quicksign.com
https://www.quicksign.com/en/

Abstract. Classification of document images is a critical step for accelerating archival of old manuscripts, online subscription and administrative procedures. Computer vision and deep learning have been suggested as a first solution to classify documents based on their visual appearance. However, achieving the fine-grained classification that is required in real-world setting cannot be achieved by visual analysis alone. Often, the relevant information is in the actual text content of the document, although this text is not available in digital form. In this work, we introduce a novel pipeline based on off-the-shelf architectures to deal with document classification by taking into account both text and visual information. We design a multimodal neural network that is able to learn both the image and from word embeddings, computed on noisy text extracted by OCR. We show that this approach allows us to improve single-modality classification accuracy by several points on the small Tobacco3482 and large RVL-CDIP datasets, even without clean text information. We release a post-OCR text classification (https://github.com/Quicksign/ocrized-text-dataset) that complements the Tobacco3482 and RVL-CDIP ones to encourage researchers to look into multi-modal text/image classification.

Keywords: Document classification · Text classification · Multimodal learning

1 Introduction

The ubiquity of computers and smartphones has incentivized governments and companies alike to digitize most of their processes. Onboarding new clients, paying taxes and proving one's identity is more and more done through a computer, as the rise of online banking has shown in the last few years. Industrial and public archives are also ongoing serious efforts to digitize their content in an effort for preservation, e.g. for old manuscripts, maps and documents with a historical value. This means that previously physical records, such as forms and identity documents, are now digitized and transferred electronically. In some cases, those records are produced and consumed by fully automated systems that rely

P. Cellier and K. Driessens (Eds.): ECML PKDD 2019 Workshops, CCIS 1167, pp. 427–443, 2020.
https://doi.org/10.1007/978-3-030-43823-4_35

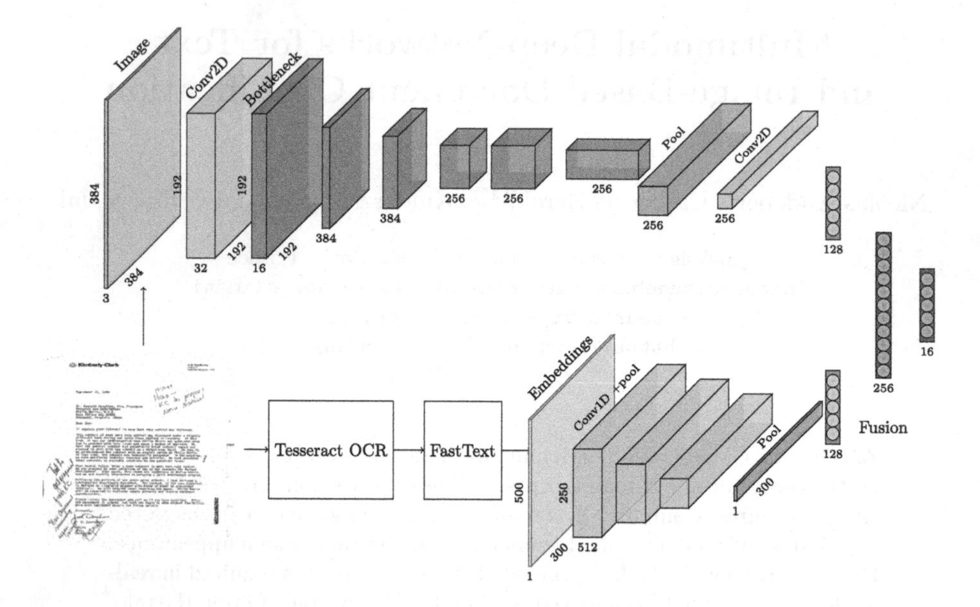

Fig. 1. Multimodal classifier for hybrid text/image classification. Training is performed end-to-end on both textual and visual features.

on machine-readable formats, such as XML or PDF with text layers. However, most of these digital copies are generated by end-users using whatever mean they have access to, i.e. scanners and cameras, especially from smartphones. For this reason, human operators have remained needed to proofread the documents, extract selected fields, check the records' consistency and ensure that the appropriate files have been submitted. Automation through expert systems and machine learning can help accelerate this process to assist and alleviate the burden of this fastidious work for human workers.

A common task involved in data filing processes is document recognition, on which depends the class-specific rules that command each file. For example, a user might be asked to upload several documents such as a filled subscription form, an ID and a proof-of-residence. In this work, we tackle the document classification task to check that all required files have been sent so that they are filed accordingly.

Yet, if discriminating between broad classes of documents can be achieved based on their appearance only (e.g. separating passports from banking information), fine-grained recognition often depends on the textual content of the documents. For example, different tax forms might share their layout, logos and templates while the content in itself vastly differs. Computer vision has been interested for some time in optical character recognition (OCR) to extract text from images. However, dealing with both the textual and visual contents remains an open problem. In the past years, deep learning has been established as the new state-of-the-art for image classification and natural language processing. For

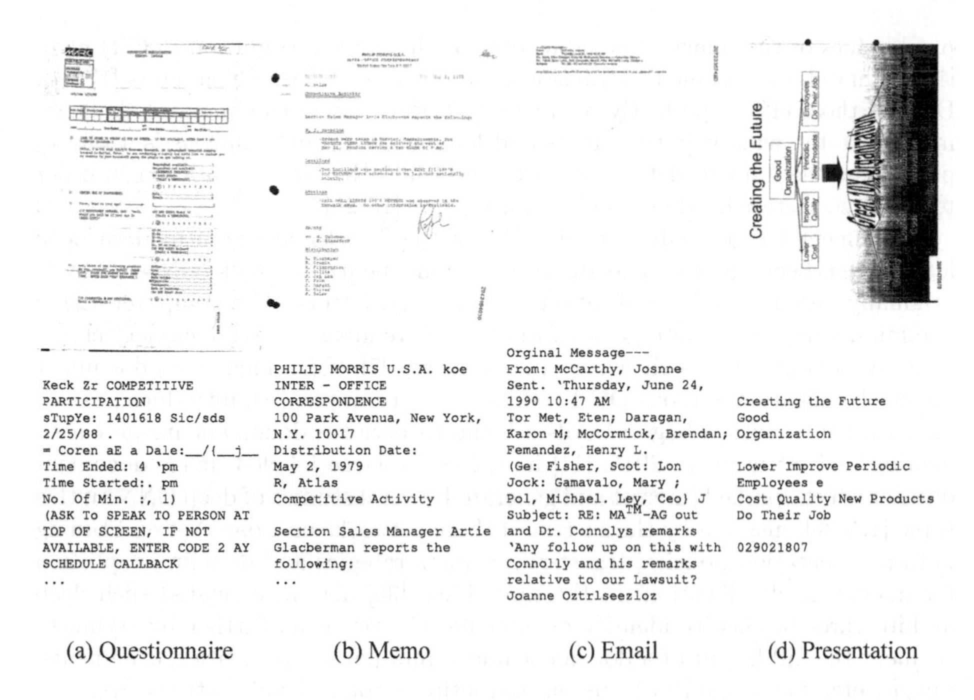

Keck Zr COMPETITIVE
PARTICIPATION
sTupYe: 1401618 Sic/sds
2/25/88 .
= Coren aE a Dale:__/(__j__
Time Ended: 4 'pm
Time Started:. pm
No. Of Min. :, 1)
(ASK To SPEAK TO PERSON AT
TOP OF SCREEN, IF NOT
AVAILABLE, ENTER CODE 2 AY
SCHEDULE CALLBACK
...
PHILIP MORRIS U.S.A. koe
INTER - OFFICE
CORRESPONDENCE
100 Park Avenua, New York,
N.Y. 10017
Distribution Date:
May 2, 1979
R, Atlas
Competitive Activity
Section Sales Manager Artie
Glacberman reports the
following:
...
Orginal Message---
From: McCarthy, Josnne
Sent. 'Thursday, June 24,
1990 10:47 AM
Tor Met, Eten; Daragan,
Karon M; McCormick, Brendan;
Femandez, Henry L.
(Ge: Fisher, Scot: Lon
Jock: Gamavalo, Mary ;
Pol, Michael. Ley, Ceo) J
Subject: RE: MA™-AG out
and Dr. Connolys remarks
'Any follow up on this with
Connolly and his remarks
relative to our Lawsuit?
Joanne Oztrlseezloz
Creating the Future
Good
Organization
Lower Improve Periodic
Employees e
Cost Quality New Products
Do Their Job
029021807
(a) Questionnaire
(b) Memo
(c) Email
(d) Presentation

Fig. 2. Document samples from the RVL-CDIP [11] dataset with corresponding text extracted by Tesseract OCR.

fine-grained document recognition, we expect the model to leverage both image and text information.

This work introduces a multimodal deep network that learns from both a document image and its textual content automatically extracted by OCR to perform its classification. We design a pragmatic pipeline for end-to-end heterogeneous feature extraction and fusion under time and cost constraints. We show that taking both the text and the document appearance into account improves both single modality baselines by several percents on two datasets from the document recognition literature. We detail some limitations of the current academic datasets and give leads for an application in an industrial setting with unclean data, such as photographed documents.

2 Related Work

Analyzing digitized documents is an old task in computer vision that was boosted by the dissemination of computers in offices and then of digital cameras and smartphones in everyday life. To allow for textual search and easy indexing, the critical part of digitization is extracting text content from documents that have been scanned or photographed. Indeed, either when scanning or taking a picture of the document, its actual text is lost, although it is implicitly embedded in the pixel values of the image. Numerous optical character recognition (OCR) algorithms have been designed to transform images into strings of characters [17,37]. Despite those efforts perfectly reading any type of document remains challenging due to the wide variety of fonts and languages. Layout analysis is a way to preprocess the data to detect text areas and find the text orientation in order to enforce a better local and global consistency [15,20].

Document image analysis is also one of the first topic where modern deep learning has been applied. The first convolutional neural network (CNN) [21] was originally designed for classification of digits and letters. The computer vision community deployed consequent efforts to achieve image-based document classification without text, as shown by a 2007 survey [7] which focuses on document image classification without OCR results. As an example, [19] introduced SURF visual features with a bag-of-words scheme to perform document image classification and retrieval. In 2015, [11] introduced a large labeled image document dataset which sparked interest and generated several studies of deep CNN on this topic [1,9,36], inspired by the success of these networks on ImageNet and tuning data augmentation policies, transfer learning strategies and domain adaptation for document classification. In the same idea, [35] also investigated such deep architectures to classify identity documents. [2] goes even further by trying to segment the full layout of a document image into paragraphs, titles, ornaments, images etc. These models focus on extracting strong visual features from the images to classify the documents based on their layout, geometry, colors and shape.

On the other hand, text-based document classification has also long been investigated. In 1963, [6] introduced an algorithmic approach to classify scientific abstracts. More recently, [23] experimented with one-class SVM for document classification based on various text features, such as TF-IDF. [33] used Latent Dirichlet Allocation to perform topic modeling and used it as a generative approach to document classification. The recent appearance of learned word embeddings approaches such as word2vec [24] or ELMo [30] paved to way to a large body of works related to recurrent and attention mechanisms for text classification. For example, [39] proposed a bidirectional recurrent network with a hierarchical attention mechanism that learns both at the word and sentence levels to improve document classification.

Some works tried to reconcile the text-based and image-based approaches to exploit both information sources. [26] performs OCR to detect keywords in images which are then encoded as colored boxes before passing the image through a CNN. While a clever trick, this does not leverage the representation power of word embeddings. Closer to our approach, [38] goes further by generating text feature maps that are combined with visual feature maps in a fully convolutional network. However, the considered documents are synthetic and the network is trained using perfectly clean texts and images, which is unrealistic for practical uses. More similar to us, [4] learns to combine bag of words and bag of visual words features for industrial document images using a statistical model combining outputs of two single-modality classifiers. While using shallow features, they show that using both information allows for a better accuracy when the OCR is unreliable, which is often the case in an industrial setting.

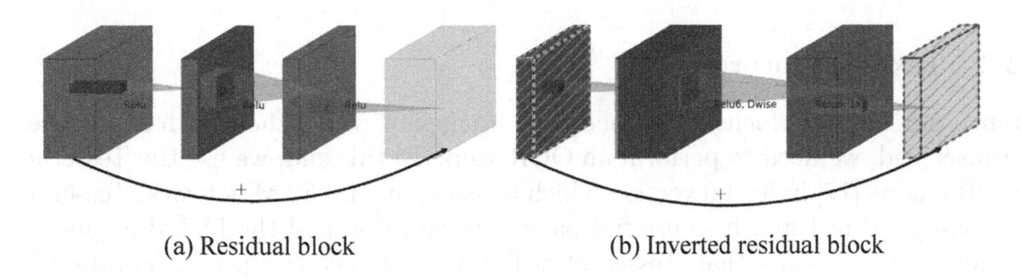

(a) Residual block (b) Inverted residual block

Fig. 3. MobileNetV2 uses inverted residual blocks to reduce the number of channels that are forwarded in subsequent layers. Figure from [34].

In this paper, we go further in this direction and propose a new baseline with a hybrid deep model. In order to classify OCRized document images, we present a pragmatic pipeline perform visual and textual feature extraction using off-the-shelf architectures. To leverage the complementary information present in both modalities, we design an efficient end-to-end network that jointly learn from text and image while keeping computation cost at its minimum. We build on existing deep models (MobileNet and FastText) and demonstrate significant improvements using our fusion strategy on two document images dataset.

3 Learning on Text and Image

3.1 Visual Features

There is a large literature both in general image recognition and in image document classification. Recent works have established deep convolutional neural networks as the *de facto* state of the art on many competitions in object recognition, detection and segmentation, e.g. ImageNet. Deep features, extracted by pretrained or fine-tuned deep CNNs, constitute a strong baseline for visual recognition tasks [32]. Based on this, we choose to fine-tune a CNN pretrained on ImageNet in order to extract visual features on our images, as suggested in several recent document classification publications [1,11,36]. As we aim to perform inference on a large volume of data with time and cost constraints, we focus on a lightweight architecture with competitive classification performance, in our case the MobileNet v2 model [34].

MobileNetV2 [34] consists in a stack of bottleneck blocks. Based on the residual learning principle [13], each bottleneck block transforms a feature map first by expanding it by increasing its number of channels with a 1×1 convolutional layer with identity activation. Then, a 3×3 depthwise convolution is performed, followed by a ReLU and a final 1×1 convolution with ReLU. For efficiency issues, this block inverts the traditional residual block since the expansion is performed inside the block, whereas residual blocks compress and then reexpand the information, as illustrated in Fig. 3. The final MobileNetV2 contains 19 residual bottleneck layers. Compared to other state of the art CNNs, MobileNetV2's accuracy is on-par with VGG-16 while being significantly faster.

3.2 Textual Features

Since our use case focuses on document images in which the text has not been transcribed, we need to perform an OCR step. To this end, we use the Tesseract OCR engine [17] in its 4.0 version which is based on an LSTM network. Tesseract is configured in English to use full page segmentation and the LSTM engine. In practice, this means that Tesseract will try to detect the text orientation in the image and perform the needed affine transformation and rotation if any. Tesseract also deals with the image binarization using Otsu's thresholding to identify black text on white background [27]. This will suffice on the datasets described in Sect. 4.1, although we found Tesseract challenging to apply on real-world images, especially pictures which are not flat and grayscale scans.

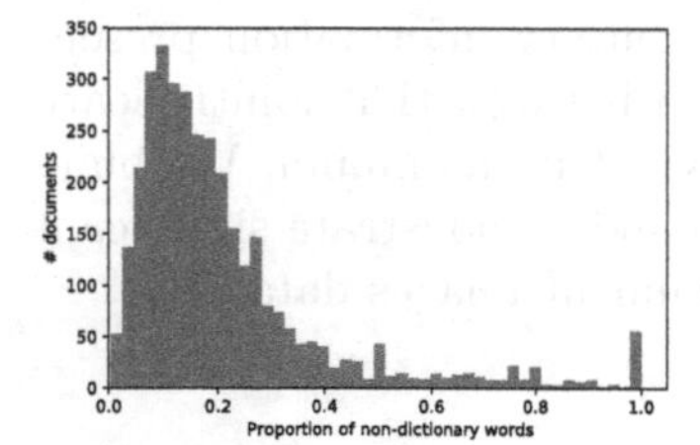

(a) Document distribution w.r.t of non-dictionary words % in the Tobacco3482-Tesseract corpus.

Word pair	Similarities		
specifically	GloVe	ELMo	FastText
Specificalily	0.71	0.68	0.96
filter	GloVe	ELMo	FastText
fiilter	0.91	0.73	0.96
alcohol	GloVe	ELMo	FastText
Aleohol	0.40	0.69	0.88
Largely	GloVe	ELMo	FastText
Largly	0.25	0.81	0.98

(b) Word embeddings similarity for misspelled words.

Fig. 4. Tesseract OCR outputs noisy text that does not entirely overlap with the assumptions usually held when training word embeddings for NLP.

Recent literature in NLP suggests that pretrained word embeddings offer a strong baseline which surpasses traditional shallow learning approaches. Many word embeddings have been designed following the initial success of *word2vec* [24], such as GloVe [29] or more recently the contextualized word embeddings from ELMo [30].

However, those word embeddings assume a good tokenization of the words, i.e. most embeddings remove digits, ignore punctuation and do not deal with out-of-vocabulary (OOV) words. Since these embeddings are learned on clean corpus (e.g. Wikipedia or novels), tokenization is fairly straightforward. OOV words are either assigned a random embedding or mapped to the closest in-vocabulary word based on the Levenshtein distance.

Unfortunately, outputs of the Tesseract OCR are noisy and not as clean as the training data from these embeddings. Even in grayscale, well-oriented documents, OCR might have trouble dealing with diacritics, exotic fonts or curved text, as illustrated by the extracts from Fig. 2. Moreover, specific user domains (e.g. banking or medieval manuscripts) might use rare words, codes, abbreviations or overall jargon that is absent from general-purpose word embeddings. Since we face many possible misspellings in the extracted text, we cannot use the previous workarounds for OOV embeddings since it would inject a lot of non-discriminant features in our text representation In average, on the Tobacco3482 corpus, a document processed by Tesseract OCR contains 136 words with 4 characters or more. Of those, only 118 in average are in the GloVe embeddings [29][1] and only 114 are in Enchant's spellchecker US English dictionary. Overall, approximately 26% of the corpus is absent from the US English dictionary and 23% from the GloVe embeddings. The document distribution with respect to the proportion of out-of-vocabulary words is shown in Fig. 4a. Although most of the documents are concentrated around 10% of OOVs, there is a significant long tail including several dozens of documents that contain only words outside of the English language.

Therefore, we turn to character-based word embeddings that are able to deal with OOV words by assigning them plausible word vectors that preserve both a semantic and a spelling similarity. One possibility was to use the mimicking networks from [31] that learn to infer word embeddings such as GloVe, but based only on subword information. More complex embeddings such as FastText [5,16] and ELMo [30], which produce vectors using respectively n-grams and subword information, can also address this problem. Finally, the Magnitude library [28] uses two alternative strategies to deal with OOV words:

- Assigning a *deterministic* random vector. These vectors do not capture semantic sense, however similar words based on the Levenshtein-Damerau distance will have similar vectors. Misspellings will therefore not be close to the original word, but similar lingo words will be close.
- Using character n-grams inspired by [5] and interpolation with in-vocabulary words, Magnitude can generate vectors for OOV words which are sensible based on existing learned embedding.

Preliminary data exploration shows that subword-aware embeddings perform better at preserving similarity despite misspellings, as illustrated in Fig. 4b. We therefore focus our interest on the FastText embedding, which is faster than ELMo since the latter requires passing the context through a bidirectionnal LSTM during inference. It is worth noting that this raises concern for characters that have not been seen by FastText. We found experimentally that Tesseract OCR generated no character that was OOV for FastText on the documents we considered.

Finally, it is necessary to convert those word embeddings into a document embedding. We consider two approaches:

- The simple baseline for sentence embedding suggested in [3], which consists in a weighted average of word embeddings altered by PCA.

[1] Based on the Wikipedia 2014 + Gigaword 5 datasets.

- Using variable-length document embeddings consisting in a sequence of word embeddings.

The first approach is suitable as generic feature while the second requires a statistical model able to deal with sequences, such as recurrent or convolutional neural networks. For both methods, we use the SpaCy small English model [14] to perform the tokenization and punctuation removal. Individual word embeddings are then inferred using FastText [5] pretrained on the Common Crawl dataset.

3.3 Multimodal Features

Once text and image features have been extracted, we feed them to a multi-layer perceptron following [10]. To do so, we need to combine both feature vectors into one. Two approaches can be envisioned:

- Adaptive averaging of both feature vectors. This aligns both feature spaces so that scalars at the same index become compatible by summation, i.e. that each dimension of the vectors have a similar semantic meaning.
- Concatenating both vectors. This does not imply that both feature spaces can be aligned and delegates to the fusion MLP the task of combining the two domains.

Both fusion strategies are differentiable, therefore the whole network can be trained in an end-to-end fashion. Moreover, the model is modular and each feature extractor can be swapped for another model, e.g. MobileNet can be exchanged with any other popular CNN and FastText could be replaced by subword-level NLP models, even differentiable ones that could allow fine-tuning the embeddings. In this work, we try to keep things simple and build on robust base networks in order to clearly understand how the data fusion impacts model performance. Preliminary experiments showed that the summation fusion significantly underperformed compared to pure image baseline. We suggest that this is provoked by the impossibility of aligning the text and image feature spaces without breaking their discriminating power, resulting in suboptimal space. Therefore, we move on with the concatenation strategy for the rest of this paper. The complete pipeline is illustrated in Fig. 1.

4 Experimental Setup

4.1 Datasets

Tobacco3482. The Tobacco3482 dataset [19] contains 3482 black and white documents, a subset from the Truth Tobacco Industry Documents[2] archives of legal proceedings against large American tobacco companies. There are annotations for 10 classes of documents (e.g. email, letter, memo...). Following common practices, we perform k-fold cross-validation using 800 documents for training and the rest for testing. Results are averaged over 3 runs.

[2] https://www.industrydocuments.ucsf.edu/tobacco/.

Table 1. Preliminary tuning of the single-modality baselines on Tobacco3482.

(a) Preliminary experiments on Tobacco3482 for the text baseline.

Model	OA	F_1
MLP (document)	70.8%	0.69
CNN 1D (word sequence)	73.9%	0.71

OA = overall accuracy, F_1 = class-balanced F_1 score.

(b) Preliminary experiments on Tobacco3482 for the image baseline.

Model	OA	F_1
MobileNetV2	84.5%	0.82
MobileNetV2 (w/ DA)	83.9%	0.82

OA = overall accuracy, F_1 = class-balanced F_1 score, DA = data augmentation.

RVL-CDIP. The RVL-CDIP dataset [11] is comprised of 400 000 grayscale digitized documents from the Truth Tobacco Industry Documents. There are annotations for 16 classes of documents (e.g. email, letter, invoice, scientific report...), each containing 25 000 samples. We use the standard train/val/test split from [11] with 320 000 documents for training, 40 000 for validation and 40 000 for testing.

Text Generation. The Tobacco3482 and RVL-CDIP are image-based datasets. In order to evaluate our multi-modal networks, we wish to learn from both visual and textual content. Therefore we use the Tesseract OCR library[3] to extract text from the grayscales images. We perform this operation on both datasets. We release the OCR text dataset openly[4] to encourage other researchers to replicate our work or test their own model for post-OCR text classification or multi-modal text/image classification.

4.2 Models

This subsection describes the implementation details of our deep networks. All models are implemented in TensorFlow 1.12 using the Keras API and trained using a NVIDIA Titan X GPU. Hyperparameters were manually selected on a subset of Tobacco3482 and fixed for all experiments.

Text Baseline. Seeing that our representation of textual data can be either a document embedding or a sequence of word embeddings, we compare two models for our text baseline.

The first model is an improved Multi-Layer Perceptron (MLP) with ReLU activations, Dropout and Batch Normalization (BN) after each layer. The network has a fixed width of 2048 neurons for all layers except the last one, which produces a 128 feature vector, classified by a softmax layer. Weights are randomly initialized using He's initialization [12]. The averaged document embedding [3] is used as an input for this classifier.

[3] https://github.com/tesseract-ocr/tesseract/.

[4] The QS-OCR dataset is available at: https://github.com/Quicksign/ocrized-text-dataset.

The second model is a one-dimensional convolutional neural network designed inspired by previous work for sentence classification [18]. The CNN is 4-layers deep and interlaces 1D convolutions with a window of size 12 with maxpooling with a stride of 2. Each layer consists in 512 channels with ReLU activation. The final feature map is processed by a max-pooling-through-time layer that extracts maximal features on the sequence on top of which we apply Dropout for regularization. A fully connected layer then maps the features to the softmax classifier. The input word sequence is zero-padded up to 500 words for documents with less 500 words.

We experiment on the Tobacco3482 dataset in order to evaluate which text model to choose. Results are reported in Table 1a. Without surprise, the CNN 1D outperforms significantly the MLP classifier. The pattern recognition abilities of the convolutional network makes it possible to interpret the word sequences by leveraging contextual information. Since only some part of the text might be relevant, averaging over all word embeddings dilute the discriminating information. Moreover, noisy embeddings due to garbage output from Tesseract (e.g. incoherent strings where OCR has failed) are included in the final document embedding. However, when dealing with word sequences, convolutional layers and temporal max-pooling help extracting only the relevant information. Therefore, we choose to include the 1D CNN as the text component in our multimodal architecture.

This model is denoted **Text** in the rest of the paper. It is optimized using Stochastic Gradient Descent with momentum for 100 epochs, with a learning rate of 0.01, a momentum of 0.9 and a batch size of 40[5].

Image Baseline. We investigate as our base CNN the lightweight MobileNetV2 [34] which focuses on computing efficiency, albeit at the cost of a slightly lower top-1 accuracy on ImageNet compared to other state of the art CNN. We train the CNN on grayscale document images resized at 384×384. Although this warps the aspect ratio, [36] reports better accuracy than when using padding at the same resolution. As the model is designed for RGB images, the grayscale channel is duplicated three times. This allows us to initialize the network by loading its pretrained weights on ImageNet, which accelerates convergence and slightly improves accuracy through transfer learning.

This model is denoted **Image** in the rest of the paper. It is optimized using Stochastic Gradient Descent with momentum for 200 epochs, with a learning rate of 0.01, a momentum of 0.9 and a batch size of 40.

As reported in Table 1b, preliminary experiments on the Tobacco3482 with random JPEG artifacts, saturation and contrast alterations did not significantly alter the classifier's accuracy compared to no augmentation. This is explained by the low variability between the grayscale document images. All images are grayscale with dark text on white background with horizontal text lines, therefore color and geometric augmentation are not necessary. However, [36] report some success using shear transform, which we did not consider in this work. It is

[5] Hyperparameters are manually tuned on a small validation set.

worth noting that compared with previous literature on the RVL-CDIP dataset, e.g. [1,11,36], we do not average predictions over multiple crops at inference time for speed concerns. This might explain why our visual baseline underperforms the current state of the art in this state (although this does not question the gains due to the multi-modal network).

Table 2. Overall accuracy on the RVL-CDIP dataset.

Model	IMAGE	TEXT	FUSION	CNNs [11]	VGG-16 [1]	AlexNet+SPP [36]
OA	89.1%	74.6%	90.6%	89.8%	90.97%	90.94%

OA = Overall Accuracy.

Fusion. For our multimodal network, we consider the same model as our baselines except that the final layers are cut-off. For the **TEXT** model, the last layer produces an output vector of dimension 128 instead of the number of classes. For the **IMAGE** model, we aggregate the last convolutional features using global average pooling on each channel, which produces a feature vector of dimension 1280. We then map this feature vector using a fully connected layer to a representation space of dimension 128.

Table 3. Overall accuracy and F_1 scores on the Tobacco3482 datasets.

Model	OA	F_1	Adv.	Email	Form	Letter	Memo	News	Notes	Report	Res.	Sci.
CNNs [11]	79.9	–	–									
TEXT	73.8	0.71	0.60	0.96	0.76	0.71	0.79	0.67	0.62	0.43	**0.97**	0.57
IMAGE	84.5	0.82	**0.94**	0.96	0.85	0.83	0.90	0.89	0.83	0.61	0.80	0.62
FUSION	**87.8**	**0.86**	0.93	**0.98**	**0.88**	**0.86**	**0.90**	**0.90**	**0.85**	**0.71**	0.96	**0.68**
Oracle	92.1	0.91	0.94	0.99	0.94	0.92	0.93	0.93	0.89	0.81	0.97	0.79

Adv. = Advertisement, Res. = Resume, Sci. = Scientific.

This model is denoted **FUSION** in the rest of the paper. It is optimized using Stochastic Gradient Descent with momentum for 200 epochs, with a learning rate of 0.01, a momentum of 0.9 and a batch size of 40.

5 Discussion

5.1 Performances

Model performances scores on Tobacco3482 and RVL-CDIP are reported in Tables 2 and 3. Behaviour of all models is consistent both on the smaller dataset and on the very large one. In both cases, the **TEXT** baseline is significantly underperforming the **IMAGE** one. Indeed, as could be seen in Fig. 2, Tesseract OCR outputs noisy text. This includes words that have been misspelled – which are correctly dealt with by the FastText embeddings – and new words that are hallucinated due to poor binarization or salt-and-pepper noise in the image. Moreover, layout and visual information tends to be more informative based on how the classes were defined: scientific papers, news and emails follow similar templates while advertisements present specific graphics. However, in both cases, this simple document embedding is enough to classify more than 70% of the documents, despite its roughness.

Using the **Image** model only, we reach accuracies competitive with the state of the art. MobileNetV2 alone does on-par is with the holistic CNN ensemble from [11] and is competitive with fine-tuned GoogLeNet and ResNet-50 [1] (90.97%).

On both datasets, the fusion scheme is able to improve the overall accuracy by $\simeq$1.5% which demonstrates the relevance of our approach. While the document embedding we chose is simple, it appears to be at least partially robust to OCR noise and to preserve enough information about the document content to boosts CNN accuracy on document image classification even further. We also report the results from an oracle, which corresponds to the perfect fusion of the **Text** and **Image** baselines, i.e. a model that would combine the predictions from both single-modality networks and always choose the right one. The oracle corresponds to the theoretical maximal accuracy boost that we could expect from the **Fusion** model. On Tobacco3482, the oracle corresponds to a 7.6% absolute improvement (9% relative). In our case, the **Fusion** model improves the best single-source baseline by an absolute 3.3% (4% relative), which is significant although still leaves the door open to further improvements. More importantly, the gains are consistent on all classes of interest, almost never underperforming one of the two base networks on any class. This confirm the proposed approach as the two sources, image and text, give complementary information to classify a document.

5.2 Processing Time

Although some applications of document image recognition can be performed offline, most of the time users upload a document and expect near real-time feedback. User experience engineering [25] indicates than less than 1 s is the maximum latency the user can suffer before the interface feels sluggish, and 10 s is the maximum delay before they start loosing their attention. On the RVL-CDIP dataset, Tesseract processes a document image in $\simeq$910 ms in average on an Intel Core i7-8550U CPU using 4 threads, including loading the image from disk. This means that every additional latency induced by the network inference time is critical since it will negatively affect the user experience.

On the same CPU, the full inference using the **Fusion** model takes $\simeq$360 ms including loading, resizing and normalizing the image. The complete process including Tesseract OCR therefore takes less than $\simeq$1300 ms which is acceptable in a system requiring user input. Of those, 130 ms are spent in the 1D CNN (including reading the file and performing FastText inference) and 230 ms in MobileNetV2 (including image preprocessing). The overhead added by the final fusion layer is negligible. We stress that this is using a standard TensorFlow without any CPU-specific compilation flags, which could speed up the inference further. On a NVIDIA Titan X GPU, the **Fusion** network runs in 110 ms (50 ms for **Text**, 60 ms for MobileNetV2), which brings the total just above the 1 s recommendation. In our case, using compute-efficient architectures allow us to avoid running on an expensive and power-hungry GPU.

As a comparison basis, other architecture choices that we dismissed earlier would have resulted in poorer performance and the network would not be usable in a near real-time user application. For example, the Xception network [8] takes 630 ms to run during inference with the same parameters and hardware. For the text model, an LSTM-based RNN with a similar depth takes many seconds to run.

Note that, although this does not reduced the perceived delay for one user, the global throughput of the system can be improved by batching the images. Two Tesseract processes can leverage the full eight cores from an Intel Core i7-8550U CPU. In this setting, processing an image takes $\simeq$660 ms in average. Thanks to the batch efficiency of neural networks, the average processing time becomes $\leq$750 ms on GPU and $\leq$1000 ms on CPU. This is particularly helpful when users have several documents to upload that can be processed concurrently.

5.3 Limitations

One of the main limitation of this work stems from the public document image datasets available. Indeed, in a real-world application, document images can be grayscale, RGB, scanned images and photographs with various rotations, brightness, contrast and hue values. The Tobacco documents are all oriented in the right way, which makes it easier for Tesseract to perform OCR. Moreover, documents have been scanned by professionals who tried to maximize their legibility while user-generated often presents poor quality.

While it was not required here, data augmentation is definitely required for practical applications to encompass the large variety of environmental conditions in which documents are digitized. This is especially true for rotations, since it is often not possible to ensure that users will capture the document with the right orientation and Tesseract does not always correctly detects it. For industrial-grade applications dealing with user-generated content, such a data augmentation is necessary to alleviate overfitting and reduce the gap between train and actual data. Preprocessing page segmentation and layout analysis tools, such as dhSegment [2] can also bring significant improvements by renormalizing image orientation and cropping the document before sending it to the classifier.

Moreover, as we have seen, the post-OCR word embeddings include lots of noisy or completely wrong words that generate OOV errors. In practical applications, we found beneficial to perform a semantic tokenization and named entity recognition using SpaCy. This allows us to perform a partial spellchecking, e.g. using symspell[6] to correct words that have been misread by Tesser-

[6] https://github.com/wolfgarbe/SymSpell.

act, without affecting proper nouns or domain-specific abbreviations and codes. If this can deal frequent mispellings of words, it might also suppress out-of-vocabulary words such as alphanumeric codes. Therefore, learning domain specific, character-based or robust-to-OCR embeddings [22] is an interesting lead for future research, as the current interest in the ICDAR2019 competition on Post-OCR Text Correction shows[7].

6 Conclusion

In this work, we tackled the problem of document classification using both image and text contents. Based only on an image of a digitized document, we try to perform a fine-grained classification using visual and textual features. To do so, we first used Tesseract OCR to extract the text from the image. We then compute character-based word embeddings using FastText on the noisy Tesseract output and generate a document embedding which represents our text features. Their counterpart visual features are learned using MobileNetv2, a standard CNN from the state of the art. Using those pragmatic approaches, we introduce an end-to-end learnable multimodal deep network that jointly learns text and image features and perform the final classification based on a fused heterogeneous representation of the document. We validated our approach on the Tobacco3482 and RVL-CDIP datasets showing consistent gains both on small and large datasets. This shows that there is a significant interest into hybrid image/text approach even when clean text is not available for document image classification and we aim to further investigate this topic in the future.

References

1. Afzal, M.Z., Kölsch, A., Ahmed, S., Liwicki, M.: Cutting the error by half: investigation of very deep CNN and advanced training strategies for document image classification. In: 2017 14th IAPR International Conference on Document Analysis and Recognition (ICDAR), vol. 01, pp. 883–888, November 2017. https://doi.org/10.1109/ICDAR.2017.149
2. Ares Oliveira, S., Seguin, B.L.A., Kaplan, F.: dhSegment: a generic deep-learning approach for document segmentation, August 2018
3. Arora, S., Liang, Y., Ma, T.: A simple but tough-to-beat baseline for sentence embeddings. In: Proceedings of the International Conference on Learning Representations (ICLR), November 2016
4. Augereau, O., Journet, N., Vialard, A., Domenger, J.: Improving classification of an industrial document image database by combining visual and textual features. In: 2014 11th IAPR International Workshop on Document Analysis Systems, pp. 314–318, April 2014. https://doi.org/10.1109/DAS.2014.44
5. Bojanowski, P., Grave, E., Joulin, A., Mikolov, T.: Enriching word vectors with subword information. Trans. Assoc. Comput. Linguist. **5**, 135–146 (2017)
6. Borko, H., Bernick, M.: Automatic document classification. J. ACM **10**(2), 151–162 (1963). https://doi.org/10.1145/321160.321165

[7] https://sites.google.com/view/icdar2019-postcorrectionocr.

7. Chen, N., Blostein, D.: A survey of document image classification: problem statement, classifier architecture and performance evaluation. Int. J. Doc. Anal. Recogn. (IJDAR) **10**(1), 1–16 (2007). https://doi.org/10.1007/s10032-006-0020-2
8. Chollet, F.: Xception: deep Learning with depthwise separable convolutions. In: Proceedings of the IEEE Conference on Computer Vision and Pattern Recognition (CVPR), Honolulu, United States, pp. 1800–1807, July 2017. https://doi.org/10.1109/CVPR.2017.195
9. Das, A., Roy, S., Bhattacharya, U., Parui, S.K.: Document image classification with intra-domain transfer learning and stacked generalization of deep convolutional neural networks. In: 2018 24th International Conference on Pattern Recognition (ICPR), pp. 3180–3185, August 2018. https://doi.org/10.1109/ICPR.2018.8545630
10. Eitel, A., Springenberg, J.T., Spinello, L., Riedmiller, M., Burgard, W.: Multimodal deep learning for robust RGB-D object recognition. In: 2015 IEEE/RSJ International Conference on Intelligent Robots and Systems (IROS), pp. 681–687, September 2015. https://doi.org/10.1109/IROS.2015.7353446
11. Harley, A.W., Ufkes, A., Derpanis, K.G.: Evaluation of deep convolutional nets for document image classification and retrieval. In: 2015 13th International Conference on Document Analysis and Recognition (ICDAR), pp. 991–995, August 2015. https://doi.org/10.1109/ICDAR.2015.7333910
12. He, K., Zhang, X., Ren, S., Sun, J.: Delving deep into rectifiers: surpassing human-level performance on ImageNet classification. In: Proceedings of the IEEE International Conference on Computer Vision, pp. 1026–1034, December 2015. https://doi.org/10.1109/ICCV.2015.123
13. He, K., Zhang, X., Ren, S., Sun, J.: Deep residual learning for image recognition. In: Proceedings of the IEEE Conference on Computer Vision and Pattern Recognition (CVPR), Las Vegas, United States, pp. 770–778, June 2016. https://doi.org/10.1109/CVPR.2016.90
14. Honnibal, M., Montani, I.: spaCy 2: natural language understanding with Bloom embeddings, convolutional neural networks and incremental parsing (2017, to appear)
15. Imade, S., Tatsuta, S., Wada, T.: Segmentation and classification for mixed text/image documents using neural network. In: Proceedings of 2nd International Conference on Document Analysis and Recognition (ICDAR 1993), pp. 930–934, October 1993. https://doi.org/10.1109/ICDAR.1993.395584
16. Joulin, A., Grave, E., Bojanowski, P., Mikolov, T.: Bag of tricks for efficient text classification. In: Proceedings of the 15th Conference of the European Chapter of the Association for Computational Linguistics: Volume 2, Short Papers, pp. 427–431. Association for Computational Linguistics (2017)
17. Kay, A.: Tesseract: an open-source optical character recognition engine. Linux J. **2007**(159), 2 (2007)
18. Kim, Y.: Convolutional neural networks for sentence classification. In: Proceedings of the 2014 Conference on Empirical Methods in Natural Language Processing (EMNLP), pp. 1746–1751, October 2014. https://doi.org/10.3115/v1/D14-1181
19. Kumar, J., Ye, P., Doermann, D.: Structural similarity for document image classification and retrieval. Pattern Recogn. Lett. **43**, 119–126 (2014). https://doi.org/10.1016/j.patrec.2013.10.030
20. Le, D.X., Thoma, G.R., Wechsler, H.: Classification of binary document images into textual or nontextual data blocks using neural network models. Mach. Vis. Appl. **8**(5), 289–304 (1995). https://doi.org/10.1007/BF01211490

21. LeCun, Y., Bottou, L., Bengio, Y., Haffner, P.: Gradient-based learning applied to document recognition. Proc. IEEE **86**(11), 2278–2324 (1998). https://doi.org/10.1109/5.726791
22. Malykh, V., Logacheva, V., Khakhulin, T.: Robust word vectors: context-informed embeddings for noisy texts. In: Proceedings of the 2018 EMNLP Workshop W-NUT: The 4th Workshop on Noisy User-Generated Text, pp. 54–63, November 2018
23. Manevitz, L.M., Yousef, M.: One-class SVMs for document classification. J. Mach. Learn. Res. **2**(Dec), 139–154 (2001)
24. Mikolov, T., Chen, K., Corrado, G., Dean, J.: Efficient estimation of word representations in vector space. In: ICLR 2013, January 2013
25. Nielsen, J.: Usability Engineering. Morgan Kaufmann Publishers Inc., San Francisco (1993)
26. Noce, L., Gallo, I., Zamberletti, A., Calefati, A.: Embedded textual content for document image classification with convolutional neural networks. In: Proceedings of the 2016 ACM Symposium on Document Engineering (DocEng 2016), pp. 165–173. ACM, New York (2016). https://doi.org/10.1145/2960811.2960814
27. Otsu, N.: A threshold selection method from gray-level histograms. IEEE Trans. Syst. Man Cybern. **9**(1), 62–66 (1979). https://doi.org/10.1109/TSMC.1979.4310076
28. Patel, A., Sands, A., Callison-Burch, C., Apidianaki, M.: Magnitude: a fast, efficient universal vector embedding utility package. In: Proceedings of the 2018 Conference on Empirical Methods in Natural Language Processing: System Demonstrations, pp. 120–126, November 2018
29. Pennington, J., Socher, R., Manning, C.: GloVe: global vectors for word representation. In: Proceedings of the 2014 Conference on Empirical Methods in Natural Language Processing (EMNLP), pp. 1532–1543. Association for Computational Linguistics (2014). https://doi.org/10.3115/v1/D14-1162
30. Peters, M., et al.: Deep contextualized word representations. In: Proceedings of the 2018 Conference of the North American Chapter of the Association for Computational Linguistics: Human Language Technologies, Volume 1 (Long Papers), pp. 2227–2237. Association for Computational Linguistics (2018). https://doi.org/10.18653/v1/N18-1202
31. Pinter, Y., Guthrie, R., Eisenstein, J.: Mimicking word embeddings using Subword RNNs. In: Proceedings of the 2017 Conference on Empirical Methods in Natural Language Processing, pp. 102–112. Association for Computational Linguistics (2017). https://doi.org/10.18653/v1/D17-1010
32. Razavian, A.S., Azizpour, H., Sullivan, J., Carlsson, S.: CNN features off-the-shelf: an astounding baseline for recognition. In: Proceedings of the IEEE Conference on Computer Vision and Pattern Recognition Workshops (CVPRW), pp. 512–519, June 2014. https://doi.org/10.1109/CVPRW.2014.131
33. Rubin, T.N., Chambers, A., Smyth, P., Steyvers, M.: Statistical topic models for multi-label document classification. Mach. Learn. **88**(1), 157–208 (2012). https://doi.org/10.1007/s10994-011-5272-5
34. Sandler, M., Howard, A., Zhu, M., Zhmoginov, A., Chen, L.: MobileNetV2: inverted residuals and linear bottlenecks. In: 2018 IEEE/CVF Conference on Computer Vision and Pattern Recognition, pp. 4510–4520, June 2018. https://doi.org/10.1109/CVPR.2018.00474

35. Sicre, R., Awal, A.M., Furon, T.: Identity documents classification as an image classification problem. In: Battiato, S., Gallo, G., Schettini, R., Stanco, F. (eds.) ICIAP 2017. LNCS, vol. 10485, pp. 602–613. Springer, Cham (2017). https://doi.org/10.1007/978-3-319-68548-9_55
36. Tensmeyer, C., Martinez, T.: Analysis of convolutional neural networks for document image classification. In: 2017 14th IAPR International Conference on Document Analysis and Recognition (ICDAR), vol. 01, pp. 388–393, November 2017. https://doi.org/10.1109/ICDAR.2017.71
37. Wong, K.Y., Casey, R.G., Wahl, F.M.: Document analysis system. IBM J. Res. Dev. **26**(6), 647–656 (1982). https://doi.org/10.1147/rd.266.0647
38. Yang, X., Yumer, E., Asente, P., Kraley, M., Kifer, D., Giles, C.L.: Learning to extract semantic structure from documents using multimodal fully convolutional neural networks. In: 2017 IEEE Conference on Computer Vision and Pattern Recognition (CVPR), pp. 4342–4351, July 2017. https://doi.org/10.1109/CVPR.2017.462
39. Yang, Z., Yang, D., Dyer, C., He, X., Smola, A., Hovy, E.: Hierarchical attention networks for document classification. In: Proceedings of the 2016 Conference of the North American Chapter of the Association for Computational Linguistics: Human Language Technologies, pp. 1480–1489. Association for Computational Linguistics (2016). https://doi.org/10.18653/v1/N16-1174

Manifold Mixing for Stacked Regularization

João Pereira[1,3(✉)], Erik S. G. Stroes[1], Albert K. Groen[1], Aeilko H. Zwinderman[2], and Evgeni Levin[1,3]

[1] Department of Cardiovascular Medicine, University Medical Center Amsterdam, Amsterdam, The Netherlands
{j.p.belopereira,e.s.stroes,a.k.groen,e.levin}@amsterdamumc.nl
[2] Department of Clinical Epidemiology, Biostatistics and Bioinformatics, University Medical Center Amsterdam, Amsterdam, The Netherlands
a.h.zwinderman@amsterdamumc.nl
[3] Horaizon BV, Delft, The Netherlands

Abstract. In many real-world learning tasks, one has access to datasets consisting of multiple modalities, for example, various omics profiles of the patients coupled with medical records and other unstructured data sources. Often, the "core mechanism" (e.g. health or disease state) is reflected in all of these modalities and so this commonality can become more evident when the source domain (e.g. proteins) can accordingly transform the local geometry of the target (e.g. lipids). In this paper, we propose a novel algorithm that takes multiple data sources, constructs corresponding manifolds, and "mixes" information across them to find the common denominators in the observable outcomes. By leveraging manifold information from these different sources we obtain more robust and accurate results in comparison to standard methods. In the empirical evaluation on a clinical cohort related to ischaemia in patients with coronary artery disease, we demonstrate the applicability and efficacy of the proposed algorithm.

Keywords: Manifold Mixing · Multi-view · Stacked regularization

1 Introduction

Exponential increase in multi-modal data, stemming from different instruments and measurements presents both an opportunity and a challenge. With a larger sheer volume of information, there is potentially more we can learn for a given process, but coherently combining different data sources with the goal of improving analysis remains a challenging and underdeveloped task. In the medical field for instance, multiple omics data such as proteins or lipids encode somewhat related biological information. Therefore, one might expect that health or disease state is reflected in both of these modalities, despite their different format. Learning frameworks such as manifold alignment [5,10] and domain adaptation [6,8] may not be directly applicable as they try to find a common latent

P. Cellier and K. Driessens (Eds.): ECML PKDD 2019 Workshops, CCIS 1167, pp. 444–452, 2020.
https://doi.org/10.1007/978-3-030-43823-4_36

manifold and learn to transfer knowledge from a source to a target domain, respectively. Orthogonally to existing methods, we present a way of "mixing" information from multiple domains, without imposing hard similarity between them. The motivation is that for a given outcome, the "core mechanism" (e.g. health or disease state) is reflected in all of these modalities and so this commonality can become more evident when the source domain (e.g. proteins) can accordingly transform the local geometry of the target (e.g. lipids).

2 Approach

We use a stacked regularization setting [11] where each level-one model is trained using "mixed manifolds" of various data modalities. In the next subsections we briefly discuss classical stacked regularization, domain alignment, adaption, and finally propose our mixing algorithm. Regarding notation, we will use capital bold, bold and no formatting for matrices, vectors and scalars or functions, respectively (e.g. $\mathbf{X}, \mathbf{x}, f/W$). We will also use calligraphic font to denote spaces (e.g. $\mathcal{X}$).

2.1 Stacking

Let $\mathbf{X}$ be a dataset of N samples whose values are sampled from an input space $\mathcal{X} = \{\mathcal{X}^1, \mathcal{X}^2, ..., \mathcal{X}^M\}$ where $\mathcal{X}^1$ to $\mathcal{X}^M$ are subspaces corresponding to different "sources" or "views" $1 \rightarrow M$ which we will refer to as "domains". Denote by y the output sampled from an output space $\mathcal{Y}$. In a supervised setting, the goal is to compute $p\left(y|\mathbf{x}^1, ..., \mathbf{x}^M\right)$, where $\mathbf{x}^i$ are the coordinates of an instance from $\mathbf{X}$ in the domain $\mathcal{X}^i$. In stacked regularization, or stacking, the input is passed to a first layer of W_0 predictors $g_1^0(\mathbf{x}), ..., g_{W_0}^0(\mathbf{x})$, with:

$$g_i^0(\mathbf{x}) = p\left(y|\mathbf{x}^1, ... \mathbf{x}^M, \boldsymbol{\theta}_i^0\right), \tag{1}$$

where $\boldsymbol{\theta}_i^0$ are the hyperparameters of the ith model. For our task, we suggest to pass one data source per model: $g_i^0(\mathbf{x}) = p\left(y|\mathbf{x}^i, \boldsymbol{\theta}_i^0\right)$, so that the width of the first layer W_0 is equal to the number of domains M. The output from this layer is then passed to one or more layers of W_k models $g_1^k, ..., g_{W_k}^k$ which blend the outputs of the previous ones:

$$g_i^k(\mathbf{x}) = p\left(y|g_1^{k-1}(\cdot), ..., g_{W_k}^{k-1}(\cdot)), \boldsymbol{\theta}_i^k\right), \; k \in [1, L], \tag{2}$$

where L is the total number of blending layers and $\boldsymbol{\theta}_i^k$ the hyperparameters of ith model from the kth layer. The last blending layer is then passed to a final model f that produces the output $f(\mathbf{x}) = p\left(y|g_1^L(\mathbf{x}), ..., g_{W_L}^L(\mathbf{x}), \boldsymbol{\theta}^{L+1}\right)$, where $\boldsymbol{\theta}^{L+1}$ are the hyperparameters of f. You can visualize the stacked model general architecture in Fig. 1. From a frequentist point of view, the goal of stacking is then to find:

$$\underset{\boldsymbol{\theta}}{argmin}\; \mathcal{L}(\mathbf{y}; f(\mathbf{X}), \boldsymbol{\theta}), \tag{3}$$

where $\boldsymbol{\theta}$ is the set of hyperparameter values from all of the stack models, $\mathbf{y}$ is the output for all of the data, and $\mathcal{L}$ is the loss function when using $f(\mathbf{x})$ to predict $\mathbf{y}$. For a fully Bayesian approach, one should compute the posterior probability of each model by integrating out the hyperparameter values:

$$p\left(g_i^k|Z\right) \propto p\left(Z|g_i^k\right) p\left(g_i^k\right) \propto \\ p\left(g_i^k\right) \int p\left(Z|\boldsymbol{\theta}_i^k, g_i^k\right) p\left(\boldsymbol{\theta}_i^k|g_i^k\right) d\boldsymbol{\theta}_i^k, \tag{4}$$

where Z is the complete dataset $(\mathbf{X}, \mathbf{y})$.

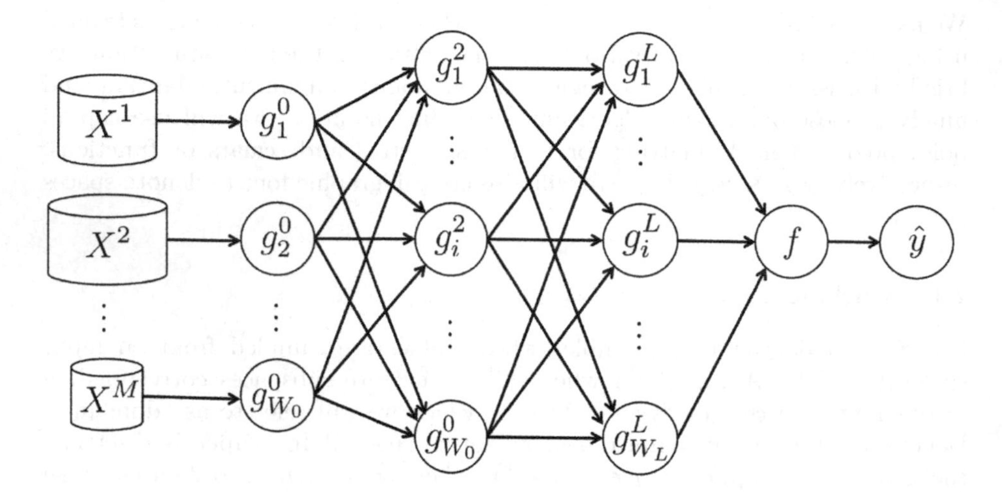

Fig. 1. Our proposed stacked setting

Although this approach is attractive because it considers the uncertainty of the model, it also incurs high computational cost for large $\boldsymbol{\theta}_i^k$.

Two important aspects are: (a) optimizing each model independently does not guarantee finding the global optimal stacked model and (b) there is an implicit assumption that each model g_i^k can learn/handle data from different sources (possibly with different formats) effectively.

2.2 Stacking Optimization

Finding an optimal stacked model can be done by optimizing each sub-model individually or by jointly optimizing all the sub-models. Optimizing each model individually has an important complexity advantage because the number of possible $\boldsymbol{\theta}$ combinations increases exponentially with the number of parameters: $k^{|\boldsymbol{\theta}|}$, where k is the number of values considered for each parameter.

Lemma 1. *For a given dataset* $\mathbf{X}, \mathbf{y}$*, stacked model* $f(x)$ *and parameters* $\boldsymbol{\theta}$*, the following relation is true:* $\mathcal{L}(\mathbf{y}, f(x), \boldsymbol{\theta}^*) \leq \mathcal{L}(\mathbf{y}, f(x), \boldsymbol{\theta}')$*, where*

$\boldsymbol{\theta}^* = \underset{\boldsymbol{\theta}}{argmin}\, \mathcal{L}\left(\mathbf{y}, f(x), \boldsymbol{\theta}\right)$, $\boldsymbol{\theta}' = \varphi_{k=1}^{L}\left(\varphi_{i=0}^{W_k}\left(\underset{\boldsymbol{\theta}_i^k}{argmin}\, \mathcal{L}\left(\mathbf{y}, g_i^k(x), \boldsymbol{\theta}_i^k\right)\right)\right)$, *and* $\varphi_{j=1}^{L}\left(\underset{\boldsymbol{\theta}_j}{argmin}\, f(\boldsymbol{\theta}_j)\right)$ *is a sequential composition of minimizations with respect to index* j*:* $\underset{\boldsymbol{\theta}_{j=L}}{argmin}\left(\underset{\boldsymbol{\theta}_{j=L-1}}{argmin}\left(...\underset{\boldsymbol{\theta}_{j=1}}{argmin}\left(f(\boldsymbol{\theta}_j)\right)\right)\right)$.

Proof. Let μ be a measure on the measurable space $(\Theta, \boldsymbol{\theta})$. Since $\boldsymbol{\theta}$ is a disjoint set, its measure is just:

$$\mu(\boldsymbol{\theta}) = \prod_{k=0}^{L+1}\prod_{i=1}^{W_k}\mu(\boldsymbol{\theta}_i^k) \tag{5}$$

Denote by $\{\boldsymbol{\theta}_i^k\}^*$ the set of values that satisfy $\underset{\boldsymbol{\theta}_i^k}{argmin}\, \mathcal{L}\left(\mathbf{y}, g_i^k(x), \boldsymbol{\theta}_i^k\right)$, and $\{\boldsymbol{\theta}_i^k\}$ the set of values $\boldsymbol{\theta}_i^k$ can take. Since $\{\boldsymbol{\theta}_i^k\}^* \subset \{\boldsymbol{\theta}_i^k\}$, then $\mu\left(\{\boldsymbol{\theta}_i^k\}^*\right) \leq \mu\left(\{\boldsymbol{\theta}_i^k\}\right), \forall\, i, k$, and so:

$$\mu\left(\boldsymbol{\theta}'\right) = \prod_{k=0}^{L+1}\prod_{i=1}^{W_k}\mu\left(\{\boldsymbol{\theta}_i^k\}^*\right) \leq \prod_{k=0}^{L+1}\prod_{i=1}^{W_k}\mu\left(\{\boldsymbol{\theta}_i^k\}\right) \tag{6}$$

$\mathcal{L}\left(\mathbf{y}, f(x), \boldsymbol{\theta}^*\right)$ is thus optimizing over a larger domain than $\mathcal{L}\left(\mathbf{y}, f(x), \boldsymbol{\theta}'\right)$ is, yielding $\mathcal{L}\left(\mathbf{y}, f(x), \boldsymbol{\theta}^*\right) \leq \mathcal{L}\left(\mathbf{y}, f(x), \boldsymbol{\theta}'\right)$

There is a trade-off between complexity and performance when it comes to optimizing the model. If performance is the goal, then the next step is to decide what form is the optimization going to take. A grid-search would quickly become unfeasible for models with multiple hyperparameters, so an attractive solution is to instead use Bayesian optimization [1].

2.3 Domain Alignment

Note that at this point there is no information sharing between the first layer's models. However, in many situations it may be desirable that some information *is* shared across these models since they are build using different modalities of the same sample set. The motivation is that even though the samples come from different distributions, the generating processes should be similar and thus they should lie in a similar low-dimensional manifold. This is the central problem of *Manifold Alignment* [7]. Our *Manifold Mixing* is based on similar motivation, with crucial difference - we consider that each domain has a contribution of its own, and therefore we will not enforce an exact match between the manifolds but merely a transformation of the local inter-sample geometry using all the domains, indirectly linking the stacked first layer models together.

2.4 Domain Adaptation

Given two domains $\mathcal{X}^s$ and $\mathcal{X}^t$, that are different but related, the goal of *Domain Adaptation* is that of learning to transfer knowledge acquired from the source $\mathcal{X}^s$ to the target $\mathcal{X}^t$. The most common setting is when there are many labeled examples in the source, but not in the target, and therefore one tries to learn an estimator h such that it minimizes the error on both the source and target distribution prediction [2]. In our setting, the source and target domains represent different modalities of the same sample. For clarity, we will use source and target domain definitions as well, and use the former to transform the latter.

2.5 Manifold Mixing

We would like to address the question: how to combine data from different domains with a similar relation to the output? Our approach consists in creating a map between each pair of domains $\mathcal{X}^s \rightarrow \mathcal{X}^t$, while deforming the local geometry of the two to become more similar. We drew inspiration from LLE [9] in that we will also use the neighbours of a point to predict its position. In our case, we will use the neighbours of this point in the other domains to predict its position in the original domain. Consider a set of points S and two mappings taking the points in S to two coordinate systems of domains $\mathcal{X}^t$ and $\mathcal{X}^s$: $\varphi : S \rightarrow \mathbb{R}^{|t|}$, $\psi : S \rightarrow \mathbb{R}^{|s|}$, and suppose the subsets $\mathbf{X}^t$, $\mathbf{X}^s$ of the dataset $\mathbf{X}$ are measured in these coordinate systems. Let us introduce an approximation $\mathbf{L}_s^t$ to the mapping $\varphi \circ \psi^{-1} : \mathbb{R}^{|s|} \rightarrow \mathbb{R}^{|t|}$ from the coordinates of domain $\mathcal{X}^s$ to the coordinates of domain $\mathcal{X}^t$: $\min_{\mathbf{L}_s^t} \sum_{i=1}^N ||\mathbf{x}_i^t - \mathbf{L}_s^t \mathbf{x}_i^s||^2$, with $\mathbf{x}_i^t, \mathbf{x}_i^s$ corresponding to the ith entry of $\mathbf{X}^t$ and $\mathbf{X}^s$, respectively. The optimal solution is then given by:

$$\begin{aligned} \frac{\partial}{\partial \mathbf{L}_s^t} \sum_{i=1}^N ||\mathbf{x}_i^t - \mathbf{L}_s^t \mathbf{x}_i^s||^2 = 0 \Leftrightarrow \sum_{i=1}^N \mathbf{L}_s^t \left(\mathbf{x}_i^s \mathbf{x}_i^{s\mathsf{T}}\right) = \sum_{i=1}^N \mathbf{x}_i^t \mathbf{x}_i^{s\mathsf{T}} \\ \mathbf{L}_s^t \left(\mathbf{X}^s \mathbf{X}^{s\mathsf{T}}\right) = \mathbf{X}^t \mathbf{X}^{s\mathsf{T}} \Leftrightarrow \mathbf{L}_s^t = \mathbf{X}^t \mathbf{X}^{s\mathsf{T}} \left(\mathbf{X}^s \mathbf{X}^{s\mathsf{T}}\right)^{-1}. \end{aligned} \tag{7}$$

Denote by $\mathbf{n}_i^t[j]$ the jth neighbour of instance $\mathbf{x}_i$ in the domain $\mathcal{X}^t$. Let the array of the points in $\mathcal{X}^s$ which are the neighbours of instance $\mathbf{x}_i^t$ in the domain $\mathcal{X}^t$ be: $\mathbf{N}_i^{s\leftarrow t} = \left[\mathbf{x}^s_{\mathbf{n}_i^t[1]}, \mathbf{x}^s_{\mathbf{n}_i^t[2]}, \ldots, \mathbf{x}^s_{\mathbf{n}_i^t[k]}\right]$. Our goal is to 'mix' information from different manifolds. This is accomplished by projecting the neighbours of $\mathbf{x}_i^t$ from the source to the target domain and then finding the linear combination of the points that best reconstructs $\mathbf{x}_i^t$ in the original domain:

$$\min_{\mathbf{w}_i} \sum_i ||\mathbf{x}_i^t - \tilde{\mathbf{x}}_i^{t\leftarrow s}||^2 = \min_{\mathbf{w}_i} \sum_i ||\mathbf{x}_i^t - L_s^t \mathbf{N}_i^{s\leftarrow t} \mathbf{w}_i||^2, \tag{8}$$

where $\tilde{\mathbf{x}}_i^{t\leftarrow s}$ is the reconstruction of $\mathbf{x}_i^t$ using domain $\mathcal{X}^s$. We visualize how substituting $\mathbf{x}_i$ by $\tilde{\mathbf{x}}_i^{t\leftarrow s}$ might affect the target manifold in Fig. 2. After setting the derivative w.r.t. $\mathbf{w}_i$ to zero, the optimal solution corresponds to:

$$\mathbf{w}_i = \left(\left(\tilde{\mathbf{N}}_i^{t\leftarrow s}\right)^{\mathsf{T}} \tilde{\mathbf{N}}_i^{t\leftarrow s}\right)^{-1} \left(\tilde{\mathbf{N}}_i^{t\leftarrow s}\right)^{\mathsf{T}} \mathbf{x}_i^t, \tag{9}$$

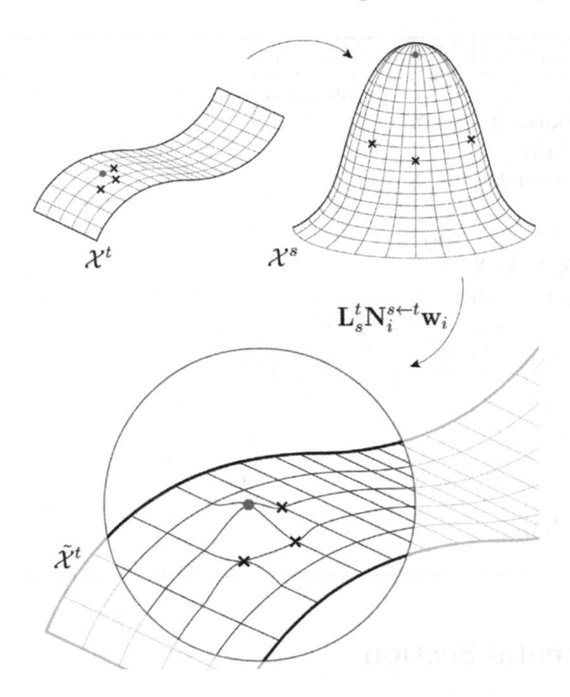

Fig. 2. Target manifold being deformed by the source manifold using the manifold mixing method. The crosses are the neighbours of point $\mathbf{x}_i$ (point in red) in the target domain. These neighbours are mapped from the source to the target domain and then used to locate $\mathbf{x}_i$. This causes the target manifold to be locally deformed by the source manifold. (Color figure online)

where $\tilde{\mathbf{N}}_i^{t\leftarrow s} = \mathbf{L}_s^t\mathbf{N}^{s\leftarrow t}$, the neighbors of $\mathbf{x}_i$ in $\mathcal{X}_t$ projected from their coordinates in $\mathcal{X}_s$ back to the coordinates in $\mathcal{X}_t$. We can now transform the original space $\mathcal{X}^t$ into the space reconstructed from the other domains $\tilde{\mathcal{X}}^t$ by computing for each instance the weighted mean of its reconstructions:

$$\tilde{\mathbf{x}}_i^t = \beta_t\mathbf{x}_i^t + \sum_{s\neq d}\beta_s\tilde{\mathbf{x}}_i^{t\leftarrow s}, \tag{10}$$

where β_j can be seen as the prior of domain $\mathcal{X}^j$'s relevance, and $\sum_j \beta_j = 1$. When evaluating a new point $\mathbf{x}_{new}$, first the nearest neighbours from the training set are found, and then the reconstruction is given by $\tilde{\mathbf{N}}_i^{s\leftarrow t}\mathbf{w}_{new}$. The complexity of the algorithm is bounded by the matrix inversion of the coordinate mapping in Eq. 7, and therefore the algorithm complexity is $\mathcal{O}(d^3)$, where d is the maximum number of features among all the domains.

Algorithm 1. Manifold Mixing Algorithm

Input: data $\mathbf{X} = [\mathbf{X}^1, \ldots, \mathbf{X}^M]$, domain weights β
Output: transformed data $\tilde{\mathbf{X}}$
for $t = 1$ **to** M **do**
  $\mathbf{n}^t \leftarrow \text{NearestNeighbours}(\mathbf{X}^t, k)$
  $\tilde{\mathbf{X}}^t \leftarrow \beta_t \mathbf{X}^t$
  for s **in** $m \in [1, M] \setminus t$ **do**
    $\mathbf{L}_s^t \leftarrow \mathbf{X}^t \mathbf{X}^{s\mathsf{T}} (\mathbf{X}^s \mathbf{X}^{s\mathsf{T}})^{-1}$
    for $\mathbf{x}_i = 1$ **to** N **do**
      $\mathbf{N}_i^{s\leftarrow t} \leftarrow \mathbf{X}^s[\mathbf{n}_i^t]$, $\tilde{\mathbf{N}}_i^{t\leftarrow s} \leftarrow \mathbf{L}_s^t \mathbf{N}_i^{s\leftarrow t}$
      $\mathbf{w}_i \leftarrow \left(\left(\tilde{\mathbf{N}}_i^{t\leftarrow s} \right)^\mathsf{T} \tilde{\mathbf{N}}_i^{t\leftarrow s} \right)^{-1} \left(\tilde{\mathbf{N}}_i^{t\leftarrow s} \right)^\mathsf{T} \mathbf{x}_i^t$
      $\tilde{\mathbf{X}}_i^t \mathrel{+}= \beta_s \tilde{\mathbf{N}}_i^{t\leftarrow s} \mathbf{w}_i$
    end for
  end for
end for
$\tilde{\mathbf{X}} \leftarrow [\tilde{\mathbf{X}}_1, , \ldots, , \tilde{\mathbf{X}}_M]$
return: $\tilde{\mathbf{X}}$

3 Experimental Section

3.1 Methods

To test our method we used a recent clinical cohort [3] containing data on patients with cardiovascular disease. There are 440 subjects in the dataset of which 56 suffered from an early cardiovascular event. For each patient, 359 protein levels and 9 clinical parameters are measured. We evaluate performance our method (stacked regularization with manifold mixing) for predicting a cardiovascular event. We compare proposed approach to that of using a standard stacked model with joint Bayesian optimization of the hyper-parameters, as well as with using random forest on the merged/ feature concatenated datasets (protein levels and clinical parameters). For both our method and the standard stacking, the architecture consisted of two larger random forest models in the first layer and a smaller one in the output.

3.2 Data Selection and Preprocessing

We perform random shuffles with 90% train size and even class distribution in the train/test set. We use remaining 10% to test the model. Since the dataset is unbalanced (much larger number of negative than positive subjects), we took a random sample from the negative class of size equal to the total number of positive class subjects, prior to the split at each shuffle. The protein were measured using a technology that uses standard panels for different proteins, meaning some of the proteins might have no relation to the outcome at all. For this reason, for each run we pre-selected 50 proteins using Univariate Feature Selection on the training set. Then, we normalized the train and test data independently, and measured the average ROC for each of the methods. We perform 5-fold cross validation for optimal hyper-parameter estimation on the train set for the random forests, and bayesian optimization for the stacked models. Once that is accomplished, we retrain the model with the optimal parameters on the complete training set and test on the remaining 10%. We repeat the this procedure multiple times and report the average ROC-AUC as well as the standard deviation. Described strategy is frequently referred to as stability selection procedure [4] The proteins were measured using OLINK technology that records expression levels of proteins via targeted and customised analysis [3].

3.3 Results

The results are presented in Fig. 3. Proposed approach (MM stacked) outperformed both the regular stacked model and the random forests (RF) using the merged data. Both stacked regularized techniques outperformed standard RF.

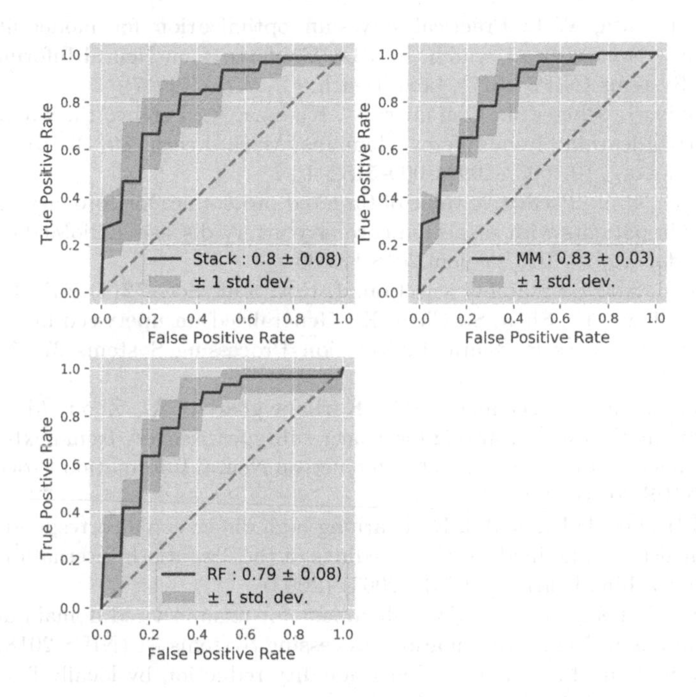

Fig. 3. Average AUC for the three methods compared. The highest performance is that of the Manifold Mixing stacked model (MM), and both stacked models outperformed using Random Forests (RF) on the merged data

4 Conclusions and Future Work

In this paper we propose the manifold mixing framework to improve the analysis of multi-modal data stemming from different sources. In our preliminary experiments, the obtained results support efficacy of our method. We outperform both standard stacked regularization and the model built on feature concatenated data. In the near future, we plan on performing further tests with larger number of shuffles, and testing on different datasets and heterogeneous domains. One pitfall of the current algorithm is the linearity of the map between manifolds which might fail in highly curved regions. A possible solution is to kernelize the method using graph kernels. Another interesting direction is to subdivide the manifold into multiple subregions based on the local curvature and create a mapping per subregion.

Acknowledgments. Supported by a European Research Area Network on Cardiovascular Diseases (ERA-CVD) grant (ERA CVD JTC2017, OPERATION). Thanks to Cláudia Pinhão for supporting with the design of the figures.

References

1. Acerbi, L., Ma, W.J.: Practical Bayesian optimization for model fitting with Bayesian adaptive direct search. In: 31st Conference on Neural Information Processing Systems (NIPS 2017), Long Beach, CA, USA (2017)
2. Ben-David, S., Blitzer, J., Crammer, K., Kulesza, A., Pereira, F., Vaughan, J.W.: A theory of learning from different domains. Mach. Learn. **79**(1), 151–175 (2009). https://doi.org/10.1007/s10994-009-5152-4
3. Bom, M.J., et al.: Predictive value of targeted proteomics for coronary plaque morphology in patients with suspected coronary artery disease. EBioMedicine (2018). https://doi.org/10.1016/j.ebiom.2018.12.033
4. Bühlmann, N.M.P.: Stability selection. J. Roy. Stat. Soc. **72**(4), 417–473 (2010)
5. Cui, Z., Chang, H., Shan, S., Chen, X.: Generalized unsupervised manifold alignment. In: Advances in Neural Information Processing Systems 27 (NIPS 2014) (2014)
6. Hajiramezanali, E., Dadaneh, S.Z., Karbalayghareh, A., Zhou, M., Qian, X.: Bayesian multi-domain learning for cancer subtype discovery from next-generation sequencing count data. In: 32nd Conference on Neural Information Processing Systems (NIPS 2018) (2018)
7. Ham, J.H., Lee, D.D., Saul, L.K.: Learning high dimensional correspondences from low dimensional manifolds. In: Proceedings of the Twentieth International Conference on Machine Learning (ICML 2003) (2003)
8. Kumar, A., et al.: Co-regularized alignment for unsupervised domain adaptation. In: Advances in Neural Information Processing Systems 31 (NIPS 2018) (2018)
9. Roweis, S., Saul, L.: Nonlinear dimensionality reduction by locally linear embedding. Science **290**(5500), 2323–2326 (2000)
10. Wang, C., Mahadevan, S.: Heterogeneous domain adaptation using manifold alignment. In: Proceedings of the Twenty-Second International Joint Conference on Artificial Intelligence (2011)
11. Wolpert, D.H.: Stacked generalization. Neural Netw. **5**, 241–259 (1992)

A Wide and Deep Neural Network for Survival Analysis from Anatomical Shape and Tabular Clinical Data

Sebastian Pölsterl[(✉)], Ignacio Sarasua, Benjamín Gutiérrez-Becker, and Christian Wachinger

Artificial Intelligence in Medical Imaging (AI-Med), Department of Child and Adolescent Psychiatry, Ludwig-Maximilians-Universität, Munich, Germany
sebastian.poelsterl@med.uni-muenchen.de

Abstract. We introduce a wide and deep neural network for prediction of progression from patients with mild cognitive impairment to Alzheimer's disease. Information from anatomical shape and tabular clinical data (demographics, biomarkers) are fused in a single neural network. The network is invariant to shape transformations and avoids the need to identify point correspondences between shapes. To account for right censored time-to-event data, i.e., when it is only known that a patient did not develop Alzheimer's disease up to a particular time point, we employ a loss commonly used in survival analysis. Our network is trained end-to-end to combine information from a patient's hippocampus shape and clinical biomarkers. Our experiments on data from the Alzheimer's Disease Neuroimaging Initiative demonstrate that our proposed model is able to learn a shape descriptor that augments clinical biomarkers and outperforms a deep neural network on shape alone and a linear model on common clinical biomarkers.

1 Introduction

Alzheimer's disease (AD) is a neurodegenarative disorder and the most common form of dementia diagnosed in people over 65 years of age. Initially, patients suffer from short memory loss, until progressive deterioration eventually requires patients to be completely dependent upon caregivers due to severe impairment of cognitive and motor abilities [1,38,45]. Mild cognitive impairment (MCI) is a pre-dementia stage which is characterized by clinically significant cognitive decline, but without impairing daily live [29,41]. Although subjects with MCI are at an increased risk of developing dementia due to AD, a significant portion of patients with MCI remain stable and do not progress [41]. The pathophysiological processes of this transition are complex and not fully understood, but previous studies showed that changes in certain biomarkers precede the onset of cognitive symptoms by many years [25]. Important biomarkers include brain atrophy measured by magnetic resonance images (MRI), levels of cortical amyloid deposition obtained from cerebrospinal fluid (CSF), and glucose uptake of

P. Cellier and K. Driessens (Eds.): ECML PKDD 2019 Workshops, CCIS 1167, pp. 453–464, 2020.
https://doi.org/10.1007/978-3-030-43823-4_37

neurons measured by fluorodeoxyglucose positron emission tomography (FDG-PET) (see [44] for a detailed overview). To stop or slow down the progression to dementia, it is vital to identify those patients that are at an increased risk for rapid progression from MCI to AD. In particular, several previous studies have established strong morphological changes in the hippocampus associated to the progression of dementia [18–20, 50, 51].

We study progression to Alzheimer's disease by explicitly modelling the timing of this transition and by considering the finite follow-up time and drop-out of patients in clinical studies using techniques from survival analysis (also called time-to-event analysis). Survival analysis differs from traditional machine learning in the fact that parts of the training data can only be partially observed – they are *censored*. If a patient withdraws from the study, is lost to follow-up, or did not develop AD during the study period, the patient's time of progression is *right censored*, i.e., it is unknown whether the patient has or has not progressed after the study ended. Only if a patient develops AD during the study period, one can record the exact time of this event – it is *uncensored*.

In this paper, we propose for the first time a wide and deep neural network for survival analysis that learns to identify patients at high risk of progressing to AD by fusing information from 3D hippocampus shape and tabular clinical data. To the best of our knowledge, no one has previously attempted to learn a deep survival model on 3D anatomical shape representations in an end-to-end fashion. In our experiments on data from the Alzheimer's Disease Neuroimaging Initiative, we demonstrate by fusing information we can more accurately predict AD converters than a baseline deep network on shapes and a Cox's proportional hazards model on clinical data.

2 Related Work

Most previous work formulates progression analysis from MCI to AD as a classification problem within a fixed time horizon such as 3 years (see e.g. [4, 9, 11, 40, 48]). The major downside of this approach is that such a model cannot generalize to other time spans, and that censored conversion times are ignored during training. Instead, it is statistically more appropriate to explicitly incorporate censored event times using methods from survival analysis. Several authors used survival analysis techniques by combining information from various modalities such as structural MRI, FDG-PET, genetics, and neuropsychological tests [3, 12–15, 27, 31, 34, 46, 49, 51, 53]. All of these approaches compute features from high-dimensional imaging data in a pre-processing step, before training a linear survival model. They differ with respect to the type and extend of computed features, which range from volume measurements of a few brain regions [15] to voxel-based analysis [49]. In addition, we note that extensive prior work aims to identify healthy controls, patients with MCI, and patients with AD by casting it as a three-way classification problem and using multi-view machine learning techniques; we refer interested readers to the review in [36].

In contrast, this work focuses on multi-view learning to predict progression from MCI to AD, which has been formulated as a classification problem within a fixed time period in [35,47,52,54]. [52] propose to use sparsity-inducing penalties to combine features extracted from MRI and PET images with CSF measurements and neuropsychological tests. MCI to AD conversion within 2 years was studied in [35]. They propose to learn from features extracted from MRI and FDG-PET, and CSF measurements by view-aligned hypergraph learning. The approach in [47] uses stability-weighted low-rank matrix completion to impute missing values in MRI and PET features, and neuropsychological tests. They consider right censored conversion times as missing values and try to impute the actual (unobserved) time of conversion via matrix completion. In [54], the authors propose a missing-data-aware approach to learn from MRI, PET, and genetics by learning a common and multiple modality-specific latent feature representations. To the best or our knowledge, the only previous work that employed multi-view learning for survival analysis was presented in [42] for predicting adverse events in cancer and heart disease.

Using neural networks for survival analysis originated in the late 1990s in the work of [2,5,16,33], who studied relatively simple networks with one hidden layer applied to tabular data. The first deep survival model was proposed in [26] and builds on the loss proposed in [16]. The only previous work that investigated deep learning for MCI to AD conversion from multi-modal data is [30,37]. Both approaches consider a classification problem within a fixed time frame, which ignores censoring of conversion times. In addition, the features in [30] were pre-computed from MRI and not learned end-to-end. In [37], a deep network is proposed that learns from 3D patches of MRI and FDG-PET at multiple scales.

Finally, [20] proposed a deep neural network operating on point clouds of multiple neuroanatomical shapes. They study diagnosis of MCI and AD patients rather than progression, and do not consider demographics or clinical biomarkers in their model.

3 Methods

We present a wide and deep neural network for learning from right censored time-to-event data (see Fig. 1). Our model takes a point cloud representation of an anatomical shape and tabular data as input. The deep part of the network is a PointNet [43] that learns features describing the 3D geometric structure of the left hippocampus. The wide part of the network takes demographics and clinical biomarkers and their interactions. The network is trained to fuse both types of information in and end-to-end fashion using a survival analysis loss appropriate for right censored event times. First, we are going to describe PointNet, which constitutes the deep part of the network, before showing how it can be integrated with tabular clinical data for survival analysis.

3.1 Learning from Anatomical Shape

We represent anatomical shapes as point clouds that represent a 3D geometric structure as a set of coordinates. Point clouds avoid the combinatorial irregularities and complexities of meshes, and thus are easier to learn from. However, the network needs to be constructed in a way to consider that a point cloud is just an unordered set of points that is invariant to permutations of its members. To this end, we employ PointNet [43], which is illustrated in Fig. 1 and described in more detail below.

The i-th point cloud $\mathcal{P}_i$ is represented by a set of K 3D coordinates $\mathcal{P}_i = \{\mathbf{p}_{i_1}, \ldots, \mathbf{p}_{i_K}\}$ with $\mathbf{p}_{i_k} \in \mathbb{R}^3$ being the x, y, and z coordinates. To be invariant to permutations of the input set, the symmetric max pooling operator across all embedding vectors of points is used. We first pass each individual coordinate vector through a multilayer perceptron $\text{MLP}_{\text{point}}$ with shared weights among all points, thus projecting each 3D point to a higher dimensional representation. These representations are aggregated using the max pooling operator across all points, which ensures that our downstream survival analysis task is invariant to permutation:

$$\text{POINTNET}(\mathcal{P}_i) = \text{MAXPOOL}\left(\text{MLP}_{\text{points}}(\mathbf{p}_{i_1}), \ldots, \text{MLP}_{\text{points}}(\mathbf{p}_{i_K})\right). \quad (1)$$

$\text{MLP}_{\text{point}}$ is a three-layer network with 64, 128, and 400 dimensional outputs, respectively, with rectified linear units (ReLU) and batch normalization [23]. Hence, we extract 400 features that globally describe the input anatomical shape.

In order to make our network invariant to rotation of the input point cloud, we use an affine transformation network that outputs a rotation matrix $\mathbf{T} \in \mathbb{R}^{3\times 3}$ which is multiplied by the raw 3D coordinates of input points. This transformation is learned in a data-dependent manner by using an additional POINTNET network that learns to predict the optimal $\mathbf{T}$ for each individual point cloud. The global feature vector computed by POINTNET is fed to three fully-connected layers with 200, 100, and 9 units, ReLU activation function and batch normalization, respectively. Finally, we modify the vanilla PointNet in (1) by transforming individual points by the output of the transformation network:

$$\begin{aligned} \text{TRANSFORM}(\mathcal{P}_i) &= \text{MAXPOOL}\left(\text{MLP}_{\text{points}}(\mathbf{p}_{i_1}), \ldots, \text{MLP}_{\text{points}}(\mathbf{p}_{i_K})\right), \\ \varphi_{i_k} &= \text{TRANSFORM}(\mathcal{P}_i)\mathbf{p}_{i_k}, \\ \text{POINTNET}(\mathcal{P}_i) &= \text{MAXPOOL}\left(\text{MLP}_{\text{points}}(\varphi_{i_1}), \ldots, \text{MLP}_{\text{points}}(\varphi_{i_K})\right). \end{aligned} \quad (2)$$

3.2 Wide and Deep Neural Network

After obtaining a global latent representation of an anatomical shape, we can further learn high-level descriptors of point clouds by feeding the output of the max pooling operation to an MLP. In addition, we can leverage routine clinical patient information to predict progression to Alzheimer's disease. Typically, such information consists of feature vectors that are either dense (e.g. biomarker concentrations), or sparse (e.g. one-hot encoded genetic alterations). Compared to individual points in a point cloud, clinical information already contains rich information for which we do not need to learn a highly abstract latent representation. In fact, most clinical research relies on linear models, which allow for easy interpretation of individual feature's contribution to the overall prediction.

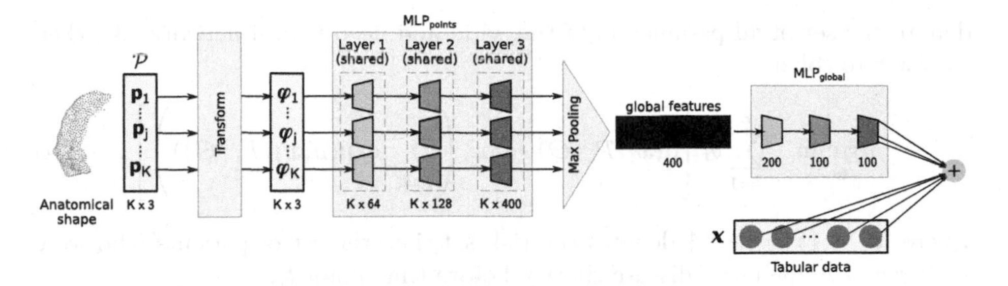

Fig. 1. Wide and Deep PointNet Architecture. The network takes a point cloud representation $\mathcal{P}$ of the left hippocampus with K points, applies a transformation, and then aggregates point features by max pooling. The global feature vector is processed by a global MLP outputting a 100-dimensional latent representation that is fused with tabular clinical data using a linear model.

Here, we jointly train a linear model on clinical information with a deep PointNet on anatomical shapes using a wide and deep architecture [8]. While the deep component learns a complex latent representation of anatomical shape, the linear component models known clinical variables $\mathbf{x} \in \mathbb{R}^d$ associated with Alzheimer's disease. In particular, we can easily incorporate gene-gene (epistasis) and gene–environment interactions by using a cross-product transformation $\phi(\mathbf{x})$ [8]. Thus, the final patient-level latent representation is given by

$$\mu(\mathbf{x}_i, \mathcal{P}_i) = \mathbf{w}_{\text{wide}}^\top \text{CONCAT}\left(\mathbf{x}_i, \phi(\mathbf{x}_i)\right) + \mathbf{w}_{\text{deep}}^\top \text{MLP}_{\text{global}}(\text{POINTNET}(\mathcal{P}_i)), \qquad (3)$$

where CONCAT denotes vector concatenation, POINTNET is the global feature vector from (2), $\text{MLP}_{\text{global}}$ is a three-layer MLP with 200, 100, and 100 units, ReLU activation and batch normalization, and $\mathbf{w}_{\text{wide}}$ and $\mathbf{w}_{\text{deep}}$ are weights to be learned.

3.3 Survival Analysis

Our overall objective is to predict progression from mild cognitive impairment to Alzheimer's disease from right censored time-to-event data, which demands for proper training algorithms that take this unique characteristic into account. More formally, we denote by $t_i > 0$ the time of an event (Alzheimer's disease), and $c_i > 0$ the time of censoring of the i-th patient. Due to right censoring, it is only possible to observe $y_i = \min(t_i, c_i)$ and $\delta_i = I(t_i \leq c_i)$ for every patient, with $I(\cdot)$ being the indicator function and $c_i = \infty$ for uncensored records. Hence, training our survival model is based on a dataset comprising quadruplets $(\mathcal{P}_i, \mathbf{x}_i, y_i, \delta_i)$ for $i = 1, \ldots, n$. After training, the survival model ought to predict a risk score of experiencing an event based on a point cloud and a set of clinical features. As loss function, we employ the loss proposed in [16], which is an extension of Cox's proportional hazards model [10] to neural networks. Let $\boldsymbol{\Theta}$

denote the set of all parameters of the wide and deep neural network (3), then we want to solve

$$\arg\min_{\boldsymbol{\Theta}} \quad \sum_{i=1}^{n} \delta_i \left[\mu(\boldsymbol{x}_i, \mathcal{P}_i \,|\, \boldsymbol{\Theta}) - \log \left(\sum_{j \in \mathcal{R}_i} \exp(\mu(\boldsymbol{x}_j, \mathcal{P}_i \,|\, \boldsymbol{\Theta})) \right) \right], \tag{4}$$

where $\mathcal{R}_i = \{j \,|\, y_j \geq t_i\}$ denotes the risk set, i.e., the set of patients who were still free of Alzheimer's disease shortly before time point t_i.

4 Experiments

4.1 Data

In our experiments, we are using data from the Alzheimer's Disease Neuroimaging Initiative (ADNI) [24]. ADNI was launched in 2003 as a public-private partnership with the primary goal to test whether longitudinal MRI and PET imaging combined with other biomarkers, clinical and neuropsychological assessments to measure the progression of MCI and early AD. For up-to-date information, see www.adni-info.org. We selected 397 subjects with MCI at baseline and at least one follow-up visit. Magnetic resonance images of all subjects were processed with FreeSurfer [17] to obtain segmentations, which were subsequently pre-processed using the grooming operations included in ShapeWorks [7] to obtain smooth hippocampi surfaces. We used left hippocampus shapes represented as point clouds comprised of 1024 points. For tabular clinical data, we used age, gender, education, CSF, FDG-PET, and AV45-PET. CSF measurements included levels of beta amyloid 42 peptides ($A\beta_{42}$), total tau protein (T-tau), and Tau phosphorylated at threonine 181 (p-Tau_{181}). We augment age to account for non-linear effects by using a natural B-spline expansion with four degrees of freedom and an interaction term between age and gender [22]. Education, which is a categorical variable, was encoded using orthogonal polynomial coding. In addition, we considered left hippocampus volume (normalized by intra-cranial volume) as estimated by FreeSurfer [17] from MRI scans of the brain.

4.2 Model Training

We trained our deep and wide network using Adam [28] for 120 epochs with weight decay. We tuned hyper-parameters (size of PointNet's global feature vector, size of $\mathbf{w}_{\text{deep}}$, weight decay, learning rate schedule, β_1 of Adam) using Bayesian black-box optimization by computing the model's performance on the validation set [32]. Data is randomly split into three parts: 80% for training, 10% for validation, and 10% for testing. We repeated this process 10 times with different splits. The performance of all methods was estimated by Harrell's concordance index (c index), which is identical to the area under the receiver operating characteristics curve if the outcome is binary and no censoring is present [21]. As baseline model, we selected a linear Cox's proportional hazards model (CoxPH) [10] trained on tabular clinical data. The baseline model was trained once on tabular clinical data only (see above), and once with the volume of left hippocampus included as additional feature. We note that CoxPH and our model optimize the same loss during training. Therefore, differences in performance stem from the ability of our model to directly incorporate 3D anatomical shape information.

5 Results

The performance of our deep and wide network and baseline models is summarized in Fig. 2. It shows that tabular clinical makers with a median c index of 0.750 are already strong predictors of conversion from MCI to AD. When including hippocampus volume as additional feature, the median c index increased to 0.803. Using a deep PointNet solely using hippocampus shape and ignoring any clinical variables resulted in a c index of 0.534. Our deep and wide network achieved a median c index of 0.780 without hippocampus volume, and 0.809 with hippocampus volume. The latter is the model with highest median c index and outperforms the linear model with hippocampus volume on 6 of 10 splits. This shows that when jointly learning a deep PointNet, it is able to learn a powerful global descriptor of hippocampus shape that augments clinical features for MCI-to-AD progression. Moreover, our results confirm that hippocampus volume is a useful independent predictor that cannot be fully captured by anatomical shape alone, as described previously [50].

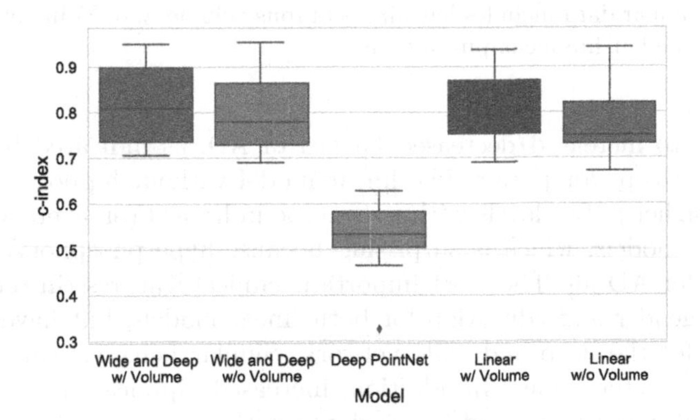

Fig. 2. Performance of individual models across ten random splits of the data. w/ Volume: tabular data includes left hippocampus volume. w/o Volume: tabular data does *not* include left hippocampus volume.

We can also compare the coefficients of the linear models with the linear part of our wide and deep neural network. The coefficients can be directly interpreted in terms of log-hazard ratio, which is a measure of effect a variable has on survival, similar to log-odds ratio in logistic regression. The coefficients across all folds are depicted in Fig. 3. All models agree with respect to which features are

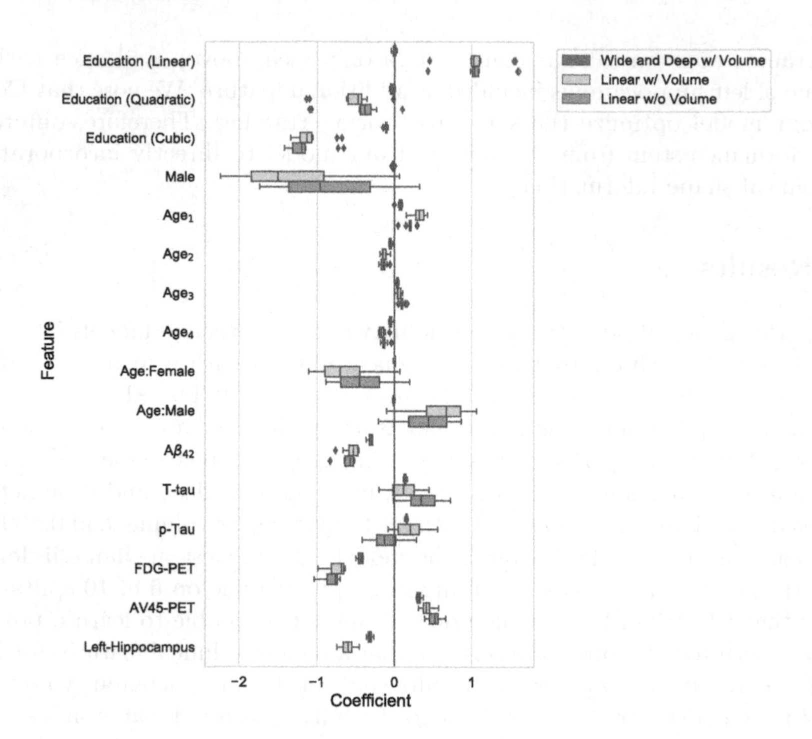

Fig. 3. Comparison of coefficients associated with tabular clinical features. Additional eight orthogonal polynomial encodings of education have been omitted from this plot. w/ Volume: tabular data includes left hippocampus volume. w/o Volume: tabular data does *not* include left hippocampus volume.

contributing to increased/decreased hazard of AD, as indicated by the coefficients' sign, except for p-Tau. The linear model without hippocampus volume associated higher p-Tau levels with a decrease in hazard (on average) compared to the other models, which is surprising because hyperphosphorylation of tau is a marker for AD [6]. The most important clinical features (in terms of magnitude) are gender and education for both linear models, but have only minor importance for the deep and wide network. Similar behavior can be observed for age-gender interactions. In addition, increased hippocampus volume has a relatively high importance and is associated with a decreased hazard of AD. It is ranked third for the deep and wide network and eleven for the linear model. FDG-PET has the biggest effect for the wide and deep network and is also among the top 4 features for the linear models. From a clinical perspective, this result is reassuring as reduction of metabolic activity in cortical regions has been associated with AD [39]. Finally, we note that the variability of coefficients across splits is smaller for the deep and wide neural network compared to the linear model. We believe this is an effect of using weight decay during optimization, which penalizes large coefficients.

6 Conclusion

We proposed a wide and deep neural network that fuses 3D anatomical shape and tabular clinical variables for the prediction of MCI-to-AD conversion. We trained a model end-to-end using a survival loss that properly accounts for right censored time of conversion. Our experiments demonstrate that the proposed architecture is able to learn a global shape descriptor that augments clinical variables and leads to improved prediction performance.

Acknowledgements. This research was partially supported by the Bavarian State Ministry of Education, Science and the Arts in the framework of the Centre Digitisation.Bavaria (ZD.B). We gratefully acknowledge the support of NVIDIA Corporation with the donation of the Quadro P6000 GPU used for this research.

References

1. Albert, M.S., et al.: The diagnosis of mild cognitive impairment due to Alzheimer's disease: recommendations from the National Institute on Aging-Alzheimer's Association workgroups on diagnostic guidelines for Alzheimer's disease. Alzheimer's Dement. J. Alzheimer's Assoc. **7**, 270–279 (2011)
2. Bakker, B., Heskes, T.: A neural-Bayesian approach to survival analysis. In: 9th International Conference on Artificial Neural Networks (ICANN), pp. 832–837 (1999)
3. Barnes, D.E., Cenzer, I.S., Yaffe, K., Ritchie, C.S., Lee, S.J.: A point-based tool to predict conversion from mild cognitive impairment to probable Alzheimer's disease. Alzheimer's Dement. **10**(6), 646–655 (2014)
4. Beheshti, I., Demirel, H., Matsuda, H., Alzheimer's Disease Neuroimaging Initiative: Classification of Alzheimer's disease and prediction of mild cognitive impairment-to-Alzheimer's conversion from structural magnetic resource imaging using feature ranking and a genetic algorithm. Comput. Biol. Med. **83**, 109–119 (2017)
5. Biganzoli, E., Boracchi, P., Mariani, L., Marubini, E.: Feed forward neural networks for the analysis of censored survival data: a partial logistic regression approach. Stat. Med. **17**(10), 1169–1186 (1998)
6. Blennow, K., Vanmechelen, E., Hampel, H.: CSF total tau, Aβ42 and phosphorylated tau protein as biomarkers for Alzheimer's disease. Mol. Neurobiol. **24**(1–3), 087–098 (2001). https://doi.org/10.1385/MN:24:1-3:087
7. Cates, J., Fletcher, P.T., Styner, M., Hazlett, H.C., Whitaker, R.: Particle-based shape analysis of multi-object complexes. In: Metaxas, D., Axel, L., Fichtinger, G., Székely, G. (eds.) MICCAI 2008. LNCS, vol. 5241, pp. 477–485. Springer, Heidelberg (2008). https://doi.org/10.1007/978-3-540-85988-8_57
8. Cheng, H.T., et al.: Wide & deep learning for recommender systems. In: Proceedings of the 1st Workshop on Deep Learning for Recommender Systems (DLRS) (2016)
9. Chételat, G., et al.: Using voxel-based morphometry to map the structural changes associated with rapid conversion in MCI: a longitudinal MRI study. NeuroImage **27**, 934–946 (2005)
10. Cox, D.R.: Regression models and life tables (with discussion). J. Roy. Stat. Soc. Ser. B (Stat. Methodol.) **34**, 187–220 (1972)

11. Cuingnet, R., et al.: Automatic classification of patients with Alzheimer's disease from structural MRI: a comparison of ten methods using the ADNI database. NeuroImage **56**, 766–781 (2011)
12. Da, X., et al.: Integration and relative value of biomarkers for prediction of MCI to AD progression: spatial patterns of brain atrophy, cognitive scores, APOE genotype and CSF biomarkers. NeuroImage. Clin. **4**, 164–173 (2014)
13. Desikan, R.S., et al.: Temporoparietal MR imaging measures of atrophy in subjects with mild cognitive impairment that predict subsequent diagnosis of Alzheimer disease. Am. J. Neuroradiol. **30**, 532–538 (2009)
14. Desikan, R.S., et al.: Automated MRI measures predict progression to Alzheimer's disease. Neurobiol. Aging **31**, 1364–1374 (2010)
15. Devanand, D.P., et al.: Hippocampal and entorhinal atrophy in mild cognitive impairment: prediction of Alzheimer disease. Neurology **68**(11), 828–836 (2007)
16. Faraggi, D., Simon, R.: A neural network model for survival data. Stat. Med. **14**(1), 73–82 (1995)
17. Fischl, B.: FreeSurfer. NeuroImage **62**(2), 774–781 (2012)
18. Frisoni, G.B., et al.: Mapping local hippocampal changes in Alzheimer's disease and normal ageing with MRI at 3 Tesla. Brain **131**(12), 3266–3276 (2008)
19. Gerardin, E., et al.: Multidimensional classification of hippocampal shape features discriminates Alzheimer's disease and mild cognitive impairment from normal aging. NeuroImage **47**, 1476–1486 (2009)
20. Gutiérrez-Becker, B., Wachinger, C.: Deep multi-structural shape analysis: application to neuroanatomy. In: Frangi, A.F., Schnabel, J.A., Davatzikos, C., Alberola-López, C., Fichtinger, G. (eds.) MICCAI 2018. LNCS, vol. 11072, pp. 523–531. Springer, Cham (2018). https://doi.org/10.1007/978-3-030-00931-1_60
21. Harrell, F.E., Califf, R.M., Pryor, D.B., Lee, K.L., Rosati, R.A.: Evaluating the yield of medical tests. J. Am. Med. Assoc. **247**, 2543–2546 (1982)
22. Hastie, T., Tibshirani, R., Friedman, J.: The Elements of Statistical Learning: Data Mining, Inference, and Prediction. SSS, 2nd edn. Springer, New York (2009). https://doi.org/10.1007/978-0-387-84858-7
23. Ioffe, S., Szegedy, C.: Batch normalization: accelerating deep network training by reducing internal covariate shift. In: Proceedings of the 32nd International Conference on Machine Learning, pp. 448–456 (2015)
24. Jack, C.R., et al.: The Alzheimer's Disease Neuroimaging Initiative (ADNI): MRI methods. J. Magn. Reson. Imaging **27**(4), 685–691 (2008)
25. Jack, C.R., et al.: Tracking pathophysiological processes in Alzheimer's disease: an updated hypothetical model of dynamic biomarkers. Lancet Neurol. **12**(2), 207–216 (2013)
26. Katzman, J.L., et al.: DeepSurv: personalized treatment recommender system using a Cox proportional hazards deep neural network. BMC Med. Res. Methodol. **18**, 24 (2018)
27. Kauppi, K., et al.: Combining polygenic hazard score with volumetric MRI and cognitive measures improves prediction of progression from mild cognitive impairment to Alzheimer's disease. Front. Neurosci. **12**, 260 (2018)
28. Kingma, D.P., Ba, J.: Adam: a method for stochastic optimization. In: 3rd International Conference on Learning Representations (ICLR) (2015)
29. Langa, K.M., Levine, D.A.: The diagnosis and management of mild cognitive impairment: a clinical review. JAMA **312**, 2551–2561 (2014)
30. Lee, G., Nho, K., Kang, B., Sohn, K.A., Kim, D.: Alzheimer's disease neuroimaging initiative: predicting Alzheimer's disease progression using multi-modal deep learning approach. Sci. Rep. **9**, 1952 (2019)

31. Li, K., O'Brien, R., Lutz, M., Luo, S., Alzheimer's Disease Neuroimaging Initiative: A prognostic model of Alzheimer's disease relying on multiple longitudinal measures and time-to-event data. Alzheimer's Dement. J. Alzheimer's Assoc. **14**, 644–651 (2018)
32. Liaw, R., Liang, E., Nishihara, R., Moritz, P., Gonzalez, J.E., Stoica, I.: Tune: A Research Platform for Distributed Model Selection and Training (2018)
33. Liestøl, K., Andersen, P.K., Andersen, U.: Survival analysis and neural nets. Stat. Med. **13**(12), 1189–1200 (1994)
34. Liu, K., Chen, K., Yao, L., Guo, X.: Prediction of mild cognitive impairment conversion using a combination of independent component analysis and the Cox model. Front. Hum. Neurosci. **11**, 33 (2017)
35. Liu, M., Zhang, J., Yap, P.T., Shen, D.: View-aligned hypergraph learning for Alzheimer's disease diagnosis with incomplete multi-modality data. Med. Image Anal. **36**, 123–134 (2017)
36. Liu, X., Chen, K., Wu, T., Weidman, D., Lure, F., Li, J.: Use of multimodality imaging and artificial intelligence for diagnosis and prognosis of early stages of Alzheimer's disease. Transl. Res.: J. Lab. Clin. Med. **194**, 56–67 (2018)
37. Lu, D., Popuri, K., Ding, G.W., Balachandar, R., Beg, M.F., Alzheimer's Disease Neuroimaging Initiative: Multimodal and multiscale deep neural networks for the early diagnosis of Alzheimer's disease using structural MR and FDG-PET images. Sci. Rep. **8**, 5697 (2018)
38. McKhann, G.M., et al.: The diagnosis of dementia due to Alzheimer's disease: recommendations from the National Institute on Aging-Alzheimer's Association workgroups on diagnostic guidelines for Alzheimer's disease. Alzheimer's Dement. J. Alzheimer's Assoc. **7**(3), 263–269 (2011)
39. Minoshima, S., Giordani, B., Berent, S., Frey, K.A., Foster, N.L., Kuhl, D.E.: Metabolic reduction in the posterior cingulate cortex in very early Alzheimer's disease. Ann. Neurol. **42**(1), 85–94 (1997)
40. Moradi, E., Pepe, A., Gaser, C., Huttunen, H., Tohka, J.: Machine learning framework for early MRI-based Alzheimer's conversion prediction in MCI subjects. NeuroImage **104**, 398–412 (2015)
41. Petersen, R.C.: Mild cognitive impairment. N. Engl. J. Med. **364**(23), 2227–2234 (2011)
42. Pölsterl, S., Conjeti, S., Navab, N., Katouzian, A.: Survival analysis for high-dimensional, heterogeneous medical data: exploring feature extraction as an alternative to feature selection. Artif. Intell. Med. **72**, 1–11 (2016)
43. Qi, C.R., Su, H., Mo, K., Guibas, L.J.: PointNet: deep learning on point sets for 3D classification and segmentation. In: The IEEE Conference on Computer Vision and Pattern Recognition (CVPR), pp. 652–660 (2017)
44. Scheltens, P., et al.: Alzheimer's disease. The Lancet **388**(10043), 505–517 (2016)
45. Sperling, R.A., et al.: Toward defining the preclinical stages of Alzheimer's disease: recommendations from the National Institute on Aging-Alzheimer's Association workgroups on diagnostic guidelines for Alzheimer's disease. Alzheimer's Dement. J. Alzheimer's Assoc. **7**(3), 280–292 (2011)
46. Teipel, S.J., Kurth, J., Krause, B., Grothe, M.J.: The relative importance of imaging markers for the prediction of Alzheimer's disease dementia in mild cognitive impairment – beyond classical regression. NeuroImage: Clin. **8**, 583–593 (2015)
47. Thung, K.-H., Adeli, E., Yap, P.-T., Shen, D.: Stability-weighted matrix completion of incomplete multi-modal data for disease diagnosis. In: Ourselin, S., Joskowicz, L., Sabuncu, M.R., Unal, G., Wells, W. (eds.) MICCAI 2016. LNCS, vol. 9901, pp. 88–96. Springer, Cham (2016). https://doi.org/10.1007/978-3-319-46723-8_11

48. Tong, T., Gao, Q., Guerrero, R., Ledig, C., Chen, L., Rueckert, D., Alzheimer's Disease Neuroimaging Initiative: A novel grading biomarker for the prediction of conversion from mild cognitive impairment to Alzheimer's disease. IEEE Trans. Bio-med. Eng. **64**, 155–165 (2017)
49. Vemuri, P., et al.: Time-to-event voxel-based techniques to assess regional atrophy associated with MCI risk of progression to AD. NeuroImage **54**, 985–991 (2011)
50. Wachinger, C., Reuter, M., Alzheimer's Disease Neuroimaging Initiative, et al.: Domain adaptation for Alzheimer's disease diagnostics. Neuroimage **139**, 470–479 (2016)
51. Wachinger, C., Salat, D.H., Weiner, M., Reuter, M., Alzheimer's Disease Neuroimaging Initiative: Whole-brain analysis reveals increased neuroanatomical asymmetries in dementia for hippocampus and amygdala. Brain **139**(12), 3253–3266 (2016)
52. Zhang, D., Shen, D., Alzheimer's Disease Neuroimaging Initiative: Multi-modal multi-task learning for joint prediction of multiple regression and classification variables in Alzheimer's disease. NeuroImage **59**, 895–907 (2012)
53. Zhou, H., Jiang, J., Lu, J., Wang, M., Zhang, H., Zuo, C.: Dual-model radiomic biomarkers predict development of mild cognitive impairment progression to Alzheimer's disease. Front. Neurosci. **12**, 1045 (2019)
54. Zhou, T., Liu, M., Thung, K.H., Shen, D.: Latent representation learning for Alzheimer's disease diagnosis with incomplete multi-modality neuroimaging and genetic data. IEEE Trans. Med. Imaging **38**, 2411–2422 (2019)

Deep Generative Multi-view Learning

Mahdi Karami[✉]

Department of Computing Science, University of Alberta, Edmonton, AB, Canada
karami1@ualberta.ca

Abstract. Deep generative networks has attracted proliferating interests recently. In this work, the linear generative multi-view model is extended to nonlinear multi-views model where the deep neural network is leveraged to model complex latent representation underlying the multi-view observation. The proposed deep multi-view model admits fast stochastic optimization for training the network and offers a model to infer the shared hidden representation and subsequently generate the second view based on the available primary view at the test time. Empirical results prove the merits of the proposed methods. Furthermore, it is shown that the proposed deep model can generate samples in the input space and suppress the background noise or other complex forms of distortions, the abilities that are not naturally available in CCA based methods.

1 Introduction

The problem of multi-view learning is studied extensively in the literature and its merits has been demonstrated in extracting richer representation from available multiple views at the training time (Chaudhuri et al. 2009; Hardoon et al. 2004; Foster et al. 2008). To capture nonlinearity in the model, one can either use kernel methods or follow the recent growing path of the deep neural network (DNN). Both of these methods have been explored in the literature and researchers proposed some advanced two-view models (Hardoon et al. 2004; Bach and Jordan 2003; Andrew et al. 2013). Kernel based methods, such as KCCA (Hardoon et al. 2004), require large memory to store a massive amount of training data to use at the test time. To overcome this issue and improve the kernel based method in terms of memory and speed, some kernel approximation techniques based on random sampling of training data are proposed in Williams and Seeger (2001) and Lopez-Paz et al. (2014). On the other hand, the main advantage of the DNN over kernel based method is that, its parametric model can be better trained with larger amount of data using the fast stochastic optimization techniques.

The proposed deep two-view methods can be mainly categorized in two groups. On one hand, there are models inspired by auto-encoder, e.g. split autoencoder (SplitAE) of Ngiam et al. (2011), in which the deep autoencoders are trained so that the reconstruction error of both views are minimized. In this methods, the encoding network of both view are shared while each view has its own (split) decoder network. On the other hand, another pathway is based

P. Cellier and K. Driessens (Eds.): ECML PKDD 2019 Workshops, CCIS 1167, pp. 465–477, 2020.
https://doi.org/10.1007/978-3-030-43823-4_38

on canonical correlation analysis (CCA), such as deep CCA (DCCA) method (Andrew et al. 2013) that extends the linear single layer CCA to deep CCA in which the model parameters are estimated to maximize the cross correlation between the projection of both views.

To combine the benefits of both deep auto-encoder (AE) and CCA for multi-view datasets and hence enhance learned representation, the idea of *deep CCA-Auto encoder (DCCAE)* is proposed in Wang et al. (2015b). This method tries to optimize the following objective function that is combination of reconstruction errors of two autoencoders and the canonical correlation between the learned bottleneck features (the output of the deep encoders)

$$\begin{aligned}
\min_{W_f, W_g, W_p, W_q, U, V} \quad & -\tfrac{1}{T}\operatorname{tr}\mathbf{U}^T f(\mathbf{X}) g(\mathbf{Y})^T \mathbf{V} \\
& + \tfrac{\lambda}{T}\sum_{i=1}^{T}\left(\|\mathbf{x}_i - p(f(\mathbf{x}_i))\|^2 + \|\mathbf{y}_i - q(g(\mathbf{y}_i))\|^2\right) \\
\text{s.t.} \quad & \tfrac{1}{T}\mathbf{U}^T f(\mathbf{X}) f(\mathbf{X})^T \mathbf{U} = \mathbf{I} \\
& \tfrac{1}{T}\mathbf{V}^T g(\mathbf{Y}) g(\mathbf{Y})^T \mathbf{V} = \mathbf{I} \\
& u_i^T f(\mathbf{X}) g(\mathbf{Y})^T v_j = 0 \quad \text{for } i \neq j
\end{aligned} \tag{1}$$

Here, the functions $\{f, g, p, q\}$ are flexible nonlinear mappings modeled by neural networks that are parameterized by the set of learnable parameters $\{W_f, W_g, W_p, W_q\}$. $\lambda > 0$ is a trade-off parameter that controls the reconstruction error and canonical correlation between the projected views in the objective function (1). In this equation, CCA term tries to maximize the mutual information between the projected views, $f(\mathbf{x}_i)$ and $g(\mathbf{y}_i)$, and AE loss tries to minimize the reconstruction error between views and their projections. This approach was shown to outperform DCCA and SplitAE for classification and clustering tasks in two-view application (Wang et al. 2015b).

On the other hand, DCCAE has some drawbacks that limits its applications. Its main drawbacks are two folds. First, the objective function and the constraints couples all the training samples through the (cross-)covariance terms, this will block the stochastic optimization method (e.g. SGD) to be applied here in its standard form. Nevertheless, it was shown in Wang et al. (2015a) that if the mini-batch size is large enough the stochastic gradient can approximate the true gradient but still this requires very large mini-batch sizes which imposes heavy computational complexity on the training algorithm. Second, it does not estimate the hidden state and a model that can generate the second view based on the observation from the primary (first) view. In addition, the empirical studies showed that the canonical term of the objective function (1) dominates in practice and hence the objective is less sensitive to the reconstruction error; this in turn result in the trained autoencoders that don't reconstruct the views very well while mainly trying to learn projected mapping $\mathbf{U}^T f(\mathbf{X})$, $\mathbf{V}^T f(\mathbf{Y})$ that are maximally correlated.

Wang et al. (2015b) also proposed a modification of their DCCAE method, in which the constraints are relaxed so that the feature dimensions are no longer required to be uncorrelated, the objective of this method, also called as *correlated autoencoder (CorrAE)*, is formulated as

$$\begin{aligned}\min_{W_f,W_g,W_p,W_q,U,V} \quad & -\tfrac{1}{T}\operatorname{tr}\mathbf{U}^T f(\mathbf{X})g(\mathbf{Y})^T\mathbf{V} \\ & +\tfrac{\lambda}{T}\sum_{i=1}^{T}\left(\|\mathbf{x}_i - p(f(\mathbf{x}_i))\|^2 + \|\mathbf{y}_i - q(g(\mathbf{y}_i))\|^2\right) \\ \text{s.t. } & \tfrac{1}{T}\mathbf{u}_i^T f(\mathbf{X})f(\mathbf{X})^T\mathbf{u}_i = \tfrac{1}{T}\mathbf{v}_i^T g(\mathbf{Y})g(\mathbf{Y})^T\mathbf{v}_i = 1. \end{aligned} \tag{2}$$

This variation of the deep multi-view model is designed to examine the importance of the correlation among the learned feature dimensions by comparing its performance with that of the original DCCAE method in some learning tasks.

Deep Generative Multi-view (DGMV) Model: On the other hand, it was shown by White et al. (2012) and Yu et al. (2014) that simple linear CCA can be expressed as a linear generative two-view form where the views are generated as perturbed linear model of the latent representation $\boldsymbol{\phi}_i$ as

$$\begin{cases}\mathbf{x}_i = \mathbf{C}\boldsymbol{\phi}_i + \epsilon_i, \\ \mathbf{y}_i = \mathbf{E}\boldsymbol{\phi}_i + \nu_i\end{cases} \tag{3}$$

where the perturbation terms are Gaussian independent and identically distributed (i.i.d.) vectors $\epsilon \sim \mathcal{N}(0, \boldsymbol{\Sigma}_\epsilon)$ and $\nu \sim \mathcal{N}(0, \boldsymbol{\Sigma}_\nu)$. This model makes the latent representation explicit and its joint model parameter estimation and latent variable inference can be expressed as a regularized loss objective function that can be reformulated as a convex optimization problem. We can generalize (3) to nonlinear model resulting in the deep nonlinear generative multi-view model

$$\begin{cases}\mathbf{x}_i = p(\boldsymbol{\phi}_i) + \epsilon_i, \\ \mathbf{y}_i = q(\boldsymbol{\phi}_i) + \nu_i\end{cases} \tag{4}$$

where the generative mappings $p(\boldsymbol{\phi}_i)$, $q(\boldsymbol{\phi}_i)$ can be modeled by deep neural networks parameterized by W_p, W_q. Therefore, given the shared latent representation $\boldsymbol{\phi}_i$, two views can be generated by a non-linear mapping plus independent Gaussian noises hence one can formulate the following regularized loss objective function

$$\min_{W_p,W_q,\Phi} \quad \frac{1}{T}\sum_{i=1}^{T}\left(\|x_i - p(\phi_i)\|^2 + \|y_i - q(\phi_i)\|^2\right) + \mathcal{R}(\Phi), \tag{5}$$

In this work, we tackle this deep multi-view subspace learning problem by introducing auto-encoders as inference model.

2 Problem Definition

As explained in the previous section, we prefer a deep multi-view network that offers a model to explicitly infer the shared latent source that generates both views and can predict the second view based on the available primary view at the test time. To this end, we introduce two auto-encoder networks with encoder (recognition) networks $f()$, $g()$ that provide latent projected views, $f_{\mathbf{x}_i} = f(\mathbf{x}_i)$ and $g_{\mathbf{y}_i} = g(\mathbf{y}_i)$, and the decoder (reconstruction) networks $p(\phi_i)$, $q(\phi_i)$ that reconstruct each view based on the latent representation. The encoders and decoders can be modeled by deep neural networks with learnable parameter matrices $\{\mathbf{W}_f, \mathbf{W}_g, \mathbf{W}_p, \mathbf{W}_q\}$ that correspond to each deep model function. Inspired by the generative interpretation of linear CCA (3), we add a generative linear two-view layer, on top of auto-encoder in the latent space, in order to obtain a shared latent representation $\boldsymbol{\phi}_i$ for the pair of encoded projected $\{f_{\mathbf{x}_i},\ g_{\mathbf{y}_i}\}$. Since the auto-encoders reconstruct each individual view, the latent variable $\boldsymbol{\phi}_i$ indeed provides a shared underlying representation of both views in a deep nonlinear form. In the other words, the deep generative two-view network (DGMV) can be expressed mathematically as the following pairs of models

$$\begin{cases} \mathbf{x}_i = p(f_{\mathbf{x}_i}) + \epsilon_i, \\ \mathbf{y}_i = q(g_{\mathbf{y}_i}) + \nu_i \end{cases},$$
$$\begin{cases} f_{\mathbf{x}_i} = \mathbf{C}\boldsymbol{\phi}_i + \epsilon'_i, \\ g_{\mathbf{y}_i} = \mathbf{E}\boldsymbol{\phi}_i + \nu'_i \end{cases} \tag{6}$$

where $\mathbf{C}, \mathbf{E}$ are the factor loading matrices (matrices of basis) for each view and the latent representations vectors $\boldsymbol{\phi}_i$ are stacked in the matrix $\varPhi$. Figure 1 depicts the graphical representation of this model. Consequently, the deep multi-view subspace learning problem can be formulated by the following combined regularized objective function

$$\min_{\mathbf{W}_f, \mathbf{W}_g, \mathbf{W}_p, \mathbf{W}_q, \mathbf{C}, \mathbf{E}, \varPhi} \underbrace{\tfrac{\lambda}{T} \sum_{i=1}^{T} \|\mathbf{x}_i - p(f(\mathbf{x}_i))\|^2 + \|\mathbf{y}_i - q(g(\mathbf{y}_i))\|^2}_{\text{autoencoder objective terms}}$$
$$+ \underbrace{\tfrac{1}{T} \sum_{i=1}^{T} \mathcal{L}_1 \left(\mathbf{C}\phi_i; f(\mathbf{x}_i)\right) + \mathcal{L}_2 \left(\mathbf{E}\phi_i; g(\mathbf{y}_i)\right) + \lambda_r \sum_{j=1}^{K} \mathcal{R}_1(\varPhi_{j:}) \mathcal{R}_2(\mathbf{C}_{:j}, \mathbf{E}_{:j})}_{\text{linear two-view objective terms}} \tag{7}$$

Here, $\{\mathcal{L}_1,\ \mathcal{L}_2\}$ are the loss functions that measure the divergences between the latent projected views $\{f_{\mathbf{x}_i}, y_{\mathbf{y}_i}\}$ and their corresponding factorized estimates $\{\mathbf{C}\boldsymbol{\phi}_i, \mathbf{E}\boldsymbol{\phi}_i\}$. These losses are assumed to be convex in their first arguments, where different noise assumptions result different loss functions, for instance the i.i.d. Gaussian noise assumption amounts to ℓ_2 losses. The regularizer terms, $\mathcal{R}_1(\varPhi_{j:}), \mathcal{R}_2(\mathbf{C}_{:j}, \mathbf{E}_{:j})$, capture special structures on the factors loading matrices and the latent features which are controlled by constant factor λ_r. On the other hands, the loss functions that measure the fitness error between each view and its reconstruction by the auto-encoder are modeled by ℓ_2 losses. Minimizing these loss terms results the latent projections that best reconstruct each view. The parameter $\lambda > 0$ balances the trade-off between the auto-encoder loss and the linear two-view loss.

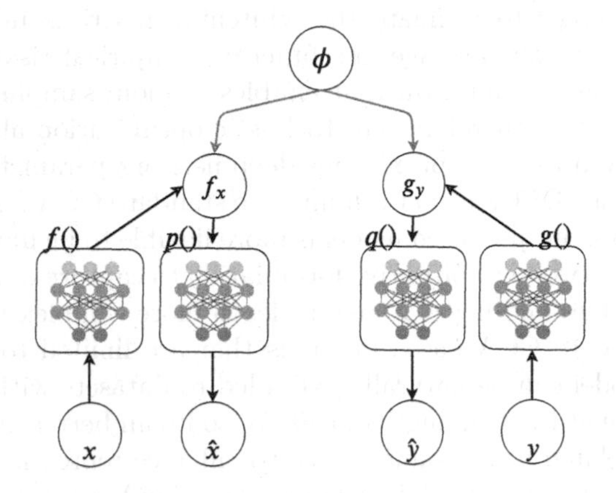

Fig. 1. Graphical representation of the deep generative two-view model.

2.1 Deep Multi-view with Conditionally Independent Views

One important assumption in multi-view learning is that the views are conditionally independent given the shared latent representation (Yu et al. 2014). This property is crucial in some applications aiming to recover a natural latent representation. As explained in White et al. (2012), this property can be encouraged by selecting regularizer terms of the form $\mathcal{R}_2(\mathbf{C}_{:j}, \mathbf{E}_{:j}) = \max\{\|\mathbf{C}_{:j}\|_2, \|\mathbf{E}_{:j}\|_2\}$ in the optimization objective (7). Using this regularizer, the basis of reconstruction models of each view are individually constrained and don't compete against each other to obtain their own share in reconstructing the views $\mathbf{x}_i$, $\mathbf{y}_i$, so this regularizer better respects the conditional independence of the views. Here, we select $\mathcal{R}_1(\boldsymbol{\Phi}_{j:}) = \|\boldsymbol{\Phi}_{j:}\|_2$ to encourage row-wise sparsity which, in turn, results in low-rank representation. Subsequently, the two-view objective terms in Eq. (7) can be reformulated as a convex optimization problem in the parameters of linear two-view model, $\{\mathbf{C}, \mathbf{E}, \boldsymbol{\Phi}\}$ (White et al. 2012; Yu et al. 2014). Although, the combined objective function of the deep generative model (7) is not convex in the parameters of deep networks, we found this convex reformulation of the linear two-view layer to be beneficial for the training of deep two-view model and final latent variable in practice.

2.2 Advantages of the Proposed Model

- As mentioned above, the proposed method provide a model for inferring the hidden representation underlying both views and subsequently predicting the second view based on the available primary view at the test time. This is in

contrast to CCA-based methods, such as DCCAE, that don't directly offer a model for generating samples from the latent variable so it is difficult to reconstruct one view based on the other one (Wang et al. 2015b).
- In addition, as opposed to CCA-based methods that require sufficiently large batch size in order to estimate the whitening matrices in the constraints and the gradients, the average loss function (empirical risk) in (7) exhibits the standard summation form that enables random sampling for stochastic gradient calculation therefore the stochastic optimization algorithms can be readily employed here to optimize for deep network parameters.
- In contrast to the DCCAE that is limited to standard CCA formulation on the projected views, our proposed model is more flexible to include different types of losses for the two-view objective formulation to capture different properties of latent variables and hence is able to learn more complex models.
- Also, dissimilar to CCA based methods that are limited to two views, this generative model can be naturally extended to datasets with more than two views available at the training (Guo 2013), so it can better integrate different information related to the same source to enhance representation learning.
- Additionally, it is expected that the reconstruction losses are more involved in deep generative multi-view training compared to DCCAE since all the objective terms in (7) has the form of losses. So, one might expect that other forms of losses can be replaced for the ℓ_2 of reconstruction error in the objective function (7) to improve reconstruction ability of the model; the property that doesn't seem practical in the DCCAE as its CCA term tends to dominate in practice while ignoring the reconstruction terms which in turn results in poor reconstructed views. This property will be investigated in the experimental studies in Sect. 3.
- Similar to the deep variational CCA model (Wang et al. 2016), we can introduce private variables that capture view-specific structures in the datasets and disentangle the underlying shared and private information in each view.

The combination of the aforementioned advantages, make the proposed deep generative two-view model a powerful and flexible candidate in multi-view settings with different downstream goals such as classification, subspace clustering, speech recognition and word pair semantic similarity. In the following section we empirically study the performance of the proposed method.

3 Experiments

Experimental Design. For the experiments, we used the two-view noisy digits datasets of Wang et al. (2015b) created based on MNIST dataset that consists of grayscale digit images of size 28×28 pixels. To synthesize the views, the pixel values are scaled to range $[0, 1]$. The first view of the dataset is generated by rotating each image at angles randomly sampled from uniform distribution $\mathcal{U}(-\pi/4, \pi/4)$ and the second view is selected from a different image of the same identity as in the first view and a random uniform noise is added, then the final

Table 1. Classification error of different multi-view learning algorithms on a two-view data set generated based on the MNIST digit images. The results of DGMV method are averaged over 3 rials. The performance of the DGMV is compared against the following benchmark methods: **Linear CCA:** linear single layer CCA, **SplitAE:** split autoencoder with Sigmoid gates (Ngiam et al. 2011), **DCCA:** deep CCA with Sigmoid gates (Andrew et al. 2013), **Randomized KCCA:** randomized kernel CCA approximation with Gaussian RBF kernels and random Fourier features (Lopez-Paz et al. 2014), **CorrAE:** deep correlated auto-encoder with Sigmoid gates (2) (Wang et al. 2015b), **DistAE:** deep minimum-distance auto-encoder with Sigmoid gates (Wang et al. 2015b), **DCCAE:** deep CCA-Auto encoder with Sigmoid gates (1) (Wang et al. 2015b), **VCCA:** deep variational CCA with ReLU gates (Wang et al. 2016), **VCCA-private:** deep variational CCA with an extra pair of latent variables for modeling the private information within each view. ReLU gates are used as the nonlinearities in all the networks (Wang et al. 2016), the performance results of the benchmark methods are from Wang et al. (2015b, 2016).

Method	Classification error (%)
Linear CCA (K = 10)	19.6
SpliAE (K = 10)	11.9
CorrAE (K = 10)	12.9
DistAE (K = 20)	16.0
KCCA (K = 10)	5.1
DCCA (K = 10)	2.9
DCCAE (K = 10)	2.2
VCCA	3.0
VCCA-private	2.4
DGMV (K = 50)	**1.32**
DGMV (K = 70)	**1.30**

value is truncated to remain in range $[0, 1]$. Following this procedure, both views are just sharing the same identity (label) of the digit but not the style of the handwriting as they are based on arbitrary images in the same class. The training set is divided into training/validation subsets of length $50K/10K$ and the performance is measured on the $10K$ images in the test set. This noisy MNIST two-view dataset was used in Wang et al. (2015b) to evaluate the performance of the multi-view model.

To make a fair comparison, we used neural network architecture for the auto-encoders with the same capacity as the one used in Wang et al. (2015b). Accordingly, for the deep network models, the encoding networks are composed of three fully-connected nonlinear layers of size 1024 units and the last linear layer of size K where K is the dimensionality of the final mapping of the encoding network. The decoding networks consist of three fully-connected layers of 1024 nonlinear units with final layer of size 784 that reconstruct the original images. Sigmoid function is used as the nonlinearity in the deep auto-encoders. Here, we used

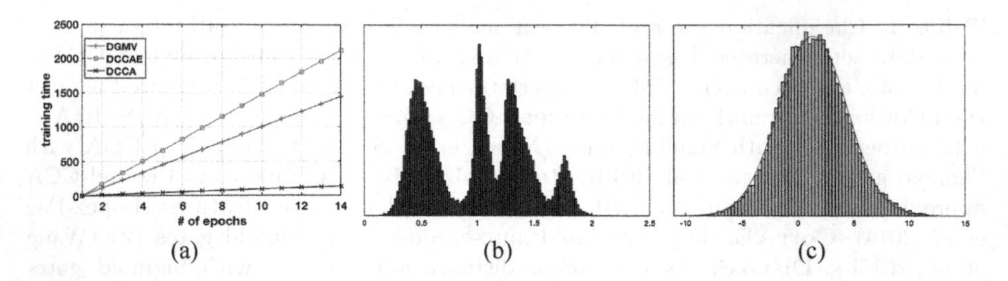

Fig. 2. (a) Running time of different learning algorithms over the rounds (epochs) of SGD optimization, (b) histogram of one dimensions of the primary projected view $f(x_i)$ of DCCAE and (c) histogram of one dimensions of the primary projected view $f(x_i)$ of DGMV.

sigmoid gate function for all the hidden units of the deep networks. In order to prevent over-fitting, we also applied stochastic drop-out to all the layers as regularization techniques.

In the experiments, the downstream task is classification and the misclassification rate is measured as the performance metric. For that goal, the one-versus-one linear SVM classification algorithm is applied on the shared latent representation ϕ of the proposed models or the projected mappings of the CCA based methods. It is worth emphasizing that the proposed DGMV model is able to infer the shared underlying representation of both views based on both encoding projections $\{f_{\mathbf{x}_i}, g_{\mathbf{y}_i}\}$. The shared latent representation is not naturally available in the CCA-based methods which are only able to construct the projection of each individual view. To tune the parameters of the SVM algorithm, cross-validation procedure is employed selecting the best performing model, averaged over 3 trials, on the validation set and the final classification error is evaluated on the test set. For the proposed deep multi-view models, we used the ℓ_2 loss function for both $\mathcal{L}_1, \mathcal{L}_2$ in the objective function (7). To train the deep generative multi-view (DGMV) model, the stochastic gradient descent is used for learning the parameters of the deep networks and accelerated proximal gradient descent (Karami et al. 2017) is employed for optimization of the latent two-view model while we alternatively switch between training of latent multi-view model and the deep AEs after each epoch of training while keeping the other set fixed. Furthermore, we practically found that the convex reformulation of the linear two-view model results in better performance than non-convex optimization algorithm for the training of the latent two-view model and inference of shared latent variable. Similar to Wang et al. (2015b), deep auto-encoders are pre-trained using the layer-wise training method of restricted Boltzmann machines (RBMs) (Hinton and Salakhutdinov 2006). The parameters of each algorithm are tuned through cross validation with grid search.

Classification performance of different methods are presented in Table 1 in bit error rate where the best dimensionality of latent variable for each method is reported in parenthesis. The results highlight that DGMV outperform the available methods in terms of the classification performance. In CCA based methods, the dimensionality of the projected latent variable, K, is selected from the set $\{5, 10, 20, 30, 50\}$ in Wang et al. (2015b) and the best results are achieved by $K = 10$ while in our experiments we found that DGMV can benefit from larger projected latent variable size and it achieves better performance with larger K.

In order to evaluate the learning behavior of the methods, we also compare the running time of different learning algorithms in CPU seconds over the rounds (epochs) of optimization in Fig. 2(a). To make a fair comparison, all experiments were rerun on the same machine using Matlab. Comparing the computation times, we can see that the training of the proposed DGMV methods is faster than DCCAE and while the running time of DCCA is shorter per epoch but it needs more epochs of training (50 epochs versus 14 epochs used for DCCAE and deep two-view models) until it converge to a reasonable result.

Moreover, the histograms of projected view, depicted in Fig. 2(b) and (c), confirm that the outputs of the encoders in DCCAE are not Gaussian distributed while CCA is known to work well in the Gaussian setting while on the other hand, the histograms of projected view of deep generative multi-view model in Fig. 2(c) shows that its distribution is approximately Gaussian.

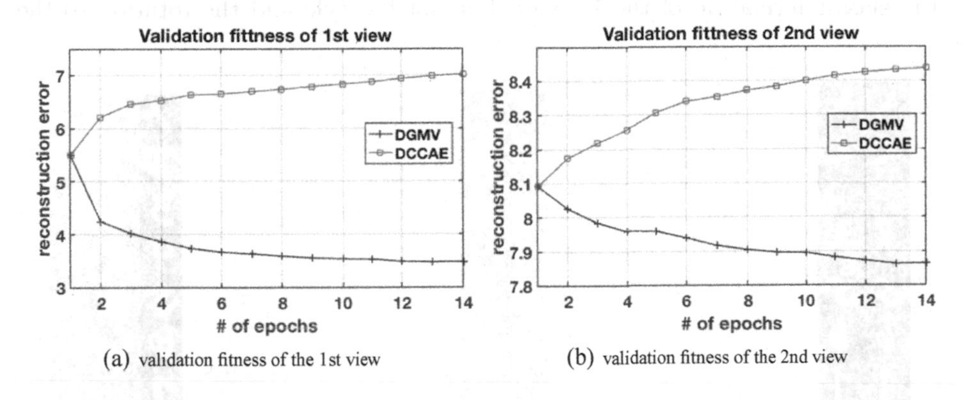

(a) validation fitness of the 1st view (b) validation fitness of the 2nd view

Fig. 3. Reconstruction fitness of both views for different learning algorithms over the rounds (epochs) of optimization.

3.1 Reconstruction Performance

To examine the sample generation behavior of the proposed method, the reconstruction performance of the proposed methods is also evaluated and compared against that of DCCAE. First, the reconstruction error of each view is evaluated for different methods with latent variable dimensionality of $K = 10$. As the validation fitness over the course of training in Fig. 3 illustrates, DGMV tends to decrease the reconstruction errors of both views as the training algorithm progresses while DCCAE leads to increased reconstruction error to achieve smaller canonical correlation among the projected views. This empirical study shows that DCCAE sacrifices the reconstruction ability and focuses on canonical correlation term in order to achieve good discrimination performance while accurate reconstruction of input signal is highly desirable in practice.

Also to illustrate the reconstruction capability of the proposed method, some training samples of digits in both views and their reconstructed images are depicted in Figs. 4(a) and (b) each reconstruction image is generated by its own autoencoder network. Figure 4(c) depicts the predicted images of the second view based on the 1st view using the combined network: *1st encoder* $(f()) \rightarrow$ *latent linear multi-view on the encoded projections* $\rightarrow$ *2nd decoder* $(q())$. Here, the network is trained with latent variable dimensionality of $K = 70$. These figures shows the reconstruction capability of DGMV method where the generated samples in the input space can denoise the noisy observation, the ability that was missing in DCCA and DCCAE. More specifically, one can observe from Fig. 4(c) that the rotations of images in the first view are eliminated from the generated images in the second view and a prototypical image of same digit is reconstructed by feeding a sample from that digit class to the network. This observation, which is also reported in Wang et al. (2016) for variational CCA (VCCA) model, can be justified by the fact that the 2nd view only contains the class information of the 1st view but not its style and the rotation so the

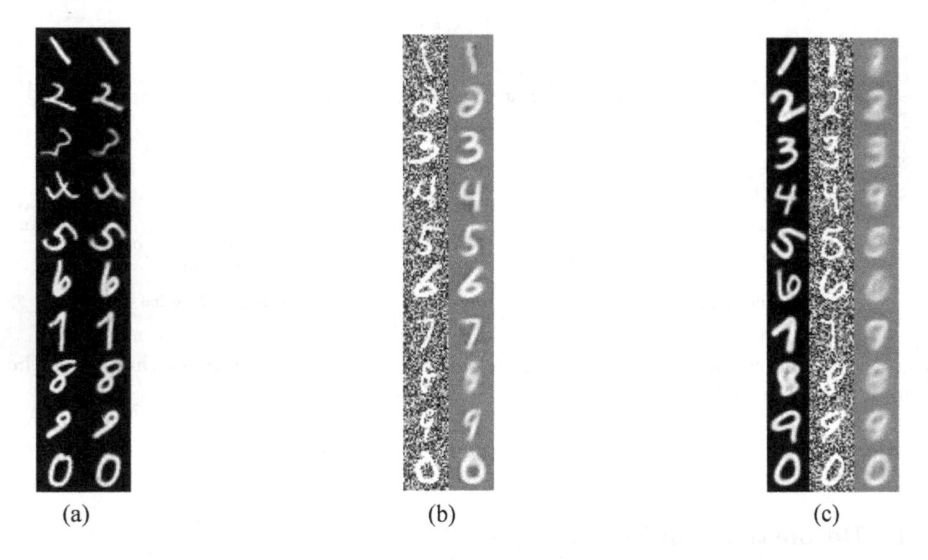

Fig. 4. (a) Samples of the training dataset in the first views and their reconstructed images generated by autoencoder network of view 1 (AE1) depicted in columns 1 and 2, respectively. (b) Samples of the training dataset in the first views and their reconstructed images generated by autoencoder network of view 2 (AE2) depicted n columns 1 and 2, respectively. (c) Column 3 is the predicted images of the second view based on the samples from the first (primary) view of the test dataset in column 1. The second column shows the observed noisy samples of the second view.

trained autoencoder of the second view (AE2) will ignore the style information of the 1st view. More generated samples from different experimental setup can be found in Appendix A.1.

4 Conclusion and Discussion

In this work, a new deep generative multi-view model is proposed that extends the linear generative interpretation of classical CCA to a nonlinear deep architecture. The proposed deep multi-view network provides a model for inferring the hidden representation underlying both views that subsequently provides better class separation and also reconstruction. Furthermore, training of the model parameters enjoys the stochastic optimization algorithms that provide fast and efficient learning. This deep network can generate samples in the input space, so it can be employed to reconstruct one view based on available primary view at the test time. In addition to its denoising capability, this method also showed the potential to suppress more complex forms of distortion, such as random rotation, from the signal. While CCA based methods achieve good discrimination performance at the expense of sacrificing the reconstruction error, the proposed method offers both class separation and sample generation in a more flexible way.

A Appendix

A.1 More Generated Samples

To illustrate the reconstruction capability of the proposed methods, we also made another two-view dataset where views are drawn not only from the same identity but also from the same digit of that identity of the MNIST dataset. Note that in the previous setting, images of the second view were sampled arbitrarily from the same class of 1st view. For these new setting, we select the main view unaltered from the MNIST dataset and synthesize the second view by adding noise and/or randomly rotating the main view. In this way, both views of each pair are originated from the same digit image (same pose), then we use the data from the main view to recover the image of second view, consequently we evaluate the ability of different non-linear two-view learning models in denoising and removing random rotation effect.

In the following figure, the reconstruction and prediction ability of the deep multiview networks are illustrated where the second view is built by adding uniform noise to the first view. Here, the deep network trained for hidden dimension size of $K = 60$ (Fig. 5).

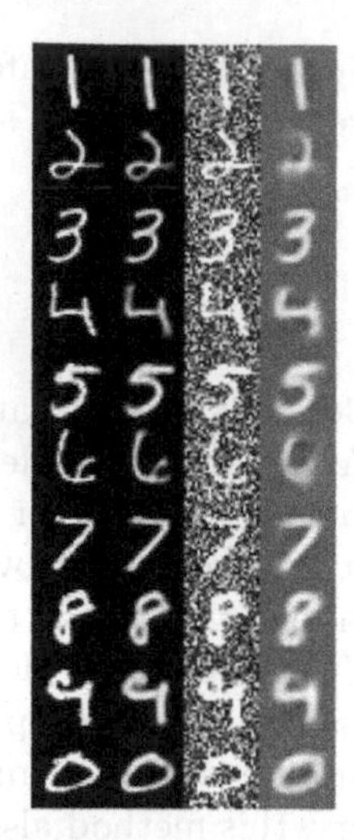

(a) Reconstruction of both views in training

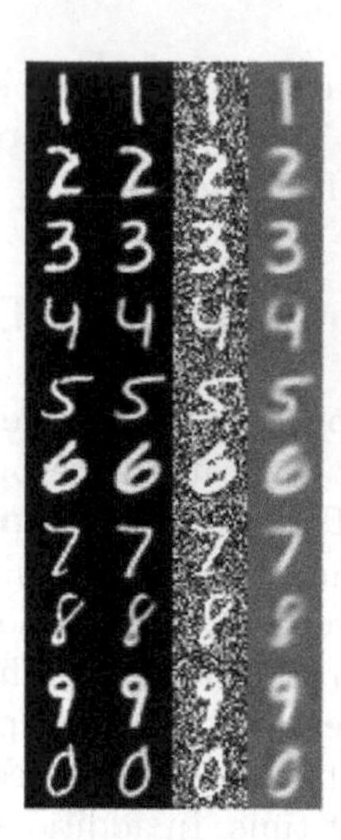

(b) Prediction of second view by the first view

Fig. 5. Column 1 and 3 are the images from 1st and 2nd view, respectively, column 2 is the reconstructed image based on view 1 using 1st autoencoder (AE1). Column 4 of (a) shows reconstructed image based on view 2 using AE2 while column 4 of (b) are predicted images based on view 1 using the network: encoder1+multiview model+decoder2. Samples of figure (a) and figure (b) are drawn from training set and test set, respectively

References

Andrew, G., Arora, R., Bilmes, J., Livescu, K.: Deep canonical correlation analysis. In: International Conference on Machine Learning, pp. 1247–1255 (2013)

Bach, F.R., Jordan, M.I.: Kernel independent component analysis. J. Mach. Learn. Res. **3**, 1–48 (2003). (ISSN 1532–4435)

Chaudhuri, K., Kakade, S.M., Livescu, K., Sridharan, K.: Multi-view clustering via canonical correlation analysis. In: Proceedings of the 26th Annual International Conference on Machine Learning, pp. 129–136. ACM (2009)

Foster, D.P., Kakade, S.M., Zhang, T.: Multi-view dimensionality reduction via canonical correlation analysis (2008)

Guo, Y.: Convex subspace representation learning from multi-view data. In: Twenty-Seventh AAAI Conference on Artificial Intelligence (2013)

Hardoon, D.R., Szedmak, S.R., Shawe-Taylor, J.R.: Canonical correlation analysis: an overview with application to learning methods. Neural Comput. **16**(12), 2639–2664 (2004). (ISSN 0899–7667)

Hinton, G.E., Salakhutdinov, R.R.: Reducing the dimensionality of data with neural networks. Science **313**(5786), 504–507 (2006)

Karami, M., White, M., Schuurmans, D., Szepesvári, C.: Multi-view matrix factorization for linear dynamical system estimation. In: Advances in Neural Information Processing Systems, pp. 7092–7101 (2017)
Lopez-Paz, D., Sra, S., Smola, A., Ghahramani, Z., Schölkopf, B.: Randomized nonlinear component analysis. In: International Conference on Machine Learning, pp. 1359–1367 (2014)
Ngiam, J., Khosla, A., Kim, M., Nam, J., Lee, H., Ng, A.Y.: Multimodal deep learning. In: Proceedings of the 28th International Conference on Machine Learning (ICML 2011), pp. 689–696 (2011)
Wang, W., Arora, R., Livescu, K., Bilmes, J.A.: Unsupervised learning of acoustic features via deep canonical correlation analysis. In: 2015 IEEE International Conference on Acoustics, Speech and Signal Processing (ICASSP), pp. 4590–4594. IEEE (2015a)
Wang, W., Livescu, K., Bilmes, J.: On deep multi-view representation learning. In: ICML, vol. 37 (2015b)
Wang, W., Lee, H., Livescu, K.: Deep variational canonical correlation analysis. arXiv preprint arXiv:1610.03454 (2016)
White, M., Yu, Y., Zhang, X., Schuurmans, D.: Convex multi-view subspace learning. In: Advances in Neural Information Processing Systems (2012)
Williams, C.K.I., Seeger, M.: Using the Nyström method to speed up kernel machines. In: Advances in Neural Information Processing Systems, pp. 682–688 (2001)
Yu, Y., Zhang, X., Schuurmans, D.: Generalized conditional gradient for sparse estimation. arXivorg (2014)

New Trends in Representation Learning with Knowledge Graphs (KGRL)

New Trends in Representation Learning with Knowledge Graphs (KGRL)

Introduction

Welcome to the First Workshop on New Trends in Representation Learning with Knowledge Graphs (KGRL) co-located with ECML-PKDD 2019. The primary goal of the workshop is to use Knowledge Graphs which are becoming the standard for storing, retrieving and querying structured data. In academia and industry, they are increasingly used to provide background knowledge. Over the last few years, several research contributions are made to show machine learning especially representation learning is successfully applied to knowledge graphs enabling inductive inference about facts with unknown truth values. In this workshop, we want to see how novel representation learning methods can be applied to flexible relational reasoning tasks and what are its advantages in terms of expressive power, interpretability, and generalization. In this first edition, we called for short papers. All the accepted ones agreed for archival are published in these proceedings.

KGRL 2019 received 4 submissions. These papers have received 2 highly-qualified double-blind reviews. Besides considering the average overall score, only papers for which none of the reviewers expressed a negative opinion (strong or weak reject) were accepted. In total, 2 papers were accepted to appear in the workshop proceedings, with an acceptance rate of 50.

The program of the workshop, besides 4 oral presentations, includes 2 invited talks by Maximilian Nickel and Mathias Niepert. The workshop received sponsorship by "Maschinelles Lernen mit Wissensgraphen" (MLwin).

The KGRL Workshop Organizers.

Organization

Organizers

Volker Tresp	Ludwig-Maximilians University and Siemens, Germany
Jens Lehmann	University of Bonn and Fraunhofer IAIS, Germany
Aditya Mogadala	Saarland University, Germany
Achim Rettinger	Trier University, Germany
Afshin Sadeghi	Fraunhofer IAIS and University of Bonn, Germany
Mehdi Ali	University of Bonn and Fraunhofer IAIS, Germany

Program Committee

Aditya Menon	Google Research, USA
Dongwoo Kim	POSTECH, South Korea
Steffen Thoma	FZI Research Center for Information Technology, Germany
Lei Zhang	FIZ Karlsruhe, Germany
Bibek Paudel	Stanford University, USA
Daniel Ruffinelli	University of Mannheim, Germany
Emir Muñoz	NUI Galway and Genesys, Ireland
Mayank Kejriwal	University of Southern California, USA

Invited Speakers

Maximilian Nickel	Facebook AI Research, USA
Mathias Niepert	NEC Labs Europe, Germany

Sponsorship

Maschinelles Lernen mit Wissensgraphen (MLwin)

SDE-KG: A Stochastic Dynamic Environment for Knowledge Graphs

Varun Ranganathan(✉) and Natarajan Subramanyam

PES University, Bangalore 560085, KA, India
varunranga1997@hotmail.com, natarajan@pes.edu
http://www.pes.edu

Abstract. State-of-the-art techniques that perform reasoning over large knowledge graphs incorporate a path-finder and a path-reasoner. The path-reasoner is a learning agent that performs the inference task by producing a relation. The path-finder is usually the knowledge graph environment that moves the agent to the next-hop entity. While the path-reasoner can work on a continuous state space, the knowledge graph environment on which it is being trained, operates on a discrete state space. This restricts the agent from deducing implicit paths. In this paper, a novel path-finder called Stochastic Dynamic Environment for Knowledge Graphs (SDE-KG) has been proposed. SDE-KG is a meta-framework that can be combined with many embedding methods to create a continuous function of the knowledge graph environment which may facilitate smarter multi-hop reasoning.

Keywords: Knowledge Graphs · Stochastic Dynamic Environment · Multihop reasoning · Reinforcement learning · Representation learning

1 Introduction

Multi-hop traversal over Knowledge Graphs (KGs) involves finding at a chain of reasoning that best describes the relation between a source and a target entity. This is better assisted by KG embedding techniques that allows for the completion of a KG by representing its components in a vector space [12]. Neural multi-hop approaches introduced by Neelakantan et al. [9] and Guu et al. [4] use KG embeddings with supervised learning techniques on data gathered using random walks. Newer approaches introduced by Xiong et al. [12] and Das et al. [2] embrace the reinforcement learning approach which improved the quality of reasoning paths. The environment moves the agent to the next-hop entity after selecting a suitable path and gives the agent a reward. These approaches train the agent to traverse over a discrete state space of the KG. This disallows the agent from combining relations thereby reducing the number of hops required to traverse from a source to the target entity [7]. Moreover, incomplete nature of KGs may cause entities and relationships to be pretermitted. A stochastic environment may allow for the implicit inclusion of such entities and relations.

P. Cellier and K. Driessens (Eds.): ECML PKDD 2019 Workshops, CCIS 1167, pp. 483–488, 2020.
https://doi.org/10.1007/978-3-030-43823-4_39

The quality of reasoning decreases as the size of the KG increases. Multi-hop traversal algorithms, presented in previous work, do not simplify the KG for the agent to focus on a portion of the graph. A dynamic environment may allow the agent to focus on a subportion of the KG. This would allow the agent to make more intelligible traversal decisions.

This paper presents a novel approach towards building a path-finder for multi-hop reasoning called SDE-KG. SDE-KG is trained using a novel objective function that takes into account the existence of an entity in the KG and the euclidean distance hopped towards the target entity. The outline of the paper is as follows. Section 2 introduces SDE-KG, a Stochastic Dynamic Environment for Knowledge Graphs along with the motivation and mathematical formulation. In Sect. 3, experiments are conducted on various knowledge graphs with several translation-based knowledge graph embedding methods. Section 4 provides the concluding remarks with the future scope of SDE-KG. The code and software for the training and evaluation of SDE-KG, along with the dataset statistics and hyperparameters can be found at github.com/varunranga/SDEKG-KGRL. Results obtained from experiments can be found at tinyurl.com/SDEKG-KGRL-Results.

2 SDE-KG: Stochastic Dynamic Environment for Knowledge Graphs

2.1 Motivation and Task

The motivation behind SDE-KG arises from the need for a smarter environment for multi-hop reasoning over large scale knowledge graphs. Knowledge graph environments adopted in previous methodologies do not explicitly assist the agent towards the required target. Given the head entity and the relation outputted by the agent, the environment searches the knowledge graph for relevant triplets and picks a random tail entity as the next-hop entity. This could prove to be harmful for relations of the 1-N type. The environment may select a 'candidate entity', a next-hop entity related to the source entity with the 1-N relation which is closest (in terms of euclidean distance) to the target entity. In doing so, the time taken to perform the reasoning task increases. The proposed path-finder is trained to move the agent as close as possible to the required target entity, while placing it on an entity that exists in the knowledge graph (Fig. 1).

The environment can be represented as a continuous function $\mathcal{E}$ which accepts the current and target entity from a state space $\mathcal{S}$, and a relation from an action space $\mathcal{A}$ and returns the next-hop entity from the state space $\mathcal{S}$. The following notations have been used: e_{src} is the source entity, r is the relation, e_{nxt} is the next-hop entity, e_{tgt} is the target entity, e_{int} is an intermediate entity, e_{cnd} is a candidate entity and d is the embedding dimension. In this problem setup, the source entity e_{src} and the target entity e_{tgt} are known. The succeeding or next-hop entity e_{nxt} is unknown. The relation r is given by the path-reasoner. The entity prediction task is to predict the next-hop entity e_{nxt}, given $(e_{src}, r, ?, e_{tgt})$.

2.2 Deriving SDE-KG

Lin et al. [8] views relations as a transformation from one entity to another. When an agent interacts with the environment using a relation, it transforms a point in space. Therefore, the next-hop entity y can be given by:

$$e_{int} = \mathcal{F}_r(e_{src}) \tag{1}$$

Two types of relations can arise: 1-1 and 1-N. For a 1-1 relation type, Eq. (1) implies that e_{int} is the next-hop entity. For a 1-N type of relation, Eq. (1) causes a mode collapse [10], since the transformation leads to several entities. To overcome this issue, the environment must assist the agent by moving it to a next-hop entity closest to the target entity. Therefore, another transformation function is used which considers the relation type, the current position of the agent and the target entity. In the case of a 1-N relationship type, e_{int} is considered as an intermediate entity. The final entity can be given by:

$$e_{nxt} = \mathcal{G}(r, e_{int}, e_{tgt}) \tag{2}$$

To allow for the representation of the environment as a continuous function, function $\mathcal{F}$ is represented by a matrix, that performs a linear transformation on the vector representation of an entity. This matrix can be formed using linear function approximators such as perceptrons [3]. A layer of d^2-perceptrons takes the vector representation of the relation, and creates an appropriate transformation matrix $\mathcal{F}$. The matrix $\mathcal{F}$ is applied on the source entity, to give the intermediate entity e_{int}. Function $\mathcal{G}$ models the difference between the intermediate entity and the next-hop entity in the direction of the given target. Inspired by skip connections from Residual Networks [5], function $\mathcal{G}$ adds an appropriate vector to vector representation of e_{int}. This vector can be approximated by a layer of d-perceptrons that take the vector representations of the intermediate entity, relation and the target entity and output the next-hop entity e_{nxt}.

To train SDE-KG, two objectives are taken into consideration. The first objective maximizes the hop towards target entity. A hop can be defined as the displacement (in terms of euclidean distance) towards a target entity given the source entity. To satisfy this objective, the difference in the distance between the target entity and the next-hop entity and the distance between the target entity and the source entity is minimized. To avoid overshooting the agent from the target entity, the absolute value, represented by $|.|$, of the difference is taken. $\mathcal{L}_{jump}$ is given by:

$$\mathcal{L}_{jump} = |\sqrt{\Sigma_{i=1}^{d}(e_{tgt_i} - e_{nxt_i})^2} - \sqrt{\Sigma_{i=1}^{d}(e_{tgt_i} - e_{src_i})^2}| \tag{3}$$

The second objective is to move the entity to a point in space corresponding to an entity that exists in the knowledge graph, which can be reached from the source entity through that relation. This is a matching objective which involves the minimization of the squared error between the predicted next-hop entity

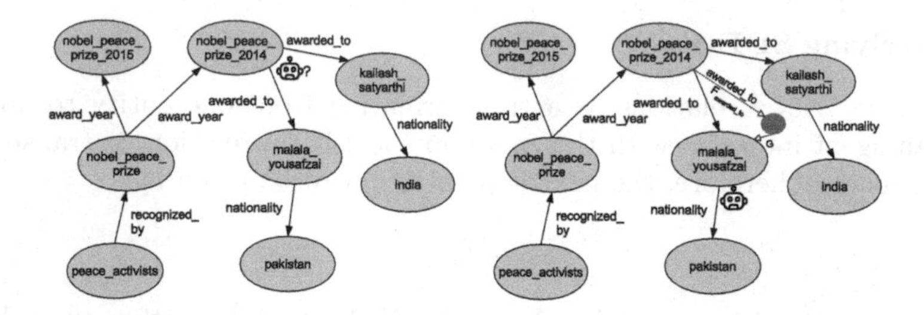

Fig. 1. Left: Example of a query to relate entity 'peace_activists' to entity 'pakistan'. A multi-hop agent that is on 'nobel_peace_prize_2014' may be shifted to 'kailash_satyarthi' which is not as close as 'malala_yousafzai' to 'pakistan', even after querying with the correct relation 'awarded_to'. This is one of the problems with random picking of tail entity by discrete environments when 1-N relationships are involved. Right: SDE-KG helps the agent move towards the target by moving it to an intermediate position based on the relationship type, and shifts it to the entity nearest to the target entity.

embedded vector e_{nxt} and a candidate entity embedded vector e_{cnd}. The candidate entity can be described as the tail entity that is closest to the target for a given head entity and the relation. $\mathcal{L}_{valid}$ is given by:

$$\mathcal{L}_{valid} = \Sigma_{i=1}^{d} (e_{cnd_i} - e_{nxt_i})^2 \tag{4}$$

The two objective functions are combined to create a loss function on which SDE-KG is trained. The overall loss function $\mathcal{L}$ is given by:

$$\mathcal{L} = \mathcal{L}_{jump} + \mathcal{L}_{valid} \tag{5}$$

3 Experiments and Results

To understand the properties of SDE-KG, experiments were performed on three small knowledge graph datasets, and two large knowledge graph datasets. To gain a better insight, four translational knowledge graph embedding methods were used to train SDE-KG. These were TransE [1], TransH [11], TransR [8], and TransD [6].

SDE-KG is trained via a random entity picking procedure. In each training step, two random entities are chosen as the source and destination entities. A random relation is also chosen. To train SDE-KG to land on an entity which exists in the knowledge graph, the candidate entity is search using a simple rule-based approach. The evaluation procedure of SDE-KG uses a random walk strategy. A random agent is used to generate paths of length L from a source entity to a destination entity by taking paths available from the knowledge graph. A random entity e_{src} is chosen as the source entity. A random triplet is selected such that its head entity matches the source entity. For the first hop, the relation r of the randomly selected triplet is stored. This process is iterated L times. The tail of the last randomly selected triplet e_{tgt} is stored as the target. For

Table 1. Performance of the predictive power of SDE-KG with respect to picking the candidate entity. TransH embedding method best represents the KG to allow complex chains of reasoning. TransR and TransD embedding methods perform indistinguishably due to the similarity in the underlying concept of their embedding methodology.

Dataset	Hop length	Embedding model							
		TransE		TransH		TransR		TransD	
		MRR	H@10	MRR	H@10	MRR	H@10	MRR	H@10
Countries	1	0.4766	**0.9340**	**0.5496**	**0.9340**	0.4412	0.7460	0.4470	0.9080
	2	0.4700	**0.9660**	**0.5984**	**0.9660**	0.4018	0.6760	0.4622	0.9360
	3	0.3270	**0.9600**	**0.3548**	0.9580	0.3383	0.6880	0.3403	0.8980
	5	0.3000	**0.9640**	**0.3499**	0.9620	0.3248	0.6640	0.3318	0.9320
UMLS	1	0.3380	0.6980	0.3146	0.6400	**0.3439**	**0.7600**	0.3022	0.5920
	2	**0.4586**	**0.7760**	0.4217	0.6860	0.4291	0.7580	0.4159	0.6700
	3	0.4563	**0.7980**	0.4156	0.7060	0.4187	0.7300	**0.4838**	0.7100
	5	0.4486	**0.8080**	0.4017	0.6580	0.3904	0.6680	**0.5088**	0.7440
Kinship	1	0.2367	0.5080	0.1866	0.4500	**0.3076**	**0.7080**	0.2826	0.6680
	2	0.2937	0.5600	0.2815	0.5420	**0.4613**	**0.7920**	0.3327	0.6860
	3	0.3118	0.5820	0.2701	0.4960	**0.4328**	**0.7600**	0.3202	0.6380
	5	0.3096	0.5520	0.2491	0.4880	**0.4424**	**0.7740**	0.3348	0.6700
NELL-995	1	0.0086	0.0182	**0.1216**	**0.2662**	0.0032	0.0047	0.0155	0.0331
	2	0.0148	0.0294	**0.0545**	**0.1291**	0.0036	0.0059	0.0117	0.0247
	3	0.0171	0.0369	**0.0641**	**0.1470**	0.0041	0.0054	0.0147	0.0300
	5	0.0204	0.0412	**0.0698**	**0.1567**	0.0045	0.0066	0.0147	0.0289
	10	0.0266	0.055	**0.0841**	**0.1967**	0.0060	0.0097	0.0176	0.0364
	20	0.0377	0.0745	**0.1466**	**0.3348**	0.0072	0.0126	0.0305	0.0625
FB15K-237	1	0.0185	0.0390	**0.0211**	**0.0453**	0.0028	0.0020	0.0089	0.0115
	2	0.0407	0.0747	**0.0659**	**0.1424**	0.0331	0.0464	0.0142	0.0237
	3	0.0304	0.0593	**0.0686**	**0.1577**	0.0092	0.0130	0.0141	0.0244
	5	0.0399	0.0774	**0.0824**	**0.1976**	0.0143	0.0205	0.0159	0.0269
	10	0.0846	0.1521	**0.1094**	**0.2536**	0.0653	0.0957	0.0206	0.0369
	20	0.0928	0.1681	**0.1173**	**0.2724**	0.0725	0.1082	0.0229	0.0443

the example (e_{src}, r, ?, e_{tgt}), the candidate entity is also selected. The entity outputted by SDE-KG is compared with the candidate entity based on their euclidean distance.

Upon inspection of results presented in Table 1, a few properties can be observed. The increase in the MRR and Hits@10 metrics can be noticed as the hop length increases. It can be inferred that, further away the agent is from the target entity, better are the predictions for the next-hop entity. SDE-KG moves the agent towards the target with exponentially increasing jump lengths. Better embedding methods help SDE-KG land the agent on valid entities present in the knowledge graph. Another noticeable property of SDE-KG is its stateless nature, that is, it does not remember information regarding previous transactions. This can allow for multiple agents, that perform various tasks, to traversal over one continuous function of the knowledge graph.

4 Conclusion and Future Scope

This paper proposes a novel path-finder for knowledge graph traversal called SDE-KG. SDE-KG converts a knowledge graph into a continuous function that can allow for efficient multi-hop logical reasoning. SDE-KG also allows for the representation of entities and relations that do not explicitly exist in the knowledge graph. The evaluation methodology provides evidence for the working of SDE-KG. Future works could make use of SDE-KG to perform the task of multi-hop logical reasoning. Since the path-finder operates on a continuous state and action space, an end-to-end differentiable approach to multi-hop reasoning can be adopted. Appropriate vector representations can be obtained for the components of the knowledge graph that will better the performance in multi-hop reasoning.

References

1. Bordes, A., Usunier, N., Garcia-Duran, A., Weston, J., Yakhnenko, O.: Translating embeddings for modeling multi-relational data. In: Advances in Neural Information Processing Systems, pp. 2787–2795 (2013)
2. Das, R., et al.: Go for a walk and arrive at the answer: reasoning over paths in knowledge bases using reinforcement learning. arXiv preprint arXiv:1711.05851 (2017)
3. Freund, Y., Schapire, R.E.: Large margin classification using the perceptron algorithm. Mach. Learn. **37**(3), 277–296 (1999). https://doi.org/10.1023/A:1007662407062
4. Guu, K., Miller, J., Liang, P.: Traversing knowledge graphs in vector space. arXiv preprint arXiv:1506.01094 (2015)
5. He, K., Zhang, X., Ren, S., Sun, J.: Deep residual learning for image recognition. In: Proceedings of the IEEE Conference on Computer Vision and Pattern Recognition, pp. 770–778 (2016)
6. Ji, G., He, S., Xu, L., Liu, K., Zhao, J.: Knowledge graph embedding via dynamic mapping matrix. In: Proceedings of the 53rd Annual Meeting of the Association for Computational Linguistics and the 7th International Joint Conference on Natural Language Processing (Volume 1: Long Papers), vol. 1, pp. 687–696 (2015)
7. Jiang, X., Wang, Q., Qi, B., Qiu, Y., Li, P., Wang, B.: Attentive path combination for knowledge graph completion. In: Asian Conference on Machine Learning, pp. 590–605 (2017)
8. Lin, Y., Liu, Z., Sun, M., Liu, Y., Zhu, X.: Learning entity and relation embeddings for knowledge graph completion. In: Twenty-Ninth AAAI Conference on Artificial Intelligence (2015)
9. Neelakantan, A., Roth, B., McCallum, A.: Compositional vector space models for knowledge base inference. In: 2015 AAAI Spring Symposium Series (2015)
10. Thanh-Tung, H., Tran, T., Venkatesh, S.: On catastrophic forgetting and mode collapse in generative adversarial networks. arXiv preprint arXiv:1807.04015 (2018)
11. Wang, Z., Zhang, J., Feng, J., Chen, Z.: Knowledge graph embedding by translating on hyperplanes. In: Twenty-Eighth AAAI Conference on Artificial Intelligence (2014)
12. Xiong, W., Hoang, T., Wang, W.Y.: DeepPath: a reinforcement learning method for knowledge graph reasoning. arXiv preprint arXiv:1707.06690 (2017)

Iterative Representation Learning for Entity Alignment Leveraging Textual Information

Weixin Zeng[1], Jiuyang Tang[1,2], and Xiang Zhao[1,2](✉)

[1] Science and Technology on Information Systems Engineering Laboratory, National University of Defense Technology, Changsha, China
xiangzhao@nudt.edu.cn

[2] Collaborative Innovation Center of Geospatial Technology, Wuhan, China

Abstract. Entity alignment (EA), which aims to find equivalent entities in different knowledge graphs (KGs), is an essential task for aggregating KGs from different sources. State-of-the-art EA solutions mainly rely on KG structure representation for judging the equivalence of entities while overlooking textual representation. Additionally, the lack of supervision signals for learning structural representation has not attracted enough attentions. In this work, we propose an iterative representation learning process that can increase the scale of training set with confident EA pairs selected from each round and generate structural representation with higher quality. Additionally, we point out that structural and textual representations are in essence two complementing views for EA and propose to integrate them to convey more comprehensive signals. The experimental results reveal that our solution outperforms the state-of-the-arts by a large margin.

Keywords: Entity alignment · Representation learning

1 Introduction

Knowledge graph (KG) is an effective means to acquire knowledge from data in unstructured or structured forms, and present them in an organized and approachable manner. Nevertheless, whichever approach is taken for construction, the resulting KG can never reach *full coverage* or being *fully correct*, and there always exists a trade-off between *coverage* and *correctness* [1].

One way to automatically increase the coverage and correctness of KGs is by utilizing knowledge from other KGs. This is intuitive, since most KGs contain complementing information. To incorporate the knowledge in external KGs into the target KG, the first, and the most crucial step, is to align KGs. Most recent research works [2–7,10] focus on the entity alignment (EA) task, since the number of unique entities is much larger than that of other unique elements [1].

State-of-the-art EA methods normally utilize KG representation, e.g., TransE [2–4,6] and graph convolutional network (GCN) [5], to make the most of

P. Cellier and K. Driessens (Eds.): ECML PKDD 2019 Workshops, CCIS 1167, pp. 489–494, 2020.
https://doi.org/10.1007/978-3-030-43823-4_40

KG structures and learn *structural* embeddings of entities. The intuition behind this is that identical entities in different KGs often have similar surrounding structures, and hence close embeddings. However, most of the state-of-the-arts neglect that, *textual* information, e.g., entity names and entity descriptions, could also offer *string* and *semantic* signals for matching entities. Furthermore, the performance of embedding based methods is also constrained by the lack of supervision signals for alignment in real-life scenarios.

To fill these gaps, we propose to learn both structural and textual representations of entities for EA. Specifically, regarding structural information, we adopt a self-training graph convolutional network (GCN) that leverages newly labeled EA pairs as training data to generate structural representation in higher quality. Noting that textual representation is actually complementing to structural representation, we utilize entity name embedding to capture textual signals and then combine them so as to provide a more comprehensive view for aligning entities. The evaluation on cross-lingual EA task against existing methods reveals the advantage of our proposed solution (East).

2 Methodology

Structural Information. In this work, we harness GCN to encode the neighbourhood information of entities as real-valued vectors. GCN is a kind of convolutional network which directly operates on graph structured data [8]. It generates node-level embeddings by encoding information about the node neighbourhoods. A GCN model normally comprises multiple stacked GCN layers. The input to l-th GCN network layer is a vertex feature matrix $\mathbf{H}^l \in \mathbb{R}^{N \times d^l}$, where N is the number of nodes and d^l is the dimensionality of feature vectors in the l-th layer. The output of the l-th layer $\mathbf{H}^{l+1} = \sigma(\hat{\mathbf{D}}^{-\frac{1}{2}}\hat{\mathbf{A}}\hat{\mathbf{D}}^{-\frac{1}{2}}\mathbf{H}^l\mathbf{W}^l)$, where $\hat{\mathbf{A}} = \mathbf{A} + \mathbf{I}$ and $\mathbf{I}$ is the identity matrix, $\hat{\mathbf{D}}$ is the diagonal node degree matrix of $\hat{\mathbf{A}}$. $\mathbf{W}^l \in \mathbb{R}^{d^l \times d^{l+1}}$ is the weight matrix of the l-th layer in GCN. d^{l+1} is the dimensionality of the feature vectors in the next layer. The activation function σ is normally set to *ReLU*.

In EA task, GCN is harnessed to generate structural representations of entities. We build two 2-layer GCNs, and each GCN processes one KG to generate embeddings of its entities. The initial feature matrix, $\mathbf{X}$, is sampled from truncated normal distribution with L2-normalization on rows [5]. It gets updated by GCN layers and the final output matrix $\mathbf{Z}$ can encode the structural information contained in each KG. Note that the dimensionality of feature vectors is fixed at d_s and kept the same for all layers.

The entity embeddings generated by two different GCNs are then aligned into the same embedding space by using pre-aligned EA pairs S. In specific, the training objective is to minimize the margin-based ranking loss function:

$$L = \sum_{(e_1,e_2)\in S} \sum_{(e_1',e_2')\in S'_{(e_1,e_2)}} [\| \mathbf{e}_1 - \mathbf{e}_2 \|_{l1} - \| \mathbf{e}_1' - \mathbf{e}_2' \|_{l1} + \gamma]_+, \tag{1}$$

where $[x]_+ = max\{0, x\}$, $S'_{(e_1,e_2)}$ denotes the set of negative EA pairs obtained by corrupting (e_1, e_2), i.e., substituting e_1 or e_2 with a randomly sampled entity from its corresponding KG. $\mathbf{e}$ denotes the (structural) embedding of entity e. γ is a positive margin that separates positive and negative EA pairs. Stochastic gradient descent (SGD) is harnessed to minimize the loss function.

Textual Information. An entity contains abundant textual information, which helps match entities in different KGs since equivalent entities have the same semantic meaning.

More specifically, we choose averaged word embeddings to capture the semantic meaning on account of its simplicity and generality. Suppose the name of entity e comprises p words, $w_1, ..., w_p$. Then the name embedding can be calculated by $ne(e) = \frac{1}{p}\sum_{i=1}^{p} \mathbf{w_i}$, where $\mathbf{w_i}$ is the word embedding of word w_i.

Considering entity name embedding and GCN entity embedding represent different views of entities, i.e., from semantic aspect and from structural aspect, we combine them to provide a more comprehensive view for bridging entities in different KGs. Concretely, the distance between two entities, $e_1 \in G_1$ and $e_2 \in G_2$, is defined as $D(e_1, e_2) = \alpha D_s(e_1, e_2) + (1-\alpha) D_t(e_1, e_2)$, where $D_s(e_1, e_2)$ represents Euclidean distance between entities $e_1 \in G_1$ and $e_2 \in G_2$ in the structural embedding space and $D_t(e_1, e_2)$ represents Euclidean distance in the textual embedding space. α is a hyper-parameter balancing the significance of two different sources of information. Theoretically, the distance would be small for equivalent entities in different KGs and the entity with the smallest D to target entity e can be regarded as the counterpart for e.

Iterative Training. Among real-life KGs, the number of existing EA pairs is limited. As thus, we propose to include newly-labeled EA pairs with high confidence into the seed EA pairs (training set) for generating more accurate structural representation.

The specific self-training procedure can be found in Algorithm 1. It takes two KGs, a set of pre-aligned EA pairs as inputs and generates final aligned entity pairs S'. The first step is to generate name embedding matrix $\mathbf{N}$ and input feature matrix $\mathbf{X}$ (line 1). By feeding $\mathbf{X}$, KGs and pre-aligned pairs into the 2-layer GCN model, the structural representation $\mathbf{Z}$ can be learned, which, together with other elements, are forwarded to a *HardAlign* procedure to generate augmented training set (line 2). Note that *HardAlign* and *SoftAlign* are two methods with different constraints for selecting confident EA pairs from the results and adding them to training set. S_H and S_S denote the augmented training set after *HardAlign* and *SoftAlign* procedures, respectively. The output structural matrix $\mathbf{Z}$ is considered as input matrix $\mathbf{X}$ for the next training round. The iteration of GCN training and *HardAlign* would continue until the number of newly selected pairs is below a given threshold, θ_1, otherwise it would take too long for the iteration to end (line 3–5). Then we loosen the constraint for adding new EA pairs into the training set and replace *HardAlign* with *SoftAlign*. Similar looping would be performed on GCN and *SoftAlign* before the number of newly added EA pairs reaches another given threshold θ_2 (line 6–9).

Algorithm 1. Self-training.

Input:
$S = \{(e_{i1}, e_{i2}) | e_{i1} \in E_1, e_{i2} \in E_2\}_{i=1}^{m}$, KGs: $G_1 = (E_1, R_1, T_1), G_2 = (E_2, R_2, T_2)$

Output:
Final aligned pairs S'

1: Initialization of entity embedding matrix $\mathbf{X}$; entity name embedding matrix $\mathbf{N}$
2: $\mathbf{Z} \leftarrow GCN(G_1, G_2, S, \mathbf{X})$, $S_H \leftarrow HardAlign(G_1, G_2, S, \mathbf{Z}, \mathbf{N}), \mathbf{X} \leftarrow \mathbf{Z}$
3: **while** $len(S_H) - len(S) > \theta_1$ **do**
4: $S \leftarrow S_H, \mathbf{Z} \leftarrow GCN(G_1, G_2, S, \mathbf{X}), S_H \leftarrow HardAlign(G_1, G_2, S, \mathbf{Z}, \mathbf{N}), \mathbf{X} \leftarrow \mathbf{Z}$
5: **end while**
6: $S \leftarrow S_H, \mathbf{Z} \leftarrow GCN(G_1, G_2, S, \mathbf{X}), S_S \leftarrow SoftAlign(G_1, G_2, S, \mathbf{Z}, \mathbf{N}), \mathbf{X} \leftarrow \mathbf{Z}$
7: **while** $len(S_S) - len(S) > \theta_2$ **do**
8: $S \leftarrow S_S, \mathbf{Z} \leftarrow GCN(G_1, G_2, S, \mathbf{X}), S_S \leftarrow SoftAlign(G_1, G_2, S, \mathbf{Z}, \mathbf{N}), \mathbf{X} \leftarrow \mathbf{Z}$
9: **end while**

The *HardAlign* process requires that, for every given entity $e_{j1} \in E_1 - S_1$ (in G_1 but not in the training set), suppose its closest entity in G_2 is e_{k2}, if for e_{k2}, its closest entity in G_1 is e_{j1}, and the distance between them is below a given threshold θ_3, (e_{j1}, e_{k2}) would be considered as a correct EA pair. This is a relatively strong constraint as it requires the distance between the two entities is the smallest from both sides and also below a certain threshold. As a result, we allow the introduction of more EA pairs via a soft alignment mechanism.

Regarding *SoftAlign*, suppose the focus is to find the counterpart for $e_{j1} \in E_1 - S_1$, we first select its top-ϵ closest entities E_{k2}, which are sorted from the smallest distance to the largest. Then for each $e_{k2} \in E_{k2}$, if e_{j1} is one of its top-ϵ closest entities, and the distance between them is below a given threshold θ_4, (e_{j1}, e_{k2}) would be regarded as a correct EA pair and the rest entities in E_{k2} would not be considered. This procedure is similar for finding the counterpart of $e_{k2} \in E_2 - S_2$.

3 Experiment

Parameter Settings. We utilize the fastText embedding as word embedding and the multilingual word embeddings are obtained from MUSE [9]. As for GCN settings, d_s is set to 300, γ is set to 3, the training epochs are 300. Five negative examples are generated for each positive pair. The hyper-parameter α is chosen as 0.3. For the self-training process, θ_1 and θ_2 are set to 100, θ_3 and θ_4 are set to 10, while ϵ is 3. The parameters are tuned on validation set.

Datasets and Competitors. For fair comparison, we adopt the WK3l60k [7] dataset, which consists of two cross-lingual datasets, English-French (En-Fr) and English-German (En-De), extracted from the subset of DBpedia. The En-Fr dataset comprises 54,205 entity pairs, while there are 55,523 entity pairs in En-De dataset. In both datasets, 20% are used for training, 10% for validation and 70% for testing (according to previous works). We utilize state-of-the-art EA methods for comparison, i.e., MTransE [2], ITransE [3], BootEA [6], KDCoE [7] and GCN [5]. We also report the results generated by name embedding, East(NE), which can reflect the importance of name information.

Evaluation Protocol. We consider Hits@k (k = 1, 10) and mean reciprocal rank (MRR) as evaluation metrics. For each target entity in test set, the entities in the other KG would be ranked according to their distance D to target entity in an ascending order. Hits@k reflects the percentage of correctly aligned entities in top-k closest entities for target entities. Unless otherwise specified, the results of Hits@k are represented in percentages.

Results. Table 1 presents the results of cross-lingual EA. ITransE merely achieves 10.14% Hits@1 score on En-Fr and 6.55% on En-De. This might be explained that it is designed for mono-lingual EA task and might not adapt well to cross-lingual EA where there is a higher inconsistency among KGs. The results of MTransE and GCN(SE) are equally matched on En-De, while MTransE outperforms GCN on En-Fr. This demonstrates that GCN is more sensitive to the consistency of KGs.

BootEA outperforms MTransE by over 0.1 on MRR, whereas it is inferior to KDCoE on En-Fr in terms of all metrics. This reveals the significance of textual information. Nevertheless, on En-De, KDCoE achieves worse results than BootEA on both Hits@10 and MRR, which indicates that entity description sometimes can bring noise and hurt the overall performance. In contrast to entity description text, entity name might be a more stable source of textual information as East(NE) exceeds KDCoE by 0.2 in terms of MRR on En-De. Integrating East(NE) with structural information and self-training framework, East further improves the performance and its Hits@1 value already doubles that of KDCoE on En-De.

Table 1. Results on Wk3l60k

	En-Fr			En-De		
	Hits@1	Hits@10	MRR	Hits@1	Hits@10	MRR
MTransE	27.4	33.98	0.309	17.9	31.59	0.225
ITransE	10.14	11.59	0.106	6.55	11.44	0.076
GCN	13.39	30.91	0.193	16.98	31.6	0.22
BootEA	33.1	56.73	0.412	29.39	48.76	0.36
KDCoE	48.32	56.95	0.496	33.52	45.47	0.349
East(NE)	39.19	59.2	0.461	48.4	67.31	0.549
East	**61.35**	**76.67**	**0.664**	**68.54**	**80.87**	**0.725**

Ablation Study. To testify the effectiveness of each component, we perform ablation study on East. Specifically, there are six variants, East-SA (removing soft alignment), East-ST (removing self-training process), East-NE (removing name embedding), East-SE (removing structural embedding), East-NE-ST (removing name embedding and self-training), East-SE-ST (removing structural embedding and self-training). As revealed in Fig. 1, all components in East contribute positively to the overall results.

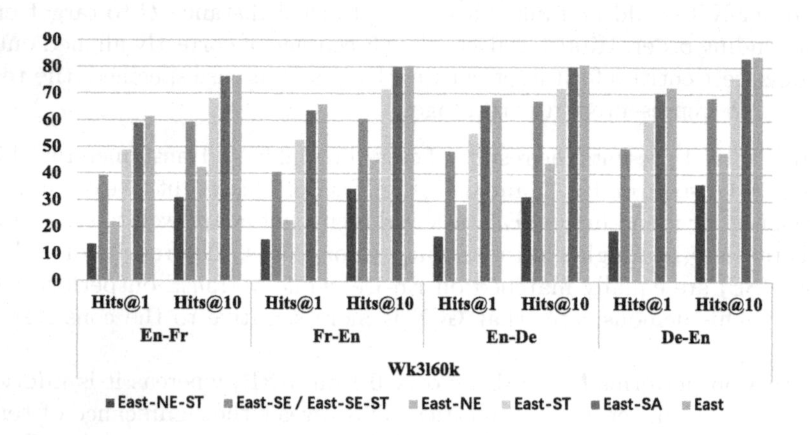

Fig. 1. Ablation study.

References

1. Paulheim, H.: Knowledge graph refinement: a survey of approaches and evaluation methods. Semant. Web **8**(3), 489–508 (2017)
2. Chen, M., Tian, Y., Yang, M., Zaniolo, C.: Multilingual knowledge graph embeddings for cross-lingual knowledge alignment. In: IJCAI, pp. 1511–1517 (2017)
3. Zhu, H., Xie, R., Liu, Z., Sun, M.: Iterative entity alignment via joint knowledge embeddings. In: IJCAI, pp. 4258–4264 (2017)
4. Sun, Z., Hu, W., Li, C.: Cross-lingual entity alignment via joint attribute-preserving embedding. In: d'Amato, C., et al. (eds.) ISWC 2017. LNCS, vol. 10587, pp. 628–644. Springer, Cham (2017). https://doi.org/10.1007/978-3-319-68288-4_37
5. Wang, Z., Lv, Q., Lan, X., Zhang, Y..: Cross-lingual knowledge graph alignment via graph convolutional networks. In: EMNLP, pp. 349–357 (2018)
6. Sun, Z., Hu, W., Zhang, Q., Qu, Y.: Bootstrapping entity alignment with knowledge graph embedding. In: IJCAI, pp. 4396–4402 (2018)
7. Chen, M., Tian, Y., Chang, K.-W., Skiena, S., Zaniolo, C.: Co-training embeddings of knowledge graphs and entity descriptions for cross-lingual entity alignment. In: IJCAI, pp. 3998–4004 (2018)
8. Kipf, T.N., Welling, M.: Semi-supervised classification with graph convolutional networks. CoRR, abs/1609.02907 (2016)
9. Conneau, A., Lample, G., Ranzato, M.A., Denoyer, L., Jégou, H.: Word translation without parallel data. CoRR, abs/1710.04087 (2017)
10. Trsedya, B.D., Qi, J., Zhang, R.: Entity alignment between knowledge graphs using attribute embeddings. In: AAAI (2019)

Fourth Workshop on Data Science for Social Good (SoGood 2019)

Workshop on Data Science for Social Good (SoGood 2019)

The *Fourth Workshop on Data Science for Social Good (SoGood 2019)* was held in conjunction with the *European Conference on Machine Learning and Principles and Practice of Knowledge Discovery in Databases (ECML PKDD 2019)* in Würzburg, Germany, on 20th September 2019. The previous three editions of the workshop were also held jointly with ECML PKDD in 2016–2018.

Data Science has a great potential for contributing to social good (also called common or public good) and benefiting communities and societies. These possibilities, however, are often not sufficiently perceived by the public at large. Emerging Data Science applications are already aiding people at the bottom of the economic pyramid and people with special needs; improving healthcare, public safety and transportation; dealing with environmental problems, disasters and climate change, and promoting sustainable development. In regular conferences and journals, papers on these topics are often scattered in sessions with names such as "Social networks", "Predictive models" or the catch-all term "Applications", which hide the social good nature of these papers. Additionally, such forums tend to have a strong bias for papers that are novel in the strictly technical sense (new algorithms, new kinds of data analysis, new technologies) rather than novel in terms of the social impact of the application.

This workshop aimed to attract papers presenting applications of Data Science to Social Good (which may or may not require new methods), or applications that take into account social aspects of Data Science methods and techniques. It also aimed to bring together researchers, students and practitioners to share their experience and foster discussion about the possible applications, challenges and open research problems, and to continue building a research community in the area of Data Science for Social Good.

There are numerous application domains; the call for papers included the following non-exclusive list:

- Government transparency and IT against corruption
- Public safety and disaster relief
- Access to food, water and utilities
- Efficiency and sustainability
- Data journalism
- Economic, social and personal development
- Transportation
- Energy
- Smart city services
- Education
- Social services, unemployment and homelessness
- Healthcare

- Ethical issues, fairness and accountability
- Topics aligned with the UN Sustainable Development Goals: http://www.un.org/sustainabledevelopment/sustainable-development-goals/

The workshop papers were selected through a peer-reviewed process in which each submitted paper was assigned to three members of the Program Committee. The main selection criteria were the novelty of the application and its social impact. Twelve papers were accepted for presentation.

The *SoGood 2019 Best Paper Award* was awarded to Tobias Bauer, Emre Devrim, William Lopez Jaramillo, Misha Glazunov, Balaganesh Mohan and Gerasimos Spanakis from the University of Maastricht in the Netherlands for their paper "#MeTooMaastricht: Building a Chatbot to Assist Survivors of Sexual Harassment".

The program included two excellent and thought-provoking keynotes:

- "How Can Data Science Make the World a Better Place – Some Examples and Personal Thoughts" by Professor Stan Matwin, Dalhousie University, Canada
- "The Pulse of a City - a Glimpse at a Locality Using Microblogs and Machine Learning" by Professor Osmar Zaiane, University of Alberta, Canada

More information about the workshop, including the slides of the keynote talks, can be found on the workshop website: https://sites.google.com/view/ecmlpkddsogood2019.

We would like to thank Stan Matwin and Osmar Zaiane for their excellent talks, the Program Committee members for their detailed and constructive reviews, the authors for their well-prepared presentations, and all workshop attendees for their engagement and participation – thank you for making this workshop a very successful event.

December 2019

Ricard Gavaldà
Irena Koprinska
João Gama

SoGood 2019 Workshop Organization

Workshop Co-chairs

Ricard Gavaldà	UPC BarcelonaTech, Spain, gavalda@cs.upc.edu
Irena Koprinska	University of Sydney, Australia, irena.koprinska@sydney.edu.au
João Gama	University of Porto, Portugal, jgama@fep.up.pt

Program Committee

Marta Arias	UPC BarcelonaTech, Spain
Albert Bifet	Telecom ParisTech, France
Itziar de Lecuona	University of Barcelona, Spain
José del Campo	University of Málaga, Spain
Jeremiah Deng	University of Otago, New Zealand
Cèsar Ferri	Technical University of Valencia, Spain
Geoffrey Holmes	University of Waikato, New Zealand
Josep-Lluís Larriba-Pey	UPC BarcelonaTech, Spain
Ana Nogueira	INESC TEC, Portugal
Maria Pedroto	INESC TEC, Portugal
Rita Ribeiro	University of Porto, Portugal
Sónia Teixeira	INESC TEC, Portugal
Emma Tonkin	University of Bristol, UK
Alicia Troncoso	University Pablo de Olavide, Spain
Evgueni Smirnov	University of Maastricht, The Netherlands
Kristina Yordanova	University of Rostock, Germany
Martí Zamora	UPC BarcelonaTech, Spain

SoGood 2019 Keynote Talks

How Can Data Science Make the World a Better Place – Some Examples and Personal Thoughts

Stan Matwin

Dalhousie University, Canada

Abstract. We will present briefly several projects that - working with various types of data - had very different social improvement goals as their objectives. In the first project, joint work with NGOs PeaceGeeks and UMATI, we analyzed twitter traffic in Kenya. Based on Susan Benesch's hate speech theory, the goal was to detect violence-inducing social media posts. In the second project we have analyzed the equality-driven social media activism of women in Saudi Arabia. In another project, starting with a gender studies framework describing different kinds of sexist language, we used Machine Learning and text mining to find sexism in social media (twitter) data. We will also discuss select cases of environmental and economic Data Science for the Social Good (DSSG). One elegant example involves the work of Trygg Mat Tracking, a Norwegian company that uses a specialized ocean big data to monitor, and effectively fight, illegal fishing in East Africa. The Data for Development (D4D) Data Challenge is another example of an interesting initiative in DSSG. We will close with some personal thoughts and recommendations as to what makes a good DSSG project.

Biography. Stan Matwin is a Professor and Canada Research Chair (Tier 1), and the Director of the Institute for Big Data Analytics at Dalhousie University, Canada. Internationally recognized for his work in Machine Learning and Artificial Intelligence, he has authored and co-authored more than 300 refereed papers, supervised more than 70 graduate students, and taught Data Science on four continents. He is the Coordinator for the Applications Area of the Springer Encyclopedia of Machine Learning, and one of the founders of Ocean Data Science Inc., a new Canadian start-up. He is a Fellow of the European Coordinating Committee for AI, a Fellow of the Canadian AI Society (CAIAC), and a recipient of the CAIAC Lifetime Achievement Award.

The Pulse of a City - a Glimpse at a Locality Using Microblogs and Machine Learning

Osmar Zaïane

University of Alberta, Canada

Abstract. Since the advent of Web 2.0 and social media, anyone with an Internet connection can create content online. Popular social media applications, such as microblogging with Twitter, are used for a number of reasons. Users can share millions of posts daily on Twitter to cover events real-time, express opinions or simply describe their daily life. Many argue that the majority of information shared this way is worthless. However, someone's trash is someone-else's treasure.

In this ongoing work, we present the Grebe social data aggregation framework for extracting geo-fenced Twitter data for analysis of user engagement in health and wellness topics. Grebe also provides various visualization tools for analyzing temporal and geographical health trends. A large dataset of geo-fenced twitter posts was collected to analyze three types of contexts: geographical context via prediction of user location using supervised learning, topical context via determining health-related tweets using various learning approaches and a six dimensional wellness model, and affective context via sentiment analysis of tweets using rule-based methods.

When location is determined, the information in tweets can be used, not only to learn about what is happening in a city, but also to understand users' emotions (e.g., love, fear) and sentiments (e.g., positive, negative) on topics and events as they unfold over time. An interactive visualization tool was developed to compare and contrast sentiments and emotions during different temporal periods at city level.

Biography. Osmar R. Zaïane is a Professor in Computing Science at the University of Alberta, Canada, and Scientific Director of the Alberta Machine Intelligence Institute (Amii). Dr. Zaiane obtained his Ph.D. from Simon Fraser University, Canada, in 1999. He has published more than 300 papers in refereed international conferences and journals. He is Associate Editor of many international journals on data mining and data analytics and served as program chair and general chair for scores of international conferences in the field of knowledge discovery and data mining. Dr. Zaiane received numerous awards including the 2010 ACM SIGKDD Service Award from the ACM Special Interest Group on Data Mining, which runs the world's premier data science, big data, and data mining association and conference.

#MeTooMaastricht: Building a Chatbot to Assist Survivors of Sexual Harassment

Tobias Bauer, Emre Devrim, Misha Glazunov, William Lopez Jaramillo, Balaganesh Mohan, and Gerasimos Spanakis(✉)

Department of Data Science and Knowledge Engineering, Maastricht University, Maastricht, The Netherlands
jerry.spanakis@maastrichtuniversity.nl

Abstract. Inspired by the recent social movement of #MeToo, we are building a chatbot to assist survivors of sexual harassment cases (designed for the city of Maastricht but can easily be extended). The motivation behind this work is twofold: properly assist survivors of such events by directing them to appropriate institutions that can offer them help and increase the incident documentation so as to gather more data about harassment cases which are currently under reported. We break down the problem into three data science/machine learning components: harassment type identification (treated as a classification problem), spatio-temporal information extraction (treated as Named Entity Recognition problem) and dialogue with the users (treated as a slot-filling based chatbot). We are able to achieve a success rate of more than 98% for the identification of a harassment-or-not case and around 80% for the specific type harassment identification. Locations and dates are identified with more than 90% accuracy and time occurrences prove more challenging with almost 80%. Finally, initial validation of the chatbot shows great potential for the further development and deployment of such a beneficial for the whole society tool.

Keywords: Chatbots · Named entity recognition · Classification

1 Introduction

As one of the most influential social movements in recent years, #MeToo has enabled sexual harassment to rise to the surface that usually does not get the attention required [1]. There are various types of sexual harassment such as verbal, physical or non-verbal issues in real life and unfortunately, those are some of the most under-reported criminal offenses. Most survivors (we intentionally use the terminology "survivors" instead of "victims") may not be willing to go to the police or reveal these issues on social media or even people around, although

---

T. Bauer, E. Devrim, M. Glazunov, W.L. Jaramillo and B. Mohan—Equal contribution.

P. Cellier and K. Driessens (Eds.): ECML PKDD 2019 Workshops, CCIS 1167, pp. 503–521, 2020.
https://doi.org/10.1007/978-3-030-43823-4_41

they are affected mentally or physically or both. There are plenty of reasons for this under reporting, for example, the feeling of shame or embarrassment [2].

In this nonprofit project, #MetooMaastricht, we aim to help sexual harassment survivors in the city of Maastricht, Netherlands. Therefore, we introduce the idea of an intelligent tool (namely a chatbot), which can retrieve crucial information from survivors' texts such as the types of harassment as well as the time and location of the event in order to suggest the best set of actions.

Bearing in mind the previous studies in sexual harassment and text mining techniques our main research questions are defined as follows:

- How can we best design and implement an intelligent chatbot in order to advise people affected by harassment cases?
- How can we successfully classify different types of harassment cases based on short texts by using text classification techniques?
- Can we extract time and location information from these texts?
- How can we use the information extracted from our models in our final product, a chatbot, for proper guidance to survivors?

2 Related Work

Most of the work in this project is based on concepts and techniques used in the domain of natural language processing (NLP), so in this section, we set the theoretical framework of our project.

2.1 Language Representation

Getting from raw text to computer-based language representations is a crucial task in NLP [3]. We briefly describe the most influential ones here: traditional sparse representations (word count vectors etc.) and modern dense representations (word embeddings etc.).

Sparse Representations. The most basic representations of text requires simply counting terms and represent different texts as rows and frequency of each possible term as columns. This approach would result in higher values for more repetitive words and longer texts, advanced techniques to find out relative importance of a term were derived such as TF-IDF vectors [4]. These vectors consist of two terms; the first one is Term Frequency (TF), which is the ratio of a specific term in a document. The second one is Inverse Document Frequency (IDF) that is equal to the logarithm of the ratio of the total number of documents over the number of documents containing such term within the corpus. Those vectors can be created based on various input types such as words, characters or combination of N terms (N-grams) [5].

Word Embeddings. The motivation behind finding better representations for categorical data comes from the limitations of the traditional use of one-hot encoding mapping of categorical variables, where each category is mapped to a high N-dimensional vector consisting of a single "one" representing a specific value in the variable category, and N-1 zeroes alongside representing the other possible values for the same variable. To overcome the limitations present in one hot encoding representations, approaches such as Word2vec models have been used in NLP. These models create a dense high dimensional vector representation for each unique word in the corpus of a text input. The vectors obtained are positioned in the vector space such that words that share the same context or are similar are close to one another in that space [6]. The two main model architectures used in the Word2vec algorithm are: continuous bag-of-word (CBOW) and skip-gram (SG) models. The main difference between the two of them is that while CBOW takes multiple context of each word as inputs and tries to predict the word corresponding to its context, skip-gram uses the target word to predict the context [7].

Document/Paragraph Embeddings. Paragraph or document vector (Doc2vec) is the extended version of Word2vec such that Word2vec learns the d-dimensional representation of words while Doc2vec aims to learn projection of documents into dimensional space. For this purpose, the authors of the Doc2vec simply introduced an additional document vector along with word vectors into Word2vec [8]. Therefore, while training the word vectors, the document vector is trained as well, that gives us the numeric representation of the document. Similar to Word2vec, Doc2vec has two main models which are Distributed Memory (DM) and Distributed Bag of Words (DBOW). DM is analogous to CBOW that uses document feature vector in addition to surrounding words to predict the target word. On the other hand, DBOW is similar to skip-gram that tries to predict randomly sampled words from the paragraph as outputs.

State-of-the-Art Language Models and Representations. By combining the latest achievements in language modelling by means of transformers based on self-attention with the idea of deep contextualized word-piece embeddings together with pretraining universal language model, several NLP and AI research groups introduced universal language models that can be subsequently fine-tuned for a specific NLP task.

Google AI group introduced the so-called bidirectional encoder representations from transformers or BERT for short [9]. Google has made BERT code and implementation available, as well as pre trained BERT models on different languages on huge amounts of data where only minor changes can be done to the model to fine tune it to the tasks needed. On top of this research several frameworks have incorporated the current state-of-the-art models such as DeepPavlov [10], a python library that builds upon BERT, and many others allowing the user to combine them to improve on many NLP tasks.

2.2 Text Classification

Text classification is widely used as part of supervised machine learning to tackle similar problems such as sentiment analysis or categorization of articles. Prior to the 1990s, the most common approach were rule-based classification systems, which were manually constructed for each class based on expert opinion [11]. Machine Learning techniques have started to dominate old-fashioned rule-based systems in the following decades, as they help to decrease a remarkable amount of engineering effort on rule construction. Text representations (as discussed in the previous paragraphs) play an important role here. Different models can be applied based on the representation basis (TF-IDF vectors, word embeddings, etc.) or the techniques (traditional machine learning algorithms like logistic regression, support vector machines, etc. or deep learning models like recurrent neural networks).

2.3 Named Entity Recognition

Named Entity Recognition (NER) is an NLP task that attempts extracting the so called "named entities" from a text. Named entities may include persons, organizations, locations, time, etc. The most common classical way of NER is based on sequence model tagging like Conditional Random Fields (CRF) [12]. State-of-the-art methods of NER are also based on the fine-tuning of pre-trained universal language models (such as BERT which was described previously).

One of the challenges in NER is disambiguation: tagging a named entity appropriately frequently implies knowledge about the world than cannot be deduced from the formal text analysis only. To that end various knowledge bases and semantic ontologies may be of use. Some of them aim at the specific lexical areas such as WordNet [13] that allows handling of synonym/antonym words together with a simple hierarchy of hypernyms and hyponyms. Other techniques aim at constructing universal knowledge graphs that represent all the possible knowledge concepts within a single graph with complex and diverse links between them like Wikidata [14] which stores information from Wikipedia in a structured way available for online querying.

2.4 Chatbots

Chatbot technology was firstly introduced with the implementation of ELIZA in 1964. It was the first program to make Natural language conversation with a computer possible [15]. ELIZA tackled five problems of a chatbot "the identification of critical words, the discovery of a minimal context, the choice of appropriate transformations, the generation of responses appropriate to the transformation or in the absence of critical words". These are the basic rules still applicable even in modern chatbots.

Today, chatbots have come a long way, and together with more complex NLP modules are used in many business setups for automatic answering and other functions. Some of the most used frameworks include Facebook's wit.ai[1] and Google's Dialogflow API[2]. The operation of modern chatbots does not require any stand-alone platforms; they can be integrated into massively used messaging platforms such as Facebook Messenger, Google Assistant or Telegram.

3 Methodology

To answer our research questions, we used data available from SafeCity[3] regarding previous harassment reports written by survivors in India. Based on this data, we have trained models with different approaches to classify the cases into different kinds of harassment. Then, by using harassment cases correctly identified by the classifier, we aimed to extract spatio-temporal subject information to properly assist the survivor. This assistance consists of a set of instructions recommended by the chatbot (our final product). All the inputs and end products of this project are designed for English language.

3.1 Dataset

The SafeCity reports contain around 12,000 precise texts in English mainly mentioning commenting, ogling and groping issues. Moreover, there are more severe physical harassment cases mentioned as well. Also, it should be underlined that a report naturally may include more than one types of harassment. Figure 1 shows the distribution of several types of harassment in such reports used for this project.

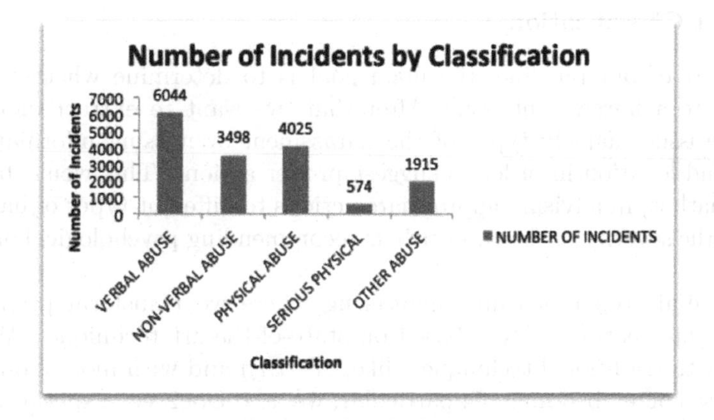

Fig. 1. Number of harassment types in SafeCity

[1] https://wit.ai/.
[2] https://dialogflow.com/.
[3] https://safecity.in/.

Text Pre-processing. We applied the following pre-processing pipeline by taking into account the nature of the reports provided by SafeCity.

- **Contraction handling:** Replacing word contractions such as *I'm* with their unabbreviated form *I am* taking into account misspellings such as *Im*. This was done using regular expressions.
- **Special character removal:** Removing special characters such as $ and double spaces. This was done using regular expressions as well.
- **Spelling correction:** Simple spelling correction function available in Python was added that uses Levenshtein distance [16].
- **Negation handling:** Simple negation handling approach was used in order to identify the word *not* and finding an antonym for the following word, then replacing both not and its following word with the antonym. This was done using the Wordnet synonym-antonym lexicon from the NLTK in Python [13] following a similar approach to [17].
- **Lemmatization:** In the feature extraction process for Text Classification models, the corpus was lemmatized in both Bag of Words and Embeddings approaches. This was done using the SpaCy [18].
- **Lower case:** For the majority of tasks (except Named-entity Recognition) the text was converted to lowercase, since this reduced the corpus size and made no difference in most of the tasks.
- **Part-of-Speech Tags:** We used SpaCy again to find out the most frequent POS tags to visualize our reports (See word clouds in the Appendix). Additionally, we created some models using only these tags but dropped this idea since we couldn't observe performance improvements.

3.2 Text Classification

In this part of our pipeline, the main goal is to determine whether a report is related to a harassment issue. After that, we want to extract more details about the issue, namely types of the harassment or missing information such as time and location in order to suggest proper actions. This would be helpful for our chatbot, in advising appropriate actions to different types of harassment based on the severity of the case such as recommending psychological or medical support.

The initial step is feature engineering where we transform pre-processed text data into feature vectors based on state-of-the-art techniques. We experimented with traditional techniques (like TF-IDF) and with more modern techniques based on embeddings. In particular, we used Doc2vec, a special version of Word2vec for documents/paragraphs [8]. Logistic Regression and Support Vector Machine models were built by using the representations and their performance are discussed in the results under Sect. 4.

Figure 2 shows a graphical representation of the workflow used to do the classification task.

3.3 Named Entity Recognition

To provide specific assistance to the survivors of harassment, we are interested in the spatial and temporal information of an incident. Spatial information (in this context) is the place where the harassment has occurred. Temporal information, on the other hand, is information about the date and time of the incident. This information can help us provide the right instructions on which actions a survivor should take and can help towards building a spatio-temporal map of harassment cases in Maastricht. To receive these types of information we applied different named entity recognition techniques.

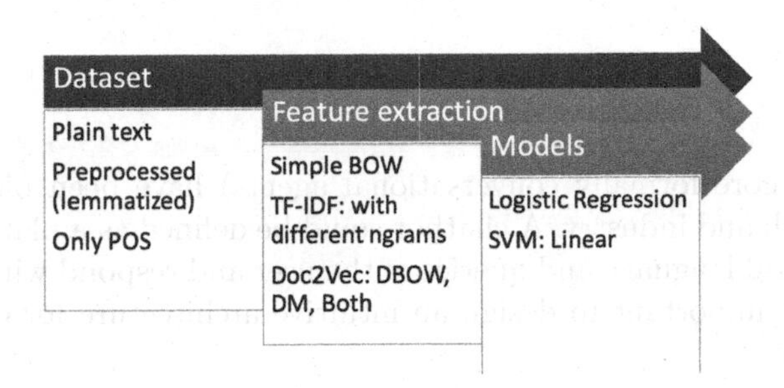

Fig. 2. Classification flow

In our project we applied state-of-the-art techniques (mainly based on CRF models) and modern pretraining/finetuning techniques. For the first part we made use of available solutions in several software packages that are freely distributed, namely the Natural Language Toolkit (NLTK) (Python), the spaCy library (Python) and the Stanford CoreNLP software (Java).

Each of the package exploits different approaches in identifying named entities, so we estimated their capabilities (e.g., entities they are able to extract, the annotation type BIO or BILUO) and identified the one that best fits our needs based on this research study [19], namely, Stanford CoreNLP. We considered entities only on the same sentence level, so no co-reference and anaphora resolution have been applied.

BERT Model Finetuning. 2018 gave a rise to new successfully applied trends in NLP, namely, unsupervised universal language model pretraining and a subsequent fine-tuning of such a model to the specific NLP task. For this task, we considered Google AI BERT encapsulated into DeepPavlov framework and which was fine-tuned on several widely-used NER datasets for benchmarking such as OntoNotes [20] and CoNLL 2003 [21]. Fine-tuning is basically a form of transfer learning: It is applied using a pre-trained generative language model [9,22]. Large neural networks have been trained on general tasks such as language modelling and then fine-tuned for classification tasks. Particularly, NLP tasks can be fine-tuned with the same single model. In our project we used approach based on universal language model fine-tuning for named entity recognition, namely, pre-trained BERT model for NER task was used for sequence tagging. The framework that is used for Bert NER is DeepPavlov[4]. The model is based on the Transformer architecture [23].

Knowledge Base Incorporation. The problem of the wrong NER labeling for cases when a location is labelled as a person has been addressed by means of Wikidata. Namely, each person entity is being queried and checked for the presence of the property related to geographical coordinates in the knowledge base. If such property is found there then the person tag is relabelled to the location.

3.4 Chatbot

Chatbots (or more formally conversational agents) have been blooming lately both in research and industry. A chatbot could be defined as a platform that can deal with natural language and queries of the user and respond with appropriate responses. It is important to design an intuitive architecture for conversational user experience.

Design Details. The conversation flow must be designed in order to gather all the data required to provide correct information. An example of incomplete information follows ("U" stands for user and "A" stands for the chatbot answer):

U: Hello
A: Hello, how are you feeling today?
U: Not very well.
A: May I ask what happened?
U: I was walking down the xyz street and a group of men called me mean things.
A: I'm so sorry that happened to you. I will try my best to help you with this.

This dialogue doesn't give detailed information such as the type of the incident as well as the exact time and location that are required to provide useful information to the user. "Mean things" cannot be classified into any kind of legit harassment type. This is why it is important for the chatbot to get direct answers from the user with clear information. To overcome this, we will employ a slot filling based chatbot architecture.

[4] http://docs.deeppavlov.ai/en/master/components/ner.html.

Slot Filling Based Dialogue Modeling. Slot filling is a way to represent the crucial components that the chatbot should extract from a conversation with any use. In a way, slots are used to represent the semantics of the dialogue. For example, consider the following dialogue (where "U" stands for the user, "A" stands for the answer of the chatbot).

U: I was walking down in Frankenstraat yesterday evening and a bunch of mean were staring at me!
P: I was walking down in {location} {time} and {harassment type}

slots:

- harassment type: a bunch of mean were staring at me
- location: Frankenstraat
- time: yesterday

A: I am sorry that happened to you! suggest appropriate action like helpline phone number

Based on the example, we define three slots for our architecture (and we also present some challenges):

@Date: Dates can be given in international formats like mm/dd/yy or verbally written like 24th of April etc.

@Time: Yesterday cannot be a valid time slot, so the system has to reply with an query for asking for exact time, e.g. I'm sorry that happened to you, I am trying to get the help you need, but I need the exact time frame of the incident. Alternatively, we can use the system time to understand the meta like yesterday and today.

@location: Frankenstraat is a valid slot location.

We also define what will the different intents of the conversation are. In our case, intents are the different type of harassment, and entities are the slots, i.e. date, time and locations. More specifically, we define three intent categories: physical abuse, verbal abuse and non-verbal abuse.

Approaches for Chatbot. Nowadays, chatbots can be broadly classified as rule-based (scripted) or end-to-end (usually based on deep learning) chatbots. For this project, we experimented with both but decided to proceed with a rule-based approach because of the lack of necessity for a deep learning chatbot and data for training a dataset being very small for deep learning to be useful.

Telegram[5] is a mass communication application used worldwide similar to alternative applications such as Facebook Messenger or WhatsApp[6]. Telegram has support where users can interact with bots by sending them messages, commands and inline requests. The bot created by the API can be specialized for our use case by integrating our NLP platform for question answering. A script was written based on the intents and entities of the several scenarios with appropriate reply vocabularies using python and Telegram API.

[5] https://telegram.org/.
[6] https://www.whatsapp.com/.

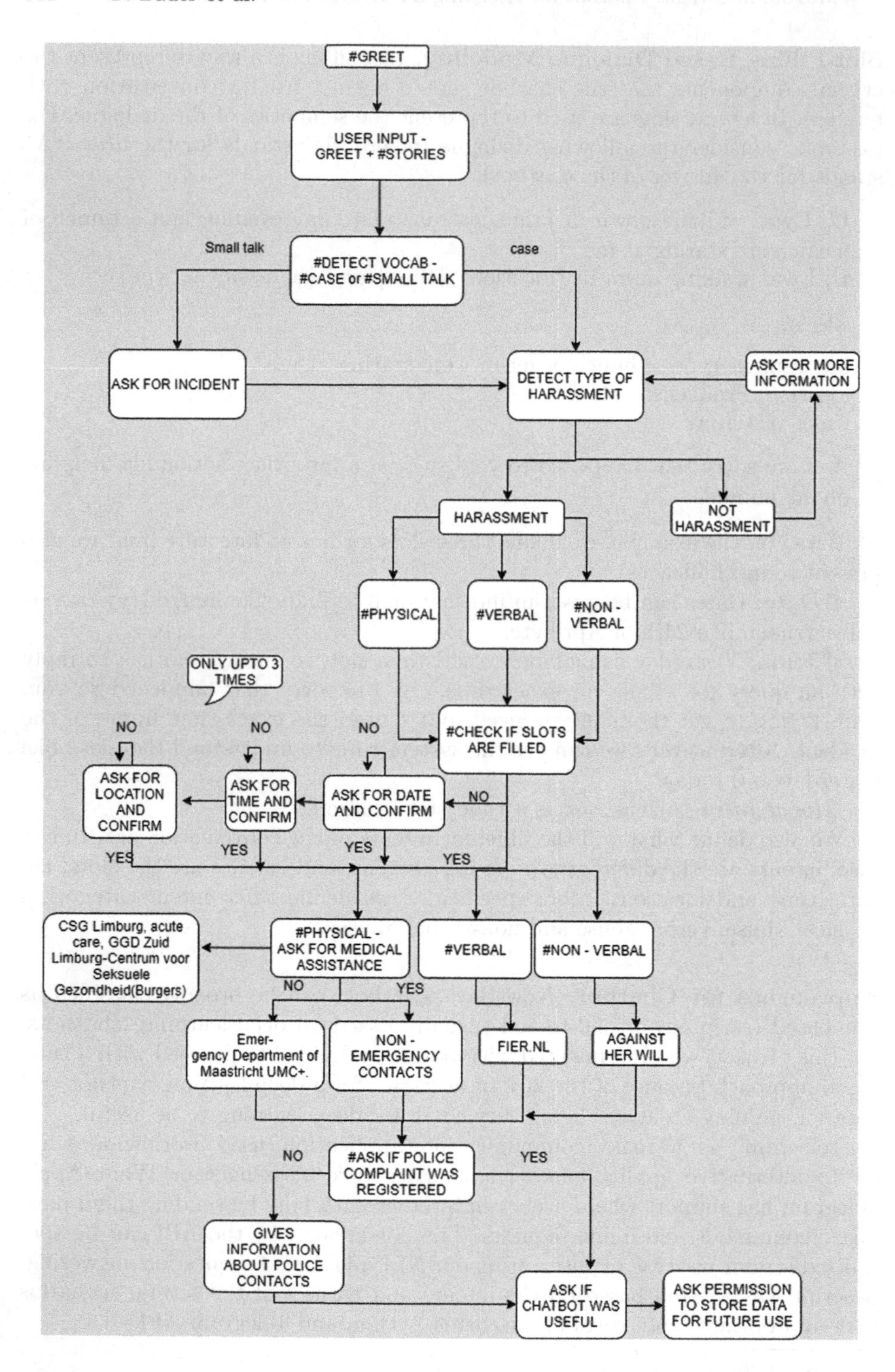

Fig. 3. Chat dialogue flow

Chatbot - Dialogue Flowchart. The ultimate goal of the chatbot is to provide the user with the necessary information based on their input. This has to be as diverse as possible and the conversations must be natural and efficient at the same time. The overall chat workflow is shown in Fig. 3 and each block will have chatbot reply with unique sentences which were framed with the help of experts[7].

Initially, the chatbot greets the user and asks for information about the possible harassment event. If the user's input is not classified as a harassment case, the chatbot continues to ask. At every step for the user the text sent by the user is concatenated to its previous inputs and it is sent to the classification and named entity recognition system for evaluation. Once the text is classified as harassment, depending on whether the location, date and time information could be retrieved, the chatbot either asks the user for that information if it was missing, or asks the user to confirm the retrieved location, date or time information from the previous input. When there is some slot (location, date or time) missing information the chatbot will ask the user for the details up to 3 times per slot and continue asking for information to fill the next slot. Once all the slots are filled or the attempts to do so have been executed, depending on the type of abuse (physical, verbal, non verbal) identified in the users input the chatbot will provide specific information to the user depending on the case.

When physical abuse is detected, the chatbot provides information for medical assistance (Emergency Department of Maastricht UMC+), Centrum Seksueel Geweld Limburg (CSG Limburg), Acute care (for crises or emergencies), GGD Zuid Limburg-Centrum voor Seksuele Gezondheid (Burgers). When verbal abuse is detected, the chatbot provides information of fier.nl[8], an online chat for support for this kind of abuse. When non-verbal abuse is detected, the chatbot provides information of "Against her will", another organization specialised in this kind of abuse. Obviously, the specific information provided for each case can be further tailored.

Finally, the user is asked if they have reported the event to the police and relevant information is provided and in the end the chatbot asks the user if they found the process useful and ask for consent to keep the user's data anonymously for further use (e.g. more training data or provide the relevant authorities with more cases).

4 Results and Validation

4.1 Classification Models

We define 4 classification (sub)problems as follows:

- **Harassment or not:** First of all, we wanted to see that at what level we can diversify a harassment case from any similar short text which is written

[7] United Nations University - Maastricht.
[8] https://www.fier.nl/chat.

by a user on the Internet. Therefore, we collected datasets consisting of some user reviews on IMDB, Amazon or tweets on Twitter as the negative class of our target.

- **Labeling verbal abuses among all harassment reports:** As a next step, we created models in order to catch verbal abuses among all harassment cases. We already had those labels thanks to the SafeCity dataset.
- **Labeling non-verbal abuses among all harassment reports:** Similar to verbal models.
- **Labeling physical abuses among all harassment reports:** Since the number of serious physical abuses was low, they were merged to physical abuses.

For these models, different datasets were created in which numbers of positive and negative classes were in balance. In order to compare candidate models properly, 30% of the data were selected as a test set which was stratified by the target. Then, combinations of various text types, feature extraction methods and modeling techniques were implemented as can be seen in Fig. 2.

In the final models, which are input for the chatbot, two models for each classification problem were created by using pre-processed (lemmatized) text. Those use TF-IDF with up to 3 n-grams and Doc2Vec with Distributed Bag of Words (DBOW) approaches respectively. We decided to use these different approaches since both resulted in a good performance in the test set and ensembling them in the chatbot would give us more robust outcomes.

As the classification model, both use Logistic Regression since it has performed better than SVM and returns the probability that gives us the flexibility to change the cutoff. The chatbot is capable of processing incoming texts through the same steps and classify them. Figure 4 shows the performance of final models on test sets.

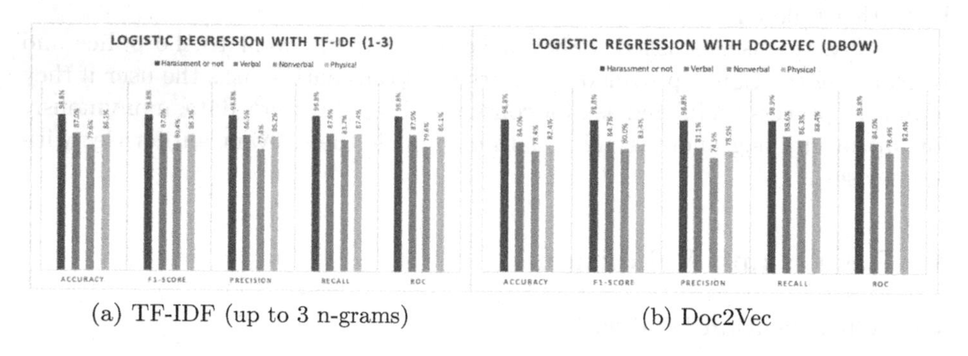

(a) TF-IDF (up to 3 n-grams)   (b) Doc2Vec

Fig. 4. Logistic regression models final performance

4.2 NER Validation

For the named entity recognition we did a validation using a self made dataset. We created this dataset by writing 5 short reports of harassment cases. In these reports we set the named entities with placeholder variables. To show that the NER model works for a variety of different named entities we downloaded a list of 12900 city names from around the world from SimpleMaps[9]. To further verify that the model is able to identify date and time information in a text we chose different formats to represent those information that can be inserted into the reports. Examples for the date format are: "yesterday", "5 months ago" or "on the 5th July 2019". On the other hand examples for a time format are: "around 10 am", "at 10 o'clock" or "at night".

In the next step we inserted these location, date and time information into the reports at the designated positions randomly. Subsequently we put the resulting reports into the different NER models and compared the results provided by these with the original named entities. To avoid cases in which the detected named entities match except for the prefix we removed prefixes from both strings.

Table 1. Validation results for accuracy

Classifier	Location	Date	Time
BERT with Ontonotes	0.92	0.934	0.798
BERT with CoNLL	0.976	–	–
Stanford	0.45	0.2	0.1

To receive comparable results for the three different used NER models namely Stanford, BERT trained on CoNLL corpora and BERT trained on Ontonotes we generated for each report template 100 variations with randomly picked named entities and used them as input for the models. Table 1 shows the result of these tests. It can be seen that both BERT models deliver reasonable results for the identification of location entities. However the BERT model trained on CoNLL corpora is not able to identify any information about the date or time. However the results produced by BERT are significantly better than the results from the Stanford NER model. The drop of accuracy for time information in the BERT model can be explained by looking at the returned values. Apparently there is some confusion between date and time information.

4.3 Chatbot Validation

Because of the complexity of the chatbot dialogue flow we were not able to validate the chatbot entirely. However, we were able to write scripts of specific showcases and compare the responses given by the chatbot with the responses we expected.

In the first scenario we don't greet the chatbot at all and just report to it an incidence that is clearly a form of physical harassment. We also provide all necessary information about the location, date and time of the incident directly

[9] https://simplemaps.com/data/world-cities.

in the first message. Thus the bot just asks us to confirm this information. In the next step we expect that the bot asks if we need medical assistance. We decline that and the bot gives us the contact details of CSG Limburg, acute care and the GGD Zuid Limburg-Centrum voor Seksuele Gezondheid. Afterwards the bot asks us if we reported the incidence to the police. We answer with yes, so the bot does not give us any additional information and just asks us if it was helpful. To try out if everything is working we answer with no. In the last step the bot asks if it can store the data anonymously. We accept this and the bot ends the conversation as expected.

In the second scenario we greet the bot and introduce ourselves as John in the first message. Thus we expect the bot to ask us about the incident. So the second message we send describes an incident that can be categorized as a form of verbal abuse. But this time we do not provide any information about the location, date or time at all. So we expect the bot to ask us about the location this incident took place. So we tell the bot that this took place "in Maastricht" and confirm with yes after the it asks us if this is correct. In the next step the bot asks us about the date on which the abuse occurred. Again we give it the answer straight away by replying with "yesterday" and confirm with yes. Lastly the bot asks us at which time it occurred and we answer with "at 10 am" and confirm once again. In the next step, since the report clearly described an incident of verbal abuse the bot gives us the contact information of fier.nl and asks us if the police was already informed. We reply with "no" and receive the contact information of the local police department. Afterwards the bot asks us again if it was helpful. We answer with yes this time and the bot then asks for permission to store our data. This time we refuse and the bot says us goodbye and ends the conversation.

In the last scenario we send the bot a message that clearly has nothing to do with any form of sexual harassment. Hence we expect the bot to ask for more information. So in the next message we report an incidence that falls under the category of non-verbal abuse. But again we do not provide any information about the location, date or time. Thus the bot asks us where and when this took place. We reply three times with a message that clearly does not contain any information about the location, date or time. Thus the bot continues by giving us information about "Against her will" and asking us if it was reported to the police, if the bot was helpful and if it can store the data.

The complete transcripts of the conversations can be found in the Appendix in Figs. 5, 6 and 7. The responses of the bot match the chat dialogue flow described in Sect. 3.4.

5 Conclusion

#MeToo is a social movement that has attracted great media attention in recent years, especially in social networks. As global awareness is rising, the goal of this work, namely #MeTooMaastricht is to provide survivors of sexual harassment a safe platform to share their experiences and get proper assistance. To this twofold purpose, we implemented a chatbot using the Telegram API. In order to provide the most appropriate help, we have taken into account various factors related to the incident, such as the type of harassment that was experienced as well as the location, date and time of the incident. The latter proved to be challenging, as it is not trivial to extract accurate spatio-temporal info from a chat text about sexual harassment.

Classification of the harassment type was successful by reusing data from SafeCity and combining two models: a TF-IDF with up to 3 n-grams and Doc2Vec with Distributed Bag of Words (DBOW) with a Logistic Regression classifier. Results gave an over 80% accuracy for identification of harassment type. Named entity recognition (NER) was implemented by finetuning BERT state-of-the-art model enhanced by the Wikidata knowledge base and delivered very accurate results for location and dates (90%) and very satisfactory results for time events (80%). Finally, a slot-filling based chatbot was implemented so as to encapsulate the classification and NER frameworks into the dialogue flow.

Initial results of this work are really encouraging into ways that survivors of harassment can be assisted by means of data science. However, there are many possible directions for improvement in the future. First of all, the interaction with the chatbot can be improved in terms of what type of language is used. On this end, we plan to further work with social scientists that can run specific focus groups on validating the script flow. Moreover, we want to explore more possibilities on the technical side (e.g. use location or map info so as to enhance the results of NER) and on the security front (e.g. guarantee anonymity and malicious use). Finally, one of our overarching goals is to have a chatbot which is adaptable to each case (e.g. show empathy when needed) and be less "linear" in its functionality (e.g. act more freely but still within the script).

Acknowledgements. We would like to thank the Safecity website for providing the dataset needed for the first part of this research. We also gratefully acknowledge the valuable contributions of Mary Kaltenberg, post-doctoral fellow at Brandeis University, in building the dialogue flow of the chatbot implemented in this paper.

Appendix

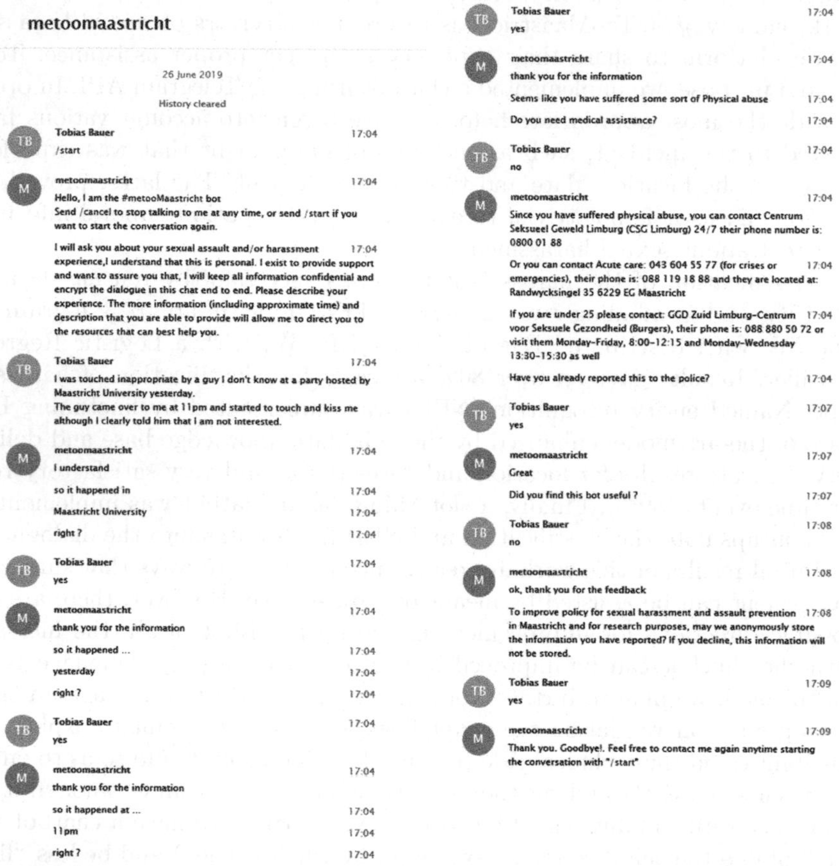

metoomaastricht

26 June 2019

History cleared

Tobias Bauer 17:04
/start

metoomaastricht 17:04
Hello, I am the #metooMaastricht bot
Send /cancel to stop talking to me at any time, or send /start if you want to start the conversation again.

I will ask you about your sexual assault and/or harassment experience,I understand that this is personal. I exist to provide support and want to assure you that, I will keep all information confidential and encrypt the dialogue in this chat end to end. Please describe your experience. The more information (including approximate time) and description that you are able to provide will allow me to direct you to the resources that can best help you. 17:04

Tobias Bauer 17:04
I was touched inappropriate by a guy I don't know at a party hosted by Maastricht University yesterday.
The guy came over to me at 11pm and started to touch and kiss me although I clearly told him that I am not interested.

metoomaastricht 17:04
I understand
so it happened in 17:04
Maastricht University 17:04
right ? 17:04

Tobias Bauer 17:04
yes

metoomaastricht 17:04
thank you for the information
so it happened ... 17:04
yesterday 17:04
right ? 17:04

Tobias Bauer 17:04
yes

metoomaastricht 17:04
thank you for the information
so it happened at ... 17:04
11pm 17:04
right ? 17:04

Tobias Bauer 17:04
yes

metoomaastricht 17:04
thank you for the information
Seems like you have suffered some sort of Physical abuse 17:04
Do you need medical assistance? 17:04

Tobias Bauer 17:04
no

metoomaastricht 17:04
Since you have suffered physical abuse, you can contact Centrum Seksueel Geweld Limburg (CSG Limburg) 24/7 their phone number is: 0800 01 88
Or you can contact Acute care: 043 604 55 77 (for crises or emergencies), their phone is: 088 119 18 88 and they are located at: Randwycksingel 35 6229 EG Maastricht 17:04
If you are under 25 please contact: GGD Zuid Limburg-Centrum voor Seksuele Gezondheid (Burgers), their phone is: 088 880 50 72 or visit them Monday-Friday, 8:00-12:15 and Monday-Wednesday 13:30-15:30 as well 17:04
Have you already reported this to the police? 17:04

Tobias Bauer 17:07
yes

metoomaastricht 17:07
Great
Did you find this bot useful ? 17:07

Tobias Bauer 17:08
no

metoomaastricht 17:08
ok, thank you for the feedback
To improve policy for sexual harassment and assault prevention in Maastricht and for research purposes, may we anonymously store the information you have reported? If you decline, this information will not be stored. 17:08

Tobias Bauer 17:09
yes

metoomaastricht 17:09
Thank you. Goodbye!. Feel free to contact me again anytime starting the conversation with "/start"

Fig. 5. Transcript of scenario 1

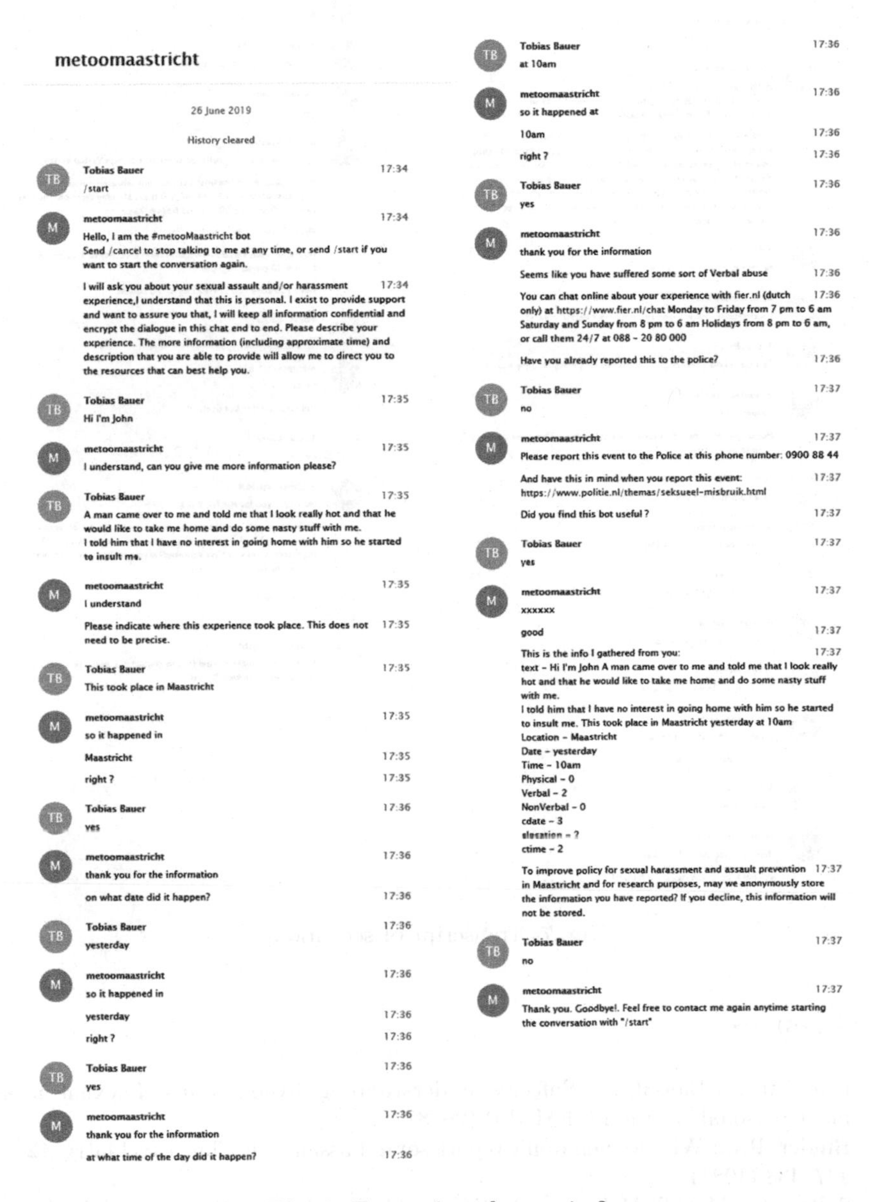

Fig. 6. Transcript of scenario 2

metoomaastricht

26 June 2019

History cleared

Tobias Bauer 18:04
/start

metoomaastricht 18:04
Hello, I am the #metooMaastricht bot
Send /cancel to stop talking to me at any time, or send /start if you want to start the conversation again.

I will ask you about your sexual assault and/or harassment experience,I understand that this is personal. I exist to provide support and want to assure you that, I will keep all information confidential and encrypt the dialogue in this chat end to end. Please describe your experience. The more information (including approximate time) and description that you are able to provide will allow me to direct you to the resources that can best help you. 18:04

Tobias Bauer 18:04
Hi I'm just checking this bot

metoomaastricht 18:04
I understand, can you give me more information please?

Tobias Bauer 18:05
This guy I know always looks at me like he's imagining me naked.

metoomaastricht 18:05
I understand

Please indicate where this experience took place. This does not need to be precise. 18:05

Tobias Bauer 18:05
How does this bot work?

metoomaastricht 18:05
Can you be more explicit please?

Tobias Bauer 18:05
I just want to find out what this bot does.

metoomaastricht 18:05
Can you be more explicit please?

Tobias Bauer 18:05
The story I told was just made up.

metoomaastricht 18:05
thank you for the information

on what date did it happen? 18:05

Tobias Bauer 18:07
I don't know

metoomaastricht 18:07
thank you for the information

at what time of the day did it happen? 18:07

Tobias Bauer 18:07
I don't know

metoomaastricht 18:07
Can you be more explicit please?

Tobias Bauer 18:07
No

metoomaastricht 18:07
Can you be more explicit please?

Tobias Bauer 18:07
No

metoomaastricht 18:07
Seems like you have suffered some sort of Non Verbal abuse

you could contact "Against her will" and talk anonymously their phone is: 0592 – 34 74 44, or visit them Monday through Thursday from 2:00 pm to 5:00 pm and from 6:00 pm to 18:07

Phone: 0592 – 34 74 44 18:07

Hours: Monday through Thursday from 2:00 pm to 5:00 pm and from 6:00 pm to 9:00 pm 18:07

Have you already reported this to the police? 18:07

Tobias Bauer 18:08
yes

metoomaastricht 18:08
Great

Did you find this bot useful ? 18:08

Tobias Bauer 18:08
no

metoomaastricht 18:08
ok, thank you for the feedback

To improve policy for sexual harassment and assault prevention in Maastricht and for research purposes, may we anonymously store the information you have reported? If you decline, this information will not be stored. 18:08

Tobias Bauer 18:08
yes

metoomaastricht 18:08
Thank you. Goodbye!. Feel free to contact me again anytime starting the conversation with "/start"

Fig. 7. Transcript of scenario 3

References

1. Karlekar, S., Bansal, M.: Safecity: understanding diverse forms of sexual harassment personal stories. In: EMNLP (2018)
2. Binder, R.L.: Why women don't report sexual assault. J. Clin. Psychiatry **42**(11), 437–438 (1981)
3. Salton, G., McGill, M.J.: Introduction to Modern Information Retrieval. Mcgraw-Hill, New York (1983)
4. Zhang, W., Yoshida, T., Tang, X.: A comparative study of TF* IDF, LSI and multi-words for text classification. Expert Syst. Appl. **38**(3), 2758–2765 (2011)

5. Cavnar, W.B., Trenkle, J.M., et al.: N-gram-based text categorization. In: Proceedings of SDAIR-94, 3rd Annual Symposium on Document Analysis and Information Retrieval, vol. 161175. Citeseer (1994)
6. Mikolov, T., Chen, K., Corrado, G., Dean, J.: Efficient estimation of word representations in vector space. arXiv preprint arXiv:1301.3781 (2013)
7. Rong, X.: word2vec parameter learning explained. arXiv preprint arXiv:1411.2738 (2014)
8. Le, Q., Mikolov, T.: Distributed representations of sentences and documents. In: International Conference on Machine Learning, pp. 1188–1196 (2014)
9. Devlin, J., Chang, M.-W., Lee, K., Toutanova, K.: Bert: pre-training of deep bidirectional transformers for language understanding. arXiv preprint arXiv:1810.04805 (2018)
10. Burtsev, M., et al.: DeepPavlov: open-source library for dialogue systems. In: Proceedings of ACL 2018, System Demonstrations, Melbourne, Australia, July 2018, pp. 122–127. Association for Computational Linguistics (2018)
11. Sebastiani, F.: Machine learning in automated text categorization. ACM Comput. Surv. (CSUR) **34**(1), 1–47 (2002)
12. Lafferty, J.D., McCallum, A., Pereira, F.C.N.: Conditional random fields: probabilistic models for segmenting and labeling sequence data. In: Proceedings of the Eighteenth International Conference on Machine Learning, ICML 2001, pp. 282–289. Morgan Kaufmann Publishers Inc., San Francisco (2001)
13. Miller, G.: WordNet: An Electronic Lexical Database. MIT Press, Cambridge (1998)
14. Vrandečić, D., Krötzsch, M.: Wikidata: A Free Collaborative Knowledgebase. Commun. ACM **57**(10), 78–85 (2014)
15. Weizenbaum, J.: Computer power and human reason: from judgment to calculation (1976)
16. Norvig, P.: How to write a spelling corrector (2007). http://norvig.com/spell-correct.html
17. Krebs, F., Lubascher, B., Moers, T., Schaap, P., Spanakis, G.: Social emotion mining techniques for Facebook posts reaction prediction. In: Proceedings of the 10th International Conference on Agents and Artificial Intelligence, pp. 211–220 (2018)
18. https://spacy.io/
19. Jiang, R., Banchs, R.E., Li, H.: Evaluating and combining name entity recognition systems. In: Proceedings of the Sixth Named Entity Workshop, Berlin, Germany, August 2016, pp. 21–27. Association for Computational Linguistics (2016)
20. Hovy, E., Marcus, M., Palmer, M., Ramshaw, L., Weischedel, R.: OntoNotes: the 90% solution. In: Proceedings of the Human Language Technology Conference of the NAACL, Companion Volume: Short Papers, NAACL-Short 2006, pp. 57–60. Association for Computational Linguistics, Stroudsburg (2006)
21. Tjong Kim Sang, E.F., De Meulder, F.: Introduction to the CoNLL-2003 shared task: language-independent named entity recognition. In: Proceedings of the Seventh Conference on Natural Language Learning at HLT-NAACL 2003 - Volume 4, CONLL 2003, pp. 142–147. Association for Computational Linguistics, Stroudsburg (2003)
22. Howard, J., Ruder, S.: Fine-tuned language models for text classification. CoRR, abs/1801.06146 (2018)
23. Vaswani, A., et al.: Attention is all you need. CoRR, abs/1706.03762 (2017)

Analysis of Vocational Education and Training and the Labour Market in Catalonia. A Data-Driven Approach

José Mena[1,2](✉), Marc Torrent-Moreno[1], Daniel González[1], Laura Portell[1], Oriol Pujol[2], and Jordi Vitrià[2]

[1] Eurecat, Centre Tecnològic de Catalunya, Barcelona, Spain
{jose.mena,marc.torrent,daniel.gonzalez,laura.portell}@eurecat.org
[2] Universitat de Barcelona, Barcelona, Spain
{oriol_pujol,jordi.vitria}@ub.edu

Abstract. In this paper, we introduce BDFP, an ongoing project developed by the Big Data Center of Excellence of Barcelona which aims at analysing the Vocational Education and Training (VET) and its demand in the labour market. The main contribution of the project is the development of a data science-based solution to assist policymakers to design effective policies that help on building the bridge between the VET educational system and the labour demand. The project combines data sources from both the job market and educational domains, leveraging machine learning for breaking the existing information silos and develop a set of visualisations, reports and dashboards that enable the combined study of both the VET and the jobs market. The present article describes the process of inception and development of the tools and details preliminary results that are currently being analysed together with domain experts of both fields. The final results will be compiled in a final report that will be publicly available.

Keywords: Vocational Education and Training · Labour market · Data science · NLP

1 Introduction

Motivated by the high potential benefits of a *data-rich society*, in February 2015 a public-private partnership launched the Big Data Center of Excellence in Barcelona[1] to assist and boost a *data culture* at all types of organisations operating in Catalonia. One of the main activities driven since then has been linking the dots among relevant stakeholders of the data economy in the region while promoting meaningful initiatives to demonstrate the advantages of putting together significant datasets, still a highly challenging task nowadays.

[1] https://www.bigdatabcn.com/.

P. Cellier and K. Driessens (Eds.): ECML PKDD 2019 Workshops, CCIS 1167, pp. 522–537, 2020.
https://doi.org/10.1007/978-3-030-43823-4_42

Led by prominent actors constituted as an advisory board, debates took place to identify meaningful societal questions that could be, nowadays, solved by data-driven projects. Vocational and Educational Training (VET)[2] was selected due to its relevance for current societal challenges (i.e., it is key to fight young unemployment [1]) as well as for the existing datasets were valuable insights could be derived from. After 6 months interviewing all relevant stakeholders, selecting the right questions to answer (mapped to 5 concrete research topics), and signing collaboration agreements to be able to access data we could kick-off the BDFP project in mid-2018, where BDFP stands for *Big Data en Formació Professional* which translates to Big Data in VET.

The present work proposes a data-driven approach with a combination of different data analysis algorithms including data mining, rule-based systems and machine learning to analyse the evolution of the labour market (extracted by the free text job vacancies posted in the leading job portal) and the VET offering (extracted by the official training curricula in the complete territory) in Catalonia during the last few years. Special attention is devoted to two main strategic market sectors for the region, namely ICT and Industry 4.0, and the transformation of the particular skill set demanded by employers.

The paper is organised as follows. Section 2 describes similar initiatives, and Sect. 3 contextualises the work described and introduces the research topics posed. Section 4 describes the data sources included and the exploratory tools developed. In Sect. 5, we describe the main challenges of the approach proposed and how we overcame them by applying ML techniques. Section 7 describes some preliminary results obtained by using the tools developed and Sect. 8 points to conclusions and future work.

2 Similar Initiatives

Analysing the relationship between the labour market and the VET is a broad field of study due to its relevance for society. In the scientific community, we can find [2], where various works were compiled that analysed VET skills from different perspectives, analysing the role of policymakers, the territorial deployment or the impact of demographical and employment patterns changes.

Focusing on the link between labour demand and VET supply, we can find similar works focused on different regions, like in [3], where they analyse the situation of VET in India, and the situation of VET graduates in the labour market. In [5], they studied in depth the relationship between the VET and jobs in Germany from different points of view like gender or type of training. In [4], they carried out a similar study in Australia but performing the analysing at the level of the skills acquired in training and how these skills were translated to the labour market.

Most of the previous works base their studies on surveys and official sources of information. In this sense, the present work is more aligned with initiatives like

[2] Training for a specific occupation through a combination of theoretical teaching and practical experience.

the project e-skills match[3], that analyse the labour market from the demands posted on job portals. In this study, we follow this approach but extending it to other types of studies and skills like those related to Industry 4.0.

3 Context, Methodology and Goals

The BDFP project has been promoted by the Big Data Center of Excellence in Barcelona, an initiative led by Eurecat (the primary Technology Center of Catalonia) with the support of the Catalan government, the City Council of Barcelona and Oracle. Thanks to the commitment and contacts of its advisory board[4] a consortium was put together with the required datasets as well as technological and domain knowledge. Namely, the following organizations and teams have contributed significantly to this project: three departments of the Catalan government (Digital Policy and Public Administration, Education, and, Business and Knowledge), the Catalan Occupation Service, the local development agency of the Barcelona City Council (Barcelona Activa), the GIPE research group of the Universitat Autònoma of Barcelona, the consulting company Everis, the job portal Infojobs, the Bertelsmann foundation aimed to improve the youth employment, the Fundació Barcelona Formació Professional aimed at improving VET, and the Big Data and Data Science department of Eurecat.

This project was launched with the aim of achieving two very different goals. First, it provides valuable insights about the evolution of the skill-sets offered in the VET contents in all Catalan territory as well as the ones demanded by the job market during the same period, 2015–2018. This information is of great value for the Catalan Education Department in charge of designing the curricula of the VET courses trying to satisfy the local job market near future requirements. Second, the project aims also to showcase the need and benefits of joining efforts by different institutions to solve societal challenges, with different knowledge and assets, ranging from datasets, data science experts, technology providers, domain experts, decision-makers and facilitators. From the one hand, all these roles are required to launch and successfully execute such a project and are impossible to find in a single organization but many. On the other hand, the potential benefits of data sharing and novel analytic approaches can only be efficiently assimilated by decision-makers when knowledge sharing processes are established among the different actors when working in common challenges, and therefore, they will be inserted in the next future agenda of the relevant stakeholders.

As a matter of fact, the first 6 months of the project were dedicated to holding several one-to-one meetings with every organization, understanding their perspectives and goals around VET in Catalonia, the existing challenges and what would be the main questions that they would find most relevant answering, taking into consideration their feasibility, and how could they help. The agreed five research topics are the following:

[3] https://www.eskillsmatch.eu/en/about.
[4] https://www.bigdatabcn.com/el-big-data-coe-barcelona/big-data-working-group/.

- T1: Geographic characterization of the labour demand, evolution of the labour demand based on the contracts registered in Catalonia during the last 5 years.
- T2: Analysis of the relationship between Dual VET and sectorial labour demand, a particular study case of the type of VET training includes an internship in a company.
- T3: Temporal evolution of the VET skills, evolution of the demanded kills focusing on ICT and Industry 4.0.
- T4: Comparison of labor supply and demand in ICT and Industry 4.0,
- T5: Identification of overqualification, required in a job post with respect to the responsibilities described.

During the following eight months, a core team was established, mainly formed by data analysts and scientists, who explored the data and created the models as explained in the next sections. On-demand meetings were done with domain experts of the organizations when needed to set the basis, describe standard definitions, and interpret the results in every step. Further, after each significant step, high-level meetings were appointed with high-level representatives to inform and validate those partial results and define the next steps. Finally, a great effort was devoted with volunteers of most organizations, first to define the rules in order to categorize the skills from the free text, and afterwards to label 100 skills in 1,117,729 job posts to train the models.

4 Exploratory Analysis

4.1 Data Collection and Processing

Concerning the datasets used in the project, we split them into two categories: the labour demand or the VET offer.

First, we start by studying the VET offer in Catalonia. In Spain, there are three types of VET: *FP INICIAL*, which corresponds to Initial VET studies that combine theoretical subjects with practical training, FP Dual, a type of VET that includes in-company training, and FP Ocupacional, that is meant for professionals that are unemployed or that want to improve their careers. For each type of VET, we obtained the number of students enrolled, and graduates by family, studies, year (for the period 2013–2017, except for Dual where only the period 2016–2017 was available) We obtained this data from the Education Department of the Local Government and the local Employment Service, SOC.

We also analyze the labour demand from two sources. On the one hand, the original contracts as registered during 2013–2017 in the Public Employment service, including the contract duration, occupation code, company activity code and geographical location, plus some demographic information like gender or age. On the other hand, for the same period, we collected jobs posted in two job portals: Infojobs, one of the leading job portals in Spain, and *Feina Activa*, the job portal hosted by the local Employment Service.

Beyond gathering all data and standard processing carried out to the different datasets, to handle outliers or missing values or to normalize some attributes, there have been some individual cases where additional processing was required.

For the VET data sources, the first issue to solve was the identification of the studies to be included in the study. The posterior analysis includes two levels of granularity: the characterization of the demand, including all the VET studies, and, on the other hand, the analysis of the matching between demand and supply focused on the two families of studies: ICT and Industry 4.0 To characterize those studies and be able to link them to the labour demand, a set of training skills definition was selected. The selection was carried out following the official definitions provided by the National Ministry of Education for each of the studies included in the study.

In the case of the contracts, we had to deal with different types of contracts depending on their duration, ranging from hours to years, so just counting the number of contracts would have led to wrong conclusions. To mitigate this issue, we complement the contracts with an index of labour turnover based on the annual reports by the Labor and Productive Model Observatory, and a study carried out by the Observatory of Industry, allowing to approximate the effective hiring from the total contracting. Besides, we selected the training skills as the link between both domains to match the contract with the VET supply. We developed together with SOC, the local public Employment Service, a dictionary of National Occupational Codes, CNO, and training skills.

Moreover, there was an additional processing step to merge the information of job averts coming from both the private portal, Infojobs, and the public one, *Feina Activa*. To have a single source of information for the demand, we defined a data model for job posts that included a common set of attributes present in both portals. To merge some of the attributes, we developed individual dictionaries of equivalences for things like the duration of the contract, the educational level or the type of working day.

4.2 Exploration

The different sources of information included in the project, both for the definition of the labour demand and the supply of VET, are stored as different Elasticsearch indexes in the system. We chose Elasticsearch because it is an indexing system that offers a very nice search API, and comes with Kibana, an excellent tool for building useful and intuitive dashboards, both of them opensource.

We developed an exploratory dashboard for each of the sources (contracts, the different types of VET and job posts) in order to deliver an exploratory tool that allows the analysis of the data sources and start answering the research questions posed, especially to non-technical users. An example of this dashboard is shown in Fig. 1.

In the case of the job posts, the results obtained by the different classification models complemented the information included from the original data sources, i.e., we were able to add the families they belong, the skills, languages required and if there was overqualification.

For some of the research topics, it was required to join some of the data sources altogether to, for example, compare the demand and the supply. We found out that Kibana was quite limiting in this aspect, as it did not allow to

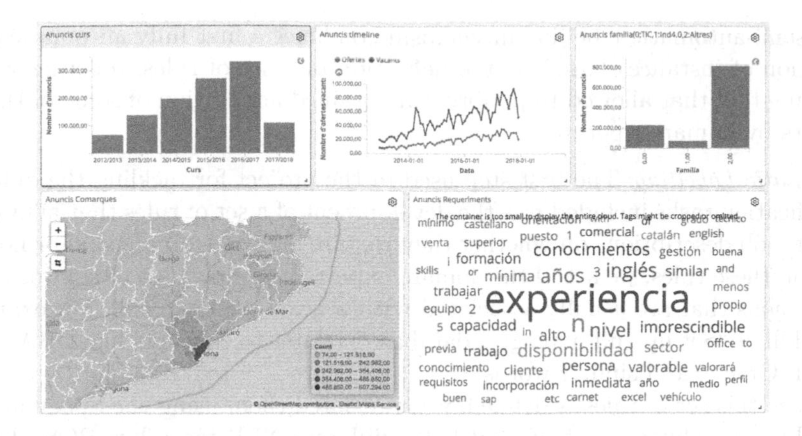

Fig. 1. Example of dashboard created using Kibana that includes some indicators related to the job posts.

join different indexes to produce combined visualizations. Thus, for some of the analysis, we had to develop custom visualizations in order to show some of the indicators required in the study.

5 Scientific Challenges

This section explains the main two challenges encountered during the execution of the project and how they are addressed thanks to knowledge discovery, data mining and machine learning techniques.

5.1 Challenge 1: Mapping Job Posts with Training Skills

Mapping skills like "Implement, verify and document web apps" or "Manage relational databases" to jobs like ".NET junior developer" or "Analyst in SQLServer and SSIS" is not straightforward. Despite some of the fields included in the job advert can help on establishing this link, they sometimes can be misleading - for example, the sector of the company may differ from the position to cover - or might not be informed if they are marked as optional.

The significant volume of job posts included in the study, more than one million, prevent the team from manually analysing them, making it necessary to adopt smarter approaches. Leveraging the presence of domain experts in the team, we used a combination of rule-based models together with ML models, based on annotated data.

The Large Scale Labelling Problem. The development of a semi-automatic tool for large scale labelling is required to automate the process of assigning job offerings to the family of studies and tagging the required skills demanded.

This semi-automatic labelling mechanism combines a first fully automatic identification of instances based on the definition of a set of rules, together with a labelling tool that allowed to perform fine-grained annotation of some of the job adverts by human experts.

Automatic Labelling: The first step used in the project for tackling the different classification tasks included was the development of a set of rules that allowed to classify job descriptions on whether they require a given training skill or not. To develop these rules, we asked the domain experts to define a set of keywords and expressions that are usually associated with a given training skill. For example, The skill of "Set up and manage a database" relates to concepts like DBA, SQL, Mysql, Oracle, and similar words.

Once this set of rules is defined, we translated them using the Spacy library. This library delivers a set of models for different NLP tasks like POS identification, NER, Lemmatization or Tokenization, and Rule-based matching, among others. In this case, we made use of the Rule-based matching tool and the POS, Lemmatization and tokenization available for the Spanish language.

This rule-based method allows having the first selection of skills and, by grouping these skills by the family of studies they belong, it also allows us to give a first tagging of the family they belong to. The same approach was used in the project to infer other characteristics of the job posts like the requirement of a foreign language and other soft skills by developing ad-hoc rules for that purpose. The main drawback of this approach is the fact that it depends on how exhaustive is the definition of the rules, making it impossible to capture all the terms and expressions that might be related to each concept.

Labelling Tool: To overcome the limitations of the rule-based model, we complement it with a ML classification system. In order to have labelled data, in the context of the project we developed a labelling tool, that aimed at enabling the domain experts to evaluate job descriptions, allowing them to identify the family of studies, training skills required and determine whether there was overqualification or not.

The annotation process run for two months with the invaluable help of more than 30 experts that annotated more than 3,000 job posts. Despite this significant effort, the annotation of some skills was not sufficient. Some of the skills had less than ten labels, preventing the corresponding classifier from training properly. To fight the lack of labels, we added some positive examples drawing a sample from the most representative examples as classified using the rule-based system for each skill. Besides complementing the positive examples with those obtained from the rule-based, we also limited the study to those skills with more than 100 labels.

Job Advertisement Topic Prediction and Skills Automatic Tagging. After the annotation process, we first trained a classifier for topic prediction, with three possible labels: ICT, Industry 4.0, and Others. Once the job advert is classified in a family, the original intention was to apply a multi-labelling

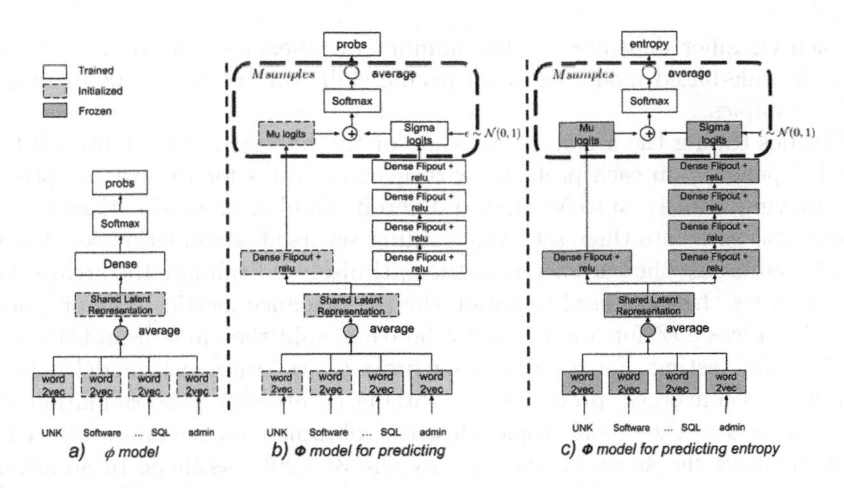

Fig. 2. Models used in the project. (a) Deep learning model used for challenge 1, (b) Uncertainty Bayesian wrapper for deep black-box models used in challenge 2.

classifier for the skills. The fact that the labelling tool stored a separated label for each skill, having no way to link them afterwards, force us to train a classifier for each of them. At this step, we trained for those skills that were more annotated, 15 for ICT and 30 for Industry 4.0.

The model used in all cases is shown in Fig. 2(a). The input for the models is the description of the job, including different attributes like the level of education, minimum requirements, description of the position, title or previous knowledge. In order to fight the lack of positive labels for some of the skills, we try different combinations of those fields for building different samples out of the same labelled job. We also combine samples obtained from the labelling tool with some from the rule-based model to obtain balanced datasets. The resulting text for each job position is transformed into a sequence of words with a limited length of 120 words, using left padding for shorter texts.

We used an artificial neural network, where the first layer of the model is an embedding layer. In this work, we use a pre-trained Word2vec embedding [6] trained with a billion of Spanish words [7]. We average the embeddings of the words included in the job description to obtain a latent representation for it. This latent representation is the input for a fully connected layer with a softmax activation, used for obtaining the probabilities of each class predicted. For some of the classifiers, we substitute the average of the embeddings for an LSTM layer plus a hidden dense layer, showing better accuracy scores. Sometimes, though, this leads to overfitting, despite having 50% of dropout, probably due to the lack of sufficient data samples, so we have to stick to the original model.

From the original 100 skills selected, 29 for ICT and 71 for Industry 4.0, we finally selected only 38, 15 for ICT and 23 for Industry 4.0, that correspond with those that received enough labels to train the classifier properly. Each classifier was trained using a specific training dataset. The number of examples for each classifier depended on the number of labels and the results obtained from the rule-based model for that specific skill, varying from 1,000 to almost 4,000 examples.

Besides tuning the architecture, some of the hyperparameters needed to be tuned depending on each problem, with learning rates for the Adam optimiser used varying from 1e−3 to 5e−4, or a different number of epochs. Each training dataset was split into three sets: the training set itself, a validation set that was used for adjusting the parameters of the optimiser and validate the architecture, and a test set that was used to obtain the performance metrics. The proportion for each set was 90% for training and validation, split then in 90% and 10% each, and 10% for testing. For each training process, we train each model until the training loss converged, preventing overfitting by observing the validation loss.

As a result, the family/topic classifier obtained an accuracy of 94.75%. Figure 3 shows the accuracy obtained by the 38 skill classifiers. In addition to the accuracy, we computed a confusion matrix to analyse the behaviour of each classifier with regards to false positives or negatives, and we performed a manual check of some examples to carry out a qualitative evaluation of the models. Even though the majority of the classifiers achieved accuracies over 80%, we observe that those with lower values correspond to skills that are hard to model using rules. For those cases, obtaining a more significant set of labels could help with improving the results.

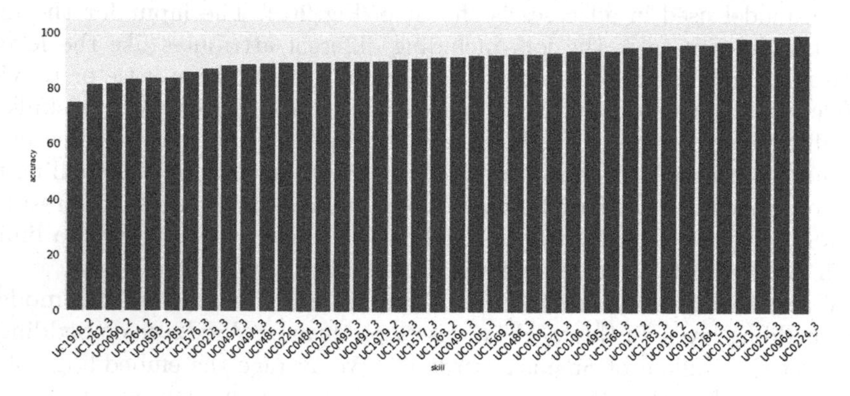

Fig. 3. Accuracies obtained in test for the 38 skills classifiers

Once trained, we employed the learned classifiers to the whole set of job adverts. First, we applied the family of studies classifier, to isolate those that belong to ICT and Industry 4.0. Later on, we used the 15 ICT skill classifiers to the ICT jobs and the 23 Industry 4.0 one to tag the job adverts of each family with the skills that are required for the position. As a result, we add a list of skills required for the described position for each ICT and Industry 4.0 job advert that can be used in the later analysis.

5.2 Challenge 2: Job Overqualification Analysis

A second valuable insight from this project consists of understanding the degree of matching between job demands and job offerings. In this second challenge, we take advantage of the data gathered to classify each job advert on whether it includes overqualification in its description or not. Similarly to the case of detecting the skills present in the job offers, in the case of detecting overqualification in demand, it is required to deal with unstructured textual information. This motivates us to use advanced NLP models.

Using a similar strategy to that explained in challenge 1, the prediction accuracy only reaches 72.28%. This value, though acceptable in some contexts, is inadequate for a careful analysis of the problem. Our hypothesis for justifying this value considers the difficulty of defining the concept of over-qualification and the subjectivity involved in those definitions. There are different levels of overqualification. For example, they are asking a university degree for a job that a VET student can perform, or asking for a high level of VET when it can be carried out by medium degree VET graduates.

These two different properties introduce noise in the labelling process, and consequently, affect the performance of the machine learning classifiers. In this setting, the degree of confidence in the prediction can help to refine the results. This is addressed by means of modeling uncertainty.

At first glance, when using artificial neural networks, observing the entropy of the probabilities resulting from the softmax output can provide an idea of how confident the predictions are. This is, high probabilities for the target class, close to 1, suggests confident predictions. However, the problem with this approach is that for some data points with low occurrences in the training dataset or with ambiguous semantics, the model can yield overconfident predictions [8]. And, thus mislead further analysis.

Estimating the Uncertainty. When talking about machine learning techniques' uncertainty we find two different concepts of uncertainty depending on its source. These are:

- **Epistemic uncertainty**, which corresponds to the uncertainty originated by the model. It can be explained as to which extent our model is able to describe the distribution that generated the data. There are two different types of uncertainties caused by whether the model has been trained with enough data, or whether the expressiveness of the model can capture the complexity of the distribution. When using an expressive enough model, this type of uncertainty can be reduced by including more samples during the training phase.
- **Aleatoric uncertainty**, that belongs to the data. This uncertainty is inherent to the data and cannot be reduced by adding more data to the training process. We can further divide this uncertainty in two classes:
  - Homoscedastic: measures the level of noise that is derived from the measurement process. This uncertainty remains constant for all the data.

- Heteroscedastic: measures the level of uncertainty caused by the data. In the case of NLP, this can be explained by the ambiguity of some words or sentences.

The different types of uncertainty must be measured differently. Consider a dataset, $D = \{x_i, y_i\}$, $i = 1 \ldots N$, that is composed by pairs of data and labels points, respectively. Given a new sample x^* we want to predict its label y^*. Our goal is to capture the distribution that generated the outputs by using a model with parameters W. Under the Bayesian setting, this description corresponds to the following marginal equation,

$$p(y^*|x^*, D) = \int_W p(y^*|f^W(x^*))p(W|D)dW \tag{1}$$

In Eq. 1 one can see that the distribution of the output depends on two terms: one that depends on the application of the model to the input data, the aleatoric component, and a second one that is measuring how the model may vary depending on the training data, the epistemic component. For the epistemic uncertainty, we model the weights as random variables by introducing Gaussian perturbations and Flipout as introduced in [10], to estimate the conditioned probability by using Montecarlo (MC) sampling. The model trained up to this model is a deterministic model, except for the epistemic components. As such, it does not allow to infer the aleatoric component of the uncertainty. Thus, for computing the aleatoric heteroscedastic uncertainty, we build an assistance a deep neural model that will complement the former ANN. We assume that the aleatoric component can be modelled using a latent layer of random variables following Gaussian distributions [9]. While the ANN output will stand for the mean value of that distribution, we will let the assistance NN to work out the standard deviation corresponding to each input sample. The details of the implementation can be found in [13]. As in the former case, we use Montecarlo approximations to sample from the latent layer and approximate the output distribution.

As a result of both Montecarlo samplings, a probability density function of the output values is obtained. This will serve for computing the overall uncertainty.

Computing the Uncertainty Score. Figure 2(b) illustrates the classifier trained to estimate both epistemic and aleatoric uncertainties. It is remarkable that just by training the model with the new architecture for 20 epochs, the resulting accuracy increases up to 84,25%.

Model in Fig. 2(c) depicts the model that is used to predict the uncertainty score. In this article, we used predictive entropy as defined in [8]. The predictive entropy, introduced by [11], measures the dispersion of the predictions around the mode. In this case, we combine the computation of the aleatoric and epistemic uncertainty. Thus it is necessary to combine the random variables that learned the variability of the model, the epistemic component, together with the random variables assigned to the output logits that model the aleatoric uncertainty.

In order to obtain the uncertainty score, we carry out two consecutive Montecarlo simulations: first, we sample a model W and then use this model to sample the output prediction for each logit, following the distribution parameterized by the outputs of the ANN and the assistance NN. Using the resulting probabilities, we compute the predictive entropy as follows,

$$\mathbb{H}[y|\mathbf{x}, D_{train}] := -\sum_{c} \mathbb{E}(p_c) \log \mathbb{E}(p_c) \quad (2)$$

Uncertainty-Based Rejection Classifier. Despite the increment in accuracy obtained after training the ANN with uncertainty, we can further exploit the uncertainty scored to improve the results by filtering out the less confident predictions. As a result, the quality of the filtered predictions obtained increases as it only outputs confident predictions. This score can be used as a rejection mechanism for the classification.

Different measurements can be defined for rejection. For example, the test dataset can be sorted by the rejection value, from higher to lower scores. If there is a correlation between the uncertainty score and the misclassification value of the input, by discarding the more uncertain data points, we will increase the performance of the classification system. We consider different rejection points corresponding to descending values of the rejector from including all points to discard all of them in the last iteration. The analysis of the three performance measures [12] for each rejection point must consider a trade-off between the number of samples rejected and the quality of the classifications.

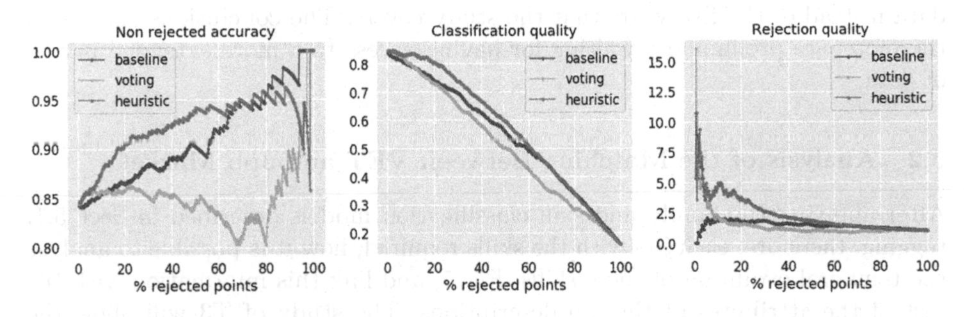

Fig. 4. Performance measures showing the accuracy of kept points, how correct predictions are kept and wrong discarded, and the ability of rejecting wrong samples.

Figure 4 compares the results obtained after applying three different models for computing uncertainty: predictive entropy for the aleatoric model, as proposed in this work, the predictive entropy of the original model, used as a baseline, and an additional uncertainty score, variation ratios, as described in [8]. The plot shows how only by rejecting the 10% of predictions with higher uncertainty scores, the model increases its performance up to 88% – reaching 90% prediction accuracy when rejecting the more uncertain 20% of the predictions.

6 Project Results Insights

The present section shows preliminary results obtained from the application of the models and techniques introduced in the previous sections. The goal of the section is to describe how these results complement the original information and allow domain experts to analyse them in order to obtain insights and explanations for the relationship between labour demand and VET supply.

6.1 Overall Analysis of the Labour Market

For answering T1, geographic characterization of the labour demand, we looked at the demand at a general level, not focusing on the selected families but considering the full picture of the hiring at the region. To do so, we look at the contracts data source, connecting it to the VET studies by using the mapping developed. For tackling this research topic, we also include additional data sources, like demographic information and about the companies, like the number of companies per sector, their number of employees, to contextualize the data about the hiring and its evolution, enabling comparisons between the number of contracts, population and number or size of companies.

For T2, we analyze the relationship between Dual VET and sector labour demand, as a specific case of T1 focusing on Dual VET. Dual VET is a particular type of training where students have the opportunity of finishing their studies doing an internship in a company. Here, we focus on aspects like the impact of gender or age range, studying the distribution of the dual VET across the families of studies and the region. For this analysis, we only had access to one year of data instead of the five years that the study covers. The conclusions extracted, therefore, are preliminary, waiting for having access to a more extended period of data.

6.2 Analysis of the Matching Between VET and Job Market

After applying the family and skill classification models described in Sect. 5.1, tagging, therefore, each job with the skills required, now it is possible to analyse the temporal evolution of these skills, Fig. 5, and link this information with the rest of the attributes of the job descriptions. The study of T3 will allow the analysis of trends in demand for the selected skills, delivering new tools for the design of VET curricula that best adapt to the real market needs.

The skills assigned to the job positions are also used to match VET studies and answer T4, checking the degree of educational coverage of the VET according to the real demand obtained from the analysis of job posts.

Figure 6 shows a comparison between the demand for job positions that require a given skill and the enrollments for studies that include the skill, aiming to study the educational coverage for those skills across the region. Again, this study can be carried out considering different aspects like the temporary evolution, the type of job positions, and so forth.

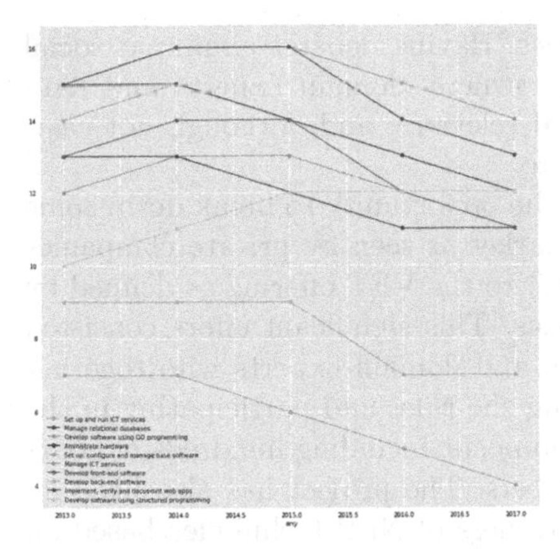

Fig. 5. Evolution of % of top 10 demanded skills with respect to the total ICT demand.

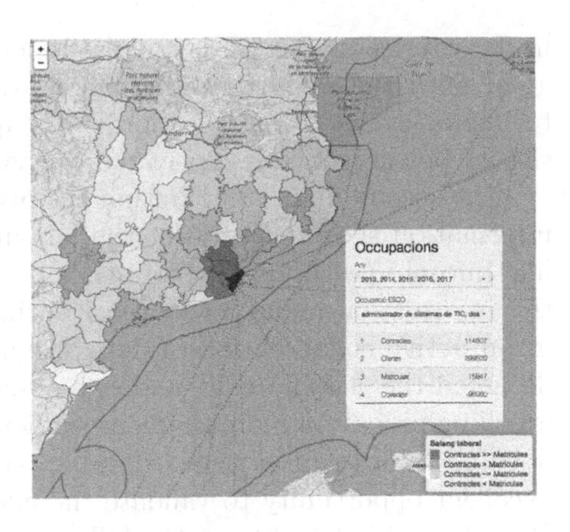

Fig. 6. Territorial analysis comparing between contracts and VET students for sys admins.

6.3 Adequacy Between Required Functions/Skills and the Level of Studies

Finally, T5 is answered based on the results obtained from the uncertainty-based rejection method described in Sect. 5.2. Taking the 222,957 job posts that correspond to ICT and Industry 4.0 positions, as indicated by the results obtained from using the family classifier, we apply a rejection ratio that, on test time, reached a 92.5% of accuracy. Thus, we discard 137,157 job descriptions, focusing the study on the remaining 85,800. From those, we estimate only 17,388 as including overqualification in the job position.

This process allows us to study the trends associated with the overqualification, its temporal evolution, analysing potential differences between ICT and Industry 4.0, or studying the phenomenon individually on each family. By examining the overqualified job positions, we would like to study the different types and levels of overqualification and determine their cause. Together with domain experts, we continue to analyse these results to obtain the final project insights.

7 Conclusions

In this paper, we have introduced the BDFP project, (*Big Data per a la Formació Professional* or Big Data for VET in English, an ongoing initiative promoted by the Center of Excellence in Big Data of Barcelona, and supported by the local government and a total of 11 public and private institutions. The project aims at analysing the evolution of the jobs market and the corresponding VET offering in the region of Catalonia since 2013 to 2018, with a strong focus on two strategic sectors, ICT and Industry 4.0.

We consider the following three as the main contributions of the project. The first one has been to enable the joint conversation and definition of common goals in data terms among all participating entities. Having debates aiming at social good with the main decision-makers, data owners, domain experts and data technologies experts in a region is of capital relevance and, although not easy, should be energetically motivated everywhere.

The second main contribution has been the opportunity to break down some information silos and connect the labour market as seen by private companies like Infojobs (with mostly free text job posts) to the VET offering as defined by the information managed by local authorities. This significant effort consisted in an active collaboration of data scientists and domain experts who together designed the classification models by defining the rules and participating in the labelling process of more than one million job posts, including hundreds of hours devoted by a team of knowledgeable volunteers. The project has also been an excellent opportunity to validate the effectiveness of NLP techniques based on Deep Learning to extract the skillsets required by employers from the free text of job posts as defined in the VET official curricula. Moreover, the complexity inherent in some tasks - e.g. the detection of overqualification - has required the application of advanced methods for improving the performance of the resulting models.

The third main contribution has been the characterisation of the evolution of a relevant part of the skill sets required by the employers in the whole Catalan territory for the two selected sectors during the period of study, and the relationship of the corresponding VET offerings. We, therefore, validated the applicability of the data sources and models selected for relevantly answering the research topics defined in the project. Although we are aware that the job vacancies from the two collaborating portals do not represent the entire job market, and it is biased to those higher profiled, it is a significant sample where concluding results can be derived from.

Currently, together with the domain experts, we are exploring the results of the project to obtain further insights and explanations for the questions posed at the beginning of the project. The complete conclusions of this work will be compiled into a report that will be publicly available and will be used by local policymakers to analyse the evolution of the labour demand, detect new trends on the demand of VET skills and study how to best adapt the training programs to the current requirements of the companies. Finally, we expect to work with some of the many organisations that have approached us during this process in order to extend it to other disciplines beyond ICT or Industry 4.0, and other regions in Spain and Europe.

Acknowledgement. The authors would like to acknowledge all organizations contributing to this project (named in Sect. 3), specially the ones that also helped financing the initiative: Catalan Government, City Council of Barcelona, Fundació Bertelsmann, Everis and Eurecat; as well as the members from the advisory board of the Big Data Center of Excellence who contributed along the whole project as individuals: Josep Lluis Cano, from ESADE Business School and Frederic Udina, from the Universitat Pompeu Fabra.

This work has been partially funded by the Spanish projects TIN2016-74946-P, TIN2015-66951-C2 (MINECO/FEDER, UE), RTI2018-095232-B-C21 and 2017 SGR 1742, and by AGAUR of the Generalitat de Catalunya through the Industrial PhD grant.

References

1. Direcció General de Formació Professional Inicial i Ensenyaments de Règim Especia: Insercio Laboral Dels Ensenyaments Professionals (2018)
2. Ryan, P. (ed.): International Comparisons of Vocational Education and Training for Intermediate Skills. Psychology Press, London (1991)
3. Agrawal, T., Agrawal, A.: Vocational education and training in India: a labour market perspective. J. Vocat. Educ. Train. **69**(2), 246–265 (2017). https://doi.org/10.1080/13636820.2017.1303785
4. Wheelahan, L., Buchanan, J., Yu, S.: Linking qualifications and the labour market through capabilities and vocational streams. Synthesis report. National Centre for Vocational Education Research Ltd. PO Box 8288, Stational Arcade, Adelaide, SA 5000, Australia (2015)
5. Witte, J.C., Kalleberg, A.L.: Matching training and jobs: the fit between vocational education and employment in the German labour market. Eur. Sociol. Rev. **11**(3), 293–317 (1995). https://doi.org/10.1093/oxfordjournals.esr.a036365
6. Mikolov, T., et al.: Efficient estimation of word representations in vector space. In: Proceedings of Workshop at ICLR (2013)
7. Cardellino, C.: Spanish Billion Words Corpus and Embeddings (2016). https://crscardellino.github.io/SBWCE/
8. Gal, Y.: Uncertainty in deep learning. Ph.D. thesis, University of Cambridge (2016)
9. Kendall, A., Gal, Y.: What uncertainties do we need in Bayesian deep learning for computer vision? In: Advances in Neural Information Processing Systems, pp. 5574–5584 (2017)
10. Wen, Y., et al.: Flipout: efficient pseudo-independent weight perturbations on mini-batches. CoRR abs/1803.04386 (2018)
11. Shannon, C.E.: A mathematical theory of communication. Bell Syst. Tech. J. **27**(3), 379–423 (1948)
12. Condessa, F., et al.: Performance measures for classification systems with rejection. CoRR (2015)
13. Mena, J., Brando, A., Pujol, O., Vitrià, J.: Uncertainty estimation for black-box classification models: a use case for sentiment analysis. In: Morales, A., Fierrez, J., Sánchez, J.S., Ribeiro, B. (eds.) IbPRIA 2019. LNCS, vol. 11867, pp. 29–40. Springer, Cham (2019). https://doi.org/10.1007/978-3-030-31332-6_3

SOS-EW: System for Overdose Spike Early Warning Using Drug Mover's Distance-Based Hawkes Processes

Wen-Hao Chiang[1], Baichuan Yuan[2], Hao Li[2], Bao Wang[2], Andrea Bertozzi[2], Jeremy Carter[1], Brad Ray[3], and George Mohler[1](✉)

[1] Indiana University - Purdue University Indianapolis, Indianapolis, USA
{chiangwe,carterjg,gmohler}@iupui.edu

[2] University of California Los Angeles, Los Angeles, USA
{byuan,lihao0809,wangbao,bertozzi}@math.ucla.edu

[3] School of Social Work, Wayne State University, Detroit, USA
bradray@wayne.edu

Abstract. Opioid addictions and overdoses have increased across the U.S. and internationally over the past decade. In urban environments, overdoses cluster in space and time, with 50% of overdoses occurring in less than 5% of the city and dozens of calls for emergency medical services being made within a 48-hour period. In this work, we introduce a system for early detection of opioid overdose clusters based upon the toxicology report of an initial event. We first use drug SMILES, one hot encoded molecular substructures, to generate a bag of drug vectors corresponding to each overdose (overdoses are often characterized by multiple drugs taken at the same time). We then use spectral clustering to generate overdose categories and estimate multivariate Hawkes processes for the space-time intensity of overdoses following an initial event. As the productivity parameter of the process depends on the overdose category, this allows us to estimate the magnitude of an overdose spike based on the substances present (e.g. fentanyl leads to more subsequent overdoses compared to Oxycontin). We validate the model using opioid overdose deaths in Indianapolis and show that the model outperforms several recently introduced Hawkes-Topic models based on Dirichlet processes. Our system could be used in combination with drug test strips to alert drug using populations of risky batches on the market or to more efficiently allocate naloxone to users and health/social workers.

Keywords: Opioid overdose · Hawkes process · Embedding · Spectral clustering · Topic model · Drug mover's distance

1 Introduction

The United States is experiencing an overdose epidemic with more than a half million drug overdose deaths since 2,000 and over 70,000 drug overdose deaths in

W.-H. Chiang and B. Yuan—Both authors contributed equally to this work.

P. Cellier and K. Driessens (Eds.): ECML PKDD 2019 Workshops, CCIS 1167, pp. 538–554, 2020.
https://doi.org/10.1007/978-3-030-43823-4_43

2017 alone [43]. A majority of these deaths have been opioid-related overdoses; however, the role of opioids has varied dramatically across three waves of the epidemic, each resulting in increasing death rates [2]. This first wave began in the 1990s and was driven by prescription opioid-related deaths [3]. The reduced availability of these prescription medications is said to have resulted in the second wave of the epidemic, which began in 2010, and was driving by heroin-related deaths [3,41,45]. The third wave started in 2013 and has largely been driven by illicit fentanyl, a synthetic opioid that is 50 to 100 times more potent than morphine [12]. National estimates suggest that in 2016 nearly half of opioid-related deaths contained fentanyl [16], and there is evidence showing that fentanyl is being mixed into heroin and cocaine which is likely contributing overdose deaths involving these substances [17,29]. Recent research has also shown that opioid overdoses cluster in space and time, where over half of opioid overdose deaths may occur in less than 5% of a city [1].

As the overdose epidemic has progressed researchers and policy makers have revealed shortcomings in official data sources, namely vital records data. One limitation is that vital records data rely on the International Classification of Diseases, 10th Revision (ICD-10) codes which do not record the specific substances related to an overdose fatality [6,15,27,48]; for example, there is no ICD code for fentanyl. Another limitation though has been the undercounting of opioid-related fatalities as 20 to 35% of drug overdose deaths are unspecified [42], meaning no substance was indicated as a primary or contributing cause of death. Moreover, rates of undercounting vary geographically as they are the result of state policies for death investigation procedures [42]. While researchers have developed measures to adjust for these limitations [42], better data collection systems are being implemented [47], and state policies are changing [11], it remains clear that we lacked sufficient data to quickly detect and identify the substances driving this overdose epidemic at the national level. However, one source of local information that can be used to address these gaps are toxicology results collected as part of an overdose death investigation. In the present study, we use a robust toxicology dataset from Marion County, Indiana [Indianapolis] that were collected as part of the CDCs Prevention for States funding initiative [28,37,38]. In the toxicology dataset, we observe spatio-temporal clustering patterns [1]. These shift patterns demonstrate that overdose events concentrate within micro places in a short time window and shift through time, which motivates our present work.

Our goal in the present work is to develop a statistical framework for modeling and prediction of opioid overdose clusters in space and time, leveraging information provided in the toxicology report of the initial overdose in the cluster. An overview of our proposed system, SOS-EW, is given in Fig. 1. We use a Hawkes process to model overdoses as a branching process. Each event may trigger offspring events nearby in space and time. The branching ratio of the process, determining the average number of offspring, depends on the drugs contained in the toxicology report of each parent event in the branching process. To reduce the dimension, we use spectral clustering with earth mover's distance

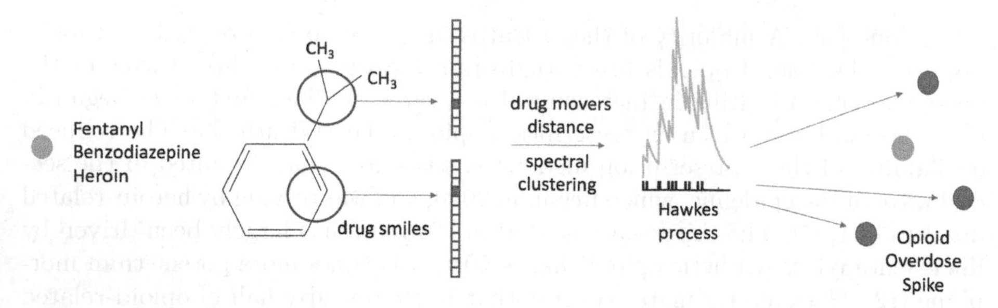

Fig. 1. Overview of the SOS − EW system for early warning of opioid spikes. The initial overdose toxicology report shows fentanyl, benzodiazepine, and heroin present. Each drug is vectorized using SMILES and the event is assigned an overdose category using spectral clustering based on earth mover's distance of the drug vectors ("drug mover's distance"). The increase in the intensity of the Hawkes process is determined by the category and allows for the prediction of an opioid overdose spike, those events triggered in the branching process by the initial overdose.

on bags of drug SMILES [14] vectors corresponding to each toxicology report (we refer to in the rest of the paper as "drug mover's distance"). The resulting method outperforms existing Dirichlet-based Hawkes topic models in the task of early warning of opioid overdose spikes (clusters) based on an initial event and its toxicology report.

The outline of the paper is as follows. In Sect. 2, we review related work on point process models of event clustering in urban environments and topic point processes for event data with high dimensional marks. In Sect. 2, we then present the details on our proposed method including clustering of the toxicology reports and the spatio-temporal Hawkes process. In Sect. 3, we provide details for several baseline models we use to benchmark SOS-EW and in Sect. 4 we present the results of our numerical experiments. We then discuss the implications of our results for practice in Sect. 5.

2 Method

SOS − EW system for early warning of opioid spikes is mainly comprised of the following two components:

1. Overdose category clustering;
2. Marked spatio-temporal Hawkes process kernel estimation and simulation.

Given a toxicology report, overdose events are first clustered into several overdose categories through spectral clustering [34]. The distance between overdose events in spectral clustering is measured based on earth mover's distance [40] of drug vectors which characterize drug's two-dimensional molecular structure (in particular we use SMILES, one hot encoded molecular substructures [14]). Drug overdose events over continuous time are then modeled through spatio-temporal

Hawkes processes. We estimate the productivity for each category based on historical overdose events and simulate future events to generate a short ranked list of hotspots containing overdose spikes. Figure 1 presents an overview of the SOS – EW system. In Sect. 2.1, we review related work on spatial self-exciting point processes, along with topic point processes. In Sect. 2.2, we present the details of our method for overdose event clustering and we introduce our approach for the estimation and simulation of spatio-temporal Hawkes processes in Sect. 2.3.

2.1 Related Work

Self-exciting (Hawkes) point processes have been used to model space-time clustering in urban crime patterns [32] and Hawkes process-based learning to rank algorithms were recently a top-performing solution in the 2017 NIJ Crime Forecasting competition [31], which focused on ranking the top crime hotspots in a city according to short-term crime risk. Other point process models, for example, log-Gaussian Cox Processes, can model spatial diffusion of events and have also proven accurate at modeling crime hotspots [8,44]. More recently, self-exciting point processes have been used to model clustering in emergency call data [25]. In more extreme security settings spatio-temporal point process models for event prediction have been applied to conflict [51] and terrorism [10] datasets.

In the above studies, the models either only used as input the spatial coordinates and time of the events, or in some cases an additional low-dimensional (<10) event category. However, event data often is accompanied by a high dimensional mark, for example, text data, imagery, sensor data, or in our case a 133 dimensional vector indicating drugs in a toxicology screen.

Recent work in the machine learning and information retrieval literature has focused on extending temporal and network-based Hawkes processes to handle text information in the events [4,21]. Dirichlet Hawkes processes [4,49] have been introduced for this purpose, where document clustering is jointly learned with a temporal Hawkes process. In the network setting, Hawkes processes have been used to model coupled information and event diffusion on networks [5]. However, these studies have not dealt with spatio-temporal data, which is critical in studying the spread of opioid overdoses.

Our work offers several contributions to the above-related literature. First, we investigate the applicability of existing Hawkes-topic models in the spatial setting and then we improve upon the accuracy of these models in several prediction tasks related to early warning of opioid overdose clusters. Second, we introduce a novel clustering method for drug overdoses based upon drug mover's distance. Related to word mover's distance [20] that has shown higher coherence than LDA based topic models, we believe our drug mover's distance-based spectral clustering may be useful in a variety of applications where sets of molecules need to be compared and clustered.

2.2 Overdose Categorization

To categorize overdose events through clustering, we first measure the similarity between two overdose events in terms of a "distance" based on the drugs involved in the events. Each event consists of a mark indicating one or more drug substances found in the victim's system. We denote an event i containing m drug substances as $\mathbf{E}_i = \{\mathbf{d}_1, \mathbf{d}_2, \cdots, \mathbf{d}_m\}$, where drug m is denoted as $\mathbf{d}_m$. Each drug is represented by a set of 2D substructures, i.e., $\mathbf{d} \in \{s_1, s_2, \cdots, s_k\}$, where the substructure k is denoted as s_k. The distance between each drug event is then calculated by earth mover's distance [40].

Earth mover's distance (EMD) is a metric to measure a distance between two distributions. EMD is based on the minimal cost that must be paid to move one distribution into the other. Given two events, $\mathbf{E}_p$ and $\mathbf{E}_q$, with m and n drugs, respectively, we want to find a transportation flow $\mathbf{F} \in \mathbb{Z}_2^{m\times n}$, where $\mathbb{Z}_2 = \{0, 1\}$, that minimizes the overall cost:

$$
\begin{aligned}
&\min \sum_{i=1}^{m}\sum_{j=1}^{n} F_{ij}C_{ij}, \\
\text{subject to } &\sum_{j=1}^{n} F_{ij} \leq 1 \quad 1 \leq i \leq m, \\
&\sum_{i=1}^{m} F_{ij} \leq 1 \quad 1 \leq j \leq n, \\
&\sum_{i=1}^{m}\sum_{j=1}^{n} F_{ij} \leq \min(m, n).
\end{aligned} \tag{1}
$$

C_{ij} is the cost for moving $\mathbf{d}_i$ to $\mathbf{d}_j$. We define such cost as Jaccard distance [23] and it can be calculated by dividing the difference of the sizes of the union and the intersection of two sets of substructure by the size of the union:

$$C_{ij} = \frac{|\,\mathbf{d}_i \cup \mathbf{d}_j\,| - |\,\mathbf{d}_i \cap \mathbf{d}_j\,|}{|\,\mathbf{d}_i \cup \mathbf{d}_j\,|}. \tag{2}$$

Such an optimization problem 1 can be further solved through the transportation simplex method [26]. Once the optimal transportation flow is found, the EMD between event $\mathbf{E}_p$ and $\mathbf{E}_q$ is defined as the resulting overall cost normalized by the total transportation flow:

$$\mathrm{EMD}(\mathbf{E}_p, \mathbf{E}_q) = \frac{\sum_{i=1}^{m}\sum_{j=1}^{n} F_{ij}C_{ij}}{\sum_{i=1}^{m}\sum_{j=1}^{n} F_{ij}}. \tag{3}$$

After calculating the EMD between each overdose events, we then construct a similarity matrix (i.e., adjacency matrix). The similarity between $\mathbf{E}_p$ and $\mathbf{E}_q$ is calculated using a radial basis function kernel, i.e., $\exp\left(\frac{-\mathrm{EMD}(\mathbf{E}_p,\mathbf{E}_q)^2}{2\epsilon^2}\right)$. To categorize drug overdose events into different clusters, we apply spectral clustering [46] on all the events. The spectral clustering algorithm takes in the adjacency matrix and uses the eigenvalues and eigenvectors from the adjacency matrix of the events to perform dimensionality reduction before clustering. Each overdose event is then assigned to a category u. Therefore, each event $\mathbf{E}_i = (t_i, x_i, y_i, u_i)$ consists of four pieces of information: t_i is the timestamp of the date of death (D.o.D) of the victim; x_i and y_i are the latitude and longitude of where the victim is found; and u_i is the drug overdose category. Our approach to overdose categorization can seamlessly integrate the molecular substructure similarities across different drug overdoses and produce more pharmacokinetic-aware categories. Figure 2 shows the top 5 overdose categories, along with the most frequent drugs in each category, computed using our drug mover's distance-based spectral clustering approach.

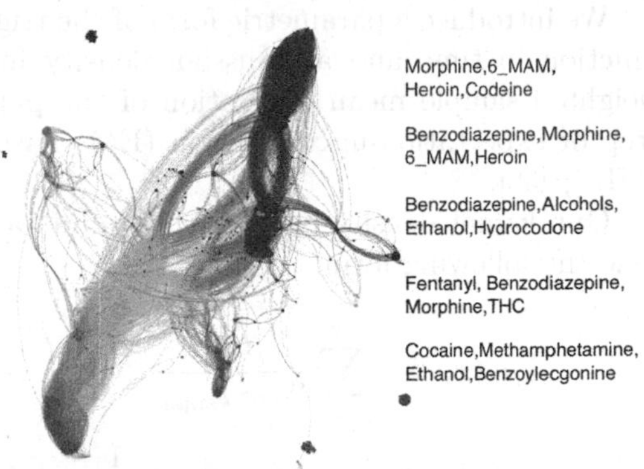

Fig. 2. Gephi visualization of graph used for spectral clustering (edges correspond to adjacency weight greater than .9) and the most frequent drugs in each of the 5 overdose categories.

2.3 Spatio-Temporal Hawkes Process

Clustering in space-time drug overdose event data may occur for a variety of reasons; for example, an increase in the prevalence of a new street drug may appear in a neighborhood leading to a spike in overdoses; or a particular batch of drugs may contain a higher than usual amount of a dangerous substance, for example, fentanyl. Motivated by the observed clustering of overdose data [1], we further characterize drug overdose events through a cross-exciting spatio-temporal Hawkes process [50] that models the contagiousness of events across overdose categories (computed using DMD spectral clustering).

Given a drug overdose sequence $\{\mathbf{E}_i\}_i^N$ with N events, we characterize a multivariate spatio-temporal Hawkes process through the following conditional intensity function for each category u:

$$\lambda_u(x, y, t) = \mu_u(x, y) + \sum_{t > t_i} K_{u_i u} g(x - x_i, y - y_i, t - t_i). \tag{4}$$

In Eq. (4), the background rate $\mu_u(x, y)$ for each category is assumed to be a constant in time, while inhomogeneous in space. The historical events increase the likelihood of the near-future events through the spatio-temporal triggering density function g. $\mathbf{K}(u_i, u_j) = K_{u_i, u_j}$ is the productivity (or triggering) matrix to quantify the self or cross-exciting impact of the events associated with category

u_i on the subsequent events in the category u_j. Specifically, K_{u_i,u_j} denotes the mean number of events in process u_j that are triggered by each event in the process u_i.

We introduce a parametric form of the triggering density with an exponential function in time and a Gaussian density in space. These choices allow for a weighted sample mean estimation of the parameters in the maximization (M) step of expectation-maximization (EM) based maximum likelihood estimation (MLE) [30].

Our kernel density-based background rate and triggering density function take the following form:

$$
\begin{aligned}
\mu_u(x,y) &= \sum_{i=1}^{N} \frac{\beta_{u_i u}}{2\pi\eta^2 T_{\text{span}}} \times \exp\left(- \frac{(x-x_i)^2 + (y-y_i)^2}{2\eta^2} \right), \\
g(x,y,t) &= \omega \exp(-\omega t) \times \frac{1}{2\pi\sigma^2} \exp(-\frac{x^2+y^2}{2\sigma^2}),
\end{aligned} \tag{5}
$$

where T_{span} denotes the time spanned through the whole training dataset; $\beta_{u_i u}$ measures the extent to which events in process u_i contribute to the background rate in the process u_j; ω controls how fast the rate $\lambda_u(x,y,t)$ returns to its baseline level $\mu_u(x,y)$ after an event occurs; and η and σ dictate the spreading scale of the triggering effect in space.

We perform the M step of the EM-type algorithm following the framework of Algorithm 1 in [50] to estimate the parameters. We use the "optimal" parameters from the previous M step to update the latent variables and alternately iterate E and M step. After parameter estimation, we utilize the branching structures [52] of self-exciting point processes to simulate self and cross-exciting events (See Algorithm 3 in [50]) for the next T days for 1,000 times. The simulated events are denoted as $\hat{\mathbf{E}} = (\hat{t}, \hat{x}, \hat{y}, \hat{u})$.

To make recommendations for early warning of overdose spikes, we generate a short ranked list of hotspots in the domain of interest. We first partition the domain of interest into $N \times N$ fine-grained grid cells by dividing the latitude and longitude span into N parts with equal length. Based on the latitude and longitude (i.e., $\hat{x}$ and $\hat{y}$) from the simulated events, we calculate the average number of the simulated events for each grid cell from 1,000 repeated simulations. We denote the average number of the simulated events in the ith and j^{th} grid in terms of latitude and longitude as $\chi(i,j)$. Finally, we sort the grids according to the average number of the simulated events in descending order and retain the top-N grids as the recommended short ranked list.

3 Comparison Methods

We compare our model with several state-of-the-art methods including the following: Non-parametric temporal Hawkes Processes; Spatio-temporal univariate Hawkes Processes; and Dirichlet Hawkes Processes that learn the category assignment while estimating the intensity function. None of the existing point process methods jointly learn the spatio-temporal self and cross-exciting density together for different overdose categories based on the drug substance structure; methods either exist for spatio-temporal point processes or for time-only topic point processes, but not both. The details of our implementation for these baseline methods are presented in the following sections.

Non-parametric Hawkes Processes: `SimpHP` [24]
Our first baseline model utilizes a non-parametric Hawkes process [24] that takes a series of time stamps and then uses a penalized MLE to simultaneously estimate the background rate $\mu(t)$ and triggering kernel $g(t)$ without prior knowledge of their form. Given a set of overdose events, we partition the training dataset into $N \times N$ subsets according to which fine-grained grid cell they belong (as defined in Sect. 2.3). Each subset of events corresponds to an independent Hawkes process. Once the estimation is done, the simulation for the next T interval is done through thinning [35]. Each Hawkes process is first simulated 1,000 times and the average number of simulated events is calculated. The top-N grids cell with the largest average number of simulated events is recommended. We denote this baseline method as `SimpHP`.

Spatial-Temporal Hawkes Processes: `SpatHP` [50]
We compare `SOS − EW` with a sub-model that only uses the geolocation and time stamps for estimation, without clustering events into different categories (univariate). The model estimation and recommendation follow the same framework in Sect. 2.3. Such a baseline model is denoted as `SpatHP`.

Dirichlet Hawkes Processes: `TopicHP` [4]
The Dirichlet Hawkes process [4] is a random process which takes into account both text information from documents and temporal dynamics of their arrival pattern to cluster the document streams. The model is estimated through an online inference algorithm that jointly learns the pattern of the clusters and the parameters of the Hawkes process for each cluster. To adapt to this model, we view each overdose event as a document and each drug as a word. Spatial information is integrated into each event by adding a grid cell index as an additional word. After model estimation, we then use thinning [35] based simulation and average the number of events for each grid cell and topic (over 1,000 simulations) to generate a recommendation of the top-N grid cells with the most number of simulated events.

4 Experiments

4.1 Data

We analyze a toxicology dataset from Marion County, Indiana that was collected as part of the CDCs Prevention for States funding initiative [28,37,38]. The dataset contains toxicology reports of 1,489 overdose death events in Indianapolis, Indiana, U.S.A. from 2010 to 2016. Each overdose event includes the date of death (D.o.D) of the victim and the geolocation (latitude and longitude) of where the victim was found. In addition, every event also contains forensic toxicology testing results that screen for 164 drug substances. A binary indicator represents whether a specific drug substance was found in the victim's body. In our analysis, we restricted to a subset of 133 drugs whose 2D chemical structure representation can be found in the chemical molecules database, Pubchem [19], for further feature generation. We also restricted our analysis to the 1,425 overdose events that include geolocation information and occurred within the city of Indianapolis boundary, where the latitude ranges from 39°37′58.8″N to 39°55′30.3″N and the longitude ranges from 87°06′41.1″W to 85°56′18.7″W. Table 1 presents the statics of the pruned dataset. Figure 4 presents the example of some overdose events. The number of overdoses is increasing in recent years (see Fig. 3).

Table 1. Statistics on overdoes event

Start date	01-14-2010
End date	12-30-2016
#event	1,425
$\overline{\#\text{d}}$	6.3698
$\overline{\#\text{ent}_\text{d}}$	68.2481

In this table, "#event" represents the number of events in the toxicology report; "$\overline{\#\text{d}}$" represents the average number of drug substances in each event; and "$\overline{\#\text{ent}_\text{d}}$" is the average number of events involved in each drug.

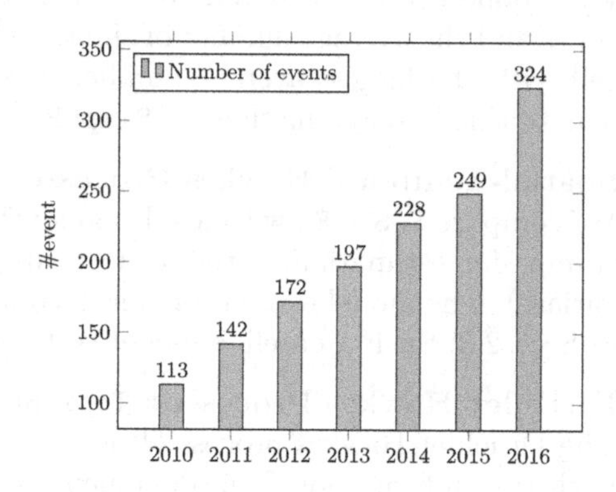

Fig. 3. Number of events per year

Features for each drug are extracted by identifying its molecular substructure fingerprints. Specifically, each drug is represented by a set of substructures s (i.e., $\mathbf{d} \in \{s_1, s_2, \cdots, s_k\}$). We further used RDKit [22], open-source software that allows us to search the substructures based on 2D chemical structures representation, to generate a feature vector of dimension 1,024 for each drug. The pruned dataset is then used for model evaluation.

4.2 Evaluation Protocols and Metrics

The domain of Indianapolis covered by the pruned dataset is first partitioned into $N \times N$ grid cells by dividing the latitude and longitude span into N parts with equal length in each direction. For each time interval t^{th}, we recommend a ranked list of grid cells based on how likely those grid cells are to have overdose events in the near future, using the history of the process up to t^{th} time interval. The performance is then evaluated through walk forward optimization

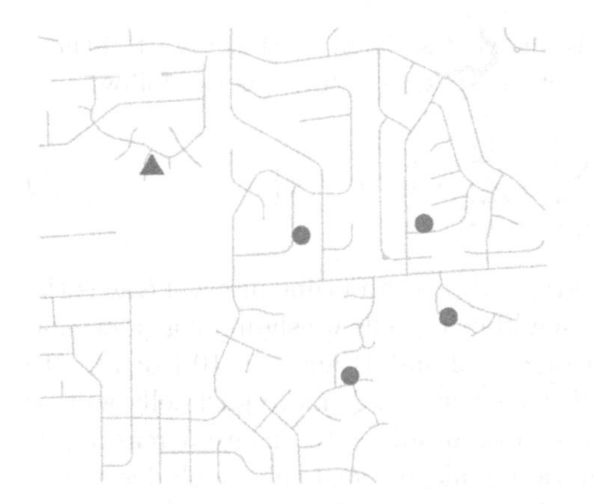

Initial Event
Alcohols, Ethanol, Benzodiazepine, Fentanyl

Triggered Events
1. Benzodiazepine, 6_MAM, Heroin_from_combo, Morphine, Codeine, Hydrocodone, Hydromorphone

2. Alcohols, Ethanol, Benzodiazepine, 6_MAM, Heroin_from_combo, Morphine, Codeine, Oxycodone, Oxymorphone

3. THC, Carboxy_THC, Oxycodone, Oxymorphone, Hydromorphone

4. Benzodiazepine, 6_MAM, Heroin_from_combo, Cocaine, Morphine, Codeine, Fentanyl, Oxycodone, Oxymorphone

Fig. 4. An illustration for an initial event and its triggered events in one of the categories (i.e., one of the Hawks processes). The initial overdose event marked in triangle symbol consists of four drug substances and it triggered four neighboring events consisting of different number of drug substances respectively.

[30]. Specifically, in our experimental setting, we first train our model over a fixed amount of the most recent historical events, which is 255 events (the number of events in the first two years). We then test the model on the next time period starting on 01/01/2012 and report the performance. Finally, the overall performance is the average from all the time periods that we have tested.

At each time interval T, models recommend a ranked list of size K for potential overdose events. In our experimental setting, we set T as 5 days and partition the domain of interest into 100×100 grid cells. The time window is consistent with the time scale on which police and health services can respond and the grid cell size is similar to those used in field trials of predictive policing [33]. The ranking performance is evaluated through normalized discounted cumulative gain at K ($NDCG@K$), which is a measurement of ranking quality and commonly used in information retrieval. $NDCG@K$ is calculated by normalizing discounted cumulative gain (denoted as $DCG@K$) with ideal $DCG@K$ (denoted as $IDCG@K$). The definition are as follows:

$$DCG@K = \sum_{i=1}^{K} \frac{2^{rel_i} - 1}{log_2(i+1)}, \qquad NDCG@K = \frac{DCG@K}{IDCG@K}, \tag{6}$$

where rel_i is the ith relevance value of the ith grid in the ranked list $\mathbf{r}$; $IDCG@K$ is the ideal $DCG@K$ when the ranked list $\mathbf{r}$ is perfectly ranked based on its relevance values; and then we define relevance value rel_i as the number of overdose events that happen in the ith grid cell in the ranked list $\mathbf{r}$ and t^{th} time interval.

In a certain time interval, a spike of overdose events may occur. To evaluate our model's ability to forecast future spikes, we first define an event spike at the tth time interval in a grid cell (i, j) as follows: If the total number of events in the neighboring cells between the $(t-1)^{\text{th}}$ and $(t+1)^{\text{th}}$ intervals is more than a threshold, then we consider that there is an event spike in (i, j) grid within these time intervals. The set of grids with an event spike is defined as the following:

$$\mathbf{s} = \{(i, j, t) \mid \sum_{\hat{i}=i-w}^{i+w} \sum_{\hat{j}=j-w}^{j+w} \sum_{\hat{t}=t-1}^{t+1} \chi(\hat{i}, \hat{j}, \hat{t}) \geq \xi\} \tag{7}$$

where $\chi(i, j, t)$ is the count of events in grid cell (i, j) and time interval t, w is the spatial window size defining how many neighboring cells we should consider; and ξ is the spike threshold: we set $\xi = 2$ (for $w = 2$ and 4) and $\xi = 10$ (for $w = 10$ and 15) in our evaluation setting. With larger w and ξ, more gird cells will be considered to have an event spike. We choose w and ξ to ensure a reasonable amount of event spikes for further evaluation while an event spike includes a huge amount of overdose events. We adopt modified reciprocal hit rank [36], precision and recall at different ranked list size K, denoted as $MRHR$, $Prec$, and Rec to evaluate the performance. $MRHR$ is a modified version of average reciprocal hit rank (ARHR), which is feasible for ranking evaluations where there are multiples relevant items (i.e., multiple spikes events), and it is calculated as the following:

$$\begin{aligned} MRHR &= \frac{1}{\mid \mathbf{s} \mid} \sum_{i=1}^{K} \left(\frac{hit_i}{rank_i}\right), \\ \text{where } hit_i &= \begin{cases} 1 & \text{if } r_i \in \mathbf{s} \\ 0 & \text{if } r_i, \notin \mathbf{s} \end{cases}, rank_i = \begin{cases} rank_{i-1} & \text{if } hit_{i-1} = 1 \\ rank_{i-1} + 1 & \text{if } hit_{i-1} = 0, \end{cases} \end{aligned} \tag{8}$$

where each hit is rewarded based on its position in the ranked list. $Prec$ and Rec are commonly used to evaluate the performance in recommendation system. $Prec$ evaluates how precisely the model can predict for future spike events while Rec measures the ability of retrieving spikes. We also evaluate average precision, denoted as APC, to account for both precision and recall without choosing K:

$$Prec = \frac{\mid \mathbf{s} \cap \mathbf{r} \mid}{\mid \mathbf{r} \mid}, \quad Rec = \frac{\mid \mathbf{s} \cap \mathbf{r} \mid}{\mid \mathbf{s} \mid}, \quad APC = \frac{\sum_{\{k:1,\cdots,K \mid r_k \in \mathbf{s}\}} Prec@k}{\mid \mathbf{s} \cap \mathbf{r} \mid}. \tag{9}$$

4.3 Experimental Results

Table 2 presents the overall performances on overdose spikes prediction under different breadth definition of spike events (Eq. 7). Our `SOS − EW` system consistently outperforms other baseline methods by a large margin in terms of $MRHR$, $Prec$, Rec, and APC. $MRHR$ is used to evaluate the ranking quality while $Prec$, Rec, and APC evaluate the retrieval for events spikes. This shows our proposed method not only can successfully recommend the regions with potential event spikes considering the ranking position but it can also precisely generate a short

Table 2. Overall performance on different spike window size w

w	mdl	$MRHR$			$Prec$			Rec			APC
		@1%	@3%	@5%	@1%	@3%	@5%	@1%	@3%	@5%	
2	SOS − EW	**.0172**	**.0188**	**.0191**	**.0277**	**.0174**	**.0124**	**.2534**	**.5038**	**.6110**	**.0451**
	SimpHP	.0088	.0089	.0090	.0034	.0019	.0018	.0289	.0496	.0842	.0103
	SpatHP	.0017	.0021	.0023	.0036	.0029	.0025	.0375	.1129	.1590	.0043
	TopicHP	.0080	.0082	.0082	.0130	.0085	.0055	.1258	.2386	.2748	.0125
4	SOS − EW	**.0218**	**.0236**	**.0240**	**.1091**	**.0724**	**.0555**	**.2690**	**.5196**	**.6699**	**.1187**
	SimpHP	.0059	.0060	.0060	.0126	.0070	.0060	.0279	.0475	.0660	.0118
	SpatHP	.0016	.0018	.0020	.0114	.0111	.0112	.0274	.0784	.1294	.0102
	TopicHP	.0082	.0089	.0090	.0474	.0315	.0205	.1089	.2226	.2434	.0250
10	SOS − EW	**.0219**	**.0254**	**.0259**	**.2000**	**.1526**	**.1229**	**.1911**	**.6734**	**.8554**	**.1851**
	SimpHP	.0029	.0031	.0032	.0189	.0119	.0111	.0128	.0662	.0854	.0125
	SpatHP	.0003	.0007	.0007	.0167	.0181	.0193	.0109	.0691	.1025	.0151
	TopicHP	.0096	.0097	.0098	.0856	.0548	.0360	.1974	.2868	.3121	.0335
15	SOS − EW	**.0620**	**.0718**	**.0726**	**.4387**	**.3275**	**.2549**	**.3234**	**.6470**	**.8025**	**.3644**
	SimpHP	.0070	.0072	.0072	.0445	.0291	.0254	.0336	.0526	.0676	.0301
	SpatHP	.0016	.0019	.0020	.0516	.0506	.0503	.0220	.0746	.1119	.0387
	TopicHP	.0083	.0091	.0092	.1739	.1212	.0802	.1035	.2081	.2267	.0622

The column "mdl" corresponds to different models. The best overall performance is **bold**.

ranked list for those event spikes precisely. As the ranking list size increases, performances of $MRHR$ remains similar after $MRHR$@3%; $Prec$ decreases while Rec increases due to the natural trade-off between these two metrics. SOS − EW estimates the model parameters and makes predictions specifically for different overdose categories compared to SpatHP which estimates the same parameters for all event data aggregated together. This indicates that strategically clustering overdose events based on the drug molecular structure can achieve better performances than the model which solely relies on spatio-temporal information. TopicHP jointly learns the clustering structure and model parameters and it can be viewed as a competitive baseline. However, only the drug distribution in each event is taken into account and drugs' chemical structure is not included in the model training. This may explain why TopicHP falls short of spikes recommendation metrics compared to SOS − EW but is still better than other baselines. Overall, SOS − EW leverages the information from geo-locations, event triggering dynamics, and drugs' high level physical and chemical properties based on 2D structures altogether and precisely makes the recommendations for future overdose event spikes.

Table 3 presents the overall model performances on $NDCG$ when only evaluating each models ability to rank grid cells (equivalent to $\omega = 0$). The ranking quality increases as the size of the ranked list grows larger (i.e., from 1% to 5%). Our proposed SOS − EW outperforms the second best baseline method TopicHP by 12.27% at $NDCG$@5%, however, TopicHP is the top performing model at 1% and 3%. These results indicate that for the very highest risk cells, spatial diffusion may play less of a role and TopicHP and SOS − EW have similar performance. However, for flagging neighborhoods instead of individual cells for spikes, SOS − EW is superior due to its ability to model spatial diffusion of risk.

Table 3. Overall $NDCG$ performance

mdl	@1%	@3%	@5%
SOS − EW	.0322	.0637	**.0842**
SimpHP	.0191	.0236	.0265
SpatHP	.0092	.0179	.0262
TopicHP	**.0492**	**.0733**	.0750

The column "mdl" corresponds to different models. The best overall performance is **bold**.

5 Implications for Practice

Results from our proposed system can be translated into more effective social service delivery and intervention programming. When flagging the top 1% of predicted spikes defined in neighborhoods of approximately $O(1\,\text{km}^2)$ in size and 5 days in length, the method captures around 25% of opioid spikes. These spatial and temporal scales are similar in size to those used in predictive policing [33] and by efficiently predicting the geographic diffusion of opioid-related toxins (such as fentanyl), social service programs and first responders can develop dynamic programs to best target areas where people face the highest risk of overdose. Further research is needed to verify whether or not the results found in Indianapolis in this study extend to other cities and rural areas.

Studies have revealed polydrug patterns whereby fentanyl is being detected alongside cocaine and methamphetamines, which is contributing to overdose deaths involving these substances [17,29]. Given the nature of this supply-side poisoning among illicit drugs, the most feasible approach may be to empower and provide persons who used drugs with the ability to test these substances. Drug testing technologies (i.e., fentanyl test strips) allow drug users to understand whether the drugs they use are contaminated with lethal substances, such as fentanyl, which can allow them to adjust behaviors and prevent a potentially fatal overdose [13]. Furthermore, the average of dispatch and response time for emergency medical services (EMS) personnel to arrive when an overdose event is reported is seven minutes on average[1] and the time to results of many drug test strips is usually less then minutes nowadays. Therefore, our system can make a prediction in a short time so that the health/social workers can react accordingly. More research is needed to extend the method in this paper, that

[1] https://www.medicalnewsbulletin.com/response-time-emergency-medical-services/.

utilizes toxicology reports, to the application of drug test strips and other drug testing tools (which may not be a thorough as a coroner's report).

Public health services can deploy syringe services, such as retractable syringes or exchange programs, that have been shown to reduce fatal opioid use [9,18]. From a policing perspective, officers can be equipped with nasal naloxone (or Narcan) within high-risk opioid locations to reduce the likelihood of death from an opioid overdose [7,39].

Acknowledgements. This work was supported by NIJ grant 2018-R2-CX-0013, NSF grants DMS-1737770, SCC-1737585, ATD-1737996, and DARPA grant FA8750-18-2-0066.

References

1. Carter, J.G., Mohler, G., Ray, B.: Spatial concentration of opioid overdose deaths in Indianapolis: an application of the law of crime concentration at place to a public health epidemic. J. Contemp. Crim. Justice **35**(2), 161–185 (2018). https://doi.org/10.1177/1043986218803527
2. Ciccarone, D.: Fentanyl in the US heroin supply: a rapidly changing risk environment. Int. J. Drug Policy **46**, 107–111 (2017)
3. Cicero, T.J., Ellis, M.S., Surratt, H.L., Kurtz, S.P.: The changing face of heroin use in the United States: a retrospective analysis of the past 50 years. JAMA Psychiatry **71**(7), 821–826 (2014)
4. Du, N., Farajtabar, M., Ahmed, A., Smola, A.J., Song, L.: Dirichlet-Hawkes processes with applications to clustering continuous-time document streams. In: Proceedings of the 21th ACM SIGKDD International Conference on Knowledge Discovery and Data Mining, pp. 219–228. ACM (2015)
5. Farajtabar, M., Wang, Y., Rodriguez, M.G., Li, S., Zha, H., Song, L.: COEVOLVE: a joint point process model for information diffusion and network co-evolution. In: Advances in Neural Information Processing Systems, pp. 1954–1962 (2015)
6. Fernandez, W., Hackman, H., Mckeown, L., Anderson, T., Hume, B.: Trends in opioid-related fatal overdoses in Massachusetts, 1990–2003. J. Subst. Abuse Treat. **31**(2), 151–156 (2006)
7. Fisher, R., O'Donnell, D., Ray, B., Rusyniak, D.: Police officers can safely and effectively administer intranasal naloxone. Prehospital Emerg. Care **20**(6), 675–680 (2016)
8. Flaxman, S., Chirico, M., Pereira, P., Loeffler, C.: Scalable high-resolution forecasting of sparse spatiotemporal events with kernel methods: a winning solution to the NIJ "real-time crime forecasting challenge". arXiv preprint arXiv:1801.02858 (2018)
9. Frost, M.C., Williams, E.C., Kingston, S., Banta-Green, C.J.: Interest in getting help to reduce or stop substance use among syringe exchange clients who use opioids. J. Addict. Med. **12**(6), 428–434 (2018)
10. Gao, P., Guo, D., Liao, K., Webb, J.J., Cutter, S.L.: Early detection of terrorism outbreaks using prospective space-time scan statistics. Prof. Geogr. **65**(4), 676–691 (2013)
11. Gilson, T.P.: The medical examiner's role in addressing the opioid crisis. US Att'ys Bull. **66**, 47 (2018)

12. Gladden, R.M.: Fentanyl law enforcement submissions and increases in syntheticopioid-involved overdose deaths—27 states, 2013–2014. MMWR Morb. Mortal. Wkly Rep. **65**, 837–843 (2016)
13. Glick, J.L., Christensen, T., Park, J.N., McKenzie, M., Green, T.C., Sherman, S.G.: Stakeholder perspectives on implementing fentanyl drug checking: results from a multi-site study. Drug Alcohol Depend. **194**, 527–532 (2019)
14. Hirohara, M., Saito, Y., Koda, Y., Sato, K., Sakakibara, Y.: Convolutional neural network based on SMILES representation of compounds for detecting chemical motif. BMC Bioinformatics **19**(19), 526 (2018)
15. Hoppe-Roberts, J.M., Lloyd, L.M., Chyka, P.A.: Poisoning mortality in the United States: comparison of national mortality statistics and poison control center reports. Ann. Emerg. Med. **35**(5), 440–448 (2000)
16. Jones, C.M., Einstein, E.B., Compton, W.M.: Changes in synthetic opioid involvement in drug overdose deaths in the United States, 2010–2016. JAMA **319**(17), 1819–1821 (2018)
17. Kandel, D.B., Hu, M.C., Griesler, P., Wall, M.: Increases from 2002 to 2015 in prescription opioid overdose deaths in combination with other substances. Drug Alcohol Depend. **178**, 501–511 (2017)
18. Karamouzian, M., Dohoo, C., Forsting, S., McNeil, R., Kerr, T., Lysyshyn, M.: Evaluation of a fentanyl drug checking service for clients of a supervised injection facility, Vancouver, Canada. Harm Reduct. J. **15**(1), 46 (2018)
19. Kim, S., Thiessen, P.A., Bolton, E.E., Chen, J., Fu, G., Gindulyte, A., Han, L., He, J., He, S., Shoemaker, B.A., et al.: PubChem substance and compound databases. Nucleic Acids Res. **44**(D1), D1202–D1213 (2015)
20. Kusner, M., Sun, Y., Kolkin, N., Weinberger, K.: From word embeddings to document distances. In: International Conference on Machine Learning, pp. 957–966 (2015)
21. Lai, E.L., et al.: Topic time series analysis of microblogs. IMA J. Appl. Math. **81**(3), 409–431 (2016)
22. Landrum, G.: RDKit: open-source cheminformatics software (2016)
23. Levandowsky, M., Winter, D.: Distance between sets. Nature **234**(5323), 34 (1971)
24. Lewis, E., Mohler, G.: A nonparametric EM algorithm for multiscale Hawkes processes. Preprint (2011)
25. Li, C., Song, Z., Wang, X.: Nonparametric method for modeling clustering phenomena in emergency calls under spatial-temporal self-exciting point processes. IEEE Access **7**, 24865–24876 (2019). https://doi.org/10.1109/ACCESS.2019.2900340
26. Lieberman, G.J., Hillier, F.: Introduction to Mathematical Programming. McGraw-Hill, New York (1995)
27. Linakis, J.G., Frederick, K.A.: Poisoning deaths not reported to the regional poison control center. Ann. Emerg. Med. **22**(12), 1822–1828 (1993)
28. Lowder, E.M., Ray, B.R., Huynh, P., Ballew, A., Watson, D.P.: Identifying unreported opioid deaths through toxicology data and vital records linkage: case study in Marion County, Indiana, 2011–2016. Am. J. Public Health **108**(12), 1682–1687 (2018)
29. McCall Jones, C., Baldwin, G.T., Compton, W.M.: Recent increases in cocaine-related overdose deaths and the role of opioids. Am. J. Public Health **107**(3), 430–432 (2017)
30. Mohler, G.: Marked point process hotspot maps for homicide and gun crime prediction in Chicago. Int. J. Forecast. **30**(3), 491–497 (2014)
31. Mohler, G., Porter, M.D.: Rotational grid, PAI-maximizing crime forecasts. Stat. Anal. Data Min. ASA Data Sci. J. **11**(5), 227–236 (2018)

32. Mohler, G.O., Short, M.B., Brantingham, P.J., Schoenberg, F.P., Tita, G.E.: Self-exciting point process modeling of crime. J. Am. Stat. Assoc. **106**(493), 100–108 (2011)
33. Mohler, G.O., et al.: Randomized controlled field trials of predictive policing. J. Am. Stat. Assoc. **110**(512), 1399–1411 (2015)
34. Ng, A.Y., Jordan, M.I., Weiss, Y.: On spectral clustering: analysis and an algorithm. In: Advances in Neural Information Processing Systems, pp. 849–856 (2002)
35. Ogata, Y.: On Lewis' simulation method for point processes. IEEE Trans. Inf. Theory **27**(1), 23–31 (1981)
36. Peker, S., Kocyigit, A.: mRHR: a modified reciprocal hit rank metric for ranking evaluation of multiple preferences in top-n recommender systems. In: Dichev, C., Agre, G. (eds.) AIMSA 2016. LNCS (LNAI), vol. 9883, pp. 320–329. Springer, Cham (2016). https://doi.org/10.1007/978-3-319-44748-3_31
37. Phalen, P., Ray, B., Watson, D.P., Huynh, P., Greene, M.S.: Fentanyl related overdose in Indianapolis: estimating trends using multilevel Bayesian models. Addict. Behav. **86**, 4–10 (2018)
38. Ray, B., Quinet, K., Dickinson, T., Watson, D.P., Ballew, A.: Examining fatal opioid overdoses in Marion County, Indiana. J. Urban Health **94**(2), 301–310 (2017)
39. Ray, B.R., Lowder, E.M., Kivisto, A.J., Phalen, P., Gil, H.: EMS naloxone administration as non-fatal opioid overdose surveillance: 6-year outcomes in Marion County, Indiana. Addiction **113**(12), 2271–2279 (2018)
40. Rubner, Y., Tomasi, C., Guibas, L.J.: The earth mover's distance as a metric for image retrieval. Int. J. Comput. Vision **40**(2), 99–121 (2000)
41. Rudd, R.A., et al.: Increases in heroin overdose deaths—28 states, 2010 to 2012. MMWR Morb. Mortal. Wkly Rep. **63**(39), 849 (2014)
42. Ruhm, C.J.: Corrected US opioid-involved drug poisoning deaths and mortality rates, 1999–2015. Addiction **113**(7), 1339–1344 (2018)
43. Seth, P., Scholl, L., Rudd, R.A., Bacon, S.: Overdose deaths involving opioids, cocaine, and psychostimulants—United States, 2015–2016. Morb. Mortal. Wkly Rep. **67**(12), 349 (2018)
44. Shirota, S., Gelfand, A.E., et al.: Space and circular time log Gaussian Cox processes with application to crime event data. Ann. Appl. Stat. **11**(2), 481–503 (2017)
45. Strickler, G.K., Zhang, K., Halpin, J.M., Bohnert, A.S., Baldwin, G., Kreiner, P.W.: Effects of mandatory prescription drug monitoring program (PDMP) uselaws on prescriber registration and use and on risky prescribing. Drug Alcohol Depend. **199**, 1–9 (2019)
46. Von Luxburg, U.: A tutorial on spectral clustering. Stat. Comput. **17**(4), 395–416 (2007)
47. Warner, M., Hedegaard, H.: Identifying opioid overdose deaths using vital statistics data (2018)
48. Wysowski, D.K.: Surveillance of prescription drug-related mortality using death certificate data. Drug Saf. **30**(6), 533–540 (2007)
49. Xu, H., Zha, H.: A Dirichlet mixture model of Hawkes processes for event sequence clustering. In: Advances in Neural Information Processing Systems, pp. 1354–1363 (2017)
50. Yuan, B., Li, H., Bertozzi, A.L., Brantingham, P.J., Porter, M.A.: Multivariate spatiotemporal Hawkes processes and network reconstruction. SIAM J. Math. Data Sci. **1**(2), 356–382 (2019)

51. Zammit-Mangion, A., Dewar, M., Kadirkamanathan, V., Sanguinetti, G.: Point process modelling of the Afghan War Diary. Proc. Natl. Acad. Sci. **109**(31), 12414–12419 (2012)
52. Zhuang, J., Ogata, Y., Vere-Jones, D.: Analyzing earthquake clustering features by using stochastic reconstruction. J. Geophys. Res. **109**, B05301 (2004). https://doi.org/10.1029/2003JB002879

Improving GP-UCB Algorithm by Harnessing Decomposed Feedback

Kai Wang[1(✉)], Bryan Wilder[1], Sze-chuan Suen[2], Bistra Dilkina[2], and Milind Tambe[1]

[1] Harvard University, Cambridge, USA
{kaiwang,bwilder,milind_tambe}@g.harvard.edu
[2] University of Southern California, Los Angeles, USA
{ssuen,dilkina}@usc.edu

Abstract. Gaussian processes (GPs) have been widely applied to machine learning and nonparametric approximation. Given existing observations, a GP allows the decision maker to update a posterior belief over the unknown underlying function. Usually, observations from a complex system come with noise and decomposed feedback from intermediate layers. For example, the decomposed feedback could be the components that constitute the final objective value, or the various feedback gotten from sensors. Previous literature has shown that GPs can successfully deal with noise, but has neglected decomposed feedback. We therefore propose a *decomposed* GP regression algorithm to incorporate this feedback, leading to less average root-mean-squared error with respect to the target function, especially when the samples are scarce. We also introduce a *decomposed* GP-UCB algorithm to solve the resulting bandit problem with decomposed feedback. We prove that our algorithm converges to the optimal solution and preserves the no-regret property. To demonstrate the wide applicability of this work, we execute our algorithm on two disparate social problems: infectious disease control and weather monitoring. The numerical results show that our method provides significant improvement against previous methods that do not utilize these feedback, showcasing the advantage of considering decomposed feedback.

Keywords: Decomposed feedback · Decomposed GP regression · D-GPUCB

1 Introduction

Many challenging sequential decision making problems involve interventions in complex physical or social systems, where the system dynamics must be learned over time. For instance, a challenge commonly faced by policymakers is to control disease outbreaks [16], but the true process by which disease spreads in the population is not known in advance. We study such problems from the perspective of online learning, where a decision maker aims to optimize an unknown expensive objective function [2]. At each step, the decision maker commits to an action and receives the objective value for that action. For instance, a policymaker may implement a disease control policy [9, 12] for a given time period and observe the number of subsequent infections. This information allows the decision maker to update their knowledge of the unknown function. The

P. Cellier and K. Driessens (Eds.): ECML PKDD 2019 Workshops, CCIS 1167, pp. 555–569, 2020.
https://doi.org/10.1007/978-3-030-43823-4_44

goal is to obtain low cumulative regret, which measures the difference in objective value between the actions that were taken and the true (unknown) optimum.

This problem has been well-studied in optimization and machine learning. When a parametric form is not available for the objective (as is often the case with complex systems that are difficult to model analytically), a common approach uses a Gaussian process (GP) as a nonparametric prior over smooth functions. This Bayesian approach allows the decision maker to form a posterior distribution over the unknown function's values. Consequently, the GP-UCB algorithm, which iteratively selects the point with the highest upper confidence bound according to the posterior, achieves a no-regret guarantee [14].

While GP-UCB and similar techniques [3, 17] have seen a great deal of interest in the purely black-box setting, many physical or social systems naturally admit an intermediate level of feedback. This is because the system is composed of multiple interacting components, each of which can be measured individually. For instance, disease spread in a population is a product of the interactions between individuals in different demographic groups or locations [19], and policymakers often have access to estimates of the prevalence of infected individuals within each subgroup [4, 18]. The true objective (total infections) is the sum of infections across the subgroups. Similarly, climate systems involve the interactions of many different variables (heat, wind, humidity, etc.) which can be sensed individually then combined in a nonlinear fashion to produce outputs of interest (e.g., an individual's risk of heat stroke) [15]. Prior work has studied the benefits of using additive models [6]. However, they only examine the special case where the target function decomposes into a sum of lower-dimensional functions. Motivated by applications such as flu prevention, we consider the more general setting where the subcomponents are full-dimensional and may be composed nonlinearly to produce the target. This general perspective is necessary to capture common policy settings which may involve intermediate observables from simulation or domain knowledge.

However, to our knowledge, no prior work studies the challenge of integrating such decomposed feedback in online decision making. Our first contribution is to remedy this gap by proposing a *decomposed GP-UCB* algorithm (D-GPUCB). D-GPUCB uses a separate GP to model each individual measurable quantity and then combines the estimates to produce a posterior over the final objective. Our second contribution is a theoretical no-regret guarantee for D-GPUCB, ensuring that its decisions are asymptotically optimal. Third, we prove that the posterior variance at each step must be less than the posterior variance of directly using a GP to model the final objective. This formally demonstrates that more detailed modeling reduces predictive uncertainty. Finally, we conduct experiments in two domains using real-world data: flu prevention and heat sensing. In each case, D-GPUCB achieves substantially lower cumulative regret than previous approaches.

2 Preliminaries

2.1 Noisy Black-Box Optimization

Given an unknown black-box function $f : \mathcal{X} \rightarrow \mathbb{R}$ where $\mathcal{X} \subset \mathbb{R}^n$, a learner is able to select an input $\boldsymbol{x} \in \mathcal{X}$ and access the function to see the outcome $f(\boldsymbol{x})$ – this encompasses one evaluation. Gaussian process regression [11] is a non-parametric method to learn the target function using Bayesian methods [5,13]. It assumes that the target function is an outcome of a Gaussian process with given kernel $k(\boldsymbol{x}, \boldsymbol{x}')$ (covariance function). Gaussian process regression is commonly used and only requires an assumption on the function smoothness. Moreover, Gaussian process regression can handle observation error. It allows the observation at point $\boldsymbol{x}_t$ to be noisy: $y_t = f(\boldsymbol{x}_t) + \epsilon_t$, where $\epsilon_t \sim N(0, \sigma^2 I)$.

2.2 Decomposition

In this paper, we consider a modification to the Gaussian process regression process. Suppose we have some prior knowledge of the unknown reward function $f(\boldsymbol{x})$ such that we can write the unknown function as a combination of known and unknown sub-functions:

Definition 1 (Linear Decomposition).

$$f(\boldsymbol{x}) = \sum\nolimits_{j=1}^{J} g_j(\boldsymbol{x}) f_j(\boldsymbol{x}) \tag{1}$$

where $f_j, g_j : \mathbb{R}^n \rightarrow \mathbb{R}$.

Here $g_j(\boldsymbol{x})$ are known, deterministic functions, but $f_j(\boldsymbol{x})$ are unknown functions that generate noisy observations. For example, in the flu prevention case, the total infected population can be written as the summation of the infected population at each age [4]. Given treatment policy $\boldsymbol{x}$, we can use $f_j(\boldsymbol{x})$ to represent the unknown infected population at age group j with its known, deterministic weighted function $g_j(\boldsymbol{x}) = 1$. Therefore, the total infected population $f(\boldsymbol{x})$ can be simply expressed as $\sum_{j=1}^{J} f_j(\boldsymbol{x})$.

Interestingly, any deterministic linear composition of outcomes of Gaussian processes is still an outcome of Gaussian process. That means if all of the f_j are generated from Gaussian processes, then the entire function f can also be written as an outcome of another Gaussian process.

Next, we generalize this definition to the non-linear case, which we call a general decomposition:

Definition 2 (General Decomposition).

$$f(\boldsymbol{x}) = g(f_1(\boldsymbol{x}), f_2(\boldsymbol{x}), ..., f_J(\boldsymbol{x})) \tag{2}$$

The function g can be any deterministic function (e.g. polynomial, neural network). Unfortunately, a non-linear composition of Gaussian processes may not be a Gaussian process, so we cannot guarantee function f to be an outcome of a Gaussian process. We will cover the result of linear decomposition first and then generalize it to the cases with general decomposition.

2.3 Gaussian Process Regression

Although Gaussian process regression does not require rigid parametric assumptions, a certain degree of smoothness is still needed to ensure its guarantee of no-regret. We can model f as a sample from a GP: a collection of random variables, one for each $\boldsymbol{x} \in \mathcal{X}$. A GP$(\mu(\boldsymbol{x}), k(\boldsymbol{x}, \boldsymbol{x}'))$ is specified by its mean function $\mu(x) = E[f(\boldsymbol{x})]$ and covariance function $k(\boldsymbol{x}, \boldsymbol{x}') = E[(f(\boldsymbol{x}) - \mu(\boldsymbol{x}))(f(\boldsymbol{x}') - \mu(\boldsymbol{x}'))]$. For GPs not conditioned on any prior, we assume that $\mu(\boldsymbol{x}) \equiv 0$. We further assume bounded variance $k(\boldsymbol{x}, \boldsymbol{x}) \leq 1$. This covariance function encodes the smoothness condition of the target function f drawn from the GP.

For a noisy sample $\boldsymbol{y}_T = [y_1, ..., y_T]^\top$ at points $A_T = \{\boldsymbol{x}_t\}_{t \in [T]}$, $y_t = f(\boldsymbol{x}_t) + \epsilon_t \ \forall t \in [T]$ with $\epsilon_t \sim N(0, \sigma^2(\boldsymbol{x}_t))$ Gaussian noise with variance $\sigma^2(\boldsymbol{x}_t)$, the posterior over f is still a Gaussian process with posterior mean $\mu_T(\boldsymbol{x})$, covariance $k_T(\boldsymbol{x}, \boldsymbol{x}')$ and variance $\sigma_T^2(\boldsymbol{x})$:

$$\mu_T(\boldsymbol{x}) = \boldsymbol{k}_T(\boldsymbol{x})^\top \boldsymbol{K}_T^{-1} \boldsymbol{k}_T(\boldsymbol{x}'), \tag{3}$$

$$k_T(\boldsymbol{x}, \boldsymbol{x}') = k(\boldsymbol{x}, \boldsymbol{x}') - \boldsymbol{k}_T(\boldsymbol{x})^\top \boldsymbol{K}_T^{-1} \boldsymbol{k}(\boldsymbol{x}'), \tag{4}$$

$$\sigma_T^2(\boldsymbol{x}) = k_T(\boldsymbol{x}, \boldsymbol{x}') \tag{5}$$

where $\boldsymbol{k}_T(\boldsymbol{x}) = [k(\boldsymbol{x}_1, \boldsymbol{x}), ..., k(\boldsymbol{x}_T, \boldsymbol{x})]^\top$, and $\boldsymbol{K}_T$ is the positive definite kernel matrix $[k(\boldsymbol{x}, \boldsymbol{x}')]_{\boldsymbol{x}, \boldsymbol{x}' \in A_T} + \text{diag}([\sigma^2(\boldsymbol{x}_t)]_{t \in [T]})$.

Algorithm 1. GP Regression

1 **Input:** kernel $k(\boldsymbol{x}, \boldsymbol{x}')$, noise function $\sigma(\boldsymbol{x})$, and previous samples $\{(\boldsymbol{x}_t, y_t)\}_{t \in [T]}$
2 **Return:** $k_T(\boldsymbol{x}, \boldsymbol{x}'), \mu_T(\boldsymbol{x}), \sigma_T^2(\boldsymbol{x})$

2.4 Bandit Problem with Decomposed Feedback

Considering the output value of the target function as the learner's reward (penalty), the goal is to learn the unknown underlying function f while optimizing the cumulative reward. This is usually known as an online learning or multi-arm bandit problem [1]. In this paper, given the knowledge of deterministic decomposition function g (Definition 1 or Definition 2), in each round t, the learner chooses an input $\boldsymbol{x}_t \in \mathcal{X}$ and observes the value of each unknown decomposed function f_j perturbed by a noise: $y_{j,t} = f_j(\boldsymbol{x}_t) + \epsilon_{j,t}, \epsilon_{j,t} \sim N(0, \sigma_j^2) \ \forall j \in [J]$. At the same time, the learner receives the composed reward from this input $\boldsymbol{x}_t$, which is $y_t = g(y_{1,t}, y_{2,t}, ..., y_{J,t}) = f(\boldsymbol{x}_t) + \epsilon_t$ where ϵ_t is an aggregated noise. The goal is to maximize the sum of noise-free rewards $\sum_{t=1}^T f(\boldsymbol{x}_t)$, which is equivalent to minimizing the cumulative regret $R_T = \sum_{t=1}^T r_t = \sum_{t=1}^T f(\boldsymbol{x}^*) - f(\boldsymbol{x}_t)$, where $\boldsymbol{x}^* = \arg\max_{\boldsymbol{x} \in \mathcal{X}} f(\boldsymbol{x})$ and individual regret $r_t = f(\boldsymbol{x}^*) - f(\boldsymbol{x}_t)$.

This decomposed feedback is related to the semi-bandit setting, where a decision is chosen from a combinatorial set and feedback is received about individual elements of the decision [10]. Our work is similar in that we consider an intermediate feedback model which gives the decision maker access to decomposed feedback about the underlying function. However, in our setting a single point is chosen from a continuous set, rather than multiple items from a discrete one. Additional feedback is received about components of the objective function, not the items chosen. Hence, the technical challenges are quite different.

3 Problem Statement and Background

Using the flu prevention as an example, a policymaker will implement a yearly disease control policy and observe the number of subsequent infections. A policy is an input $\boldsymbol{x}_t \in \mathbb{R}^n$, where each entry $x_{t,i}$ denotes the extent to vaccinate the infected people in age group i. For example, if the government spends more effort $x_{t,i}$ in group i, then the people in this group will be more likely to get a flu shot.

Given the decomposition assumption and samples (previous policies) at points $\boldsymbol{x}_t \ \forall t \in [T]$, including all the function values $f(\boldsymbol{x}_t)$ (total infected population) and decomposed function values $f_j(\boldsymbol{x}_t)$ (infected population in group j), the learner attempts to learn the function f while simultaneously minimizing regret. Therefore, we have two main challenges: (i) how best to approximate the reward function using the decomposed feedback and decomposition (non-parametric approximation), and (ii) how to use this estimation to most effectively reduce the average regret (bandit problem).

3.1 Regression: Non-parametric Approximation

Our first aim is to fully utilize the decomposed problem structure to get a better approximation of $f(x)$. The goal is to learn the underlying disease pattern faster by using the decomposed problem structure. Given the linear decomposition assumption that $f(\boldsymbol{x}) = \sum_{j=1}^{J} g_j(\boldsymbol{x}) f_j(\boldsymbol{x})$ and noisy samples at points $\{\boldsymbol{x}_t\}_{t\in[T]}$, the learner can observe the outcome of each decomposed function $f_j(\boldsymbol{x}_t)$ at each sample point $\boldsymbol{x}_t \ \forall t \in [T]$. Our goal is to provide a Bayesian update to the unknown function which fully utilizes the learner's knowledge of the decomposition.

3.2 Bandit Problem: Minimizing Regret

In the flu example, each annual flu-awareness campaign is constrained by a budget, and we assume policymaker does not know the underlying disease spread pattern. At the beginning of each year, the policymaker chooses a new campaign policy based on the previous years' results and observes the outcome of this new policy. The goal is to minimize the cumulative regret (all additional infections in prior years) while learning the underlying unknown function (disease pattern).

We will show how a decomposed GP regression, with a GP-UCB algorithm, can be used to address these challenges.

4 Decomposed Gaussian Process Regression

First, we propose a decomposed GP regression (Algorithm 2). The idea behind decomposed GP regression is as follows: given the linear decomposition assumption (Definition 1), run Gaussian process regression for each $f_j(\boldsymbol{x})$ individually, and get the aggregated approximation by $f(\boldsymbol{x}) = \sum_{j=1}^{J} g_j(\boldsymbol{x}) f_j(\boldsymbol{x})$ (illustrated in Fig. 1).

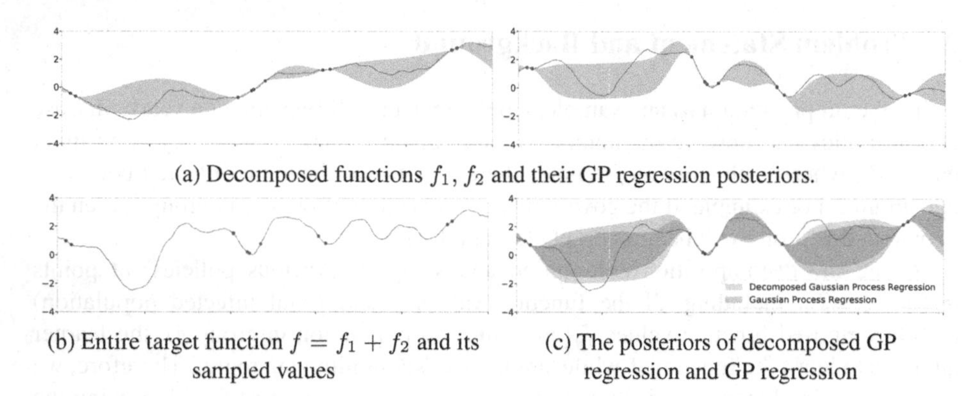

(a) Decomposed functions f_1, f_2 and their GP regression posteriors.

(b) Entire target function $f = f_1 + f_2$ and its sampled values

(c) The posteriors of decomposed GP regression and GP regression

Fig. 1. Illustration of the comparison between decomposed GP regression (Algorithm 2) and standard GP regression. Decomposed GP regression shows a smaller average variance (0.878 v.s. 0.943) and a better estimate of the target function.

Assuming we have T previous samples with input $\boldsymbol{x}_1, \boldsymbol{x}_2, ..., \boldsymbol{x}_T$ and the noisy outcome of each individual function $\boldsymbol{y}_{j,t} = f_j(\boldsymbol{x}_t) + \epsilon_{j,t}\ \forall j \in [J], t \in [T]$, where $\epsilon_{j,t} \sim N(0, \sigma_j^2)$, the outcome of the target function $f(x)$ can be computed as $y_t = \sum_{j=1}^{J} g_j(\boldsymbol{x}_t) y_{j,t}$. Further assume the function $f_j(\boldsymbol{x})$ is an outcome of $GP(0, k_j)\ \forall j$. Therefore the entire function f is also an outcome of $GP(0, k)$ where $k(\boldsymbol{x}, \boldsymbol{x}') = \sum_{j=1}^{J} g_j(\boldsymbol{x}) k_j(\boldsymbol{x}, \boldsymbol{x}') g_j(\boldsymbol{x}')$.

We are going to compare two ways to approximate the function $f(\boldsymbol{x})$ using existing samples. (i) Directly use Algorithm 1 with the composed kernel $k(\boldsymbol{x}, \boldsymbol{x}')$ and noisy samples $\{(\boldsymbol{x}_t, y_t)\}_{t \in [T]}$ – the typical GP regression process. (ii) For each $j \in [J]$, first run Algorithm 1 with kernel $k_j(\boldsymbol{x}, \boldsymbol{x}')$ and noisy samples $\{(\boldsymbol{x}_t, y_{j,t})\}_{t \in [T]}$. Then compose the outcomes with the deterministic weighted function $g_j(\boldsymbol{x})$ to get $f(\boldsymbol{x})$. This is shown in Algorithm 2.

In order to analytically compare Gaussian process regression (Algorithm 1) and decomposed Gaussian process regression (Algorithm 2), we are going to compute the variance (uncertainty) returned by both algorithms. We will show that the latter variance is smaller than the former. Proofs are in the Appendix for brevity.

Proposition 1. *The variance returned by Algorithm 1 is*

$$\sigma_{T,entire}^2(\boldsymbol{x}) = k(\boldsymbol{x}, \boldsymbol{x}) - \sum_{i,j} \boldsymbol{z}_i^\top \Big(\sum_l \boldsymbol{D}_l \boldsymbol{K}_{l,T} \boldsymbol{D}_l\Big)^{-1} \boldsymbol{z}_j \tag{6}$$

where $\boldsymbol{D}_j = diag([g_j(\boldsymbol{x}_1), ..., g_j(\boldsymbol{x}_T)])$ *and* $\boldsymbol{z}_i = \boldsymbol{D}_i \boldsymbol{k}_{j,T}(\boldsymbol{x}) g_j(\boldsymbol{x}) \in \mathbb{R}^T$.

Algorithm 2. Decomposed GP Regression

1 **Input:** kernel functions $k_j(\boldsymbol{x}, \boldsymbol{x}')$ to each $f_j(\boldsymbol{x})$ and previous samples $(\boldsymbol{x}_t, y_{j,t})\ \forall j \in [J], t \in [T]$
2 **for** $j = 1, 2..., J$ **do**
3 Let $\mu_{j,T}(\boldsymbol{x}), k_{j,T}(\boldsymbol{x}, \boldsymbol{x}'), \sigma^2_{j,T}(\boldsymbol{x})$ be the output of GP regression with $k_j(\boldsymbol{x}, \boldsymbol{x}')$ and $(\boldsymbol{x}_t, y_{j,t})$.
4 **Return:** $k_T(\boldsymbol{x}, \boldsymbol{x}') = \sum_{j=1}^{J} g_j^2(\boldsymbol{x}) k_{j,T}(\boldsymbol{x}, \boldsymbol{x}') g_j^2(\boldsymbol{x}')$, $\mu_T(\boldsymbol{x}) = \sum_{j=1}^{J} g_j(\boldsymbol{x}) \mu_{j,T}(\boldsymbol{x})$, $\sigma_T^2(\boldsymbol{x}) = k_T(\boldsymbol{x}, \boldsymbol{x})$

Proposition 2. *The variance returned by Algorithm 2 is*

$$\sigma^2_{T,decomp}(\boldsymbol{x}) = k(\boldsymbol{x}, \boldsymbol{x}) - \sum_l \boldsymbol{z}_l^\top (\boldsymbol{D}_l \boldsymbol{K}_{l,T} \boldsymbol{D}_l)^{-1} \boldsymbol{z}_l \tag{7}$$

In order that our approach has lower variance, we first recall the matrix-fractional function and its convex property.

Lemma 1. *Matrix-fractional function $h(\boldsymbol{X}, \boldsymbol{y}) = \boldsymbol{y}^\top \boldsymbol{X}^{-1} \boldsymbol{y}$ is defined and also convex on dom $f = \{(\boldsymbol{X}, \boldsymbol{y}) \in \mathbf{S}_+^T \times \mathbb{R}^T\}$.*

Now we are ready to compare the variance provided by Propositions 1 and 2.

Theorem 1. *The variance provided by decomposed Gaussian process regression (Algorithm 2) is less than or equal to the variance provided by Gaussian process regression (Algorithm 1), which implies the uncertainty by using decomposed Gaussian process regression is smaller.*

Proof (Proof sketch). In order to compare the variance given by Propositions 1 and 2, we calculate the difference of Eqs. 6 and 7. Their difference can be rearranged as a Jensen inequality with the form of Matrix-fractional function (Lemma 1), which turns out to be convex. By Jensen inequality, their difference is non-negative, which implies the variance given by decomposed GP regression is no greater than the variance given by GP regression.

Theorem 1 implies that decomposed GP regression provides a posterior with smaller variance, which could be considered the uncertainty of the approximation. In fact, the posterior belief after the GP regression is still a Gaussian process, which implies the underlying target function is characterized by a joint Gaussian distribution, where a smaller variance directly implies a more concentrated Gaussian distribution, leading to less uncertainty and smaller root-mean-squared error. Intuitively, this is due to Algorithm 2 adopts the decomposition knowledge but Algorithm 1 does not. This contribution for handling decomposition in the GP regression context is very general and can be applied to many problems. We will show some applications of this idea in the following sections, focusing first on how a linear and generalized decompositions can be used to augment the GP-UCB algorithm for multi-armed bandit problems.

5 Decomposed GP-UCB Algorithm

The goal of a traditional bandit problem is to optimize the objective function $f(\boldsymbol{x})$ by minimizing the regret. However, in our bandit problem with decomposed feedback, the learner is able to access samples of individual functions $f_j(\boldsymbol{x})$. We first consider a linear decomposition $f(\boldsymbol{x}) = \sum_{j=1}^{J} g_j(\boldsymbol{x}) f_j(\boldsymbol{x})$.

In [14], they proposed the GP-UCB algorithm for classic bandit problems and proved that it is a no-regret algorithm that can efficiently achieve the global optimal objective value. A natural question arises: can we apply our decomposed GP regression (Algorithm 2) and also achieve the no-regret property? This leads to our second contribution: the decomposed GP-UCB algorithm, which uses decomposed GP regression when decomposed feedback is accessible. This algorithm can incorporate the decomposed feedback (the outcomes of decomposed function f_j), achieve a better approximation at each iteration while maintaining the no-regret property, and converge to a globally optimal value.

Algorithm 3. Decomposed GP-UCB

1 **Input:** Input space $\mathcal{X}$; GP priors $\mu_{j,0}, \sigma_{j,0}, k_j \ \forall j \in [J]$
2 **for** t = *1,2,...* **do**
3 Compute all mean $\mu_{j,t-1}$ and variance $\sigma_{j,t-1}^2 \forall j$
4 $\mu_{t-1}(\boldsymbol{x}) = \sum_{j=1}^{J} g_j(\boldsymbol{x}) \mu_{j,t-1}(\boldsymbol{x})$
5 $\sigma_{t-1}^2(\boldsymbol{x}) = \sum_{j=1}^{J} g_j^2(\boldsymbol{x}) \sigma_{j,t-1}^2$
6 Choose $\boldsymbol{x}_t = \arg\max_{\boldsymbol{x} \in \mathcal{X}} \mu_{t-1}(\boldsymbol{x}) + \sqrt{\beta_t} \sigma_{t-1}(\boldsymbol{x})$
7 Sample $y_{j,t} = f_j(\boldsymbol{x}_t) \ \forall j \in [J]$
8 Perform Bayesian update to obtain $\mu_{j,t}, \sigma_{j,t} \ \forall j \in [J]$

Theorem 2. *Let* $\delta \in (0,1)$ *and* $\beta_t = 2\log(|\mathcal{X}| t^2 \pi^2 / 6\delta)$. *Running decomposed GP-UCB (Algorithm 3) for a composed sample* $f(\boldsymbol{x}) = \sum_{j=1} g_j(\boldsymbol{x}) f_j(\boldsymbol{x})$ *with bounded variance* $k_j(\boldsymbol{x}, \boldsymbol{x}) \leq 1$ *and each* $f_j \sim GP(0, k_j(\boldsymbol{x}, \boldsymbol{x}'))$, *we obtain a regret bound of* $\mathcal{O}(\sqrt{T \log |\mathcal{X}| \sum_{j=1}^{J} B_j^2 \gamma_{j,T}})$ *with high probability, where* $B_j = \max_{\boldsymbol{x} \in \mathcal{X}} |g_j(\boldsymbol{x})|$. *Precisely,*

$$Pr\{R_T \leq \sqrt{C_1 T \beta_T \sum_{j=1}^{J} B_j^2 \gamma_{j,T}} \ \forall T \geq 1\} \geq 1 - \delta \tag{8}$$

where $C_1 = 8 / \log(1 + \sigma^{-2})$ *with noise variance* σ^2.

We present Algorithm 3, which replaces the Gaussian process regression in GP-UCB with our decomposed Gaussian process regression (Algorithm 2). According to Theorem 1, our algorithm takes advantage of decomposed feedback and provides a more accurate and less uncertain approximation at each iteration. We also provide a regret bound in Theorem 2, which guarantees no-regret property to Algorithm 3.

According to the linear decomposition and the additive and multiplicative properties of kernels, the entire underlying function is still an outcome of GP with a composed kernel $k(\boldsymbol{x}, \boldsymbol{x}') = \sum_{j=1}^{J} g_j(\boldsymbol{x}) k_j(\boldsymbol{x}, \boldsymbol{x}') g_j(\boldsymbol{x}')$, which implies that GP-UCB algorithm can achieve a similar regret bound by normalizing the kernel $k(\boldsymbol{x}, \boldsymbol{x}') \leq \sum_{j=1}^{J} B_j^2 = B^2$. The regret bound of GP-UCB can be given by:

$$Pr\{R_T \leq \sqrt{C_1 T \beta_T B^2 \gamma_{\text{entire},T}} \ \forall T \geq 1\} \geq 1 - \delta \tag{9}$$

where $\gamma_{\text{enitre},T}$ is the upper bound on the information gain $I(y_T; f_T)$ of the composed kernel $k(\boldsymbol{x}, \boldsymbol{x}')$.

But due to Theorem 1, D-GPUCB can achieve a lower variance and more accurate approximation at each iteration, leading to a smaller regret in the bandit setting, which will be shown to empirically perform better in the experiments.

5.1 No-Regret Property and Benefits of D-GPUCB

Previously, in order to guarantee a sublinear regret bound to GP-UCB, we require an analytical, sublinear bound $\gamma_{\text{entire},T}$ on the information gain. [14] provided several elegant upper bounds on the information gain of various kernels. However, in practice, it is hard to give an upper bound to a composed kernel $k(\boldsymbol{x}, \boldsymbol{x}')$ and apply the regret bound (Inequality 9) provided by GP-UCB in the decomposed context.

Instead, D-GPUCB and the following generalized D-GPUCB provide a clearer expression to the regret bound, where their bounds (Theorems 2 and 3) only relate to upper bounds $\gamma_{j,T}$ of the information gain of each kernel $k_j(\boldsymbol{x}, \boldsymbol{x}')$. This resolves the problem of computing an upper bound of a composed kernel. We use various sublinear upper bounds of different kernels, which have been widely studied in prior literature [14].

5.2 Generalized Decomposed GP-UCB Algorithm

We now consider the general decomposition (Definition 2):

$$f(\boldsymbol{x}) = g(f_1(\boldsymbol{x}), f_2(\boldsymbol{x}), ..., f_J(\boldsymbol{x}))$$

To achieve the no-regret property, we further require the function g to have bounded partial derivatives $|\nabla_j g(\boldsymbol{x})| \leq B_j \ \forall j \in [J]$. This corresponds to the linear decomposition case, where $|\nabla_j g| = |g_j(\boldsymbol{x})| \leq B_j$.

Since, a non-linear composition of Gaussian processes is no longer a Gaussian process, the standard GP-UCB algorithm does not have any guarantees for this setting. However, we show that our approach, which leverages the special structure of the problem, still enjoys a no-regret guarantee:

Theorem 3. *By running generalized decomposed GP-UCB with hyperparameter* $\beta_t = 2\log(|\mathcal{X}|Jt^2\pi^2/6\delta)$ *for a composed sample* $f(\boldsymbol{x}) = g(f_1(\boldsymbol{x}), ..., f_J(\boldsymbol{x}))$ *of GPs with bounded variance* $k_j(\boldsymbol{x}, \boldsymbol{x}) \leq 1$ *and each* $f_j \sim GP(0, k_j(\boldsymbol{x}, \boldsymbol{x}'))$*. we obtain a regret bound of* $\mathcal{O}(\sqrt{T \log |\mathcal{X}| \sum_{j=1}^{J} B_j^2 \gamma_{j,T}})$ *with high probability, where* $B_j = \max_{\boldsymbol{x} \in \mathcal{X}} |\nabla_j g(\boldsymbol{x})|$*. Precisely,*

$$Pr\{R_T \leq \sqrt{C_1 T \beta_T \sum_{j=1}^{J} B_j^2 \gamma_{j,T}} \ \forall T \geq 1\} \geq 1 - \delta \tag{10}$$

Algorithm 4. Generalized Decomposed GP-UCB

1 **Input:** Input space $\mathcal{X}$; GP priors $\mu_{j,0}, \sigma_{j,0}, k_j \ \forall j \in [J]$
2 **for** t = *1,2,...* **do**
3 Compute the aggregated mean and variance bound:
4 $\mu_{t-1}(\boldsymbol{x}) = g(\mu_{1,t-1}(\boldsymbol{x}), ..., \mu_{J,t-1}(\boldsymbol{x}))$
5 $\sigma_{t-1}^2(\boldsymbol{x}) = J \sum_{j=1}^{J} B_j^2 \sigma_{j,t-1}^2(\boldsymbol{x})$
6 Choose $\boldsymbol{x}_t = \arg\max_{\boldsymbol{x} \in \mathcal{X}} \mu_{t-1}(\boldsymbol{x}) + \sqrt{\beta_t}\sigma_{t-1}(\boldsymbol{x})$
7 Sample $y_{j,t} = f_j(\boldsymbol{x}_t) \ \forall j \in [J]$
8 Perform Bayesian update to obtain $\mu_{j,t}, \sigma_{j,t} \ \forall j \in [J]$

where $C_1 = 8/\log(1+\sigma^{-2})$ *with noise variance* σ^2.

The intuition is that so long as each individual function is drawn from a Gaussian process, we can still perform Gaussian process regression on each function individually to get an estimate of each decomposed component. Based on these estimates, we compute the corresponding estimate to the final objective value by combining the decomposed components with the function g. Since the gradient of function g is bounded, we can propagate the uncertainty of each individual approximation to the final objective function, which allows us to get a bound on the total uncertainty. Consequently, we can prove a high-probability bound between our algorithm's posterior distribution and the target function, which enables us to bound the cumulative regret by a similar technique as Theorem 2.

The major difference for general decomposition is that the usual GP-UCB algorithm no longer works here. The underlying unknown function may not be an outcome of Gaussian process. Therefore the GP-UCB algorithm does not have any guarantees for either convergence or the no-regret property. In contrast, D-GPUCB algorithm still works in this general case if the learner is able to attain the decomposed feedback.

Our result greatly enlarges the feasible functional space where GP-UCB can be applied. We have shown that the generalized D-GPUCB preserves the no-regret property even when the underlying function is a composition of Gaussian processes. Given the knowledge of decomposition and decomposed feedback, based on Theorem 3, the functional space that generalized D-GPUCB algorithm can guarantee no-regret is closed under arbitrary bounded-gradient function composition. This leads to a very general functional space, showcasing the contribution of our algorithm.

5.3 Continuous Sample Space

All the above theorems are for discrete sample spaces $\mathcal{X}$. However, most real-world scenarios have a continuous space. [14] used the discretization technique to reduce the compact and convex continuous sample space to a discrete case by using a larger exploration constant:

$$\beta_t = 2\log(2t^2\pi^2/(3\delta)) + 2d\log(t^2 dbr\sqrt{\log(4da/\delta)})$$

while assuming $\Pr\{\sup_{\boldsymbol{x}\in\mathcal{X}} |\partial f/\partial \boldsymbol{x}_i| > L\} \le ae^{-(L/b)^2}$. (In the general decomposition case, $\beta_t = 2\log(2Jt^2\pi^2/(3\delta)) + 2d\log(t^2dbr\sqrt{\log(4da/\delta)})$). All of our proofs directly follow using the same technique. Therefore the no-regret property and regret bound also hold in continuous sample spaces.

6 Experiments

In this section, we run several experiments to compare decomposed Gaussian process regression (Algorithm 2), D-GPUCB (Algorithm 3), and generalized D-GPUCB (Algorithm 4). We also test on both discrete sample space and continuous sample space. All of our examples show a promising convergence rate and also improvement against the GP-UCB algorithm, again demonstrating that more detailed modeling reduces the predictive uncertainty.

6.1 Decomposed Gaussian Process Regression

For the decomposed Gaussian process regression, we compare the average standard deviation (uncertainty) provided by GP regression (Algorithm 1) and decomposed GP regression (Algorithm 2) over varying number of samples and number of decomposed functions. We use the following three common types of stationary kernel [11]:

- Square Exponential kernel is $k(\boldsymbol{x}, \boldsymbol{x}') = \exp(-(2l^2)^{-1}\|\boldsymbol{x} - \boldsymbol{x}'\|^2)$, l is a length-scale hyper parameter.
- Matérn kernel is given by $k(\boldsymbol{x}, \boldsymbol{x}') = (2^{1-\nu}/\Gamma(\nu))r^{\nu}B_{\nu}(r), r = (\sqrt{2\nu}/l)\|\boldsymbol{x} - \boldsymbol{x}'\|$, where ν controls the smoothness of sample functions and B_ν is a modified Bessel function.
- Rational Quadratic kernel is $k(\boldsymbol{x}, \boldsymbol{x}') = (1 + \|\boldsymbol{x} - \boldsymbol{x}'\|^2/(2\alpha l^2))^{-\alpha}$. It can be seen as a scale mixture of square exponential kernels with different length-scales.

For each kernel category, we first draw J kernels with random hyper-parameters. We then generate a random sample function f_j from each corresponding kernel k_j as the target function, combined with the simplest linear decomposition (Definition 1) with $g_j(\boldsymbol{x}) \equiv 1 \forall j$. For each setting and each $T \le 50$, we randomly draw T samples as the previous samples and perform both GP regression and decomposed GP regression. We record the average improvement in terms of root-mean-squared error (RMSE) against

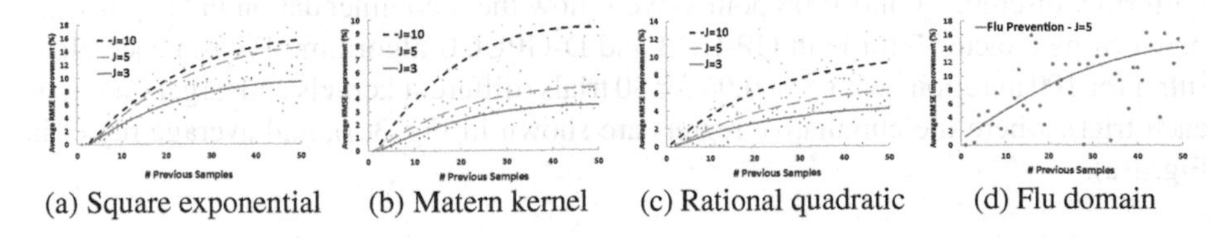

(a) Square exponential (b) Matern kernel (c) Rational quadratic (d) Flu domain

Fig. 2. Average improvement for different kernels (with trend line) using decomposed GP regression and GP regression, in RMSE

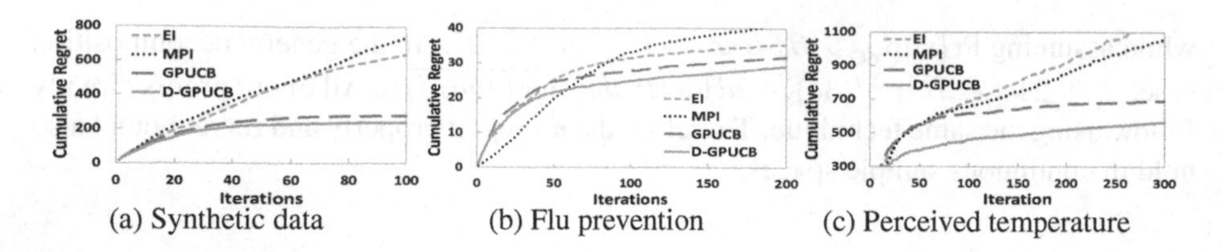

(a) Synthetic data (b) Flu prevention (c) Perceived temperature

Fig. 3. Comparison of cumulative regret: D-GPUCB, GP-UCB, and various heuristics on synthetic (a) and real data (b, c)

the underlying target function over 100 independent runs for each setting. We also run experiments on flu domain with square exponential kernel based on real data and SIR model [4], which is illustrated in Fig. 2(d).

Empirically, our method reduces the RMSE in the model's predictions by 10–15% compared to standard GP regression (without decomposed feedback). This trend holds across kernels, and includes both synthetic data and the flu domain (which uses a real dataset). Such an improvement in predictive accuracy is significant in many real-world domains. For instance, CDC-reported 95% confidence intervals for vaccination-averted flu illnesses for 2015 range from 3.5M–7M and averted medical visits from 1.7M–3.5M. Reducing average error by 10% corresponds to estimates which are tighter by hundreds of thousands of patients, a significant amount in policy terms. These results confirm our theoretical analysis in showing that incorporating decomposed feedback results in more accurate estimation of the unknown function.

6.2 Comparison Between GP-UCB and D-GPUCB

We now move the online setting, to test whether greater predictive accuracy results in improved decision making. We compare our D-GPUCB algorithm and generalized D-GPUCB with GP-UCB, as well as common heuristics such as Expected Improvement (EI) [8] and Most Probable Improvement (MPI) [7]. For all the experiments, we run 30 trials on all algorithms to find the average regret.

Synthetic Data (Linear Decomposition with Discrete Sample Space): For synthetic data, we randomly draw $J = 10$ square exponential kernels with different hyper-parameters and then sample random functions from these kernels to compose the entire target function. The sample noise is set to be 10^{-4}. The sample space $\mathcal{X} = [0, 1]$ is uniformly discretized into 1000 points. We follow the recommendation in [14] to scale down β_t by a factor 5 for both GP-UCB and D-GPUCB algorithm. We run each algorithm for 100 iterations with $\delta = 0.05$ for 30 trials (different kernels and target functions each trial), where the cumulative regrets are shown in Fig. 3(a), and average regret in Fig. 4(a).

Flu Prevention (Linear Decomposition with Continuous Sample Space): We consider a flu age-stratified SIR model [4] as our target function. The population is stratified

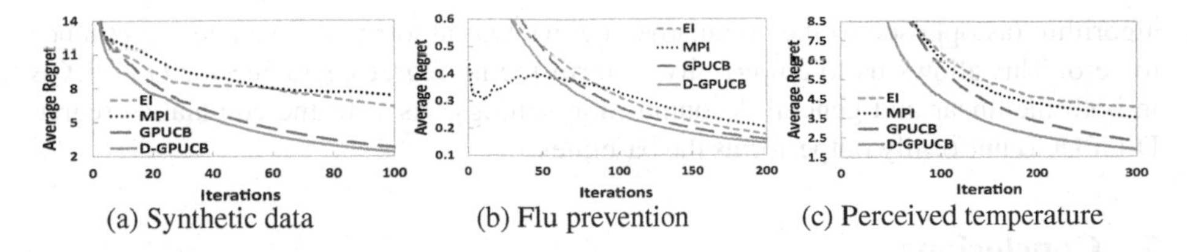

(a) Synthetic data (b) Flu prevention (c) Perceived temperature

Fig. 4. Comparison of average regret: D-GPUCB, GP-UCB, and various heuristics on synthetic (a) and real data (b, c)

into several age groups: young (0–19), adult (20–49), middle aged (50–64), senior (65–69), elder (70+). The SIR model allows the contact matrix and susceptibility of each age group to vary. Our input here is the vaccination rate $\boldsymbol{x} \in [0, 1]^5$ with respect to each age group. Given a vaccination rate $\boldsymbol{x}$, the SIR model returns the average sick days per person $f(\boldsymbol{x})$ within one year. The model can also return the contribution to the average sick days from each age group j, which we denote as $f_j(\boldsymbol{x})$. Therefore we have $f(\boldsymbol{x}) = \sum_{j=1}^{5} f_j(\boldsymbol{x})$, a linear decomposition. The goal is to find the optimal vaccination policy which minimizes the average sick days subject to budget constraints. Since we do not know the covariance kernel functions in advance, we randomly draw 1000 samples and fit a composite kernel (composed of square exponential kernel and Matérn kernel) before running UCB algorithms. We run all algorithms and compare their cumulative regret in Fig. 3(b) and average regret in Fig. 4(b).

Perceived Temperature (General Decomposition with Discrete Sample Space): The perceived temperature is a combination of actual temperature, humidity, and wind speed. When the actual temperature is high, higher humidity reduces the body's ability to cool itself, resulting a higher perceived temperature; when the actual temperature is low, the air motion accelerates the rate of heat transfer from a human body to the surrounding atmosphere, leading to a lower perceived temperature. All of these are nonlinear function compositions. We use the weather data collected from 2906 sensors in United States provided by OpenWeatherMap. Given an input location $\boldsymbol{x} \in \mathcal{X}$, we can access to the actual temperature $f_1(\boldsymbol{x})$, humidity $f_2(\boldsymbol{x})$, and wind speed $f_3(\boldsymbol{x})$. In each test, we randomly draw one third of the entire data to learn the covariance kernel functions. Then we run generalized D-GPUCB and all the other algorithms on the remaining sensors to find the location with highest perceived temperature. The result is averaged over 30 different tests and is also shown in Figs. 3(c) and 4(c).

Discussion: In the bandit setting with decomposed feedback, Fig. 3 shows a $10\%-20\%$ improvement in cumulative regret for both synthetic (Fig. 3(a)) and real data (Fig. 3(b), (c)). As in the regression setting, such improvements are highly significant in policy terms; a 10% reduction in sickness due to flu corresponds to hundreds of thousands of infections averted per year. The benefit to incorporating decomposed feedback is particularly large in the general decomposition case (Fig. 3(c)), where a single GP is a poor fit to the nonlinearly composed function. Figure 4 shows the average regret of each algorithm (as opposed to the cumulative regret). Our algorithm's average regret tends to zero. This allows us to empirically confirm the no-regret guarantee for D-GPUCB in both the linear and general decomposition settings. As with the cumulative regret, D-GPUCB uniformly outperforms the baselines.

7 Conclusions

We propose algorithms for nonparametric regression and online learning which exploit the decomposed feedback common in real world sequential decision problems. In the regression setting, we prove that incorporating decomposed feedback improves predictive accuracy (Theorem 1). In the online learning setting, we introduce the D-GPUCB algorithms (Algorithm 3 and Algorithm 4) and prove corresponding no-regret guarantees. We conduct experiments in both real and synthetic domains to investigate the performance of decomposed GP regression, D-GPUCB, and generalized D-GPUCB. All show significant improvement against GP-UCB and other methods that do not consider decomposed feedback, demonstrating the benefit that decision makers can realize by exploiting such information.

References

1. Auer, P.: Using confidence bounds for exploitation-exploration trade-offs. J. Mach. Learn. Res. **3**, 397–422 (2002)
2. Brochu, E., Cora, V.M., De Freitas, N.: A tutorial on Bayesian optimization of expensive cost functions, with application to active user modeling and hierarchical reinforcement learning. arXiv preprint arXiv:1012.2599 (2010)
3. Contal, E., Perchet, V., Vayatis, N.: Gaussian process optimization with mutual information. In: International Conference on Machine Learning, pp. 253–261 (2014)
4. Del Valle, S.Y., Hyman, J.M., Chitnis, N.: Mathematical models of contact patterns between age groups for predicting the spread of infectious diseases. Math. Biosci. Eng. MBE **10**, 1475 (2013)
5. Jones, D.R., Schonlau, M., Welch, W.J.: Efficient global optimization of expensive black-box functions. J. Global Optim. **13**(4), 455–492 (1998)
6. Kandasamy, K., Schneider, J., Póczos, B.: High dimensional Bayesian optimisation and bandits via additive models. In: International Conference on Machine Learning, pp. 295–304 (2015)
7. Kushner, H.J.: A new method of locating the maximum point of an arbitrary multipeak curve in the presence of noise. J. Basic Eng. **86**(1), 97–106 (1964)
8. Močkus, J.: On Bayesian methods for seeking the extremum. In: Marchuk, G.I. (ed.) Optimization Techniques 1974. LNCS, vol. 27, pp. 400–404. Springer, Heidelberg (1975). https://doi.org/10.1007/3-540-07165-2_55
9. Mullikin, M., Tan, L., Jansen, J.P., Van Ranst, M., Farkas, N., Petri, E.: A novel dynamic model for health economic analysis of influenza vaccination in the elderly. Infect. Dis. Ther. **4**(4), 459–487 (2015). https://doi.org/10.1007/s40121-015-0076-8
10. Neu, G., Bartók, G.: An efficient algorithm for learning with semi-bandit feedback. In: Jain, S., Munos, R., Stephan, F., Zeugmann, T. (eds.) ALT 2013. LNCS (LNAI), vol. 8139, pp. 234–248. Springer, Heidelberg (2013). https://doi.org/10.1007/978-3-642-40935-6_17

11. Rasmussen, C.E.: Gaussian processes in machine learning. In: Bousquet, O., von Luxburg, U., Rätsch, G. (eds.) ML 2003. LNCS (LNAI), vol. 3176, pp. 63–71. Springer, Heidelberg (2004). https://doi.org/10.1007/978-3-540-28650-9_4
12. Sah, P., Medlock, J., Fitzpatrick, M.C., Singer, B.H., Galvani, A.P.: Optimizing the impact of low-efficacy influenza vaccines. Proc. Natl. Acad. Sci. **115**(20), 5151–5156 (2018)
13. Snoek, J., Larochelle, H., Adams, R.P.: Practical Bayesian optimization of machine learning algorithms. In: Advances in Neural Information Processing Systems, pp. 2951–2959 (2012)
14. Srinivas, N., Krause, A., Kakade, S.M., Seeger, M.: Gaussian process optimization in the bandit setting: no regret and experimental design. arXiv preprint arXiv:0912.3995 (2009)
15. Staiger, H., Laschewski, G., Grätz, A.: The perceived temperature–a versatile index for the assessment of the human thermal environment. Part A: scientific basics. Int. J. Biometeorol. **56**(1), 165–176 (2012)
16. Vynnycky, E., Pitman, R., Siddiqui, R., Gay, N., Edmunds, W.J.: Estimating the impact of childhood influenza vaccination programmes in England and Wales. Vaccine **26**(41), 5321–5330 (2008)
17. Wang, Z., Zhou, B., Jegelka, S.: Optimization as estimation with Gaussian processes in bandit settings. In: Artificial Intelligence and Statistics, pp. 1022–1031 (2016)
18. Wilder, B., Suen, S.C., Tambe, M.: Preventing infectious disease in dynamic populations under uncertainty (2018)
19. Woolthuis, R.G., Wallinga, J., van Boven, M.: Variation in loss of immunity shapes influenza epidemics and the impact of vaccination. BMC Infect. Dis. **17**(1), 632 (2017)

Optimizing Waste Collection: A Data Mining Approach

Guilherme Londres[1,2(✉)], Nuno Filipe[2], and João Gama[1,2]

[1] LIAAD - INESC TEC, Porto, Portugal
guilherme.l.londres@inesctec.pt
[2] FEP, University of Porto, Porto, Portugal
jgama@fep.up.pt

Abstract. The smart cities concept - use of connected services and intelligent systems to support decision making in cities governance - aims to build better sustainability and living conditions for urban spaces, which are more complex every day. This work expects to optimize the waste collection circuits for non-residential customers in a city in Portugal. It is developed through the implementation of a simple, low-cost methodology when compared to commercial-available sensor systems. The main goal is to build a classifier for each client, being able to forecast the presence or absence of containers and, in a second step, predict how many containers of glass, paper or plastic would be available to be collected. Data were acquired during the period of one year, from January to December 2017, from more than 100 customers, resulting in a 26.000+ records dataset. Due to its degree of interpretability, we use Decision trees, implemented with a sliding window, which ran through the months of the year, stacking it one-by-one and/or merging few groups aiming the best correct predictions score. This project results in more efficient waste-collection routes, increasing the operation profits and reducing both costs and fuel-consumption, therefore diminishing it environmental footprint.

Keywords: Data mining for social good · Smart cities · Waste collection

1 Introduction

As the concentration of people increases in cities all over the world [1], more important becomes the policies to deal with waste. The mean waste weight produced by every person in European Union during 2010 was 5.2 tons. In the specific case of Portugal, 1.35 tons were produced per person in 2012, where 69% was recovered [4]. This process of finding a new destination for what was discarded is also called Circular Economy. It can be done not only by revamping used aluminum cans into new ones, but, for example, composting organic leftovers, transforming it in powerful fertilizers.

In Northern Portugal, one company is responsible for dealing with the waste collection and treatment over several cities. One service it provides is the door-to-door non-residential collection, where the signing customers receive three different colored containers (rigid or plastic bags), which they should separately fill

P. Cellier and K. Driessens (Eds.): ECML PKDD 2019 Workshops, CCIS 1167, pp. 570–578, 2020.
https://doi.org/10.1007/978-3-030-43823-4_45

with papers and cartons, plastic and general packages, and glass. In the city and collection circuits analyzed in this study, 120-L container bags were distributed to the customers. Those bags were picked-up via appropriate container vehicles that follows a pre-determined route. This way of picking up the waste is reportedly more efficient when compared with the clients having to move the waste to another place [2]. The pre-scheduled itinerary is sometimes not followed, due to the overfilling of the trucks. Occasionally, some customers do not have any full bag to deliver, turning inefficient the route. The collection cost itself counts for up to 70% of the total cost, according to [3].

Intending to optimize the collection routes this project was built. First, trying to predict the existence or not of waste to be gathered. Then, in a second step, forecasting how many bags would be available to be picked up. Both predictions were made for each customer. There are commercially available routing optimizer systems, which are used for this purpose. However, such schemes usually depend on sensor readings (e.g., to check how full the truck is), what would not be possible in this application due the fact that it uses plastic bags as containers. Another limitation are their elevated costs.

The proposed predictor was developed in a low-cost way, using artificial intelligence and the data already registered by the employees responsible for the waste collection. The results obtained by the predictor should be fed into the company route design tool.

2 Methodology

2.1 Preprocessing

All data used in this project was gathered by the people responsible for the waste collection, namely the truck driver and its assistant. They should manually register the date, client's name, address, and type of business, if there were delivered any bags or not, and, if positive, how many bags of each type. The data was logged for each one of the 141 customers during the period of one year, from January to December 2017, generating more than 26.000 records. This dataset was then adjusted, first, the costumers' addresses were converted into a new feature called centrality. This categorical variable with 3 classes, describes how centralized the client is in a current collection area. Another change was the transformation of the date, originally in the format dd-mm-yyyy, into two variables: weekday and month. Other features were also introduced:

– Climate - cold, warm or hot;
– Week number - 1, 2, 3 or 4;
– Proximity to a holiday or extended weekend - yes or no.

2.2 Model Training

The technique chosen to be used was Decision Trees, due to the main factor its results could be easily plotted and interpreted. It was implemented using the scikit-learn [5] library in Python [6]. The response-variable for the first training was imbalanced, as there was way more days of waste delivered by the costumers than the opposite. Hence, the most appropriate scoring method are Sensitivity, Recall and F1-Score. As input, the full dataset was used for training. In this case it uses Leave One Out to validate the model, as there were some months with few examples to be used. Sliding window concept was also used during the model training. First, it was fed with January and predicted the results for February. Then, fed with February to predict March, and so on following this pattern. The second and third approaches used the two and the three previous months, respectively, to predict the next one (e.g., train with March and April to predict May, train with March, April, and May to predict June).

3 Results and Discussion

The results are presented in three parts: The first is a fast analysis of the dataset. The second concerns the primary objective, the prediction of the presence or not of waste to be collected. Then, the second objective is discussed, the forecast of the quantity of containers.

3.1 Analysis of the Dataset

When analyzing the dataset regarding the day with higher collection, Friday is the first one, followed by Wednesday and Monday. It is important to mention that there are no collections on weekends. Monday could be expected to be a peak day, especially for restaurants that tend to have more customers over the weekend. However it does not happen. This can be explained by the fact that many of these establishments, in the studied area, close early on Saturdays and do not open on Sundays. Also, there are no relevant peaks which could be related to the proximity to holidays or extended weekends. On the other hand, there is a clear trend of waste increasing during summer vacations - from the end of July until the end of August. Despite those trends, it could not be observed other traces of seasonality in the dataset.

3.2 First Objective - Presence or Absence of Waste

As the model is trained individually for each one of the 141 customers, it was decided that the best way to present the results is using a histogram counting the number of customers and their score tiers and to create a table dividing the percentage of customers in scores above as: 95%, 90%, 85% and 80%. The results of the predictor trained with the whole dataset at once, i.e., training the model with all months at once, is presented in the Table 1 and Fig. 1.

It can be seen that 80% of the data was predicted scoring more than 80% on F1 score, and only 46.67% reached more than 95%. Looking at the histogram it is possible to see a spike around the 100% bin, and a concentration around the 80% score.

Table 1. Training with full data - scores.

	Full Year		
	Precision	Recall	F1 Score
>95%	46.67	46.67	46.67
>90%	55.24	55.24	55.24
>85%	66.67	66.67	66.67
>80%	80.00	80.00	80.00

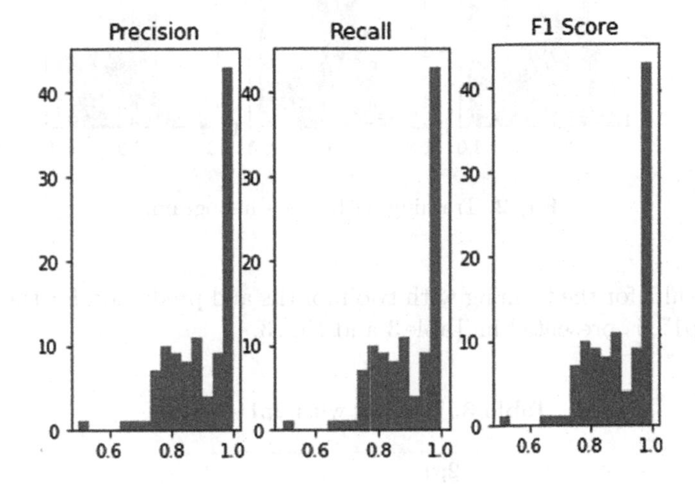

Fig. 1. Training with full data - histogram.

When feeding the training with one month and prediction the following, named here as "1p1", the result improve significantly, as shown in Table 2 and Fig. 2.

Table 2. Training with 1p1 - scores

	1p1		
	Precision	Recall	F1 Score
>95%	21.90	20.95	20.95
>90%	64.76	72.38	58.10
>85%	97.14	96.19	96.19
>80%	100.00	99.05	99.05

Note that 64.76% of the predictions reached more than 90% in precision, and 100% scored above 80%. Now it is possible to see that regarding precision, there is a wider concentration around the 90% score when comparing to the concentration around 90% recall score. However, the F1 results have presented distribution more similar to the precision score.

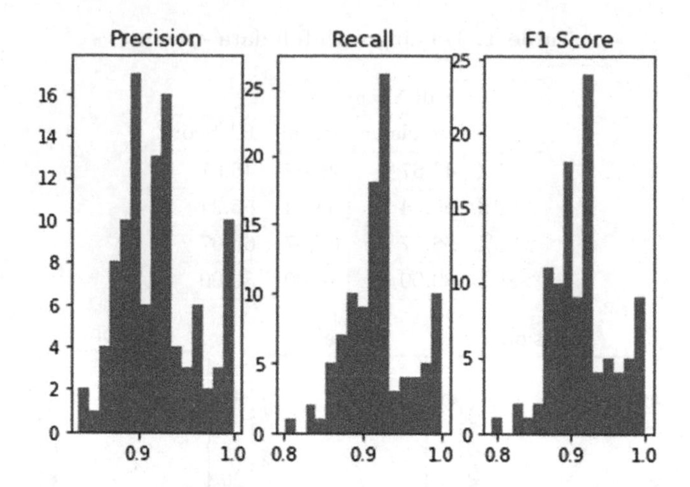

Fig. 2. Training with 1p1 - histogram.

The results for the training with two months and prediction for the next one, named "2p1", is presented in Table 3 and Fig. 3.

Table 3. Training with 2p1 - scores.

	2p1		
	Precision	Recall	F1 Score
>95%	20.95	19.05	18.10
>90%	45.71	52.38	43.81
>85%	85.71	84.76	83.81
>80%	100.00	99.05	100.00

All customers reached more than 80% precision score, while 20.95% were above 95%. It is possible to note that precision histogram has an elevated concentration immediately bellow the 90% tier, while recall and F1 score depicts similar distributions.

At Table 4 and Fig. 4 are presented the results for the case when three months were used for training and predicting the following month, named here "3p1".

It can be seen 80.95% of the predictions reached more than 85% of precision. Looking at the F1 histogram it can be noted a concentration around 90% score while both precision and recall show a more spiked trend.

Analyzing the results, it is interesting to note that when training the model with all months at once it is reached the highest concentration of predictions above 95%, summing 46.67% of forecasts in this group. However, its results among the other tiers are poor when compared to the other models which used the sliding window approach.

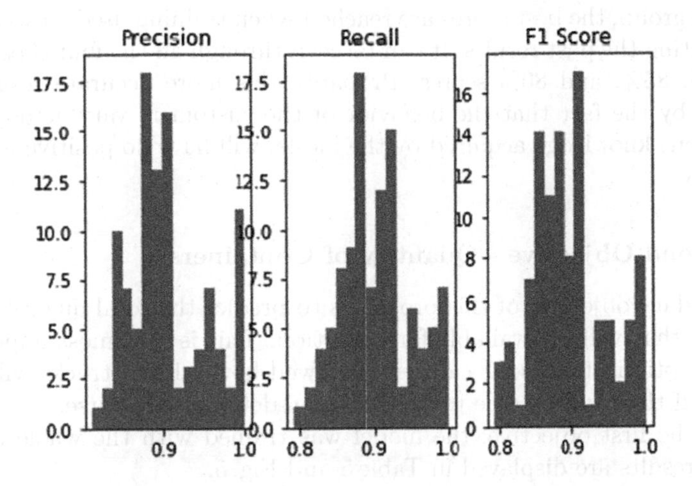

Fig. 3. Training with 2p1 - histogram.

Table 4. Training with 3p1 - scores.

	3p1		
	Precision	Recall	F1 Score
>95%	18.10	20.95	20.00
>90%	41.90	53.33	41.90
>85%	80.95	81.90	78.10
>80%	97.14	98.10	94.29

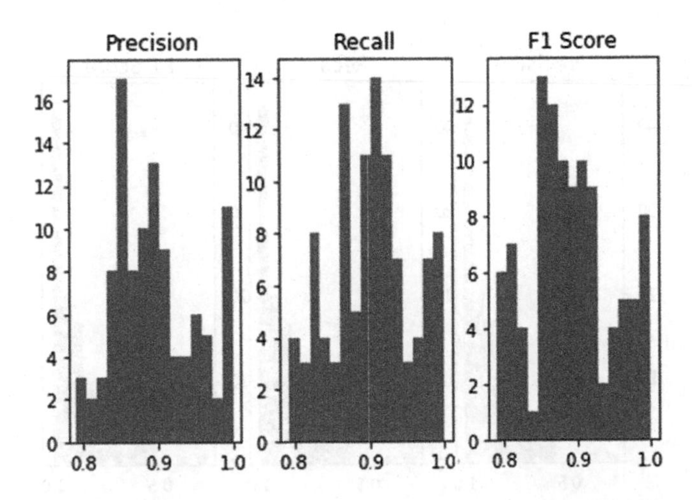

Fig. 4. Training with 3p1 - histogram.

In this group, the best scores are reached when training used only one month, i.e., forgetting the past results. It can be seen through all the four chosen ranges: 95%, 90%, 85%, and 80% scores. Probably this more accurate result can be explained by the fact that the behavior of the customers vary across the year, and previous knowledge acquired by the model will have no positive influence in the results.

3.3 Second Objective - Quantity of Containers

The secondary objective of this project is to predict the total quantity of waste containers that will be available for collection. This is of utmost importance in the route optimization, so it can be previewed how full the trucks will be, and, therefore, if they will be able to finish the predetermined course.

As in the first objective, the model was trained with the whole dataset at once, the results are displayed in Table 5 and Fig. 5.

Table 5. Training with full data - quantity scores.

	Quantity - 1p1		
	Precision	Recall	F1 Score
>95%	40.95	40.95	40.95
>90%	62.86	62.86	62.86
>85%	76.19	76.19	76.19
>80%	85.71	85.71	85.71

It can be noticed that despite having a high concentration of good scores, above 95%, it does not ensure that 100% of the results are above the lower set limit, in 80%.

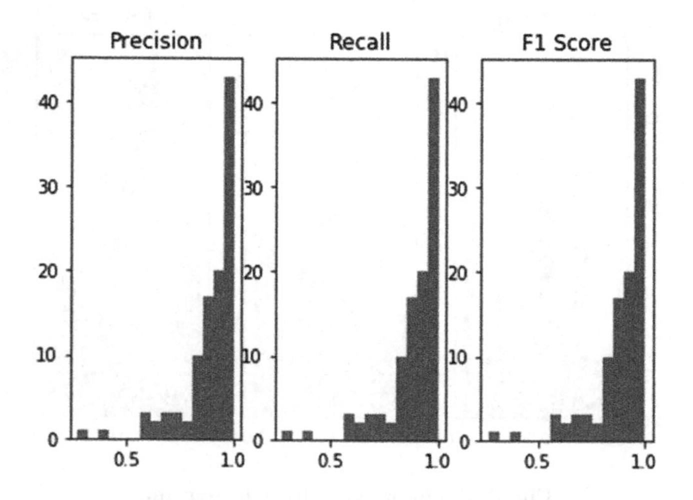

Fig. 5. Training with full - histogram.

The results for the quantity estimation for the model trained with 1 month to predict the next one, is shown in Table 6 and Fig. 6.

Table 6. Training with 1p1 data - quantity scores.

	Quantity - 1p1		
	Precision	Recall	F1 Score
>95%	34.29	41.90	39.05
>90%	58.10	65.71	58.10
>85%	75.24	76.19	74.29
>80%	84.76	85.71	83.81

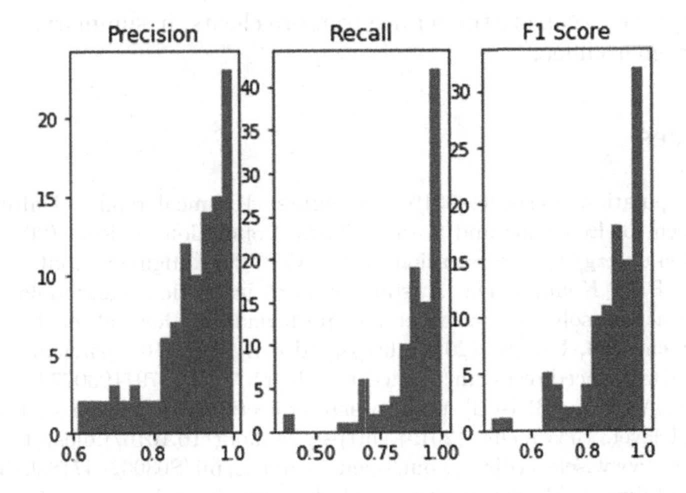

Fig. 6. Training with 1p1 - histogram.

It can be seen that a higher number of customers have reached +90%, i.e., 58.10% is above 90% of precision score. Moreover, just 86.76% of the clients are above 80% in the same metric. This result was expected to be higher, therefore, in a first approach it is acceptable.

4 Conclusion

What could be seen during the progress of this work is that despite the higher concentration of predictions scoring above 95% being reached when the model was trained with the full year of data, the stratified results were better using the 1p1 approach. For this reason, it is important to analyze the case to each customer, as it was intended for. In a macro perspective, the 1p1 would certainly be the best solution. On the other hand, if it can be analyzed in a closer viewpoint, it will depend if the customer belongs to the +95% tier of the first model or not.

Following the methodology, it was supposed to train all 3 schemes: 1p1, 2p1 and 3p1 for the quantity prediction. However, due to the small difference between the approaches and the lowest scores of 1p1, it was decided not to include it here. Also, it does make sense to have a fairer forecast in this situation, as it is more specific and probably more related to the short past, than with a long past time, as two or three months.

To improve the averages of both first and second objective, it may be necessary to analyze individually the lowest scorers. Maybe a different approach can be taken with this group and the predictions will be enhanced.

The results obtained by the model developed are satisfactory and mean a significant advance in the waste collection routing theme. This forecast data can be used right away. In a near future it could be fed to the company's new routing system to help deciding which and when to visit a customer. Therefore, saving costs, being able to expand the service to more clients, in summary, contributing to a better environment.

References

1. World population prospects 2019: Highlights. Technical report, United Nations, Department of Economic and Social Affairs, Population Division (2019). https://population.un.org/wpp/Publications/Files/WPP2019_Highlights.pdf
2. Calabrò, P.S., Komilis, D.: A standardized inspection methodology to evaluate municipal solid waste collection performance. Journal of Environmental Management **246**, 184–191 (2019). https://doi.org/10.1016/j.jenvman.2019.05.142. http://www.sciencedirect.com/science/article/pii/S0301479719307704
3. Ferrer, J., Alba, E.: BIN-CT: urban waste collection based on predicting the container fill level. Biosystems (2019). https://doi.org/10.1016/j.biosystems.2019.04.006. http://www.sciencedirect.com/science/article/pii/S0303264718301333
4. de Freitas Filipe, N.M.: Smart cities - agendamento dinamico de recolhas de residuos porta-a-porta (2018). https://hdl.handle.net/10216/116449
5. Pedregosa, F., et al.: Scikit-learn: machine learning in Python. J. Mach. Learn. Res. **12**, 2825–2830 (2011)
6. Python Software Foundation: Python 3.6.9rc1 documentation. https://docs.python.org/3.6/

Mobile Game Theory with Street Gangs

Sarah Cooney[1(✉)], Wendy Gomez[2], Kai Wang[3], Jorja Leap[2], P. Jeffrey Brantingham[2], and Milind Tambe[1]

[1] University of Southern California, Los Angeles, CA 90089, USA
{cooneys,tambe}@usc.edu
[2] University of California Los Angeles, Los Angeles, CA 90095, USA
wgomez@leapassociates.net, {jleap,branting}@@ucla.edu
[3] Harvard University, Cambridge, MA 02138, USA
kaiwang@g.harvard.edu

Abstract. Gang violence remains a persistent public safety problem in Los Angeles. Gang interventionists and community organizers are turning to *proactive peacekeeping*, a process of addressing the underlying structures that cause young people to join gangs such as pervasive poverty and marginalization. Given the increasing prevalence and decreasing cost of mobile technology, there may be opportunities for interventionists to employ technological solutions in their work. However, before such solutions can be deployed, it is necessary to have accurate models of the target users—in this case, gang-involved youth. Of particular interest with regard proactive peacekeeping is their propensity for cooperation. However, given the unique circumstances surrounding the lives of gang-involved youth, traditional laboratory-based experiments measuring cooperation are infeasible. In this paper, we present a novel method of collecting experimental data from gang-involved youth in the Los Angeles area. We design a mobile application based on the classic Prisoner's Dilemma model, which has been used to collect almost 3000 data points on cooperation from more than 20 participants. We present initial results that show despite their unique life circumstances gang-involved youth cooperate at roughly the same rate as university students in classic studies of cooperation. We conclude by addressing the implications of this result for future work and proactive peacekeeping endeavors.

Keywords: Game theory · Experimental design · Data collection

1 Introduction

In his book *Tattoos on the Heart*, Father Gregory Boyle speaks of riding his bike between the poorest neighborhoods of Los Angeles during the late 1980s negotiating peace treaties between rival street gangs [3]. The process was informal and tenuous at best, and although gang violence has declined since the early 1990s, it remains a chronic public safety issue in Los Angeles. While a proper census does

P. Cellier and K. Driessens (Eds.): ECML PKDD 2019 Workshops, CCIS 1167, pp. 579–589, 2020.
https://doi.org/10.1007/978-3-030-43823-4_46

not exists, estimates suggest that there are hundreds of unique gangs and tens-of-thousands gang-affiliated individuals in the city [29]. These are distributed throughout the city with particular concentrations in the San Fernando Valley and South Los Angeles. Many of these gangs are territorial in nature, claiming some area as their home turf. As in Chicago, this feature sets Los Angeles apart from many other cities where territoriality appears to be less important. As in other settings, however, Los Angeles gangs appear to be responsible for a disproportionate share of crime, particularly violent crime. Nearly 60% of homicides in Los Angeles are thought to be gang related [5].

Father Boyle has since stopped this kind of negotiation, writing in *Tattoos on the Heart*, "Though I don't regret having orchestrated these truces and treaties, I'd never do it again. The unintended consequence of it all was that it legitimized the gangs and fed them oxygen" [3]. Today, community organizers and gang interventionists, some of whom are former gang members themselves, are turning to *proactive peacekeeping*. Proactive peacekeeping aims to address the root causes that drive youth into gangs, such as generational poverty, marginalization, abuse, and a sense of hopelessness. It is about giving them options and opportunities beyond violence and building community outside of gangs [16,28]. Two exemplars of the proactive peacekeeping process include the late Darren "Bo" Taylor, a former gang member who founded Unity One, an organization dedicated to community building and citizen empowerment, and civil rights attorney Connie Rice, who spent decades fighting against problematic policing policies by the Los Angeles Police Department and co-founded the Advancement Project, a racial justice organization that works directly in impacted communities of Los Angeles to build grassroots organizing around public policy change [28]. Part of the proactive peacekeeping process also involves dismantling the stigmas associated with the gang label, which can serve as a barrier to peacekeeping efforts. Therefore, for the rest of this paper we will refer to our study population, gang-involved youth from Los Angeles, as "gamers", in reference to our use of game-theory and mobile games to study their behavior. In addition, we do not want to further stigmatize youth in our study whose gang involvement may be peripheral or transitory.

The world and our day-to-day interactions are increasingly moving online, and technologies like smart phones are becoming cheaper and more accessible even in areas with pervasive poverty. We feel that technology can help play a role in proactive peacekeeping activities, for instance by giving resource-limited interventionists a new way to reach gamers and provide services on demand. In order to better understand how to best utilize technology in processes such as proactive peacekeeping, it is important to have a clear model of the target users. This paper focuses on the process of collecting data from gamers about their propensity for cooperation using a mobile game.

We focus on understanding the gamers propensity for cooperation as a first step as cooperation is one of the main values associated with proactive peacekeeping. There are also well known game-theoretic models for studying cooperation, the most notable being the Prisoner's Dilemma, which we utilize in this work. Given the rich history of Prisoner's Dilemma experiments, it also provides a well-established baseline against which we can compare our data.

Despite this rich history, we cannot directly assume that the gamers propensity for cooperation will align with the accepted baseline since experiments on the propensity for cooperation have typically been limited to populations of university students. Typical members of this population are distinctly different from the typical gamer in terms of socioeconomic status and lived experiences. McCullough et al. found that individuals who experience neglect and personal violence, and are exposed to high levels of neighborhood crime, are more antisocial and tend to cooperate at lower rates [19]. Given these are particularly common experiences among the gamers, we theorize that we may need special behavioral models, requiring new, population specific data. However, due to the unique ecological circumstances surrounding gamers' lives, and a desire to study territorial influences as well, traditional lab-based experiments would be all but impossible to execute. Thus we develop a novel mobile application-based approach to collect the desired data.

In the rest of this paper we describe the mobile phone based experiment which implemented a one-shot prisoner's dilemma game in order to collect data from gamers. We then present initial results which show that counter to our hypothesis, in spite of the unique ecological circumstances surrounding the lives of gamers, we do not need special models to account for their patterns of cooperation. Finally, we discuss areas for future work and implications of this finding for proactive peacekeeping efforts.

2 Related Work

Gang Violence. Current approaches to negotiating peace between gangs are typically informal, short-lived (but see [4]), and are often precipitated by some major violent act such as the March 2019 shooting of Los Angeles-based rapper and activist Nispey Hussle [16,17]. One potential solution is Just-in-Time Adaptive Interventions, which are designed to deliver targeted, personalized interventions at just the right moment, often via technology such as a mobile device, and is already being explored in public health and education [2,20,21]. Patton et al. suggest that threats of retaliation and violence on gang members' Twitter accounts could be used to inform new intervention strategies [23]. However, in contrast to this kind of intervention, we are interested in proactive peacekeeping, which means making a concentrated effort to prevent violence from occurring in the first place, not just stopping retaliation once a violent event has occurred.

Game Theory in the Wild. This field is defined by the study of interactions between independent agents in which the payoff or utility to one agent depends on the actions of the other player(s) [10]. Classic games such as prisoner's dilemma, used in this study, and the ultimatum game can be used to experimentally gauge a population's propensity for traits such as cooperation and fairness. The prisoner's dilemma, although universal and timeless in its abstract form, was formalized using the well-known prisoner scenario in the early 1950s by researchers from the RAND group [25].

As previously mentioned, there is a rich history of experimentation with the prisoner's dilemma scenario and a variety of related models. However, the difficulties that surround working with the gamer population, particularly a lack of trust in authority [3,16], create a barrier to traditional lab-based experiments, so we conduct our experiments "in the wild". Game theoretic experiments in the wild have been conducted in a variety of contexts. Henrich et al. took traditional ultimatum game experiments to the field, conducting them in small-scale societies across the globe [14]. Other studies have used "natural experiments" such as the choices made by Swedish lottery players and the decisions of movie executives about whether or not to "cold-open" a film [6,22]. Additionally, there are experiments such as that by Delle Fave et al., which uses a smartphone application to eld test a schedule for metro patrols designed using the theory of Stackelberg security games [8]. There is also an attempt to understand the interaction among rangers and patrollers protecting wildlife in the field within a game theoretic framework [12,30]. Our work falls between the Henrich et al. and Delle Fave work, using a classic game, the one-shot prisoner's dilemma (PD), embedded in a mobile application. This allows us to compare our results to an established baseline, while collecting data from an otherwise hard to reach population. We are also able to collect location data during game play, which we hypothesize may influence gamers' propensity for cooperation given the significance of territory in their lives.

One-Shot Prisoner's Dilemma. The propensity for humans to cooperate with strangers has presented a long-standing paradox for game theorists [15,26]. The expected rational behavior of an individual in many common games is to eschew cooperation in favor of a selfish action that maximizes their own utility, often at the expense of the other player. This non-cooperative equilibrium is well-known in the two-person, one-shot Prisoner's Dilemma (PD) game where both players would be better off cooperating with one another, but this strategy is strictly dominated by mutual defection [27]. In numerous experiments stretching back over decades, however, it is clear that cooperation is common in the one-shot PD, in spite of the tactical vulnerability it creates [1]. One possible explanation for the prevalence of cooperation when it is predicted to be rare is that individuals have prior expectations about the likelihood that partners will cooperate (or that failure to cooperate will incur punishment) and that these expectations interfere with the incentives of the experiment [1,9,13]. This "homemade altruism" is thought to derive from the role that cooperation plays in routine life experiences that are rooted in repeated interactions and unique social circumstances [14]. One-shot games thus reveal prior expectations precisely because they are artificial. They also illustrate that prior expectations are subject to change, sometimes quite quickly. The one-shot PD, when played repeatedly with random strangers, shows that players adjust their strategies through a sequence equilibria with decreasing frequency of cooperation.

3 The Gamers

Gang membership is not a one-size-fits all problem. Gang researchers now typically think of gang-involvement in terms of degrees of embeddedness [7]. Individuals may be central to the activities of a gang (i.e., high embeddedness), peripheral to it (i.e., low-embeddedness), or occupy various positions between. Individuals may also readily move between social roles that are clearly identified with the gang (e.g., calling shots) and independent of the gang (e.g., parenting). Gang involvement also varies by age and gender, with the degree of involvement higher for young men between the ages of 15–25 [18].

We used an existing network of community members and outreach workers to identify and recruit active gamers to participate in the study. We made a concerted effort to ensure that gamers' privacy was respected and that they were willing participants in the study. Gamers were able to discontinue participation in the experiment at any time with no questions asked. Gamer recruitment and consent procedures were governed by UCLA IRB Protocol #16001755. Gamers were paid for their participation in the study according to the payoff scheme described in Sect. 4.

We recruited a population of 22 gamers—8 females and 14 males—between the ages of 16 and 25 from four different regions of Los Angeles which have high levels of gang activity. The gamers ranged in their level of gang affiliation and involvement. Ten of the gamers are fully initiated members of a gang with levels of engagement given by "very active", "active", or "not very active". The affiliated gamers are members of five different gangs. The remaining 12 are "not affiliated". These individuals are not officially initiated in gang life, but are familiar with it and have friends who are active.

4 Mobile One-Shot Prisoner's Dilemma

The current study aims to achieve a high degree of ecological validity, reflecting decision-making in the real-world settings experienced by gamers. Traditionally, studies in behavioral game theory have been conducted with participants brought into a controlled setting such as a research laboratory. However, it has been shown that tendencies shown by participants in the lab are in line with their behavior outside this setting [11]. Therefore we argue that we can compare the findings from our study "in the wild" to studies which have been carried out in a lab setting.

4.1 Game Design

The mobile one-shot PD application consists of a simple card game with a payoff matrix following the PD form [27]. Cards were chosen because they are a neutral object not belonging to any one particular gang. Figure 1a shows the basic game interface. The game consists of a choice between two playing cards, a king representing cooperation, and a queen representing betrayal. After the gamer chooses a card, the opponent's choice is revealed and the gamer is awarded points according to the matrix shown in Table 1. Gamers received a \$50 incentive payment for signing up to play and earned a maximum of \$0.25 per game, obtained when the gamer defected against a cooperating opponent (i.e., the temptation payoff). The gamers played against a simple algorithm, where cooperation was deployed as a Bernoulli trial with probability $p = 0.5$.

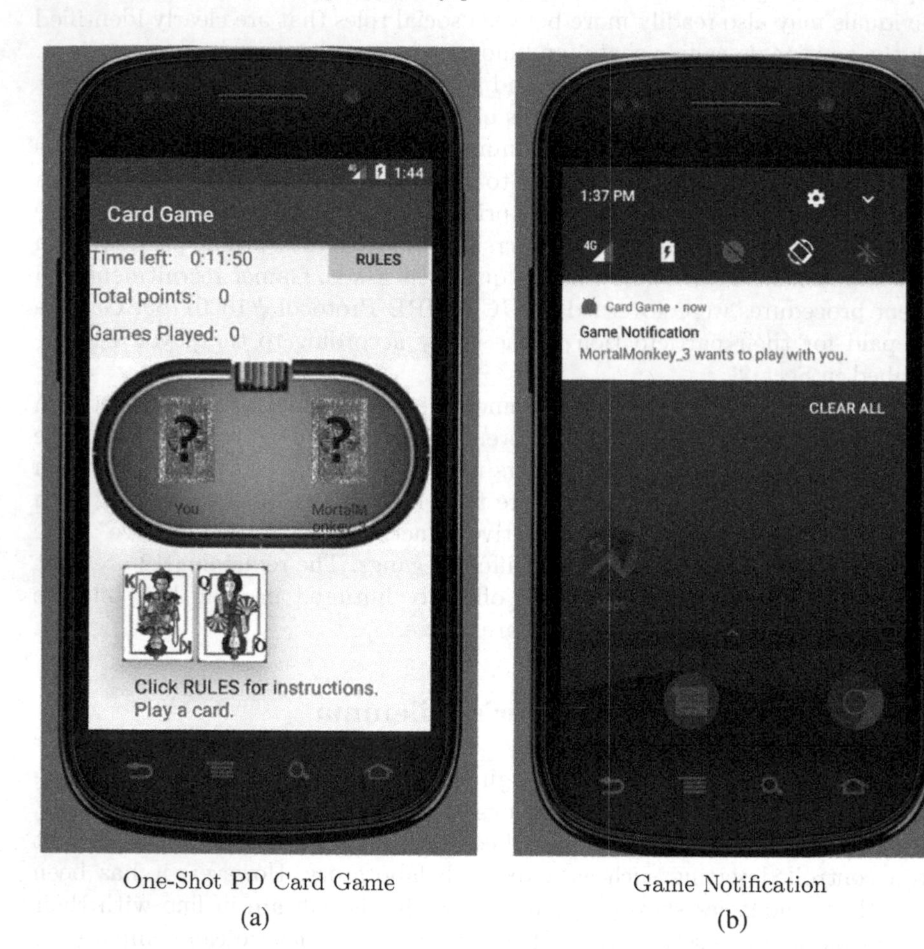

Fig. 1. Screenshots of (a) the game interface and (b) a game notification from the one-shot PD mobile application

The game was installed as an application on inexpensive android smart phones, which were given to the gamers by coordinators from their communities. Each time the gamers played a game, we collected a unique ID associated with their phone, their move (cooperate or defect), the computer's move, the date, time, and their location in latitude and longitude coordinates. In order to constrain payouts and increase the variability of location data collected, gamers were given a limited number of games spaced throughout each day.

Table 1. The payoff matrix for the mobile one-shot PD card game.

Card selection		Payout	
You	Opponent	You	Opponent
King	King	3000	3000
King	Queen	1000	4000
Queen	King	4000	1000
Queen	Queen	2000	2000

4.2 Pilot Test

The game was piloted with four gamers for two months in the fall of 2017. In the pilot, games were spaced evenly from 9 AM to 4 PM, coming in at the top of each hour. Gamers were given 30 min to play each game. If a game was not played within the allotted time, it was forfeit, with no points lost or gained. The gamer then had to wait for the next incoming game notification to play. During the two month pilot, data was collected from 125 games with one of the four gamers accounting for 86 of those instances. During the pilot, the gamers tended to play infrequently and very quickly. Twenty-four percent of games were played within the first 15 s of the hour, and 57.6% were played within the first 30 s. Although the game is not complicated, we felt that this might indicate a lack of attention on the part of the gamers. It became evident that the game needed to be more engaging to better capture the attention of the youth population.

4.3 Changes and Redeployment

After the pilot concluded, several updates were made to make the game more engaging. Rather than sending game notifications at the top of each hour, games were allocated randomly between 9 AM and 9 PM based on a Poisson distribution with $\lambda = 1/30$ to space games approximately half an hour apart, and a reminder notification was added five minutes before the end of unplayed games to encourage more play. Although gamers were still playing against the computer algorithm, randomly generated usernames were given to the "opponent" for each game to make it feel more realistic. Gamers were also given the opportunity to submit their own username before playing the game for the first time, although for the purpose of keeping identities, these usernames were not recorded or stored. Figure 1b shows a game notification with a randomly generated username—"MortalMonkey_3". The updated game was introduced into the field in February of 2018 for approximately five months of data collection. Throughout this time, 22 gamers played the game with varying levels of engagement.

Gamers in both the pilot and final experiment were paid at the end of the end of the experimental period. The results of the one-shot PD experiment are described in the next section.

5 Initial Results

A total of 2945 games were played during the study period, with the individual level of gamer engagement (number of games played) varying greatly. The number of games played by any one of the 22 gamers ranged from 0 to 551, with a mean of 134 ($\pm$135). The median number of games played was 76, with Q1 = 48 and Q3 = 211. We did not find any significant results with regard to the spatial distribution of cooperate and defect plays, however, our findings with regard to the general propensity for cooperation were both interesting and somewhat surprising to the authors.

Figure 2 depicts the patterns of cooperation observed in the one-shot mobile PD experiment. Plot A shows the Gamer IDs on the x-axis, in descending order of number of games played (y-axis). Each gamer is represented by two bars showing the number of games in which they defected (blue) and cooperated (red), respectively. Overall, gamers tended to defect at higher rates than they cooperated, particularly as the number of games played increased. The overall rate of cooperation ranged from zero to 69%, with a mean of 15 ($\pm$20). Fifteen of the twenty-two gamers engaged in more than 50 games. These gamers had an average cooperation rate of 0.15 ($\pm$0.18). Nine of the gamers played more than 100 games, and had a mean cooperation rate of just 0.10 ($\pm$0.08).

This decrease in cooperation over the number of games played is reflected in Fig. 2 plot C. This plot shows the fraction of games on which each subject cooperated as well as a five-game moving average for the first 80 games.

Finally, plot B shows the first 200 or so games for Gamer L, an unaffiliated female gamer, who played 282 games—the third most active gamer overall. This plot also reflects the deterioration of cooperation over time. During the first 50 or so games, she cooperated at a rate of about 50%, but this quickly deteriorated to less than 10%, consistent with the Andreoni and Miller findings.

6 Conclusion and Implications for Future Work

The most striking finding from these gamers "in the wild" is that they cooperate at quite high levels, at least initially. Indeed, the moving average shown in Fig. 2C is consistent with Andreoni and Miller [1], who found that initial cooperation rates of around 38% in the repeated one-shot PD with strangers, declined to less than 20% within 10 rounds of play. Over the long-run, cooperation among strangers deteriorated to less than 10% of all moves, but remained relatively stable at this low level. Our results are consistent with the conclusion that altruism exists at a natural baseline among individuals with considerable exposure to gangs. This cooperation is maintained even under conditions that are particularly inhospitable to cooperation such as in the one-shot PD [24]. We conclude not only that we do not need special models to understand cooperative tendencies among active gang members and gang-adjacent individuals, but also that their levels of cooperation are entirely consistent with other normative populations.

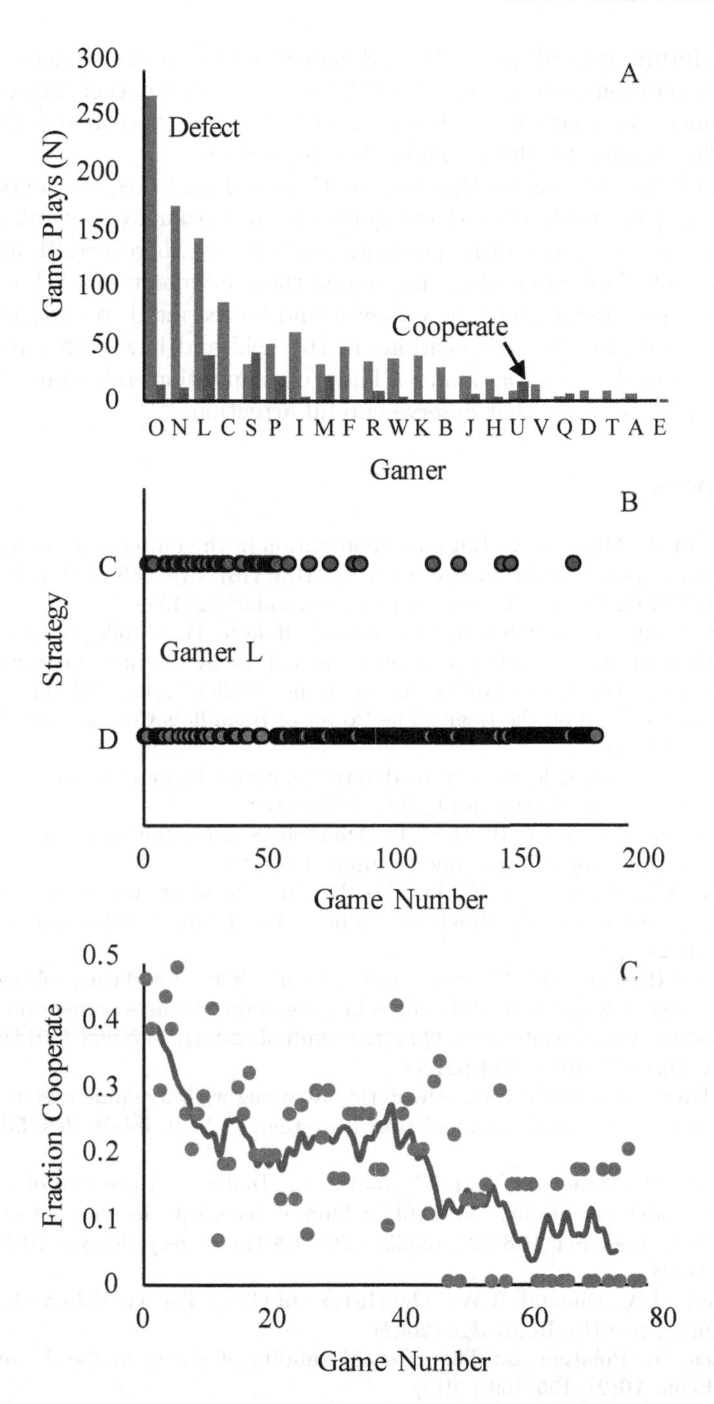

Fig. 2. Cooperation varies across gang-involved individuals and evolves over repeated exposure to one-shot PD games. (A) Number of games in which each subject cooperated and defected. (B) Shift to defection over a collection of one-shot games by Gamer L. (C) Fraction of subjects cooperating over the first 80 games. Line shows a five-game moving average.

In the future, we wish to conduct additional studies of the gamers' propensities for cooperation such as a repeated-PD experiment. Another area of interest is the gamers' inclinations for fairness, which can be measured using classic frameworks such as the ultimatum or dictator games.

Our initial results suggest that interventions seeking to reduce the risk of violence among gang-involved youth can generally start from a very similar baseline propensity to cooperate as other populations. However, there are still many open questions about how to develop and deploy these interventions. Who would be eligible for such interventions, how they would be recruited to participate, who would be responsible for interventions in the field and how such interventions would be received by the community? These open questions raise important legal and ethical implications that deserve careful attention.

References

1. Andreoni, J., Miller, J.H.: Rational cooperation in the finitely repeated prisoner's dilemma: experimental evidence. Econ. J. **103**(418), 570–585 (1993). https://doi.org/10.2307/2234532. http://www.jstor.org/stable/2234532
2. Bae, S., Chung, T., Ferreira, D., Dey, A.K., Suffoletto, B.: Mobile phone sensors and supervised machine learning to identify alcohol use events in young adults: implications for just-in-time adaptive interventions. Addict. Behav. **83**, 42–47 (2018)
3. Boyle, G.: Tattoos on the Heart: The Power of Boundless Compassion. Simon and Schuster (2011)
4. Braga, A.A.: Pulling levers focused deterrence strategies and the prevention of gun homicide. J. Crim. Justice **36**(4), 332–343 (2008)
5. Brantigham, P.J., Yuan, B., Herz, D.: Differences in retaliatory dynamics between gang and non-gang violent crime p. submitted (2019)
6. Brown, A.L., Camerer, C.F., Lovallo, D.: To review or not to review? limited strategic thinking at the movie box office. Am. Econ. J. Microeconomics **4**(2), 1–26 (2012)
7. Decker, S.H., Pyrooz, D.C., Sweeten, G., Moule, R.K.: Validating self-nomination in gang research: assessing differences in gang embeddedness across non-, current, and former gang members. J. Quant. Criminol. **30**(4), 577–598 (2014). https://doi.org/10.1007/s10940-014-9215-8
8. Delle Fave, F.M., et al.: Game-theoretic patrolling with dynamic execution uncertainty and a case study on a real transit system. J. Artif. Intell. Res. **50**, 321–367 (2014)
9. Delton, A.W., Krasnow, M.M., Cosmides, L., Tooby, J.: Evolution of direct reciprocity under uncertainty can explain human generosity in one-shot encounters. Proc. Nat. Acad. Sci. **108**(32), 13335–13340 (2011). https://doi.org/10.1073/pnas.1102131108
10. Dimand, M.A., Dimand, R.W.: The History of Game Theory, Volume 1: From the Beginnings to 1945. Routledge (2002)
11. Franzen, A., Pointner, S.: The external validity of giving in the dictator game. Exp. Econ. **16**(2), 155–169 (2013)
12. Gholami, S., et al.: Taking it for a test drive: a hybrid spatio-temporal model for wildlife poaching prediction evaluated through a controlled field test. In: Altun, Y., et al. (eds.) ECML PKDD 2017. LNCS (LNAI), vol. 10536, pp. 292–304. Springer, Cham (2017). https://doi.org/10.1007/978-3-319-71273-4_24

13. Hayashi, N., Ostrom, E., Walker, J., Yamagishi, T.: Reciprocity, trust, and the sense of control: a cross-societal study. Rationality Soci. **11**(1), 27–46 (1999). https://doi.org/10.1177/104346399011001002
14. Henrich, J., et al.: "Economic man" in cross-cultural perspective: behavioral experiments in 15 small-scale societies. Behav. Brain Sci. **28**(6), 795–815 (2005). https://doi.org/10.1017/S0140525X05000142
15. Johnson, D.D.P., Stopka, P., Knights, S.: The puzzle of human cooperation. Nature **421**(6926), 911–912 (2003). https://doi.org/10.1038/421911b
16. Leap, J.: Jumped In: What Gangs Taught Me About Violence, Drugs, Love, and Redemption. Beacon Press (2012)
17. Levin, S.: 'This is historic': how nipsey hussle's death inspired peace talks among rival la gangs, April 2019. https://www.theguardian.com/music/2019/apr/30/nipsey-hussle-los-angeles-gangs
18. Maxson, C.L.: Street Gangs, pp. 158–182. Oxford University Press, New York (2011)
19. McCullough, M.E., Pedersen, E.J., Schroder, J.M., Tabak, B.A., Carver, C.S.: Harsh childhood environmental characteristics predict exploitation and retaliation in humans. Proc. Roy. Soc. B Biol. Sci **280**(1750), 20122104 (2013). https://doi.org/10.1098/rspb.2012.2104
20. McQuillin, S.D., Lyons, M.D., Becker, K.D., Hart, M.J., Cohen, K.: Strengthening and expanding child services in low resource communities: the role of task-shifting and just-in-time training. Am. J. Community Psychol. **63**(3–4), 355–365 (2019)
21. Nahum-Shani, I., et al.: Just-in-time adaptive interventions (jitais) in mobile health: key components and design principles for ongoing health behavior support. Ann. Behav. Med. **52**(6), 446–462 (2017)
22. Östling, R., Wang, J.T.Y., Chou, E.Y., Camerer, C.F.: Testing game theory in the field: Swedish lupi lottery games. Am. Econ. J. Microeconomics **3**(3), 1–33 (2011)
23. Patton, D.U., Lane, J., Leonard, P., Macbeth, J., Smith Lee, J.R.: Gang violence on the digital street: case study of a south side Chicago gang member's twitter communication. New Media Soc. **19**(7), 1000–1018 (2017)
24. Peysakhovich, A., Nowak, M.A., Rand, D.G.: Humans display a 'cooperative phenotype' that is domain general and temporally stable. Nature Commun. **5**, 4939 (2014)
25. Poundstone, W.: Prisoner's Dilemma/John von Neumann. Game Theory and the Puzzle of the Bomb, Anchor (1993)
26. Rand, D.G., Nowak, M.A.: Human cooperation. Trends Cogn. Sci. **17**(8), 413–425 (2013). https://doi.org/10.1016/j.tics.2013.06.003. http://www.sciencedirect.com/science/article/pii/S1364661313001216
27. Rapoport, A., Chammah, A.M., Orwant, C.J.: Prisoner's dilemma: a study in conflict and cooperation, vol. 165. University of Michigan press (1965)
28. Rice, C.: Power Concedes Nothing: One Woman's Quest for Social Justice in America, From the Courtroom to the Kill Zones. Simon and Schuster (2012)
29. Villaraigosa, A.: City of Los Angeles Gang Reduction Strategy. The City of Los Angeles (2007)
30. Xu, H., et al.: Optimal patrol planning for green security games with black-box attackers. In: Rass, S., An, B., Kiekintveld, C., Fang, F., Schauer, S. (eds.) International Conference on Decision and Game Theory for Security, pp. 458–477. Springer, Cham (2017). https://doi.org/10.1007/978-3-319-68711-7_24

Paired-Consistency: An Example-Based Model-Agnostic Approach to Fairness Regularization in Machine Learning

Yair Horesh(✉), Noa Haas, Elhanan Mishraky, Yehezkel S. Resheff, and Shir Meir Lador

Intuit Inc., Mountain View, USA
{yair_horesh,noa_haas,elhanan_mishraky,hezi_resheff, shir_lador}@intuit.com

Abstract. As AI systems develop in complexity it is becoming increasingly hard to ensure non-discrimination on the basis of protected attributes such as gender, age, and race. Many recent methods have been developed for dealing with this issue as long as the protected attribute is explicitly available for the algorithm. We address the setting where this is not the case (with either no explicit protected attribute, or a large set of them). Instead, we assume the existence of a fair domain expert capable of generating an extension to the labeled dataset - a small set of example pairs, each having a different value on a subset of protected variables, but judged to warrant a similar model response. We define a performance metric - paired consistency. Paired consistency measures how close the output (assigned by a classifier or a regressor) is on these carefully selected pairs of examples for which fairness dictates identical decisions. In some cases consistency can be embedded within the loss function during optimization and serve as a fairness regularizer, and in others it is a tool for fair model selection. We demonstrate our method using the well studied *Income Census* dataset.

Keywords: Fairness · AI · Machine learning · Social responsibility

1 Introduction

The notion of fairness is deeply rooted in human kind [8,9,13] and even in other intelligent species [2,3]. In practice, fairness is elusive. Due to the nature of complex systems we operate within, both conscious and unconscious cognitive biases, and lack of complete knowledge, it is extremely hard to guarantee fairness even in the presence of sufficient good will.

When considering large scale machine learning systems we must proceed with caution. On the one hand the current trend of increased adoption of machine learning is a unique opportunity to clean the slate and utilize automation for objectivity and fairness. On the other hand, it is often unclear how to operate when labeled data is derived from historic processes with questionable fairness.

P. Cellier and K. Driessens (Eds.): ECML PKDD 2019 Workshops, CCIS 1167, pp. 590–604, 2020.
https://doi.org/10.1007/978-3-030-43823-4_47

Furthermore, models are typically optimized with respect to some measure of performance on the task they are designed to do, a process that has no relation to fairness and almost always favors the average outcomes.

Arguably, there are three levels of adherence to ethical and fair practice of AI. In the best case, a system designer is clearly and unequivocally fair. This option is unusual if at all possible (for instance because of the often mutually-exclusive notions of fairness). Failing that, fairness disputes could be based on the notion of what is fair. In this case there should be little or no doubt about the integrity and intentions of the designer. For instance, when trading off individual fairness in order to obtain better group fairness. Finally, a system can be outright discriminatory.

Too often systems already in use are discovered to be outright discriminatory. It has been claimed that the Correctional Offender Management Profiling for Alternative Sanctions (COMPAS) system – a system widely used by courts for predicting a defendant's risk of recidivism within 2 years using 137 features, has low prediction power and a strong racial bias [5,12].

While explicit discrimination is easy to detect and remove, features that are correlated to discriminating attributes are much harder to detect. Consider a classification or a regression task via some method $f(\cdot)$, with a dataset at hand $\{(d^{(i)}, x^{(i)}, y^{(i)})\}_{i=1}^{N}$, where Y is the target variable, and D and X are separate feature spaces, D contains the protected variables. Restricting the fitting of $f(\cdot)$ solely through X clearly eliminates explicit discrimination with respect to features in D. However, although $Y \perp\!\!\!\perp D|X$, we might still observe association between the predictions and D, since $Y \not\perp\!\!\!\perp D$ in the general case, even when D is not included in the fitting stage [17]. Hence, even if the protected attributes *is* completely removed from the input data, this does not guarantee fairness.

What characterizes a fair system? Several competing notions of fairness have been recently proposed in the machine learning literature. The simplest notion of fairness is *demographic parity* [4] (Table 1). To satisfy demographic parity the underlying proportion of the protected variable should be preserved within the classification process (for example, an equal number of male and female candidates should pass the exam). This criteria is meant to preserve *group fairness*, and as such has several drawbacks.

First, demographic parity can be naively achieved through random assignment of the target $\hat{Y}$ in the underprivileged group according to the distribution in the privileged group. This clearly achieves demographic parity, but misses the original objective of achieving a useful prediction of Y in the entire population. This sort of unfair selection in the underprivileged group leads to two detrimental consequences. Not only is it unfair to deserving individuals in the underprivileged group, since they have a smaller probability of being selected than similar individuals in the majority group, but this process also leads to a selection of less appropriate individuals from the underprivileged group, setting them up for failure, and reinforcing stigma. This behavior is prone to happen for instance when D represents minority groups, and there is little or no training data available for one of the demographics [11].

Second, the demographic parity approach assumes that the population affiliation and the target are independent. For example, consider the case of a hiring process for a job associated primarily with males. It is possible that the few females that do submit an application are on average more qualified than the male applicants. In such a case, we would expect a fair process not to preserve the original proportions, and indeed accept a higher proportion of the female applicants.

Metrics which asses how well a model maintain demographic parity are disparate impact and parity difference which are the ratio and difference between the conditional probability of the positive class given the binary protected variable, and *prejudice index*, which quantifies the mutual information between the target Y and D [14] (Table 1).

Other notions of fairness focus on the individual rather than on the group, and try to assure that an *individual* is treated fairly irrespective of D. These measures are based on the notion that similar individuals should be treated similarly by the system. One approach for achieving individual fairness is to aim at removing the information about D from the original data representation X. This however is not an easy thing to do, for instance, studies on gender bias show that removing bias from word embedding is extremely hard [10]. In another study it was shown that removing demographic information from representations of text is also not an easy task [7]. Recently the adversarial learning framework has been suggested to reduce bias in learned representations for fair models [20], and in the context of fair and private recommendations [18].

Metrics for evaluating a system's individual fairness include average odds difference and equal opportunity difference [11] which attempt to guarantee uniform aggregate behavior of the predictor with respect to a binary protected variable, and consistency, which compares a model's classification prediction of a given data item x to its k-nearest neighbors [19] (see Table 1 for a glossary of definitions and metrics in the fairness literature).

The aim of research on fair AI methods and metrics is to help design systems that adhere to the notion of fairness the system designer chooses to adopt. This is the *how*, not the *what.* Assuming good intentions, the normative question of what we consider to be fair is a separate issue that should be addressed by a much wider community. All of the above notions rely on the clear, categorical definition of the discriminatory variable D, and its presence in the data. In this paper we address the question of designing fair models with any specific notion of individual fairness.

Unlike the methods described above, we deal in a setting where there is no simple categorical variable (or small number thereof) that defines demographic groups for which fairness should be guaranteed. This can be the case when there are *no* explicit protected attributes (but still discrimination danger from demographic-correlated attributes). Alternatively there may be *many* protected attributes, with either many categories or continuous values. In these cases the existing methods do not apply or are infeasible to use. The proposed method uses an expert to mine a small auxiliary dataset that refines the desired notion of fairness, a performance metric, and a regularization method to obtain it.

The core idea is that if we had many pairs with similar *merit*, in the sense that with respect to the chosen notion of fairness they should get the same treatment, we could force the model to behave that way. To this end we assume the existence of a (fair) domain expert who is able to label pairs of instances. Each pair has a different value in a subset of protected variables D, and the expert asserts that a fair model should output a similar response for them. Note that this methodology doesn't require a defined similarity metric between samples, a property which allows more flexibility in applying it.

The proposed method is general in two aspects. While previous fairness inducing methods require explicit access to the protected attribute D, the pairs generated by the expert in our method can be selected on the basis of any implicit idea of a potentially discriminatory variable, that doesn't have to be directly measurable. The second aspect of generality is the wide applicability to machine learning models. We suggest a tree-training variant, and a gradient-descent training variant, together covering the majority of widely used machine learning methods.

The rest of the paper is structured as follows: in the next section we describe the proposed method of paired-consistency for fairness. Next, we describe experiments and results on the "Census Income" dataset, comparing the proposed method to alternatives that do require direct access to the restricted variables, using a large set of fairness criteria. We finish with a discussion on the pros and cons of the proposed method and future direction of research.

2 Methods

In this section we present the method of paired-consistency. The setting we operate in is a dataset: $\left\{(d^{(i)}, x^{(i)}, y^{(i)})\right\}_{i=1}^{N}$, where each example consists of features x, an additional (and possibly empty) set of explicitly given restricted variables d, and a target y. In addition, access to a fair domain expert is assumed. The expert may be a literal human expert, or an algorithm or method used as a surrogate.

The fair domain expert comes equipped with a notion of fairness, and of the potential attributes that must be protected from discrimination. These attributes may be explicit (i.e. contained in d – for example gender or age), or more complex constructs that the expert is able to determine based on a sample (d, x, y) (for example being of an underprivileged background). Upon request, the expert returns pairs:

$$\left\{(x_1^{(j)}, x_2^{(j)})\right\}_{j=1}^{M}$$

denoted as the *consistency set*. Each of these pairs consists of the features from two examples of the original dataset, that obey two requirements. First, the pair represents two examples which are different with respect to the protected attribute or construct, as determined by the expert. Second, based on the remainder of the information the expert is able to judge that the two samples warrant a similar response by the model.

An interesting property of the paired-consistency method is that it is able to protect from discrimination not only in the absence of the explicit protected variable, but even when the construct of interest is not directly measurable, as long as the fair domain expert is able to match pairs which are different with respect to it. Cases when this may be of use include when individuals with certain special circumstances are historically under-represented and a fair selection process might therefore attempt to take this into consideration. Furthermore, this method is able to mix and combine fairness with respect to different potential sources of discrimination, by combining the sets of pairs derived from each one.

In this setting, we suggest a simple model-agnostic method which can be used to assess (if used for model selection) or help assure fairness (if used as a regularizer) of a classification or regression model for predicting y. We define a paired-consistency score, which measures how similar is an output (in terms of assigned class, or predicted score) a model produces for paired members, for classification:

$$\frac{1}{M}\sum_{j=1}^{M} I[\hat{y}_1^{(j)} = \hat{y}_2^{(j)}] \tag{1}$$

where $\hat{y}_1^{(j)} = f(x_1^{(j)})$ is the model output, and $I[\cdot]$ is the indicator function. This measures the fraction of the pairs on which the model agrees. Likewise for regression:

$$1 - \frac{1}{M \cdot \delta_{max}} \sum_{j=1}^{M} (\hat{y}_1^{(j)} - \hat{y}_2^{(j)})^2 \tag{2}$$

where δ_{max} is the maximal square difference, used to normalize the measure into $[0, 1]$ (this is necessary only when comparing models, otherwise the measure to minimize becomes $\frac{1}{M}\sum_{j=1}^{M}(\hat{y}_1^{(j)} - \hat{y}_2^{(j)})^2$).

The consistency score is embedded within the loss function as a fairness regularization term, to make the model consistency aware. This is done by adding the measure (Eq. 2) to the objective, multiplied by a trade-off parameter to determine the relative importance of the main objective and the paired-consistency. Any algorithm trained via gradient-descent (and variants) can be adapted to incorporate this additional loss component. In addition, we suggest a variant for training of trees, where the local optimization criterion is augmented in a similar way to include the fraction of pairs kept intact in each split. Results of both these types are presented below (Sect. 3).

In addition (or alternatively for fairness-based model selection), the score is calculated *post-hoc*, and can be aggregated with other performance metrics, or used as part of a performance-fairness trade-off. A good classifier will be accurate but also consistent in the scoring of the pairs. To this end we define the *PRC score* as the weighted Harmonic Mean of Precision, Recall, and Paired-Consistency, which as an F1-score analogue it is a natural candidate for integrating consistency in evaluation of models.

The proposed method also allows a natural integration of the certainty of the expert. Suppose that together with the pairs, the expert also produces a weight reflecting how sure they are that the pair is indeed a fairness-match – different on some subset of the protect variables or constructs, and deserving of the same treatment – so that the expert now outputs $\{(x_1^{(j)}, x_2^{(j)}, w^{(j)})\}_{j=1}^{M}$. The classification paired-fairness measure (Eq. 1) will thus become:

$$\frac{\sum_{j=1}^{M} w^{(j)} \cdot I[\hat{y}_1^{(j)} = \hat{y}_2^{(j)}]}{M \cdot \sum_{j=1}^{M} w^{(j)}} \tag{3}$$

Table 1. Glossary: several common definitions and measures in the fairness literature. (F/TPR - false/true positive rate, D - protected variable, Y - the target, $\hat{Y}$ - model prediction, knn - k nearest neighbors).

Name	Definition
Demographic parity	$Pr(\hat{Y}=1\|D=0) = Pr(\hat{Y}=1\|D=1)$
Parity difference	$Pr(\hat{Y}=1\|D=0) - Pr(\hat{Y}=1\|D=1)$
Disparate impact	$\frac{Pr(\hat{Y}=1\|D=0)}{Pr(\hat{Y}=1\|D=1)}$
Equalized odds [11]	$TPR_{D=0} = TPR_{D=1}; FPR_{D=0} = FPR_{D=1}$
Average odds difference	$\frac{1}{2}[(FPR_{D=0} - FPR_{D=1}) + (TPR_{D=0} - TPR_{D=1}))]$
Equal opportunity [11]	$TPR_{D=0} = TPR_{D=1}$
Equal opportunity difference	$TPR_{D=0} - TPR_{D=1}$
Consistency [19]	$1 - \frac{1}{N}\sum_{i=1}^{N} \|\hat{y}_i - \frac{1}{k}\sum_{j\in knn(i)} \hat{y}_j\|$
Prejudice index [14]	$\sum \hat{p}(y,d) ln \frac{\hat{p}(y,d)}{\hat{p}(y)\hat{p}(d)}$
Paired-consistency (ours)	$\frac{1}{M}\sum_{j=1}^{M} I[\hat{y}_1^{(j)} = \hat{y}_2^{(j)}]$

3 Results

We demonstrate the paired-consistency method using a well-known dataset, and both for tree-based and gradient-based model training. The dataset we use to demonstrate the method is the "Census Income" dataset [6,15] derived from the 1994 census in the US. In this dataset the set of discriminatory variables D appears explicitly in the data. We proceed to generate consistency pairs in order to emulate the case where an expert is called upon to generate pairs in the absence of explicit information. In some of the experiments below we also leave the protected attributes in the set of features used by the model in order to test the effect of paired-consistency regularization on the utilization of restricted information by the model. This setting emulates the standard case where the outright discriminatory features are indeed excluded from the model (gender, age, race, etc.), but other highly correlated features are included.

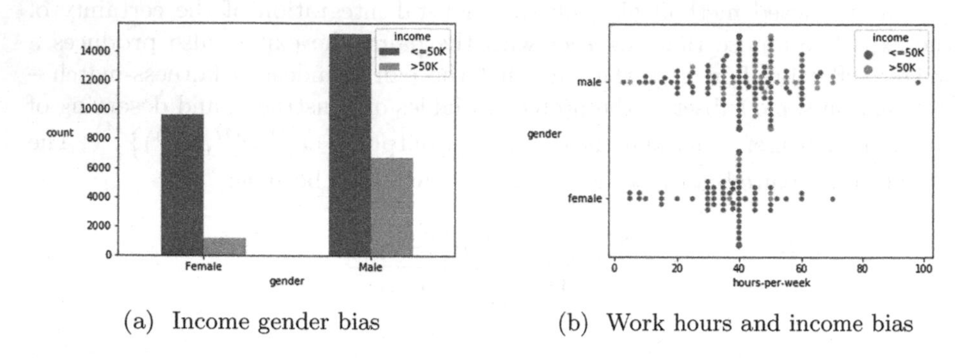

(a) Income gender bias

(b) Work hours and income bias

Fig. 1. The gender-income bias and interaction with number of weekly work hours as reflected in the *census income* dataset.

The "Census Income" dataset was chosen because it contains a combination of attributes a person is born with or has no control over (gender, race, age, native-country) and attributes that reflect their preferences and decisions in life (occupation, weekly work hours, education, martial status). The Census Income dataset contains data pertaining to over 32,000 individuals. The dataset also contains a binary field indicating high income (over $50K$ as of the 1994 census) which will be used as the target variable for our tests. The overall fraction of high-income individuals in the dataset is 26%.

In this experiment we model the likelihood of being a high-income individual based on individual traits. The setting we have in mind is one where the output of a model of this sort will impact the way people are treated. As such, we would need to take care not to discriminate on the bases of certain properties of individuals. While it is clear that if left untreated, attributes such race, gender and native-country will have predictive power for income level, some attributes are both relevant and at the same time a proxy of discriminating attributes. Figure 1 illustrates this ambiguity. The gender income imbalance reflected in the census data is captured by Fig. 1(a). However, the swarm-plot figure (Fig. 1(b)) shows there is a gender difference in the probability of being in the high-income group, and also a difference in distribution of weekly work hours. As a result, the otherwise innocent (and intuitively relevant) variable of number of work hours, gives away some information about the protected variable (which is gender).

In order to test the effect of paired-consistency on the fairness and performance of a predictive model, we use a decision tree and a Logistic Regression model. The motivation for using these simple models is that the readily interpretable outcome lets us better understand the effect of the fairness regularization, and at the same time these are representatives of the two major classes of machine learning models at this time (i.e. tree based and gradient based training). Paired-consistency is added to the Logistic Regression model by inserting the mean square deviation in output among pairs (Eq. 2) directly to the loss function, via a trade-off parameter.

For tree training, we add the fairness metric as an extension to the Gini Index used in the tree creation. In order to adapt the measure (Eq. 1) to the local criterion of tree growing, for a given split we seek to maximize the number of pairs that go in the same direction. To this end we add to the Gini Index a term that is the percent of the pairs arriving at the node that are kept intact following the split (i.e. both examples in the pair go to the same side). This term is multiplied by a trade-off parameter that controls the relative importance of the fairness regularization in the tree construction. As expected when training trees, this is a local optimization criterion. Feature importance in the resulting model was measured using the column permutation method (and using the *eli5* Python package [16]). Experiments were conducted using a 80–20 train-test split, making sure original pairs are kept in the same set. All categorical features are encoded as dummies, leading to a total of 58 features. For regularization, and to ensure an interpretable result, we limit decision tree depth to 5 and the minimal items in a leaf to 5.

Baseline. The tree baseline consists of a regular decision tree, achieving an accuracy level of 82.6%. Figure 2 shows the most important features resulting from this model. Interestingly the list is topped by the "married civil spouse" indicator, followed by occupation and education indicators. We choose to focus on the next most important variable – age, which we chose as the discriminating factor we want to mitigate in the following experiments with consistency pairs. It is important to note that in a real use-case the protected variables would undoubtedly be removed from the model themselves, but this blindness would

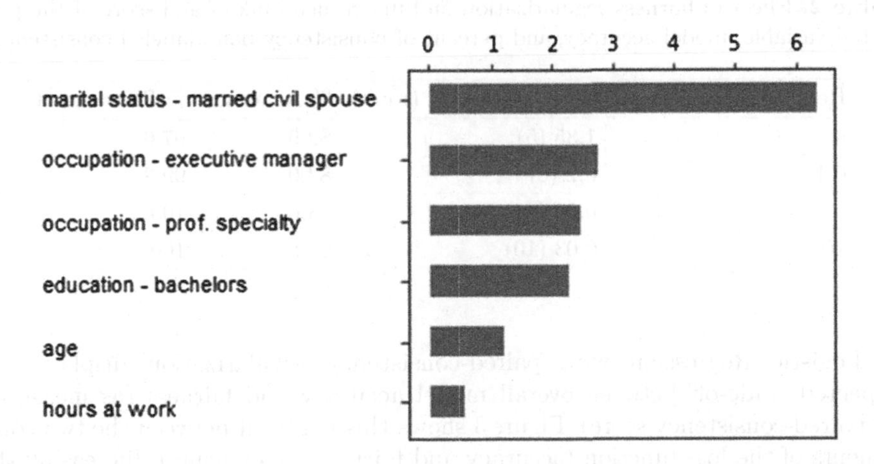

Fig. 2. Top-6 feature importance in the basic tree model for *census income* (arbitrary units).

not suffice to achieve fairness because of correlated features that remain in the input. We keep the age variable in the model in order to emulate the case of additional information correlated with the protected variable(s). The Logistic Regression baseline achieves an accuracy level of 82.9%.

Consistency Pairs. We automatically created 3,062 consistency pairs by selecting pairs of individuals who are similar in all other aspects except for age (while ignoring income). We picked pairs where the age gap is of 10 years or more. Obviously this is a toy example, and in a more complicated model a fair domain expert will likely be necessary for this purpose.

To minimize the paired-consistency fairness penalty the model must predict for each pair the same predicted income and avoid discriminating on the basis of age. We test the model with four levels of the fairness-regularization trade-off parameter. Tables 2 and 3 summarizes the results of this experiment. Table 2 shows that the importance rank of the variable under consideration is reduced monotonically as the weight of the fairness-regularization is increased, from rank 5 in the naive model to rank 10 with larger weights, reaching a plateau with a weight of 1. The effect flattens out when the percent of pairs classified together is 100% after which the fairness penalty is 0 and therefore further increasing the weight is irrelevant. Overall accuracy of the model is virtually unaffected, and even slightly improved together with increased fairness. Table 3 shows this effect – as the number of pairs used for the consistency regularization increases, the importance of the age feature in the model decreases. We note that even a relatively small number of pairs (500 pairs, versus the 32, 561 examples in the dataset) was sufficient to significantly mitigate the age bias, although the change obtained in importance of the restricted variable from rank-5 to rank 7 may not be sufficient.

Table 2. Effect of fairness regularization on importance rank of and score of the protected variable, model accuracy, and percent of consistency pairs labeled consistently.

Regularization weight	Age importance (rank)	% Accuracy	% Pairs intact
0	1.35 (5)	82.9	97.6
0.1	0.2 (8)	83.0	99.8
1	0.03 (10)	83.0	100
10	0.03 (10)	83.8	100

Logistic Regression with paired-consistency regularization displays the expected trade-off between overall model accuracy and fairness (as measured by paired-consistency score). Figure 3 shows this trade-off between the two components of the loss function (accuracy and fairness components). Increasing the trade-off parameter η shifts the weight towards the fairness objective, and in turn leads to a decrease in the paired-consistency component of the objective,

Table 3. Effect of the number of consistency pairs on importance rank and score of the protected variable, model accuracy, and percent of consistency pairs labeled consistently. The fairness-regularization weight (eta) is fixed to 0.5.

# Pairs	Age importance (rank)	% Accuracy	% Pairs intact
100	1.50 (5)	82.7	100
500	0.58 (7)	82.7	100
1000	0.33 (7)	82.8	100
3062	0.03 (10)	83.0	100

together with an increase in the original Logistic Regression loss component. The effect of the trade-off parameter is shown as the fractional change in each of the loss components, compared to the baseline ($\eta = 0$; regular Logistic Regression). Results indicate that for the price of a modest decline in accuracy, the fairness component of the loss can be reduced by as much as half. This favorable trade-off can be seen in the relative slopes of the lines in Fig. 3 for eta in the range of 0–0.5.

We further compare the fairness-accuracy trade-off in various methods for predicting the target variable using the dataset. The compared methods include both classification methods without any fairness regularization or constraints, and methodologies with the objective of a creating a fair model. We applied our paired-consistency regularization to Logistic Regression and decision tree models, and a prejudice remover [14] regularization (with $\eta = 10$) to a Logistic Regression model (using the *AI Fairness 360* [1] python package). Methods were compared both in accuracy and in fairness. Accuracy was used to measure utility, and the metrics in Table 1, as well as our paired consistency metric were used to measure various aspects of model fairness.

Such comparisons provides a clear understanding with regard to the potential trade-off between predictive modeling utility and fairness. The ultimate result would be to achieve high fairness, while maintaining the model performance with respect to the prediction objective. As theoretically expected, almost all fairness-regularization methods hindered the model's accuracy, but this effect is not dramatic for the tested dataset and methods. All fairness regularization methods show improvements in the fairness metrics over the respective baselines. The consistency-paired regularized tree seems like the fairest model available here (both in group and individual fairness), but under-performs in terms of accuracy. Another aspect to learn from these results is the differentiation between the various fairness metrics – while the overall trend is to improve fairness for all methods, each methodology outperform in a different fairness metric. This is of course expected. Each method optimizes with respect to a specific notion of fairness, and in general is likely therefore to do best on that, while being less competitive on others (this is especially the case when considering contradictory metrics such as group vs. individual fairness, where it is not possible generally to be optimal in both).

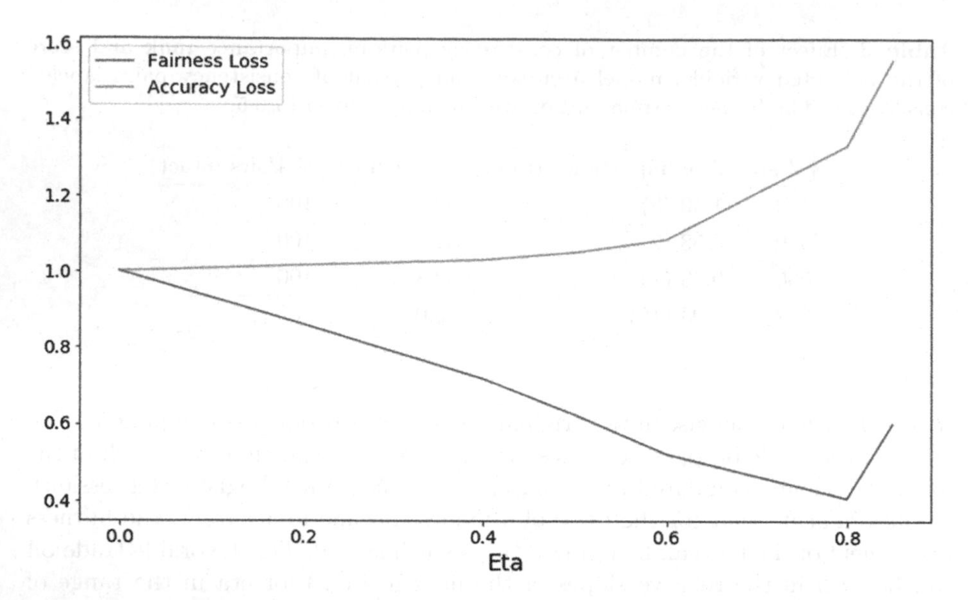

Fig. 3. Trade-off of Logistic Regression loss and paired-consistency loss components as a function of the trade-off parameter eta. Values are normalized and presented as fraction of the respective loss components for $\eta = 0$.

Finally, we test the effect of the number of consistency pairs available on the accuracy-fairness trade-off when used as a fairness regularization in Logistic Regression. The importance of this stems from the high cost and effort involved in generating fairness pairs in some real-world situations. Unlike in our current experiment, it is not always possible to generate this auxiliary data automatically, and instead a human expert is used to label data pairs. Ideally, we would want to know how many pairs are necessary, and how the number of pairs is likely to impact the fairness measures.

Results are summarized in Table 5. Logistic Regression models are trained with paired-consistency regularization ($\eta = 0.4$). As expected, as the number of consistency-pairs used is increased, the paired-consistency score increases as well, from 0.705 with 100 pairs, to 0.945 with 1000 pairs. However, 500 pairs are enough to obtain a score of 0.912, not significantly less than the optimal value. A similar picture is reflected also in the other fairness measures. The accuracy of the fairness-regularized Logistic Regression models is seen to increase overall with the number of pairs. This can be explained by the arbitrary effect each pair has on the overall the model, which may average out when many pairs are applied. An analytic understanding of this phenomenon will be necessary in future research, as well as testing on additional datasets (Table 4).

Table 4. Census Income: Comparison of different methodologies (with and without fairness constraints), in terms of performance and various fairness metrics. LR – Logistic Regression. (prej.) – Prejudice Remover (Table 1). tree/LR+pairs – tree/LR with our method of paired-consistency.

	Tree	Tree+pairs	LR	LR [14] (prej.)	LR+pairs eta=0.4	LR+pairs eta=0.5
Paired consistency score	0.976	1.000	0.912	0.913	0.927	0.932
Classification accuracy	0.832	0.834	0.829	0.826	0.824	0.815
Disparate impact	0.250	0.299	0.193	0.213	0.212	0.225
Statistical parity diff	−0.164	−0.160	−0.314	−0.314	−0.304	−0.318
Equal opportunity diff	−0.149	−0.091	−0.248	−0.227	−0.234	−0.220
Average odds diff	−0.103	−0.073	−0.215	−0.205	−0.204	−0.207

Table 5. Logistic Regression with paired-consistency regularization ($\eta = 0.4$). Effect of the number of consistency pairs on various performance and fairness scores.

# Pairs	Accuracy	Paired consistency	Parity difference	Average odds difference
100	0.759	0.705	−0.490	−0.477
500	0.804	0.912	−0.376	−0.269
1000	0.797	0.945	−0.322	−0.191
3062	0.824	0.927	−0.304	−0.204

4 Discussion and Conclusion

With the rise in popularity of AI across many domains, questions of ethical use and fairness are revisited with renewed vigor. Many methods have previously been proposed to help create fair machine learning algorithms, when the variable which leads to potential discrimination is explicitly available in the data. However, this is not always the case.

We present a simple yet powerful method to help mitigate discrimination in machine learning models, without using an explicit partitioning of the data with respect to a protected variable. Our approach relies on the ability of a fair domain expert to generate a set of pairs of examples which are equivalent based on all attributes except for a subset of the protected variables. We then assert that a fair model should treat the two examples in each of these pairs in a similar way, and define a measure of consistency that when added to a models loss function helps enforce fairness via consistency. This fairness regularization technique is shown to reduce the extent to which a decision tree model uses a forbidden feature in classification, and has favorable outcomes also with respect to other measures of fairness.

The proposed method of paired-consistency is related to several existing techniques. In a broad sense, statistically defined group fairness methods try to ensure that on the group level the minority group is treated by the machine learning algorithm in a similar way to the majority group. In that case our method is similar by reducing the size of the groups to 1 and having many such pairs.

Experiments on a well-studied dataset in the fair model literature demonstrates the viability of our method, both for tree-based and gradient-based training (with Logistic Regression). It is interesting to note that in our experiments we see little to no decline in accuracy as we increasingly enforce fairness by adjusting the trade off parameter in the loss function. This sort of degenerate trade-off is likely not the general case. When the trade-off takes on a more substantial form, the additional paired-consistency term added to the loss function can be seen as a regularization mechanism against bias, in as much as it restricts the search during optimization to regions of higher fairness. The result in the general case will inevitably be some loss in overall model accuracy.

One of the merits of the proposed approach is that it enables domain experts to take part in the fairness efforts and mitigate discrimination without the need to understand how the model works or what features or information it is based on. Even better, by using examples, the expert bypasses the need to formalize the sometimes elusive notion of fairness. In fact, the fairness labelling can and should be done by an expert prior to and independently from machine learning work. Since the labeling is independent from the methods used to make predictions, it can be seen as an extension of labeling for supervised learning rather than of the process of evaluating results of a model. However, new consistency pairs can be generated after a model is created to further evaluate its fairness properties with respect to discriminating variable of interest. Adding new consistency pairs doesn't require the model itself to be changed, only to be re-trained.

There are several limitations to paired-consistency. First, our method assumes the existence and availability of a fair domain expert capable of generating consistency pairs. In many cases this is not a huge stretch, but other times may be infeasible due to time, cost, or trust. The current experiments do however suggest that a relatively small number of pairs (several hundred) are already sufficient to achieve most of the benefit.

Even when such an expert is available, there is still a problem in agreeing on the notion of fairness to be used in the pairing of examples. This final issue is a fundamental problem of fair machine learning (and possibly fairness in general). The inability to agree on what is fair is inherently a limitation on the ability to design fair systems. We note that this question is outside of the scope of machine learning and engineering in general, and is rather a question to be tackled by a wider community in the broad spectrum of the humanities and social sciences.

Future work will focus on extending the ideas brought here to other types of models and domains, and provide theoretical performance guarantees. In the case of deep learning (or more generally gradient optimized models), it is relatively straight forward to add the consistency term as specified in Eq. 2, as is demonstrated for the Logistic Regression case here. It remains to be seen how this will effect different types of models, and how the effect varies between datasets. For other types of models it may be more difficult to incorporate this penalty, but the method can still be used independently for the purpose of fair model selection (since in that case it is a *post-hoc* calculation on the model output, that doesn't depend on the model's cost function itself).

An additional question of interest that we do not cover here is the effect of the number of consistency pairs necessary to achieve the goal. While we were able to generate a relatively large number for the current datasets (since it was an automatic process), in the more general case a human expert will manually pick consistency pairs, a potentially costly and time consuming effort. The cost and effort required limit the number of pairs that are feasible for any given dataset.

Finally, we note that this method can be applied synergistically with other fairness techniques for model construction and evaluation. For example, this method can be used in conjunction with adversarial techniques for removing unwanted information from deep learning representations [7,20] to obtain a model that is based on a representation devoid of the information about the protected variables on the one hand, and that enforces fairness in the notion of consistency on the other hand. Future work will focus on the interplay between the various trade-off parameters that emerge from such a construction. Similarly, it is interesting to investigate the effect of the pair sampling done by the fair domain expert, and cases when specific types of sampling lead to paired-consistency converging back to one of the previously proposed statistical notions of fairness.

References

1. Bellamy, R.K., et al.: AI fairness 360: an extensible toolkit for detecting, understanding, and mitigating unwanted algorithmic bias. arXiv preprint arXiv:1810.01943 (2018)
2. Bräuer, J., Call, J., Tomasello, M.: Are apes really inequity averse? Proc. Roy. Soc. B Biol. Sci. **273**(1605), 3123–3128 (2006)
3. Brosnan, S.F., De Waal, F.B.: Monkeys reject unequal pay. Nature **425**(6955), 297 (2003)
4. Calders, T., Kamiran, F., Pechenizkiy, M.: Building classifiers with independency constraints. In: 2009 IEEE International Conference on Data Mining Workshops, pp. 13–18. IEEE (2009)
5. Dressel, J., Farid, H.: The accuracy, fairness, and limits of predicting recidivism. Sci. Adv. **4**, eaao5580 (2018). https://doi.org/10.1126/sciadv.aao5580
6. Dua, D., Graff, C.: UCI machine learning repository (2017). http://archive.ics.uci.edu/ml
7. Elazar, Y., Goldberg, Y.: Adversarial removal of demographic attributes from text data. arXiv preprint arXiv:1808.06640 (2018)
8. Fehr, E., Schmidt, K.M.: A theory of fairness, competition, and cooperation. Q. J. Econ. **114**(3), 817–868 (1999)
9. Forsythe, R., Horowitz, J.L., Savin, N.E., Sefton, M.: Fairness in simple bargaining experiments. Games Econ. Behav. **6**(3), 347–369 (1994)
10. Gonen, H., Goldberg, Y.: Lipstick on a pig: debiasing methods cover up systematic gender biases in word embeddings but do not remove them. CoRR abs/1903.03862 (2019). http://arxiv.org/abs/1903.03862

11. Hardt, M., Price, E., Srebro, N., et al.: Equality of opportunity in supervised learning. In: Advances in Neural Information Processing Systems, pp. 3315–3323 (2016)
12. Angwin, J., Larson, J., Mattu, S., Kirchner, L.: Machine bias: there's software used across the country to predict future criminals. And it's biased against blacks. ProPublica, May 2016. www.propublica.org/article/machine-bias-risk-assessments-in-criminal-sentencing
13. Kahneman, D., Knetsch, J.L., Thaler, R.H.: Fairness and the assumptions of economics. J. Bus. **59**, S285–S300 (1986)
14. Kamishima, T., Akaho, S., Sakuma, J.: Fairness-aware learning through regularization approach. In: 2011 IEEE 11th International Conference on Data Mining Workshops, pp. 643–650. IEEE (2011)
15. Kohavi, R.: Scaling up the accuracy of Naive-Bayes classifiers: a decision-tree hybrid. In: KDD, vol. 96, pp. 202–207. Citeseer (1996)
16. Mikhail Korobov, K.L.: (2016). https://pypi.org/project/eli5/
17. Pedreshi, D., Ruggieri, S., Turini, F.: Discrimination-aware data mining. In: Proceedings of the 14th ACM SIGKDD International Conference on Knowledge Discovery and Data Mining, pp. 560–568. ACM (2008)
18. Resheff, Y.S., Elazar, Y., Shahar, M., Shalom, O.S.: Privacy-adversarial user representations in recommender systems. arXiv preprint arXiv:1807.03521 (2018)
19. Zemel, R., Wu, Y., Swersky, K., Pitassi, T., Dwork, C.: Learning fair representations. In: International Conference on Machine Learning, pp. 325–333 (2013)
20. Zhang, B.H., Lemoine, B., Mitchell, M.: Mitigating unwanted biases with adversarial learning. In: Proceedings of the 2018 AAAI/ACM Conference on AI, Ethics, and Society, AIES 2018, pp. 335–340. ACM, New York (2018)

Transferring Clinical Prediction Models Across Hospitals and Electronic Health Record Systems

Alicia Curth[1,2(✉)], Patrick Thoral[2], Wilco van den Wildenberg[3], Peter Bijlstra[3], Daan de Bruin[1], Paul Elbers[2], and Mattia Fornasa[1,2]

[1] Pacmed B.V., Amsterdam, The Netherlands
aliciacurth@gmail.com
[2] Department of Intensive Care Medicine, Amsterdam UMC, Location VUmc, Vrije Universiteit Amsterdam, Amsterdam, The Netherlands
[3] Department of Intensive Care Medicine, Elisabeth-TweeSteden Hospital, Tilburg, The Netherlands

Abstract. Recent years have seen a surge in studies developing clinical prediction models based on electronic health records (EHRs) as a result of advances in machine learning techniques and data availability. Yet, validation and implementation of such models in practice are rare, in part because EHR-based clinical prediction models are more difficult to apply to new data sets than results of classical clinical studies due to less controlled clinical environments.

In this paper we propose to use the theoretical framework of *domain adaptation* to analyze the problem of transferring machine-learning-based clinical prediction models across different hospitals and EHR systems. Using the model of Thoral et al. [12] predicting patient-level risk of readmission and mortality after intensive care unit discharge as a case study, we discuss, apply and compare multiple domain adaptation methods. We transfer the model from the original *source* data set to two new *target* data sets. We find that, while model performance deteriorates substantially when applying a model developed for one data set to another directly, updating models with training data from the target set and using methods that explicitly model differences in data sets always improves model performance. In a simulation experiment, we show that having access to data or model parameters from another hospital can substantially reduce the amount of data required to build an accurate prediction model for a new hospital. We also show that these performance gains diminish with increasing availability of data from the target hospital.

Keywords: Clinical prediction models · Domain adaptation · Transfer learning · Electronic Health Records · Intensive Care Medicine

1 Introduction

The increased availability and quality of electronic health records (EHRs) and the development of sophisticated learning algorithms have opened up the

P. Cellier and K. Driessens (Eds.): ECML PKDD 2019 Workshops, CCIS 1167, pp. 605–621, 2020.
https://doi.org/10.1007/978-3-030-43823-4_48

possibility of developing machine learning models to support doctors in clinical decision making [5]. These models can offer valuable patient-level information about the risk of adverse events to clinicians, particularly in highly complex and high-resource environments with large amounts of routinely collected data. Yet, only a small proportion of machine-learning-based clinical prediction models presented in studies are re-used after their original publication, and even fewer are ever implemented in clinical practice [9]. In part, this is due to a lack of validation studies and transferability of such models.

Unfortunately, transfer of EHR-based risk prediction models to new EHR-based data sets is inherently more difficult than that of models based on curated data from classical clinical trials and cohort studies: the data is less structured, the patient samples are less homogeneous, and often the amount of predictor variables is much larger while their definitions can be much less precise [5]. In addition to differences in patient populations and data quality, differences in other institutional factors, such as standards in clinical practice [7], can also lead to models that perform well in one hospital but perform substantially worse at another. Therefore, it is crucial to investigate how clinical prediction models can be safely transferred to new data sets so that they can be validated and ultimately be implemented in clinical practice to actually have an impact on patient outcomes.

With this paper, we aim to explore theory and methods that enable the transfer of clinical prediction models. For this purpose, we consider the model of [12], which uses EHRs to predict a patient's risk of readmission and mortality after discharge from the intensive care unit (ICU), as a case study. As this model is currently in the process of being implemented as a clinical decision-support software-tool at the ICU of the Amsterdam UMC, location VUmc (hereafter: VUmc), we investigate how to perform validation of this model within the VUmc, and how to use it to facilitate implementation of ICU software at other hospitals as well. To do so, we transfer the model from the original *source* data set to two new *target* data sets: a new data set obtained from the current EHR system of the VUmc, and a data set from a new hospital.

Some domain adaptation and transfer learning methods have already been employed in related work to transfer clinical prediction models across hospitals: pooling of multiple data sets using fixed weight schemes was used in the context of ICU readmission [4] and in-hospital mortality [3], also illustrating the potential of data-set pooling on reducing data-size requirements [3]. More complex methods formalizing dependence between source and target hospitals within the model structure have been used to predict *Clostridium difficile* infections [13] and surgical mortality [7]. While these are examples of successful applications of transfer methods in a clinical setting, they lack a unified theoretical framework and consequentially, do not facilitate the comparison of different methods.

This paper fills this gap in existing literature by making two contributions: first, we apply the theoretical framework of domain adaptation to formalize the problem of transferring clinical prediction models across data sets, and place different methods that have been used in clinical predictive modeling and elsewhere into one coherent framework. Second, we empirically compare their performance by applying them to the problem of transferring ICU readmission models between our data sets. We also evaluate their performance when artificially decreasing the amount of available data from the target data sets to simulate moving towards implementation of a model at a new hospital, showing that the added value of different domain adaptation methods is sensitive to the amount of available target data.

We proceed as follows: In Sect. 2, we discuss the theoretical framework of domain adaptation as well as methods that can be used to overcome shifts in patient populations and conditional outcome probabilities between data sets. In Sect. 3, we discuss our empirical strategy for testing these methods and in Sect. 4, we present our results. Section 5 summarizes and concludes.

2 Theoretical Framework

In this paper, we consider transferring a clinical prediction model from a *source* data set, on which said model was first developed and trained, to another, *target*, data set as a *domain adaptation* problem. Domain adaptation covers problems where input feature spaces and outcome definition are identical across data sets (domains), while the probability densities over the feature space and outcome may differ.[1]

In Sect. 2.1, we introduce the theoretical framework of domain adaptation and discuss issues common to domain adaptation problems. In Sects. 2.2 and 2.3, we review strategies to handle covariate shift and concept shift.

2.1 Formalizing Domain Adaptation Problems

To assess the theoretical consequences of learning from different domains, we closely follow the general framework and notation of [1]. We define a domain d to consist of (1) a distribution $\mathcal{D}_d$ over the k-dimensional feature space $\mathcal{X}$, where $\phi_d : \mathcal{X} \rightarrow \mathbb{R}$ is the probability density function of $\mathcal{D}_d$, and (2) a labelling function $f_d : \mathcal{X} \rightarrow [0, 1]$. In clinical prediction models, $\phi_d(x)$ captures the distribution of patient characteristics in the patient population of domain d, while $f_d(x)$ is $p_d(y|x)$, the true (unobserved) probability of the clinical outcome y, which in our application is readmission or mortality after ICU discharge, conditional on a patient's observed characteristics. To build a clinical prediction model, we aim to find a hypothesis function h that approximates the true underlying outcome probability as closely as possible. To do so, we define the probability that a hypothesis h disagrees with any labelling function f, given distribution $\mathcal{D}_d$ over $\mathcal{X}$, as:

$$\epsilon_d(h, f) = \mathbb{E}_{x \sim \mathcal{D}_d} [|h(x) - f(x)|] = \int |h(x) - f(x)| \phi_d(x) dx \quad (1)$$

[1] If we would also allow feature spaces and outcome definitions to differ across domains, then the problem would become a more general *transfer learning* problem [6]. We restrict ourselves to the assumption that we can map correspondence between features across hospitals and EHRs reasonably well.

Of special interest is $\epsilon_d(h, f_d)$, which is the error of the given classification problem in domain d. For notational convenience, we will refer to this as $\epsilon_d(h)$. To solve the binary classification problem at hand, we aim to find h from a hypothesis class $\mathcal{H}$ such that

$$h = \arg\min_{h \in \mathcal{H}} \epsilon_d(h) \tag{2}$$

Assume now that we shift our attention from one domain to another: a source domain $\mathcal{S}$ for which we already have created a good model, and a target domain $\mathcal{T}$, for which we aim to create a model. We consider moving to a new hospital as well as moving EHR systems within one hospital as such a change in domain, as for both cases the underlying patient populations or the conditional outcome probability could differ. We can relate the error on source and target domain as follows:

$$\epsilon_{\mathcal{T}}(h) = \epsilon_{\mathcal{S}}(h) + \underbrace{\epsilon_{\mathcal{T}}(h, f_{\mathcal{T}}) - \epsilon_{\mathcal{S}}(h, f_{\mathcal{T}})}_{\text{'Covariate shift'}} + \underbrace{\epsilon_{\mathcal{S}}(h, f_{\mathcal{T}}) - \epsilon_{\mathcal{S}}(h, f_{\mathcal{S}})}_{\text{'Concept shift'}} \tag{3}$$

When trying to transfer models across hospitals or EHR systems, there are three cases of interest:

1. $\phi_{\mathcal{T}} = \phi_{\mathcal{S}}$ and $f_{\mathcal{T}} = f_{\mathcal{S}}$: If the underlying patient populations are identical, and the true conditional readmission probabilities are equal across domains, then $\epsilon_{\mathcal{T}}(h) = \epsilon_{\mathcal{S}}(h)$ and the classifier that minimizes the source error is also optimal for the target domain. In practice this would mean that we could then directly re-use the model build for one hospital for the other, and performance on both data sets should be equally good. Classical clinical studies facilitate this by strongly restricting included patient characteristics and controlling the environment, ensuring replicability of the exact settings at the cost of applicability to other patient populations and to daily practice.
2. $\phi_{\mathcal{T}} \neq \phi_{\mathcal{S}}$ and $f_{\mathcal{T}} = f_{\mathcal{S}}$: The underlying patient populations differ, yet the unobserved conditional readmission probability is the same across domains. This phenomenon is referred to as *covariate shift*[8]. Intuitively, the consequence of this covariate shift is that during training, too much emphasis is given to patient groups that are not important during testing as they are less represented in the target data set. In this case, re-weighted source data can still be used to estimate a target model. To see this, note that

$$\epsilon_{\mathcal{T}}(h) = \int |h(x) - f_{\mathcal{T}}(x)| \phi_{\mathcal{T}}(x) \frac{\phi_{\mathcal{S}}(x)}{\phi_{\mathcal{S}}(x)} dx = \mathbb{E}_{x \sim \mathcal{D}_{\mathcal{S}}} \left[|h(x) - f_{\mathcal{S}}(x)| \frac{\phi_{\mathcal{T}}(x)}{\phi_{\mathcal{S}}(x)} \right]$$

where we used that $f_{\mathcal{T}} = f_{\mathcal{S}}$. To solve this covariate shift problem, there are many weighting algorithms available, which will be discussed in Sect. 2.2.
3. $f_{\mathcal{T}} \neq f_{\mathcal{S}}$: The unobserved conditional readmission probabilities (also) differ between data sets, a phenomenon referred to as *concept shift*[8]. Clearly, many observed patient characteristics can be expected to have a generalizable effect across hospitals - e.g. risk factors such as high age. If, however,

there are differences in institutional factors associated with the change in domain [7], for example, the quality of care, clinical practice or accuracy of feature measurement, it is possible that certain features contribute differently to the probability of adverse clinical outcomes. In this case, there is no guarantee that a good source model will perform well also on a new data set, and training a model only on source data is not sufficient to build a good target model. Methods to optimally exploit data from more than one domain are discussed in Sect. 2.3.

Note that there are also the related but conceptually slightly different issues *covariate drift* and *concept drift*. Both refer to the fact that there might be *gradual* changes to the underlying distributions along a temporal dimension t, such that $\phi_{d,t} \neq \phi_{d,t+1}$ and/or $f_{d,t} \neq f_{d,t+1}$, resulting in deteriorating model performance *within one domain* over time. We do not consider this case here[2]. Further, we would like to point out that this paper is concerned purely with predictive models; any model with the objective to establish a universal causal relationship should of course control for all confounding factors that result in concept shift, and define underlying patient populations well enough.

2.2 Strategies to Handle Covariate Shift

In this section we discuss how to solve issues related to covariate shift, i.e. patient populations differing between source and target. In unsupervised estimation (i.e. when we can train only on source data), under the assumption of no concept shift, we focus on estimating the so-called *importance weight* of a source observation, giving weight to patients in the source data set based on their similarity to patients in the target data set. The goal is to find a weight such that:

$$w(x_i) = \frac{\phi_{\mathcal{T}}(x_i)}{\phi_{\mathcal{S}}(x_i)} \; for \; i \in \mathcal{S} \tag{4}$$

Generally, there are two approaches to estimate this weight: (a) first estimate the two distributions $\phi_d(x)$ separately, which is a hard problem in high-dimensional feature spaces [10], and then compute their ratio for each observation $i \in \mathcal{S}$ or (b) estimate the density ratio $\frac{\phi_{\mathcal{T}}(x)}{\phi_{\mathcal{S}}(x)}$ directly. We considered the latter, i.e. *Direct Importance Estimation*, and as an exemplary re-weighting method we used the well-established Kullback-Leibler Importance Estimation Procedure (KLIEP) [10]. As the assumption of no concept shift is very unlikely to hold for our data sets, our attempts at unsupervised estimation using re-weighting resulted in negligible model improvements. We therefore exclude this method in the empirical applications later in this paper, yet results are available upon request.

[2] A change in EHR system within a hospital, strictly speaking, also leads to a change in distributions over time. However, that is not a *gradual* change and we decide to treat such a situation as a *shift* in distributions, not a *drift*.

When there is target data available to update the model, then training on combined data should mitigate some of the concerns related to covariate shift as the correct regions of the feature space are represented in the sample. Giving relatively more weight to target samples may then be a simple solution to set the focus on the correct regions of the feature space.

2.3 Strategies to Handle Concept Shift

In this section we present methods that can be applied in the presence of concept shift, i.e. differences in conditional outcome probabilities. This list is by no means exhaustive, and we have selected these methods because they can easily be incorporated into already existing modelling strategies. We consider the following three strategies:

1. Pool the data sets: Simply exploit increases in available training data and minimize an upper bound on the target error by considering a convex combination of source and target errors, using an empirical alpha error [1]:

$$\epsilon_{\alpha}(h) = \alpha\epsilon_{\mathcal{T}}(h) + (1-\alpha)\epsilon_{\mathcal{S}}(h) \tag{5}$$

   Intuitively, this means that with increasing alpha, we give more weight to target patients over source patients. Given source and target sample sizes $n_{\mathcal{S}}$ and $n_{\mathcal{T}}$, each patient from the target data gets weight $\alpha * \frac{n_{\mathcal{T}}+n_{\mathcal{S}}}{n_{\mathcal{T}}}$ and conversely, source patients get weight $(1-\alpha) * \frac{n_{\mathcal{T}}+n_{\mathcal{S}}}{n_{\mathcal{S}}}$. There is a theoretically optimal α^* which approaches 1 (which corresponds to training on target data only) with increasing difference of underlying distributions, increasing $n_{\mathcal{T}}$ and decreasing $n_{\mathcal{S}}$[1]. As the upper bound on the error underlying the derivation of α^* is in general computationally intractable [1], we will not compute the theoretically optimal value, rather, we wish to show that non-trivial values of alpha can be useful by tuning α as an additional hyperparameter of the learning algorithm. For the problem of transferring knowledge across ICUs, this pooling and re-weighting method has been applied by [3] and [4].
2. Sequential modeling: use the model trained on source data as a prior[3] to regularize the target model towards [2]. Intuitively, this means that we believe that a model for a new ICU will be similar to the one we already know, but is allowed to learn differences from the target data. For generalized linear models of the form $h_{\beta}(x) = g(x\beta)$, where β is a vector of coefficients, e.g. linear or logistic regressions, this translates to empirically solving

$$\min_{\beta} \sum_{i \in \mathcal{T}} l(h_{\beta}(x_i), y_i) + \lambda \sum_{k} \frac{(\beta_k - \hat{\beta}_{k,\mathcal{S}})^2}{2} \tag{6}$$

[3] The notion of a prior might be considered more natural within a Bayesian framework. We do not consider Bayesian techniques here, but note that the given approach with cross-entropy loss for binary classification results in an estimate equal to the Bayesian maximum a posteriori estimate with normal prior.

where $l(h_\beta(x_i), y_i)$ denotes the empirical loss of hypothesis h_β on observation i and $\hat{\beta}_\mathcal{S}$ is the optimal parameter vector estimated from the source domain. Note that with $\hat{\beta}_\mathcal{S} = 0$, this is equivalent to standard estimation with shrinkage enforced through a L2-penalty. For highly non-linear models, such as gradient boosting models, regularizing towards a prior might not be feasible. In those cases, we suggest another approach discussed by [2]: include the probability prediction from the source model as an additional feature into the target model. Intuitively, this corresponds to starting with a 'source risk-score' and focusing during modeling on improving it along dimensions where it does not perform well yet. Both sequential methods can be particularly useful when source hospitals are not able to share the data used to create their model, e.g. due to data protection regulations, and can only transfer the model itself. Such a sequential modeling approach using priors for support vector machines, has, in our context, been used to transfer surgical mortality models across hospitals [7].

3. Hierarchical modeling: Impose a hierarchy on the model structure. This assumes that there is a global ICU model $f_*(h)$ that underlies all hospital specific ICU models $f_d(h)$. For generalized linear models, this means that the predictive effect for variable k in domain d is given by $\beta_{k,d} = \beta_{k,*} + \xi_{k,d}$, where $\beta_{k,*}$ captures its global effects and $\xi_{k,d}$ captures domain-specific differences. The empirical optimization problem is similar to Eq. (6):

$$\min_{\beta_*, \xi_\mathcal{T}, \xi_\mathcal{S}} \sum_{d \in \{\mathcal{T}, \mathcal{S}\}} \left(\sum_{i \in d} l(h_{\beta,d}(x_i), y_i) + \sum_k \lambda_{k,d} \frac{(\xi_{k,d})^2}{2} \right) + \sum_k \lambda_{k,*} \frac{(\beta_{k,*})^2}{2} \quad (7)$$

In fact, the main difference to (6) is that we train model (7) on both data sets at the same time. Formulating $\beta_{k,d}$ as the sum of two components has the advantage that estimation of this hierarchical model can be greatly simplified by using the approach of [2]: augment the feature space $\mathcal{X} \subseteq \mathbb{R}^k$ to $\tilde{\mathcal{X}} \subseteq \mathbb{R}^{3k}$ such that any observation x_i can be represented as $\tilde{x}_i = \langle x_i, I[i \in \mathcal{T}] * x_i, I[i \in \mathcal{S}] * x_i \rangle$, where $I[i \in d]$ is an indicator specifying whether observation i originates in domain d. In this augmented representation, we can estimate $\tilde{\beta} = \langle \beta_*, \xi_\mathcal{T}, \xi_\mathcal{S} \rangle$ using standard estimation methods. We set the regularization parameters $\lambda_{k,*} < \lambda_{k,d}$ due to our belief that between-hospital differences should be small. For features that we believe have mainly domain-specific effects, we reverse this relationship. In our implementation of this model, we only estimate $\langle \beta_*, \xi_\mathcal{T} \rangle$ and thus only augment the feature space to $\mathbb{R}^{2k}$ to ensure identification of all parameters in the otherwise very large model.

In principle, both sequential and hierarchical approaches would allow to add features into the model that are only available in the target domain, similar to the approach used by [13] to transfer models for *Clostridium difficile* infections across hospitals. They use a variation of (7) where they allow variables j that are available only in the target domain to have only target-specific effects (i.e. they set $\beta_{j,*} = 0$). We do not investigate this further, but note that relaxing the assumption of perfectly coinciding feature spaces is a possibility to improve domain-specific versions of models further.

3 Experimental Set-Up: Data and Methods

3.1 Data Description and Feature Engineering

As a source data set, we consider the original set of VUmc admissions (hereafter: VUmc MV) used by [12]. The data is extracted from the VUmc Patient Data Management System (MetaVision, iMDsoft, Tel Aviv, Israel) and contains observations gathered between 2004 and March 2016. We consider two different data sets as target data:

- *VUmc Epic*: A new data set of VUmc admissions, gathered from March 2016 to December 2018. This set is extracted from the EpicCare EHR (Epic System, Verona, WI, USA), the current EHR system of the VUmc, adopted in March 2016. This transition in EHR system is to some extent associated with a change in clinical practice, e.g. due to different standardization of lab test orders.
- *ETZ*: Data from the Elisabeth-TweeSteden hospital (ETZ), a large non-university teaching hospital in Tilburg, the Netherlands. The data set contains data from two locations of the hospital: we use admissions from 2012 through March 2018 from the first location (ETZ Elisabeth) while for the second (ETZ TweeSteden) we use admissions from 2015 through March 2018. The Patient Data Management System used by ETZ is also MetaVision.

All data are pseudo-anonymized and signals deemed relevant are extracted from the three data sets[4]. Where possible, we extract the same signals across all data sets, yet the available signals do not coincide perfectly. For each source-target combination, we use only features that are available in both data sets. They include:

- patient demographics (e.g. age and sex)
- characteristics of the admission (e.g. length of stay, department of origin)
- clinical observations (e.g. nursing scores and Glasgow Coma Scale)
- automated physiological measurements from devices (e.g. patient monitor and ventilator)
- laboratory studies
- medications (e.g. sedatives and vasopressors)
- other support (e.g. enternal feeding)

Signals that can be measured more than once during the admission undergo special feature engineering. In particular, we identify 3 time windows to capture a patient's clinical condition at different points in time (the first 24 h, the last

[4] The clinical data used in this study was collected at the VUmc and ETZ and transferred to Pacmed's servers in a de-identified format. They are not publicly available, and restrictions apply to their use.

24 h and the whole ICU stay) and, for each window, we compute 8 features for each signal: the average of the measurements within a window, the standard deviation around the average, the first and last values, the minimum and the maximum value, the number of available measurements and an indicator whether there is at least one measurement. For measurements that are characterized by a start and end time (e.g. medications or interventions), we compute the following features: time spent while receiving the medication/intervention, time passed between the end of the window and the last time the medication/intervention was administered, the number of times the medication/intervention was provided and the total dosage. Some engineered features can be highly correlated with other aggregations of the same signal especially when the signal is measured infrequently. Therefore, we remove features that have correlation of above 97.5% with another aggregation of the same signal.

The distributions of all features have been visualized and inspected. We notice the presence of covariate shift in the form of different patient populations between hospitals. One example of this is the higher proportion of neurological patients at ETZ than at VUmc. We suspect concept shift, in, for example, the features measuring if and how many times a specific signal was recorded for an individual patient. These features can capture otherwise unobserved clinicians' judgment of a patients condition, yet standards differ vastly across the three data sets, making it unlikely that the features generalize well.

3.2 Cohort and Task Specification

For all domains we include only patients of 18 years and older who did not die during their ICU admission. We also remove ICU admissions shorter than 12 h and longer than 30 days, as well as patients who received palliative care. After applying these criteria, our cohort consists of 14,105 admissions in the source domain (VUmc MV) and 2,847 (VUmc Epic) and 13,300 (ETZ) admissions in the target domains.

To model the risk of readmission and death after ICU discharge, we identify admissions that are followed by another admission (for the same patient) or by death between 12 h and 7 days as the adverse outcome of interest.[5] The lower bound is implemented to remove unusually early readmissions, which are most often administrative errors, while the upper bound removes readmissions that are probably not related to the first admission. The proportion of adverse outcomes in our sample range from 5.3% (VUmc MV) to 6.1% (ETZ) and 7.3%(VUmc Epic). A summary of the sample characteristics can be found in Table 1.

[5] VUmc also has a High-dependency unit (HDU): we only consider strictly ICU admissions as initial admissions (not admissions to the HDU) but if the patient, after having been discharged by the ICU, is readmitted to the HDU, we consider this a readmission, too.

Table 1. Sample compositions of the three cohorts

	VUmc MV	VUmc Epic	ETZ
	Source	*Target*	*Target*
Period of collection	01/2004–03/2016	03/2016–12/2018	01/2012–03/2018
Hospital	VUmc	VUmc	ETZ
EHR system	Metavision	Epic	Metavision
Number of admissions	14,105	2,847	13,300
Readmission/post-discharge mortality rate	5.3 %	7.3 %	6.1 %
Number of common features used for modelling		1342	1258

3.3 Model Training

For each source-target combination we concatenate the two data sets prior to training, impute missing values by hospital median, standardize all values across the combined data set and randomly shuffle the data. We train and test all models using stratified 10-fold cross-validation, where the testing folds only contain data from the target domain and the training folds contain the full source data and/or the remaining target data, depending on which method is used. All code used for this paper is built on top of the machine learning library scikit-learn[6].

We incorporate a feature-selection step into our modeling strategy to reduce the high dimensionality of our feature space. To do so, we fit a logistic regression model with L1-penalty, and include only features with non-zero coefficient into the final model [11]. The penalty parameter is chosen based on cross-validated performance. For simplicity, we choose from a fixed menu of three values that encourage different degrees of sparsity of the model. To prevent leakage, feature selection is performed within each training fold.

As the final prediction model, after feature selection, we consider Logistic Regressions and Gradient Boosted Classifiers. We set our main focus on Logistic Regressions because we aim to show the *relative* effect the different domain adaptation methods can have, without taking a whole battery of other hyperparameters into account. We include Gradient Boosted Classifiers because we also wish to show that the availability of more information improves model performance, which is more relevant for highly non-linear machine-learning models.

When training Logistic Regressions, we impose a L2-penalty to punish overfitting. As for the feature selection step, we consider a discrete menu of different values for the penalty parameter that shrink the model coefficients by different degrees. We train Gradient Boosted Classifiers with fixed hyperparameters: 1000 trees, a learning rate of 0.01 and allowing maximally 5 splits by tree, where only 20% of all features are considered at each split.

We make some modifications to this general training procedure within some of the methods discussed in Sect. 2.3:

[6] See https://scikit-learn.org/stable/.

- *Prior*: when training with a prior, we skip the feature selection step and instead include only features selected for the source model.
- *Prediction-feature*: When including the prediction as a new feature into the gradient boosting model, we consider multiple values for the fraction of features inspected per split, because we want to allow the prediction to be considered more often than a 'regular' feature.
- *Hierarchy*: To implement this model, we first perform feature selection using the normal data set, and afterwards augment the feature space using the dummy method described in Sect. 2.3.

3.4 Experimental Procedures

Experiment 1: Comparing Model Performance on the Full Data Sets. We compare the performance of different strategies to create a clinical prediction model for the two target data sets. Next to the performance of the source model on the source data set, we compute the target performance of models trained on *source only* and on *target only* as baselines. We compare this to the performance of:

- *Pooled data*: training on the combined data-set, both un-weighted and weighted with the best alpha, where alpha is chosen from a fixed menu of values.
- *Prior*: training with the *source only* model as prior. Logistic Regression only.
- *Prediction-feature*: training with a standardized probability prediction from the *source only* model as additional feature.
- *Hierarchy*: Imposing a hierarchy on the model structure that regularizes the domain-specific parts of the model more heavily than the general parts, and reverses this relationship for features capturing the presence and count of signals. Logistic Regression only.

Experiment 2: Simulating Introduction of the Model at New Hospitals. To simulate the effect the different methods can have on data requirements when moving towards implementation of clinical prediction models at a new hospital, we remove all target observations from the training folds and gradually increase the proportion of target data available for training. This also allows us to evaluate model performance for different regimes of target sample size. We do so for n increments by randomly choosing $n * 250$ observations from the target data in each original training fold until we reach the original target set size. To perform this analysis, we fix all hyperparameter settings to those chosen using the full data set[7]. This approach is similar to the methods used by [3] to simulate a learning curve. We choose to exclude the α-weighted method from this experiment since α^* depends on the sample size. We found that fixing any ratio of target to source weight gives a curve that is almost identical to the un-weighted pooling.

[7] We choose this approach for computational feasibility of the simulation exercise. For the very small data sets considered at the beginning of the learning curve, different hyperparameter settings would have probably resulted in better performance.

3.5 Model Evaluation

As clinicians are mainly interested in probability (risk) predictions, we evaluate the performance of our models based on the area under the receiver-operating curve (AUROC). To ensure stable results, we repeat the 10-fold cross validation 10 times for different random seeds, yielding 100 different AUROC values. In Sect. 4 we report the mean of this metric m across the 100 runs, and use the standard error of this mean, i.e. $\frac{\sigma_m}{\sqrt{100}}$, to quantify uncertainty.

4 Results

4.1 Experiment 1: Comparing Model Performance on the Full Data Sets

Table 2 presents the results of the first experiment discussed in Sect. 3.4. We find that, for both target data sets, target performance is significantly below source performance when applying the model trained on source data to the target data directly. This is in line with the expectations we derived theoretically in Sect. 2.1. This performance drop is relatively larger when using ETZ as target[8], which is

Table 2. Model performance (AUROC) for different methods

Method	VUmc Epic		ETZ	
	LR	GB	LR	GB
*(1) Source performance**	*0.795 (0.002)*	*0.793 (0.002)*	*0.790 (0.002)*	*0.791 (0.002)*
(2) Source only	0.764 (0.006)	0.767 (0.008)	0.697 (0.003)	0.688 (0.003)
(3) Target only	0.767 (0.005)	0.763 (0.006)	0.742 (0.003)	0.744 (0.002)
(4) Pooled, no weight	0.797 (0.005)	**0.796 (0.005)**	0.743 (0.002)	**0.751 (0.002)**
(5) Pooled, best α	0.799 (0.005)	**0.796 (0.005)**	0.745 (0.002)	**0.751 (0.002)**
(6) Prior	0.799 (0.005)		0.733 (0.003)	
(7) Prediction-feature	0.789 (0.005)	0.781 (0.005)	0.745 (0.003)	0.747 (0.002)
(8) Hierarchy	**0.800 (0.005)**		**0.746 (0.002)**	

Area under the receiver-operating cure (AUROC) averaged over 10 random runs of 10-fold cross-validation for Logistic Regression (LR) and Gradient Boosted Classifier (GB), with standard errors in parentheses. *: Note that this is trained and evaluated on only source data to provide a reference point, and that, due to differences in data availability, slightly different subsets of features are used for VUmc Epic (columns 2 and 3) and ETZ (columns 4 and 5), resulting in slight differences in the respective source performance.

[8] Regardless of the method used, our classifiers exhibit much lower performance on ETZ data than on the VUmc data set using the same features (row (1), columns 4 and 5), despite the high number of admissions included in modeling. We postulate two possible explanations for this: First, it could be that for patient groups present at the ETZ, the underlying prediction problem is simply more difficult and readmissions are less predictable from observable patient characteristics. Second, the ETZ data set has many more missing values than the two VUmc data sets, and we hypothesize that lower data quality could be another reason for the drop in performance.

also in line with expectations because the difference in institutional factors and patient populations is larger between source and this target. Using only target data for training improves model performance significantly compared to using only source data for the ETZ case, but not for VUmc Epic.

We gain a number of useful insights from the performance of the different domain adaptation approaches. For both target data sets, there is some significant gain in using also the source data by pooling the data sets. As expected, this increase in the amount of training data results in gains that are larger for the non-linear gradient boosting model (when comparing the two classifiers), and for the VUmc Epic data (when comparing the relative improvement in model performance across the two target data sets). The latter can be attributed to VUmc MV and VUmc Epic sharing many institutional factors, and the VUmc Epic set being substantially smaller than the ETZ data set. We also find that simple re-weighting schemes based on α can improve model performance, yet these improvements fall within one standard error of the average AUROC. Our results also show that some of the sequential and in particular the hierarchical method can outperform the data pooling approach, yet, also only by a small margin that does not exceed two standard errors of the pooled data AUROC.

4.2 Experiment 2: Simulating Introduction of the Model at New Hospitals

The results presented above indicate that the effects of using more sophisticated domain-adaptation methods is comparable to the effect of the rather simple approach of pooling data. However, domain adaptation methods are made for the case where target data sets are small, and both our target data sets, the ETZ set in particular, are already relatively large. Therefore, we now investigate the relative performance of these methods for different sizes of target data sets.

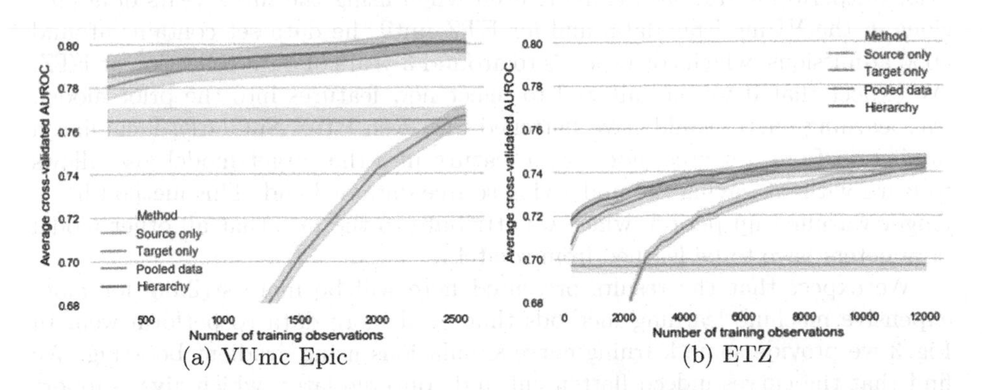

Fig. 1. Average AUROC by number of available target observations, using logistic regressions and pooled data. Shaded area indicates one standard error.

Figure 1 shows parts of the learning curves for methods requiring access to both data sets, based on Logistic Regressions. For both target samples, the experiment above illustrates that access to source data in addition to target data substantially reduces the amount of target data needed to create a model that performs well in the target domain. When there is little target data available, the hierarchical model substantially outperforms the simple pooling of data. With increasing data availability, the two approaches converge.

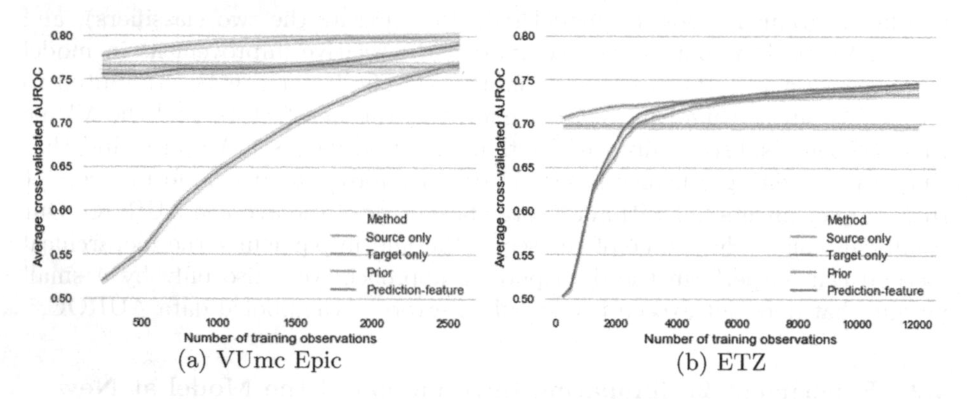

(a) VUmc Epic (b) ETZ

Fig. 2. Average AUROC by number of available target observations, using logistic regressions and only target data. Shaded area indicates one standard error.

The learning curves in Fig. 2 give insights into the case where source data is unavailable for training, which can often be the case in practice due to legal restrictions on data use. The results using the prior method are particularly striking, as they show that we can significantly improve target predictions by simply using the source model as the regularization objective. Training with a prior outperforms standard training even when using the full 2 years of admissions in the VUmc Epic data, and for ETZ until the data set contains around 6000 admissions, which corresponds to around 3 years of data collection at ETZ. We expect that if we had allowed to select new features into the prior model, this learning curve would have flattened out even later. Similarly, including a prediction from a source model as a feature into the target model also allows to learn without having the underlying source data at hand. This method has a longer warming up period, which we attribute to the fact that all other model parameters have to be learned from scratch.

We expect that the results presented here will be more striking for more expensive machine learning methods that need more data to perform well. In Fig. 3 we provide some learning curve simulations using gradient boosting. We find that the curves indeed flatten out and converge later, which gives support for the claim that more advanced machine learning techniques will benefit more from the pooling of data sets and domain adaptation methods.

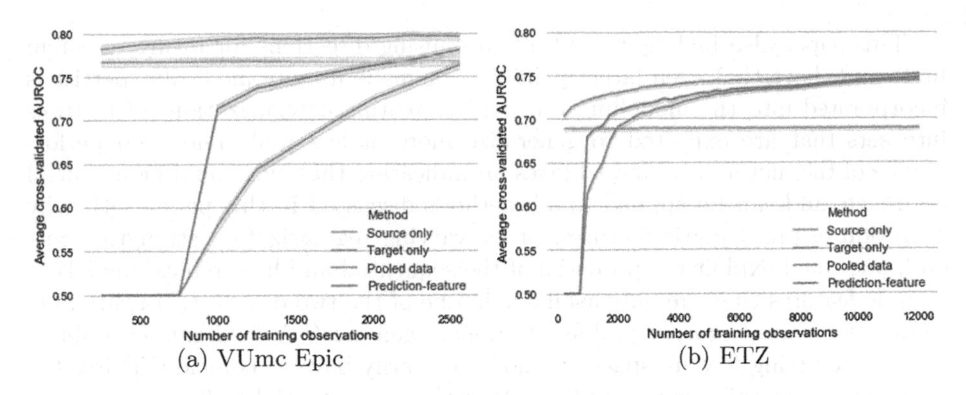

(a) VUmc Epic (b) ETZ

Fig. 3. Average AUROC by number of available target observations, for different gradient boosting methods. Shaded area indicates one standard error.

5 Conclusions and Directions for Future Research

In this paper, we analyze the problem of transferring EHR-based clinical prediction models across hospitals and EHR systems using the theoretical framework of domain adaptation. We discuss and apply different domain adaptation methods to illustrate their benefit when validating models on new data sets, and when moving towards implementation at new hospitals. Both the theoretical considerations and the empirical results have provided us with insights on transferring clinical prediction models to new domains.

We discuss that validation studies applying existing EHR-based machine learning models directly to new data sets are very likely to report deteriorated model performance if there are any differences in underlying patient populations or institutional factors and confirm this empirically. We show empirically that updating these models by adding some data from the target cohort to the training set can lead to substantial increases in model performance. We also find that having access to data from both target and source domain during training leads to better model performance than training on target data alone. As this is mainly due to an increased amount of available training examples, we find larger gains in performance for smaller amounts of available target data, for more similar target and source data sets and for more non-linear model specifications.

Our empirical experiments illustrate some important practical implications for the process of creating hospital-specific clinical decision support tools. We show that when implementing prediction models in new hospitals, having a large data set from another hospital at hand substantially reduces the amount of target data required to build a good model. If sharing of this patient-level data is not possible, then merely having access to the underlying model parameters of another hospital's model can have a similar effect. Both findings give motivation to centralize data collection and model development with cross-institutional research groups or external parties that can create and maintain large collections of EHR data and/or models for a large collection of hospitals.

This paper also highlights multiple promising directions for future research: first, we believe that even larger gains can be made if more medical expertise is incorporated into the modelling process by creating categorizations of features into sets that are expected to generalize more or less well. The good performance of the hierarchical model gives an indication that this could be a fruitful approach, and can be applied to all methods discussed in this paper, either by exclusion of problematic features, or by varying regularization strengths. Second, one could exploit the potential of the sequential and hierarchical models to include features that are only available in one of the two domains, transitioning from a *domain adaptation* problem to a more general *transfer learning* problem where underlying feature spaces do not necessarily have to coincide. Third, the flattened out learning curves indicate that there is potential to harvest the gain of increasing sample size by moving towards more expensive non-linear machine learning models that could improve model performance for all hospitals in the sample.

References

1. Ben-David, S., Blitzer, J., Crammer, K., Kulesza, A., Pereira, F., Vaughan, J.W.: A theory of learning from different domains. Mach. Learn. **79**(1–2), 151–175 (2009). https://doi.org/10.1007/s10994-009-5152-4
2. Daumé III, H.: Frustratingly easy domain adaptation. In: Conference of the Association for Computational Linguistics (ACL) (2007)
3. Desautels, T., et al.: Using transfer learning for improved mortality prediction in a data-scarce hospital setting. Biomed. Inform. Insights **9**, 1–8 (2017)
4. Desautels, T., et al.: Prediction of early unplanned intensive care unit readmission in a UK tertiary care hospital: a cross-sectional machine learning approach. BMJ Open **7**(9), e017199 (2017)
5. Goldstein, B.A., Navar, A.M., Pencina, M.J., Ioannidis, J.: Opportunities and challenges in developing risk prediction models with electronic health records data: a systematic review. J. Am. Med. Inform. Assoc. **24**(1), 198–208 (2017)
6. Kouw, W.M., Loog, M.: An introduction to domain adaptation and transfer learning. arXiv preprint arXiv:1812.11806 (2018)
7. Lee, G., Rubinfeld, I., Syed, Z.: Adapting surgical models to individual hospitals using transfer learning. In: 2012 IEEE 12th International Conference on Data Mining Workshops, pp. 57–63. IEEE (2012)
8. Moreno-Torres, J.G., Raeder, T., Alaiz-RodríGuez, R., Chawla, N.V., Herrera, F.: A unifying view on dataset shift in classification. Pattern Recogn. **45**(1), 521–530 (2012)
9. Siontis, G.C., Tzoulaki, I., Castaldi, P.J., Ioannidis, J.P.: External validation of new risk prediction models is infrequent and reveals worse prognostic discrimination. J. Clin. Epidemiol. **68**(1), 25–34 (2015)
10. Sugiyama, M., Suzuki, T., Nakajima, S., Kashima, H., von Bünau, P., Kawanabe, M.: Direct importance estimation for covariate shift adaptation. Ann. Inst. Stat. Math. **60**(4), 699–746 (2008)
11. Talenti, L., Luck, M., Yartseva, A., Argy, N., Houzé, S., Damon, C.: L1 logistic regression as a feature selection step for training stable classification trees for the prediction of severity criteria in imported malaria. arXiv preprint arXiv:1511.06663 (2015)

12. Thoral, P., Fornasa, M., Hovenkamp, H., Driessen, R., Girbes, A., Elbers, P.: Right data, right now: developing a big data machine-learning based prediction model to prevent ICU readmission. Intensive Care Med. Exp. **6**(2), 40 (2018). https://doi.org/10.1186/s40635-018-0201-6
13. Wiens, J., Guttag, J., Horvitz, E.: A study in transfer learning: leveraging data from multiple hospitals to enhance hospital-specific predictions. J. Am. Med. Inform. Assoc. **21**(4), 699–706 (2014)

Linking Physicians to Medical Research Results via Knowledge Graph Embeddings and Twitter

Afshin Sadeghi[1,2,3(✉)] and Jens Lehmann[1,2,3]

[1] Smart Data Analytics Group (SDA), University of Bonn, Bonn, Germany
{sadeghi,jens.lehmann}@cs.uni-bonn.de
[2] Fraunhofer Institute for Intelligent Analysis and Information Systems, Sankt Augustin, Germany
{afshin.sadeghi,jens.lehmann}@iais.fraunhofer.de
[3] Fraunhofer Institute for Intelligent Analysis and Information Systems, Dresden, Germany

Abstract. Informing professionals about the latest research results in their field is a particularly important task in the field of health care, since any development in this field directly improves the health status of the patients. Meanwhile, social media is an infrastructure that allows public instant sharing of information, thus it has recently become popular in medical applications. In this study, we apply Multiple Distance Knowledge Graph Embeddings (MDE) to link physicians and surgeons to the latest medical breakthroughs that are shared as the research results on Twitter. Our study shows that using this method physicians can be informed about the new findings in their field given that they have an account dedicated to their profession.

Keywords: Knowledge graph embeddings · Social media · Social good · Health care · Twitter · Machine learning

1 Introduction

Twitter is a projection of the interactions of a society connected to the internet, which is in constant evolution. The dynamic aspect of this social media allows manifold applications. From the rise of social media, Twitter was used to measure campaign impacts, collect opinions, analyze trends and to study crisis. However, recently, its applications are more individualized. Particularly, because Twitter has become the most popular form of social media used for health care communication [15], and it is reshaping health care [10], it has become the center of many studies in the field of health care. For example, a study suggests Twitter for knowledge exchange in academic medicine [7] and it was argued that disease-specific hashtags and the creation of Twitter medical communities [13] has improved the uniformity of medical discussions. Another study is dedicated to the influence of specific medical hashtags on social media platforms [5].

P. Cellier and K. Driessens (Eds.): ECML PKDD 2019 Workshops, CCIS 1167, pp. 622–630, 2020.
https://doi.org/10.1007/978-3-030-43823-4_49

Problem Statement: Pershad et al. [14] point out the potential of Twitter to reshape public health efforts, including disseminating health updates, sharing information about diseases. Especially, they emphasize on the role of Twitter to make research advances more accessible for physicians. They argue that connecting researchers and clinicians is crucial and useful since clinicians can use new information they discover from this closer contact with researchers to guide decision-making about patient treatments in such a field that is in constant progress.

In this study, we target this problem by providing a method that suggests physicians and clinicians the recent research breakthroughs in their specialized field based on their current social activity. As the first step to reach this goal, we extract a subset of Twitter network and we generate a knowledge graph (KG) from the extracted data. Figure 1 depicts a schema of the KG with example user instances and the relations between them. In this figure, it is shown that our method recommends a Tweet of Jane, who is a researcher about her latest findings to Bob who is a surgeon. The method calculates a probability that such a Tweet will be useful to Bob based on his previous favored Tweets and the relation to other physicians that work in the same field.

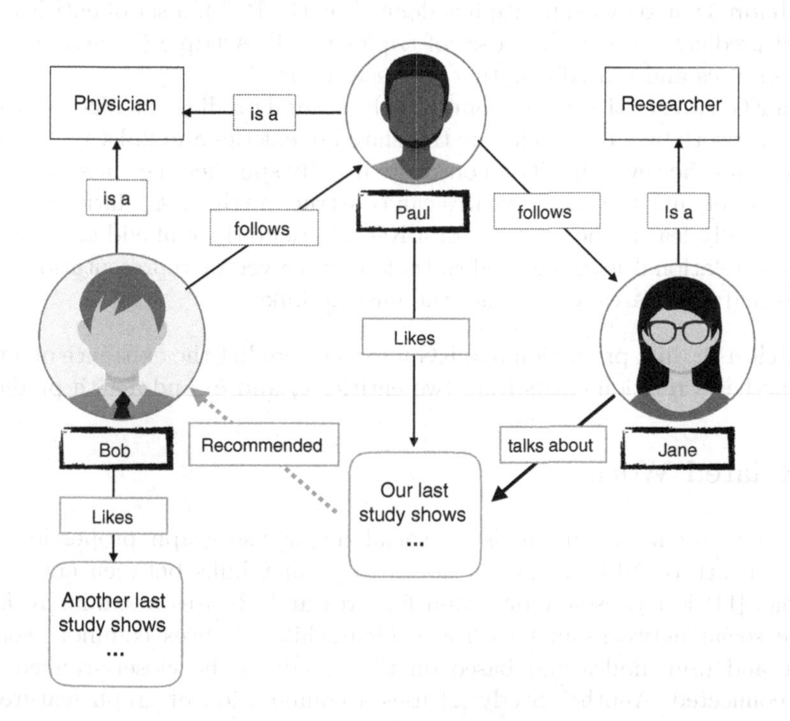

Fig. 1. A schema of the medical professional knowledge graph on Twitter with example user instances. An orange dot line depicts a new link suggested by the proposed method. (Color figure online)

We then apply an embedding method to predict links that are likely to be serving to the physicians. The proposed application is different from the user recommendation service of Twitter [9] which recommends users to follow or the works that discover similar users [8]. Here, we focus our study and evaluation on suggesting related Tweets.

The main contribution of this study is the application of knowledge graph embeddings for a new field, the extraction of a KG from Twitter for the proof of concept and experiments targeted at physicians to help them stay up-to-date in their field.

2 Background

In a social network, a node of the graph represents a person while edges that link the nodes correspond to relationships between people. The edges are also called "connections", "links". Examples of social networks are graphs that describe Facebook and Twitter. Link prediction, in general, is the task of predicting whether a link exists between a given pair of nodes or not.

Definition 1: a knowledge graph is defined by (E, P, T), a set of entities e ∈ E, a set of predicates p ∈ P and a set of triples t ∈ T. A triple (e_i, p_k, e_j) is made of two entities and a predicate that connects them.

In a KG, two entities can be connected by several predicates. When describing a social network by a KG, nodes are translated to entities and links are translated to predicates, however, in KG an ontology usually specifies the class of describes what types of entities and predicates can construct a triple. A relational learning model usually learns the relations of a KG. Particularly, embedding models are a class of relational learning models that produce vector representations of the entities and predicates and predict the missing links.

Definition 2: link prediction in a KG means to predict the existence of a triple, i.e., whether a relation exists from two entities e_i and e_j and a k-th predicate.

3 Related Work

Classic link prediction methods on social media use graph properties of the social network or NLP feature of nodes to predict links between entities. For example, [11] is base solely on graph features and [3] uses a similar technique for the social networks in healthcare. Meanwhile, [1] uses common words to cluster and rank nodes and based on that predicts the closely-ranked nodes to be connected. Another Study [2] uses a combination of graph features and keyword matches to train classifiers (SVM, Naive Bayes, etc) to predict if a link exists between two nodes.

Most of the studies on link prediction of social networks focus on the problem of link existence. Where some methods attempt to find link weights and the number of links between the nodes [17]. An advantage of link prediction using KG embedding is that the type of links are also predicted since these KG embedding models distinguish the type of links.

TransE [4] is an embedding model that is popular because of its simplicity and efficiency. It represents the entities in a KG by a relation between the vectors representing them. The score function describing these vectors in TransE is:

$$Score_{TransE} = \| h_i + r_i - t_i \|_p \tag{1}$$

where n refers to L_1 or L_2 norm and h_i and t_i are the vector representations of an entity and r_i is the vector representations of a predicate. For training, TransE uses margin ranking loss as the loss function. The following Section describes embedding a KG extracted from Twitter using MDE model.

4 KG Embeddings for Twitter Link Prediction

Knowledge graph embedding models usually generate a prediction based on their score function. Nickel et al. [12] suggests performing link prediction by comparing the score of a triple with some given threshold θ or by ranking the entries according to their likelihood that the link in question exists. We similarly use the Multiple-Distance Embedding (MDE) model [16]. In comparison to TransE, this model can learn several relational patterns and thus more can more accurately learn the hidden relation between the entities. Specifically, MDE can learn relations with symmetry, antisymmetry, transitive, inversion and composition patterns. The score function of this model is as follows:

$$Score_{MDE} = w_1 \| h_i + r_i - t_i \|_p + w_2 \| h_j + t_j - r_j \|_p + w_3 \| t_k + r_k - h_k \|_p - \psi \tag{2}$$

where $\psi \in \mathbb{R}^+$ is a positive constant. The loss function of this model is:

$$loss = \beta_1 \sum_{\tau \in \mathbb{T}^+} [f(\tau) - \gamma_1]_+ + \beta_2 \sum_{\tau' \in \mathbb{T}^-} [\gamma_2 - f(\tau')]_+ \tag{3}$$

where γ_1, γ_2 are small positive values and $\delta_0, \delta_0' = 0$. $\beta_1, \beta_2 > 0$ are constraints. The given loss minimizes the score of the positive samples. Therefore, the smaller the score of a triple, that relation is more probable. Base on this property of the loss function, we define a measure to estimate the existence of a predicate such that the more probable triples are given a higher score.

We designate the division of the maximum score of a triple in the training set to the score of a triple A as the probability of the existence of A:

$$P_a = \frac{max(Score_{training-triples})}{Score_A} \tag{4}$$

This definition is based upon the assumption that after the training, the model accurately predicates the triples of the training set.

The equation compares only the triples of the same type (with the same predicate). Thus, in predicting the triples for linking physicians to medical Tweets, we consider only triples with *like_research_Tweet_id* predicates.

- A research has shed light on the causes of #SpinalStenosis with ties connecting to the body's #genetic...
- New #research is proving that #stemcells can act as a living bandage for damaged tissue. https...
- Active #research is underway to make #hipreplacement surgeries safer and more effective. Insights...
- How new research on #stemcells could help patients in avoiding #kneereplacements...
- A recent study uses stem cells in the treatment of knee injuries...
- Collaborating with Rare Disease organizations to increase medical research ...
- A recent study looks at videotaped SCAs (sudden cardiac arrests) in athletes ...
- Inspire posts forward medical research in adverse drug reactions, new study shows...
- Immunotherapy empowers the immune system to fight cancer. New research on microbiome...
- What I told researchers trying to find a cure for my rare disease...
- More and more research indicates that a cancer diagnosis can cause PTSD, not only in patients...
- Paradigm shifting research!! New research shows how a blood test to detecting circulating tumor DNA...
- Patient-focused Drug Development or PFDD is an effort to increase the patients' voice in clinical research...
- New research indicates remission of type2diabetes is possible w/diet T2D ...
- A recent study conducted in Germany assessed post traumatic stress disorders in women diagnosed with brea...
- Parkinson's Disease (PD) affects ~10 million people worldwide. Recent research is close to...

Fig. 2. A sample of the extracted Tweets about the recent medical studies. Each row shows the content of one of the extracted Tweets.

To perform link prediction on Twitter, we train MDE over an extracted KG. In the following, we explain the procedure to extract the dataset from which we later generate a KG using it.

Knowledge Graph Extraction: We extract a set of Tweets about the latest medical studies using Python scripting and the Tweepy library[1]. We filter our search by medical keywords and time in order to only obtain medical research related Tweets which were created from the beginning of the year 2019. Figure 2 shows a sample of the extracted Tweets. To keep the privacy of users, we removed the user and Tweet identifiers from the figure.

With the same tools, we search for Twitter users who are physicians, surgeons, nurses, and researchers in the medical fields which have written about these topics or favored such Tweets. Our continues inquiry which took 8 hours, provided us 5996 Twitter users. Between these users, the job title of 69 instances was deductible (researcher in the medical field or physician) based on the medical job titles in their profile descriptions. This step reduced the users to 69 instances. We then extract the relations among these users and the relations among the users and the gathered Tweets. We also extract the users who follow or are followed by these users so we gain the neighbors of these users in the social network.

We then generate a multi-relational knowledge graph from scraped data by converting these relations to triples. To create these triples, we first define an ontology for the social KG. This ontology includes five types of relations. Table 1 lists these relation types. We also anticipate two classes for users in the ontology. Table 2 presents these classes. The created knowledge graph (TW52) includes 4439 entities which are comprised of 1021 users and 3418 Tweets. The final constructed KG includes 4791 triples. The anonymised dataset is openly available for research purposes in https://git.io/fj6h8.

[1] https://www.tweepy.org/.

Table 1. Relation types in the Social Ontology

Relation Id	Relation
0	`is_talking_about`
1	`is_followed_by`
2	`is_following`
3	`job_title_type_is`
4	`likes_research_Tweet_id`

Table 2. Class of users in the Social Ontology

Class Id	User entity class
0	`job_title_medical_researcher`
1	`job_title_physician`

5 Experiments

We set up two experiments. We firstly evaluate how well the MDE method performs on the social media dataset against a baseline in the task of link prediction. We then analyze the suggestion results of the model in different situations.

5.1 Performance Evaluation

We set up an experiment to evaluate the link prediction performance of MDE against TransE as the baseline.

Evaluation Setup: We dedicate 80% of the knowledge graph extracted from Twitter as the training dataset and set the rest as the test dataset. We randomly choose triples by uniform random selection to separate them for the test set. We perform ranking the score of each test triple against its versions with replaced head, and once with a replaced tail. We then compute the hit at N (hit@N), mean rank (MR) and mean reciprocal rank (MRR) of these rankings. We set the vector size of TransE to 20 and choose the vector size of 10 for MDE. We use L_2 normalization to normalize their score function and train them by 700 iterations. For MDE, we set the hyperparameters as follows: $\gamma_1 = \gamma_2 = 3$ and $\psi = 1.2$.

Results: Table 3 lists the evaluation results of TransE and MDE on the extracted knowledge graph. Due to the sparsity of the graph, TransE gains very low ranking scores while MDE produces superior results for all the MR and MRR and hit@N tests. The results suggest the positive influence of relation patterns learning in MDE.

Table 3. Results on Twitter extracted dataset (TW52). Better results are in bold.

Model	MR	MRR	Hit@1	Hit@3	Hit@10
TransE	1327	0.021	0.005	0.019	0.048
MDE	**1287**	**0.148**	**0.071**	**0.161**	**0.332**

5.2 Link Prediction Analysis

In this section rather than studying the performance of the model, we establish an experiment to analyze the suggestion results of the model to find out whether it creates sound suggestions in different situations. We apply the model to learn on the constructed KG and then we use it to suggest the possible interesting research results for the physicians suggested. We then study the suggested results.

Considering the physicians in the KG and Tweets which include research results, we calculate the probability that such a Tweet is favorable for physicians using Eq. 4. In our experiment, the hit@1 of the training triples was 99.8%, therefore, assuming maximum probability for the training triples in the formula holds for the experiment.

The observation of relations and entities in the KG shows that it is structured with the small world network patterns [18]. Particularly, it includes hub users and Tweets which are connected to other nodes with a number of links that greatly exceed the average degree in the network.

We select a subset of physicians in the KG and classify them according to their relation to other users and Tweets into 4 groups of 5 users. We particularly inspected their relation to hub users, which we call them User type A. Users of type A are followed by a large number of users (at least 200), they are active users and have favored variant Tweets. We consider also Users of type B which follow a small number of users (25) who are also physicians or researchers. Table 4 lists these groups of users and the mean of their probability to like a Tweet C that includes a research study. We consider two Tweets similar if their representative vectors have a small angle. These Tweets are usually favored by the same group of people.

Table 4. Mean probability of linking to a Tweet C for users with different communities and liked Tweets

User group	Mean probability of C
Users U that follow A. A and U like a Tweet similar to C	0.205
Users U that follow A. A likes a Tweet similar to C	0.134
Users U that follow B. A and B like a Tweet similar to C	0.975
New users U that still follow nobody and like no Tweet	0.127

It is observable from Table 4 that in the proposed model, users that follow a diverse group of users and topics, are less likely to be interested in an inquired Tweet than those with less diverse connections. This effect is even stronger than when the user has liked a similar Tweet before. This suggests that the model performs better if a Twitter account is dedicated only to social communications related to her profession.

Additionally, the new users that have not favored any Tweet are expected the least among the users to favor a Tweet.

6 Discussion of the Specificity of the Problem

The proposed experiment in the study has two major components. The first is data extraction and KG construction section which we specify it to the problem by data cleaning and filtering the extracted data and creating an ontology specific to the physicians and research related tweets. The result of this part is TW52 knowledge graph which is sparse in comparison to the conventional benchmark datasets of embedding models, i.e., WordNet18 and FB15K.

The second part of the study is the MDE embedding model. Although MDE is a general method for the link prediction problems, the evaluations showed that it is capable of embedding the sparse dataset much better than the state-of-the-art TransE model. Therefore we consider both components appropriate for the proposed problem.

7 Conclusion

We proposed the usage of multiple-distance knowledge graph embeddings (MDE) to suggest Tweets about medical breakthroughs to physicians. We extracted a KG of medical research Tweets and their relations to the users which medical researcher or physicians.

We evaluated MDE against TransE as the baseline in a link prediction test for the social network KG. Our experiment shows the superior ranking performance of MDE over the baseline. We defined a probability for link suggestion and provided an analytic study for it. We thereby conclude that the model can be suggested to serve in connecting the physicians and the up-to-date advances in the medical studies. Considering the time constraints of physicians on social media [6], automating such suggestions can help physicians to find news and trends relevant for medical research results more easily and in less time.

As future work, it would be interesting to extend this study on a large scale and provide it as a live service. In addition, future studies may investigate the social effect of such application to find its effect benefits for patients besides the physicians.

Acknowledgements. This study is partially supported by project MLwin (Maschinelles Lernen mit Wissensgraphen, grant no. 01IS18050F) (https://mlwin.de/.) and Cleopatra (grant no. 812997). The authors gratefully acknowledge financial support from the Federal Ministry of Education and Research of Germany (BMBF) which is funding MLwin and European Union Marie Curie ITN that funds Cleopatra, as well as Fraunhofer IAIS.

References

1. Adafre, S.F., de Rijke, M.: Discovering missing links in Wikipedia. In: Proceedings of the 3rd International Workshop on Link Discovery, pp. 90–97. ACM (2005)

2. Al Hasan, M., Chaoji, V., Salem, S., Zaki, M.: Link prediction using supervised learning. In: SDM06: Workshop on Link Analysis, Counter-Terrorism and Security (2006)
3. Almansoori, W., et al.: Link prediction and classification in social networks and its application in healthcare and systems biology. Network Model. Anal. Health Inf. Bioinf. **1**(1–2), 27–36 (2012)
4. Bordes, A., Usunier, N., Garcia-Duran, A., Weston, J., Yakhnenko, O.: Translating embeddings for modeling multi-relational data. In: Advances in Neural Information Processing Systems, pp. 2787–2795 (2013)
5. Brady, R., et al.: # colorectalsurgery. Br. J. Surg. **104**(11), 1470–1476 (2017)
6. Campbell, L., Evans, Y., Pumper, M., Moreno, M.A.: Social media use by physicians: a qualitative study of the new frontier of medicine. BMC Med. Inform. Decis. Mak. **16**(1), 91 (2016)
7. Choo, E.K., et al.: Twitter as a tool for communication and knowledge exchange in academic medicine: a guide for skeptics and novices. Med. Teach. **37**(5), 411–416 (2015). https://doi.org/10.3109/0142159X.2014.993371
8. Goel, A., Sharma, A., Wang, D., Yin, Z.: Discovering similar users on Twitter. In: 11th Workshop on Mining and Learning with Graphs (2013)
9. Gupta, P., Goel, A., Lin, J., Sharma, A., Wang, D., Zadeh, R.: WTF: the who to follow service at Twitter. In: Proceedings of the 22Nd International Conference on World Wide Web, WWW 2013, pp. 505–514. ACM, New York (2013). https://doi.org/10.1145/2488388.2488433, http://doi.acm.org/10.1145/2488388.2488433
10. Hawn, C.: Take two aspirin and tweet me in the morning: how Twitter, Facebook, and other social media are reshaping health care. Health Aff. **28**(2), 361–368 (2009)
11. Martincic-Ipsic, S., Mocibob, E., Perc, M.: Link prediction on Twitter. PLoS ONE **12**(7), e0181079 (2017)
12. Nickel, M., Tresp, V., Kriegel, H.P.: A three-way model for collective learning on multi-relational data. ICML, vol. 11, pp. 809–816 (2011)
13. Pemmaraju, N., Thompson, M.A., Qazilbash, M.: Disease-specific hashtags and the creation of twitter medical communities in hematology and oncology. In: Seminars in Hematology, vol. 54, pp. 189–192. Elsevier (2017)
14. Pershad, Y., Hangge, P., Albadawi, H., Oklu, R.: Social medicine: Twitter in healthcare. J. Clin. Med. **7**(6), 121 (2018)
15. Raghupathi, W., Raghupathi, V.: Big data analytics in healthcare: promise and potential. Health Inf. Sci. Syst. **2**(1), 3 (2014)
16. Sadeghi, A., Graux, D., Shariat Yazdi, H., Lehmann, J.: MDE: multiple distance embeddings for link prediction in knowledge graphs. In: ECAI (2020)
17. Vartak, S.: A survey on link prediction. State University of New York, Binghamton, NY-13902, USA (2008)
18. Watts, D.J., Strogatz, S.H.: Collective dynamics of 'small-world' networks. Nature **393**(6684), 440 (1998)

Prediction of Frequent Out-Of-Hours' Medical Use

Duncan Wallace(✉) and Tahar Kechadi

University College Dublin, Belfield, Ireland
duncan.wallace@insight-centre.org

Abstract. The thesis of this research is that through the mining of Electronic Medical Records containing mixed types of data, and extracting patterns from the processed data, patients can be successfully categorised through means of supervised machine learning early in their engagement with health care providers. This categorisation has quite narrow parameters: the aim of which is identify patients that are less suitable to the health care provider being examined in the course of this research; specifically that of an out-of-hours health care cooperative (OOHC). The motivation for this is to provide potential means for interventionist healthcare, in line with the increasingly role that decentralised regional programmes are having in the avenues of treatment available for patients [19] and the increasing emphasis on community based intervention [24]. The patients in question are frequent users of the OOHC, and represent a small cohort within the dataset as a whole. Our classification methodology, based upon recurrent neural networks, achieves an Area Under the Curve of between 0.81 and 0.92 in the identification of these patients.

Keywords: Medical informatics · Electronic health record · Deep learning

1 Introduction

The context of this research is treatment provided by an out-of-hours health care (OOHC) cooperative. OOHC acts as an ad-hoc delivery of triage and treatment, where interactions occur without recourse to a full medical history of the patient in question. We are motivated by the prediction of a small cohort of patients who have very frequent usage of the OOHC under investigation. This paper will first describe the setting of OOHC, the way this form of medical care informs our research, and the manner in which data is recorded in these types of organisations. We will discuss the prevailing research concerning frequent users and why their prediction is an important topic. This paper will briefly describe the dataset available to our research before explaining the methodology employed to predict cases which are likely to belong to this cohort. Finally we will provide a post-hoc explanation of what features were most significant in the determination of these cases.

Supported by Science Foundation Ireland, grant:12/RC/2289_P2.

P. Cellier and K. Driessens (Eds.): ECML PKDD 2019 Workshops, CCIS 1167, pp. 631–646, 2020.
https://doi.org/10.1007/978-3-030-43823-4_50

2 Problem Statement

Our research is based upon the early identification of patients who have underlying conditions which will cause them to repeatedly require medical attention, far beyond what would be witnessed in the general population. Such frequent patients pose a significantly increased financial and temporal demand on health care providers than that posed by non FA cases. However, a much more substantial concern is that these patients are a poor match to the services provided by telemedical OOH organisations, which are predominantly designed to treat acute and emergency cases rather than chronic illnesses. We define frequent users as patients with over 24 interactions with the OOHC in question over the course of a year, and those with over 50 interactions as high frequent users, for this same period. Relative to the threshold being considered (relating to frequent and high-frequent users) the aim of this research was to provide an accurate classification of individual cases as either positive (frequent) or negative (non-frequent) during testing using a single case entry relating to the given patient. This research represents an example of outlier detection due to the relative scarcity of these patients. Consequently, meaningful testing in relation to this problem necessitates the use of an imbalanced dataset (thereby making the detection of true positive cases a challenge).

3 Out-Of-Hours Health-Care

High level OOHC management in the form of cooperatives is becoming an increasingly common means of primary health care provision. Electronic Health Records (EHRs) are habitually used in primary care such as this for the recording of patient data [25]. However, medical histories relating to people contacting an OOHC organisation may reside in several distinct EHR systems in multiple hospitals or surgeries which may be unavailable to the OOHC provider in question [34].

OOHC cooperatives are a relatively modern health care delivery system, forming a hybridisation of traditional primary care and telemedicine. Similar to the structure adopted by the United Kingdom's National Health Service, out-of-hours care in Ireland features a plethora of services, including walk-in centres, out-of-hours centres, telephone consultation, and the emergency department (A&E) [6].

The scope of Caredoc's integrated care model is nominally quite broad, but fundamentally it is underpinned by its operation of a call centre which provides the hub for out-of-hours care for quite a wide geographical area. It has been envisioned since its inculcation, that nurse operated phones, providing both advice and triage, would reduce the burden on other areas of the health service during out-of-hours operation [21].

However, the telemedicine and triage provided is not diagnostic in nature. Numerous OOHC take advantage of software for clinical decision making, typically known as clinical decision support systems (CDSS), and Caredoc is no

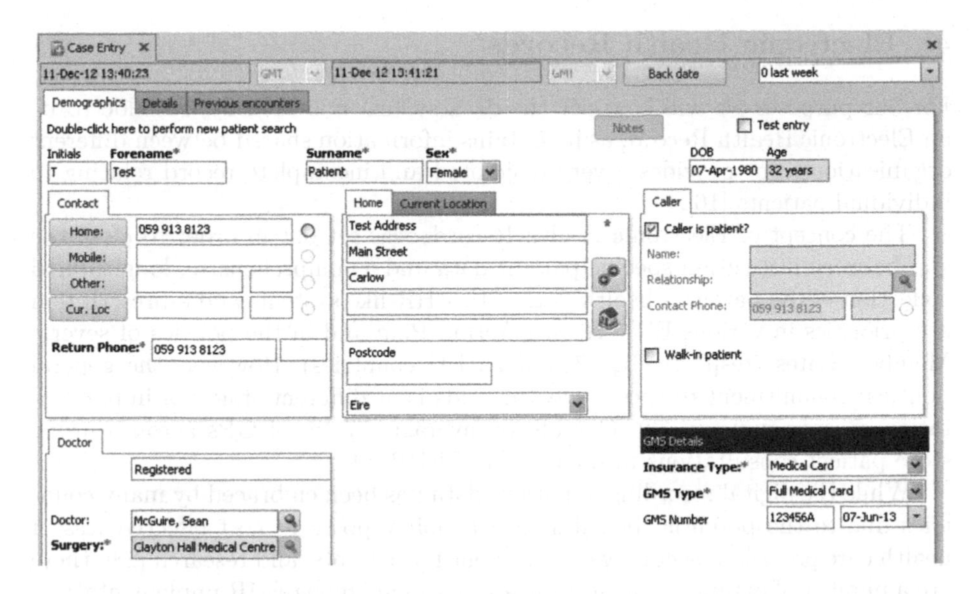

Fig. 1. Graphical User Interface used by staff at OOHC, showing text boxes used to record case data.

exception in this regard [20]. CDSS take in symptoms input by phone operators, and make suggestions about the types of conditions the patient may be suffering from. This software is useful is narrowing down the scope of what phone operators should consider when dealing with patients, but neither the values input by phone operators, nor the suggested comorbidities derived by the CDSS are actually recorded.

The patient records treated in this research may be presented *in media res*, as patients will have had prior interaction with healthcare that is not recorded, and indeed may have possible further interaction with health infrastructure, that is likewise unavailable within the scope of this project. The data flow within Caredoc is independent of any information relating to patients which may exist in health records in other health care organisations (such as in hospitals, or with the patient's own GP). While Caredoc will transfer data to a patient's GP (or public health nurse, where appropriate), the reverse is not true. As such, if diagnoses are made in relation to these patients in subsequent analysis, these diagnoses are unlikely to feature within the data possessed by the co-op, unless specifically mentioned by the patient in potential subsequent interaction between the co-op and the patient.

As such, data relating to patients often form little more than snapshots. The incomplete nature of patient medical histories is a typical feature of OOHC [1]. A decentralised solution with respect to OOHC patient medical informatics is thus a key motivation of this research. The software used to record each of episode of care is Ad Astra^{TM}. Most of the OOHC in both Ireland and the UK use this particular software (or at least some version of it) [18].

4 Electronic Health Records

For our purposes we will consider the data system managed by Caredoc to be an Electronic Health Record, as it contains information shared between different organisations, but provides a very disjointed and incomplete record relating to individual patients [16].

The concept of Electronic Health Records was set out in order to close the gap between institution-specific patient data and a comprehensive, longitudinal collection of the patient's health data [31]. EHR-like systems and e-prescription are priorities in various EU e-Health Action Plan and in the policies of several Member States (respectively, 27 and 22 EU countries). However, the general political commitment to these e-health fields is at different stages of implementation across countries [33]. Overall, on average, 77.4% of GPs across Europe store patient consultations in some form of EHR [9].

While the digital recording of patient data has been embraced by many countries due to the potential benefits such a policy poses to cost effectiveness of health care provision, accuracy of treatment for patients, and research [28], there are a number of extant problems that are common among EHR implementation. Most EHR systems used in health centres are proprietary systems built with different architectures, business rules, information technologies and models, in addition to incompatible clinical terminology. These facts hinder the interoperability among the Health Information Systems (HIS), making it difficult for health professionals to provide adequate care [13].

Electronic Health Records used in the operation of OOH cooperatives are composed of both structured, parameterized fields, and unstructured, free-text clinical notes. Knowledge discovery currently has very limited application in Caredoc. Identification of patterns within this data, at either a population or individual level, is limited to shallow treatment and narrow parametrisation [7,15]. Like many HIS, each call handled by Caredoc is treated as a unique encounter (or case) [26]. However, phone operators are able to automatically fill in the parameterised demographic fields related to the patient being treated. This is achieved by the phone number that is being used to call Caredoc being on record, or the operator manually searching for the patient by name.

EHR documentation is thus encumbered by a number of challenges. In the current system, each provider writes his or her own encounter-based notes, leading to redundancy, fragmentation, and lack of a single shared clinical narrative. This problem is further aggravated when a patient receives care across organisations whose EHRs are not interoperable [34]. EHRs generally lack standard templates to document additional inputs in structured data fields, and the EHR system that Caredoc operates is no different in relation to this shortcoming. This limitation makes it difficult for practices to find, extract, and track relevant behavioural health and physical health information to monitor quality and improve the delivery of integrated care [5].

Patient demographic details, as seen in Fig. 1, have a large number of fields, including General Medical Services (GMS) Number (if applicable), home address, and telephone number. Most of these are sensitive data, and subject to restricted access based upon data protection legislation. Parametric information also contains details about the call itself, such as the time of day and date that the call was made. However, virtually all information relating to the case in question is treated in non-sanitised free-text boxes.

Generally, case free-text records are written by highly skilled physicians and nurses using specialised terms. As is typical in EHR, case record text is very domain specific, depending on which medical discipline it is written in. Each discipline or domain within medicine uses its own set of terms that can be incomprehensible to other disciplines [8]. Patient records are primarily written for hospital internal use and for mnemonic reasons. Daily running notes might contain more spelling errors or noisiness than discharge letters that are read by a larger audience [11].

Text mining of medical information can extract features from clinical digital reports. Features from clinical data typically represent medical concepts, such as symptoms, diagnoses and prescriptions. Using this data, partial medical histories can be constructed for individuals.

5 Frequent Users

The problem of high recurring patients has long been acknowledged in healthcare. High recurring patients are, however, a complicated subset of subjects that are difficult to classify. Not only do these patients have disparate demographic details, but the symptoms with which they present to primary care staff are diverse, and rarely indicate their belonging to this subgroup. This paper will give an overview of the extant literature concerning frequent users of healthcare, why the prediction of such patients could be a significant contribution to healthcare delivery, and how general principles relating to frequent users ties into our research. In particular, this paper will discuss what measures currently exist for predicting such patients, and how our proposed model improves upon these approaches.

While frequent users of healthcare facilities has been a perennial issue, relatively little research has been conducted in relation to frequent use in the context of telemedicine. Most extant health-care management documentation relating to frequent use has focused exclusively upon frequent attendance in secondary healthcare, particularly that of emergency departments (ED). Such research has largely been conducted with the motivation of moving these types of patients to primary care (e.g. GPs or ambulatory healthcare centres). There is growing understanding that interventionist measures, while an area of critical importance, should be patient focused, and not merely shift responsibility for care of such patients. It is accepted that patients who repeatedly use either primary or secondary healthcare have ongoing medical issues which are not being resolved, despite their repeated use of healthcare facilities.

There is no standard definition of what constitutes a high use patient in any sector of healthcare provision [3]. Despite it being self evident that frequent users are characterised by the high frequency with which they interact with healthcare provision, the terminology relating to such patients is nonetheless volatile. The actual threshold for what is considered to be 'high' use varies between institutions, and usually depends on the type of healthcare being considered. For instance, the number of attendances deemed to constitute a Frequent Attender (FA) of secondary healthcare is typically significantly lower than the number of phone calls used to define a Frequent Caller (FC) [10]. Furthermore, the definition of a frequent user may depend on the manner in which healthcare is offered on a nationwide level, while the specific threshold used to determine how many contacts constitutes "frequent use" fluctuates significantly between different countries, regions, and even particular departments. In countries where public healthcare is free, such as in Denmark, Ireland, and the United Kingdom, any difference in the proportion of frequent attenders must be explained by other factors than economic [27].

A growing tendency within research into frequent users has been to create delineations between frequent and high frequent use of health care facilities, as this can help identify divergent characteristics between different types of frequent usage. For instance a study in 2019 by Bhroin et al. in the A&E department of Mercy University Hospital in Ireland (in an administrative region adjacent to the area that is covered by the OOHC we are examining) classified high frequent attender as patients with between 13 to 30 Emergency Department visits per year, and very high frequent attenders as those with over 30 Emergency Department visits [2]. Helplines on the other hand typically use a threshold of one call a week to define FC. No study has shown a threshold number at which striking differences in resources, demographics, or clinical import are observed in relation to a specific threshold for emergency department FA [23].

While mental and psychological disease, and drug abuse, have long been attributed to FA of ED, recent literature has pointed to a far more complicated set of morbidities and co-morbidities that are present in patients that are classified as frequent users. Frequent users also tend to originate from a wide range of backgrounds. There is significant disagreement between researchers on whether demographic details have any significant predictive power in relation to such patients.

Healthcare staff have described both the psychological and temporal burden that these patients pose on their facilities. Frequent use has been associated with frustration both on the part of the patient and also the healthcare staff [17]. However, it is erroneous to view such patients as merely "time wasters" [29]. The negative viewpoint that these patients may have historically been subject to reflects the difficulties of treating such patients, as they invariably present with underlying issues which are not easily resolvable by the staff that are treating them. Additionally they may present with increased psychological requirements, and interaction may be complicated by the nominal reason for their contacting the healthcare provider.

Frequent use of helplines, emergency departments, and primary care is heavily associated with serious medical conditions, the requirements of which are often not being met in the recourse offered to these patients. Emergency and

OOHC prove to be ill adapted at treating many of these patients. Although these facilities are adept at handling acute episodes, by necessity these healthcare providers are limited to the short-term, superficial treatment that will not engage with the primary issues facing this cohort. A growing body of research has suggested the creation of a specific arm of healthcare provision, featuring staff specifically trained to treat frequent users cases [3]. Moreover, strategies need to be developed to attempt to tackle underlying issues which are bringing these types of patients into contact with healthcare provision.

Intervention specifically designed to target and treat frequent users has shown significant promise, not only in terms of a reduction in the frequency with which such patients present to healthcare operators, but also in terms of the acuity of treatment and satisfaction of patients [3]. However, the means to develop ways of identifying these patients is non-trivial. If the healthcare facility is using EHR to record data, a frequent user of the same healthcare facility can be identified simply by searching for how many previous encounters the healthcare facility has had with that patient. This is nonetheless an undesirable approach, as it necessitates that a patient already be established as a FP before any sort of interventionist approach can be adopted. Furthermore, the lack of interoperability between the EHR of different institutions is a widespread and ongoing problem [32]. Interactions between a patient and a given health care provider is typically isolated from any other interaction that patient may have had with other health care provision. This is not only true in terms of types of healthcare provision (e.g. GP, OOHC, ED) but even between different institutions providing the same type of treatment. Consequently frequent users are almost exclusively considered in terms of their interactions with a single institution.

The primary complaint presented to healthcare staff is typically only tangentially related to ongoing reasons for such patients contacting the healthcare provider. As a result of this there tends to be obfuscation of the main issues facing these patients, which adds to difficulties of discoverability. Even where literature agrees that certain diseases have high correlation with frequency of presentation, major issues arise in the episodic nature of treatment in OOHC. The specific, or at least nominal reason for the patient appearing in an ED, or contacting an OOHC centre by phone, may be different with each visit. This can hide underlying conditions. Frequent users are at risk of becoming serial users (having consistent patterns of usage over multiple years). Other frequent users, on the other hand, may be acute (having a large number of contacts over a relatively short period of time). Attrition rates of those who remain frequent users decrease over time, making them an ideal group for targeted interventions [22].

While there were many factors that differentiated non-FAs from FAs in general, persistent frequent attendance was specifically associated with gender, baseline reports of depression, self-reported physical conditions and disability, and medication use [30].

6 Data-Set

Our data-set is derived from interactions that took place in the calendar year of 2014. Frequent users are an usual, but significant subset of patients in our dataset. The distribution of cases relative to patient frequency can be seen in Fig. 2, showing that the vast majority of interactions with the OOHC are "non-frequent".

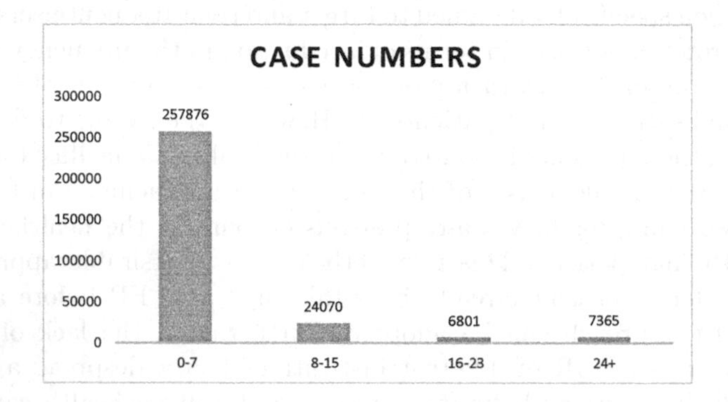

Fig. 2. Case distribution of dataset.

The dataset consists of 294336 cases, featuring some 131841 unique lexemes. The top seventy words in positive (threshold of twenty-four cases) and negative cases can be seen in Fig. 3, excluding the NLTK set of stopwords [4]. A significant overlap of high-occurring words for both frequent and non frequent users is observable in this context.

The volume of free-text used for cases was not particularly consistent (see Table 2 where average word length (w), and character length (c) is described). There were four different fields where free-text may be recorded. A single case may have free-text data in multiple fields. The different fields (labelled on the system as relating to history, diagnosis, treatment, and teleguides), while only loosely corresponding to their described purposes were nonetheless done so in this particular temporal order. Consequently, if simultaneously present for a given case, these data were appended together when creating datasets for our classifier. We considered a word length of 100 to be a good length to capture the majority of these cases. However also tested against an input length of 200 to ascertain whether any information was being inadvertently discarded which could potentially improve classification performance.

positive

'pt', 'per', 'pain', 'advised', 'dr', 'see', 'meds', 'hx', 'back', 'gp', 'chest', 'advice', 'call', 'c', 'o', '2', 'home', 'nkda', 'notes', 'patient', 'x', 'today', 'special', 'last', 'feels', 'please', 're', 'feeling', 'given', 'take', 'copd', 'says', 'visit', 'nurse', 'sob', 'phone', 'advise', 'happy', '1', 'taken', 'ago', 'took', 'appt', 'prn', 'left', 'since', 'bp', '7', 'normal', 'temp', 'ring', 'paracetamol', 'tonight', 'cough', 'nil', 'e', 'caredoc', 'spoke', '3', 'night', 'med', 'get', 'well', 'wants', 'steroids', 'days', 'v', 'also', 'go', 'seen', 'leg'

negative

'pain', 'per', 'pt', 'hx', 'x', 'temp', 'nkda', 'meds', 'chest', '2', 'nil', '7', 'c', 'gp', 'advised', 'throat', 'back', '1', 'o', 'clear', 'nad', 'appt', 'normal', 'days', 'cough', 'last', 'mum', 'left', '5', 'rash', 'since', 'e', '3', 'prn', 'today', 'sore', 'given', 'ago', 'med', 'tds', 'vomiting', 'red', 'bp', 'right', 'r', 'urine', 'see', 'well', '36', 'dr', 'review', 'ent', 'bd', 'fever', 'mg', 'tender', 'abdo', '4', 'ear', 'calpol', 'ears', 'night', 'ok', 'yesterday', 'home', 'week', 'call', 'neck', 'symptoms', 'infection', 'patient'

Fig. 3. Top seventy words in positive and negative cases respectively, excluding stop-words.

Table 1. Classification using bag-of-word model

	Naive Bayes	SVM	RF
Accuracy	0.26 ± 0.51	0.66 ± 0.385	0.68 ± 0.045
PPV	0.89 ± 0.53	0.52 ± 0.459	0.37 ± 0.015
NPV	0.24 ± 0.019	0.49 ± 0.412	0.69 ± 0.044
TPR	0.013 ± 0.001	0.01 ± 0.0049	0.006 ± 0.001

7 Methodology

We initially attempted to classify cases as either frequent or non-frequent users based upon a bag-of-words representation of the data, relating to the top 100 words in the dataset, using three different algorithms; namely Support Vector Machines (SVM), Random Forest (RF) and Naive Bayes (NB). These results, relating to positive predictive rate (PPV), negative predictive rate (NPV), and true positive rate (TPR) are visible in Table 1. This provided a decent spread of results and provided suitable baselines from which to work when developing a case classification methodology.

Unsupervised neural networks can be used to create dense vector representation of lexemes, typically referred to as word embeddings. We created word embeddings from patient free-text notes using Word2Vec, by applying the Skip-Gram model [14]. For this we trained the unsupervised network on a version of the corpus itself, which had been carefully processed in order to remove noise and provide sentence disambiguation.

Long Short-Term Memory (LSTM), originally developed to help solve the vanishing gradient problem common in simple Recurrent Neural Networks [12], is a block that has the capacity to store representations of recent input events.

Table 2. Free-text data in preprocessed corpus

Attribute	Entries	$\|\bar{c}\|$	$\|\bar{w}\|$
olc_history	15226	212.86	34.01
olc_examination	11326	148.13	22.65
olc_diagnosis	120433	36.04	5.13
olc_treatment	123517	122.08	17.11
teleguides	58906	315.17	49.95

This has proven application in natural language processing problems due to capacity of the ANN to remember term dependencies, and could be useful in the interpretation of contextual information in patient cases.

The output of the ANNs was a continuous value reflecting determined likelihood that the patient case being tested belonged to someone who would become a frequent user. Training data was produced using downsampling in order to produce a dataset evenly balanced between positive and negative cases. While this approach was necessary, insofar that domination by a majority class had to be avoided during training, this produced a significant prospect for overfitting. Positive cases for training, validation, and testing sets were randomly allocated in a 50:25:25 ratio, where testing was performed against an unbalanced dataset. While dropout was considered as part of the search space of hyperparameters that were subject to Bayesian hyperparameter optimization (along with the number of layers, learning rate, activation function, and optimisation function used within the ANN), we also sought another potential means to counter overfitting. Our approach was to deliberately prepend the vector data input with six channels of noise, to see if this would improve ultimate testing results. This was compared to the addition of normalized features derived from demographic detail recorded through the OOHC software (see Fig. 1) in the corpus. Although these normalized features were quite limited in scope, it was hypothesized that the introduction of these features, such as patient age and gender, might improve classification performance.

The structure and set of hyperparameters determined through Bayesian optimization to be the most successful, and used pursuant to the ultimate classification of patients in relation to this paper, was a Recurrent Neural Network featuring a four layer LSTM with a learning rate of 0.001, dropout of 0.109, batch size of 100, and using the Adam optimizer. It was uncertain whether increasing the length of input (maximum number of lexemes considered in each case) and channels (the dimensionality of word embeddings) would improve results, and as such, these were also tested.

8 Results

Long-Short Term Memory, using Word2Vec, trained on the corpus, and using the hyperparameters described above overall performed strongly when given 100 lexemes of input, coupled with a dimensionality of 100 channels.

We use receiver operating characteristic (ROC) curve and the area under curve (AUC) to evaluate the effectiveness of the classifier. The ROC curve shows the trade-off between the true positive rate (TPR) and the false positive rate (FPR), where the TPR and FPR are defined as follows:

$$TPR = \frac{\text{True Positives}}{\text{True Positives} + \text{False Negatives}} \tag{1}$$

$$TNR = \frac{\text{True Negatives}}{\text{True Positives} + \text{False Positives}} \tag{2}$$

If the ROC curve is closer to the top left corner of the graph, the model is better. The AUC is the area under the curve generated. In medical data, more attention is typically paid to recall rather than accuracy. While this metric is often employed in relation to the prediction of a cohort that are, or will, suffer a particular disease, in this instance the metric describes the capacity of the model to classify a cohort suffering from a non-specific set of conditions that have forced them to become frequent users of the OOHC being examined.

Results were obtained based on the criteria outlined above on 5-fold cross validated testing sets. A distinction between frequent users (using a threshold equal or above 24 cases) and high frequent users (over 50 cases) was made in testing (relating to 7365 and 2922 cases respectively). While our model provided best results with the most extreme of outliers, namely high frequent users, it did not perform quite as well on those at a threshold of over 24 cases. A linear degradation of performance was observed when more generalized types of patients were included (from an AUC of 0.92 for a threshold of 50 cases, when noise was added, to an AUC of 0.79 for a threshold of 17 cases, when noise was added). Nevertheless our model provided accurate results during testing despite a setting involving significantly imbalanced data.

Looking at Table 3, it is interesting to observe that the inclusion of features provided no significant improvement in performance by the recurrent neural network architecture. In counterpoint, the inclusion of noise had the effect of often reducing the propensity of the classifiers to overfit (which remained an issue, even with dropout).

Increasing the length of input or number of channels did not necessarily have a beneficial effect. Even where a higher percentage of true classifications were achieved in one field, there would be a corresponding decrease in true predictions in another. In particular, doubling both input length and channel size (C) tended towards far more unstable models.

A high AUC was achieved for both frequent usage and high frequent usage with our LSTM model (using 100 channels and 100 input length based on W2V word embeddings trained on preprocessed corpus), visible in Fig. 4. High FAs

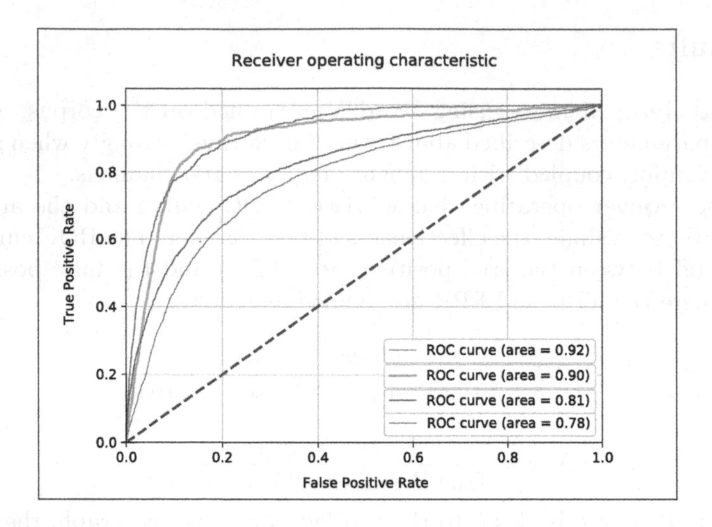

Fig. 4. ROC curve over both High FA patients and FA patients with difference in performance when including noise recorded as the red, and blue lines, for high FA and FA cases respectively. (Color figure online)

achieved an AUC of 0.9 (or 0.92 with noise added) and FAs achieved an AUC of 0.78 (or 0.81 with noise added).

9 Discussion

One issue with ANNs is their problem of interpretability. In order to improve this aspect of our program, we produced a post-hoc analysis by measuring lexemes related to cases, based upon whether these lexemes were within cases correctly, or incorrectly, classified by our ANN. The predictive value output by our ANN was summed for each lexeme for each of the related cases, with the count being inversely proportional to how frequent each lexeme was in the corpus as a whole. Finally, only the lexemes which collectively represented 80% of the entire number of words in the particular dataset were kept in order to reduce the long tail of insignificant lexemes. The resultant graph is viewable in Fig. 5.

True positives strongly featured the terms 'depressed', 'angina', 'suicidal', 'gauze', 'neuralgia', and 'diabetic'. It is worth noting that these terms may often be subject to contextual negation in individual cases (like 'patient is not suicidal'). In the case of 'suicidal', approximately 25% of the instances of this term were subject to negation. When considering the course of a patient interaction that results in these terms appearing in free text notes, it is perhaps no surprise that they bear significance, even if they are negated. While words that have strong association with psychological disorders are apparent here (including 'anxiety' and 'depressed') it is worth noting the terms that also seem to strongly indicate chronic disease (such as 'angina', 'gauze', and 'diabetic'). A further

Table 3. Architecture and input comparison

T	Length	C	LSTM			
			Features		Noise	
			PPV	NPV	PPV	NPV
24	100	100	0.71 ± 0.006	0.76 ± 0.005	0.75 ± 0.033	0.75 ± 0.047
24	100	200	0.73 ± 0.021	0.75 ± 0.003	0.72 ± 0.047	0.76 ± 0.013
24	200	100	0.71 ± 0.018	0.72 ± 0.012	0.54 ± 0.21	0.89 ± 0.081
24	200	200	0.78 ± 0.098	0.63 ± 0.21	0.38 ± 0.33	0.91 ± 0.042
50	100	100	0.88 ± 0.009	0.78 ± 0.008	0.86 ± 0.012	0.88 ± 0.014
50	100	200	0.85 ± 0.017	0.83 ± 0.026	0.88 ± 0.019	0.84 ± 0.025
50	200	100	0.80 ± 0.083	0.69 ± 0.23	0.79 ± 0.015	0.71 ± 0.17
50	200	200	0.89 ± 0.048	0.75 ± 0.165	0.82 ± 0.14	0.72 ± 0.21

investigation may be merited to the end of finding the connection between such terms in the free text notes.

There were also true positive terms that were more surprising, such as 'driver', 'wondering', and 'list'. In particular the term 'said' would conventionally seem too frequent to pose much significance. However, the nature of the medical notes is important in this regard. For instance the term 'said' appears a total of 2967 times in our corpus, as opposed to 2323 times for a term like 'diabetic'. In other textual environments (such as social media) the relative prevalence of two terms like these would be striking. True negatives for their part were strongly associated with the terms 'runny', 'viral', 'tonsillitis', 'tract', and 'rash',

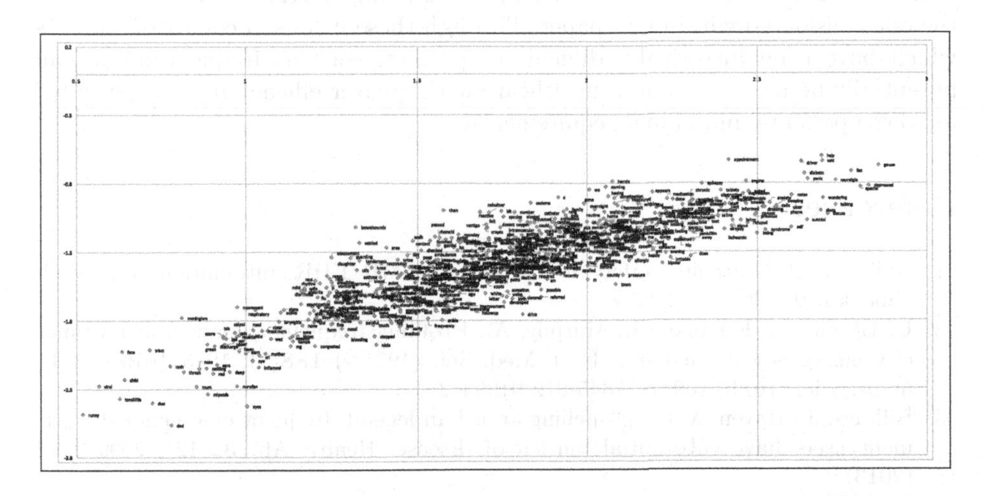

Fig. 5. Scatter-plot of the top 80% of words used in relation to cases correctly classified, with the X-axis representing positive predictions, and the Y-axis representing negative predictions

clearing indicating infections and acute diseases. True negative cases were also strongly connected to family-orientated words, such as 'mum', 'dad', and 'child'. It is worth pointing out that 'mum' and 'inflamed' also stood out among false negatives. Interestingly, 'dementia' and 'cancer' were two terms most strongly associated with false positives.

It is also the case that, notwithstanding efforts to improve the features derived from such notes, some textual notes have very little data (perhaps a couple of words at most) making the correct classification of these, in isolation, very difficult.

10 Conclusion

This paper has outlined a system which can provide accurate prediction of high use patients given a very limited amount of information relating to individual patients. The way that this was achievable was by training a model that could successfully learn patterns that were likely to represent such patients. In our investigation we learned that these patterns were likely to be informed by terms relating not only to psychological distress, but also chronic conditions. Given that the seriousness of the conditions and signs related to cases that were likely to relate to high use, or future high use patients, the value of providing potential means to intervene in the medical welfare of such patients is underscored. Like all predictive analysis in the medical domain, absolute accuracy is impossible to guarantee. These models can be used to indicate patients that may warrant further investigation in order to determine if they require elevated care than that conventionally available through OOHC provision, but cannot substitute clinician evaluation. Consequently, this type of prediction is potentially a valuable tool in the suite of services available within existing OOHC structures, such as the one considered within this paper. Through these means, a cohort of patients which have been historically difficult to predict, such as frequent users, can potentially be focused on, and healthcare with greater efficacy may be provided for these patients' individual requirements.

References

1. Aldosari, B.: Patients' safety in the era of EMR/EHR automation. Inf. Med. Unlocked **9**, 230–233 (2017)
2. Uí Bhroin, S., Kinahan, J., Murphy, A.: Profiling frequent attenders at an inner city emergency department. Ir. J. Med. Sci. (1971 -) **188**(3), 1013–1019 (2019). https://doi.org/10.1007/s11845-019-01964-2
3. Billings, J., Raven, M.C.: Dispelling an urban legend: frequent emergency department users have substantial burden of disease. Health Aff. **32**(12), 2099–2108 (2013)
4. Bird, S., Klein, E., Loper, E.: Natural language processing with Python: analyzing text with the natural language toolkit. O'Reilly Media, Inc., Sebastopol (2009)

5. Cifuentes, M., Davis, M., Fernald, D., Gunn, R., Dickinson, P., Cohen, D.J.: Electronic health record challenges, workarounds, and solutions observed in practices integrating behavioral health and primary care. J. Am. Board Fam. Med. **28**(Supplement 1), S63–S72 (2015)
6. Coombes, R.: How to fix out of hours care. BMJ **353**, i2356 (2016)
7. Cunniffe, M., Burke, M., Curran, M., Collier, D.: Developing people-centeredness in the Irish healthcare system-continuous awareness and communication are key enablers to success. Int. J. Integr. Care **16**(6) (2016)
8. Dalianis, H.: Characteristics of patient records and clinical corpora. In: Clinical Text Mining, pp. 21–34. Springer, Cham (2018). https://doi.org/10.1007/978-3-319-78503-5_4
9. De Rosis, S., Seghieri, C.: Basic ICT adoption and use by general practitioners: an analysis of primary care systems in 31 European countries. BMC Med. Inform. Decis. Mak. **15**(1), 70 (2015)
10. Edwards, M.J., Bassett, G., Sinden, L., Fothergill, R.T.: Frequent callers to the ambulance service: patient profiling and impact of case management on patient utilisation of the ambulance service. Emerg. Med. J. **32**(5), 392–396 (2015)
11. Ehrentraut, C., Tanushi, H., Dalianis, H., Tiedemann, J.: Detection of hospital acquired infections in sparse and noisy Swedish patient records. A machine learning approach using Naïve Bayes, Support Vector Machines and C4.5 (2012)
12. Gers, F.A., Schmidhuber, J., Cummins, F.: Learning to forget: continual prediction with ISTM. In: Proceedings of the 9th International Conference on Artificial Neural Networks, pp. 850–855. IET (1999)
13. Gomes, F., Paiva, J., Bezerra, A., Moura, C., Oliveira, M., Andrade, O.: MARCIA: applied clinical record management: eletronic health record applied with EHRServer. In: 2018 IEEE 20th International Conference on e-Health Networking, Applications and Services (Healthcom), pp. 1–6. IEEE (2018)
14. Guthrie, D., Allison, B., Liu, W., Guthrie, L., Wilks, Y.: A closer look at skip-gram modelling. In: Proceedings of the 5th International Conference on Language Resources and Evaluation (LREC-2006), pp. 1–4 (2006)
15. Advanced Health and Care Ltd.: Helpsheet ce-cen (2014)
16. Heart, T., Ben-Assuli, O., Shabtai, I.: A review of PHR, EMR and EHR integration: a more personalized healthcare and public health policy. Health Policy Technol. **6**(1), 20–25 (2017)
17. Holmström, I.K., Krantz, A., Karacagil, L., Sundler, A.J.: Frequent callers in primary health care-a qualitative study with a nursing perspective. J. Adv. Nurs. **73**(3), 622–632 (2017)
18. HSE: National review of GP out of hours' services (2010)
19. Iyengar, S., Katz, A., Durham, J.: Role of institutional entrepreneurship in building adaptive capacity in community-based healthcare organisations: realist review protocol. BMJ Open **6**(3), e010915 (2016)
20. Kasem, A.Y.: Exploring the views of parents of children aged two years and under following telephone advice from nurses working in a GP out-of-hours service in Ireland. Ph.D. thesis, University of Southampton (2017)
21. Khistriya, R., Main, P., Curtis, A., Irish, B.: NHS direct out-of-hours service for general practitioner registrars: trainees' experiences of a learning opportunity. Educ. Primary Care **21**(3), 186–193 (2010)
22. Krieg, C., Hudon, C., Chouinard, M.C., Dufour, I.: Individual predictors of frequent emergency department use: a scoping review. BMC Health Serv. Res. **16**(1), 594 (2016)

23. LaCalle, E., Rabin, E.: Frequent users of emergency departments: the myths, the data, and the policy implications. Ann. Emerg. Med. **56**(1), 42–48 (2010)
24. Mahato, K., Srivastava, A., Chandra, P.: Paper based diagnostics for personalized health care: emerging technologies and commercial aspects. Biosens. Bioelectron. **96**, 246–259 (2017)
25. Michiels, B., Nguyen, V.K., Coenen, S., Ryckebosch, P., Bossuyt, N., Hens, N.: Influenza epidemic surveillance and prediction based on electronic health record data from an out-of-hours general practitioner cooperative: model development and validation on 2003–2015 data. BMC Infect. Dis. **17**(1), 84 (2017)
26. Middleton, A., Gunn, J., Bassilios, B., Pirkis, J.: The experiences of frequent users of crisis helplines: a qualitative interview study. Patient Educ. Couns. **99**(11), 1901–1906 (2016)
27. Pasgaard, A.A., Mæhlisen, M.H., Overgaard, C., Ejlskov, L., Torp-Pedersen, C., Bøggild, H.: Social capital and frequent attenders in general practice: a register-based cohort study. BMC Public Health **18**(1), 310 (2018)
28. Peckham, D.: Electronic patient records, past, present and future. Paediatr. Respir. Rev. **20**, 8–11 (2016)
29. Pirkis, J., et al.: Frequent callers to telephone helplines: new evidence and a new service model. Int. J. Mental Health Syst. **10**(1), 43 (2016)
30. Pymont, C., Butterworth, P.: Longitudinal cohort study describing persistent frequent attenders in australian primary healthcare. BMJ Open **5**(10), e008975 (2015)
31. Quaglio, G., et al.: E-health in Europe: current situation and challenges ahead. Health Policy Technol. **5**(4), 314–317 (2016)
32. Reisman, M.: EHRs: the challenge of making electronic data usable and interoperable. Pharm. Ther. **42**(9), 572 (2017)
33. Stroetmann, K.A., et al.: European Countries on Their Journey Towards National eHealth Infrastructures. Office for Official Publications of the European Communities, Luxembourg (2011)
34. Warner, J.L., Smith, J., Wright, A.: It's time to wikify clinical documentation: how collaborative authorship can reduce the burden and improve the quality of the electronic health record. Acad. Med. **94**(5), 645–650 (2019)

Forecast of Study Success in the STEM Disciplines Based Solely on Academic Records

Lukas Pensel(✉) and Stefan Kramer

Johannes Gutenberg-Universität Mainz, Saarstraße 21, 55122 Mainz, Germany
pensel@uni-mainz.de

Abstract. We present an approach to the forecast of the study success in selected STEM disciplines (computer science, mathematics, physics, and meteorology), solely based on the academic record of a student so far, without access to demographic or socioeconomic data. The purpose of the analysis is to improve student counseling, which may be essential for finishing a study program in one of the above mentioned fields. Technically, we show the successful use of propositionalization on relational data from educational data mining, based on standard aggregates and basic LSTM-trained aggregates.

1 Introduction

In our today's world a good higher education is required for a multitude of positions in the economy and it is a necessity in academia. But there are multiple hurdles students have to overcome during their study in order to successfully graduate. As an American study [12] shows, almost a third of students change their major at least once. Additionally, many students, especially enrolled in STEM majors, take longer than the scheduled three years to finish their bachelors. One cause for that may be the need of many students to work in addition to their study in order to sustain themselves. This takes up some amount of their preparation time for their courses, which can lead to failed exams and thus eventually to longer study times.

Those struggles lead to longer study times and therefore a higher financial burden for many students. In order to minimize the time spent by a student to graduate and therefore minimize the financial burden for the student, many universities have student counseling facilities. But often the troubled students do not visit the counselors early or even at all by themselves and rely on the counselors to find and invite them. Since searching for those students at risk by hand is a quite tedious task and often software solutions only offer very simple queries, many of those students can only be found late or not at all.

We show how educational data mining (EDM) [17] can be used to build predictive models, which can detect students at risk with a high accuracy, while minimizing the amount of regular students being predicted as risky. Additionally we show that we can achieve those high predictive performances without

P. Cellier and K. Driessens (Eds.): ECML PKDD 2019 Workshops, CCIS 1167, pp. 647–657, 2020.
https://doi.org/10.1007/978-3-030-43823-4_51

the use of any socioeconomic or demographic features and therefore without any bias related to the background, ethnicity or gender of a student, thus the prediction is solely reliant on the study history of a student. The focus of our study is on multiple STEM disciplines, in particular computer science, mathematics, physics, and meteorology. Those models are trained and validated on real student and study data of Johannes Gutenberg University Mainz (JGU)[1] and are developed to be applied by the student counselors, in order to improve their success rate in the future. The original structure of the data is relational, so relational data mining or machine learning methods are called for.

While there exists some literature on the detection of students at risk, related approaches are not applicable to our application scenario: They either focus on online course or learning systems [14,18], single departments and courses [5,8], different levels of education [13], or they are either heavily based on non-academic data [8,13,19] or hand-selected or hand-crafted features [3]. Also relational data has not really been used in EDM so far, therefore we have to apply techniques new to the context of EDM in order to optimally solve our problem.

2 Student Monitoring

2.1 Problem Statement

In order to improve the success rate of the student counseling, the discovery rate for students at risk has to be improved. Especially the students who study for several years, but drop out before they can obtain any degree, are important to discover as early as possible. Without early counseling those students go on to study an unsuitable subject for them or in a non purposeful way, instead of studying an appropriate subject in a purposeful way.

In addition to discovering those students, we also want to know *why* they are at risk. Therefore we want to find common study patterns for those students and investigate their significance to compile a list of *risk factors* for students. And in order to improve the study quality, it is of high importance for the university to find risk factors induced by the structural construction of the different studies.

2.2 Data

The data used in this project is gathered from the student management system of the JGU JOGU-StINe. It is stored in a relational database with tables for students, studies, enrollment status, courses and exams. We just consider those bachelor studies where the student enrolled between 2009 and 2013 and either successfully finished their degree or dropped out from that study. Additionally, we only looked at bachelor of science studies with computer science, math, physics or meteorology as major.

[1] The study was carried out in compliance with the EU General Data Protection Regulation (GDPR).

The subset of the features we use is represented in Table 1 and Fig. 1 shows the relations between entries. To minimize any form of bias or discrimination, we just use the entrance qualification, which can be either general or subject-specific, as student-dependent feature. For each semester of all student and study pairs, the ECTS credit points gained that semester, the credit points accumulated so far, and the enrollment status are used as features. Additionally, for each exam the type (such as oral, written, presentation, etc.), the passing status, and the numeric grade (1.0, 1.3, ... 5.0) are used.

Table 1. Data structure

Table	Attribute name	Type	About
Student and study data	student_study_id	integer	key
	university entrance qualification	categorical	used as feature
	major	categorical	used as feature
Semester data	student_study_id	integer	foreign key
	semester_id	integer	key
	credits for this semester	integer	used as feature
	cumulative credits	integer	used as feature
	enrollment status	categorical	used as feature
Exam data	student_study_id	integer	foreign key
	semester_id	integer	foreign key
	exam_id	integer	key
	type of exam	categorical	used as feature
	passing status	boolean	used as feature
	grade	numeric	used as feature

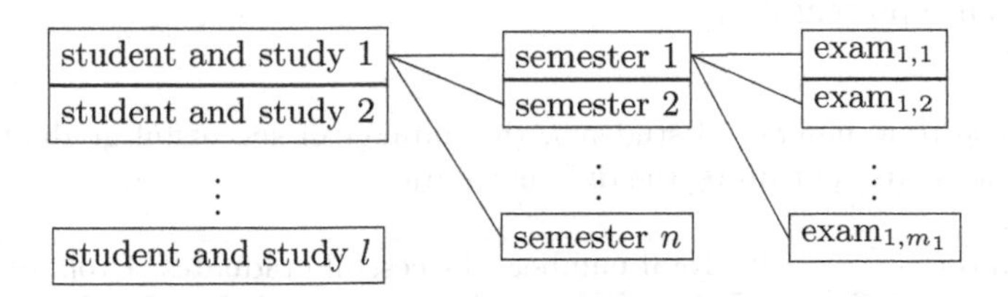

Fig. 1. Relational representation

The data used so far is quite homogeneous, since it just contains bachelor of science studies in STEM disciplines, but the system should be used for the whole university, where there are many different studies with very dissimilar structures and there are some studies with vast changes in their examination regulations throughout the years, so this has to be considered as well. Also the data before 2009 is rather inconsistent and has plenty of missing values, since JOGU-StINe was introduced in that year and prior to that system, the study records were organized by the different departments and not by a common software system.

2.3 Challenges

As described above, there are multiple challenges to cope with. First, we want to migrate as much information as possible from our database to the final models, so we need to incorporate some relational data mining techniques [16]. Second, we want to use as consistent and complete data as possible. Therefore, we just use the data from 2009 and onward. The last challenge, the differences in the structure of studies from different departments, has not been tackled yet.

3 Experiments

3.1 Data Preprocessing

From all student and study combinations, we only consider those which are not active anymore. So the student has either successfully completed the study or the student dropped from it. Further, we only consider the combinations, where the student has taken at least one exam, since it is trivial to predict the failure of a student who earns no credit points. We gather the data from those combinations as our data set X and give each entry $x \in X$ the target label $y = 1$ if the student successfully graduates and $y = 0$ otherwise. From the whole data set X multiple subsets X_n, which contain the entries of the first n semesters, are taken. The distributions of the two classes for the considered majors are presented in Table 2.

As mentioned above, the data is stored in a relational database and can therefore not be handled by standard data mining or machine learning algorithms. Our approach to solve this problem is the use of propositionalization [9] techniques, where the relational representation of the data is transformed into a propositional representation.

Table 2. The total number of students, the number of successful graduates and the number of dropouts split up by the different majors

Major	Total number	Successful graduates	Dropouts
Computer science	339	106	233
Math	380	186	194
Physics	383	219	164
Meteorology	59	29	30
Combined	1161	540	621

The first propositionalization technique we use is relational aggregations (RELAGGS) [10]. Starting from the target table, this algorithm uses foreign key relationships to discover all entries related to a specific instance. To combine those entries into a single row of data, a variety of different aggregation functions are used. We use the maximum, minimum, mean, standard deviation and sum as aggregation functions in our experiments. The schema in which the tables are combined is shown in Fig. 2.

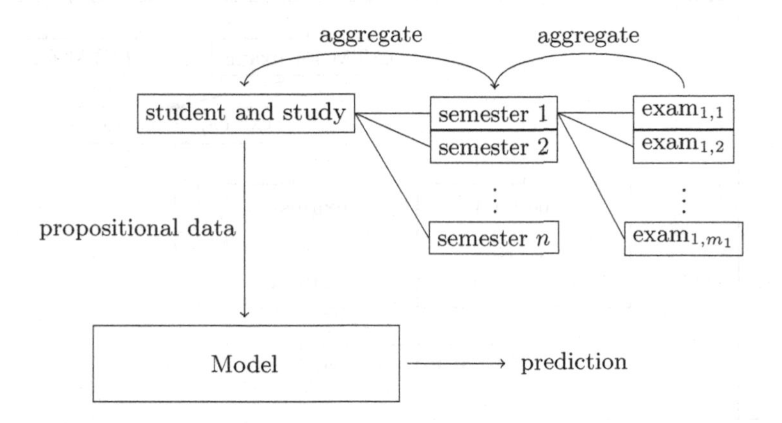

Fig. 2. Aggregation schema for the propositionalization of the data

Additionally, we try to learn useful aggregation functions, to better fit the data and therefore improve the quality of the results. Our approach for this task is the use of long short-term memory (LSTM) [6,7] networks. We feed all corresponding entries from a table, in the order in which they occur temporally, as a sequence into the LSTM and use the final output as aggregated representation of those entries. So in this case we feed all exam entries for a specific semester into an LSTM, concatenate the output with the corresponding semester entry and feed those semester entries into another LSTM, whose output is then concatenated with the student and study entry, as shown in Fig. 3. Since we can implement the LSTMs together with a multilayer perceptron (MLP) in a single network, we are able to jointly train the classifier and the aggregation functions. Therefore we should be able to increase the predictive performance in contrast to the generic aggregation performed by the RELAGGS algorithm. Unfortunately, we can only use this technique with a MLP as classifier so far.

3.2 Classification

Our goal is to find students at risk of dropping out with a high rate of success, which is the task to optimally classify students as either successful graduates ($y = 1$) or dropouts ($y = 0$). So we use random forests [2], linear support vector

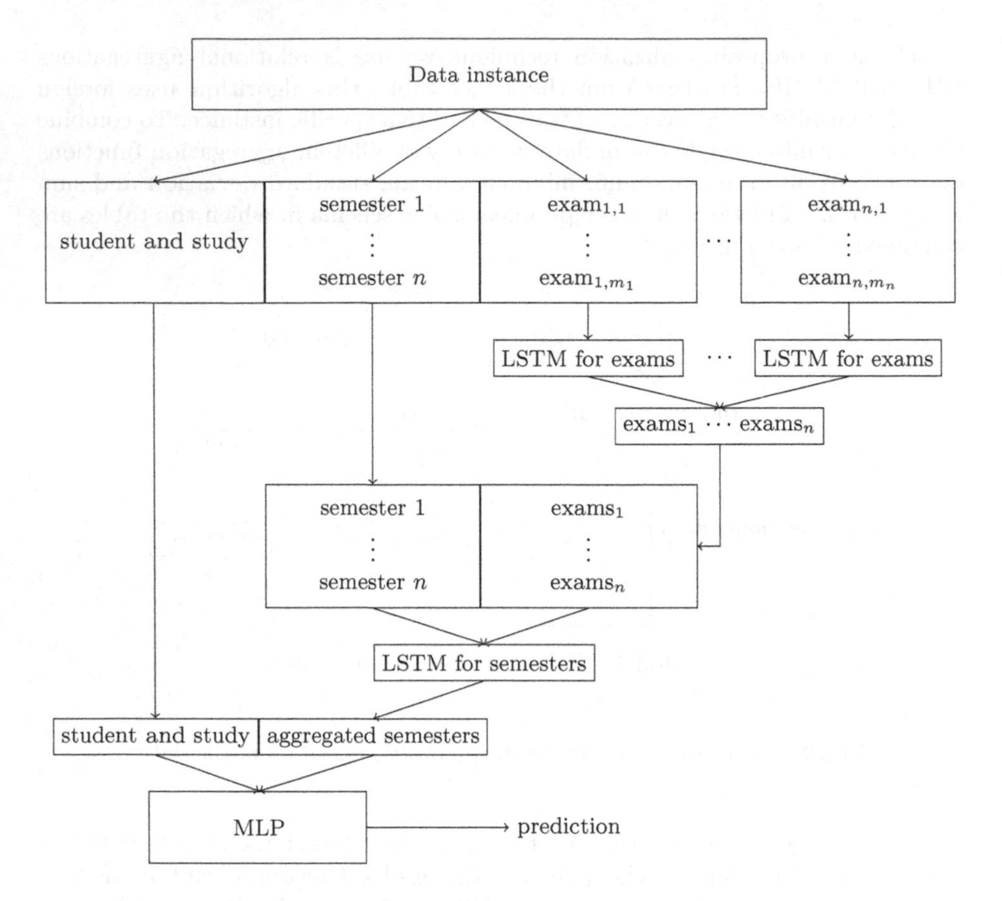

Fig. 3. Aggregation-Network using LSTMs

machines (SVM) and MLPs as classifiers in conjunction with the data propositionalized using RELAGGS and MLPs together with the LSTMs for propositionalization. For the random forests and SVMs we use the scikit-learn [15] implementations and the MLPs and LSTMs are implemented using Keras [4] with TensorFlow [1] as backend.

To validate our results. We use a ten-fold cross validation (CV) with a small grid search for hyper parameter tuning, which are described in Table 3. The hyper parameters for each fold are chosen by the area under the Receiver Operating Characteristic curve (ROC AUC) over a three-fold CV. The ten-fold CV is run for each of the first four semesters as cutoff (X_1, X_2, X_3 and X_4) and for each classifier setup the mean accuracy, ROC AUC, accuracy restricted to $y = 0$ and restricted to $y = 1$ are calculated. Since we want to have a high purity of our classification results, we additionally calculate the mean positive predictive value

(PPV), also called precision, defined by Eq. 1, and the mean negative predictive value (NPV), analogously defined, by Eq. 2.

$$\text{PPV} = \text{Precision} = \frac{\text{number of true positives}}{\text{number of true positives} + \text{number of false negatives}} \quad (1)$$

$$\text{NPV} = \frac{\text{number of true negatives}}{\text{number of true negatives} + \text{number of false positives}} \quad (2)$$

Table 3. Tested hyper parameters

Algorithm	Parameter	Values
Random forest	Number of trees	100, 1000, 10000
	Number of features	"sqrt", "log2", 0.1, 0.33
SVM	C value	0.01, 0.1, 1, 10
MLP	Dense layers	(100, 100, 50, 25), (200, 100, 100, 50, 25)
	Number of training epochs	10, 20
LSTM	Size of exam LSTMs	1×, 2× size of exam entry
	Size of semester LSTMs	1×, 2× size of semester entry

In Table 4, the results for each tested data set and algorithm are presented. As one would expect, the results improve with the number of considered semesters, so that we find over 90% of all dropouts and have under 10% of future graduates in our risk group after four semesters. But already after one semester, we can correctly predict about 80% of all dropouts and only 20% of the predicted dropouts are actually successful graduates. In Fig. 4a and b we can see that the improvement of the results diminishes with higher semester cutoffs. This is probably caused by the higher difference in passed exams between the future graduates and the future dropouts.

The results for all algorithms are quite close to each other and there is no clear best algorithm found for this task. Considering the rather small hyper parameter space that was searched during optimization and the small size of the data set in contrast to the large number of trainable parameters, especially for the LSTM and MLP combination, further experiments with larger parameter spaces and optimally more data have to be conducted, in order to come to a definite conclusion about the best algorithm for the task.

3.3 Reasoning

In addition to finding students at risk we also want know what is the reasoning behind the prediction. To achieve this we look at the feature importance given by the random forest and the coefficients of the SVM. The five features with the highest importance, hence the features with the biggest influence on the random

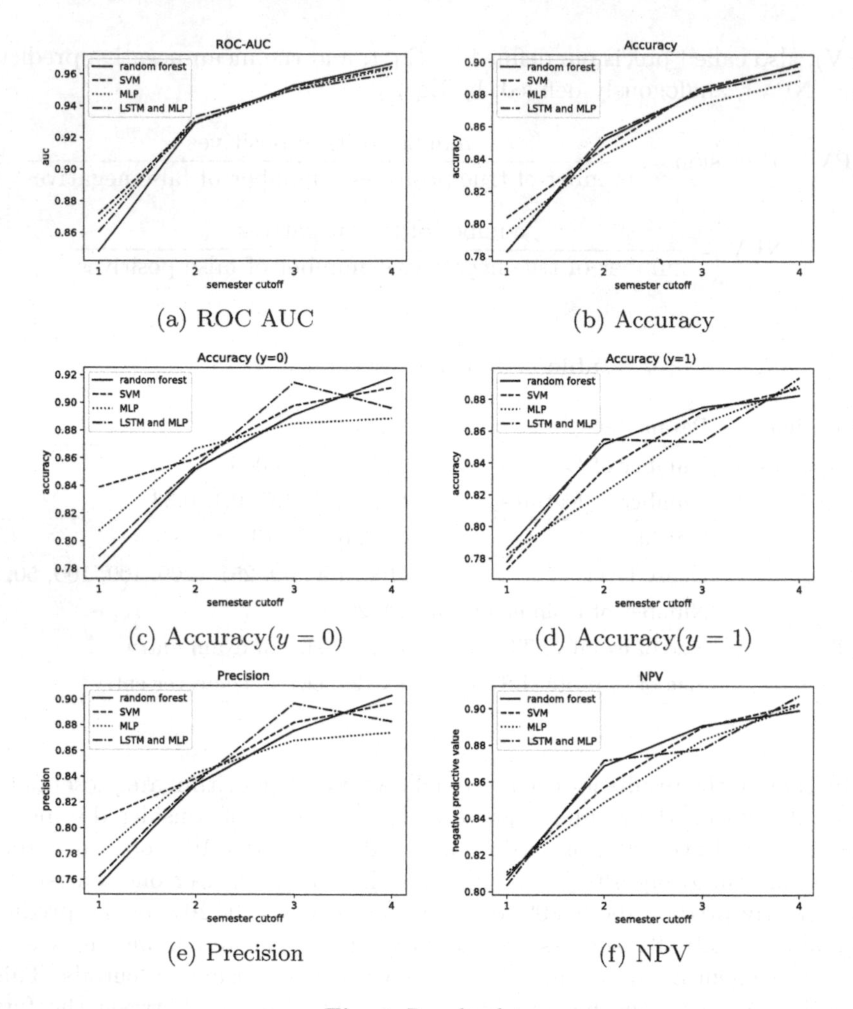

(a) ROC AUC (b) Accuracy

(c) Accuracy($y = 0$) (d) Accuracy($y = 1$)

(e) Precision (f) NPV

Fig. 4. Result plots

forest classification, as well as the sign of the corresponding SVM coefficient, which is also the sign of the correlation between the feature and the target, are presented in Table 5. Since high numeric grades are worse in Germany, it is reasonable that the grade is negatively correlated to the successful graduation. The passing status is encoded in such a way that 0 indicates a success and 1 a fail, and therefore also negatively correlated with the graduation. Interesting is the positive coefficient of the written exam for the first three semester cutoffs, which changes into a negative coefficient in the fourth. This anomaly is probably caused by the more frequent attending of repetitive exams by the students at risk compared to successful graduating students.

Table 4. Results

Data set	Algorithm	ROC AUC	Accuracy	Accuracy ($y = 0$)	Accuracy ($y = 1$)	Precision	NPV
X_1	Random forest	0.848	0.783	0.78	0.786	0.756	0.807
	SVM	0.872	0.804	0.839	0.773	0.807	0.809
	MLP	0.867	0.794	0.807	0.782	0.779	0.811
	LSTM and MLP	0.86	0.783	0.789	0.778	0.762	0.803
X_2	Random forest	0.929	0.852	0.852	0.852	0.833	0.869
	SVM	0.93	0.847	0.859	0.836	0.838	0.857
	MLP	0.929	0.842	0.867	0.821	0.843	0.849
	LSTM and MLP	0.933	0.854	0.854	0.855	0.835	0.872
X_3	Random forest	0.953	0.883	0.892	0.875	0.876	0.891
	SVM	0.952	0.885	0.898	0.873	0.882	0.89
	MLP	0.95	0.874	0.885	0.865	0.868	0.883
	LSTM and MLP	0.95	0.882	0.915	0.853	0.897	0.878
X_4	Random forest	0.967	0.899	0.919	0.882	0.903	0.899
	SVM	0.965	0.898	0.911	0.887	0.897	0.903
	MLP	0.964	0.889	0.889	0.889	0.874	0.902
	LSTM and MLP	0.96	0.895	0.896	0.894	0.883	0.907

4 Discussion

The results show that successfully identifying students at risk is very doable, even without almost any knowledge about the background of a student, just by using data about the course of the respective study. This is very much in contrast to other research in that field [5,8,11,13,19], where demographic and socioeconomic data plays a large role. And compared with the results of other related work, our approach performs equally or better regarding the range of several performance measures. Another special feature of our approach is the inclusion of the relational structure into the process. Usually just a few aggregated features, such as the grade point average (GPA), are used in the classification of students at risk, but we use a rather extensive amount of aggregated features derived from the structure of the data by the RELAGGS algorithm or the even more sophisticated LSTM aggregation.

The current student counseling at the JGU is mostly voluntary for students. Therefore, some sort of risk potential shown to the students could increase the rate of students who use the voluntary counseling. Additionally, simple and conclusive rules could be extracted from the models and those could be added to the regulations as deciding factors for mandatory student counseling.

Table 5. Results

Data set	Top features ranked by importance	SVM coefficient sign
X_1	Grade	-
	Cumulative credit points	+
	Credit points per semester	+
	Type of exam: written exam	+
	Passing status	-
X_2	Cumulative credit points	+
	Credit points per semester	+
	Type of exam: written exam	+
	Grade	-
	Passing status	-
X_3	Cumulative credit points	+
	Credit points per semester	+
	Type of exam: written exam	+
	Grade	-
	Passing status	-
X_4	Cumulative credit points	+
	Credit points per semester	+
	Grade	-
	Type of exam: written exam	-
	Type of exam: active participation	-

5 Future Work and Conclusion

Our goal is to build a system for the whole university, therefore more and especially structural different studies have to be incorporated. The next step in that direction will be the incorporation of some two subject bachelors, which have a big structural difference to the so far used single subject bachelors.

Another important next step is the continued research on the learned aggregation functions using LSTMs. To exploit the full potential of this method, further experiments on different relational data sets have to be conducted and other network topologies and improved implementations have to be tested.

Acknowledgements. This research has been funded by the Federal Ministry of Education and Research of Germany in the framework of Lehren, Organisieren, Beraten: Gelingensbedingungen von Bologna (LOB) (project number 01PL17055).

References

1. Abadi, M., et al.: TensorFlow: large-scale machine learning on heterogeneous systems (2015). Software available from https://www.tensorflow.org/

2. Breiman, L.: Random forests. Mach. Learn. **45**(1), 5–32 (2001). https://doi.org/10.1023/A:1010933404324
3. Chanlekha, H., Niramitranon, J.: Student performance prediction model for early-identification of at-risk students in traditional classroom settings. In: Proceedings of the 10th International Conference on Management of Digital EcoSystems, MEDES 2018, pp. 239–245. ACM, New York (2018). https://doi.org/10.1145/3281375.3281403
4. Chollet, F., et al.: Keras (2015). https://keras.io
5. Dekker, G.W., Pechenizkiy, M., Vleeshouwers, J.M.: Predicting students drop out: a case study. In: International Working Group on Educational Data Mining (2009)
6. Gers, F.A., Schmidhuber, J., Cummins, F.: Learning to forget: continual prediction with LSTM. Neural Comput. **12**, 2451–2471 (1999)
7. Hochreiter, S., Schmidhuber, J.: Long short-term memory. Neural Comput. **9**, 1735–1780 (1997). https://doi.org/10.1162/neco.1997.9.8.1735
8. Kovai, Z.J.: Predicting student success by mining enrolment data. Res. High. Educ. J. **15**, 1–20 (2012)
9. Kramer, S., Lavrač, N., Flach, P.: Propositionalization approaches to relational data mining. In: Džeroski, S., Lavrač, N. (eds.) Relational Data Mining, pp. 262–291. Springer, Heidelberg (2001). https://doi.org/10.1007/978-3-662-04599-2_11
10. Krogel, M.A., Wrobel, S.: Facets of aggregation approaches to propositionalization. In: Horvath, T., Yamamoto, A. (eds.) Work-in-Progress Track at the Thirteenth International Conference on Inductive Logic Programming (ILP) (2003)
11. Lauría, E.J.M., Baron, J.D., Devireddy, M., Sundararaju, V., Jayaprakash, S.M.: Mining academic data to improve college student retention: an open source perspective. In: Proceedings of the 2nd International Conference on Learning Analytics and Knowledge, LAK 2012, pp. 139–142. ACM, New York (2012). https://doi.org/10.1145/2330601.2330637
12. Leu, K.: Beginning college students who change their majors within 3 years of enrollment. Data Point. NCES 2018–434. National Center for Education Statistics (2017)
13. Márquez-Vera, C., Cano, A., Romero, C., Ventura, S.: Predicting studentfailure at school using genetic programming and different data miningapproaches with high dimensional and imbalanced data. Appl. Intell. **38**(3), 315–330 (2013). https://doi.org/10.1007/s10489-012-0374-8
14. Olive, D.M., Huynh, D.Q., Reynolds, M., Dougiamas, M., Wiese, D.: A quest for a one-size-fits-all neural network: early prediction of students at risk in online courses. TLT **12**(2), 171–183 (2019). https://doi.org/10.1109/TLT.2019.2911068
15. Pedregosa, F., et al.: Scikit-learn: machine learning in Python. J. Mach. Learn. Res. **12**, 2825–2830 (2011)
16. Raedt, L.D.: Logical and Relational Learning. Cognitive Technologies. Springer, Heidelberg (2008). https://doi.org/10.1007/978-3-540-68856-3
17. Romero, C., Ventura, S.: Educational data mining: a review of the state of the art. IEEE Trans. Syst. Man Cybern. Part C (Appl. Rev.) **40**(6), 601–618 (2010)
18. Shelton, B.E., Yang, J., Hung, J.-L., Du, X.: Two-stage predictive modeling for identifying at-risk students. In: Wu, T.-T., Huang, Y.-M., Shadieva, R., Lin, L., Starčič, A.I. (eds.) ICITL 2018. LNCS, vol. 11003, pp. 578–583. Springer, Cham (2018). https://doi.org/10.1007/978-3-319-99737-7_61
19. Zhou, Q., Quan, W., Zhong, Y., Xiao, W., Mou, C., Wang, Y.: Predicting high-risk students using internet access logs. Knowl. Inf. Syst. **55**(2), 393–413 (2018). https://doi.org/10.1007/s10115-017-1086-5

Improving Access to Science for Social Good

Mehdi Ali[1,2](✉), Sahar Vahdati[1,3](✉), Shruti Singh[4], Sourish Dasgupta[4], and Jens Lehmann[1,2]

[1] Smart Data Analytics Group (SDA), University of Bonn, Bonn, Germany
{mehdi.ali,vahdati,jens.lehmann}@cs.uni-bonn.de
[2] Fraunhofer IAIS, St. Augustin, Dresden, Germany
{mehdi.ali,jens.lehmann}@iais.fraunhofer.de
[3] University of Oxford, Oxford, UK
sahar.vahdati@cs.ox.ac.uk
[4] Rygbee Inc., Delaware City, DE, USA
{shruti.singh,sourish.dasgupta}@raxter.io
http://sda.tech
http://iais.fraunhofer.de

Abstract. One of the major goals of science is to make the world socially a good place to live. The old paradigm of scholarly communication through publishing has generated enormous amount of heterogeneous data and metadata. However, most of the scientific results are not easily discoverable, in particular those results which benefit social good and are also targeted by non-scientists. In this paper, we showcase a knowledge graph embedding (KGE) based recommendation system to be used by students involved in activities aiming at social good. The proposed recommendation system has been trained on a scholarly knowledge graph constructed for this specific goal. The obtained results highlight that the KGEs successfully encoded the structure of the KG, and therefore, our system could provide valuable recommendations.

Keywords: Machine learning · Knowledge graph embeddings · Social good

1 Introduction

People with different backgrounds ranging from school students to high profile professionals around the world are engaged in several initiatives such as political movements, environmental protection and fund-raising with the goal to achieve individual, community and society well-being [21]. One example is the *Fridays For Future* movement which was initiated by the young student Greta Thunberg to demonstrate against Swedens climate policy [40]. One of her main demands has been that the actions of the government of Sweden should become sufficient in order to comply with the essence of the Paris Agreement. Her initiative has quickly gained a lot of attention and initiated demonstrations

P. Cellier and K. Driessens (Eds.): ECML PKDD 2019 Workshops, CCIS 1167, pp. 658–673, 2020.
https://doi.org/10.1007/978-3-030-43823-4_52

all over Europe, and later in different countries around the world. Greta Thunberg is an illustrative example of a young school student who recognized some of the scientific findings with regards to the climate change and understood its importance for the social good: "We want politicians to listen to the scientists"[1], "Why should I be studying for a future that soon may be no more, when no one is doing anything to save that future?". While scientists increasingly have been called to share research findings about climate change [47], many other topics that are relevant to social good do not have a comparable media presence. For this reason, the information needs of activists that are non-experts may remain unsatisfied with regards to these topics. However, information technology and the digitization of scientific artifacts haves increased the amount of available scientific resources and offer a great potential to fulfill the information needs of activists that are concerned about social good. An overwhelming amount of scientific artifacts such as publications and their metadata have been made available independent of any geographical or temporal constraints on the web [6,21,52]. However, for non-experts the effective access to these artifacts is limited. While there are already existing services such as Google Scholar (GS) to explore and retrieve scientific publications, they alone are not sufficient to effectively fulfill the information needs of non-expert activists. One of the main reasons is the discrepancy between their search behaviors and the functionality of these services: GS expects specific search queries in order to provide relevant content on the first result page whereas non-experts (for instance undergraduate students) tend to use simple keyword or phrase queries, do not refine their search queries (e.g. by analyzing metadata), and usually ignore retrieved results beyond the first result page [10,20]. In addition, search engines and services such as Google Scholar are not developed with the specific goal of providing access to content related to social good. Therefore, there is a need for a domain-specific system that can be effectively used by non-experts to access scientific content related to social good.

An approach to structure related knowledge that can be used to perform concept-based retrieval instead of string matching are knowledge graphs (KGs) [6,25] which represent information as a set of triples of the form $(h, r, t) \in KG$ where h and t represent entities and r their relation. Recently, knowledge graph embeddings (KGEs) that encode the entities and relations of a KG into vector spaces while maintaining structural characteristics of the KG became popular. These embeddings can be used for several downstream machine learning tasks including recommendation systems.

In this paper, we present a recommender system that suggests for an entity of interest (i.e., publication, author, domain and venue) a set of related entities which helps users to effectively find relevant content related to the topic of social good from the large amount of available information. Our contributions are: (i.) a KG that contains information about publications, domains, authors and venues. We focused on publications that are related to real-world problems such as climate change, marine litter, right movement and cyber security, (ii.) a

[1] https://www.fridaysforfuture.org/greta-speeches#greta_fullspeech_feb21_2019.

baseline recommender system that exploits KGEs to provide recommendations. We trained four different KGE models i.e., TransE, TransR, TransD and ComplEx, and selected TransE to provide recommendations that have been manually evaluated. While the general approach can be transferred to different domains, the proposed recommender system is domain-specific.

In the following, we give an overview of the related work (Sect. 2), explain the KGE models that are relevant in the context of this work (Sect. 3), describe the process of creating our KG (Sect. 4), present our recommendation system (Sect. 5), explain our performed experiments (Sect. 6), discuss the limitations of our system and point out future work (Sect. 7), and finally, we give a short summary of this work (Sect. 8).

2 Related Work

Through the development of specialized search engines, digital libraries, databases and social networks for the scholarly domain, the availability of scientific artifacts and their metadata has been facilitated. Google Scholar[2] is an online search engine that has been realized in 2004 and enables users to search for both, the printed and digital version of articles. Aminer[3] provides a faceted browser on top of its mining service for researchers. *ResearchGate*[4] is a social network for researchers in which they can present their scientific profiles, their publications and interact with each other. *Mendeley*[5] is a desktop service with a web program created by Elsevier for managing and sharing research papers. There are several efforts to provide enhanced services by representing metadata of scholarly artifacts in a structured form. A crowd-sourcing platform for metadata management of scholarly artifacts is introduced in [43], and the representation of metadata in a semantic format is proposed in [3]. In Chi *et al.* [6] a knowledge graph and a metadata management system for smart education is presented. However, most of these services either lack a systematic recommendation service or provide specialized suggestions based on user profiles. To the best of our knowledge (apart from dedicated journals and university libraries [48]) the domain of social science lacks a comprehensive and specialized knowledge graph with analytical and recommendation services on top. In a recent work, an embedding based recommendation system for books has been proposed. However, the recommendations are limited to a single entity type, i.e. books. In this study and the follow up work, we aim to provide a comprehensive and domain-specific system in order to assist users in finding relevant artifacts of different types. Through the use of machine learning approaches, the system proposes recommendations that are beyond simple keyword-matching based recommendations.

[2] https://scholar.google.de/.
[3] https://www.aminer.org/.
[4] https://www.researchgate.net/.
[5] https://www.mendeley.com/.

3 Knowledge Graph Embeddings

Knowledge graph embedding models can be roughly divided into *translational distance models* and *semantic matching models.* Translational distance models compute the plausibility of a triple based on distance function (e.g. based on the Euclidean distance) and semantic matching models determine the plausibility of a triple by comparing the similarity of the latent features of the entities and relations [45]. In the following, we describe KGE models that are relevant in the context of this work, however many others have been proposed.

TransE. An established *translational distance model* is TransE [5] that models a relation r as the translation from head entity h to the tail entity t:

$$h + r \approx t \tag{1}$$

To measure the plausibility of a triple, following scoring function is defined:

$$f_r(h,t) = -\|h + r - t\| \tag{2}$$

Besides its simplicity, TransE is computational efficient, and can therefore be applied to large scale KGs. However, TransE is limited in modeling 1-N, N-1 and N-M relations. For this reason, several extensions have been proposed [45].

TransH. TransH [45] is an extension of TransE that addresses the limitations of TransE in modeling N-M relations. Each relation is represented by an additional hyperplane, and the translation from the head to the tail entity is performed in the relation specific hyperplane. First, the head and tail entities are projected into the relation specific hyperplane:

$$h_\perp = h - w_r^\top h w_r \tag{3}$$

$$t_\perp = t - w_r^\top t w_r \tag{4}$$

where w_r is the normal vector of the hyperplane. After projecting the head and tail entity, the plausibility of the triple *(h,r,t)* is computed:

$$f_r(h,t) = -\|h_\perp + d_r - t_\perp\|_2^2 \tag{5}$$

where d_r is the relation specific translation vector lying in the relation specific hyperplane.

TransR. TransR [45] is an extension of TransH that encodes entities and relations in contrast to TransE and TransH, in different vector spaces. Each relation is represented by a matrix M_r that is used to project the entities into the relational specific space:

$$h_r = hM_r \tag{6}$$

$$t_r = tM_r \tag{7}$$

Consequently, the scoring function is defined as:

$$f_r(h,t) = -\|h_r + r - t_r\|_2^2 \tag{8}$$

TransD. TransD [15] is an extension of TransR that uses fewer parameters than TransR. It also eliminates the involvement of matrix-vector multiplications. Entities and relations are represented by two vectors, of which h, r, t encode the semantics of the entities/relations, and h_p, r_p, t_p are used to construct projection matrices which project the entities in relation specific spaces:

$$M_{rh} = r_p h_p^T + I^{m \times n} \tag{9}$$

$$M_{rt} = r_p t_p^T + I^{m \times n}, \tag{10}$$

where I is a matrix where the values of the diagonal elements are 1 and 0 elsewhere (in case of $m = n$, I is the identity matrix). These matrices are used to compute the projections of the head and tail entity:

$$h_\perp = M_{rh} h \tag{11}$$

$$t_\perp = M_{rt} t \tag{12}$$

Based on the projected entities, the score of the triple (h, r, t) is computed:

$$f_r(h, t) = -\|h_\perp + r - t_\perp\|_2^2 \tag{13}$$

RESCAL. RESCAL [24] is a *semantic matching model* that represents each entity as a vector and each relation as a matrix, M_r. It uses the following scoring function:

$$f_r(h, t) = h^T M_r t \tag{14}$$

The relation matrix, M_r, encodes pairwise interactions between the features of the head and tail entities.

DistMult. DistMult [50] simplifies RESCAL by allowing only diagonal matrices:

$$f_r(h, t) = h^T diag(r) t \tag{15}$$

where $r \in R^d$ and $M_r = diag(r)$. The restriction to diagonal matrices makes DistMult more computationally efficient than RESCAL, but also less expressive compared to RESCAL.

ComplEx. ComplEx [42] is an extension of DistMult into the complex space. Considering the scoring function of DistMult (Eq. 15), it can be observed that it has a limitation in representing anti-symmetric relations since $h^T diag(r) t$ is equivalent to $t^T diag(r) h$. Equation 15 can be written in terms of the Hadamard product of h, r, t: $< h, r, t > = \sum_{i=1}^{d} h_i * r_i * t_i$, where $h, r, t \in R^d$. The scoring function of ComplEx uses the Hadamard product in the complex space, i.e. $h, r, t \in C^d$:

$$f_r(h, t) = \Re(\sum_{i=1}^{d} h_i * r_i * \overline{t_i}) \tag{16}$$

where $\Re(x)$ represents the real part of a complex number and $\overline{x}$ its conjugate. It is straightforward to show that $f_r(h, t) \neq f_r(t, h)$, i.e. ComplEx is capable of modeling anti-symmetric relations.

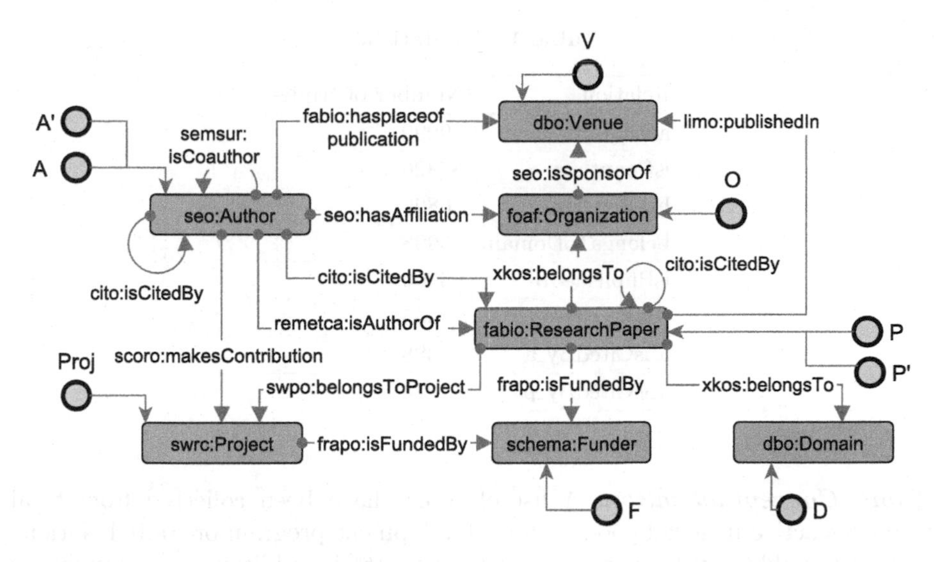

Fig. 1. KG schema for social good. The graph shows a snapshot of schema for our KG with core entities and relations between them

4 Knowledge Graph Creation

As a first step, we created a scientific KG that gathers information relevant for social good which we used as a basis for providing recommendations. We defined the following requirements for the KG:

- R1 The KG should contain publications with a focus on topics related to social good (e.g. climate change, social initiatives, political movements etc.)
- R2 The KG should contain sufficient metadata to provide qualitative recommendations.
- R3 The KG should be sufficiently large to allow conclusive insights about the applicability of modern machine learning methods.

To create the KG, the following steps were performed: (i.) *Domain Conceptualization*, (ii.) *Topic Conceptualization*, (iii.) *Data collection* and *Data Curation.*

Domain Conceptualization. Reusing already existing ontologies, we modeled possible characteristics of KGs related to social good (see Fig. 1). The model is defined generic enough to support researchers gaining an overview of the domain, to define new KGs. The model can be exploited by machines as an additional source of knowledge. Due to the lack of FAIR data [49] in scientific artifacts of social good topics, currently our KG does not contain all types and relations described in the schema. Overall, seven core classes have been identified, namely *Papers*, *Venues*, *Authors*, *Organizations*, *Funders*, *Domains* and *Projects*. Furthermore, eight relationship types have been defined between these classes (see Fig. 1) (Table 1).

Table 1. KG Statistics

Relation	Number of triples
authorOf	9090
isCoauthor	37326
hasPaperIn	6820
belongsToDomain	3998
isPublishedIn	3000
p_isCitedBy_p	355
a_isCitedBy_a	4388
a_isCitedBy_p	1225

Topic Conceptualization. A list of topics have been collected from focal resources active in social good such as development program of United Nation[6] and sustainable development goals for 2030 [16] in addition to a systematic exploration on the Web. The topics have been short listed into four distinct categories as *climate change, political movements, marine/sea litter and cyber security.* This list have been used in the follow up steps of this work.

Listing 1.1. Raw metadata 1. JSON representation of original metadata.


```
*Paper1: {"title": T1,  "publication_venue": V1,
"citation_number": "50","doc_id": 7931d391-...dd32e50e8959,
"source_name": S1, "venue_id": 34544,
"raw_text": RW1, "authors": [A1, A2, A3],
"keywords":[ Social Science, ..., Climate Change],
"publisher": P1,  literature_type": Journal,
"source_url": [U1, U2, U3, U4],
"date": 2015-01-01,  "doi": 10.1016/...,
"references": [R1, R2, R3, R4 ]}*
*Paper2: { ...  }*
...
```


Data Collection. The data was collected using web crawlers of the RAx[7] platform which has reached to index metadata of 160+ million research paper. Based on the keywords, an exemplary dataset of 4004 matched papers has been extracted. The data was initially stored in JSON format (Listing 1.1), which we converted into a set of triples (Listing 1.2) representing our KG. KGs not only enable to represent data in form of triples, but also the metadata. For instance, for an entity representing a paper, we created triples of the form *(Paper1, belongsToDomain, Environmental Studies)* or *(Author1, authorOf, Paper1).*

[6] https://www.undp.org/.
[7] https://raxter.io.

Listing 1.2. TSV representation of metadata. The KG in TSV format is used as input for the embedding models.

```
e9391a29-.... "belongsToDomain" Environmental studies.
Alan C. York "isCoauthor" G. J. Cary
Alan Manning "authorOf" 7604c5dc-...
Alark Saxena "hasPaperIn" Journal of Resources, Energy,
                          and Development
05607dab-... "p_isCitedBy_p" 635c28c3-...
05832950-... "isPublishedIn" International Womens Studies
A Allen "a_isCitedBy_a" Caroline S.E. Homer
```

5 System Description

The input to our workflow is a KG based on which a set of recommendations are computed in two major steps (Fig. 2): (i.) learning the KGEs and (ii.) generating the recommendations based on the KGEs.

Learning the KGEs. In order to learn KGEs on the constructed scholarly KG for social good, we utilize the software package PyKEEN [1] which integrates several KGE models. The learned embeddings encode structured knowledge represented in the KG. In the context of this work, we focused on the models TransE, TransD, TransR and ComplEx. The learned embeddings have been used as a basis for computing the recommendations.

Generating Recommendations. For each seed entity that can be any entity in the KG (a publication, an author or a venue), the n nearest neighbors have been computed using the Euclidean norm (however, any similarity measure can

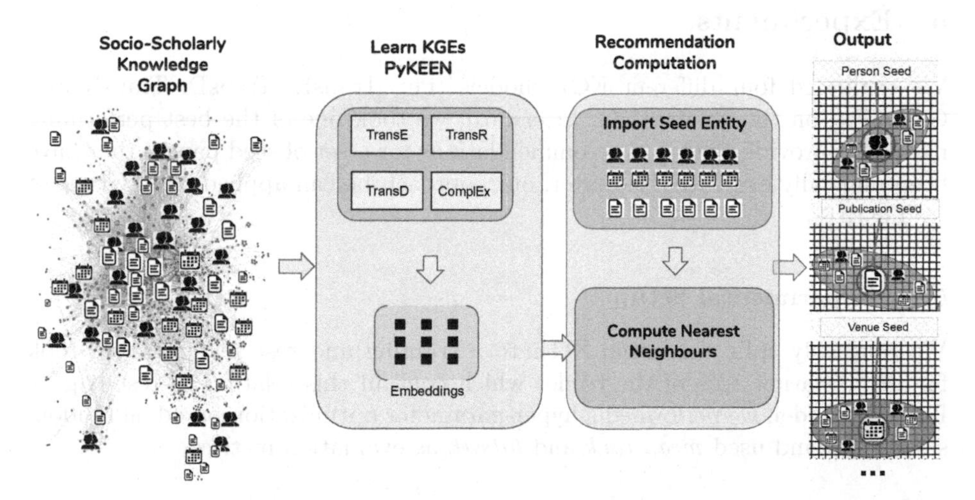

Fig. 2. A pipeline of recommendation services. (i) embedded KG into latent feature space, (ii) filter publications based on KGEs, (iii) filter publications based on embeddings of their abstracts.

be applied) and provided as recommendations. The recommendations for a seed publication can be for example the list of researchers who co-authored other publications with the authors in the seed publication, related publications or venues. The system is able to provide recommendations that represent n-hop dependencies in the KG. In turn, the provided recommendations can be used as seed entities to access information that represents long-term dependencies in the KG. The described steps don't require any complex traversing of the graph, instead, simple arithmetic operations are applied on the learned embeddings (Fig. 3).

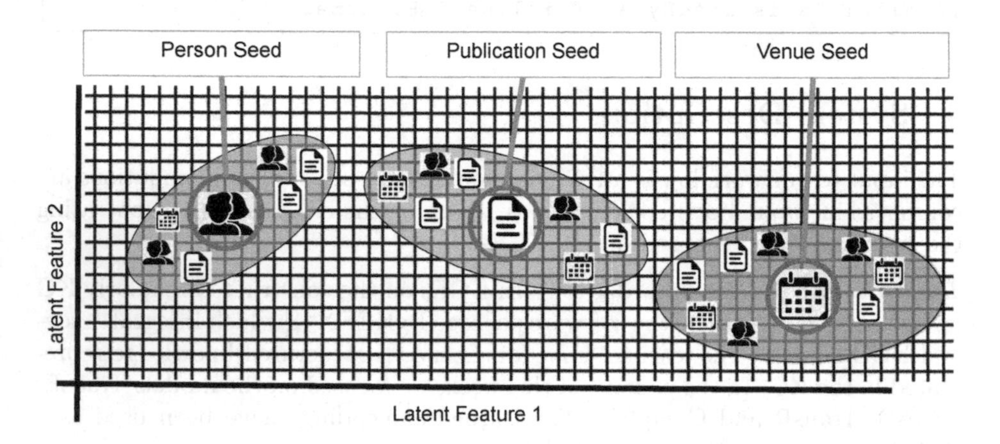

Fig. 3. Recommendations per seed entities. For every seed entity type, a number of different recommendations are given.

6 Experiments

We evaluated four different KGE models (i.e., TransE, TransD, TransR and ComplEx) on the created KG. Afterward, we took one of the best performing models to provide the top n recommendations for a set of seed papers that have been manually evaluated. However, our approach be can applied on any type of seed entities.

6.1 Experimental Setup

We randomly split the initial KG into a training and test set where we took for each relation 10% of the triples which contain this relation as test triples. For each model, we performed a hyper-parameter optimization based on random search [11] and used *mean rank* and *hits@k* as evaluation metrics.

6.2 Evaluation of the KGE Models

All the models have been trained based on the *open world assumption*, i.e., triples that are not part of the KG are not considered as non-existing, but as unknowns [25]. Therefore, we created artificial negative samples based on the negative sampling approach described by Bordes *et al.* [5]. For TransE, TransR and TransD the *margin ranking loss* that maximizes the distance between a positive and a corresponding negative triple [25] was applied, and for ComplEx and ComplEx* the *softplus loss* [42] was used. Furthermore, for all models except for ComplEx* one negative per each positive example, and for ComplEx* 10 negatives per each positive example were created in every forward step (Table 2).

Table 2. HPO results.

Model	Mean rank	Hits@10
TransE [5]	90.63	91.22%
TransD [15]	443.84	6.43%
TransR [17]	397.02	43.63%
ComplEx [42]	267.91	83.00%
ComplEx* [42]	141.64	93.66%

It can be observed that TransE and ComplEx* performed very well (Fig. 1). The high performance of TransE can be explained due to the fact that for most of the unique (subject, relation) and (relation, object)-pairs, there exists exactly one corresponding entity (subject/object) (77,72%/70.05% of the unique pairs). TransE even outperformed ComplEx when using only one negative for each positive example. However, for ComplEx only a few iterations of hyper-parameter optimization have been performed, and therefore, it is worthy to extend the hyper-parameter search. Similarly, the results of TransR and TransD might improve when applying a more extensive hyper-parameter search.

6.3 Recommendation of Related Information

Based on the results of the experiments, the TransE model has been selected to be used to compute and evaluate recommendations for a set of seed publications (Table 3 shows the titles, domains and venues of our seed papers). We chose TransE instead of ComplEx*, because it performed similarly and ComplEx(*) provides for each entity two vector representations those efficient combination should be investigated in more depth in a future work.

Table 4 includes the validated recommendations for two of our seed papers from which one belongs to the domain of *Environmental Studies* and the second to the domain of *Social Science*. The recommendations are sorted according to their scores in descending order, i.e. the first recommendation received the highest score. For each recommended artifact, we performed a manual evaluation

Table 3. Selected seed publications.

Domain	Title	Venue
Social Science	Cyber Bullying Detection Using Social and Textual Analysis [14]	System Analysis And Modeling
Social Science	Social Media, Indian Youth and Cyber Terrorism Awareness: A Comparative Analysis [23]	Journal of Mass Communication and Journalism
Social Science	Expansion of Social Assistance: Does Politics Matter? [30]	Economic and Political Weekly
Environmental studies	Reducing the impact of climate change [13]	Bulletin of The World Health Organization
Environmental studies	General Chemistry Students' Understanding of Climate Change and the Chemistry Related to Climate Change [44]	Journal of Chemical Education

by looking them up in Google Scholar (the most used search engine for scholarly artifacts), and analysing their metadata. Among the recommendations there were obvious recommendations such as the authors of the seed papers (which we removed from the list of recommendations), irrelevant recommendations such as recommendation (1) for the first seed paper, related publications (e.g. recommendation (2) and (3) for the first seed paper), co-authors of the authors of a seed paper (such as "Manfred Hauswirth") for the fist seed paper). Similar patterns can be detected in the recommendations for the second seed paper. The results highlight that relevant artifacts are recommended by the system. The recommendations indicate that the KGEs preserved the structure of the KG, for instance: (i) "Manfred Hauswirth" is a co-author of the authors of first seed paper, (ii) recommendation (1) that represents a publication, cites two of the authors of the seed paper ("Cory Andrew Henson", and "Vivek Kumar Singh"). Furthermore, it seems that the model has been able to distinguish entity types since the top recommendations usually represented publications for seed publications. While our evaluation approach indicates that the system is capable of providing relevant recommendations, involving external participants in the evaluation procedure will provide important insights regarding the effectiveness of our proposed system. In particular, we aim to perform a user study with expert and non-expert participants in order to analyse whether their information needs to topics related to social good can be fulfilled more effectively by using the proposed system. Because our work represents a preliminary work and such an evaluation requires an extensive preparation, we plan to target the described evaluation in a future work.

Table 4. Recommendation for selected seed publications.

Recommendations for Cyber Bullying Detection Using Social and Textual Analysis [14]	Type
(1) Physical-cyber-social computing: An early 21st century approach [37]	Paper
(2) Physical cyber social computing for human experience [37]	Paper
(3) Physical-Cyber-Social Computing (Dagstuhl Reports 13402) [38]	Paper
(4) Transatlantic Social Politics: 1800-Present [34]	Paper
(5) System-level design optimization for security-critical cyber-physical-social systems [53]	Paper
(6) Cybermatics: Cyber–physical–social–thinking hyperspace based science and technology [27]	Paper
(7) A cloud-edge computing framework for cyber-physical-social services [46]	Paper
(8) Guest Editorial Data Mining in Cyber, Physical, and Social Computing [18]	Paper
(9) Cyber-physical-social based security architecture for future internet of things [26]	Paper
(10) Towards a politics of collective empowerment: Learning from hill women in rural Uttarakhand, India [35]	Paper
(11) Manfred Hauswirth	Author
(12) Payam M. Barnaghi	Author
(13) Steffen Staab	Author
(14) Markus Strohmaier	Author
(15) Ramesh Jain	Author
(16) Amit P. Sheth	Author
(17) Social machine politics are here to stay [28]	Paper
(18) IEEE Internet Computing Journal	Venue
Recommendations for: General Chemistry Students' Understanding of Climate Change and the Chemistry Related to Climate Change [44]	
(1) Journal of Chemical Education	Venue
(2) Marine Transportation and the Environment [19]	Paper
(3) Stalinism and British Politics [41]	Paper
(4) Piracy and the politics of social media [2]	Paper
(5) Climate Change, Public Health and Sustainable Development: The Interlinkages [33]	Paper
(6) Moisture dynamics in walls: response to micro-environment and climate change [12]	Paper
(7) Diagenesis and Geochemistry of Sediments in Marine Environment [36]	Paper
(8) Power, norms and institutional change in the European Union: The protection of the free movement of goods [8]	Paper
(9) Adapting to climate change in Bangladesh: Good governance barriers [4]	Paper
(10) Improving US Highway Safety: Have We Taken the Right Road? [29]	Paper
(11) Climate change: the biggest challenge in the next decade?	Report
(12) Social-Historical Transformations in Russia [22]	Paper
(13) Fuller and Rouse on the legitimation of scientific knowledge [32]	Paper
(14) High Politics, Low Politics, and Global Health [51]	Paper
(15) Climate Change: A Serious Threat to Our Welfare and Environment [39]	Paper
(16) Australian developments in marine science [7]	Paper
(17) Pathways out of patronage politics: new roles for communities, new rules for politics in the Philippines [9]	Paper
18) Effects of climate change and variability on population dynamics in a long-lived shorebird [31]	Paper

7 Limitations and Future Work

The approach presented in this paper represents a preliminary work that will be extended in future. Although the created KG contains already valuable information that we exploited to provide recommendations, it can benefit from several extensions. Currently, it contains only four entity and eight relationship types. We aim to augment this KG with additional information. In particular, we want to add entities that represent NGOs and other organizations, public speakers and events that are related to the topic of social good. Moreover, we want to provide major supporters/sponsors behind these organizations and events in order to provide more insights. Furthermore, we want to include relationship types that represent connections between (public/private) organizations to events and venues. The extended KG would contain more complex information that could be used to find non-obvious dependencies and to provide more diverse recommendations. For this work, we made use of KGE models that only consider triples of the form *(h, r, t)* where both h and t represent entities of the KG. However, there is a trend to develop multimodal KGE models that incorporate different types of information such as textual, numerical and visual information. In our future work, we plan to develop a multimodal KGE model in order to exploit textual information (e.g. abstracts of the papers) and numerical information (e.g. publication date, number of citations) which are available for our KG and might help to provide better recommendations.

Here, we provided recommendations by computing the nearest neighbors of a seed entity in the embedding space. Although this approach is easy to realize and provides interesting recommendations, it should serve as a baseline system for more sophisticated systems. As a next step, we aim to explore reinforcement learning based approaches in which feedback of the recommendations are taken into account during the training.

8 Conclusion

In this paper, we presented a socio-scholarly knowledge graph which contains information about scientific artifacts that are related to the topic of social good. A specific knowledge graph embedding-based recommendation system has been developed for this KG. The system provides recommendations for any given seed entity (publication, author, venue, domain) by returning related entities. Our results show a great potential to leverage the system in broader scale of scholarly recommendations for active members of social good movements.

Acknowledgement. This work is supported by the EPSRC grant EP/M025268/1, the WWTF grant VRG18-013, the EC Horizon 2020 grant LAMBDA (GA no. 809965), the CLEOPATRA project (GA no. 812997), and the German national funded BmBF project MLwin.

References

1. Ali, M., Jabeen, H., Hoyt, C.T., Lehmann, J.: The KEEN universe. In: Ghidini, C., et al. (eds.) ISWC 2019. LNCS, vol. 11779, pp. 3–18. Springer, Cham (2019). https://doi.org/10.1007/978-3-030-30796-7_1
2. Almqvist, M.: Piracy and the politics of social media. Soc. Sci. **5**(3), 41 (2016)
3. Auer, S., Kovtun, V., Prinz, M., Kasprzik, A., Stocker, M., Vidal, M.E.: Towards a knowledge graph for science. In: Proceedings of the 8th International Conference on Web Intelligence, Mining and Semantics, p. 1. ACM (2018)

4. Bhuiyan, S.: Adapting to climate change in Bangladesh: good governance barriers. South Asia Res. **35**(3), 349–367 (2015)
5. Bordes, A., Usunier, N., Garcia-Duran, A., Weston, J., Yakhnenko, O.: Translating embeddings for modeling multi-relational data. In: Advances in Neural Information Processing Systems, pp. 2787–2795 (2013)
6. Chi, Y., Qin, Y., Song, R., Xu, H.: Knowledge graph in smart education: a case study of entrepreneurship scientific publication management. Sustainability **10**(4), 995 (2018)
7. Coffin, M.F.: Australian developments in marine science. In: Advanced Earth and Space Science (2012)
8. Dimitrakopoulos, D.G.: Power, norms and institutional change in the European Union: the protection of the free movement of goods. Eur. J. Polit. Res. **42**(2), 249–270 (2003)
9. Esguerra III, J., Villanueva, E.: Pathways out of patronage politics: new roles for communities, new rules for politics in the Philippines. IDS Bull. **40**(6), 13–21 (2009)
10. Georgas, H.: Google vs. the library (part II): student search patterns and behaviors when using Google and a federated search tool. Portal Libr. Acad. **14**(4), 503–532 (2014)
11. Goodfellow, I., Bengio, Y., Courville, A.: Deep Learning. MIT Press, Cambridge (2016)
12. Hall, C., Hamilton, A., Ho, W.D., Viles, H.A., Eklund, J.A.: Moisture dynamics in walls: response to micro-environment and climate change. Proc. Roy. Soc. A Math. Phys. Eng. Sci. **467**(2125), 194–211 (2010)
13. https://www.who.int/bulletin/volumes/85/11/07-011107.pdf
14. Huang, Q., Singh, V.K., Atrey, P.K.: Cyber bullying detection using social and textual analysis. In: Proceedings of the 3rd International Workshop on Socially-Aware Multimedia, pp. 3–6. ACM (2014)
15. Ji, G., He, S., Xu, L., Liu, K., Zhao, J.: Knowledge graph embedding via dynamic mapping matrix. In: Proceedings of ACL, pp. 687–696 (2015)
16. Lee, B.X., et al.: Transforming our world: implementing the 2030 agenda through sustainable development goal indicators. J. Public Health Policy **37**(1), 13–31 (2016)
17. Lin, Y., Liu, Z., Sun, M., Liu, Y., Zhu, X.: Learning entity and relation embeddings for knowledge graph completion. In: Twenty-Ninth AAAI Conference on Artificial Intelligence, February 2015
18. Liu, J., Yan, Z., Vasilakos, A.V., Yang, L.T.: Guest editorial data mining in cyber, physical, and social computing. IEEE Syst. J. **11**(1), 194–196 (2017)
19. Meyer, M.D.: Marine transportation and the environment (2010)
20. Monchaux, S., Amadieu, F., Chevalier, A., Mariné, C.: Query strategies during information searching: effects of prior domain knowledge and complexity of the information problems to be solved. Inf. Process. Manag. **51**(5), 557–569 (2015)
21. Mor Barak, M.E.: The practice and science of social good: emerging paths to positive social impact. Res. Soc. Work Pract. (2018). https://doi.org/10.1177/1049731517745600
22. Nagapetova, A.G., Novikova, O.S., Pokhilko, A.D., Shmatko, A.A., Vetrov, Y.P.: Social-historical transformations in Russia. Int. J. Hum. Cult. Stud. (IJHCS), 1439–1444 (2016). ISSN 2356-5926
23. Narula, S., Jindal, N.: Social media, Indian youth and cyber terrorism awareness: a comparative analysis. J. Mass Commun. Journal. **5**(246), 2 (2015)

24. Nickel, M., Tresp, V., Kriegel, H.-P.: A three-way model for collective learning on multi-relational data. In: Proceedings of the 28th International Conference on Machine Learning (ICML 2011), pp. 809–816 (2011)
25. Nickel, M., Murphy, K., Tresp, V., Gabrilovich, E.: A review of relational machine learning for knowledge graphs. Proc. IEEE **104**(1), 11–33 (2015)
26. Ning, H., Liu, H.: Cyber-physical-social based security architecture for future internet of things. Adv. Internet Things **2**(01), 1 (2012)
27. Ning, H., Liu, H., Ma, J., Yang, L.T., Huang, R.: Cybermatics: cyber-physical-social-thinking hyperspace based science and technology. Future Gener. Comput. Syst. **56**, 504–522 (2016)
28. O'Hara, K.: Social machine politics are here to stay. IEEE Internet Comput. **17**(2), 87–90 (2013)
29. O'Neill, B.: Improving US highway safety: have we taken the right road? TR News **239** (2005)
30. Pellissery, S., Barrientos, A.: Expansion of social assistance: does politics matter? Econ. Polit. Wkly., 47–54 (2013)
31. Van de Pol, M., et al.: Effects of climate change and variability on population dynamics in a long-lived shorebird. Ecology **91**(4), 1192–1204 (2010)
32. Remedios, F.: Fuller and Rouse on the legitimation of scientific knowledge. Philos. Soc. Sci. **33**(4), 444–463 (2003)
33. Ruhil, R.: Climate change, public health and sustainable development: the inter-linkages. Indian J. Public Health Res. Dev. **7**(3), 141–146 (2016)
34. Scroop, D., Heath, A.: Transatlantic Social Politics: 1800-Present. Palgrave Macmillan, New York (2014)
35. Sharma, D., Sudarshan, R.M.: Towards a politics of collective empowerment: learning from hill women in rural Uttarakhand, India. IDS Bull. **41**(5), 43–51 (2010)
36. Sharma, G.D.: Diagenesis and geochemistry of sediments in marine environment. AAPG Bull. **50**(3), 634 (1966)
37. Sheth, A., Anantharam, P., Henson, C.: Physical-cyber-social computing: an early 21st century approach. IEEE Intell. Syst. **28**(1), 78–82 (2013)
38. Sheth, A.P., Barnaghi, P., Strohmaier, M., Jain, R., Staab, S.: Physical-cyber-social computing (Dagstuhl Reports 13402). Dagstuhl Rep. **3**(9) (2014)
39. Singh, J., Agarwal, A., Singh, A.: Climate change: a serious threat to our welfare and environment. Imperial J. Interdisc. Res. (IJIR) **2**(12), 2044–2048 (2016)
40. Thomson, D., et al.: European left launches climate emergency manifesto. Green Left Weekly **7**(1219), 16 (2019)
41. Thorpe, A.: Stalinism and British politics. History **83**(272), 608–627 (1998)
42. Trouillon, T., Welbl, J., Riedel, S., Gaussier, É., Bouchard, G.: Complex embeddings for simple link prediction. In: International Conference on Machine Learning, pp. 2071–2080 (2016)
43. Vahdati, S., Arndt, N., Auer, S., Lange, C.: OpenResearch: collaborative management of scholarly communication metadata. In: Blomqvist, E., Ciancarini, P., Poggi, F., Vitali, F. (eds.) EKAW 2016. LNCS (LNAI), vol. 10024, pp. 778–793. Springer, Cham (2016). https://doi.org/10.1007/978-3-319-49004-5_50
44. Versprille, A.N., Towns, M.H.: General chemistry students' understanding of climate change and the chemistry related to climate change. J. Chem. Educ. **92**(4), 603–609 (2015)
45. Wang, Q., Mao, Z., Wang, B., Guo, L.: Knowledge graph embedding: a survey of approaches and applications. IEEE Trans. Knowl. Data Eng. **29**(12), 2724–2743 (2017)

46. Wang, X., Yang, L.T., Xie, X., Jin, J., Deen, M.J.: A cloud-edge computing framework for cyber-physical-social services. IEEE Commun. Mag. **55**(11), 80–85 (2017)
47. Wihbey, J., Ward, B.: Communicating about climate change with journalists and media producers. In: Oxford Research Encyclopedia of Climate Science (2016)
48. Wikipedia contributors: List of academic databases and search engines (2019). https://en.wikipedia.org/wiki/List_of_academic_databases_and_search_engines. Accessed 28 June 2019
49. Wilkinson, M.D., et al.: The FAIR guiding principles for scientific data management and stewardship. Sci. Data **3** (2016)
50. Yang, B., Yih, W.-T., He, X., Gao, J., Deng, L.: Embedding entities and relations for learning and inference in knowledge bases. arXiv preprint arXiv:1412.6575 (2014)
51. Youde, J.: High politics, low politics, and global health. J. Glob. Secur. Stud. **1**(2), 157–170 (2016)
52. Zegura, E., DiSalvo, C., Meng, A.L.: Care and the practice of data science for social good. In: Proceedings of the 1st ACM SIGCAS Conference on Computing and Sustainable Societies, p. 34. ACM (2018)
53. Zeng, J., Yang, L.T., Lin, M., Shao, Z., Zhu, D.: System-level design optimization for security-critical cyber-physical-social systems. ACM Trans. Embed. Comput. Syst. (TECS) **16**(2), 39 (2017)

Author Index

Printed in the United States
By Bookmasters

Printed in the United States
By Bookmasters